MW01011613

THE ILLUSTRATED
BATTLE CRY
of FREEDOM
☆ ☆ ☆ ☆ ☆
The Civil War Era

JAMES M. McPHERSON

THE ILLUSTRATED
BATTLE CRY
of FREEDOM

☆ ☆ ☆ ☆ ☆

The Civil War Era

JAMES M. McPHERSON

OXFORD
UNIVERSITY PRESS
2003

OXFORD
UNIVERSITY PRESS

Oxford   New York

Auckland   Bangkok   Buenos Aires   Cape Town   Chennai
Dar es Salaam   Delhi   Hong Kong   Istanbul   Karachi   Kolkata
Kuala Lumpur   Madrid   Melbourne   Mexico City   Mumbai   Nairobi
São Paulo   Shanghai   Taipei   Tokyo   Toronto

Published by Oxford University Press, Inc.
198 Madison Avenue, New York, New York, 10016
www.oup.com

Oxford is a registered trademark of Oxford University Press

Library of Congress Cataloging-in-Publication Data is available.
McPherson, James M.
    The illustrated Battle cry of freedom : the Civil War era / James M.
McPherson.
        p. cm.
Rev. ed. of: Battle cry of freedom.
Includes bibliographical references (p.) and index.
    ISBN 0-19-515901-2 (acid-free paper)—ISBN 0-19-516828-3 (signed
leather ed. : acid-free paper)
    1. United States—History—Civil War, 1861–1865—Campaigns. 2.
United States—History—Civil War, 1861–1865—Campaigns—Pictorial works. 3.
United States—History—Civil War, 1861–1865. 4. United States—History—Civil
War, 1861–1865—Pictorial works. I. McPherson, James M. Battle cry of freedom. II.
Title.
E470 .M46 2003
973.7'3'0222—dc21   2003009267

Pages 784–86 constitute an extension of this copyright page.

Pages ii–iii: Members of the color guards of the 35th and 36th Massachusetts Infantry
stand one last time with their shot-torn battle flags before returning home after Appomattox.
These two regiments lost 259 men killed and mortally wounded in action during the Civil War.

1 3 5 7 9 10 8 6 4 2
Printed in Hong Kong
on acid-free paper

To Willie

and to the

memory of

Glenn, Vann, and Bill

Who introduced me to the world

of history and academia in the

good old days at Hopkins

Battle Cry of Freedom

★ ★ ★ ★ ★

VERSE 3

Union: We will wel - come to our num - bers the loy - al, true and brave,
Confederate: They have laid down their— lives on the blood - y bat - tle field,

Shout - ing the bat - tle cry of Free - dom, And al - though he may be poor Not a
Shout, shout the bat - tle cry of Free - dom; Their— mot - to is re - sis - tance, To

man shall be a slave, Shout - ing the bat - tle cry of Free - dom.
ty - rants we'll not yield! Shout, shout the bat - tle cry of Free - dom.

CHORUS

The Un - ion for - ev - er, Hur - rah, boys, Hur - rah!
Our Dix - ie for - ev - er, she's never at a loss

Down with the trai - tor, up with the star; While we ral - ly 'round the flag, boys,
Down with the ea - gle, up with the cross, We'll— ral - ly 'round the bonnie flag,

ral - ly once a - gain, Shout - ing the bat - tle cry of Free - dom.
we'll rally once a - gain, Shout, shout the bat - tle cry of Free - dom.

The original words and music of this sprightly song were written in the summer of 1862 by George F. Root, one of the North's leading Civil War composers. So catchy was the tune that southern composer H. L. Schreiner and lyricist W. H. Barnes adapted it for the Confederacy. The different versions became popular on both sides of the Mason-Dixon line. Reproduced here are Verse 3 and the Chorus of each version.

CONTENTS

MAPS

PREFACE
TO THE ILLUSTRATED EDITION

The original edition of *Battle Cry of Freedom* caught a rising wave of interest in the American Civil War that has not yet crested. The numbers of Civil War books, movies, television documentaries, popular magazines, battle reenactments, and round tables have continued to grow during the past fifteen years. Much new scholarship has appeared, especially about the experiences of people on the home fronts and about women in the war effort. If I were writing *Battle Cry* today, I could benefit from this scholarship to enrich some of my findings and interpretations. In rereading the book, however, I have been gratified by how well it stands up in the light of new scholarship. This new edition, therefore, is not a revision of the original in the usual sense. With the expert assistance of James Wade, for which I am most grateful, we have abridged the text to about 80 percent of its original length. We further reduced the length by eliminating the footnotes (readers interested in documentation should consult the original edition). I have taken the opportunity provided by this new illustrated edition to correct a few errors and clarify or update some of the numerical data in the original. Hal Just has skillfully redrawn the maps for sharper and more attractive visual impact. But the narrative and interpretation remain the same as in the original edition. What is most decidedly new about this edition is more than seven hundred illustrations and their captions. Much of the expanded interest in the Civil War during the past fifteen years has been inspired by the visual impact of contemporary photographs, paintings, drawings, and other images. The millions who have watched Ken Burns's video documentary *The Civil War* were powerfully moved by such images. The blending of modern and contemporary visuals in *Civil War Journal* on the Arts and Entertainment Network—now on the History Channel—has been remarkably successful. Videotapes such as Smithsonian's *Great Battles of the Civil War* and movies like *Glory* and *Gettysburg* have reached large audiences. The old adage that a picture is worth a thousand words may not be literally true. It nevertheless expresses an essential truth. Thus I hope that the illustrations in this edition of *Battle Cry* will immeasurably enhance the reader's enjoyment and understanding of the narrative. The illustrations are of many types: photographs; woodcut engravings from illustrated newspapers, many based on drawings by such famous artists as Winslow Homer, Thomas Nast, Edwin Forbes, and Alfred R. Waud; lithographs and steel engravings, some of them hand colored; paintings by nineteenth-century artists; and cartoons. I am indebted to Susan Day for her industry and skill in finding and helping me select the best illustrations from a variety of sources. These images appear throughout the text to provide a visual reinforcement and amplification of words on the page. My explanatory captions often go beyond both text and image to provide additional information and interpretations. The illustrations and captions together constitute a substantial enrichment of the original *Battle Cry*. Those who enjoyed that edition will, I hope, like this one even better. And a new generation of readers will find here a blending of words and pictures intended to bring the Civil War alive in a unique manner.

PRINCETON   JAMES M. McPHERSON
FEBRUARY 2003

PREFACE
TO THE FIRST EDITION

Both sides in the American Civil War professed to be fighting for freedom. The South, said Jefferson Davis in 1863, was "forced to take up arms to vindicate the political rights, the freedom, equality, and State sovereignty which were the heritage purchased by the blood of our revolutionary sires." But if the Confederacy succeeded in this endeavor, insisted Abraham Lincoln, it would destroy the Union "conceived in Liberty" by those revolutionary sires as "the last, best hope" for the preservation of republican freedoms in the world. "We must settle this question now," said Lincoln in 1861, "whether in a free government the minority have the right to break up the government whenever they choose."

Northern publicists ridiculed the Confederacy's claim to fight for freedom. "Their motto," declared poet and editor William Cullen Bryant, "is not liberty, but slavery." But the North did not at first fight to free the slaves. "I have no purpose, directly or indirectly, to interfere with slavery in the States where it exists," said Lincoln early in the conflict. The Union Congress overwhelmingly endorsed this position in July 1861. Within a year, however, both Lincoln and Congress decided to make emancipation of slaves in Confederate states a Union war policy. By the time of the Gettysburg Address, in November 1863, the North was fighting for a "new birth of freedom" to transform the Constitution written by the founding fathers, under which the United States had become the world's largest slaveholding country, into a charter of emancipation for a republic where, as the northern version of "The Battle Cry of Freedom" put it, "Not a man shall be a slave."

The multiple meanings of slavery and freedom, and how they dissolved and re-formed into new patterns in the crucible of war, constitute a central theme of this book. That same crucible fused the several states bound loosely in a federal *Union* under a weak central government into a new *Nation* forged by the fires of a war in which more Americans lost their lives than in all of the country's other wars combined.

Americans of the Civil War generation lived through an experience in which time and consciousness took on new dimensions. "These are fearfully critical, anxious days, in which the destinies of the continent for centuries will be decided," wrote one contemporary in a sentence typical of countless others that occur in Civil War diaries and letters. "The excitement of the war, & interest in its incidents, have absorbed everything else. We think and talk of nothing else," wrote Virginia's fire-eater Edmund Ruffin in August 1861, a remark echoed three days later by the Yankee sage Ralph Waldo Emerson: "The war . . . has assumed such huge proportions that it threatens to engulf us all—no preoccupation can exclude it, & no hermitage hide us." The conflict "crowded into a few years the emotions of a lifetime," wrote a northern civilian in 1865. After Gettysburg, General George Meade told his wife that during the past ten days "I have lived as much as in the last thirty years." From faraway London, where he served his father as a private secretary at the American legation, young Henry Adams wondered "whether any of us will ever be able to live contented in times of peace and laziness. Our generation has been stirred up from its lowest layers and there is that in its history which will stamp every member of it until we are all in our graves. We cannot be commonplace. . . . One does every day and without a second thought, what at another time would be the event of a year, perhaps of a life." In 1882 Samuel Clemens found that the Civil War remained at the center of southern consciousness: it was "what A.D. is elsewhere; they date from it." This was scarcely surprising, wrote Twain, for the war had "uprooted institutions that were centuries old . . . transformed the social life of half the country, and wrought so profoundly upon the entire national character that the influence cannot be measured short of two or three generations."

Five generations have passed, and that war is still with us. Hundreds of Civil War Round Tables and Lincoln Associations flourish today. Every year thousands of Americans dress up in blue or gray uniforms and take up their replica Springfield muskets to reenact Civil War battles. A half-dozen popular and professional history magazines continue to chronicle every conceivable aspect of the war. Hundreds of books about the conflict pour off the presses every year, adding to the more than fifty thousand titles on the subject that make the Civil War by a large margin the most written-about event in American history. Some of these books—especially multivolume series on the Civil War era—have achieved the status of classics: James Ford Rhodes's seven-volume *History of the United States* from the Compromise of 1850 to the Compromise of 1877; Allan Nevins's four-volume *Ordeal of the Union* from 1847 to 1861, and four more on *The War for the Union*; David M. Potter's 600-page study *The Impending Crisis, 1848–1861*; Bruce Catton's three volumes on the Army of the Potomac (*Mr. Lincoln's Army; Glory Road*; and *A Stillness at Appomattox*), his three additional volumes, *The Centennial History of the Civil War*, plus two volumes on Ulysses S. Grant's Civil War career; Douglas Southall Freeman's magnificent four-volume biography *R. E. Lee* and his additional three-volume *Lee's Lieutenants*; and Shelby Foote's *The Civil War*, three engrossing volumes totaling nearly three thousand pages.

Alongside these monumental studies the present effort to compress the war and its causes into a single volume seems modest indeed. Nevertheless, I have tried to integrate the political and military events of this era with important social and economic developments to form a seamless web synthesizing up-to-date scholarship with my own research and interpretations. Except for Chapter 1, which traces the contours of American society and economy in the middle decades of the nineteenth century, I have chosen a narrative framework to tell my story and point its moral. This choice proceeds not only from the overall design of the *Oxford History* but also from my own convictions about how best to write the history of these years of successive crises, rapid changes, dramatic events, and dynamic transformations. A topical or thematic approach could not do justice to this dynamism, this complex relationship of cause and effect, this intensity of experience, especially during the four years of war when developments in several spheres occurred almost simultaneously and impinged on each other so powerfully and immediately as to give participants the sense of living a lifetime in a year.

As an example: the simultaneous Confederate invasions of Maryland and Kentucky in the late summer of 1862 occurred in the context of intense diplomatic activity leading toward possible European intervention in the war, of Lincoln's decision to issue an emancipation proclamation, of antiblack and antidraft riots and martial law in the North, and of hopes by Peace Democrats to capture control of the Union Congress in the fall elections. Each of these events directly affected the others; none can be understood apart from the whole. A topical or thematic approach that treated military events, diplomacy, slavery and emancipation, antiwar dissent and civil liberties, and northern politics in separate chapters, instead of weaving them together as I have attempted to do here, would leave the reader uninformed about how and why the battle of Antietam was so crucial to the outcome of all these other developments.

The importance of Antietam and of several other battles in deciding "the destinies of the continent for centuries" also justifies the space given to military campaigns in this book. Most of the things that we consider important in this era of American history—the fate of slavery, the structure of society in both North and South, the direction of the American economy, the destiny of competing nationalisms in North and South, the definition of freedom, the very survival of the United States—rested on the shoulders of those weary men in blue and gray who fought it out during four years of ferocity unmatched in the Western world between the Napoleonic Wars and World War I.

The most pleasant task in writing a book is the expression of gratitude to people and institutions that have helped the author. The resources of the Firestone Library at Princeton University and of the Henry E. Huntington Library in San Marino, California, provided most of the research material on which this book is based. A year at the Center for Advanced Study in the Behavioral Sciences at Stanford, where part of this book was written, supplemented an earlier sabbatical year at the Huntington to give me the time and opportunity for reading, research, and writing about the Civil War era. These two rich and rewarding years in California were financed in part by Princeton University, in part by fellowships funded by the National Endowment for the Humanities, and in part by the Huntington Library and the Behavioral Sciences Center. To all of them I am especially indebted for the support that made the writing of *Battle Cry of Freedom* possible. To Gardner Lindzey, Margaret Amara, and the staff of the Behavioral Sciences Center who helped me gain access to the riches of the Stanford and Berkeley libraries I also express my appreciation. The staff of the Manuscripts Collection of the Library of Congress, and Richard Sommers as Archivist-Historian at the U.S. Army Military History Institute at Carlisle, Pennsylvania, extended me every courtesy and assistance during research visits to these superb repositories. I also thank the staffs of the photographs and prints divisions at the libraries where I obtained photographs for the illustrations in this book.

George Fredrickson read an early draft of this book and offered valuable suggestions for improvement, as did my colleague Allan Kulikoff who kindly read Chapters 1 and 20. Sheldon Meyer, Senior Vice President of Oxford University Press, has been in on the project from the beginning and has shepherded it through to conclusion with an expert helping hand. Managing Editor Leona Capeless at Oxford refined the manuscript with her careful editing and cheerful encouragement. To Vann Woodward I owe more than I can express. Teacher, friend, scholar, editor, he has guided my growth as an historian for nearly thirty years, offered the highest example of craftmanship, and done more than anyone else to bring this book to fruition. To Willie Lee Rose also I owe much as a friend and fellow graduate student at Johns Hopkins who did more than anyone else except Vann to introduce me to the mysteries of the guild.

Without the love and companionship of my wife Patricia this volume could never have come into existence. Not only did she help with some of the research and read early drafts with a sharp eye for confused or overblown rhetoric; she also joined me in the tiresome but essential task of correcting proofs, and suggested the title. Finally to Jenny, and to Dahlia and her friends, I express warm appreciation for helping me understand the potential as well as problems of Civil War cavalry.

PRINCETON   JAMES M. McPHERSON
JUNE 1987

THE ILLUSTRATED
BATTLE CRY
of FREEDOM

✦ ✦ ✦ ✦ ✦

The Civil War Era

JAMES M. McPHERSON

From the Halls of Montezuma

On the morning of September 14, 1847, brilliant sunshine burned off the haze in Mexico City. A mild breeze sprang up to blow away the smell of gunpowder lingering from the bloody battle of Chapultepec. Unshaven, mud-stained soldiers of the United States army in threadbare uniforms marched into the Plaza de Armas, formed a ragged line, and stood at weary attention as a shot-torn American flag rose over the ancient capital of the Aztecs. Civilians looked on in disappointed wonder. Were these tattered gringos the men who had vanquished the splendid hosts of Santa Anna?

Martial music suddenly blared from a street entering the plaza. Jaunty dragoons with drawn sabers cantered into the square escorting a magnificent bay charger ridden by a tall general resplendent in full-dress uniform with gold epaulets and white-plumed chapeau. The Mexicans broke into involuntary applause. If they must endure the humiliation of conquest, they preferred their conquerors to look the part. As the band played "Yankee Doodle" and "Hail to the Chief," General Winfield Scott dismounted and accepted formal surrender of the city. Cross-belted U.S. marines soon patrolled the Halls of Montezuma while at nearby Guadalupe Hidalgo the American envoy Nicholas Trist negotiated a treaty that enlarged the territory of the United States by nearly one-quarter and reduced that of Mexico by half. During the sixteen previous months, American forces under Generals Scott and Zachary Taylor had won ten major battles, most of them against larger Mexican armies defending fortified positions. The Duke of Wellington had pronounced Scott's campaign against Mexico City the most brilliant in modern warfare.

But ironies and squabbles marred the triumphs. The war had been started by a Democratic president in the interest of territorial expansion and opposed by Whigs whose antiwar position helped them wrest control of the House in the congressional elections of 1846. Yet the two commanding generals in this victorious war were Whigs. Democratic President James K. Polk relieved Whig General Scott of command after Scott had ordered the court-martial of two Democratic generals who had inspired newspaper articles claiming credit for American victories. The president recalled his own envoy for appearing to be too soft toward the Mexicans; Trist

Opposite page: The artist's rendition of General Winfield Scott's triumphal entry into Mexico City the day after the U.S. victory in the battle of Chapultepec takes some liberties with historical reality. Having fought the previous day and marched to the walls of the city, American soldiers had hacked their way through the walls overnight. Their uniforms would not have been as clean and pressed as they appear here.

JUSTICE. PEACE

UNION

General Zachary Taylor commanded the American troops that invaded Mexico overland from Texas in 1846–47, and won the first four battles of the war, listed here on the bunting twisted around the pillars. These victories made the apolitical Taylor an irresistible candidate for the presidential nomination in 1848. So famous was he that this poster did not need to mention his name.

ignored the recall and negotiated a treaty which obtained all of Mexico that Polk had hoped for originally but less than he now wanted. Polk nevertheless sent the treaty to the Senate, where a combination of Whigs who wanted no Mexican territory and Democrats who wanted more came within four votes of defeating it. The antiwar party nominated war hero Zachary Taylor for president in 1848 and won; the same party nominated war hero Winfield Scott for president four years later and lost. Congressmen from northern states tried to enact a proviso banning slavery from the territories acquired by a war in which two-thirds of the volunteer soldiers had come from slave states. General Taylor was a slaveholder but opposed the expansion of slavery when he became president. The discord generated by the Mexican War erupted fifteen years later in a far larger conflict whose foremost hero was elected president two decades after he, as Lieutenant Sam Grant, had helped win the decisive battle of Chapultepec in a war that he considered "one of the most unjust ever waged by a stronger against a weaker nation."

The bickering Americans won the Mexican War because their adversaries were even more riven by faction. They won also because of the marksmanship and élan of their mixed divisions of regulars and volunteers and above all because of the professionalism and courage of their junior officers. Yet the competence of these men foreshadowed the ultimate irony of the Mexican War, for many of the best of them would fight against each other in the next war. Serving together on Scott's staff were two bright lieutenants, Pierre G. T. Beauregard and George B. McClellan. Captain Robert E. Lee's daring reconnaissances behind Mexican lines prepared the way for two crucial American victories. In one of his reports Captain Lee commended Lieutenant Grant. The latter received official thanks for his role in the attack on Mexico City; these thanks were conveyed to him by Lieutenant John Pemberton, who sixteen years later would surrender to Grant at Vicksburg. Lieutenants James Longstreet and Winfield Scott Hancock fought side by side in the battle of Churubusco; sixteen years later Longstreet commanded the attack against Hancock's corps at Cemetery Ridge, an attack led by George Pickett, who doubtless recalled the day that he picked up the colors of the 8th Infantry in its assault on Chapultepec when Lieutenant Longstreet fell wounded while carrying these colors. Albert Sidney Johnston and Joseph Hooker fought together at Monterrey; Colonel Jefferson Davis's Mississippi volunteers broke a Mexican charge at Buena

Vista while artillery officers George H. Thomas and Braxton Bragg fought alongside each other in this battle with the same spirit with which they would fight against each other as army commanders at a ridge a thousand miles away in Tennessee. Lee, Joseph E. Johnston, and George Gordon Meade served as Scott's engineer officers at the siege of Vera Cruz, while offshore in the American fleet Lieutenant Raphael Semmes shared a cabin with Lieutenant John Winslow, whose U.S.S. *Kearsarge* would sink Semmes's C.S.S. *Alabama* seventeen years later and five thousand miles away.

The Mexican War fulfilled for the United States its self-proclaimed manifest destiny to bestride the continent from sea to shining sea. But by midcentury the growing pains of this adolescent republic threatened to tear the country apart before it reached maturity.

CHAPTER ONE

★ ★ ★ ★ ★

The United States at Midcentury

I

In 1850, Zachary Taylor—the last president born before the Constitution—could look back on vast changes during his adult life. The population of the United States had doubled and then doubled again. Pushing relentlessly westward and southward, Americans had similarly quadrupled the size of their country by settling, conquering, annexing, or purchasing territory that had been occupied for millennia by Indians and claimed by France, Spain, Britain, and Mexico. During the same half-century the gross national product increased sevenfold. No other nation in that era could match even a single component of this explosive growth. The combination of all three made America the *Wunderkind* nation of the nineteenth century.

Regarded as "progress" by most Americans, this unparalleled and unrestrained growth had negative as well as positive consequences. For Indians it was a story of contraction rather than expansion, of decline from a vital culture toward dependence and apathy. The one-seventh of the population that was black also bore much of the burden of progress while reaping few of its benefits. Slave-grown crops sustained part of the era's economic growth and much of its territorial expansion. The cascade of cotton from the American South dominated the world market, paced the industrial revolution in England and New England, and fastened the shackles of slavery more securely than ever on Afro-Americans.

Even for white Americans, economic growth did not necessarily mean unalloyed progress. Although per capita income doubled during the half-century, not all sectors of society shared equally in this abundance. While both rich and poor enjoyed rising incomes, their inequality of wealth widened significantly. More dangerous was the specter of ethnic conflict. After 1830 waves of immigrants, most of them Roman Catholic, alarmed some Protestant Americans, sparking nativist organizations that resisted cultural pluralism.

The greatest danger to American survival at midcentury, however, was neither class tension nor ethnic division. Rather it was sectional conflict between North and

Opposite page: This 1857 painting by Robert S. Duncanson, whose grandfather had been a slave, portrays an Arcadian America before railroads and industry invaded the countryside.

"Our Peculiar Domestic Institutions."

Northern Hospitality—New-York nine months law. [The Slave steps out of the Slave State, and his chains fall. A Free State, with another chain, stands ready to re-enslave him.]

Burning of McIntosh at St. Louis, in April, 1836.

Showing how slavery improves the condition of the female sex.

The Negro Pew, or "Free" Seats for black Christians.

Mayor of New-York refusing a Carman's license to a colored Man.

Servility of the Northern States in arresting and returning fugitive Slaves.

Selling a Mother from her Child.

Hunting Slaves with dogs and guns. A Slave drowned by the dogs.

"Poor things, 'they can't take care of themselves.'"

Mothers with young Children at work in the field.

A Woman chained to a Girl, and a Man in irons at work in the field.

Branding Slaves.

Cutting up a Slave in Kentucky.

Paid.   Unpaid.

When abolitionists founded the American Anti-Slavery Society in 1833, they first appealed to the Christian conscience of slaveowners to persuade them to cease sinning against their fellow human beings by holding them in bondage. Few slaveowners responded, so by 1840 the antislavery movement publicized atrocities against slaves in an effort to rouse the northern people to condemn the South's "peculiar institution." Lynching, whipping, branding, and mutilation of slaves as well as the cruelty of northern race prejudice are all condemned in these illustrations.

South over the future of slavery. To many Americans, human bondage seemed incompatible with the founding ideals of the republic. If all men were created equal and endowed by the creator with certain inalienable rights including liberty and the pursuit of happiness, what could justify the enslavement of several millions of these men (and women)? The generation that fought the Revolution abolished slavery in states north of the Mason-Dixon line; the new states north of the Ohio River came into the Union without bondage. South of those boundaries, however, slavery became essential to the region's economy and culture.

Meanwhile, a wave of Protestant revivals known as the Second Great Awakening swept the country during the first third of the nineteenth century. In New England, upstate New York, and those portions of the Old Northwest above the 41st parallel populated by the descendants of New England Yankees, this evangelical enthusiasm generated a host of moral and cultural reforms. The most dynamic and divisive of them was abolitionism.

By midcentury this antislavery movement had gone into politics and had begun to polarize the country. Slaveholders did not consider themselves egregious sinners. And they managed to convince most nonslaveholding whites in the South (two-thirds of the white population there) that emancipation would produce economic ruin, social chaos, and racial war. The slavery issue would probably have caused an eventual showdown between North and South in any circumstances. But it was the country's sprawling growth that made the issue so explosive. Was the manifest destiny of those two million square miles west of the Mississippi River to be free or slave? Like King Solomon, Congress had tried in 1820 to solve that problem for the Louisiana Purchase by splitting it at the latitude of 36° 30' (with slavery allowed in Missouri as an exception north of that line). But this only postponed the crisis. In 1850 Congress postponed it again with another compromise. By 1860 it could no longer be deferred. The country's territorial growth might have created a danger of dismemberment by centrifugal force in any event. But slavery brought this danger to a head at midcentury.

II

At the time of the Louisiana Purchase in 1803 the United States was an insignificant nation on the European periphery. Its population was about the same as Ireland's. Thomas Jefferson thought that the Empire for Liberty he had bought from Napoleon was sufficient to absorb a hundred generations of America's population growth. By 1850, two generations later, Americans were not only filling up this empire but were spilling over into a new one on the Pacific coast. A few years after 1850 the United States surpassed Britain to become the most populous nation in the Western world save Russia and France. By 1860 the country contained nearly thirty-two million people, four million of them slaves. During the previous half-century the American population had grown four times faster than Europe's and six times the world average.

Three factors explained this phenomenon: a birth rate half again as high as Europe's; a death rate slightly lower; and immigration. All three were linked to the relative abundance of the American economy. The ratio of land to people was much greater than in Europe, making food supply more plentiful and enabling couples to marry earlier and to have more children. Though epidemics frequently ravaged North America, they took a lesser toll in its largely rural environment than among Europe's denser population. The land/people ratio in the United States raised wages and offered opportunities that attracted five million immigrants during that half-century.

Although the United States remained predominantly rural in this period, the urban population (defined as those living in towns or cities with 2,500 or more people) grew three times faster than the rural population from 1810 to 1860, going from 6 percent to 20 percent of the total. This was the highest *rate* of urbanization in American history. During those same decades the percentage of the labor force engaged in nonagricultural pursuits grew from 21 to 45 percent. Meanwhile the rate of natural increase of the American population, while remaining higher than Europe's, began to slow as parents, desiring to provide their children with more nurture and education, decided to have fewer of them. From 1800 to 1850 the American birth rate declined by 23 percent. The death rate also decreased slightly—but probably no more than 5 percent. Yet the population continued to grow at the same pace through the whole period—about 35 percent each decade—because rising immigration offset the decline of the birth rate. For the half-century as a whole, the margin of births over deaths caused three-quarters of the population increase while immigration accounted for the rest.

Economic growth fueled these demographic changes. The population doubled

An outstanding example of the rapid pace of urbanization in this period, Chicago grew almost overnight from a rural village in the 1830s to a major city by the 1850s—the hub of several railroads, a bustling Lake Michigan port, and the marketing and processing center for a large agricultural hinterland. In 1847 the nation's leading farm implement manufacturer, the McCormick Harvesting Machinery Company, established its plant in Chicago.

every twenty-three years; the gross national product doubled every fifteen. At some point after the War of 1812—probably following recovery from the depression of 1819–23—the economy began to grow faster than the population. Although most Americans benefited from this rise of income, those at the top benefited more than those at the bottom. While average income rose 102 percent, real wages for workers increased by somewhere between 40 and 65 percent. This widening disparity between rich and poor appears to have characterized most capitalist economies during their early decades of intensive growth and industrialization.

*　*　*　*　*

Improved transportation was a prerequisite of economic development in a country as large as the United States. Before 1815 the only cost-efficient means of carrying freight long distances were sailing ships and downriver flatboats. Most American roads were rutted dirt paths all but impassable in wet weather. The cost of transporting a ton of goods thirty miles inland from an American port equaled the cost of carrying the same goods across the Atlantic. To travel from Cincinnati to New York took a minimum of three weeks; the only feasible way to ship freight between the same two cities was down the Ohio and Mississippi rivers to New Orleans and then by salt water along the Gulf and Atlantic coasts—a trip of at least seven weeks. It is not surprising, therefore, that America's transatlantic trade exceeded internal commerce, that most manufactured goods purchased in the United States came from Britain, that artisans sold mainly custom goods in local markets, that farmers living more than a short distance from navigable water consumed most of what they raised—and that the economy grew little if any faster than population.

All this changed after 1815 as a result of what historians, without exaggeration, have called a transportation revolution. Private companies, states, even the national government financed the construction of all-weather macadamized roads. More important, New York state pioneered the canal era by building the Erie Canal from Albany to Buffalo, linking New York City to the Northwest by water and setting off a frenzy of construction that produced 3,700 miles of canals by 1850. During those same years, steamboats made Robert Fulton's dream come true by churning their way along every navigable river from Bangor to St. Joseph. The romance and economic importance of steamboats were both eclipsed by the iron horse in the 1850s. The 9,000 miles of rail in the United States by 1850 led the world but paled in comparison with the 21,000 additional miles laid during the next decade, which gave to the United

When New York's Governor De Witt Clinton committed his state to construction of the Erie Canal from Albany to Buffalo, skeptics said it could never be done. They labeled it "Clinton's Ditch" and "Clinton's Folly." But he proved them wrong. The largest engineering project yet undertaken in the United States, the 364-mile canal was completed in 1825. It repaid New York's $7.5 million investment many times over, ensured New York City's standing as the nation's leading port, and began a reorientation of internal commerce from a north-south to a primarily east-west axis.

States in 1860 a rail network larger than the rest of the world's combined. By 1861 the telegraph leaped beyond the railheads to span the continent.

These marvels profoundly altered American life. They halved overland transport costs by road to fifteen cents a ton-mile. But even improved, all-weather macadamized roads soon became unimportant except for short hauls and local travel. Canal rates dropped to less than one cent a ton-mile, river rates even lower, and rail charges to less than three cents by 1860. Towns bypassed by the tracks shriveled; those located on the iron boomed, especially if they also enjoyed water transport. Springing from the prairie shores of Lake Michigan, Chicago became the terminus for fifteen rail lines by 1860, its population having grown by 375 percent during the previous decade. Racing at breakneck speeds of thirty miles an hour, the iron horse cut travel time between New York and Chicago from three weeks to two days. Along with the railroad and with technological innovations in printing and paper-making, the telegraph vastly increased the influence of newspapers, the country's principal medium of communication. The price of a single issue dropped from six cents in 1830 to one or two cents by 1850. Circulation increased twice as fast as population. The "latest news" became hours rather than days old. Fast trains carried weekly editions of metropolitan newspapers (like Horace Greeley's *New York Tribune*) to farmers a thousand miles away, where they shaped political sentiments. In 1848 several major newspapers pooled resources to form the Associated Press for the handling of telegraphic dispatches.

The transportation revolution refashioned the economy. As late as 1815 Americans produced on their farms or in their homes most of the things they consumed, used, or wore. Blacksmiths forged the tools and farm implements used in the community. Even firearms were built with handicraft skill and pride by a nearby craftsman. In larger towns and cities, master tailors or shoemakers or cabinetmakers or wheelwrights presided over small shops where they worked with a few journeymen and an apprentice or two who turned out fine custom or "bespoke" goods for wealthier purchasers. In an

The iron horse was the most important development in overland transportation since the domestication of the flesh-and-blood horse several millennia earlier. Without the rapid expansion of the railroad network, the economic development and the integration of markets in such a large country as the United States would not have been possible. And as a glance at the maps (overleaf) indicates, the railroads bound the midwestern states more firmly to those of the Northeast—which would be of no small consequence when war came in 1861.

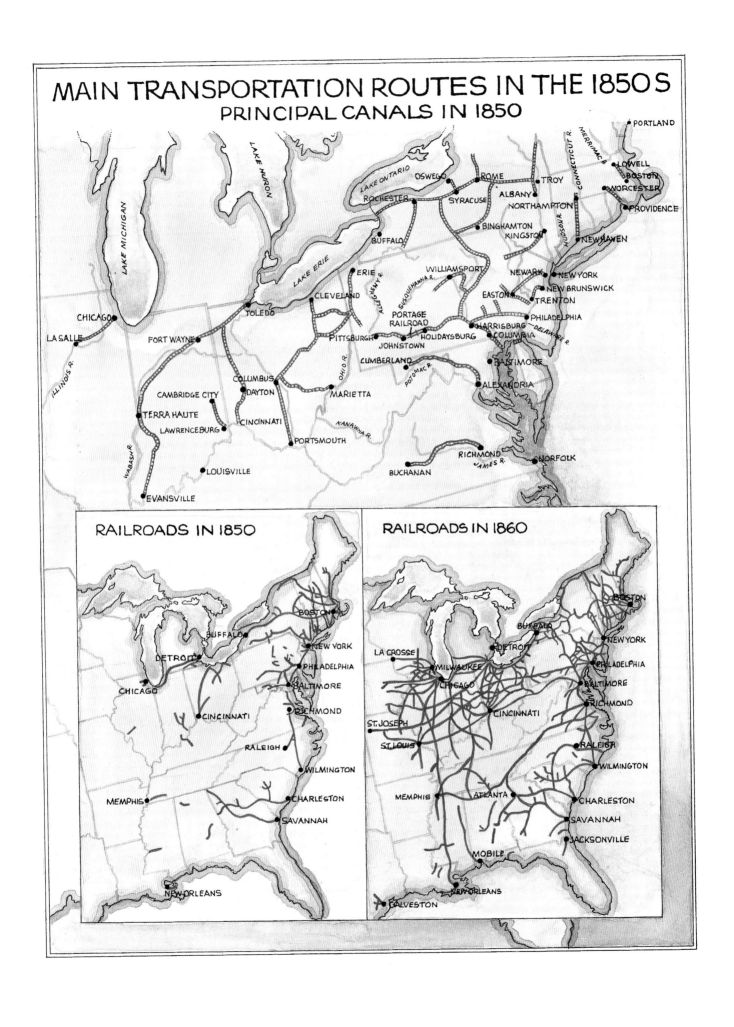

MAIN TRANSPORTATION ROUTES IN THE 1850S
PRINCIPAL CANALS IN 1850

PORTLAND

LAKE HURON

LAKE MICHIGAN

LAKE ONTARIO

OSWEGO   ROME   TROY   LOWELL   BOSTON
ROCHESTER   SYRACUSE   ALBANY   NORTHAMPTON   WORCESTER
BINGHAMTON   KINGSTON   PROVIDENCE
BUFFALO   NEW HAVEN

LAKE ERIE

ERIE R.   WILLIAMSPORT   NEWARK   NEW YORK
CLEVELAND   ALLEGHENY R.   SUSQUEHANNA R.   EASTON   NEW BRUNSWICK
TRENTON
PORTAGE   HARRISBURG   PHILADELPHIA
CHICAGO   TOLEDO   RAILROAD   DELAWARE R.
PITTSBURGH   HOLIDAYSBURG   COLUMBIA
LA SALLE   FORT WAYNE   JOHNSTOWN   BALTIMORE
OHIO R.   CUMBERLAND   POTOMAC R.
ILLINOIS R.   COLUMBUS   MARIETTA   ALEXANDRIA
CAMBRIDGE CITY   DAYTON
TERRA HAUTE   CINCINNATI   KANAWHA R.
LAWRENCEBURG   PORTSMOUTH
WABASH R.   RICHMOND   NORFOLK
LOUISVILLE   BUCHANAN   JAMES R.
EVANSVILLE

CONNECTICUT R.   MERRIMAC R.   HUDSON R.

RAILROADS IN 1850

BOSTON
BUFFALO   NEW YORK
DETROIT   PHILADELPHIA
CHICAGO   BALTIMORE
CINCINNATI   RICHMOND
RALEIGH
WILMINGTON
MEMPHIS   CHARLESTON
SAVANNAH
NEW ORLEANS

RAILROADS IN 1860

BOSTON
BUFFALO   NEW YORK
LA CROSSE   DETROIT   PHILADELPHIA
MILWAUKEE   BALTIMORE
CHICAGO   RICHMOND
ST. JOSEPH   CINCINNATI
ST. LOUIS   RALEIGH
WILMINGTON
MEMPHIS   ATLANTA   CHARLESTON
SAVANNAH
JACKSONVILLE
MOBILE
NEW ORLEANS
GALVESTON

age of slow and expensive overland transport, few of these items were sold more than twenty miles from where they were made.

This preindustrial world could not survive the transportation revolution, which made possible a division of labor and specialization of production for ever larger and more distant markets. More and more farmers specialized in crops for which their soil and climate were most suitable. With the cash from sale of these crops they bought food and clothing and hardware previously made locally or by themselves but now grown, processed, or manufactured elsewhere and shipped in by canal or rail. To sow and reap these specialized crops, farmers bought newly invented seed drills, cultivators, mowers, and reapers that a burgeoning farm machinery industry turned out in ever-increasing numbers.

In towns and cities, entrepreneurs who became known as "merchant capitalists" or "industrialists" reorganized and standardized the production of a variety of goods for large-volume sale in regional and eventually national markets. Some of these new entrepreneurs came from the ranks of master craftsmen who now planned and directed the work of employees to whom they paid wages by the day or by the piece instead of sharing with them the work of fabricating a product and the proceeds of its sale. Other merchant capitalists and industrialists had little or no prior connection with the "trade" (shoemaking, tailoring, etc.). They were businessmen who provided capital and organizing skills to restructure an enterprise in a more efficient manner. These restructurings took various forms, but all had one dominant feature in common: the process of making a product (shoes or furniture, for example), which had previously been performed by one or a few skilled craftsmen, was broken

This illustration portrays a typical shoemaker's shop as it would have looked in the first third of the nineteenth century. The master shoemaker is fitting a woman for a custom pair of shoes, which he will make by hand with the help of the two apprentices working in the background. After 1830 this craft process would break down into the manufacture of standardized shoe sizes by semiskilled or unskilled workers each cutting or stitching separate parts of shoes, increasingly by means of specialized machines as time went on.

This 1859 advertisement for a mechanical reaper illustrates the revolution in agriculture that occurred in the antebellum generation. Note the men standing at the left and right of the main picture holding a sickle and a scythe, the traditional means of cutting grain. By the 1850s two men and a pair of horses could harvest as much grain in a day as eight men with scythes or twenty men with sickles.

Even as the older states of the Northeast were crisscrossed with railroads carrying the products of commercialized farming and the new factories, regions farther west still depended on older forms of transportation and self-sufficient farming, as shown here in this idealized painting.

The leading edge of American industrialization in the antebellum era was the manufacture of cloth by power-driven machinery. The power looms shown here were first introduced in 1815. They soon replaced skilled handloom weavers for all but the most expensive fabrics. Handloom weavers were men; most operators of power looms were women or girls, as portrayed here, though the foremen (called overseers) were males.

down into numerous steps each requiring limited skills and performed by a separate worker. Sometimes the worker did his task with hand tools, but increasingly with the aid of power-driven machinery.

Highly mechanized industries like textiles went early to the factory system, where all operations were housed under one roof with a single source of power (usually water, sometimes steam) to drive the machines. This system enabled the New England textile industry to increase its annual output of cotton cloth from 4 million yards in 1817 to 308 million in 1837. In less mechanized enterprises like garment-sewing, operations took place in smaller shops with part of the process being "put out" to semiskilled workers—often women and children—in their homes and returned to the shop for finishing. This remained true even after the invention in the 1840s of the sewing machine, which could be operated in the home as well as in a factory.

Whatever the precise mixture of power machinery and hand tools, of central shop and putting out, the main characteristics of this new mode of production were division and specialization of labor, standardization of product, greater discipline of the labor force, improved efficiency, higher volume, and lower costs. These factors reduced wholesale commodity prices by 45 percent from 1815 to 1860. During the same years consumer prices declined even more, by an estimated 50 percent.

By 1860 the nascent outline of the modern American economy of mass consumption, mass production, and capital-intensive agriculture was visible. Its development had been uneven across different regions and industries. It was far from complete even in the most advanced sections of the country like New England, where many village blacksmiths and old-time shoemakers could still be found. On the frontier west of the Mississippi and on many internal frontiers in the older sections where the transportation revolution had not yet penetrated—the upland and piney woods regions of the South, for example, or the forests of Maine and the Adirondacks—it had scarcely begun. Many Americans still lived in a nearly self-sufficient handicraft, premarket economy not much different from what their grandparents had known. But the more advanced sectors of the economy had already given the United States the world's highest standard of living and the second-highest industrial output, closing in fast on their British cousins despite the latter's half-century head start in the industrial revolution.

Those cousins had begun to sit up and take notice. It was not so much the quality of American muskets, reapers, locks, and revolvers that impressed Britons, but the way in which they had been produced by machine-made interchangeable parts. The concept of interchangeability was not new in 1851. Nor was it exclusively American. The French arms industry had pioneered interchangeable parts for muskets as early as the 1780s. But most of those parts had been fashioned by skilled craftsmen working with hand tools. Their interchangeability was at best approximate. What was new to European observers in 1851 was the American technique of making each part by a special-purpose machine, which could reproduce an endless number of similar parts within finer tolerances than the most skilled of craftsmen could achieve. The British named this process "the American system of manufactures," and so it has been known ever since.

It was no coincidence that interchangeability was first perfected in small-arms manufacture. In wartime an army needs a large number of weapons in a hurry and must be able to replace damaged parts in an equal hurry. The U.S. government armories at Springfield and Harper's Ferry had gradually developed the process during the generation before 1850. The British imported American machinery to establish the Enfield Armoury during the Crimean War. Samuel Colt also set up a revolver factory in London stocked with machinery from Connecticut. These events symbolized a transfer of world leadership in the machine-tool industry from Britain to the United States. "There is nothing that cannot be produced by machinery," Colt told a committee of Parliament in 1854—and by then the British were ready to believe him.

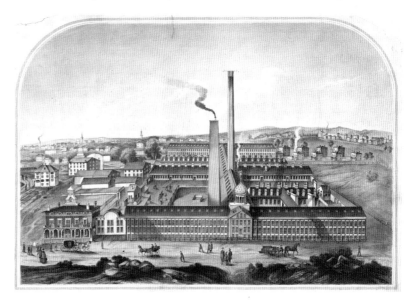

The Colt firearms plant in Hartford on the Connecticut River was the most advanced factory in the world in the 1850s, using specialized machinery to fabricate interchangeable parts. The machines were driven by water power, which supplied most of the energy for antebellum American industry.

The principles of mass production in America extended to what seemed unlikely practices: for example, the building of houses. To meet the needs of instant cities the first balloon-frame buildings appeared during the 1830s in Chicago and in Rochester, a boom town on the Erie Canal. These houses were constructed with the now familiar combination of machine-sawed boards fastened together with factory-produced nails to form the skeleton of a frame house. Machine-sawed siding and shingles and factory-made doors and window parts filled in the frame. Skeptics scoffed that these "balloon frames" would blow away in the first high wind. But in fact they were remarkably strong, for the boards were nailed together in such a way that every strain went against the grain of the wood. These houses could be put up in a fraction of the time and at a fraction of the cost of houses built by traditional methods used to build log, timber-frame, brick, or stone structures. So successful was this "Chicago construction" that it spread quickly to every part of the country.

Balloon-frame houses illustrated four of the factors cited then and later to explain the emergence of the American system of manufactures. The first was what economists call demand and what social historians might call a democracy of consumption: the need or desire of a growing and mobile population for a variety of ready-made consumer goods at reasonable prices. European visitors who commented (not always favorably) on the relationship between a political system of universal (white) manhood suffrage and a socioeconomic system of standardized consumption were right on the mark. Grinding poverty and luxurious wealth were by no means absent from the United States, but what impressed most observers was the broad middle.

Another factor that gave rise to the American system was the shortage and consequent high cost of labor. A deficiency of skilled carpenters, for example, had spawned the balloon-frame house. Europeans found surprisingly little opposition to mechanization among American workers. With labor scarce in the first place, new machines, instead of displacing workers, as they often did elsewhere, tended rather to multiply each worker's productivity. American "workmen hail with satisfaction

A typical schoolhouse in the lower Hudson Valley in the 1830s. Note the male teacher standing in the doorway. Most teachers at that time were indeed men, but within the next generation women would begin to dominate the teaching profession. Perhaps some of those future teachers would include the girls in the foreground of this engraving.

all mechanical improvements," reported a British industrialist (with exaggeration), "the importance and value of which, as releasing them from the drudgery of unskilled labour, they are enabled by education to understand and appreciate."

While not rejecting this labor-scarcity thesis, some historians emphasize a third reason for the capital-intensive nature of the American system—the high resource endowment of the United States. Resources are a form of capital; three outstanding examples in this period were land, wood, and abundant water-power sites, especially in New England. The high ratio of land to people encouraged a form of agriculture that would have been wasteful elsewhere but made economic sense in the United States, where the use of machinery achieved a modest yield per acre but a high yield per man-hour of labor. Wood was as plentiful in America as it was scarce in Europe; machined products were far more wasteful of wood than handcrafted items, but economically rational where wood was cheap and labor expensive. The American lead in woodworking machines laid the groundwork for an emerging superiority in metal-working machines after 1850. Fast-flowing streams provided a cheap source of energy for American mills that enabled water to retain its status as the principal source of industrial power in the United States until 1870.

A fourth reason offered by British observers to explain American economic efficiency was an educational system that had produced widespread literacy and "adaptative versatility" among American workers. By contrast a British workman trained by long apprenticeship "in the trade" rather than in schools lacked "the ductility of mind and the readiness of apprehension for a new thing" and was "unwilling to change the methods which he has been used to," according to an English manufacturer. The craft apprenticeship system was breaking down in the United States, where most children in the Northeast went to school until age fourteen or fifteen. "Educated up to a far higher standard than those of a much superior social grade in the Old World . . . every [American] workman seems to be continually devising some new thing to assist him in his work, and there is a strong desire . . . to be 'posted up' in every new improvement."

Elias Howe of Boston patented the first workable sewing machine in 1846. Other inventors soon introduced modifications, creating a jungle of patent infringement suits. In 1851 the intinerant inventor Isaac Merritt Singer patented the most significant improvements on the basic pattern. Through victories in patent infringement cases and the superiority of his product, Singer soon emerged as the leading producer of sewing machines. This 1857 drawing shows the central sales office of the Singer Company in New York City. Two women in the foreground are trying out the latest models.

This was perhaps putting it a bit strongly. But many American technological innovations were indeed contributed by workers themselves. Elias Howe, a journeyman machinist in Boston who invented a sewing machine, was one of many examples. This was what contemporaries meant when they spoke of Yankee ingenuity. They used "Yankee" in all three senses of the word: Americans; residents of northern states in particular; and New Englanders especially. Of 143 important inventions patented in the United States from 1790 to 1860, 93 percent came out of the free states and nearly half from New England alone—more than twice that region's proportion of the free population. Much of the machine-tool industry and most of the factories with the most advanced forms of the American system of manufactures were located in New England.

The connection made by British observers between Yankee "adaptative versatility" and education was accurate. New England led the world in educational facilities and literacy at midcentury. More than 95 percent of its adults could read and write; three-fourths of the children aged five to nineteen were enrolled in school, which they attended for an average of six months a year. The rest of the North was not far behind. The South lagged with only 80 percent of its white population literate and one-third of the white children enrolled in school for an average of three months a year. The slaves, of course, did not attend school, and only about one-tenth of them could read and write. Even counting the slaves, nearly four-fifths of the American population was literate in the 1850s, compared with two-thirds in Britain and northwest Europe and one-fourth in southern and eastern Europe. Counting only the free population, the literacy rate of 90 percent in the United States was equaled only by Sweden and Denmark.

The rise of schooling in these countries since the seventeenth century had grown out of the Protestant Reformation. The priesthood of all believers needed to know how to read and understand God's word. In the nineteenth century, religion continued to play an important role in American education. Most colleges and many secondary schools were supported by church denominations. Even the public schools still reflected their Protestant auspices. Since 1830 a rapid expansion and rationalization of the public school system had spread westward and southward from New England—though it had not yet penetrated very far below the Ohio. An important purpose of these schools remained the inculcation of Protestant-ethic values "of regularity, punctuality, constancy and industry" by "moral and religious instruction daily given," according to the Massachusetts superintendent of schools in 1857. These values, along with cognitive skills and knowledge, also served the needs of a growing capitalist economy. Schools were "the grand agent for the development or augmentation of national resources," wrote Horace Mann in 1848, "more powerful in the production and gainful employment of the total wealth of a country than all the other things mentioned in the books of the political economists."

III

Recent scholarship has challenged the observations quoted earlier that American workers readily embraced the new industrial order. Skilled artisans in particular appear to have resisted certain features of capitalist development. They formed trade unions and workingmen's parties which attained considerable strength in the 1830s, when tensions caused by the transition from a localized craft economy to an expanding capitalism were most acute. Disputes about wages and control of the work process provoked strikes and other forms of conflict. Worker activism declined after 1837 as the depression generated unemployment which drew the fangs of militancy. After recovery from the depression, vastly increased immigration intensified ethnic and religious divisions within the working class.

Nativism, temperance, and the growing sectional conflict took precedence over the economic issues that had prevailed in the 1830s. Nevertheless, frictions persisted in the workplace and occasionally erupted, as in the Massachusetts shoemakers' strike of 1860.

Technological innovation was not the main cause of worker unrest. To be sure, machines displaced some craftsmen or downgraded their skills. But most machines during this era executed simple repetitive motions previously performed by unskilled or semiskilled workers. And even when more complex machine tools replaced some artisans, they expanded other categories of highly skilled workers—machinists, tool-and-die makers, millwrights, civil and mechanical engineers—whose numbers doubled during the 1850s. The transportation and communications revolutions created whole new occupations, some of them skilled and well paid—steamboat pilots, railroad men, telegraphers. The latter two categories increased fivefold in the 1850s. The rapid westward expansion of the urban frontier, the extraordinary mobility of the American population, and regional differentials in the pace of technological development meant that skilled workers who were displaced by new technology in one part of the country could go west and find a job.

Despite the generally rising trend of real wages, workers at the bottom of the scale, especially women, children, and recent immigrants, labored long hours in sweatshops or airless factories for a pittance. They could make a living only if other members of their families also worked. For some of these laborers, however, the pennies they earned as domestic servants or factory hands or stevedores or seamstresses or hod-carriers or construction workers represented an improvement over the famine conditions they had left in Ireland. Nevertheless, poverty was widespread and becoming more so among laborers in large cities with a substantial immigrant population. New York packed an immense populace of the poor into noisome tenements, giving the city a death rate nearly twice as high as London's.

Although the working poor of New York would explode into the worst riot of American history in 1863, these people did not provide the cutting edge of labor protest in the antebellum era. It was not so much the level of wages as the very concept of wages itself that fueled much of this protest. Wage labor was a form of

These daguerreotypes of a group of shoemakers, a cooper, and a blacksmith date from about 1850. Already these ancient crafts were less honored and remunerated than in former times, and within another generation or two a rapidly changing economy would make them obsolescent or obsolete.

By the 1850s the rapid growth of New York City, fueled in part by heavy immigration from Ireland, had turned Manhattan into one of the most densely populated areas in the world. Many of the overcrowded tenement houses were firetraps, as illustrated by this drawing of a tenement fire on 15th Street on March 28, 1860, in which two women and eight children lost their lives.

dependency that seemed to contradict the republican principles on which the country had been founded. The core of republicanism was liberty, a precious but precarious birthright constantly threatened by corrupt manipulations of power. The philosopher of republicanism, Thomas Jefferson, had defined the essence of liberty as independence, which required the ownership of productive property. A man dependent on others for a living could never be truly free, nor could a dependent class constitute the basis of a republican government. Women, children, and slaves were dependent; that defined them *out* of the polity of republican freemen. Wage laborers were also dependent; that was why Jefferson feared the development of industrial capitalism with its need for wage laborers. Jefferson envisaged an ideal America of farmers and artisan producers who owned their means of production and depended on no man for a living.

But the American economy did not develop that way. Instead, skilled craftsmen who owned their tools and sold the products of their labor for a "just price" found themselves gradually drawn into a relationship where they sold their labor. Instead of working for themselves, they worked for someone else. Instead of earning a just price for their skill, they earned wages whose amount was determined not by the intrinsic value of their labor but by what an increasingly distant "market" would bear. The emergence of industrial capitalism from 1815 to 1860 thus began to forge a new system of class relations between capitalists who owned the means of production and workers who owned only their labor power. Journeymen artisans who experienced this process did not like it. They and their spokesmen offered a sharp critique of emerging capitalism as well as its constraints—"wage slavery" and work rules that were imposed on employees.

Capitalism was incompatible with republicanism, they insisted. Dependence on wages robbed a man of his independence and therefore of his liberty. Wage labor was no better than slave labor—hence "wage slavery." In the new regimen all laborers worked in lockstep; the system turned them into machines; they became slaves to the clock. Manufacturers encouraged the temperance movement that gathered force after 1830 because its Protestant-ethic virtues of sobriety, punctuality, reliability, and thrift were precisely the values needed by disciplined workers in the new order. Some employers banned drinking on the job and tried even to forbid their workers to drink *off* the job. For men who considered their thrice-daily tipple a right, this was another mark of slavery.

In the eyes of labor reformers, capitalism also violated other tenets of republicanism: virtue, commonweal, and equality. Virtue required individuals to put the community's interest above their own; capitalism glorified the pursuit of self-interest in the quest for profits. Commonweal specified that a republic must benefit all the people, not just favored classes. But by granting charters and appropriating money to establish banks, create corporations, dig canals, build railroads, dam streams, and undertake other projects for economic development, state and local governments had favored certain classes at the expense of others. They had created *monopolies*, concentrations of power that endangered liberty. They had also fostered a growing inequality of wealth (defined as ownership of real and personal property). In the largest American cities by the 1840s, the wealthiest 5 percent of the population owned about 70 percent of the taxable property, while the poorest half owned almost nothing. Although wealth was less unequal in the countryside, in the nation as a whole by 1860 the top 5 percent of free adult males owned 53 percent of the wealth and the bottom half owned only 1 percent. Age as well as class accounted for this disparity—most twenty-one-year-olds owned little or nothing while most sixty-year-olds owned something, and the average man could expect to increase his wealth fivefold during the passage from youth to maturity. Nevertheless, ownership of property was becoming an elusive goal for Americans at the lower end of the economic scale.

Denunciations of this state of affairs rang with republican rhetoric. The factory bound its workers "hand and foot by a system of petty despotism as galling as ever oppressed the subjects of tyranny in the old world." A versifier drew the parallel between America's fight for liberty in 1776 and the workers' struggle a half-century later:

> For liberty our fathers fought
> Which with their blood they dearly bought,
> The Fact'ry system sets at nought. . . .
> Great Britain's curse is now our own,
> Enough to damn a King and Throne.

To counter the power of this new tyranny a worker had only the right to withdraw his labor—to quit and go elsewhere, or to strike. This was more power than chattel slaves had, but whether it was sufficient to redress the balance with capital was endlessly debated then and ever since. Radicals did not think so. They proposed a variety of schemes to equalize wealth and property or to circumvent the wage system by producers' cooperatives. But these were pinpricks on the periphery of capitalism. Closer to the center was an antimonopoly crusade that channeled itself through the Jacksonian Democratic party. This movement united trade unions and labor spokesmen with yeoman farmers, especially those in the upland South and lower Northwest who stood on the edge of the market revolution apprehensive of being drawn into it. These groups evinced a producers' consciousness based on the labor theory of value: all genuine wealth is derived from the labor that produced it, and the proceeds of that wealth should go to those who created it. These "producing classes" did not include bankers, lawyers, merchants, speculators, and other "capitalists" who were "bloodsuckers" or "parasites" that "manipulated 'associated wealth'" and "have grown fat upon the earnings of the toil worn laborer." Of all the "leeches" sucking the lifeblood of farmers and workers, bankers were the worst. Banks in general and the Second Bank of the United States in particular became the chief symbol of capitalist development during the 1830s and the chief scapegoat for its perceived ills.

Part of the capital for the American industrial revolution came from state and local governments, which financed roads, canals, and education. Part came from foreign investors who sought higher yields in the fast-growing American economy than they could get at home. Part came from retained earnings of American companies. But state-chartered banks were a growing source of capital. Their numbers tripled while their assets increased fivefold from 1820 to 1840. After standing still during the depression of the 1840s, the number and assets of banks doubled again from 1849 to 1860. Their notes constituted the principal form of money in the antebellum era.

Important as banks were to economic development, they were even more significant as a political issue. A two-party system of Democrats and Whigs formed around Andrew Jackson's veto of the recharter of the Second Bank of the United States in 1832. For a dozen years or more after the Panic of 1837 the banking question remained the most polarizing issue in state politics, pitting probanking Whigs against antibanking Democrats. The latter portrayed the concentration of wealth in banks as the gravest threat to liberty since George III. "Banks have been the known enemies of our republican government from the beginning," they proclaimed, "the engine of a new form of oppression . . . a legacy that the aristocratic tendencies of a

This rare photograph from 1850 shows Wall Street in lower Manhattan. The old post office is in the right distance, across from the U.S. Treasury building, a part of which appears at the extreme right. Although few corporation stocks were publicly traded at that time, Wall Street had already become the nerve center of American financial institutions.

bygone age has left, as a means to fill the place of baronial usurpation and feudal exactions." Banks caused "the artificial inequality of wealth, much pauperism and crime, the low state of public morals, and many of the other evils of society. . . . In justice to equal rights let us have no banks."

In reply, supporters of banks ridiculed such sentiments as puerile and reactionary. The "credit system," they declared, was "the offspring of free institutions," an agency of economic growth that had brought unprecedented prosperity to all Americans. Northern Whigs and their Republican successors after 1854 elaborated a free-labor rationale for their vision of capitalist development. To the artisan argument that the system of wages and division of labor alienated workers from employers, Whigs replied that greater efficiency benefited both alike by raising wages as well as profits. To the claim that all wealth was created by labor, Whigs replied that the banker who mobilized capital, the entrepreneur who put it to work, and the merchant who organized markets were "laborers" who created wealth just as surely as did the farmer or craftsman who worked with his hands. To the proposition that wages turned the worker into a slave, the free-labor ideology replied that wage dependency need be only temporary; that in an economy of rapid growth and a society of equal opportunity and free public education, a young man who practiced the virtues of hard work, self-discipline, self-improvement, thrift, and sobriety could pull himself up by his own bootstraps and become self-employed or a successful employer himself.

Americans in the mid-nineteenth century could point to plenty of examples, real as well as mythical, of self-made men who by dint of "industry, prudence, perseverance, and good economy" had risen "to competence, and then to affluence." With the election of Abraham Lincoln they could point to one who had risen from a log cabin to the White House. "I am not ashamed to confess that twenty five years ago I was a hired laborer, mauling rails, at work on a flat-boat—just what might happen to any poor man's son!" Lincoln told an audience at New Haven in 1860. But in the free states a man knew that "he can better his condition . . . there is no such thing as a freeman being fatally fixed for life, in the condition of a hired laborer." "Wage slave" was a contradiction in terms, said Lincoln. "The man who labored for another last year, this year labors for himself, and next year he will hire others to labor for him." If a man "continue through life in the condition of the hired laborer, it is not the fault of the system, but because of either a dependent nature which prefers it, or improvidence, folly, or singular misfortune." The "*free* labor system," concluded Lincoln, "opens the way for all—gives hope to all, and energy, and progress, and improvement of condition to all." It was precisely the lack of this hope, energy, and progress in the slave South that made the United States a House Divided.

However idealized Lincoln's version of the American Dream may have been, this ideology of upward mobility mitigated class consciousness and conflict in the United States. The Gospel of Success produced an outpouring of self-improvement literature advising young men how to get ahead. This imparted a dynamism to American life, but also a frenetic pace and acquisitive materialism that repelled some Europeans and troubled many Americans.

Whigs and Republicans supported all kinds of "improvements" to promote economic growth and upward mobility—"internal improvements" in the form of roads, canals, railroads, and the like; tariffs to protect American industry and labor from low-wage foreign competition; a centralized, rationalized banking system. Many of them endorsed the temperance crusade, which sobered up the American population to the extent of reducing the per capita adult consumption of liquor from the equivalent of seven gallons of 200-proof alcohol annually in the 1820s to less than two gallons by the 1850s. During the same years the per capita consumption of coffee and tea doubled. Whigs also supported public schools as the great lever of upward mobility. Common schools, said New York's Whig Governor William H. Seward, were "the great levelling institutions of the age . . . not by levelling all to the condition of the base, but by elevating all to the association of the wise and good." Horace Mann believed that education "does better than to disarm the poor of their hostility toward the rich; it prevents their being poor."

People who subscribed to these Whig-Republican principles tended to be those who had succeeded in the market economy, or aspired to. Numerous studies of antebellum voting patterns have shown that Whigs and Republicans did best among upwardly mobile Protestants in white-collar and skilled occupations and among farmers who lived near transportation networks that drew them into the market economy. These were "insiders" who welcomed the capitalist transformation of the nineteenth century and for the most part benefited from it. Although some Democrats, especially in the South, were also insiders, the greatest Democratic support came from "outsiders": workers who resented the deskilling of artisan occupations and the dependency of wage labor; Catholic immigrants at the bottom of the status and occupational ladder who took umbrage at Yankee Protestant efforts to reform their drinking habits or force their children into public schools; heirs of the Jefferson-Jackson distrust of banks, corporations, or other concentrations of wealth that threatened republican liberty; yeoman farmers in the upcountry or backcountry who disliked city slickers, merchants, banks, Yankees, or anybody else who might interfere with their freedom to live as they pleased.

Given the illogicality of American politics, these generalizations are subject to numerous qualifications. Despite their marginality, the tiny number of black men who lived in the half-dozen northern states that allowed them to vote formed a solid Whig bloc. The Democratic party's professed egalitarianism was for whites only. Its commitment to slavery and racism was blatant in the North as well as the South, while Whiggery grew in part from the same evangelical reformism that had generated the abolitionist movement. At the other end of the social scale, Democratic leaders in New York included many bankers and merchants who had nothing in common with the Irish-American masses in the tenements except their allegiance to the same party. The generalizations in the preceding paragraph, therefore, describe a tendency, not an axiom.

That tendency was perhaps most visible in the older states of the Northwest—Ohio, Indiana, and Illinois. Most of the initial settlers there had come from the upper South and Pennsylvania. They populated the southern part of the region and evolved a corn-hog-whiskey economy, selling their small surplus in markets accessible by the

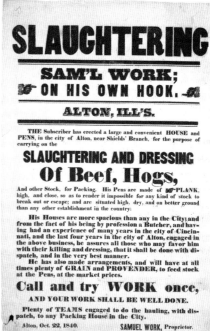

Ohio-Mississippi river network. They were called Buckeyes, Hoosiers, Suckers; they dressed in homespun clothes dyed with the oil of walnut or butternut trees, and hence acquired the generic name Butternuts. They remained rural, southern, and localist in their orientation, hostile toward "Yankees" of New England heritage who settled the northern portions of these states made accessible by the Erie Canal after 1825. These Yankees established a wheat-cattle-sheep-dairy farming economy linked to eastern markets by the burgeoning rail network after 1850. The railroads and the rapidly multiplying banks, industries, towns and cities owned or controlled by the "Yankees" caused these parts of the states to grow faster than the Butternut sections. Needless to say the Butternut districts were overwhelmingly Democratic while the Yankee counties voted Whig and after 1854 Republican.

Another Democratic voting bloc were literal outsiders—the immigrants. During the first forty years of the republic, immigrants had not come in large numbers. Even in the 1820s arrivals averaged fewer than 13,000 each year. In the next decade, however, this figure quadrupled. The pressure of a growing population on limited resources in Britain, Ireland, and western Germany squeezed thousands into ships bound for higher wages or cheap land in the new world. Despite economic depression in America during the early 1840s, the annual number of immigrants jumped 40 percent over the boom years of the thirties. Recovery from the depression in the United States coincided with the potato-famine years in Ireland and political unrest on the Continent associated with the revolutions of 1848. These push-pull forces impelled three million immigrants across the Atlantic in the decade after 1845. This was the largest proportionate influx of foreign-born in American history.

Before 1840 three-quarters of the immigrants were Protestants, mainly from Britain. Half of all newcomers who joined the labor force went into skilled or white-collar occupations, and another third became farmers. But as immigration

Americans ate more meat than any other people, and by the antebellum generation the slaughtering and processing of meat had become a big business, with Cincinnati the main center for this activity. The left-hand illustration shows the assembly-line technique for butchering hogs. Meat was preserved by salting rather than refrigeration; because salt pork both tasted and kept better than salt beef, Americans consumed more pork and bacon than steaks and roasts.

Most of the three million immigrants who arrived in the United States from 1845 through 1854 came on crowded sailing ships similar to the one shown here. During daylight hours in good weather they could remain on deck, but much of the time they were confined in fetid conditions below deck.

Tensions between Protestants and Catholics in Philadelphia erupted into violence in May 1844 when shots fired from the Hibernia Hose Company killed George Shiffler, a member of the anti-Catholic American Republican Association, shown below holding the American flag as he is dying. In retaliation, Protestants burned the Hibernia Hose firehouse and St. Michael's Catholic Church. Two months later another riot broke out, with militia trying to separate the combatants (below right).

increased sixfold during the next two decades, its religious and occupational mix changed dramatically. Two-thirds of the new immigrants were Catholics from Ireland and Germany. And while the proportion of farmers (mostly German) held up, the percentage of every other category declined except unskilled and semiskilled laborers, mainly Irish, who jumped to nearly half of the total.

The poverty, religion, and cultural alienation of the Irish made them triple outsiders. Anti-Catholic and ethnic riots occurred in several northeastern cities during the 1830s and 1840s. The worst erupted in 1844 at Philadelphia, where a pair of three-way battles among Protestants, Irish Catholics, and the militia left at least sixteen dead, scores wounded, and two churches and dozens of other buildings destroyed. "Nativist" political parties sprang up in various cities with the goals of lengthening the period of naturalization before immigrants could become citizens and voters, and of restricting officeholding to natives. These parties managed to

elect a mayor of New York and three congressmen from Philadelphia. This nativism was actually more anti-Catholic than anti-immigrant. Indeed, Protestant immigrants (especially from northern Ireland) were among the most violent "nativists." Although the movement drew on middle-class leaders, it recruited a large following among skilled Protestant workers. Their ethnic hostility toward fellow laborers did much to abort the Jacksonian birth of worker solidarity. But because of the Whiggish overtones of nativism, it cemented the Democratic allegiance of Catholic immigrants more firmly than ever. Political nativism would explode even more destructively in the 1850s, when it contributed to the breakdown of the two-party system that preceded the Civil War.

The economic transformation had an ambiguous impact on another group of political outsiders—women. The shift of manufacturing from household to shop or factory altered the functions of many families from units of production to units of consumption. The transition of agriculture from subsistence to cash crops had a similar though less pronounced effect on farm families. These changes modified the primary economic roles of most free women from producers to consumers. (Slave women, of course, continued to work in the fields as they had always done.) Instead of spinning yarn, weaving cloth, or making soap and candles and the like at home, women increasingly bought these things at the store.

To be sure, some women took jobs in textile mills or did outwork as seamstresses, milliners, shoe binders, and so on. Though few if any women (except slaves) were

The "Yankee peddler" was a ubiquitous institution in antebellum America, forerunner of the traveling salesman of later generations. The itinerant peddler presided over a retail store on wheels, bringing clocks, music boxes, flatware, needles, thread, and many other products of burgeoning American industry to small towns and rural areas across the land.

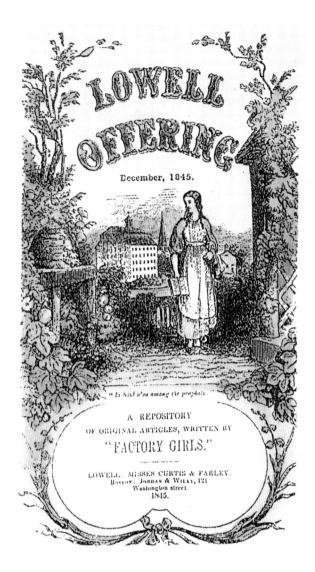

From about 1820 to 1845 one of the most famous experiments in American social and economic history took place. The proprietors of the new textile mills in Lowell, Massachusetts, decided to employ mostly young unmarried women in their factories and to house them in clean, well-run dormitories. From 1841 to 1845 these "factory girls" published their own magazine of poetry, short stories, and essays, the Lowell Offering, *the first periodical in the world to be written exclusively by women. Pictured here is the final issue. After 1845 immigrants began to replace these native-born young women in the mills.*

counted in the labor force of agriculture (though farm women certainly worked hard), construction, mining, or transportation, many continued to work as domestic servants and laundresses. At midcentury one-fourth of the employees in manufacturing were women, while in the textile industry women and girls constituted nearly two-thirds of the wage workers. Nevertheless, only 25 percent of white women worked outside the home before marriage, and fewer than 5 percent did so while married. Many young single women—like the famous Lowell girls who worked in the textile mills of that city—were part of the labor force for only two or three years while they built a dowry for marriage. The middle-class ideal for women was home and motherhood. And the enormously popular women's magazines (more than a hundred existed during this era, led by the renowned *Godey's Lady's Book*) diffused this ideal through society.

The economic transformation took men as producers *out* of the home into office or factory. This separation of job from home evoked a notion of separate "spheres" for men and women. Man's sphere was the bustling, competitive, dynamic world of business, politics, affairs of state. Woman's world was the home and family; her role was to bear and nurture children and to make the home a haven to which the husband returned from work each day to find love and warmth at the hearth. To the extent that this "cult of domesticity" removed women from the "real world" and confined them to an inferior sphere, it was a setback to any quest for equal rights and status.

But did domesticity constitute a real setback? Historians have begun to qualify this interpretation. The economic transformation coincided with—and in part caused—a change in the quality of family life as well as the quantity of children. As the family became less an economic unit it ripened into a covenant of love and nurturance of children. The ideal of romantic love increasingly governed the choice of a marriage partner, a choice made more and more by young people themselves rather than by their parents. And if wives now had a lesser economic role, they enjoyed a larger familial one. Patriarchal domination of wife and children eroded in urban areas as fathers went away from home for most waking hours and mothers assumed responsibility for socializing and educating the children. Affection and encouragement of self-discipline replaced repression and corporal punishment as the preferred means of socialization in middle-class families. These families became more child-centered—a phenomenon much noted by European visitors. Childhood emerged as a separate stage of life. And as parents lavished more love on their children, they had fewer of them and devoted more resources to their education by sending them to school in greater numbers for longer periods of time.

This helps explain the simultaneous decline of the birth rate and the rise of education in the nineteenth century. Women played a crucial part in these developments and derived significant benefits from them. Middle-class marriages became more of an equal partnership than ever before. In some respects women attained a superior position in the partnership. If men ruled outside the home, women tended to rule within it. The decision to have fewer children was a mutual one but probably most often initiated by women. It required some sacrifice of traditional male sexual prerogatives. The principal means of contraception—continence and *coitus interruptus*—placed the responsibility of restraint on males. Fewer children meant that middle-class women in 1850 were less continuously burdened by pregnancy, childbirth, and nursing than their mothers and grandmothers had been. This not only enabled them to give each child more affection; it also freed them for activities outside the home.

For, in an apparent paradox, the concept of a woman's sphere *within* the family became a springboard for extension of that sphere beyond the hearth. If women were becoming the guardians of manners and morals, the custodians of piety and child-training, why should they not expand their demesne of religion and education outside the home? And so they did. Women had long constituted a majority of church members; during the Second Great Awakening they increased their prevalence in that realm. This evangelical revival also produced a "benevolent empire" of Bible societies, moral reform organizations, and social uplift associations of all kinds—most notably the temperance and abolitionist movements. Women were active in all of these efforts, first in separate female societies but increasingly in "mixed" associations after women abolitionists made this breakthrough in the 1830s.

Women's advances in education were even more impressive. Before the nineteenth century, girls in America, as everywhere else, received much less formal education than boys, and a considerably higher proportion of women than men was illiterate. By 1850 that had changed in the United States, where girls went to elementary school and achieved literacy in virtually the same proportions as boys—the only country where that was yet true. Higher education was still a male domain, but several female "seminaries" for advanced secondary schooling were founded during the second quarter of the

This lithograph is an idealized illustration of the "sphere" of motherhood that had become such a powerful image in domestic ideology by the 1840s. The absent father is obviously at work producing the wealth that sustains this upper-class family. Although farmers and most lower- and middle-class urban families could not afford this lifestyle, it nevertheless represented an ideal toward which they were expected to aspire. The portrayal of children as small adults was still an artistic convention, although childhood and adolescence were already beginning to emerge as separate stages of life.

nineteenth century. Oberlin College admitted both women and men soon after its founding in 1833. Even more important, perhaps, was the feminization of the teaching profession. Like most other social and economic changes, this process began in New England and spread gradually westward and southward. By 1850 nearly three-quarters of the public school teachers in Massachusetts were women.

Another educating profession was opening to women during this era—writing for publication. The new emphasis on home and family created a huge audience for articles and books on homemaking, child-rearing, cooking, and related subjects. Women's magazines proliferated to meet the need. A paying profession arose for female writers. The expanded literacy and leisure of women, combined with the romanticism and sentimentalism of Victorian culture, also spawned a lucrative market for fiction which focused on the tribulations of love, marriage, home, family, and death. A bevy of authors turned out scores of sentimental best-sellers—"that damned mob of scribbling women," Nathaniel Hawthorne called them, perhaps in envy of their royalty checks.

Therefore, while the notion of a domestic sphere closed the front door to women's exit from the home into the real world, it opened the back door to an expanding world of religion, reform, education, and writing. Inevitably, women who could write or speak or teach or edit magazines began to ask why they should not be paid as much as men for these services and why they could not also preach, practice law or medicine, hold property independently of their husbands—and vote. Thus "domestic feminism"—as some historians label it—led by an indirect route to a more radical feminism that demanded equal rights in all spheres. In 1848 a convention in the upstate New York village of Seneca Falls launched the modern women's rights movement. Its Declaration of Sentiments, modeled on the Declaration of Independence, proclaimed "that all men and women are created equal" and deserved their "inalienable rights" including the elective franchise. The convention met in a church; one of its two foremost organizers, Elizabeth Cady Stanton, had been educated in the first women's seminary, at Troy, New York; the other, Lucretia Mott, had started her adult life as a schoolteacher; both had been active in the abolitionist movement. These activities constituted part of the back door of domestic feminism which in 1848 nudged open the front door a tiny crack.

Elizabeth Cady Stanton with her sons Daniel and Henry in 1848, the same year she organized the Seneca Falls Convention, the first women's rights meeting in American history. Stanton was well educated and had studied Greek and Latin in the hope that she might be admitted to a college, but none was open to her. Neither was the right to vote, nor access to most professions. It was to challenge these barriers that she founded the women's rights movement.

IV

The evolution of the child-centered nurturing family during this era helped inspire abolitionists to focus on the greatest perceived sin of American slavery: the tragic irony that caused the institution simultaneously to encourage the slave family and to threaten it with destruction.

Slave marriages had no legal basis in the United States. More than half of the bondsmen in 1850 lived on farms or plantations with fewer than twenty slaves where they had difficulty finding marital partners in the same quarters. But slaves nevertheless married and raised large families. Most slaveowners encouraged this process, in part because abolition of the African slave trade after 1807 made them dependent on natural increase to meet the labor demands of an expanding cotton kingdom. In contrast to the United States, slave economies in most other parts of the western hemisphere reached their peak development while the African slave trade flourished. Thus they relied mainly on imports to keep up their labor supply. They also imported twice as many males as females and discouraged their slaves from forming families. In consequence, while the slave population of the United States doubled by natural reproduction every twenty-six years, slaves in other new-world societies experienced a net natural *decrease*.

But North American slavery undermined the same family structure that it simultaneously encouraged. Responsible masters did their best to avoid breaking up slave families by sale or removal. Not all masters felt such a responsibility, however, and in any case they could not reach beyond the grave to prevent sales to satisfy creditors in settlement of an estate. The continual expansion of the plantation economy to new frontiers uprooted many slaves who left behind family members as they trekked westward. Recent studies of slave marriages have found that about one-fourth of them were broken by owners or heirs who sold or moved husband or wife apart from the other. The sale of young children apart from parents, while not the normal pattern, also occurred with alarming frequency.

This breakup of families was the largest chink in the armor of slavery's defenders. Abolitionists thrust their swords through the chink. One of the most powerful moral attacks on the institution was Theodore Weld's *American Slavery as It Is*, first published in 1839 and reprinted several times. Made up principally of excerpts from advertisements and articles in southern newspapers, the book condemned slavery out of the slaveowners' own mouths. Among hundreds of similar items in the book were reward notices for runaway slaves containing such statements as "it is probable he will aim for Savannah, as he said he had children in that vicinity," or advertisements like the following from a New Orleans newspaper: "NEGROES FOR SALE.—A negro woman 24 years of age, and two children, one eight and the other three years. Said negroes will be sold separately or together as desired."

Harriet Beecher Stowe used Weld's book as a source for scenes in the most influential indictment of slavery of all time, *Uncle Tom's Cabin* (of which more later). Written in the sentimental style made popular by best-selling women novelists, *Uncle Tom's Cabin* homed in on the breakup of families as the theme most likely to pluck the heartstrings of middle-class readers who cherished children and spouses of their own. Eliza fleeing across the ice-choked Ohio River to save her son from the slave trader and Tom weeping for children left behind in Kentucky when he was sold South are among the most unforgettable scenes in American letters.

The slaves in this photograph from Virginia in 1861 appear to be either an extended family or two nuclear families. Slaveowners encouraged large families among their slaves, especially in upper-South states like Virginia, because slave children were a capital asset that could be realized when they grew up. The owner of these particular assets could not know that within four years they would own themselves.

Although many northern readers shed tears at Tom's fate, the political and economic manifestations of slavery generated more contention than moral and humanitarian indictments. Bondage seemed an increasingly peculiar institution in a democratic republic experiencing a rapid transition to free-labor industrial capitalism. In the eyes of a growing number of Yankees, slavery degraded labor, inhibited economic development, discouraged education, and engendered a domineering master class determined to rule the country in the interests of its backward institution. Slavery undermined "intelligence, vigor,

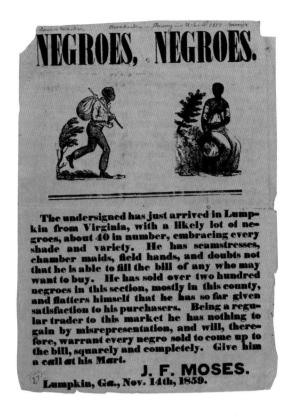

NEGROES, NEGROES.

The undersigned has just arrived in Lumpkin from Virginia, with a likely lot of negroes, about 40 in number, embracing every shade and variety. He has seamstresses, chamber maids, field hands, and doubts not that he is able to fill the bill of any who may want to buy. He has sold over two hundred negroes in this section, mostly in this county, and flatters himself that he has so far given satisfaction to his purchasers. Being a regular trader to this market he has nothing to gain by misrepresentation, and will, therefore, warrant every negro sold to come up to the bill, squarely and completely. Give him a call at his Mart.

J. F. MOSES.
Lumpkin, Ga., Nov. 14th, 1859.

and energy," asserted New York's antislavery Whig leader William Henry Seward in the 1840s. It had produced in the South "an exhausted soil, old and decaying towns, wretchedly-neglected roads . . . an absence of enterprise and improvement." The institution was "incompatible with all . . . the elements of the security, welfare, and greatness of nations." Slavery and free labor, said Seward in his most famous speech, were "antagonistic systems" between which raged an "irrepressible conflict" that must result in the destruction of slavery.

But whether or not slavery was backward and inefficient, as Seward maintained, it was extraordinarily productive. The yield of raw cotton doubled each decade after 1800, the greatest increase for any agricultural commodity. Cotton from the American South grown mostly by slave labor furnished three-fourths of the world's supply. Southern staples provided three-fifths of all American exports, earning foreign exchange that played an important part in American economic growth. And while slavery certainly made the Old South "different" from the North, the question whether differences outweighed similarities and generated an

One way to achieve wealth in the ante-bellum South was through the trade in slaves. The trader who placed this advertisement could probably sell these forty slaves in the rich cotton country of Georgia's Chattahoochee Valley for twice what he paid for them in Virginia. Southern planters professed disdain for slave traders, but without the traders their economy and society could not have functioned.

The scene portrayed in this illustration occurred more often than defenders of slavery liked to admit. The auctioneer is selling a mother and daughter separately, perhaps never to see each other again. Another mother sits nursing her child while she too waits to be sold.

Eli Whitney's invention of the cotton gin in 1793 made possible the rise of the antebellum cotton kingdom. Before then, the amount of hand labor required to separate the seeds from the tenacious cotton fibers made the growing of short-staple cotton unprofitable. A simple device with a spiked cylinder rotating through a grid of bars, the "gin" (short for engine) could clean hundreds of pounds of cotton in a day.

irrepressible conflict remains a matter of interpretation. North and South, after all, shared the same language, the same Constitution, the same legal system, the same commitment to republican institutions, the same predominantly Protestant religion and British ethnic heritage, the same history, the same memories of a common struggle for nationhood.

Yet by the 1850s Americans on both sides of the line separating freedom from slavery came to emphasize more their differences than similarities. Yankees and Southrons spoke the same language, to be sure, but they increasingly used these words to revile each other. The legal system also became an instrument of division, not unity: northern states passed personal liberty laws to defy a national fugitive slave law supported by the South; a southern-dominated Supreme Court denied the right of Congress to exclude slavery from the territories, a ruling that most northerners considered infamous. As for a shared commitment to Protestantism, this too had become divisive rather than unifying. The two largest denominations—Methodist and Baptist—had split into hostile northern and southern churches over the question of slavery, and the third largest—Presbyterian—split partly along sectional lines and partly on the issue of slavery. The ideology of republicanism had also become more divisive than unifying, for most northerners interpreted it in a free-labor mode while most southerners insisted that one of the most cherished tenets of republican liberty was the right to property—including property in slaves.

People on both sides began pointing with pride or alarm to certain quantitative differences between North and South. From 1800 to 1860 the proportion of the northern labor force in agriculture had dropped from 70 to 40 percent while the southern proportion had remained constant at 80 percent. Only one-tenth of southerners lived in what the census classified as urban areas, compared with one-fourth of northerners. Seven-eighths of the immigrants settled in free states. Among antebellum men prominent enough to be later chronicled in the *Dictionary of American Biography*, the military profession claimed twice the percentage of southerners as northerners, while the ratio was reversed for men distinguished in literature, art, medicine, and education. In business the proportion of Yankees was three times as great, and among engineers and inventors it was six times as large. Nearly twice the percentage of northern youth attended school. Almost half of the southern people (including slaves) were illiterate, compared to 6 percent of residents of free states.

Many conservative southerners scoffed at the Yankee faith in education. The *Southern Review* asked: "Is this the way to produce producers? To make every child in the state a literary character would not be a good qualification for those who must live by manual labor." The South, replied Massachusetts clergyman Theodore Parker in 1854, was "the foe to Northern Industry—to our mines, our manufactures, and our commerce . . . to our democratic politics in the State, our democratic culture in the school, our democratic work in the community." Yankees and Southrons could no more mix than oil and water, agreed Savannah lawyer and planter Charles C. Jones, Jr. They "have been so entirely separated by climate, by morals, by religion, and by estimates so totally opposite of all that constitutes honor, truth, and manliness, that they cannot longer exist under the same government."

Underlying all of these differences was the peculiar institution. "On the subject of slavery," declared the *Charleston Mercury* in 1858, "the North and South . . . are not only two Peoples, but they are rival, hostile Peoples." This rivalry concerned the future of the republic. To nineteenth-century Americans the West represented the future. Expansion had been the country's lifeblood. So long as the slavery controversy focused on the morality of the institution where it already existed, the two-party system managed to contain the passions it aroused. But when in the 1840s the controversy began to focus on the expansion of slavery into new territories it became irrepressible.

This nostalgic Currier and Ives lithograph from 1884 depicts slavery as many southern whites wanted to remember it. Well-dressed slaves pick cotton in leisurely fashion while others haul it to the gin and a steamboat passes up the river in the background. The whole scene portrays an idyllic world of orderly tranquility and happy slaves.

* * * * *

"Go West, young man," advised Horace Greeley during the depression of the 1840s. And westward did they go, by millions in the first half of the nineteenth century, in obedience to an impulse that has never ceased. From 1815 to 1850 the population of the region west of the Appalachians grew nearly three times as fast as that of the original thirteen states. During that era a new state entered the Union on the average of every three years. By the 1840s the states between the Appalachians and the Mississippi had passed the frontier stage. It had been a frontier of rivers, mainly the Ohio-Mississippi-Missouri network with their tributaries, which had carried settlers to their new homes and provided their initial links with the rest of the world.

After pushing into the first tier of states beyond the Mississippi, the frontier in the 1840s leapfrogged more than a thousand miles over the semi-arid Great Plains and awesome mountain ranges to the Pacific coast. This was first a frontier of overland trails and of sailing routes around the horn; of trade in beaver skins from the mountains, silver from Santa Fe, and cattle hides from California. By the 1840s it had also become a farming frontier as thousands of Americans sold their property at depression prices, hitched their oxen to Conestoga wagons, and headed west over the Oregon, California, and Mormon trails to a new future—on land that belonged to Mexico or was claimed by Britain. That was a small matter, however, because most Americans considered it their "manifest destiny" to absorb these regions into the United States.

By all odds the most remarkable westward migration before the California gold rush of 1849 was the Mormon hegira to the Great Salt Lake basin. The first indigenous American religion, Mormonism sprang from the spiritual enthusiasm aroused

by the Second Great Awakening among second-generation New England Yankees in the "burned-over district" of upstate New York. Founder and Prophet Joseph Smith built not only a church but also a utopian community, which like dozens of others in that era experimented with collective ownership of property and unorthodox marital arrangements. Unlike most other utopias, Mormonism survived and flourished.

But the road to survival was filled with obstacles. The Mormons' theocratic structure was both a strength and a weakness. Claiming direct communication with God, Smith ruled his band with iron discipline. Marshaled into phalanxes of tireless workers, true believers created prosperous communities wherever they settled. But Smith's messiah complex, his claim that Mormonism was the only true religion and would inherit the earth, his insistence on absolute obedience, spawned schisms within the movement and resentment without. Harried from New York and Ohio, the Mormons migrated west to create their Zion in Missouri. But Missourians had no use for these Yankee Saints who received revelations from God and were suspected of abolitionist purposes. Mobs massacred several Mormons in 1838–39 and drove the remainder across the Mis-

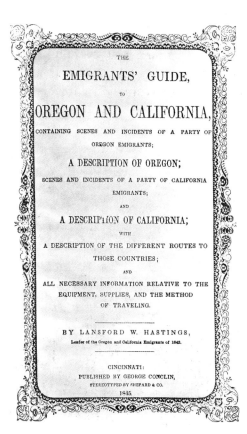

sissippi to Illinois. There the faithful prospered for several years despite the economic depression. Peripatetic missionaries converted thousands to the faith. They built the river town of Nauvoo into a thriving New England city of 15,000 souls. But Gentile neighbors envied the Saints' prosperity and feared their private army, the Nauvoo Legion. When yet another schismatic offshoot disclosed Smith's latest revelation sanctioning polygamy, the Prophet ordered the dissenters' printing press destroyed. Illinois officials arrested Smith and his brother; in June 1844 a mob broke into the jail and murdered them.

Smith's successor, Brigham Young, recognized that the Saints could not build their Zion among hostile unbelievers. Thus he led an exodus in 1846–47 to the basin of the Great Salt Lake in Mexican territory, a region apparently so inhospitable that no other white men wanted it. There the only neighbors would be Indians, who according to Mormon theology were descendants of one of Israel's lost tribes whom it was their duty to convert.

Brigham Young proved to be one of the nineteenth century's most efficient organizers. Like Joseph Smith, he had been born in Vermont. What Young lacked in the way of Smith's charisma he more than compensated for with an iron will and extraordinary administrative ability. He organized the Mormon migration down to the last detail. Under his theocratic rule, centralized planning and collective irrigation from mountain streams enabled Mormons to survive their starving time during the first two winters at Salt Lake and to make the desert literally bloom—not as a rose, but with grain and vegetables. As thousands of new converts arrived each year from Europe as well as the United States, the Great Basin Zion attained a population of 40,000 by 1860. Young even managed to prevent the faithful from joining the various gold rushes to California in 1849 and to the Virginia City and Denver regions in 1859. The Mormons earned more from trade with prospectors on their way to the gold fields than most of the miners did after they got there.

Born into a New England Congregationalist family, Brigham Young questioned many tenets of the Calvinist theology. In 1824 he joined the Methodist Church, but continued his quest for religious answers. In 1830 he read the Book of Mormon and found his answers. Without Young, Mormonism might have gone the way of many other sects that sprang up in the 1830s. Joseph Smith founded the Church of Jesus Christ of Latter-day Saints; Brigham Young turned it into a thriving institution.

Brigham Young led an advance party of Mormon migrants from Iowa to what was then Mexican territory in 1847. From a pass in the Wasatch Mountains, they looked down on the Great Salt Lake and the barren desert surrounding it. "This is the Place!" Young exclaimed. Harnessing the mountain streams for irrigation, the Mormons made the desert bloom and founded a city on the shores of the lake. When a plague of locusts threatened to devour their crops, a huge flock of seagulls—sent by God, Mormons believed—appeared and devoured the insects.

The greatest threat to the Saints was conflict with the United States government, which acquired the Great Basin from Mexico just as the Mormons were founding their Zion at Salt Lake. In 1850 Young persuaded Washington to name him governor of the new territory of Utah. This united church and state at the top and preserved peace for a time. But Gentile territorial judges and other officials complained that their authority existed in name only; the people obeyed laws handed down and interpreted by the church hierarchy. Tensions between Mormons and Gentiles sometimes escalated to violent confrontations. American opinion turned sharply against the Saints in 1852 when the church openly embraced plural marriage as divinely ordained (Brigham Young himself took a total of fifty-five wives). In 1856 the first national platform of the Republican party branded polygamy a "barbarism" equal to slavery. In 1857 President James Buchanan declared the Mormons to be in rebellion and sent troops to force their submission to a new governor. During the Saints' guerrilla warfare against these soldiers in the fall of 1857, a group of Mormon fanatics massacred 120 California-bound emigrants at Mountain Meadows. This prompted the government to send more troops. A realist, Young accepted the inevitable, surrendered his civil authority, restrained his followers, and made an uneasy peace with the United States. When the next president, Abraham Lincoln, was asked what he intended to do about the Mormons, he replied that since they were the least of his problems "I propose to let them alone."

Like so much of American history, the westward movement seems to be a story of growth and success. But for the original Americans—the Indians—it was a bitter tale of contraction and defeat. By 1850 the white man's diseases and wars had reduced the Indian population north of the Rio Grande to half of the estimated one million who had lived there two centuries earlier. In the United States all but a few thousand Indians had been pushed west of the Mississippi. Democratic administrations in the 1830s had carried out a forced removal of 85,000 Indians of the five "civilized nations"—Cherokee, Choctaw, Creek, Chickasaw, and Seminole—from

the southeastern states to an Indian territory set aside for them just west of Arkansas. Also in the 1830s a ruthless repression of Black Hawk's attempt to reclaim ancestral homelands in Illinois and the final suppression of Seminole resistance in Florida brought more than two centuries of Indian warfare east of the Mississippi to an end.

By then the government had decided to establish a "permanent Indian frontier" along roughly the 95th meridian (the western borders of Arkansas and Missouri). Beyond this line, Indians could roam freely in what explorer Zebulon Pike had labeled the Great American Desert. But the idea of a permanent Indian frontier lasted scarcely a decade. The overland westward migrations, the conquest of Mexican territory, and the discovery of gold in California opened this vast region to the manifest destiny of white Americans. So the government revived the burlesque of negotiations with Indian chiefs for cessions of huge chunks of territory in return for annuity payments that were soon soaked up by purchases of firewater and other white man's goods from wily traders. Since there was no more western frontier beyond which to push the Indians of the Pacific coast, a policy evolved to place them on "reservations" where they could learn the white man's ways or perish. Most reservations were located on poor land, and a good many Indians had little inclination to learn the white man's ways. So they perished—in California alone disease, malnutrition, firewater, and homicide reduced the Indian population from an estimated 150,000 in 1845 to 35,000 by 1860. Although the Great Plains and the desert Southwest remained as yet uncoveted by white settlers, the reservation policy foretokened the fate of the proud warriors of these regions a decade or two later.

The manifest destiny that represented hope for white Americans thus spelled doom for red Americans. And it also lit a slow fuse to a powder keg that blew the United States apart in 1861.

The Sauk leader Black Hawk refused to recognize the cession by tribal leaders of ancestral lands in Illinois to the United States. When promised government payments of corn to the Sauks in Iowa failed to come through in the winter of 1831–32, Black Hawk led a band across the Mississippi River to plant crops in their former Illinois land. Defeated in the ensuing "war," Black Hawk toured eastern cities in 1833 to be seen by large crowds eager to view a "noble savage." The medallion he is wearing in this portrait appears to be a likeness of Secretary of War Lewis Cass.

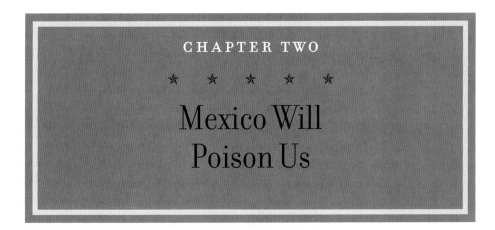

CHAPTER TWO

★ ★ ★ ★ ★

Mexico Will Poison Us

I

James K. Polk presided over the acquisition of more territory than any other president in American history. During his one-term administration the country expanded by two-thirds with the annexation of Texas, the settlement of the Oregon boundary, and the seizure of all Mexican provinces north of 31°. Having been elected in 1844 on a platform demanding that Oregon extend to a northern boundary of 54° 40' and Texas to a southern boundary of the Rio Grande River, Polk compromised with Britain on 49° but went to war against Mexico for Texas—with California and New Mexico thrown in for good measure. And thereby hung a tale of sectional conflict that erupted into civil war a decade and a half later.

"Mr. Polk's War" evoked opposition from Whigs in Congress, who voted against the resolution affirming a state of war with Mexico in May 1846. After the Democratic majority passed this resolution, however, most Whigs supported appropriations for the armies confronting enemy forces. Having witnessed the disappearance of the Federalist party after it opposed the War of 1812, a Whig congressman said sardonically that he now favored "war, pestilence, and famine." Nevertheless, Whigs continued to accuse Polk of having provoked the conflict by sending American troops into territory claimed by Mexico. They sniped at the administration's conduct of the war and opposed territorial acquisition as a result of it. Encouraged by the elections of 1846 and 1847, in which they picked up thirty-eight seats and gained control of the House, Whigs intensified their attacks on Polk. One of these new Whig congressmen, a lanky, craggy Illinoisian with gray eyes, disheveled black hair, and ill-fitting clothes, introduced resolutions calling for information about the exact spot where Mexicans had shed American blood to start the war. Though the House tabled Abraham Lincoln's resolutions, it did pass one sponsored by another Whig declaring that the war had been "unnecessarily and unconstitutionally begun by the President."

Like the war, Manifest Destiny was mainly a Democratic doctrine. Since the day when Thomas Jefferson overcame Federalist opposition to the purchase of Louisiana, Democrats had pressed for the expansion of American institutions across

Opposite page: The westward movement of white settlement was a dominant motif of nineteenth-century America. The railroad and schoolhouse were prominent symbols of this seemingly inexorable process.

Although James K. Polk was the first president to be photographed while in office, the most familiar image of him is this portrait painted by the American artist George P. A. Healy in 1846. Polk complained that the many hours he had to sit for the artist were a waste of time, but when he saw the finished product, which made him look years younger, he expressed himself "heartily rejoiced at it."

When Commodore John D. Sloat, commander of the U.S. fleet in the Pacific, received word on July 7, 1846, of the first fighting between Americans and Mexicans along the Rio Grande, he immediately seized the virtually defenseless Mexican capital of California at Monterey. Three days later he likewise captured San Francisco. This lithograph shows Monterey with American ships anchored offshore and two American officers standing on the bluffs.

the whole of North America whether the residents—Indians, Spaniards, Mexicans, Canadians—wanted them or not. Whigs were not averse to extending the blessings of American liberty, even to Mexicans and Indians. But they looked askance at doing so by force. Befitting the evangelical origins of much Whig ideology, they placed their faith in mission more than in annexation. "'As a city set upon a hill,'" the United States should inculcate the ideas of "true republicanism" by example rather than conquest, insisted many Whigs.

Acquisition of Mexican territory was Polk's principal war aim. The desire of American settlers in Oregon and California for annexation to the United States had precipitated the dual crises with Britain and Mexico in 1846. Praising these emigrants as "already engaged in establishing the blessings of self-government in valleys of which the rivers flow to the Pacific," Polk had pledged to extend American law to "the distant regions which they have selected for their homes." A treaty with Britain secured Oregon north to the 49th parallel. But efforts to persuade Mexico to sell California and New Mexico had failed. So Polk decided to use force. Soon after becoming president he ordered the Pacific fleet to stand ready to seize California's ports in the event of war with Mexico. In the fall of 1845 Polk instructed the U.S. consul at Monterey to encourage annexation sentiment among American settlers and disaffected Mexicans.

Americans in California needed little encouragement, especially when they had among them a glory-hunting captain of the army topographical corps, John C. Frémont. Famous for his explorations of the West, Frémont was also the son-in-law of Missouri's powerful Senator Thomas Hart Benton. When rumors of war with Mexico reached the Sacramento valley, Frémont took it upon himself to assist settlers in an uprising that proclaimed an independent California. This "bear flag republic" (its flag bore the image of a grizzly bear) enjoyed a brief existence before its citizens celebrated official news of the war that ensured their annexation by the United States.

While these proceedings unfolded, Missouri volunteers and a regiment of regulars were marching over the Santa Fe Trail to seize the capital of New Mexico. Commanded by Stephen Watts Kearny, these tough dragoons occupied Santa Fe on August 18, 1846, without firing a shot. After raising the American flag, Kearny left behind a garrison and pushed across the desert to California with a hundred

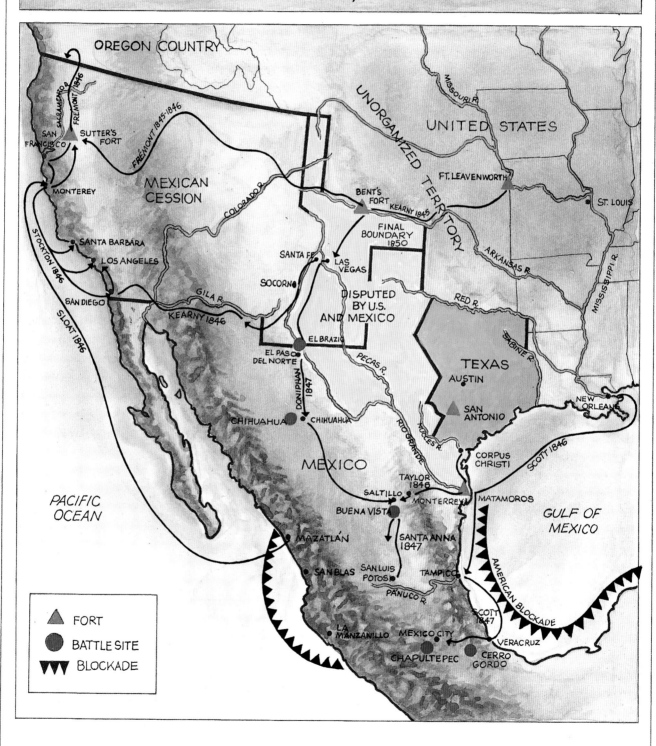

PRINCIPAL CAMPAIGNS OF THE MEXICAN WAR, 1846-1847

men who joined a few hundred sailors, marines, and volunteers to subdue Mexican resistance there by January 1847. During the next several months a string of stunning American victories south of the Rio Grande culminating in the capture of Mexico City ensured the permanence of these American conquests. The only remaining question was how much territory to take.

Polk's appetite was originally sated by New Mexico and California. In April 1847 he sent Nicholas Trist to Mexico as a commissioner to negotiate a treaty for these provinces. But the ease of American conquest made Polk suddenly hungry for more territory. By the fall of 1847 a Democratic movement to annex "all Mexico"—or at least several additional provinces—was in full cry. The whipsaw cuts and rasps of all-Mexico Democrats and no-territory Whigs left Trist on a precarious limb three thousand miles away in Mexico City where the proud Santa Anna proved reluctant to yield up half his country. Polk sided with the hard-liners in Washington and recalled Trist in October 1847. But a breakthrough in negotiations appeared possible just as Trist received the recall dispatch, so he disobeyed orders and signed a treaty that fulfilled Polk's original instructions. In return for a payment by the United States of $15 million plus the assumption of Mexican debts to American citizens, Mexico recognized the Rio Grande boundary of Texas and ceded New Mexico and upper California to the United States. When this Treaty of Guadalupe Hidalgo reached Washington in February 1848, Polk initially spurned it. On second thought, however, he submitted it to the Senate, where the Whigs would have enough votes to defeat any treaty that sliced off more Mexican territory but might approve one that avoided the appearance of conquest by paying Mexico for California and New Mexico. The strategy worked; the Senate ratified the treaty by a vote of 38 to 14, with five of the opposition votes coming from Democrats who wanted more territory and seven from Whigs who wanted none.

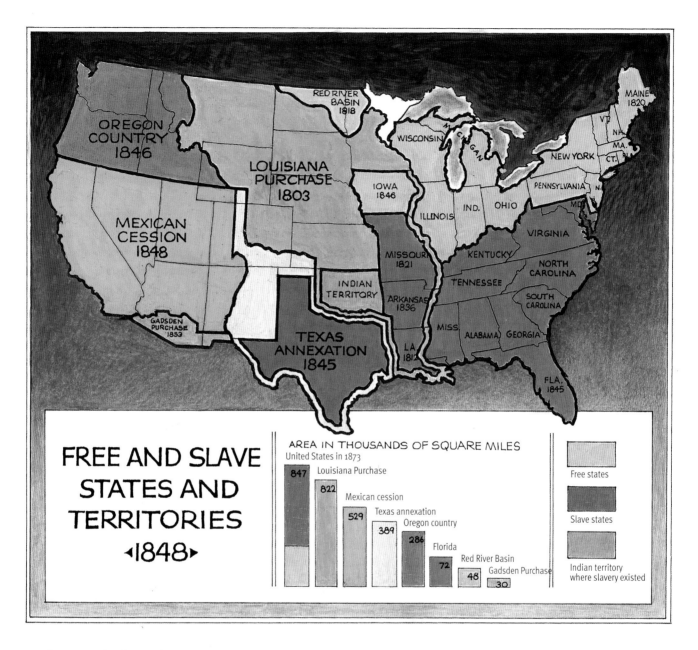

FREE AND SLAVE STATES AND TERRITORIES ◄1848►

AREA IN THOUSANDS OF SQUARE MILES

United States in 1873

- 847 Louisiana Purchase
- 822 Mexican cession
- 529 Texas annexation
- 389 Oregon country
- 286 Florida
- 72 Red River Basin
- 48 Gadsden Purchase
- 30

Free states

Slave states

Indian territory where slavery existed

This triumph of Manifest Destiny may have reminded some Americans of Ralph Waldo Emerson's prophecy that "the United States will conquer Mexico, but it will be as the man swallows the arsenic, which brings him down in turn. Mexico will poison us." He was right. The poison was slavery. Jefferson's Empire for Liberty had become mostly an empire for slavery. Territorial acquisitions since the Revolution had added the slave states of Louisiana, Missouri, Arkansas, Florida, and Texas to the republic, while only Iowa, just admitted in 1846, had increased the ranks of free states. Many northerners feared a similar future for this new southwestern empire. They condemned the war as part of a "slave-power conspiracy" to expand the peculiar institution. Was not President Polk a slaveholder? Had he not been elected on a platform of enlarging slave territory by annexing Texas? Were not proslavery southerners among the most aggressive proponents of Manifest Destiny? Did not most of the territory (including Texas) wrested from Mexico lie south of the old Missouri Compromise line of 36° 30'—a traditional demarcation between freedom and slavery?

Polk could not understand what the fuss was about. "In connection with the Mexican War," he wrote in his diary, slavery was "an abstract question. There is no probability that any territory will ever be acquired from Mexico in which slavery would ever exist." Agitation was thus "not only mischievous but wicked." But a good many congressmen—even some in Polk's own party—did not share the president's conviction. They believed agitation of the question necessary. This issue overshadowed all others from 1846 to 1850. Hundreds of congressmen felt moved to speak on the matter. More than half expressed confidence (if southern) or fear (if northern) that slavery would go into the new territories if allowed to do so. Many of them conceded that the institution was unlikely to put down deep roots in a region presumed to be covered with deserts and mountains. But to make sure, northern congressmen voted for a resolution to exclude slavery therefrom. This was the fateful Wilmot Proviso. As Congress neared adjournment on the sultry Saturday night of August 8, 1846, Pennsylvania's first-term Representative David Wilmot rose during the debate on an appropriations bill for the Mexican War and moved an amendment: "that, as an express and fundamental condition of the acquisition of any territory from the Republic of Mexico . . . neither slavery nor involuntary servitude shall ever exist in any part of said territory."

More lay behind this maneuver than met the eye. Antislavery conviction motivated Wilmot and his allies, but so did a desire to settle old political scores. Wilmot acted for a group of northern Democrats who were vexed with Polk and fed up with southern domination of the party. Their grievances went back to 1844 when southerners had denied New York's Martin Van Buren the presidential nomination because he refused to endorse the annexation of Texas. The administration's compromise on the 49th parallel for the Oregon boundary incensed the many Democrats who had chanted the slogan "Fifty-four forty or fight!" Having voted for the annexation of Texas with its disputed Rio Grande border at risk of war with Mexico, they felt betrayed by Polk's refusal to risk war with Britain for all of Oregon. "Our rights to Oregon have been shamefully compromised," declared an Ohio Democrat. "The administration is Southern, Southern, Southern! . . . Since the South have fixed boundaries for free territory, let the North fix boundaries for slave territories."

When Wilmot introduced his proviso, therefore, he released the pent-up ire of northern Democrats, many of whom cared less about slavery in new territories than about their power within the party. Northern Whigs, who had a more consistent antislavery record, were delighted to support the proviso. This bipartisan northern coalition in the House passed it over the united opposition of southern Democrats and Whigs. This was a dire omen. The normal pattern of division in Congress had occurred along party lines on issues such as the tariff, the Bank, federal aid to internal improvements, and the like. The Wilmot Proviso wrenched this division by parties into a conflict of sections. The political landscape would never again be the same.

"As if by magic," commented the *Boston Whig*, "it brought to a head the great question that is about to divide the American people."

The full impact of the proviso did not become apparent immediately, for Congress adjourned in 1846 before the Senate could vote on it. But northern Democrats reintroduced it at the next session, prompting an anguished lament from the president, who began to comprehend the whirlwind he was reaping as the result of his war. "The slavery question is assuming a fearful . . . aspect," wrote Polk in his diary. It "cannot fail to destroy the Democratic party, if it does not ultimately threaten the Union itself." The House again passed Wilmot's amendment by a sectional vote. But the South's greater power in the Senate (fifteen slave states and fourteen free states composed the Union in 1847) enabled it to block the proviso there. Arm-twisting by the administration eventually compelled enough northern Democrats in the House to change their votes to pass the appropriations bill without the proviso. But the crisis had not been resolved—only postponed.

Free-soil sentiment in 1847 can be visualized in three concentric circles. At the center was a core of abolitionists who considered slavery a sinful violation of human rights that should be immediately expiated. Surrounding and drawing ideological nourishment from them was a larger circle of antislavery people who looked upon bondage as an evil—by which they meant that it was socially repressive, economically backward, and politically harmful to the interests of free states. This circle comprised mainly Whigs (and some Democrats) from the Yankee belt of states and regions north of the 41st parallel who regarded this issue as more important than any other in American politics.

This daguerreotype is the earliest known photograph of Abraham Lincoln. It was made in 1846, about the time Lincoln was elected to Congress. The photographer was probably N. H. Shepherd of Springfield, Illinois.

The outer circle contained all those who had voted for the Wilmot Proviso but did not necessarily consider it the most crucial matter facing the country and were open to compromise. This outer circle included such Whigs as Abraham Lincoln, who believed slavery "an unqualified evil to the negro, the white man, and the State" which "deprives our republican example of its just influence in the world—enables the enemies of free institutions, with plausibility, to taunt us as hypocrites," but who also believed that "the promulgation of abolition doctrines tends rather to increase than to abate its evils" by uniting the South in defense of the institution. The outer circle also included Democrats, like Martin Van Buren, who cared little about the consequences of slavery for the slaves and had been allied with the "slave power" until it had blocked Van Buren's nomination in 1844.

All free soilers—except perhaps some of the Van Burenites—concurred with the following set of propositions: free labor was more efficient than slave labor because it was motivated by the inducement of wages and the ambition for upward mobility rather than by the coercion of the lash; slavery undermined the dignity of manual work by associating it with servility and thereby degraded white labor wherever bondage existed; slavery inhibited education and social improvements and kept poor whites as well as slaves in ignorance; the institution therefore mired all southerners except the slaveowning gentry in poverty and repressed the development of a diversified economy; slavery must be kept out of all new territories so that free labor could flourish there.

This woodcut portrays slavery as southern defenders of the institution wanted others to see it. Well-fed and well-dressed bondspeople enjoy their leisure on Sunday by singing, dancing, and playing. What other working class, this illustration seems to ask, enjoys so much of the good life?

For some members of the two outer circles these propositions did not spring from a "squeamish sensitiveness . . . nor morbid sympathy for the slave," as David Wilmot put it. If slavery goes into the new territories, wrote free-soil editor and poet William Cullen Bryant, "the free labor of all the states will not." But if slavery is kept out, "the free labor of all the states [will go] there . . . and in a few years the country will teem with an active and energetic population."

Southerners bristled at these attacks on their social system. At one time a good many of them, like Thomas Jefferson, had shared the conviction that slavery was an evil—albeit a "necessary" one for the time being because of the explosive racial consequences of emancipation. But the sense of evil had faded by 1830 as the growing world demand for cotton fastened the tentacles of a booming plantation economy on the South. Abolitionist attacks on slavery placed southerners on the defensive and goaded them into angry counterattacks. By 1840 slavery was no longer a necessary evil; it was "a great moral, social, and political blessing—a blessing to the slave, and a blessing to the master." It had civilized African savages and provided them with cradle-to-grave security that contrasted favorably with the miserable poverty of "free" labor in Britain and the North. It created a far superior society to that of the "vulgar, contemptible, counter-jumping" Yankees. Indeed, said Senator Robert M. T. Hunter of Virginia, "there is not a respectable system of civilization known to history whose foundations were not laid in the institution of domestic slavery." "Instead of an evil," said John C. Calhoun in summing up the southern position, slavery was "a positive good . . . the most safe and stable basis for free institutions in the world."

Proponents of slavery naturally wished to offer the blessings of this institution to the new territories. Even those who did not expect bondage to flourish there resented the northern effort to exclude it as an insult to southern honor. The Wilmot Proviso pronounced "a degrading inequality" on the South, declared a Virginian. "No true Southron," said scores of them, would submit to such "social and sectional degradation. . . . Death is preferable to acknowledged inferiority."

In addition to their sacred honor, slaveholders had "the lives and fortunes of ourselves and families" at stake. Enactment of the Wilmot Proviso would yield ten new free states, warned James Hammond of South Carolina. The North would then "ride over us rough shod" in Congress, "proclaim freedom or something equivalent to it to our slaves and reduce us to the condition of Hayti. . . . Our only safety is in *equality* of POWER. If we do not act now, we deliberately consign our children, not our posterity, but our *children* to the flames."

Southerners challenged the constitutionality of the Wilmot Proviso. Admittedly, precedent seemed to sanction congressional exclusion of slavery from territories. The first Congress under the Constitution had reaffirmed the Northwest Ordinance of 1787 banning the institution from the Northwest Territory. Subsequent Congresses reenacted the ordinance for each territory carved out of the region. The Missouri Compromise of 1820 (which allowed Maine to be admitted as a free state and Missouri as a slave state) prohibited slavery north of 36° 30' in the Louisiana Purchase. Southern congressmen had voted for these laws. But in February 1847 South Carolina's Senator John C. Calhoun introduced resolutions denying the right of Congress to exclude slave property from the territories. "Tall, careworn, with fevered brow, haggard cheek and eye, intensely gazing," as Kentucky's Henry Clay described him, Calhoun insisted that territories were the "common property" of sovereign states. Acting as the "joint agents" of these states, Congress could no more prevent a slaveowner from taking his human property to the territories than it could prevent him from taking his horses or hogs there. If the North insisted on ramming through the Wilmot Proviso, warned Calhoun in sepulchral tones, the result would be "political revolution, anarchy, civil war."

The Senate did not pass the Calhoun resolutions. As the presidential election of 1848 neared, both major parties sought to heal the sectional rifts within their ranks. One possible solution, hallowed by tradition, was to extend the Missouri Compromise line through the middle of the new territories to the Pacific. Polk and his cabinet endorsed this policy. Ailing and prematurely aged, the president did not seek renomination. Secretary of State James Buchanan made 36° 30' the centerpiece of his drive for the nomination. Several times in 1847–48 the Senate passed a version of this proposal, with the backing of most southern senators, who yielded the principle of slavery in all the territories for the sake of securing its legality in some. But the northern majority in the House voted it down.

Another idea emerged from the maelstrom of presidential politics. This one came to be known as popular sovereignty. It was identified in 1848 mainly with Michigan's Senator Lewis Cass, Buchanan's main rival for the Democratic presidential nomination. Maintaining that settlers in territories were as capable of self-government as citizens of states, Cass proposed that they should decide for themselves whether to have slavery. This idea had the political charm of ambiguity, for Cass did not specify *when* voters might choose for or against slavery—during the territorial stage or only when adopting a state constitution. Most contemporaries presumed the former—including Calhoun, who therefore opposed popular sovereignty because it could violate the property rights of southern settlers. But enough southerners saw merit in the approach to enable Cass to win the nomination—though significantly the platform did

This Whig cartoon satirizes the Democratic presidential candidate, sixty-six-year-old Lewis Cass, who had been a general in the War of 1812. Flourishing a sword labeled "Manifest Destiny," holding a spear, and riding a cannon carriage, Cass and his party would provoke another war with their appetite for Cuba and for more Mexican territory—or so the Whigs wanted voters to believe.

Although many Whigs had opposed the Mexican War, they knew where their political bread was buttered, and were eager to latch on to a war hero as their presidential candidate. The antislavery, anti-war Conscience Whigs could not stomach Taylor's candidacy, and bolted the party to help found the Free Soil party in 1848.

not endorse popular sovereignty. It did reject the Wilmot Proviso and the Calhoun resolutions, however. The Democratic party continued the tradition of trying to preserve intersectional unity by avoiding a firm position on slavery.

So did the Whigs. Indeed they adopted no platform at all and nominated the hero of a war that most of them had opposed. Nothing illustrated better the strange-bedfellow nature of American politics than Zachary Taylor's candidacy. A thickset man with stubby legs and heavy brows contracted into a perpetual frown, careless in dress, a career army officer (but not a West Pointer) with no discernible political opinions, Taylor seemed unlikely presidential timber. The handsome, imposing General in Chief Winfield Scott, a dedicated professional with a fondness for dress uniforms, and an articulate Whig, looked like a better choice if the antiwar party felt compelled to mend its image by nominating a military candidate. But Scott had the defects of his virtues. His critics considered him pompous. He had a penchant for writing foot-in-mouth public letters which made him vulnerable to ridicule. His nickname—Old Fuss and Feathers—conveys the nature of his political liabilities. And Taylor had the virtues of his defects, as the image conveyed by *his* sobriquet of Rough and Ready illustrates. Many voters in this new age of (white) manhood suffrage seemed to prefer their candidates rough-hewn. As a war hero Taylor claimed first priority on public affection. Although Scott had planned and led the campaign of 1847 that captured Mexico City, Taylor's victories of 1846 along the Rio Grande and his extraordinary triumph against odds of three to one at Buena Vista in February 1847 had made his reputation before Scott got started.

Buena Vista launched a Taylor bandwagon that proved unstoppable. Rough and Ready's main rival for the nomination (besides Scott) was Henry Clay. Urbane, witty, popular, the seventy-year-old Clay was Mr. Whig—a founder of the party and architect of its "American System" to promote economic growth by a protective tariff, a national bank, and federal aid to internal improvements. As a three-time loser in presidential contests, however, Clay carried the liabilities as well as assets of a long political career. Like a majority of his party he had opposed the annexation of Texas and the Mexican War. But the Whigs could not hope to win the election without carrying some states where annexation and the war had been popular. Taylor seemed to be the answer.

The general was also a godsend to southern Whigs, who faced an erosion of strength at home because of the persistent support by northern Whigs for the Wilmot Proviso. (Most northern Democrats had abandoned Wilmot's proviso for Cass's formula of popular sovereignty.) Southern Whig leaders, especially Senator John J. Crittenden of Kentucky and Congressman Alexander Stephens of Georgia, maneuvered the Taylor boom into a southern movement. Taylor's ownership of Louisiana and Mississippi plantations with more than a hundred slaves seemed to assure his safety on the issue of most importance to southerners. "The truth is," declared Robert Toombs of Georgia, Clay "has sold himself body and soul to the Northern Anti-Slavery Whigs." Southern delegates to the Whig convention provided the votes to deny Clay the nomination on the first ballot and then to award it to Taylor on the fourth.

Taylor's candidacy brought to a head a long-festering schism in northern Whiggery. "Of course, we cannot & will not under any circumstances support General Taylor," wrote Charles Sumner of Massachusetts. "We cannot support any body who is not known to be against the extension of Slavery." Sumner spoke for a faction of the party known as "Conscience Whigs." They challenged a more conservative group labeled "Cotton Whigs" because of the prominence of textile magnates in their ranks. The Cotton faction had opposed the Mexican War and favored the Wilmot Proviso. But their position on these issues seemed lukewarm, and in 1848 they wished to join hands with southern Whigs in behalf of Taylor and victory. Unable to sanction this alliance of "lords of the loom" with "lords of the lash," Conscience Whigs bolted the party. Their purpose, in Sumner's words, was no less than "a new crystallization of parties, in which there shall be one grand Northern party of Freedom."

The time appeared ripe for such a movement. In New York the Van Buren faction of Democrats was ready for revolt. Dubbed "Barnburners" (after the legendary Dutch farmer who burned his barn to rid it of rats), this faction sent a separate delegation to the national Democratic convention. When the convention voted to seat both New York delegations, the Barnburners stomped out and held their own conclave to nominate Van Buren on a Wilmot Proviso platform. Antislavery Democrats and Whigs from other northern states cheered. The Barnburner convention provided the spark for an antislavery political blaze; the Liberty party offered itself as kindling.

A humorous Free Soil cartoon showing Martin Van Buren and his son John as "Barnburner" Democrats setting fire to Lewis Cass's regular Democratic barn (Cass is on the roof ready to jump) in order to rid it of its proslavery rats, shown leaping from the burning structure.

Founded in 1839 by simon-pure abolitionists, the Liberty party had managed to win only 3 percent of the northern votes for its first presidential candidate, in 1844. Since that election, party leaders had been debating future strategy. A radical faction wanted to proclaim a new doctrine that the Constitution empowered the government to abolish slavery *in the states*. But a more pragmatic majority under the leadership of Salmon P. Chase wanted to move in the other direction—toward a coalition with antislavery Whigs and Democrats. An astute lawyer who had defended fugitive slaves, Chase combined religious conviction and humorlessness with unquenchable ambition and shrewd political insight. Although Liberty men must continue to proclaim the goal of ending slavery everywhere, said Chase, they could best take the first step toward that goal by joining with those who believed in keeping it out of the territories—whatever else they believed. If such a coalition gained enough leverage in Ohio to elect Chase to the U.S. Senate, so much the better. Chase put out feelers to Conscience Whigs and Barnburner Democrats in the spring of 1848. These ripened into a Free Soil convention in August, after the major-party nominations of Cass and Taylor had propelled antislavery men out of their old allegiances.

The Free Soil convention at Buffalo resembled nothing so much as a camp meeting. Fifteen thousand fervent "delegates" thronged into the sweltering city while an executive committee of 465 met in a church to do the real work. This committee accomplished something of a miracle by fusing factions from three parties that held clashing opinions and created its new fusion party by nominating a Barnburner for president and a Conscience Whig for vice president on a Liberty platform drafted mainly by Chase. The "mass convention" in the park roared its approval of the committee's work.

Van Buren, formerly a proslavery Jacksonian, endorsed exclusion of slavery from the territories and abolition of slavery in the District of Columbia. His Barnburner backers proclaimed bondage "a great moral, social, and political evil—a relic of barbarism which must necessarily be swept away in the progress of Christian civilization." Speaking to fellow Whigs, Sumner said that "it is not for the Van Buren of 1838 that we are to vote, but the Van Buren of *to-day*." With Charles Francis Adams as vice-presidential nominee, the ticket strengthened its Conscience image. Charles Francis inherited the antislavery mantle from his father, John Quincy, who had died earlier in the year.

Free Soilers made slavery the campaign's central issue. Both major parties had to abandon their strategy of ignoring the question. Instead, they tried to win support in each section by obfuscating it. Democrats circulated different campaign biographies of Cass in North and South. In the North they emphasized popular sovereignty as the best way to keep slavery out of the territories. In the South Democrats cited Cass's pledge to veto the Wilmot Proviso and pointed with pride to the party's success (over Whig opposition) in acquiring territory into which slavery *might* expand.

Having no platform to explain and a candidate with no political record to defend, Whigs had an easier time appearing to be all things to all men. In the North they pointed to Taylor's pledge *not* to veto whatever Congress decided to do about slavery in the territories. Those antislavery Whigs who supported Taylor in the belief

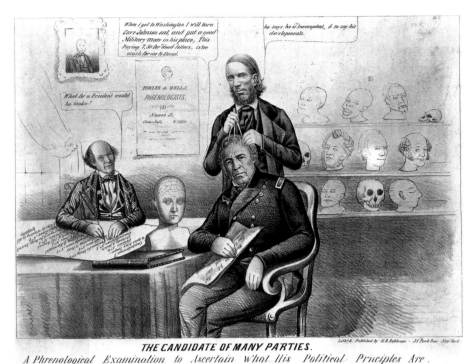

THE CANDIDATE OF MANY PARTIES.

A Phrenological Examination to Ascertain What His Political Principles Are.

This Democratic cartoon ridiculing Taylor's supposed lack of political convictions and knowledge was typical of the complicated caricatures of that era. A well-known "phrenologist" examines Taylor's head to determine his political principles as Whig editor Horace Greeley looks on. Phrenology was a pseudoscience of the day that purported to determine human characteristics from the shape of the skull. The phrenologist finds Taylor to be "incompetent," "obstinate and mulish," and "combative."

that he would take their side—William H. Seward and Abraham Lincoln, for example—turned out to be right. Southerners should have paid more attention to a speech by Seward at Cleveland. Affable, artful, sagacious, an instinctive politician but also a principled opponent of slavery, Seward would soon emerge as one of Taylor's main advisers. "Freedom and slavery are two antagonistic elements of society," he told a Cleveland audience. "Slavery can be limited to its present bounds"; eventually "it *can* and *must* be abolished."

But in the South, Taylor's repute as the hero of Buena Vista and his status as a large slaveholder dazzled many eyes. Taylor carried eight of the fifteen slave states with a majority of 52 percent. He also carried seven of fifteen free states, though the Whig popular vote in the North dropped to 46 percent because of Free Soil inroads. But while they won 14 percent of the northern vote and supplanted Democrats as the second party in Vermont, Massachusetts, and New York, the Free Soilers did not carry a single state. Despite stresses produced by the slavery issue, the centripetal forces of party overcame the centrifugal forces of section. Nevertheless, those stresses had wrenched the system almost to the breaking point.

II

Almost unnoticed in the East during the presidential campaign, another dramatic event of 1848 presaged further strains on the two-party system. Workers constructing a sawmill for John Sutter near Sacramento in January discovered flecks of gold in the river bed. Despite Sutter's attempt to keep the news quiet, word spread to San Francisco. Gold fever turned the port into a ghost town by June as the population headed for the Sierra foothills. In August the news reached the Atlantic coast,

In the first year or two of the California gold rush, many prospectors worked alone, panning for gold in the streams with the primitive technique of separating the gravel from heavier gold dust by shaking a pan. By the early 1850s, when this picture was painted, groups of miners worked cooperatively to wash the gravel by sluicing it through these "long Tom" troughs.

where it encountered skepticism from a public surfeited with fabulous tales from the West. But in December the whole country took notice when Polk's last annual message to Congress included a reference to the "extraordinary" finds in California. As if on cue, a special agent from the gold fields arrived in Washington two days later with a tea caddy containing 320 ounces of pure gold. Doubt disappeared; everyone became a true believer; many dreamed of striking it rich; and a hundred thousand of them headed west. The trickle of migrants to California during the previous decade became a flood in the great gold rush of '49. By the census year of 1850 California had a larger population than Delaware or Florida. The territory's quest to become the thirty-first state sparked a renewed sectional crisis back east.

California needed a territorial government. So did New Mexico with its substantial Hispanic and Indian population and its growing Mormon settlement next to the Great Salt Lake. In December 1848 President Polk urged the lame-duck Congress to create territorial governments for California and New Mexico. To resolve the vexing slavery question, Polk recommended extension of the 36° 30' line to the Pacific.

But Congress, during the short session that expired on March 4, 1849, did little

compromise Whigs endured the slings and arrows of both sides. The hostility of Taylor toward Clay and Webster became especially caustic.

Into this volatile atmosphere came a new crisis in late June. A handful of civilians and soldiers had convened a convention in Santa Fe to write a free-state constitution. It was ratified by an electorate casting fewer than eight thousand votes. Taylor urged the admission of New Mexico along with that of California, thereby doubling the insult to southern honor. Meanwhile the governor of Texas threatened to uphold with force his state's claim to Santa Fe and all the rest of New Mexico east of the Rio Grande. A clash between Texans and the U.S. army seemed imminent. As July 4 approached, southerners bristled with threats to fight for Texas. Taylor did not flinch. After preparing orders for the Santa Fe garrison to stand firm, he spent a hot Fourth of July listening to speeches at the unfinished Washington Monument, assuaging his hunger and thirst with large quantities of raw vegetables, cherries, and iced milk. The president fell ill next day and died on July 9 of acute gastroenteritis.

Whether for weal or woe, Taylor's death marked a turning point in the crisis. The new president, Millard Fillmore, was a New York Whig hostile to the Seward faction in his own state. Sympathetic to the Compromise, this northern president tilted almost as far South as the southern President Taylor had tilted North. Fillmore shelved New Mexico's application for statehood and gave his support to the omnibus. Nevertheless, the Senate spent a month passing a bewildering series of amendments and rescindments of amendments before sending Clay's measure down to defeat on July 31. Exhausted and disillusioned, the once-redoubtable Kentuckian left Washington to recuperate at Newport. His younger colleagues remained in the cauldron on Capitol Hill to pick up the pieces.

And it was by pieces that the Compromise finally passed. Representing the new generation, Stephen A. Douglas came on stage to star in the third act. A man whose capacity for liquor was exceeded only by his capacity for work (the combination would kill him eleven years later at the age of forty-eight), Douglas earned the sobriquet Little Giant for his great political prowess contained in a frame five feet four inches tall. Never a believer in the omnibus strategy, Douglas stripped the vehicle down to its component parts and put together a majority for each of those parts. Northerners of both parties and border-state Whigs supplied the votes for admission of California, prohibition of the slave trade in the

A man of great ambition and energy, Stephen A. Douglas was described as a "steam engine in britches." At the age of twenty-seven he had become a judge on the Illinois Supreme Court; he was elected to the U.S. House of Representatives two years later, in 1843, and in 1846, at the age of thirty-three, to the Senate. His leadership in forging a coalition to pass the separate parts of the Compromsie of 1850 represented not only the emergence of a new political generation but also the rise to political maturity of the Midwest (then called the Old Northwest).

These songs, composed to celebrate the Compromise of 1850, demonstrate how widespread was the belief that the fate of the Union had been at stake in the crisis resolved by the Compromise. The composer of "The National Union" dedicated the song to Henry Clay. The unbroken chain circling the Capitol, each link a state, represents the indissoluble Union. In the cover illustration for "The Flag of Our Union" two female figures, North and South, stand together holding the flag symbolizing an unbroken Union.

District, and payment of $10 million to Texas (quickly accepted) to settle the border dispute with New Mexico. Many northern Democrats joined southerners of both parties to enact a stronger fugitive slave law and organize Utah and New Mexico as territories without restrictions on slavery. Fillmore helped the cause by persuading enough northern Whigs to abstain from the votes on the fugitive slave and territorial bills to allow their passage. On all these measures the divisions occurred mainly along sectional rather than party lines, another sign that the existing two-party system was crumbling under the weight of slavery.

Nevertheless, Douglas's achievement seemed to have broken the deadlock that had paralyzed government and threatened the republic since 1846. It lanced the boil of tension that had festered in Congress during one of its longest and most contentious sessions in history. Most of the country gave a sigh of relief. President Fillmore christened the Compromise "a final settlement" of all sectional problems, and this phrase soon became the hallmark of political orthodoxy. Only Calhounites and Free Soilers challenged its finality.

But these curmudgeons of the right and left were temporarily isolated. When the Nashville Convention met again in November only half of the delegates—from seven states—showed up. Even these true believers seemed to recognize the futility of their proceedings. They passed resolutions denouncing the Compromise and affirming the right of secession but finally agreed only to meet again at some unspecified time and place. South Carolina fire-eaters, disgusted at this timidity, determined that next time they would act alone in the expectation that other states would follow.

Free soilers also condemned "the consummation of the iniquities of this most disgraceful session of Congress"—as Charles Francis Adams expressed it. Salmon P. Chase believed that "the question of slavery in the territories has been avoided. It has not been settled." He was right. In its final form the legislation organizing Utah and New Mexico specified that when admitted as states "they shall be received into the Union, with or without slavery, as their constitution may prescribe at the time of their admission." This said nothing about slavery *during the territorial stage*. The omission was deliberate. Congress passed the buck by expediting the appeal of territorial laws to the Supreme Court. As it happened, no slavery case came up from these territories. Several slaveholders carried their property to Utah, where Governor Brigham Young and his legislature obliged them by legalizing the institution in 1852 (the same year that the Saints openly endorsed polygamy). New Mexico also enacted a slave code in 1859. But neither territory was likely to strengthen the South in Congress. The census of 1860 counted twenty-nine slaves in Utah and none in New Mexico; in any event, statehood for either was distant. California furnished an irony that may have settled Calhoun more comfortably in his grave. Court decisions in that state permitted the "sojourn" (sometimes for several years) of slaveowners with their property. For a time in the 1850s California probably had more slaves than Utah and New Mexico combined. And this new free state did not tip the Senate balance against the South, for its senators were Democrats of a decidedly doughface cast, sympathetic to Southern principles.

Although one of the least-debated parts of the Compromise, the fugitive slave law turned out to be the most divisive legacy of the "final settlement"—because the Fillmore administration rigorously enforced it.

CHAPTER THREE

★ ★ ★ ★ ★

An Empire for Slavery

I

On all issues but one, antebellum southerners stood for state's rights and a weak federal government. The exception was the fugitive slave law of 1850, which gave the national government more power than any other law yet passed by Congress. This irony resulted from the Supreme Court's decision in *Prigg v. Pennsylvania* (1842).

In the typical oblique language of the Constitution on slavery, Article IV, Section 2, stipulated that any "person held to service or labor in one state" who escaped to another "shall be delivered up on claim of the party to whom such service or labor shall be due." The Constitution did not specify how this provision should be enforced. A federal law of 1793 authorized slaveowners to cross state lines to recapture their property and bring it before any local magistrate or federal court to prove ownership. This law provided the fugitive with no protection of habeas corpus, no right to a jury trial, no right to testify in his own behalf. Some northerners believed that the law amounted to an invitation for kidnappers to seize free blacks. And indeed, professional slave catchers did not always take pains to make sure they had captured the right man, nor did every judge go out of his way to ensure that a supposed fugitive matched the description on the affidavit. A good many slave catchers did not bother to take their captured prey before a court but simply spirited it south by the quickest route.

To remedy such abuses, several northern states enacted personal liberty laws. These measures variously gave fugitives the rights of testimony, habeas corpus, and trial by jury, or they imposed criminal penalties for kidnapping. In the hands of antislavery officials, some of these laws could be used to inhibit the capture of fugitives. In 1837 Pennsylvania convicted Edward Prigg of kidnapping after he had seized a slave woman and her children and returned them to their Maryland owner. Prigg's lawyers appealed the case to the U.S. Supreme Court, which in 1842 rendered a complex decision. Declaring the Pennsylvania antikidnapping law of 1826 unconstitutional, the Court upheld the fugitive slave law of 1793 and affirmed that a

Opposite page: The famous landscape artist Thomas Moran painted this dramatic picture of slaves escaping through a swamp with bloodhounds almost literally at their heels.

After the Civil War many northern whites professed to have been active in the underground railroad, that shadowy and romanticized network of "stations" that hid escaped slaves and helped them on their way to freedom. One genuine "conductor" on this railroad, the Quaker merchant Levi Coffin, is shown in this painting standing in the wagon and wearing a broad-brimmed hat. Coffin's homes in central Indiana (depicted here) and, after 1847, in Cincinnati were havens for fugitives seeking freedom. Coffin and his wife Catherine reportedly helped a hundred slaves a year on their way north.

slaveholder's right to his property overrode any contrary state legislation. At the same time, however, the Court ruled that enforcement of the fugitive slave clause of the Constitution was a federal responsibility and that states need not cooperate in any way. This opened the floodgates for a new series of personal liberty laws (nine between 1842 and 1850) that prohibited the use of state facilities in the recapture of fugitives.

In some areas of the North, owners could not reclaim their escaped property without the help of federal marshals. Black leaders and sympathetic whites in numerous communities formed vigilance committees to organize resistance to such efforts. These committees cooperated with the legendary underground railroad that carried fugitives north toward freedom. Magnified by southerners into an enormous Yankee network of lawbreakers who stole thousands of slaves each year, the underground railroad was also mythologized by its northern conductors who related their heroic deeds to grandchildren. The true number of runaway slaves is impossible to determine. Perhaps several hundred each year made it to the North or to Canada. Few of these fugitives had escaped from the lower South, the region that clamored loudest for a stronger fugitive slave law—less for practical advantage than as a matter of principle. Like a free California, northern aid to escaping slaves was an insult to southern honor. "Although the loss of property is felt," said Senator James Mason of Virginia, "the loss of honor is felt still more." The fugitive slave law, commented another politician, was "the only measure of the Compromise [of 1850] calculated to secure the rights of the South."

To secure these rights the law seemed to ride roughshod over the prerogatives of northern states. Yankee senators had tried in vain to attach amendments to the bill guaranteeing alleged fugitives the rights to testify, to habeas corpus, and to a jury trial. Southerners indignantly rejected the idea that these American birthrights

$200 Reward.

RANAWAY from the subscriber, on the night of Thursday, the 30th of Sepember,

FIVE NEGRO SLAVES,

To-wit: one Negro man, his wife, and three children.

The man is a black negro, full height, very erect, his face a little thin. He is about forty years of age, and calls himself *Washington Reed*, and is known by the name of Washington. He is probably well dressed, possibly takes with him an ivory headed cane, and is of good address. Several of his teeth are gone.

Mary, his wife, is about thirty years of age, a bright mulatto woman, and quite stout and strong.

The oldest of the children is a boy, of the name of FIELDING, twelve years of age, a dark mulatto, with heavy eyelids. He probably wore a new cloth cap.

MATILDA, the second child, is a girl, six years of age, rather a dark mulatto, but a bright and smart looking child.

MALCOLM, the youngest, is a boy, four years old, a lighter mulatto than the last, and about equally as bright. He probably also wore a cloth cap. If examined, he will be found to have a swelling at the navel. Washington and Mary have lived at or near St. Louis, with the subscriber, for about 13 years.

It is supposed that they are making their way to Chicago, and that a white man accompanies them, that they will travel chiefly at night, and most probably in a covered wagon.

A reward of $150 will be paid for their apprehension, so that I can get them, if taken within one hundred miles of St. Louis, and $200 if taken beyond that, and secured so that I can get them, and other reasonable additional charges, if delivered to the subscriber, or to THOMAS ALLEN, Esq., at St. Louis. Mo. The above negroes, for the last few years, have been in possession of Thomas Allen, Esq., of St. Louis.

WM. RUSSELL.

ST. LOUIS, Oct. 1, 1847.

A typical advertisement offering a reward for apprehension of fugitive slaves. Note the assumption that the underground railroad aided the escape of these slaves: "a white man accompanies them . . . travel chiefly at night . . . in a covered wagon." There were undoubtedly many people in Illinois ready to earn the $200 reward; whether anyone did so is unknown.

applied to slaves. The fugitive slave law of 1850 put the burden of proof on captured blacks but gave them no legal power to prove their freedom. Instead, a claimant could bring an alleged fugitive before a federal commissioner (a new office created by the law) to prove ownership by an affidavit from a slave-state court or by the testimony of white witnesses. If the commissioner decided against the claimant he would receive a fee of five dollars; if in favor, ten dollars. This provision, supposedly justified by the paperwork needed to remand a fugitive to the South, became notorious among abolitionists as a bribe to commissioners. The 1850 law also required U.S. marshals and deputies to help slaveowners capture their property and fined them $1,000 if they refused. It empowered marshals to deputize citizens on the spot to aid in seizing a fugitive, and imposed stiff criminal penalties on anyone who harbored a fugitive or obstructed his capture. The expenses of capturing and returning a slave were to be borne by the federal treasury.

The operation of this law confirmed the impression that it was rigged in favor of claimants. In the first fifteen months after its passage, eighty-four fugitives were returned to slavery and only five released. During the full decade of the 1850s, 332 were returned and only eleven declared free. Nor did the law contain a statute of limitations. Some of the first fugitives returned to slavery had been longtime residents of the North. In September 1850 federal marshals arrested a black porter who had lived in New York City for three years and took him before a commissioner who refused to record the man's insistence that his mother was a free Negro and remanded him to his claimant owner in Baltimore. Several months later slave catchers seized a prosperous black tailor who had resided in Poughkeepsie for many years and carried him back to South Carolina. In February 1851 agents arrested a black man in southern Indiana, while his horrified wife and children looked on, and returned him to an owner who claimed him as a slave who had run away nineteen years earlier. A Maryland man asserted ownership of a Philadelphia woman who he said had run away twenty-two years previously. For good measure he also claimed her six children born in Philadelphia. In this case the commissioner found for the woman's freedom. And in the cases of the Poughkeepsie

This antislavery lithograph from 1850 shows the anticipated tragic consequences of the fugitive slave law. A white posse has chased down four black men. Their dress indicates that the artist intended them to be free blacks out for a stroll; the posse, intent on kidnapping them, shoots them down when they fail to stop. The fugitive slave law did in fact provide cover for an increase in the kidnapping of free blacks for sale into slavery.

Holy Bible

Effects of the Fugitive-Slave-Law.

Declaration of independence

This photograph of five elderly blacks was taken in Ontario in 1850. Fearing recapture or kidnapping if they remained in the northern United States, thousands of blacks headed for Canada after passage of the Fugitive Slave Act. These five people are unidentified, so we do not know whether they were escaped slaves or free African-Americans. In either case they were taking no chances.

tailor and the New York porter, black and white friends raised money to buy their freedom. But most fugitives who were carried south stayed there.

Antislavery lawyers challenged the fugitive slave law, but in 1859 the U.S. Supreme Court upheld it. Long before this, however, blacks and their white allies had done everything they could to nullify the law by flight and resistance. The quick seizures of blacks who had long lived in the North sent a wave of panic through northern Negro communities. Many black people fled to Canada—an estimated three thousand in the last three months of 1850 alone. During the 1850s the Negro population of Ontario doubled to eleven thousand.

Boston remained the cockpit for the struggle against the fugitive slave law. A young couple, William and Ellen Craft, had escaped from Georgia and were much celebrated by abolitionists. As soon as the law was passed their owner sent two agents to recapture them. The Crafts had joined the church of Theodore Parker, head of a local vigilance committee. Under the "higher law" doctrine, blacks and whites in Boston had vowed to resist the fugitive slave law. "We must trample this law under our feet," said the abolitionist orator Wendell Phillips. It "is to be denounced, resisted, disobeyed," declared the local antislavery society. "As moral and religious men, [we] cannot obey an immoral and irreligious statute." When the slave catchers arrived in Boston on October 25, 1850, Parker and others hid the Crafts and, through active resistance, forced the would-be captors to leave Boston.

The vigilance committee, responding to President Fillmore's pledge to send in federal troops and do whatever was necessary to recapture the Crafts, put them on a ship bound for England. Parker sent a defiant missive to Fillmore by way of a parting shot. "I would rather lie all my life in jail, and starve there, than refuse to protect one of these parishioners of mine," the pastor told the president. "I must reverence the laws of God, come of that what will come. . . . You cannot think that I am to stand by and see my own church carried off to slavery and do nothing."

In February 1851 Bostonians again defied Washington's authority, snatching a fugitive slave from Virginia, a waiter named Shadrach, from the custody of federal marshals and sending him via the underground railroad to Canada, where he opened a restaurant. Daniel Webster denounced it as an act of treason, Henry Clay demanded an investigation to find out "whether we shall have a government of white men or black men in the cities of this country," and Fillmore saw to it that those responsible were indicted. But a Boston jury refused to convict them. While abolitionists cheered, a Savannah newspaper editor expressed a more common opinion—perhaps in the North as well as in the South—when he denounced Boston as "a black speck on the map—disgraced by the lowest, the meanest, the *blackest* kind of *nullification.*"

Also in February 1851, another slave escaped to Boston, where he too found work as a waiter. This time the mayor of Boston allowed policemen to be deputized as marshals, and Thomas Sims was apprehended in April. All legal maneuvers by

CAUTION!!

COLORED PEOPLE

OF BOSTON, ONE & ALL,

You are hereby respectfully CAUTIONED and advised, to avoid conversing with the

Watchmen and Police Officers of Boston,

For since the recent **ORDER OF THE MAYOR & ALDERMEN,** they are empowered to act as

KIDNAPPERS

AND

Slave Catchers,

And they have already been actually employed in **KIDNAPPING, CATCHING, AND KEEPING SLAVES.** Therefore, if you value your LIBERTY, and the *Welfare of the Fugitives* among you, *Shun* them in every possible manner, as so many *HOUNDS* on the track of the most unfortunate of your race.

Keep a Sharp Look Out for KIDNAPPERS, and have TOP EYE open.

APRIL 24, 1851.

THOMAS SIMS, THE SLAVE.

vigilance committee members were in vain; 250 U.S soldiers stood guard as Sims was put on a ship and sent back to slavery.

Boston's mercantile elite had upheld law and order—and vulnerable blacks fled the city. The scene of resistance shifted elsewhere for a time. So far this resistance had produced no casualties except a few cuts and bruises. Most abolitionists had traditionally counseled nonviolence. Some of them, like William Lloyd Garrison, were pacifists. But the fugitive slave law eroded the commitment to nonviolence. "The only way to make the Fugitive Slave Law a dead letter," said black leader Frederick Douglass in October 1850, "is to make half a dozen or more dead kidnappers." In Springfield, Massachusetts, a white wool merchant named John Brown with the glint of a Biblical warrior in his eye organized a black self-defense group which he named the Gileadites.

Then, in a Pennsylvania village near the Maryland border that welcomed fugitive slaves, a slave owner and three deputy marshals, despite the warnings of two Quaker townsmen, engaged in a shootout with armed black men protecting two of the Maryland owner's slaves. When it was over the owner was dead, his son seriously wounded, and the black men vanished into the countryside, while their three leaders went to Canada via the underground railroad.

The "Battle of Christiana" became a national event. "Civil War—The First Blow Struck," proclaimed a Lancaster, Pennsylvania, newspaper. The *New York Tribune* pronounced the verdict of many Yankees: "But for slavery such things would not be; but for the Fugitive Slave Law they would not be in the free States." Southerners announced that "unless the Christiana rioters are hung . . . *we leave you!* . . . If you fail in this simple act of justice, *the bonds will be dissolved.*"

This time Fillmore called out the marines. Together with federal marshals they

Boston was a hotbed of resistance to the recapture of fugitive slaves. After several instances of attempted seizures, the vigilance committee posted broadsides like this one (left) all over the city. This woodcut illustration (right) of Thomas Sims appeared in a magazine after Sims's rendition to slavery. His owner sold him at auction. Sims eventually wound up in Mississippi, where he escaped to Union lines during the Vicksburg campaign in 1863. General Grant gave him a pass to return to Boston, where he arrived in time to watch the presentation of colors to the 54th Massachusetts Infantry, the first black regiment recruited in the North. After the war, Sims became a clerk and messenger in the office of the U.S. attorney general, the agency that had remanded him to slavery in 1851.

scoured the countryside and arrested more than thirty black men and a half-dozen whites. The government sought extradition of the three fugitives who had escaped to Ontario, but Canadian officials refused. To show that it meant business, the administration prosecuted alleged participants not merely for resisting the fugitive slave law but for treason. A federal grand jury so indicted thirty-six blacks and five whites. In another victory for abolitionism, after a local jury acquitted the first defendant, one of the Quakers, the government dropped the remaining indictments and decided not to press other charges.

In Syracuse, New York, William McHenry, a cooper who had escaped from Missouri, was plucked from his owner's agents by a large group of blacks and whites who broke McHenry out of jail and got him safely to Canada along with some of the black participants. The plan had been hatched by two of the North's most prominent abolitionists, Gerrit Smith and Samuel J. May, a Unitarian clergyman, who told his congregation that God's law took precedence over the fugitive slave law, which "we must trample . . . under foot, be the consequences what they may." Ultimately only one person was convicted—of riot, not treason—and he died before he could appeal the verdict.

Northern resistance to the fugitive slave law fed the resentment of fire-eaters still seething over the admission of California. But already a reaction was setting in. The highest cotton prices in a decade and the largest cotton crop ever caused many a planter to think twice about secession. Whig unionism reasserted itself under the leadership of Toombs and Stephens. Old party lines temporarily dissolved as a minority of Democrats in Georgia, Alabama, and Mississippi joined Whigs to form Constitutional Union parties to confront Southern Rights Democrats. Unionists won a majority of delegates to the state conventions, where they advocated "cooperation" with other states rather than secession by individual states. As the Nashville Convention had demonstrated, cooperation was another word for inaction. Unionists won the governorships of Georgia and Mississippi (where Jefferson Davis ran as the Southern Rights candidate) and the legislatures of Georgia and Alabama, and elected fourteen of the nineteen congressmen from these three states. Even in South Carolina the separatists suffered a setback. This denouement of two years of disunion rhetoric confirmed the belief of many northerners that secession threats had been mere "gasconade" to frighten the government into making concessions.

But a closer analysis would have qualified this conclusion. In several states unionists adopted the "Georgia Platform," which declared that while the South did "not wholly approve" of the Compromise of 1850 she would "abide by it as a permanent adjustment of this sectional controversy"—so long as the North similarly abided. *But*—any action by Congress against slavery in the District of Columbia, or any refusal to admit a new slave state or to recognize slavery in the new territories, would cause Georgia (and other states) to resist, with secession "as a last resort." Above all, "upon a faithful execution of the *Fugitive Slave Law* . . . depends the preservation of our much beloved Union."

Southern unionism, in other words, was a perishable commodity. It would last only so long as the North remained on good behavior. With Fillmore in the White House, the situation seemed stabilized for the time being. But northern Whigs were restless. Most of them were having a hard time swallowing the fugitive slave law. The party was sending a growing number of radical antislavery men to Congress: Thaddeus Stevens of Pennsylvania and George W. Julian of Indiana entered the House in 1849; Benjamin Wade of Ohio came to the Senate in 1851. If such men as these gained control of the party it would splinter along North-South lines. Southern Whigs had barely survived Taylor's apostasy; another such shock would shatter them.

The situation appeared to ease somewhat; fewer than one-third as many blacks were returned from the North to slavery in 1852 as in the first year of the law's operation. Democrats, conservative Whigs, mercantile associations, and other forces of moderation organized public meetings throughout the North to affirm support of the Compromise including the fugitive slave law.

These same forces, aided by the Negrophobia that characterized much of the northern population, went further than this. In 1851 Indiana and Iowa and in 1853 Illinois enacted legislation barring the immigration of any black persons, free or slave. Three-fifths of the nation's border between free and slave states ran along the southern boundaries of these states. Intended in part to reassure the South by denying sanctuary to fugitive slaves, the exclusion laws also reflected the racist sentiments of many whites, especially Butternuts. Although Ohio had repealed its Negro exclusion law in 1849, many residents of the southern tier of Ohio counties wanted no part of black people and were more likely to aid the slave catcher than the fugitive.

Nevertheless, resentment of the fugitive slave law continued to simmer among many Yankees. It was intensified by the publication of an extraordinary book. Its author, Harriet Beecher Stowe, daughter, sister, and wife of Congregational clergymen, had breathed the doctrinal air of sin, guilt, atonement, and salvation since childhood. She could clothe these themes in prose that throbbed with pathos as well as bathos. After running serially in an antislavery newspaper for nine months, *Uncle Tom's Cabin* came out as a book in the spring of 1852. Within a year it sold three hundred thousand copies in the United States alone—comparable to at least three million today. The novel enjoyed equal popularity in Britain and was translated into several foreign languages. Within a decade it had sold more than two million copies in the United States, making it the best seller of all time in proportion to population.

Although Stowe said that God inspired the book, the fugitive slave law served as His mundane instrument. "Hattie, if I could use a pen as you can, I would write something that will make this whole nation feel what an accursed thing slavery is," said her sister-in-law after Congress passed the law. "I will if I live," vowed Harriet. And she did, writing by candlelight in the kitchen after putting her six children to bed and finishing the household chores. Unforgettable characters came alive in these pages despite a contrived plot and episodic structure that threatened to run away with the author. "That triumphant work," wrote Henry James, who had been moved by it in his youth, was "much less a book than a state of vision." Drawing on her observance of bondage in Kentucky and her experiences with runaway slaves during a residence of eighteen years in Cincinnati, this New England woman made the image of Eliza running across the Ohio River on ice floes or Tom enduring the beatings of Simon Legree in Louisiana more real than life for millions of readers. Nor was the book simply an indictment of the South. Some of its more winsome characters were southerners, and its most loathsome villain, Simon Legree, was a transplanted Yankee. Mrs. Stowe (or perhaps God) rebuked the whole nation for the sin of slavery. She aimed the novel at the evangelical conscience of the North. And she hit her mark.

It is not possible to measure precisely the political influence of *Uncle Tom's Cabin*. One can quantify its sales but cannot point to votes that it changed or laws that it inspired. Yet few contemporaries doubted its power. "Never was there such a literary *coup-de-main* as this," said Henry Wadsworth Longfellow. In England, Lord Palmer-

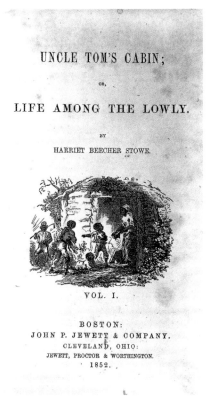

When Harriet Beecher Stowe, shown here, first published chapters of Uncle Tom's Cabin *as weekly installments in an antislavery newspaper in 1851, they attracted little attention outside antislavery circles. But when they came out in 1852 as a book, two huge presses running twenty-four hours a day could not keep up with demand.*

UNCLE TOM'S CABIN;

OR,

LIFE AMONG THE LOWLY.

BY

HARRIET BEECHER STOWE.

VOL. I.

BOSTON:
JOHN P. JEWETT & COMPANY.
CLEVELAND, OHIO:
JEWETT, PROCTOR & WORTHINGTON.
1852.

ston, who as prime minister a decade later would face a decision whether to intervene on behalf of the South in the Civil War, read *Uncle Tom's Cabin* three times and admired it not so much for the story as "for the statesmanship of it." As Abraham Lincoln was grappling with the problem of slavery in the summer of 1862, he borrowed from the Library of Congress *A Key to Uncle Tom's Cabin*, a subsequent volume by Stowe containing documentation on which she had based the novel. When Lincoln met the author later that year, he reportedly greeted her with the words: "So you're the little woman who wrote the book that made this great war."

Uncle Tom's Cabin struck a raw nerve in the South. Despite efforts to ban it, copies sold so fast in Charleston and elsewhere that booksellers could not keep up with the demand. The vehemence of southern denunciations of Mrs. Stowe's "falsehoods" and "distortions" was perhaps the best gauge of how close they hit home. "There never before was anything so detestable or so monstrous among women as this," declared the *New Orleans Crescent*. The editor of the *Southern Literary Messenger* instructed his book reviewer: "I would have the review as hot as hellfire, blasting and searing the reputation of the vile wretch in petticoats who could write such a volume." Within two years proslavery writers had answered *Uncle Tom's Cabin* with at least fifteen novels whose thesis that slaves were

A measure of the impact of Uncle Tom's Cabin *in Britain is this note in the* Illustrated London News *referring to the songs and stage plays that the novel had inspired there within less than a year of its publication.*

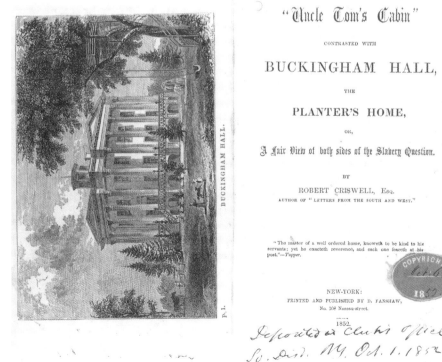

One of the many novels written by southern whites to refute Uncle Tom's Cabin *was* Uncle Tom's Cabin Contrasted with Buckingham Hall, the Planter's Home, *by Robert Criswell, of which the title page and frontispiece illustration are shown here. All of these novels together had a tiny fraction of the impact of* Uncle Tom's Cabin, *and their authors are forgotten today.*

better off than free workers in the North was capsulized by the title of one of them: *Uncle Robin in His Cabin in Virginia and Tom Without One in Boston*. A decade later during the Civil War a South Carolina diarist with doubts of her own about slavery reflected the obsession of southerners with *Uncle Tom's Cabin* by using it as a constant benchmark to measure the realities of life in the South.

In a later age "Uncle Tom" became an epithet for a black person who behaved with fawning servility toward white oppressors. This was partly a product of the ubiquitous Tom shows that paraded across the stage for generations and transmuted the novel into comic or grotesque melodrama. But an obsequious Tom was not the Uncle Tom of Stowe's pages. That Tom was one of the few true Christians in a novel intended to stir the emotions of a Christian public. Indeed, Tom was a Christ figure. Like Jesus he suffered agony inflicted by evil secular power. Like Jesus he died for the sins of humankind in order to save the oppressors as well as his own people. Stowe's readers lived in an age that understood this message better than ours. They were part of a generation that experienced not embarrassment but inspiration when they sang the words penned a decade later by another Yankee woman after she watched soldiers march off to war:

> As he died to make men holy,
> Let us die to make men free.

II

The South's defensive-aggressive temper in the 1850s stemmed in part from a sense of economic subordination to the North. The census of 1850 alarmed many southerners. During the previous decade, population growth had been 20 percent greater in the free states than in the slave states. Lack of economic opportunity seemed to account for this ominous fact. Three times as many people born in slave states had migrated to free states as vice versa, while seven-eighths of the immigrants from abroad settled in the North, where jobs were available and competition with slave labor nonexistent. The North appeared to be racing ahead of the South in crucial indices of economic development. In 1850 only 14 percent of the canal mileage ran through slave states. In 1840 the South had possessed 44 percent of the country's railroad mileage, but by 1850 the more rapid pace of northern construction had dropped the southern share to 26 percent.

Worse still were data on industrial production. With 42 percent of the population, slave states possessed only 18 percent of the country's manufacturing capacity, a decline from the 20 percent of 1840. More alarming, nearly half of this industrial capital was located in the four border states whose commitment to southern rights was shaky.

The one bright spot in the southern economy was staple agriculture. By 1850 the price of cotton had climbed back to nearly double its low of 5.5 cents a pound in the mid-1840s. But states that grew cotton kept less than 5 percent of it at home for manufacture into cloth. They exported 70 percent of it abroad and the remainder to

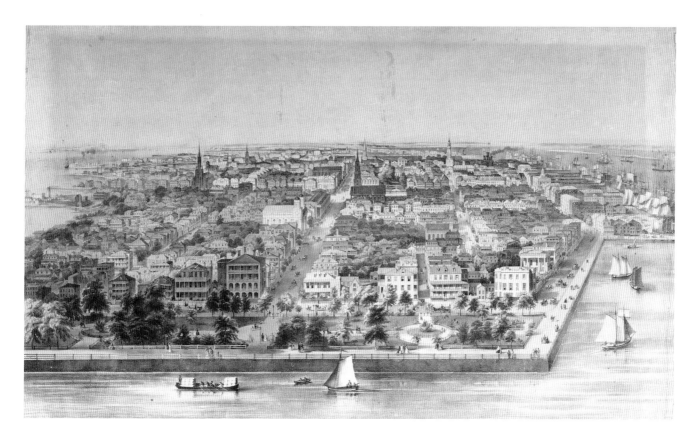

northern mills, where the value added by manufacture equaled the price that raw cotton brought the South, which in turn imported two-thirds of its clothing and other manufactured goods from the North or abroad. Compounding the problem, some 15 or 20 percent of the price of raw cotton went to "factors," largely representing northern or British firms, who arranged credit, insurance, warehousing, and shipping for planters. Nearly all the ships that carried cotton from southern ports and returned with manufactured goods were built and owned by northern or British companies. On their return voyages from Europe they usually put in and unloaded their cargo at northern ports, thereby increasing freight charges on imported goods to the South.

Southern self-condemnation of this "degrading vassalage" to Yankees became almost a litany during the sectional crisis from 1846 to 1851. "Our whole commerce except a small fraction is in the hands of Northern men," complained a prominent Alabamian in 1847. "Financially we are more enslaved than our negroes." Yankees "abuse and denounce slavery and slaveholders," declared a southern newspaper four years later, yet "we purchase all our luxuries and necessaries from the North." How could the South expect to preserve its power, asked the young southern champion of economic diversification James B. D. De Bow, when "the North grows rich and powerful whilst we at best are stationary?"

In 1846 De Bow had established a magazine in New Orleans with the title *Commercial Review of the South and West* (popularly known as *De Bow's Review*) and a hopeful slogan on its cover, "Commerce is King." The amount "lost to us annually by our vassalage to the North," said De Bow in 1852, was "one hundred million dollars." De Bow demanded "action! ACTION!! *ACTION!!!*—not in the rhetoric of

With one of the finest harbors in the United States and a rich agricultural hinterland, Charleston had stagnated by 1850, the year of this view of the city. From 1820 to 1850 South Carolina's population had increased by only 33 percent compared with 141 percent for the United States as a whole and 59 percent for the northeastern states. Although old families and the proud planter class in South Carolina professed disdain for the bustle and materialism of the North, they keenly felt—and resented—their languishing demographic and economic position.

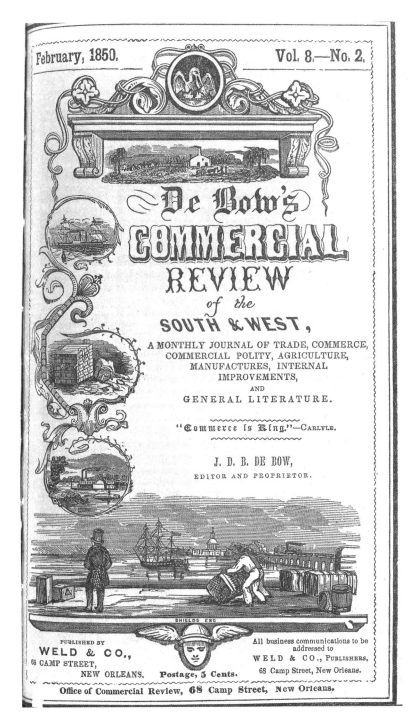

February, 1850.   Vol. 8.—No. 2.

De Bow's

COMMERCIAL

REVIEW

of the

SOUTH & WEST,

A MONTHLY JOURNAL OF TRADE, COMMERCE,
COMMERCIAL POLITY, AGRICULTURE,
MANUFACTURES, INTERNAL
IMPROVEMENTS,
AND
GENERAL LITERATURE.

"Commerce is King."—CARLYLE.

J. D. B. DE BOW,
EDITOR AND PROPRIETOR.

PUBLISHED BY
WELD & CO.,
68 CAMP STREET,
NEW ORLEANS.   Postage, 5 Cents.

SHIELDS ENG

All business communications to be
addressed to
WELD & CO., PUBLISHERS,
68 Camp Street, New Orleans.

Office of Commercial Review, 68 Camp Street, New Orleans.

Cover page of an issue of De Bow's
Review

Congress, but in the busy hum of mechanism, and in the thrifty operations of the hammer and anvil."

De Bow also revived the southern commercial conventions that had first met in the 1830s to urge the end of "the degrading shackles of our commercial dependence" on the North by establishing southern-owned shipping lines for trade with Europe and railroad connections between the lower Mississippi valley and the south Atlantic coast. But these had not materialized by 1852, so De Bow helped orchestrate a meeting at New Orleans that year. Thereafter a similar gathering met at least once a year through 1859 in various southern cities.

These conventions, prolific in oratory and resolutions, pressed southerners to emulate Yankees in the building of factories. The delegates also devoted some attention to cultural matters, noting that, apart from newspapers, most of what southerners read was published in the North. Not only did many of the South's brightest sons attend northern colleges; a shocking number of southern college presidents, professors, schoolteachers, and even newspaper editors were natives of Yankeedom. The conventions called for a reversal of such pernicious trends.

But the industrial gospel aroused the most enthusiasm. Textiles seemed the South's most logical route to industrialization. "Bring the spindles to the cotton," became a rallying cry of southern promoters. William Gregg, who had established a large textile mill at Graniteville in the South Carolina piedmont, firmly stated the case. "Have we not the raw material on the spot, thus saving the freight of a double transportation? Is not labor cheaper with us than with our northern brethren?"

Next to industry as the South's salvation stood railroads. The slave states did take significant strides in the 1850s, more than quadrupling their railroad mileage. Capital invested in southern manufacturing rose 77 percent, exceeding the rate of population growth so that the amount invested per capita increased 39 percent. The value of southern-produced textiles increased 44 percent. But like Alice in Wonderland, the faster the South ran, the farther behind it seemed to fall. While the slave states' proportion of national railroad mileage increased to 35 percent in 1860, this was less than the 44 percent of 1840. The North remained more than twice as well supplied with rail transportation in 1860.

While per capita investment in manufacturing increased no faster in the North than in the South during the 1850s, the population of free states grew more than that of slave states (40 percent to 27 percent) so that the southern share of national manufacturing capacity dropped from 18 to 16 percent. The effort to bring the spindles to the cotton failed: in 1860 the value of cotton textiles manufactured in the slave states was only 10 percent of the American total. The city of Lowell, Massachusetts, operated more spindles in 1860 than all eleven of the soon-to-be Confederate states combined. Two-fifths of all southern manufacturing capital in 1860 was in the four border states. Proponents of industrial development below the Potomac confessed frustration. Southerners were "destitute of every feature which characterizes an industrious people," mourned William Gregg.

Contemporaries and historians have advanced several explanations for this industrial inferiority. Following the lead of Adam Smith, classical economists considered free labor more efficient than slave labor because the free worker is stimulated by the fear of want and the desire for betterment. The northern journalist and landscape architect Frederick Law Olmsted made three extensive trips through the South in the 1850s, which resulted in three books that portrayed a shiftless, indolent, rundown society as the fruit of bondage. The subsistence level at which slaves and many "poor whites" lived discouraged the development of a market for consumer goods that could have stimulated southern manufacturing.

These explanations for southern "backwardness" have some merit. Yet they are not entirely convincing. The successful employment of slaves as well as white workers in southern textile mills, in iron foundries like the Tredegar Works in Richmond, and in other industries demonstrated a potential for industrialization on a greater scale. As for the lack of a home market, southern consumers generated a significant demand for *northern*-made shoes, clothing, locomotives, steamboats, and farm implements—to name just a few products—that encouraged such promoters as Gregg and De Bow to believe that a market for southern manufactures existed if it could only be exploited.

Other accounts of southern industrialization have focused not on deficiencies of labor or of demand but on a lack of capital. Capital was abundant in the South, to be sure: in 1860, according to the census measure of wealth (real and personal property), the average southern white male was nearly twice as wealthy as the average northern white man. The problem is that most of this wealth was invested in land and slaves. A northerner succinctly described the investment cycle of the southern economy: "To sell cotton in order to buy negroes—to make more cotton to buy more negroes, 'ad infinitum,' is the aim and direct tendency of all the operations of the thorough going cotton planter."

Was this preference for reinvestment in slaves economically rational? No,

As this advertisement indicates, by 1859 the major cities of the South were linked by rail and one could buy a through ticket from New York to New Orleans. What the advertisement does not specify, however, is that the trip would take several days and involve several changes of trains.

The dominant image of the antebellum South is that of slaves picking cotton. Here is one of the many illustrations that have made that image so familiar. Note that the slaves are doing all the work while the white overseer, with a whip tucked under his arm, chats with the planter.

answered an earlier generation of historians following the lead of Ulrich B. Phillips, who found plantation agriculture a decreasingly profitable enterprise that southern whites preserved for cultural rather than economic reasons. Yes, answered a more recent generation of historians, who have analyzed bushels of data and concluded that slave agriculture yielded as great a return on capital as potential alternative investments. Maybe, is the answer of still another group of economic historians, who suggest that investments in railroads and mills might have yielded higher returns than agriculture, that cotton was living on the borrowed time of an almost saturated market, and that whatever the rationality of individual planter reinvestment in agriculture the collective result inhibited the economic development of the South as a whole.

Some evidence points to the South's agrarian value system as an important reason for lack of industrialization. Although the light of Jeffersonian egalitarianism may have dimmed by 1850, the torch of agrarianism still glowed. "Those who labor in the earth are the chosen people of God . . . whose breasts He has made His peculiar deposit for substantial and genuine virtue," the husbandman of Monticello had written. The proportion of urban workingmen to farmers in any society "is the proportion of its unsound to its healthy parts" and adds "just so much to the support of pure government, as sores do to the strength of the human body." The durability of this conviction in the South created a cultural climate unfriendly to industrialization. An Englishman traveling through the South in 1842 found a widespread feeling "that the labours of the people should be confined to agriculture, leaving manufactures to Europe or to the States of the North."

Defenders of slavery contrasted the bondsman's comfortable lot with the misery of wage slaves so often that they began to believe it. Beware of the "endeavor to imitate . . . Northern civilization" with its "filthy, crowded, licentious factories," warned a planter in 1854.

By the later 1850s southern agrarians had mounted a counterattack against the gospel of industrialization. After all, trade was a lowly calling fit for *Yankees*, not for gentlemen. "That the North does our trading and manufacturing mostly is true," wrote an Alabamian in 1858, "and we are willing that they should. Ours is an agricultural people, and God grant that we may continue so. It is the freest, happiest, most independent, and with us, the most powerful condition on earth."

Many planters did invest in railroads and factories, of course, and these enterprises expanded during the 1850s. But the trend seemed to be toward even greater concentration in land and slaves. Southerners had a larger portion of their capital invested in land and slaves in 1860 than in 1850.

Although the persistence of Jeffersonian agrarianism may help explain this phenomenon, the historian can discover pragmatic reasons as well. The 1850s were boom years for cotton and for other southern staples. Low cotton prices in the 1840s had spurred the crusade for economic diversification. But during the next decade the price of cotton jumped more than 50 percent to an average of 11.5 cents a pound. The cotton crop consequently doubled to four million bales annually by the late 1850s. Sugar and tobacco prices and production similarly increased. The apparent insatiable demand for southern

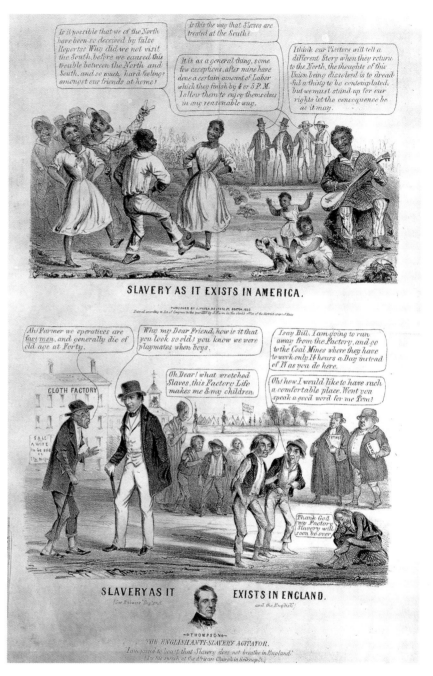

SLAVERY AS IT EXISTS IN AMERICA.

SLAVERY AS IT EXISTS IN ENGLAND.

staples caused planters to put every available acre into these crops. The per capita output of the principal southern food crops actually declined in the 1850s, and this agricultural society headed toward the status of a food-deficit region.

Although these trends alarmed some southerners, most expressed rapture over the dizzying prosperity brought by the cotton boom. The advocates of King Commerce faded; King Cotton reigned supreme.

By the later 1850s southern commercial conventions had reached the same conclusion. The merger of this commercial convention movement with a parallel series of planters' conventions in 1854 reflected the trend. Thereafter slave agriculture and its defense became the dominant theme of the conventions. Even *De Bow's Review* moved in this direction. Though De Bow continued to give lip service to industrial-

One of the principal themes in the southern defense of slavery was the alleged contrast between the well-fed, well-treated, and happy-go-lucky slaves and the nasty, brutish, and short lives of wage slaves in free society, especially England. In these paired cartoons, slaves dance and sing in the upper panel while, in the lower panel, miserable factory workers in England lament their lot and wait for the early death they welcome as a better alternative.

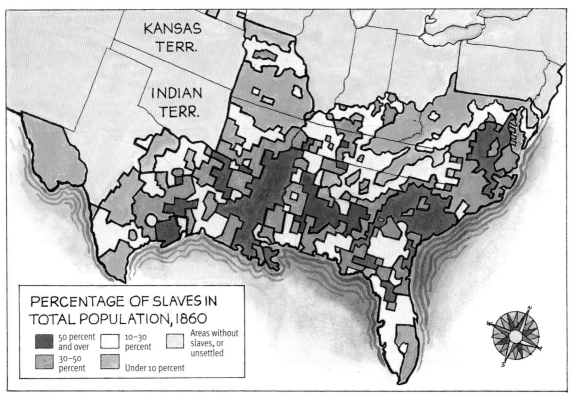

PERCENTAGE OF SLAVES IN TOTAL POPULATION, 1860

- 50 percent and over
- 30-50 percent
- 10-30 percent
- Under 10 percent
- Areas without slaves, or unsettled

KANSAS TERR.

INDIAN TERR.

THE SOUTHERN ECONOMY

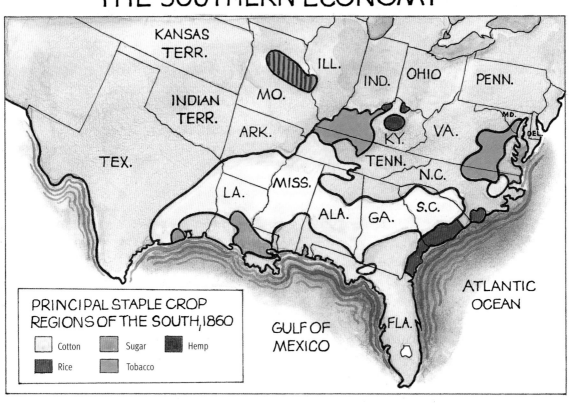

KANSAS TERR.

INDIAN TERR.

ILL.

MO.

IND.

OHIO

PENN.

MD.

DEL.

ARK.

KY.

VA.

TEX.

TENN.

N.C.

LA.

MISS.

ALA.

GA.

S.C.

FLA.

ATLANTIC OCEAN

GULF OF MEXICO

PRINCIPAL STAPLE CROP REGIONS OF THE SOUTH, 1860

- Cotton
- Rice
- Sugar
- Tobacco
- Hemp

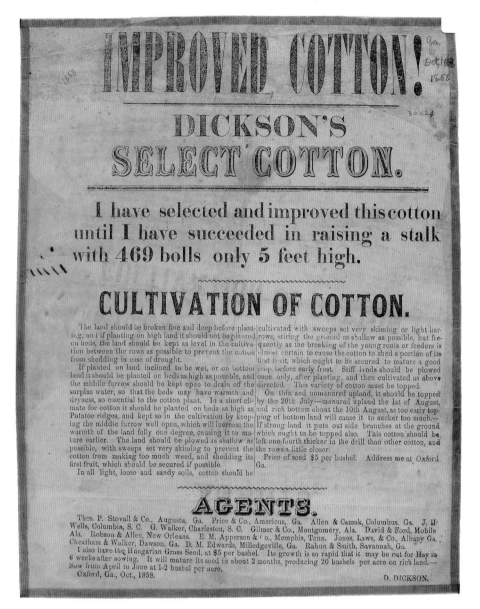

ization, his *Review* devoted more and more space to agriculture, proslavery polemics, and southern nationalism. By 1857 the politicians had pretty well taken over these "commercial" conventions. And the main form of commerce they now advocated was a reopening of the African slave trade.

Federal law had banned this trade since the end of 1807. Smuggling continued on a small scale after that date; in the 1850s the rising price of slaves produced an increase in this illicit traffic and built up pressure for a repeal of the ban. Political motives also actuated proponents of repeal. Agitation of the question, said one, would give "a sort of spite to the North and defiance of their opinions." A delegate to the 1856 commercial convention insisted that "we are entitled to demand the opening of this trade from an industrial, political, and constitutional consideration. . . . With cheap negroes we could set the hostile legislation of Congress at defiance. The slave population after supplying the states would overflow into the territories, and nothing could con-

The demand for cotton helped fuel the movement to reopen the slave trade. High slave prices also resulted in an increase of the illegal slave trade from Africa. This illustration from 1860 shows Africans being landed at Key West after the capture of a smuggler by a U.S. naval ship.

trol its natural expansion." For some defenders of slavery, logical consistency required a defense of the slave trade as well. "Slavery is right," said a delegate to the 1858 convention, "and being right there can be no wrong in the natural means of its formation." Or as William L. Yancey put it: "If it is right to buy slaves in Virginia and carry them to New Orleans, why is it not right to buy them in Africa and carry them there?"

Why not indeed? But most southerners failed to see the logic of this argument. In addition to moral repugnance toward the horrors of the "middle passage" of slaves across the Atlantic, many slaveowners in the upper South had economic reasons to oppose reopening of the African trade. Their own prosperity benefited from the rising demand for slaves; a growing stream of bondsmen flowed from the upper South to the cotton states. Nevertheless, the commercial convention at Vicksburg in 1859 (attended by delegates from only the lower South) called for repeal of the ban on slave imports. Proponents knew that they had no chance of success in Congress. But they cared little, for most of them were secessionists who favored a southern nation that could pass its own laws. In the meantime they could try to circumvent federal law by bringing in "apprentices" from Africa. De Bow became president of an African Labor Supply Association formed for that purpose. In 1858 the lower house of the Louisiana legislature authorized the importation of such apprentices. But the senate defeated the measure.

Frustrated in their attempts to change the law, fire-eaters turned their efforts to breaking it. The most famous example of the illicit slave trade in the 1850s was the schooner *Wanderer*, owned by Charles A. L. Lamar, member of a famous and powerful southern family. Lamar organized a syndicate that sent several ships to Africa for slaves. One of these was the *Wanderer*, a fast yacht that took on a cargo of five hundred Africans in 1858. The four hundred survivors of the voyage to Georgia earned Lamar a large profit. But federal officials had got wind of the affair and arrested Lamar along with several crew members. Savannah juries acquitted all of them. Lamar repurchased the *Wanderer* at public auction and went on with his slave-trading ventures until the Civil War, in which he was killed at the head of his regiment.

III

Those who wanted to import more slaves also wanted to acquire more slave territory. For this purpose a good many southerners looked not to the rather unpromising regions already part of the United States but to lands south of the border. At the 1856 commercial convention a delegate from Texas proposed a toast that was drunk with enthusiasm: "To the Southern republic bounded on the north by the Mason and Dixon line and on the south by the Isthmus of Tehuantepec, including Cuba and all other lands on our southern shore."

This version of Manifest Destiny was not new in 1856. Eight years earlier, just after the Senate had approved the treaty acquiring California and New Mexico, President Polk had outlined his next goal: "I am decidedly in favour of purchasing Cuba & making it one of the States of [the] Union." This idea appealed particularly to southerners as a way to expand their political power. "The Pearl of the West Indies," proclaimed one annexationist pamphlet, "with her thirteen or fifteen representatives in Congress, would be a powerful auxiliary to the South."

Polk authorized his minister to Spain to offer $100 million for the island. But this effort died stillborn. The American minister's clumsy efforts both amused and angered Spanish officials. The Spanish foreign minister declared that sooner than sell Cuba, Spain "would prefer seeing it sunk in the ocean." In any case it was unlikely that Congress, with its Whig and Wilmot Proviso majority in the House, would have appropriated funds to buy a territory containing nearly half a million slaves. Whig victory in the 1848 presidential election ended official efforts to acquire Cuba—for the time being.

Annexationists were not surprised by this failure. After all Texas, California, and New Mexico had been won only by revolution and war; they were willing to apply the same methods in Cuba. Their champion was a handsome, charismatic Cuban soldier of fortune named Narciso Lopez who had fled to New York in 1848 after Spanish officials foiled his attempt to foment an uprising of Cuban planters. Lopez recruited an army of several hundred adventurers, Mexican War veterans, and Cuban exiles for an invasion of the island. But the Taylor administration got wind of the enterprise and sent a naval force to seize Lopez's ships and block his departure in September 1849.

Undaunted, Lopez began to organize a new expedition of "filibusters" (from the Spanish *filibustero*, meaning freebooter or pirate). Believing northerners too "timid and dilatory" for this venture, Lopez left New York for New Orleans, where he planned to "rest his hopes on the men of the bold West and chivalric South." On the way he stopped in Mississippi to ask Governor John Quitman to command the invasion force. Quitman was a veteran of the Mexican War, in which he had risen to major general and commanded the assault that took Mexico City. A fire-eater who scattered threats of secession during the crisis of 1850, Quitman was tempted by the offer but turned it down because he felt compelled to remain at his post in Mississippi. He did

This cartoon lampoons Lopez's filibustering expedition to Cuba. After being driven out of Cardenas, Lopez runs for his ship carrying a bag marked $50,000, a much exaggerated reference to the small sum his men took from the customs house. The cartoon has Lopez say: "Well! We have not Revolutionized Cuba, but then we Got what we came for, my Comrades came for Glory, I came for Cash, I've Got the Cash, they've Got the Glory."

Pub⁴ & for Sale by J L Magee 34 Mott S⁵ NY

GENˡ LOPEZ THE CUBAN PATRIOT GETTING HIS CASH

LOPEZ. Well, we have not Revolutionized Cuba, but then we have Got what we came for, my Comrades came for Glory, I came for Cash, I've Got the Cash, they've Got the Glory, & I suppose we're all satisfied. Im O. P. H. for the United States again. Can't Live under a Military Despotism help Lopez recruit men and raise money to buy weapons. Lopez obtained arms and volunteers from similar sources in Louisiana. In May 1850 his army of six hundred men sailed from New Orleans to the accompaniment of cheering crowds and the "winking encouragement" of public officials. Lopez landed on the northwest coast of Cuba, captured the town of Cardenas, and burned the governor's mansion. But the expected uprising of Cuban revolutionaries failed to materialize. When Spanish troops closed in on Cardenas the filibusters retreated to their ship, which barely out-raced a pursuing Spanish warship to Key West, where the expeditionary force ingloriously dissolved.

Nevertheless, Lopez received a hero's welcome in the lower South. Dozens of towns and organizations offered him salutes, parades, toasts, and banquets. Southern senators demanded American action to punish Spain. "I want Cuba, and I know that sooner or later we must have it," declared Jefferson Davis's fellow senator from Mississippi, Albert Gallatin Brown. But Brown would not stop there. "I want Tamaulipas, Potosi, and one or two other Mexican States; and I want them all for the same reason—for the planting and spreading of slavery." Indeed, pronounced *De Bow's Review*, "we have a destiny to perform, 'a manifest destiny' over all Mexico, over South America, over the West Indies."

Zachary Taylor's administration, then trying to bring in California and New Mexico as free states, was unmoved by this rhetoric. The government indicted Lopez, Quitman, and several other southerners for violation of the neutrality laws. Like Lamar, Quitman and his confederates were not convicted by local juries. Wild celebrations marked this denouement. "If the evidence against Lopez were a thousand fold stronger," commented a New Orleans newspaper, "no jury could be impaneled to convict him because public opinion makes a law."

Thus vindicated, the filibusters tried again in 1851. William J. Crittenden of Kentucky, nephew of the attorney general, commanded a "regiment" of southern volunteers in the invasion force of 420 men. Once again port officials in New Orleans colluded with the filibusters to allow their departure on August 3, 1851, in a ship loaded to the gunwales. But this time Spanish troops were ready and waiting. They had already suppressed a premature local uprising intended to cooperate with the invaders. In several engagements the Spaniards killed two hundred of the filibusters and captured the rest. Cuban officials sent 160 of the prisoners to Spain, garroted Lopez in front of a large crowd in Havana, and lined up fifty American prisoners including Crittenden in the public square and executed them by firing squad.

When this news reached New Orleans, mobs rioted out of control. They destroyed the Spanish consulate and sacked shops owned by Spaniards. But the Fillmore administration, embarrassed by its negligent failure to stop the filibusters before they reached Cuba, confined its activities to a successful diplomatic effort to release the remaining American prisoners from Spain.

Filibustering died down for a time while expansionists concentrated on winning a friendly administration in the election of 1852. The spread-eagle nationalism of the "Young America" element in the Democratic party made Cuba an important issue in this election. The Young Americans were by no means all southerners. Stephen Douglas of Illinois was their foremost champion. But expansion remained preeminently a southern priority. The election of Franklin Pierce as president caused Young Americans to celebrate with bonfires and torchlight parades brandishing such banners as "The Fruits of the Late Democratic Victory—Pierce and Cuba."

Pierce's first actions pleased these partisans. "The policy of my Administration will not be controlled by any timid forebodings of evil from expansion," the new president promised in his inaugural address. "Our position on the globe, render[s] the acquisition of certain possessions . . . eminently important for our protection. . . . [The] future is boundless." Pierce filled his cabinet and the diplomatic corps with votaries of Manifest Destiny. Of all these appointments, that of Pierre Soulé as minister to Spain offered the clearest signal of the administration's intentions. A native of France whose republicanism had forced him to emigrate to Louisiana in 1825, the firebrand Soulé hailed the European revolutions of 1848 to free the continent from monarchy even as he supported filibusters to Cuba to bring that island into the Union as a slave state. Within a year of his arrival at Madrid, Soulé denounced the monarchy, wounded the French ambassador in a duel, presented a forty-eight-hour ultimatum (which Spain ignored) over an incident involving an American ship at Havana, and began intriguing with Spanish revolutionaries.

Despite all this, the only expansionist achievement of the Pierce administration was the Gadsden Purchase. And even that came to less than southerners had hoped. A railroad promoter from South Carolina, James Gadsden became minister to Mexico with the purpose of buying additional territory for a railroad route from New Orleans to the Pacific. Antislavery Yankees suspected that he had another purpose in mind as well: to acquire territory suitable for future admission as slave states. They may have been right. Gadsden initially offered Santa Anna up to $50 million for nearly 250,000 square miles of northern Mexico. The canny Mexican leader needed the money, as always, but could not see his way clear to selling off almost one-third of what was left of his country. Santa Anna finally made a $15 million deal with Gadsden to sell 55,000 square miles, but northern senators cut out 9,000 of these before enough northern Democrats joined southern senators to approve the treaty in 1854.

Gadsden's efforts were crowded out of the limelight by Cuba. Determined to acquire the island one way or

Historians rank Franklin Pierce as one of the weakest presidents because his deference to southern Democrats produced proslavery policies that sharpened sectional polarization and pushed the country down the slippery slope toward war. Personal tragedy may have accounted for part of Pierce's want of energetic leadership. Between his election and inauguration his only surviving son, eleven years old, was killed in a railroad accident witnessed by both parents. Pierce's wife never fully recovered from this shock.

This Mathew Brady photograph of Pierre Soulé captures some of the driving energy and imperious determination of the man. His appointment to a diplomatic post created an oxymoron, for he was anything but diplomatic. Almost everything he did as minister to Spain proved counterproductive to his own goals, including American acquisition of Cuba.

another, Pierce knew that Spain was no more willing to sell in 1853 than five years earlier. Surviving evidence indicates that the administration therefore hoped to foster a Texas-style revolution in Cuba supported by another filibuster invasion. The secretary of state's instructions to Soulé in Madrid stated that, while a renewed effort to purchase Cuba was "inopportune," the United States expected the island to "release itself or be released from its present Colonial subjection." Pierce apparently met with John Quitman in July 1853 and encouraged him to go ahead with a filibuster expedition, this time with more men backed by more money than Lopez's ill-fated invasions. Quitman needed little encouragement. "We have been swindled . . . out of the public domain," he declared. "Even a portion of Texas, supposed to be secured as slaveholding, has been wrested from us [by settlement of the boundary dispute in favor of New Mexico]. . . . The golden shore of the Pacific . . . is denied to Southern labor. . . . We are now hemmed in on the west as well as the north." Thus it was time "to strike with effect" in Cuba "after the fashion of Texas."

Prominent southerners endorsed Quitman's project. The governor of Alabama actively supported it. Numerous political leaders in Texas helped organize the expedition, which was scheduled, like the others, to depart from New Orleans. "Now is the time to act," wrote Alexander Stephens from Georgia, "while England and France have their hands full" with the Crimean War and could not interfere. By the spring of 1854 Quitman had recruited several thousand volunteers. Cuban exiles made contacts with revolutionary groups on the island to coordinate yet another uprising. Senator John Slidell of Louisiana, backed by other southern senators, introduced a resolution to suspend the neutrality law. The foreign relations committee was about to report this resolution favorably when, with apparent suddenness in May 1854, the administration turned negative and reined in Quitman.

What had happened? Apparently the administration, which had spent all of its political capital in obtaining passage of the Kansas-Nebraska Act, decided to back off from a second proslavery enterprise that might wreck the northern half of the party. On May 31, the day after he signed the Kansas-Nebraska Act, Pierce issued a proclamation enjoining filibustering on pain of suffering the full penalties of the neutrality law.

But this did not end efforts to acquire Cuba. Deciding in 1854 to exploit the sorry financial plight of the Spanish government, Pierce authorized Soulé to offer as much as $130 million for the island. If Spain turned this down, Soulé was then to direct his effort "to the next desirable object, which is to detach that island from the Spanish dominion." Whatever this cryptic instruction may have meant, if the administration expected Soulé to operate through the quiet channels of diplomacy they had mistaken their man. In October 1854 he met at Ostend in Belgium with his fellow ministers to Britain and France, James Buchanan and John Mason. The volatile Louisianian somehow persuaded the normally cautious Buchanan as well as the naive Mason to sign a memorandum that became known as the Ostend Manifesto. "Cuba is as necessary to the North American republic as any of its present . . . family of states," proclaimed this document. If the United States decided that its security required possession of the island, and Spain persisted in refusing to sell, then "by every law, human and Divine, we shall be justified in wresting it from Spain."

In his usual fashion, Soulé had failed to keep the Ostend meeting secret from the European press. An American newspaper also picked up details of the "Manifesto" and broke the story in November 1854. Antislavery newspapers denounced the "shame and dishonor" of this "Manifesto of the Brigands," this "highwayman's plea" to "grasp, to rob, to murder, to grow rich on the spoils of provinces and toils of slaves." The House subpoenaed the diplomatic correspondence and published it. Already reeling from a Kansas-Nebraska backlash that had cost the Democrats sixty-six of their ninety-one northern congressmen in the 1854 elections, the shell-shocked administration forced Soulé's resignation and abandoned all schemes to obtain Cuba. Quitman nevertheless renewed plans for a filibustering expedition in the spring of 1855. Pierce finally persuaded him to desist—a task made easier when Spanish troops in January 1855 arrested and executed several Cuban revolutionaries, an unpleasant reminder of what might be in store for leaders of another invasion.

Meanwhile, public attention shifted a few hundred miles west by south of Havana where the most remarkable and successful filibuster leader was tracing his meteoric career. Born in Nashville in 1824, William Walker bore few outward signs of the ambition for power that burned within him. Shy and taciturn, ascetic, sandy-haired and freckled, five feet five inches tall and weighing less than 120 pounds, his only distinctive feature was a pair of luminous, transfixing, grey-green eyes. After graduating *summa cum laude* from the University of Nashville at the age of fourteen, this restless prodigy studied medicine in Europe, earned a medical degree from the University of Pennsylvania at the age of nineteen, but practiced for only a short time before moving to New Orleans to study law. After a brief career as a lawyer, Walker turned to journalism and became an editor of the *New Orleans Crescent*.

In 1849 Walker joined the stream of humanity moving to California. But his restive soul found no repose in that golden state. As a journalist he attacked crime and helped inspire the vigilante movement in San Francisco. He fought three duels and was twice wounded. In 1853 Walker finally found his avocation. With forty-five heavily armed men he sailed from San Francisco to "colonize" Baja California and Sonora. His professed intent was to subdue the Apaches, bring the blessings of American civilization and Anglo-Saxon energy to these benighted Mexican provinces, and incidentally to exploit Sonora's gold and silver deposits.

This was neither the first nor last of many American filibustering expeditions south of the border during the unquiet years following the Mexican War. The chronic instability and frequent overthrows of the government in Mexico City created power vacuums filled by bandit chieftains and gringo invaders who kept the border in a constant state of upheaval. Walker's expedition enjoyed more initial success than most such enterprises. His filibusters captured La Paz, the sleepy capital of Baja California. Walker proclaimed himself president of this new republic and

This photograph captures the extraordinarily penetrating eyes of William Walker. Boyish-looking, slight, and shy, he nevertheless possessed a strange charisma that attracted soldiers of fortune to his filibustering banner.

proceeded to annex Sonora without having set foot in that richer province. This bold action attracted more recruits from California. Walker's army of footloose Forty-niners, with few supplies and less military experience, marched through rugged mountains, rafted across the Colorado River, and invaded Sonora. Exhausted, starving, and mutinous, fifty of Walker's men deserted and the rest retreated in the face of a superior force that killed several of them. With thirty-four survivors Walker fled across the border and surrendered to American authorities at San Diego in May 1854. Hailed as a hero by many San Franciscans, Walker stood trial for violating the neutrality law and was acquitted by a jury that took eight minutes to reach its verdict.

This Sonoran exercise was merely a warm-up for the real game. American attention in the early 1850s focused on the Central American isthmus as a land bridge between the Atlantic and Pacific oceans. A canal through these jungles would shorten the passage between California and the rest of the United States by weeks. Nicaragua seemed to offer the best route for such a canal, but the difficulty and cost of construction would be great. Meanwhile the New York transportation tycoon Cornelius Vanderbilt established the Accessory Transit Company to carry passengers and freight between New York and San Francisco via Nicaragua. Attracted by the tropical climate with its potential for the production of fruit, cotton, sugar, and coffee, other American investors began casting covetous eyes on the region. But the political climate discouraged investment; Nicaragua seemed in a constant state of revolution, having suffered through fifteen presidents in the six years before 1855. The temptation for filibustering there was almost irresistible; William Walker proved unable to resist it.

In 1854 Walker signed a contract with the rebels in Nicaragua's current civil war and in May 1855 sailed from San Francisco with the first contingent of fifty-seven men to support this cause. Because Britain was backing the other side and American-British tensions had escalated in recent years, U.S. officials looked the other way when Walker departed. With financial support from Vanderbilt's transit company, Walker's filibusters and their rebel allies defeated the "Legitimists" and gained control of the government. Walker appointed himself commander in chief of the Nicaraguan army as Americans continued to pour into the country—two thousand by the spring of 1856. President Pierce granted diplomatic recognition to Walker's government in May.

Although Walker himself and half of his filibusters were southerners, the enterprise thus far did not have a particularly prosouthern flavor. By mid-1856, however, that was changing. While much of the northern press condemned Walker as a pirate, southern newspapers praised him as engaged in a "noble cause. . . . It is our cause at bottom." In 1856 the Democratic national convention adopted a plank written by none other than Pierre Soulé endorsing U.S. "ascendancy in the Gulf of Mexico." Proponents of slavery expansion recognized the opportunities there for plantation agriculture. Indeed, Central America offered even more intriguing possibilities than Cuba, for its sparse mixed-blood population and weak, unstable governments seemed to make it an easy prey. Of course, the Central American republics had abolished slavery a generation earlier. But this was all the better, for it would allow southerners to establish slave plantations without competition from local planters.

During 1856 hundreds of American would-be planters took up land grants in Nicaragua. In August, Pierre Soulé himself arrived in Walker's capital and negotiated a loan for him from New Orleans bankers. The "grey-eyed man of destiny," as the press now described Walker, needed this kind of help. His revolution was in trouble. The other Central American countries had formed an alliance to overthrow him. They were backed by Cornelius Vanderbilt, whom Walker had angered by siding with an anti-Vanderbilt faction in the Accessory Transit Company. The president of Nicaragua defected to the enemy, whereupon Walker installed himself as president in July 1856. The Pierce administration withdrew its diplomatic recognition. Realizing that southern backing now represented his only hope, Walker decided "to bind the Southern States to Nicaragua as if she were one of themselves," as he later put it. On September 22, 1856, he revoked Nicaragua's 1824 emancipation edict and legalized slavery again.

This bold gamble succeeded in winning southern support. "No movement on the earth" was as important to the South as Walker's, proclaimed one newspaper. "In the name of the white race," said another, he "now offers Nicaragua to you and your slaves, at a time when you have not a friend on the face of the earth." The commercial convention meeting at Savannah expressed enthusiasm for the "efforts being made to introduce civilization in the States of Central America, and to develop these rich and productive regions by the introduction of slave labor." Several shiploads of new recruits arrived from New Orleans and San Francisco during the winter of 1856–57 to fight for Walker. But they were not enough. Some of them reached Nicaragua just in time to succumb to a cholera epidemic that ravaged

The tight formation of Walker's volunteer "army" as they march from their ship to land on Nicaraguan soil is probably a product of the artist's imagination. While his ragtag forces were good fighters, they were hardly disciplined soldiers. In the end they were decimated not by enemy soldiers but by cholera.

Walker's army even as the Central American alliance overwhelmed it in battle. On May 1, 1857, Walker surrendered his survivors to a United States naval commander whose ship carried them back to New Orleans. They left behind a thousand Americans dead of disease and combat.

This did not end the matter. Indeed, in the South it had barely begun. A wild celebration greeted Walker's return. Citizens opened their hearts and purses to the "grey-eyed man of destiny" as he traveled through the South raising men and money for another try. In November 1857 Walker sailed from Mobile on his second expedition to Nicaragua. But the navy caught up with him and carried his army back to the states. Southern newspapers erupted in denunciation of this naval "usurpation of power." Alexander Stephens urged the court-martial of the commodore who had detained Walker. Two dozen southern senators and congressmen echoed this sentiment in an extraordinary congressional debate. "A heavier blow was never struck at southern rights," said a Tennessee representative, "than when Commodore Paulding perpetrated upon our people his high-handed outrage." The government's action proved that President Buchanan was just like other Yankees in wanting to "crush out the expansion of slavery to the South." In May 1858 a hung jury in New Orleans voted 10 to 2 to acquit Walker of violating the neutrality law.

This outpouring of southern sympathy swept Walker into a campaign to organize yet another invasion of Nicaragua. A second tour of the lower South evoked an almost pathological frenzy among people who believed themselves locked in mortal combat with Yankee oppressors. Walker's third expedition sailed from Mobile in December 1858, but their ship hit a reef and sank sixty miles from the Central American coast. Despite the humiliation of returning to Mobile in the British ship that rescued them, the filibusters received their customary tumultuous welcome.

But Walker's act was growing stale. When he set out again to recruit support for a fourth try, the crowds were smaller. Ninety-seven filibusters traveled in small groups to a rendezvous in Honduras where they hoped to find backing for a new invasion of Nicaragua. Instead they found hostility and defeat. Walker surrendered to a British navy captain, expecting as usual to be returned to the United States. Instead the captain turned him over to local authorities. On September 12, 1860, the grey-eyed man met his destiny before a Honduran firing squad.

His legacy lived on, not only in Central American feelings about gringos but also in North American feelings about the sectional conflict that was tearing apart the United States. When Senator John J. Crittenden proposed to resolve the secession crisis in 1861 by reinstating the 36° 30' line between slavery and freedom in all territories "now held, or hereafter acquired," Abraham Lincoln and his party rejected the proposal on the ground that it "would amount to a perpetual covenant of war against every people, tribe, and State owning a foot of land between here and Tierra del Fuego."

This was only a slight exaggeration. Having begun the decade of the 1850s with a drive to defend southern rights by economic diversification, many southerners ended it with a different vision of southern enterprise—the expansion of slavery into a tropical empire controlled by the South.

George Bickley, a Virginian, sought to turn this vision into reality by organizing

the Knights of the Golden Circle, founded in the mid-1850s to promote a "golden circle" of slave states from the American South through Mexico and Central America to the rim of South America, curving northward again through the West Indies to close the circle at Key West. "With this addition to either our *system*, the *Union*, or to a Southern Confederacy," wrote Bickley in 1860, "we shall have in our hands the Cotton, Tobacco, Sugar, Coffee, Rice, Corn, and Tea lands of the continent, and the world's great storehouse of mineral wealth."

Thus had Thomas Jefferson's Empire for Liberty become transmuted by 1860 into Mississippi Congressman L.Q.C. Lamar's desire to "plant American liberty with southern institutions upon every inch of American soil." But the furor over this effort to plant the southern version of liberty as slavery along the Gulf of Mexico took a back seat to the controversy sparked by the effort to plant it in Kansas.

After his expulsion from Nicaragua in 1857, Walker toured the South to raise funds for another invasion to plant "American institutions"—especially slavery—in Central America. Large crowds turned out to hear Walker, as in the case of this speech from the portico of the St. Charles Hotel in New Orleans.

CHAPTER FOUR

✶ ✶ ✶ ✶ ✶

Slavery, Rum, and Romanism

I

The year 1852 turned out to be the last one in which the Whig party contested a presidential election. Millard Fillmore's efforts to enforce the fugitive slave law won him the support of southern Whigs for renomination. But the president had alienated antislavery Whigs, especially the Seward faction in Fillmore's own state of New York. Seward favored the nomination of Winfield Scott, a Virginian (but not a slaveholder). The Whig convention presented the curious spectacle of most southern delegates favoring a northern candidate, and vice versa, while many antiwar Whigs of four years earlier once again backed a general who had led American troops to victory in the war these Whigs had opposed. Maneuvers at the convention heightened the impression of Whig stultification. Southerners obtained enough support from northern moderates to adopt a plan pledging to "acquiesce in" the Compromise of 1850 "as a settlement in principle and substance" of the "dangerous and exciting" slavery question. All votes against this plank came from those northern Whigs who provided half of Scott's delegate support. Balloting for a presidential nominee ground through fifty-two roll calls as Yankee delegates furnished 95 percent of Scott's vote and southern delegates cast 85 percent of Fillmore's. On the fifty-third ballot a dozen southern moderates switched to Scott and put him over the top.

This denouement dismayed many southern Whigs. Suspecting that Seward had engineered the outcome, they feared a reprise of the Taylor debacle. When Scott's acceptance letter included only a lukewarm endorsement of the platform, they were sure of it. "If we support him," wrote a North Carolinian, "we must expect to constitute a tail to the army of abolitionists in front." As the campaign proceeded, defections of southern Whigs became a stampede. On election day Scott won 35 percent of the popular vote in the lower South (compared with Taylor's 50 percent four years earlier) and carried only Kentucky and Tennessee among the fifteen slave states. In the eleven future Confederate states the Whigs in 1852–53 elected no governors and merely fourteen of sixty-five congressmen while maintaining control of only the

Opposite page: Next to abolitionism, the temperance movement was the paramount reform effort of the age. This lithograph portrays the dire consequences of drink as men and women together get drunk and gamble in a noisome dive.

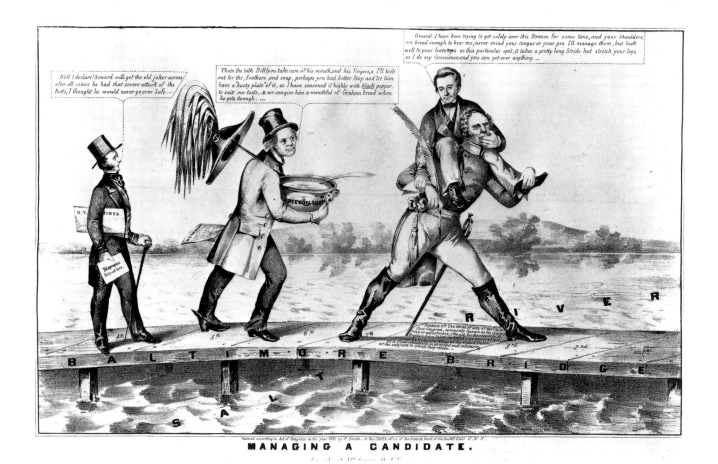

MANAGING A CANDIDATE.

This Democratic cartoon portrays Winfield Scott as the puppet of a trio of powerful New York antislavery Whigs: Senator William H. Seward, who is riding on Scott's shoulders, followed by Horace Greeley and Henry J. Raymond, editors of the New York Tribune *and* New York Times. *Seward is steering Scott along the planks of the Whig platform, forcing him to step over plank number 8, an endorsement of the Compromise of 1850, which Seward had opposed.*

Tennessee legislature. Alexander Stephens's pronouncement that "the Whig party is dead" seemed no exaggeration in the lower South.

The transmigration of southern Whigs into Democrats was made easier by the increasing friendliness of northern Democrats toward the South. Even the return of Barnburners to the Democratic fold seemed not to hinder this process. The Democratic national convention adopted no fewer than three planks pledging fidelity to the Compromise of 1850, and affirmed that "Congress has no power . . . to interfere with questions of slavery"—except of course to help masters recover fugitives. Because of the party rule requiring a two-thirds majority to nominate a president, southern delegates were able to block the candidacies of Lewis Cass and Stephen Douglas, whose notions about popular sovereignty made them suspect. But the southerners could not nominate their own candidate, the pliable James Buchanan. Through forty-eight ballots the party remained apparently as deadlocked as the Whigs. On the forty-ninth they nominated dark horse Franklin Pierce of New Hampshire, a former senator and a Mexican War veteran, who was acceptable to all factions and safe on slavery despite his Yankee background. Going into the campaign more united than in any election since Jackson's day, the Democrats won by a landslide.

Pierce fulfilled southern expectations. Although his efforts to acquire Cuba failed, the administration enforced the fugitive slave law vigorously and opened the remainder of the Louisiana Purchase north of 36° 30' to slavery. But it did so at great cost to domestic tranquility, to the structure of the Democratic party, and ultimately to the Union itself.

On May 24, 1854, in Boston a fugitive slave from Virginia, Anthony Burns, was arrested and placed under heavy guard in the federal courthouse. A biracial group of abolitionists led by thirty-year-old Unitarian clergyman Thomas Wentworth Higginson made an unsuccessful attempt to break in and rescue Burns. President Pierce ordered several companies of marines, cavalry, and artillery to Boston, where they joined state militia and local police to keep the peace while a federal commissioner determined Burns's fate. "Incur any expense," Pierce wired the district attorney in Boston, "to insure the execution of the law." The president also ordered a revenue cutter to stand by to carry Burns back to Virginia. Although Burns's owner was amenable, the offer by Bostonians to purchase Burns's freedom was not sanctioned by the U.S. attorney, who saw to it that Burns was marched to the cutter through streets crowded with people angered by his decision and returned to Virginia—at a cost of $100,000 (equal to more than two million 2003 dollars). The Pierce administration had upheld the majesty of the law.

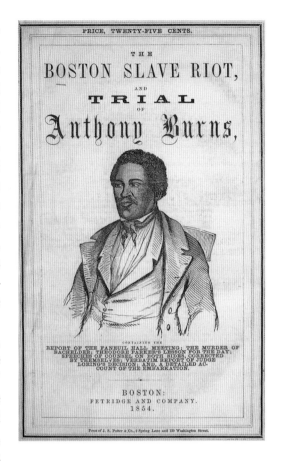

THE
BOSTON SLAVE RIOT,
AND
TRIAL
OF
Anthony Burns,

CONTAINING THE
REPORT OF THE FANEUIL HALL MEETING; THE MURDER OF BACHELDER; THEODORE PARKER'S LESSON FOR THE DAY; SPEECHES OF COUNSEL ON BOTH SIDES, CORRECTED BY THEMSELVES; VERBATIM REPORT OF JUDGE LORING'S DECISION; AND, A DETAILED ACCOUNT OF THE EMBARKATION.

BOSTON:
FETRIDGE AND COMPANY.
1854.

Press of J. S. Potter & Co., 2 Spring Lane and 130 Washington Street.

The fallout from this affair radiated widely. "When it was all over, and I was left alone in my office," wrote a heretofore conservative Whig, "I put my face in my hands and wept. I could do nothing less." The textile magnate Amos A. Lawrence said that "we went to bed one night old fashioned, conservative, Compromise Union Whigs & waked up stark mad Abolitionists." A federal grand jury indicted Higginson, Theodore Parker, Wendell Phillips, and four other white and black abolitionists for riot and inciting to riot, but ultimately the government abandoned its prosecution, because it was deemed impossible to win a jury trial in Massachusetts. William Lloyd Garrison publicly burned a copy of the Constitution on the Fourth of July while thousands breathed Amen to his denunciation of this document as a covenant with death. The New England states passed new personal liberty laws that collided in various ways with federal law.

Ohio, Michigan, and Wisconsin also passed stronger personal liberty laws after fugitive slave controversies in those states. Even more important than the fugitive slave issue in arousing northern militancy was the Kansas-Nebraska Act passed by Congress in May 1854. Coming at the same time as the Anthony Burns case, this law may have been the most important single event pushing the nation toward civil war. Kansas-Nebraska finished off the Whig party and gave birth to a new, entirely northern Republican party.

Restless settlers and land speculators had begun to cast covetous eyes on the fertile soil of the Kansas and Platte river valleys. By 1852, also, the idea of a transcontinental railroad through the region had become the dream of entrepreneurs, politicians, and frontiersmen alike. But until the government extracted land cessions from the Indians and organized the area as a territory, the region could not be surveyed and farmers could not settle there. Southerners were in no hurry to organize this territory, for it lay north of 36° 30', where slavery was excluded by the Missouri Compromise. Besides, they preferred a southern route for a Pacific railroad through the already organized territory of New Mexico, with New Orleans as its eastern terminus.

The Virginia slave Anthony Burns escaped in March 1854 and made his way to Boston, where he found a job in a clothing store. But he made the mistake of writing a letter to his brother, still a slave. His owner intercepted the letter, thereby learning of Burns's whereabouts. Burns's "trial" (really a hearing before a federal commissioner) and the failed rescue attempt in which one man was killed attracted national attention. When federal troops and state militia marched Burns to a ship to carry him back to slavery, thousands of sullen Bostonians lined the streets draped with the American flag hanging upside down, and church bells tolled a dirge to liberty in the cradle of the American Revolution. A year later a committee did manage to buy Burns's freedom and send him to Oberlin College.

It so happened that two Illinois Democrats—William A. Richardson and Stephen A. Douglas—were chairmen respectively of the House and Senate committees on territories. Both were champions of Young America's manifest destiny to expand ever westward. A large investor in Chicago real estate, Douglas had enhanced the value of his property by securing a federal land grant for a railroad from that city to Mobile. Perhaps hoping to enable construction of a railroad from Chicago to San Francisco along a similar land grant, Douglas and Richardson in 1853 reported bills to organize Nebraska Territory, embracing most of the remaining land in the Louisiana Purchase north of 36° 30', land that would remain free soil. The House quickly passed the measure, but opposition from southern senators tabled it in March 1853. To get his bill enacted, Douglas needed the support of at least a half-dozen southern senators. And they let him know exactly what it was going to cost.

The most powerful Senate bloc was a quartet of southerners who boarded together at a house on F Street. This "F Street Mess," as they called themselves, consisted of James M. Mason and Robert M. T. Hunter of Virginia, Andrew P. Butler of South Carolina, and David R. Atchison of Missouri—chairmen respectively of the foreign relations, finance, and judiciary committees, and president pro tem. In this last capacity Atchison was next in line for the presidency because Pierce's vice president had died during his second month in office. Intemperate, profane, and bellicose, Atchison was the most outspoken defender of southern rights in the Senate. His slaveholding constituents opposed the organization of Nebraska territory, for Missouri would thenceforth "be surrounded by free territory. . . . With the emissaries of abolitionists around us . . . this species of property would become insecure." Atchison announced that he would see Nebraska "sink in hell" before voting to organize it as free soil. From the F Street Mess the word came to Douglas: if he wanted Nebraska he must repeal the ban on bondage there and place "slaveholder and non-slaveholder upon terms of equality."

Douglas knew that such action would "raise a hell of a storm" in the North. So he first tried to outflank the Missouri Compromise instead of repealing it. His initial version of the Nebraska bill in January 1854 reproduced the language of the Utah and New Mexico legislation four years earlier, providing that Nebraska, when admitted as a state or states, would come in "with or without slavery, as their constitutions may prescribe." But for southerners this did not meet the case. If the Missouri Compromise prevailed during the territorial stage, slavery could never gain a foothold. Atchison turned the screws, whereupon Douglas discovered that a "clerical error" had omitted a section of the bill stating that "all questions pertaining to slavery in the Territories . . . are to be left to the people residing therein." But this was not yet good enough, for the Missouri Compromise still lived despite the implicit circumvention of it by the clerical-error clause. So Douglas took the

One of the few senators to have both a town and a railroad (The Atchison, Topeka, and Santa Fe) named after him, David R. Atchison considered himself the successor of John C. Calhoun as a defender of slavery and southern rights. His aggressive tactics, however, did more than anything else to provoke the northern opposition that eventually destroyed everything he stood for.

fateful step. He added an explicit repeal of the ban on slavery north of 36° 30'. More than that, his new version of the bill organized two territories—Nebraska west of Iowa, and Kansas west of Missouri. This looked like a device to reserve Kansas for slavery and Nebraska for freedom, especially since the climate and soil of eastern Kansas were similar to those of the Missouri River basin in Missouri, where most of the slaves in that state were concentrated.

This did indeed provoke a hell of a storm that made the debates of 1850 look like a gentle shower. The first clouds blew up from the Pierce administration itself. The president feared the political consequences of repudiating a covenant sanctified by thirty-four years of national life. Except for Secretary of War Jefferson Davis and Secretary of the Navy James Dobbin of North Carolina, the cabinet opposed the repeal clause. The administration drafted a vague alternative that would have referred the whole question of slavery in the territories to the Supreme Court. But this did not satisfy the F Street Mess. They confronted the president with an ultimatum: endorse repeal or lose the South. Pierce surrendered. Moreover, he agreed to make the revised Kansas-Nebraska bill "a test of party orthodoxy."

Northern Democrats and Whigs were stunned by Douglas's bill. But Free Soilers were not surprised. It was just what they had expected from the "slave power." And they were ready with a response to rally the North against this "gross violation of a sacred pledge," this "atrocious plot" to convert free territory into a "dreary region of despotism, inhabited by masters and slaves." These phrases came from the collaborative pens of Salmon P. Chase, Charles Sumner, Joshua Giddings, and three other Free Soil congressmen who published an "Appeal of the Independent Democrats" in the *National Era*—the same paper that had serialized *Uncle Tom's Cabin*.

This appeal set the keynote for an outpouring of angry speeches, sermons, and editorials in Congress and across the North. The moderate *New York Times* predicted that the northern backlash could "create a deep-seated, intense, and ineradicable hatred of the institution [slavery] which will crush its political power, at all hazards, and at any cost." Hundreds of "anti-Nebraska" meetings sent resolutions and petitions to Congress. "This crime shall not be consummated," declared a typical resolution. "Despite corruption, bribery, and treachery, Nebraska, the heart of our continent, shall forever continue free." Of ten northern state legislatures in session during the first months of 1854, the five controlled by Whigs denounced the bill and four of the five controlled by Democrats refused to endorse it. Only the Illinois legislature, under pressure from Douglas, approved the measure. In Congress northern Whigs unanimously opposed it. Douglas insisted that repeal of the ban on slavery north of 36° 30' was nothing new. The Compromise of 1850, he declared, had superseded that restriction by allowing popular sovereignty in former Mexican territory north as well as south of that line.

The Kansas-Nebraska Act's repeal of the ban on slavery in Northern territories galvanized angry opposition. All over the North "anti-Nebraska" rallies took place in the summer of 1854, leading to the founding of the Republican party that year.

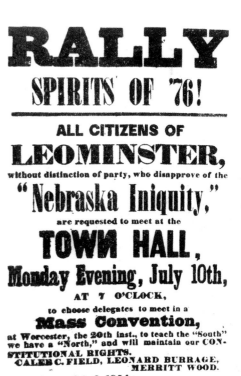

RALLY

SPIRITS OF '76!

ALL CITIZENS OF

LEOMINSTER,

without distinction of party, who disapprove of the

"Nebraska Iniquity,"

are requested to meet at the

TOWN HALL,

Monday Evening, July 10th,

AT 7 O'CLOCK,

to choose delegates to meet in a

Mass Convention,

at Worcester, the 20th inst., to teach the "South" we have a "North," and will maintain our CONSTITUTIONAL RIGHTS.

CALEB C. FIELD, LEONARD BURRAGE, MERRITT WOOD.

Leominster, July 8, 1854.

Northern senators exposed the speciousness of this argument. The Compromise of 1850 applied only to the Mexican cession, not to the Louisiana Purchase, and no one at the time—Douglas included—had thought otherwise. The supersedence theory emerged as a rationalization for a policy forced on Douglas by southern pressure. Nevertheless, Democratic party discipline and Douglas's parliamentary legerdemain pushed the bill through the Senate in March by a vote of 41 to 17 with only five of the twenty free-state Democrats joining northern Whigs and Free Soilers in opposition.

Northern Democrats in the House who had to face elections in the fall proved more resistant to administration pressure. Nevertheless Alexander Stephens, floor manager of the bill, applied "whip and spur" and drove it to passage on May 22 by a vote of 115 to 104. "I feel as if the *Mission* of my life was performed," wrote an exultant Stephens. Perhaps so, but only by giving the *coup de grâce* to the intersectional two-party system. Every northern Whig in the two houses voted against the bill, while 25 of 34 southern Whigs voted or were paired for it. Of 75 southern Democrats, 72 voted or were paired for the measure while 49 of 108 northern Democrats voted or were paired against it. Many of the latter knew that an affirmative vote meant defeat for reelection, while a negative vote meant an end to influence in the party establishment. Only seven of the northern representatives who voted Aye won reelection, while several who voted Nay left the Democratic party never to return. For northern and southern Whigs the bitter divisions caused a final parting of the ways. "The Whig party has been killed off effectually by that miserable Nebraska business," wrote Truman Smith of Connecticut, who resigned in disgust from the Senate. "We Whigs of the North are unalterably determined never to have even the slightest political correspondence or connexion" with southern Whigs. Adding insult to injury, southern senators killed a bill passed by a predominantly northern vote in the House to provide settlers with a 160-acre homestead grant on public lands. Such a law, explained one southerner, "would prove a most efficient ally for Abolition by encouraging and stimulating the settlement of free farms with Yankees and foreigners pre-committed to resist the participancy of slaveholders in the public domain."

The question was, who would pick up the pieces of the smashed political parties? In the lower South, Democrats would soon sweep most of the remaining shards of Whiggery into their own dustbin. In the upper South, Whigs clung to a precarious existence—under different names—for a few more years. In the North, matters were more complicated. Some antislavery Whigs like William H. Seward hoped to rejuvenate the party for the 1854 state and congressional elections by absorbing Free Soilers and anti-Nebraska Democrats. But the latter groups declined to be absorbed. Instead, along with many Whigs they proposed to abandon "mere party names, and rally as one man for the reestablishment of liberty and the overthrow of the Slave Power." New antislavery coalitions thus formed throughout the North to contest the fall elections. These coalitions called themselves by various names—Anti-Nebraska, Fusion, People's, Independent—but the one name that emerged most prominently was Republican. An anti-Nebraska rally at a church in Ripon, Wisconsin, seems to have been the first to adopt this label. A meeting of thirty congressmen in Washington

endorsed the name on May 9. The new party in Michigan officially designated itself Republican in July. Conventions in numerous congressional districts, especially in the Old Northwest, chose this name that resonated with the struggle of 1776. "In view of the necessity of battling for the first principles of republican government," resolved the Michigan convention, "and against the schemes of aristocracy the most revolting and oppressive with which the earth was ever cursed, or man debased, we will co-operate and be known as Republicans."

The campaigns in the North were intense and bitter, nowhere more than in Douglas's own state of Illinois. Douglas opened the canvass with a speech on September 1 in Chicago, where a hostile crowd shouted him down for two hours until he strode angrily off the platform and headed for friendlier districts downstate. Meanwhile, Abraham Lincoln was "aroused . . . as he had never been before" by the Kansas-Nebraska Act. Still calling himself a Whig, Lincoln took the stump in behalf of anti-Nebraska candidates for the legislature, hoping that victory would forge a legislative majority to elect him to the U.S. Senate. Lincoln and Douglas confronted each other on the same platform in speeches at Springfield and Peoria during October. In these addresses Lincoln set forth the themes that he would carry into the presidency six years later.

The founding fathers, said Lincoln, had opposed slavery. They adopted a Declaration of Independence that pronounced all men created equal. They enacted the Northwest Ordinance of 1787 banning slavery from the vast Northwest Territory. To be sure, many of the founders owned slaves. But they asserted their hostility to slavery in principle while tolerating it temporarily (as they hoped) in practice. That was why they did not mention the words "slave" or "slavery" in the Constitution, but referred only to "persons held to service." "Thus, the thing is hid away, in the constitution," said Lincoln, "just as an afflicted man hides away a wen or a cancer, which he dares not cut out at once, lest he bleed to death; with the promise, nevertheless, that the cutting may begin at the end of a given time." The first step was to prevent the spread of this cancer, which the fathers took with the Northwest Ordinance, the prohibition of the African slave trade in 1807, and the Missouri Compromise restriction of 1820. The second was to begin a process of gradual emancipation, which the generation of the fathers had accomplished in the states north of Maryland.

Lincoln denied "that there CAN be MORAL RIGHT in the enslaving of one man by another." But he did not want to pass judgment on southern people. When they "tell us they are no more responsible for the origin of slavery, than we, I acknowledge the fact. . . . They are just what we would be in their situation. . . . When it is said that the institution exists, and that it is very difficult to get rid of it," Lincoln acknowledged that fact also. "I surely will not blame them for not doing what I should not know how to do myself. If all earthly power were given me, I should not know what to do, as to the existing institution. My first impulse would be to free all the slaves, and send them to Liberia." But a moment's reflection convinced him of the impossibility of that. "What then, free them and keep them among us as underlings? Is it quite certain that this betters their condition? . . . What next? Free them, and make them politically and socially, our equals?" Even if Lincoln's own feelings would accept this, "we well know that those of the great mass of white people will not. . . . A universal feeling, whether well or ill-founded, cannot be safely disregarded."

In any case, the Constitution protected slavery where it already existed. But that "furnishes no more excuse for permitting slavery to go into our own free territory, than it would for reviving the African slave trade." The great "moral wrong and injustice" of the Kansas-Nebraska Act was that it opened territory previously closed to slavery, thus putting the institution "on the high road to extension and perpetuity" instead of restricting it in order gradually to end it. Popular sovereignty was false in principle and pernicious in practice, said Lincoln. Its assumption that the question of slavery in a territory concerned only the people who lived there was wrong. It affected the future of the whole nation. "Is not Nebraska, while a territory, a part of us? Do we not own the country? And if we surrender the control of it, do we not surrender the right of self-government?" For his own part, "I can not but hate" this "*declared* indifference, but as I must think, covert *real* zeal for the spread of . . . the monstrous injustice of slavery." Douglas's assertion that natural conditions would prevent bondage from taking root in Kansas was a "LULLABY argument." Temperature, rainfall, and soil in eastern Kansas were the same as in Missouri and Kentucky. Five slave states already existed north of the 36° 30' line. "Climate will not . . . keep slavery out of these territories . . . nothing in *nature* will." Lincoln knew that Missourians had already taken slaves to Kansas. The only way to stop them was for Congress to vote slavery out.

But such action, Douglas had protested, would be contrary to the settlers' "sacred right of self-government." Nonsense, replied Lincoln. *Slavery* was contrary to that right. "When the white man governs himself that is self-government; but when he governs himself, and also governs another man . . . that is despotism. . . .

The negro is a *man*. . . . There can be no moral right in connection with one man's making a slave of another. . . . Let no one be deceived," concluded Lincoln:

> The spirit of seventy-six and the spirit of Nebraska, are utter antagonisms. . . .
> Little by little . . . we have been giving up the old for the new faith. Near
> eighty years ago we began by declaring that all men are created equal; but now
> from that beginning we have run down to the other declaration, that for some
> men to enslave others is a "sacred right of self-government." These principles
> cannot stand together. . . . Our republican robe is soiled, and trailed in the
> dust. Let us repurify it. . . . Let us re-adopt the Declaration of Independence,
> and with it, the practices, and policy, which harmonize with it. . . . If we do
> this, we shall not only have saved the Union; but we shall have so saved it, as
> to make, and to keep it, forever worthy of the saving.

This eloquent speech expressed the platform of the new Republican party. Lincoln did not formally become a Republican for another year or more, after the Whig party had crumbled beyond salvation. Nor did he go as far as many other Republicans who called for abolition of slavery in the District of Columbia and repeal of the fugitive slave law. But Lincoln's affirmation of moral opposition to slavery, his belief that the national government had a right and duty to exclude it from the territories, and his conviction that this "cancer" must eventually be cut out became hallmarks of the Republican party. The historical basis of Lincoln's argument, of course, had some holes in it, and Douglas lost no time in driving his own oratory through the largest of them. The same supposedly antislavery fathers who had excluded slavery from the Northwest Territory had allowed it to expand into southwest territories, laying the groundwork for seven new slave states and the great cotton kingdom of the lower South. But free soilers brushed this problem aside; if the republicans of the Jeffersonian era had fallen short of the mark in some things, the new Republicans of the 1850s would not repeat the same mistake. Slavery must not expand; the party that had passed the Kansas-Nebraska Act must be repudiated.

A majority of northern voters in 1854 seemed to agree. The elections were a stunning rebuke to the Democrats. After carrying all but two northern states in 1852, they lost control of all but two free-state legislatures in 1854. The number of northern Democrats in the House would drop from ninety-three to twenty-three, who would be far outnumbered by their fifty-eight southern Democratic colleagues. Perhaps one-quarter of northern Democratic voters deserted their party in this election.

Having elected 150 congressmen under various labels, opponents of the Democrats would control the next House—if they could come together under the same political umbrella. But that was a big if. The difficulty of doing so was illustrated by Lincoln's fortunes in Illinois, where the anti-Nebraska coalition had a substantial majority on a joint ballot of the legislature. Lincoln's fellow Whigs constituted about three-quarters of this coalition. But a half-dozen anti-Nebraska Democrats refused to vote for a Whig for U. S. senator, causing Lincoln to fall short of a majority in ballot after ballot. Finally, to prevent the election of a Douglas Democrat,

Lincoln threw his support to an anti-Nebraska Democrat, Lyman Trumbull, who thereby won on the tenth ballot.

The muddy waters in Illinois were quite translucent compared with the murky depths of northern politics elsewhere. Up from the great deep came a tidal wave of nativism that seemed to swamp even the anti-Nebraska movement in some areas, especially in states east of Ohio. "Nearly everybody appears to have gone altogether deranged on Nativism," yelped a Pennsylvania Democrat in 1854. A Connecticut politician lamented that nativists "are making havoc with the Democratic party here," while a Whig leader in upstate New York warned that his district was "very badly infected with Knownothingism." Variously described as a "tornado," a "hurricane," and a "freak of political insanity," these "Know Nothings" swept the state elections of 1854 in Massachusetts and Delaware, polled an estimated 40 and 25 percent of the vote in Pennsylvania and New York, and made impressive showings in other parts of the Northeast and the border states. Who were these mysterious Know Nothings, where did they come from, and what did they stand for?

II

The nativist parties that had flared up in the early 1840s died back to embers after the elections of 1844. In the 1852 presidential election the Whigs, led by anti-nativist William H. Seward, tried to appeal for the Irish and Catholic vote. General Scott, Whig presidential candidate, was a high-church Episcopalian who had educated his daughters in a convent. As commander of American forces in Mexico he had protected Church property. In 1852 the Whigs planted friendly Irish questioners in audiences addressed by Scott, giving the candidate a chance to declare how much he "loved to hear that rich Irish brogue." But this clumsy effort backfired, for while Irish Americans as usual voted Democratic, many Whigs were offended by

New York City has always been the chief entry port for immigrants. Before the opening of the processing facilities at Ellis Island in 1892, Castle Garden served that function for almost forty years. This old stone circular building on the Battery at the tip of Manhattan had been a fort, an amusement park, and most recently an aquarium before it became a reception hall for arriving immigrants in 1855.

the appeal to "paddies" and stayed home on election day. As the slavery issue knocked southern Whigs loose from their party, a renewal of ethnic hostilities did the same in a number of northern states.

Several causes contributed to this revival of nativism. Immigration during the first five years of the 1850s reached a level five times greater than a decade earlier. Most of the new arrivals were poor Catholic peasants or laborers from Ireland and Germany who crowded into the tenements of large cities.

The Five Points neighborhood on Manhattan's Lower East Side was notorious as a slum district where many Irish immigrants lived. This caricature drawing presents some of the stereotypes about immigrants and their living conditions—filthy streets with pigs and dogs running loose, discarded whiskey bottles and a building labeled "Old Brewery," a drunk on the ground, boys fighting.

Crime and welfare costs soared. Cincinnati's crime rate, for example, tripled between 1846 and 1853, and its murder rate increased sevenfold. Boston's expenditures for poor relief rose threefold during the same period. Native-born Americans attributed these increases to immigrants, especially the Irish, whose arrest rate and share of relief funds were several times their percentage of the population. Natives were not necessarily the most nativist. Earlier Protestant immigrants from England, Scotland, and especially Ulster had brought their anti-Catholic sentiments with them and often formed the vanguard of anti-Irish rioters and voters in the United States. Radicals and agnostics among the Forty-eighters who had fled Germany after suppression of the 1848 revolutions carried to America a bitter enmity toward the Catholic Church which had sided with the forces of counter-revolution. In a period of reaction during the papacy of Pius IX (1846–78) Pius proclaimed the doctrine of papal infallibility and issued his Syllabus of Errors

THE PROPAGATION SOCIETY.___ MORE FREE THAN WELCOME.

This Currier and Ives lithograph of 1855 reflects the anti-Catholic sentiments that fueled the Know Nothing movement. Pope Pius IX steps ashore on American soil bearing a sword in one hand and a cross in the other, while five bishops hold his boat. The Pope tells "Young America," holding a King James Bible, and "Brother Jonathan," leaning on the staff of the American flag, that he has come "to take charge of your spiritual welfare . . . Kneel then! And kiss our big toe in token of submission." They reply: "No you don't, Mr. Pope. . . . You can neither coax or frighten our boys. "

condemning socialism, public education, rationalism, and other such iniquities. Taking his cue from the Pope, Archbishop John Hughes of New York attacked abolitionists, Free Soilers, and various Protestant reform movements as kin to the "Red Republicanism" of Europe.

Immigration had caused Catholic church membership to grow three times faster than Protestant membership in the 1840s. Pointing with pride to this fact (which Protestants viewed with alarm), Archbishop Hughes in 1850 delivered a well-publicized address, *The Decline of Protestantism and Its Causes*. "The object we hope to accomplish," said Hughes, "is to convert all Pagan nations, and all Protestant nations." The archbishopric's newspaper proclaimed that "Protestantism is effete, powerless, dying out . . . and conscious that its last moment is come when it is fairly set, face to face, with Catholic truth."

Such words fanned the embers of anti-Catholicism; the Puritan war against popery had gone on for two and one-half centuries and was not over yet. In 1852 the first Plenary Council of American bishops, meeting in Baltimore, attacked the godlessness of public education and decided to seek tax support for Catholic schools or tax relief for parents who sent their children to such schools. During 1852–53 this effort set off bitter campaigns in a dozen northern cities and states (including Maryland). "Free School" tickets drawn from both major parties, but especially from the Whigs, won several elections on the platform of defending public schools as the nursery of republicanism. Archbishop Hughes branded public schools as wellsprings of "Socialism, Red Republicanism, Universalism, Infidelity, Deism, Atheism, and Pantheism."

Adding fuel to the fire, a controversy arose over church property. Contrary to European tradition, U.S. Catholic churches in many areas were owned by a lay board of trustees representing the congregation rather than outright by the Church itself. The clergy's unsuccessful attempts to rectify this situation through legislation led to Vatican intervention. In July 1853 Monsignor Gaetano Bedini arrived in the United States as a papal nuncio to adjudicate the property dispute in certain dioceses in favor of the clergy and toured the country bestowing the papal blessing on American Catholics. Much of the Protestant and nativist press erupted in frenzied attacks on the Papacy—"the most fierce tyranny the world knows." The Church's role in suppressing Italian nationalist uprisings in 1848–49 also aroused radical expatriates from several Catholic countries against Bedini. As his tour continued, riots broke out in several cities that he visited, and upon his departure for Italy in February 1854 he had to be smuggled aboard a ship in the New York harbor to escape a mob.

The temperance movement also exacerbated ethnic tensions. Before 1850 this movement had been successful as, primarily, one of self-denial and moral suasion aimed at persuading the Protestant middle and working classes

This temperance print dated 1855 is typical of the genre. From roots labeled Gin, Brandy, Beer, and so on grow the gnarled tree Intemperance whose limbs are labeled Crime, Vice, Disease, Immorality, and so on. A serpent with an apple in its mouth and a mug of beer on its head twists around the tree. On the right are drunken men and women, while on the left a group of prohibitionists march with a banner proclaiming "Hurrah! For the Maine Law." One reformer chops the tree's roots.

TREE OF INTEMPERANCE

BY A. D. FILLMORE.

to cast out demon rum. Irish and German immigrants, for whom taverns and beer gardens were centers of social and political life, were less than receptive to such exhortations. A perceived rise of drunkenness, brawling, and crime especially among the Irish population helped turn temperance reform into a coercive movement aimed at this recalcitrant element. Believing that liquor was a cause of social disorder, prohibitionists sought passage of state laws to ban the manufacture and sale of alcoholic beverages. They achieved their first major victory in Maine in 1851. This success set off a wave of "Maine law" debates in other legislatures. The Democratic party generally opposed temperance laws while the Whigs were divided. Fearful of alienating "wet" voters, Whigs refused to take a stand and thereby estranged the large temperance component in their ranks. Coalitions of drys from all parties captured control of enough legislatures from 1852 to 1855 to enact Maine laws in a dozen additional states including all of New England, New York and Delaware, and several midwestern states.

Reform movements were the main venue for public activities by women in antebellum America. Believing that wives of drinking husbands were the main victims of intemperance, many women became active in temperance organizations. This remarkable daguerreotype portrays a member of the Daughters of Temperance, which had some twenty thousand members in 1848.

These laws, like Prohibition in a later generation, were frequently honored in the breach. Nonenforcement was widespread; legislatures or courts in several states subsequently repealed the laws or restricted their scope. By 1861 only three of the thirteen states that had legislated prohibition were still dry. The larger significance of the prohibition movement in the 1850s was not the laws it enacted but the impetus it gave to nativism. A Catholic newspaper classified prohibition with "State Education Systems, Infidelity, Pantheism," abolitionism, socialism, women's rights, and "European Red Republicanism." Temperance advocates replied in kind. "It is liquor which fills so many Catholic (as well as other) homes with discord and violence . . . fills our prisons with Irish culprits, and makes the gallows hideous with so many Catholic murderers," declared Horace Greeley's *New York Tribune*.

Buffeted by the winds of anti-Nebraska, anti-liquor, anti-Catholic, and anti-immigrant sentiments, the two-party system in the North was ready for collapse by 1854. And it was not only the antislavery Republicans who picked up the pieces. In several states a new and powerful nativist party seemed to glean even more from the wreckage. A number of secret fraternal societies restricted in membership to native-born Protestants had sprung up by the 1850s. Two of them in New York, the Order of United Americans and the Order of the Star Spangled Banner, had merged in 1852 under the leadership of James Barker. Against the background of Protestant-Catholic clashes over public schools, the Bedini visit, and temperance campaigns, the dynamic Barker organized hundreds of lodges all over the country with an estimated membership ranging up to a million or more. Members were pledged to vote for no one except native-born Protestants for public office. In secret councils the Order endorsed certain candidates or nominated its own. When asked by outsiders about the Order, members were to respond "I know nothing." Because of their secrecy and tight-knit organization, these "Know Nothings" became a potentially powerful voting bloc.

They drew their membership mainly from young men in white-collar and skilled blue-collar occupations. A good many of them were new voters. One analysis showed that men in their twenties were twice as likely to vote Know Nothing as men over thirty. Their leaders were also "new men" in politics who reflected the social backgrounds of their constituency. In Pittsburgh more than half of the Know Nothing leaders were under thirty-five and nearly half were artisans and clerks. Know Nothings elected to the Massachusetts legislature in 1854 consisted mainly of skilled workers, rural clergymen, and clerks in various enterprises. Maryland's leaders were younger and less affluent than their Democratic counterparts.

As a political movement, the Know Nothings had a platform as well as prejudices. They generally favored temperance and always opposed tax support for parochial schools. Their main goal was to reduce the power of foreign-born voters in politics. Under federal law, immigrants could become naturalized citizens after five years in the United States. In a few large cities Democratic judges obligingly issued naturalization papers almost as soon as immigrants got off the boat. Most states limited the vote to citizens, though several allowed immigrants to vote within a year of establishing residence. By the early 1850s the heavy wave of immigration that had begun in 1846 was showing up in voting rolls. Since immigrants were preponderantly young adults, the number of foreign-born voters grew faster than their proportion of the population. In Boston, for example, immigrant voters increased by 195 percent from 1850 to 1855 while the native-born vote rose only 14 percent. Because this "foreign" vote was mainly Democratic, Catholic, and wet, its rapid growth had alarming implications to Whigs, Protestants, and temperance reformers—and even to some native-born Democrats of the working class who found themselves competing with foreign-born laborers willing to work for lower wages. Rural residents also resented the growing power of the immigrant vote in the cities. The Know Nothings called for an increase of the waiting period for naturalization to twenty-one years. In some states they wished to restrict officeholding to native-born citizens and to impose a waiting period of several years after naturalization before immigrants could vote. They did not propose limits on immigration per se, though some Know Nothings probably hoped that by making citizenship and political rights more difficult to obtain they might discourage immigrants from coming to the United States.

Nativists charged that urban Democratic political machines like Tammany Hall illegally issued naturalization papers to immigrants so they could vote for the party—"early and often" in some cases. Such accusations were not without foundation. This 1856 drawing illustrates the process at Tammany Hall.

Most Know Nothings in northern states also opposed the Kansas-Nebraska Act. In some areas they joined anti-Nebraska coalitions in 1854. This raised the complex question of the relationship between Know Nothings and the new Republican party. The antislavery movement grew from the same cultural soil of evangelical Protestanism as temperance and nativism. Some free soilers viewed slavery and Catholicism alike as repressive institutions. The support of immigrant Catholic voters for the proslavery "Hunker" wing of the Democratic party cemented this perceived identity of slavery and Catholicism. So did frequent

editorials in the Catholic press branding the free-soil movement as "wild, lawless, destructive fanaticism." Competing with free blacks at the bottom of the social order, Irish-Americans were intensely anti-Negro and frequently rioted against black people in northern cities. In 1846 a solid Irish vote had helped defeat a referendum to grant equal voting rights to blacks in New York state. In 1854 a Massachusetts free soiler summarized the issues in the forthcoming elections as "freedom, temperance, and Protestantism against slavery, rum, and Romanism."

A Know Nothing cartoon from about 1850 picturing stereotypical Irish and German immigrants stealing the ballot box while their fellows in the background provoke a brawl at the polls.

On the other hand, many antislavery leaders recognized the incongruity of nativism with their own ideology. "I do not perceive," wrote Abraham Lincoln, "how any one professing to be sensitive to the wrongs of the negroes, can join in a league to degrade a class of white men." William H. Seward had battled the nativists in his state for more than a decade. The New York Republican platform in 1855 declared that "we repudiate and condemn the proscriptive and anti-republican doctrines of the order of Know-Nothings." An "anti-slavery man," said George W. Julian, founder of the Republican party in Indiana, "is, of necessity, the enemy of [this] organized scheme of bigotry and proscription." Other Republicans declared, "we are also against . . . [this] system of Northern Slavery to be created by disfranchising the Irish and Germans."

Genuine free soilers also deplored the Know Nothing craze as a red herring that diverted attention from "the real question of the age," slavery. "Neither the Pope nor the foreigners ever can govern the country or endanger its liberties," wrote Charles A. Dana, managing editor of Greeley's *New York Tribune*, "but the slave-breeders and slavetraders do govern it." Nevertheless, as a matter of political expediency, free-soil leaders in several states formed alliances with the Know Nothings in 1854 and 1855. In some cases they did so with the intention of taking over the movement in order to channel it in an antislavery direction. Massachusetts provided the clearest example of this. In that state the issues of the Mexican War and Wilmot Proviso had reshuffled political alignments so that a coalition of Free Soilers (including Conscience Whigs) and Democrats had gained control of the legislature from 1850 to 1852. The coalition elected Charles Sumner to the Senate and proposed or passed a number of reforms: a mechanic's lien law, a ten-hour law for laborers, general banking and incorporation laws, prohibition legislation, and reapportionment of the legislature to shift some power from Boston (with its Cotton Whigs and its large Irish vote) to central and western Massachusetts. The conservative Whig and Boston vote narrowly defeated reapportionment in a referendum in 1853. This provided the main spark for the Know Nothing fire of 1854 that swept out of western Massachusetts and kindled the whole state, electing the governor, an over-

A friend of many New England intellectuals and reformers, Charles Sumner became the foremost national spokesman for these constituencies when he was elected to the U.S. Senate in 1851. Sumner used that position as a podium for learned orations more than for practical political and legislative achievements.

whelming majority of the legislature, and all of the congressmen. The Whig establishment was traumatized by this conflagration. "I no more suspected the impending result," wrote a Whig journalist, "than I looked for an earthquake which would level the State House and reduce Faneuil Hall to a heap of ruins."

Free Soil/Republican leaders like Charles Francis Adams and Charles Sumner were taken equally by surprise. But that was not true of all free soilers. Indeed one of them, Henry Wilson, had much to do with the outcome. Like many of the younger Know Nothing voters, Wilson had been an apprentice and journeyman shoemaker in his youth. The "Natick Cobbler," as he was called, became a shoe manufacturer, went into politics as a Whig, and in 1848 helped found the Free Soil party. In 1854 the new Republican party nominated Wilson for governor. Whigs, Democrats, and Know Nothings also nominated candidates. Shrewdly perceiving that the nativist frenzy would overwhelm the other parties, Wilson joined the Know Nothing movement in the hope of controlling it. Some free soilers expressed disgust with this strategy. "When the freedom of an empire is at issue," wrote one of them, "Wilson runs off to chase a paddy!" Wilson remained on the ticket as Republican candidate but came in a distant fourth, having persuaded most of his free-soil followers to vote Know Nothing.

There was method in Wilson's apparent madness, as a choleric Cotton Whig recognized. The Know Nothings, he wrote, "have been controlled by the most desperate sort of Free Soil adventurers. Henry Wilson and Anson Burlingame have ruled the hour. . . . Our members of Congress are one and all of the ultra-agitation Anti-Slavery Stamp." The Know Nothing legislature elected Wilson to the Senate, where he did nothing for nativism but much for the antislavery cause. The only nativist laws passed by this legislature were a literacy qualification for voting and a measure disbanding several Irish militia companies—and the latter was in part an antislavery gesture, since these companies had provided much of the manpower that returned Anthony Burns to bondage. The legislature also enacted a new personal liberty law and a bill forbidding racial segregation in public schools—the first such law ever passed. In addition, these Know Nothing lawmakers passed a series of reform measures that earned them an ironic reputation as one of the most progressive legislatures in the state's history: abolition of imprisonment for debt, a married women's property act, creation of an insurance commission, compulsory vaccination of schoolchildren, expansion of the power of juries, and homestead exemption from seizure for debt.

Republicans and Know Nothings had succeeded in breaking down the Whigs and weakening the Democrats in most parts of the North. But in 1855 it remained uncertain which of these two new parties would emerge as the principal alternative to the Democrats. In about half of the states, Republicans had become the second major party. In the other half the American party, as the Know Nothings now named their political arm, seemed to prevail. But a development of great significance occurred in 1855. The center of nativist gravity began to shift southward. While the Know

Nothings added Connecticut, Rhode Island, New Hampshire, and California to the state governments they controlled, they also won elections in Maryland and Kentucky, gained control of the Tennessee legislature, polled at least 45 percent of the votes in five other southern states, and did better in the South as a whole than the Whigs had done since 1848.

In much of the South the American party was essentially the Whig party under a new name. To be sure, a tradition of nativism existed in the South despite the relatively small number of immigrants and Catholics there. This nativism undergirded the American party in Maryland, Louisiana, Missouri, and to some degree in Kentucky—states that contained cities with large immigrant populations. Nativist riots and election-day violence figured more prominently in southern cities than in the North. In some areas of the upper South, especially Maryland, the American party appealed equally to Democrats and Whigs. But elsewhere in the South it drew mainly from former Whigs who preferred the political company of nativists to that of Democrats. And the Know Nothings' nationalism became a unionist counterweight to the increasingly sectionalist Democrats.

The slavery issue soon split the Know Nothings along sectional lines. At the first national council of the American party, in June 1855 at Philadelphia, Henry Wilson led a bolt of most northern delegates when southerners and northern conservatives passed a plank endorsing the Kansas-Nebraska Act. From this time forth the party wasted away in the North while it grew stronger in the South. The logical place for antislavery Know Nothings to go was into the Republican party, which stood ready to receive them if it could do so without sanctioning nativism. Abraham Lincoln voiced the Republican dilemma in this matter. "Of their principles," Lincoln said of the Know Nothings, "I think little better than I do of the slavery extensionists. . . . Our progress in degeneracy appears to me to be pretty rapid. As a nation, we began by declaring that *'all men are created equal.'* We now practically read it 'all men are created equal, *except negroes.'* When the Know-Nothings get control, it will read 'all men are created equal, except negroes, *and foreigners, and catholics.'* When it comes to this I should prefer emigrating to some country where they make no pretence of loving liberty—to Russia, for instance, where despotism can be taken pure, and without the base alloy of hypocrisy." Nevertheless, in central Illinois the Know Nothings "are mostly my old political and personal friends." Without them "there is not sufficient materials to combat the Nebraska democracy." Lincoln was willing "to 'fuse' with anybody I can fuse on ground which I think is right." The only hope of carrying Illinois was to "get the elements of this organization" on our own terms after "Know-Nothingism has . . . entirely tumbled to pieces."

In Ohio, Salmon P. Chase showed how this might be done. After winning all of the congressional districts in 1854, the Ohio anti-Nebraska coalition looked forward to electing Chase governor in the state elections of 1855. But could they do it without Know Nothing support? Militant free soilers like Joshua Giddings thought so. The nativists, he said, were "unjust, illiberal, and un-American. We will never unite with such a party, in any compact whatever." Chase seemed to agree. "I cannot proscribe men on account of their birth," he wrote. "I cannot make religious faith a political test." He therefore recognized in January 1855 that the strength of "the Know-Nothing movement . . . may make the election of a man in my position impossible."

But Chase's ambition soon caused him to waffle. He privately expressed a willingness to work with antislavery Know Nothings if he could do so without "sacrificing principle." In effect, Chase wanted Republicans to spurn nativist *policies* while recognizing nativism as a cultural impulse. In particular, he was willing to make a gesture toward anti-Catholicism but not to alienate Protestant immigrants, especially the large German vote, whose support Republicans wanted and needed. This shading toward anti-Romanism but away from a generalized nativism became a way for Republicans to absorb some Know Nothings without feeling that they were "sacrificing principle."

Chase managed to walk this tightrope without falling. The conservative Know Nothings nominated a separate ticket in Ohio. Radical free soilers threatened to do the same if Chase made any concessions to the nativists. The Republican state convention nominated Chase on an antislavery platform that, in the candidate's words, did not "contain a squint toward Knism." The nominees for other state offices, however, were men of Know Nothing background—though Chase considered them "honest men . . . sincerely opposed to slavery" who "adhere but slightly to their order." Proclaiming that "there is nothing before the people but the vital issue of slavery," Chase privately predicted that Know Nothingism would "gracefully give itself up to die."

Perhaps. In any case, the main ethnocultural issue in the campaign was antiblack racism injected by the Democrats, who rapidly perfected the technique

of tarring "Black Republicans" with the brush of Negro equality. Labeling the Chase candidacy "Sambo's State Ticket," Ohio Democrats proclaimed that Republicans intended to sacrifice the interests of more than twenty millions of people . . . to those of three millions of blacks." Chase survived such onslaughts and won the governorship with 49 percent of the vote to 43 percent for the Democrats and 8 percent for the separate American ticket. Though they could not have won without Know Nothing support, Republicans came to power in Ohio committed to an antislavery platform and not bound by promises to nativists. They demonstrated this political legerdemain once again in the prolonged battle over the speakership of the national House of Representatives that convened in December 1855.

The chaos of parties at the opening of this Congress reflected the devastation wrought by the 1854–55 elections. Most estimates counted somewhere in the neighborhood of 105 Republican congressmen, 80 Democrats, and 50 Americans. Of the last, thirty-one came from slave states and a half-dozen of the rest were conservatives on the slavery question. Of the Democrats, only twenty-three came from free states, and a few of these were uncomfortable in the traces with southern colleagues. Of the Republicans (not all of whom yet acknowledged that label), perhaps two-thirds had at least a nominal connection with Know Nothingism, though half or more of these placed a higher priority on antislavery than on nativism. One of the latter was Nathaniel P. Banks of Massachusetts, a one-time Democrat and then a Know Nothing who like his colleague Henry Wilson in the Senate now wanted to harness the Know Nothing cart to the Republican horse. The Republicans nominated Banks for speaker, but in ballot after ballot during two increasingly tense months Banks fell short of the 118 votes needed for election. The process, however, crystallized his supporters as Republicans, and when the House on February 2, 1856, finally changed the rules to allow a plurality to prevail, Banks won the speakership with 103 votes on the 133rd ballot. If any one moment marked the birth of the Republican party, this was it.

A moment of confrontation in the House of Representatives during the interminable contest for the speakership in January 1856. None of the congressmen here has drawn a weapon, but some look angry or disgusted enough to do so.

What made possible this remarkable eclipse of Know Nothings and surge of Republicans to become the North's majority party within less than two years? Part of the answer lay in a dramatic decline of immigration, which during the years after 1854 fell to less than half of the level it had attained in the first half of the decade. But the main reason could be expressed in two words: Bleeding Kansas. Events in that far-off territory convinced most northerners that the slave power was after all a much greater threat to republican liberty than the Pope was.

CHAPTER FIVE

✶ ✶ ✶ ✶ ✶

The Crime Against Kansas

I

Having lost the battle in Congress for a free Kansas, antislavery men determined to wage the war on the prairie itself. "Since there is no escaping your challenge," William H. Seward told southern senators on May 25, 1854, "I accept it in behalf of the cause of freedom. We will engage in competition for the virgin soil of Kansas, and God give the victory to the side which is stronger in numbers as it is in right." In Massachusetts the erstwhile conservative Amos Lawrence was chief financial backer of the New England Emigrant Aid Company, formed in the summer of 1854 to promote free-soil settlement of Kansas. Few New Englanders actually went there, but the company did provide aid to farmers from midwestern states who began to trickle into Kansas. Lawrence's role was reflected in the name of the town that became headquarters of the free-state forces in the territory.

At the outset, however, Missourians from just across the border were stronger in numbers than the free soilers and at least equal in determination. "We are playing for a mighty stake," Senator David Atchison of Missouri assured Virginia's Robert M. T. Hunter. "The game must be played boldly. . . . If we win we carry slavery to the Pacific Ocean, if we fail we lose Missouri Arkansas Texas and all the territories." Fifteen years earlier Missourians had harried and burned the Mormons out of the state; Atchison was confident of their ability to give free soilers the same treatment in Kansas. When Andrew Reeder, a Pennsylvania Democrat, arrived in Kansas as territorial governor in the fall of 1854 he called an election for a delegate to Congress. This became the first of many Kansas elections in which the normal rowdiness of frontier politics was magnified a hundredfold by the contest over slavery. In November 1854, Atchison and other prominent Missourians led an invasion of "border ruffians" into Kansas to swell the vote for the proslavery candidate. The border ruffians won the first round. Casting more than 1,700 ballots that a subsequent congressional committee found to be fraudulent, they elected a proslavery delegate to Congress.

They probably could have won in a fair election. Governor Reeder took a census in preparation for the next election (of a territorial legislature) in March 1855. Of

Opposite page: The main street of Lawrence, Kansas, in 1856. Lawrence became the "capital" of the free-state forces in Kansas in their battles with proslavery Missourians.

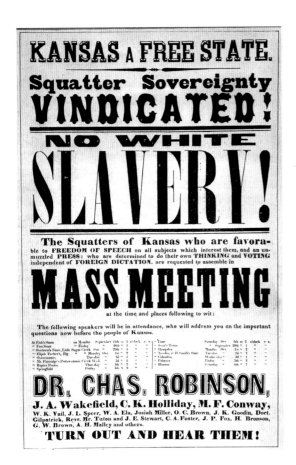

Left: Charles Robinson was a Massachusetts physician who went to Kansas in 1854 as one of the first settlers sponsored by the New England Emigrant Aid Company. He became a leader of the free-state party, speaking out against the efforts by Missourians to foist slavery on the territory. When Kansas came in as a state in 1861, Robinson was its first governor.

Right: This antislavery print depicts the border ruffians, lubricated with whiskey, who had ridden over from Missouri to vote for proslavery candidates. Note the sign below the window of the polling booth: "Down with the Abolitionists."

8,501 *bona fide* residents (including 242 slaves), 2,905 were legal voters, of whom three-fifths had come from Missouri and other slave states. Nevertheless Atchison wanted to make sure of victory. "Mark every scoundrel among you that is the least tainted with free-soilism, or abolitionism, and exterminate him," the senator's lieutenant in Missouri exhorted a crowd at St. Joseph. "Enter every election district in Kansas . . . and vote at the point of a Bowie knife or revolver!" Taking a leave from the Senate, Atchison again led a band of border ruffians into Kansas. "There are eleven hundred men coming over from Platte County to vote," he told his followers, "and if that ain't enough we can send five thousand—enough to kill every God-damned abolitionist in the Territory." Five thousand was about the number that came—4,908 according to a congressional investigation—and cast illegal ballots to elect a territorial legislature composed of thirty-six proslavery men and three free soilers. "Missourians have nobly defended *our* rights," stated an Alabama newspaper. "All hail!" declared the proslavery *Leavenworth Herald*. "Come on, Southern men! Bring your slaves and fill up the Territory. Kansas is saved."

Governor Reeder was appalled by these proceedings. He had come to Kansas sympathetic toward slavery, but the Missourians' threats against his life if he interfered with their activities converted him to the other side. He ordered new elections in one-third of the districts. Free-soil candidates won most of them, but when the legislature met in July 1855 it contemptuously seated the original proslavery victors. Reeder had meanwhile gone to Washington, where he pleaded with Pierce to repudiate this burlesque. But the president was swayed by arguments of Atchison, Douglas, and other Democrats that the Emigrant Aid Company had provoked the problem and Republican newspapers had blown it out of proportion. Atchison also persuaded Pierce to replace Reeder with someone more pliable, who turned out to be Wilson Shannon from Ohio. One of Shannon's first responsibilities was to enforce a slave code enacted by the legislature that imposed a fine and imprisonment for expressing opinions against slavery, authorized the death penalty for encouraging slave revolts or helping slaves to escape, required all voters to take an oath to uphold these laws, and retroactively legalized the border-ruffian ballots by requiring no prior residence in Kansas in order to vote.

FREE STATE CONVENTION!

All persons who are favorable to a union of effort, and a permanent organization of all the Free State elements of Kansas Territory, and who wish to secure upon the broadest platform the co-operation of all who agree upon this point, are requested to meet at their several places of holding elections, in their respective districts on the 25th of August, instant, at one o'clock, P. M., and appoint five delegates to each representative to which they were entitled in the Legislative Assembly, who shall meet in general Convention at

Big Springs, Wednesday, Sept. 5th '55,

at 10 o'clock A. M., for the purpose of adopting a Platform upon which all may act harmoniously who prefer Freedom to Slavery.
The nomination of a Delegate to Congress, will also come up before the General Convention.
Let no sectional or party issues distract or prevent the perfect co-operation of Free State men. Union and harmony are absolutely necessary to success. The pro-slavery party are fully and effectually organized. No jars nor minor issues divide them. And to contend against them successfully, we also must be united.— Without prudence and harmony of action we are certain to fail. Let every man then do his duty and we are certain of victory.
All Free State men, without distinction, are earnestly requested to take immediate and effective steps to insure a full and correct representation for every District in the Territory. "United we stand; divided we fall."
By order of the Executive Committee of the Free State Party of the Territory of Kansas, as per resolution of the Mass Convention in session at Lawrence, Aug 15th and 16th, 1855.
J. K. GOODIN, Sec'y.   C. ROBINSON, Chairman.
                                                                           Herald of Freedom, Print.

Free-soil Kansans—who by the fall of 1855 outnumbered *bona fide* proslavery settlers—had no intention of obeying these laws or of recognizing the "bogus legislature" that had passed them. Northern settlers armed themselves with new Sharps breechloading rifles sent from New England. Free soilers organized politically and called a convention to meet at Topeka in October. They drew up a free-state constitution and called elections for a new legislature and governor. Proslavery voters of course boycotted these elections. By January 1856 Kansas had two territorial governments: the official one at Lecompton and an unofficial one at Topeka representing a majority of actual residents.

Partisans of both sides in the territory were walking arsenals; it was only a matter of time until a shooting war broke out. The murder of a free-soil settler by a proslavery man in November 1855 set off a series of incidents that seemed likely to start the war. Some 1,500 Missourians crossed the border to march on the free-soil

The slavery controversy in Kansas politicized the whole population and produced almost nonstop conventions in one town after another.

The earnest delegates to a free-state constitutional convention in Topeka on October 23, 1855, shown in this drawing, adopted a constitution requesting admission as a free state. Congress ignored it, and for the next two years Kansas had rival pro- and antislavery territorial governments, often engaged in violent conflict.

stronghold of Lawrence, where a thousand men waited to receive them with Sharps rifles and a howitzer. Federal troops stood by idly because they had received no orders from the inert Pierce administration. Governor Shannon went to Lawrence and persuaded both sides to disband their forces. With Atchison's help he managed to prod the reluctant Missourians homeward. "If you attack Lawrence now," Atchison told them, "you attack as a mob, and what would be the result? You could cause the election of an abolition President, and the ruin of the Democratic party. Wait a little. You cannot now destroy these people without losing more than you would gain."

A severe winter cooled passions somewhat until, in the spring of 1856, proslavery Judge Samuel Lecompte instructed a grand jury to indict members of the free-state government for treason. Some eight hundred Missourians, deputized as a posse, laid siege to Lawrence, home of many members of the free-state government. Even though those the posse had come to "apprehend" decided not to resist in order to avoid further contempt of law, the "posse" thereupon poured into Lawrence, demolished its two newspaper offices, burned the hotel and the home of the elected free-soil governor, and plundered shops and houses.

All of this occurred against the backdrop of a national debate about Kansas. Both

After the "sack of Lawrence," free-state Kansans decided they needed more firepower. Somehow they acquired this six-pound howitzer and made it clear to their adversaries that they were prepared to use it. They did not have occasion to do so, but its existence may have had a deterrent effect against the border ruffians.

Republicans and Democrats in Congress introduced bills for the admission of Kansas as a state—the former under the Topeka free-state constitution, the latter after an election of a new constitutional convention to be administered by the Lecompton territorial government. Southerners viewed this matter as crucial to their future. "The admission of Kansas into the Union as a slave state is now a point of honor," wrote Congressman Preston Brooks of South Carolina in March 1856. "The fate of the South is to be decided with the Kansas issue."

Since Republicans controlled the House, and Democrats the Senate, neither party's Kansas bill could become law. Both parties focused on the propaganda value of the issue looking toward the presidential election. Republicans gained more from this strategy because Democratic support of proslavery excesses in Kansas offered a ready-made opportunity to dramatize yet another slave-power attack on northern rights. Republican newspapers exploited Bleeding Kansas for all it was worth.

Southerners continued to give them plenty to exploit. Hard on the heels of the "Sack of Lawrence" came shocking news from the U.S. Capitol itself. All spring Charles Sumner had been storing up wrath toward what he considered "The Crime Against Kansas"—the title of a two-day address he delivered to crowded Senate galleries May 19–20. "I shall make the most thorough and complete speech of my life," Sumner informed Salmon P. Chase a few days before the address. "My soul is wrung by this outrage, & I shall pour it forth." So he did, with more passion than good taste. "Murderous robbers from Missouri," Sumner declared, "hirelings picked from the drunken spew and vomit of an uneasy civilization" had committed a "rape of a virgin territory, compelling it to the hateful embrace of slavery." Sumner singled out members of the F Street Mess for specific attack, including South Carolina's Andrew P. Butler, who had "discharged the loose expectoration of his speech" in demanding the disarming of free-state men in Kansas. Butler's home state with "its shameful imbecility from Slavery" had sent to the Senate in his person a "Don Quixote who had chosen a mistress to whom he has made his vows, and who . . . though polluted in the sight of the world, is chaste in his sight—I mean the harlot, Slavery."

Sumner's speech produced an uproar—in the Senate, where several Democrats rebuked him, and in the press, where even Republican praise was tempered by reservations about the rhetoric. The only thing that prevented some southerner from challenging Sumner to a duel was the knowledge that he would refuse. Besides, dueling was for social equals; someone as low as this Yankee blackguard deserved a horsewhipping—or a caning. So felt Congressman Preston Brooks, a cousin of Andrew Butler. Two days after the speech Brooks walked into the nearly empty Senate chamber after adjournment and approached the desk where Sumner was writing letters. Your speech, he told the senator, "is a libel on South Carolina, and Mr. Butler, who is a relative of mine." Sumner started to rise, and the frenzied Brooks beat him over the head thirty times or more with a gold-headed cane as Sumner, his legs trapped under the bolted-down desk, finally wrenched it loose from the floor and collapsed with his head covered by blood.

This incident incensed even those Yankees who had little use for Sumner. "Bleeding Sumner" joined Bleeding Kansas as a symbol of the slave power's iniquities.

Few events that took place on the floor of the U.S. Senate have had such an impact as Preston Brooks's caning of Charles Sumner, pictured here by the artist for Frank Leslie's Illustrated Newspaper. *A Richmond newspaper praised Brooks:* "The vulgar Abolitionists in the Senate are getting above themselves. They must be lashed into submission." *For many northerners this was the last straw.* "Are we too slaves," *asked one,* "a target for their brutal blows, when we do not comport ourselves to please them?"

The South, declared one newspaper, "cannot tolerate free speech anywhere, and would stifle it in Washington with the bludgeon and the bowie-knife, as they are now trying to stifle it in Kansas by massacre, rapine, and murder."

Adding insult to injury, the South lionized Brooks as a hero. Although some southerners regretted the affair for its galvanizing effect on the North, public approval of Brooks's act far outweighed qualms. Newspapers in his own state expressed pride that Brooks had "stood forth so nobly in defense of . . . the honor of South Carolinians." A Louisiana planter and former army officer, Braxton Bragg, wrote that the House should pass a vote of thanks to Brooks. "You can reach the sensibilities of such dogs" as Sumner, wrote Bragg, "only through their heads and a big stick." Brooks himself boasted that "every Southern man sustains me. The fragments of the stick are begged for as *sacred relics*." After southerners blocked the House from expelling him, Brooks resigned anyway and returned home, where he was overwhelmingly reelected. From all over the South Brooks received dozens of new canes, some inscribed with such mottoes as "Hit Him Again" and "Use Knock Down Arguments."

This southern response outraged northern moderates even more than the caning had done. "It was not the attack itself (horrible as that was) that excited me," wrote an old-line Whig who thereafter voted Republican, "but the tone of the Southern Press, & the approbation, apparently, of the whole Southern People." Republican organizers reported that they had "never before seen anything at all like the present state of deep, determined, & desperate feelings of hatred, & hostility to the further extension of slavery, & its political power."

Brooks's only punishment was a $300 fine levied by a district court. Sumner's injuries, complicated by a post-traumatic syndrome that turned psychogenic neurosis into physical debility, kept him away from the Senate most of the time for the next four years. During that time the Massachusetts legislature reelected him as a symbolic rebuke to the "barbarism of slavery." A good many Yankees wanted to go beyond such passive protest. "If the South appeal to the rod of the slave for argument with the North," wrote a New York clergyman in his diary, "no way is left for the North, but to strike back, or be slaves." Out in Kansas lived a fifty-six-year-old abolitionist who also believed in this Old Testament injunction of an eye for an eye. Indeed, John Brown looked much like the Biblical warrior who slew his enemies with the jawbone of an ass— though Brown favored more up-to-date weapons like rifles, and, on one infamous occasion, broadswords.

"Without shedding blood there is no remission of sins." John Brown, pictured here, quoted this Biblical injunction frequently, and acted on it. The sin of slavery must be atoned in blood. And he considered himself God's chosen instrument to carry out the task, first in Kansas and three years later at Harper's Ferry in Virginia.

The father of twenty children, Brown had enjoyed little success over the years in his various business and farming enterprises. In 1855 he joined six of his sons and a son-in-law who had taken up claims in Kansas. A zealot on the subject of slavery with an almost mesmeric influence over many of his associates, Brown enlisted in a free-state military company (which included his sons) for service in the guerrilla conflict that was spreading during the spring of 1856. On their way to help defend Lawrence against the Missourians in May, this company learned that the unresisting town had been pillaged. The news threw Brown into a rage at the proslavery forces and contempt for the failure of Lawrence men to fight. That was no way to make Kansas free, he told his men. We must "fight fire with fire," must "strike terror in the hearts of the proslavery people." When further word reached Brown's party of the caning of Sumner in Washington, Brown "went crazy—*crazy*," according to witnesses. "Something must be done to show these barbarians that we, too, have rights," Brown declared. He reckoned that proslavery men had murdered at least five free soilers in Kansas since the troubles began. Brown conceived of a "radical, retaliatory measure" against "the slave hounds" of his own neighborhood near Pottawatomie Creek—none of whom had anything to do with those murders. With four of his sons and three other men, Brown abducted five proslavery settlers from their cabins on the night of May 24–25 and coolly split open their skulls with broadswords. An eye for an eye.

This shocking massacre went unpunished by legal process. Federal officials did manage to arrest two of Brown's sons who had *not* taken part in the affair, while proslavery bands burned the Brown homesteads. The twin traumas of Lawrence and Pottawatomie escalated the bushwhacking war in Kansas. One of Brown's sons was among some two hundred men killed in this conflict. Considering themselves soldiers in a holy war, Brown and his other sons somehow evaded capture and were never indicted for the Pottawatomie killings. And despite strenuous efforts by the U.S. army to contain this violence, the troops were too few to keep up with the hit-and-run raids that characterized the fighting.

As news of the Pottawatomie massacre traveled eastward, a legend grew among antislavery people that Brown was not involved or that if he was he had acted in self-defense. Not surprisingly, Republican newspapers preferred to dwell on the "barbarism" of border ruffians and Preston Brooks rather than on the barbarism of a free-state fighter. In any event, the Pottawatomie massacre was soon eclipsed by stories of other "battles" under headlines in many newspapers featuring "The Civil War in Kansas." More than anything else, that civil war shaped the context for the presidential election of 1856.

II

It was by no means certain when the year opened that the Republicans would become the North's second major party. The American party held a national convention in February with hopes of healing its sectional breach of the previous year. Some of the northern delegates who had walked out in June 1855 returned. But once more an alliance of southerners with New York and Pennsylvania conservatives defeated a resolution calling for repeal of the Kansas-Nebraska Act. Seventy Yankee delegates thereupon exited to organize a "North American" party. The remaining delegates nominated Millard Fillmore as the American party candidate for president.

The North Americans called a convention to meet a few days before the Republican gathering in June. Their intent was to nominate an antislavery nativist whom the Republicans would be compelled to endorse in order to avoid splitting the antislavery vote. But the outcome demonstrated the impossibility of the nativist tail wagging the antislavery dog. Once again Nathaniel Banks, who had just consolidated Republican control of the House by his election as speaker, served as a stalking horse for Republican absorption of North Americans. Still in good standing among nativists, Banks allowed his name to be put in nomination as the North American presidential candidate. After the Republicans nominated their candidate, Banks would withdraw in his favor, leaving the North Americans little choice but to endorse the Republican nominee. Several delegates to the North American convention were privy to this plot. It worked just as planned. Banks received the nomination, whereupon all eyes turned to Philadelphia, where the Republicans convened their first national convention.

Republican leaders like ex-Whig Thurlow Weed of New York and ex-Democrat Francis Preston Blair of Maryland were shrewd men. They welcomed delegates "without regard to past political differences or divisions, who are opposed to the repeal of the Missouri Compromise [and] to the policy of the present Administration." The platform and candidate would have to be carefully crafted to attract as many and alienate as few voters as possible. Especially delicate was the task of winning both nativists and immigrants (at least Protestant immigrants). Almost as difficult was the fusion of former Whigs and Democrats. The platform pursued these goals by concentrating on issues that united disparate elements and ignoring or equivocating on those that might divide them. Four-fifths of the platform dealt with slavery; it damned the administration's policy in Kansas, asserted the right of Congress to ban slavery in the territories, called for admission of Kansas as a free state, denounced the Ostend Manifesto, and quoted the Declaration of Independence as authority for free-soil principles. Two brief planks echoed the ancient Whig program of government financing for internal improvements by endorsing such aid for a transcontinental railroad and for rivers and harbors improvements—projects that would also attract Democratic support in areas benefiting from them (Pierce had vetoed three rivers and harbors bills). The final plank, relating to nativism, was a masterpiece of ambiguity. By opposing all legislation that might restrict "liberty of conscience and equality of rights among citizens," the platform seemed to rebuke nativism. But by specifying "citizens" it apparently did not preclude the Know Nothing plan (which Republicans had no real intention of carrying out) to lengthen the waiting period for naturalization to twenty-one years. And "liberty of conscience" was also a code phrase for Protestants who resented Catholic attempts to ban the reading of the King James Bible in public schools.

COL. JOHN C. FREMONT.
Hoisting the American Flag on the highest Peak of the Rocky Mountains

Because the Republican party was new, its platform was more important than usual in American politics. But of course the candidate would do even more to shape the party's image. The ideal "available man" was one who had not, like Seward and Chase, made enemies among nativists, antislavery Democrats, or conservative Whigs. The most "available" man, precisely because he had almost no political experience and therefore no record to defend, was John C. Frémont. The dashing image of this "Pathfinder" of the West was a political asset. Frémont would win votes, predicted one Republican strategist, "from the romance of his life and position." His marriage to the headstrong Jessie Benton, daughter of the legendary Jacksonian Thomas Hart Benton, who was an enemy of the Atchison faction in Missouri, provided Frémont with important connections among ex-Democrats. His role in promoting a free California in 1849 and his endorsement of a free Kansas in 1856 gave him good antislavery credentials. Frémont thus won the nomination on the first ballot. Ex-Whigs received a sop with the selection of New Jersey's William Dayton for vice president.

Dayton's nomination threatened to upset the delicate scheme to secure North American endorsement of the Republican candidates. Banks declined the North American nomination as planned, but in return for backing Frémont the nativists expected Republican endorsement of their vice-presidential nominee. When the Republicans refused, North Americans made angry noises for a time but finally

In two respects John C. Frémont seemed an unlikely candidate for a northern antislavery party that quietly courted the votes of former Know Nothings. He had been born in South Carolina and attended the College of Charleston. His father was a French émigré and a nominal Catholic. But Frémont had long since left his southern and Catholic roots behind and had earned fame and popularity as head of several western exploring and mapping expeditions, planting the flag high in the mountains as depicted here. As a senator from California in 1850–51 he had voted for antislavery measures.

JAMES BUCHANAN,
DEMOCRATIC CANDIDATE FOR PRESIDENT OF THE UNITED STATES.

accepted Dayton. Their endorsement of the Republican ticket required them to swallow an extra-large slice of humble pie, for Frémont's father had been a Catholic and the Pathfinder had been married by a priest. As an organized political movement, nativism went into a long eclipse after 1856. Hostility to Romanism (as well as Rum) remained a subterranean current within Republicanism. But for mainstream Republicans the Slave Power, not Catholicism, was the danger that threatened American liberties. "You are here today," the party chairman had told delegates to the Republican convention, "to give direction to a movement which is to decide whether the people of the United States are to be hereafter and forever chained to the present national policy of the extension of slavery."

In all respects the Democratic candidate was Frémont's opposite. The Pathfinder at forty-three was the youngest presidential nominee thus far; James Buchanan at sixty-five was one of the oldest. While the colorful Frémont and his ambitious wife had made numerous enemies as well as friends over the years, the dour Presbyterian bachelor Buchanan seemed colorless and safe. But Buchanan shared one political attribute with Frémont—availability. He had been out of the country as minister to Britain during the Kansas-Nebraska furor. Unlike Pierce and Douglas, the other candidates for the nomination, he carried no taint of responsibility for the mess in Kansas. Buchanan also came from Pennsylvania, which was shaping up as the crucial battleground of the election.

At the Democratic national convention Pierce and Douglas drew much of their support from southern delegates grateful for their role in repealing the Missouri Compromise. Most of Buchanan's votes came from the North—an irony, for Buchanan would turn out to be more prosouthern than either of his rivals. As the balloting went on through more than a dozen roll calls, Pierce and then Douglas withdrew for the sake of harmony, enabling Buchanan to win on the seventeenth ballot. Reversing the proportions of the Republican platform, the Democratic document devoted little more than a fifth of its verbiage to the slavery issue. It endorsed popular sovereignty and condemned the Republicans as a "sectional party" inciting "treason and armed resistance to law in the Territories." Other planks in the platform reasserted old Jacksonian chestnuts: state's rights; a government of limited powers; no federal aid to internal improvements; no national bank, so "dangerous to our republican institutions and the liberties of the people."

The campaign evolved into two separate contests: Buchanan *vs.* Fillmore in the South and Buchanan *vs.* Frémont in the North. Electioneering was lackluster in most parts of the South because the outcome was a foregone conclusion. Though Fillmore won 44 percent of the popular vote in slave states, he carried only Maryland. Frémont won all of the upper North—New England plus Michigan and Wisconsin—with a lopsided margin of 60 percent of the popular vote to 36 percent for Buchanan and 4 percent for Fillmore. Large Republican majorities in the Yankee regions of upstate New York, northern Ohio, and northern Iowa ensured a Frémont victory in those states as well. The vital struggle took place in the lower-North states of Pennsylvania, Indiana, Illinois, and New Jersey. Pennsylvania and any of the others, or all of them except Pennsylvania, when added to the almost solid South would give Buchanan the presidency.

Democrats concentrated their efforts on the lower North, where they presented an image of Union-saving conservatism as an alternative to Republican extremism. The old issues of banks, internal improvements, and the tariff seemed of little interest in this election. Even the newer ones of temperance and nativism affected only regional pockets. Democrats of course went through the motions of branding Republicans as neo-Whig promoters of banks and protective tariffs or as bigoted heirs of the Know Nothings. But the salient issues were slavery, race, and above all

THE GREAT REPUBLICAN REFORM PARTY,
Calling on their Candidate.
For Sale at N? 2 Spruce St N.Y.

Democrats sought votes in 1856 by tarnishing the Republicans with guilt by association with every radical "ism" that was around in the 1850s. This cartoon shows Frémont promising to carry out the reforms of black equality, Roman Catholicism, Free Love, socialism (represented by the bearded man in the battered hat), woman suffrage, and temperance.

Union. On these matters northern Democrats could take their stand not necessarily as defenders of slavery but as protectors of the Union and the white race against the disunionist Black Republicans.

These Yankee fanatics were a sectional party, charged Democrats. That was quite true. In only four slave states (all in the upper South) did Frémont tickets appear, and the Republicans won considerably less than 1 percent of the vote in these states. If Frémont won the presidency by carrying a solid North, warned Democrats, the Union would crumble. As Buchanan himself put it, "the Black Republicans must be . . . boldly assailed as disunionists, and this charge must be re-iterated again and again." Southerners helped along the cause by threatening to secede if the Republicans won. "The election of Frémont," declared Robert Toombs, "would be the end of the Union, and ought to be."

These warnings proved effective. Many old-line Whigs—including the sons of Henry Clay and Daniel Webster—announced their support for Buchanan as the only way to preserve the Union. Even Frémont's father-in-law, Thomas Hart Benton, despite his hatred of the Democratic leadership, urged his followers to vote for Buchanan. Other Whig conservatives in crucial states like New York, Pennsylvania, and Illinois voted for Fillmore (whose campaign the Democrats secretly helped to finance), thereby dividing the anti-Democratic vote and helping place the latter two states in the Democratic column.

Not only would a Republican victory destroy the Union, said Democrats, but by disturbing slavery and race relations it would also menace white supremacy in both North and South. "Black Republicans," an Ohio Democratic newspaper told voters, intended to "turn loose . . . millions of negroes, to elbow you in the workshops, and compete with you in the fields of honest labor." Indiana Democrats organized a parade which included young girls in white dresses carrying banners inscribed "Fathers, save us from nigger husbands!"

These charges of disunionism and racial equality placed Republicans on the defensive. In vain did they respond that the real disunionists were the southerners threatening to secede. In vain also did Republicans insist that they had no intention to "elevate the African race to complete equality with the white man." On the contrary, said a good many Republicans, the main purpose of excluding slavery from the territories was to protect white settlers from degrading competition with black labor. To refute the charge of egalitarian abolitionism, the free-state "constitution" of Kansas contained a provision excluding free blacks as well as slaves. "It is not so much in reference to the welfare of the Negro that we are here," Lyman Trumbull told the Republican convention, but "for the protection of the laboring whites, for the protection of ourselves and our liberties." Abolitionists like Lewis Tappan and William Lloyd Garrison denounced the Republican party precisely because it "had no room for the slave or the free man of color. . . . Its morality . . . is bounded by 36 deg. 30 min. . . . It is a complexional party, exclusively for white men, not for all men."

But Republican denials failed to convince thousands of voters in the lower North that the party was not, after all, a "Black Republican" communion ruled by "a wild and fanatical sentimentality toward the black race." Democrats could

point to many Republicans who had spoken in behalf of equal rights for blacks. They noted that most men now calling themselves Republicans had voted recently for the enfranchisement of blacks in New York, Wisconsin, and elsewhere, and that the Massachusetts legislators who had ended school segregation now backed Frémont. Democrats could also point to endorsements of Republicans by prominent black men like Frederick Douglass. Next to the taint of disunion, the tar-brush of black equality was the biggest obstacle to Republican success in large parts of the North.

Republicans knew that to win they must attack, not defend. They perceived the Achilles' heel of the opposition to be subservience to the slave power. "The slave drivers," declared an Ohio Republican, "seek to make our country a great slave empire: to make slave breeding, slave selling, slave labor, slave extension, slave policy, and slave dominion, FOREVER THE CONTROLLING ELEMENTS OF OUR GOVERNMENT."

The precise point of Republican attack was Kansas. Should he speak of "the tariff, National Bank, and internal improvements, and the controversies of the Whigs and Democrats?" asked Seward rhetorically in a campaign speech. "No," he answered, "they are past and gone. What then, of Kansas? . . . Ah yes, that is the theme . . . and nothing else." A lifelong Democrat who decided to vote Republican explained that "had the Slave Power been less *insolently aggressive*, I would have been content to see it extend . . . but when it seeks to extend its sway by fire & sword [in Kansas] I am ready to say hold, enough!"

The campaign generated a fervor unprecedented in American politics. Young Republicans marched in huge torchlight parades chanting a hypnotic slogan: "Free Soil, Free Speech, Free Men, Frémont!" The turnout of eligible voters in the North was an extraordinary 83 percent. The northern people seemed to be "on the tiptoe of Revolution," wrote one awestruck politician, and a journalist confirmed that "the process now going on in the politics of the United States is a *Revolution*."

While this passion mobilized a large Republican vote, it deepened the foreboding that drove many ex-Whigs to vote for Buchanan or Fillmore. The Pierce administration also took steps to defuse the Kansas time bomb. Overwhelmed by his inability to control the violence there, territorial governor Wilson Shannon resigned in August. Pierce replaced him with John W. Geary, whose six-foot-five frame and fearless manner made him a commanding figure. Only thirty-six years old, Geary had pursued several careers with success: attorney, civil engineer, Mexican War officer who had led an assault at Chapultepec, and the first mayor of San Francisco, where he had subdued outlaws in that wide-open city. If anyone could pacify Kansas in time to save the Democrats, Geary was the man. He reportedly said that he went to Kansas "carrying a Presidential candidate on his shoulders." By facing down guerrilla bands from both sides and using federal troops (whose numbers in Kansas reached 1,300) with boldness and skill, Geary suppressed nearly all of the violence by October. Kansas ceased to bleed—temporarily at least.

The dawn of peace in Kansas brought some disaffected northern Democrats back into the fold as they saw that popular sovereignty, given the preponderance of northern settlers, might make Kansas a free state after all. From only 25 seats in the House following the disaster of 1854, northern Democrats rebounded to 53, though they were still outnumbered by 75 southern Democrats and 92 Republicans. Most important, while Frémont carried eleven northern states with 114 electoral votes, Buchanan carried the remaining five (Pennsylvania, New Jersey, Indiana, and Illinois along with California) with 62, which added to his 112 from the South gave him a comfortable margin. Buchanan was a minority president in the popular vote, however, having won 45 percent of that vote nationally—56 percent in the South and 41 percent in the North.

This photograph shows John W. Geary as a major general in the Union army. No picture of him in the 1850s is available.

Southerners did not intend to let Buchanan forget that he owed his election mostly to them. "Mr. Buchanan and the Northern Democracy are dependent on the South," noted a Virginia judge after the election as he outlined his idea of a southern program for the next four years. "If we can succeed in Kansas, keep down the Tariff, shake off our Commercial dependence on the North and add a little more slave territory, we may yet live free men under the Stars and Stripes."

III

Success in Kansas would require a bold strategy to overcome the estimated two-to-one majority of free-soil settlers. The proslavery legislature, elected by border ruffians in 1855 and still the official lawmaking body, was equal to the occasion. Meeting in January 1857, it ignored Governor Geary's request to modify the draconian slave code that prescribed the death penalty for certain antislavery acts. Instead, the legislature enacted a bill for what amounted to a rigged constitutional convention. Specifying the election of delegates in June, the measure entrusted county sheriffs (all proslavery) with the registration of voters and designated county commissioners (also proslavery) to choose judges of election. Given the record of previous elections in Kansas, little acumen was needed to discern the purpose of these provisions. To top them off, the bill specified that the new constitution drawn up by the convention would go into effect without a referendum.

Geary was appalled. He had come to Kansas as a Democrat who "heartily despised" the "pernicious" doctrines of abolition. But he soon became convinced of the "criminal complicity of public officials" in trying to make Kansas a slave state "at all hazards." This started him on the path to free soil and a career as a fighting general in the Civil War and Republican governor of Pennsylvania afterwards. In 1857 he vetoed the convention bill. The legislature promptly passed it over his veto. At loggerheads with territorial officials, his life threatened almost daily, without support from the lame-duck Pierce administration, Geary resigned on March 4, 1857. After leaving Kansas he gave an interview in which he condemned its "felon legislature." Geary had put down lawless elements in the nation's toughest town, San Francisco, but Kansas proved too much for him.

Faced during his first days in office with the same Kansas problem that had wrecked the Pierce administration, Buchanan was determined that it should not ruin his. He prevailed upon Robert J. Walker, a Mississippian who had served with Buchanan in Polk's cabinet, to go to Kansas as territorial governor and give it a state constitution drafted by orderly process and approved by a referendum. More than a foot shorter than Geary in height, Walker was his equal in courage. But he too found Kansas more than he could handle. Though a southerner, he acknowledged that the free-state men had a majority in any fair election. The problem was that the election of delegates scheduled for June would not be fair. Arriving in Kansas at the end of May—too late to change the electoral procedures—Walker urged free-state men to participate anyway. Not wishing to sanction the legitimacy of this election, they refused. With only 2,200 of 9,250 registered voters participating, proslavery delegates won all the seats to the convention scheduled to meet at Lecompton in September.

These farcical proceedings got Walker's governorship off on the wrong foot. His sharpest critics were fellow southerners. They opposed a referendum on the forthcoming constitution; Walker favored one. From the moment he arrived in the territory, therefore, he had to endure hostility from southerners on the ground and back east. When word came from Washington that Buchanan backed the governor's insistence on a referendum, southern Democrats rose in righteous indignation. *"We are betrayed,"* they cried, "by an administration that went into power on [southern] votes." All four southern members of the cabinet turned against Walker. Several state legislatures and Democratic state conventions censured him.

This pressure caused Buchanan to cave in. The South won yet another of its Pyrrhic victories. Before this happened, however, Kansans went to the polls yet again, to elect a new territorial legislature. Walker persuaded free soilers to vote this time by promising to enforce strict fairness. But lo and behold, the initial

Only five feet two inches tall, Robert J. Walker had a very large head, which inspired confidence that he made up in brains what he lacked in brawn. A native of Pennsylvania, Walker had called Mississippi home for thirty-one years in 1857. As a senator from that state he had supported all the orthodox prosouthern and proslavery measures of the era. He had been Polk's secretary of the treasury and had favored the annexation of even more of Mexico than the United States acquired in 1848. His experience in Kansas, however, helped to change his opinions almost 180 degrees. He became an opponent of slavery and supported the Union in the Civil War.

returns seemed to indicate an astonishing proslavery victory. Closer investigation uncovered the curious phenomenon of two remote districts with 130 legal voters having reported almost 2,900 ballots. In one case some 1,600 names had been copied onto the voting rolls from an old Cincinnati city directory. Throwing out the fraudulent returns, Walker certified a free-state majority in the next territorial legislature. This action provoked more bitter outcries from southerners against "tampering" with the returns.

While this furor continued, the constitutional convention completed its work at Lecompton. The document that emerged was in most respects conventional. But it declared that "the right of property is before and higher than any constitutional sanction, and the right of the owner of a slave to such slave and its increase is the same and as inviolable as the right of the owner of any property whatever." No amendment to the constitution could be made for seven years, and even after that time "no alteration shall be made to affect the rights of property in the ownership of slaves." Here was the solution of a problem of urgent national interest, offered by a convention representing one-fifth of the potential voters in Kansas. And to make sure that those voters did not reject its handiwork, the convention decided to send the constitution and a petition for statehood to Congress without a referendum—in defiance of all pledges by Walker and Buchanan.

With Democratic control of Congress, and southern control of the Democratic party, proslavery forces believed that this desperate gambit would succeed. But it was too barefaced for most Democrats, including some southerners, who sought a way to preserve the form of a referendum without its substance. On November 7 the convention modified its position. It now mandated a referendum, not on the whole constitution, but only on two alternative slavery clauses designated as the "Constitution with Slavery" or the "Constitution with no Slavery." This seemed fair enough—except that the constitution with no slavery specified that, while "Slavery shall no longer exist" in Kansas, "the right of property in slaves now in this Territory shall in no manner be interfered with." In effect, the constitution with no slavery merely prohibited the future importation of slaves into Kansas. Free soilers saw this choice as a "heads you win, tails I lose" proposition. They therefore denounced it as "The Great Swindle." Much of the northern Democratic press joined their Republican rivals in expressing outrage at this "dirty piece of work." Even if free-state men voted for the constitution with no slavery, they asked, what would stop slaveowners from smuggling human property across the two-hundred-mile border with Missouri? Once in Kansas this property would be as "inviolable" as any other. Several southern states banned the importation of slaves, but such laws had proved meaningless. And in any case, the chances of defeating the constitution *with* slavery were problematical, because the convention put the polling machinery for the referendum in the hands of the same officials who had shown so much previous skill in rigging elections.

Governor Walker denounced the outcome at Lecompton as "a vile fraud, a bare counterfeit." It was "impossible" that Buchanan would accept it, said Walker, for as recently as October 22 the president had reiterated his support for a fair referendum. But proslavery men who smiled and said that Buchanan had changed his mind were

right. To one northern Democrat who bitterly protested the president's reversal, Buchanan said he had no choice: if he did not accept the results of the Lecompton convention, southern states would either "secede from the Union or take up arms against him." Walker left Kansas never to return—the fourth governor in three years to be ground between the millstones of slavery and free soil.

On December 3, 1857, Walker's friend Stephen A. Douglas stormed into the White House to confront Buchanan on the "trickery and juggling" of this Lecompton constitution. To give Kansas statehood under such a travesty of popular sovereignty, Douglas warned the president, would destroy the Democratic party in the North. Douglas swore to oppose Buchanan in Congress if he insisted on going through with it. In return Buchanan warned Douglas that his disagreeing with "an administration of his own choice" would be political suicide. The gage was down for a duel that would split the Democratic party and ensure the election of a Republican president in 1860.

The "fraudulent submission" (Douglas's words) of the Lecompton constitution to Kansas voters occurred on December 21. Free soilers refused to participate in this referendum, which thereby approved the constitution "with slavery" by a vote of 6,226 to 569. (As usual, an investigation found 2,720 of the majority votes to have been fraudulent.) Meanwhile the new free-soil territorial legislature scheduled its own referendum for January 4, 1858. Voters this time would have an opportunity to accept or reject the whole constitution. Proslavery voters boycotted this referen-

Even though the proslavery party with its capital at Lecompton had become a minority in Kansas, it still had the support of the Buchanan administration. The Lecompton governor's "mansion" pictured here was perhaps in keeping with the amount of genuine support and respect he commanded.

dum, which resulted in a poll of 138 for the constitution "with slavery," 24 for it "with no slavery," and 10,226 against the constitution.

Congress now had two referenda to choose from. Fire-eaters below the Potomac heated up their rhetoric to ensure the correct choice. Governors and legislatures stood by to call conventions to consider secession if Congress refused to admit Kansas under the "duly ratified" Lecompton constitution. "If Kansas is *driven out of the Union for being a Slave State*," asked South Carolina's Senator James Hammond, "can any Slave State remain in it with honor?" These threats stiffened Buchanan's backbone. On February 2, 1858, he sent the Lecompton constitution to Congress with a message recommending admission of a sixteenth slave state. Kansas, proclaimed the president, "is at this moment as much a slave state as Georgia or South Carolina."

The Lecompton issue gripped Congress for several months. It evoked more passion than even the initial Kansas-Nebraska Act four years earlier. The lineup was the same now as then—with two significant differences: this time Douglas led the opposition; and the new Republican party dominated northern representation in the House. Douglas's political future hung in the balance. If he had supported Lecompton, southern backing for his presidential nomination in 1860 would have been assured. But in those circumstances the nomination would have been worth little. The millstone of Lecompton would sink Democratic chances of carrying any northern state. Douglas did not hesitate in his choice. He could never vote, he told the Senate, to "force this constitution down the throats of the people of Kansas, in opposition to their wishes and in violation of our pledges." Douglas had the novel experience of seeing himself lionized by such members of the opposition as Horace Greeley, who wanted to adopt him as a good Republican.

From the South, however, came little but eternal damnation. Southerners professed "astonishment" that the Illinoisian had turned against them. "Douglas was with us until the time of trial came," said a Georgian, "then he deceived and betrayed us." As the controversy sharpened, southern rhetoric toward Douglas became more heated: he was "at the head of the Black column . . . stained with the dishonor of treachery without a parallel."

With its southern-dominated Democratic majority, the Senate approved admission of Kansas as a slave state on March 23, 1858. In the House the administration could count on at least half of the northern Democrats, as in 1854. But this time that was not enough to win the battle. "Battle" was not too strong a word for events in the House. On one occasion during an all-night session, Republican Galusha Grow of Pennsylvania and Democrat Lawrence Keitt of South Carolina got into a fight, and other congressmen from both sides rushed into the melee. Although this fracas resulted in no real harm to any aging participant, Alexander Stephens believed that "if any weapons had been on hand it would probably have been a bloody one. All things here are tending my mind to the conclusion that the Union cannot and will not last long." On April 1, in a dramatic roll call, twenty-two (of fifty-three) northern Democrats joined the Republicans and a handful of Americans to defeat Lecompton by a vote of 120 to 112. "The agony is over," wrote a Douglas Democrat, "and thank God, the right has triumphed!"

To save face, the administration supported a compromise by which Kansans would vote again on acceptance or rejection of Lecompton under the guise of a referendum on an adjustment in the size of the customary land grant to be received upon admission to statehood. Rejection of the land grant would defer statehood for at least two years. Spurning this subterfuge as a bribe, Kansans defeated it on August 2 by a vote of 11,300 to 1,788. During this time Kansas had resumed bleeding from a number of wounds. Free Soilers and border ruffians raided and ambushed each other with considerable ferocity. In May 1858, almost on the second anniversary of the Pottawatomie massacre, a proslavery band evened the score by seizing nine free-state settlers from their cabins and shooting them by firing squad (four survived their wounds). John Brown himself reappeared in the territory. His band invaded Missouri, killed a slaveholder, and liberated eleven slaves and a good many horses and took them to Canada.

Free-state Kansans organized a Republican party and elected two-thirds of the delegates to a new constitutional convention in 1859. Kansas finally came in as a free state in January 1861, joining California, Minnesota, and Oregon, whose entry since the Mexican War had given the North a four-state edge over the South. Kansas also became one of the most Republican states in the Union. Though most of the free-state settlers had originally been Democrats, the struggle with the slave power pushed them into the Republican party, which regularly rolled up two- or three-to-one majorities during the early years of statehood.

With enemies like the Democrats, Republicans scarcely needed friends. As if Kansas were not enough, the Buchanan administration, the Supreme Court, and southern Democrats ventured several other actions seemingly designed to ensure Republican victory in the presidential election of 1860.

LINCOLN AND DOUGLAS DEBATE IN 1858.

CHAPTER SIX

★ ★ ★ ★ ★

Mudsills and Greasy Mechanics for A. Lincoln

I

D red Scott lived all but two of his sixty-odd years in obscurity. The fame he achieved late in life was not for himself but for what he represented. Scott had been a slave of army surgeon John Emerson, who had taken him from Missouri to posts in Illinois and at Fort Snelling in the northern part of the Louisiana Purchase (now Minnesota) for several years in the 1830s. At Fort Snelling, Scott married a slave also owned by Emerson. She gave birth to a daughter in territory made free by the Missouri Compromise while Emerson was returning the Scotts to Missouri. After Emerson died and his widow inherited the Scotts, white friends of Dred Scott in St. Louis advised him in 1846 to sue for freedom on grounds of prolonged residence in a free state and a free territory. Scott did so. Thus began an eleven-year saga that started as a simple freedom suit and escalated into the most notorious *cause célèbre* in American constitutional history.

Scott first lost his suit but then won it on retrial in St. Louis county court in 1850. On appeal the Missouri supreme court overturned this decision in 1852 and remanded the Scotts to slavery. The case was beginning to acquire political significance. Missouri courts had previously granted freedom to slaves in cases similar to Scott's. In overturning those precedents and asserting that Missouri law prevailed despite Scott's residence in free territory, the state supreme court was reacting to proslavery pressures. Scott's lawyers, who now included a Vermont-born resident of St. Louis, thought they could win the case if they could get it before a federal court. Scott's owner having moved to New York, the lawyers appealed to the federal circuit court under the diverse-citizenship clause of the Constitution, which gives federal courts jurisdiction over cases involving citizens of different states. In 1854 the circuit court for Missouri accepted the case (thereby affirming Scott's status as a citizen) but upheld the Missouri court's denial of his suit for freedom. Scott's lawyers appealed to the U.S. Supreme Court. Proslavery elements welcomed this move. The potential of the case for resolving crucial constitutional issues had become clear. And the Supreme Court had a southern majority.

Opposite page: Knox College in Galesburg was the site of the fifth Lincoln-Douglas debate, on October 7, 1858. Strongly antislavery, Galesburg was friendly territory for Lincoln.

DRED SCOTT.

HARRIET, WIFE OF DRED SCOTT.

Dred Scott married Harriet Robinson at Fort Snelling in what was then Wisconsin Territory in 1837. Before returning to St. Louis in 1840 they had a daughter. A second daughter was later born in St. Louis. An antislavery lawyer who had moved to Missouri from Illinois in 1846 and the pastor of the Second African Baptist Church in St. Louis, where Harriet Scott was a member, sponsored the Scotts' suit for freedom. Meanwhile the Scotts' owner, the widow of Dr. Emerson, had remarried. Her new husband was an abolitionist who was horrified to learn, from the Supreme Court's decision in 1857, that his wife was a slaveholder. He immediately freed the Scotts. Dred lived only a year and a half in freedom, dying of tuberculosis in September 1858; history does not record what happened to Harriet.

The justices first heard arguments on the case in 1856 and held it over for reargument in the 1856–57 session—perhaps to avoid rendering a decision before the presidential election. Three main questions were before the Court: 1) As a black man, was Scott a citizen with a right to sue in federal courts? 2) Had prolonged residence (two years in each place) in a free state and territory made Scott free? 3) Was Fort Snelling actually free territory—that is, did Congress in 1820 have the right to ban slavery in the Louisiana Purchase north of 36° 30'? The Court could have ducked questions one and three by merely reaffirming the decisions of the Missouri supreme court and the federal circuit court that Missouri law governed Scott's status. Precedents existed for doing so; the Supreme Court itself in *Strader v. Graham* (1851) had refused to accept an appeal from the Kentucky supreme court ruling that slaves from Kentucky taken temporarily to Ohio remained slaves under Kentucky law. And indeed, for a time it appeared that the Court would take this way out. On February 14, 1857, a majority of justices voted to reaffirm the *Strader* principle and let it go at that. Justice Samuel Nelson of New York began to write the decision. But a few days later the majority reversed itself and decided to issue a comprehensive ruling covering all aspects of the case.

Why did the Court take this fateful step? Answers to this question have been uncertain and partisan. Only fragmentary accounts of the justices' confidential discussions leaked out, some of them years later. One interpretation of this evidence maintains that the two non-Democrats on the Court, John McLean of Ohio and Benjamin Curtis of Massachusets, stated their intention to dissent from the narrow decision prepared by Nelson. Their dissent would not only uphold Scott's freedom but would also affirm black citizenship and endorse the right of Congress to prohibit slavery in the territories. Not wishing these dissents to stand as the Court's only statement on such contentious issues, the southern majority reconsidered its decision to ignore them and voted to have Chief Justice Roger B. Taney write a comprehensive ruling. Thus, according to this interpretation, McLean and Curtis were responsible for provoking the vexatious Dred Scott decision that superseded Nelson's innocuous opinion.

But the truth appears to be more complex. For a decade the question of slavery in the territories had threatened the Union. Politicians had been trying to pass the buck to the courts since the Compromise of 1850, which had provided for expedited appeal to the Supreme Court of any suit concerning slave property in the territories of Utah and New Mexico—a provision repeated verbatim in the Kansas-Nebraska Act of 1854. The problem was that because these territories did not prohibit slavery, no such suit materialized. But here, conveniently, came a suit from another part of the Louisiana Purchase. The yearning for settlement of this question by "judicial statesmanship" was widespread in Washington during the winter of 1856–57, especially among southerners. Alexander Stephens, a friend of Justice James M. Wayne of Georgia and a distant cousin of Justice Robert Grier of Pennsylvania, wrote privately in December 1856: "I have been urging all the influence I could bring to bear upon the Sup. Ct. to get them no longer to postpone the case on the Mo. Restriction. . . . I have reason to believe they will [decide] that the restriction was unconstitutional." Other southerners exerted similar pressures on the Court. They seemed to be succeeding. Two weeks later Stephens reported that "from what I hear *sub rosa* [the decision] will be according to my own opinions upon every point. . . . The restriction of 1820 will be held to be unconstitutional. The Judges are all writing out their opinions I believe *seriatim*. The Chief Justice will give an elaborate one."

The five southern justices did want to rule against Congress's right to ban slavery from the territories. Some of them had indeed begun writing opinions to that effect. But the difficulty was in getting the two northern Democratic justices, Grier and Nelson, to go along with them. This was why the southerners had reluctantly decided to sidestep the issue with Nelson's narrow ruling. Word that McLean and Curtis would raise the broader questions in their dissents gave southern justices the pretext they needed to change their minds. They approved a motion by Wayne that Taney should prepare a decision covering all aspects of the case.

There still remained the problem of cajoling a concurrence from at least one northern justice to avoid the appearance of a purely sectional ruling. Nelson could not be persuaded—he had already written his opinion and was probably miffed by his colleagues' intent to bypass it. But Grier was pliable. He was also from

Roger Brooke Taney was born during the American Revolution (1777) and lived through most of the Civil War, dying in 1864. His tenure as chief justice of the United States (1836–64) was longer than that of any other chief justice except John Marshall. Although the Taney Court rendered many important decisions concerning economic regulation, incorporation laws, and federal-state relations, it is remembered mostly for its notorious proslavery rulings, especially the Dred Scott decision.

Buchanan's home state. The president-elect was anxious to have the territorial question resolved. In response to a suggestion from Justice John Catron of Tennessee, Buchanan brought highly improper but efficacious influence to bear on Grier, who succumbed. Taney had his northern justice and could proceed with his ruling.

It was an opinion he had long wanted to write. Eighty years old, the chief justice was frail and ill. The death of his wife and daughter two years earlier in a yellow fever epidemic had left him heart-stricken. Yet he clung to life determined to defend his beloved South from the malign forces of Black Republicanism. In his younger days Taney had been a Jacksonian committed to liberating American enterprise from the shackles of special privilege. As Jackson's secretary of the treasury he had helped destroy the Second Bank of the United States. His early decisions as chief justice had undermined special corporate charters. But the main theme of his twenty-eight-year tenure on the Court was the defense of slavery. Taney had no great love of the institution for its own sake, having freed his own slaves. But he did have a passionate commitment "to southern life and values, which seemed organically linked to the peculiar institution and unpreservable without it." In private letters Taney expressed growing anger toward "northern aggression." "Our own southern countrymen" were in great danger, he wrote; "the knife of the assassin is at their throats." Taney's southern colleagues on the Court shared this apprehension, according to historian Don Fehrenbacher; Justice Peter Daniel of Virginia was "a brooding proslavery fanatic" and the other three were "unreserved defenders of slavery." Because of this "emotional commitment so intense that it made perception and logic utterly subservient," the Dred Scott decision was "essentially visceral in origin . . . a work of unmitigated partisanship, polemical in spirit [with an] extraordinary cumulation of error, inconsistency, and misrepresentation."

Taney's opinion took up first the question whether Dred Scott, as a black man, was a citizen with the right to sue in federal courts. Taney devoted more space to this matter than to anything else. Why he did so is puzzling, for in the public mind this was the least important issue in the case. But southern whites viewed free blacks as an anomaly and a threat to the stability of slavery; Taney's own state of Maryland contained the largest free Negro population of any state. The chief justice's apparent purpose in negating U.S. citizenship for blacks, wrote Fehrenbacher, was "to launch a sweeping counterattack on the antislavery movement and . . . to meet every threat to southern stability by separating the Negro race absolutely from the federal Constitution and all the rights that it bestowed." To do so, however, he had to juggle history, law, and logic in "a gross

---

NOW READY:

THE

Dred Scott Decision.

OPINION OF CHIEF-JUSTICE ROGER B. TANEY,

WITH AN INTRODUCTION,

BY DR. J. H. VAN EVRIE.

ALSO,

AN APPENDIX,

BY SAM. A. CARTWRIGHT, M.D., of New Orleans,

ENTITLED,

"Natural History of the Prognathous Race of Mankind."

ORIGINALLY WRITTEN FOR THE NEW YORK DAY-BOOK.

THE GREAT WANT OF A BRIEF PAMPHLET, containing the famous decision of Chief-Justice Taney, in the celebrated Dred Scott Case, has induced the Publishers of the DAY-BOOK to present this edition to the public. It contains a Historical Introduction by Dr. Van Evrie, author of "Negroes and Negro Slavery," and an Appendix by Dr. Cartwright, of New Orleans, in which the physical differences between the negro and the white races are forcibly presented. As a whole, this pamphlet gives the *historical, legal,* and *physical* aspects of the "Slavery" Question in a concise compass, and should be circulated by thousands before the next presidential election. All who desire to answer the arguments of the abolitionists should read it. In order to place it before the masses, and induce Democratic Clubs, Democratic Town Committees, and all interested in the cause, to order it for distribution, it has been put down at the following low rates, for which it will be sent, free of postage, to any part of the United States. Dealers supplied at the same rate.

Single Copies	$0 25
Five Copies	1 00
Twelve Copies	2 00
Fifty Copies	7 00
One Hundred Copies	12 00
Every additional Hundred	10 00

Address

VAN EVRIE, HORTON, & CO.,

Publishers of DAY-BOOK,

No. 40 Ann Street, New York.

---

perversion of the facts." Negroes had not been part of the "sovereign people" who made the Constitution, Taney ruled; they were not included in the "all men" whom the Declaration of Independence proclaimed "created equal." After all, the author of that Declaration and many of the signers owned slaves, and for them to have regarded members of the enslaved race as potential citizens would have been "utterly and flagrantly inconsistent with the principles they asserted." For that matter, wrote Taney, at the time the Constitution was adopted Negroes "had for more than a century before been regarded as beings of an inferior order . . . so far inferior, that they had no rights which a white man was bound to respect."

This was false, as Curtis and McLean pointed out in their dissents. Free blacks in 1788 and later had many legal rights (to hold and bequeath property, make contracts, seek redress in courts, among others). In five of the thirteen states that ratified the Constitution black men were legal voters and participated in the ratification process. No matter, said Taney, these were rights of state citizenship and the question at issue was United States citizenship. A person might "have all of the rights and privileges of the citizen of a State," opined the chief justice, and "yet not be entitled to the rights and privileges of a citizen in any other State"—a piece of judicial legerdemain that contradicted Article IV, Section 2, of the Constitution: "The citizens of each state shall be entitled to all privileges and immunities of citizens in the several states."

Having established to his satisfaction that blacks were not citizens, Taney could have stopped there and refused jurisdiction because the case was not properly before the Court. That he did not do so rendered the remainder of his decision, in the opinion of many contemporaries and the earliest generations of historians, *obiter dictum*—a statement in passing on matters not formally before the Court and therefore without force of law. But Taney insisted that because the circuit court had considered all aspects of the case and decided them "on their merits," the whole case including the constitutionality of the Missouri Compromise restriction on which Scott based part of his suit for freedom *was* properly before the Court. Modern scholars agree. Whatever else Taney's ruling was, it was not *obiter dictum*.

Taney and six other justices (with only Curtis and McLean dissenting) concurred that Scott's "sojourn" for two years in Illinois and for a similar period at Fort Snelling, *even if the latter was free territory*, did not make him free once he returned to Missouri. To this matter Taney devoted only one of the fifty-five pages of his opinion. The constitutionality of the Missouri Compromise received twenty-one pages of labored prose arguing that Congress never had the right to prohibit slavery in a territory. That the Constitution (Article IV, Section 3) gave Congress the power to "make all needful rules and regulations" for the territories was not relevant, said the chief justice in a typical example of hair-splitting, because rules and regulations were not laws. The Fifth Amendment protected persons from being deprived of life, liberty, or property without due process; slavery was no different from other property, and a ban on slavery was therefore an unconstitutional deprivation of property. "And if Congress itself cannot do this," continued Taney in what he intended as a blow against popular sovereignty, "it could not authorize a territorial government to exercise" such a power. This clearly was *obiter dictum*, since the question of the power of a territorial government over slavery was not part of the case.

Republicans adopted the dissents by Curtis and McLean as their official position on the case. Not only was Scott a free man by virtue of his prolonged residence in free territory, said the dissenters, but he was also a citizen under the Constitution. And that Constitution did empower Congress to prohibit slavery in the territories. "*All* needful rules and regulations" meant precisely what it said. The first Congress under the Constitution had reaffirmed the Northwest Ordinance of 1787 banning slavery in the Northwest Territory. Subsequent Congresses down through 1820 excluded slavery from specific territories on four additional occasions. Many framers of the Constitution were alive during this period, and none objected to these acts. Indeed, several framers served in Congress and voted for them or, as presidents of the United States, signed them into law! If the exclusion of slavery from a territory violated due process, asked Curtis, what of the 1807 law ending importation of slaves from Africa? Indeed, what of laws in *free states* banning slavery? In any case, to prevent a slaveowner from taking his slaves into a territory did not deprive him of that property.

Instead of removing the issue of slavery in the territories from politics, the Court's ruling encouraged northern Democrats, who saw it as devastating to the antislavery platform, and gratified southerners, who regarded it as a reaffirmation of the constitutionality of slavery and a lethal blow to Black Republicans. But the Republican party declined to die. Its press condemned this "jesuitical decision" based on "gross historical falsehoods" and a "willful perversion" of the Constitution. If this ruling "shall stand for law," wrote William Cullen Bryant, slavery was no longer the "peculiar institution" of fifteen states but "a Federal institution, the common patrimony and shame of all the States." Republican state legislatures passed resolutions asserting that the ruling was "not binding in law and conscience."

The *New York Tribune* declared contemptuously that this decision by "five slaveholders and two doughfaces" was a "*dictum* . . . entitled to just as much moral weight as would be the judgment of a majority of those congregated in any Washington barroom." The *dictum* theory justified Republican refusal to recognize the ruling as a binding precedent. They proclaimed an intent to "reconstitute" the Court and to overturn *Dred Scott*. "The remedy," said the *Chicago Tribune*, was "the ballot box. . . . Let the next President be Republican, and 1860 will mark an era kindred with that of 1776."

It soon dawned on northern Democrats that Taney had aimed to discomfit them as well as the Republicans. Although the question of popular sovereignty had not been directly before the Court, the principle of *Dred Scott* was not merely that Congress had

Many public meetings expressed outrage over the Dred Scott decision. This broadside advertised a protest meeting in Philadelphia to be addressed by leading black and white abolitionists.

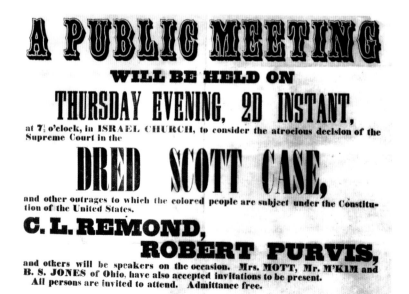

A PUBLIC MEETING

WILL BE HELD ON

THURSDAY EVENING, 2D INSTANT,

at 7½ o'clock, in ISRAEL CHURCH, to consider the atrocious decision of the Supreme Court in the

DRED SCOTT CASE,

and other outrages to which the colored people are subject under the Constitution of the United States.

C. L. REMOND,

ROBERT PURVIS,

and others will be speakers on the occasion. Mrs. MOTT, Mr. M'KIM and B. S. JONES of Ohio, have also accepted invitations to be present. All persons are invited to attend. Admittance free.

no power to exclude slavery from a territory, but that slave property *could not be excluded*. Douglas grasped this nettle fearlessly. Yes, he said in a speech at Springfield, Illinois, in June 1857, the Dred Scott decision was law and all good citizens must obey it. A master's right to take slaves into any territory was irrevocable. *But*—citizens of a territory could still control this matter. How? The right of property in slaves "necessarily remains a barren and worthless right," said Douglas, "unless sustained, protected and enforced by appropriate police regulations and local legislation" which depended on "the will and the wishes of the people of the Territory."

This anticipated the famous Freeport doctrine enunciated by Douglas more than a year later in his debates with Lincoln. It was an ingenious attempt to enable both northern and southern Democrats to have their cake and eat it. It might have worked had not Lecompton crumbled Democratic unity. When that happened, southern Democrats insisted on another dessert. They agreed with Douglas that the Dred Scott decision would not enforce itself. "The Senator from Illinois is right," conceded Senator Albert G. Brown of Mississippi. "By non-action, by unfriendly action . . . the Territorial Legislature can exclude slavery." But that would amount to a denial of the "right of protection for our slave property in the Territories. The Constitution as expounded by the Supreme Court, awards it. We demand it; we mean to have it." Congress must pass a federal slave code for the territories, said Brown, and enforce it with the United States army if necessary. If those in the North "deny to us rights guaranteed by the Constitution . . . then, sir . . . the Union is a despotism [and] I am prepared to retire from the concern."

Thus instead of crippling the Republican party as Taney had hoped, the Dred Scott decision strengthened it by widening the sectional schism among Democrats. Republicans moved quickly to exploit their advantage by depicting the decision as the consequence of a slave-power conspiracy. Seward and Lincoln were two of the foremost advocates of a conspiracy theory. Citing "whisperings" between Taney and Buchanan at the inaugural ceremony plus other unnamed evidence, Seward charged collusion between the president-elect and the chief justice. Seward's accusations provoked an uproar. Some historians have echoed Democratic opinion that they were "venomous" and "slanderous." But in fact Seward hit uncomfortably close to the mark. He might almost have read the letter from Buchanan to Grier urging the Pennsylvania justice to go along with the southern majority.

Seward's insinuations enraged Taney. The chief justice said later that if the New Yorker had won the presidency in 1860 he would have refused to administer the oath. Ironically, Taney did administer the oath to a man who had made a similar accusation. In a speech after his nomination for senator from Illinois in 1858, Abraham Lincoln reviewed the process by which Democrats had repealed the Missouri Compromise in 1854 and then declared it unconstitutional in 1857. We cannot *know* that all of this was part of a conspiracy to expand slavery, conceded Lincoln. "But when we see a lot of framed timbers . . . which we know have been gotten out at different times and places by different workmen—Stephen, Franklin, Roger and James, for instance—and when we see these timbers joined together, and see they exactly make the frame of a house . . . we find it impossible to not *believe* that Stephen and Franklin and Roger and James . . . all worked upon a common *plan*."

The same speech included a more famous house metaphor. "'A house divided against itself cannot stand,'" said Lincoln quoting Jesus. "I believe this government cannot endure, permanently half *slave* and half *free*." The opponents of slavery hoped to stop the spread of the institution and "place it where the public mind shall rest in the belief that it is in the course of ultimate extinction." But advocates of slavery—including those conspiring carpenters—were trying to "push it forward, till it shall become lawful in *all* the States . . . *North* as well as *South*." How could they do this? "Simply [by] the next Dred Scott decision. It is merely for the Supreme Court to decide that no State under the Constitution can exclude it, just as they have already decided that . . . neither Congress nor the Territorial Legislature can do it." Article VI of the Constitution affirms that the Constitution and laws of the United States "shall be the supreme law of the land . . . anything in the Constitution or laws of any State to the contrary notwithstanding." If, therefore, the U.S. Constitution protected "the right of property in a slave," noted Lincoln, then "nothing in the Constitution or laws of any State can destroy the right of property in a slave." Lincoln himself believed that "the right of property in a slave is *not* distinctly and expressly affirmed in the Constitution." But Democrats including Douglas believed that it was. If they had their way, Lincoln told Illinois Republicans in June 1858, "we shall *lie down* pleasantly dreaming that the people of *Missouri* are on the verge of making their State *free*; and we shall *awake* to the *reality*, instead, that the *Supreme* Court has made *Illinois* a *slave* State."

Did Lincoln and other Republicans really believe that the Dred Scott decision was part of a conspiracy to expand slavery into free *states*? Or were they creating a bugaboo to frighten northern voters? Stephen Douglas presumed the latter. "A school boy knows" that the Court would never make "so ridiculous a decision," said Douglas. "It is an insult to men's understanding, and a gross calumny on the Court." A good many historians have echoed Douglas's words. But was the Republican claim ridiculous? In November 1857 the *Washington Union*, organ of the Buchanan administration, carried an article asserting that the abolition of slavery in northern states had been an unconstitutional attack on property. In private correspondence and in other contexts not conducive to propaganda, Republicans expressed genuine alarm at the implications of *Dred Scott*. "The Constitution of the United States is the paramount law of every State," Senator James Doolittle of Wisconsin pointed out, "and if that recognizes slaves as property, as horses are property, no State constitution or State law can abolish it." Noting that Scott had lived as a slave in Illinois for two years, the New York legislature denounced the doctrine that "a master may take his slave into a Free State without dissolving the relation of master and slave. . . . [This] will bring slavery within our borders, against our will, with all its unhallowed, demoralizing, and blighting influences."

The legislature's concern was not abstract. Pending in the New York courts was a case concerning a slaveholder's right to retain ownership of his slaves while in transit through a free state. *Lemmon v. The People* had originated in 1852 when a New York judge upheld the freedom of eight slaves who had left their Virginia owner while in New York City on their way to Texas. Most northern states had earlier granted slaveowners the right of transit or temporary sojourn with their slaves. But by the 1850s all except New Jersey and Illinois had laws on the books offering freedom to any slave brought by a master within their borders. The Dred Scott decision challenged the principle of these laws. Virginia therefore decided to take the Lemmon case to the highest New York court (which upheld the state law in 1860) and would undoubtedly have appealed it to Taney's Supreme Court had not secession intervened. The Lemmon case might well have become Lincoln's "next Dred Scott decision" and opened the door to some form of slavery in free states.

II

Thus in the context of *Dred Scott*, Lincoln's "warning that slavery might become lawful everywhere was . . . far from absurd." His attempt to identify Douglas with this proslavery conspiracy ("Stephen and Franklin and Roger and James") was part of Lincoln's campaign for the Senate in 1858.

During the Lecompton debate Douglas had said that he cared not whether slavery was voted down or up in Kansas—his concern was that Kansas have a fair vote. This "care not" policy, said Lincoln, had been prolific of evil, for it enabled the proponents of slavery to push forward their program of expansion without effective opposition. The only way to stop them was to elect Republicans "whose hearts are in the work—who *do care* for the result," who "consider slavery a moral, social, and political wrong," who "will oppose . . . the modern Democratic idea that slavery is as good as freedom, and ought to have room for expansion all over the continent."

This was the message that Lincoln carried to Illinois voters in dozens of speeches during that summer of '58. Douglas traversed the same territory branding Lincoln a Black Republican whose abolition doctrines would destroy the Union and flood Illinois with thousands of thick-lipped, bullet-headed, degenerate blacks. Lincoln "believes that the Almighty made the Negro equal to the white man," said Douglas at Springfield in July. "He thinks that the Negro is his brother. I do not think the Negro is any kin of mine at all. . . . This government . . . was made by white men, for the benefit of white men and their posterity, to be executed and managed by white men."

Desiring to confront Douglas directly, Lincoln proposed a series of debates. Douglas agreed to seven confrontations in various parts of the state. These debates are deservedly the most famous in American history. They matched two powerful logicians and hard-hitting speakers, one of them nationally eminent and the other little known outside his region. To the seven prairie towns came thousands of farmers, workers, clerks, lawyers, and people from all walks of life to sit or stand outdoors for hours in sunshine or rain, heat or cold, dust or mud. The crowds participated in the debates by shouted questions, pointed comments, cheers, and groans. The stakes were higher than a senatorial election, higher even than the looming presidential contest of 1860, for the theme of the debates was nothing less than the future of slavery and the Union. Tariffs, banks, internal improvements,

This rare photograph shows the crowd that turned out for Lincoln's speech outside the courthouse in Paris, Illinois, on September 7, 1858. In the speech Lincoln charged that Douglas's policy of "popular sovereignty" was really an ill-disguised scheme to foist slavery on Kansas in violation of the will of the majority there.

corruption, and other staples of American politics received not a word in these debates—the sole topic was slavery.

In the fashion of debaters, Douglas and Lincoln opened with slashing attacks designed to force the other man to spend his time defending vulnerable positions. Lincoln's main thrust was the accusation that Douglas had departed from the position of the founding fathers, while the Republicans were upholding that position. Like the fathers, Republicans "insist that [slavery] should as far as may be, be treated as a wrong, and one of the methods of treating it as a wrong is to make provision that *it shall grow no larger.*" Lincoln reiterated that the country could not exist forever half slave and half free; it had existed in that condition so far only because until 1854 most Americans shared the founders' faith that restricting slavery's growth would put it on the path to ultimate extinction. But Douglas not only *"looks to no end of the institution of slavery,"* he looks to its *"perpetuity and nationalization."* He is thus "eradicating the light of reason and the love of liberty in this American people."

In one respect Lincoln's celebrated Freeport question was a departure from this strategy of linking Douglas to the slave power. Was there any lawful way, Lincoln asked at Freeport, that the people of a territory could exclude slavery if they wished to do so? The point of the question, of course, was to nail the contradiction between *Dred Scott* and popular sovereignty. Folklore history has portrayed this question as the stone that slew Goliath. If Douglas answered No, he alienated Illinois voters and jeopardized his reelection to the Senate. If he answered Yes, he alienated the South and lost their support for the presidency in 1860. The problem with this thesis is that Douglas had already confronted the issue many times. Lincoln knew how he would answer the question: "He will instantly take ground that slavery can not actually exist in the territories, unless the people desire it, and so give it protective territorial legislation. If this offends the South he will let it offend them; as at all events he means to hold on to his chances in Illinois. . . . He cares nothing for the South—he knows he is already dead there" because of his opposition to Lecompton. Lincoln asked the question anyway; Douglas answered as expected. His answer became famous in retrospect as the Freeport doctrine. It did play a role in prompting the southern demand for a territorial slave code—an issue that split the Democratic party in 1860. But this would have happened anyway. Lincoln did not press the question in subsequent debates, for its tendency to highlight Douglas's differences from southern Democrats ran counter to Lincoln's effort to highlight their similarities.

Douglas's counterattack smote Lincoln's house-divided metaphor. Why cannot the country continue to "exist divided into free and slave States?" asked Douglas. Whatever their personal sentiments toward slavery, the founding fathers "left each State perfectly free to do as it pleased on the subject." If the nation "cannot endure thus divided, then [Lincoln] must strive to make them all free or all slave, which will inevitably bring about a dissolution of the Union." To talk about ultimate extinction of slavery "is revolutionary and destructive of the existence of this Government." No, said Douglas, "I would not endanger the perpetuity of this Union. I would not blot out the great inalienable rights of the white men for all the negroes that ever existed."

The Lincoln-Douglas debates drew large crowds in most of the seven towns where they were held. The crowds sensed that the future of the nation might be at stake in the outcome of this election: free or slave, united or divided. Note the presence of women in the audience. Though women could not vote, many of them avidly followed political events.

THE CAMPAIGN IN ILLINOIS.

THE LAST JOINT DEBATE.

DOUGLAS AND LINCOLN AT ALTON.

5,000 TO 10,000 PERSONS PRESENT!

LINCOLN AGAIN REFUSES TO ANSWER WHETHER HE WILL VOTE TO ADMIT KANSAS IF HER PEOPLE APPLY WITH A CONSTITUTION RECOGNIZING SLAVERY.

APPEARS IN HIS OLD CHARACTER OF THE "ARTFUL DODGER."

TRIES TO PALM HIMSELF OFF TO THE WHIGS OF MADISON COUNTY AS A FRIEND OF HENRY CLAY AND NO ABOLITIONIST, AND IS EXPOSED!!

GREAT SPEECHES OF SENATOR DOUGLAS.

Lincoln's inclusion of blacks among those "created equal" was a "monstrous heresy," said Douglas. "The signers of the Declaration had no reference to the negro . . . or any other inferior and degraded race, when they spoke of the equality of men." Did Thomas Jefferson "intend to say in that Declaration that his negro slaves, which he held and treated as property, were created his equals by Divine law, and that he was violating the law of God every day of his life by holding them as slaves? ('No, no.')"

Douglas hit his stride in exploitation of the race issue. He considered it a sure winner in southern and central Illinois. The Negro "must always occupy an inferior position," shouted Douglas to cheering partisans. "Are you in favor of conferring upon the negro the rights and privileges of citizenship? ('No, no.') Do you desire to strike out of our State Constitution that clause which keeps slaves and free negroes out of the State . . . in order that when Missouri abolishes slavery she can send one hundred thousand emancipated slaves into Illinois, to become citizens and voters on an equality with yourselves? ('Never,' 'no.') . . . If you desire to allow them to come into the State and settle with the white man, if you desire them to vote . . . then support Mr. Lincoln and the Black Republican party, who are in favor of the citizenship of the negro. ('Never, never.')"

How did Douglas know that Lincoln favored these things? Black speakers were campaigning for him in the Yankee districts of northern Illinois, showing "how much interest our colored brethren [feel] in the success of their brother Abe. (Renewed laughter.) . . . Those of you who believe that the negro is your equal . . . of course will vote for Mr. Lincoln. ('Down with the negro,' no, no, &c.)"

Douglas's harping on this theme exasperated Lincoln. "Negro equality! Fudge!!" he wrote privately. "How long . . . shall there continue knaves to vend, and fools to gulp, so low a piece of demagougeism?" But try as he might, Lincoln could not ignore the issue. As he emerged from his hotel for the fourth debate at Charleston in southern Illinois, a man asked him if he was "really in favor of producing a perfect equality between negroes and white people." Placed on the defensive, Lincoln responded defensively. "Anything that argues me into his idea of a perfect social and political equality," complained Lincoln of Douglas's innuendoes, "is but a specious and fantastic arrangement of words, by which a man can prove a horse chestnut to be a chestnut horse." Lincoln admitted that he believed black people "entitled to all the natural rights enumerated in the Declaration of Independence, the right to life, liberty, and the pursuit of happiness." But "I do not understand that because I do not want a negro woman for a slave I must necessarily have her for a wife. (Cheers and laughter.)" So that his horse chestnut should no longer be mistaken for a chestnut horse, Lincoln spelled out his position with clarity: "that I am not, nor ever have been in favor of bringing about in any way the social and political equality of the white and black races, (applause)—that I am not nor ever have been in favor of making voters or jurors of negroes, nor of qualifying them to hold office, nor to intermarry with white people; and I will say in addition to this that there is a physical difference between the races which I believe will for ever forbid the two races living together on terms of social and political equality."

So far Lincoln would go in concession to the prejudices of most Illinois voters. But no farther. "Let us discard all this quibbling about this man and the other man— this race and that race and the other race being inferior," he said in Chicago. Instead let us "unite as one people throughout this land, until we shall once more stand up declaring that all men are created equal." Whether or not the black man was equal to the white man in mental or moral endowment, "in the right to eat the bread, without leave of anybody else, which his own hand earns, *he is my equal and the equal of Judge Douglas, and the equal of every living man.* (Great applause.)" As for political rights, racial intermarriage, and the like, these were matters for the state legislature, "and as Judge Douglas seems to be in constant horror that some such danger is rapidly approaching, I propose as the best means to prevent it that the Judge be kept at home and placed in the State Legislature where he can fight the measures. (Uproarious laughter and applause.)"

Despite Lincoln's wit, Douglas scored points on this issue. The Little Giant also backed Lincoln into a corner on the matter of slavery's "ultimate extinction." More than once Lincoln had said: "I have no purpose directly or indirectly to interfere with the institution of slavery in the States where it exists." "Well, if he is not in favor of that," asked Douglas, "how does he expect to bring slavery in a course of ultimate extinction? ('Hit him again.')" With such obfuscatory rhetoric, charged Douglas, the Black Republicans tried to conceal their purpose to attack slavery and break up the Union. Like the abolitionists, Lincoln refused to be drawn into discussion of a "plan" for ending slavery. He hoped that southerners would once again come to regard bondage as an evil, just as Washington, Jefferson, and the other founders had regarded it. And just as they had limited its expansion as a first step toward ending the evil, "I have no doubt that it *would* become extinct, for all time to come, if we but re-adopted the policy of the fathers."

In any case the questions of "a perfect social and political equality . . . upon which Judge Douglas has tried to force the controversy . . . are false issues," said

Lincoln in the concluding debate. The true issue was the morality and future of slavery. "That is the issue that will continue in this country when these poor tongues of Judge Douglas and myself shall be silent. It is the eternal struggle between these two principles—right and wrong—throughout the world . . . from the beginning of time. . . . The one is the common right of humanity and the other the divine right of kings. . . . No matter in what shape it comes, whether from a king who seeks to bestride the people of his own nation and live by the fruit of their labor, or from one race of men as an apology for enslaving another race, it is the same tyrannical principle."

In the judgment of history—or at least of most historians—Lincoln "won" the debates. The judgment of Illinois voters in 1858 is more difficult to discover. Republican and Democratic candidates for the legislature won virtually the same number of votes statewide—125,000 for each party. Democrats carried all but three of the fifty-four southern counties and Republicans all but six of the forty-eight northern counties. Because the legislature had not been reapportioned to reflect the faster growth of northern counties in the 1850s, and because eight of the thirteen holdover senators not up for election were Democrats, that party had a majority of fifty-four to forty-six in the next legislature and elected Douglas. It was a significant triumph for the Little Giant. He confirmed his standing as leader of his party in the North and its strongest candidate for the next presidential nomination. For Lincoln the election was a victory in defeat. He had battled the famous Douglas on at least even terms, clarified the issues between Republicans and northern Democrats more sharply than ever, and emerged as a Republican spokesman of national stature.

Democrats also carried five of the nine congressional districts in Illinois. That made the state one of the few northern bright spots for the party in 1858. Elsewhere Democrats suffered almost as great a debacle as in 1854. In the next House of Representatives the number of northern Democrats would drop from fifty-three to thirty-two. In the four lower-North states carried by Buchanan in 1856 (Pennsylvania, Indiana, Illinois, and New Jersey) the party balance shifted in 1858 from twenty-nine Democratic and twenty-one Republican congressmen to sixteen Democrats and thirty-four Republicans. The Republican share of the vote in these four states jumped from 35 percent in 1856 (when the American party was in the field) to 52 percent in 1858. Buchanan had invited a few friends to an ele-

This photograph was taken in Macomb, Illinois, a day before Lincoln's second debate with Douglas in Freeport. Lincoln could scarcely be considered handsome; he joked that he was the ugliest man he had ever known. The beard that he decided two years later to grow filled out his face but could not conceal his large ears.

gant White House dinner on election night. As telegrams bearing tidings of the returns from Pennsylvania came in, "we had a merry time of it," wrote the president next day, "laughing among other things over our crushing defeat. It is so great that it is almost absurd."

Lecompton and *Dred Scott* accounted for much of this Republican gain. Once again, victories by the "slave power" had produced a backlash that strengthened its deadliest enemies in the North. Other issues also worked in favor of the Republicans. The disappearance of the American party in the North pushed most of the remaining nativists into Republican ranks because they continued to perceive Democrats as the party of Romanism. In manufacturing regions the Democratic tariff policy and the depression following the Panic of 1857 intensified voter backlash. Republicans also benefited from continued southern opposition to homestead legislation and to federal aid for construction of a transcontinental railroad.

III

A dozen years of growth and prosperity came to a jolting halt in 1857–58. The Panic of 1857 had both foreign and domestic roots. The Crimean War (1854–56) had cut off Russian grain from the European market. American exports mushroomed to meet the need. This intensified a surge of speculation in western lands. The decade-long expansion of all economic indices had also produced rapid rises in the prices of stocks and bonds. From 1848 to 1856 the number of banks increased 50 percent and their notes, loans, and deposits doubled. Railroad mileage and capital grew threefold from 1850 to 1857. Textile mills, foundries, and factories ran at full tilt to meet an apparently insatiable demand. California gold continued to pump millions of dollars monthly into the economy. By 1856, however, pessimists began to discern some cracks in this economic structure. Much of the capital invested in American railroads, insurance companies, and banks came from Europe, especially Britain. The Crimean War plus simultaneous British and French colonial ventures in the Far East drained specie from the banks of those countries. This brought a doubling and even tripling of interest rates in Britain and France, causing European investors to sell lower-yielding American securities to reinvest at home. The resulting decline in the prices of some American stocks and bonds in 1856–57 in turn reduced the assets of American banks holding these securities. Meanwhile British banks increased the ratio of reserves to liabilities, causing some American banks to do the same. And a buildup of unsold inventories caused several American textile mills to shut down temporarily.

By the summer of 1857 the combination of speculative fever in some parts of the economy and ominous cutbacks in others created a climate of nervous apprehension. "What can be the end of all this but another general collapse like that of 1837?" asked the financial writer of the *New York Herald.* "The same premonitory symptoms that prevailed in 1835–36 prevail in 1857 in a tenfold degree . . . paper bubbles of all descriptions, a general scramble for western lands and town and city sites, millions of dollars, made or borrowed, expended in fine houses and gaudy

THE BANKS ON A "BUST."

This cartoon satirizes the bank failures that set off the Panic of 1857. The banks had overexpanded (gone on a "bust") and could not meet their obligations. The implication is that once this bust had run its course the economy would experience a hangover that would be good for it; the banks would be more conservative in the future.

furniture. . . . That a storm is brewing on the commercial horizon there can be no doubt."

Given this mood, any financial tremor was likely to become an earthquake through the mechanism of self-fulfilling prophecy. On August 24 came the tremor: the New York branch of an Ohio investment house suspended payments because the cashier had embezzled its funds. The crisis of confidence set off by this event reverberated through the economy. Financial markets in most parts of the country were now connected by telegraph; the novelty of instant communication charged these markets with a volatility that caused a rumor in one region to become a crisis somewhere else. Depositors made runs on banks, which had to call in loans to obtain specie. This caused overextended speculators and entrepreneurs to go under. A wave of panic selling hit Wall Street. As the ripple of these failures began to spread through the country in September, a ship carrying $2 million in gold from California went to the bottom in a storm. By mid-October all but a handful of the nation's banks had suspended specie payments. Factories shut down; business failures multiplied; railroads went bankrupt; construction halted; crop prices plummeted; the intricate structure of land speculation collapsed like a house of cards; immigration dropped in 1858 to its lowest level

The Panic extended from banks to some of the retail establishments that depended on them for credit. This illustration from Harper's Weekly *depicts a crowd of shoppers on Broadway taking advantage of a liquidation sale at a dry goods store satirically labeled "O.L.D. PINCHPENCE."*

in thirteen years; imports fell off; and the federal treasury (whose revenues came mainly from tariffs and land sales) ran a deficit for the first time in a decade. Men and women by hundreds of thousands lost their jobs and others went on short time or took wage cuts as the winter of 1857–58 came on.

Remembering that some of the European revolutions in 1848 (which had been preceded by a financial downturn) had taken a radical turn toward class warfare, Americans wondered if they would experience similar events. Unemployed workers in several cities marched in demonstrations carrying banners demanding work or bread. In New York a large crowd broke into the shops of flour merchants. On November 10 a mob gathered in Wall Street and threatened forced entry into the U.S. customs house and subtreasury whose vaults contained $20 million. Soldiers and marines dispersed them, but unrest persisted through the winter, causing more than one anxious citizen to apprehend that "a nightmare broods over society."

Though often militant in rhetoric, these demonstrations generated little violence. No one was killed and few were injured—in sharp contrast to the Know Nothing riots a few years earlier and the ongoing guerrilla warfare in Kansas. Relief and public works in northern cities helped alleviate hardships over the winter. One of the most striking consequences of the depression was a religious revival that brought people of all occupations together in prayer meetings at which they contemplated God's punishment for the sins of greed and high living that had caused the crash.

Perhaps the Lord took pity. The depression of 1857–58 turned out to be milder and shorter than expected. California gold came east in large quantities during the fall and winter. Banks in New York resumed specie payments by December 1857, and those elsewhere followed suit during the next few months. The stock market rebounded in the spring of 1858. Factories reopened, railroad construction resumed its rapid pace, and unemployment declined. By early 1859 recovery was almost complete. Trade unions, which had all but disappeared under the impact of the depression, revived in 1859 and began a series of strikes to recoup predepression wages. In February 1860 the shoemakers of Lynn, Massachusetts, went out in what became the largest strike in American history to that time, eventually involving twenty thousand workers in the New England shoe industry.

The political effects of the depression may have equaled its economic consequences. It took time, however, for political crosscurrents to settle into a pattern that benefited Republicans. The initial tendency to blame banks for the panic seemed to give Democrats an opportunity to capitalize on their traditional antibank posture. They did reap some political profits in the Old Northwest. But elsewhere the issue had lost much of its old partisan salience because Democrats had become almost as probank as the opposition. Republicans of Whig origin pointed the finger of blame at the absence of a national bank to ride herd over irresponsible practices of state banks. Several Republicans called for revival of something like the Second Bank of the United States from the grave in which Andrew Jackson had buried it two decades earlier. Democratic tariff policies also came under indictment from Whiggish Republicans.

Although no modern historian has attributed the depression of 1857–58 to low

The shoemakers' strike was mostly peaceful, but on this occasion a mob led by a man with the apt name of Napoleon Wood attacked a wagon carrying boxes containing leather destined for strike-breaking outworkers. The strike lasted six weeks and won modest increases for many workers. A substantial number of strikers were women; indeed, without their participation the strike could not have succeeded.

tariffs, Horace Greeley and his fellow protectionists did so. Republicans made tariff revision one of their priorities, especially in Pennsylvania, where recovery of the iron industry lagged behind other sectors. The argument that the lower 1857 duties had enabled British industry to undersell American railroad iron carried great weight among workers as well as ironmasters. Indeed, Republicans pitched their strongest tariff appeals to labor, which had more votes than management, arguing that higher tariffs would lead to more and better jobs. Such arguments seemed to work, for in the 1858 elections Republicans scored large gains in Pennsylvania industrial districts.

The tariff issue provides an illustration of how political fallout from the depression exacerbated sectional tensions. In each of three congressional sessions between the Panic and the election of 1860, a coalition of Republicans and protectionist Democrats tried to adjust the 1857 duties slightly upward. Every time an almost solid South combined with half or more of the northern Democrats to defeat them. With an economy based on the export of raw materials and the import of manufactured goods, southerners had little interest in raising the prices of what they bought in order to subsidize profits and wages in the North. Thus Congress remained, in the view of one bitter Republican, "shamelessly prostituted, in a base subserviency to the Slave Power." A Pennsylvanian discerned a logical connection between the South's support for the Lecompton constitution and its opposition to tariff adjustment: "popular rights disregarded in Kansas; free industry destroyed in the States."

Sectional alignments were even more clear on three land-grant measures of the 1850s: a homestead act, a Pacific railroad act, and grants to states for the establishment of agricultural and mechanical colleges. The idea of using the federal government's vast patrimony of land for these purposes had been around for a decade or more. All three measures took on added impetus from the depression of 1857–58. Free land would help farmers ruined by the Panic get a new start. According to the theories of labor reformer George Henry Evans, homesteads would also give unemployed workingmen an opportunity to begin new lives as independent landowners and raise the wages of laborers who remained behind. Construction of a transcontinental railroad would tap the wealth of the West, bind the country together, provide employment, and increase the prosperity of all regions. Agricultural and mechanical colleges would make higher education available to farmers and skilled workingmen. All three measures reflected the Whig ideology of a harmony of interests between capital and labor, which would benefit mutually from economic growth and improved education. Along with a tariff to protect American workers and entrepreneurs, these land-grant measures became the new Republican free-labor version of Henry Clay's venerable American System. Republicans could count on more northern Democratic support for the land bills than for the tariff, especially from Douglas Democrats in the Old Northwest.

But most southerners opposed these measures. The homestead act would fill up the West with Yankee settlers hostile to slavery. Southerners also had little interest in using the public lands to establish schools most of whose students would be Yankees. Nor did they have much stake in the construction of a Pacific railroad with an expected eastern terminus at St. Louis or Chicago. Southern senators provided most of the votes in 1858 to postpone consideration of all three bills. At the next session of Congress a series of amendments to the railroad bill whittled it down to a meaningless provision for preliminary bids. In February 1859 Republicans and two-thirds of the northern Democrats in the House passed a homestead act. Vice President Breckinridge of Kentucky broke a tie vote in the Senate to defeat it. But enough northern Democrats joined Republicans in both Senate and House to pass the land-grant college act. Buchanan paid his debts to southern Democrats by vetoing it.

A somewhat different path led to a similar outcome in the first session of the 36th

By 1856, the date of this illustration, Chicago had become the great railroad hub in the central part of the country. This new station served trains going and coming to and from the East and South. Chicago also aspired to be the eastern terminus of the proposed railroad to the Pacific coast.

1. Brother Jonathan proceeds to annex the lovely Miss Cuba, in obedience to the laws of manifest destiny.

2. The first consequence of the measure is an enormous increase in the size and number of the cigars smoked by Young America.

3. The market for young niggers is so tremendously affected that a couple of those interesting objects are sold for a cent, with guarantee.

5. The United States Treasury, depleted by the transmission of $30,000,000 to Madrid, incontinently stops payment.

This panel of cartoons satirizes the enthusiasm for annexing Cuba in 1859— at the cost of bankrupting the Treasury.

Congress (1859–60), elected in 1858 and containing more Republicans than its predecessor. Disagreement over a northern *vs.* a southern route once again killed the Pacific railroad bill. The South also continued to block passage of a land-grant college act over Buchanan's veto. But a homestead act reached the president's desk. The House had passed it by a vote in which 114 of the 115 Ayes came from northern members and 64 of the 65 Nays from southern members. After much parliamentary maneuvering the Senate passed a modified version of the bill. A conference committee worked out a compromise, but Buchanan vetoed it as expected. Southern opposition in the Senate blocked an attempt to pass it over his veto.

The southern checkmate of tariff, homestead, Pacific railroad, and land-grant college acts provided the Republicans with vote-winning issues for 1860. During the effort to pass the homestead bill in 1859, Republicans tangled with Democrats over another measure that would also become an issue in 1860—the annexation of Cuba. Manifest Destiny was a cause that united most Democrats across sectional lines. Whatever they thought of slavery in Kansas, they agreed on the desirability of annexing Cuba with its 400,000 slaves. Both Douglas and Buchanan spoke in glowing terms of Cuba; the signs seemed to point to a rapprochement of warring Democratic factions, with Cuba as the glue to piece them together. In his December 1858 message to Congress, Buchanan called for new negotiations with Spain to purchase Cuba. Senator John Slidell of Louisiana introduced a bill to appropriate $30 million for a down payment. The foreign relations committee approved it in February 1859. For the next two weeks the $30 million bill was the main topic of Senate debate. Republicans rang all the changes on the slave-power conspiracy, prompting southerners to reply in kind while northern Democrats kept a low profile. Republican strategy was to delay the bill until adjournment on March 4, 1859. At the same time they hoped to bring the homestead bill, already passed by the House, to a vote. Democrats refused to allow this unless Republicans permitted a vote on Cuba. The question, said the irreverent Ben Wade of Ohio, was "shall we give niggers to the niggerless, or land to the landless?" In the end the Senate did neither, so each party prepared to take the issues to the voters in 1860.

Meanwhile a clash between Douglas and southern Democrats over the issue of a federal slave code for territories had reopened the party's Lecompton wounds. The

Senate Democratic caucus fired the first round by removing Douglas from his chairmanship of the committee on territories. Then on February 23, 1859, southern senators lashed out at Douglas in language usually reserved for Black Republicans. The Little Giant's sin was an assertion that he would never vote for a slave code to enforce bondage in a territory against the will of a majority living there. Popular sovereignty, said Jefferson Davis, who led the attack on Douglas, was "full of heresy." A refusal to override it would make Congress "faithless to the trust they hold at the hands of the people of the States." "We are not . . . to be cheated," the Mississippian declared, by men who "seek to build up a political reputation by catering to the prejudice of a majority to exclude the property of a minority." For such men, said Davis as he looked Douglas in the eye, the South had nothing but "scorn and indignation."

This debate registered the rise in rhetorical temperature during the late 1850s. Southern aggressiveness was bolstered by self-confidence growing out of the Panic of 1857. The depression fell lightly on the South. Cotton and tobacco prices dipped only briefly before returning to their high pre-Panic levels. The South's export economy seemed insulated from domestic downturns. This produced a good deal of boasting below the Potomac, along with expressions of mock solicitude for the suffering of unemployed wage slaves in the North. "Who can doubt, that has looked at recent events, that cotton is supreme?" asked James Hammond of South Carolina in his celebrated King Cotton speech to the Senate on March 4, 1858. The South "poured in upon you one million six hundred thousand bales of cotton just at the moment to save you from destruction. . . . We have sold it for $65,000,000, and saved you." Slavery demonstrated the superiority of southern civilization, continued Hammond. "In all social systems there must be a class to do the menial duties, to

New Orleans was the leading port for the export of cotton to Europe and even to the textile mills of New England. At any given time the levee was lined with steamboats landing cotton from upriver for transshipment to seagoing vessels.

perform the drudgery of life. . . . It constitutes the very mudsill of society. . . . Such a class you must have, or you would not have that other class which leads progress, civilization, and refinement. . . . Your whole hireling class of manual laborers and 'operatives,' as you call them, are essentially slaves. The difference between us is, that our slaves are hired for life and well compensated . . . yours are hired by the day, not cared for, and scantily compensated."

This mudsill theme was becoming increasingly visible in southern propaganda. The most extreme expression of it occurred in the writings of George Fitzhugh. A frayed-at-the-elbows scion of a Virginia First Family, Fitzhugh wrote prolifically about "the failure of free society." In 1854 and 1857 he gathered his essays into books entitled *Sociology for the South* and *Cannibals All!* The latter was published a few weeks before the Panic of 1857 and seemed almost to predict it. Free labor under capitalism was a war of each against all, wrote Fitzhugh, a sort of social cannibalism. "Slavery is the natural and normal condition of society," he maintained. "The situation of the North is abnormal and anomalous." To bestow "upon men equality of rights, is but giving license to the strong to oppress the weak" because "capital exercises a more perfect compulsion over free laborers than human masters over slaves; for free laborers must at all times work or starve, and slaves are supported whether they work or not." Therefore "we slaveholders say you must recur to domestic slavery, the oldest, the best, the most common form of Socialism" as well as "the natural and normal condition of the laboring men, white or black."

Fitzhugh's ideas flowed a bit outside the mainstream of the proslavery argument, which distinguished sharply between free whites and slave blacks and assigned an infinite superiority to the former *because* they were white. But while Fitzhugh's notions were eccentric they were not unique. Some proslavery proponents drew a distinction between southern yeomen and northern workers or farmers. Southerners were superior because they lived in a slave society. Yankees *were* perhaps fit only to be slaves. To explain this, southerners invented a genealogy that portrayed Yankees as descendants of the medieval Anglo-Saxons and southerners as descendants of their Norman conquerors. These divergent bloodlines had coursed through the veins of the Puritans who settled New England and the Cavaliers who colonized Virginia. "The Southern people," concluded an article in the *Southern Literary Messenger*, "come of that race . . . recognized as Cavaliers . . . directly descended from the Norman Barons of William the Conqueror, a race distinguished in its earliest history for its warlike and fearless character, a race in all times since renowned for its gallantry, chivalry, honor, gentleness, and intellect." If matters came to a fight, therefore, one Norman southerner could doubtless lick ten of those menial Saxon Yankees.

Whether or not southern superiority resulted from "the difference of race between the Northern people and the Southern people," as the *Southern Literary Messenger* would have it, the vaunted virtues of a free-labor society were a sham. "The great evil of Northern *free* society," insisted a South Carolina journal, "is that it is burdened with a *servile class of mechanics and laborers*, unfit for self-government, yet clothed with the attributes and powers of citizens." A Georgia newspaper was even more emphatic in its distaste. "Free Society! we sicken at the name. What is it but a conglomeration of greasy mechanics, filthy operatives, small-fisted farmers, and moon-struck theorists? . . . The prevailing class one meets with [in the North] is that of mechanics struggling to be genteel, and small farmers who do their own drudgery, and yet are hardly fit for association with a Southern gentleman's body servant."

Northern newspapers picked up and reprinted such articles. Yankees did not seem to appreciate southern sociology. Sometimes the response was good-humored, as demonstrated by a banner at one of the Lincoln-Douglas debates: "SMALL-FISTED FARMERS, MUD SILLS OF SOCIETY, GREASY MECHANICS, FOR A. LINCOLN." Other reactions were angrier and sometimes unprintable. No doubt some of the soldiers who marched through Georgia and South Carolina with Sherman a few years later had read these descriptions of themselves as greasy mechanics and servile farmers.

In any event, northerners gave as good as they got in this warfare of barbs and insults. In a famous campaign speech of 1858, William H. Seward derided the southern doctrine that "labor in every society, by whomsoever performed, is necessarily unintellectual, groveling, and base." This idea had produced the backwardness of the South, said Seward, the illiteracy of its masses, the dependent colonial status of its economy. In contrast "the free-labor system educates all alike, and by opening all the fields of industrial employment to . . . all classes of men . . . brings into the highest possible activity all the physical, moral and social energies of the whole State." A collision between these two systems impended, "an irrepressible conflict between opposing and enduring forces, and it means that the United States must and will . . . become either entirely a slave-holding nation, or entirely a free-labor nation."

Southerners claimed that free labor was prone to unrest and strikes. Of course it was, said Abraham Lincoln during a speaking tour of New England in March 1860 that coincided with the shoemakers' strike. "*I am glad to see that a system prevails in New England under which laborers CAN strike when they want to (Cheers). . . . I like the system which lets a man quit when he wants to, and wish it might prevail every-*

This man standing next to machinery in a northern factory was one of the "greasy mechanics" disdained by champions of the rural southern way of life.

where (Tremendous applause)." The glory of free labor, said Lincoln, lay in its open competition for upward mobility, a competition in which most Americans finished ahead of where they started in life. "I want every man to have the chance—and I believe a black man is entitled to it—in which he *can* better his condition." That was the significance of the irrepressible conflict and of the house divided, concluded Lincoln, for if the South got its way "free labor that *can* strike will give way to slave labor that cannot!"

The harshest indictment of the South's social system came from the pen of a white southerner, Hinton Rowan Helper. A self-appointed spokesman for nonslaveholding whites, Helper was almost as eccentric in his

own way as George Fitzhugh. Of North Carolina yeoman stock, he had gone to California in the gold rush to make his fortune but returned home disillusioned. Brooding on the conditions he perceived in the Carolina upcountry, Helper decided that "slavery lies at the root of all the shame, poverty, ignorance, tyranny and imbecility of the South." The peculiar institution "is hostile to general education," Helper declared in his 1857 book *The Impending Crisis*. "Its very life, is in the ignorance and stolidity of the masses." Data from the 1850 census—which had alarmed the southern elite itself a few years earlier—furnished Helper information that, used selectively, enabled him to "prove" the superior productivity of a free-labor economy. The hay crop of the North alone, he claimed, was worth more than the boasted value of King Cotton and all other southern staples combined. Helper urged nonslaveholding whites to use their votes—three-fourths of the southern total—to overthrow "this entire system of oligarchical despotism" that had caused the South to "welter in the cesspool of ignorance and degradation. . . . Now is the time for them to assert their rights and liberties . . . [and] strike for Freedom in the South."

If Helper had published this book in North Carolina or in Baltimore, where he was living when he completed it, *The Impending Crisis* might have languished in obscurity. Endless recitals of statistics dulled its cutting edge of criticism. But no southern publisher would touch it. So Helper lugged his manuscript to New York, where it was published in the summer of 1857. The *New York Tribune* recognized its value to Republicans and printed an eight-column review. This caused readers both North and South to take notice. Helper had probably overstated the disaffection of nonslaveholders from the southern social system. Outside the Appalachian highlands many of them were linked to the ruling class by ties of kinship, aspirations for slave ownership, or mutual dislike of Yankees and other outsiders. A caste system as well as a form of labor, slavery elevated all whites to the ruling caste and thereby reduced the potential for class conflict. However poor and illiterate some whites may have been, they were still white. If the fear of "nigger equality" caused most of the northern working class to abhor Republicans even where blacks constituted only 2 or 3 percent of the population, this fear operated at much higher intensity where the proportion of blacks was tenfold greater. But while Helper exaggerated yeoman alienation in the South, so also did many slaveholders who felt a secret foreboding that nonslaveowners in regions like Helper's Carolina upcountry might turn against their regime. Several southern states therefore made it a crime to circulate *The Impending Crisis*. This of course only attracted more attention to the book. A Republican committee raised funds to subsidize an abridged edition in 1859 to be scattered far and wide as a campaign document. The abridgers ensured a spirited southern reaction by adding such captions as "The Stupid Masses of the South" and "Revolution—Peacefully if we can, Violently if we must." Sixty-eight Republican congressmen endorsed a circular advertising the book.

One of them was John Sherman of Ohio, a moderate ex-Whig who later confessed that he had signed the endorsement without reading the book. Sherman's signature caused another donnybrook over the election of a speaker of the House when the 36th Congress convened in December 1859. Though Republicans, who nominated Sherman, outnumbered Democrats 113 to 101 in the House, upper-

South Americans held the balance of power. Through two months and forty-four ballots the House remained deadlocked on the edge of violence. Southerners denounced Helper, his book, and anyone connected with either as "a traitor, a renegade, an apostate . . . infamous . . . abominable . . . mendacious . . . incendiary, insurrectionary." Most congressmen came armed to the sessions; the sole exception seemed to be a former New England clergyman who finally gave in and bought a pistol for self-defense. Partisans in the galleries also carried weapons. One southerner reported that a good many slave-state congressmen expected and wanted a shootout on the House floor: they "are willing to fight the question out, and to settle it right there. . . . I can't help wishing the Union were dissolved and we had a Southern confederacy." The governor of South Carolina informed one of his state's congressmen on December 20, 1859: "If . . . you upon consultation decide to make the issue of force in Washington, write or telegraph me, and I will have a regiment in or near Washington in the shortest possible time."

Tensions between North and South were as great in the Senate as in the House during this session. In this cartoon Senators Jefferson Davis and William H. Seward square off against each other in a debate over Davis's resolution calling for a federal slave code in the territories, which has knocked Stephen Douglas (the Little Giant) and his popular sovereignty to the floor. Editor Horace Greeley of the New York Tribune stands behind Seward.

Through all this the Republicans supported Sherman, who consistently fell a few votes short of a majority. Having organized the Senate with sixteen of the twenty-two committees headed by southern chairmen, southerners were quite ready to keep the House unorganized until they got their way. To prevent this outcome, Sherman finally withdrew, and the Republicans nominated lackluster William Pennington of New Jersey, who because of his support of the fugitive slave law a decade earlier picked up enough border-state support to win the speakership.

Nothing yet had so dramatized the parting bonds of Union as this struggle in the House. The hair-trigger temper of southerners is easier to understand if one keeps in mind that the contest opened just three days after John Brown was hanged in Virginia for trying to incite a slave insurrection. Brown's raid at Harper's Ferry was an ominous beginning to the fateful twelve months that culminated in the presidential election of 1860.

CHAPTER SEVEN

The Revolution
of 1860

I

Like Dred Scott, John Brown lived the first fifty-odd years of his life in obscurity. Unlike Scott, he attained notoriety not through the law but by lawlessness. Except for a brief reappearance in the Kansas wars, however, Brown's activities for three years after 1856 were more mysterious than notorious. He made several trips east to raise money for the freedom fight in Kansas. As he shuttled back and forth, Brown evolved a plan to strike against slavery in its heartland. Like the Old Testament warriors he admired and resembled, he yearned to carry the war into Babylon. He studied books on guerrilla warfare and on slave revolts. Fascinated by the ability of small bands to hold off larger forces in mountainous terrain, Brown conceived the idea of a raid into the Appalachian foothills of Virginia. From there he would move southward along the mountains attracting slaves to his banner. In May 1858 Brown journeyed with eleven white followers to a community of former slaves in Chatham, Canada. Thirty-four blacks met secretly with Brown's group to adopt a "provisional constitution" for the republic of liberated slaves to be established in the mountains. The delegates elected Brown commander in chief of the army of this new nation.

John Brown had never shared the commitment of most abolitionists to nonviolence. "Without shedding of blood there is no remission of sin" was his favorite New Testament passage (Hebrews 9:22). Bondage was "a most barbarous, unprovoked, and unjustifiable war" of masters against slaves, declared the preamble of Brown's Chatham constitution. Victory over these "thieves and murderers" could be won only by a revolution.

Events during the 1850s had converted some abolitionists to Brown's view. The fugitive slave law did more than anything else to discredit nonviolence. Before 1850 Frederick Douglass had been a pacifist. "Were I asked the question whether I would have my emancipation by the shedding of one single drop of blood," he said in the 1840s, "my answer would be in the negative. . . . The only well grounded hope of the slave for emancipation is the operation of moral force." But a month

Opposite page: This painting of John Brown by Ole Peter Hansen Balling captures the grim determination of this warrior against slavery.

after enactment of the fugitive slave law he changed his tune and advocated "forcible resistance" to the law. "Slave-holders . . . tyrants and despots have no right to live," said Douglass now. "The only way to make the fugitive slave law a dead letter is to make half a dozen or more dead kidnappers." Only through violence, Douglass came to believe, could the oppressed earn self-respect and the respect of their oppressors.

Many free soilers in Kansas also concluded that as the slave power had lived by the sword, it must die by the sword. In 1855 a New England Garrisonian and pacifist, Charles Stearns, went to Lawrence, Kansas, to open a store and soon found pacifism untenable. In a letter to Garrison he wrote: "The cold-blooded murder, last night, of one of our best citizens, has decided me. I am sorry to deny the principles of Jesus Christ, after contending for them so long, but it is not for myself that I am going to fight. It is for God and the slaves." Another convert was Gerrit Smith, wealthy landowner and philanthropist of upstate New York. A vice president of the American Peace Society, Smith declared in 1856 that "hitherto I have opposed the bloody abolition of slavery." But when the slave power "begins to march its conquering bands into [Kansas] . . . I and ten thousand other peace men are not only ready to have it repulsed with violence, but pursued even unto death with violence."

Smith became a member of the "Secret Six" who backed John Brown's scheme to invade the South. Like Smith, the other five were men of means and standing: Thomas Wentworth Higginson, Transcendental clergyman and writer; Theodore Parker, leading intellectual light of Unitarianism; Samuel Gridley Howe, a physician of international repute for his work with the blind and the deaf; George L. Stearns, a prosperous manufacturer; and Franklin B. Sanborn, a young educator and protégé of Emerson. The cause that bonded these men was their support for the free-state activists in Kansas. Most of them had also participated in resistance to the fugitive slave law. Parker headed the vigilance committee in Boston, while Higginson had led the abortive attack to free Anthony Burns in 1854. Several of the Secret Six had stood by in impotent rage while the police, militia, army, and marines had marched Burns back to slavery.

This scene burned in their memories. Their work for Kansas fanned the flames. It also brought them into contact with John Brown. They were ready for his message of action. Like Frederick Douglass, they had come to believe that the slaves could achieve manhood and liberation only by striking a blow themselves. Slavery "is destined, as it began in blood, so to end," wrote Higginson in 1858. "Never in history was there an oppressed people who were set free by others." Perhaps unconscious of the irony, the Secret Six (all white men) considered John Brown (also white) the ideal leader of the slaves in their strike for freedom. In 1858 Brown revealed to the Secret Six his plans for an invasion of the southern Appalachians. With varying degrees of enthusiasm or skepticism they agreed to support him. Stearns diverted funds intended for Kansas to the purchase of guns and pikes to arm the slaves that Brown expected to flock to his standard. Under an assumed name Brown rented a farm in Maryland across the Potomac River from Harper's Ferry, Virginia. He planned to seize the U.S. armory and arsenal there and distribute its arms to the slaves as they joined up with him. Brown's shock troops for this purpose ultimately consisted of five black men and seventeen whites, including three of his sons. This was a pitifully small "army" to invade slave territory and attack U.S. property.

Brown did try to attract more black recruits. In August 1859 he urged his old friend Frederick Douglass to join him as a sort of liaison officer to the slaves. But Douglass refused. He was convinced that Brown had embarked on a suicidal mission, "an attack on the federal government" that "would array the whole country against us." Harper's Ferry was a "perfect steel-trap," said Douglass. Situated on a peninsula formed by the confluence of the Potomac and Shenandoah rivers, surrounded on all sides by commanding heights, it was indefensible against a counterattack. You will "never get out alive," Douglass warned Brown. As summer turned to fall and additional recruits did not arrive, Brown decided to go with what he had. A sort of fatalism stole over him. He wrote a "Vindication of the Invasion" in the past tense as if it had already failed. When he finally moved, in mid-October, he did so without previous notice to the slaves he expected to join him, without rations, without having scouted any escape routes from Harper's Ferry, with no apparent idea of what to do after capturing the armory buildings. It was almost as if he knew that failure with its ensuing martyrdom would do more to achieve his ultimate goal than any "success" could have done. In any event, that was how matters turned out.

Leaving three men to guard his base, Brown led the other eighteen into Harper's Ferry after dark on October 16. They quickly captured the armory complex defended

In the summer of 1859 John Brown rented this vacant farmhouse (photographed a year later) seven miles from Harper's Ferry. Here he gathered his troops and weapons and made his plans for the attack on the armory. He left behind in this house many letters and papers that implicated his New England supporters. The house still stands and is administered by the National Park Service.

A view of Harper's Ferry in 1860 from the Maryland side of the Potomac River. The Shenandoah River flows into the Potomac from the left. The armory is located along the Baltimore and Ohio Railroad tracks running alongside the Potomac from the center of the picture toward the right.

by a single watchman. Brown sent a patrol into the countryside to pass the word among slaves and bring in several hostages, including a great-grandnephew of George Washington. Having done this much, Brown sat down to wait—presumably for slaves to rally to the cause. But the only ones to come in were a few brought by the patrol. Ironically, the first casualty was a free Negro baggage-master at the railroad station who was killed by Brown's bridge guard in the dark when he walked out on the trestle looking for the night watchman. Brown stopped the eastbound midnight train and held it for several hours, but then unaccountably let it proceed—to spread the alarm.

By midmorning on October 17, residents of Harper's Ferry were sniping at Brown's men while Virginia and Maryland militia converged on the town. During the afternoon eight of Brown's men (including two of his sons) and three townsmen were killed while seven of the raiders escaped (two of them were later captured). Brown retreated with his survivors and prisoners to the thick-walled fire-engine house, where he made a stand. During the night a company of U.S. marines arrived, commanded by two cavalry officers, Colonel Robert E. Lee and Lieutenant J.E.B. Stuart. After the militia had declined the honor of storming the engine house, Lee sent in the marines. They attacked with battering ram and bayonets, not firing a shot in order to avoid risk to the hostages. With the loss of one man the marines killed two raiders and captured the others including Brown, who was wounded by an officer's dress sword. Less than thirty-six hours after it started, John Brown's strange effort to free the slaves was over.

But the repercussions resounded for years. Passions ran high in Virginia, where mobs clamored for Brown's blood. To forestall a lynching the state of Virginia hastily indicted, tried, and convicted Brown of treason, murder, and fomenting insurrection. The judge sentenced him to hang one month later, on December 2. The other six captured raiders also received swift trials; four of them (including two blacks) were hanged on December 16 and the remaining two on March 16, 1860. The matter of Brown's northern supporters provoked great interest. Brown had left behind at the Maryland farmhouse a carpetbag full of documents and letters, some of them revealing his relationship with the Secret Six. Of those gentlemen, Parker was in Europe

This illustration portrays the interior of the fire-engine house at Harper's Ferry just before it was stormed and captured by U.S. marines. The man sitting in the center is Colonel Lewis Washington, one of the hostages. Other hostages stand along the wall to the left. Brown is standing with his rifle in the left center, while his followers both black and white fight to the last.

dying of tuberculosis, and Higginson stood firm in Massachusetts, making no apology for his role and defying anyone to arrest him. But the other four beat an abject retreat. Stearns, Howe, and Sanborn fled to Canada, while Gerrit Smith suffered a breakdown and was confined for several weeks in the Utica insane asylum.

The Canadian exiles returned after Brown was hanged, but when the Senate established an investigating committee chaired by James Mason of Virginia, Sanborn again headed north to avoid testifying. From Canada he wrote Higginson imploring him "in case you are summoned . . . do not tell what you know to the enemies of the cause." Higginson expressed contempt toward such behavior. "Sanborn, is there no such thing as *honor* among confederates? . . . Can your clear moral sense . . . justify holding one's tongue . . . to save ourselves from all share in even the reprobation of society when the nobler man whom we have provoked on into danger is the scapegoat of that reprobation—& the gallows too?"

Sanborn refused a summons from the Mason committee and resisted an attempt by the sergeant at arms of the Senate to arrest him. Massachusetts Chief Justice Lemuel Shaw voided the arrest warrant on a technicality. Howe and Stearns did go to Washington and faced the Mason committee. For some reason the committee never called Higginson—probably because by February 1860 Mason's resolve to uncover a northern conspiracy had weakened, and he did not want to give Higginson a national platform to proclaim his sentiments. Ultimately the Mason committee found no conspiracy, and no one except the men actually present with Brown at Harper's Ferry was ever indicted.

Reaction in the South to Brown's raid brought to the surface a paradox that lay near

Under heavy security to prevent a rescue attempt, John Brown was hanged at Charles Town, Virginia, on December 2, 1859. Brown had discouraged all talk of a rescue. His dignity during and after his trial and his quiet acceptance of the verdict impressed even Virginians. To many in the North he was not a criminal but a martyr to freedom.

Although many southern whites professed gratification that no slaves had flocked to John Brown's banner, this scene reflected southern imagination rather than reality. Few if any planters were likely to give their slaves weapons, especially if invasion by "Yankee fanatics" impended. But the illustration did reinforce the wishful thinking that the slaves were happy in slavery.

the heart of slavery. On the one hand, many whites lived in fear of slave insurrections. On the other, southern whites insisted that slaves were well treated and cheerful in their bondage. The news of Harper's Ferry sent an initial wave of shock and rage through the South, especially when newspapers reported that among the papers found in Brown's carpetbag were maps of seven southern states designating additional targets. For several weeks wild rumors circulated of black uprisings and of armed abolitionists marching from the North to aid them. By the time of Brown's execution, however, many in the South uttered a sigh of relief. Not only had the rumors proved false, but southerners also gradually realized that not a single slave had voluntarily joined Brown. The South's professed belief in the slaves' tranquility was right after all! It was only Yankee fanatics who wanted to stir up trouble.

The problem of those Yankee fanatics would soon cause southern opinion to evolve into a third phase of unreasoning fury, but not until the antislavery reaction to Harper's Ferry had itself gone through two phases. The first northern response was a kind of baffled reproach. The *Worcester Spy*, an antislavery paper in Higginson's hometown, characterized the raid as "one of the rashest and maddest enterprises ever." To William Lloyd Garrison the raid, "though disinterested and well intended," seemed "misguided, wild, and apparently insane." But such opinions soon changed into a perception of Brown as a martyr to a noble cause. His behavior during and after his trial had much to do with this transformation. In testimony, letters, interviews, and above all in his closing speech to the court he exhibited a dignity and fortitude that impressed even Virginia's Governor Henry Wise and the fire-eater Edmund Ruffin. In that speech prior to sentencing, Brown rose to a surpassing eloquence that has echoed down the years:

> I deny everything but what I have all along admitted: of a design on my part to free slaves. . . . Had I interfered in the manner which I admit . . . in behalf of the rich, the powerful, the intelligent, the so-called great . . . every man in this Court would have deemed it an act worthy of reward rather than punishment.

This Court acknowledges, too, as I suppose, the validity of the law of God. I see a book kissed, which I suppose to be the Bible, or at least the New Testament, which teaches me that all things whatsoever I would that men should do to me, I should do even so to them. It teaches me, further, to remember them that are in bonds as bound with them. I endeavored to act up to that instruction. . . . Now, if it is deemed necessary that I should forfeit my life for the furtherance of the ends of justice, and mingle my blood further with the blood of my children and with the blood of millions in this slave country whose rights are disregarded by wicked, cruel, and unjust enactments, I say, let it be done.

These words moved Theodore Parker to pronounce Brown "not only a martyr . . . but also a SAINT." They inspired Ralph Waldo Emerson to prophesy that the old warrior would "make the gallows as glorious as the cross." Brown understood his martyr role, and cultivated it. Like Christ, to whom Brown unabashedly compared himself, he would accomplish in death the salvation of the poor he had failed while living to save. Brown spurned all schemes to cheat the hangman's rope by rescue or by pleading insanity. "I am worth inconceivably more to hang," he told his brother, "than for any other purpose."

Extraordinary events took place in many northern communities on the day of Brown's execution. Church bells tolled; minute guns fired solemn salutes; ministers preached sermons of commemoration; thousands bowed in silent reverence for the martyr to liberty. "I have seen nothing like it," wrote Charles Eliot Norton of Harvard. More than a thousand miles away in Lawrence, Kansas, the editor of the *Republican* wrote that "the death of no man in America has ever produced so profound a sensation. A feeling of deep and sorrowful indignation seems to possess the masses." Young William Dean Howells said that "Brown has become an idea, a thousand times purer and better and loftier than the Republican idea"; Henry David Thoreau pronounced Brown "a crucified hero."

What can explain this near-canonization of Brown? Some Yankees professed to admire Brown for daring to strike the slave power that was accustomed to pushing the North around with impunity. "This will be a great day in our history," wrote Henry Wadsworth Longfellow in his diary on the day of Brown's execution, "the date of a new Revolution,—quite as much needed as the old one." When the Virginians hanged Brown they were "sowing the wind to reap the whirlwind, which will come soon." This was the spirit that two years later made "John Brown's Body" the favorite marching song of the Union army. But there was more to it than that. John Brown had drawn his sword in an attempt to cut out the cancer of shame that tainted the promise of America. No matter that his method was misguided and doomed to failure. "History, forgetting the errors of his judgment in the contemplation of his unfaltering course . . . and of the nobleness of his aims," said William Cullen Bryant, "will record his name among those of its martyrs and heroes." Though "Harper's Ferry was insane," stated the religious weekly *The Independent*, "the controlling motive of his demonstration was sublime."

The distinction between act and motive was lost on southern whites. They saw only that millions of Yankees seemed to approve of a murderer who had tried to set the slaves at their throats. This perception provoked a paroxysm of anger more intense than the original reaction to the raid. The North "has sanctioned and applauded theft, murder, treason," cried *De Bow's Review*. Could the South afford any longer "to live under a government, the majority of whose subjects or citizens regard John Brown as a martyr and a Christian hero?" asked a Baltimore newspaper. No! echoed from every corner of the South. "The Harper's Ferry invasion has advanced the cause of disunion more than any event that has happened since the formation of the government," agreed two rival Richmond newspapers. It had "wrought almost a complete revolution in the sentiments . . . of the oldest and steadiest conservatives. . . . Thousands of men . . . who, a month ago, scoffed at the idea of a dissolution of the Union . . . now hold the opinion that its days are numbered."

To reassure the South that sympathy for Brown was confined to a noisy minority, northern conservatives organized large anti-Brown meetings. They condemned "the recent outrage at Harper's Ferry" as a crime "not only against the State of Virginia, but against the Union itself. . . . [We] are ready to go as far as any Southern men in putting down all attempts of Northern fanatics to interfere with the constitutional rights of the South." Democrats saw an opportunity to rebuild their bridges to the South and to discredit Republicans by linking them to Brown. Harper's Ferry, said Stephen Douglas, was the "natural, logical, inevitable result of the doctrines and teachings of the Republican party." Democrats singled out Seward for special attack, for they expected him to win the Republican presidential nomination. Seward was the "arch agitator who is responsible for this insurrection," they asserted. His "bloody and brutal" irrepressible-conflict speech had inspired Brown's bloody and brutal act.

Fearing political damage, Republican leaders hastened to disavow Brown. Seward condemned the old man's "sedition and treason" and pronounced his execution "necessary and just." Even though Brown "agreed with us in thinking slavery wrong," said Lincoln, "that cannot excuse violence, bloodshed, and treason."

To southern people the line separating Lincoln's moral convictions from Brown's butchery was meaningless. "We regard every man," declared an Atlanta newspaper, "who does not boldly declare that he believes African slavery to be a social, moral, and political blessing" as "an enemy to the institutions of the South." As for the supportive resolutions of northern conservatives, they were so much "gas and vaporing." "Why have not the conservative men at the North frowned down the infamous black-republican party?" asked *De Bow's Review*. "They have forborne to crush it, till now it overrides almost everything at the North." On the Senate floor Robert Toombs warned that the South would "never permit this Federal government to pass into the traitorous hands of the Black Republican party."

John Brown's ghost stalked the South as the election year of 1860 opened. Keyed up to the highest pitch of tension, many slaveholders and yeomen alike were ready for war to defend hearth and home against those Black Republican brigands. Thousands joined military companies; state legislatures appropriated funds for the purchase of arms. Every barn or cotton gin that burned down sparked new rumors of slave insurrections and abolitionist invaders. Every Yankee in the South became *persona non grata*. Some of them received a coat of tar and feathers and a ride out of town on a rail. A few were lynched. The northern-born president of an Alabama college had to flee for his life. In Kentucky a mob drove thirty-nine people associated with an antislavery church and school at Berea out of the state. Thirty-two representatives in the South of New York and Boston firms arrived in Washington reporting "indignation so great against Northerners that they were compelled to return and abandon their business." In this climate of fear and hostility, Democrats prepared for their national convention at Charleston in April 1860.

II

Most southern Democrats went to Charleston with one overriding goal: to destroy Douglas. In this they were joined by a scattering of administration Democrats from the North. Memories of Lecompton and the Freeport doctrine thwarted all efforts to heal the breach. Some lower-South Democrats even preferred a Republican president to Douglas in order to make the alternatives facing the South starkly clear: submission or secession. And they ensured this result by proceeding to cleave the Democratic party in two.

The Alabama Democratic convention took the first step in January 1860 by instructing its delegates to walk out of the national convention if the party refused to adopt a platform pledging a federal slave code for the territories. Other lower-South Democratic organizations followed suit. In February, Jefferson Davis presented the substance of southern demands to the Senate in resolutions affirming that neither Congress nor a territorial legislature could "impair the constitutional right

OUR POLITICAL SNAKE-CHARMER.

DOUGLAS.—You perceive, ladies and gentlemen, that the creatures are entirely under my control. *(Aside)* Say, Forney, hope the brutes wont bite!

The humorous weekly Vanity Fair *shows Stephen Douglas's political skills as well as the problems he faced in 1860 in this cartoon. The snakes represent political parties and factions, each of which might prove fatal to Douglas's presidential prospects. While John Forney, editor of the* Philadelphia Press *and a key Douglas supporter, plays the oboe, Douglas declares: "You perceive, ladies and gentlemen, that the creatures are entirely under my control." But in an aside to Forney, Douglas says he hopes they won't bite. Unfortunately for Douglas, they did.*

of any citizen of the United States to take his slave property into the common territories. . . . It is the duty of the federal government there to afford, for that as for other species of property, the needful protection." The Senate Democratic caucus, dominated by southerners, endorsed the resolutions and thereby threw down the gauntlet to Douglas at Charleston.

In the fevered atmosphere of 1860, Charleston was the worst possible place for the convention. Douglas delegates felt like aliens in a hostile land. Fire-eating orators held forth outdoors each evening. Inside the convention hall, northerners had a three-fifths majority because delegates were apportioned in the same way as electoral votes rather than by party strength. Douglas's supporters were as determined to block a slave-code plank as southerners were to adopt one. There was thus an "irrepressible conflict" in the party, wrote the brilliant young journalist from Cincinnati, Murat Halstead, whose reports provide the best account of the convention. "The South will not yield a jot of its position. . . . The Northern Democracy . . . are unwilling to submit themselves to assassination or to commit suicide."

The crisis came with the report of the platform committee, in which each state had one vote. California and Oregon joined the slave states to provide a majority of 17 to 16 for a slave-code plank similar to the Jefferson Davis resolutions. The minority report reaffirmed the 1856 platform endorsing popular sovereignty and added a pledge to obey a Supreme Court decision on the powers of a territorial legislature. This was not good enough for southerners. They accepted the axiom of the Freeport doctrine that a Court decision would not enforce itself. Slave property needed federal protection, said the committee chairman, a North Carolinian, so that when the United States acquired Cuba, Mexico, and Central America any slaveholder could take his property there with perfect security. The foremost orator for southern rights, William Lowndes Yancey, gave a rousing speech in favor of the majority report. The galleries rang with cheers as Yancey launched into his peroration: "We are in a position to ask you to yield," he said to northern delegates. "What right of yours, gentlemen of the North, have we of the South ever invaded? . . . Ours are the institutions which are at stake; ours is the property that is to be destroyed; ours is the honor at stake."

After this eloquence the replies of northern delegates sounded futile, indeed almost funereal. "We cannot recede from [popular sovereignty] without personal dishonor," said a Douglas Democrat from Ohio, "*never, never, never,* so help us God." And they did not. After two days of bitter parliamentary wrangling, Douglas men pushed through their platform by a vote of 165 to 138 (free states 154 to 30, slave states 11 to 108). Fifty delegates from the lower South thereupon walked out. Everything that followed was anticlimax. Douglas could not muster the two-thirds

After fifty southern delegates walked out of the Democratic convention in Charleston, they met in another hall and adopted the slave-code platform rejected by the main convention. Not sure what to do next, they stood around and talked for several days, as shown here, waiting to see whether the main convention would nominate Douglas. When it did not, everybody went home to try again in Baltimore six weeks later.

majority required for nomination. Nor could the convention agree on anyone else during fifty-seven acrimonious ballots. Exhausted and heartsick, the delegates adjourned to try again six weeks later in the more hospitable clime of Baltimore. Attempts to reunite the party seemed hopeless. Delegates from the Northwest went home angry toward their southern brethren. "I never heard Abolitionists talk more uncharitably and rancorously of the people of the South than the Douglas men," wrote a reporter. "They say they do not care a d—n where the South goes. . . . 'She may go out of the Convention into hell,' for all they care." But most southern bolters aimed to seek readmission at Baltimore. Their strategy was "to rule or ruin," wrote Alexander Stephens, who had moved toward moderation during the past year and was now supporting Douglas. If readmitted, the bolters intended to insist again on a slave-code platform and if defeated to walk out again, this time with the promise of most upper-South delegates to join them. If they were denied admission, the same upper-South delegates would bolt and help their cotton-state compatriots form a new party.

But Douglas's supporters in several lower-South states organized rival delegations to Baltimore. The fate of the Democratic party hung on the credentials fight there. After sober second thoughts about their willingness to let the bolters go to hell, most northern delegates were willing to compromise by seating some of the bolters and some of the challengers. But anti-Douglas southerners wanted all or nothing. They walked out once more, followed by most delegates from the upper South and a handful of proslavery northerners—more than one-third of the total. The bolters quickly organized their own convention and nominated John C. Breckinridge of Kentucky (the current vice president) for president on a slave-code platform. The dispirited loyalists nominated Douglas and returned home with renewed bitterness in their hearts toward the rebels who had all but ensured the election of a Black Republican president.

Republicans helped along that cause by adroit action at their national convention

The Chicago photographer Alexander Hesler traveled to Springfield to take this photograph on June 3, 1860, two weeks after Lincoln's nomination. Undoubtedly retouched, this picture makes Lincoln look younger and more handsome than any other from that period. Lincoln wrote that the photograph "is, I think, a very true one; though my wife, and many others, do not. My impression is that their objection rises from the disordered condition of the hair." Lincoln's hair was usually "disordered."

in Chicago. The basic problem confronting the party was the need to carry nearly all of the free states in order to win. Expecting to lose California, Oregon, and perhaps New Jersey, they must capture Pennsylvania and either Indiana or Illinois among the states they had lost in 1856 to achieve an electoral majority. William H. Seward's weakness in these lower-North states formed a growing cloud on the horizon of his anticipated nomination. To carry these states, a Republican had to attract support from many of the Fillmore voters of 1856. Seward's long record of hostility to nativism would undercut this effort. More important, his higher-law and irrepressible-conflict speeches had given him a radical reputation that daunted old Whig conservatives. Despite Seward's repudiation of John Brown and his ideals, some Harper's Ferry mud clung to his coattails. In addition, years of internecine Whig warfare in New York had earned Seward numerous enemies, among them Horace Greeley. A Seward nomination might also rob Republicans of the issue of corruption that scandals in the Buchanan administration had given them the opportunity to exploit. The bad smell of recent franchise grants by the New York legislature that could be traced to Seward's political manager Thurlow Weed tainted his candidate's repute. The rowdy, hard-drinking claque of gallery supporters that the Seward delegation brought to Chicago did nothing to improve the New Yorker's image.

Coming into the convention with a large lead based on strength in upper-North states, Seward hoped for a first-ballot nomination. But Republicans were sure to win those states no matter whom they nominated. Pragmatists from all regions and politicians from the doubtful states combined in a stop-Seward movement. They had plenty of potential candidates: favorite sons from Vermont and New Jersey, and four men with state or regional backing whose aspirations went beyond favorite-son status: Salmon P. Chase of Ohio, Simon Cameron of Pennsylvania, Edward Bates of Missouri, and Abraham Lincoln of Illinois. But Chase shared Seward's handicap of a radical reputation and did not command unanimous support from even his own state. Cameron's notoriety as a spoilsman who had been a Democrat, then a Know Nothing, and had flirted with Whiggery, militated against his candidacy among delegates concerned that the party should appear to be as pure as Caesar's wife. Bates seemed for a time Seward's strongest challenger because Greeley and the influential Blair family backed him in the hope that he might carry even a few border states as well as the lower North. But the colorless sixty-seven-year-old Missourian had been a slaveholder and a Know Nothing, and in 1856 he had supported Fillmore. He therefore alienated too many constituencies whose support was essential—especially German Protestants. The belief that a Republican might carry a border state was fanciful, and Bates wound up with delegate support mainly from marginal states where Republican prospects were bleak or hopeless: Missouri, Maryland, Delaware, and Oregon.

This left Lincoln. By the time the convention's opening gavel came down on May 16, Lincoln had emerged from a position as the darkest of horses to become Seward's main rival. Party leaders gradually recognized that the Illinoisian had most of the strengths and few of the weaknesses of an ideal candidate. He was a former antislavery Whig in a party made up mostly of former antislavery Whigs.

THE REPUBLICAN WIGWAM.

But despite his house-divided speech, he had a reputation as a moderate. Many former Democrats in the party could not stomach Seward, but they remembered with appreciation Lincoln's gesture in stepping aside to permit the election of antislavery Democrat Lyman Trumbull to the Senate in 1855. Lincoln had opposed the Know Nothings, which would help him with the German vote, but not so conspicuously as to drive away former American voters who would refuse to support Seward. Already known popularly as Honest Abe, Lincoln had a reputation for integrity that compared favorably with the dubious image of Thurlow Weed's New York machine. Of humble origins, Lincoln personified the free-labor ideology of equal opportunity and upward mobility. He *had* been born in a log cabin. In a stroke of political genius, one of Lincoln's managers exhibited at the Illinois state convention a pair of weatherbeaten fence rails that Lincoln had supposedly split thirty years earlier. From then on, Lincoln the railsplitter became the symbol of frontier, farm, opportunity, hard work, rags to riches, and other components of the American Dream embodied in the Republican self-image. Finally, Lincoln was from a state and region crucial to Republican chances, particularly if Douglas as expected became the nominee of northern Democrats. Except for William Henry Harrison, who died after a month in office, no president had been elected from the Old Northwest. The fastest-growing part of the country, this region believed that its turn had come. The selection of Chicago as the convention site incalculably strengthened Lincoln's candidacy. Huge, enthusiastic crowds composed mostly of Illinoisians turned up at the large hall built for the convention and nicknamed the "Wigwam." Counterfeit tickets enabled thousands of leather-lunged Lincoln men to pack the galleries.

Lincoln was not an unknown factor in national politics before 1860. His contest

The city of Chicago put up this large building specifically to host the Republican convention in 1860. Rectangular in shape, 180 by 100 feet, it could seat ten thousand people. It was named the Wigwam because, like the Indian prototype, it was not intended to be permanent.

Horace Greeley had once been a political ally of William H. Seward but turned against him and came to the Chicago convention determined to block Seward's nomination. This Vanity Fair *cartoon portrays Greeley as Brutus assassinating Caesar/Seward while the bearded Henry Raymond, editor of the* New York Times, *who also opposed Seward, lurks in the background as Mark Antony. For reasons that are not clear, Lincoln is depicted as a black man; at this time he as less liberal on racial issues than Seward.*

"ET TU, GREELEY?"

with Douglas had won wide attention; the publication of the debates early in 1860 enhanced his reputation. In 1859 Lincoln had given political speeches in a half-dozen midwestern states. In February 1860 he addressed a large audience in New York's Cooper Institute and went on to New England, where he gave eleven speeches. This first appearance of Lincoln in the Northeast was a triumph, enabling his supporters back in Illinois to crow that "no man has ever before risen so rapidly to political eminence in the United States." Partly on the basis of these speeches Lincoln picked up delegate support in New England, winning nineteen votes from this Seward stronghold on the first ballot at Chicago.

Yet so obscure was Lincoln in certain circles before his nomination that some pundits had not included his name on their lists of seven or a dozen or even twenty-one potential candidates. Several newspapers spelled his first name Abram. But not for long. The turning point came when Indiana decided to join Illinois to give Lincoln solid first-ballot support from two of the most important lower-North states. This

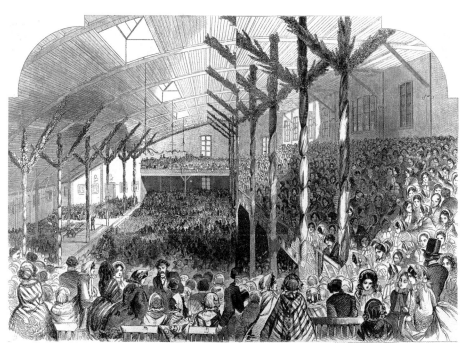

The interior of the Wigwam during the Republican convention. Although all the delegates were men, some of the spectators were women, as shown here—though the illustrator may have chosen to feature women prominently more for reasons of aesthetics than of realism.

gave Lincoln's managers, a little known but brilliant group of Illinoisians, the chance to win a pledge from Pennsylvania to cast most of its second-ballot votes for Lincoln after the first-ballot gesture to Cameron. All through the feverish night of May 17–18 the Illinois politicos worked to line up other scattered second-ballot support for Lincoln. The belief that Lincoln could carry the lower North and Seward could not was the most powerful Lincoln weapon. And delegates from other states were influenced by the actions of Indiana and Pennsylvania because they knew that the party must capture them to win.

The first ballot revealed Seward's weakness and Lincoln's surprising strength. With 233 votes needed to nominate, Seward fell sixty short at 173½ while Lincoln polled 102. The direction of the wind became clear on the second ballot as Seward gained fewer than a dozen votes while Vermont, Pennsylvania, and scattered votes from other states including some of Ohio's switched to Lincoln, bringing him almost even with Seward at 181 votes. During these ballots the Wigwam was electric with an excitement unprecedented in American politics. Ten thousand spectators, most of them for Lincoln, jammed the galleries. The crowd communicated a palpable impulse to delegates, reinforcing the dramatic growth of Lincoln's second-ballot total to convey an impression of irresistible momentum. As the third ballot began, suspense stretched nerves almost to the breaking point. Six more New England votes switched to Lincoln, along with eight from New Jersey, nine from Maryland, and four more from his native Kentucky. When another fifteen Chase votes from Ohio went to Lincoln, the rafters literally shook with reverberation. Scores of pencils added the total before the clerk announced it: Lincoln had 231½ votes. Amid a sudden silence the Ohio chairman leaped onto his chair and announced the change of four more votes to Lincoln. With this "there was the rush of a great wind in the van of a storm—and in another breath, the storm was there . . . thousands cheering with the energy of insanity."

None of the forty thousand people in and around the Wigwam ever forgot that moment. All except the diehard Seward delegates were convinced that they had selected the strongest candidate. Few could know that they had also chosen the best man for the grim task that lay ahead. To balance the ticket the convention nominated for vice president Hannibal Hamlin of Maine, a former Democrat and one of Lincoln's earliest supporters in New England but also a friend of Seward. The Republican platform was one of the most effective documents of its kind in Ameri-

Note how short this platform was compared with modern party platforms. But in contrast with today, voters actually read the platform in 1860 and expected their party to carry it out if elected.

can history. While abating none of the antislavery convictions expressed in the 1856 platform, it softened the language slightly and denounced John Brown's raid as "the gravest of crimes." Gladly accepting the issues handed to Republicans by the opposition, the platform pledged support for a homestead act, rivers and harbors improvements, and federal aid for construction of a transcontinental railroad. For Pennsylvania, and for the Whiggish elements of the party in general, the platform contained a tariff plank that called for an "adjustment" of rates "to encourage the development of the industrial interests of the whole country" and "secure to the workingmen liberal wages." Another plank tilted the party away from nativism by declaring opposition to "any change in our naturalization laws or any state legislation by which the rights of citizens . . . from foreign lands shall be abridged or impaired." To southern disunionists the platform issued a warning against "contemplated treason, which it is the imperative duty of an indignant people sternly to rebuke and forever silence."

III

The excitement and optimism at Chicago carried over into the Republican campaign. This young party exuded the ebullience of youth. First-time voters flocked to the Republican standard. Thousands of them enrolled in "Wide-Awake" clubs and marched in huge parades carrying torches mounted on the ubiquitous fence rails that became a symbol of this campaign. One advantage the Republicans enjoyed over their opponents was party unity. The disappointed Sewardites followed their leader's example and stumped with enthusiasm for Lincoln. Only a handful of abolitionists on the left and a rather larger number of Whig-Americans on the right showed signs of alienation. The latter represented the main obstacle to Republican hopes of sweeping the North. Like the mythical phoenix, the Whig party kept rising from its own ashes. In 1860 it did so in the guise of the Constitutional Union party, which had held its convention a week before the Republicans. These conservatives decided that the best way to avoid the calamity of disunion was to take no stand at all on the issues that divided North and South. Instead of a platform, therefore, they adopted a pious resolution pledging "to recognize no political principle other than *the Constitution . . . the Union . . . and the Enforcement of the Laws.*" The convention nominated wealthy slaveholder John Bell of Tennessee for president and venerable Cotton Whig Edward Everett of Massachusetts for vice president.

Songs and rallies had been a part of American elections since 1840, but the Republicans carried these techniques to new heights in 1860. The "'Wigwam' Grand March" was one of many Republican marching songs. The most impressive feature of this campaign was the Wide-Awake Clubs that marched to music like this, carrying torches as if they were rifles. A year later many of these same men were marching with the real things.

Few delegates were under sixty years of age; this "Old Gentlemen's Party" became a butt of gentle ridicule by Republicans, who described the Bell-Everett ticket as "worthy to be printed on gilt-edged satin paper, laid away in a box of musk, and kept there." At the same time, southern Democrats accused Constitutional Unionists of "insulting the intelligence of the American people" by trying to organize a "party which shall ignore the slavery question. That issue must be met and settled."

Constitutional Unionists did not expect to win the election. The best they could hope for was to carry several upper-South states and weaken Lincoln sufficiently in the lower North to deny him an electoral majority. This would throw the election of a president into the House, where each state had one vote but no party controlled a majority of states. Democrats might then combine with Whig-American-Unionists to elect Breckinridge, a Kentuckian who could perhaps be weaned away from his extremist southern-rights backers. Or the Constitutional Unionists might have enough leverage to elect Bell. Or if the House failed to name a president by March 4, 1861, the vice president elected by the Democratic Senate would become acting president. That worthy individual would be either Breckinridge's running mate Joseph Lane of Oregon, a proslavery native of North Carolina, or the Constitutional Unionists' own Edward Everett.

But this spoiling strategy backfired. In several southern states the Constitutional Unionists felt compelled to prove themselves just as faithful to southern rights as the Democrats by embracing a federal slave code for the territories. This provoked many conservative ex-Whigs in the North to vote for Lincoln as the lesser of evils. The Bell-Everett ticket won less than 3 percent of the northern vote and took no states out of the Lincoln column.

The election of 1860 was unique in the history of American politics. The campaign resolved itself into two separate contests: Lincoln *vs.* Douglas in the North; Breckinridge *vs.* Bell in the South. Republicans did not even have a ticket in ten southern states, where their speakers would have been greeted with a coat of tar and feathers—or worse—if they had dared to appear. In the remaining five slave states—all in the upper South—Lincoln received 4 percent of the popular votes, mostly from antislavery Germans in St. Louis and vicinity. Breckinridge fared a little better in the North, where he won 5 percent of the popular vote, enough to deny California and Oregon to Douglas. Lincoln carried these states by a plurality and all other free states except New Jersey by a majority of the popular vote.

This was accomplished only by hard work. Though repudiated by the South and by the Buchanan administration, Douglas remained a formidable opponent. At the outset of the campaign he appeared to have a chance of winning eight northern and one or two border states with some 140 of the 303 electoral votes. To prevent this, Republicans mounted a campaign unprecedented in energy and oratory. Lincoln himself observed the customary silence of presidential candidates, but all other

As this campaign poster for John Bell and Edward Everett indicates, the Constitutional Union party was long on symbolism but short on substance. The two candidates stand with their hands resting on the Constitution, while the American eagle caries several unionist slogans in its beak. Below the candidates are streamers forming a loop enclosing clasped hands with the words "The Union must and shall be preserved."

Stephen Douglas broke tradition and took to the campaign trail himself in 1860. Lincoln stuck with tradition, however, and remained quietly at home in Springfield. On August 8 a Republican crowd stopped at his house to greet him and then went on to a great torchlight procession that evening. Six feet four inches tall, Lincoln (in white suit) towers above the crowd just to the right of the front door.

party leaders great and small took to the stump and delivered an estimated fifty thousand speeches. Republicans made a special effort headed by Carl Schurz to reduce the normal Democratic majority among German-Americans. They achieved some success among German Protestants—enough, perhaps, to make a difference in the close states of Illinois and Indiana—though the lingering perceptions of Republican dalliance with nativism and temperance kept the Catholic vote overwhelmingly Democratic.

In a bold break with tradition, Douglas campaigned for himself. In ill health, his voice hoarse, he nevertheless ranged through the whole country (except the west coast) from July to November in an exhausting tour that undoubtedly did much to bring on his death a year later. It was a courageous effort, but a futile one. Douglas carried the message to both North and South that he was the only *national* candidate, the only leader who could save the country from disunion. But in reality, Douglas Democrats were scarcely more a national party than the Republicans. Most southern Democrats painted Douglas nearly as black as Lincoln, and a traitor to boot. Douglas wound up with only 12 percent of the southern popular vote.

If the Democratic charge of sectionalism against Republicans lacked credibility this time, the old standby of branding them racial egalitarians retained its potency. Republicans had increased their vulnerability on this issue by placing a constitutional amendment to enfranchise blacks on the ballot in New York state. A Democratic float in a New York parade carried life-size effigies of Horace Greeley and a "good looking nigger wench, whom he caressed with all the affection of a true Republican." A banner proclaimed that "free love and free niggers will certainly

elect Old Abe." The *New York Herald*, largest Democratic newspaper in the country, predicted that if Lincoln was elected "hundreds of thousands" of fugitive slaves would "emigrate to their friends—the Republicans—North, and be placed by them side by side in competition with white men. . . . African amalgamation with the fair daughters of the Anglo Saxon, Celtic, and Teutonic races will soon be their portion under the millennium of Republican rule."

This onslaught wilted a good many Republicans. Although most party newspapers in New York endorsed the equal suffrage amendment, few speakers mentioned it, and the party made little effort in its behalf. Nearly one-third of the Republican voters joined virtually all Democrats in voting against it, sending the measure to a resounding defeat, even though Lincoln carried New York. And in the lower North generally, Republicans played down the moral issue of slavery while emphasizing other matters of regional concern. In Pennsylvania and New Jersey they talked about the tariff; from Ohio to California the Republicans portrayed themselves as a homestead party, an internal improvements party, a Pacific railroad party. This left Democrats with less opportunity to exploit the race issue. "The Republicans, in their speeches, say nothing of the nigger question," complained a Pennsylvania Democrat, "but all is made to turn on the Tariff." Of course the Republican position on these issues constituted a flank attack on the slave power. After Buchanan had vetoed the homestead act, even a Democratic paper in Iowa denounced the president as an "old sinner" and his northern associates as "pimps and hirelings" of "the Slave Propagandists."

The Buchanan administration handed Republicans another issue: corruption. Americans had always viewed malfeasance and abuse of power as the gravest dangers to republican liberty. Not only was Buchanan, in Republican eyes, the pliant tool of the slave power, but his administration also, in the words of historian Michael Holt, "was undoubtedly the most corrupt before the Civil War and one of the most corrupt in American history." An exposure of frauds filled a large volume

On October 23 the Democrats held a "Union procession" in New York City. Two of the floats portrayed the issues on which they hoped to carry the state for Douglas: the prediction that the election of the "railsplitter" Lincoln would split the Union, and the notion that the Republicans would promote racial equality, as exemplified by "Horace Greeley" driving a black woman in a cart pulled by a mule.

Horace Greeley's cherubic countenance gave little hint of his shrewdness and success in the rough-and-tumble world of journalism. The son of a poor Vermont farmer, he learned the trade of printer, moved to New York City at the age of twenty, and started the New York Tribune *as a Whig party paper in 1841. Within a decade he had built it into the country's most powerful newspaper, always taking an advanced antislavery position. In 1854 Greeley left the Whig party and made the* Tribune *the foremost Republican paper.*

compiled by a House investigating committee. The committee's report came off the presses in June 1860, just in time for an abridged edition to be distributed as a Republican campaign document.

This report topped off a series of previous investigations that disclosed a sorry record of graft and bribery in government contracts, the civil service, and Congress itself. The War and Navy departments had awarded contracts without competitive bidding to firms that made contributions to the Democratic party. Postmasters in New York and Chicago under both Pierce and Buchanan had siphoned public funds into party coffers for years. Democrats had used some of this money in congressional contests in 1858. They had also bribed judges to naturalize immigrants prematurely so they could vote in the crucial states of Pennsylvania and Indiana in 1856 and had "colonized" Irish railroad construction workers in Indiana to help swing that state to Buchanan. The New York postmaster fled the country in 1860 when auditors found his accounts $155,000 short. The House committee also dug up evidence that the administration had bribed congressmen to vote for admission of Kansas under the Lecompton constitution. Government printing contracts, long a lucrative source of patronage, became a greater scandal than ever under Buchanan. Kickbacks from payments exceeding by several times the printing cost found their way into the party treasury.

Secretary of War John Floyd presented the biggest target to graft hunters. He had sold government property for much less than its real value to a consortium headed by cronies. He had also signed padded bills presented to the War Department by a contractor in financial difficulties who then used these signed bills as collateral for bank loans and for negotiable bonds from an Interior Department Indian trust fund. Although partially revealed before the election, Floyd's full complicity in this matter did not come out until December 1860, when Buchanan allowed him to resign without punishment. A Virginian, Floyd pronounced himself a secessionist and returned home, where he was fêted by like-minded compatriots who praised one of his final acts in office—an order (subsequently countermanded) to transfer 125 cannon from Pittsburgh to arsenals in Mississippi and Texas.

Republicans made big capital out of these scandals. To be sure, Buchanan was not running for reelection, and most northern Democrats had already repudiated his administration. But some Douglas Democrats had also been caught with their hands in the till, and the whole party was tarnished by the image of corruption. Republican campaigners combined a crusade to "throw the rascals out" with denunciations of the slave power. The revelations of malfeasance, said Charles Francis Adams, had shown how "the slaveholding interest has been driven to the expedient of attempting to bribe the people of the Free States with their own money in order to maintain itself in control of the government." The future would reveal that a good many Republican politicians were none too honest themselves. But in 1860 the party carried an unsullied banner of reform and freedom against the tired old corrupt proslavery Democrats.

To some members of their constituency, however, the Republican message seemed sour. When party orators discussed slavery, especially in the lower North, they often took pains to describe Republicanism as the true "White Man's Party." Exclusion of slavery from the territories, they insisted, meant exclusion of black competition with white settlers. This caused several abolitionists to denounce the Republicans as no better than Douglas Democrats. William Lloyd Garrison believed that "the Republican party means to do nothing, can do nothing, for the abolition of slavery in the slave states." Wendell Phillips even went so far as to call Lincoln "the Slave Hound of Illinois" because he refused to advocate repeal of the fugitive slave law.

But some Republicans came almost up to the abolitionist standard. In the upper North the old evangelical fervor against bondage infused their rhetoric. After the Republican convention Seward rediscovered the irrepressible conflict. Even in Missouri he boldly proclaimed that freedom "is bound to go through . . . for the simple reason that it is going through all the world."

In the eyes of Republicans, Secretary of War John B. Floyd was the most notorious member of the Buchanan administration. To corruption he added the crime of treason. Floyd went on to an inglorious career as a Confederate general.

Gubernatorial candidates John Andrew of Massachusetts and Austin Blair of Michigan, Senators Charles Sumner, Salmon P. Chase, and Benjamin Wade, Congressmen George W. Julian and Thaddeus Stevens, nearly the whole Republican party of Vermont, and a host of other party leaders were abolitionists in all but name. Many of them *did* favor repeal of the fugitive slave law, along with the abolition of slavery in the District of Columbia and the prohibition of the interstate slave trade.

Believing that these men embodied the progressive spirit and future thrust of the Republican party, many abolitionists supported it in 1860. "Lincoln's election will indicate growth in the right direction," wrote one, while Frederick Douglass acknowledged that a Republican victory "must and will be hailed as an anti-slavery triumph." Southerners thought so too. Democrats below the Potomac considered Lincoln "a relentless, dogged, free-soil border ruffian . . . a vulgar mobocrat and a Southern hater . . . an illiterate partisan . . . possessed only of his inveterate hatred of slavery and his openly avowed predilections of negro equality." As the election neared, the increasing likelihood that a solid North would make Lincoln president brewed a volatile mixture of hysteria, despondency, and elation in the South. Whites feared the coming of new John Browns encouraged by triumphant Black Republicans; unionists despaired of the future; secessionists relished the prospect of southern independence. Even the weather during that summer of 1860 became part of the political climate: a severe drought and prolonged heat wave withered southern crops and frayed nerves beyond the point of endurance.

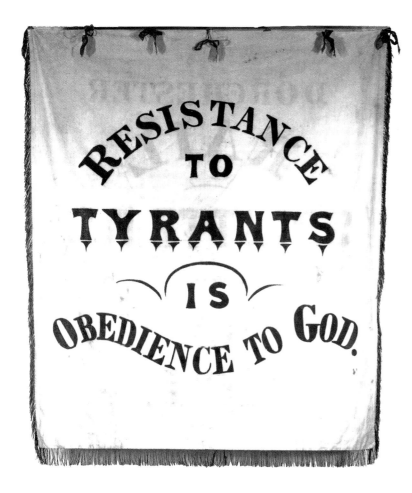

In Dorchester, Massachusetts, Republicans carried such banners as this one in a parade, proclaiming a favorite antislavery slogan in this strongly antislavery community. In many other parts of the North, however, Republicans shied away from such slogans, which might have seemed to align them too closely with John Brown's style of attacking slavery.

Stories of slave uprisings that followed the visits of mysterious Yankee strangers, along with reports of arson and rapes and poisonings by slaves, crowded the southern press. Somehow these horrors never seemed to happen in one's own neighborhood. Many of them, in fact, were reported from faraway Texas. And curiously, only those newspapers backing Breckinridge for president seemed to carry such stories. Bell and Douglas newspapers even had the effrontery to accuse Breckinridge Democrats of getting up "false-hoods and sensation tales" to "arouse the passions of the people and drive them into the Southern Disunion movement." But this accusation must have been wrong. No less a personage than R. S. Holt, a wealthy Mississippi planter and brother of the U.S. postmaster general, reported that "we have constantly a foretaste of what Northern brother-hood means, in almost daily conflagrations & in discovery of poison, knives & pistols distributed among our slaves by emissaries sent out for that purpose." Fortunately, Holt added, "Miracles & Providence" had prevented the accomplishment of their "hellish" designs.

In vain, then, did a southern conservative point out that most of these atrocity stories "turned out, on examination, to be totally false, and *all of them* grossly exaggerated." On the eve of the election a Mississippian observed that "the minds of the people are aroused to a pitch of excitement probably unparalleled in the history of our country." A writer in a Texas Methodist weekly was sure that "the designs of the abolitionists are . . . poison [and] fire" to "deluge [the South] in blood and flame . . . and force their fair daughters into the embrace of buck negroes for wives." However irrational these fears, the response was real—vigilante lynch law that made the John Brown scare of the previous winter look like a Sunday School picnic. "It is better for us to hang ninety-nine innocent (suspicious) men than to let one guilty one pass," wrote a Texan, "for the guilty one endangers the peace of society."

This mass hysteria caused even southern unionists to warn Yankees that a Republican victory meant disunion. "The Election of Lincoln is Sufficient Cause for Secession," a Bell supporter in Alabama entitled his speech. The moderate Benjamin H. Hill of Georgia insisted that "this Government and Black Republicanism cannot live together. . . . At no period of the world's history have four thousand millions of property debated whether it ought to submit to the rule of an enemy." The fever spread to the border states. John J. Crittenden, Kentucky's elder statesman of unionism, heir of Henry Clay's mantle of nationalism, gave a speech just before the election in which he denounced the "profound fanaticism" of Republicans who

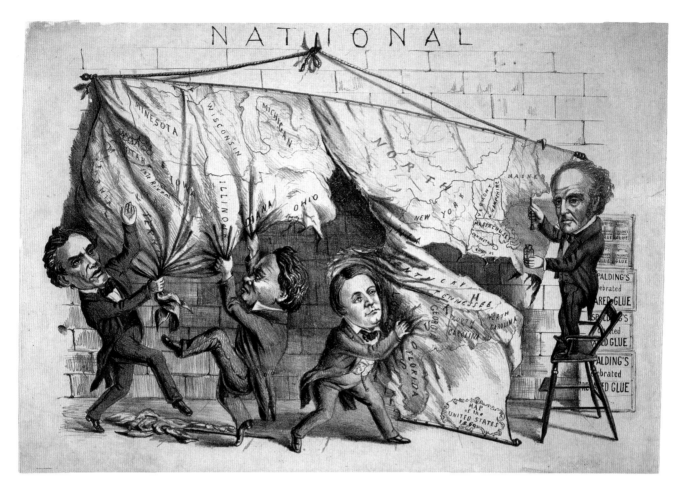

This cartoon satirizes all four presidential candidates. At the left, Lincoln and Douglas both try to grab as many midwestern states as possible, while Breckinridge rips away all the southern states. Bell tries to hold the Northeast together with Spalding's glue. The message seems to be that three of the candidates are threatening to tear the country apart and the fourth can think of nothing better than glue to hold it together.

"think it their duty to destroy . . . the white man, in order that the black might be free. . . . [The South] has come to the conclusion that in case Lincoln should be elected . . . she could not submit to the consequences, and therefore, to avoid her fate, will secede from the Union."

Republicans refused to take these warnings to heart. They had heard them before, a dozen times or more. In 1856 Democrats had used such threats to frighten northerners into voting Democratic. Republicans believed that the same thing was happening in 1860. In a speech at St. Paul, Seward ridiculed this new southern effort "to terrify or alarm" the North. "Who's afraid? (Laughter and cries of 'no one.') Nobody's afraid; nobody can be bought." Nor did Lincoln expect "any formidable effort to break up the Union. The people of the South have too much sense," he thought, "to attempt the ruin of the government."

Hindsight was to reveal that southerners meant what they said. Yet it is hard to see what Republicans could have done to allay southern anxieties short of dissolving their party and proclaiming slavery a positive good. It was not so much what Republicans might do as what they stood for that angered southerners. As a committee of the Virginia legislature put it, "the very existence of such a party is an offense to the whole South." A New Orleans editor regarded every northern vote cast for Lincoln as *a deliberate, cold-blooded insult and outrage*" to southern honor. Lincoln rejected pleas from conservatives that he issue a statement to mollify the South. "What is it I could say which would quiet alarm?" he asked in October. Hav-

Daily Enquirer.

BY TYLER, WISE & ALLEGRE.

SATURDAY MORNING, NOVEMBER 10.

Reading Matter on Every Page.

In our Daily edition to-day may be found the following:
On First Page—News and other articles of general interest. On Second Page—Editorials, communications, late news, &c. On Third Page—Local and State news, telegraphic despatches, marine news, &c. On Fourth Page—Poetry and a variety of news items.

The Result in Virginia.

The returns show, that in the cities and counties heard from, Breckinridge has 2,743 majority over Bell. The remaining counties gave Letcher 1,098 majority over Goggin. The Democratic majority in this State will be over three thousand.

The Presidential Election—Opinions of the Press.

That this condition of things brings the country, and necessarily so, into the jaws of fearful convulsions, is, we think, perfectly certain. To state this is but to restate what distinguished men of all parties, in the North and in the South, have again and again laid down as axiomatic truths.

Secession Movement at Savannah.

SAVANNAH, Nov. 8, 11 P. M.—A mass meeting of citizens was held here to-night, the largest gathering ever held here, to express their sentiments in regard to the present political crisis.

ing made such conciliatory statements before, he felt any repetition would simply encourage "bold bad men . . . who are eager for something new upon which to base new misrepresentations—men who would like to frighten me, or, at least, to fix upon me the character of timidity and cowardice. They would seize upon almost any letter I could write, as being an '*awful coming down.*'"

Douglas did speak out. On his first foray into the South he told crowds in North Carolina that he would "hang every man higher than Haman who would attempt . . . to break up the Union by resistance to its laws." Campaigning in Iowa when he learned that Republicans had swept the October state elections in Pennsylvania, Ohio, and Indiana, Douglas said to his private secretary: "Mr. Lincoln is the next President. We must try to save the Union. I will go South." Go he did, to Tennessee, Georgia, and Alabama, at some risk to his deteriorating health and even to his life. Douglas courageously repeated his warnings against secession. The whole North would rise up to prevent it, he said pointedly. "I hold that the election of any man on earth by the American people, according to the Constitution, is no justification for breaking up this government." Southerners listened to him, but they did not hear.

The only shred of hope for Democrats was a "fusion" of the three opposition parties in key northern states to deny Lincoln their electoral votes and throw the election into the House—but all efforts to effect this failed. Lincoln won majorities over the combined opposition in New York, Pennsylvania, and Rhode Island; the three fusion electors in New Jersey gave Douglas his only northern electoral votes. He also carried Missouri, while Bell won Virginia, Kentucky, and his native Tennessee. Breckinridge carried the rest of the South, winning 45 percent of the section's popular votes to Bell's 39 percent. Though Lincoln won only 40 percent of the national popular vote (54 percent in the North), his 180 electoral votes gave him a comfortable cushion over the necessary minimum of 152. Even if the opposition had combined against him in every free state he would have lost only New Jersey, California, and Oregon and still would have won the presidency with 169 electoral votes.

To southerners the election's most ominous feature was the magnitude of Republican victory north of the 41st parallel. Lincoln won more than 60 percent of the vote in that region, losing scarcely two dozen counties. Three-quarters of the Republican congressmen and senators in the next

Congress would represent this "Yankee" and antislavery portion of the free states. These facts were "full of portentous significance," declared the *New Orleans Crescent*. "The idle canvass prattle about Northern conservatism may now be dismissed," agreed the *Richmond Examiner*. "A party founded on the single sentiment . . . of hatred of African slavery, is now the controlling power." No one could any longer "be deluded . . . that the Black Republican party is a moderate" party, pronounced the *New Orleans Delta*. "It is, in fact, essentially a revolutionary party."

Whether or not the party was revolutionary, antislavery men concurred that a revolution had taken place. "We live in revolutionary times," wrote an Illinois free soiler, "& I say God bless the revolution." Charles Francis Adams, whose grandfather and father had been defeated for reelection to the presidency by slaveowners, wrote in his diary the day after Lincoln's victory: "The great revolution has actually taken place. . . . The country has once and for all thrown off the domination of the Slaveholders."

For weeks before the presidential election on November 6, it had been clear that Lincoln was the likely victor. Once that anticipation became fact, secession sentiments burst all restraints in the lower South. Newspapers in the upper South, such as the Richmond Enquirer *(opposite page), expressed grave apprehensions about the future. Residents of the lower South went into the streets to cheer secession speakers and approve resolutions demanding disunion. The mass meeting in Savannah on November 8 (above) was one of the first of many such rallies.*

★ ★ ★ ★ ★

CHAPTER EIGHT

The Counterrevolution
of 1861

I

The second Continental Congress had deliberated fourteen months before declaring American independence in 1776. To produce the United States Constitution and put the new government into operation required nearly two years. In contrast, the Confederate States of America organized itself, drafted a constitution, and set up shop in Montgomery, Alabama, within three months of Lincoln's election.

The South moved so swiftly because, in seeming paradox, secession proceeded on a state-by-state basis rather than by collective action. Remembering the lesson of 1850, when the Nashville Convention had turned into a forum of caution and delay, fire-eaters determined this time to eschew a convention of states until the secession of several of them had become a *fait accompli*. Not surprisingly, South Carolina acted first. "There is nothing in all the dark caves of human passion so cruel and deadly as the hatred the South Carolinians profess for the Yankees," wrote the correspondent of the London *Times* from Charleston. The enmity of Greek for Turk was child's play "compared to the animosity evinced by the 'gentry' of South Carolina for the 'rabble of the North.'" In this mood the South Carolina legislature called a convention to consider secession. By a vote of 169 to 0 the convention enacted on December 20 an "ordinance" dissolving "the union now subsisting between South Carolina and other States."

In a chain reaction by conventions in other lower-South states, Mississippi adopted a similar ordinance on January 9, 1861, followed by Florida on January 10, Alabama on January 11, Georgia on January 19, Louisiana on January 26, and Texas on February 1. Although none of these conventions exhibited the unity of South Carolina's, their average vote in favor of secession was 80 percent. This figure was probably a fair reflection of white opinion in those six states. Except in Texas, the conventions did not submit their ordinances to the voters for ratification. This led to charges that a disunion conspiracy acted against the will of the people. But in fact the main reason for nonsubmission was a desire to avoid delay. The voters had just

Opposite page: The Confederate flag is raised over Fort Sumter on April 14, 1861.

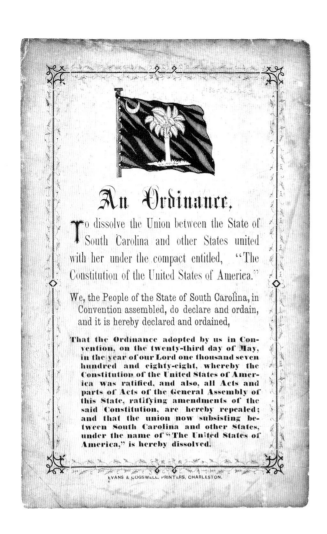

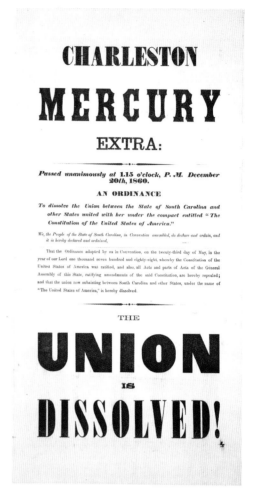

CHARLESTON
MERCURY
EXTRA:

Passed unanimously at 1.15 o'clock, P. M. December
20th, 1860.

AN ORDINANCE

*To dissolve the Union between the State of South Carolina and
other States united with her under the compact entitled "The
Constitution of the United States of America."*

We, the People of the State of South Carolina, in Convention assembled, do declare and ordain, and
it is hereby declared and ordained,

That the Ordinance adopted by us in Convention, on the twenty-third day of May, in the
year of our Lord one thousand seven hundred and eighty-eight, whereby the Constitution of the
United States of America was ratified, and also, all Acts and parts of Acts of the General
Assembly of this State, ratifying amendments of the said Constitution, are hereby repealed;
and that the union now subsisting between South Carolina and other States, under the name of
"The United States of America," is hereby dissolved.

THE
UNION
IS
DISSOLVED!

Above: Since the 1830s South Carolina had been a hotbed of disunion convictions, so it was not surprising that the Palmetto State was the first to pass an ordinance of secession, unanimously, on December 20, 1860. The fire-eating Charleston Mercury *hailed the event in an extra published the same day. One of the state's few unionists said disgustedly that South Carolina was too small for a republic and too large for an insane asylum.*

Opposite: The first seven states to secede, plus two more that seceded later (Arkansas and North Carolina), were carried by Breckinridge in 1860; his own state of Kentucky was not. Kentucky did not secede, but Breckinridge nevertheless went with the Confederacy and rose to the rank of major general in its army.

elected delegates who had made their positions clear in public statements; another election seemed superfluous. The Constitution of 1787 had been ratified by state conventions, not by popular vote; withdrawal of that ratification by similar conventions satisfied a wish for legality and symmetry. In Texas the voters endorsed secession by a margin of three to one; there is little reason to believe that the result would have been different in any of the other six states.

Divisions in the lower South occurred mainly over tactics and timing, not goals. A majority favored the domino tactics of individual state secession followed by a convention of independent states to form a new confederacy. But a significant minority, especially in Alabama, Georgia, and Louisiana, desired some sort of cooperative action throughout the South *preceding* secession to ensure unity among at least the cotton-South states. But these "cooperationists" were not agreed on strategy and were overwhelmed by the secessionist tidal wave which produced a league of a half-dozen seceded states within six weeks of South Carolina's secession. The radical cooperationists supported secession but argued that a united South would present a stronger front; those who might be labeled "ultimatumists" urged a convention of southern states to draw up a list of demands for presentation to the incoming Lincoln administration—including enforcement of the fugitive slave law, repeal of personal liberty laws, guarantees against interference with slavery in the District of Columbia

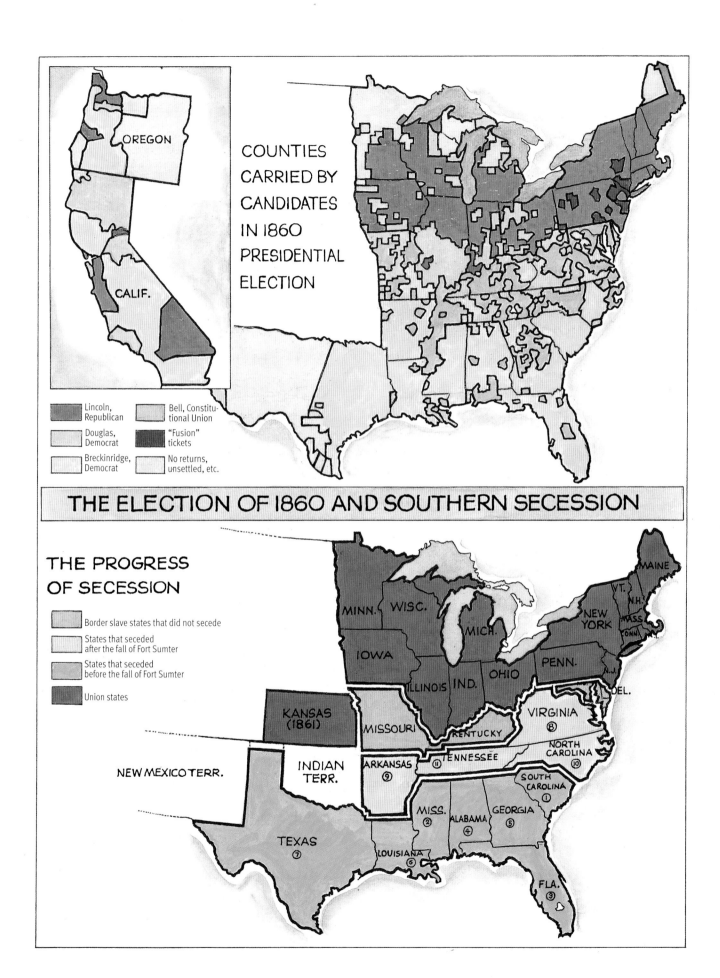

COUNTIES
CARRIED BY
CANDIDATES
IN 1860
PRESIDENTIAL
ELECTION

OREGON

CALIF.

Lincoln, Republican	Bell, Constitutional Union
Douglas, Democrat	"Fusion" tickets
Breckinridge, Democrat	No returns, unsettled, etc.

THE ELECTION OF 1860 AND SOUTHERN SECESSION

THE PROGRESS OF SECESSION

Border slave states that did not secede

States that seceded after the fall of Fort Sumter

States that seceded before the fall of Fort Sumter

Union states

MINN. WISC. MICH. NEW YORK MAINE VT. N.H. MASS. CONN.

IOWA ILLINOIS IND. OHIO PENN. N.J. DEL.

KANSAS (1861) MISSOURI KENTUCKY VIRGINIA ⑧

NEW MEXICO TERR. INDIAN TERR. ARKANSAS ⑨ TENNESSEE ⑪ NORTH CAROLINA ⑩

SOUTH CAROLINA ①

MISS. ② ALABAMA ④ GEORGIA ⑥

TEXAS ⑦ LOUISIANA ⑥

FLA. ③

A PROTEST

AGAINST THE

ORDINANCE OF SECESSION,

Passed by the Louisiana Convention, on the 26th January, 1861, presented to the Convention on that day, by JAMES G. TALIAFERRO, *the Delegate from the Parish of Catahoula, who asked that it might be entered upon the journal of the Convention, which was refused.*

THE delegate from the parish of Catahoula opposes unqualifiedly the separate secession of Louisiana from the federal Union, and asks leave to place upon the records of the convention his reasons for that opposition. They are as follow:

I oppose the act of secession because, in my deliberate judgment, the wrongs alleged as the cause of the movement might be redressed under the constitution by an energetic execution of the laws of the United States, and that, standing upon the guarantees of the constitution, in the Union, southern rights might be triumphantly maintained under the protection and safeguards which the constitution affords.

Because, in secession I see no remedy for the actual and present evils complained of, and because the *prospective* evils depicted so gloomily may never come; and if they should, the inalienable right to resist tyranny and oppression might then be exercised as well and as successfully as now.

Because I see no certainty that the seceding states will ever be confederated again; none that the border states will secede at all; and if they should, I see no reliable ground for believing that they would incorporate themselves with the gulf or cotton states in a new government. I see no surety either that Texas would unite with them.

Because the gulf or cotton states alone, were they to unite in a separate confederacy, would be without the elements of power, indispensable in the formation of a government to take a respectable rank among the nations of the earth.

Because I believe that peaceable secession is a right unknown to the constitution of the United States; that it is a most dangerous and mischievous principle in the structure of any government and when carried into the formation of the contemplated confederacy of the gulf states, will render it powerless for good, and complete its incapacity to afford to the people permanent security for their lives, liberties and property.

Because it is my solemn and deliberate conviction that the distraction of the southern states by separate secession will defeat the purpose it is intended to accomplish, and that its certain results will be to impair instead of strengthen the security of southern institutions.

Because the proper status of Louisiana is with the border states, with which nature has connected her by the majestic river which flows through her limits; and because an alliance in a weak government with the gulf states east of her, is unnatural and antagonistic to her obvious interests and destiny.

Because by separate secession the state relinquishes all its rights within the government, it surrenders its equal rights to the common territories, to the vast public domain of the United States and the public property of every kind belonging to the nation. And for this reason I oppose secession as being emphatically submission.

Because, secession may bring anarchy and war, as it will assuredly bring ruinous exactions upon property in the form of direct taxation, a withering blight upon the prosperity of the state, and a fatal prostration of all its great interests.

Because, the act of dissolving the ties which connect Louisiana with the federal Union is a revolutionary act that this convention is, of itself, without legitimate power to perform. Convened without authority of the people of the state, and refusing to submit its action to them for their sanction in the grave and vital act of changing their government, this convention violates the great fundamental principle of American government, that the will of the people is supreme.

JAMES G. TALIAFERRO,

DELEGATE FROM THE PARISH OF CATAHOULA

Not every delegate to the conventions that voted to take their states out of the Union agreed to this action. In Louisiana, where the final vote for secession was 113 to 17, delegate James G. Talliaferro felt so strongly about what he considered a disastrous decision that he wrote this formal protest and asked that it be entered in the journal of the convention. His request was denied. Many of Talliaferro's dire prophesies came true, especially his prediction that secession would bring "a withering blight upon the prosperity of the state . . . a fatal prostration of all its great interests."

or with the interstate slave trade, and protection of slavery in the territories, at least those south of 36° 30'. If Republicans refused this ultimatum, then a united South would go out. Since Republicans seemed unlikely to promise all of these concessions and most southerners would not trust them even if they did, the ultimatumists commanded little support in secession conventions.

The third and most conservative group of cooperationists were conditional unionists, who asked fellow southerners to give Lincoln a chance to prove his moderate intentions. Only if Republicans committed some "overt act" against southern rights should the South resort to the drastic step of secession. But while the ranks of conditional unionists contained influential men like Alexander Stephens, they too were swept along by the pace of events. Secession was an unequivocal act which relieved the unbearable tension that had been building for years. It was a catharsis for pent-up fears and hostilities. It was a *joyful* act that caused people literally to dance in the streets. Their fierce gaiety anticipated the celebratory crowds that gathered along the Champs-Elysées and the Unter den Linden and at Picadilly Circus in that similarly innocent world of August 1914. Not that the flag-waving, singing crowds in Charleston and Savannah and New Orleans wanted or expected war; on the contrary, they believed that "the Yankees were cowards and would not fight"—or said they did, to assure the timid that there was no danger. "So far as civil war is concerned," remarked an Atlanta newspaper blithely in January 1861, "we have no fears of that in Atlanta." It became a common saying in the South during the secession winter that "a lady's thimble will hold all the blood that will be shed."

Cooperationists were not so sure about this. "War I look for as almost certain," wrote Alexander Stephens, who also warned that "revolutions are much easier started than controlled, and the men who begin them [often] . . . themselves become the victims." But Stephens's prescient warning was lost in the wind, and he joined the revolution himself when his state went out. Before that happened, however, the cooperationists had demonstrated considerable strength in each state except South Carolina and Texas. In elections for convention delegates, candidates representing some kind of cooperationist position polled at least 40 percent of the vote in those five states. Many eligible voters had not gone to the polls in these elections, leading to a belief that the potential cooperationist electorate was even larger. In Alabama and Georgia, 39 and 30 percent respectively of the delegates voted against the final resolution of secession despite the enormous pressures brought on them to go along with the majority.

This caused many northerners and some historians to exaggerate the strength of unionism in the lower South. As late as July 1861, Lincoln expressed doubt "whether there is, to-day, a majority of the legally qualified voters of any State, except perhaps South Carolina, in favor of disunion." A century later several historians echoed this faith in a silent majority of southern unionists. One of them concluded that "the secessionists succeeded less because of the intrinsic popularity of their program than because of the extreme skill with which they utilized an emergency psychology."

Though an emergency psychology certainly existed, the belief in a repressed unionist majority rests on a misunderstanding of southern unionism. As a Mississippi "unionist" explained after Lincoln's election, he was no longer "a Union man in the sense in which the North is Union." His unionism was conditional; the North had violated the condition by electing Lincoln. Cooperationists in Alabama who voted against secession cautioned outsiders not to "misconstrue" their action. "We scorn the Black Republicans," they declared. "The State of Alabama cannot and will not submit to the Administration of Lincoln. . . . We intend to resist . . . but our resistance is based upon . . . unity of action, with the other slave states." Or as a Mississippi cooperationist put it: "Cooperation before secession was the first object of my desire. Failing this I am willing to take the next best, subsequent cooperation or cooperation after secession." This was the position of most delegates who initially opposed immediate secession. It was a weak foundation on which to build a faith in southern unionism.

Was secession constitutional? Or was it an act of revolution? The Constitution is silent on this question. But most secessionists believed in the legality of their action. State sovereignty, they insisted, had preceded national sovereignty. When they had ratified the Constitution, states delegated some of the functions of sovereignty to a federal government but did not yield its fundamental attributes. Having ratified the Constitution by a convention, a state could reassert total sovereignty in the same manner. This theory presented a slight problem for states (five of the seven) that had come into the Union after 1789. But they too, despite the appearance of being creatures rather than creators of the Union, could assert the prior sovereignty of their states, for each had formed a state constitution (or in the case of Texas, a national constitution) *before* petitioning Congress for admission to the Union.

Those southerners (mostly conditional unionists) who found this theory a bit hard to swallow could fall back on the right of revolution. Senator Alfred Iverson of Georgia conceded that, while no state had a constitutional right to secede, "each State has the right of revolution. . . . The secession of a State is an act of revolution." Sporting blue cockades (the symbol of secession), some of these enthusiastic revolutionaries even sang "The Southern Marseillaise" in the streets of Charleston and New Orleans. Ex-governor Henry Wise of Virginia, who urged the formation of committees of public safety, gloried in his reputation as the "Danton of the Secession Movement in Virginia."

But the American Revolution, not the French, was the preferred model for secessionists. *Liberté* they sought, but not *égalité* or *fraternité*. Were not "the men of 1776 . . . Secessionists?" asked an Alabamian. From "the high and solemn motive of defending and protecting the rights . . . which our fathers bequeathed to us," declared Jefferson Davis, let us "renew such sacrifices as our fathers made to the holy cause of constitutional liberty."

What were these rights and liberties for which Confederates contended? The right to own slaves; the liberty to take this property into the territories; freedom from the coercive powers of a centralized government. Black Republican rule in Washington threatened republican freedoms as the South understood them. The ideology for which the Fathers had fought in 1776 posited an eternal struggle between liberty and power. Because the Union after March 4, 1861, would no longer be controlled by southerners, the South could protect its liberty from the assaults of hostile powers only by going out of the Union. "On the 4th of March, 1861," declared a Georgia secessionist, "we are either *slaves in the Union or freemen out of it*." The question, agreed Jefferson Davis and a fellow Mississippian, was "Will you be slaves or will be independent? . . . Will you consent to be robbed of your property" or will you "strike bravely for liberty, property, honor and life?"

What stake did nonslaveholding whites have in this crusade for the freedom of planters to own slaves? Some secessionists worried a great deal about this question. What if Hinton Rowan Helper was right? What if nonslaveowners were potential Black Republicans? "The great lever by which the abolitionists hope to extirpate slavery in the States is the aid of non-slaveholding citizens in the South," fretted a Kentucky editor. How would they ply this lever? By using the patronage to build up a cadre of Republican officeholders among nonslaveowners—first in the border states and upcountry, where slavery was most vulnerable, and then in the heart of the cotton kingdom itself. Governor Joseph E. Brown of Georgia feared that some whites would be "bribed into treachery to their own section, by the allurements of office." When Republicans organized their "Abolition party . . . of Southern men," echoed the *Charleston Mercury*, "the contest for slavery will no longer be one between the North and the South. It will be in the South, between the people of the South."

The elections of delegates to secession conventions seemed to confirm this fear. Many upcountry districts with few slaves sent cooperationist delegates. In the conventions, delegates supporting delay or cooperation owned, on the average, less wealth and fewer slaves than immediate secessionists. The implications of these data should not be pushed too far. A good many low-slaveholding Democratic counties voted for immediate secession, while numerous high-slave-holding Whig counties backed cooperation. And of course cooperationism did not necessarily mean unionism. Nevertheless, the partial correlation of cooperationism with low slaveholding caused concern among secessionists.

So they undertook a campaign to convince nonslaveholders that they too had a stake in disunion. The stake was white supremacy. In this view, the Black Republican program of abolition was the first step toward racial equality and amalgamation. Georgia's Governor Brown carried this message to his native uplands of north Georgia, whose voters idolized him. Slavery "is the poor man's best Government," said Brown. "Among us the poor white laborer . . . does not belong to the menial class. The negro is in no sense his equal. . . . He belongs to the only true aristocracy, the race of *white men*." Thus yeoman farmers "will never consent to submit to abolition rule," for they "know that in the event of the abolition of slavery, they would be greater sufferers than the rich, who would be able to protect themselves." Much secessionist rhetoric played variations on this theme. The election of Lincoln, declared an Alabama newspaper, "shows that the North [intends] to free the negroes and force amalgamation between them and the children of the poor men of the South." "Do you love your mother, your wife, your sister, your daughter?" a Georgia secessionist asked nonslaveholders. If Georgia remained in a Union "ruled by Lincoln and his crew . . . in TEN years or less our CHILDREN will be the *slaves* of negroes." To defend their wives and daughters, presumably, yeoman whites therefore joined planters in "rallying to the standard of Liberty and Equality for white men" against "our Abolition enemies who are pledged to prostrate the white freemen of the South down to equality with Negroes." Most southern whites could agree, according to secessionists, that "democratic liberty exists solely because we have black slaves" whose presence "promotes equality among the free." Hence "freedom is not possible without slavery."

This Orwellian definition of liberty as slavery provoked ridicule north of the Potomac. For disunionists to compare themselves to the Revolutionary fathers "is a libel upon the whole character and conduct of the men of '76," declared William Cullen Bryant's *New York Evening Post*. The founders fought "to establish the rights of man . . . and principles of universal liberty." The South was rebelling "not in the interest of general humanity, but of a domestic despotism. . . . Their motto is not liberty, but slavery." Thomas Jefferson's Declaration of Independence spoke for "Natural Rights against Established Institutions," added the *New York Tribune*, while "Mr. Jeff. Davis's caricature thereof is made in the interest of an unjust, outgrown, decaying Institution against the apprehended encroachments of Natural Human Rights." It was, in short, not a revolution for liberty but a counterrevolution "reversing the wheels of progress . . . to hurl everything backward into deepest darkness . . . despotism and oppression."

In the nineteenth century, any large political or social movement soon generated an outpouring of songs, poems, and other forms of popular expression. The secession movement was no exception, as illustrated by this title page of the sheet music to the "Secession Quick Step." Note the symbolic connection to the American Revolution in the dedication to the "Minute Men of Georgia" and the snake with the slogan, in Latin, "Don't Tread on Me."

Without assenting to the rhetoric of this analysis, a good many disunionists in effect endorsed its substance. The signers of the Declaration of Independence were wrong if they meant to include Negroes among "all men," said Alexander Stephens after he had become vice president of the Confederacy. "Our new government is founded upon exactly the opposite idea; its foundations are laid, its cornerstone rests, upon the great truth that the negro is not equal to the white man; that slavery . . . is his natural and normal condition." Black Republicans were the real revolutionaries. They subscribed to "tenets as radical and revolutionary" as those of the abolitionists, declared a New Orleans newspaper. Therefore it was "an abuse of language" to call secession a revolution, said Jefferson Davis. We left the Union "to save ourselves from a revolution" that threatened to make "property in slaves so insecure as to be comparatively worthless." In 1861 the Confederate secretary of state advised foreign governments that southern states had formed a new nation "to preserve their old institutions" from "a revolution [that] threatened to destroy their social system."

This is the language of counterrevolution. But in one respect the Confederacy departed from the classic pattern of the genre. Most counterrevolutions seek to restore the *ancien régime*. The counterrevolutionaries of 1861 made their move before the revolutionaries had done anything—indeed, several months before Lincoln even took office. In this regard, secession fit the model of "preemptive counterrevolution" developed by historian Arno Mayer. Rather than trying to restore the old order, a preemptive counterrevolution strikes first to protect the status quo before the revolutionary threat can materialize. "Conjuring up the dangers of leaving revolutionaries the time to prepare their forces and plans for an assault on *their* terms," writes Mayer, "counterrevolutionary leaders urge a preventive thrust." To mobilize support for it, they "intentionally exaggerate the magnitude and imminence of the revolutionary threat."

Though Mayer was writing about Europe in the twentieth century, his words also describe the immediate secessionists of 1860. They exaggerated the Republican threat and urged preemptive action to forestall the dangers they conjured up. The South could not afford to wait for an "overt act" by Lincoln against southern rights, they insisted. "If I find a coiled rattlesnake in my path," asked an Alabama editor, "do I wait for his 'overt act' or do I smite him in his coil?"

II

Seldom in history has a counterrevolution so quickly provoked the very revolution it sought to preempt. This happened because most northerners refused to condone disunion. On that matter, if on little else, the outgoing and incoming presidents of the United States agreed.

In his final message to Congress, on December 3, 1860, James Buchanan surprised some of his southern allies with a firm denial of the right of secession. The Union was not "a mere voluntary association of States, to be dissolved at pleasure by any one of the contracting parties," said Buchanan. "We the People" had adopted the Constitution to form "a *more* perfect Union" than the one existing under the Articles of Confederation, which had stated that "the Union shall be perpetual." The framers of the national government "never intended to implant in its bosom the seeds of its own destruction, nor were they guilty of the absurdity of providing for its own dissolution." State sovereignty was *not* superior to national sovereignty, Buchanan insisted. The Constitution bestowed the highest attributes of sovereignty exclusively on the federal government: national defense; foreign policy; regulation of foreign and interstate commerce; coinage of money. "This Constitution," stated that document, "and the laws of the United States . . . shall be the supreme law of the land . . . any thing in the constitution or laws of any State to the contrary notwithstanding." If secession was legitimate, warned the president, the Union became "a rope of sand" and "our thirty-three States may resolve themselves into as many petty, jarring, and hostile republics. . . . By such a dread catastrophe the hopes of the friends of freedom throughout the world would be destroyed. . . . Our example for more than eighty years would not only be lost, but it would be quoted as a conclusive proof that man is unfit for self-government."

Thousands of northern editorials and speeches echoed these themes. Fears of a domino effect were especially pervasive. "A successful rebellion by a few States now," ran an editorial typical of hundreds, "will be followed by a new rebellion or secession a few years hence." This was not mere alarmism. Some Americans were already speculating about a division of the country into three or four "confederacies" with an independent Pacific coast republic thrown in for good measure. Several New York merchants and Democrats with ties to the South were talking of setting up as a free city. A prominent New York lawyer secretly informed railroad president George B. McClellan in December 1860 that "when secession is fairly inaugurated at the South, we mean to do a little of the same business here & cut loose from the fanatics, of New England & of the North generally, including most of our own State." In January 1861 Mayor Fernando Wood brought this matter into the open with a message to the aldermen advocating the secession of New York City. The project went nowhere, but it did plant seeds of copperheadism that germinated a couple of years later.

"The doctrine of secession is anarchy," declared a Cincinnati newspaper. "If any minority have the right to break up the Government at pleasure, because they have not had their way, there is an end of all government." Lincoln too considered secession the "essence of anarchy." He branded state sovereignty a "sophism." "The Union is older than any of the States," Lincoln asserted, "and, in fact, it created them as States." The Declaration of Independence transformed the "United Colonies" into the United States; without this union then, there would never have been any "free and independent States." "Having never been States, either in substance, or in name, *outside* the Union," asked Lincoln, "whence this magical omnipotence of 'State rights,' asserting a claim of power to lawfully destroy the Union itself?" Perpetuity was "the fundamental law of all national governments." No government "ever had provision in its organic law for its own termination. . . . No State, upon its own mere motion, can lawfully get out of the Union. . . . They can only do so against law, and by revolution."

Neither Lincoln nor any other northerner denied the right of revolution. After all, Yankees shared the legacy of 1776. But there was no "right of revolution at *pleasure*," declared a Philadelphia newspaper. Revolution was "a moral right, when exercised for a morally justifiable cause," wrote Lincoln. But "when exercised without such a cause revolution is no right, but simply a wicked exercise of physical power." The South had no just cause. The event that precipitated secession was the election of a president by a constitutional majority. The "central idea" of the Union cause, said Lincoln, "is the necessity . . . of proving that popular government is not an absurdity. We must settle this question now, whether in a free government the minority have the right to break up the government whenever they choose."

But how was it to be settled? This problem was compounded by the lame-duck syndrome in the American constitutional system. During the four-month interval between Lincoln's election and inauguration, Buchanan had the executive power but felt little responsibility for the crisis, while Lincoln had responsibility but little power. The Congress elected in 1860 would not meet in regular session for thirteen months, while the Congress that did meet in December 1860 experienced an erosion of authority as members from the lower South resigned when their states seceded. Buchanan's forceful denial of the legality of disunion ended with a lame confession of impotence to do anything about it. Although the Constitution gave no state the right to withdraw, said the president, it also gave the national government no power "to coerce a State into submission which is attempting to withdraw."

Republicans ridiculed this reasoning. Buchanan had demonstrated that "no state has the right to secede unless it wishes to," jibed Seward, and that "it is the President's duty to enforce the laws, unless somebody opposes him." But Republicans seemed unable to come up with any better alternative. Several options presented themselves: coercion, compromise, or allowing "the erring sisters to depart in

John Rarey, a native of Ohio, was the most famous horse trainer of the nineteenth century. His method of gaining an animal's confidence and appealing to its intelligence through gentler, less cruel methods than the traditional "make them fear you" method anticipated modern techniques. This cartoon implies that Buchanan's conciliatory approach, however, would never work with such an obstreperous animal as South Carolina.

A NEW APPLICATION OF THE RAREY SYSTEM.

Mr. *Rarey* Buchanan doesn't see why he can't put the Federal straps on that spunky little colt Miss South Carolina. When he tries to pat her—she bites; when he tries to apply the strap—she kicks. He really doesn't see what is to be done with her—s'poses she'll have to have her own way. To which remark Miss Carolina doesn't say, neigh !

194   BATTLE CRY OF FREEDOM

peace." Although various Republican leaders sanctioned each of these approaches at one time or another, none of the options commanded a majority before April 1861. Instead, a rather vague fourth alternative emerged—described as "masterly inactivity" or a "Fabian policy"—a position of watchful waiting, of making no major concessions but at the same time avoiding needless provocation, in the hope that the disunion fever would run its course and the presumed legions of southern unionists would bring the South back to its senses.

When Congress convened in December several Republicans, especially from the Old Northwest, "swore by everything in the Heavens above and the Earth beneath that they would convert the rebel States into a wilderness." "Without a little blood-letting," wrote Michigan's radical, coarse-grained Senator Zachariah Chandler, "this Union will not . . . be worth a rush." The danger of losing access to the lower Mississippi valley may have accounted for the bellicosity of many midwesterners. The people of the Northwest, said the *Chicago Tribune*, would never negotiate for free navigation of the river. "It is *their right*, and they will assert it to the extremity of blotting Louisiana out of the map."

And how would customs duties be collected at southern ports? Whose customs houses were they—American or Confederate? In the nullification crisis of 1832, Andrew Jackson had vowed to use force to collect duties in South Carolina and to hang the nullification leaders. "Oh, for one hour of Jackson!" exclaimed many Yankee Republicans who developed a sudden retrospective affection for this Tennessee Democrat. If letters received by Republican congressmen were any indication, their constituents stood ready to "coerce" the rebels. "We elected Lincoln," wrote an Illinoisian, "and are just as willing, if necessity requires, to fight for him. . . . Little Boone [County] can be relied on for 500 Wide Awakes, well armed and equipped." Lincoln "must *enforce the laws of the U. States against all rebellion*," added an Ohioan, "no matter what the consequences."

Lincoln seemed to agree. In December 1860 he told his private secretary that the very existence of government "implies the legal power, right, and duty . . . of a President to execute the laws and maintain the existing government." Lincoln quietly passed word to General in Chief Winfield Scott to make ready to collect the customs and defend federal forts in seceded states, or to retake them if they had been given up before his inauguration. In Springfield the *Illinois State Journal*, quasi-official spokesman for Lincoln during this period, warned that "disunion by armed force is treason, and treason must and will be put down at all hazards. . . . The laws of the United States must be executed—the President has no discretionary power on the subject—his duty is emphatically pronounced in the Constitution."

Republicans preferred to distinguish between "coercion"—which had a harsh ring—and enforcement of the laws. "It is not making war upon a State to execute the laws," insisted the *Boston Advertiser*. But to southerners this was a distinction without a difference. To "execute the laws" in a foreign country—the Confederacy—would mean war. In any event the whole question was hypothetical until March 4, for Buchanan intended no "coercion." And even if he had, the resources were pitifully inadequate. Most of the tiny 16,000-man army was scattered over two

In 1861 the tiny U.S. army of fewer than 16,000 men was scattered at many posts, mainly in the western states and territories. Thus the militias of seceding states were able easily to seize the unguarded or lightly guarded federal installations in those states: arsenals, mints, and forts. Here the castle-like federal arsenal in Charleston is guarded by a militia company, the Washington Light Infantry, waiting for the action of the secession convention, whereupon they took it over.

thousand miles of frontier, while most of the navy's ships were patrolling distant waters or laid up for repair. The strongest armed forces during the winter of 1860–61 were the militias of seceding states. Moreover, upper-South unionists who had managed to keep fire-eaters in their states at bay made an impression on Republicans with warnings that anything which smacked of coercion would tip the balance toward secession. For a time, therefore, Republican opinion drifted uncertainly while other groups sought to fashion a compromise.

Buchanan's message to Congress set the agenda for these efforts. He first blamed the North in general and Republicans in particular for "the incessant and violent agitation of the slavery question" which had now "produced its natural effects" by provoking disunion. Because of Republicans, said the president, "many a matron throughout the South retires at night in dread of what may befall herself and children before morning." Buchanan stopped short of asking the Republican party to dissolve; instead he asked northerners to stop criticizing slavery, repeal their "unconstitutional and obnoxious" personal liberty laws, obey the fugitive slave law, and join with the South to adopt a constitutional amendment protecting slavery in all territories. Unless Yankees proved willing to do these things, said Buchanan, the South would after all "be justified in revolutionary resistance to the Government." As an additional sign of northern good will, Buchanan also advised support for his long-standing effort to acquire Cuba, which would further placate southern fears by adding a large new slave state to the Union.

Republican responses to these suggestions may be readily imagined. The printable comments included "pharasaical old hypocrite . . . bristling with the spirit of a rabid slaveocracy . . . wretched drivel . . . truckling subserviency to the Cotton Lords . . . gross perversion of facts . . . brazen lies." After the voters had just rejected the Breckinridge platform by a margin of 4,000,000 to 670,000 in the presidential election, Buchanan "proposes an unconditional surrender . . . of six-sevenths of the people to one-seventh . . . by *making the Breckinridge platform a part of the Constitution!*"

Although few of the compromise proposals introduced in Congress went so far as Buchanan's, they all shared one feature: Republicans would have to make all the concessions. Republicans refused to succumb to what they considered blackmail. Indeed, the possibility that a coalition of Democrats and Constitutional Unionists might patch together a "shameful surrender" and call it compromise caused some Republicans to prefer the alternative of letting the cotton states "go in peace." Having long regarded the Union as a "covenant with death," Garrisonian abolitionists were glad that slaveholders had broken the covenant. Even non-Garrisonians agreed, in Frederick Douglass's words, that "if the Union can only be maintained by new concessions to the slaveholders [and] a new drain on the negro's blood, then . . . let the Union perish." Several radical Republicans initially took a similar position. If South Carolina wanted to leave, said the *Chicago Tribune* in October 1860, "let her go, and like a limb lopped from a healthy trunk, wilt and rot where she falls." Horace Greeley's *New York Tribune* prominently advocated the go-in-peace approach. "If the Cotton States shall become satisfied that they can do better out of the Union than in it, we insist on letting them go," wrote Greeley in a famous editorial three days after Lincoln's election. "We hope never to live in a republic whereof one section is pinned to the residue by bayonets."

A genuine desire to avoid war accounted in part for this attitude. But other motives were probably more important, for all of these Republicans subsequently endorsed war to preserve the Union. Greeley's go-in-peace editorials represented a dual gambit, one part aimed at the North and the other at the South. Like most Republicans, Greeley believed at first that southern states did not really intend to secede; "they simply mean to bully the Free States into concessions." Even after

As soon as Alabama seceded on January 11, 1861, these men of the Perote Guards seized the Perote Sand Batteries, a federal fortification guarding the approaches to Mobile Bay. This is one of the earliest photographs of a military unit that became part of the Confederate army.

South Carolina went out, Greeley wrote to Lincoln that "I fear nothing . . . but another disgraceful backdown of the free States. . . . Another nasty compromise, whereby everything is conceded and nothing secured, will so thoroughly disgrace and humiliate us that we can never again raise our heads." To advise the North to let the disunionists go, therefore, became a way of deflecting compromise. Toward the South, Greeley expected his gambit to operate like the strategy of parents who tell an obstreperous adolescent son, after his repeated threats to run away from home, "There's the door—go!" By avoiding talk of coercion it might also allow passions to cool and give unionists breathing room to mobilize their presumed silent majority below the Potomac.

Go-in-peace sentiment faded as it became clear that the dreaded alternative of compromise would not come to pass. To sift all the compromise proposals introduced in Congress, each house set up a special committee. The Senate "Committee of Thirteen" included powerful men: William H. Seward, Benjamin Wade, Stephen Douglas, Robert Toombs, Jefferson Davis, and John J. Crittenden. It was Crittenden who cobbled together a plan which he proposed as a series of amendments to the Constitution. In their final form these amendments would have guaranteed slavery in the states against future interference by the national government; prohibited slavery in territories north of 36° 30' and protected it south of that line in all territories "now held, or *hereafter acquired*" (italics added); forbidden Congress to abolish slavery on any federal property within slave states (forts, arsenals, naval bases, etc.); forbidden Congress to abolish slavery in the District of Columbia without the consent of its inhabitants *and* unless it had first been abolished by both Virginia and Maryland; denied Congress any power to interfere with the interstate slave trade;

In this cartoon the Republican "patient" is holding a copy of the party's platform while three members of Congress try to force an oversize pill labeled "Crittenden Compromise" down his throat. On the floor sits a basket of several more "constitutional remedies" pills, implying that once the patient has swallowed the first pill he will be forced to accept more.

A CURE FOR REPUBLICAN LOCK-JAW

and compensated slaveholders who were prevented from recovering fugitives in northern states. These constitutional amendments were to be valid for all time; no future amendment could override them.

Despite the one-sided nature of this "compromise," some Republican businessmen who feared that a secession panic on Wall Street might deepen into another depression urged party leaders to accept it. Thurlow Weed—and by implication Seward—gave signs in December of a willingness to do so. But from Springfield came word to stand firm. "Entertain no proposition for a compromise in regard to the *extension* of slavery," Lincoln wrote to key senators and congressmen. "The tug has to come, & better now, than any time hereafter." Crittenden's compromise, Lincoln told Weed and Seward, "would lose us everything we gained by the election. . . . Filibustering for all South of us, and making slave states would follow . . . to put us again on the high-road to a slave empire." The very notion of a territorial compromise, Lincoln pointed out, "acknowledges that slavery has equal rights with liberty, and surrenders all we have contended for. . . . We have just carried an election on principles fairly stated to the people. Now we are told in advance, the government shall be broken up, unless we surrender to those we have beaten. . . . If we surrender, it is the end of us. They will repeat the experiment upon us *ad libitum*. A year will not pass, till we shall have to take Cuba as a condition upon which they will stay in the Union."

Following Lincoln's advice, all five Republicans on the Senate Committee of Thirteen voted against the Crittenden compromise. Although Crittenden's compromise resurfaced again later, Republican opposition and lower-South indifference continued to doom it.

Did this mean that Republicans killed the last, best hope to avert disunion? Probably not. Neither Crittenden's nor any other compromise could have stopped secession in the lower South. No compromise could undo the event that triggered disunion: Lincoln's election by a solid North. "We spit upon every plan to compromise," wrote one secessionist. "No human power can save the Union, all the cotton states will go," said Jefferson Davis, while Judah Benjamin agreed that "a settlement [is] totally out of our power to accomplish." On December 13, before any compromises had been debated—indeed, before any states had actually seceded—more than two-thirds of the senators and representatives from seven southern states signed an address to their constituents: "The argument is exhausted. All hope of relief in the Union, through the agency of committees, Congressional legislation, or constitutional amendments, is extinguished. . . . The honor, safety, and independence of the Southern people are to be found in a Southern Confederacy." Delegates from seven states who met in Montgomery on February 4, 1861, to organize a new nation paid no attention to the compromise efforts in Washington.

But it was significant that only seven slave states were represented at Montgomery. By February 1861 the main goal of compromise maneuvers was to keep the other eight from going out. The legislatures of five of these states had enacted provisions for the calling of conventions. But thereafter the resemblance to events below the 35th parallel ceased. Voters in Virginia, Arkansas, and Missouri elected a majority of unionists to their conventions. Voters in North Carolina and Tennessee, given the choice of voting for or against the holding of a convention, voted against doing so. Although the Confederate states sent commissioners to the upper-South conventions with appeals to join their southern sisters, the Missouri and Arkansas conventions rejected secession in March (Arkansas by a narrow margin), and Virginia did the same by a two-to-one margin on April 4. The main reason for this outcome was the lesser salience of slavery in the upper South. Slaves constituted 47 percent of the population in the Confederate states but only 24 percent in the upper South; 37 percent of the white families in Confederate states owned slaves compared with 20 percent of the families in the upper South.

This failure of secession in the upper South seemed to confirm the Republican belief in the region's basic unionism. But much of that unionism was highly conditional. The condition was northern forbearance from any attempt to "coerce" Confederate states. The Tennessee legislature resolved that its citizens "will as one man, resist [any] invasion of the soil of the South at any hazard and to the last extremity." To put teeth into a similar admonition by the Virginia legislature, the convention of that commonwealth remained in session to watch developments after initially voting down secession. Moderate Republicans heeded these warnings and trod softly during the first three months of 1861. This was the time of "masterly inactivity," of limited concessions to strengthen that silent majority of lower-South unionists so they could begin a "voluntary reconstruction" of their states. Seward in particular had abandoned the irrepressible conflict to become chief of the conciliationists. "Every thought that we think," he wrote to Lincoln on January 27, "ought to be conciliatory, forbearing and patient, and so open the way for the rising of a Union Party in the seceding States which will bring them back into the Union." Although less optimistic than Seward, Lincoln approved of this approach so long as it involved "no compromise which *assists* or *permits* the extension" of slavery.

Republicans on the special House Committee of Thirty-Three (one for each state) had first demonstrated the possibilities of such a "Fabian policy." Charles Francis Adams sponsored a proposal to admit New Mexico (which included present-day Arizona) as a state. This maneuver had a deep purpose: to divide the upper and lower South and cement the former to the Union by the appearance of concession on the territorial question. New Mexico had a slave code and a few slaves. But everyone recognized that the institution would not take root there; as Crittenden noted, the ultimate consequence of New Mexico's admission would be to give the North another free state. Lower-South members of the committee scorned the proposal while several upper-South members approved it, thereby accomplishing Adams's intention. He persuaded nine of the fifteen Republicans on the committee to endorse this apparent violation of the party's platform. The measure therefore obtained committee approval on December 29. When it finally reached a floor vote two months later, however, a three-to-one negative Republican margin defeated it. Nevertheless, during those two months the New Mexico scheme had played a part in keeping the upper South in the Union.

Two other recommendations from the Committee of Thirty-Three helped along this cause. Both received Seward's active and Lincoln's passive endorsement. The first was a resolution calling for faithful obedience to the fugitive slave law and repeal of personal liberty laws in conflict with it. This passed the House on February 27 with the support of about half the Republican representatives. Next day the House adopted a proposed Thirteenth Amendment to the Constitution guaranteeing slavery in the states against any future interference by the federal government. This was too much for three-fifths of the Republicans to swallow, but the two-fifths who did vote for it in both House and Senate gave this amendment the bare two-thirds majority needed to send it to the states for ratification. Before that process got anywhere, however, other matters intervened to produce four years later a Thirteenth Amendment that abolished slavery.

Seward's conciliation policy also bore fruit in the form of a "peace convention" that assembled in Washington on February 4, the same day that the Confederate constitutional convention met in Montgomery. Called by the Virginia legislature, the peace convention further divided the upper and lower South. The seceded states plus Arkansas refused to send delegates. Five northern states also failed to participate—California and Oregon because of distance; Michigan, Wisconsin, and Minnesota because their Republican leaders distrusted the enterprise. Many Republicans in other states shared this distrust, but Seward persuaded them to support the project as a gesture of good will. Taking the Crittenden compromise as a starting point, this "Old Gentlemen's Convention" accomplished little except to mark time. Many of the delegates belonged to a past era, typified by the chairman, seventy-one-year-old ex-president John Tyler of Virginia. Debates were aimless or acrimonious; Republican participation was perfunctory or hostile. After three weeks of labor, the convention brought forth the Crittenden compromise modified to make it slightly more palatable to the North. Extension of the 36° 30' line would apply only to "present territory," and a majority vote of senators from both the free and slave states would be required to obtain any new territory. When this recommendation went before Congress, it suffered an unceremonious defeat, mainly by Republican votes.

* * * * *

Six hundred miles distant the Confederate convention appeared by contrast to be a triumph of efficiency. In six days the delegates at Montgomery drafted a temporary constitution, turned themselves into a provisional Congress for the new government, elected a provisional president and vice president, and then spent a more leisurely month fashioning a permanent constitution and setting the machinery of government in motion. Elections for a bicameral Congress and for a president and vice president to serve the single six-year term prescribed by the Constitution were to be held in November 1861.

Although Barnwell Rhett and a few other fire-eaters came to Montgomery as delegates, they took a back seat at a convention that did its best to project a moderate image to the upper South. Befitting the new Confederacy's claim to represent the true principles of the U.S. Constitution which the North had trampled upon,

The state capitol in Montgomery, Alabama, became the site for the convention that created the Confederate States of America in February 1861. Once they had completed their work, the delegates proclaimed themselves the Provisional Congress of the Confederacy, and Montgomery became the new nation's capital for three months until it moved to Richmond in May.

most of the provisional constitution was copied verbatim from that venerable document. The same was true of the permanent Confederate Constitution, adopted a month later, though some of its departures from the original were significant. The preamble omitted the general-welfare clause and the phrase "a more perfect Union" and added a clause after "We the People": "each State acting in its sovereign and independent character." Instead of the U.S. Constitution's evasions on slavery ("persons held to service or labor"), the Confederate version called a slave a slave. It guaranteed the protection of bondage in any new territory the Confederacy might acquire. The Constitution did forbid the importation of slaves from abroad, to avoid alienating Britain and especially the upper South, whose economy benefited from its monopoly on export of slaves to the lower South. The Constitution permitted a tariff for revenue but not for protection of domestic industries, though what this distinction meant was unclear since the clause did not define it. Another clause forbade government aid for internal improvements. The Constitution also nurtured state's rights by empowering legislatures to impeach Confederate officials whose duties lay wholly within a state. After weakening the executive by limiting the president to a single six-year term, the Constitution strengthened that branch by giving the president a line-item veto of appropriations and granting cabinet officers a potential nonvoting seat on the floor of Congress (this was never put into effect).

Most interest at Montgomery focused on the choice of a provisional president. There was no shortage of aspirants, most notably Robert Toombs of Georgia, but the final nod went to a reluctant West Point graduate who would have preferred to become commander of the Confederacy's army. Jefferson Davis became the major-

Chosen provisional president and vice president of the Confederacy (they would win election to these offices under the Confederate Constitution in November 1861), neither Jefferson Davis nor Alexander H. Stephens possessed robust health. Davis was virtually blind in one eye and suffered from neuralgia and dyspepsia. Weighing only ninety-five pounds, Stephens suffered throughout his life from headaches, diarrhea, arthritis, and colitis. Both long outlived the nation they led, however, Stephens dying in 1883 at the age of seventy-one and Davis in 1889 at the age of eighty-one.

ity choice after word came from Richmond that Virginia's prosecession senators Mason and Hunter favored him. Austere, able, experienced in government as a senator and former secretary of war, a Democrat and a secessionist but no fire-eater, Davis was the ideal candidate; the delegates elected him unanimously on February 9. His sense of duty—and destiny—bid him accept. To console Georgia and strengthen the Confederacy's moderate image, one-time Whig and more recently Douglas Democrat Alexander Stephens received the vice presidency. To satisfy geographical balance, Davis apportioned the six cabinet posts among each state of the Confederacy except his own Mississippi, with the top position of secretary of state going to the sulking Georgian Toombs.

"The man and the hour have met!" So said a genial William L. Yancey as he introduced Jefferson Davis to a cheering crowd in Montgomery on February 16. It was on this occasion that "Dixie" began its career as the unofficial Confederate anthem. Perhaps inspired by the music, Davis made a brief, bellicose speech. "The time for compromise has now passed," he said. "The South is determined to maintain her position, and make all who oppose her smell Southern powder and feel Southern steel." His inaugural address two days later was more pacific. He assured everyone that

Jefferson Davis arrived at Montgomery late in the evening on February 16, after an exhausting five-day trip from his home in Mississippi, stopping in almost every town to speak and endure a reception. A huge crowd had been waiting for hours in a light drizzle but had lost none of their enthusiasm; they cheered Davis when he appeared on the balcony of the Exchange Hotel at 11 p.m. and William Yancey proclaimed, "The man and the hour have met!"

These were the men responsible for launching the Confederate government. From left to right they were Judah P. Benjamin, the attorney general who later served briefly as secretary of war and then for three years as secretary of state; Secretary of the Navy Stephen R. Mallory, who remained in that position for the whole life of the Confederacy; Secretary of the Treasury Christopher G. Memminger, who may have had the Confederacy's toughest job in raising money to finance the war; Vice President Stephens; Secretary of War Leroy P. Walker, who proved a failure and lasted less than seven months; President Davis; Postmaster General John H. Reagan, who served through the entire war; and Secretary of State Robert Toombs, who soon resigned to become a brigadier general.

the Confederacy wished to live in peace and extended a warm invitation to any states that "may seek to unite their fortunes to ours." Davis then settled down to the heavy responsibilities of organizing a new nation—and of enlarging its borders.

*   *   *   *   *

Abraham Lincoln's chief concern was to prevent that enlargement. And part of the energy expended in building *his* cabinet was directed to that end. Putting together a cabinet gave Lincoln no end of trouble. The infant Republican party was still a loose coalition of several previous parties, of down-east Yankees and frontiersmen, radicals and conservatives, ideologues and pragmatists, of upper North and lower North and border-state tycoons like the Blairs of Maryland, of strong leaders several of whom still considered themselves better qualified for the presidency than the man who won it. Lincoln had to satisfy all of these interests with his seven cabinet appointments, which would also indicate the direction of his policy toward the South.

With an aplomb unparalleled in American political history, the president-elect appointed his four main rivals for the nomination to cabinet posts. Lincoln did not hesitate in his choices of Seward for secretary of state and Bates for attorney general. Cameron represented a more formidable problem. The Pennsylvanian believed that he had a commitment from Lincoln's convention managers. In any case, to leave him out would cause disaffection. But putting him in provoked an outcry from many Republicans when word leaked that Lincoln had offered Cameron the treasury. Taken aback, Lincoln withdrew the offer, whereupon Cameron's friends mobilized a campaign in his behalf that distracted the party as the inauguration neared. Lincoln finally settled the matter—but not the controversy—by giving Cameron the War Department. The treasury went to Chase, who had become a leader of the "iron-back" Republicans opposed to any hint of concession to the

South. Chase's appointment so offended Seward that he withdrew his acceptance as secretary of state—an obvious attempt to make Lincoln dump Chase. This was the first test of Seward's ambition to be "premier" of the administration. "I can't afford to let Seward take the first trick," Lincoln told his private secretary. The president-elect persuaded Seward to back down and remain in the cabinet with Chase—though one more confrontation lay ahead before Seward was convinced that Lincoln intended to be his own premier.

Paying a debt to Indiana for early support of his nomination, Lincoln named Caleb Smith secretary of the interior. The fussy, bewigged Connecticut Yankee Gideon Welles received the Navy Department. Lincoln wanted to appoint a non-Republican from the upper South as a gesture of good will to hold this region in the Union. He offered a portfolio to Congressman John Gilmer of North Carolina. But to join a Black Republican administration was too much of a political risk, so Gilmer turned down the offer on grounds that Lincoln's refusal to compromise on slavery in the territories made it impossible for him to accept. Lincoln thereupon rounded out his cabinet with Montgomery Blair as postmaster general. Though a resident of Maryland, Blair was a Republican and an "iron-back."

Even more important than the cabinet as a sign of future policy would be Lincoln's inaugural address. Knowing that the fate of the upper South, and of hopes for voluntary reconstruction of the lower South, might rest on what he said on March 4, Lincoln devoted great care to every phrase of the address. It went through several drafts after consultation with various Republican leaders, especially Seward. This process began in Springfield two months before the inauguration and continued through Lincoln's twelve-day roundabout trip by rail to Washington, during which he made dozens of speeches to trackside crowds and official receptions. The president-elect felt an obligation to greet the multitudes who lined his route to catch a glimpse of their new leader. In effect, Lincoln was making a whistle-stop tour *after* his election.

This tour may have been a mistake in two respects. Lincoln's deliberately bland speeches made an unfavorable impression on those predisposed to see him as a commonplace prairie lawyer. Second, Lincoln's mail and the national press had for weeks been full of threats and rumors of assassination; such a public tour entailed severe risks. Reliable intelligence warning that an assassination attempt would be made in Baltimore led to his being secretly taken through the city in the dead of night. Lincoln thereafter regretted the decision—it embarrassed many of his supporters and enabled opposition cartoonists to ridicule him. The whole affair started his administration off on the wrong foot at a time when it needed the appearance of firmness and command.

Lincoln put the finishing touches on his inaugural address during his first days in Washington. While he had been composing it, seven states were not only seceding but were also seizing federal property within their borders—customs houses, arsenals, mints, and forts. The first draft of the inaugural therefore had one theme and two variations. The theme was Lincoln's determination to preserve an undivided Union. The variations contrapuntally offered a sword and an olive branch. The sword was an intention to use "all the powers at my disposal" to "reclaim the public property and places which have fallen; to hold, occupy, and possess these, and all other property and places belonging to the government, and to collect the duties on imports." The olive branch was a reiteration of his oft-repeated pledge not "to interfere with the institution of slavery where it exists" and to enforce the constitutional injunction for the return of fugitive slaves. Lincoln also promised the South that "the government will not assail *you*, unless you *first* assail *it*."

Seward and Lincoln's Illinois confidant Orville Browning found the sword too prominent in this draft. The upper South, not to mention the Confederate government, was sure to regard any attempt to "reclaim" forts and other property as "coercion." And even the promise not to assail these states unless they first assailed the government contained a veiled threat. Seward persuaded Lincoln to delete "unless you *first* assail *it*" and to soften a few other phrases. He also drafted a peroration appealing to the historic patriotism of southern people. The president-elect added a passage assuring southerners that whenever "in any interior locality" the hostility to the United States was "so great and so universal, as to prevent competent resident citizens from holding the Federal offices," he would suspend government activities "for the time." Most significantly, perhaps, Browning prevailed on Lincoln to drop his threat to *reclaim* federal property, so that the final version of

In the nineteenth century, presidential inaugurations took place on the west front of the Capitol instead of on the east front as they do today. Lincoln's first inauguration occurred against the unfinished dome of the Capitol during its expansion. This unfinished dome came to symbolize the unfinished Union now threatened with permanent division. Work on the dome continued during the war, and it was completed in time for Lincoln's second inauguration, five weeks before the Union was made permanent by northern victory in the war.

the address vowed only to "hold, occupy, and possess" such property and to "collect duties and imposts."

These phrases were ambiguous. How would the duties be collected? By naval vessels stationed offshore? Would this be coercion? How could the government "hold, occupy, and possess" property that was under control of Confederate forces? Of the few installations remaining in Union hands Fort Sumter, on an island in Charleston harbor, had become a commanding symbol of national sovereignty in the very cradle of secession, a symbol that the Confederate government could not tolerate if it wished its own sovereignty to be recognized by the world. Would Lincoln use force to defend Sumter? The ambiguity was intentional. Hoping to avoid provocation, Lincoln and Seward did not wish to reveal whether the velvet glove enclosed an iron fist.

There was no ambiguity about the peroration, revised and much improved from Seward's draft. "I am loth to close," said Lincoln. "We are not enemies, but friends. We must not be enemies. Though passion may have strained, it must not break our bonds of affection. The mystic chords of memory, stretching from every battlefield, and patriot grave, to every living heart and hearthstone, all over this broad land, will yet swell the chorus of the Union, when again touched, as surely they will be, by the better angels of our nature."

Contemporaries read into the inaugural address what they wished or expected to see. Republicans were generally satisfied with its "firmness" and "moderation." Confederates and their sympathizers branded it a "Declaration of War." Douglas Democrats in the North and conditional unionists in the South formed the constituencies that Lincoln most wanted and needed to reach. From these quarters the verdict was mixed but encouraging. "I am with him," said Douglas. Influential Tennesseans commended the "temperance and conservatism" of the address. And John Gilmer of North Carolina, though he had been unwilling to join Lincoln's cabinet, approved the president's first act in office. "What more does any reasonable Southern man expect or desire?" Gilmer asked.

Lincoln had hoped to cool passions and buy time with his inaugural address—time to organize his administration, to prove his pacific intent, to allow the seeds of voluntary reconstruction to sprout. But when the new president went to his office for the first time on the morning after the inauguration, he received a jolt. On his desk lay a dispatch from Major Robert Anderson, commander of the Union garrison at Fort Sumter. Anderson reported that his supplies would last only a few more weeks. Time was running out.

III

Fort Sumter stood on a man-made granite island four miles from downtown Charleston at the entrance to the bay. With brick walls forty feet high and eight to twelve feet thick, designed to mount 146 big guns, this new fort when fully manned by 650 soldiers could stop anything trying to enter or leave the harbor. But at the beginning of December 1860 Fort Sumter was untenanted except by workmen completing the construction of its interior. Most of the eighty-odd soldiers of the U.S. garrison at Charleston occupied Fort Moultrie, an obsolete installation a mile across the bay from Sumter on an island easily accessible from the mainland and exposed to capture from the rear. The Carolinians had expected to get Moultrie along with Sumter and all other United States property in Charleston for the asking. Even before seceding, South Carolina officials began pressing the Buchanan administration on this matter. After declaring its independence, the republic of South Carolina sent commissioners to Washington to negotiate for the forts and the arsenal. Their quest was backed by hundreds of militiamen in Charleston who vowed to drive the Yankees out if they did not leave voluntarily.

The garrison at Fort Moultrie was not commanded by a Yankee, however. Major Robert Anderson was a Kentuckian, a former slaveowner who sympathized with the South but remained loyal to the flag he had served for thirty-five years. A man haunted by a tragic vision, Anderson wanted above all to avert a war that would divide his own family as well as his state and nation. Yet he knew that if war came, it was likely to start on the spot where he stood. Carolina hotspurs were straining at the leash; if they attacked, honor and his orders would require him to resist. Once the flag was fired upon and blood shed, there would be no stopping the momentum of war.

Like Anderson, President Buchanan keenly desired to prevent such a calamity— at least until he left office on March 4. Once way to forestall a clash, of course, was to withdraw the garrison. Though urged to do so by three southern members of his cabinet, Buchanan refused to go this far. He did promise South Carolina congressmen on December 10 not to send the reinforcements Anderson had requested. In return, South Carolina pledged not to attack Anderson while negotiations for transfer of the forts were going on. The Carolinians also understood Buchanan to have agreed not to change the military status quo at Charleston in any way.

While Buchanan dithered, Anderson acted. Interpreting ambiguous orders from

A satirical Currier and Ives print showing Governor Francis Pickens of South Carolina preparing to fire a cannon labeled "Peacemaker," which is aimed directly at his stomach. Pickens tells a pitiful President Buchanan, "Mr. President, if you don't surrender that fort at once, I'll be 'blowed' if I don't fire." Buchanan throws up his hands and cries, "Oh don't, Governor Pickens, don't fire! Till I get out of office." When Lincoln became president, the situation was no laughing matter and the cannons were pointed at Fort Sumter.

the War Department as giving him authority to move his command from weak Fort Moultrie to powerful Fort Sumter if necessary to deter an attack, Anderson did so with stealth and skill after dark on the evening of December 26. Having made this move to preserve the peace, Anderson awoke next morning to find himself a hero in the North for thumbing his nose at the arrogant Carolinians and a villain to angry southerners who branded the occupation of Sumter as a violation of Buchanan's pledge. The harried Buchanan almost succumbed to southern insistence that he must order the garrison back to Moultrie. But he knew that if he did so,

Major Robert Anderson did his best to avoid starting a war but became the victim of the circumstances that started it during his watch at Fort Sumter. He became a hero in the North for his gallant resistance against overwhelming odds. The worst moment in his life was on April 14, 1861, when the American flag that had flown over the fort was lowered in surrender. Perhaps his best moment came exactly four years later when he raised the same flag triumphantly over the ruined fort.

he and his party would lose their last shred of respect in the North. A cabinet reshuffle also stiffened Buchanan's backbone. The southern members and one infirm Yankee resigned during December and early January. Into their places stepped staunch unionists, especially Secretary of War Joseph Holt (a Kentuckian), Attorney General Edwin M. Stanton, and Secretary of State Jeremiah Black. Stanton and Black drafted for Buchanan a reply to the South Carolina commissioners rejecting their demand for Sumter. Buoyed by this new experience of firmness, Buchanan went further—he approved a proposal by General in Chief Scott to reinforce Anderson.

In an effort to minimize publicity and provocation, Scott sent the reinforcements (200 soldiers) and supplies on the unarmed merchant vessel *Star of the West.* Bungling marred the whole enterprise, however. Word of the mission leaked to the press, while the War Department failed to get notice of it to Anderson, so that the garrison at Sumter was about the only interested party that lacked advance knowledge of the *Star of the West*'s arrival at the harbor entrance January 9. South Car-

Harper's Weekly *combat artist Theodore R. Davis drew this sketch of Major Anderson's stealthy transfer of the Fort Moultrie garrison to Fort Sumter at dusk on December 26, 1860. Having spiked the guns and cut down the flagstaff at Moultrie, on the right in this picture, the men rowed across the bay to Sumter, pictured at left. The crew on the South Carolina patrol vessel approaching from Charleston thought the boats were merely carrying laborers to the yet unfinished Fort Sumter and passed by without investigation.*

South Carolina militia fired on the Star of the West *from Morris Island, south of the entrance to Charleston Bay, and forced her to turn back. If the guns of Fort Sumter had returned fire, the Civil War might have started then and there. But they did not.*

olina artillery fired on the ship and scored one hit before her civilian captain, discretion eclipsing valor, turned around and headed out to sea. These could have been the opening shots of a civil war. But they were not—because Anderson did not fire back. Lacking information and orders, he did not want to start a war on his own responsibility. So the guns of Sumter remained silent.

Wrath in both North and South rose almost to the bursting point. But it did not burst. Despite mutual charges of aggression, neither side wanted war. Secessionists from other states quietly warned South Carolinians to cool down lest they provoke a conflict before the new Confederacy was organized and ready. A tacit truce emerged whereby the Carolinians left the Sumter garrison alone so long as the government did not try again to reinforce it. A similar (and explicit) arrangement prevailed at Fort Pickens at the mouth of Florida's Pensacola Bay—where, in contrast to Sumter, the navy could have landed reinforcements on the island at any time well out of range of southern guns.

Fort Pickens, however, remained something of a sideshow. The spotlight of history focused on Charleston and Fort Sumter. Anderson and his men became in northern eyes the defenders of a modern Thermopylae. James Buchanan and Governor Francis Pickens of South Carolina handed the fate of these men over to Abraham Lincoln and Jefferson Davis. The new Confederate president sent another trio of commissioners to Washington to negotiate for the transfer of Forts Sumter and Pickens to his government. He also sent newly commissioned General Pierre G. T. Beauregard, a Louisianian, to take command of the thousands of militia and several dozen big seacoast guns and mortars ringing Charleston harbor and pointing at the lonely soldiers inside Fort Sumter.

This was the situation when Lincoln learned on March 5 that the garrison was running short of supplies. The new president faced some hard choices. He could scrape together every available warship and soldier to shoot their way into the bay with supplies and reinforcements. But this would burden him with the onus of start-

ing a war. It would divide the North and unite the South including most of the not-yet-seceded states. Or Lincoln could prolong peace and perhaps keep the upper South in the Union by withdrawing the garrison and yielding Sumter. But this too would divide the North, demoralize much of the Republican party, perhaps fatally wreck his administration, constitute an implicit acknowledgment of the Confederacy's independence, and send a signal to foreign governments whose diplomatic recognition the Confederacy

Pierre Gustave Toutant Beauregard, of French Creole ancestry, was born and raised in Louisiana. He did his best to live up to his reputation as "Napoleon in Gray," but never quite made it. He had graduated second in his West Point class of 1838 and was the first military hero of the Confederacy. But his career and reputation stagnated after 1861.

was earnestly seeking. Or Lincoln could play for time, hoping to come up with some solution to preserve this vital symbol of sovereignty without provoking a war that would divide his friends and unite his enemies. Lincoln had six weeks at the outside to find a solution, for by then Anderson's men would be starved out of Sumter. These pressures sent the untried president to a sleepless bed with a sick headache more than once during those six weeks.

Lincoln's dilemma was made worse by conflicting counsels and cross purposes within his government. General Scott said that reinforcement was now impossible without a large fleet and 25,000 soldiers. The government had neither the ships nor the men. Scott's advice to pull out swayed the war and navy secretaries. Seward also concurred. He wanted to give up Sumter for political as well as military reasons. Such a gesture of peace and good will, he told Lincoln, would reassure the upper South and strengthen unionists in Confederate states. Seward was playing a deep and devious game. In line with his aspirations to be premier of this administration, he established independent contact through an intermediary with the Confederate commissioners. On his own authority, and without Lincoln's knowledge, Seward passed the word to these commissioners that Sumter would be yielded. He also leaked this news to the press. Within a week of Lincoln's inauguration, northern papers carried "authoritative" stories that Anderson's men would be pulled out.

Lincoln had made no such decision—though the nearly unanimous advice of those who were paid to advise him nearly persuaded him to do so. But what then would become of his inaugural pledge to "hold, occupy, and possess" federal property? At the very least he could reinforce Fort Pickens; on March 12 General Scott issued orders for that purpose. When Lincoln polled his cabinet on March 15 concerning Sumter, however, five of the seven secretaries recommended evacuation. A sixth, Chase, advised resupplying the garrison only if it could be done without risking war. Montgomery Blair alone wanted to hold on to the fort whatever the risk.

Lincoln's cabinet was filled with experienced political leaders, several of whom (especially Seward and Chase) believed themselves better qualified to lead the country than the less experienced Lincoln. The president soon demonstrated his mastery, however, especially in the decision about Fort Sumter. From left to right: Postmaster-General Montgomery Blair; Secretary of the Interior Caleb Smith; Secretary of the Treasury Salmon P. Chase; Lincoln; Secretary of State William H. Seward; Secretary of War Simon Cameron; Attorney General Edward Bates; and Secretary of the Navy Gideon Welles.

He believed that instead of encouraging southern unionists, surrender would discourage them. Only "measures which will inspire respect for the power of the Government and the firmness of those who administer it" could sustain them, said Blair. To give up the fort meant giving up the Union.

Lincoln was inclined to think so too. And Blair offered the president more than supportive advice. He introduced Lincoln to his brother-in-law Gustavus V. Fox, a thirty-nine-year-old Massachusetts businessman and former navy lieutenant. Fox was the first of many such men who would surge into prominence during the next four years: daring, able, fertile with ideas for doing things that the creaking old military establishment said could not be done. Fox proposed to send a troop transport escorted by warships to the bar outside Charleston harbor. Men and supplies could there be transferred to tugs or small boats which could cross the bar after dark for a dash to Sumter. Warships and the Sumter garrison would stand by to suppress attempts by Confederate artillery to interfere.

It might just work; in any case, Lincoln was willing to think about it. For he was now hearing from the constituency that had elected him. Many Republicans were outraged by reports that Sumter was to be surrendered. "HAVE WE A GOVERNMENT?" shouted newspaper headlines. Even Democrats called for reinforcement. The prolonged uncertainty was stretching nerves to the breaking point. "The Administration *must have a policy of action*," proclaimed the *New York Times*. "Better almost anything than additional suspense," echoed other northern papers. "The people want *something* to be decided on [to] serve as a rallying point for the abundant but discouraged loyalty of the American heart."

These signs of northern opinion hardened Lincoln's resolve. Meanwhile, however, Seward continued to tell Confederate commissioners that Sumter would be given up. One of the three emissaries that Lincoln sent to Charleston to appraise matters, his old friend Ward H. Lamon, seems to have told Carolinians and Anderson himself that evacuation was imminent. Hawks and doves within the administration were clearly on a collision course. The crash came on March 28. That day

Located at the tip of Santa Rosa Island at the entrance to Pensacola Bay, Fort Pickens, pictured here, was far less vulnerable to Confederate artillery on the mainland than was Fort Sumter. And because Florida then was less populous than any other Confederate state and much less important symbolically than South Carolina, Fort Pickens did not become the potential trigger for starting a war that Fort Sumter did.

Lincoln learned that General Scott wanted to evacuate *both* Forts Pickens and Sumter. His grounds for urging this were political rather than military: "The evacuation of both the forts," wrote the general, "would instantly soothe and give confidence to the eight remaining slave-holding States, and render their cordial adherence to this Union perpetual." Lincoln called his cabinet into emergency session after a state dinner that evening. "Blank amazement" registered on most faces as an obviously nettled president read to them Scott's memorandum. The general (a Virginian) was advising unconditional surrender to the Confederacy. Whether or not influenced by Seward (as most cabinet members assumed), Scott's politically motivated recommendation rendered suspect his initial opinion that reinforcement of Sumter was impossible. The cabinet reversed its vote of two weeks earlier. Four of the six members (Caleb Smith still went along with Seward; Cameron was absent) now favored resupply of Sumter. All six supported additional reinforcement of Pickens. Lincoln issued orders for a secret expedition to carry out the latter task. More momentously, he also instructed Fox to ready ships and men for an attempt to reinforce Sumter.

Having served four years as governor of New York and twelve years as a U.S. senator, William H. Seward expected to dominate the Lincoln administration as "premier." Undeterred by Seward's hawk-like countenance, effectively captured in this photograph, Lincoln soon set him straight on who would be running the administration.

This backed Seward into a corner. His assurances to southern commissioners, his peace policy of voluntary reconstruction, his ambitions to be premier—all appeared about to collapse. To recoup his position Seward acted boldly—and egregiously. He intervened in the Fort Pickens reinforcement and managed to divert the strongest available warship from the Sumter expedition, with unfortunate consequences. Then on April 1 he sent an extraordinary proposal to Lincoln. In mystifying fashion, Seward suggested that to abandon Sumter and hold Pickens would change the issue from slavery to Union. Beyond that, the secretary of state would "demand explanations" from Spain and France for their meddling in Santo Domingo and Mexico, and declare war if their explanations were unsatisfac-

Confederate artillery fired on Fort Sumter from four directions on April 12 and 13, 1861. The undermanned fort returned the fire, but with little effect. The most destructive Confederate shots came from batteries at Fort Moultrie, at the right in this illustration, and from Cumming Point at the tip of Morris Island, at the left. Note that Confederate shells have set the interior of Fort Sumter on fire but the American flag is still flying. It would soon be lowered in surrender, however, as the flames crept toward the powder magazine.

tory. Presumably this would reunite the country against a foreign foe. "Whatever policy we adopt," Seward pointed out, "it must be somebody's business to pursue and direct it incessantly." He left little doubt whom he had in mind.

Lincoln's astonishment when he read this note can well be imagined. Not wanting to humiliate Seward or lose his services, however, the president mentioned the matter to no one and wrote a polite but firm reply the same day. He had pledged to hold, occupy, and possess federal property, Lincoln reminded his secretary of state, and he could not see how holding Sumter was any more a matter of slavery or less a matter of Union than holding Pickens. Ignoring Seward's idea of an ultimatum to Spain or France, Lincoln told him that whatever policy was decided upon, "*I* must do it." A chastened Seward said nothing more about this and served as one of Lincoln's most loyal advisers during the next four years.

Seward made one last effort to salvage the situation. The Virginia convention, still in session, would undoubtedly vote to secede if a clash of arms occurred. Seward persuaded Lincoln to meet with a Virginia unionist in Washington on April 4. The purpose was to see if a bargain could be struck: evacuation of Sumter in return for adjournment of the convention without secession. Just before his inauguration Lincoln had expressed interest in this idea. Whether he explicitly offered such a deal in his private conversation with John Baldwin on April 4 has long been a matter of controversy. In any event nothing came of this meeting, from which Lincoln emerged with a soured view of Virginia unionism. That very day he gave the go-ahead for the Sumter expedition.

The nature of that enterprise had changed subtly but significantly from Fox's first proposal. Instead of trying to shoot its way into the harbor, the task force would first attempt only to carry supplies to Anderson. Warships and soldiers would stand by for action, but if Confederate batteries did not fire on the supply boats they would not fire back, and the reinforcements would remain on shipboard. Lincoln would notify Governor Pickens in advance of the government's peaceful intention to send in provisions only. If Confederates opened fire on the unarmed boats carrying "food for hungry men," the South would stand convicted of an aggressive act. On its shoulders would rest the blame for starting a war. This would unite the North and, perhaps, keep the South divided. If southerners allowed the supplies to go through, peace and the status quo at Sumter could be preserved and the Union government would have won an important symbolic victory. Lincoln's new conception of the resupply undertaking was a stroke of genius. In effect he was telling Jefferson Davis, "heads I win, tails you lose." It was the first sign of the mastery that would mark Lincoln's presidency.

When the formal surrender of Fort Sumter took place on April 14, this palmetto flag—the state flag of South Carolina—was first raised over the fort. The Confederate militia who subdued the fort were all South Carolinians. Then the Confederate flag went up.

On April 6, Lincoln sent a special messenger to Charleston to inform Governor Pickens that "an attempt will be made to supply Fort-Sumter with provisions only; and that, if such attempt be not resisted, no effort to throw in men, arms, or ammunition, will be made, without further notice, [except] in case of an attack on the Fort." This put the ball in Jefferson Davis's court. The Confederate president was also under great pressure to "do something." Even if the seven lower-South states held together, the Confederacy's future was precarious without the upper South. After talking with Virginia secessionists, the fire-eater Louis Wigfall urged a prompt attack on Sumter to bring that commonwealth into the fold. The hot-blooded Edmund Ruffin and Roger Pryor, vexed by the lingering unionism in their native state of Virginia, echoed this exhortation. "The shedding of blood," wrote Ruffin, "will serve to change many voters in the hesitating states, from the submission or procrastinating ranks, to the zealous for immediate secession." If you want us to join you, Pryor told Charlestonians, *"strike a blow!"* The *Charleston Mercury* was willing. "Let us be ready for war. . . . The fate of the Southern Confederacy hangs by the ensign halliards of Fort Sumter."

Therefore to Abraham Lincoln's challenge—Shall it be Peace or War?—Jefferson Davis replied, War. A fateful cabinet meeting in Montgomery on April 9 endorsed Davis's order to Beauregard: reduce the fort *before* the relief fleet arrived, if possible. Anderson rejected Beauregard's ritual summons to surrender, but remarked in passing that he would be starved out in a few days if help did not arrive. The Confederates knew that help was about to arrive, so they opened fire at 4:30 A.M. on April 12. Fox's fleet, scattered by a gale and prevented by high seas from launching the supply boats, was helpless to intervene. After thirty-three hours of bombardment by four thousand shot and shells, which destroyed part of the fort and set the interior on fire, Anderson's exhausted garrison surrendered.

Scenes like this one were duplicated hundreds of times in North and South in 1861. The 1st Michigan Volunteer Infantry stands at attention in Detroit on May 1, 1861, for the formal presentation of its colors before a large crowd that has gathered to cheer them off to the front. The 1st Michigan became part of the Army of the Potomac, fought through the war to Appomattox in twenty-seven battles and many smaller actions, and had 187 men killed in action—125 in 1862 alone.

Able to man only a few of Sumter's forty-eight mounted guns, they had fired a thousand rounds in reply—without much effect. On April 14 the American flag came down and the Confederate stars and bars rose over Sumter.

This news galvanized the North. On April 15 Lincoln issued a proclamation calling 75,000 militiamen into national service for ninety days to put down an insurrection "too powerful to be suppressed by the ordinary course of judicial proceedings." The response from free states was overwhelming. War meetings in every city and village cheered the flag and vowed vengeance on traitors. "The heather is on fire," wrote a Harvard professor who had been born during George Washington's presidency. "I never knew what a popular excitement can be. . . . The whole population, men, women, and children, seem to be in the streets with Union favors and flags."

From Ohio and the West came "one great Eagle-scream" for the flag. "The people have gone stark mad!" In New York City, previously a nursery of pro-southern sentiment, a quarter of a million people turned out for a Union rally. The "time before Sumter" was like another century, wrote a New York woman. "It seems as if we never were alive till now; never had a country till now."

Democrats joined in the Eagle-scream of patriotic fury. Stephen Douglas paid a well-publicized national unity call to the White House and then traveled home to Chicago, where he told a huge crowd: "There are only two sides to the question. Every man must be for the United States or against it. There can be no neutrals in this war, *only patriots—or traitors*." A month later Douglas was dead—a victim probably of cirrhosis of the liver—but for a year or more his war spirit lived on among most Democrats. "Let our enemies perish by the sword" was the theme of Democratic editorials in the spring of 1861. "All squeamish sentimentality should be discarded, and bloody vengeance wreaked upon the heads of the contemptible traitors who have provoked it by their dastardly impertinence and rebellious acts."

To the War Department from northern governors came pleas to increase their states' quotas of troops. Lincoln had called on Indiana for six regiments; the governor offered twelve. Having raised the requisitioned thirteen regiments, Ohio's governor wired Washington that "without seriously repressing the ardor of the people, I can hardly stop short of twenty." From Governor John Andrew of Massachusetts came a terse telegram two days after Lincoln's call for troops: "Two of our regiments will start this afternoon—one for Washington, the other for Fort Monroe; a third will be dispatched tomorrow, and the fourth before the end of the week." It began to appear that something larger than a lady's thimble might be needed to hold the blood shed in this war.

A typical recruiting poster appealing for Union volunteers to avenge the attack on Fort Sumter and to restore the Union. The company formed in Bucks County north of Philadelphia in response to this appeal became part of the 11th Pennsylvania Volunteer Infantry and fought through the entire war, in twenty-four battles and countless skirmishes. The regiment had 236 men and one dog—its mascot, Sallie—killed in action during the war.

CHAPTER NINE

Facing Both Ways:
The Upper South's Dilemma

I

The outbreak of war at Fort Sumter confronted the upper South with a crisis of decision. Its choice could decide the fate of the Confederacy. These eight states contained most of the South's resources for waging war: more than half of its population, two-thirds of its white population, three-quarters of its industrial capacity, half of its horses and mules, three-fifths of its livestock and food crops. In addition, men of high potential as military leaders hailed from these states: Robert E. Lee, Thomas J. Jackson, Joseph E. Johnston, James E. B. Stuart, and Ambrose Powell Hill of Virginia; Daniel H. Hill of North Carolina; Albert Sidney Johnston and John Bell Hood of Kentucky; Nathan Bedford Forrest of Tennessee.

The upper South's response to Lincoln's April 15 militia requisition seemed to promise well for the Confederacy. The governors of Kentucky, Tennessee, and Missouri not only refused to furnish any troops but sharply rebuffed Lincoln's requisition, finding it coercive and unconstitutional, a violation of the rights of their states and those of their southern brothers. Virginia, North Carolina, and Arkansas sent similar replies, while the governors of Maryland and Delaware remained ominously silent.

These references to "our rights" and "southern brothers" suggest the motives that impelled four of the eight states into the Confederacy and left three others with large secessionist minorities. "We must either identify ourselves with the North or the South," wrote a Virginian, while two former North Carolina unionists expressed the view of most of their fellows: "The division must be made on the line of slavery. The South must go with the South. . . . Blood is thicker than Water." In the eyes of southern unionists, this tragic war was mainly Lincoln's fault. What the president described in his proclamation of April 15 calling out the militia as a necessary measure to "maintain the honor, the integrity, and the existence of our National Union" was transmuted south of the Potomac into an unconstitutional coercion of sovereign states. Unionists claimed that Lincoln had made their position untenable. John Bell, the 1860 presidential candidate of the Constitutional Union party from whom many moderates in the upper South took their cue, announced in Nashville on April 23 his

Opposite page: The firing on Fort Sumter forced a decision on the upper-South states—would they stay in the Union or go with the Confederacy? These Tennesseeans chose the Confederacy and became officers and noncoms in an artillery battery.

support for a "united South" in "the unnecessary, aggressive, cruel, unjust wanton war which is being forced upon us" by Lincoln's mobilization of militia.

Such explanations for conversion to secession were undoubtedly sincere. But their censure of Lincoln had a certain self-serving quality. The claim that his call for troops was the cause of the upper South's decision to secede is misleading. As the telegraph chattered reports of the attack on Sumter April 12 and its surrender next day, huge crowds poured into the streets of Richmond, Raleigh, Nashville, and other upper-South cities to celebrate this victory over the Yankees and demanded that their own states join the cause. Scores of such demonstrations took place from April 12 to 14, *before* Lincoln issued his call for troops. Many conditional unionists were swept along by this powerful tide of southern nationalism; others were cowed into silence.

News of Sumter's fall reached Richmond on the evening of April 13. A jubilant procession marched on the state capitol, where a battery fired a hundred-gun salute "in honor of the victory." The crowd lowered the American flag from the capitol building and ran up the Confederate stars and bars. Citizens of Wilmington, North Carolina, reacted to the news of Sumter with "the wildest excitement," flew Confederate flags from public buildings, and fired salutes to them. These outbursts were not merely a defensive response to northern aggression. Rather they took on the character of a celebration, a joyous bonding with southern brothers who had scored a triumph over the Black Republican Yankees.

The Virginia convention moved quickly to adopt an ordinance of secession. On April 17 ex-governor Henry Wise electrified the convention with a fiery speech. He announced that Virginia militia were *at that instant* seizing the federal armory at Harper's Ferry and preparing to seize the Gosport navy yard near Norfolk. At such a moment no true Virginian could hesitate; the convention passed an ordinance of secession by a vote of 88 to 55.

Although Wise's announcement was slightly premature, he knew whereof he spoke: he had planned the Harper's Ferry expedition himself. A hard-bitten secessionist whose long white hair and wrinkled face made him look older than his fifty-four years, Wise had been governor when John Brown attacked Harper's Ferry. Perhaps this experience turned Wise's mind to the importance of the rifle works there, one of the two armories owned by the United States government (the other was at Springfield, Massachusetts). Without consulting Virginia's current Governor John Letcher, whom he considered lukewarm on secession, Wise met with militia officers on April 16 to set their regiments in motion for Harper's Ferry and Norfolk. Letcher belatedly approved these moves. On April 18, one day after passage of the secession ordinance, several companies of militia closed in on Harper's Ferry, defended by forty-seven U.S. army regulars. To prevent capture of the valuable rifle machinery, the soldiers set fire to the works and fled. The Virginians moved in and saved most of the machinery, which they shipped to Richmond, where it soon began turning out guns for the Confederacy.

An even greater prize was the Gosport navy yard, the country's premier naval base and the largest shipbuilding and repair facility in the South. Of the twelve hundred cannon and ten ships there in April 1861, many of the guns and four of

the warships were modern and serviceable, including the powerful forty-gun steam frigate *Merrimack*. Most of the civilian workers and naval officers at the yard were southerners; a majority of the officers would soon resign to join the Confederacy. Commanding the eight hundred sailors and marines stationed at the yard was Commodore Charles McCauley, a bibulous sixty-eight-year-old veteran who had gone to sea before Abraham Lincoln and Jefferson Davis were born. McCauley proved unequal to the crisis posed by several thousand Virginia militia reported to be heading for the navy yard. He refused to allow the *Merrimack* and the other three ships to escape when they had a chance to do so on April 18. The next day, just before reinforcements arrived aboard two warships from Washington, McCauley ordered all facilities at the yard burned, the cannon spiked, the ships scuttled. Even these unnecessary actions were bungled; the dry dock, ordnance building, and several other structures failed to burn; most of the cannon remained salvageable and were soon on their way to forts throughout the South; the hull of the *Merrimack* survived intact and ready for its subsequent conversion into the famous ironclad C.S.S. *Virginia*.

These events occurred before Virginia officially seceded, because the ordinance would not become final until ratified in a referendum on May 23. But the mood of the people predestined the outcome. For all practical purposes Virginia joined the Confederacy on April 17. A week later Governor Letcher and the convention concluded an alliance with the Confederacy that allowed southern troops to enter the state and placed Virginia regiments under Confederate control. On April 27 the convention invited the Confederate government to make Richmond its permanent capital. The southern Congress, tired of the inadequate, overcrowded facilities in Montgomery and eager to cement Virginia's allegiance, accepted the invitation on May 21. When Virginians went to the polls on May 23 they ratified a *fait accompli* by a vote of 128,884 to 32,134.

Virginia brought crucial resources to the Confederacy. Her population was the

South's largest. Her industrial capacity was nearly as great as that of the seven original Confederate states combined. The Tredegar Iron Works in Richmond was the only plant in the South capable of manufacturing heavy ordnance. Virginia's heritage from the generation of Washington, Jefferson, and Madison gave her immense prestige that was expected to attract the rest of the upper South to the Confederacy. And as events turned out, perhaps the greatest asset that Virginia brought to the cause of southern independence was Robert E. Lee.

Lee was fifty-four years old in 1861, the son of a Revolutionary War hero, scion of the First Families of Virginia, a gentleman in every sense of the word, without discernible fault unless a restraint that rarely allowed emotion to break through the crust of dignity is counted a fault. He had spent his entire career in the U.S. army since graduating second in his West Point class of 1829. Lee's outstanding record in the Mexican War and his experience as an engineer officer, as a cavalry officer, and as superintendent of West Point had earned him promotion to full colonel on March 16, 1861. General in Chief Winfield Scott considered Lee the best officer in the army. In April, Scott urged Lincoln to offer Lee field command of the newly levied Union army. As a fellow Virginian Scott hoped that Lee, like himself, would remain loyal to the service to which he had devoted his life. Lee had made clear his dislike of slavery, which he described in 1856 as "a moral and political evil." Until the day Virginia left the Union he had also spoken against secession. "The framers of our Constitution never exhausted so much labor, wisdom, and forbearance in its formation," he wrote in January 1861, "if it was intended to be broken up by every member of the [Union] at will. . . . It is idle to talk of secession."

But with Virginia's decision, everything changed. "I must side either with or against my section," Lee told a northern friend. His choice was foreordained by birth and blood: "I cannot raise my hand against my birthplace, my home, my chil-

No photograph of Robert E. Lee in 1861 is known to exist. Several engravings and woodcut illustrations of Lee were published in 1861, but all of them were retouched from a photograph by Mathew Brady taken sometime between 1850 and 1852. The earliest known wartime photograph of Lee is this one made in early 1862.

dren." On the very day he learned of Virginia's secession, April 18, Lee also received the offer of Union command. He told his friend General Scott regretfully that he must not only decline, but must also resign from the army. "Save in defense of my native State," said Lee, "I never desire again to draw my sword." Scott replied sadly: "You have made the greatest mistake of your life, but I feared it would be so." Five days later Lee accepted appointment as commander in chief of Virginia's military forces; three weeks after that he became a brigadier general in the Confederate army. Most officers from the upper South made a similar decision to go with their states, some without hesitation, others with the same bodeful presentiments that Lee expressed on May 5: "I foresee that the country will have to pass through a terrible ordeal, a necessary expiation perhaps for our national sins."

Scores of southern officers, however, like Scott remained loyal to nation rather than section. Some of them played key roles in the eventual triumph of nation over section: Virginian George H. Thomas, who saved the Union Army of the Cumberland at Chickamauga and destroyed the Confederate Army of Tennessee at Nashville; Tennessean David G. Farragut, who captured New Orleans and damned the torpedoes at Mobile Bay; North Carolinian John Gibbon, who became one of the best division commanders in the Army of the Potomac while three of his brothers fought for the South. At the same time a few northern-born officers who had married southern women chose to go with their wives' section rather than with their own, and rose to high positions in the Confederacy: New Jersey's Samuel Cooper, who married a Virginian and became adjutant general in the Confederate army; Pennsylvanian John Pemberton, who also married a Virginia woman and rose to command of the Army of Mississippi, which he surrendered to Grant at Vicksburg; and Josiah Gorgas, also of Pennsylvania, who married the daughter of an Alabama governor and became chief of ordnance for the Confederacy, where he created miracles of improvisation and instant industrialization to keep Confederate armies supplied with arms and ammunition.

II

The example of Virginia—and of Robert E. Lee—exerted a powerful influence on the rest of the upper South. Arkansas was the next state to go. Its convention had adjourned in March without taking action, subject to recall in case of emergency. Lincoln's call for troops supplied the emergency; the convention reassembled on May 6. Even before the delegates arrived in Little Rock, however, prosecession Governor Henry Rector aligned his state with the Confederacy by seizing federal arsenals at Fort Smith and Little Rock and by allowing Confederate forces to place artillery to command the Mississippi at Helena. The convention met in an atmosphere of high emotion, the galleries packed with spectators waving Confederate flags. Within minutes an ordinance of secession came to the floor. A motion to submit this ordinance to a referendum—a test vote of unionist strength at the convention—was defeated 55 to 15. Most of the fifteen minority delegates came from the Ozark Plateau of northwest Arkansas, where few slaves lived. After defeat of this motion, the convention passed the ordinance of secession by a vote of 65 to 5.

North Carolina and Tennessee also went out during May. Even before calling the legislature into special session, the governor of North Carolina ordered the militia to seize three federal forts on the coast and the arsenal in Fayetteville. The legislature met on May 1 and authorized an election on May 13 for a convention to meet on May 20. During these weeks everyone in the state, even in the previously unionist mountain counties, seemed to favor secession. "This furor, this moral epidemic, swept over the country like a tempest, before which the entire population seemed to succumb," wrote a participant. After a test vote on a procedural matter showed that the moderates were a minority, the delegates on May 20 unanimously enacted an ordinance of secession. Meanwhile the Tennessee legislature short-circuited the convention process by adopting a "Declaration of Independence" and submitting it to a referendum scheduled for June 8. Tennessee imitated the action of Virginia by concluding a military alliance with the Confederacy and allowing Confederate troops to enter the state several weeks before the referendum. That election recorded 104,913 for secession and 47,238 against. Significantly, however, the voters of mountainous east Tennessee cast 70 percent of their ballots against secession.

Although speeches and editorials in the upper South bristled with references to rights, liberty, state sovereignty, honor, resistance to coercion, and identity with southern brothers, such rhetoric could not conceal the fundamental issue of slavery. The following table shows the correlation between slaveholding and support for secession in the Virginia and Tennessee conventions.

	MEDIAN NO. OF SLAVES OWNED BY DELEGATES		DELEGATES FROM COUNTIES WITH FEWER THAN 25% SLAVES		DELEGATES FROM COUNTIES WITH MORE THAN 25% SLAVES	
	VA.	TENN.	VA.	TENN.	VA.	TENN.
Voting for Secession	11.5	6.5	34	30	53	23
Voting against Secession	4	2	39	20	13	2

The popular vote in secession referendums illustrated the point even more graphically. The voters in thirty-five Virginia counties with a slave population of only 2.5 percent opposed secession by a margin of three to one, while voters in the remainder of the state, where slaves constituted 36 percent of the population, supported secession by more than ten to one. The thirty counties of east Tennessee that rejected secession by more than two to one contained a slave population of only 8 percent, while the rest of the state, with a slave population of 30 percent, voted for secession by a margin of seven to one. Similar though less dramatic correlations existed in Arkansas and North Carolina, where moderate delegates had a median slaveholding about half that of the all-out secessionists.

The *Nashville Patriot* of April 24, 1861, was conscious of no irony when it cited the "community of interest existing in all the slaveholding States" as the reason why these states must unite to defend "justice and liberty." The upper South, like the lower, went to war to defend the freedom of white men to own slaves and to take them into the territories as they saw fit, lest these white men be enslaved by Black Republicans who threatened to deprive them of these liberties.

III

In the four border states the proportion of slaves and slaveowners was less than half what it was in the eleven states that seceded. But the triumph of unionism in these states was not easy and the outcome (except in Delaware) by no means certain. Maryland, Kentucky, and Missouri contained large and resolute secessionist minorities. A slight twist in the chain of events might have enabled this faction to prevail in any of these states. Much was at stake in this contest. The three states would have added 45 percent to the white population and military manpower of the Confederacy, 80 percent to its manufacturing capacity, and nearly 40 percent to its supply of horses and mules. For almost five hundred miles the Ohio River flows along the northern border of Kentucky, providing a defensive barrier or an avenue of invasion, depending on which side could control and fortify it. Two of the Ohio's navigable tributaries, the Cumberland and Tennessee rivers, penetrate through Kentucky into the heart of Tennessee and northern Alabama. Little wonder that Lincoln was reported to have said that while he hoped to have God on his side, he must have Kentucky.

Control of Maryland was even more immediately crucial, for the state enclosed Washington on three sides (with Virginia on the fourth) and its allegiance could determine the capital's fate at the outset of the war. Like the lower South, Maryland had voted for Breckinridge in the presidential election. Southern-Rights Democrats controlled the legislature; only the stubborn refusal of unionist Governor Thomas Hicks to call the legislature into session forestalled action by that body. The tobacco counties of southern Maryland and the eastern shore of the Chesapeake Bay were secessionist. The grain-growing counties of northern and western Maryland, containing few slaves, were safe for the Union. But the loyalty of Baltimore, with a third of the state's population, was suspect. The mayor's unionism was barely tepid, and the police chief sympathized with the South. Confederate flags appeared on many city homes and buildings during the tense days after Sumter. The traditional role of mobs in Baltimore politics created a volatile situation. Only a spark was needed to ignite the state's secessionists; such a spark hit the streets of Baltimore on April 19.

On that day the 6th Massachusetts Regiment—the first fully equipped unit to respond to Lincoln's call for troops—entered Baltimore on its way to Washington. No rail line passed through Baltimore, so the troops had to detrain at the east-side station and cross the city to board a train to the capital. As they marched, a mob gathered and a violent confrontation ensued. When it was over four soldiers and twelve Baltimoreans lay dead and several score groaned with wounds. They were the first of more than 700,000 combat casualties during the next four years.

Maryland flamed with passion. Here was coercion in deadly earnest. Worst of all, the soldiers who had killed Baltimore citizens were from the blackest of Black Republican states. To prevent more northern regiments from entering Baltimore, the mayor and the chief of police, with the reluctant approval of Governor Hicks, ordered the destruction of bridges on the railroads from Philadelphia and Harrisburg. Secessionists also tore down telegraph lines from Washington through Maryland. The national capital was cut off from the North. For several days, rumors were the only form of information reaching Washington. They grew to alarming proportions. Virginia regiments and armed Maryland secessionists were said to be converging on the capital. Washington was gripped by a siege mentality. Citizens' groups and government clerks formed themselves into volunteer companies. At General Scott's orders, these units sandbagged and barricaded

Baltimore was notorious for its election riots carried out by the street fighters for political factions with such names as "Plug Uglies" and "Blood Tubs." It was scarcely surprising, therefore, that the first blood in the Civil War was spilled on the streets of Baltimore on April 19, 1861. This date was the eighty-sixth anniversary of Lexington and Concord, where Massachusetts militia had also shed the first blood of the American Revolution.

public buildings and prepared the imposing Treasury edifice for a last-stand defense.

Reports filtered through of an aroused North and of more regiments determined to force their way through Maryland at any cost. Lincoln feared Virginia would attack the city before more troops arrived. But on April 25 a train carrying the crack New York 7th puffed into Washington, followed by more trains bearing additional regiments from northeastern states. They had arrived over a circuitous route via Annapolis under the command of Benjamin F. Butler, who thereby achieved one of the few military successes of his contentious career. A clever lawyer and shrewd politician whose paunchy physique, balding head, drooping mustache, and cocked left eye gave him a shifty appearance that matched his personality, Butler was a Massachusetts Democrat soon to become a Republican. From Governor Andrew he had wrested an appointment as brigadier general of the militia that Andrew had mobilized upon Lincoln's call for troops. The 6th Massachusetts had been the first regiment of this brigade to leave for Washington. When Butler, following with the 8th Massachusetts, learned of the riot in Baltimore and the burning of railroad bridges, he detrained the 8th at the head of Chesapeake Bay, commandeered a steamboat, and landed the regiment at Annapolis. The 8th Massachusetts contained several railwaymen and mechanics in its ranks. Finding that secessionists had ripped up tracks and destroyed rolling stock on the line from Annapolis to Washington,

The 7th Regiment of New York State Militia, shown here parading through New York on its way to Washington, was composed of the elite of the city. This regiment saw almost no action in the war, though many of its members enlisted in other regiments and saw a great deal of action. One of these was Robert Gould Shaw, who became a captain in the 2nd Massachusetts Infantry and in 1863 the colonel of the 54th Massachusetts, the first black regiment recruited in the North. Shaw was killed leading that regiment in the attack on Fort Wagner. The 7th New York made its greatest contribution to the Union cause by giving the Lincoln administration a psychological boost when it arrived in Washington on April 25.

Butler called for volunteers to repair the rusting derelict of a locomotive he found in the Annapolis yards. A private stepped forward: "That engine was made in our shop; I guess I can fit her up and run her." Setting a pattern for the feats of railroad construction that helped the North win the war, Butler's troops and the 7th New York reopened the line over which thousands of northern soldiers poured into Washington.

Although Baltimore remained tense, the buildup of Union military strength along Maryland's railroads and a declaration of martial law in the city on May 13 dampened secession activities. Though Governor Hicks succumbed to pressures to call the legislature into session, that body ultimately accepted the governor's recommendation of "a neutral position between our brethren of the North and of the South."

As a means of avoiding a difficult choice, "neutrality" was a popular stance in the border states during the first weeks after Sumter. But given Maryland's strategic location and the thousands of northern soldiers stationed in the state or passing through it, neutrality soon became an impossible dream. Indigenous Maryland unionism began to assert itself. The state's economic health was based on rail and water connections with the North. President John W. Garrett of the Baltimore and Ohio Railroad was a firm unionist and offered the railroad's facilities to carry troops and supplies from the West. Unionist candidates won all six seats in a special congressional election on June 13. By that time the state had also organized three Union regiments. Marylanders who wanted to fight for the Confederacy had to depart for Virginia to organize Maryland regiments on Confederate soil.

Union officials nonetheless continued to worry about underground

Benjamin Butler was a Massachusetts Democrat who had supported Jefferson Davis for the Democratic presidential nomination in 1860. When the war came, he quickly changed his politics and eventually became an influential Republican. He hardly fit the image of a modern major general, and indeed, as a military leader he proved to be a good politician.

In addition to fixing the locomotive they found at Annapolis, the men of the 8th Massachusetts relaid the tracks and repaired the bridges between that city and Washington. These militiamen may not have been very professional as soldiers, but as civilians in uniform they could do almost anything they turned their hand to.

Confederate activities in Baltimore. Army officers overreacted by arresting a number of suspected secessionists and imprisoning them in Fort McHenry. One of those arrested was John Merryman, a wealthy landowner and lieutenant in a secessionist cavalry unit that had burned bridges and torn down telegraph wires during the April troubles. Merryman's lawyer petitioned the federal circuit court in Baltimore for a writ of habeas corpus. The senior judge of this court was none other than Roger B. Taney, who on May 26 issued a writ ordering the commanding officer at Fort McHenry to bring Merryman before the court to show cause for his arrest. The officer refused, citing Lincoln's April 27 suspension of the writ of habeas corpus in portions of Maryland.

This confrontation became the first of several celebrated civil liberties cases during the war. Article I, Section 9, of the Constitution stipulates that the privilege of the writ of habeas corpus "shall not be suspended, unless when in cases of rebellion or invasion the public safety may require it." In a circuit court ruling on May 28, Taney denied the president's right to suspend the writ. The provision authorizing the suspension, he pointed out, appears in the article of the Constitution specifying the powers of Congress; therefore only Congress can exercise the power. Moreover, Taney continued, the Constitution does not authorize the arrest of civilians by army officers without the sanction of civil courts, nor does it permit a citizen to be held in prison indefinitely without trial.

The Republican press denounced Taney's opinion as a new species of proslavery sophistry. Lincoln refused to obey it. The particular location of the habeas corpus clause in the Constitution was irrelevant, several prominent constitutional lawyers maintained; suspension was an emergency power to be exercised in case of rebellion; the president was the only person who could act quickly enough in an emergency, especially when Congress was not in session. The whole purpose of suspending the writ, said these legal scholars, was to enable army officers to arrest and detain without trial suspected traitors when civil authorities and courts were potentially sympathetic with treason, as in Baltimore.

In his message to the special session of Congress on July 4, 1861, Lincoln took note of the Merryman case. The president considered his primary duty to be the suppression of rebellion so that the laws of the United States could be executed in the South. Suspension of the writ was a vital weapon against rebellion. "Are all the laws, *but one* [the right of habeas corpus], to go unexecuted," asked the president rhetorically, "and the government itself go to pieces, lest that one be violated?" Whatever the respective merits of Taney's and Lincoln's positions, Taney commanded no troops and could not enforce his opinion, while Lincoln did and could. Merryman was released after seven weeks at Fort McHenry and indicted in the U.S. circuit court, but his case never came to trial because the government knew that a Maryland jury would not convict him.

While lawyers continued to argue, the army arrested the Baltimore police chief, four police commissioners, and several prominent citizens for their roles in the April 19 riot and their alleged continuing subversive activities. More was yet to come. After Confederate victory in the battle of Manassas on July 21, secessionists in Maryland became bold again. A special session of the legislature in August rang with rhetoric denouncing the "gross usurpation, unjust, tyrannical acts of the President of the United States." By the time another extra session was scheduled to meet on September 17, the administration was

alarmed by reports of a plot for a simultaneous Confederate invasion of Maryland, insurrection in Baltimore, and enactment of secession by the legislature. Lincoln decided to take drastic action. Union troops sealed off Frederick (where the legislature was meeting) and arrested thirty-one secessionist members along with numerous other suspected accessories to the plot, including Mayor George Brown of Baltimore. All were imprisoned for at least two months, until after the election of a new legislature in November.

Not surprisingly, this balloting resulted in a smashing victory for the Union party. After the election, prisoners were gradually released after taking an oath of allegiance to the United States, the last of them in December 1862. Although Lincoln justified the prolonged detention of these men on grounds of "tangible and unmistakable evidence" of their "substantial and unmistakable complicity with those in armed rebellion," the government never revealed the evidence or brought any of the prisoners to trial. Some of them, probably including Mayor Brown, were guilty of little more than southern sympathies or lukewarm unionism. They were victims of the obsessive quest for security that arises in time of war, especially civil war.

A thousand miles to the west of Maryland, events equally dramatic and more violent marked the struggle to keep Missouri in the Union. Dynamic personalities polarized this struggle even more than the situation warranted. On one extreme stood Governor Claiborne Fox Jackson, a proslavery Democrat and onetime leader of the border ruffians. On the other stood Congressman Francis P. Blair, Jr., whose connections in Washington included a brother as postmaster general and a father as an adviser of Lincoln. Blair had used his influence to secure the appointment of Captain Nathaniel Lyon as commander of the soldiers stationed at the U.S. arsenal in St. Louis—the largest arsenal in the slave states, with 60,000 muskets and other arms in storage. A Connecticut Yankee and a twenty-year veteran of the army, Lyon was a free soiler whose intense blue eyes, red beard, and commanding voice offered

This drawing in Frank Leslie's Illustrated Newspaper *depicts the arrest of the Baltimore police chief, George P. Kane, at three o'clock in the morning of June 17, 1861. An alleged Confederate sympathizer, Kane found himself incarcerated in Fort McHenry. He was indicted for treason by a federal grand jury but never tried. The government finally released Kane in November 1862. He returned to Baltimore and after the war was elected mayor.*

Many Missourians considered Nathaniel Lyon a fanatic, but uncompromising unionists there and in the North called him a hero for the decisive action he took in May 1861 to disarm the pro-Confederate militia in St. Louis. Three months later he became the first Union general killed in action, at the battle of Wilson's Creek.

better clues than his small stature to the zeal and courage that made him an extraordinary leader of men. Lyon had served in Kansas when Claiborne Fox Jackson had led proslavery invaders from Missouri. In 1861 the Lyon and the Fox once again faced each other in a confrontation of greater than Aesopian proportions.

In his inaugural address as governor on January 5, 1861, Jackson insisted that Missouri "stand by her sister slave-holding States." The lieutenant governor, the speaker of the house, and a majority of the controlling Democratic party in the legislature took the same position. The unionism of the state convention elected to consider secession had frustrated their hopes. In the aftermath of Sumter, however, Jackson moved quickly to propel Missouri into the Confederacy. He took control of the St. Louis police and mobilized units of the prosouthern state militia, which seized the small U.S. arsenal at Liberty, near Kansas City. On April 17, the same day that the governor spurned Lincoln's call for troops, he wrote to Jefferson Davis asking for artillery to assist in the capture of the St. Louis arsenal. The requested artillery appeared that May in a grove on the edge of St. Louis, "Camp Jackson," where the southern militia was drilling.

Blair and Lyon matched Jackson's every move. Lyon mustered into federal service several regiments organized by the German-American population, the hard core of unionism in St. Louis. To reduce the danger of secessionist capture of surplus arms in the arsenal, Lyon and Blair arranged for the secret transfer of 21,000 muskets across the river to Illinois. Lyon was not content to remain on the defensive and allow passions to cool, as conditional unionists advised. He decided to capture the 700 militiamen and their artillery at Camp Jackson. On May 9 he made a personal reconnaissance by carriage through the camp disguised in a dress and shawl as Frank Blair's mother-in-law. The next day he surrounded Camp Jackson with four regiments of German-Americans and two companies of regulars. The militia surrendered without firing a shot. The shooting started later. As Lyon marched the prisoners through the city, a raucous crowd lined the road and grew to dangerous size. Shouting "Damn the Dutch" and "Hurrah for Jeff Davis," the mob threw brickbats and rocks at the German soldiers. When someone shot an officer, the soldiers began firing back. Before they could be stopped, twenty-eight civilians and two soldiers lay dead or dying, with uncounted scores wounded. That night mobs roamed the streets and murdered several lone German-Americans. Next day another clash took the lives of two soldiers and four civilians.

Panic reigned in St. Louis, while anger ruled the state capital at Jefferson City, where the legislature quickly passed Governor Jackson's bills to place the state on a war footing. The events in St. Louis pushed many conditional unionists into the ranks of secessionists. The most prominent convert was Sterling Price, a Mexican War general and former governor, whom Jackson appointed as commander of the prosouthern militia. Missouri appeared headed for a civil war within its own borders. Moderates made one last effort to avert fighting by arranging a June 11 confer-

This sketch shows the mob in St. Louis attacking Union troops just before the enraged soldiers decided they could take no more and began shooting back. Note that many of the civilian rioters were well dressed.

Born into a wealthy slaveholding family in Virginia, Sterling Price moved with them to Missouri in 1830, where he prospered as a tobacco planter. He served as governor and congressman and rose to the rank of brevet brigadier general in the Mexican War. Angered by what he considered the extremist tactics of Nathaniel Lyon, Price offered his services to the Confederacy. He is photographed here as a major general in the Confederate army.

ence between Jackson and Price on one side and Blair and Lyon (now a brigadier general) on the other. Jackson and Price offered to disband their regiments and prevent Confederate troops from entering Missouri if Blair and Lyon would do the same with respect to Union regiments. After four hours of argument about these terms, Lyon rose angrily and declaimed: "Rather than concede to the State of Missouri for one single instant the right to dictate to my Government in any matter . . . I would see you . . . and every man, woman, and child in the State, dead and buried. *This means war.*"

Lyon was as good as his word. Four days after this conference he occupied Jefferson City. Price's militia and the legislature abandoned the capital without resistance. Relentlessly pursued by Lyon, Price's defeated forces retreated all the way to the southwest corner of Missouri by early July. Lyon became the North's first war hero. With little outside help he had organized, equipped, and trained an army, won the first significant Union victories of the war, and gained control of most of Missouri.

But he had stirred up a hornets' nest. Although guerrilla bands would have infested Missouri in any case, the polarization of the state by Lyon's and Blair's actions helped turn large areas into a no-man's land of hit-and-run raids, arson, ambush, and murder. More than any other state, Missouri suffered the horrors of internecine warfare and the resulting hatreds which persisted for decades after Appomattox.

None of this fighting dislodged Union political control of most of the state. This control was exercised in a unique manner. The governor and most of the legislature had decamped. The only unionist body with some claim to sovereignty was the state convention that had adjourned

THE BATTLE OF BOONEVILLE, OR THE GREAT MISSOURI "LYON" HUNT.

A Currier and Ives print celebrating a minor Union victory at Boonville on the Missouri River on June 17 that forced Governor Claiborne Fox Jackson and General Sterling Price to yield temporary control of Missouri to Union forces. General Lyon is portrayed as a lion chasing the effete Jackson and Price to the far corner of the state.

in March after rejecting secession. On July 22, therefore, a quorum of the convention reassembled, constituted itself the provisional government of Missouri, declared the state offices vacant and the legislature nonexistent, and elected a new governor and other state officials. Known as the "Long Convention" (to establish the analogy with the Long Parliament of the English Civil War), the convention ruled Missouri until January 1865, when a government elected under a new free-state constitution took over.

Meanwhile Claiborne Jackson called the prosouthern legislature into session at Neosho near the Arkansas border. Less than a quorum showed up, but on November 3, 1861, this body enacted an ordinance of secession. The Congress in Richmond admitted Missouri as the twelfth Confederate state on November 28. Although Missouri sent senators and representatives to Richmond, its Confederate state government was driven out of Missouri shortly after seceding and existed as a government in exile for the rest of the war.

Nearly three-quarters of the white men in Missouri and two-thirds of those in Maryland who fought in the Civil War did so on the side of the Union. Kentucky was more evenly divided between North and South; at least two-fifths of her white fighting men wore gray. Kentucky was the birthplace of both Abraham Lincoln and Jefferson Davis. Heir to the nationalism of Henry Clay, Kentucky was also drawn to the South by ties of kinship and culture. Three slave states and three free states touched its borders. Precisely because Kentucky was so evenly divided in sentiment and geography, its people were loath to choose sides. A month after Lincoln's call for troops, the legislature resolved that "this state and the citizens thereof shall take no part in the Civil War now being waged [but will] occupy a position of strict neutrality."

Kentuckians took pride in their traditional role as mediator between North and

South. Governor Beriah Magoffin appealed to the governors of the three midwestern states on Kentucky's northern border for a conference to propose mediation between the warring parties. He sent emissaries to Tennessee and Missouri for the same purpose. If all six states formed a united front, thought Magoffin, they could compel North and South to make peace. But the Republican midwestern governors, busy mobilizing their states for war, refused to have anything to do with the idea, while Tennessee soon made its commitment to the Confederacy. A border states conference held in Frankfort on June 8 attracted delegates from only Kentucky and Missouri. They adjourned in futility after passing unnoticed resolutions.

In theory, neutrality was little different from secession. "Neutrality!!" exclaimed a Kentucky unionist in May 1861. "Why, Sir, this is a declaration of State Sovereignty, and is the very principle which impelled South Carolina and other States to secede." Lincoln agreed—in theory. But he, like other pragmatic unionists, recognized that neutrality was the best they could expect for the time being. The alternative was actual secession. His interim policy was to turn a blind eye to the many Kentuckians slipping into Tennessee to join the Glorious Cause,

Kentucky was the most divided of the border states. The Union Press *was an uncompromising newspaper in Louisville which proclaimed the rebellion a "crime" that must be "suppressed" by "all the means necessary." The soldiers in the photograph belonged to a Louisville unit of the Kentucky State Guard, which declared for the Confederacy in 1861 and became part of John Hunt Morgan's dashing cavalry brigade.*

GOVERNOR MAGOFFIN'S NEUTRALITY means holding THE COCK OF THE WALK (*Uncle Sam*) while THE CONFEDERATE CAT (*Jeff Davis*) kills off his Chickens.

The cartoonist has taken a decidedly skeptical view of Kentucky Governor Beriah Magoffin's "neutrality." With a bottle of bourbon strapped to his belt, Magoffin holds back the rooster Uncle Sam while Jefferson Davis kills the unionist chickens.

ignore Confederate recruiting of others, and promise not to send troops into the state if it refrained from using force against the Union. Lincoln carried this promise to the extreme of allowing an immense trade through the state to the Confederacy. Horses, mules, food, leather, salt, and other military supplies, even munitions, entered Tennessee via Kentucky. Even though Lincoln had declared a blockade of Confederate ports, he hesitated to impose a land blockade against Kentucky lest he violate her "neutrality." Not until August 16, after state elections had shown that unionists were in firm control of Kentucky, did Lincoln issue a proclamation banning all trade with the Confederacy. Even this did not entirely halt the trade, but at least it made such commerce illegal and drove it underground.

Lincoln's forbearance toward Kentucky paid off. Unionists became more outspoken, and fence-sitters jumped down onto the Union side. The legacy of the great compromiser Henry Clay began to assert itself. Unionist "home guard" regiments sprang up to counter the pro-southern "state guard" militia organized by Governor Magoffin. Union agents clandestinely ferried 5,000 muskets across the river from Cincinnati to arm the home guards. Kentuckian Robert Anderson, of Fort Sumter fame, established Union recruiting camps for Kentucky volunteers on the Ohio side of the river to match the Confederate camps just across the Tennessee line. At a special election on June 20, unionists won more than 70 percent of the votes and gained control of five of Kentucky's six congressional seats. This balloting understated pro-Confederate sentiment, for many southern-rights voters refused to participate in an election held under the auspices of a government they rejected. Nevertheless, the regular election of the state legislature on August 5 resulted in an even more conclusive Union victory: the next legislature would have a Union majority of 76 to 24 in the House and 27 to 11 in the Senate.

This legislative election marked the beginning of the end of neutrality in Kentucky. Military activities along the state's borders soon forced the new legislature to declare its allegiance. Several northern regiments were stationed in Cairo, Illinois, at the confluence of the Ohio and Mississippi rivers. An equally large Confederate force occupied northwest Tennessee, fewer than fifty miles away. Key to the control of the Mississippi between these two forces was the high bluff at the rail terminal of Columbus, Kentucky. Both rival commanders cast covetous eyes on Columbus, and each feared—correctly—that the other intended to seize and fortify the heights there.

The Confederate commander was Leonidas Polk, tall and soldier-like in appearance, member of a distinguished southern family, a West Point graduate near the top of his class who had left the army in 1827 to enter the ministry and rise to a bishopric of the Episcopal church. When war came in 1861, he doffed his clerical robes and donned a major general's uniform. An officer of high reputation, Polk never measured up to his early military promise and did not survive the war. The opposing Union commander was Ulysses S. Grant, slouchy and unsoldier-like in appearance, of undistinguished family, a West Point graduate from the lower half of his class who had resigned from the army in disgrace for drunkenness in 1854 and had failed in several civilian occupations before volunteering his services to the Union in 1861. "I feel myself competent to command a regiment," Grant had diffidently informed the adjutant general in a letter of May 24, 1861—to which he received no reply. Grant's commission as colonel and his promotion to brigadier general came via the congressman of his district and the governor of Illinois, who were scraping the barrel for officers to organize the unwieldy mass of Illinois volunteers. A man of no reputation and little apparent promise, Grant would rise to the rank of lieutenant general commanding all the Union armies and become president of the United States.

Polk moved first to grasp the prize of Columbus. On September 3, troops from his command entered Kentucky and occupied the town. Grant responded by occupying Paducah and Smithland at the mouths of the strategically crucial Tennessee and Cumberland rivers. Both sides had invaded Kentucky, but by moving first the Confederates earned the stigma of aggressor. This converted the legislature from lukewarm to warlike unionism. On September 18 the American flag rose over the capitol and legislators resolved by a three-to-one margin that Kentucky having been "invaded by the forces of the so-called Confederate States . . . the invaders must be expelled." Governor Magoffin and Senator Breckinridge resigned to cast their lot with the Confederacy. Other Kentuckians followed them. On November 18 a convention of two hundred delegates passed an ordinance of secession and formed a provisional government, which the Congress in Richmond admitted as the thirteenth Confederate state on December 10. By the end of the year 35,000 Confederate troops occupied the southwest quarter of Kentucky, facing more than 50,000 Federals who controlled the rest of the state.

This Mathew Brady photograph of Leonidas Polk in his clerical robe was made before he became a major general in the Confederate army. A wealthy Louisiana planter and slaveholder as well as an Episcopal bishop, Polk declared that God was on the side of the Confederacy.

War had finally come to Kentucky. And here more than anywhere else it was literally a brothers' war. Four grandsons of Henry Clay fought for the Confederacy and three others for the Union. One of Senator John J. Crittenden's sons became a general in the Union army and the other a general in the Confederate army. The

This photograph of Grant as a brigadier general in 1861 was made before he became famous. Later and more familiar photographs show him with a shorter and more neatly trimmed beard and without the jaunty turned-up brim on his hat.

Kentucky-born wife of the president of the United States had four brothers and three brothers-in-law fighting for the South—one of them a captain killed at Baton Rouge and another a general killed at Chickamauga. Kentucky regiments fought each other on several battlefields; in the battle of Atlanta, a Kentucky Breckinridge fighting for the Yankees captured his rebel brother.

IV

The unionism of the fourth border state, tiny Delaware, was never in doubt. For all practical purposes Delaware was a free state. Less than 2 percent of its people were slaves, and more than 90 percent of its black population was free. In January 1861 the legislature had expressed "unqualified disapproval" of secession, and it never again considered the question. The state's few slaveholders and Confederate sympathizers lived mainly in the southern counties, bordering Maryland's eastern shore.

Each of the four upper-South states that seceded contained a large area with little more commitment to slavery and the Confederacy than Delaware—western Virginia, western North Carolina, eastern Tennessee, and northern Arkansas. The economy and society of two of these upland regions were so distinct from the remainder of their states as to produce wartime movements for separate statehood. West Virginia managed to secede from the Confederacy and rejoin the Union. A similar effort in east Tennessee failed, leaving a legacy of bitterness that persisted long after the war.

The thirty-five counties of Virginia west of the Shenandoah Valley and north of the Kanawha River contained a quarter of Virginia's white population in 1860. Slaves and slaveowners were rare among these narrow valleys and steep mountainsides. The region's culture and economy were oriented to nearby Ohio and Pennsylvania rather than to the faraway lowlands of Virginia. The largest city, Wheeling, was only sixty miles from Pittsburgh but 330 miles from Richmond. For decades the plebeian mountaineers, underrepresented in a legislature dominated by slaveholders, had nursed grievances against the "tidewater aristocrats" who governed the state. Slaves were taxed at less than a third of their market value while other property was taxed at full value. The lion's share of state internal improvements went to the eastern counties, while the northwest cried out in vain for more roads and railroads.

The events of 1861 brought to a head the long-standing western sentiment for separate statehood. Only five of the thirty-one delegates from northwest Virginia voted for the secession ordinance on April 17. Voters in this region rejected ratification by a three-to-one margin. Mass meetings of unionists all over the northwest coalesced into a convention at Wheeling on June 11. The main issue confronting this convention was immediate versus delayed steps toward separate statehood for western Virginia. The stumbling block to immediate action was Article IV, Section 3, of the U.S. Constitution, which requires the consent of the legislature to form a new state from the territory of an existing one. The Confederate legislature of Vir-

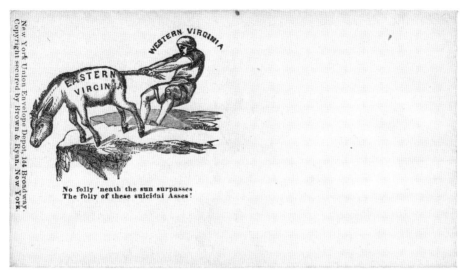

New York Union Envelope Depot, 144 Broadway.
Copyright secured by Brown & Ryan, New York.

No folly 'neath the sun surpasses
The folly of these suicidal Asses!

Once the war broke out, many envelopes with patriotic illustrations quickly appeared in both North and South. This one depicts a loyal unionist of western Virginia trying to hold back the ass of eastern Virginia from committing suicide by jumping off the cliff of secession. Interestingly, this envelope anticipated Senator Charles Sumner's constitutional argument that by seceding, Confederate states had committed "state suicide" and had reverted to the status of territories.

ginia would not consent to a separate state, of course, so the Wheeling convention formed its own "restored government" of Virginia. Branding the Confederate legislature in Richmond illegal, the convention declared all state offices vacant and on June 20 appointed new state officials, headed by Francis Pierpoint as governor. Lincoln recognized the Pierpoint administration as the de jure government of Virginia. A rump legislature, theoretically representing the whole state but in practice representing only the northwestern counties, thereupon elected two U.S. senators from Virginia, who were seated by the Senate on July 13, 1861. Three congressmen from western Virginia also took their seats in the House.

When the Wheeling convention reconvened, in August 1861, a prolonged debate took place between separatists and conservatives. The latter found it difficult to swallow the idea that a legislature representing only one-fifth of Virginia's counties could act for the whole state. But the convention finally adopted an "ordinance of dismemberment" on August 20, subject to ratification by a referendum on October 24, 1861, at which the voters would also elect delegates to a constitutional convention for the new state of "Kanawha." All of these proceedings occurred against the backdrop of military operations in which a Union army invaded western Virginia and defeated a smaller Confederate army. This achievement was crucial to the success of the new-state movement; without the presence of victorious northern troops, the state of West Virginia could not have been born.

Union forces moved into western Virginia for strategic as well as political reasons. The Baltimore and Ohio Railroad and the Ohio River ran through this region and along its border for two hundred miles. The most direct rail link between Washington and the Midwest, the B&O would play an important role in Civil War logistics. In May 1861 the Confederates at Harper's Ferry had already cut the railroad while rebel militia in northwest Virginia occupied the line at Grafton and burned bridges west of there. Western Virginia unionists pleaded with Washington for troops; preoccupied with defense of the capital, General Scott could offer little help. But across the Ohio River, Governor William Dennison of Ohio came to the rescue. Like many other states, Ohio raised more regiments than called for in Lincoln's April 15 proclamation. Dennison was

particularly fortunate to have the assistance of George B. McClellan, William S. Rosecrans, and Jacob D. Cox, all of them destined for prominent Civil War commands. McClellan and Rosecrans had graduated near the top of their West Point classes and had gone on to successful civilian careers in business and engineering after resigning from successful careers in the army. Cox was an Oberlin graduate, an outstanding lawyer, a founder of the Republican party in Ohio, and a brigadier general of Ohio militia. These three men organized the regiments raised by Governor Dennison and his equally energetic neighbor, Governor Oliver P. Morton of Indiana. Taking command of these troops, McClellan sent a vanguard across the Ohio River on May 26 to link up with two unionist Virginia regiments.

Their initial objective was the B&O junction at Grafton, sixty miles south of Wheeling. The colonel commanding the Confederate detachment of 1,500 at Grafton withdrew his outnumbered forces to Philippi, fifteen miles farther south and then hastily retreated twenty-five more miles south, pursued by 3,000 Union soldiers. On June 21, McClellan arrived at Grafton to take personal command of the campaign. Thirty-four years old, possessing charm, culture, great ability and an even greater ego, McClellan exhibited in West Virginia a nascent Napoleonic complex that manifested itself in the writing of dispatches and proclamations, though not in the handling of troops in battle. "Soldiers!" he declaimed in an address to his troops at Grafton. "I have heard that there was danger here. I have come to place myself at your head and to share it with you. I fear now but one thing—that you will not find foemen worthy of your steel."

Robert E. Lee also hoped that McClellan's soldiers would meet worthy foemen. But Lee, functioning in Richmond as a sort of commander in chief of Virginia's armed forces, had few men and less steel to spare for faraway western Virginia. He scraped together a few thousand reinforcements and sent them to Beverly under the command of Robert S. Garnett. With 4,500 men "in a most miserable condition as to arms, clothing, equipment, and discipline," Garnett fortified the passes through which ran the main roads from the Shenandoah Valley to Wheeling and Parkersburg.

By the end of June, McClellan had 20,000 men in trans-Allegheny Virginia.

OPERATIONS IN WESTERN VIRGINIA, 1861

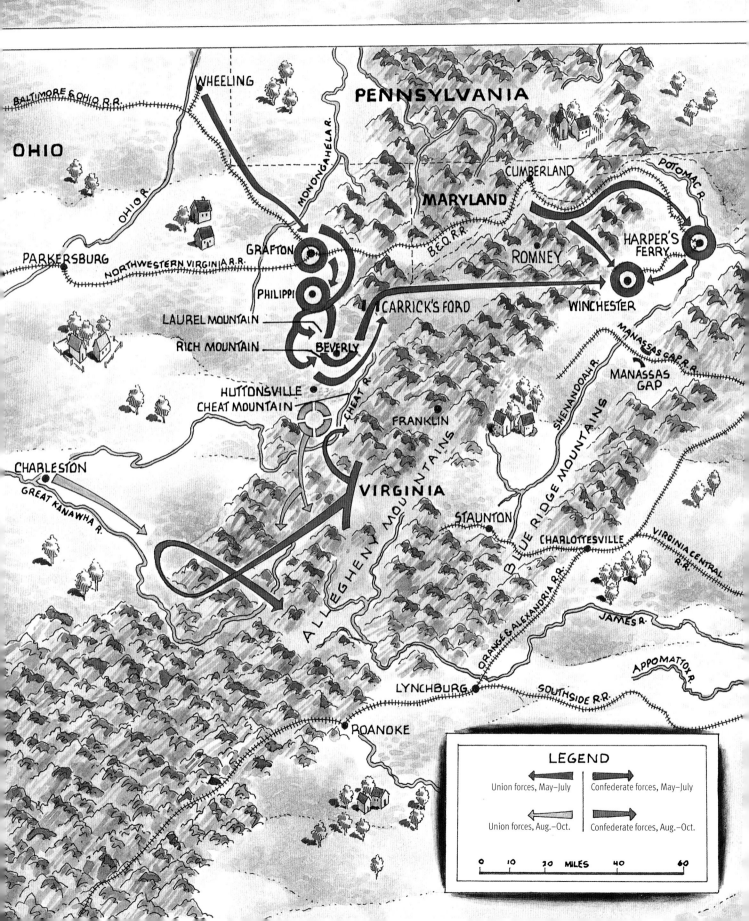

LEGEND

Union forces, May–July | Confederate forces, May–July

Union forces, Aug.–Oct. | Confederate forces, Aug.–Oct.

0   10   20   MILES   40   60

When Confederates occupied Harper's Ferry in April 1861, they did not destroy the Baltimore and Ohio Railroad bridge over the Potomac River because they hoped that Maryland would secede and join the Confederacy. When that prospect did not materialize, and when the advance of Union troops under McClellan into western Virginia threatened to cut off the Confederates at Harper's Ferry, they blew up the bridge on June 15 and retreated to Winchester. This was one of the first of many bridges destroyed during the war.

Five or six thousand of them guarded the B&O, which had been reopened to Washington. McClellan sent another 2,500 men under Jacob Cox to move up the Kanawha River to Charleston. With the remaining 12,000, McClellan planned to encircle and trap Garnett's little army. Leaving 4,000 men to make a feint against Laurel Mountain, McClellan took three brigades to launch the main attack at Rich

Major General George B. McClellan became one of the Union's first heroes because of his well-advertised success in western Virginia. The press began calling him "the young Napoleon," an image that McClellan was glad to reinforce by his pose in this Mathew Brady photograph in 1861.

Mountain eight miles to the south. Rather than assault the Confederate trenches head-on, McClellan accepted Rosecrans's plan for a flank attack by one brigade while McClellan with two others stood ready to exploit whatever success Rosecrans achieved. Guided by a local unionist over a narrow mountain track, Rosecrans's Ohio and Indiana regiments rolled up the rebel flank on July 11 and killed, wounded, or captured 170 of the 1,300 Confederates at a cost of about sixty casualties to themselves. Misinterpreting the sounds of battle through the woods and laurel thickets, McClellan feared that Rosecrans was losing; he therefore failed to launch the follow-up attack and allowed most of the rebels to escape. Jacob Cox, writing later as a historian of the campaign, pointed out that McClellan in West Virginia "showed the same char-

acteristics which became well known later. There was the same overestimate of the enemy, the same tendency to interpret unfavorably the sights and sounds in front, the same hesitancy to throw in his whole force when he knew that his subordinate was engaged."

Despite McClellan's timidity, Rosecrans's attack sent the Confederates into a pell-mell retreat. Five hundred of them were subsequently captured, while Garnett's main force of 3,000 at Laurel Mountain, with the Federals now in their rear, fled over bad roads to the north and east. Union brigades pursued and on July 13 attacked Garnett's rear guard at Corrick's Ford, where Garnett lost his life—the first Civil War general killed in action. Although most of the rebels got away, the campaign cleared northwest Virginia of organized southern forces. Northern newspapers hailed this as a stunning success. McClellan did not hesitate to take the credit. McClellan's victories enabled the reconvened Wheeling convention to enact the separate statehood ordinance in August. Before the referendum on October 24 took place, however, the Confederates made a determined effort to recapture western Virginia. By August they had managed to get 20,000 troops into the trans-Allegheny region, outnumbering the Federals there for the only time in the war. But most of these men were untrained, many were armed with unreliable old smoothbore muskets or even with squirrel rifles and shotguns, and one-third of them were on the sick list—mostly with measles and mumps, which struck down farm boys who had never before been exposed to these childhood diseases. Sick or well, 5,000 of the Confederate troops served in two independent commands headed by John B. Floyd

This rendering of the Union attack on the Confederate flank at the Rich Mountain pass was drawn by an artist who was not there. It shows General McClellan cheering on the attackers, but McClellan was not there either. He remained idle with two brigades three miles away while General William S. Rosecrans with one brigade rolled up the Confederate flank. The cloth covering the cap and neck of several soldiers was called a "havelock" after Sir Henry Havelock, a British general in India, designed to protect the neck against the sun. Civil War soldiers found that the havelocks trapped the humidity inside the cloth, and soon discarded them.

and Henry A. Wise, former governors of Virginia and eager secessionists who now thirsted after military glory. In July, Jacob Cox's Ohioans had maneuvered Wise's brigade all the way up the Kanawha River to White Sulphur Springs, a hundred miles east of Charleston. Floyd's brigades reinforced Wise, but the two men cordially hated each other and spent more time feuding than planning a counterattack against Cox.

Meanwhile the government in Richmond sent Robert E. Lee to take overall command of Confederate forces in western Virginia. Lee went personally to Huntersville, where 10,000 wet, sick, hungry Confederate soldiers confronted 3,000 Union troops dug in on the high ground of Cheat Mountain, a few miles south of the Rich Mountain pass from which Rosecrans had driven the rebels in July. The southern people expected great things of Lee. But this time he disappointed them. His complicated plan for a convergence of five separate columns against two Union positions was frustrated by the difficult terrain, the inexperience of his officers, the fatigue and sickness of his men—and by the protracted rainy weather prevailing before Lee's troops moved out on September 10. Mud slowed their movements to a crawl. After some skirmishing that cost each side fewer than a hundred casualties had eliminated all chance of surprise, Lee gave up and called off the operation on September 15. The Federals remained in control of the Allegheny passes. Supply problems prevented further Confederate operations in this area.

Lee took most of his troops south to the Kanawha Valley to reinforce Floyd and Wise, whose advance had been checked by Rosecrans at Carnifex Ferry on September 10. Jefferson Davis finally resolved the disputes between these two political generals by recalling Wise to Richmond. When Lee arrived in the Kanawha region his troops outnumbered the Federals, but once again rain, sickness, and terrain—plus Rosecrans's effective generalship—foiled a Confederate attempt to trap the enemy. Rosecrans pulled his forces back to a more defensible position on October 6. Seeing no chance to attack them successfully, Lee returned to Richmond at the end of

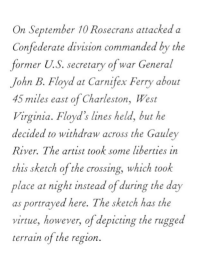

On September 10 Rosecrans attacked a Confederate division commanded by the former U.S. secretary of war General John B. Floyd at Carnifex Ferry about 45 miles east of Charleston, West Virginia. Floyd's lines held, but he decided to withdraw across the Gauley River. The artist took some liberties in this sketch of the crossing, which took place at night instead of during the day as portrayed here. The sketch has the virtue, however, of depicting the rugged terrain of the region.

October. He soon went to South Carolina to shore up Confederate coastal defenses, leaving behind a damaged reputation. In August, Richmond newspapers had predicted that he would drive the Yankees back to Ohio; in October, they mocked him as "Granny Lee" and "Evacuating Lee." The acerbic *Richmond Examiner* pronounced Lee "outwitted, outmaneuvered, and outgeneraled."

During the first half of November, Rosecrans resumed his offensive. With much maneuvering but little fighting, he forced Floyd to withdraw entirely from what is today West Virginia. The Kanawha Valley as well as northwest Virginia thereafter remained under Union military control—except for periodic rebel raids and constant guerrilla warfare. Most of the Kanawha Valley had voted for secession in the May 23 referendum; Confederate sentiment persisted there even after this region became part of the new state of West Virginia. Like Missouri and other parts of the border South, West Virginia suffered from a savage war within the larger war—neighbor against neighbor, bushwhacker against bushwhacker. Rebel guerrillas tied down thousands of Union troops, whose counterinsurgency efforts enjoyed little more success than similar efforts in recent wars. The exasperated Union infantry

Although a slaveholder and a defender of slavery before the war, William S. Brownlow denounced the slaveholders' rebellion and defied the Confederates to arrest him. They did, but found him such a feisty prisoner that they deported him from Tennessee in March 1862. Brownlow returned to Knoxville in triumph when Union troops finally gained control of east Tennessee in the fall of 1863. As postwar governor, he waged war against the Ku Klux Klan as vigorously as he had against rebels a few years earlier.

commander Robert H. Milroy declared in October 1862: "We must inaugurate a system of Union guerrillas to put down the rebel guerrillas." Milroy suited action to words. He carried out such ruthless counterguerrilla warfare that the Confederates put a price on his head.

Union military control of western Virginia was firm enough to permit the statehood referendum to take place as scheduled on October 24, 1861. The voters overwhelmingly endorsed a new state, but the turnout was small. Pro-Confederate voters in more than a dozen counties boycotted the election. Nevertheless, the constitutional convention in January 1862 established boundaries that included fifty counties, and the "restored state legislature of Virginia" sanctioned the creation of the new state of West Virginia on May 23, 1862. About 4 percent of the people in the proposed new state were slaves. Recognizing that a Republican Congress was unlikely to admit another slave state, the constitutional convention included an emancipation provision in the constitution, clearing the way for West Virginia to come into the Union on June 20, 1863. Slaves born after July 4, 1863, would be freemen, and all others emancipated on their twenty-fifth birthday.

Republicans in 1861 viewed events in western Virginia as a model for the reconstruction of Union governments in other parts of the upper South. East Tennessee seemed the most promising locale for this effort. Unionists there held two conventions in 1861, at Knoxville on May 30–31 and at Greeneville on June 17–20. Former Whigs and Democrats cooperated warily in this effort against the greater enemy. Their leaders were Andrew Johnson, a lifelong Democrat, and William G. Brownlow, a former Methodist clergyman turned fighting editor of the *Knoxville Whig* whose profane language toward secessionists belied his nickname of "Parson" Brownlow. Johnson was the only U.S. senator from a seceding state who remained loyal to the Union. Brownlow stayed at the helm of his newspaper, flew the American flag over his home, and vowed to "fight the Secession leaders till Hell freezes over, and then fight them on the ice." Of plebeian origins, Johnson and Brownlow expressed the resentments of their nonslaveholding constituents against the secessionist gentry. "A cheap purse-proud set they are," said Johnson, "not half as good as the man who earns his bread by the sweat of his brow." Brownlow insisted that east Tennessee yeomen "can never live in a Southern Confederacy and be made hewers of wood and drawers of water for a set of aristocrats and overbearing tyrants."

Unionists in east Tennessee could accomplish little without northern military support. Lincoln continually pressed his generals for action in this theater. But distance, logistical difficulties, and Kentucky stood in the way. So long as Lincoln was nursing unionism in Kentucky by respecting her neutrality, no northern troops could cross the state to reach east Tennessee. Even after Union forces moved into Kentucky in September 1861, the forbidding terrain and lack of transport facilities

over the Cumberland Mountains made military operations difficult, especially in winter. While two railroads, a navigable river, and a macadamized turnpike carried troops and supplies from Ohio to the main theaters of operations in western Virginia, no such routes ran from Union bases in eastern Kentucky 150 miles over the mountains to Knoxville.

In November, however, word of a northern invasion reached Union partisans in east Tennessee. With arms smuggled to them by northern agents they went into action, burning five railroad bridges and ambushing Confederate outposts. But the Yankees did not come. The reason was William Tecumseh Sherman. Commander of Union forces in Kentucky, the volatile, red-haired Sherman had not yet developed the *sangfroid* he displayed later in the war. Apprehensive about a buildup of Confederate forces in central Kentucky, Sherman called off the planned invasion of east Tennessee by a small army under General George H. Thomas, who had approached within forty miles of the Tennessee border. Sherman's inflated estimates of Confederate strength and his waspish comments to reporters caused hostile newspapers to call him insane. The administration relieved him of command and transferred him to an obscure post in Missouri. Sherman's career, like Robert E. Lee's, was almost eclipsed by failure before the war was seven months old.

Sherman's successor, Don Carlos Buell, reluctantly yielded to administration

A typically stylized Currier and Ives lithograph depicting the successful Union counterattack at the battle of Mill Springs (or Logan's Cross Roads), Kentucky. The Union commander, General George Thomas, watches on horseback in the distance.

pressure and ordered Thomas to renew his advance. A Union-loyal Virginian, large and imposing in appearance, methodical and deliberate in his movements, Thomas led his 4,000-man army over almost nonexistent mountain roads in winter rains and sleet. On January 19, 1862, a Confederate army of equal size attacked Thomas at Logan's Cross Roads near Mill Springs, Kentucky, but was repulsed and then routed by a Union counterattack. Despite his victory, Thomas could advance no farther in the harsh mountain winter. By spring, Union advances in western and central Tennessee would divert all efforts to that quarter. Ironically, while northern armies "liberated" the Confederate portion of Tennessee they left the unionist portion to fend for itself—to Lincoln's chagrin.

Without northern help, east Tennessee unionists suffered grievously for their loyalty. Confederate troops cracked down after the bridge burnings in November. They declared martial law, executed five bridge-burners, arrested Brownlow and turned his printing office into an arms factory, and imprisoned hundreds of unionists—a much more thorough suppression of dissent than northern forces had carried out in Maryland. Brownlow's genius for self-dramatization turned him into a martyr and an embarrassment to the Confederates, who therefore released him and escorted him to Union lines in March 1862.

Many other east Tennesseans made individual and group escapes to join the Union army. Even though that army did not occupy east Tennessee until September 1863, more than halfway through the war, 30,000 white Tennesseans fought for the North—more than from any other Confederate state.

V

The actions of the eight upper-South states in 1861 had an important but equivocal impact on the outcome of the war. One can begin to measure that impact by noting the possible consequences of what did *not* happen. If all eight states (or all but Delaware) had seceded, the South might well have won its independence. If all eight had remained in the Union, the Confederacy surely could not have survived as long as it did. As it was, the balance of military manpower from these states favored the South. The estimated 425,000 soldiers they furnished to southern armies comprised half of the total who fought for the Confederacy. These same states furnished some 235,000 white soldiers and eventually 85,000 blacks to the Union armies—together amounting to only 15 percent of the men who fought for the Union. Nevertheless, the ability of the North to mobilize this much manpower from slave states gave an important impetus to the Union war effort. And the strategic importance of the rivers, railroads, and mountains of the border states (including West Virginia) can hardly be exaggerated. On the other hand, guerrilla warfare and the problems of administering sizable regions with populations of doubtful loyalty tied down large numbers of Union troops in the border states.

The divided allegiance of the upper South complicated the efforts by both sides to define their war aims and to find a strategy for achieving these aims. For while the Union and Confederate governments were contending for the upper South, they were also mobilizing their armed forces and deciding how to use them.

CHAPTER TEN

★ ★ ★ ★ ★

Amateurs
Go to War

I

War fever during the months after Sumter overrode sober reflections on the purpose of the fighting. Most people on both sides took for granted the purpose and justice of their cause. Yankees believed that they battled for flag and country. "We must fight now, not because we want to subjugate the South . . . but because we *must*," declared a Republican newspaper in Indianapolis. "The Nation has been defied. The National Government has been assailed. If either can be done with impunity . . . we are not a Nation, and our Government is a sham." Nor did northern Democratic editors fall behind their Republican rivals in patriotism. "We were born and bred under the stars and stripes," wrote a Pittsburgh Democrat. Although the South may have had just grievances against Republicans, "when the South becomes an enemy to the American system of government . . . and fires upon the flag . . . our influence goes for that flag, no matter whether a Republican or a Democrat holds it."

Scholars who have examined thousands of letters and diaries written by Union soldiers found them expressing similar motives; "fighting to maintain the best government on earth" was a common phrase. It was a "grate strugle for the Union, Constitution, and law," wrote a New Jersey soldier. "Our glorious institutions are likely to be destroyed. . . . We will be held responsible before God if we don't do our part in helping to transmit this boon of civil & religious liberty down to succeeding generations." Americans of 1861 felt responsible to their forebears as well as to God and posterity. "I know . . . how great a debt we owe to those who went before us through the blood and sufferings of the Revolution," wrote a New England officer to his wife on the eve of the first battle of Bull Run (Manassas). "I am willing—perfectly willing—to lay down all my joys in this life, to help maintain this government, and to pay that debt."

One of Lincoln's qualities of greatness as president was his ability to articulate these war aims in pithy prose. "Our popular government has often been called an experiment," Lincoln told Congress on July 4, 1861. "Two points in it, our people have already settled—the successful *establishing*, and the successful *administering* of it. One

Opposite page: Virginia militia entrain at Martinsburg to capture the federal arsenal at Harper's Ferry.

still remains—its successful maintenance against a formidable internal attempt to overthrow it. . . . This issue embraces more than the fate of these United States. It presents to the whole family of man, the question, whether a constitutional republic, or a democracy . . . can or cannot, maintain its territorial integrity, against its own domestic foes."

The flag, the Union, the Constitution, and democracy—all were symbols or abstractions, but nonetheless powerful enough to evoke a willingness to fight and die for them. Southerners also fought for abstractions—state sovereignty, the right of secession, the Constitution as *they* interpreted it, the concept of a southern "nation" different from the American nation whose values had been corrupted by Yankees. "Thank God! we have a country at last," said Mississippian L.Q.C. Lamar in June 1861, a country "to live for, to pray for, to fight for, and if necessary, to die for." A North Carolinian was "willing to give up my life in defence of my Home and Kindred. I had rather be dead than see the Yanks rule this country." He got his wish—at Gettysburg.

Although southerners later bridled at the official northern name for the conflict—"The War of the Rebellion"—many of them, comparing themselves to their forefathers who had rebelled against British rule, proudly wore the label of rebel during the war itself.

＊   ＊   ＊   ＊   ＊

Jefferson Davis said repeatedly that the South was fighting for the same "sacred right of self-government" that the Revolutionary fathers had fought for. In his first message to Congress after the fall of Sumter, Davis proclaimed that the Confederacy would "seek no conquest, no aggrandizement, no concession of any kind from the States with which we were lately confederated; all we ask is to be let alone."

Both sides believed they were fighting to preserve the heritage of republican liberty; but Davis's last phrase ("all we ask is to be let alone") specified the most immediate, tangible Confederate war aim: defense against invasion. Regarding Union soldiers as vandals bent on plundering the South and liberating the slaves, many southerners literally believed they were fighting to defend home, hearth, wives, and sisters. "Our men *must* prevail in combat, or lose their property, country, freedom, everything," wrote a southern diarist. "On the other hand, the enemy, in yielding the contest, may retire into their own country, and possess everything they enjoyed before the war began." Southern women brought irresistible pressure on men to enlist. "If every man did not hasten to battle, they vowed they would themselves rush out and meet the Yankee vandals. In a land where women are worshipped by the men, such language made them war-mad." A Confederate soldier captured early in the war put it simply. His tattered homespun uniform and even more homespun speech made it clear that he was not a member of the planter class. His captors asked why he, a nonslaveholder, was fighting to uphold slavery. He replied: "I'm fighting because you're down here."

For this soldier, as for many other southerners, the war was not about slavery. But without slavery there would have been no Black Republicans to threaten the South's way of life, no special southern civilization to defend against Yankee invasion. This paradox plagued southern efforts to define their war aims. In particular, slavery handicapped Confederate foreign policy. The first southern commissioners to Britain reported in May 1861 that "the public mind here is entirely opposed to the Government of the Confederate States of America on the question of slavery. . . . The sincerity and universality of this feeling embarrass the Government in dealing with the question of our recognition." In their explanations of war aims, therefore,

NORTH CAROLINA.
A CALL TO ARMS!!!

Ye sons of Carolina! awake from your dreaming!
The minions of Lincoln upon us are streaming!
Oh! wait not for argument, call, or persuasion,
To meet at the onset this treach'rous invasion!

Oh! think of the maidens, the wives, and the mothers,
Fly ye to the rescue, sons, husbands and brothers,
And sink in oblivion all party and section,
Your hearthstones are looking to you for protection!

" Her name stands the foremost in Liberty's story,"
Oh! tarnish not now her fame and her glory!
Your fathers to save her their swords bravely yielded,
And she never yet has to tyranny yielded.

The babe in its sweetness—the child in its beauty,
Unconsciously urge you to action and duty!
By all that is sacred, by all to you tender,
Your country adjures, arise and defend her!

" The Star Spangled Banner," dishonored is streaming
O'er bands of fanatics ; their swords are now gleaming ;
They thirst for the life-blood of those you most cherish ;
With brave hearts and true, then, arouse! or they perish !

Round the flag of the South, oh! in thousands now rally,
For the hour's departed when freemen may dally ;
Your all is at stake, then go forth, and God speed you !
And onward to glory and victory lead you !

Thompson & Co., Printers, Raleigh, 1861.

A typical recruiting poster in the southern states during the spring of 1861, appealing to the manhood of North Carolina to defend home, women, and liberty against "the minions of Lincoln" presumably coming South for beauty and booty.

Confederates rarely mentioned slavery except obliquely in reference to northern violations of southern rights. Rather, they portrayed the South as fighting for liberty and self-government—blithely unmindful of Samuel Johnson's piquant question about an earlier generation of American rebels: "How is it that we hear the loudest *yelps* for liberty among the drivers of negroes?"

For reasons of their own most northerners initially agreed that the war had nothing to do with slavery. In his message to the special session of Congress on July 4, 1861, Lincoln reaffirmed that he had "no purpose, directly or indirectly, to interfere with slavery in the States where it exists." The Constitution protected slavery in those states; the Lincoln administration fought the war on the theory that secession was unconstitutional and therefore the southern states still lived under the Constitution. Congress concurred. On July 22 and 25 the House and Senate passed similar resolutions sponsored by John J. Crittenden of Kentucky and Andrew Johnson of Tennessee affirming that the United States fought with no intention "of overthrowing or interfering with the rights or established institutions of [the seceded] States" but only "to defend and maintain the supremacy of the Constitution and to preserve the Union with all the dignity, equality, and rights of the several States unimpaired."

Republicans would soon change their minds about this. But in July 1861 even radicals who hoped that the war *would* destroy slavery voted for the Crittenden-Johnson resolutions (though three radicals voted No and two dozen abstained). Most abolitionists at first also refrained from open criticism of the government's neutral course toward slavery. Assuming that the "death-grapple with the Southern slave oligarchy" must eventually destroy slavery itself, William Lloyd Garrison advised fellow abolitionists in April 1861 to "'stand still, and see the salvation of God' rather than attempt to add anything to the general commotion."

A concern for northern unity underlay this decision to keep a low profile on the slavery issue. Lincoln had won less than half of the popular vote in the Union states (including the border states) in 1860. Some of those who had voted for him, as well as all who had voted for his opponents, would have refused to countenance an anti-slavery war in 1861. By the same token, an explicit avowal that the defense of slavery was a primary Confederate war aim might have proven more divisive than unifying in the South. Both sides, therefore, shoved slavery under the rug as they concentrated their energies on mobilizing eager citizen soldiers and devising strategies to use them.

II

The United States has usually prepared for its wars after getting into them. Never was this more true than in the Civil War. The country was less ready for what proved to be its biggest war than for any other war in its history. In early 1861 most of the tiny 16,000-man army was scattered in seventy-nine frontier outposts west of the Mississippi. Nearly a third of its officers were resigning to go with the South. The War Department slumbered in ancient bureaucratic routine. Most of its clerks, as well as the four previous secretaries of war, had come from the South. All but one of the heads of the eight army bureaus had been in service since the War of 1812. General in Chief Winfield Scott, seventy-four years old, suffered from dropsy and vertigo, and sometimes fell asleep during conferences. Many able young officers, frustrated by drab routine and cramped opportunities, had left the army for civilian careers. The "Winnebago Chief" reputation (an allusion to his reportedly having cheated Indians in a supply contract) of Secretary of War Cameron did not augur well for his capacity to administer with efficiency and honesty the huge new war contracts in the offing.

The army had nothing resembling a general staff, no strategic plans, no program for mobilization. Although the army did have a Bureau of Topographical Engineers, it possessed few accurate maps of the South. Only two officers had commanded as much as a brigade in combat, and both were over seventy. Most of the arms in government arsenals (including the 159,000 muskets seized by Confederate states) were old smoothbores, many of them flintlocks of antique vintage.

The navy was little better prepared for war. Of the forty-two ships in commission when Lincoln became president, most were patrolling waters thousands of miles from the United States. Fewer than a dozen warships were available for immediate service along the American coast. But there were some bright spots in the naval outlook. Although 373 of the navy's 1,554 officers and a few of its 7,600 seamen left to go with the South, the large merchant marine from which an expanded navy would draw experienced officers and sailors was overwhelmingly northern. Nearly all of the country's shipbuilding capacity was in the North. And the Navy Department, unlike the War Department, was blessed with outstanding leadership. Gideon Welles, whose long gray beard and stern countenance led Lincoln to call him "Father Neptune," proved to be a capable administrator. But the real dynamism in the Navy Department came from Assistant Secretary Gustavus V. Fox, architect of the Fort Sumter expedition. Within weeks of Lincoln's proclamation of a blockade against Confederate ports on April 19, the Union navy had bought or chartered scores of merchant ships, armed them, and dispatched them to blockade duty. By the end of 1861 more than 260 warships were on duty and 100 more (including three experimental ironclads) were under construction.

The northern naval outlook appeared especially bright in contrast to the southern. The Confederacy began life with no navy and few facilities for building one. The South possessed no adequate shipyards except the captured Gosport naval yard at Norfolk, and not a single machine shop capable of building an engine large enough to power a respectable warship. While lacking material resources, however, the Confederate navy possessed striking human resources, especially Secretary of the Navy Stephen R. Mallory and Commanders Raphael Semmes and James D. Bulloch.

Mallory, a former U.S. senator from Florida with experience as chairman of the Senate naval affairs committee, proved equal to the task of creating a navy from scratch. He bought tugboats, revenue cutters, and river steamboats to be converted into gunboats for harbor patrol. Recognizing that he could never challenge the Union navy on its own terms, Mallory decided to concentrate on a few specialized

This photograph of General Winfield Scott shows him at the pinnacle of his powers as general in chief of the United States army in the 1850s. In 1861 the stern visage and force of character remained, but energy and ambition had declined.

Although a state's-rights Democrat, Stephen R. Mallory initially opposed secession. When Florida went out, however, he like most southerners "went with his state." Many contemporaries considered him inefficient as secretary of the Confederate navy, and polite Richmond society snubbed him because of his penchant for women of questionable virtue. But historians appraise Mallory as an innovative leader who did a great deal with limited resources.

tasks that would utilize the South's limited assets to maximum advantage. He authorized the development of "torpedoes" (mines) to be planted at the mouths of harbors and rivers; by the end of the war such "infernal devices" had sunk or damaged forty-three Union warships. He encouraged the construction of "torpedo boats," small half-submerged cigar-shaped vessels carrying a contact mine on a bow-spar for attacking blockade ships. It was only one step from this concept to that of a fully submerged torpedo boat. The Confederacy sent into action the world's first combat submarine, the C.S.S. *Hunley*, which sank three times in trials, drowning the crew each time (including its inventor Horace Hunley) before sinking a blockade ship off Charleston in 1864 and then going down itself for the fourth and last time.

Mallory knew of British and French experiments with iron-clad warships. He believed that the South's best chance to break the blockade was to build and buy several of these revolutionary vessels, equip them with iron rams, and send them out to sink the wooden blockade ships. In June 1861 Mallory authorized the rebuilding of the half-destroyed U.S.S. *Merrimack* as the Confederacy's first ironclad, rechristened the C.S.S. *Virginia*. The Confederacy began converting other vessels into ironclads, but its main source for these and other large warships was expected to be British shipyards. For the sensitive task of exploiting this source, Mallory selected James D. Bulloch of Georgia.

With fourteen years' experience in the U.S. navy and eight years in commercial shipping, Bulloch knew ships as well as anyone in the South. He also possessed the tact, social graces, and business acumen needed for the job of getting warships built in a country whose neutrality laws threw up a thicket of obstacles. Arriving at Liverpool in June 1861, Bulloch quickly signed contracts for two steam/sail cruisers that eventually became the famed commerce raiders *Florida* and *Alabama*. In the fall of 1861 he bought a fast steamer, loaded it with 11,000 Enfield rifles, 400 barrels of gunpowder, several cannons, and large quantities of ammunition, took command of her himself, and ran the ship through the blockade into Savannah. The steamer was then converted into the ironclad ram C.S.S. *Atlanta*. Bulloch returned to England, where he continued his undercover efforts to build and buy warships. His activities prompted one enthusiastic historian to evaluate Bulloch's contributions to the Confederacy as next only to those of Robert E. Lee.

The commerce raiders built in Britain represented an important part of Confederate naval strategy. In any war, the enemy's merchant shipping becomes fair game. The Confederates sent armed raiders to roam the oceans in search of northern vessels. At first the South depended on privateers for this activity. An ancient form of wartime piracy, privateering had been practiced with great success by Americans in the Revolution and the War of 1812. In 1861 Jefferson Davis proposed to turn this weapon against the Yankees. On April 17 Davis offered letters of marque to any southern shipowner who wished to turn privateer. About twenty such craft were

soon cruising the sea lanes off the Atlantic coast, and by July they had captured two dozen prizes.

Panic seized northern merchants, whose cries forced the Union navy to divert ships from blockade duty to hunt down the "pirates." They enjoyed some success, but in doing so caused a crisis in the legal definition of the war. Lincoln's proclamation on April 19, 1861, refusing to recognize the Confederacy as a legitimate government and threatening to hang captured privateers as pirates—to which Jefferson Davis responded by warning that one Union prisoner would hang for each "pirate" executed—was on shaky ground. By imposing a blockade Lincoln had implicitly recognized the conflict as a war rather than merely a domestic insurrection, so privateers had to be considered prisoners of war. By 1862, however, Confederate privateers had become ineffective, so the Confederacy turned to commerce raiders—warships manned by naval personnel and designed to sink rather than to capture enemy shipping. The transition from privateering to commerce raiding actually began in June 1861, when the five-gun steam sloop C.S.S. *Sumter* evaded the blockade at the mouth of the Mississippi and headed toward the Atlantic. Her captain was Raphael Semmes of Alabama, a thirty-year veteran of the U.S. navy who now launched his career as the chief nemesis of that navy and terror of the American merchant marine. During the next six months the *Sumter* captured or burned eighteen vessels before Union warships finally bottled her up in the harbor at Gibraltar in January 1862. Semmes sold the *Sumter* to the British and made his way across Europe to England, where he took command of the C.S.S. *Alabama* and went on to bigger achievements.

Despite ingenuity and innovations, however, the Confederate navy could never

Next to the ironclads C.S.S. Virginia *(Merrimac) and U.S.S.* Monitor, *the* H. L. Hunley *(named after its inventor) was the most famous Civil War vessel. It has recently been raised from its watery grave off the South Carolina coast, where it went to the bottom after sinking a Union warship in 1864. This postwar painting by Conrad Wise Chapman was based on technical drawings of the* Hunley. *The propeller was driven by crew members inside the hull turning cranks.*

The C.S.S. Sumter, *pictured here, was the first commerce raider commissioned by the Confederate navy. Converted from a merchant ship, she carried five guns and was commanded by Captain Raphael Semmes, a former U.S. navy lieutenant from Alabama. The* Sumter *escaped through the Union blockade off New Orleans in June 1861. Over the next six months she captured or destroyed eighteen American merchant vessels before three Union warships bottled her up at Gibraltar. The* Sumter *was sold to a British buyer, and Semmes went on to even greater exploits as captain of the C.S.S.* Alabama.

A South Carolina artillery squad photographed in the spring of 1861, ironically wearing the blue uniforms of their militia company, the "Flying Artillery." These soldiers manned one of the guns that fired on Fort Sumter. They would soon exchange their blue uniforms for Confederate gray.

overcome Union supremacy on the high seas or along the coasts and rivers of the South. The Confederacy's main hopes rode with its army. A people proud of their martial prowess, in 1861 southerners felt confident, even though they were outnumbered, of their ability to whip the Yankees in a fair fight—or even an unfair one. Expecting a short and glorious war, southern boys rushed to join the colors before the fun was over. Even though the Confederacy had to organize a War Department and an army from the ground up, the South got an earlier start on mobilization than the North. As each state seceded, it took steps to consolidate and expand militia companies into active regiments. By the 1850s the old idea of militia service as an

obligation of all males had given way to the volunteer concept. Volunteer military companies with distinctive names—Tallapoosa Grays, Jasper Greens, Floyd Rifles, Lexington Wild Cats, Palmetto Guards, Fire Zouaves—sprang up in towns and cities across the country. But the training, capability, discipline, and equipment of these units varied widely. Nevertheless, it was these volunteer companies that first answered the call for troops in both South and North.

By early spring 1861 South Carolina had 5,000 men under arms, most of them besieging Fort Sumter. Other southern states were not far behind. The Confederate Congress in February created a War Department, and President Davis appointed Leroy P. Walker of Alabama as secretary of war. Though a politician like his Union counterpart Simon Cameron, Walker had a better reputation for honesty and efficiency. More important, perhaps, Jefferson Davis himself was a West Point graduate, a combat veteran of the Mexican War, and a former secretary of war in the U.S. government. Although Davis's fussy supervision of Confederate military matters eventually led to conflict with some army officers, the president's martial expertise helped speed southern mobilization in 1861.

On March 6 the Confederate Congress authorized an army of 100,000 volunteers for twelve months. Most of the militia regiments already organized were sworn into the Confederate army, while newly formed units scrambled for arms and equipment. At first the states, localities, and individuals rather than the Confederate government equipped these regiments. Although the South selected cadet gray as its official uniform color, each regiment initially supplied its own uniforms, so that Confederate armies were garbed in a confusing variety of clothing that defied the concept of "uniform." Cavalrymen and artillery batteries provided their own horses. Some volunteers brought their own weapons, ranging from bowie knives and Colt revolvers to shotguns and hunting rifles. Many recruits from planter families brought their slaves to wash clothes and cook for them. Volunteer companies, following the venerable militia tradition, elected their own officers (captain and lieutenants). State governors officially appointed regimental officers (colonel, lieutenant colonel, and major), but in many regiments these officers were actually elected either by the men of the whole regiment or by the officers of all the companies. In practice, the election of officers was often a *pro forma* ratification of the role that a prominent planter, lawyer, or other individual had taken in recruiting a company or a regiment. Sometimes a wealthy man also paid for the uniforms and equipment of a unit he had recruited. Wade Hampton of South Carolina, reputed to be the richest planter in the South, enlisted a "legion" (a regiment-size combination of infantry, cavalry, and artillery) that he armed and equipped at his own expense—and of which, not coincidentally, he became colonel.

By the time Lincoln called for 75,000 men after the fall of Sumter, the South's do-it-yourself mobilization had already enrolled 60,000 men. But these soldiers were beginning to experience the problems of logistics and supply that would plague the southern war effort to the end. Even after the accession of four upper-South states, the Confederacy had only one-ninth the industrial capacity of the Union. The Union had more than twice the density of railroads per square mile as the Confederacy, and several times the mileage of canals and macadamized roads. The South

This model shows the official Confederate infantry uniform complete with accoutrements. In practice, one or more accoutrements were nonregulation or missing. As indicated here, the uniforms were more often homespun butternut than gray wool in material and color.

These men of Company B of the 9th Mississippi have not yet received any kind of uniforms in 1861. Even when they did, their uniforms would not be "uniform." Appearances can be deceiving, however; while these men do not look like soldiers, and most of them never would, the 9th Mississippi became a crack regiment. By the end of the war several of the men in this photograph would be dead.

could produce enough food to feed itself, but the transport network, adequate at the beginning of the war to distribute this food, soon began to deteriorate because of a lack of replacement capacity. Nearly all of the rails had come from the North or from Britain; of 470 locomotives built in the United States during 1860, only 19 had been made in the South.

The Confederate army's support services labored heroically to overcome these deficiencies. But with the exception of the Ordnance Bureau, their efforts always seemed too little and too late. The South experienced a hothouse industrialization during the war, but the resulting plant was shallow-rooted and poor in yield. Quartermaster General Abraham Myers could never supply the army with enough tents, uniforms, blankets, shoes, or horses and wagons. Consequently Johnny Reb often had to sleep in the open under a captured blanket, to wear a tattered homespun butternut uniform, and to march and fight barefoot unless he could liberate shoes from a dead or captured Yankee.

Soldiers also complained about the poor quality and meager quantity of their food and held Commissary General Lucius B. Northrop responsible; civilians damned him for rising prices at home and for the transportation nightmares that left produce rotting in warehouses while the army starved. Nevertheless, Jefferson Davis kept him in office until almost the end of the war, a consequence, it was whispered, of cronyism stemming from their friendship as cadets at West Point. Northrop's unpopularity besmudged Davis when the war began to go badly for the South.

The Ordnance Bureau was the one bright spot of Confederate supply. When Josiah Gorgas accepted appointment as chief of ordnance in April 1861 he faced an apparently more hopeless task than did Myers or Northrop. The South already grew plenty of food, and the capacity to produce wagons, harness, shoes, and clothing seemed easier to develop than the industrial base to manufacture gunpowder, cannon, and rifles. No foundry in the South except the Tredegar Iron Works had the capability to manufacture heavy ordnance. There were no rifle works except small arsenals at Richmond and at Fayetteville, North Carolina, along with the captured machinery from the U.S. armory at Harper's Ferry, which was transferred to Richmond. The du Pont plants in Delaware produced most of the country's gunpowder; the South had manufactured almost none, and this heavy, bulky product would be difficult to smuggle through the tightening blockade. The principal ingredient of gunpowder, saltpeter (potassium nitrate, or "niter"), was also imported.

But Gorgas proved to be a genius at organization and improvisation. He almost literally turned plowshares into swords. He sent Caleb Huse to Europe to purchase all available arms and ammunition. Huse was as good at this job as James Bulloch was at his task of building Confederate warships in England. The arms and other supplies Huse sent back through the blockade were crucial to Confederate survival during the war's first year. Meanwhile Gorgas began to establish armories and foundries in several states to manufacture small arms and artillery. He created a Mining and Niter Bureau headed by Isaac M. St. John, who located limestone caves containing saltpeter in the southern Appalachians, and appealed to southern women to save the contents of chamber pots to be leached for niter. The Ordnance Bureau also built a huge gunpowder mill at Augusta, Georgia, which under the superintendency of George W. Rains began production in 1862. Ordnance officers roamed the South buying or seizing stills for their copper to make rifle percussion caps; they melted down church and plantation bells for bronze to build cannon; they gleaned southern battlefields for lead to remold into bullets and for damaged weapons to repair.

Gorgas, St. John, and Rains were unsung heroes of the Confederate war effort. The South suffered from deficiencies of everything else, but after the summer of 1862 it did not suffer seriously for want of ordnance—though the quality of Confederate artillery and shells was always a problem. Gorgas could write proudly in his diary on the third anniversary of his appointment: "Where three years ago we were not making a gun, a pistol nor a sabre, no shot nor shell (except at the Tredegar Works)—a pound of powder—we now make all these in quantities to meet the demands of our large armies."

But in 1861 these achievements still lay in the future. Shortages and administrative chaos seemed to characterize the Ordnance Bureau as much as any other department of the army. Despite the inability to equip men already in the army, the

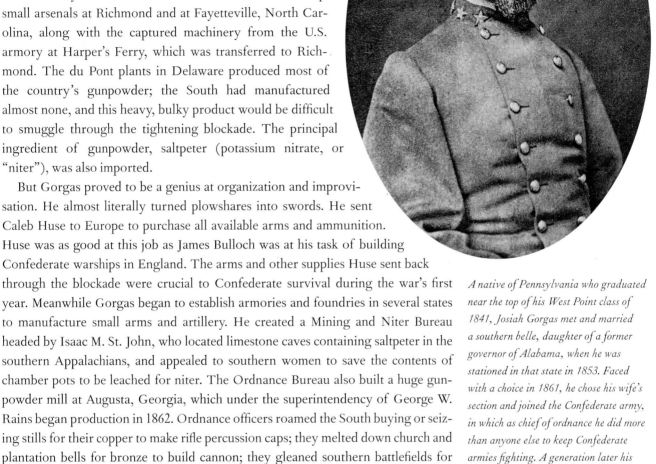

A native of Pennsylvania who graduated near the top of his West Point class of 1841, Josiah Gorgas met and married a southern belle, daughter of a former governor of Alabama, when he was stationed in that state in 1853. Faced with a choice in 1861, he chose his wife's section and joined the Confederate army, in which as chief of ordnance he did more than anyone else to keep Confederate armies fighting. A generation later his son, Colonel William C. Gorgas of the U.S. army, led the effort to eradicate yellow fever and malaria in Panama to make possible the construction of the Panama Canal.

Built from scratch in less than a year, this gunpowder plant in Augusta, Georgia, became a shining example of the hothouse industrialization of an agricultural economy. This factory produced almost three million pounds of gunpowder plus small arms, ammunition, and artillery.

Confederate Congress in May 1861 authorized the enlistment of up to 400,000 additional volunteers for three-year terms. Recruits came forward in such numbers that the War Department, by its own admission, had to turn away 200,000 for lack of arms and equipment. One reason for this shortage of arms was the hoarding by state governors of muskets seized from federal arsenals when the states seceded. Several governors insisted on retaining these weapons to arm regiments they kept at home (instead of sending them to the main fronts in Virginia or Tennessee) to defend state borders and guard against potential slave uprisings. This was an early manifestation of state's-rights sentiment that handicapped centralized efforts. As such it was hardly the Richmond government's fault, but soldiers in front-line armies wanted to blame somebody, and Secretary of War Walker was a natural scapegoat. "The opinion prevails throughout the army," wrote General Beauregard's aide-de-camp at Manassas on June 22, "that there is great imbecility and shameful neglect in the War Department." Although Beauregard's army won the battle of Manassas a month later, criticism of Walker rose to a crescendo. Many southerners believed that the only thing preventing the Confederates from going on to capture Washington after the victory was the lack of supplies and transportation for which the War Department was responsible. Harassed by criticism and overwork, Walker resigned in September and was replaced by Judah P. Benjamin, the second of the five men who eventually served in the revolving-door office of war secretary.

III

Walker—like his successors—was a victim of circumstances more than of his own ineptitude. The same could not be said of his counterpart in Washington. Although Simon Cameron was also swamped by the rapid buildup of an army that exceeded the capacity of the bureaucracy to equip it, he was more deserving of personal censure than Walker.

The North started later than the South to raise an army. The Union had more than 3.5 times as many white men of military age as the Confederacy. But when adjustments are made for the disloyal, the unavailable (most men from the western territories and Pacific coast states), and the white workers released for the Confederate army by the existence of slavery in the South, the actual Union manpower superiority was about 2.5 to 1. From 1862 onward the Union army enjoyed

approximately this superiority in numbers. But because of its earlier start in creating an army, the Confederacy in June 1861 came closer to matching the Union in mobilized manpower than at any other time in the war.

Lincoln's appeal for 75,000 ninety-day militiamen had been based on a law of 1795 providing for calling state militia into federal service. The government soon recognized that the war was likely to last more than three months and to require more than 75,000 men. On May 3 Lincoln called for 42,000 three-year army volunteers and 18,000 sailors, besides expanding the regular army by an additional 23,000 men. The president did this without congressional authorization, citing his constitutional power as commander in chief. When Congress met in July it not only retroactively sanctioned Lincoln's actions but also authorized another one million three-year volunteers. In the meantime some states had enrolled *two-year* volunteers (about 30,000 men), which the War Department reluctantly accepted. By early 1862 more than 700,000 men had joined the Union army. Some 90,000 of them had enlisted in the ninety-day regiments whose time had expired. But many of these men had reenlisted in three-year regiments, and several ninety-day regiments had converted themselves into three-year units.

The confusing patchwork of enlistment processes at the national level was offset by enterprise and vigor at the local and state levels. "Twenty-four hundred men in camp and less than half of them armed," Indiana's Governor Morton wrote to Secretary of War Cameron early in the war. "Why has there been such delay in sending arms? . . . No officer here yet to muster troops into service. Not a pound of powder or a single ball sent us, or any sort of equipment. Allow me to ask what is the cause of all this?" By the end of June, Cameron was turning away offers of regiments. As

This sketch shows a navy recruiting office in lower Manhattan with scores of men crowding the entrance intending to enlist in May 1861. The patriotic fervor in the North that followed the attack on Fort Sumter ensured that the Union navy as well as the army would make—and even exceed—its quota.

Lincoln ruefully admitted in his July 4 message to Congress, "one of the greatest perplexities of the government, is to avoid receiving troops faster than it can provide for them."

States, cities, and individuals took up the slack left by the national government. Individual states bore the costs of supplying and equipping regiments until the army could absorb them. Governors sent purchasing agents to Europe, where they competed with each other and with Confederate agents to bid up the price of the Old World's surplus arms to supply the armies of the New. The states contracted with textile mills and shoe factories for uniforms and shoes. Municipalities raised money to organize and supply "their" regiments. Voluntary associations such as the Union Defense Committee of New York sprang into existence to recruit regiments, equip them, and charter ships or trains to transport them to Washington. A group of northern physicians and women formed the United States Sanitary Commission to supplement the inadequate and outdated facilities of the Army Medical Bureau.

The earliest northern regiments, like the southern, were clad in a colorful variety of uniforms: blue from Massachusetts and Pennsylvania; gray from Wisconsin and Iowa; gray with emerald trim from Vermont; black trousers and red flannel shirts from Minnesota; and gaudy "Zouave" outfits from New York with their baggy red breeches, purple blouses, and red fezzes. The Union forces gathering in Washington looked like a circus on parade. The variety of uniforms in both Union and Confederate armies, and the similarity of some uniforms on opposite sides, caused tragic mixups in early battles when regiments mistook friends for enemies or enemies for friends. As fast as possible the northern government overcame this situation by clothing its soldiers in the standard light blue trousers and dark blue blouse of the regular army.

By the latter part of 1861 the War Department had taken over from the states the responsibility for feeding, clothing, and arming Union soldiers. But this process was marred by inefficiency, profiteering, and corruption. To fill contracts for hundreds of thousands of uniforms, textile manufacturers compressed the fibers of recycled woolen goods into a material called "shoddy." This noun soon became an adjective to describe uniforms that ripped after a few weeks of wear, shoes that fell apart, blankets that disintegrated, and poor workmanship in general on items necessary to equip an army of half a million men and to create its support services

The first eight Wisconsin regiments that marched off to war in 1861 initially wore gray uniforms such as those in this photograph (one has faded to brown), evidently because of a shortage of blue dye. The confusion caused by this "Wisconsin gray" led on at least one occasion at the first battle of Bull Run to the second Wisconsin being fired upon simultaneously by Union and Confederate units.

within a few short months. Railroads overcharged the government; some contractors sold muskets back to the army for $20 each that they had earlier bought as surplus arms at $3.50; sharp horse traders sold spavined animals to the army at outrageous prices. Simon Cameron became the target of just as well as unjust criticism of such transactions. He signed lucrative contracts without competitive bidding and gave a suspiciously large number of contracts to firms in his home state of Pennsylvania. The War Department routed a great deal of military traffic over the Northern Central Railroad and the Pennsylvania Railroad, in which Cameron and Assistant Secretary of War Thomas Scott had direct financial interests.

The House created an investigatory committee on contracts that issued a report in mid-1862 condemning Cameron's management. By then Lincoln had long since gotten rid of Cameron by sending him to St. Petersburg as minister to Russia. The new secretary of war was Edwin M. Stanton, a hard-working, gimlet-eyed lawyer from Ohio who had served briefly as attorney general in the Buchanan administration. A former Democrat with a low opinion of Lincoln, Stanton radically revised both his politics and his opinion after taking over the war office in January 1862. He also became famous for his incorruptible efficiency and brusque rudeness toward war contractors—and toward everyone else as well.

Even before Stanton swept into the War Department with a new broom, the headlong, helter-skelter, seat-of-the pants mobilization of 1861 was just about over. The army's logistical apparatus had survived its shakedown trials and had even achieved a modicum of efficiency. The northern economy had geared up for war production on a scale that would make the Union army the best fed, most lavishly

The tired, lugubrious countenance of Simon Cameron and the determined, confident mien of Edwin M. Stanton speak volumes about their respective performances as secretary of war. Lincoln replaced Cameron with Stanton in January 1862 because in ten months on the job Cameron had made a mess of things; in cleaning up the mess Stanton did not make himself popular with war contractors, but he got the job done.

Montgomery Meigs's no-nonsense style of administration is captured by this photograph. As quartermaster general, he was the star performer of Union military logistics.

Opposite: This photograph of a Union infantry regiment in camp illustrates the logistical support necessary for Union military operations in enemy territory. At least nineteen wagons are visible in the photograph, each with its complement of two or four horses or mules.

supplied army that had ever existed. Much of the credit for this belonged to Montgomery Meigs, who became quartermaster general of the army in June 1861. Meigs had graduated near the top of his West Point class and had achieved an outstanding record in the corps of engineers. He supervised a number of large projects including the building of the new Capitol dome and construction of the Potomac Aqueduct to bring water to Washington. His experience in dealing with contractors enabled him to impose some order and honesty on the chaos and corruption of early war contracts. Meigs insisted on competitive bidding whenever possible, instead of the cost-plus system favored by manufacturers who liked to inflate profits by padding costs.

Nearly everything needed by an army except weapons and food was supplied by the Quartermaster Bureau: uniforms, overcoats, shoes, knapsacks, haversacks, canteens, mess gear, blankets, tents, camp equipage, barracks, horses, mules, forage, harnesses, horseshoes and portable blacksmith shops, supply wagons, ships when the army could be supplied by water, coal or wood to fuel them, and supply depots for storage and distribution. The logistical demands of the Union army were much greater than those of its enemy. Most of the war was fought in the South, where Confederate forces operated close to the source of many of their supplies. Invading northern armies, by contrast, had to maintain long supply lines of wagon trains, railroads, and port facilities. A Union army operating in enemy territory averaged one wagon for every forty men and one horse or mule (including cavalry and artillery horses) for every two or three men. A campaigning army of 100,000 men therefore required 2,500 supply wagons and at least 35,000 animals, and consumed 600 tons of supplies each day. Although in a few noted cases—Grant in the Vicksburg campaign, Sherman in his march through Georgia and the Carolinas—Union armies cut loose from their bases and lived off the country, such campaigns were the exception.

Meigs furnished these requirements in a style that made him the unsung hero of northern victory. He oversaw the spending of $1.5 billion, almost half of the direct cost of the Union war effort. He compelled field armies to abandon the large, heavy Sibley and Adams tents in favor of portable shelter tents known to Yankee soldiers as "dog tents"—and to their descendants as pup tents. The Quartermaster Bureau furnished clothing manufacturers with a series of graduated standard measurements for uniforms. This introduced a concept of "sizes" that was applied to men's civilian clothing after the war. The army's voracious demand for shoes prompted the widespread introduction of the new Blake-McKay machine for sewing uppers to soles. In these and many other ways, Meigs and his bureau left a permanent mark on American society.

IV

In the North as in the South, volunteer regiments retained close ties to their states. Companies and even whole regiments often consisted of recruits from a single township, city, or county. Companies from neighboring towns combined to form a regiment, which received a numerical designation in chronological order of organization: the 15th Massachusetts Infantry, the 2nd Pennsylvania Cavalry, the 4th Volunteer Battery of Ohio Artillery, and so on. Ethnic affinity also formed the basis of some companies and regiments: the 69th New York was one of many Irish regiments; the men of the 79th New York were Highland Scots complete with kilted dress uniforms; numerous regiments contained mostly men of German extraction. Sometimes brothers, cousins, or fathers and sons belonged to the same company or regiment. Localities and ethnic groups retained a strong sense of identity with "their" regiments. This helped to boost morale on both the home and fighting fronts, but it could mean sudden calamity for family or neighborhood if a regiment suffered 50 percent or more casualties in a single battle, as many did.

The 9th Massachusetts Infantry was composed mainly of Irish-Americans from Boston and vicinity. It became one of the best regiments in the Army of the Potomac, but at great cost. Nearly half of its men were killed or wounded in the war. This photograph was taken on a Sunday morning in 1861 while the regiment was still in its training camp near Washington. The priest standing near the cross in front of the tent is preparing to say mass to the regiment's officers in dress uniform.

The normal complement of a regiment in both the Union and Confederate armies was a thousand men formed in ten companies. Within a few months, however, deaths and discharges because of sickness significantly reduced this number. Medical examinations of recruits were often superficial. A subsequent investigation of Union enlistment procedures in 1861 estimated that 25 percent of the recruits should have been rejected for medical reasons. Many of these men soon had to be invalided out of the army. Within a year of its organization a typical regiment was reduced to half or less of its original number by sickness, battle casualties, and desertions. Instead of recruiting old regiments up to strength, states preferred to organize new ones with new opportunities for patronage in the form of officers' commissions and pride in the number of regiments sent by the state. Of 421,000 new three-year volunteers entering the Union army in 1862, only 50,000 joined existing

This painting depicts the castle-like barracks of Virginia Military Institute. On February 22, 1861, after the formation of the Confederacy but while Virginia was still in the Union, the cadets made clear their allegiance: instead of the stars and stripes, one of the flagpoles flew a hand-lettered banner proclaiming, "Hurrah for South Carolina."

regiments. Professional soldiers criticized this practice as inefficient and wasteful. It kept regiments far below strength and prevented the leavening of raw recruits by seasoned veterans. In 1862 and 1863, many old regiments went into combat with only two or three hundred men while new regiments suffered unnecessary casualties because of inexperience.

On both sides there were conflicts between the discipline of military professionalism and the independent spirit of volunteers, with their concomitant belief that citizen soldiers ought to have a say about who led them into battle. This admirably democratic idea was a disaster in war, one compounded by political appointments of officers, many of them inexperienced or incapable or both. This was less of a problem for the Confederacy because its leadership core was made up of the 313 trained officers who had resigned from the Union army as well as the products of military colleges like Virginia Military Institute. One-third of the field officers of Virginia regiments in 1861 were V.M.I. alumni. Of the 1,902 men who had ever attended V.M.I., 1,781 fought for the South. When Confederate regiments elected officers, they usually chose men with some military training. Most northern officers from civilian life had to learn their craft by experience, with its cost in defeat and casualties.

✻ ✻ ✻ ✻ ✻

On July 22, the day after the defeat at Bull Run, when officers panicked and left their men to fend for themselves, the Union Congress authorized the creation of military boards to examine officers and remove those found to be unqualified. Over the next few months hundreds of officers were discharged or resigned voluntarily rather than face an examining board. This did not end the practice of electing officers, nor of their appointment by governors for political reasons, but it went partway toward establishing minimum standards of competence for those appointed. As the war lengthened, promotion to officer's rank on the basis of merit became increasingly the rule in veteran regiments. By 1863 the Union army had pretty well ended the practice of electing officers.

This practice persisted longer in the Confederacy. Nor did the South establish examining boards for officers until October 1862. Yet Confederate officers, at least in the Virginia theater, probably did a better job than their Union counterparts during the first year or two of the war. Two factors help to explain this. First, Union General in Chief Winfield Scott decided to keep the small regular army together in 1861. These officers and enlisted men, with the military experience so vital to training raw recruits, would not be dispersed among the volunteer army. In contrast, the Confederate forces had a much larger core of experienced officers well placed in the initial phases of the war.

Political criteria continued to play a role in the appointment of generals as well as lesser officers. In both North and South the president commissioned generals, subject to Senate confirmation. Lincoln and Davis found it necessary to consider factors of party, faction, and state as carefully in appointing generals as in naming cabinet officers or postmasters. Many politicians coveted a brigadier's star for themselves or their friends. Lincoln was particularly concerned to nurture Democratic support for the war, so he commissioned a large number of prominent Democrats as generals—among them Benjamin F. Butler, Daniel E. Sickles, John A. McClernand, and John A. Logan. To augment the loyalty of the North's large foreign-born population, Lincoln also rewarded ethnic leaders with generalships—Carl Schurz, Franz Sigel, Thomas Meagher, and numerous others. Davis had to satisfy the aspirations for military glory of powerful state politicians; hence he named such men as Robert A. Toombs of Georgia and John B. Floyd and Henry A. Wise of Virginia as generals.

These appointments made political sense but sometimes produced military calamity. "It seems but little better than murder to give important commands to such men as Banks, Butler, McClernand, Sigel, and Lew Wallace," wrote the West Point professional Henry W. Halleck, "yet it seems impossible to prevent it." "Political general" became almost a synonym for incompetency, especially in the North. But this was often unfair. Some men appointed for political reasons became first-class Union corps commanders—Frank Blair and John Logan, for example. West Pointers Ulysses S. Grant and William T. Sherman received their initial commissions through the political influence of Congressman Elihu Washburne of Illinois and Senator John Sherman (William's brother) of Ohio. And in any case, West Point professionals held most of the top commands in both North and South—and some of them made a worse showing than the political generals. Generals appointed from civilian life sometimes complained bitterly that the "West Point clique" ran the armies as closed corporations, controlling promotions and reserving the best commands for themselves.

The appointment of political generals, like the election of company officers, was an essential part of the process by which a highly politicized society mobilized for war. Democracy often characterized the state of discipline in Civil War armies as well. As late as 1864 the inspector general of the Army of Northern Virginia complained of "the difficulty of having orders properly and promptly executed. There is not that spirit of respect for and obedience to general orders which should pervade a military organization." Just because their neighbors from down the road back home now wore shoulder straps, Johnny Reb and Billy Yank could see no reason why their orders should be obeyed unless the orders seemed reasonable. "We have tite Rools over us, the order was Red out in dress parade the other day that we all have to pull off our hats when we go to the coln or genrel," wrote a Georgia private. "You know that is one thing I wont do. I would rather see him in hell before I will pull off my hat to any man and tha Jest as well shoot me at the start." About the same time a Massachessetts private wrote that "drill & saluting officers & guard duty is played out."

Many officers did little to inspire respect. Some had a penchant for drinking and carousing—which of course set a fine example for their men. Such officers were in the minority, however, and over time a number of them were weeded out by resignation or by examining boards. The best officers from civilian life took seriously their new profession. Many of them burned the midnight oil studying manuals on drill and tactics. They avoided giving petty or unreasonable orders and compelled obedience to reasonable ones by dint of personality and intellect rather than by threats. They led by example, not prescript. And in combat they led from the front, not the rear. In both armies the proportion of officers killed in action was about 15 percent higher than the proportion of enlisted men killed. Generals suffered the highest combat casualties; their chances of being killed in battle were 50 percent greater than the privates'.

Civil War regiments learned on the battlefield to fight, not in the training camp. In keeping with the initial lack of professionalism, the training of recruits was superficial. It consisted mainly of the manual of arms (but little target practice), company and regimental drill in basic maneuvers, and sometimes brigade

Raw recruits learning the basics of soldiering in front of the east side of the unfinished U.S. Capitol in May 1861. At least this company had been issued muskets, which are stacked at the left while the men learn the fundamentals of changing from column into line, facing left, right, front, and rear, and other maneuvers.

drill and skirmishing tactics. Rarely did soldiers engage in division drill or mock combat. Indeed, brigades were not combined into divisions until July 1861 or later, nor divisions into corps until the spring and summer of 1862. Regiments sometimes went into combat only three weeks after they had been organized, with predictable results. General Helmuth von Moltke, chief of the Prussian general staff, denied having said that the American armies of 1861 were nothing but armed mobs chasing each other around the countryside—but whether he said it or not, he and many other European professionals had reason to believe it. By 1862 or 1863, however, the school of experience had made rebel and Yankee veterans into tough, combat-wise soldiers whose powers of endurance and willingness to absorb punishment astonished many Europeans who had considered Americans all bluster and no grit. A British observer who visited the Antietam battlefield ten days after the fighting wrote that "in about seven or eight acres of wood there is not a tree which is not full of bullets and bits of shell. It is impossible to understand how anyone could live in such a fire as there must have been here."

V

Amateurism and confusion characterized the development of strategies as well as the mobilization of armies. Most officers had learned little of strategic theory. The curriculum at West Point slighted strategic studies in favor of engineering, mathematics, fortification, army administration, and a smattering of tactics. The assignment of most officers to garrison and Indian-fighting duty on the frontier did little to encourage the study of strategy. Few if any Civil War generals had read Karl von Clausewitz, the foremost nineteenth-century writer on the art of war. A number of officers had read the writings of Antoine Henry Jomini, a Swiss-born member of Napoleon's staff who became the foremost interpreter of the great Corsican's campaigns. All West Point graduates had absorbed Jominian principles from the courses of Dennis Hart Mahan, who taught at the military academy for nearly half a century. Henry W. Halleck's *Elements of Military Art and Science* (1846), essentially a translation of Jomini, was used as a textbook at West Point. But Jomini's influence on Civil War strategy should not be exaggerated, as some historians have done. Many Jominian "principles" were common-sense ideas hardly original with Jomini: concentrate the mass of your own force against fractions of the enemy's; menace the enemy's communications while protecting your own; attack the enemy's weak point with your own strength; and so on. There is little evidence that Jomini's writings influenced Civil War strategy in a direct or tangible way; the most successful strategist of the war, Grant, confessed to having never read Jomini.

The trial and error of experience played a larger role than theory in shaping Civil War strategy. The experience of the Mexican War governed the thinking of most officers in 1861. But that easy victory against a weak foe in an era of smoothbore muskets taught some wrong lessons to Civil War commanders who faced a determined enemy armed (after 1861) largely with rifled muskets. The experience necessary to fight the Civil War had to be gained in the Civil War itself. As generals and civilian leaders learned from their mistakes, as war aims changed from limited to total war, as political demands and civilian morale fluctuated, military strategy evolved and adjusted. The Civil War was preeminently a *political* war, a war of peoples rather than of professional armies. Therefore political leadership and public opinion weighed heavily in the formation of strategy.

In 1861 many Americans had a romantic, glamorous idea of war. "I am absent in a glorious cause," wrote a southern soldier to his homefolk in June 1861, "and glory in being in that cause." Many Confederate recruits echoed the Mississippian who said he had joined up "to fight the Yankies—all fun and frolic." A New York volunteer wrote home soon after enlisting that "I and the rest of the boys are in fine spirits . . . feeling like larks." Regiments departing for the front paraded before cheering, flag-waving crowds, with bands playing martial airs and visions of glory dancing in their heads. Many people on both sides believed that the war would be short—one or two battles and the cowardly Yankees or slovenly rebels would give up.

In 1861 the photographer arranged these men of the 1st Massachusetts Light Artillery in various poses illustrating how soldiers spent their spare time. One man tickles another with a feather. The other four are playing poker; the soldier on the right has a newspaper draped over his arm, perhaps for reading if he dropped out of a hand. Even a small bird cooperated by standing on the sponge used to extinguish sparks in the cannon's barrel after each shot.

With such confidence in quick success, thoughts of strategy seemed superfluous. Responsible leaders on both sides did not share the popular faith in a short war. Yet even they could not foresee the kind of conflict this war would become—a total war, requiring total mobilization of men and resources, destroying these men and resources on a massive scale, and ending only with unconditional surrender. In the spring of 1861 most northern leaders thought in terms of a limited war. Their purpose was not to conquer the South but to suppress insurrection and win back the latent loyalty of the southern people. The faith in southern unionism lingered long.

A war for limited goals required a strategy of limited means. General in Chief Winfield Scott's preference was not to invade and conquer the South, something he thought would require a large and ruinously expensive army of occupation, one possibly deployed for many years, but to "envelop" it with a blockade by sea and a fleet of gunboats supported by soldiers along the Mississippi. Thus sealed off from the world, the rebels would suffocate and the government "could bring them to terms with less bloodshed than by any other plan."

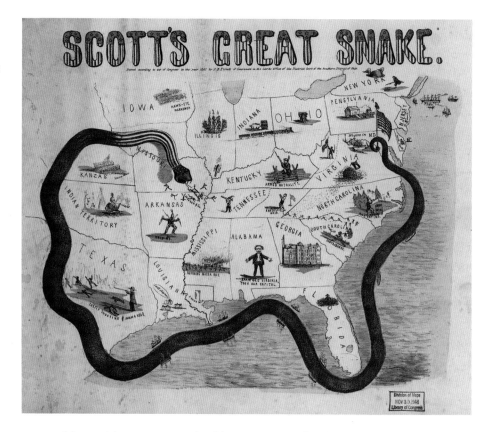

General Winfield Scott's "Anaconda Plan" gave cartoonists a field day. This cartoon was more sympathetic than most. It implies that Scott's snake will indeed squeeze the rebellion to death in short order. The cartoonist used the opportunity to lampoon some of the southern states: for example, a comic figure in Alabama exclaims, "Dam old Virginia, Took our Capital."

But this would require considerable time—time for the navy to acquire enough ships to make the blockade effective, time to build the gunboats and train the men for the expedition down the Mississippi. Scott recognized that carrying out such a plan would be made impossible by "the impatience of our patriotic and loyal Union friends. They will urge instant and vigorous action, regardless, I fear, of the consequences." Indeed they did. Northern public opinion demanded an invasion to "crush" the rebel army covering Manassas, a rail junction in northern Virginia linking the main lines to the Shenandoah Valley and the deep South. Newspapers scorned Scott's strategy as the "Anaconda Plan." The Confederate government having accepted Virginia's invitation to make Richmond its capital, the southern Congress scheduled its next session to begin there on July 20. Thereupon Horace Greeley's *New York Tribune* blazoned forth with a standing headline:

FORWARD TO RICHMOND! FORWARD TO RICHMOND!

The Rebel Congress Must Not be
Allowed to Meet There on the
20th of July

BY THAT DATE THE PLACE MUST BE HELD
BY THE NATIONAL ARMY

Other newspapers picked up the cry of "On to Richmond." Some hinted that Scott's Anaconda Plan signified a traitorous reluctance to invade his native state. Many northerners could not understand why a general who with fewer than 11,000 men had invaded a distant country of eight million people, marched 175 miles, defeated larger enemy armies, and captured their capital would shy away from invading Virginia and fighting the enemy twenty-five miles from the United States capital. The stunning achievements of an offensive strategy in Mexico tended to make both Union and Confederate commanders offensive-minded in the early phases of the Civil War. The success of Lyon in Missouri and of McClellan in western Virginia seemed to confirm the value of striking first and striking fast.

Scott remained unconvinced. He considered the ninety-day regiments raw and useless; the three-year regiments would need several months' training before they were ready for a campaign. But Scott was out of step with the political imperatives of 1861. Public pressure made it almost impossible for the government to delay military action on the main Virginia front. Scott's recommended blockade of southern seaports had begun, and his proposed move down the Mississippi became part of Union strategy in 1862. But events ultimately demonstrated that the North could win the war only by destroying the South's armies in the field. In that respect the popular clamor for "smashing" the rebels was based on sound if oversanguine instinct. Lincoln thought that an attack on the enemy at Manassas was worth a try. Such an attack came

GENERAL SCOTT.

THE HERCULES OF THE UNION,
SLAYING THE GREAT DRAGON OF SECESSION.

This cartoon departed from the usual depiction of General in Chief Winfield Scott. Instead of the author of the Anaconda Plan, he is a heroic dragon slayer wielding a club labeled "Liberty and Union" to smash the hydra-headed serpent of secession. Each of the seven heads, labeled in the neck with such crimes as Blasphemy, Perjury, Treason, etc., represents a leading Confederate official. The second and third heads from the top are Vice President Alexander Stephens and President Jefferson Davis.

within his conception of limited war aims. If successful it might discredit the secessionists; it might lead to the capture of Richmond; but it would not destroy the social and economic system of the South; it would not scorch southern earth.

By July 1861 about 35,000 Union troops had gathered in the Washington area. Their commander was General Irvin McDowell, a former officer on Scott's staff with no previous experience in field command. A teetotaler who compensated by consuming huge amounts of food, McDowell did not lack intelligence or energy— but he turned out to be a hard-luck general for whom nothing went right. In response to a directive from Lincoln, McDowell drew up a plan for a flank attack on the 20,000 Confederates defending Manassas Junction. An essential part of the plan required the 15,000 Federals near Harper's Ferry under the command of Robert Patterson, a sixty-nine-year-old veteran of the War of 1812, to prevent the 11,000 Confederates confronting him from reinforcing Manassas.

McDowell's plan was a good one—for veteran troops with experienced officers. But McDowell lacked both. At a White House strategy conference on June 29, he pleaded for postponement of the offensive until he could train the new three-year men. Scott once again urged his Anaconda Plan. But Quartermaster General Meigs, when asked for his opinion, said that the only way to win was to beat the enemy on the field of battle and do so expeditiously. "To make the fight in Virginia was cheaper and better as the case now stood." Lincoln agreed. As for the rawness of McDowell's troops, Lincoln seemed to have read the mind of a rebel officer in Virginia who reported his men to be so deficient in "discipline and instruction" that it would be "difficult to use them in the field. . . . I would not give one company of regulars for the whole regiment." The president ordered McDowell to begin his offensive. "You are green, it is true," he said, "but they are green, also; you are all green alike."

*   *   *   *   *

The southern commander at Manassas was Pierre G. T. Beauregard, the dapper, voluble hero of Fort Sumter, Napoleonic in manner and aspiration. Heading the rebel forces in the Shenandoah Valley was Joseph E. Johnston, a small, impeccably attired, ambitious but cautious man with a piercing gaze and an outsized sense of dignity. In their contrasting offensive- and defensive-mindedness, Beauregard and Johnston represented the polarities of southern strategic thinking. The basic war aim of the Confederacy, like that of the United States in the Revolution, was to defend a new nation from conquest. Confederates looked for inspiration to the heroes of 1776, who had triumphed over greater odds than southerners faced in 1861. The South could "win" the war by not losing; the North could win only by winning. The large territory of the Confederacy—750,000 square miles, as large as Russia west of Moscow, twice the size of the thirteen original United States—would make Lincoln's task as difficult as Napoleon's in 1812 or George III's in 1776. Early in the war Jefferson Davis seems to have envisaged a strategy like that of George Washington in the Revolution. Washington traded space for time; he retreated when necessary in the face of a stronger enemy; he counterattacked against isolated British outposts or detachments when such an attack promised success; above all, he tried to avoid full-scale battles that would have risked annihilation of his army and defeat of his cause. This has been called a strategy of attrition—a strategy of winning by not losing, of wearing out a better-equipped foe and compelling him to give up by prolonging the war and making it too costly.

But two main factors prevented Davis from carrying out such a strategy except in a limited, sporadic fashion. Both factors stemmed from political as well as military realities. The first was a demand by governors, congressmen, and the public for troops to defend every portion of the Confederacy from penetration by "Lincoln's abolition hordes." Thus in 1861 small armies were dispersed around the Confederate perimeter along the Arkansas-Missouri border, at several points on the Gulf and Atlantic coasts, along the Tennessee-Kentucky border, and in the Shenandoah Valley and western Virginia as well as at Manassas. Historians have criticized this "cordon defense" for dispersing manpower so thinly that Union forces were certain to break through somewhere, as they did at several points in 1862.

The second factor inhibiting a Washingtonian strategy of

A classmate of Robert E. Lee in the West Point class of 1829, Joseph E. Johnston had risen to the staff rank of brigadier general and the post of quartermaster general of the U.S. army in 1860. A Virginian like Lee, he also followed Lee's example and resigned from the U.S. army on April 22, 1861, to cast his lot with the Confederacy. There were times during the next four years when Jefferson Davis may have secretly wished that Johnston had stayed in the old army.

attrition was the temperament of the southern people. Believing that they could whip any number of Yankees, many southerners scorned the notion of "sitting down and waiting" for the Federals to attack. The southern press clamored for an advance against Washington in the same tone that northern newspapers cried "On to Richmond." Beauregard devised several bold plans for an offensive against McDowell. But the question became moot when Beauregard learned of McDowell's offensive against him.

The Confederates eventually synthesized these various strands of strategic theory and political reality into what Davis called an "offensive-defensive" strategy. This consisted of defending the Confederate homeland by using interior lines of communication (a Jominian but also common-sense concept) to concentrate dispersed forces against an invading army and, if opportunity offered, to go over to the offensive, even to the extent of invading the North. No one ever defined this strategy in a systematic, comprehensive fashion. Rather, it emerged from a series of major campaigns in the Virginia-Maryland and Tennessee-Kentucky theaters during 1862 and culminated at Gettysburg in 1863. It almost emerged, in embryonic form, from the first battle of Manassas (Bull Run) in July 1861, a small battle by later Civil War standards but one that would have important psychological consequences in both the North and the South.

CHAPTER ELEVEN

✯ ✯ ✯ ✯ ✯

Farewell
to the Ninety Days' War

I

General McDowell had good reason for his reluctance to march green troops "On to Richmond" in July 1861. Circumstances beyond his control plagued the campaign from its outset. Scheduled to begin July 8, the movement of McDowell's 30,000 men was delayed by shortages of supply wagons and by the necessity to organize late-arriving regiments into brigades and divisions. When the army finally began to move out on July 16, the terms of several ninety-day men were about to expire. Indeed, an infantry regiment and artillery battery went home on the eve of the ensuing battle. The longer enlistments of Confederate soldiers gave them a psychological advantage, for the recruit whose time was almost up seemed less motivated to fight.

Out in the Shenandoah Valley, General Robert Patterson likewise feared that the ninety-day recruits in his army of 15,000 would not stand fast in a real battle against Joseph E. Johnston's 11,000 Confederates. This was one of several reasons why Patterson failed in his task of pinning down Johnston in the Valley while McDowell attacked Beauregard at Manassas. Patterson was also confused by orders from Washington that left it unclear whether he should attack or merely maneuver against Johnston. Wrongly believing himself outnumbered by the enemy, Patterson chose the safer course of maneuver. Unfortunately, he maneuvered himself right out of the campaign. On July 18 and 19 Johnston's army gave him the slip, marched from Winchester to the railroad at Piedmont, and entrained for Manassas. With their arrival the Confederate forces at Manassas became equal in size to McDowell's invading army.

Beauregard had been forewarned of McDowell's advance by his espionage network in Washington, headed by Rose O'Neal Greenhow, a friend of several northern politicians but also a Confederate spy. In the best romantic tradition, coded messages carried by southern belles riding fast steeds brought word of Union plans. Even with this advance knowledge, Johnston could not have reinforced Beauregard in time if McDowell's army had moved faster than a snail's pace. At this stage of the

Opposite page: This detail of a painting of the Army of the Potomac by James Hope shows the mighty instrument created by General George B. McClellan, riding at the head of his staff.

A forty-six-year-old widow who lived in Washington, Maryland-born Rose O'Neal Greenhow cultivated her contacts with northern politicians to pass along military information to General Beauregard. Placed under house arrest in August 1861, she continued her spying activities, which landed her in Old Capitol Prison in January 1862. She was photographed there with her daughter before she was deported to the Confederacy in June 1862. In October 1864 a blockade runner on which she was returning from England was driven aground by Union warships off the North Carolina coast. She tried to wade ashore carrying heavy gold bars she was smuggling into the Confederacy. A wave knocked her over, and she drowned when the weight of the gold held her underwater.

war, soldiers without marching experience carrying fifty pounds of equipment took three days to cover a distance that road-wise veterans later slogged in one day. When the Yankees finally reached Centreville, three miles from the Confederate defenses behind Bull Run, they had eaten all their food and had to delay another day while more rations were brought up. Lacking trained cavalry, McDowell personally scouted enemy lines and discovered that rugged terrain and strong defenses on the Confederate right ruled out his original plan to turn that flank. Another day went by as he planned an attack on the left flank and scouted the roads in that direction. While this was going on, the overworked railroad was bringing Johnston's troops to Manassas. By the time McDowell launched his assault on the morning of July 21, three Valley brigades had arrived and the fourth was on its way.

Despite all the delays, McDowell's attack came within an ace of success. Beauregard had distributed his troops along the south bank of Bull Run, a sluggish, tree-choked river a few miles north of Manassas. Confederate regiments guarded the railroad bridge on the right, the Warrenton turnpike bridge six miles upstream on the left, and a half-dozen fords between the bridges. Expecting McDowell to attack toward the railroad, Beauregard placed nine of his ten and one-half brigades on that flank, from which he planned to anticipate the Yankees by launching his own surprise assault on the morning of July 21. Instead, the roar of artillery and crack of musketry several miles upstream shortly after sunrise indicated that McDowell had sprung his surprise first.

The Union attacking column, 10,000 strong, had roused itself at 2:00 A.M. and stumbled through the underbrush and ruts of a cart track on a six-mile flanking march while other regiments made a feint at the turnpike bridge. The flanking column forded Bull Run two miles upriver from the bridge, where no Confederates expected them. The commander of rebel forces at the bridge was Colonel Nathan "Shanks" Evans (so called because of his spindly legs), a hard-bitten, hard-drinking South Carolinian. Recognizing the Union shelling of the bridge as a feint and seeing the dust cloud from the flanking column to his left, Evans took most of his troops to meet the first Yankee brigade pouring across the fields. Evans slowed the Union attack long enough for two brigades of Confederate reinforcements to come up.

For two hours 4,500 rebels gave ground grudgingly to 10,000 Yankees north of the turnpike. Never before under fire, the men on both sides fought surprisingly well. But lack of experience prevented northern officers from coordinating simultaneous assaults by different regiments. Nevertheless, the weight of numbers finally pushed the Confederates across the turnpike and up the slopes of a commanding hill. Several southern regiments broke and fled to the rear; McDowell appeared to be on the verge of a smashing success. A multitude of northern reporters, congressmen, and other civilians had driven out from Washington to watch the battle. They could see little but smoke from their vantage point two miles from the fighting. But

they cheered reports of Union victory, while telegrams to Washington raised high hopes in the White House.

The reports were premature. Johnston and Beauregard had sent additional reinforcements to the Confederate left and had arrived personally on the fighting front, where they helped rally broken Confederate units. For several hours during the afternoon, fierce but uncoordinated attacks and counterattacks surged back and forth across Henry House Hill (named for the home of Judith Henry, a bedridden widow who insisted on remaining in her house and was killed by a shell). Men whom the war would make famous were in the thick of the fighting: on the Union side Ambrose E. Burnside, William Tecumseh Sherman, and Oliver O. Howard, each of whom commanded a brigade and would command an army before the war was over; on the Confederate side Beauregard and Johnston, the former in field command and the latter in overall command; along with James E. B. ("Jeb") Stuart, the dashing, romantic, bearded, plumed, and deadly efficient colonel of a cavalry regiment that broke one Union infantry attack with a headlong charge; Wade Hampton, whose South Carolina legion suffered heavy casualties; and Thomas J. Jackson, a former profes-

THE DISPOSITION OF FORCES
JULY 16, 1861

■ Union concentrations

■ Confed. concentrations

0   MILES   20

MARTINSBURG

FREDERICK

WEST VIRGINIA (1863)

HARPERS FERRY

MARYLAND

PATTERSON

APPALACHIAN MOUNTAINS

SHENANDOAH VALLEY

WINCHESTER

LEESBURG

JOHNSTON

POTOMAC RIVER

SHENANDOAH RIVER

STRASBURG

BLUE RIDGE MOUNTAINS

McDOWELL

WASHINGTON

FRONT ROYAL

MANASSAS GAP R.R.

BULL RUN

FAIRFAX CT. HO.

SUDLEY SPRING

ALEXANDRIA

GAINESVILLE

GROVETON

CENTREVILLE

MANASSAS JCT.

WARRENTON

ORANGE & ALEXANDRIA R.R.

BEAUREGARD

VIRGINIA

POTOMAC RIVER

CULPEPER CT. HO.

FREDERICKSBURG

ORANGE CT. HO.

THE BATTLE OF BULL RUN (MANASSAS)
JULY 21, 1861

← Confed. movements   → Union movements

← Confed. retreat   → Union retreat

■ Confed. concentrations

0   MILE   1

SUDLEY SPRINGS

CENTREVILLE

TO WASHINGTON 20 MI.

CATHARPIN RUN

McDOWELL

STONE BRIDGE

UNFINISHED R.R.

GROVETON

BEAUREGARD

BULL RUN

HENRY HOUSE HILL

JOHNSTON

WARRENTON TURNPIKE

MANASSAS GAP R.R.

ORANGE & ALEXANDRIA R.R.

UNION MILLS

MANASSAS JUNCTION

sor at V.M.I. now commanding a brigade of Virginians from the Shenandoah Valley. Humorless, secretive, eccentric, a stern disciplinarian without tolerance for human weaknesses, a devout Presbyterian who ascribed Confederate successes to the Lord and likened Yankees to the devil, Jackson became one of the war's best generals, a legend in his own time.

The legend began there on Henry House Hill. As the Confederate regiments that had fought in the morning retreated across the hill at noon, Jackson brought his fresh troops into line just behind the crest. General Barnard Bee of South Carolina, trying to rally his broken brigade, pointed to Jackson's men and shouted something like: "There is Jackson standing like a stone wall! Rally behind the Virginians!" But at least one observer placed a different construction on Bee's remark, claiming that the South Carolinian gestured angrily at Jackson's troops standing immobile behind the crest, and said: "Look at Jackson standing there like a damned stone wall!" Whatever Bee said—he could not settle the question by his own testimony, for a bullet killed him soon afterward—Jackson's brigade stopped the Union assault and suffered more casualties than any other southern brigade this day. Ever after, Jackson was known as "Stonewall," and his men who had stood fast at Manassas became the Stonewall Brigade.

Much confusion of uniforms occurred during the battle. On numerous occasions regiments withheld their fire for fear of hitting friends, or fired on friends by mistake. The same problem arose with the national flags carried by each regiment. With eleven stars on a blue field set in the corner of a flag with two red and one white horizontal bars, the Confederate "stars and bars" could be mistaken for the stars and stripes in the smoke and haze of battle. Afterwards Beauregard designed a new battle flag, with white stars embedded in a blue St. Andrew's Cross on a red field, which became the familiar banner of the Confederacy.

One mixup in uniforms affected the outcome of the battle. At the height of the fighting for Henry House Hill, two Union artillery batteries were blasting gaps in the Confederate line. Suddenly a blue-clad regiment emerged from the woods seventy yards to the right of two of the guns. Thinking the regiment might be its requested infantry support, the artillery withheld fire for fatal minutes while the regiment, which turned out to be the 33rd Virginia of Jackson's brigade, leveled mus-

The flag below left was the first Confederate national flag designated by the Confederate Congress in 1861. This flag was carried by Confederate regiments at the first battle of Manassas and other early battles, but its similarity in design and color to the American flag (which had thirteen alternating red and white stripes, as today, compared with the red/white/red bars of the Confederate flag) caused confusion on the battlefield. General Beauregard designed a battle flag to be carried instead of the national flag by Confederate regiments—it is this battle flag with its white stars on a blue St. Andrew's Cross set against a red background that has come down to us as the familiar symbol of the Confederacy. Below right is the American flag that flew over Fort Sumter in April 1861. It was lowered on April 14 and replaced by a Confederate flag with its seven stars for the seven states then constituting the Confederacy.

This lithograph dating from 1889 depicts the climax of the battle when the Confederate counterattack in late afternoon drove back the Union troops, some of whom are fleeing across the bridge. Note the colorful Zouave uniforms of many Union soldiers and the havelocks worn by those in the lower left corner. Both accoutrements would disappear later in the war.

kets and fired. The guns were wiped out, and the Union attack lost cohesion in that sector of the battlefield.

Indeed, by midafternoon the northern army lost what little cohesion it had everywhere, as regiments continued to fight in a disconnected manner, stragglers began melting to the rear, and McDowell failed to get two reserve brigades into the action. Johnston and Beauregard, by contrast, had brought up every unit within reach, including the last brigade from the Valley, just off the train and marching onto the field about 4:00 P.M. By that time the rebels had an equal number of men in the battle zone (about 18,000 were eventually engaged on each side) and a decisive superiority in fresh troops. Most of the Union regiments had been marching or fighting for the better part of fourteen hours with little food or water on a brutally hot, sultry day. Seeing Confederate reinforcements appear in front of them, some northern soldiers asked: "Where are *our* reserves?" At this moment, sensing his advantage, Beauregard ordered a counterattack all along the line. As Confederate units surged forward a strange, eerie scream rent the air. Soon to be known as the rebel yell, this unearthly wail struck fear into the hearts of the enemy, then and later. "There is nothing like it on this side of the infernal region," recalled a northern veteran after the war. "The peculiar corkscrew sensation that it sends down your backbone under these circumstances can never be told. You have to feel it."

Startled by this screaming counterattack, the discouraged and exhausted Yankee soldiers, their three-months term almost up, suddenly decided they had fought enough. They began to fall back, slowly and with scattered resistance at first, but with increasing panic as their officers lost control, men became separated from their companies, and the last shred of discipline disappeared. The retreat became a rout as men threw away guns, packs, and anything else that might slow them down in the wild scramble for the crossings of Bull Run. Some units of Sherman's brigade and several companies of regulars maintained their discipline and formed a rear guard that slowed the disorganized rebel pursuit.

Fleeing Union soldiers became entangled with panic-stricken civilians. Some congressmen tried in vain to stop wild-eyed soldiers, now miles from the battlefield, who had no intention of stopping short of the far side of the Potomac. "The further they ran, the more frightened they grew," stated one of the congressmen.

Back on the other side of Bull Run, jubilant rebels celebrated their victory and rounded up hundreds of Union prisoners. Jefferson Davis himself had turned up at the moment of victory having traveled by train and on horseback, only to encounter a swelling stream of wounded and stragglers who cried out, "Go back! We are whipped!" Though Davis knew that the rear areas of a battlefield always presented a scene of disorder and defeat no matter what was going on at the front, he rode on with a sinking heart. Was this to be the fate of his Confederacy? As he neared Johnston's headquarters, however, the sounds of battle rolled away to the north. Johnston came forward with the news of southern triumph. Elated, Davis urged vigorous pursuit of the beaten enemy. Although some Confederate units had gone a mile or two beyond Bull Run, Johnston and Beauregard believed that no full-scale pursuit was possible. In Johnston's words, "our army was more disorganized by victory than that of the United States by defeat."

When the magnitude of Confederate victory sank in during the following weeks, southern newspapers began to seek scapegoats for the failure to "follow up the victory and take Washington." But the prospect of "taking" Washington in July 1861 was an illusion, as Davis, Johnston, and Beauregard recognized at the time. McDowell formed a defensive line of unbloodied reserves at Centreville on the night of July 21. Early next morning a heavy rain began to turn the roads into soup. Confederate logistics were inadequate for a sustained advance even in good weather. The army depots at Manassas were almost bare of food. Despite a mood of panic in Washington, the rebels were not coming—and could not have come.

In July 1861 the controversy about failure to pursue lay in the future. The South erupted in joy over a victory that seemed to prove that one Southron could indeed lick any number of Yankees. It was easy to forget that the numbers engaged were equal, that Confederate troops had fought on the defensive for most of the battle (easier than attacking, especially for green troops), and that the Yankees had come close to winning. In any case the battle of Manassas (or Bull Run, as the North named it) was one of the most decisive tactical victories of the war. Although its strategic results came to seem barren to many in the South, the battle did postpone for eight months any further Union efforts to invade Virginia's heartland. And the price in casualties was small compared with later battles. About 400 Confederates were killed and 1,600 wounded, of whom some 225 would die of their wounds. The Union forces also lost about 625 killed and mortally wounded, 950 nonmortally wounded, and more than 1,200 captured.

Perhaps the most profound consequences of the battle were psychological. But

these consequences were full of paradox. The South's gleeful celebration generated a cockiness heedless of the Biblical injunction that pride goeth before a fall. Manassas was *"one of the decisive battles of the world,"* wrote political leader Thomas R. R. Cobb of Georgia. It *"has* secured our independence." Edmund Ruffin considered "this hard-fought battle virtually the close of the war." The *Mobile Register* predicted that the Union army would "never again advance beyond cannon shot of Washington." The *Richmond Whig* went even further: "The breakdown of the Yankee race, their unfitness for empire, forces dominion on the South. We are compelled to take the sceptre of power. We must adapt ourselves to our new destiny."

Immediately after the battle the shame and despair of many northerners almost caused them to agree with these southern assessments. Horace Greeley, whose *New York Tribune* had done so much to prod the government into premature action, endured a week of self-reproachful, sleepless nights before writing a despondent letter to Lincoln: "On every brow sits sullen, scorching, black despair. . . . If it is best for the country and for mankind that we make peace with the rebels, and on their own terms, do not shrink even from that."

Yet the deep, long-lasting impact of Bull Run on the North was not defeatism, but renewed determination. In a sermon on a text from Proverbs—"adversity kills only where there is a weakness to be killed"—one of the North's leading clergymen expressed this new mood of grim resolution. It was echoed by a soldier in the ranks:

More than a thousand Union soldiers were captured at Bull Run. These prisoners from the 11th New York were confined in a makeshift prison at Castle Pinckney in Charleston harbor. After several months they were exchanged to fight again.

"I shall see the thing played out, or die in the attempt." Even as Greeley was writing despairingly to Lincoln, an editorial in the *Tribune* by another hand maintained that "it is not characteristic of Americans to sit down despondently after a defeat. . . . Reverses, though stunning at first, by their recoil stimulate and quicken to unwonted exertion. . . . Let us go to work, then, with a will."

Lincoln agreed with this editorial rather than with Greeley's letter. Though shaken by the news of Bull Run, the president and General Scott did not panic. They worked through the night to salvage some order from the chaos of defeat." The day after Bull Run, Lincoln signed a bill for the enlistment of 500,000 three-year men. Three days later he signed a second bill authorizing another 500,000. Volunteers thronged recruiting offices during the next few weeks; offers of new regiments poured in from northern governors; and soon the regiments themselves began to crowd into the training camps surrounding Washington, where they found a dynamic, magnetic general to command them: George B. McClellan.

At 2:00 A.M. on the morning after Bull Run, a telegram summoned McClellan to take command of this new army of three-year volunteers, soon to be named the Army of the Potomac. When McClellan arrived in Washington on July 26 he found "no army to command—only a mere collection of regiments cowering on the banks of the Potomac, some perfectly raw, others dispirited by the recent defeat." Whatever self-serving overtones one might detect in these words, McClellan did accomplish all that was expected of him in his first two months of command. His military police rounded up stragglers and combed their officers out of Washington barrooms. His examining boards weeded incompetent officers out of the army. McClellan was a

The 96th Pennsylvania Infantry, one of the three-year regiments organized after the defeat at Bull Run, was photographed in its camp near Washington in the late fall of 1861 before disease, detachments, and casualties began to whittle away its original 1,000-man enrollment. McClellan drilled these and other new regiments for months before they ever fired a shot in anger.

The wife of a former U.S. senator from South Carolina who became a military aide to Jefferson Davis, Mary Boykin Chesnut moved in high circles of power and society in the Confederacy. She kept a detailed diary, much of which was later lost or destroyed, but not before she used it to write a revised and polished diary after the war that sometimes benefited from hindsight. That rewritten diary is an important source for Confederate history.

superb organizer and administrator. He was a professional with regard to training. He turned recruits into soldiers. He instilled discipline and pride in his men, who repaid him with an admiration they felt toward no other general. McClellan forged the Army of the Potomac into a fighting machine second to none—this was his important contribution to ultimate Union victory—but he proved unable to run this machine at peak efficiency in the crisis of battle.

Not all southerners shared the post-Manassas conviction of Confederate invincibility. Mary Boykin Chesnut perceived that the victory "lulls us into a fool's paradise of conceit" while it "will wake every inch of [northern] manhood." A diary-keeping clerk in the Confederate War Department fumed a month after the battle: "We are resting on our oars, while the enemy is drilling and equipping 500,000 or 600,000 men." With the benefit of hindsight, participants on both sides agreed after the war that the one-sided southern triumph in the first big battle "proved the greatest misfortune that could have befallen the Confederacy." Such an interpretation has become orthodoxy in Civil War historiography.

This orthodoxy contains much truth, but perhaps not the whole truth. The confidence gained by the men who won at Manassas imbued them with an *esprit de corps* that was reinforced by more victories in the next two years. At the same time the Union defeat instilled a gnawing, half-acknowledged sense of martial inferiority among northern officers in the Virginia theater. Thus the battle of Manassas, and more importantly the collective southern and northern memories of it, became an important part of the psychology of war in the eastern theater. This psychology helps explain why McClellan, having created a powerful army, was reluctant to commit it to all-out battle. He always feared, deep down, that the enemy was more powerful than he. And the Confederates, armed with the morale of victory, enjoyed an edge that went far toward evening the material odds against them in Virginia. Hence the paradox of Bull Run: its legacy of confidence both hurt and helped the South; the humiliation and renewed determination both hurt and helped the North.

II

Two days after Bull Run, Lincoln penned a memorandum on future Union strategy. Efforts to make the blockade effective were to be pushed forward; Maryland was to be held "with a gentle[!], but firm, and certain hand"; Union troops in Virginia were to be reinforced, thoroughly trained, and prepared for a new invasion; the inept Patterson was to be replaced by a new commander of the army at Harper's Ferry (Nathaniel P. Banks); Union armies in the western theaters were to take the offensive, "giving rather special attention to Missouri."

Lincoln had high expectations of his newly appointed commander of the Western Department (mainly Missouri), John C. Frémont, famed as the Pathfinder of the West. Frémont's eleven years' experience in the army's topographical corps gave him a military reputation unmatched by most other political generals. But the formidable difficulties of a Missouri command—a divided population, guerrilla warfare, impending Confederate invasions from Arkansas and Tennessee—quickly brought out the weaknesses in Frémont's character. He was showy rather than solid. His naiveté and his ambition to build quickly a large army and navy for a grand sweep down the Mississippi made him easy prey for contractors whose swollen profits produced a new crop of scandals. Frémont could have survived all this if he had produced victories. But instead, soon after he arrived in St. Louis on July 25, Union forces in Missouri suffered reverses that came as aftershocks to the earthquake at Bull Run.

Frémont's appointment brought Nathaniel Lyon under his command. After chasing Sterling Price's militia to the southwest corner of the state, Lyon's small army of 5,500 men occupied Springfield at the end of a precarious supply line nearly two hundred miles from St. Louis. Lyon faced a motley southern force composed of Price's 8,000 Missourians and 5,000 other Confederate troops under General Ben McCulloch, a rough-hewn frontiersman who had won his spurs as an Indian fighter, Mexican War officer, and Texas Ranger. Price was eager to redeem Missouri from the Yankee and "Dutch" troops under Lyon. McCulloch distrusted the reliability of Price's poorly armed Missourians but finally yielded, with great reluctance, to Price's entreaties for an offensive.

In the meantime, Lyon learned that Frémont could send him no reinforcements. All Union troops seemed to be needed elsewhere to cope with guerrillas and to counter a rebel incursion into southeast Missouri that threatened the Union base at Cairo, Illinois. Outnumbered by more than two to one, with the ninety-day enlistments of half his men about to expire, Lyon's only choice seemed to be retreat. But the fiery red-haired general could not bear to yield southwest Missouri without a fight. He decided to attack McCulloch and Price before they could attack him.

Disregarding the maxims of military textbooks (just as Robert E. Lee later did to win his greatest victories), Lyon divided his small army in the face of a larger enemy and sent a flanking column of 1,200 men under Franz Sigel on a night march around to the south of the Confederate camp along Wilson's Creek, ten miles south of Springfield. While Sigel came up on the Confederate rear, Lyon would attack from the front with the main Union force. The Federals carried out this difficult maneuver successfully, achieving surprise in a two-pronged attack at sunrise on August 10. But McCulloch and Price kept their poise and rallied their men for a stand-up, seesaw firefight at short range along the banks of Wilson's Creek and on the slopes of a nearby hill.

The battle was marked by two turning points that finally enabled the rebels to prevail. First, after initially driving back the Confederates on the southern flank, Sigel's attack came to a halt after another incident of mistaken identity. A Louisiana regiment clad in uniforms similar to the militia gray of Lyon's 1st Iowa approached close enough to Sigel's vanguard to pour in a murderous volley before the unionists recognized them as enemies. Sigel's attack disintegrated. The Louisianians and Arkansans in this part of the field then joined the Missourians fighting Lyon's main force, whom they now outnumbered by three to one. In the thick of the fighting, Lyon was twice wounded slightly and his horse was shot from under him before a bullet found his heart. This demoralized the unionists, who in addition had almost run out of ammunition. Slowly they pulled back,

This mural of the battle of Wilson's Creek was painted by N.C. Wyeth (father of the artist Andrew Wyeth) for the Missouri state capitol in Jefferson. Several Missouri regiments fought against each other in this small but vicious battle. The Union commander, Nathaniel Lyon, was the first northern general killed in battle in the war.

yielding the battlefield to the enemy and withdrawing to Springfield unpursued by the equally battered southerners.

Each side in this bloody battle suffered about 1,300 casualties, a considerably higher proportion of losses than at Bull Run. Although the Confederates' tactical victory at Wilson's Creek was much less decisive than at Manassas and its impact on public opinion outside Missouri was small, its strategic consequences at first seemed greater. The Union forces retreated all the way to Rolla, a hundred miles north of Springfield. Having gained confidence and prestige, Price marched northward to the Missouri River, gathering recruits on the way. With 18,000 troops he surrounded the 3,500-man garrison at Lexington, the largest city between St. Louis and Kansas City. Frémont scraped together a small force to reinforce the garrison, but it could not break through Price's ring. After three days of resistance, Lexington surrendered on September 20.

Price's reputation soared, while Frémont's plummeted. In two months of command he appeared to have lost half of Missouri. Confederate guerrillas stepped up their activities. And then a bold step that Frémont had taken to reverse the decline of his fortunes backfired and helped to seal his fate.

On August 30 Frémont issued a startling proclamation. As commanding general he took over "the administrative powers of the State," declared martial law, announced the death penalty for guerrillas caught behind Union lines, and confiscated the property and freed the slaves of all Confederate activists in Missouri. Two motives seem to have impelled this rash action: first, the felt need for draconian measures to suppress guerrillas and to intimidate rebel sympathizers; second, a desire to win favor with antislavery Republicans. Frémont accomplished his second goal, but at the cost of alienating Lincoln, who was engaged in sensitive efforts to keep Kentucky in the Union. The president wrote privately to Frémont ordering

Hemp for the making of rope was Missouri's chief cash crop. It also proved to have military value: Confederates besieging the Union garrison at Lexington used hemp bales for protection as they pushed forward to tighten the ring around enemy defenses, as shown in this illustration.

him to shoot no guerrillas "without first having my approbation," for if he were to execute captured guerrillas indiscriminately, "the Confederates would very certainly shoot our best men in their hands, in retaliation; and so, man for man, indefinitely." Second, Lincoln warned Frémont that freeing the slaves of rebels would "alarm our Southern Union friends, and turn them against us—perhaps ruin our rather fair prospect for Kentucky." The president asked (not ordered) Frémont to modify this part of his proclamation to conform with an act passed by Congress on August 6, which confiscated only the property (including slaves) used directly in the Confederate war effort.

A wiser man would have treated Lincoln's request as an order. But with a kind of proconsular arrogance that did not sit well with Lincoln, Frémont refused to modify his proclamation without a public order to do so. He also sent his high-spirited wife to Washington to persuade Lincoln of his error. Jessie Frémont offended the president by hinting at her husband's superior wisdom and greater prestige. She did Frémont's cause considerable harm. Even as she spoke, letters from border-state unionists were arriving at the White House expressing alarm and disaffection. "We could stand several defeats like that at Bulls Run, better than we can this proclamation if endorsed by the Administration," wrote Kentuckian Joshua Speed, Lincoln's oldest and best friend. "Do not allow us by the foolish action of a military popinjay to be driven from our present active loyalty." On the day after Jessie Benton Frémont's visit, Lincoln publicly ordered her husband to modify his emancipation edict.

After this, Frémont's days as commander in Missouri were numbered. Knowing that he could save himself only by a military victory, he pulled together an army of 38,000 men and set forth to destroy Price's militia. Since capturing Lexington, Price discovered that he

This cartoon provides a dramatic visual metaphor of Lincoln's reasons for rescinding Fremont's emancipation edict in Missouri. The shipwrecked president desperately tries to save himself and the Union. To take on the black man (emancipation), Lincoln fears, would sink them both.

lacked the manpower and logistical capacity to turn his raid into a successful occupation of captured territory. More than half of his troops melted away to harvest crops or to go off bushwhacking on their own. Price retreated again to the southwest corner of the state. Before the Federals caught up with him, Lincoln removed Frémont from command. Union forces would eventually defeat and scatter Price's army, but when that happened Frémont would be far away in western Virginia about to embark on another failure.

III

Lincoln's revocation of Frémont's emancipation order and his removal of the general from command stirred up a controversy. The issue was slavery. During the weeks after congressional passage in July of the Crittenden-Johnson resolutions disavowing antislavery war aims, many Republicans began to change their minds. Abolitionists who had earlier remained silent began to speak out. An important catalyst of this change was the Union defeat at Bull Run. "The result of the battle was a fearful blow," wrote an abolitionist, but "I think it may prove the means of rousing this stupid country to the extent & difficulty of the work it has to do." A rebellion sustained *by* slavery in defense *of* slavery could be suppressed only by moving *against* slavery. As Frederick Douglass expressed this conviction: "To fight against slaveholders, without fighting against slavery, is but a half-hearted business, and paralyzes the hands engaged in it. . . . Fire must be met with water. . . . War for the destruction of liberty must be met with war for the destruction of slavery."

Recognizing that racism or constitutionalism would prevent many northerners from accepting moral arguments for emancipation as a war aim, antislavery spokesmen developed the argument of "military necessity." Southerners boasted that slavery was "a tower of strength to the Confederacy" because it enabled the South "to place in the field a force so much larger in proportion to her population than the North." Precisely, agreed emancipationists. Slaves constituted more than half of the South's labor force and were so important to the southern war effort that the government impressed slaves into support service before it began drafting white men as soldiers. "The very stomach of this rebellion is the negro in the form of a slave," said Douglass. "Arrest that hoe in the hands of the negro, and you smite the rebellion in the very seat of its life."

How could this be done under the Constitution, which protected slavery? Rebels had forfeited their constitutional rights, answered emancipationists. Their property was liable to confiscation as a punishment for treason. Moreover, while in theory the South was engaged in domestic insurrection, in practice it was waging a war. The Lincoln administration had already recognized this by proclaiming a blockade and by treating captured rebel soldiers as prisoners of war. Having thus conceded belligerent status to the Confederacy, the Union could also confiscate enemy property as a legitimate act of war.

Benjamin Butler was the first prominent figure to act on these arguments. Back in

May, three slaves who had been working on southern fortifications escaped to Butler's lines at Fortress Monroe, Virginia. Butler informed their owner that since Virginia claimed to be out of the Union, the fugitive slave law did not apply. He labeled the escaped slaves "contraband of war" and put them to work in his camp. Northern newspapers picked up the "contraband of war" phrase, and thereafter the slaves who came into Union lines were known as contrabands.

The administration, after some hesitation, approved Butler's policy. By July nearly a thousand contrabands had rejoined the Union at Fortress Monroe. Their legal status was ambiguous. Butler decided to clarify it by addressing pointed questions to the War Department. In a letter of July 30 which soon appeared in

Almost every Confederate unit had black orderlies, cooks, and servants in about the same proportion as this South Carolina squad photographed in 1861. Two slaves are standing in the rear on the left behind the lieutenant standing with his sword touching the ground. In the illustration below, a squad of slaves overseen by white officers works on Confederate fortifications at Corinth, Mississippi.

The arrival of the Original Contraband at Fortress Monroe

After General Butler labeled three slaves who came into his lines at Fortress Monroe contraband of war and gave them protection, word spread quickly among slaves in the region. They flocked to Fortress Monroe in large numbers, as shown in this pen-and-ink drawing of the main entrance to the fort.

the newspapers, he asked Secretary of War Cameron: "Are these men, women, and children, slaves? Are they free? . . . What has been the effect of the rebellion and a state of war upon [their] status? . . . If property, do they not become the property of the salvors? But we, their salvors, do not need and will not hold such property . . . has not, therefore, all proprietary relation ceased?"

Hard questions, these, and explosive ones. While Butler wrote, Congress was wrestling with the same questions in debate on a bill to confiscate property used in aid of the rebellion. John J. Crittenden of Kentucky insisted that Congress had no more right to legislate against slavery in the states during wartime than in peacetime. True, agreed Republicans, but Congress *can* punish treason by confiscation of property, a penalty that operated against the individual but not the institution. In this tentative, limited fashion the Republicans enacted a confiscation act on August 6. Butler had his answer, such as it was. The contrabands were no longer slaves if—and only if—they had been employed directly by the Confederate armed services. But were they then free? The law did not say. This was hardly the ringing endorsement of emancipation that abolitionists had begun to call for. But it went too far for Democratic and border-state congressmen. All but three of them voted against the bill while all but six Republicans voted for it. This was the first breach in bipartisan support for Union war measures. It was a signal that if the conflict became an antislavery war it would thereby become a Republican war.

Such a prospect worried Lincoln in 1861. That was why he had revoked Frémont's emancipation edict, which went well beyond the confiscation act by apply-

DARK ARTILLERY; OR, HOW TO MAKE THE CONTRABANDS USEFUL.

In a cartoon by the artist for Frank Leslie's Illustrated Newspaper, *which readers no doubt found humorous, Union officers discover a military use for the "contrabands" who had come into Union lines.*

ing to *all* slaves owned by rebels and by declaring those slaves *free*. The president's action was unpopular with most Republicans. "It is said we must consult the border states," commented an influential Connecticut Republican. "Permit me to say *damn* the border states. . . . A thousand Lincolns cannot stop the people from fighting slavery." Even Orville Browning, a conservative senator from Illinois and Lincoln's close friend, criticized the revocation of Frémont's edict. Stung by this response, Lincoln chose to reply in a private letter to Browning. Frémont's action, he said, was "not within the range of *military* law, or necessity." He could have confiscated enemy property including slaves as Butler had done, "but it is not for him to fix their permanent future condition [by declaring them free]. That must be settled according to laws made by law-makers, and not by military proclamations." Browning had endorsed Frémont's policy as "the only means of saving the government." On the contrary, said Lincoln, "it is itself the surrender of government." When a company of Union soldiers from Kentucky heard about Frémont's edict, said Lincoln, they "threw down their arms and disbanded." If the order had not been modified, "the very arms we had furnished Kentucky would be turned against us. I think to lose Kentucky is nearly the same as to lose the whole game. Kentucky gone, we can not hold Missouri, nor, as I think, Maryland. These all against us, and the job on our hands is too large for us. We would as well consent to separation at once, including the surrender of this capitol." And in any case, "can it be pretended that it is any longer [a] . . . government of Constitution and laws, wherein a General, or a President, may make permanent rules of property by proclamation?"

One wonders if Lincoln remembered these words when a year later he did endeavor to make a permanent rule of property with his Emancipation Proclamation declaring the slaves "forever free." But a lifetime of change was compressed into that one year. The slavery issue just would not fade away. The slaves them-

Many slaves not only confiscated themselves by coming into Union lines; they also confiscated mules and wagons and thereby "liberated" those items as well from slaveowners, as shown in this photograph of contrabands coming into Union lines in Virginia.

selves would not let it fade away. By ones and twos, dozens and scores, they continued to convert themselves to "contrabands" by coming into Union lines.

By October 1861 some radical Republicans were urging not only freeing the contrabands but also arming them to fight for the Union. Secretary of War Cameron endorsed such action in his annual report: "Those who make war against the Government justly forfeit all rights of property. . . . It is as clearly a right of the Government to arm slaves, when it may become necessary, as it is to use gun-powder taken from the enemy." Cameron released his report to the press on December 1 without prior approval from the president. When an astonished Lincoln read these words he ordered Cameron to recall the report and delete this paragraph. But some newspapers had already published it. Cameron's precipitate action, like Frémont's, contributed to a widening rift between Lincoln and the radical wing of his party. Soon Cameron, like Frémont, lost his job. In both cases the main reason for removal was inefficiency, not abolitionism, but few radicals believed that the slavery issue had nothing to do with it.

In his annual message on December 3, 1861, Lincoln said: "I have been anxious and careful" that the war "shall not degenerate into a violent and remorseless revolutionary struggle." But abolitionists and some Republicans were already viewing it as a revolutionary conflict between two social systems. *"We are the revolutionists!"* wrote Virginia-born, New England-educated Moncure Conway in 1861. Although the Confederates "justify themselves under the right of revolution," Conway continued, their cause "is not a revolution but a rebellion against the noblest of revolutions." Thaddeus Stevens, the grim-visaged Cromwellian leader of radical Republicans in the House, called for precisely the kind of violent, remorseless struggle Lincoln hoped to avoid: "Free every slave—slay every traitor—burn every rebel mansion, if these things be necessary to preserve this temple of freedom." We must "treat this [war] as a radical revolution," said Stevens, "and remodel our institutions." On December 4, by a solid Republican vote, the House refused to reaffirm the Crittenden resolution disavowing an antislavery purpose in the war.

IV

The slavery issue played a part in a growing Republican disenchantment with McClellan. But more important than slavery were McClellan's defects of character and generalship.

"McClellan is to me one of the mysteries of the war," said Ulysses S. Grant a dozen years after the conflict. Historians are still trying to solve that mystery. Life seemed to have prepared McClellan for greatness. His birth into a well-to-do Philadelphia family and his education at the best private schools prepared him for admission to West Point by special permission when he was two years under the minimum age. After graduating second in his class, McClellan won renown at the age of twenty for engineering achievements in the Mexican War. His subsequent army career included assignment as an American observer of the Crimean War. In 1857 he resigned his commission to become chief engineer and vice president of a railroad at the age of thirty and president of another railroad two years later. In May 1861, at the age of thirty-four, he became the second-ranking general in the U.S. army and in July he took command of the North's principal field army. McClellan came to Washington, in the words of the London *Times* correspondent, as "the man on horseback" to save the Union; the press lionized him; a sober-minded contemporary wrote that "there is an indefinable *air of success* about him and something of the 'man of destiny.'"

But perhaps McClellan's career had been too successful. He had never known, as Grant had, the despair of defeat or the humiliation of failure. He had never learned the lessons of adversity and humility. The adulation he experienced during the early weeks in Washington went to his head. McClellan's letters to his wife revealed the beginnings of a messiah complex. "I find myself in a strange position here: President, Cabinet, Genl. Scott & all deferring to me," he wrote the day after arriving in Washington. "By some strange operation of magic I seem to have become *the* power of the land." The next week McClellan reported that he had received "letter after letter—have conversation after conversation calling on me to save the nation—alluding to the Presidency, Dictatorship, etc." McClellan said he wanted no part of such powers, but he did revel in the cheers of his soldiers as he rode along their lines—cheers that reinforced his Napoleonic self-image. "You have no idea how the men brighten up now when I go among them. I can see every eye glisten. . . . You never heard such yelling. . . . I believe they love me. . . . God has placed a great work in my hands. . . . I was called to it; my previous life seems to have been unwittingly directed to this great end."

The first victim of McClellan's vainglory was General in Chief Scott. More than twice McClellan's age, Scott was America's foremost living soldier, a hero of two wars, second only to George Washington in military reputation. But Scott's fame belonged to past wars. McClellan aspired to be the hero of this one. A rivalry with the "old general," as McClellan privately called Scott, soon developed. In truth, there could be only one head of the post–Bull Run military buildup. McClellan set about this task with great energy. He complained that Scott was frustrating his plans to expand and prepare the army for an early offensive. "I am leaving nothing undone to increase our force," McClellan wrote to his wife in early August, "but that confounded old Gen'l always comes in my way. He is a perfect incubus. He understands nothing, appreciates nothing. . . . If he *cannot* be taken out of my path, I . . . will resign and let the admin[istration] take care of itself. . . . The people call upon me to save the country—I *must* save it and cannot respect anything that is in the way." Lincoln tried to mediate between the two generals, but finally succumbed to pressure from Republican senators and allowed Scott to retire on November 1 "for reasons of health." McClellan succeeded him as general in chief. Lincoln cautioned McClellan that the dual jobs of general in chief and commander of the Army of the Potomac "will entail a vast labor upon you." Replied McClellan: "I can do it all."

The senators helped force Scott's retirement because McClellan convinced them that the "old general" was mainly responsible for the army's inactivity. When McClellan had first arrived in Washington he expressed an intent to "carry this thing 'en grand' & crush the rebels in one campaign." Republicans thought this had the right ring. But McClellan soon began to express fears that Beauregard was about to march forward with a huge army to crush *him*. A curious lack of confidence began to creep into McClellan's words and deeds, even as he continued to think of himself as God's chosen instrument to save the republic. The first signs appeared of a chronic tendency to overestimate enemy strength and to use this estimate as an excuse to remain on the defensive. In October, McClellan had 120,000 men while Beauregard and Johnston had only 45,000 in and near Manassas. But McClellan professed to believe that the enemy numbered 150,000 and was preparing to attack him.

The Confederates had pushed their picket posts within sight of Washington. They had also established batteries on the lower Potomac to interdict river traffic to the capital. In late September the southerners withdrew from one exposed position on Munson's Hill a few miles southwest of Washington. When the Federals moved in, instead of the large cannon they had expected they found a log shaped and painted to resemble a cannon. This "Quaker gun" embarrassed McClellan and called into question his reports of superior Confederate forces. The patience of northern people with the lack of action against the saucy rebels had begun to wear thin. The Quaker gun incident further dissipated the once-enormous reservoir of support and adulation for McClellan. As the fine, dry days of October wore away and the Army of the Potomac still made no advance, some Republicans began to suspect McClellan's competence and even his loyalty. The daily telegraphic bulletin "All quiet along the Potomac," which had reassured northerners just after Bull Run, now became a phrase of derision aimed at McClellan. Lyman Trumbull said in November that if McClellan's army went into winter quarters without fighting a battle "I very much fear the result would be recognition of the Confederacy by foreign governments [and] the demoralization of our own people. . . . Action, action is what we want and must have."

Action did temporarily break the quiet along the Potomac on October 21, but not the kind the North was hoping for. The rebels held the town of Leesburg, Virginia, forty miles upriver from Washington. Hoping to dislodge them, McClellan ordered General Charles P. Stone to make a "slight demonstration" from the Maryland side of the river while other Union regiments marched upriver on the Virginia side to threaten the Confederate flank. Stone assigned the mission to Colonel Edward Baker, a former Illinois politician and old friend of Lincoln, who had named his second son after him. Baker sent most of his brigade across the river, where it ran into a Confederate brigade posted in the woods at the top of a hundred-foot bank called Ball's Bluff. With no previous combat experience, Baker and his men took poorly chosen positions. After some lively skirmishing, in which Baker was killed, the Confederates drove the Yankees in disorder down the bank and into the river, where some of those who escaped bullets were drowned. More than half of Baker's 1,700 men were killed, wounded, or captured.

This humiliating disaster evoked from Lincoln tears of grief for Baker's death and provoked among Republicans an angry search for a scapegoat. When Congress met in December it established a Joint Committee on the Conduct of the War to investigate the causes for defeat at Ball's Bluff and Bull Run. Benjamin Wade chaired the committee and radical Republicans dominated it as the hunt for scapegoats got underway. The committee's first victim was General Stone. This officer had acquired a proslavery reputation because of a bitter exchange of letters with Governor Andrew of Massachusetts concerning the return to slavery of contrabands who had sought refuge with Massachusetts regiments under Stone's command. Several witnesses before the committee vaguely described alleged contacts between Stone and Confederate officers. Even though this testimony built a case of

The young artist Alfred Wordsworth Thompson was present with Union troops as they shelled Confederate positions and prepared to cross the Potomac from Maryland to Virginia in a maneuver that led to the battle of Ball's Bluff on October 21, 1861. A landscape painter, Thompson subordinated the soldiers and artillery to the fall foliage and corn shocks in a scene that is ironically pastoral.

treason against Stone, whom the committee suspected of sending his men into a trap, the general was given no opportunity to confront his accusers or even to read their testimony. While McClellan tried for a time to protect his subordinate, he soon realized that Stone was a surrogate for the committee's real target—himself. When additional dubious evidence of Stone's supposed dealings with the enemy came to McClellan, he turned it over to Secretary of War Stanton, who ordered Stone's arrest. For six months this luckless—and probably innocent—general was imprisoned at Fort Lafayette. No formal charges were ever brought against him. He was finally released and restored to minor commands, but his career was ruined.

Whether or not McClellan threw Stone to the wolves to protect himself, he had clearly gotten into deep political waters by the end of 1861. McClellan was a Democrat. Some of his closest army comrades in prewar days had been southerners, including Joseph Johnston, whose army at Manassas McClellan seemed reluctant to attack. Although no admirer of slavery, McClellan liked abolitionists even less. He had political ties with New York Democrats who had begun to mention him as the party's next presidential candidate. To one of these Democrats, McClellan wrote in November: "Help me to dodge the nigger—we want nothing to do with him. *I* am fighting to preserve the integrity of the Union. . . . To gain that end we cannot afford to mix up the negro question."

Lincoln at this time would have agreed with McClellan's expression of war aims. The president also did his best to shield McClellan from the growing criticism of the army's inactivity. "I intend to be careful and do as well as possible," McClellan told Lincoln during one of their early discussions. "Just don't let them hurry me, is all I ask." Lincoln replied: "You shall have your own way in the matter." The president borrowed books on military science from the Library of Congress and sat up late trying to master the elements of strategy. As an amateur he was willing to defer to McClellan the professional. At the same time, as a professional in his own field the president tried to educate the general in the realities of politics—especially the danger of ignoring political pressures in a people's war. At one of their frequent meetings, Lincoln tried to make McClellan see that the demands of Republican leaders for action were "a reality, and must be taken into account."

McClellan not only resisted such realities; in private he also expressed his contempt for all Republican politicians—including Lincoln. In letters to his wife he wrote that "I can't tell you how disgusted I am becoming with these wretched politicians—they are a most despicable set of men. . . . The presdt. is nothing more than a well meaning baboon . . . 'the original gorilla.' . . . It is sickening in the extreme . . . [to] see the weakness and unfitness of the poor beings who control the destinies of this great country."

One evening in November, Lincoln and Seward called on McClellan at home. He was out at a wedding party; when he returned an hour later and learned of his visitors, McClellan ignored them and went upstairs. Half an hour later a servant informed the president and secretary of state that the general had gone to bed. Lincoln's private secretary was furious, but the president reportedly said: "I will hold McClellan's horse if he will only bring us success."

But that was the rub. Military success could be achieved only by taking risks; McClellan seemed to shrink from the prospect. He lacked the mental and moral courage required of great generals—the will to *act*, to confront the terrible moment of truth on the battlefield. Having experienced nothing but success in his career, he was afraid to risk failure. He also suffered from what might be termed the "Bull Run syndrome"—a paralysis that prevented any movement against the Confederates until the army was thoroughly prepared. McClellan excelled at preparation, but it was never quite complete. The army was perpetually *almost* ready to move—but the enemy was always larger and better prepared.

To cover his fears, McClellan tried to shift the blame to others. In November, when McClellan had nearly three times the number of men and more than three times the weight of artillery as the Confederates in his front, he complained: "I cannot move without more means. . . . I have left nothing undone to make this army what it ought to be. . . . I am thwarted and deceived by these incapables at every turn. . . . It now begins to look as if we are condemned to a winter of inactivity. If it is so the fault will not be mine; there will be that consolation for my conscience, even if the world at large never knows it."

V

Jefferson Davis was also having problems with the *amour propre* of his generals. On August 31 the Confederate president named five men to the rank of full general. Joseph E. Johnston and Pierre G. T. Beauregard were fourth and fifth on the list, below Adjutant General Samuel Cooper, Albert Sidney Johnston, and Robert

E. Lee. When Joseph Johnston learned of this, he erupted in outrage. Not only was this ranking illegal, he informed Davis in a hotly worded letter, it was also an insult to his honor. Among his many complaints was that Robert E. Lee had won no battles and was even then floundering in West Virginia; while he, Joe Johnston, had won the battle of Manassas. Davis had committed a "violation of my rights as an officer," Johnston told the president.

Insulted by the tone of Johnston's letter, Davis sent an icy reply: "Sir, I have just received and read your letter of the 12th instant. Its language is, as you say, unusual; its arguments and statements utterly one sided, and its insinuations as unfounded as they are unbecoming." Not until later did Davis deem it necessary to explain his decision. The main effect of this graceless dispute was to plant a seed of hostility between Davis and Johnston that was to bear bitter fruit for the Confederacy. It also demonstrated an important difference between Davis and Lincoln as war leaders. A proud man sensitive of his honor, Davis could never forget a slight or forgive the man who committed it. Not for him was Lincoln's willingness to hold the horse of a haughty general if he would only win victories.

Davis also quarreled with Beauregard. The jaunty Louisianian's report on the battle of Manassas became public in October. It implied that Davis had delayed Johnston's reinforcement of Beauregard almost to the point of disaster. It noted Davis's rejection of Beauregard's grandiose plan for an offensive *before* the battle in a manner that caused the press to confuse this issue with the then-raging controversy over responsibility for failing to follow up the victory by capturing Washington. Throughout the report Beauregard's flamboyant prose tended to magnify his own role. Miffed, Davis reprimanded the general for writing an account that "seemed to be an attempt to exalt yourself at my expense." One way to deal with Beauregard, who had grown restless in his role as second in command to Johnston in Virginia, was to send him as far away from Richmond as possible. In January 1862 Davis transferred Beauregard to the Tennessee-Kentucky theater, where he could try to help the other Johnston—Albert Sidney—cope with the buildup of Union forces in Kentucky.

Despite quarrels with his generals, Davis faced the New Year with more confidence than Lincoln. Since mid-July the Confederacy had won most of the important land battles in the war: Manassas, Wilson's Creek, Lexington (Mo.), Ball's Bluff. Although the Union navy had achieved some significant victories, these had not yet led anywhere. One of the apparent naval triumphs—the capture of southern commissioners James Mason and John Slidell from the British ship *Trent*—had even produced a Yankee backdown in the face of British threats. Northern banks had suspended specie payments, and the government faced a financial crisis. Northern morale was at its lowest ebb since the days after Bull Run. The London *Times* correspondent in Washington reported that every foreign diplomat but one agreed that "the Union is broken for ever, and the independence of the South virtually established." The Army of the Potomac went into winter quarters having done nothing to dislodge enemy outposts within sight of that river; worse still, McClellan fell ill with typhoid fever in mid-December, leaving the army without a functioning commander for nearly a month. Lincoln had assigned two promising generals, Henry W. Halleck and Don Carlos Buell, to command of the Missouri and Kentucky theaters, but in January both reported an early advance impossible. "It is exceedingly discouraging," wrote Lincoln on a copy of Halleck's letter to him. "As everywhere else, nothing can be done." On the day he wrote these words, January 10, 1862, the president dropped into Quartermaster General Meigs's office. "General, what shall I do?" he asked despondently. "The people are impatient; Chase has no money; . . . the General of the Army has typhoid fever. The bottom is out of the tub. What shall I do?"

But January 1862 proved to be the darkness before dawn for the Union cause. Although other dark nights would follow, the four months after January turned out to be one of the brightest periods of the war for the North.

CHAPTER TWELVE

Blockade and Beachhead: The Salt-Water War, 1861–1862

I

The navy achieved some of the Union's most important military successes in 1861. The primary naval task was the blockade. It was no easy task. The Confederacy's 3,500 miles of coastline included ten major ports and another 180 inlets, bays, and river mouths navigable by smaller vessels. By June 1861 three dozen blockade ships were patrolling this coastline. Additional blockaders were commissioned or chartered every week—some of them old sailing brigs, others converted sidewheeler ferryboats—which joined the modern steam frigates and sloops of war in the ceaseless, tedious cruising off southern ports.

At first these ships were too few to apprehend more than one out of every dozen merchant vessels running the blockade. Even as the blockaders gained in numbers and effectiveness, another difficulty became obvious. The navy had only two bases in the South: Hampton Roads at the mouth of the James River opposite Confederate-held Norfolk; and Key West, Florida. Some ships spent nearly as much time going to and from these bases for supplies and repairs as they did on blockade duty. To remedy the problem, the navy decided to seize additional southern harbors to serve as bases. While plans for the first such operation went forward, the navy scored its initial victory of the war at Hatteras Inlet in North Carolina.

For two hundred miles along the North Carolina coast runs a series of barrier islands penetrated by a half-dozen inlets, of which Hatteras Inlet was the only one navigable by large ships. Behind this barrier lay the Albemarle and Pamlico sounds, inland seas with rail and canal connections to the interior. This transport network served as Richmond's back door to the Atlantic, the front door being closed by Union control of Hampton Roads. Numerous blockade runners passed through Hatteras Inlet during the war's early months. The North Carolina sounds also served as a haven for privateers that dashed through the inlets to capture unwary merchant vessels. What the privateers failed to snatch, the frequent storms off Cape Hatteras sometimes wrecked, for the rebels had dismantled the lighthouse and removed all navigation buoys from this treacherous coast.

Opposite page: This detail of a painting by an unknown artist shows the Confederate ironclad C.S.S. Virginia *sinking the U.S.S.* Cumberland *at Hampton Roads on March 8, 1862. (See full painting on page 310.)*

This drawing of the Union naval attacks on Fort Clark and Fort Hatteras on August 28–29 was done by Alfred R. Waud, one of the foremost Civil War artists. The steam-powered warships, five of which are labeled in the drawing, moved in an oval pattern to present a moving target to the fort's smoothbore guns while concentrating a heavy return fire from longer-range rifled guns. These innovative tactics inaugurated a new era in warfare between ships and forts.

No self-respecting navy could tolerate this "nest of pirates." Commodore Silas Stringham of the Atlantic blockading squadron put together a flotilla of seven ships carrying 141 guns to wipe it out. Two transports carrying 900 soldiers and marines under Benjamin Butler's command accompanied the task force. After a sustained bombardment of the unfinished forts on August 28–29 their 679 defenders surrendered without Butler's landing force having fired a shot. When news of this victory reached the North it took some of the sting out of Bull Run and Wilson's Creek. In North Carolina panic reigned along the tidewater as Tarheels expected additional assaults on all their coastal towns. But the bluejackets were not ready to follow up their victory—yet.

The next naval success required scarcely any effort at all. Off the coast of Mississippi halfway between New Orleans and Mobile lies Ship Island. In September 1861 the Confederates obligingly abandoned its half-completed fortifications after a token shelling by the U.S.S. _Massachusetts_. The Federals occupied the island and built up a base for the Gulf blockade squadron and for a campaign to capture New Orleans.

Meanwhile a formidable fleet was heading down the Atlantic coast toward Port Royal, South Carolina. This task force consisted of seventeen warships, twenty-five colliers, and thirty-three transports carrying 12,000 infantry, 600 marines, and their supplies. A gale off Cape Hatteras on November 1 scattered the fleet and foundered several transports carrying much of the army's ammunition and most of its landing boats. This mishap canceled the original plan for troops to land and assault the two forts guarding the entrance to Port Royal Bay. Once again the navy would have to do the job alone.

This was not a pleasant prospect for Flag Officer Samuel du Pont, nephew of the founder of the du Pont gunpowder company and a veteran of forty-six years in the navy. The traditional belief that one gun on shore was equal to four on shipboard seemed to give the forty-three guns in the forts a better than even chance against 157 in the fleet. But on November 7 du Pont, using tactics made possible by steam power, ordered his ships to steam back and forth past the forts in an oval pattern, pounding them with heavy broadsides while presenting moving targets in return. Both forts were knocked out after only four hours of firing. The Confederate defenders and white civilians fled the coastal sea islands connected by waterways radiating out from Port Royal Bay. Union forces occupied this region of rich long-staple cotton plantations. Left behind by their owners were some ten thousand contrabands who soon became part of an abolitionist experiment in freedmen's education and cotton planting with free labor.

At the cost of thirty-one casualties, the Union navy secured the finest natural harbor on the south Atlantic coast. More than that, the navy acquired a reputation of invincibility that depressed morale along the South's salt-water perimeter. The day after the capture of Port Royal, Robert E. Lee arrived in Savannah as the newly appointed commander of the south Atlantic coastal defenses. He recognized that sea power gave Yankees the option of striking when and where they pleased. "There are so many points to attack, and so little means to meet them on water," he sighed, "that there is but little rest." Lee had little choice but to concentrate Confederate defenses at strategic points, yielding most of the coastline to the enemy. During the next few months, bluejackets seized several other harbors and ports as far south as St. Augus-

After their liberation from slavery by the Union capture of Port Royal, former slaves tilled the ground as free farm laborers on the South Carolina and Georgia sea islands. This photograph from 1862 shows contrabands on Edisto Island posing in traditional working postures, but now as free people rather than slaves.

This photograph of Ambrose E. Burnside was made after his promotion to major general as a reward for his successful campaign in North Carolina. These victories earned Burnside a high reputation that he was unable to sustain in his subsequent Civil War career.

tine, Florida. In April 1862, siege guns planted on an island at the mouth of the Savannah River battered down Fort Pulaski, giving the Federals control of the entrance to Savannah.

Another joint army-navy expedition—in which the army for once did most of the fighting—sealed off all harbors in North Carolina except Wilmington. This expedition launched the checkered career of Ambrose E. Burnside, a handsome, florid, personable Rhode Islander whose imposing mutton-chop whiskers would contribute a new word to the language with an anagram (sideburns) of his name. After leading a brigade at Bull Run, Burnside had gone home to organize a division of soldiers accustomed to working around water and boats. They would need such skills, for their objective was to follow up the capture of Hatteras Inlet by gaining control of the North Carolina sounds. The Yankees' toughest foe in this enterprise turned out not to be the rebels but the weather. Burnside's flotilla of makeshift gunboats, coal scows, and passenger steamboats carrying his 12,000 troops was scattered by a gale off Hatteras on January 13 that wrecked three of his vessels. Two more weeks of gale-force winds forced the expeditionary force to hunker down in misery just inside Hatteras Inlet. When the weather finally moderated, seasick soldiers welcomed the prospect of combat as a lesser evil.

Their first target was Roanoke Island, a swampy piece of land ten miles long by two miles wide. Controlling the passage between Pamlico Sound and Albemarle Sound, Roanoke Island was the key to Richmond's back door. Commander of the 3,000 Confederate soldiers, four batteries with thirty-two guns, and seven one-gun gunboats defending the island was Henry A. Wise, the political general, transferred here as a result of his feuds with fellow Virginian John Floyd in West Virginia. Wise had learned enough about war to recognize the inadequacy of his "mosquito-fleet" gunboats, badly sited batteries, and poorly trained, outnumbered troops. He pleaded with Richmond for more men and more guns, but Richmond seemed strangely indifferent.

This indifference cost them dearly. On February 7–8, Burnside's sixteen gunboats mounting sixty-four guns drove off the mosquito fleet and neutralized the Confederate shore batteries while steamers towed landing boats through the surf and 7,500 soldiers waded ashore on Roanoke Island. There they plunged through "impenetrable" knee-deep swamps and smashed through rebel entrenchments, suffering only 264 casualties. For this price they captured the island's 2,675 defenders. General Wise escaped, but his son, an infantry captain, was killed in the fighting. Next day Union gunboats destroyed the mosquito fleet and seized Elizabeth City on the mainland. During the next several weeks, Yankees captured all the North Carolina ports on the sounds, including New Berne and Beaufort with their rail connections to the interior and Beaufort's fine harbor, which became another base for the blockade fleet.

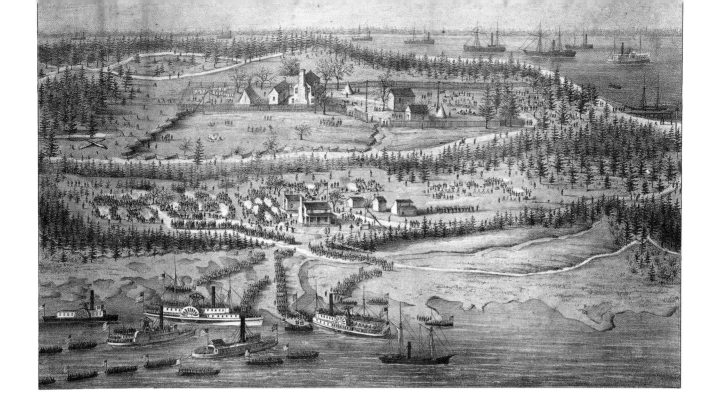

Here was amphibious warfare with style. It won a promotion to major general for Burnside. It raised northern morale and dampened southern spirits. The Confederate Congress set up a committee to investigate the Roanoke Island disaster. The hue and cry forced Judah Benjamin to resign as secretary of war (though Davis, who liked Benjamin, promptly appointed him secretary of state). By April 1862 every Atlantic coast harbor of importance except Charleston and Wilmington (N.C.) was in Union hands or closed to blockade runners. Because of this, and because of the increasing number of Union warships, the blockade tightened considerably during the first half of 1862. Moreover, southern hopes to breach the blockade with their (not so) secret weapon—the ironclad C.S.S. *Virginia*—had been dashed by the U.S.S. *Monitor*.

Having no traditions and few old-navy prejudices to overcome, the rebels got a head start into the new era of ironclad warships. In July 1861 they began grafting an armorplated casemate onto the salvaged hull of the frigate *Merrimack*. The capacity of the Tredegar Iron Works was stretched to the limit to construct two layers of two-inch iron plate sufficient to protect a superstructure 178 feet long and 24 feet high above the waterline and one-inch plate covering the 264-foot hull down to three feet below the waterline. The superstructure sloped at an angle of 36° to give added protection by causing enemy shots to ricochet.

This contemporary lithograph of the landing and deployment of Union troops at Roanoke Island on February 7, 1862, makes the process look more orderly than it actually was. Nevertheless, it was a successful operation that went forward almost without a hitch. Union warships, shown at upper right, had driven away the outgunned Confederate "mosquito fleet" that morning, enabling Union troops to land without opposition. Next day they attacked the Confederate infantry through swamps (not shown here) and routed them.

Despite a rocky tenure as secretary of war from September 1861 to March 1862, Judah P. Benjamin was one of Jefferson Davis's closest advisers and confidants. He served the rest of the war as secretary of state. Benjamin had been the first acknowledged Jew elected to the U.S. Senate (in 1852, from Louisiana). After hot words in a Senate debate, Benjamin challenged Senator Jefferson Davis to a dual. The future Confederate president apologized instead, and the two men thereafter became good friends. At the end of the war, Benjamin escaped to England and built a new career as an international lawyer.

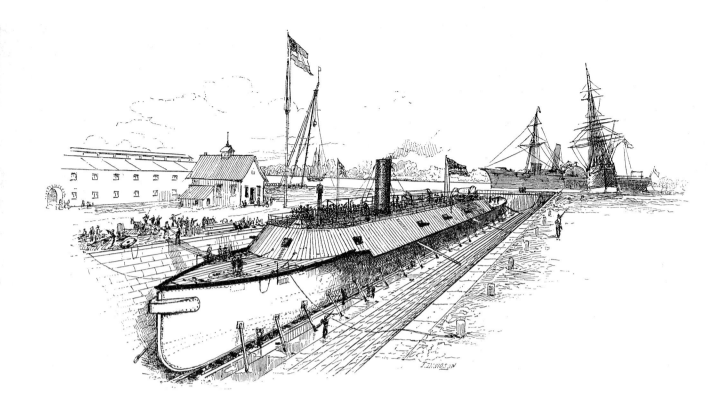

An accurate drawing of the conversion of the former forty-four-gun steam frigate U.S.S. Merrimack *into the ironclad C.S.S.* Virginia *at Gosport Navy Yard near Norfolk. Workmen laid iron plating over the salvaged wooden hull of the* Merrimack. *Note the iron ram bolted to the prow.*

The strange appearance of this craft, rechristened the *Virginia*, reminded observers of a barn floating with only its roof above water. The *Virginia* was armed with ten guns, four on each broadside plus fore and aft seven-inch pivot rifles. Attached to her prow was an iron ram to stave in the hulls of wooden warships. But she had major vulnerabilities—the ship's two old, reconditioned engines were inadequate, limiting her speed to four or five knots, and the weight of her armor gave her a draft of twenty-two feet. This prevented operations in shallow water while her unseaworthiness prevented her from venturing into the open sea. She was so unmaneuverable that a 180-degree turn took half an hour. Some of these problems would not become apparent until the *Virginia* was launched; in the meantime she inspired hope in the South and fear in the North.

This fear was the main factor in overcoming northern inertia on the ironclad question. With a conventional navy superior to anything the Confederates could construct, and preoccupied with the need to build up the blockade fleet, Secretary of the Navy Welles did not at first want to experiment with newfangled notions. But rumors of rebel activities caused Congress to force his hand with a law of August 3, 1861, directing the construction of three prototype ironclads. Welles set up a naval board to assess the dozens of proposals submitted by shipbuilders. The board accepted two, which resulted in the building of the *Galena* and the *New Ironsides*, ships of conventional design overlaid by iron plating.

No bid came from John Ericsson, the irascible genius of marine engineering who had contributed the screw propeller and several other innovations to ship design. Bitter about earlier feuds with the navy, Ericsson sulked in his New York office until a shipbuilder persuaded him to submit his radical design to the Navy Department.

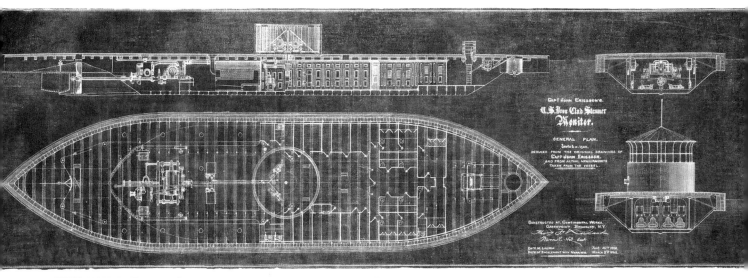

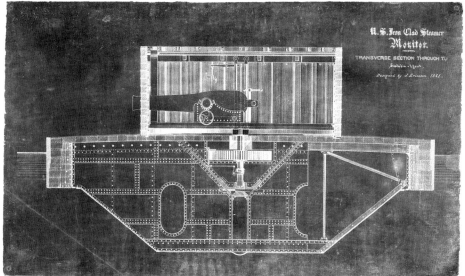

These drawings of the Monitor *show the ingenuity of its design. Steam from the boilers that drove the two synchronized engines also provided the power to turn the turret and hoist the 180-pound shells from the magazine to the guns. The slight protuberance above the deck near the bow was the pilothouse. It was the most vulnerable part of the* Monitor. *During the fight with the* Virginia, *the pilothouse took a direct hit that wounded Lieutenant John Worden, skipper of the* Monitor.

Ericsson's proposal incorporated several novel features. A wooden hull sheathed with thin iron plate would be overlaid by a flat deck 172 feet long with perpendicular sides extending below the waterline and protected by 4.5 inch armor plating. The propeller, the anchor, and all vital machinery would be protected by this shell, which was designed to float with less than two feet of freeboard, giving the craft the appearance of a raft—and also presenting a small target to enemy fire. Sitting on the deck was Ericsson's most important innovation: a revolving turret encased in eight inches of armor and containing two eleven-inch guns. This turret, along with the shallow draft (eleven feet), light displacement (1,200 tons, about one-fourth of the *Virginia*'s displacement), and eight-knot speed would give Ericsson's ship maneuverability and versatility. She could almost literally dance around a heavier enemy and fire in any direction.

Lincoln and Welles were impressed by Ericsson's design. But would it float? More specifically, would it stay afloat in a heavy sea? Some members of the naval board were skeptical. They had never seen anything like this cheesebox on a raft.

This painting by an unknown artist shows the C.S.S. Virginia *backing away after ramming the U.S.S.* Cumberland. *The U.S.S.* Minnesota *and U.S.S.* Congress *are maneuvering in the background. The* Congress *would become the* Virginia's *next victim.*

These reservations forced Ericsson to accept a contract providing for a full refund of the $275,000 allocated for construction if the ship did not prove a "complete success" (whatever that meant). Ericsson had confidence in his creation. He subcontracted the work to several firms to save time and supervised almost every detail personally. Starting three months later than the South, northern industry launched Ericsson's ironclad on January 30, 1862, two weeks before the Confederates launched the *Virginia*. Doubters present at each launching predicted that these crazy craft would never float but cheered the disproof of their predictions. Several more weeks were required to finish the fittings of both ships. Ericsson named his vessel *Monitor* (one who admonishes and corrects wrongdoers). There was no time for test runs to determine whether she fulfilled the terms of the contract; the *Monitor*'s test would be trial by combat.

On March 8 the *Virginia* steamed out from Norfolk on what her crew assumed was a test run. But this too was to be the real thing. Five Union ships mounting a total of 219 guns guarded the mouth of the James River at Hampton Roads: the *Minnesota, Roanoke, St. Lawrence, Congress,* and *Cumberland.* The last three were sailing ships—pride of the navy in the 1840s but already made obsolescent by steam. The first two were steam frigates (the *Roanoke* was disabled by a broken shaft), pride of the navy in 1862. But the fighting this day would make them obsolescent as well. Rumors that the *Merrimack* (as the Federals continued to call the *Virginia*) was coming out had circulated for weeks. Today she came, heading first for the twenty-four-gun *Cumberland*, sending several shells into her side before ramming and tearing a seven-foot hole in her hull that sent her to the bottom. While this was happening the *Cumberland* and *Congress* fired numerous broadsides at the *Virginia*, which "struck and glanced off," in the words of a northern observer, "having no more effect than peas from a pop-gun." This was not quite accurate; before the day was over two of the *Virginia*'s guns were knocked out, every fitting on deck and part of her smokestack were shot away, her ram was wrenched off by the collision with the *Cumberland*, and two of her crew were killed and several wounded. But none of the ninety-eight shots that struck her penetrated the armor or did any disabling damage.

After sinking the *Cumberland*, the *Virginia* went after the fifty-gun *Congress*, raking the helpless vessel with broadsides which started fires that eventually reached the powder magazine and blew her up. The *Minnesota* having run aground in an effort to help her sister ships, the *Virginia* turned her attention to this flagship of the fleet that had captured Hatteras Inlet the previous August. But the *Virginia*'s deep draft prevented her from closing with the *Minnesota* as night came on. The rebels left the *Minnesota* and the other ships for the morrow, and called it a day.

And what a day—the worst in the eighty-six-year history of the U. S. navy. The *Virginia* sank two proud ships within a few hours—a feat no other enemy would accomplish until 1941. At least 240 bluejackets had been killed, including the captain of the *Congress*—more than the navy suffered on any other day of the war. The whole Union fleet at Hampton Roads—still the main blockade base—was threatened with destruction. A taste of panic flavored the telegrams to Washington that night. The cabinet met in emergency session next morning. Secretary of the Navy Welles tried to calm Secretary of War Stanton's nerves with news that the *Monitor* was on its way from Brooklyn to Hampton Roads to confront the *Virginia*. But would she get there in time? And even if she did, was this two-gun "tin can on a shingle" any match for the rebel monster?

She did, and she was. The *Monitor* had arrived alongside the *Minnesota* the night before, her crew exhausted from fighting a storm that had almost sunk them on the way from Brooklyn. The prospect of fighting the *Virginia*, however, started their adrenaline pulsing again. When the Confederate ship steamed out on the morning of March 9 to finish off the Federal fleet, her crew spied a strange craft next to the *Minnesota*. "We thought at first it was a raft on which one of the *Minnesota*'s boilers was being taken to shore for repairs," said a *Virginia* midshipman. But, to the crew's shock, the boiler ran out a gun and fired and then began circling the sluggish *Virginia* "like a fice dog" and hurling 180-pound shot from her eleven-inch guns. For two hours the ironclads slugged it out. Neither could punch through the other's armor, though the *Monitor*'s heavy shot cracked the *Virginia*'s outside plate at several places. At one point the southern ship grounded. As the shallower-draft *Monitor* closed in, many aboard the *Virginia* thought they were finished. But she broke loose and continued the fight, trying without success to ram the *Monitor*. By this time the *Virginia*'s wheezy engines were barely functioning, and one of her lieutenants found her "as unwieldly as Noah's Ark." The *Monitor* in turn tried to ram the *Virginia*'s stern to disable her rudder or propeller, but just missed. Soon after this a shell from the *Virginia* struck the *Monitor*'s pilothouse, wounding her captain. The Union ship stopped fighting briefly; the *Virginia*, in danger of running aground again, steamed back toward Norfolk. Each crew thought they had won the battle, but in truth it was a draw. The exhausted men on both sides ceased fighting—almost, it seemed, by mutual consent.

This day saw the completion of a revolution in naval warfare begun a generation

No photographer was on hand to record the epic shootout between the Monitor *and* Merrimack (Virginia) *on March 9, 1862. Yet that first battle between ironclad ships has probably been portrayed in more illustrations and paintings than any other event of the Civil War. This dramatic painting by an unknown artist, who claimed to have been an eyewitness, was owned by Franklin D. Roosevelt and hangs today in the Roosevelt Library at Hyde Park, New York.*

The turret and deck of the Monitor *photographed on July 9, 1862. Note the dents in the turret from the Virginia's solid shots. Some of these shots caused rivets inside the turret to shear off with bullet-like speed, but no crew members were injured by these flying rivets.*

earlier by the application of steam power to warships. Doomed were the graceful frigates and powerful line-of-battle ships with their towering masts and sturdy oak timbers. The world's premier naval power realized, as the London *Times* declared, that it would be folly to employ any British warship, apart from the experimental ironclads *Warrior* and *Ironside*, in "an engagement with that little *Monitor*."

Of more immediate interest in Washington, the Union fleet at Hampton Roads was saved. For the next two months the *Monitor* and *Virginia* eyed each other warily but did not fight. With no ironclads in reserve, neither side could risk losing its indispensable weapon. When McClellan's army invaded the Virginia peninsula and forced the Confederates back toward Richmond in May 1862, Norfolk fell to the Federals and the *Virginia* was stranded. Too unseaworthy to fight her way into open water and too deep-drafted to retreat up the James River, the plucky ironclad was blown up by her crew on May 11, less than three months after she had been launched. The *Monitor* also failed to live until her first birthday. On the last day of 1862 she sank in a gale off Cape Hatteras while being towed south for a blockade assignment.

Despite their defects, the *Virginia* and *Monitor* were prototypes for the subsequent ironclads built or begun by both sides during the war: twenty-one by the Confederacy and fifty-eight by the Union. Many of these never saw action; all were designed for bay and river fighting; none achieved the fame of their progenitors, and they had little effect on the course of the war. Steam/sail warships built of wood remained the mainstay of the Union's deep-water navy. But in the last third of the nineteenth century the world's navies converted to iron and steel, incorporating the principal features of "Ericsson's folly": low profiles, speed and maneuverability, revolving gun turrets, and a few guns of heavy caliber rather than multiple-gun broadsides.

II

Blockade duty in the Union navy offered few opportunities for glory. The main enemy was boredom. About 500 ships took part in the blockade during the war, with perhaps an average of 150 on duty at a given time over the four years of fighting. These ships captured or destroyed about 1,500 blockade runners. Assuming that for every runner captured, a blockade ship sighted or chased a dozen, this meant that the average blockader sighted a runner once every three or four weeks and participated in one or two captures a year.

Only the chance to strike it rich kept blockade sailors sane and alert. The crew shared half and half with the government the proceeds from every prize they captured. This amounted to about 7 percent of the prize's value for the captain, a lesser portion for each officer, and 16 percent shared among the seamen. The dream of hitting the jackpot in this system sometimes came true: within nine days in the fall of 1864 the little gunboat *Aeolus* captured two runners unassisted, earning $40,000 for her captain, $8,000 to $20,000 for each of her officers, and $3,000 for each seaman.

Potential profits as well as actual excitement were greater for the crews of blockade runners. But in the first year of the war the blockade resembled a sieve more

than a cordon; the small risk of running it raised cargo prices and insurance rates but offered few thrills. By the summer of 1862, though, things were different. With most of the South's ports sealed off or occupied, the blockade fleet could concentrate on the few ports remaining open. Tactics were developed that worked reasonably well against slow or large blockade runners in conditions of good visibility. But such craft trying to run the blockade in these conditions soon disappeared from southern shores. In their place came sleek, fast, shallow-drafted vessels built (mostly in Britain) for the purpose, painted gray for low visibility, burning smokeless anthracite, with low freeboard, telescoping smokestacks, and underwater steam-escape valves. With pilots on board who knew every inch of the coast, these ships chose moonless, foggy, or stormy nights to make their dash into or out of a channel from which all navigation markers had been removed except coded shore lights to guide the pilots. Under such circumstances, a runner might pass within two hundred yards of a warship without being detected. Some runners carried signal rockets identical to those used by the Union navy, which they fired in a wrong direction to confuse pursuit.

Nassau, Bermuda, and Havana became the principal bases for blockade runners. There they took on cargoes of guns, ammunition, shoes, army blankets, medicines, salt, tea, liquor, hoop skirts, and corset stays. When the Union navy acquired enough ships it established a third cordon of blockaders patrolling these ports (despite British and Spanish protests) to intercept runners hundreds of miles from southern shores. The blockade runners usually escaped these patrols, however, and

made the run to Wilmington, Charleston, Mobile, or some other port where they picked up cotton for the return run.

Wilmington and Nassau became wartime boom towns—rowdy, violent, bawdy, awash with wealth and greed. The chance of profits from a successful voyage outweighed the one chance in three (by 1864) of capture. Owners could make back their investment in one or two round trips, clearing pure profit with every subsequent voyage. Cotton prices in European markets soared to six, eight, ten times their prewar levels, enabling speculators who bought cotton in the South and shipped it out to earn a return of several hundred percent. By 1864 captains of blockade runners received $5,000 or more in gold for a round trip, other officers from $750 to $3,500, and common seamen $250. In addition, captains reserved part of the cargo space for their own cotton (outgoing) or high-value goods (incoming), which they sold at auction. Many of the owners, captains, and crews were British, including some former Royal Navy officers who had resigned to pursue this more lucrative career. Although patriotism actuated the numerous southerners who also owned and operated blockade runners, the profit motive was not entirely absent. The North treated captured southern crews as prisoners of war but could not risk the diplomatic consequences of imprisoning foreign crew members, so let them go.

How effective was the blockade? There are two ways of answering this question. One way is to point out that during the war an estimated five out of six blockade runners got through (nine out of ten in 1861 scaling down to one out of two by 1865). They shipped out half a million bales of cotton and brought in a million pairs

This painting shows several blockade runners anchored in the harbor at St. George, Bermuda, awaiting transfer of cargo from larger ships arriving from Europe. Painted light gray to blend with the horizon, burning smokeless anthracite, with raked telescoping smokestacks, these fast vessels were almost invisible as they slipped through the blockade.

The British blockade runner Dee *photographed in the harbor at Hamilton, Bermuda, in 1863. On February 5, 1864, she ran aground trying to escape blockade ships off Masonboro Inlet, North Carolina, and was destroyed by the U.S.S.* Cambridge.

of shoes, half a million rifles, a thousand tons of gunpowder, several hundred cannon, and so on. The dollar value of Charleston's foreign trade was greater in 1863 than in the last year of peace. Confederate envoys to Britain compiled long lists of ships that had run the blockade to prove that it was a "paper blockade" entitled to no recognition by international law. In January 1863 Jefferson Davis pronounced the "so-called blockade" a "monstrous pretension."

But most southerners who lived through the blockade gave a different answer. "Already the blockade is beginning to shut [ammunition] out," wrote Mary Boykin Chesnut on July 16, 1861. It was "a stockade which hems us in," she added in March 1862. In July 1861 a Charleston merchant noted in his diary that the "blockade is still carried on and every article of consumption particularly in the way of groceries are getting very high." Four months later he wrote: "Business perfectly prostrated everything enormously high salt selling at 15 and 20 cents a quart hardly any shoes to be had dry goods of every kind running out." A southern naval officer conceded after the war that the blockade "shut the Confederacy out from the world, deprived it of supplies, weakened its military and naval strength."

Historical opinion leans toward this latter view. While it was true that five out of six runners got through, that is not the crucial statistic. Rather, one must ask how many ships carrying how much freight *would have* entered southern ports if there had been no blockade. Eight thousand trips were made through the blockade during four years of war, but more than twenty thousand vessels had cleared into or out of southern ports during the four prewar years. The blockade runners were built for speed, not capacity, and when pursued they sometimes jettisoned part of their cargo. The blockade reduced the South's seaborne trade to less than a third of normal. And of course the Confederacy's needs for all kinds of supplies were much greater than the peacetime norm. As for cotton exports, 1861 must be disregarded because the South voluntarily embargoed cotton in an attempt to influence British foreign policy.

After the end of this embargo in 1862 the half-million bales shipped through the blockade during the last three years of war compared rather poorly with the ten million exported in the last three antebellum years. As far as the greater dollar volume of Charleston's wartime trade is concerned, there were two reasons for this: Charleston was one of the principal ports for blockade runners because they were shut out of the other ports; and inflation so eroded the Confederate dollar that by March 1863 it required ten such dollars to buy what one had bought two years earlier. Indeed, the blockade was one of the causes of the ruinous inflation that reduced the Confederate dollar to 1 percent of its original value by the end of the war.

To maintain that the blockade "won the war" for the North, as naval historians are wont to do, goes entirely too far. But it did play an important role in Union victory. Although naval personnel constituted only 5 percent of the Union armed forces, their contribution to the outcome of the war was much larger.

III

The question of the blockade's effectiveness became a critical foreign policy issue during the war's first year. The international law governing blockades was part of the Declaration of Paris, acceded to by European powers (but not the United States) in 1856 after the Crimean War: "Blockades, in order to be binding, must be effective; that is to say, maintained by forces strong enough to prevent access." Southern diplomats insisted that the ease of running the blockade in 1861 proved its ineffectiveness; therefore no nation need respect it. This had been the traditional American position toward British blockades, especially during the Napoleonic wars when the United States defied the British and traded with both sides. But now the shoe was on the other foot. A major goal of Confederate diplomacy in 1861 was to persuade Britain to declare the blockade illegal as a prelude to intervention by the Royal Navy to protect British trade with the South.

Cotton was the principal weapon of southern foreign policy. Britain imported three-quarters of its cotton from the American South. The textile industry dominated the British economy. The inevitability of British intervention to obtain cotton became an article of faith in the South during 1861. In July 1861 Vice President Alexander Stephens expressed certainty that "in some way or other [the blockade will] be raised, or there will be revolution in Europe. . . . Our cotton is . . . the tremendous lever by which we can work our destiny."

To ply this lever, southerners decided to embargo cotton exports. The *Memphis Argus* instructed planters to "keep every bale of cotton on the plantation. Don't send a thread to New Orleans or Memphis till England and France have recognized the Confederacy—not one thread." Although the Confederate government never officially sanctioned the embargo, so powerful was public opinion that it virtually enforced itself. Most of the 1860 crop had been shipped before the war began. The shipping season for 1861 would normally have begun in September, but despite the looseness of the blockade little cotton went out. In the spring of 1862 southerners planted about half their usual cotton acreage and devoted the rest of the land to

Cotton bales on the wharf at Charleston awaiting shipment to Europe. Most of the 1860 crop was shipped, but an embargo in 1861 plus the Union blockade caused most of that year's crop to remain on the plantations or to pile up in southern ports.

food production. British imports of cotton from the South in 1862 amounted to about 3 percent of the 1860 level.

King Cotton diplomacy seemed promising at first. British and French officials exchanged worried views about the probable impact of a cotton famine. In October 1861 Prime Minister Viscount Palmerston and Foreign Minister Lord Russell anticipated that "the cotton question may become serious by the end of the year. . . . We cannot allow some millions of our people to perish to please the Northern States." British and French diplomats discussed the possibility of joint action to lift the blockade.

But in the end several factors prevented such action. The first was Russell's and Palmerston's desire to avoid involvement in the war. Even without Secretary of State Seward's bellicose warnings against intervention—which the British regarded as insolent blustering—Britain recognized that any action against the blockade could lead to a conflict with the United States more harmful to England's interests than the temporary loss of southern cotton. Our "true policy," Palmerston told Russell on October 18, was "to go on as we have begun, and to keep quite clear of the conflict." Napoleon III of France leaned toward intervention but was unwilling to take any action without British cooperation.

If Britain took umbrage at Seward's "bullying," many Englishmen resented even more the Confederacy's attempt at economic blackmail. If southerners "thought they could extort our cooperation by the agency of king cotton," declared the *Times*, they had better think again. To intervene on behalf of the South "because they keep cotton from us," said Lord Russell in September 1861, "would be ignominious beyond measure. . . . No English Parliament could do so base a thing."

Because of British (and French) sensitivity on this issue, southern diplomats could not admit the existence of a cotton embargo. But this trapped them in a paradox, for how could they proclaim the blockade ineffective if no cotton was reaching Europe? In reply to a question on this matter by the French foreign minister in February 1862, the Confederate commissioner to Paris conceded that "although a very large proportion of the vessels that attempted to run the blockade . . . had succeeded in passing, the risk of capture was sufficiently great to deter those who had not a very adventurous spirit from attempting it." Fatal admission! Eight days later Foreign Minister Russell announced Britain's position on the blockade: "The fact that various ships may have successfully escaped through it . . . will not of itself prevent the blockade from being an effective one by international law" so long as it was enforced by a number of ships "sufficient really to prevent access to [a port] *or to create an evident danger of entering or leaving it.*" By February the northern blockade certainly met this criterion. Britain also discounted southern arguments about the ineffectiveness of the blockade because, as the crown's solicitor general put it, Britain must resist "new fangled notions and interpretations of international law which might make it impossible for us effectively at some future day to institute any blockade, and so destroy our naval authority."

YE CONFERENCE

"NOT ANY, WE THANK YOU MR DAVIS."

This cartoon expresses a northern slant on the Confederacy's quest for foreign recognition and assistance. A bowing Jefferson Davis offers a tray of "bonds" to Emperor Louis Napoleon of France. Davis also holds a tray of cotton, presumably to entice Napoleon, who turns away with a gesture of refusal. In the background stands Britain's Queen Victoria holding a document labeled "Proclamation," probably her proclamation of neutrality in the American war dated May 13, 1861.

Southern expectations of foreign intervention to break the blockade were betrayed by a double irony: first, the "success" of the cotton embargo seemed only to prove the success of the blockade; and second, the huge cotton exports of 1857–60 led to excess inventories in textile mills in 1861 which, despite production cuts, produced a satiated market for cloth. Inventories of raw cotton and finished cloth in Britain and France were higher in December 1861 than in any previous December. The cotton famine from which the South expected so much did not really take hold until the summer of 1862. By then the Confederacy had scuttled its embargo and was trying desperately to export cotton through the tightening blockade to pay for imported supplies. By then, too, the stimulus of high prices had brought about an increase of cotton acreage in Egypt and India, which supplied most of Europe's cotton imports for the next three years.

The worst time of unemployment in the British textile industry occurred from the summer of 1862 to the spring of 1863. But the impact of this did not measure up to southern hopes or British fears. Even before the war, textiles had been losing their dominant role in the British economy. The war further stimulated growth in the iron, shipbuilding, armaments, and other industries. This offset much of the decline in textiles. The manufacture of woolen uniforms and blankets for American armies absorbed some of the slack in cotton manufacturing. A flourishing trade in war matériel with the North as well as blockade running to the South helped convince British merchants of the virtues of neutrality. Crop failures in western Europe from 1860 through 1862 increased British dependence on American grain and flour. During the first two years of the Civil War the Union states supplied nearly half of British grain imports, compared with less than a quarter before the war. Yankees exulted that King Corn was more powerful than King Cotton. And because Confederate commerce raiders drove much of the U.S. merchant marine from the seas, most of this expanded trade with the North was carried by British ships—another economic shot in the arm that helped discourage British intervention in the war.

By the summer of 1862 the "cotton famine" had caused serious unemployment in British textile mills. Charity helped to allay the suffering of unemployed workers, some of whom are shown in this Illustrated London News *drawing of people queuing up for distribution of food.*

By the second year of the conflict, Britain was willing to tolerate extraordinary northern extensions of the blockade. In April 1862 Union warships began seizing British merchant vessels plying between England and Nassau or Bermuda, on the grounds that their cargoes were destined ultimately for the Confederacy. The first ship so captured was the *Bermuda*, which was confiscated by a U.S. prize court. The navy bought her and put her to work as a blockade ship. This added insult to the injury that had already provoked a jingoistic response in Britain. But American diplomats cited British law justifying seizures by the Royal Navy during the Napoleonic wars of American ships carrying cargoes to a neutral port with the intention of reexporting them to France ("continuous voyage"). When this chicken came home to roost in 1862, Whitehall could hardly repudiate its own precedent.

In February 1863 a Union warship captured the British vessel *Peterhoff* in the Caribbean, where she was on her way to Matamoros, Mexico, with a cargo of military supplies clearly destined for transfer over the border to the Confederacy. The prize court upheld the navy's extension of "continuous voyage" to include reexport of contraband across land frontiers as well as from neutral ports. This time a large portion of the British public railed against Yankee "overbearing and domineering insolence." But the Foreign Office merely recorded the precedent, which Britain cited a half-century later to justify seizure of American ships carrying contraband to neutral Holland intended for overland transshipment to Germany.

IV

Next to obtaining British intervention against the blockade, the main goal of Confederate foreign policy was to secure diplomatic recognition of the South's nationhood. In the quest for recognition, the Confederate State Department sent to Europe a three-man commission headed by William L. Yancey. As a notorious fire-eater and an advocate of reopening the African slave trade, Yancey was not the best choice to win friends in antislavery Britain. Nevertheless, soon after the southerners arrived in London the British government announced an action that misled Americans on both sides of the Potomac to anticipate imminent diplomatic recognition of the Confederacy.

Lincoln had proclaimed the rebels to be insurrectionists. Under international law this would deny the Confederacy status as a belligerent power. But the North's declaration of a blockade constituted an act of war affecting neutral powers. On May 13

Britain therefore declared her neutrality in a proclamation issued by the queen. This would seem to have been unexceptionable—except that it automatically recognized the Confederacy as a belligerent power. Other European nations followed the British lead. Status as a belligerent gave Confederates the right under international law to contract loans and purchase arms in neutral nations and to commission cruisers on the high seas with the power of search and seizure. Northerners protested this British action with hot words; Charles Sumner later called it "the most hateful act of English history since Charles 2nd." But northern protests rested on weak legal grounds, for the blockade was a virtual recognition of southern belligerency. Moreover, in European eyes the Confederacy with its national constitution, its army, and its effective control of 750,000 square miles of territory and a population of nine million people was a belligerent power in practice no matter what it was in northern theory. As Lord Russell put it: "The question of belligerent rights is one, not of principle, but of fact."

Northern bitterness stemmed in part from the context and timing of British action. The proclamation of neutrality came just after two "unofficial" conferences between Lord Russell and the Confederate envoys. And it preceded by one day the arrival in London of Charles Francis Adams, the new United States minister. The recognition of belligerency thus appeared to present Adams with a *fait accompli* to soften him up for the next step: diplomatic recognition of southern nationhood. As Seward viewed it, Russell's meetings with Yancey and his colleagues were "liable to be construed as recognition"—and the South did so construe them.

All spring Seward had been growing more agitated by British policy. When he learned of Russell's meetings with the rebel commissioners, he exploded in anger. "God damn them, I'll give them hell," he told Sumner. On May 21 Seward sent an undiplomatic dispatch to Adams instructing him to break off relations if the British government had any more dealings with southern envoys. Lincoln had told Seward to allow Adams to present the substance of the dispatch verbally to Lord Russell. After reading Seward's bellicose words, Adams decided that in this case discretion was indeed the better part of valor. Adams had been a superb choice for the London legation. His grandfather and father had preceded him there; Charles had spent much of his youth in the St. Petersburg and London legations. His reserve and self-restraint struck an empathic chord among Englishmen, who were offended by the braggadocio they attributed to American national character. Adams and Lord Russell took each other's measure at their first meeting and liked what they saw. Adams concealed Seward's iron fist in a velvet glove. Equally urbane, Russell assured the American minister that Britain had no present intention of granting diplomatic recognition to the Confederacy. The foreign secre-

Bearing a distinct resemblance to his father and grandfather, the second and sixth presidents of the United States, Charles Francis Adams proved an ideal choice for minister to Great Britain during the Civil War. He deserved much of the credit for preventing British intervention in the conflict.

CAPTURE OF SECESSION VARMINTS.

BULL—"*What are you about, sir ? Picking pockets, eh ?*"
JONATHAN—"*Don't get wrathy, now ! You shouldn't be carryin' skunks about with you, John !*"

(And Jonathan necks the varmints accordingly).

This cartoon shows the initial gleeful reaction in the North to Captain Wilkes's capture of Mason and Slidell. "Jonathan" (the United States) picks the pockets of John Bull to pluck away the southern "varmints" carried by the Trent.

tary conceded that he had twice met with the southern commissioners but "had no expectation of seeing them any more."

Nor did he. It took some time for this message to sink into the minds of the southern envoys, who continued to send optimistic reports to Richmond. In September 1861, however, Yancey grew restless and he resigned. At the same time the Confederate government decided to replace the commissioners with ministers plenipotentiary in major European capitals. Richmond sent James Mason of Virginia to London and John Slidell of Louisiana to Paris.

By so doing the South unwittingly set in motion a series of events that almost brought Anglo-American relations to a rupture. The departure of Mason and Slidell from Charleston by blockade runner was scarcely a secret. The U.S. navy was embarrassed by its failure to intercept their ship before it reached Havana, where the diplomats transferred to the British steamer *Trent*. Captain Charles Wilkes decided to redeem the navy's reputation. A forty-year veteran now commanding the thirteen-gun sloop U.S.S. *San Jacinto*, Wilkes was a headstrong, temperamental man who fancied himself an expert on maritime law. Diplomatic dispatches could be seized as contraband of war; Wilkes decided to capture Mason and Slidell as the "embodiment of despatches." This novel interpretation of international law was never tested, for instead of capturing the *Trent* as a prize after stopping her on the high seas on November 8, Wilkes arrested Mason and Slidell and let the ship go on.

The northern public greeted Wilkes's act with applause, and the House of Representatives passed a resolution lauding him. But after the first flush of jubilation, second thoughts began to arise. The British press expressed outrage at Wilkes's "impressment" of Mason and Slidell; the possibility of an ugly confrontation had a decidedly negative impact on America's financial markets. Prime Minister Palmerston told his cabinet: "You may stand for this but damned if I will." The cabinet voted to send Washington an ultimatum demanding an apology and release of the Confederate diplomats. Britain ordered troops to Canada and strengthened the western Atlantic fleet. War seemed imminent.

Although the Anglophobe press in America professed to welcome this prospect, cooler heads recognized the wisdom of Lincoln's reported words: "One war at a time." The Union army's capacity to carry on even that one war was threatened by an aspect of the *Trent* crisis unknown to the public and rarely mentioned by historians. In 1861 British India was the Union's source of saltpeter, the principal ingredient of gunpowder. The war had drawn down saltpeter stockpiles to the danger

point. In the fall of 1861 five ships were being loaded with 2,300 tons of the mineral in England when news of the *Trent* reached London. The government clamped an embargo on all shipments to the United States until the crisis was resolved. No settlement, no saltpeter.

Given the consequences involved, Seward and Lincoln sought to defuse the crisis without the humiliation of bowing to an ultimatum. In an uncharacteristic mood of moderation, Seward expressed a willingness to yield Mason and Slidell on the grounds that Wilkes had acted without instructions. Diplomatic hints had come from London that this face-saving compromise would be acceptable to the British. In a crucial Christmas Day meeting, Lincoln and his cabinet concluded that they had no choice but to let Mason and Slidell go—and press and public supported the decision. Mason and Slidell resumed their interrupted trip to Europe, where they never again came so close to winning foreign intervention as they had done by being captured in November 1861. Their release punctured the war bubble. The saltpeter left port and was soon turned into gunpowder for the Union army.

The afterglow of this settlement left Anglo-American relations in better shape than before the crisis. "The first effect of the release of Messrs. Mason and Slidell has been extraordinary," wrote young Henry Adams from the American legation in London, where he served as secretary to his father. "The current which ran against us with such extreme violence six weeks ago now seems to be going with equal fury in our favor." This new current was strengthened by reports of the northern victories along the Atlantic coast—and even more by news of remarkable Union military successes in the West.

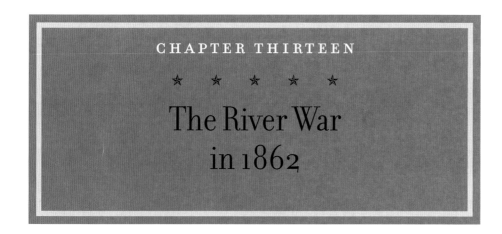

I

Before February 1862 there had been little fighting along the rivers south of Cairo, Illinois. But in the next four months these rivers became the scene of decisive action. The strategic value of the river network radiating from Cairo had been clear from the outset. This southernmost city in the free states grew into a large military and naval base. From there, army-navy task forces launched invasions up the Tennessee and Cumberland rivers (southward) and down the Mississippi in 1862.

One reason for the success of these offensives lay in the harmonious teamwork of the navy and army commanders at Cairo: the God-fearing, teetotaling, antislavery Connecticut Yankee Flag Officer Andrew H. Foote; and Brigadier General Ulysses S. Grant, who may have feared God but was indifferent toward slavery and not noted for abstinence. It was lucky for the North that Grant and Foote worked well together, because the institutional arrangements for army-navy cooperation left much to be desired. On the theory that inland operations—even on water—were the army's province, the War Department built the first gunboats for western river operations. Naval officers commanded the vessels, but army officers controlled their operations. Crews for these gunboats were a mixed lot—volunteer riverboatmen, soldiers detailed from the army, civilian steamboat pilots and engineers, and a few Jack Tars recruited from the salt-water navy. Not until the autumn of 1862 did Congress rectify this anomalous arrangement by placing the river squadrons under navy control. Yet the river fleet won its greatest victories during the early, makeshift months.

The gunboats of this navy were the creation of James B. Eads, the Ericsson of the fresh-water navy. A native of Indiana who had established a boat-building business in St. Louis, Eads contracted in August 1861 to construct seven shallow-draft gunboats for river work. When completed before the end of the year, these craft looked like no other vessel in existence. They were flat-bottomed, wide-beamed, and paddle-wheeled, with their machinery and crew quarters protected by a sloping casemate sheathed in iron armor up to 2.5 inches thick. Because this casemate, designed by naval constructor Samuel Pook, reminded observers of a turtle

Opposite page: The U.S.S. General Lyon *with a twelve-pound howitzer on the foredeck. The gunboats of the Union river navy were so shallow-drafted that, as Lincoln later put it, they could go wherever the ground was a little damp.*

Cairo, Illinois, was the southernmost city in the free states, farther south than Richmond, the Confederate capital. Located at the confluence of the Ohio and Mississippi rivers, its strategic importance was great. This photograph shows the beginnings of the buildup of Cairo as a military base in 1861, with the Mississippi River and the Missouri shore in the background.

shell, the boats were nicknamed "Pook's turtles." Although strange in appearance, these formidable craft each carried thirteen guns and were more than a match for the few converted steamboats the South could bring against them.

For defense against river-borne invasions the Confederacy relied mainly on forts. These were particularly strong on the Mississippi. At Columbus, Kentucky, only fifteen miles below Cairo, General Leonidas Polk had fortified the heights with 140 heavy guns. Well might the Confederates boast about this "Gibraltar of the West," for nothing that floated, not even Pook's turtles, seemed likely to get past those guns. Just to make sure, though, the southerners fortified several other strongpoints along the 150 miles of river down to Memphis. In strange contrast to these Gibraltars, the forts protecting the Tennessee and Cumberland rivers just south of the Kentucky border were poorly sited and unfinished at the end of 1861. Perhaps this was because the Mississippi loomed so large in southern consciousness, while the Tennessee and the Cumberland seemed less important. Yet these rivers penetrated one of the principal grain-growing, mule- and horse-breeding, and iron-producing areas of the Confederacy. The ironworks at Clarksville on the Cumberland were second in the South only to Tredegar at Richmond, while Nashville on the same river was a major producer of gunpowder and the main supply depot for Confederate forces in the West.

Fifty-five years old when this photograph was made in 1862, Andrew Hull Foote had served in the U.S. navy since the age of fourteen. Strongly religious and opposed to drinking, he banned liquor on the ships he commanded, and managed to make the ban stick. His influence led to the abolition of the grog ration on all naval ships in 1862.

These forces were commanded by Albert Sidney Johnston, the highest-ranking field officer in the Confederacy. A native of Kentucky who had fought for both Texas and the United States against Mexico, Johnston was commander of the Pacific Department in California when the Civil War began. Like Robert E. Lee, he declined a high commission in the Union army and made his way across the Southwest, dodging Apaches and Union patrols on his way to join the Confederacy. Tall, well-built, possessing a sense of humor and a manner of quiet authority, Johnston looked like the great soldier he was reputed to be. Jefferson Davis had admired him as a fellow student at Transylvania University and West Point in the 1820s and had fought with him in the Black Hawk and Mexican wars. While Davis was forming a low opinion of the other Johnston—Joseph—he pronounced Albert Sidney "the greatest soldier, the ablest man, civil or military, Confederate or Federal."

Johnston's Western Military Department stretched from the Appalachians to the Ozarks. By early 1862 he had about 70,000 troops on this five-hundred-mile line facing half again as many Federals stretched along a line of similar length from eastern Kentucky to southwest Missouri. The northerners, however, were handicapped by divided authority. In November, Henry W. Halleck had replaced Frémont as commander of the Department of Missouri. Halleck's authority extended as far east as the Cumberland River. Beyond it, Don Carlos Buell headed the Department of the Ohio, with headquarters in Louisville.

The outbreak of war had found Halleck and Buell, like Johnston, in California. Their prewar careers had also produced reputations that led their countrymen to expect great things of them. Halleck had graduated near the top of his West Point class. He wrote *Elements of Military Art and Science*, essentially a paraphrase of Jomini's writings, and translated Jomini's *Life of Napoleon*. These works earned Halleck renown as a strategic theorist. Old Brains, as he was sometimes called (though not to his face), had resigned from the army in 1854 to become a business-man and lawyer in California, where he wrote two books on mining law and

One of the "Pook's turtles" built by James Eads, the ironclad U.S.S. Cincinnati *helped Union forces gain control of the western river network almost as far south as Vicksburg in 1862. She was not invulnerable, however; in an attack against the river defenses of Vicksburg on May 27, 1863, she took several hits below the waterline and sank with the loss of two dozen sailors.*

This wartime sketch shows some of the Confederate fortifications on the lower slopes of the bluffs on the Mississippi River at Columbus, Kentucky. At the top of the bluffs, additional earthworks (not shown here) protected this strongpoint against land attack. Columbus did not succumb to enemy attacks; the Confederates evacuated it in March 1862 after the Union capture of Forts Henry and Donelson cut its communications.

declined a judgeship on the state supreme court. Although balding and paunchy, with a double chin, goggle eyes, and an irritable temper, Halleck inspired confidence as a military administrator. In his early months of command he performed up to expectations, bringing order out of the chaos left by Frémont and organizing efficiently the logistical apparatus for 90,000 soldiers and the fresh-water navy in his department. Buell also proved himself an able administrator. Like McClellan, who sponsored his assignment to Louisville, Buell was a firm disciplinarian who knew how to turn raw recruits into soldiers. But unlike McClellan, he lacked charisma and was never popular with his men.

Lincoln believed that the North would win this war only by using its superior numbers to attack "different points, at the *same* time" to prevent the enemy from shifting troops from quiet to threatened sectors. But he could not get Halleck and Buell to cooperate. Buell was prepared to attack the main Confederate force at Bowling Green if supported with a diversionary attack by Halleck up the Tennessee River, but Halleck demurred. "I am not ready to cooperate" with Buell, he informed Lincoln on January 1, 1862. "Too much haste will ruin everything."

Lincoln was beginning to suspect that whatever merits Halleck possessed as an administrator and theorist, he was not a fighting soldier. But Halleck had a fighter under his command: Ulysses S. Grant at Cairo. He urged Halleck to permit him to take his troops and Foote's new gunboats up the Tennessee to capture Fort Henry. Halleck hesitated, refused permission, then reversed himself at the end of January and ordered Grant to go ahead.

Once unleashed, Grant moved with speed and force. This was his first real opportunity to dispel doubts stemming from the drinking problems that had forced his army resignation in 1854. Since reentering the army in June 1861, Grant had served an apprenticeship in command that had increased his self-confidence. He had discovered that his laconic, informal, commonsense manner inspired respect and obedience from his men. Unlike so many other commanders, Grant rarely clamored for reinforcements, rarely complained, rarely quarreled with associates, but went ahead and did the job with the resources at hand.

Despite the Napoleonic pose, General Henry W. Halleck was more administrator than soldier, more at home behind a desk than in the field.

Grant's first assignment as colonel of the 21st Illinois had been to attack the camp of a rebel regiment in Missouri. Grant had proved his personal courage as a junior officer in the Mexican War. But now he was in command; he was *responsible*. He had learned a valuable lesson when he prepared to attack the Missouri regiment and found that they had decamped. Grant suddenly realized that the enemy colonel "had been as much afraid of me as I had been of him. This was a view of the question I had never taken before; but it was one I never forgot. . . . The lesson was valuable." It was a lesson that McClellan and many other Union commanders, especially in the East, never learned.

A few months after this incident, Grant had taken five regiments from Cairo down the Mississippi to create a diversion in aid of another Union operation in Missouri by attacking a Confederate camp at Belmont, across the river from the southern Gibraltar at Columbus. On November 7 Grant's troops routed a rebel force of equal size but were in turn counterattacked and surrounded by reinforcements from Columbus. While some of his officers advocated surrendering, Grant cut his way out and got his troops back to their transports—not without loss, but having inflicted greater losses on the enemy. This action, though hardly a Union victory, taught Grant more valuable lessons and demonstrated his coolness under pressure. Lincoln did not know it yet, but he had found the general he desperately needed.

Grant and Foote proposed to attack Fort Henry because they considered it the weak point in Albert Sidney Johnston's line. They were right. Built on a low bank dominated by surrounding hills and threatened with flooding by every rise in the river, the fort did no credit to southern engineering. Preoccupied with the need to defend Columbus and Bowling Green, where he believed the main Union attacks would come, Johnston neglected to strengthen Fort Henry until too late. On February 5 transports protected by four of Foote's ironclads and three wooden gunboats landed Grant's 15,000 troops several miles below Fort Henry. The plan was for the foot soldiers to attack the fort from the rear while the gunboats shelled it from the river. Heavy rain slowed down Grant's troops but also caused the river to flood the fort's lower level. When the Union flotilla hove into sight on February 6, only nine of the fort's guns bore on the enemy, while the boats could fire twice as many guns in return from their bows-on position. Recognizing the odds as hopeless, the fort's commander sent its 2,500-man garrison cross-country to Fort Donelson, twelve miles away on the Cumberland, remaining behind with one artillery company to fight a delaying action against the gunboats.

Under the circumstances the rebel cannoneers performed well, slugging it out with the fleet and putting one ironclad out of commission, but with half of their men killed or wounded and most guns disabled they were forced to surrender to the gunboats even before Grant's men arrived on the scene. The three wooden gunboats steamed upriver to knock out a railroad bridge on the line linking Johnston's forces at Columbus with those at Bowling Green. The gunboats continued another 150 miles all the way to Muscle Shoals in Alabama, destroying or capturing nine Confederate vessels including one powerful steamboat the rebels had been turning into an ironclad. This captured vessel became part of the invading fleet that made the Tennessee a Union highway into the deep South.

This Currier and Ives lithograph of the attack on Fort Henry (shown in the left distance) exaggerates the height of the gunboat smokestacks. Compare this illustration with the photograph of the Cincinnati on p. 327.

"Fort Henry is ours," Grant telegraphed Halleck on February 6. "I shall take and destroy Fort Donelson on the 8th." But bad weather delayed the supplying and marching of his troops overland, while Foote had to repair his battered gunboats before they could steam back down the Tennessee and up the Cumberland to Donelson. This delay bought Johnston some time, if only to consider his unenviable position. The one-two punch of capturing Fort Henry and cutting the railroad south of it had put Grant between Johnston's two main forces. The Yankees could now attack Columbus from the rear, or overwhelm the 5,000 Confederates at Fort Donelson and then steam upriver to take Nashville, or come up behind Johnston's 25,000 at Bowling Green while Buell's 50,000 attacked them from the front. Johnston's only options seemed to be the concentration of all available men (about 35,000) to defend Donelson and perhaps counterattack to regain Fort Henry, or to give up Kentucky and concentrate his whole army to defend the vital factories and depots at Nashville.

Beauregard arrived for an emergency meeting of Confederate brass at Bowling Green on February 7; his departure from Virginia had been a great relief for Jefferson Davis. Ebullient as ever, Beauregard wanted to smash Grant and Buell in turn. Johnston demurred. He feared that his entire army, instead of being able to fight the two enemy forces separately, would be flattened between Grant's hammer and Buell's anvil. Johnston preferred retreat to the Nashville-Memphis line, leaving a token force at Donelson to delay Grant and saving the bulk of the army to fight another day under more favorable conditions. In effect, Johnston proposed to abandon the strategy of dispersed defensive in favor of concentration for a possible offensive-defensive stroke. It was a good plan. But Johnston unaccountably changed his mind and decided to make a real fight at Fort Donelson. Instead of taking his whole available force there, however, he sent 12,000 men and retreated with the rest to Nashville. To command at Donelson, Johnston assigned none other than John Floyd, who had been transferred to Kentucky after helping to lose West Virginia. Floyd's presence made Donelson an even bigger plum for Federal picking, since he was a wanted man in the North for fraud and alleged transfer of arms to southern arsenals as Buchanan's secretary of war.

"Fort" Donelson was not really a fort; rather, it was a an earthwork enclosing fifteen acres of soldiers' huts and camp equipment, plus two batteries of twelve heavy guns dug into the side of a hundred-foot bluff on the Cumberland to repel attack by water, and three semicircular miles of trenches to repel it by land. Southern soldiers were strengthening these trenches as Grant's confident 15,000 Yankees approached on February 12. Probing attacks next day were repulsed, convincing Grant that Donelson would not topple without a fight. Ten thousand Union reinforcements arrived on February 14 along with four of Foote's ironclads and two wooden gunboats. Hoping to repeat the Fort Henry experience, Grant ordered the navy to shell the fort while his troops closed the ring to prevent the garrison's escape. But this time the navy met more than its match. Foote brought his ironclads too close, causing them to overshoot their targets and giving the shorter-range Confederate guns a chance to inflict severe damage on them. One by one these crippled monsters drifted downstream out of the fight. Each had taken some forty or more hits; fifty-four sailors were dead or wounded while not a gun or man in the rebel batteries had been lost. The morale of the southerners, who had believed the gunboats invincible, soared.

Their elation was premature, for they were still surrounded on three sides by better-armed foot soldiers and on the fourth by floating artillery which, though bruised, yet controlled the river. The besieged defenders had three apparent choices: to surrender now; to sit tight and hope for a miracle; or to cut their way out and escape to Nashville. That night, while Union soldiers who had thrown away blankets and overcoats on a previous balmy day shivered and caught pneumonia in driving sleet and snow, Confederate generals held a council of war to decide what to do. Floyd's division commanders, the self-important Tennessee politician Gideon Pillow and the darkly handsome West Pointer Simon Bolivar Buckner, agreed to try a breakout attack on the morrow. All night they shifted troops to Pillow's sector on the left. These movements were masked by the snow and howling winds.

As chance would have it, Grant was downstream conferring with Foote when the rebel attack exploded soon after dawn. The north wind blew the sound of battle away and kept him in ignorance of what was happening five miles to the south. Not expecting any fighting that day "unless I brought it on myself," Grant had told his division commanders merely to hold their positions until further notice. These instructions anticipated a pattern in Grant's generalship: he always thought more about what he planned to do to the enemy than what his enemy might do to him. This offensive-mindedness eventually won the war, but it also brought near disaster to Grant's forces more than once. On this occasion his orders to sit tight inhibited the two division commanders on the left and center from doing much to help General John A. McClernand's division on the right, which bore the full fury of the Confederate assault. McClernand was an ambitious Democrat from Illinois whose

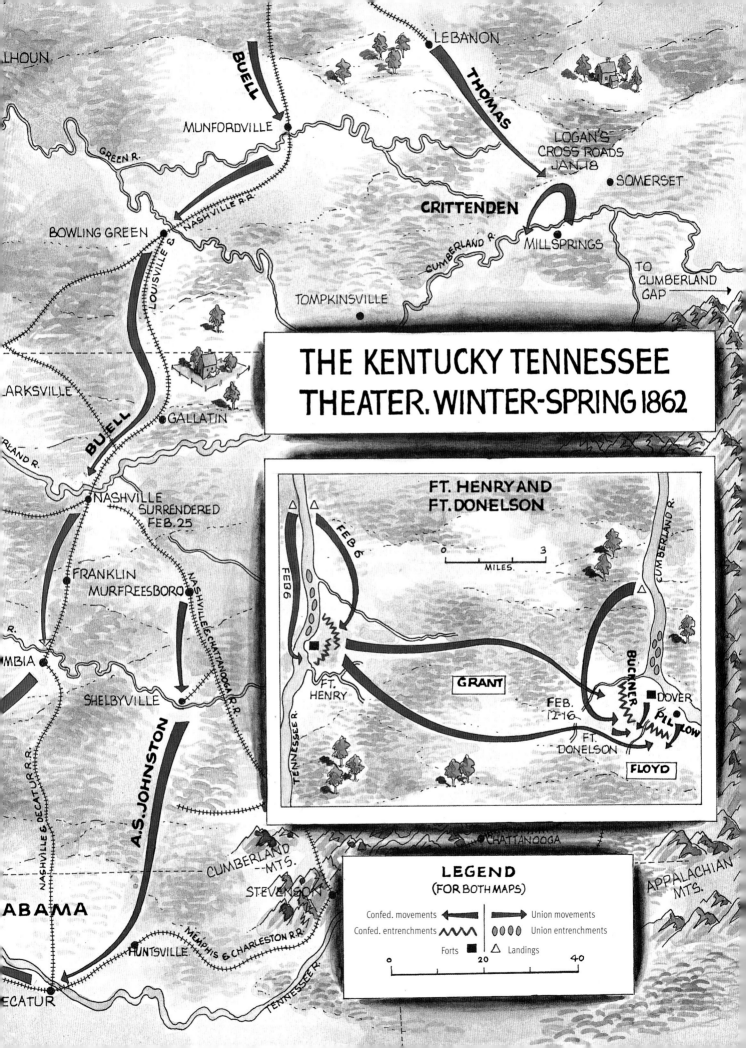

THE KENTUCKY TENNESSEE THEATER. WINTER-SPRING 1862

LHOUN

BUELL

LEBANON

THOMAS

MUNFORDVILLE

LOGAN'S CROSS ROADS JAN.18

GREEN R.

SOMERSET

NASHVILLE R.R.

CRITTENDEN

BOWLING GREEN

MILLSPRINGS

CUMBERLAND R.

LOUISVILLE &

TOMPKINSVILLE

TO CUMBERLAND GAP →

RLAND R.

BUELL

ARKSVILLE

GALLATIN

NASHVILLE SURRENDERED FEB. 25

FRANKLIN
MURFREESBORO

R.

NASHVILLE & CHATTANOOGA R.R.

MBIA

SHELBYVILLE

FT. HENRY AND FT. DONELSON

0   3
MILES.

FEB 6

FEB 6

FEB 6

CUMBERLAND R.

BUCKNER

GRANT

DOVER

FT. HENRY

FEB. 12-16

PILLOW

TENNESSEE R.

FT. DONELSON

FLOYD

A.S. JOHNSTON

NASHVILLE & DECATUR R.R.

CHATTANOOGA

CUMBERLAND MTS.

APPALACHIAN MTS.

ABAMA

STEVENSON

LEGEND
(FOR BOTH MAPS)

Confed. movements ⟵

Union movements ⟶

Confed. entrenchments ∿∿∿

Union entrenchments ⬭⬭⬭

Forts ■

Landings △

MEMPHIS & CHARLESTON R.R.

HUNTSVILLE

TENNESSEE R.

ECATUR

0   20   40

This splendid painting by the French artist Paul Philippoteaux shows Grant at Fort Donelson as his men counterattack on February 15 to close the breach opened by the Confederate assault on the Union right. Note the wounded men at lower left being tended by surgeons while two black orderlies carry a wounded soldier at lower right.

thirst for glory had earned Grant's mistrust. On this frosty morning of February 15 McClernand got his chance to fight, but the odds were against him. Many of his regiments performed well, but after several hours of hard fighting five brigades on the Union right had been driven back nearly a mile. Demoralized and out of ammunition, they were in no condition to stop the rebels from escaping through the breach.

Couriers had dashed off to find Grant, who returned post-haste to the battlefield. Meanwhile General Pillow was taken aback by the exhaustion and disorganization of his victorious soldiers, who had suffered heavy casualties. He concluded that they could not march cross-country and fight off a possible flank attack by the Union reinforcements that his scouts reported were gathering. Pillow persuaded Floyd, over Buckner's agonized protest, to call off the breakout attempt and order the troops back to the relative safety of their trenches.

During this lull of Confederate indecision, Grant arrived on the scene. As at Belmont, he refused to panic. "The position on the right must be retaken," he told his officers. Grant, reckoning that the enemy must be more demoralized than his men, given their aborted breakout attempt, declared that "the one who attacks first now will be victorious and the enemy will have to be in a hurry if he gets ahead of me." Grant had Foote's gunboats lob a few shells at the rebels to give the infantry moral support while Union officers reorganized their brigades, counterattacked, and regained the ground lost in the morning.

Night fell on a dismal scene. Nearly a thousand Yankees and rebels had been killed and three thousand wounded, many of the latter suffering and dying in the thickening cold. A chill also fell on southern headquarters, where mutual recriminations hung heavy in the air. A planned nighttime escape of the garrison was aborted when scouts reported Union regiments camped near the only practicable road. Pillow still wanted the garrison to fight its way out, but Floyd and Buckner, convinced that such false heroics would sacrifice three-fourths of their men, considered surrender the only alternative. As political generals, however, Floyd and Pillow did not want to surrender their own persons. Remembering his prewar record, Floyd anticipated little mercy from his captors. He commandeered two steamboats docked near Donelson and escaped upriver with 1,500 of his Virginia troops in the darkness before dawn. The disputatious Pillow was no more eager than Floyd to become a prisoner of war. Having proclaimed "liberty or death" as his slogan, he chose liberty—and escaped with his staff across the Cumberland in a small boat. Before leaving, Floyd had turned the command of Fort Donelson over to Pillow, who in turn passed it to West Pointer Buckner. Disgusted by this *opéra bouffe*, Buckner intended to share the fate of his men.

Before surrendering, however, Buckner permitted another disgusted commander to escape with his men—Nathan Bedford Forrest, head of a cavalry battalion that had fought with distinction that day. A self-made man who had grown rich from slave trading and planting, Forrest enlisted as a private in June 1861 and rose to lieutenant-colonel of the battalion he raised and equipped at his own expense. Self-educated, with no previous military experience, Forrest became one of the South's most innovative and hard-driving commanders. He developed combined mounted and dismounted tactics not mentioned in military textbooks—which he had never read—but ideal for the wooded terrain of western Tennessee and northern Mississippi. A large, powerful, and fearless man, Forrest possessed a killer instinct toward Yankees and toward blacks in any capacity other than slave. Before daybreak on February 16 he led 700 troopers out of Fort Donelson across an icy stream too deep for infantry to ford, and escaped without encountering a single Union picket.

Soon after dawn on February 16, Buckner sent a proposal to Grant for discussion of surrender terms. Back came a blunt reply: "No terms except an unconditional and immediate surrender can be accepted. I propose to move immediately on your works." Buckner was nettled by these "ungenerous and unchivalrous" words. After all, he had lent the down-and-out Grant money to help him get home after his resignation from the army in 1854. Nevertheless, Buckner now had no choice but to surrender his twelve or thirteen thousand men. When this news reached the North, church bells rang and cannons fired salutes to celebrate the great victory. Lincoln promoted Grant to major general, making him second in command only to Halleck in the West. Eight months earlier Grant had been an obscure ex-captain of dubious reputation; now his name was celebrated by every newspaper in the land.

The strategic consequences of this campaign were the most important of the war so far. Nearly a third of Johnston's forces in the Tennessee-Kentucky theater were *hors de combat*. Half of the remainder were at Nashville and half at Columbus, two hundred miles apart with a victorious enemy between them in control of the rivers

The Civil War brought to the fore a good many men with no previous military experience who turned out to be gifted leaders of men in battle. Of these, Nathan Bedford Forrest was surely the most notable—and notorious. Enlisting as a private, he rose to the rank of lieutenant general before the war's end. Along the way, however, he made his lethal hatred of both blacks and whites in arms against the Confederacy infamously clear. After the war, Forrest was the reputed "Grand Wizard" of the Ku Klux Klan.

and railroads. Buell's unbloodied Army of the Ohio was bearing down on Nashville from the north, while a newly organized Union Army of the Mississippi commanded by John Pope threatened Columbus from across the Mississippi River. Johnston had to evacuate Nashville on February 23, making it the first Confederate state capital and important industrial center to fall. A few days later the garrison at Columbus also pulled out. All of Kentucky and most of Tennessee came under Union military control—save for guerrilla activity and periodic rebel cavalry raids, which thenceforth became endemic in this theater. Confederate forts still guarded the Mississippi along Tennessee's western border, but they seemed doomed as well. The *New York Tribune*, a good barometer of northern opinion, rose as high as it had fallen low after Bull Run: "The cause of the Union now marches on in every section of the country," declared the *Tribune*. "Every blow tells fearfully against the rebellion. The rebels themselves are panic-stricken, or despondent. It now requires no very far-reaching prophet to predict the end of the struggle."

Many rebels were indeed despondent. Southern newspapers and diarists lamented the "disgraceful . . . shameful . . . catalogue of disasters." Mary Boykin Chesnut suffered "nervous chills every day. Bad news is killing me." From London, James Mason reported that "the late reverses at Fort Henry and Fort Donelson have had an unfortunate effect upon the minds of our friends here." In the midst of these gloomy tidings, Jefferson Davis was inaugurated for his six-year presidential term on February 22, 1862. Davis and his Negro footmen in the inaugural procession wore black suits. When asked why, the coachman replied dryly: "This, ma'am, is the way we always does in Richmond at funerals and sichlike." The rain that poured down during the ceremony added to the funereal atmosphere. In his inaugural address, Davis conceded that "after a series of successes and victories, we have recently met with serious disasters."

Like their northern counterparts after Bull Run, however, southern spokesmen urged renewed dedication to the task. The losses of Forts Henry and Donelson "were for our own good!" according to Richmond newspapers. "Days of adversity prove the worth of men and of nations. . . . We must go to the work with greater earnestness than we have yet shown."

But southerners were fated to endure several more defeats before they could next celebrate a victory. Johnston's defensive line east of the Mississippi having collapsed in February, his line west of the river caved in the following month. A new general had taken command of the rebel forces in Arkansas—Earl Van Dorn, a diminutive but hard-bitten Mississippian who had been wounded five times in the Mexican War and in frontier Indian fighting. Van Dorn had dazzled Johnston with visions of an invasion through Missouri to capture St. Louis and then to descend on Grant's forces from the north. To do this, however, he first had to defeat a Union army of 11,000 men that had pushed Sterling Price's Missourians out of their home state during the winter. Van Dorn put together a motley force numbering 16,000, consisting of the divisions under Price and Ben McCulloch that had won at Wilson's Creek the previous August plus three regiments of Indians from the Five Civilized Nations in Indian Territory. The latter, mostly Cherokees, served under tribal chiefs who had made treaties of alliance with the Confederacy in the hope of achieving

greater independence within a southern nation than they enjoyed in the United States—an ironic hope, since it was mostly southerners who had driven them from their ancestral homeland a generation earlier. In any event, with Indian help the old Indian fighter Van Dorn intended to "make a reputation and serve my country.... I must have St. Louis—then Huzza!"

The small Union army standing in Van Dorn's way just south of Pea Ridge on the Arkansas-Missouri border was commanded by Samuel R. Curtis, a colorless but competent West Pointer who had fought in Mexico and subsequently served three terms as an Iowa congressman. Rather than attack Curtis's entrenched troops frontally, Van Dorn led his army on a long flanking march to cut Union supply lines and attack them from the rear. Alert northern scouts, including "Wild Bill" Hickok, detected the move. When Van Dorn attacked what he expected to be the enemy rear on the bleak, overcast morning of March 7, he found that Curtis had faced his troops about and was ready for him. On the Union left, artillery fire scattered the Indian regiments while Yankee riflemen killed McCulloch and his second in command and captured the third-ranking southern officer on that part of the field, taking all the steam out of the rebel attack. Meanwhile, Union infantry on the right three miles to the east, outnumbered by more than two to one, had grudgingly given ground in fierce fighting around Elkhorn Tavern at a critical road junction.

Next morning Van Dorn discovered that when you get in the enemy's rear, he is also in yours. Confederate troops had run short of ammunition, but the Union army now stood between them and their ammunition wagons. Both armies concentrated near Elkhorn Tavern, where a Federal artillery barrage knocked out southern batteries that did not have enough shells for effective counterfire. Seven thousand Union infantrymen swept forward in a picture-book charge led by Franz Sigel's division of German-American regiments from Missouri and Illinois. The rebels turned tail and ran. It was as inglorious a rout in reverse as Bull Run. Although each side suffered about 1,300 casualties, the battle of Pea Ridge was the most one-sided victory won by an outnumbered Union army during the war. Van Dorn's forces

The battle of Pea Ridge has sometimes been called the battle of Elkhorn Tavern. This painting shows the climax of the battle on the second day, March 8, 1862, as Union troops advanced across the valley in the middle distance against a Confederate brigade on Pea Ridge at the upper right and against the main Confederate position around Elkhorn Tavern in the right foreground. The man on horseback with his arm in a sling from a flesh wound is General Sterling Price, commander of the Missouri Confederate troops in the battle.

scattered in every direction. It took nearly two weeks to reassemble them. Johnston then ordered Van Dorn to bring his 15,000 men across the Mississippi to Corinth, a rail junction in northern Mississippi. But they did not arrive in time to take part in the ensuing battle near a small log church named Shiloh.

II

Criticism of Sidney Johnston rose to a crescendo after the losses in Tennessee, almost as if in mockery of the earlier praise for him. But Davis was not stampeded by this "senseless clamor." "If Sidney Johnston is not a general," said the president, "we had better give up the war, for we have no general." Johnston refused to reply to his critics. "The test of merit, in my profession . . . is success," he wrote privately. "It is a hard rule, but I think it right. . . . What the people want is a battle and a victory."

Depressed in spirit, Johnston seemed to have little hope of achieving that victory. Beauregard stepped into the breach and helped Johnston concentrate 42,000 men at Corinth, Mississippi—27,000 from the reunited wings of Johnston's army plus 15,000 brought up from New Orleans and Mobile. Commander of the latter was Braxton Bragg, a quick-tempered martinet whose arrival injected some discipline into an army dispirited by defeat. Bragg's departure from the Gulf Coast left that region denuded of infantry and vulnerable to an amphibious attack, but southern strategists considered it essential to defend Corinth, the junction of the Confederacy's main north-south and east-west railroads in the Mississippi Valley. Beauregard wanted to do more than that; he hoped to march north and sweep the Yankees out of

Tennessee. "We must do something," said Beauregard, "or die in the attempt, otherwise, all will be shortly lost." Johnston caught Beauregard's vision and energy. Together they planned an offensive to regain Tennessee.

Having taken credit (as department commander) for his subordinates' victories, Halleck had been promoted to the command of all Union troops west of the Appalachians. He sent Grant forward to Pittsburg Landing on the Tennessee River, twenty miles north of Corinth, and ordered Buell to join him there with 35,000 additional troops. When the two armies were united, Halleck intended to take field command of their 75,000 men and lead them against Corinth. But the rebels meant to hit Grant before Buell arrived. Beauregard drew up plans for a march by four different corps on converging roads to deploy for battle on April 4. The plans were better suited for veterans than for green troops and inexperienced staff officers. Few of these southern soldiers had made a one-day march of twenty miles, and fewer still had been in combat. In these respects Johnston's troops resembled the Federals that McDowell had led to Bull Run nine months earlier—and their fate was similar. The march turned into a nightmare of confusion and delays, aggravated by heavy rain that bogged down wagons and artillery. It was late on April 5 before the army had deployed in position.

By this time Beauregard was in despair and wanted to call off the attack. The two-day delay, he said, would mean that Buell had reinforced Grant. Beauregard was also certain that the noise made by rebel soldiers firing off their guns to see if rain-dampened powder still worked had eliminated all chance of surprise. But at a council of war on the afternoon of April 5, Johnston overruled his objections. Having finally gotten the army into position to fight, Johnston was not about to back down. Confederate colonels had already read out to their regiments Johnston's address pledging to lead them to "a decisive victory." No matter if Buell had reinforced Grant, said Johnston, "I would fight them if they were a million." He ordered his corps commanders to finish their preparations: "Gentlemen, we shall attack at daylight tomorrow."

The facts on which Beauregard based his counsel of caution should have been true—but they were not. Buell's lead division had indeed arrived at Savannah, Grant's headquarters nine miles downriver from Pittsburg Landing. But neither Grant nor Buell felt a sense of urgency, so they did not send this division forward or hurry the arrival of the others. Five of Grant's six divisions were camped on the tableland west of Pittsburg Landing. The sixth, under General Lew Wallace (future author of *Ben-Hur*), was stationed five miles to the north guarding the army's supply depots at another river landing. As he had done at Fort Donelson, Grant again focused his mind so intently on plans for attacking the rebels that he could spare no thoughts for what the rebels might be planning to do to him. His troops were equally offensive-minded and shared Grant's conviction that defeat had so demoralized and fatigued Johnston's army that "Corinth will fall much more easily than Donelson did when we do move." Grant did not entrench his men at Pittsburg Landing because he did not expect to fight there and did not want to

General Albert Sidney Johnston never had a chance to prove whether he could justify Jefferson Davis's extravagant faith in his generalship. After being forced out of his native state of Kentucky and losing most of Tennessee, he was killed while trying to recoup these losses in the battle of Shiloh.

rob them of their aggressive spirit. The two divisions nearest Corinth, which would receive the first thrust of any attack, were composed of new troops untried by combat. Commanding one of these divisions was William Tecumseh Sherman, recently restored to command. Like Grant, Sherman was overconfident. Five months earlier the press had labeled him insane because he had exaggerated the rebel threat in Kentucky. Now, perhaps to prove that he had recovered from his attack of nerves, Sherman underestimated the enemy threat.

Some northern newspapers claimed that the Union army was so surprised by the attack at Shiloh that their camps were overrun before many soldiers could get out of their tents. This illustration might seem to support the accusation, but in fact it shows part of Prentiss's division making a stand after a fighting retreat from their original line a quarter mile in advance of their camp. Eventually the Confederates captured Prentiss's camp.

Some of his front-line colonels thought that the increased noise and activity off to the south on April 4 and 5 indicated the buildup of something big. But Sherman dismissed this activity as nothing more "than some picket firing. . . . I do not apprehend anything like an attack on our position." For his part, Grant interpreted the signs of rebel movements as a possible threat to Wallace's isolated division downriver and warned Wallace to be alert. Grant wrote to Halleck on April 5 that he had "scarcely the faintest idea of an attack (general one) being made upon us, but will be prepared should such a thing take place."

But he was not prepared for the thousands of screaming rebels who burst out of the woods near Shiloh church next morning. They hit first the two green divisions

This lithograph of Shiloh Methodist Church illustrates the terrible irony of war. The peaceful, pastoral setting became the focal point of heavy fighting and many deaths on the morning of April 6 and again on the afternoon of the following day.

of Sherman and of Benjamin M. Prentiss, an Illinois political general with Mexican War experience. Against all odds, Johnston had achieved a surprise—but not a total one. Long before dawn one of Prentiss's brigade commanders had sent out a patrol that discovered advance units of the Confederate battle line. The patrol fell back slowly, skirmishing noisily to warn Prentiss's division, which scrambled into formation. Sherman's men also jumped up from breakfast and grabbed their muskets. As their commander rode forward to see what was happening, a volley rang out and Sherman's orderly fell dead at his side. "My God, we're attacked!" cried the general, finally convinced. After the initial shock, Sherman performed this day with coolness and courage. The next twelve hours proved to be the turning point of his life. What he learned that day at Shiloh—about war and about himself—helped to make him one of the North's premier generals. Sherman was everywhere along his lines at Shiloh, shoring up his raw troops and inspiring them to hurl back the initial assaults—with staggering losses on both sides. Sherman himself was wounded slightly (twice) and had three horses shot under him. On his left Prentiss's men also stood fast at first, while up from the rear came reinforcements from the other three divisions, two of which had fought at Donelson.

Waiting for Buell's arrival at army headquarters nine miles downriver, Grant heard the firing as he sat down to breakfast. Commandeering a dispatch boat, he steamed up to Pittsburg Landing and arrived on the battlefield about 9:00 A.M. The fighting by this time had reached a level unprecedented in the war. Johnston and

This lithograph portrays part of the Union line at Shiloh under attack on the morning of April 6. Note the soldier in the foreground running away while the officer, sword in hand, yells at him in vain to stop. Another officer, sword held high, leads reinforcements forward. The artist was Thure de Thulstrup, a native of Sweden who had served in the Swedish army and the French Foreign Legion before coming in the 1870s to the United States, where he had a successful career as a painter of military subjects, including many Civil War scenes.

Beauregard committed all six of their divisions early in the day; all of Grant's soldiers in the vicinity also double-timed to the front, which stretched six miles between the Tennessee River on the Union left and Owl Creek on the right. Grant sent a courier to summon Lew Wallace's division to the battlefield. But Wallace took the wrong road and had to countermarch, arriving too late to participate in the battle on April 6. For better or worse, Grant's five divisions on the field had to do all the fighting that first day at Shiloh.

For thousands of them the shock of "seeing the elephant" (the contemporary expression for experiencing combat) was too much. They fled to the rear and cowered under the bluffs at the landing. Fortunately for the Union side, thousands of southern boys also ran from the front with terror in their eyes. One of the main tasks of commanders on both sides was to reorganize their shattered brigades and plug holes caused by this leakage to the rear and mounting casualties. Grant visited each of his division commanders during the day and established a line of reorganized stragglers and of artillery along the ridge west of Pittsburg Landing to make a last-ditch stand if the rebels got that far. Johnston went personally to the front on the Confederate right to rally exhausted troops by his presence. There in midafternoon he was hit in the leg by a bullet that severed an artery and caused him to bleed to death almost before he realized he had been wounded.

Beauregard took command and tried to keep up the momentum of the attack. By this time the plucky southerners had driven back the Union right and left two miles from their starting point. In the center, though, Prentiss with the remaining fragments of his division and parts of two others had formed a hard knot of resistance along a country lane that northern soldiers called the sunken road and rebels called the hornets' nest. Grant had ordered Prentiss to "maintain that position at all

Part of "Grant's Last Line" at Shiloh, a concentration of big guns along the ridge above Pittsburg Landing. The Confederates did not test the power of this line. This photograph of a twenty-four-pounder cannon was taken after the battle.

hazards." Prentiss obeyed the order literally. Instead of containing and bypassing this position (a tactical maneuver not yet developed), southern commanders launched a dozen separate assaults against it. Although 18,000 Confederates closed in on Prentiss's 4,500 men, the uncoordinated nature of rebel attacks enabled the Yankees to repel each of them. The southerners finally pounded the hornets' nest with sixty-two field guns and surrounded it with infantry. Prentiss surrendered his 2,200 survivors at 5:30, an hour before sunset. Their gritty stand had bought time for Grant to post the remainder of his army along the Pittsburg Landing ridge.

Part of the "hornets' nest," a farm road on the Shiloh battlefield defended against repeated Confederate attacks on April 6 until the remnants of the Union brigades that fought here were surrounded and captured. This photograph was taken after the bodies had been buried, the wounded removed, and the detritus of battle cleaned up. Blasted trees and vegetation bear witness to the fierceness of the fighting here.

By then, Lew Wallace's lost division was arriving and Buell's lead brigade was crossing the river. Beauregard did not know this yet, but he sensed that his own army was disorganized and fought out. He therefore refused to authorize a final assault in the gathering twilight. Although partisans in the endless postwar postmortems in the South condemned this decision, it was a sensible one. The Union defenders had the advantages of terrain (many of the troops in a Confederate assault would have had to cross a steep backwater ravine) and of a large concentration of artillery—including the eight-inch shells of two gunboats. With the arrival of reinforcements, Yankees also gained the advantage of numbers. On the morrow Buell and Grant would be able to put 25,000 fresh troops into action alongside 15,000 battered but willing survivors who had fought the first day. Casualties and straggling had reduced the number of Beauregard's effectives to about 25,000. Sensing this, Grant never wavered in his determination to counterattack on April 7. When some of his officers advised retreat before the rebels could renew their assault in the morning, Grant replied: "Retreat? No. I propose to attack at daylight and whip them."

Across the lines Beauregard (who had sent a victory telegram to Richmond) and his men were equally confident. They had won; tomorrow's task would be simply one of mopping up. If Beauregard had been aware of Grant's reinforcements he would not have been so confident, but the rebel high command had been misled by a report from cavalry in northern Alabama that Buell was heading that way. But Nathan Bedford Forrest's scouts watched boats ferry Buell's brigades across the river all through the night. Forrest tried to find Beauregard. Failing in this, he gave

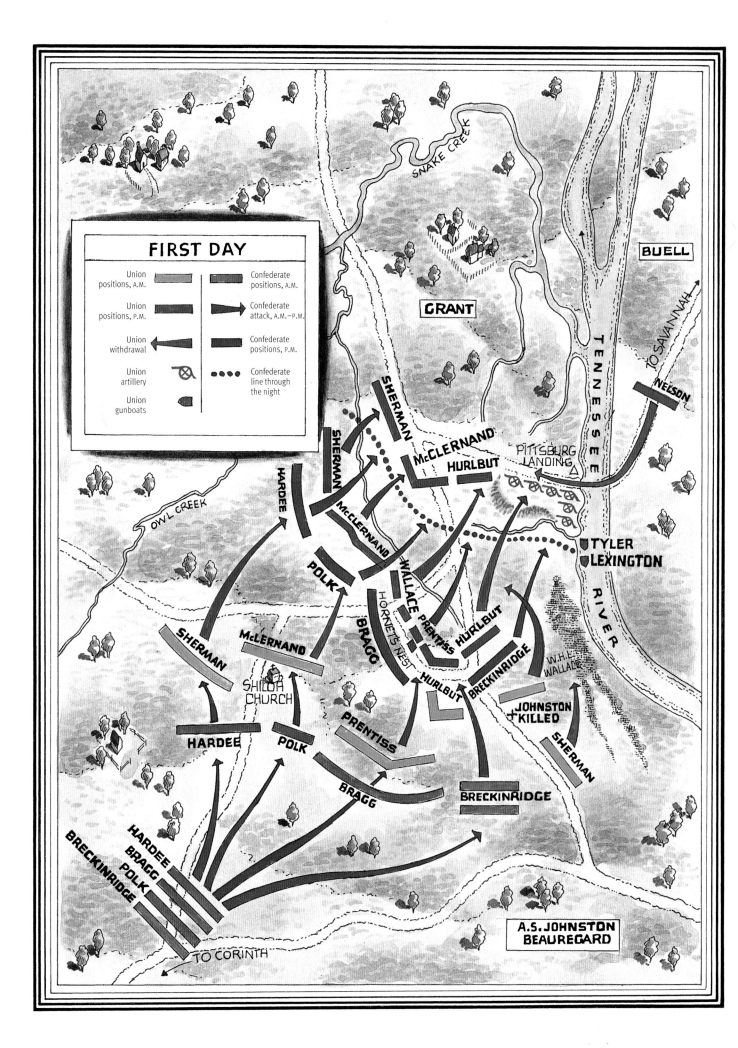

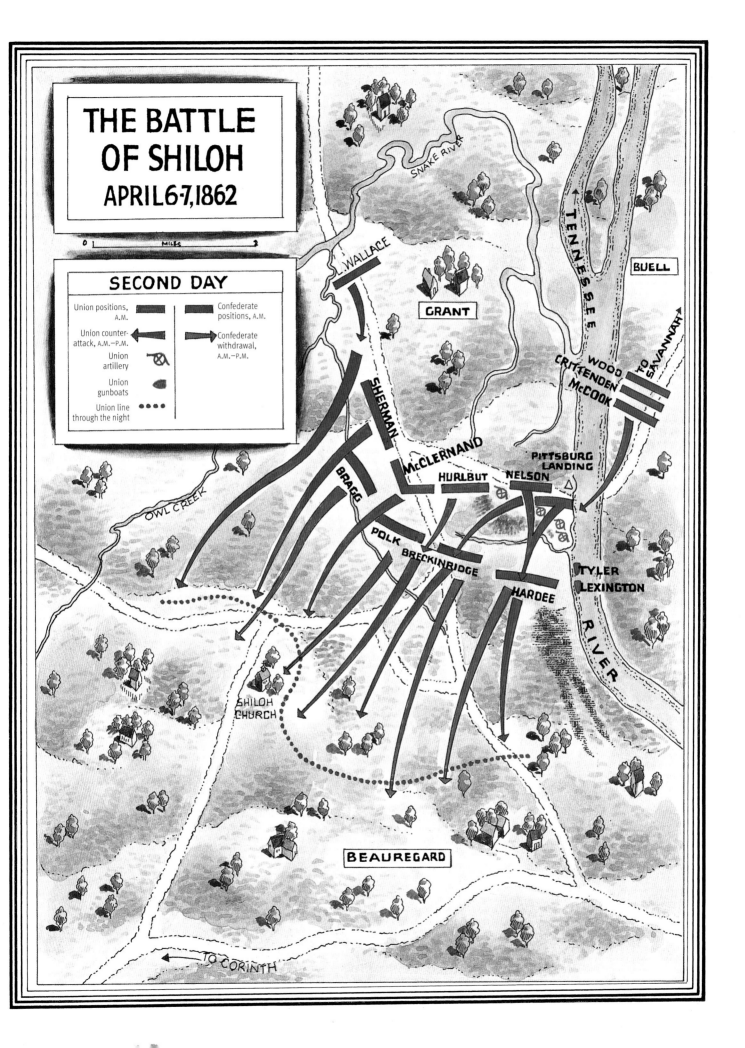

THE BATTLE OF SHILOH
APRIL 6-7, 1862

0 — MILES — 2

SECOND DAY

Union positions, A.M.

Confederate positions, A.M.

Union counter-attack, A.M.–P.M.

Confederate withdrawal, A.M.–P.M.

Union artillery

Union gunboats

Union line through the night

SNAKE RIVER

TENNESSEE

BUELL

WALLACE

GRANT

WOOD
CRITTENDEN
McCOOK

TO SAVANNAH

SHERMAN

McCLERNAND

PITTSBURG LANDING

BRAGG

HURLBUT

NELSON

OWL CREEK

POLK
BRECKINRIDGE

TYLER
LEXINGTON

HARDEE

RIVER

SHILOH CHURCH

BEAUREGARD

TO CORINTH

Taken a few days after the battle, this photograph shows several steamboats tied up at Pittsburg Landing, where Buell's troops crossed from the other side of the Tennessee River to reinforce Grant. The boat at the right is the Tycoon, *sent by the Cincinnati Sanitary Commission with medical supplies and hospital beds for the wounded. Next to it is the* Tigress, *Grant's headquarters boat, on which he had rushed to the battlefield on the morning of April 6.*

up in disgust when other southern generals paid no attention to his warnings. "We'll be whipped like Hell" in the morning, he predicted.

Soldiers on both sides passed a miserable night. Rain began falling and soon came down in torrents on the 95,000 living and 2,000 dead men scattered over twelve square miles from Pittsburgh Landing back to Shiloh church. Ten thousand of the living were wounded, many of them lying in agony amid the downpour. Lightning and thunder alternated with the explosions of shells lobbed by the gunboats all night long into Confederate bivouacs. Despite their exhaustion, few soldiers slept on this "night so long, so hideous." Grant spent the night on the field with his men, declining the comfort of a steamboat cabin. Four miles away Beauregard slept comfortably in Sherman's captured tent near Shiloh church. Next morning he had a rude awakening. A second day at Shiloh began with a surprise attack, but now the Yankees were doing the attacking. All along the line Buell's Army of the Ohio and Grant's Army of Western Tennessee swept forward, encountering little resistance at first from the disorganized rebels. In midmorning the southern line stiffened, and for a few hours the conflict raged as hotly as on the previous day. A particularly unnerving sight to advancing Union troops was yesterday's casualties. Some

One Union soldier stands guard and another nurses a fire while others try to get some sleep during a downpour at the Shiloh battlefield on the night of April 6–7.

wounded men had huddled together for warmth during the night. "Many had died there, and others were in the last agonies as we passed," wrote a northern soldier. "Their groans and cries were heart-rending."

By midafternoon the relentless Union advance had pressed the rebels back to the point of their original attack. Not only did the Yankees have fresh troops and more men, but the southerners' morale had suffered a letdown when they realized they had not won a victory after all. About 2:30 Beauregard issued the order to retreat. The bluecoats, too fought out and shot up for effective pursuit over muddy roads churned into ooze by yet another downpour, flopped down in exhaustion at the recaptured camps. Next day Sherman did take two tired brigades in pursuit four miles down the Corinth road, but returned after a brief skirmish with Forrest's cavalry that accomplished little more than the wounding of Forrest. Both the blue and the gray had had enough fighting for a while.

And little wonder. Coming at the end of a year of war, Shiloh was the first battle on a scale that became commonplace during the next three years. The 20,000 killed and wounded at Shiloh (about equally distributed between the two sides) were nearly double the 12,000 battle casualties at Manassas, Wilson's Creek, Fort Donelson, and Pea Ridge *combined*. Gone was the romantic innocence of Rebs and Yanks who had marched off to war in 1861. "I never realized the 'pomp and circumstance' of the thing called glorious war until I saw this," wrote a Tennessee private after the battle. "Men . . . lying in every conceivable position; the dead . . . with their eyes wide open, the wounded begging piteously for help. . . . I seemed . . . in a sort of daze." Sherman

The walking wounded of Grant's army and stragglers pretending to be wounded are making their way to the rear at Pittsburg Landing while ammunition wagons are going to the front. These men had "seen the elephant" and no longer had any notions of romance or glory about war.

described "piles of dead soldiers' mangled bodies . . . without heads and legs. . . . The scenes on this field would have cured anybody of war."

Shiloh disabused Yankees of their notion of a quick Confederate collapse in the West. After the surrender of Donelson, a Union soldier had written: "My opinion is that this war will be closed in less than six months." After Shiloh he wrote: "If my life is spared I will continue in my country's service until this rebellion is put down, should it be ten years." Before Shiloh, Grant had believed that one more Union victory would end the rebellion; now he "gave up all idea of saving the Union except by complete conquest." Shiloh launched the country onto the floodtide of total war.

III

Although Grant had snatched victory from the jaws of defeat at Pittsburg Landing, northern opinion at first focused more on those jaws than on victory. Newspapers reported Union soldiers bayoneted in their tents and Grant's army cut to pieces before being saved by the timely arrival of Buell. A hero after Donelson, Grant was now a bigger goat than Albert Sidney Johnston had been in the South after his retreat from Tennessee. What accounted for this fickleness of northern opinion? The reverses of the first day at Shiloh and the appalling casualties furnish part of the explanation. The self-serving accounts by some of Buell's officers, who talked more freely to reporters than did Grant and his subordinates, also swayed opinion. False rumors circulated that Grant was drunk at Shiloh. The disgraced captain of 1854 seemed unable to live down his reputation. Then, too, the magnitude of northern victory at Shiloh was not at first apparent. Indeed, Beauregard persevered in describing the battle as a southern triumph. Only "untoward events," he reported, had saved the Yankees from annihilation; the Confederate withdrawal to Corinth was part of a broader strategic plan!

After the recognition of Confederate failure at Shiloh finally sank in, many southerners turned against Beauregard. They blamed him for having snatched defeat from the jaws of victory by refusing to order a final twilight assault on the first day. About the time this shift occurred in southern opinion, Illinoisians began coming to Grant's defense. When a prominent Pennsylvania Republican went to Lincoln and said that Grant was incompetent, a drunkard, and a political liability to the administration, the president heard him out and replied: *"I can't spare this man; he fights."* Grant made mistakes before the battle that all of his undoubted coolness and indomitable will during the fighting barely redeemed. But in the end the Union armies won a strategic success of great importance at Shiloh. They turned back the Confederacy's supreme bid to regain the initiative in the Mississippi Valley. From then on it was all downhill for the South in this crucial region. On the very day, April 7, that Beauregard's battered army began its weary retreat to Corinth, a Union army-navy team won another important—and almost bloodless—triumph on the Mississippi.

When the Confederates evacuated their Gibraltar at Columbus in February, they left a garrison of 7,000 men and fifty-two big guns at Island No. 10 fifty miles downriver. This strongpoint blocked northern shipping as completely as Columbus had done. Halleck ordered Andrew Foote's river fleet to shell the island batteries while John Pope's newly formed Army of the Mississippi closed in by land from the Mis-

From March 15 to April 7, 1862, Union gunboats and mortar boats hammered Confederate positions on Island No. 10, strategically located at a sharp bend in the Mississippi. The Eads ironclads are in the foreground of this Harper's Weekly *illustration while the mortar boats sheltered behind a point at the bend send their big shells arching through the air toward the island.*

During a storm on the night of April 1–2, fifty sailors from the Union gunboat fleet and fifty soldiers from the 42nd Illinois carried out a daring raid to spike Confederate cannons at Island No. 10. The purpose of the raid was to improve the chances for a successful run past the island by the U.S.S. Carondelet *three nights later.*

souri side of the river. Foote's seven ironclads and ten mortar boats (large scows, each mounting a thirteen-inch mortar) bombarded the rebel defenses at long range without much effect. Meanwhile Pope gained control of the Missouri bank below the island and brought several shallow-draft transports through a cutoff canal dug by his troops with the aid of contrabands. This penned in the Confederates from three sides, leaving open only a precarious supply line through the swamps on the Tennessee bank of the river. Pope pleaded with Foote for a gunboat to run the gauntlet of guns on the island and protect a downriver troop crossing to close this fourth side. The *Carondelet* did so during a spectacular thunderstorm on the night of April 4 and was fol-

The U.S.S. Carondelet *is tied up on the bank after her spectacular run past the Confederate batteries on Island No. 10 during another storm on the night of April 4–5. Enemy gunners fired forty-nine shots at her and missed every time.*

lowed by a second gunboat two nights later during another storm. Spearheaded by the gunboats, Pope's army crossed the Mississippi, surrounded the garrison, and on April 7 captured 4,500 men along with guns and equipment the South could ill afford to lose. With only a handful of casualties, Pope achieved what Halleck considered a more brilliant success than Grant at Donelson, and the North acquired a new hero.

After this success, Halleck ordered Pope to join Grant and Buell at Pittsburg Landing, where Halleck took personal command of the combined armies numbering more than 100,000 men. Assembled there was the greatest concentration of military talent in the war, including four future generals in chief of the United States army: Halleck, Grant, Sherman, and Philip Sheridan (then a captain); and five other present or future commanders of whole armies: Buell, Pope, Rosecrans, George H. Thomas, and James B. McPherson. Halleck could scarcely find a use for all this talent, particularly for Grant. Old Brains still undervalued Grant's worth and put him on the shelf by appointing him to a meaningless post as second in command of the combined forces. An unhappy Grant requested transfer, but in the end he stayed on.

Halleck inched forward toward Corinth, entrenching the whole army at every skirmish with Confederate outposts. If Halleck's precautions made sure that Beauregard could not attack him, they made equally sure that he could not effectively attack Beauregard. Halleck waged war by the book—his book. It was an eighteenth-century Jominian war of maneuver and siege against "strategic points," not a modern war of all-out combat to destroy or cripple an enemy army. Halleck would be happy if he could maneuver Beauregard out of Corinth without a fight. Grant, for one, could not see "how the mere occupation of places was to close the war while large and effective rebel armies existed." But Halleck wanted no part of Grant's kind of war.

Confederate leaders also considered Corinth a crucial strategic point. "If defeated here," wrote Beauregard two weeks after Shiloh, "we lose the whole Mississippi Valley and probably our cause." The South scraped up reinforcements from eastern

Soldiers of the 31st Ohio fording Chambers Creek during the advance toward Corinth in May 1862. This lithograph is based on a sketch by a soldier in that regiment. Most soldiers removed their shoes and tied them around their necks before wading the stream. The soldier in the right foreground lifting his leg to let the water drain from his shoe probably wishes he had done so.

Tennessee and from as far away as the south Atlantic coast. Van Dorn brought 15,000 from Arkansas. By the beginning of May Beauregard had 70,000 men at Corinth. But many of them were recovering from wounds while, because of a befouled, inadequate water supply, others died of typhoid and dysentery. Given this attrition and the prospect of being surrounded by a siege, Beauregard changed his mind about the need to hold Corinth at all costs. As Halleck was extending his lines around the city and hauling forward his siege guns, Beauregard on May 29 decided to pull out. He did so with great skill and stealth, leaving behind only a few stragglers and a pestilential town as spoils for Halleck. Fifty miles to the south at his new base in Tupelo, Mississippi, Beauregard pronounced the evacuation of Corinth "equivalent to a great victory." But a shocked and angry Jefferson Davis believed that another such victory would sink the Confederacy. Although Beauregard talked of resuming the offensive, Davis had enough of his Napoleonic plans and Lilliputian execution. When Beauregard took an unauthorized leave of absence to recuperate his broken health, Davis seized the opportunity and replaced him with Braxton Bragg.

With the capture of Corinth, the Union army stood astride the railroad to Memphis. Before Halleck's bluecoats could take the Confederacy's fifth largest city, however, a hybrid fleet on the river did the job. It had not been easy. After the loss of Island No. 10, the next rebel strongpoint on the Mississippi was Fort Pillow, fifty miles above Memphis. In addition to the fort's forty guns, the southerners had a new river defense fleet of eight steamboats converted into armed rams. On May 10 this makeshift navy had surprised the Union fleet at Plum Run Bend above Fort Pillow with a hit-and-run attack that put two ironclads temporarily out of action with gaping holes below the waterline. The elated southern fleet captain assured Beauregard that the Yankees "will never penetrate farther down the Mississippi."

But the bluejackets soon got some rams of their own. The ram concept was a

On the night of May 29–30 the Confederates pulled out of Corinth, setting warehouses and the railroad station on fire. Union troops entered the town the next morning, as shown in this woodcut illustration from Frank Leslie's Illustrated Newspaper. *The crossing of the Mobile and Ohio and the Memphis and Charleston railroads at the extreme right of the illustration gave Corinth its strategic value.*

revival of naval tactics from the days of galleys, before the advent of gunpowder and sailing ships (which could rarely be maneuvered to ram another ship) had converted navies to broadside firepower. The development of steam propulsion made ramming feasible again. Several hundred tons of warship with a reinforced prow moving at even a slow speed could be far more lethal than any shot or shell then in existence. The *Virginia* had proved this at Hampton Roads, and the Confederate river fleet proved it again at Plum Run Bend. The most enthusiastic proponent of ram power was a thin, frail-looking, fifty-seven-year-old civil engineer from Pennsylvania, Charles Ellet. Having failed to interest the Union navy in his ideas, Ellet took them to Secretary of War Stanton, who expressed enthusiasm. Stanton made Ellet a colonel and sent him west to develop a ram fleet for river fighting.

Ellet rebuilt nine steamboats according to his own calculations for maximum strength. Preferring riverboat men to naval personnel for his crews, he signed them up for special service. Ellet commanded the flagboat himself and placed his brother Alfred in command of the second boat. Seven other Ellets—brothers, nephews, and a son—also joined the enterprise, some as captains. This remarkable family and its even more remarkable flotilla wanted to prove their mettle by attacking the rebel fleet at Fort Pillow. Beauregard forestalled them by ordering the evacuation of the fort when his withdrawal from Corinth made it vulnerable to land attack. But the Confederates decided to make a stand at Memphis. At sunrise on June 6 the southern river fleet steamed out to challenge five Union ironclads and four of Ellet's rams. Thousands of Memphis residents lined the bluffs to cheer on their side.

But in less than two hours the home team had lost. Charles and Alfred Ellet headed their rams downriver at fifteen knots against the rebel van. The shock of collision between Charles's boat and the leading Confederate ram could be felt on the bluffs. Charles's attack punched a huge hole in the rebel bow, while Alfred's boat squeezed between two southern rams converging on her, causing them to collide with each other. Alfred then circled back and rammed the rebel boat that had sur-

This illustration of the battle of Memphis on June 6, 1862, is based on a sketch by Captain Henry Walke of the U.S.S. Carondelet. *The defeated Confederate fleet is in the foreground. Looming in the left front is the C.S.S.* Bragg, *on fire and soon to be captured. Only the twin stacks of the C.S.S.* Beauregard *can be seen above the surface at the right center. The only Confederate vessel to escape was the C.S.S.* Van Dorn, *depicted here at the extreme left heading downriver as fast as her paddle wheels and the current could take her.*

vived this crash. Meanwhile the Union gunboats had gotten into the action. Their salvos finished off two crippled Confederate boats, sank another, and captured three others after disabling them. Only one southern vessel escaped downriver. The rebel fleet existed no more. Residents of Memphis watched in sullen silence as Ellet's son Charles, Jr., led a four-man detachment to raise the stars and stripes over the post office. His doughty father, the only significant Union casualty of the conflict, died of his wound two weeks later. Charles, Jr., became the army's youngest colonel at nineteen and subsequently took command of the ram fleet. A year later he too was dead.

The Yankees occupied Memphis and turned it into a base for future operations, while the fleet steamed three hundred miles downriver to the Confederacy's next bastion at Vicksburg. Meanwhile the spectacular achievements of the river fleet had been eclipsed by the salt-water navy, which captured New Orleans and pushed upriver to plant the American flag deep in the heart of Dixie.

The capture of New Orleans illustrated the strategic wisdom of Lincoln's desire to attack several places simultaneously. Union pressure in Tennessee had forced southern leaders to strip Louisiana of an army division (which fought at Shiloh) and eight gunboats (the fleet destroyed at Memphis). Left to defend New Orleans were 3,000 short-term militia, some river batteries just below the city where Andrew Jackson had beaten the British in 1815, a mosquito fleet of a dozen small gunboats, two unfinished ironclads, and two forts mounting 126 guns astride the Mississippi seventy-five miles below the city. The defenders relied mainly on these forts, which were expected to blow out of the water any wooden warships foolish enough to breast the three-knot current in an attempt to pass them. But the Union navy had already shown that enough ships with enough big guns commanded by an intrepid sailor were more than a match for brick forts. The navy was about to prove it again; the sailor this time was the most intrepid of all, Flag-Officer David Glasgow Farragut.

Sixty years old, Farragut had gone to sea at the age of nine and fought in the War of 1812 and the Mexican War. Like Grant, he possessed great force of character rather than a subtle intellect. Although he had been born in Tennessee and was married to a Virginian, Farragut's loyalty to the flag he had served for half a century was unswerving. When fellow southerners tried to persuade him to defect, he rejected their entreaties with the words: "Mind what I tell you: You fellows will catch the devil before you get through with this business." They would catch much of it from Farragut himself. In February 1862 he took command of a task force comprising eight steam sloops (frigates drew too much water to get over the bars at the mouth of the Mississippi), one sailing sloop, and fourteen gunboats. Accompanying this force were nineteen mortar schooners to soften up the forts with high-angle fire before the fleet ran past them. To deal with any resistance on land, transports carried to the Gulf 15,000 soldiers commanded by the ubiquitous Benjamin Butler.

By early April, Farragut got his fleet over the bars and up to an anchorage a couple of miles below the forts. From there the mortar schooners began to pound the forts at the rate of three thousand shells a day. Although this blitz dismounted a few guns and created a great deal of rubble, it did little to reduce enemy firepower. Farragut had never believed much in the mortar attack; after six days of it he decided to run the gauntlet without further delay. Two Union gunboats crept up under the forts one night to cut the chain holding a boom of hulks across the river; though discovered and fired upon, their crews succeeded in making an opening large enough for the fleet to squeeze through single file. At 2:00 A.M. on April 24, seventeen of Farragut's warships weighed anchor and began to steam upriver. The forts opened fire with eighty or ninety guns; the ships replied with twice as many; the mortar fleet recommenced its bombardment; the Confederate ironclad *Louisiana*, moored to the bank with her engines not yet working, cut loose with as many of her sixteen guns as would bear. Three of the rebel gunboats entered the fray and tried to ram Union warships (one of them succeeded, sinking the ten-gun sloop *Varuna*) while the civilian captains of the other rebel boats fled upstream or scuttled their craft. Confederate tugs pushed fire-rafts heaped with flaming pine and pitch into the current to float down on Yankee ships. With all this happening in a space of scarcely a square mile, it was the greatest fireworks display in American history.

Every Union ship that got through, as well as the four that did not, took a heavy pounding; the fleet lost thirty-seven men killed and 147 wounded during the hour and a half it took to pass the forts. The rebels suffered fewer casualties, but their mosquito fleet was gone, the unfinished ironclads were destroyed by their crews to prevent capture, the garrisons in the forts later mutinied and surrendered, and the militia scampered for the hinterland. On the morning of April 25, Farragut's ships silenced the river batteries below New Orleans with a broadside or two. The fleet

The thin lips and piercing eyes of David Glasgow Farragut give evidence of his grim determination. With the capture of New Orleans at the end of April 1862, he won perhaps the most spectacular victory of the war so far. As a reward, Farragut was promoted to rear admiral, in July 1862. In December 1862 he was promoted to vice admiral and in July 1866 he became the first full admiral in American history.

This famous painting by Mauritz F. H. de Haas depicts Farragut's fleet passing Forts St. Philip and Jackson and shows the Confederate ram C.S.S. Manassas *pushing a fire-raft alongside Farragut's flagship, the U.S.S.* Hartford. *The* Hartford's *crew doused the flames while the Confederate tug* Mosher, *which had towed the raft downriver, sank in the right foreground—one of eight Confederate vessels lost in the battle.*

then steamed up to a city filled with burning cotton and cursing mobs brandishing pistols against the eleven-inch guns trained on their streets. A lad of seventeen at the time, George Washington Cable later recalled that on this bleak day "the crowds on the levee howled and screamed with rage. The swarming decks answered never a word; but one old tar on the *Hartford*, standing with lanyard in hand beside a great pivot-gun, so plain to view that you could see him smile, silently patted its big black breech and blandly grinned." On April 29 Farragut had marines raise the flag over public buildings; two days later Butler's unscathed troops moved in to begin an efficient but remorseless rule of the occupied city.

During the next two months most of Farragut's ships twice ascended the Mississippi, receiving the surrender of Baton Rouge and Natchez along the way. But Vicksburg proved another matter. Summoned to surrender, the military governor of the city replied: "Mississippians don't know, and refuse to learn, how to surrender. . . . If Commodore Farragut . . . can teach them, let [him] come and try." He came, he tried, but he did not conquer. In the last week of June the Union fleets that had subdued New Orleans and Memphis met at Vicksburg with the plan of crushing its defenses between the combined weight of more than two hundred guns and twenty-three mortars. But the rebel batteries emplaced on the sides and top of the two-hundred-foot bluff on which the city was built gave as good as they got. Farragut soon concluded that while naval bombardment might level the town and drive its inhabitants underground, the ship's guns could not alone overcome a determined defense. And the South was determined to defend this last barrier to Union control of the Mississippi. Earl Van Dorn had arrived to command ten thousand soldiers entrenched at Vicksburg by the end of June. A Union infantry assault up the bluffs from the river would be suicidal. The only way to crack the defenses was to attack with a large land force from the rear while maintaining the naval blockade on the river. How to do this was a knotty problem in strategy that the Union army would not solve for nearly a year.

Farragut had brought 3,000 of Butler's soldiers up to Vicksburg. Too few in number for operations against Van Dorn, these men set to work (with the help of 1,500 contrabands) to dig a canal across an oxbowed neck of land out of range of Vicksburg's guns, in the hope that the river would cut a new channel and leave the Confederate fortress high and dry. But the Mississippi, dropping several inches every day in the summer drought, refused to cooperate. Farragut became alarmed that his deep-draft vessels would be stranded by the falling river. Three-fourths of the Union soldiers and half of the sailors fell ill with typhoid, dysentery, or malaria, with several dying each day.

The Yankees finally gave up the attempt to take Vicksburg this summer, but not before the rebels gave them a parting black eye. The weapon that delivered this blow was the C.S.S. *Arkansas* commanded by the South's own sea-dog counterpart of Farragut, Kentuckian Isaac Newton Brown. This thirty-year veteran of the U.S. navy had been overseeing the completion of a homemade ironclad up the Yazoo River while the Union fleet was shelling Vicksburg. Propelled by balky engines, carrying ten guns, and resembling the *Virginia* in appearance, the *Arkansas* steamed down to challenge the combined Federal fleets in mid-July. She first encountered and crippled the famed *Carondelet*, then swooped down between the two surprised Union flotillas

For three weeks (July 15–August 6, 1862), the C.S.S. Arkansas *raised southern hopes of regaining control of the lower Mississippi River. After giving Union fleets a black eye at Vicksburg, she steamed downriver by fits and starts until her balky engines gave out and she met an early end near Baton Rouge.*

tied up on either bank with their steam down and guns unloaded. They remedied the latter quickly and peppered the iron intruder with a hailstorm of shot. The *Arkansas* fired back "to every point of the circumference, without the fear of hitting a friend or missing an enemy." Despite suffering sixty casualties and extensive damage, the *Arkansas* disabled one of the Ellet rams and finally drifted to safety under the guns of Vicksburg.

Angry as a hornet, Farragut tried in vain to destroy the rebel monster. He finally gave up in disgust and on July 26 started his fleet downstream before low water grounded it. The Union river gunboats returned to Helena, Arkansas. For the time being, Confederates controlled two hundred river miles of the Mississippi from Vicksburg to Port Hudson, Louisiana, where they built fortifications second in strength only to Vicksburg's. The South took heart at the *Arkansas*'s exploits. Van Dorn decided to attack the Union garrison at Baton Rouge, "and then, Ho! for New Orleans." He ordered the *Arkansas* downriver to neutralize the Union gunboats at Baton Rouge while an army division attacked by land. But the *Arkansas*'s faltering engines kept her from arriving before the bluecoats had repulsed the rebel assault on August 5. Next day the ironclad's engines failed again as Union warships bore down on her. The crew blew her up to prevent capture.

This event served as a coda to what the *New York Tribune* had described in May as "A Deluge of Victories" in the West. From February to May, Union forces conquered 50,000 square miles of territory, gained control of 1,000 miles of navigable rivers, captured two state capitals and the South's largest city, and put 30,000 enemy soldiers out of action. The decline of southern morale in consequence of these reverses can be measured in the diary entries of Mary Boykin Chesnut during April and May:

> Battle after battle—disaster after disaster. . . . How could I sleep? The power they are bringing to bear against our country is tremendous. . . . Every morning's paper enough to kill a well woman [or] age a strong and hearty one. . . . New Orleans gone—and with it the Confederacy. Are we not cut in two? . . . I have nothing to chronicle but disasters. . . . The reality is hideous.

IV

In the view from Richmond the threat of McClellan's splendidly equipped army loomed even larger than disasters in the West. After much anxious prodding from Lincoln, McClellan had finally submitted a plan for a spring offensive against Joseph E. Johnston's army defending Manassas. Instead of attacking the rebels directly, McClellan proposed to transport his army by water down the Chesapeake Bay to the mouth of the Rappahannock River, eighty miles southeast of Manassas. This would place the Federals between Johnston and Richmond, thereby forcing the Confederates to race southward to defend their capital. McClellan anticipated either the capture of Richmond before Johnston could get there or a battle on a field of McClellan's choice where his men would not have to assault enemy trenches.

Lincoln did not like this plan, for if it placed McClellan's army between Johnston and Richmond it also left Johnston's army between McClellan and Washington. While Lincoln did not yet share the suspicion that as a Democrat McClellan was "soft" on the rebels and did not really want to smash them, he was not happy with McClellan's concept of strategy. Like Grant, the president believed in attacking the enemy's *army* rather than in maneuvering to capture *places*. By "going down the Bay in search of a field, instead of fighting near Manassas," Lincoln told McClellan, "[you are] only shifting, and not surmounting, a difficulty. . . . [You] will find the same enemy, and the same, or equal, intrenchments, at either place."

Joseph Johnston's hasty evacuation of the Confederate base at Manassas Junction on March 9, 1862, required the destruction of mountains of supplies and equipment the Confederates could ill afford to lose. When Union troops moved in, they found acres of ruins, as shown in this photograph taken several months later.

Before McClellan could launch his maneuver, Johnston anticipated it by withdrawing from Manassas in early March to a more defensible position behind the Rappahannock forty miles to the south. While perhaps prudent militarily, this retreat had adverse political consequences. Coming amid other Confederate reverses, it added to the depression of public morale. And it also drove deeper the wedge of distrust between Johnston and Davis. The latter was not persuaded of the necessity for pulling back; when he learned that Johnston had done so with a haste that required the destruction of huge stockpiles of supplies which could not be moved over muddy roads, Davis was mortified and angry.

He was no more mortified than Lincoln was by the discovery that the evacuated Confederate defenses were not as strong or extensive as McClellan had claimed. Newspaper correspondents found more Quaker guns at Centreville. One reporter wrote that "the fancied impregnability of the position turns out to be a sham." There had clearly been no more than 45,000 rebels on the Mansassas-Centreville line, fewer than half the number McClellan had estimated. "Utterly dispirited, ashamed, and humiliated," wrote another northern reporter, "I return from this visit to the rebel stronghold, feeling that their retreat is *our defeat.*"

The question was, what to do now? Johnston's retreat ruined McClellan's plan for flanking the enemy via the Rappahannock. But the Union commander was loath to give up the idea of transporting his army by water to a point east of Richmond. He proposed a landing at Fortress Monroe on the tip of the Virginia Peninsula, formed by the York and James rivers. With a secure seaborne supply line, the Union army could then drive seventy miles up the Peninsula, crossing only two rivers before reaching Richmond. This seemed to McClellan much better than Lincoln's idea of an overland invasion, which would have to advance one hundred miles from Washington to Richmond with a half-dozen rivers to cross and was dependent on a railroad vulnerable to cavalry raids. Nevertheless, Lincoln remained skeptical. Operating on interior lines, the Confederates could shift troops to the Peninsula and

McClellan would still "find the same enemy, and the same, or equal, intrenchments." But the president reluctantly consented to McClellan's plan, provided he left behind enough troops to defend Washington from a sudden rebel strike. McClellan promised.

Quartermaster General Montgomery Meigs assembled 400 ships and barges to transport McClellan's army of more than 100,000 men, 300 cannon, 25,000 animals, and mountains of equipment to the Peninsula. It was an awesome demonstration of the North's logistical capacity. But from the outset an ill fate seemed to upset McClellan's plans. Having lost full confidence in his commander, Lincoln reduced McClellan's authority. On March 8 he appointed four corps commanders for the Army of the Potomac after consulting the Committee on the Conduct of the War but without consulting McClellan. Three days later he demoted McClellan from general in chief to commander only of the Army of the Potomac. Lincoln justified this on the ground that McClellan's duties as a field commander would prevent him from giving attention to other theaters. Although this made sense, it also signaled Lincoln's reservations about McClellan. On March 11 the president also created a new military department in West Virginia for General Frémont. Republican pressure had compelled this move to give the antislavery Frémont an important command. Three weeks later the same

By 1862 the northern economy was pouring forth a huge amount of supplies and weapons for the war effort. Quartermaster General Montgomery Meigs had organized transportation for this mountain of material, part of which is photographed near the wharfs in Alexandria, ready for shipment to the Virginia Peninsula. What use McClellan would make of all this ordnance remained to be seen.

One of the forts ringing Washington in 1862, Fort Slemmer protected northern approaches to the capital. This 1862 photograph shows Union soldiers marching out of the sally port through a break in the abatis, a barrier of felled trees with branches interlaced to form an obstacle to attacking troops. Fort Slemmer was never attacked.

pressure induced Lincoln to detach a division from McClellan's army and send it to Frémont.

The president subsequently withheld other divisions from McClellan because he discovered that the general had left behind fewer troops than promised for the defense of Washington. McClellan was correct in his belief that the rebels had no intention of launching a strike against Washington and that even if they did, General Nathaniel P. Banks's 23,000 men in the Shenandoah Valley could be shifted in time to meet them. But in his impatience with civilian interference McClellan failed to explain to Lincoln his arrangements for defending the capital. Lincoln's concern for the safety of Washington was excessive. Yet if by some chance the rebels did threaten the city, the president would stand convicted of criminal negligence in the eyes of the northern people.

Lincoln's concern was heightened by a clash in the Shenandoah Valley on March 23. Stonewall Jackson commanded a small Confederate army there. His mission was to harass Banks's force near Winchester and to prevent the transfer of Union troops from the Valley to McClellan. When Jackson learned that two of Banks's three divisions were about to be transferred, he attacked, but ran into a full division and was badly mauled at Kernstown, just south of Winchester. A tactical defeat effectively became an important strategic victory when Lincoln canceled the transfer of Banks's divisions upon discovering there were fewer troops in place to defend Washington than McClellan had indicated. He also ordered Irvin McDowell's large corps of 35,000 men to remain in northern Virginia, temporarily depriving McClellan of some 50,000 of the 150,000 men he had expected to become part of his army on the Peninsula.

An embittered McClellan later charged that the administration did not want him,

Union forces counterattacking Stonewall Jackson's small army in the battle of Kernstown on March 23, 1862. Badly outnumbered, Jackson's troops suffered the only real defeat experienced by that general in the Civil War. But this tactical defeat turned into a strategic victory by preventing the reinforcement of McClellan with Union divisions drawn from the Shenandoah Valley.

A photograph of part of the Confederate defenses at Yorktown, with Union soldiers standing on the parapet after the Confederates evacuated the position on the night of May 3–4. The southerners had reinforced their earthworks with cotton bales, which were effective at absorbing enemy shots but had to be soaked with water to prevent them from being set afire by exploding shells.

Three of the huge mortars that McClellan intended to use to blast the Confederates out of their Yorktown defenses. Before they could do so, General Johnston withdrew the army to a new line close to Richmond.

a Democrat, to succeed—but the Republicans fumed at the general's apparent lack of will to succeed. During the first week of April about 55,000 of McClellan's troops approached the Confederate defenses near the old Revolutionary War battlefield at Yorktown. Dug in behind the Warwick River were fewer than 13,000 rebels commanded by John B. Magruder. By making a show of moving his infantry and artillery around to give the impression of having more men than he actually had, Magruder convinced McClellan that he could take Yorktown only by a siege. This news distressed Lincoln. "I think you had better break the enemies' line . . . at once," the president wired McClellan. "By delay the enemy will relatively gain upon you."

Lincoln tried to warn McClellan about growing Republican doubts of his loyalty, telling him that the public would not accept a repetition of Manassas. Never, Lincoln declared, had he more fervently supported him—"*But you must act.*"

McClellan did not act; instead he brought up his sappers and siege guns. Week after week went by as Union artillery prepared to blast the rebels from their trenches with mortars and two-hundred-pound shells. Lincoln felt driven to distraction by this "indefinite procrastination." As he had warned, the Confederates used the delay to shift Johnston's whole army to the Peninsula.

An inspection of the Yorktown defenses convinced Johnston that they were hopelessly weak: "No one but McClellan could have hesitated to attack." Johnston recommended withdrawal all the way to prepared defenses just outside Richmond itself. But Jefferson Davis and Robert E. Lee vetoed this proposal and ordered Johnston to defend the Yorktown line as long as possible. Lee's role in this matter was a measure of Davis's loss of confidence in Johnston. The president had recalled Lee from Savannah in March and installed him in Richmond as a sort of assistant commander in chief. Johnston hung on at Yorktown until the beginning of May, when he knew that McClellan was about to pulverize the defenses with his siege guns. Rather than wait for this, Johnston evacuated the trenches on the night of May 3–4 and retreated up the Peninsula. Davis was as dismayed by this further loss as Lincoln was by the consumption of a month's time in accomplishing it. On May 5 a strong Confederate rear guard commanded by James Longstreet fought a delaying action near the old colonial capital of Williamsburg. At the cost of 1,700 casualties the rebels inflicted 2,200 and delayed the Union pursuit long enough to enable the rest of the army to get away with its artillery and wagons.

Frequent rains had impeded operations during April; even heavier rains bogged down the armies during May. The only significant action took place on the water. With Johnston's retreat, Norfolk and its navy yard were no longer tenable. The Confederates blew up everything there of military value—including the *Virginia*—and pulled out. The *Monitor* led a flotilla of five gunboats up the James River. Their captains dreamed of emulating Farragut by running the river batteries and steaming on to level their guns at Richmond. Confederate officials began packing the archives and preparing to leave the city. But they soon unpacked. On May 15 the batteries at Drewry's Bluff seven miles below Richmond stopped the gunboats. The *Monitor* proved ineffective because her guns could not be elevated enough to hit the batteries on the ninety-foot bluff. Rebel cannons punished the other boats with a plunging fire while sharpshooters along the banks picked off Yankee sailors. The fleet gave up; Richmond breathed a collective sigh of relief.

Despite the gleam of cheer afforded by the battle of Drewry's Bluff, a sense of impending doom pervaded the South. McClellan's army approached to within six miles of Richmond, while reports of defeats and retreats arrived almost daily from the West. In the crisis atmosphere created by these setbacks during the spring of 1862, the southern Congress enacted conscription and martial law. Internal disaffection increased; the Confederate dollar plummeted. During these same months a confident Union government released political prisoners, suspended recruiting, and placed northern war finances on a sound footing. In contrapuntal fashion, developments on the home front responded to the rhythm of events on the battlefield.

In addition to establishing artillery batteries at a bend in the James River at Drewry's Bluff seven miles downriver from Richmond, Confederates sank several vessels in the channel to block Union warships trying to go upriver. The Drewry's Bluff batteries proved a more effective obstacle than these obstructions.

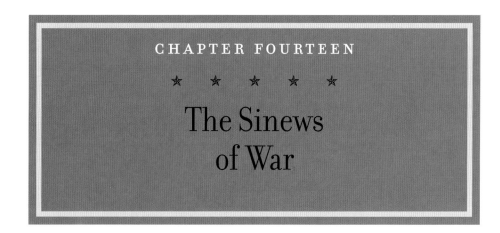

CHAPTER FOURTEEN

✯ ✯ ✯ ✯ ✯

The Sinews
of War

I

So long as the South seemed to be winning the war, Jefferson Davis was an esteemed leader. But after the fall of Forts Henry and Donelson, Davis had lost "the confidence of the country," according to the *Richmond Whig*. George W. Bagby, editor of the *Southern Literary Messenger* and a Richmond correspondent for several newspapers, wrote during the spring of 1862: "We have reached a very dark hour. . . . Cold, haughty, peevish, narrow-minded, pig-headed, *malignant*, he [Davis] is the cause. While he lives, there is no hope."

Austere and humorless, Davis did not suffer fools gladly. He lacked Lincoln's ability to work with partisans of a different persuasion for the common cause. Lincoln would rather win the war than an argument; Davis seemed to prefer winning the argument. Although he rarely defended himself in public, he sometimes privately lashed back at critics in a manner that only increased their hostility. Suffering from dyspepsia and a neuralgia that grew worse under wartime pressures and left him blind in one eye, Davis was wracked by constant pain that exacerbated his waspish temper. He recognized and regretted his thin-skinned defensiveness: "I wish I could learn just to let people alone who snap at me," Davis said to his wife in May 1862, "in forbearance and charity to turn away as well from the cats as the snakes."

He was under increasing pressure from the cats to wage total war, which would necessitate conscription, an assault on liberties cherished by the several states of the Confederacy. The Congress had continued to rely on volunteerism; in December 1861 it enacted legislation granting a fifty-dollar bounty and a sixty-day furlough to one-year men who reenlisted, with the additional proviso that they could join new regiments and elect new officers if they wished. But furloughs could weaken the army even more than the alarming disinclination of soldiers to reenlist—and their election of officers would likely favor the selection of "good ol' boys" rather than effective disciplinarians. Even Robert E. Lee, who had gone to war to prevent the coercion of individual states by a central government, insisted that the war would be lost unless the government could draft men into the army. Davis agreed and, on

Opposite page: Once the northern economy geared up for war, it produced both guns and butter in unprecedented quantities. These cannons, limber chests, and caissons have been offloaded at Broadway Landing, Virginia, ready to go to the front.

TO ARMS! TO ARMS!

$50 BOUNTY.

Do not wait to be Drafted, but Volunteer!!

The subscribers wish to get sixty Recruits for

CAPT. STICLEMAN'S COMPANY VIRGINIA VOLUNTEERS.

Persons wishing to enlist will find it greatly to their advantage to join this Company, as we can offer superior inducements.

You will receive pay and subsistence from the time your names are enrolled; your bounty of 50 dollars, and 25 dollars for clothing, as soon as you can be examined by an Army Surgeon.

For further particulars apply to us at Floyd Court House, Va.

LIUT. G. M. HELMS, } Recruiting
Sergt. J. W. SHELTON. } Officers.

February 22, 1862.

WE WILL ATTEND THE

PUBLIC MEETINGS

to be held at the following places

Indian Valley, Saturday, March 1st: Jackson Harriss' Stillhouse, Monday, 3rd; Jacob S. Harman's Store, Friday, 7th; Oil Mills Saturday, 8th; Copper Hill, Friday, 14th; Locust Grove, Saturday, 15th, and at Floyd Court House, March, 20th (Court day.)

Even before the Confederate Congress enacted a conscription law in April 1862, Virginia had mandated a militia draft. This broadside appealing for volunteers and promising a bounty anticipated similar action by other southern states.

March 28, 1862, sent a special message to Congress recommending conscription. Responding to the objections of state's righters and libertarians, the blunt, hot-tempered Senator Louis Wigfall of Texas took the floor and warned his colleagues: "The enemy are in some portions of almost every State in the Confederacy. . . . Virginia is enveloped by them. We need a large army. How are you going to get it? . . . No man has any individual rights, which come into conflict with the welfare of the country."

More than two-thirds of the congressmen and senators concurred. On April 16 they enacted the first conscription law in American history. It declared all able-bodied white male citizens between the ages of eighteen and thirty-five liable to service for three years. One-year volunteers must remain in the army two more years.

There was a crucial loophole: a drafted man could hire a substitute from the pool of "persons not liable for duty"—men outside the specified age group or immigrant aliens. This dispensation had deep roots in European as well as American history. Its justification was that the talents of men who could afford substitutes might be of more value organizing and producing the matériel of war on the home front. But recognizing that substitution would not exempt all men necessary for behind-the-lines duty, Congress on April 21 passed a supplementary law specifying several exempt categories: Confederate and state civil officials, railroad and river workers, telegraph operators, miners, several categories of industrial laborers, hospital personnel, clergymen, apothecaries, and teachers. Congress resisted planter pressure to exempt overseers—but that issue would rise again.

Hiring a substitute was the most controversial form of exemption. The rich could simply buy their way out of the army while the poor might become rich—if they survived—by selling themselves as substitutes, particularly if they deserted as soon as they could, and sold themselves again—and again, and again. One man in Richmond was said to have sold himself thirty times. The price of substitutes rose by late 1863 to as high as $6,000 (the equivalent of $300 in gold, or three years' wages for a skilled workingman). The abuses of substitution became so obnoxious that Congress abolished the privilege in December 1863.

The main purpose of conscription was to stimulate volunteering by the threat of coercion rather than by its actual use. To a degree this carrot-and-stick method worked. During 1862 the total number of men in the Confederate army increased from about 325,000 to 450,000. Since about 75,000 men were lost from death or wounds during this period, the net gain was approximately 200,000. Fewer than half of these new men were conscripts and substitutes; the remainder were considered volunteers even though their motive for enlisting may not have been unalloyed patriotism.

THE VOLUNTARY MANNER IN WHICH SOME OF THE SOUTHERN VOLUNTEERS ENLIST.

Despite its success in getting more men into the army, conscription was the most unpopular act of the Confederate government. Yeoman farmers who could not buy their way out of the army voted with their feet and escaped to the woods or swamps. Enrollment officers met bitter resistance in the upcountry and in other regions of lukewarm or nonexistent commitment to the Confederacy. Armed bands of draft-dodgers and deserters ruled whole counties. Conscription represented an unprecedented extension of government power among a people on whom such power had rested lightly in the past. Even some soldiers, who might have been expected to welcome a law that forced slackers to share their hardships, instead considered it a repudiation of what they were fighting for.

Conscription dramatized a fundamental paradox in the Confederate war effort: the need for Hamiltonian means to achieve Jeffersonian ends. The Confederate Constitution, Davis argued, gave Congress the power "to raise and support armies" and to "provide for the common defence." It also contained another clause (likewise copied from the U.S. Constitution) empowering Congress to make all laws "necessary and proper for carrying into execution the foregoing powers." In Hamiltonian language, Davis insisted that the "necessary and proper" clause legitimized conscription. No one could doubt the necessity "when our very existence is threatened by armies vastly superior in numbers." Therefore, he told the Jeffersonians, "the true and only test is to enquire whether the law is intended and calculated to carry out the object. . . . If the answer be in the affirmative, the law is constitutional."

Most southerners probably agreed—especially if they lived in Virginia or western Tennessee or Mississippi or Louisiana, which were threatened by invasion in 1862. The draft was upheld by every court in which it was tested.

Another challenge to state's rights was martial law. In his February 22 inaugural address Davis had contrasted the Confederacy's refusal "to impair personal liberty or the freedom of speech, of thought, or of the press" with Lincoln's imprisonment without trial of "civil officers, peaceful citizens, and gentlewomen" in vile "Bastilles." He did not mention the suppression of civil liberties in parts of the Confederacy, especially east Tennessee, where several hundred civilians languished in southern "Bastilles" and five had been executed. Only five days after Davis's inaugural address, Congress authorized him to suspend the writ of habeas corpus and declare martial law in areas that were in "danger of attack by the enemy." Davis promptly proclaimed martial law in Richmond and other Virginia cities. He did so not only because of Union invasion but also because of rising crime and violence among the war-swollen population of the capital. General John H. Winder, provost marshal of the Richmond district, created an efficient but ruthless corps of military police. Winder not only established a pass system and arrested soldiers and civilians for the usual crimes and misdemeanors but also jailed without trial several "disloyal" citizens including two women and John Minor Botts, a venerable Virginia unionist and former U.S. congressman. When the *Richmond Whig* compared these actions to Lincoln's suppression of civil liberties, Winder threatened to shut down the newspaper. Although he refrained, his threat was sufficiently "chilling" to stifle such dissent.

Some newspapers, however, thought these measures were needed to encourage patriotism, secure tranquility, and protect property. The *Richmond Examiner* believed that in an emergency "the Government must do all these things by military order. . . . To the dogs with Constitutional questions and moderation! What we want is an effectual resistance."

Some commanders of military districts far from Richmond took it upon themselves to proclaim martial law. Davis, reacting to sharp protests, forbade generals to suspend the writ or impose martial law on their own authority. But they sometimes honored his prohibition in the breach. Suspension of the writ proved an especially effective device to enforce conscription in parts of the South where state judges issued writs of habeas corpus ordering the release of draftees.

Civil libertarians linked martial law with conscription in their condemnations of Davis's "despotism." A triumvirate of Georgians emerged as leaders of an anti-administration faction on these issues: Governor Brown, Vice President Stephens, and Robert Toombs—now an ambitious but frustrated brigadier general. Even though the Confederate Constitution sanctioned suspension of the writ in case of invasion, Stephens considered such action "unconstitutional" and a direct threat to liberty. Brown warned that "we have more to fear from military despotism than from subjugation by the enemy." Bending to such protests, Congress in April limited the scope of martial law and specified that the authority to impose it would expire in September. In October Congress renewed Davis's power to suspend the writ—but provided for expiration of this power in February 1863. Draft resistance caused Congress to renew the power for a third time in February 1864, but once more it expired at the end of July.

Davis therefore possessed the authority to suspend the writ of habeas corpus for a total of only sixteen months. During most of that time he exercised this power more sparingly than did his counterpart in Washington. The rhetoric of southern libertarians about executive tyranny thus seems overblown. The Confederacy did not have the North's problem of administering captured territory with its hostile population. Nor did the South have as large a disloyal population—sizable though it was—in its disaffected upland regions as the Union contained in the border states. These areas accounted for most of the Lincoln administration's suspension of civil liberties.

For a few months in the spring of 1862, however, the rise in Union military fortunes caused a relaxation of northern procedures. Since July 1861, Secretary of State Seward had been in charge of internal security and in his zeal to ferret out treason brooked no restraint by rules of evidence. His power to imprison virtually anyone outraged Republicans as well as Democrats. Perhaps it was necessary to arrest pro-Confederate legislators in Maryland, wrote Horace Greeley, but when the government imprisoned such a prominent northern Democrat as James Wall of New Jersey (soon to be elected to the Senate) "you tear the whole fabric of society."

Lincoln recognized the harm done to the Union and the justice of these protests. The appointment of Edwin M. Stanton as secretary of war provided an opportunity for Lincoln to transfer enforcement of internal security to the War Department on February 14, 1862, and initiate the release of some two hundred political prisoners. At the outbreak of the rebellion, Lincoln explained, harsh measures had been necessary because "every department of the Government was paralyzed by treason." Now that the government had established itself and possessed armed forces sufficient to suppress rebellion, it was time to "return to the normal course of the administration." Lincoln therefore ordered the release of all political prisoners upon their taking an oath of loyalty. Stanton appointed a review board that applied liberal criteria for determining loyalty. Confident of imminent victory, the North released most of its political prisoners during the spring of 1862. The *New York Tribune* rejoiced that "the reign of lawless despotism is ended." Stanton won praise as a humane civil libertarian—an ironic preview to his subsequent reputation as a ruthless tyrant.

Stanton was also responsible for another optimistic policy decision in the spring of 1862. On April 3 he ordered all recruiting offices closed. The public perceived this as a sign that the armies were large enough to win the war. Stanton may have shared this belief; in any case he considered the existing system of raising troops inefficient. State governors, prominent individuals, and officers on detached service from active regiments were all beating the same bushes for recruits. Stanton closed down these operations in order to reorganize and rationalize them—if necessary. With the rebellion evidently collapsing in the West and McClellan poised for the final thrust up the Peninsula, many northerners believed it would not be necessary. By July they realized their mistake.

II

Events on the battlefields affected each side's ability to finance the war. The grave structural problems of the Confederate economy, with most of its capital tied up in the nonliquid form of land and slaves, became all too manifest. While the

The most valuable property in the South were the slaves. But they were untaxed by the Confederate government and taxed at a low rate by the states. These ex-slaves on Cockspur Island, Georgia, were photographed after Union forces occupied this and other coastal islands in November 1861.

Confederate states possessed 30 percent of the national wealth (in the form of real and personal property), they had only 12 percent of the circulating currency and 21 percent of the banking assets. The cotton embargo prevented the South from cashing in on its principal asset in 1861–62. Instead of possessing money to invest in Confederate bonds, most planters were in debt—mainly to factors who in turn were financed by northern merchants or banks.

The South initially hoped to turn that planter debt into a means of making Yankee bankers pay for the war. A law enacted by the Confederate Congress on May 21, 1861, requiring Confederate citizens to pay into the treasury the amount of debts owed to U.S. citizens, in return for which they would receive Confederate bonds (as well as a later measure confiscating "alien property") yielded disappointing results—no more than $12 million, a far cry from the estimated $200 million owed to northern creditors. Enforcement was difficult and concealment of debts easy. And some planters preferred to retain their credit rating with northern factors as an aid to selling cotton illegally across the lines.

Of the three principal methods to finance a war—taxation, borrowing, and fiat money—taxation is the least inflationary. But it also seemed the least desirable to southerners in 1861. A rural society in which one-third of the people were slaves, and which required few public services, had a per capita tax burden only half of that in the free states. Except for tariff duties—which despite southern complaints were lower in the late 1850s than they had been for almost half a century—virtually all taxes were collected by state and local governments. The Confederate government possessed no machinery for levying internal taxes, and its constituents had no tradi-

tion of paying them. Congress enacted a tiny tariff in 1861, but it brought in only $3.5 million during the entire war. In August 1861 a direct tax of one-half of 1 percent on real and personal property became law. The Richmond government relied on states to collect this levy. Only South Carolina actually did so; Texas confiscated northern-owned property to pay its assessment; all the other states paid their quotas not by collecting the tax but by borrowing the money or printing it in the form of state notes!

The glorious cause relied, therefore, on a debt that could be paid off only by future generations. The first bond issue of $15 million was quickly subscribed. Subsequent action by Congress in May and August of 1861 authorized the issuance of $100 million in bonds at 8 percent interest. But these sold slowly in a cash-poor economy with a rate of inflation that had already reached 12 percent a *month* by the end of 1861. A "produce loan," the brainchild of Treasury Secretary Christopher Memminger, which allowed investors to pledge the proceeds from cotton, tobacco, and other crops in return for bonds, was more ingenious in concept than successful in results. Only $34 million was eventually realized from it.

Investors bought most of the remainder of the $100 million bond issue with treasury notes. These notes came off the printing presses in ever-increasing volume. The South resorted to this method of financing the war from necessity, not choice. Memminger warned in 1862 that the printing of notes was "the most dangerous of all methods of raising money. . . . The large quantity of money in circulation today must produce depreciation and final disaster." Indeed it did. But from the onset of war, bills accumulated on Memminger's desk faster than he could pay them with the

The Confederate treasury was not the only agency to print money. State governments, banks, and private businesses issued a bewildering variety of notes that came to be known as "shinplasters" because they were worth nothing except as bandages for cuts and bruises. A growing shortage of paper in the South sometimes forced printers to use wallpaper, as in this example of the 50¢ note issued by the Greensboro Mutual Life Insurance Company.

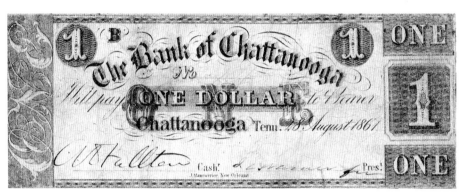

proceeds of loans or taxes. He had no choice but to ask Congress to authorize treasury notes. Congress did so in amounts of $20 million in May 1861, another $100 million in August, a further $50 million in December, and yet another $50 million in April 1862. During the first year of its existence the Confederate government obtained three-quarters of its revenues from the printing press, nearly a quarter from bonds (purchased in part with these same treasury notes), and less than 2 percent from taxes. Although the proportion of loans and taxes increased slightly in later years, the Confederacy financed itself primarily with a billion and a half paper dollars that depreciated from the moment they came into existence.

These notes were to be redeemable in specie at face value within two years of the end of the war. In effect they were backed by the public's faith in the Confederacy's potential for survival. Some congressmen wanted to make the notes legal tender—to require by law all persons to accept them in payment for debts and obligations. But a majority of Congress, along with Memminger and President Davis, considered this unconstitutional, inexpedient, or both. The promise to redeem in specie after the war, said Memminger, was a better way to assure acceptability.

Southern states, counties, cities, even private businesses also began to issue notes and small-denomination "shinplasters." Awash in a sea of paper, much of it easily counterfeited, the South experienced runaway inflation. At first the currency depreciated slowly, because Confederate victories in the summer of 1861 bolstered confidence. In September the price index stood only 25 percent above its January level. But the issuance of new notes caused the index to jump 35 percent in the next three months. Military reverses in the spring of 1862 moved the index up 100 percent in

the first half of the year; continued expansion of the currency caused it to double again in the second half. By the beginning of 1863 it took seven dollars to buy what a dollar had bought two years earlier.

This kind of inflation became, in effect, a form of confiscatory taxation whose burden fell most heavily on the poor. It exacerbated class tensions and caused a growing alienation of the white lower classes from the Confederate cause. Wage increases lagged far behind price increases. In 1862 wages for skilled and unskilled workers increased about 55 percent while prices rose 300 percent. Conditions on the small farms where most southern whites lived were little better. Although farm families grew much of what they consumed, the absence of adult males from many of the farms reduced crop yields and caused severe hardship.

The worst problem on many farms was the shortage of salt (the only means of preserving meat) and its catastrophic rise in price—from two dollars a bag before the war to sixty dollars in some places by the fall of 1862. Despite the emergency development of southern salt mines, wartime transportation problems and shortages of labor kept supplies scarce and prices high. An outraged Mississippian in December 1862 asked: "In the name of God . . . is this war to be carried on and the Government upheld at the expense of the Starvation of the Women and children?"

A rise in desertions from the army in 1862 resulted in part from the distress of the men's families. A soldier from Mississippi who had overstayed his furlough wrote to the governor on December 1, 1861: "Poor men have been compelled to leave the army to come home to provide for their families. . . . We are poor men and are willing to defend our country but our families [come] first."

Anguished southerners sought scapegoats to blame for their woes. They accused "speculators" and "extortioners" of cornering the market in essential items to force prices up to levels that enabled them to sell commodities for fantastic profits. In September 1862 a Georgia newspaper asserted that "Whilst our brave soldiers are off battling the Abolitionists . . . a conscienceless set of vampires are at home warring upon their indigent families." The *Richmond Examiner* lamented in July 1862 that "native Southern merchants have outdone Yankees and Jews. . . . The whole South stinks with the lust of extortion."

Despite this condemnation of "native" merchants, the *Examiner* and many other southerners focused on Jews as the worst "extortioners." Jewish traders had "swarmed here as the locusts of Egypt," declared a congressman. "They ate up the substance of the country, they exhausted its supplies, they monopolized its trade." As in other times and places, people suffering from causes beyond their comprehension fastened on an identifiable minority as scapegoats. There were Jewish merchants in the South, of course, and some of them speculated in consumer goods. So did a much larger number of southern-born Gentiles. But most merchants—Jewish and Gentile—were as much victims as perpetrators of shortages and inflation. To be sure, many of them sold goods at markups of 50 percent or more. But when inflation was running at 10 or 15 percent a month, they made little if any profit in real terms on much of what they sold.

By 1862 the Confederate economy had become unmanageable. The futility of trying to bring it under control was illustrated by the attempts of several states to curb "monopolies" or fix maximum prices. Antimonopoly laws were aimed at speculators who tried to corner markets in any of several necessities, or to charge "exorbitant" prices for them. But these laws proved unenforceable, for they either created a black market or further exacerbated shortages. Richmond's czar of martial law, General John Winder, established maximum prices for several categories of food in April 1862. Farmers and fishermen immediately ceased to sell at these prices. After three weeks Winder admitted failure and lifted the controls, whereupon prices doubled or tripled. Under the pressures of blockade, invasion, and a flood of paper money, the South's unbalanced agrarian economy simply could not produce both guns and butter without shortages and inflation.

This cartoon of a rattlesnake in the form of a dollar sign seems to suggest that tapping northern wealth was the key to winning the war.

The northern economy proved more adaptable to the demands of war. But for a time in the winter of 1861–62, fiscal problems threatened to overwhelm the Union cause. Lincoln's administration entered the war with at least two financial advantages over the Confederacy: an established treasury and an assured source of revenue from the tariff. But declining revenues and budget deficits, as well as the secession-induced drain on specie from the treasury, presented Lincoln with impediments that included the highest national debt in forty years. Unlike his Confederate counterpart Memminger, an expert in commercial and financial law, Secretary of the Treasury Salmon P. Chase was a political appointee without prior financial experience who proved to be an adept learner and a good treasury secretary. His principal tutor was Jay Cooke, head of a Philadelphia banking firm, whose brother had been an ally of Chase in Ohio politics. Chase kept the treasury afloat

in the war's early months with short-term bank loans at 7.3 percent. Cooke persuaded some of his moneyed associates to buy longer-term bonds at 6 percent. Chase and Cooke pioneered the concept of selling "war bonds" to ordinary people, as well as to bankers, in denominations as small as $50 to be paid in monthly installments. Cooke eventually achieved great success in selling $400 million of "five-twenties"—6 percent bonds redeemable in not less than five or more than twenty years—and nearly $800 million of "seven-thirties"—three-year notes at 7.3 percent. Despite newspaper charges of profiteering because Cooke's firm earned $4 million for marketing these bonds, the actual commission amounted to about three-eighths of 1 percent, out of which Cooke paid all expenses for agents and advertising, leaving a net profit of about $700,000. This was a cheaper and more efficient means of selling bonds to the masses than any other the government could have employed.

Unlike the Confederacy, which relied on loans for less than two-fifths of its war finances, the Union raised two-thirds of its revenues by this means. And while the South ultimately obtained only 5 or 6 percent of its funds by actual taxation, the northern government raised 21 percent in this manner. Congress revised the tariff upward several times during the conflict, but wartime customs duties averaged only $75 million a year—scarcely more, after adjustment for inflation, than the $60 million annually in the mid-1850s. Far more important in potential, though not at first in realization, were the new internal taxes levied in the North, beginning with the first

This illustration from Frank Leslie's Illustrated Newspaper *in September 1861 portrays ordinary northern citizens, including a black man and several women, buying war bonds in New York City. Although this drawing exaggerated the popular demand for bonds at this early stage of the war, by 1865 nearly one out of four northern families had purchased government bonds.*

federal income tax in American history enacted on August 5, 1861. This revolutionary measure grew from a need to assure the financial community that sufficient revenue would be raised to pay interest on bonds. The Republican architects of the 1861 income tax made it modestly progressive by imposing the 3 percent tax on annual incomes over $800 only, thereby exempting most wage-earners. This was done, explained Senate Finance Committee Chairman William Pitt Fessenden, because the companion tariff bill was regressive in nature. "Taking both measures together, I believe the burdens will be more equalized on all classes of the community."

Most of these taxes would not be collected until 1862. Meanwhile the government would have to depend on loans. But the legacy of the Jacksonian divorce of government from banking created complications. Gold for purchase of bonds had to be literally deposited in a government subtreasury. An ambiguous amendment to the war-loan act of August 5 seemed to repeal this requirement and permit the treasury to leave the gold on deposit to the government's credit in banks, where it would form part of the legal reserves to support the banks' notes. But Chase, something of a hard-money Jacksonian in his fiscal views, chose not to proceed in this manner. Instead, he required banks and other purchasers of bonds to pay in specie, which then sometimes remained idle for weeks in government vaults while bank reserves dropped toward the danger point.

Union defeat at the battle of Ball's Bluff in October 1861 and McClellan's failure to advance on Richmond eroded confidence in northern victory. Then came the threat of war with Britain over Captain Wilkes's seizure of Mason and Slidell from the *Trent*. The panic on financial exchanges caused a run on banks, whose specie reserves plummeted. The sequel was inevitable. On December 30 the banks of New York suspended specie payments. Banks elsewhere followed suit. Deprived of specie, the treasury could no longer pay suppliers, contractors, or soldiers. The war economy of one of the world's richest nations threatened to grind to a halt. As Lincoln lamented on January 10, "the bottom is out of the tub. What shall I do?"

What indeed? Lincoln, no financial expert, played little role in congressional efforts to resolve the crisis. Chase proposed the chartering of national banks authorized to issue notes secured by government bonds. This would free the currency from direct specie requirements, pump new money into the economy, and create a market for the bonds. These ideas eventually bore fruit in the National Banking Act of 1863.

The immediate problem was solved, however, by issuance of treasury notes—fiat money. But a great deal of opposition to the measure had to be overcome. The bill introducing it seemed to imitate the dubious Confederate example—but with a crucial difference. The U.S. notes were to be legal tender—receivable for all debts public or private except interest on government bonds and customs duties. The exemption of bond interest was intended as an alternative to selling the bonds below par, with the expectation that the payment of 6 percent interest in specie would make the bonds attractive to investors at face value. Customs duties were to be payable in specie to assure sufficient revenue to fund the interest on bonds. In all other transactions individuals, banks, and government itself would be required to accept U.S. notes—soon to be called greenbacks—as lawful money.

Opponents who insisted on a narrow interpretation of the constitutional power to "coin" money maintained it meant just that—coins. But the attorney general and most Republican congressmen favored a broad construction of the coinage and the "necessary and proper" clauses of the Constitution. "The bill before us is a war measure," Elbridge G. Spaulding of New York told the House, "a *necessary means* of carrying into execution the power granted in the Constitution 'to raise and *support* armies.' . . . These are extraordinary times, and extraordinary measures must be resorted to in order to save our Government and preserve our nationality."

Opponents also questioned the expediency, morality, even the theology of the legal tender bill. Such notes would depreciate, they said, as the Revolutionary continentals had done and as Confederate notes were even then depreciating. Inflation, a decline in real wages, and a decline in real value of savings and fixed-value securities would be the doleful consequences of this measure. One banker insisted that "gold and silver are the only true measure of value. These metals were prepared by the Almighty for this very purpose."

Supporters of the bill exposed the hollowness of such arguments. The fact was that coinage was not the effective currency of the country. State banknotes—many of them depreciated and irredeemable—were the principal medium of exchange. The issue before Congress was whether the notes of a sovereign government had "as much virtue . . . as the notes of banks which have suspended specie payments."

By early February most businessmen and bankers had become convinced of the necessity for the legal tender bill. So had Treasury Secretary Chase and Finance Committee Chairman Fessenden. "I came with reluctance to the conclusion that the legal tender clause is a necessity," Chase informed Congress on February 3, 1862. *"Immediate action is of great importance. The Treasury is nearly empty."* Fessenden considered the measure "of doubtful constitutionality. . . . It is bad faith. . . . It shocks all my notions of political, moral, and national honor." But he voted for the bill. So did three-fourths of his Republican colleagues in Congress, who readily overcame the three-fourths of the Democrats who voted against it. With Lincoln's signature on February 25, the Legal Tender Act became law.

This act created a national currency and altered the monetary structure of the United States. It asserted national sovereignty to help win a war fought to preserve that sovereignty. It provided the treasury with resources to pay its bills, restored investor confidence to make possible the sale at par of the $500 million of new 6 per-

The famous greenback dollar issued under authority of the Legal Tender Act passed in February 1862. Secretary of the Treasury Chase's portrait is on the bill. This dollar bill was the great-great-grandfather of the money we carry in our wallets today.

Almost everything became the subject of a popular song during the Civil War, including money, as illustrated by this cover page of the sheet music for the "Legal Tender Polka."

cent bonds authorized at the same time, and unlocked the funds that had gone into hoarding during the financial crisis of December. All these good things came to pass without the ruinous inflation predicted by opponents, despite the authorization of another $150 million of greenbacks in July 1862. This brought the total to $300 million, nearly equal to the amount of Confederate treasury notes then in circulation. But while the southern price index rose to 686 (February 1861 = 100) by the end of 1862, the northern index then stood only at 114. For the war as a whole the Union experienced inflation of only 80 percent (contrasted with 9,000 percent for the Confederacy), which compares favorably to the 84 percent of World War I (1917–20) and 70 percent in World War II (1941–49, including the postwar years after the lifting of wartime price controls). While the greenbacks' lack of a specie backing created a speculator's market in gold, the "gold premium" did not rise drastically except in periods of Union military reverses. During the four months after passage of the Legal Tender Act, the gold premium rose only to 106 (that is, 100 gold dollars would buy 106 greenback dollars).

Three main factors explain the success of the Legal Tender Act. First: the underlying strength of the northern economy. Second: the fortuitous timing of the law. It went into effect during the months of Union military success in the spring of 1862, floating the greenbacks on a buoyant mood of confidence in victory. The third reason was the enactment of a comprehensive tax law on July 1, 1862, which soaked up much of the inflationary pressure produced by the greenbacks. The Union ultimately raised half again as much war revenue from taxes as from the issuance of paper money—in sharp contrast with the Confederate experience.

The Internal Revenue Act of 1862 taxed almost everything but the air northerners breathed—taxes on a great variety of products and services; taxes on gross receipts of businesses and banks as well as dividends and interest paid to investors; an inheritance tax; and an income tax. The law also created a Bureau of Internal Revenue, which remained a permanent part of the federal government even though most of these taxes (including the income tax) expired several years after the end of the war. The relationship of the American taxpayer to the government was never again the same.

The Internal Revenue Act was strikingly modern in several respects. It withheld the tax from the salaries of government employees and from dividends paid by corporations. It expanded the progressive aspects of the earlier income tax by exempting the first $600, levying 3 percent on incomes between $600 and $10,000, and 5 percent on incomes over $10,000. The first $1,000 of any legacy was exempt from the inheritance tax. Businesses worth less than $600 were exempt from the value-added and receipts taxes. Excise taxes fell most heavily on products purchased by the affluent. In explanation of these progressive features, Chairman Thaddeus Stevens of the House ways and means committee said that its burdens would fall fairly and largely on the rich, not on workers and farmers and the poor.

Whether northern wage-earners appreciated this solicitude is hard to tell. By the time the Internal Revenue Act went into effect many of them were suffering the pinch of inflation. While far less serious than in the South, price increases did cause an average decline of 20 percent in real wages of northern workers by 1863 or 1864. In classical economic theory, the labor shortage caused by a wartime decline of immigration and by the enlistment of workers in the army should have enabled wages to keep up with the cost of living, if not exceed it. Three factors seem to have prevented this from happening. The first was some slack in the economy left from the aftershocks of the Panic of 1857 and a renewed panic and downturn caused by secession in 1861, which meant that a labor surplus did not become a labor shortage until 1862. Second, a wartime speedup in mechanization of certain key industries helped alleviate the tight labor market: for example, more reapers and mowers for harvesting grain and hay were produced during the war than ever before, easing the demand for agricultural labor; the sewing machine multiplied the productivity of seamstresses making army uniforms and other clothing; and the Blake-McKay machine for sewing uppers to the soles of shoes reduced the time consumed in that process a hundredfold. Third was a great increase in the employment of women, in occupations ranging from government civil service and army nursing to agricultural field work and manufacturing. In agriculture, the increased use of farm machinery enabled women to fill much of the gap left by the enlistment of nearly a million northern farmers and farm laborers in the army. In northern industry women worked mainly in occupations where they were already prominent—textiles, clothing, shoemaking—but increased their proportion of the manufacturing labor force from one-fourth to one-third during the war. Because women earned much less than men for the same or similar jobs, their expanded proportion of the wartime labor force kept down the average of wage increases.

The wage lag behind cost-of-living increases fueled protests and strikes, especially in 1863–64. A good many strikes succeeded in winning substantial wage gains, especially in skilled trades and heavy industries where machinery and women could do little to redress a now-acute labor shortage. By the last year of the war real wages in many of these trades had returned to prewar levels and were poised for postwar increases. For unskilled workers and women, however, low wages and inflation remained a searing grievance. Wartime activism and strikes, combined with labor's pride in its contribution to northern victory, caused an increase of worker militancy and organization. Several new national trade unions were organized during the war,

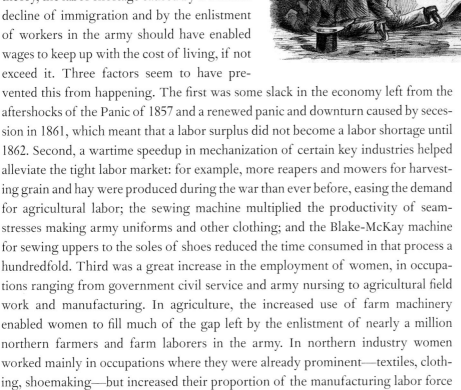

This cartoon satirizes the Internal Revenue Act signed by Lincoln on July 1, 1862. Tax agents are snooping every corner of the Scroggs home looking for things to tax. Mr. Scroggs says he is willing to pay any amount of tax, but please leave his wife's crinoline alone.

and a number of labor newspapers sprang into existence, paving the way for the founding of the umbrella National Labor Union in 1866. The wartime impetus helped drive union membership to its highest proportion of the industrial labor force in the nineteenth century by the eve of the Panic of 1873.

III

The second session of the 37th Congress (1861–62) was one of the most productive in American history. Not only did the legislators revolutionize the country's tax and monetary structures and take several steps toward the abolition of slavery; they also enacted laws of far-reaching importance for the disposition of public lands, the future of higher education, and the building of transcontinental railroads. These achievements were all the more remarkable because they occurred in the midst of an all-consuming preoccupation with war. Yet it was the war—or rather the absence of southerners from Congress—that made possible the passage of these Hamiltonian-Whig-Republican measures for government promotion of socioeconomic development.

Having appealed to voters in the Northwest with a homestead plank in the 1860 platform, Republicans easily overcame feeble Democratic and border-state opposition to pass a homestead act on May 20, 1862. This law granted 160 acres of public land to a settler after five years' residence and improvements on his (or her, since the law made no distinction of sex) claim. Although the Homestead Act never measured up to the starry-eyed vision of some enthusiasts who had hoped to "give every poor man a farm," it did become an important part of the explosive westward expansion after the war. Even before Appomattox, twenty-five thousand settlers had staked claims to more than three million acres, forerunners of some half-million farm families who eventually settled eighty million acres of homesteaded land.

For years Vermont's Justin Morrill—the architect of Republican tariff legislation in 1861 and chairman of the House subcommittee that framed the Internal Revenue Act—had sponsored a bill to grant public lands to the states for the promotion of higher education in "agriculture and the mechanic arts." When Morrill brought his measure before Congress again in 1861, regional tensions within the Republican party delayed its passage. The bill proposed to grant every state (including southern states if and when they returned) thirty thousand acres of public land for each congressman and senator. Since New York, Pennsylvania, and other populous eastern states would get the lion's share of the bounty while all of the public land they would receive was located in the West, the plan did not sit well with many westerners. Nevertheless a

A farmhouse on a homestead in Minnesota near the Iowa border after the Civil War. The farmer sitting on his doorstep may have been a Civil War veteran.

sufficient number of western Republicans supported the
bill—partly as a *quid pro quo* for eastern support of the
Homestead Act—to pass the Morrill Act on July 2,
1862. For good measure, Congress also created a
Department of Agriculture. The success of the
land-grant college movement was attested by
the later development of first-class institutions
in many states and world-famous universities
at Ithaca, Urbana, Madison, Minneapolis, and
Berkeley.

Freed of impediments once imposed by the
southern states, Yankee legislators highballed
forward in 1862 to create a transcontinental railroad. On July 1, the same day that the Internal Revenue Act became law, Lincoln signed the Pacific Railroad
Act granting 6,400 acres of public land (later doubled) per mile
and lending $16,000 per mile (for construction on the plains) and $48,000

The University of Wisconsin was founded in 1848, the year Wisconsin became a state. This photograph of the university dates from 1865. The land grant received by Wisconsin helped this university became one of the nation's most illustrious educational institutions.

per mile (in the mountains) of government bonds to corporations organized to build
a railroad from Omaha to Sacramento. Intended to prime the pump of private capital, this measure succeeded in spectacular fashion. The first rails were laid eastward
from Sacramento in 1863; six years later the golden spike linked the Central Pacific
and Union Pacific at Promontory, Utah. Other land grants to transcontinental railroads followed the first one, eventually totaling 120 million acres. Although these
railroads became a source of corruption and of corporate power in politics, most
Americans in 1862 viewed government aid as an investment in national unity and
economic growth that would benefit all groups in society.

This was the philosophy that underlay all three of the land-grant laws of 1862.
To some degree these laws functioned at cross purposes, for settlers, universities,
and railroads competed for portions of the same land in subsequent years. Yet the
225 million acres that the government ultimately gave away under these laws constituted only a fraction of the two billion acres of public land. And despite waste, corruption, and exploitation, these land grants did help to people a vast domain,
sprinkle it with schools, and span it with steel rails.

By its legislation to finance the war, emancipate the slaves, and invest public land
in future growth, the 37th Congress did more than any other in history to change
the course of national life. As one scholar has aptly written, this Congress drafted
"the blueprint for modern America." It also helped shape what historians Charles
and Mary Beard labeled the "Second American Revolution"—that process by
which "the capitalists, laborers, and farmers of the North and West drove from
power in the national government the planting aristocracy of the South . . . making
vast changes in the arrangement of classes, in the accumulation and distribution of
wealth, in the course of industrial development, and in the Constitution inherited
from the Fathers." This new America of big business, heavy industry, and capital-
intensive agriculture that surpassed Britain to become the foremost industrial
nation by 1880 and became the world's breadbasket for much of the twentieth cen-

This famous illustration commemorates the joining of the Union Pacific and Central Pacific railroads at Promontory, Utah, in 1869, thus fulfilling the hopes of the Congress that passed the Pacific Railroad Act seven years earlier.

tury probably would have come about even if the Civil War had never occurred. But the war molded the particular configuration of this new society, and the legislation of the 37th Congress that authorized war bonds to be bought with greenbacks and repaid with gold and thereby helped concentrate investment capital, that confiscated southern property and strengthened northern industry by expanding internal markets, protecting those markets with tariffs, and improving access to them with subsidies to transportation, that settled the public domain and improved its cultivation, and that rationalized the country's monetary and credit structure—this legislation did indeed help fashion a future different enough from the past to merit the label of revolution.

The revolution abounded in ironies, to be sure. Congressmen from western states had been the strongest proponents of the Legal Tender Act and the National Banking Act, in order to remedy the instability and regional imbalance of the monetary and credit system from which western states suffered most. Eastern congressmen and bankers, more satisfied with the existing system, had been lukewarm or opposed. Westerners had also been the prime supporters of federal aid to construct a transcontinental railroad, while easterners, already served by a good transportation system, were less enthusiastic. Yet the consequences of these acts were to *increase* the domination of the country's credit, transportation, and marketing structure by eastern bankers, merchants, and investors. By the 1890s the farmers of the West and South revolted against their "slavery" to an eastern "money power" that was allegedly squeezing their life blood from them. Back in the 1830s Jacksonian artisans and yeomen had viewed with suspicion the transportation revolution, the growth of banks, and the evolution of wage-labor capitalism that seemed to threaten their republican independence. By the 1890s this economic system had penetrated the farthest reaches of the country. For the last time, perhaps, aggrieved Americans rose in the name of Jeffersonian republicanism in a counterrevolution against the second American revolution of free-labor capitalism. Once again the country rang with rhetoric of sectional conflict—this time the South and West against the Northeast—in a presidential election with the Populist ticket headed by a former Union general teamed with a former Confederate major as his running mate.

But before the "Second American Revolution" could draft the "blueprint for modern America," the North must win the war. Its prospects for doing so took a sudden turn for the worse in the summer of 1862, when Stonewall Jackson and Robert E. Lee derailed the Union war machine.

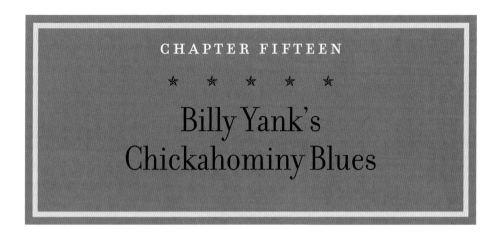

CHAPTER FIFTEEN

Billy Yank's Chickahominy Blues

I

In May 1862, with some 100,000 Union troops closing in on Richmond, prospects for the Confederacy's survival seemed bleak. Joseph E. Johnston could bring about two-thirds that number to defend the capital. Although McClellan's past performance suggested that he would lay siege to Richmond rather than attack Johnston's army, the fall of the Confederate capital seemed only a matter of time.

The next act in this drama took place not in front of Richmond but a hundred miles to the northwest in the Shenandoah Valley. Commanding the rebel forces in that strategic region, Stonewall Jackson had been reinforced to a strength of 17,000 men by a division from Johnston's army. Its commander was Richard S. Ewell, an eccentric, balding, forty-five-year-old bachelor whose beaked nose and habit of cocking his head to one side reminded observers of a bird. Everything about Ewell seemed odd, from his ulcer-induced diet of hulled wheat boiled in milk with raisins and egg yolk to his manner of cursing with a lisp. But while Ewell was an unfailing source of jokes around soldier campfires, Jackson seemed even more peculiar. Attired in an old army coat he had worn in the Mexican War and a broken-visored V.M.I. cadet cap, Jackson constantly sucked lemons to palliate his dyspepsia and refused to season his food with pepper because (he said) it made his left leg ache. A disciplinary martinet, Jackson had tarnished some of the fame won at Manassas by an aborted winter campaign into West Virginia that provoked a near mutiny by some of his troops. A devout Presbyterian, Jackson came across to some colleagues as a religious fanatic. Taciturn, humorless, and secretive, he rarely explained to subordinates the purpose of his orders. His rule of strategy—"always mystify, mislead, and surprise the enemy"—seemed to apply to his own officers as well. Before May 8, 1862, many of his soldiers considered him crazy and called him "Old Tom Fool." Events during the next month, however, showed them that he was crazy like a fox. These events made Jackson the South's premier hero for a time—until eclipsed by an even wilier fox with no tinge of fanaticism, Robert E. Lee.

Serving as Jefferson Davis's military adviscr, Lee conceived the idea of a diversion in the Shenandoah Valley to prevent McDowell's Union corps from reinforcing

Opposite page: A Union wagon train descends a treacherous road into the Shenandoah Valley, where many of the wagons will be gobbled up by Stonewall Jackson's army.

383

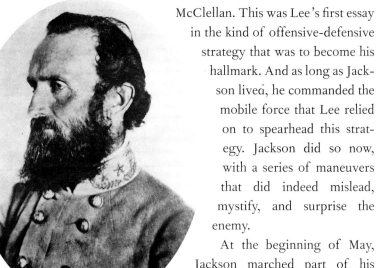

McClellan. This was Lee's first essay in the kind of offensive-defensive strategy that was to become his hallmark. And as long as Jackson lived, he commanded the mobile force that Lee relied on to spearhead this strategy. Jackson did so now, with a series of maneuvers that did indeed mislead, mystify, and surprise the enemy.

At the beginning of May, Jackson marched part of his army east across the Blue Ridge. Federal scouts reported that he was heading toward the Richmond front. Jackson's own troops believed the same. But when they arrived at the railroad near Charlottesville, Jackson put them on trains that carried them back west over the Blue Ridge to Staunton. From there Jackson led 9,000 men a few miles farther over mountain passes to the hamlet of McDowell, where on May 8 they fought and defeated a Union force half as large. These bluecoats were part of an army of 25,000 men that John C. Frémont was assembling in West Virginia for a drive 250 miles southward to capture Knoxville. This impracticable plan was a compound of Frémont's romanticism and Lincoln's desire to liberate east Tennessee. Jackson's surprise attack disrupted the campaign before it got started.

Stonewall marched his men back into the Shenandoah Valley at Harrisonburg. Nathaniel Banks had dispatched two divisions to aid McClellan; his sole remaining division had recently retreated northward from there to Strasburg, where they dug

In their Shenandoah Valley campaign of May–June 1862, Generals Stonewall Jackson (at right) and Richard Ewell made an odd pair, but they were the Confederacy's most successful team since Beauregard and Joseph Johnston at Manassas the previous July. When Ewell was first assigned to Jackson's command, he considered Stonewall "crazy as a March hare." Ewell soon changed his mind.

A postwar photograph of Massanutten Mountain, looking west from the Luray Valley. Fifty miles long from Harrisonburg in the south to Front Royal in the north, Massanutten can be crossed from the Shenandoah Valley to the Luray Valley at two gaps. Relying on maps prepared by his superb topographical officer, Jedediah Hotchkiss, Jackson used the mountain and these gaps to confuse the enemy, moving so fast that his infantry became known as "Jackson's foot cavalry."

in. Jackson made as if to follow, but at New Market he suddenly swerved eastward across Massanutten Mountain, which at that point divided the Shenandoah into two smaller valleys. Jackson was about to exploit his unsurpassed knowledge of the terrain. While Jackson's hell-for-leather cavalry under Turner Ashby kept up a feint along the pike toward Strasburg, deceiving Banks into thinking that the rebels were coming that way, the main Confederate thrust came in the Luray Valley east of Massanutten Mountain. Here on May 23 Jackson's and Ewell's combined force overwhelmed the small Union outpost at Front Royal. Jackson was now on Banks's flank only ten miles away with a force more than double the size of the Union division.

In all of these swift, deceptive movements Jackson was aided by local scouts and spies who knew every foot of the country. Banks had to contend not only with Jackson's army but also with a hostile civilian population—a problem confronted by every invading Union army, and one that helped make this a war of peoples as well as of armies.

Impatient toward weaknesses of the flesh, Jackson had driven his infantry at a killing pace. Ewell caught the spirit and ordered his marching columns stripped to the minimum. "We can get along without anything but food and ammunition," he stated. "The road to glory cannot be followed with much baggage." Although barefoot, blistered, and broken down from marching 160 miles and fighting two battles in two weeks, Jackson's men no longer called him Old Tom Fool. Now he was Old Jack, and they were proud to be known as his foot cavalry.

They would need this pride to keep them going, for even harder marching and fighting lay ahead. The truth of his predicament having dawned on him, Banks retreated at top speed from Strasburg to his base at Winchester twenty miles north. Jackson's tired troops pressed after him on May 24, slicing into Banks's wagon train and capturing a cornucopia of supplies. Banks's main body won the race to Winchester, where they turned to fight. At foggy daybreak on May 25, some 15,000 rebels assaulted 6,000 Yankees on the hills south and west of town. After some sharp

The Virginia artist John Adams Elder served as a draftsman in the Confederate War Department and painted several military scenes during the war. The importance of scouts in gathering intelligence, especially in the Shenandoah Valley, is the theme of this painting.

fighting the Federals broke and streamed northward for the safety of the Potomac thirty-five miles away. Ashby's undisciplined cavalry had disintegrated into looters, plundering Union camps or leading captured horses to the troopers' nearby homes. Without cavalry and with worn-out infantry, Jackson could not pursue the routed bluecoats. Nevertheless his victories at Front Royal and Winchester had reaped at least 2,000 prisoners, 9,000 rifles, and such a wealth of food and medical stores that Jackson's men labeled their opponent "Commissary Banks."

Jackson's campaign accomplished the relief of pressure against Richmond that Lee had hoped for. When Lincoln learned on May 24 of Jackson's capture of Front Royal, he made

Nathaniel P. Banks had served in the Massachusetts legislature, in Congress (where he was Speaker of the House), and as governor of Massachusetts before he donned the uniform of a major general of volunteers in May 1861. A year later, after Stonewall Jackson had outmarched and outfought him, Banks may have wished he had stuck to politics.

two swift decisions. First he ordered Frémont to push his troops eastward into the Valley at Harrisonburg, from where they could march north and attack Jackson's rear. Second, he suspended McDowell's movement from Fredericksburg toward Richmond and ordered him to send two divisions post haste to the Valley to smash into Jackson's flank. Both McClellan and McDowell protested that this action played into the enemy's hand. It was "a crushing blow to us," McDowell wired Lincoln. "I shall gain nothing for you there, and shall lose much for you here." Nevertheless, McDowell obeyed orders. Back to the Valley he sent James Shields's division, which Banks had sent to him only a few days earlier. McDowell himself followed with another division. Sitting in the War Department telegraph office in Washington, Lincoln fired off telegrams to the three separate commands of Frémont, Banks, and McDowell, hoping to move them like knights and bishops on the military chessboard. But his generals moved too slowly, or in the wrong direction. Instead of crossing into the Valley at Harrisonburg, Frémont found the passes blocked by small enemy forces and marched forty miles northward to cross at a point northwest of Strasburg. This angered Lincoln; as he feared, it opened the way for Jackson's 16,000 to escape southward through Strasburg before Frémont's 15,000 and Shields's 10,000 (with another 10,000 close behind) converged on them from west and east.

After the battle of Winchester, Jackson had marched to within a few miles of Harper's Ferry to give the impression that he intended to cross the Potomac. On May 30 his force was nearly twice as far from Strasburg as the converging forces of Frémont and Shields. Nothing but a few cavalry stood in the way of the Union pincers. But a strange lethargy seemed to paralyze the northern commanders. Jackson's foot cavalry raced southward day and night on May 30 while the bluecoats tarried. The

Edwin Forbes was one of the most prolific illustrators of the war, producing hundreds of drawings for Frank Leslie's Illustrated Newspaper. *One of his first assignments was the Shenandoah Valley campaign of 1862, during which he accompanied Frémont's army in its largely futile pursuit of Jackson.*

JACKSON'S SHENANDOAH VALLEY CAMPAIGN MAY-JUNE 1862

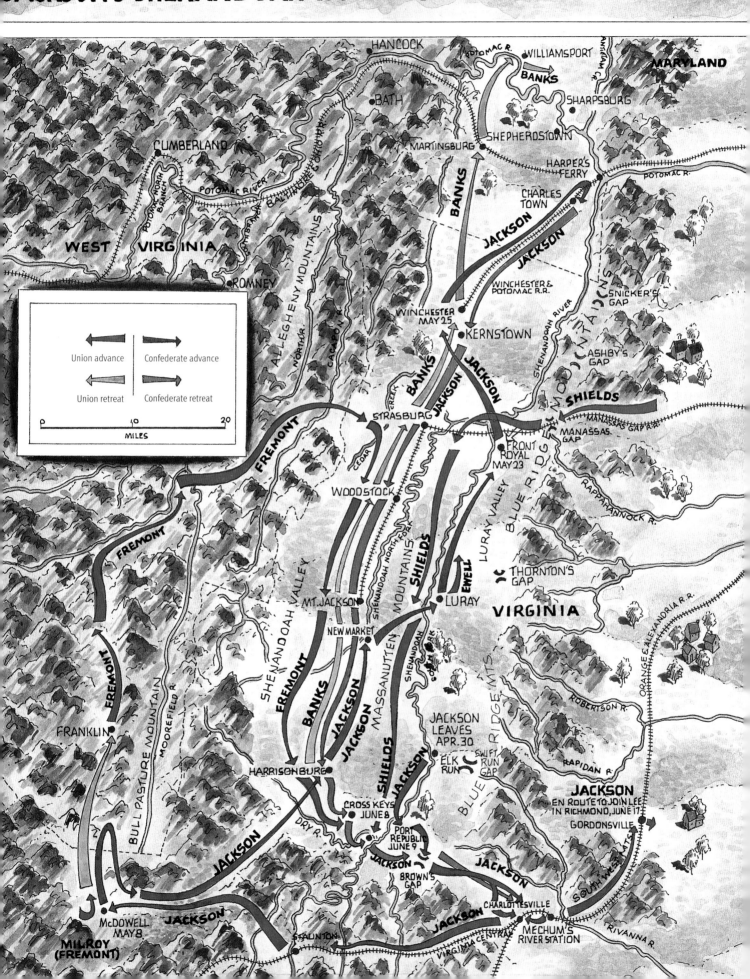

Union advance
Confederate advance
Union retreat
Confederate retreat

0   10   20
MILES

MARYLAND
WILLIAMSPORT
BANKS
SHARPSBURG
HANCOCK
POTOMAC R.
SHEPHERDSTOWN
BATH
MARTINSBURG
HARPER'S FERRY
POTOMAC R.
CUMBERLAND
BALTIMORE & OHIO R.R.
POTOMAC RIVER
POTOMAC NORTH BRANCH
CHARLES TOWN
BANKS
JACKSON
JACKSON
WEST VIRGINIA
SOUTH BRANCH
SNICKER'S GAP
ROMNEY
NORTH R.
WINCHESTER & POTOMAC R.R.
SHENANDOAH RIVER
ASHBY'S GAP
CACAPON R.
ALLEGHENY MOUNTAINS
WINCHESTER MAY 25
KERNSTOWN
BANKS
JACKSON
JACKSON
SHIELDS
FREMONT
STRASBURG
JACKSON
MANASSAS GAP R.R.
CEDAR CREEK
FRONT ROYAL MAY 23
MANASSAS GAP
BLUE RIDGE MOUNTAINS
RAPPAHANNOCK R.
WOODSTOCK
SHENANDOAH NORTH FORK
SHIELDS
LURAY VALLEY
THORNTON'S GAP
SHENANDOAH VALLEY
MT. JACKSON
MASSANUTTEN MOUNTAINS
EWELL
LURAY
VIRGINIA
NEW MARKET
FREMONT
BANKS
JACKSON
SHENANDOAH SOUTH FORK
SOUTH FORK
JACKSON LEAVES APR. 30
ORANGE & ALEXANDRIA R.R.
FRANKLIN
FREMONT
SHIELDS
JACKSON
ELK RUN
SWIFT RUN GAP
ROBERTSON R.
RAPIDAN R.
HARRISONBURG
DRY R.
CROSS KEYS JUNE 8
BLUE RIDGE MTS.
JACKSON EN ROUTE TO JOIN LEE IN RICHMOND, JUNE 17
GORDONSVILLE
BULL PASTURE MOUNTAIN
MOOREFIELD R.
PORT REPUBLIC JUNE 9
JACKSON
JACKSON
BROWN'S GAP
SOUTH WEST MTS.
McDOWELL MAY 8
JACKSON
STAUNTON
CHARLOTTESVILLE
JACKSON
MILROY (FREMONT)
VIRGINIA CENTRAL
MECHUM'S RIVER STATION
RIVANNA R.

Confederate troops burning a footbridge over the north fork of the Shenandoah River to slow the Union pursuit of Jackson during the first week of June 1862.

rebels cleared Strasburg on June 1 and slogged southward while Frémont and Shields, finally aroused, nipped at their heels. For the next few days it became a stern chase, with Frémont pursuing Jackson on the Valley pike and Shields trudging southward on a parallel course east of Massanutten Mountain. Ashby's cavalry burned four bridges to delay Union pursuit. Several rear-guard cavalry fights took place, one of them resulting in the death of Ashby, who had become a romantic hero in the South. Jackson kept pushing his men to the edge of collapse. They won the race to the only undamaged bridge left on the Shenandoah River, at Port Republic near the south end of the Valley where Jackson had launched his epic campaign five weeks earlier. During those weeks Jackson's own division had marched more than 350 miles (Ewell's had marched 200 miles) and won three battles. Now they stopped to fight again.

On June 8 Frémont's troops advanced against Ewell's division stationed three miles north of Port Republic near the tiny village of Cross Keys. Frémont handled this attack poorly. Although outnumbering Ewell by 11,000 to 6,000, he committed only a fraction of his infantry to an attack on the Confederate right. After its repulse, Frémont settled down for an artillery duel that accomplished nothing. Reacting to this feeble effort, Jackson made a typically bold decision. His army of 15,000 was caught between two enemy forces whose combined strength he believed to be at least 50 percent greater than his own. The safe course was retreat to the nearest defensible pass in the Blue Ridge. But the two Federal armies under Frémont and Shields were separated by unfordable rivers, while Jackson's troops held the only bridge. On the night of June 8–9, Jackson ordered Ewell to leave a token force confronting Frémont and march the rest of his division to Port Republic. Jackson intended to overwhelm Shields's advance force and then face about to attack Frémont. But the stubborn resistance of Shields's two brigades at Port Republic frustrated the plan. Three thousand blue-coats held off for three hours the seven or eight thousand men that Jackson finally got into action. The weight of numbers eventually prevailed, but by then Jackson's army was too battered to carry out the attack against Frémont, who had remained quiescent during this bloody morning of June 9. Both sides pulled back and regrouped. That night Jackson withdrew to Brown's Gap in the Blue Ridge.

Jackson's Valley campaign won renown and is still studied in military schools as an example of how speed and use of terrain can compensate for inferiority of numbers. Jackson's army of 17,000 men had outmaneuvered three separate enemy forces with a combined strength of 33,000 and had won five battles, in all but one of which (Cross Keys) Jackson had been able to bring superior numbers to the scene of combat. Most important, Jackson's campaign had diverted 60,000 Union soldiers from other tasks and had disrupted two major strategic movements—Frémont's east

Tennessee campaign and McDowell's plan to link up with McClellan's right wing before Richmond. Jackson's victories in the Valley created an aura of invincibility around him and his foot cavalry. Stonewall became larger than life in the eyes of many northerners; he had gotten the drop on them psychologically, and kept it until his death a year later.

Lincoln's diversion of McDowell's corps to chase Jackson was probably a strategic error—perhaps even the colossal blunder that McClellan considered it. But if Union commanders in the Valley had acted with half the energy displayed by Jackson they might well have trapped and crippled Jackson's army. And even if McDowell's corps had joined McClellan as planned, the latter's previous record offered little reason to believe that he would have moved with speed and boldness to capture Richmond.

II

Rising a few miles north of Richmond, the Chickahominy River flows southeast until it empties into the James halfway down the Peninsula. The Chickahominy became an important factor in the defense of Richmond. Normally sluggish and shallow, the river had swollen to a raging torrent during the abnormal May rains. It bisected the ring of Union troops closing in on Richmond. McClellan had placed more than half of his army on the north side of the Chickahominy to protect his base of supplies and to hook up with McDowell's expected advance from the north. Several makeshift bridges threatened by the flooding river provided the only links between the two wings of McClellan's army.

Prodded by an apprehensive Jefferson Davis, Johnston finally decided to attack the weaker Union left wing south of the river. Reinforcements from North Carolina had brought his strength to nearly 75,000 men. A torrential downpour on May 30 seemed providential to the Confederates, for it washed out most of the Chickahominy bridges and gave southern troops numerical superiority over the two isolated Union corps south of the river.

But from the beginning of Johnston's planned early-morning attack on May 31, things went wrong. A misunderstood verbal order caused James Longstreet to advance his oversize division on the wrong road, where it entangled parts of two other divisions and delayed the attack until midafternoon. In an ill-coordinated assault, the Confederates managed to drive the Union left a mile through the

During the last three weeks of May 1862, Union troops spent more time building bridges across the Chickahominy River than they spent marching or fighting. Because the frequent heavy rains during this period turned the river's bottomlands into a swamp, the bridges had to extend hundreds of feet beyond the stream itself. On May 27–28 the 5th New Hampshire built this "Grapevine Bridge."

crossroads village of Seven Pines, about seven miles east of Richmond. On the Union right, however, the leather-lunged commander of the 2nd Corps, sixty-five-year-old Edwin "Bull" Sumner, got one of his divisions across the Chickahominy on swaying bridges with ankle-deep water coursing over them and brought the rebel left to a bloody halt in the dusk near the railroad station of Fair Oaks. Next day, indecisive fighting sputtered out as additional Union reinforcements from across the Chickahominy forced the Confederates to yield the ground they had won the first day.

Seven Pines (or Fair Oaks, as the Yankees called it) was a confused battle, "phenomenally mismanaged" on the Confederate side according to Johnston's chief of ordnance. Most of the 42,000 men engaged on each side fought in small clusters amid thick woods and flooded clearings where wounded soldiers had to be propped against fences or stumps to prevent them from drowning in the muck. If either side gained an advantage it was the Federals, who inflicted a thousand more casualties (6,000) than they suffered. The most important southern casualty was Joe Johnston, wounded by a shell fragment and a bullet through the shoulder on the evening of May 31. To replace him Davis appointed Robert E. Lee, who recognized the futility of further fighting by breaking off the engagement on June 1.

When Lee took command of the newly designated Army of Northern Virginia, few shared Davis's high opinion of the quiet Virginian. McClellan voiced pleasure at the change in southern command, for he considered Lee "cautious and weak under grave responsibility . . . likely to be timid and irresolute in action."

A psychiatrist trying to understand what made McClellan tick might read a great deal into these words, which described McClellan himself but could not have been more wrong about Lee. The latter ignored criticism and set about reorganizing his army for a campaign that would fit his offensive-defensive concept of strategy. Lee's first actions emphasized the defensive. He put his soldiers to work strengthening the fortifications and trenches ringing Richmond, which earned him new derision as "the king of spades." But it soon became clear that Lee's purpose was not to

This sketch by Alfred R. Waud depicts a bayonet charge by the 71st New York across a soggy clearing against a Confederate position in the woods. Confederate skirmishers fire at the Yankees from the edge of the woods before falling back to their main line, which stopped the Yankee advance.

hunker down for a siege. On the contrary, he told Davis, "I am preparing a line that I can hold with part of our forces" while concentrating the rest for a slashing attack on McClellan's exposed right flank north of the Chickahominy.

Lee knew that this flank was "in the air" (unprotected by natural or man-made obstacles such as a river, right-angle fortifications, etc.) because a remarkable reconnaissance by Jeb Stuart's cavalry had discovered the fact. Twenty-nine years old, Stuart had already won modest fame in the war but had an insatiable appetite for more. Dressed in knee-high cavalry boots, elbow-length gauntlets, red-lined cape with a yellow sash, and a felt hat with pinned-up brim and ostrich-feather plume, Stuart looked the dashing cavalier he aspired to be. He was also a superb leader of cavalry, especially in gathering information about enemy positions and movements. In this as in other tasks assigned to the cavalry—screening the army from enemy horsemen, patrolling front and flanks to prevent surprise attacks, raiding enemy supply lines, and pursuing defeated enemy infantry—the rebel troopers were superior to their adversaries at this stage of the war. Having grown up in the saddle, sons of the Virginia gentry quite literally rode circles around the neophyte Yankee horsemen. When Lee told Stuart on June 10 that he wanted a reconnaissance to discover the strength and location of the Union right, Stuart was ready.

With 1,200 picked men he rode north from Richmond on June 12 and swung east across the headwaters of the Chickahominy, brushing aside the small enemy patrols he encountered. Stuart's progress was helped by the fragmented organization of Union cavalry, which was sprinkled by companies and regiments throughout the army instead of consolidated into a separate division as the southern cavalry was. Stuart's troopers discovered the location of Fitz-John Porter's 5th Corps, which McClellan had kept north of the Chickahominy while transferring the rest of

This formal portrait of Jeb Stuart captures some but not all of the qualities that contemporaries called "dashing." Some historians have said that Stuart grew such a full beard to hide a weak chin. That is not true; a photograph of him as a cadet at West Point in 1854, before he grew a beard, shows a strong chin.

This painting of Stuart and his cavalry on the ride around McClellan's army was done in 1900 by Henry A. Ogden. It reflects the romantic image of Stuart that began with this raid.

the army to the other side. Stuart had accomplished his mission. But he determined to make glorious history by continuing in a complete circuit around McClellan's army to foil the pursuit. He pushed on, winning skirmishes, capturing 170 enemy soldiers and nearly twice as many horses and mules, destroying wagonloads of Union supplies, traveling day and night over byways guided by troopers who had grown up in these parts, and crossed the swollen Chickahominy on an improvised bridge which the rebels burned behind themselves minutes before pursuing Union cavalry reined up impotently on the north bank. Stuart's horsemen evaded further clashes and completed the circuit to Richmond by June 16, four days and a hundred miles after setting out. This exploit won Stuart all the acclaim he could have desired. He also gained great personal satisfaction from the enterprise, for one of the opposing cavalry commanders was his father-in-law, Philip St. George Cooke, a Virginian whose decision to remain loyal to the Union had vexed Stuart. "He will regret it but once," Jeb had vowed, "and that will be continuously."

Lee had the information he needed. And he knew whom he wanted to lead the attack: Jackson. He would bring Jackson's army secretly from the Valley to hit Porter's corps on the flank while three divisions of the Richmond army crossed the Chickahominy and simultaneously attacked its front. The danger in this, of course, was that while Lee concentrated 60,000 men against Porter's 30,000 north of the Chickahominy, the 75,000 bluecoats south of the

This cartoon satirizing the inability of Union cavalry to stop Stuart's ride around McClellan's army appeared in the Southern Illustrated News.

river might smash through the 27,000 Confederates on their front and walk into Richmond. But Lee had already taken McClellan's measure. The Union commander, as usual, believed himself outnumbered south as well as north of the Chickahominy.

All this time McClellan was sending a steady stream of telegrams to Washington explaining why he was not quite ready to launch his own offensive: the roads were too wet; his artillery was not all up; it took time to reorganize the divisions crippled in the Seven Pines/Fair Oaks fighting, and to incorporate the one division of reinforcements finally received from McDowell; and when, asked McClellan, was the rest of McDowell's corps going to join him? By June 24 McClellan had penetrated the rebel smokescreen to learn of Jackson's approach; on June 25 he wired Stanton: "The rebel force is stated at 200,000, including Jackson [it was actually less than 90,000. . . . I shall have to contend against vastly superior odds. . . . If [the army] is destroyed by overwhelming numbers . . . the responsibility cannot be thrown on my shoulders; it must rest where it belongs."

Lee attacked next day, June 26, the second day of what became known as the Seven Days battles. The fighting began inauspiciously for the rebels. Lee's plan called for Jackson to hit Porter's flank early in the morning. The sun passed the meridian while the silence continued and Lee fretted in frustration. Where was Jackson? Unable to wait longer, the impulsive A. P. Hill sent his division forward in a late-afternoon assault against an equal number of Federals (16,000) entrenched behind Beaver Dam Creek near Mechanicsville, about six miles northeast of Richmond. The result was a slaughter: nearly 1,500 rebels killed and wounded by Yankees who suffered only 360 casualties. All this time Jackson's three divisions were only a few miles to the north, but their commander made no effort to hasten to Hill's aid.

No single explanation for Jackson's lethargy is satisfactory. Union cavalry had harassed his advance. Northern axemen had felled trees across the road and burned bridges across creeks. But Jackson's foot cavalry had brushed this sort of thing aside in the Valley; why did it slow them now? The best answer seems to be the exhaustion of men not fully recovered from the rigors of the Valley campaign and the subsequent bone-jarring railroad travel followed by marching in unaccustomed heat. Jackson, operating on little sleep for weeks, was probably suffering from what today would be called stress fatigue. Intolerant of weakness in others, he refused to recognize it in himself or to do anything about it—except to collapse into unscheduled naps at crucial times during the Seven Days fighting.

Despite having won what he described as a "complete victory" at Mechanicsville, McClellan had no thought of going over to the offensive. Aware of Jackson's arrival near his right flank, he instructed Porter on the night of

This photograph of Ellison's Mill on Beaver Dam Creek was taken just after the war. The heaviest fighting in the battle of Mechanicsville on June 26, 1862, took place in the vicinity of this mill. It was an inauspicious beginning for Lee's counteroffensive; the Confederates suffered a repulse with heavy losses.

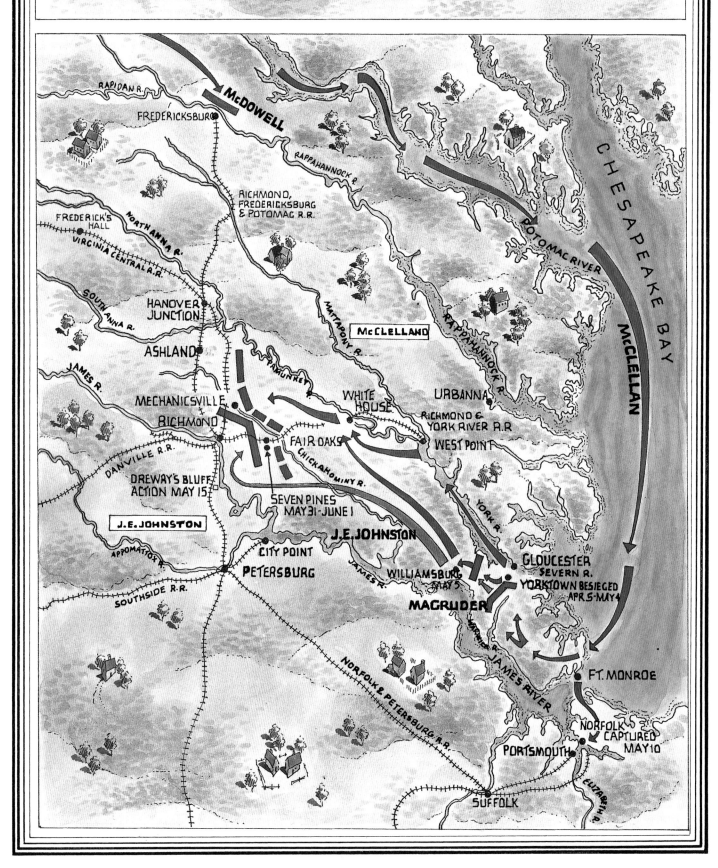

THE PENINSULA CAMPAIGN
APRIL- MAY 1862

THE SEVEN DAYS BATTLES
JUNE 25-JULY 1, 1862

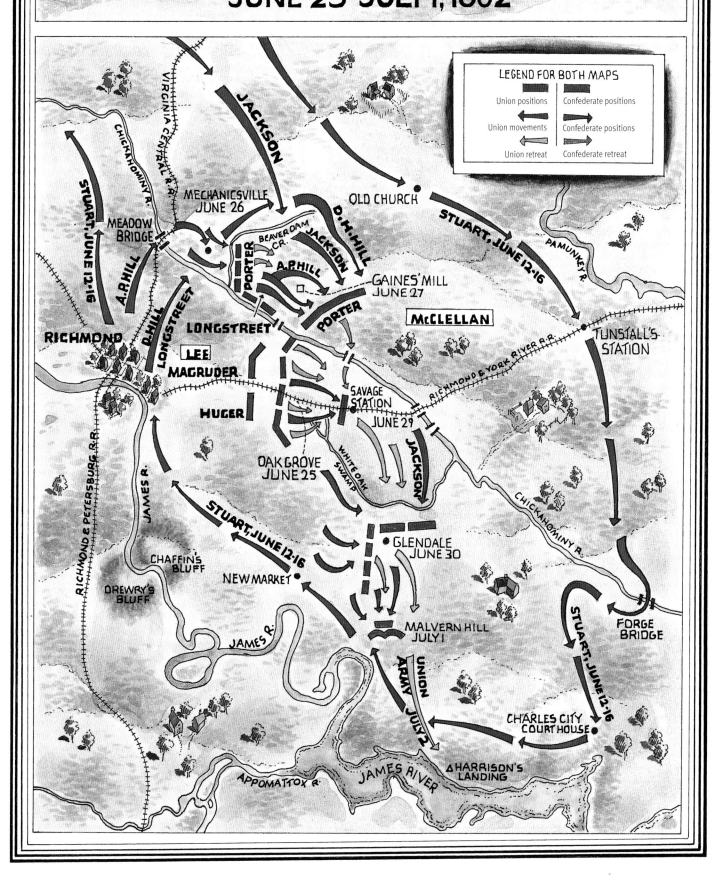

LEGEND FOR BOTH MAPS

Union positions | Confederate positions
Union movements | Confederate positions
Union retreat | Confederate retreat

JACKSON

STUART, JUNE 12-16

CHICKAHOMINY R.

VIRGINIA CENTRAL R.R.

MEADOW BRIDGE

MECHANICSVILLE JUNE 26

OLD CHURCH

STUART, JUNE 12-16

PAMUNKEY R.

A.P. HILL

PORTER

BEAVER DAM CR.

JACKSON

D.H. HILL

A.P. HILL

GAINES' MILL JUNE 27

McCLELLAN

RICHMOND

D. HILL

LONGSTREET

LONGSTREET

PORTER

LEE

MAGRUDER

TUNSTALL'S STATION

RICHMOND & YORK RIVER R.R.

HUGER

SAVAGE STATION JUNE 29

JACKSON

RICHMOND & PETERSBURG R.R.

JAMES R.

OAK GROVE JUNE 25

WHITE OAK SWAMP

CHICKAHOMINY R.

STUART, JUNE 12-16

CHAFFIN'S BLUFF

NEW MARKET

GLENDALE JUNE 30

DREWRY'S BLUFF

JAMES R.

MALVERN HILL JULY 1

UNION ARMY JULY 2

STUART, JUNE 12-16

FORGE BRIDGE

CHARLES CITY COURT HOUSE

APPOMATTOX R.

JAMES RIVER

△ HARRISON'S LANDING

June 26–27 to fall back four miles to an even stronger position on the high ground behind Boatswain's Swamp, near Gaines's Mill. Believing that his rail supply line north of the Chickahominy was threatened by the Confederate drive against his right, McClellan also decided to shift his base and all of his supplies to the James River on the south side of the Peninsula. This meant giving up his original plan of capturing Richmond by a siege and artillery bombardment, for his siege guns could travel overland only by rail and there was no railroad from the James. McClellan thenceforth fought only to protect his retreat, euphemistically called a "change of base." Thus while the battle of Mechanicsville had been a tactical defeat for the South, it turned out to be a strategic victory. It accomplished Lee's first goal of dislodging McClellan's siege operations. It gave the Confederate commander a psychological edge over his adversary—which Lee never yielded. Even though Jackson had failed to attack on June 26, his appearance near the battlefield and his reputation from the Valley gave him the drop on the Yankees once again.

Before Lee could reap the harvest of this advantage, however, he must drive Porter's corps from its rifle pits behind Boatswain's Swamp. This proved costly. The rebel attack on June 27 again suffered from poor coordination between Lee and his division commanders. Lee's plan called for A. P. Hill to attack Porter's center while Longstreet made a feint against the left and Jackson with four divisions assaulted the Union right. If Porter shifted troops to meet Jackson's threat, Longstreet was to convert his feint into an attack and all 55,000 rebels would go forward together against Porter's 35,000. But once more Jackson was slow getting into position and lethargic in attacking. Once again A. P. Hill's division fought almost alone for several hours on a hot afternoon, attacking across a deep ravine and through entangling woods against well-placed Union defenders who punished Hill's brigades. Disjointed assaults by Longstreet and by portions of Jackson's command relieved some of the pressure on Hill. Finally, near sundown, Lee got all his divisions to go forward in concert. In the middle of the line a brigade of Texans commanded by a tall, tawny-bearded, gladiatorial brigadier named John Bell Hood achieved a breakthrough. Pierced in the center, Porter's line collapsed. Fresh Union brigades from across the Chickahominy formed a rear guard and prevented a rout, enabling Porter to get most of his men and guns across the river during the night. Nevertheless, 2,800 bluecoats were captured and 4,000 were killed or wounded. But the Confederate triumph cost Lee close to 9,000 casualties—nearly as many, in six hours of fighting, as the South had lost in two days at Shiloh.

McClellan had sent Porter 6,000 men from the south side of the Chickahominy. The remaining 69,000 Federals on that side had remained quiet during the two days of bloody

A southern cartoon satirizing McClellan's "change of base" to the James River, which the Union general tried to justify as a "strategic movement" rather than a retreat. Both McClellan and the wounded American eagle express a desire to get to the protection of Union gunboats on the James—a common theme in southern editorials and other commentaries on the Yankees' alleged lack of courage.

conflict north of the river. Their officers were transfixed by a repeat performance of Prince John Magruder's theatrics. Left by Lee in charge of 27,000 men holding the line east of Richmond, Magruder had ordered his troops to bristle with aggressive intent. These gray-costumed thespians responded enthusiastically. Artillery fired salvos; infantry lined up in attack formations and probed Union defenses; officers with stentorian voices called out orders to imaginary regiments in the woods. Several Union generals took the bait and informed McClellan that the rebels were strong and threatening on their front. The Federals thus missed an opportunity to counterattack with their overwhelming superiority south of the Chickahominy on June 27. Indeed, at 8:00 P.M. McClellan telegraphed Stanton that he had been "attacked by greatly superior numbers" on *both* sides of the Chickahominy!

In reality the Army of the Potomac was still in good shape despite the defeat at Gaines's Mill. But McClellan was a whipped man mentally. After midnight he again wired Stanton: "I have lost this battle because my force was too small. . . . The Government has not sustained this army. . . . If I save this army now, I tell you plainly that I owe no thanks to you or to any other persons in Washington. You have done your best to sacrifice this army." That McClellan escaped removal from command after sending such a dispatch was owing to an astonished colonel in the telegraph office, who excised the last two sentences before sending the message to Stanton.

As McClellan pulled his army back toward the James River, Lee hoped to hit them in the flank while they were on the move. He improvised a new plan that called for nine Confederate divisions to converge by six different roads against the retreating bluecoats. But poor staff work, faulty maps, geographical obstacles, timid division commanders (especially Magruder and Benjamin Huger), stout Yan-

Confederate burial details hastily interred Union dead in shallow graves after the battle of Gaines's Mill. Over time, erosion and animals exposed their bodies, several of which are shown here in a photograph that was probably made in April 1865.

kee resistance, and—yet again—Jackson's slowness frustrated Lee's efforts. The first failure occurred on June 29 at Savage's Station just three miles south of the Chickahominy. Three Union divisions formed a rear guard there to protect a field hospital and the southward passage of a huge wagon train. Lee ordered Magruder to attack this position from the west while Jackson came down on its right from the north. But Jackson dawdled all day rebuilding a bridge instead of fording the river. Magruder finally went forward alone with less than half of his division. The Yankees repulsed this feeble attack, then withdrew during the night leaving behind 2,500 sick and wounded men (from earlier fighting) and several surgeons who volunteered to share their captivity.

Next day another of Lee's complicated plans for a concentric assault by seven divi-

A rear-guard battle at Savage's Station on June 29 enabled the rest of the retreating Army of the Potomac to get away and bought time for McClellan to destroy supplies that he could not remove. The explosion in the distance is a Union ordnance train going up. Union skirmishers are in action at the upper left; the main infantry line is in the middle distance, the artillery behind them, and reserves in the foreground.

sions near the village of Glendale came to grief. Only Longstreet and Hill managed to get their men into action, fighting a fierce stand-up battle against parts of five Union divisions in late afternoon. The rebels gained a little ground and took a thousand prisoners but lost 3,500 killed and wounded, twice as many as the Yankees. With 25,000 men, Jackson made no contribution to the outcome except a negative one of failing to do his part. Approaching White Oak Swamp from the north, he sent a crew to rebuild the bridge over the creek. When Union artillery and sharpshooters prevented this, Jackson lay down and took a nap. Meanwhile his officers found fords practicable for infantry, but Jackson, seemingly in a trance, did nothing while Longstreet's and Hill's men bled and died two miles to the south. Jackson's failure, in the words of one historian, was "complete, disastrous and unredeemable."

Yet Lee still hoped to redeem something from his attempt to destroy "those people" (his term for the enemy). Lee's temper on the morning of July 1 was frayed. If those people got away, he snapped to one unwary brigadier, it would happen "because I cannot have my orders carried out!" The Federals had taken up another defensive position—the strongest one yet—three miles south of Glendale, on Malvern Hill near the James River. One hundred and fifty feet high and flanked by deep ravines a mile apart, Malvern Hill would have to be attacked frontally and uphill across open fields. Four Union divisions and one hundred guns covered this front with four additional divisions and 150 guns in reserve. Unless these troops were utterly demoralized, it seemed suicidal to attack them. But Lee perceived many apparent signs of demoralization. The route of Union retreat was littered with abandoned equipment and arms. Confederate quartermasters and ordnance officers had reaped a rich harvest of captured matériel—including thirty thousand small arms and fifty cannon.

The rebels had also captured 6,000 Yankees in the previous six days, and continued to pick up scores of stragglers on the morning of July 1. In the end it turned out that the Army of the Potomac, with a resilience in the face of adversity that became its hallmark, was not demoralized after all. But its commander was. McClellan wired Washington that he had been "overpowered" by "superior numbers" and that "I fear I shall be forced to abandon my material to save my men under cover of the gunboats." With his uncanny ability to read the opposing commander's mind, Lee sensed McClellan's unnerved state but mistakenly projected it upon the men in the ranks as well.

A portion of White Oak Swamp a dozen miles east of Richmond, where Jackson failed to advance against Union defenders on June 30.

In any event, Lee's frustration made him ready to grasp at any opportunity to strike "those people" once more. Longstreet—who had emerged as Lee's most reliable subordinate in this campaign—untypically shared this aggressive mood. On the morning of July 1 Longstreet found two elevated positions north of Malvern Hill from which he thought artillery might soften up Union defenses for an infantry assault. Lee ordered the artillery to concentrate on the two knolls. But staff work broke down again; only some of the cannoneers got the message, and their weak fire was soon silenced by Union batteries. Lee nevertheless ordered the assault to go forward. Confusion in the delivery of these orders meant that the attack was disjointed, with brigades advancing individually rather than together. This enabled Union artillery to pulverize nearly every attacking unit, allowing only a few enemy regiments to get close enough for infantry to cut them down. For perhaps the only time in the war, artillery fire caused more enemy casualties than rifle fire.

This panoramic sketch of the Confederate attack against Union infantry and artillery in the middle distance accurately portrays the futility of this frontal assault. Union gunboats on the James River, shown at upper right, helped pulverize the attackers. Note that many Confederate units are still carrying the national flag ("stars and bars") rather than the more familiar battle flag.

D. H. Hill's division was one of the most severely mauled; Hill later wrote that the battle of Malvern Hill "was not war—it was murder." The 5,500 Confederates killed and wounded in this battle were more than double the Union total.

Aware that the rebels had been hurt, some Union generals wanted to mount a counterattack next day. Even McClellan's protégé Fitz-John Porter favored such a move. When McClellan instead ordered a continuation of the retreat to Harrison's Landing on the James, one of his most pugnacious brigadiers—Philip Kearny of New Jersey, who had lost an arm in the Mexican War—burst out to fellow officers: "Such an order can only be prompted by cowardice or treason. . . . We ought instead of retreating to follow up the enemy and take Richmond."

For his part Lee recognized the futility of any more attacks. Twenty thousand southerners—nearly a quarter of his army—had fallen dead and wounded during the previous week, twice the Union total. Rebels and Yankees paused to lick their wounds. While the bluecoats had suffered only one tactical defeat in the Seven Days—at Gaines's Mill—they had constantly retreated, and the campaign had resulted in a strategic Confederate victory, with all that meant for morale in the respective armies and on the home fronts. Nonetheless, Lee was dissatisfied. "Our success has not been as great or as complete as I could have desired," he wrote. "Under ordinary circumstances the Federal Army should have been destroyed." Destroyed! This Napoleonic vision would continue to govern Lee's strategic thinking until that moment a year later when the vision was itself destroyed on the gentle slope of Cemetery Ridge near a small Pennsylvania town.

In the immediate aftermath of the Seven Days, Lee took several steps to remedy the defects in his command structure revealed by the campaign. Because Jackson's divisions and several other brigades had joined Lee's force only on the eve of these battles, the Army of Northern Virginia had never before fought as a unit and Lee had no time to forge its chain of command into an extension of his will. To do so now he shuffled several officers, exiled the weaker division commanders to Texas and Arkansas, and promoted abler subordinates to their places. Because the problem of communicating directly with eight or nine division commanders had proven insuperable during the Seven Days, Lee reorganized the army into two corps (though they were not officially designated as such until later) under Longstreet and Jackson. No evidence exists that Lee reproached Jackson for his dismal performance during the Seven Days, though the assignment of the larger corps to Longstreet may have implied a rebuke. In any case, Jackson soon recovered from his stress fatigue and went on to justify the confidence expressed by Lee's giving him corps command.

III

The 5th Corps, commanded by Major General Fitz-John Porter who is shown here, did the heaviest fighting on the Union side and suffered the most casualties in the Seven Days battles, especially at Gaines's Mill and Malvern Hill.

The thirty thousand men killed and wounded in the Seven Days equaled the number of casualties in *all* the battles in the western theater—including Shiloh—during the first half of 1862. The Seven Days established a pattern for harder fighting and greater casualties in battles between the Army of Northern Virginia and the Army of the Potomac than between any other armies. Most soldiers in the Army of the Potomac were from northeastern states, while most men in the western Union armies hailed from the Old Northwest. The western farm boys and outdoorsmen regarded themselves as tougher soldiers than the effete "paper-collar" soldiers from the Northeast. But in truth the "pasty-faced" clerks and mechanics of the East proved to be more immune to the diseases of camp life and more capable in combat of absorbing and inflicting punishment than western Union soldiers. For the war as a whole the death rate from disease was 43 percent higher among Union soldiers from states west of the Appalachians than among the effete easterners, while the latter experienced combat mortality rates 23 percent higher than the westerners. The number of combat deaths in the Army of the Potomac was greater than in all the other Union armies combined. Forty-one of the fifty Union regiments with the highest percentage of combat casualties fought in this army. In the South, forty of the fifty highest-casualty regiments served in the Army of Northern Virginia. Of all the army commanders on both sides, Lee had the highest casualty rate. One reason for this was Lee's concept of the offensive-defensive, which he applied to tactics as well as to strategy. Lee probably deserves his reputation as the war's best tactician, but his success came at great cost. In every one of the Seven Days battles the Confederates attacked, and consequently lost a higher proportion of killed and wounded than the defenders. The same was true in several of Lee's subsequent battles. Even in 1864–65, when their backs were to the wall and they had barely strength enough to parry their adversary's heavier blows, the Army of Northern Virginia essayed several offensive

A typical scene in an Army of the Potomac winter camp in Virginia. The mud and filth and crowded conditions in such camps were a breeding ground for disease. "Corduroyed" roads made of small logs (right foreground) and elevated walkways to the log huts represented a feeble effort to keep men and horses out of the mud.

counterstrokes. The incongruity between Lee's private character as a humane, courteous, reserved, kindly man, the very model of a Christian gentleman, and his daring, aggressive, but costly tactics as a general is one of the most striking contrasts in the history of the war.

Several battles in the western theater, of course, also produced a ghastly harvest of death. One reason for the high casualties of Civil War battles was the disparity between traditional tactics and modern weapons. The tactical legacy of eighteenth-century and Napoleonic warfare had emphasized close-order formations of soldiers trained to maneuver in concert and fire by volleys. To be sure, some of the citizen-soldiers of the American Revolution fought Indian-style from behind trees or rocks, and the half-trained *levée en masse* of the French Revolution advanced in loose order like "clouds of skirmishers." But they did so mainly because they lacked training and discipline; the ideal for Washington's Continentals and Napoleon's veterans as well as Frederick's Prussians and Wellington's redcoats remained the compact, cohesive columns and lines of automatons who moved and fired with machine-like efficiency.

These tactics also stressed the offensive. Assault troops advanced with cadenced step, firing volleys on command and then double-timing the last few yards to pierce the enemy line with a bayonet charge. Napoleon used his artillery in conjunction with infantry assaults, moving the field guns forward with the foot soldiers to blast holes in enemy ranks and soften them up for the final charge. Americans used these tactics with great success in the Mexican War. West Point teaching stressed the tacti-

cal offensive. Most of the top Civil War officers had fought in Mexico and/or had attended West Point; from both experiences they had absorbed the message that the tactical offensive based on close-order infantry assaults supported by artillery won battles.

In Mexico this happened without high casualties because the basic infantry weapon was the single-shot muzzle-loading smoothbore musket. The maximum range of this weapon was about 250 yards; its effective range (the distance at which a good marksman could hit a target with any regularity) was about eighty yards on a still day. The close-order formation was therefore necessary to concentrate the firepower of these inaccurate weapons; artillery could accompany charging infantry because cannoneers were relatively safe from enemy musket fire until they came within a couple of hundred yards or less; bayonet charges could succeed because double-timing infantry could cover the last eighty yards during the twenty-five seconds it took defending infantrymen to reload their muskets after firing a volley.

Rifling a musket increased its range fourfold by imparting a spin to a conical bullet that enabled it literally to bore through the air. This fact had been known for cen-

Officers required soldiers to practice close-order drill as much as possible in winter camp, to keep them busy and to teach discipline and efficiency in preparation for close-order tactics in battle.

The Model 1822 musket is shown here with its cartridge containing powder and a round .69 caliber ball wrapped in paper, which served as wadding when the gun was fired. Most troops were equipped with these obsolete smoothbore weapons in the first year and even more of the war.

turies, but before the 1850s only special regiments or one or two companies per regiment were equipped with rifles. These companies were used as skirmishers—that is, they operated in front and on the flanks of the main body, advancing or withdrawing in loose order and shooting at will from long range at enemy targets of opportunity. Given the rifle's greater range and accuracy, why were not all infantrymen equipped with it? Because a bullet large enough to "take" the rifling was difficult to ram down the barrel. Riflemen sometimes had to pound the ramrod down with a mallet. After a rifle had been fired a few times a residue of powder built up in the grooves and had to be cleaned out before it could be fired again. Since rapid and reliable firing was essential in a battle, the rifle was not practicable for the mass of infantrymen.

Until the 1850s, that is. Although several people contributed to the development of a practicable military rifle, the main credit belongs to French army Captain Claude E. Minié and to the American James H. Burton, an armorer at the Harper's Ferry Armory. In 1848 Minié perfected a bullet small enough to be easily rammed down a rifled barrel, with a wooden plug in the base of the bullet to expand it upon firing to take the rifling. Such bullets were expensive; Burton developed a cheaper and better bullet with a deep cavity in the base that filled with gas and expanded the rim upon firing. This was the famous "minié ball" of Civil War rifles. The superiority of the rifle was demonstrated by British and French soldiers who carried them in the Crimean War. As secretary of war in 1855, Jefferson Davis converted the United States army to the .58-caliber Springfield rifled musket. Along with the similar British Enfield rifle (caliber .577, which would take the same bullet as the Springfield), the Springfield became the main infantry arm of the Civil War.

Because they were single-shot weapons loaded from the muzzle, these rifles were still awkward to load. Even the most dextrous soldier could fire no more than three shots per minute. Several inventors had developed breechloading rifles by 1861, but with the paper-wrapped cartridges (containing bullet and powder) then in use, gas and sometimes flame escaped from the breech and made the weapon unreliable and even dangerous to the user. Progress in solving this problem made the single-shot Sharps carbine and rifle popular with the Union cavalry and sharpshooter units that managed to obtain them. The development of metal cartridges enabled the northern army to equip its cavalry and some infantry units with repeaters by 1863, of which the seven-shot Spencer carbine was most successful. These weapons had a smaller powder charge and therefore a shorter range than the paper-cartridged Springfield and Enfield and were more prone to

The Springfield (bottom) and British-made Enfield rifled muskets were the workhorse weapons of the Civil War. Both took the same .58-caliber cartridge, even though the Enfield's caliber was .577. That tiny difference made the Springfield more popular with Union soldiers because it seemed ever so slightly less likely to foul and jam.

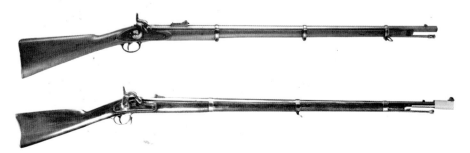

malfunction. The muzzle-loaders thus remained the principal infantry weapons throughout the war.

Northern industry geared up to manufacture more than two million rifles during the war; unable to produce more than a fraction of this total, the South relied mainly on imports through the blockade and on capture of Union rifles. In 1861 neither side had many rifles, so most soldiers carried old smoothbores taken from storage in arsenals. During 1862 most Union regiments received new Springfields or Enfields, while many Confederate units still had to rely on smoothbores. This was one reason for the two-to-one excess of Confederate casualties in the Seven Days. By 1863 nearly all infantrymen on both sides carried rifles.

The transition from smoothbore to rifle had two main effects: it multiplied casualties; and it strengthened the tactical defensive. Officers trained and experienced in the

The Army of the Potomac organized two sharpshooter regiments composed of soldiers who were crack shots. The men in the 1st and 2nd Sharpshooters came from eight different states. They were used mainly as skirmishers and snipers, and did more damage to the enemy than any other Union infantry units of comparable size. This painting of a sharpshooter in a tree near Yorktown in May 1862 is one of Winslow Homer's best war paintings, based on a sketch he drew for Harper's Weekly.

These soldiers of the 3rd Georgia Infantry pose with their smoothbore muskets, bayonets fixed, looking calm and determined. The variety of headgear was typical in the Confederate army.

old tactics were slow to recognize these changes. Time and again generals on both sides ordered close-order assaults in the traditional formation. With an effective range of three or four hundred yards, defenders firing rifles decimated these attacks. Artillery declined in importance as an offensive weapon, because its accuracy and the reliability of shells at long range were poor, and the guns could no longer advance with the infantry toward enemy lines, for marksmen could pick off the cannoneers and especially the horses at distances up to half a mile. Sharpshooters also singled out enemy officers, which helps to explain why officers and especially generals had higher casualty rates than privates. Officers on both sides soon began to stay off horseback when possible and to wear a private's uniform with only a sewn-on shoulder patch to designate their rank. The old-fashioned cavalry charge against infantry, already obsolescent, became obsolete in the face of rifles that could knock down horses long before their riders got within saber or pistol range. The Civil War hastened the evolution of dismounted cavalry tactics in which the horse was mainly a means of transportation rather than a weapon in its own right.

As time went on, experience taught soldiers new tactics adapted to the rifle. Infantry formations loosened up and became a sort of large-scale skirmish line in which men advanced by rushes, taking advantage of cover offered by the ground to reload before dashing forward another few yards, working in groups of two or three to load and shoot alternately in order to keep up a continuous rather than a volley fire. But officers had difficulty maintaining control over large units employing such tactics in that preradio age. This limited the employment of loose-order tactics and compelled the retention of close-order assaults in some instances to the end of the war.

And while loose-order tactics occasionally succeeded in carrying enemy lines, they did not restore dominance to the tactical offensive, especially when defenders began digging trenches and throwing up breastworks at every position, as they did by 1863 and 1864. It became a rule of thumb that attacking forces must have a numerical superiority of at least three to one to succeed in carrying trenches defended by alert troops. Robbed by the rifle of some of its potency as an offensive weapon, the artillery functioned best on the defensive by firing at attacking infantry with grapeshot and canister (as at Malvern Hill) in the manner of a huge sawed-off shotgun. Despite the occasional success of head-on tactical assaults such as the Confederate victories at Gaines's Mill, Chancellorsville, and Chickamauga or Union triumphs at Missionary Ridge and Cedar Creek, the defense usually prevailed against frontal attacks. Even when an assault succeeded, it did so at high cost in killed and wounded. Steeped in romantic martial traditions, glorying in the "charge" and in "valor," southern soldiers in the Seven Days suffered grievously from their assaults.

The most common type of cannon in both armies was the twelve-pound Napoleon gun howitzer, named after Emperor Napoleon III, who introduced this gun in the French army in the 1850s. Made of bronze, durable and versatile, it could fire almost any kind of shell or cannonball, grapeshot, and canister. These Confederate Napoleons were captured in the Union attack on Missionary Ridge (Chattanooga) in 1863.

Well might D. H. Hill reflect in later years on the bodies piled in front of Union lines at Gaines's Mill: "It was thought to be a great thing to charge a battery of artillery or an earthwork lined with infantry. . . . We were very lavish of blood in those days."

During 1862 and 1863, Confederate armies went on the tactical offensive in six of the nine battles in which the killed and wounded of both sides together exceeded 15,000. Although they won two of these six battles (Chancellorsville and Chickamauga) and achieved a strategic success in a third (the Seven Days), their total casualties in these six contests exceeded Union casualties by 20,000 men (89,000 to 69,000). In the spring of 1864 the situation was reversed as Grant's men suffered nearly twice the casualties of Lee's army when the Yankees took the offensive from the Wilderness to Petersburg. The quest of both sides for victory through tactical assaults in the old manner proved a chimera in the new age of the rifle. The tactical predominance of the defense helps explain why the Civil War was so long and bloody. The rifle and trench ruled Civil War battlefields as thoroughly as the machine gun and trench ruled those of World War I.

IV

In the fog-enshrouded gloom at Malvern Hill on the morning of July 2, 1862, a Union cavalry officer looked over the field of the previous day's conflict. "Over five thousand dead and wounded men were on the ground . . . enough were alive and moving to give to the field a singular crawling effect." Soon the two armies agreed on a truce to bury the dead and succor the wounded. These tasks etched the horrors of war even more indelibly than the actual fighting. "The sights and smells that assailed us were simply indescribable," wrote a southern soldier on burial detail, "corpses swollen to twice their original size, some of them actually burst asunder with the pressure of foul gases. . . . The odors were nauseating and so deadly that in a short time we all sickened and were lying with our mouths close to the ground, most of us vomiting profusely."

Many civilians on both sides, especially in the South, experienced these sights and smells of war directly as well as through soldiers' letters. Much of the fighting in May and June 1862 occurred almost on Richmond's doorstep. Many of the 21,000 wounded Confederates from Seven Pines and the Seven Days were brought into the city. "We lived in one immense hospital, and breathed the vapors of the charnel house," wrote a Richmond woman. Churches, hotels, warehouses, shops, barns, even private homes were pressed into service as temporary hospitals. White women volunteered by the hundreds as nurses; slaves were mobilized as orderlies and gravediggers.

Like the Union army, the Confederates gave first aid and emergency treatment of wounded in field hospitals near or on the battlefield. The South was slow to establish general hospitals for the treatment and convalescence of the badly wounded and of soldiers with long-term illnesses. At first such hospitals were maintained primarily by local or private initiative. By late 1861 the Confederate Medical Department had taken over this function. The army established several general hospitals in Richmond; the principal one, on an east-side hill, was Chimborazo Hospital, which became the largest such facility in the world, with 250 pavilion buildings each housing forty to sixty patients and 100 tents with space for eight to ten convalescents each. But only a fraction of these structures had been completed by June 1862, when thousands of wounded poured into the city and many died in the streets because there was nowhere else to put them. The shock of the Seven Days and of subsequent battles in Virginia compelled the expansion and modernization of southern general hospitals.

This shock plus the vital example of women volunteers in Richmond and at Corinth, Mississippi, also forced a reversal of the Medical Department's initial hostility to female nurses. Prior to the Civil War, Florence Nightingale had forced a reform of the inadequate British army medical services in the Crimea, dignified nursing as a profession, and, in 1860, established the world's first school of nursing at St. Thomas's Hospital in London. She was the inspiration for several southern white women who volunteered their services as nurses or founded small hospitals

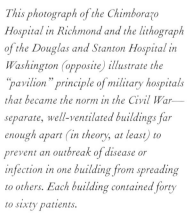

This photograph of the Chimborazo Hospital in Richmond and the lithograph of the Douglas and Stanton Hospital in Washington (opposite) illustrate the "pavilion" principle of military hospitals that became the norm in the Civil War— separate, well-ventilated buildings far enough apart (in theory, at least) to prevent an outbreak of disease or infection in one building from spreading to others. Each building contained forty to sixty patients.

for soldiers. One of the best such hospitals was established in Richmond by Sally Louisa Tompkins, whom Jefferson Davis eventually commissioned as a captain so that her infirmary could qualify as an army hospital.

While it was permissible for white women to make bandages and nurse the sick at home or even in the slave quarters, it was previously unthinkable that they be exposed to the horrors of an army hospital. Twenty-seven-year-old Kate Cumming of Mobile was one of the numerous southern women from good families who defied this ban and proved more than equal to dealing with the appalling conditions in such places when, in April 1862, she went to Corinth where Beauregard's battered army was trying to recover after Shiloh. She arrived at a Corinth hotel that had been turned into a hospital and immediately realized that nothing she "had ever heard or read had given me the faintest idea of the horrors witnessed here." But she and her sisters in mercy fought down the desire to run away and went immediately to work. "I sat up all night, bathing the men's wounds, and giving them water," she wrote in her diary. "The men are lying all over the house, on their blankets, just as they were brought in from the battlefield. . . . The foul air from this mass of human beings at first made me giddy and sick, but I soon got over it. We have to walk, and when we give the men anything kneel, in blood and water; but we think nothing of it."

Cumming and other white women who nursed in Confederate military hospitals during the summer of 1862 were volunteers. The official army nurses were soldiers detailed for the purpose (many of them convalescents themselves) and slave "attendants" impressed as cooks, laundresses, and cleanup workers. Some genteel volunteers were Lady Bountiful types who played at nursing for a few days and then departed. But most women rendered valuable service, and thereby overcame the prejudices of many army surgeons who had initially opposed the presence of white women. These hardy volunteers proved to be both nurturing and effective, knowl-

After her volunteer nursing in makeshift Confederate hospitals in Corinth, Kate Cumming became one of the foremost army nurses and hospital matrons in the Confederacy. She served in both field and general hospitals at Vicksburg and Chattanooga in 1863 and several hospitals in Georgia during 1864 when the Confederates were forced to retreat repeatedly as Sherman drove toward Atlanta. After the war Cumming published her journal, which is a valuable source on Confederate medicine.

edgeable, and indefatigable. In September 1862 the Confederate Congress enacted a law providing for civilian matrons and nurses in army general hospitals, "giving preference in all cases to females where their services may best subserve the purpose." A good many white women became part of the official army medical service under this law and were deservedly honored for contributions to "the lost cause" equal to that of Confederate soldiers. Other women made crucial contributions by organizing soldiers' aid or hospital relief societies throughout the South to provide supplies, services, and money to aid sick and wounded soldiers or their families. This projection of southern women into public activities on an unprecedented scale was not only an essential part of the shift to total war in 1862 but also an emancipation from the pedestal of ethereal femininity that had constricted their lives.

* * * * *

Their northern sisters, arguably more emancipated when the war began, threw themselves into the fray with equal energy and in greater numbers. Their efforts were channeled through a powerful organization, the United States Sanitary Commission, the largest voluntary association yet formed in a country noted for such enterprises. Within days of the war's outbreak the Commission grew out of a fusion of local soldiers' aid societies which had been largely created by women previously active in societies advocating the abolition of slavery, women's rights, temperance, education, missions, and the like. Elizabeth Blackwell, the first American woman to brave male derision to earn an M.D. (1849), took the lead in organizing a meeting of three thousand women at Cooper Institute in New York on April 29, 1861. Several prominent men also participated in this meeting, which formed the Women's Central Association for Relief to coordinate the work of numerous smaller associations.

Members of the Women's Central Association for Relief in New York in their Manhattan office tallying shipments of medical supplies to the front.

The initial task of the W.C.A.R. was to establish a training program for nurses—the first such venture in the United States. The W.C.A.R. also became the nucleus of the United States Sanitary Commission.

The "Sanitary," as it came to be called, was inspired by the reforms achieved through the efforts of the British Sanitary Commission in the Crimean War. That organization exposed the filthy and primitive conditions which, through resulting disease and infection, decimated the Allied armies. A number of American medical men and women wanted to organize a similar commission to alleviate such problems in the Union army. On May 15 a delegation of distinguished physicians (all men) headed by Henry Bellows, a prominent Unitarian clergyman interested in medical problems, traveled to Washington as representatives of the W.C.A.R. and affiliated organizations. After initially encountering opposition from the Army Medical Bureau (whose head, the surgeon general, had served in the regular army for forty-three years and did not welcome interference by busybody civilians, much less female nurses), the delegation bypassed that department and met with Secretary of War Cameron and the president. At first Lincoln could see little use for a civilian auxiliary to the Medical Bureau, referring to such as a "fifth wheel to the coach." But he acquiesced nevertheless, and on June 13 signed the order creating the U.S. Sanitary Commission.

The commission's official powers were investigatory and advisory only. But the decentralized, do-it-yourself nature of northern mobilization in 1861 offered an opportunity for a voluntary association to create its own powers. With Bellows as president and the talented Frederick Law Olmsted as executive secretary, the Sanitary did precisely that. It enlisted physicians and other prominent citizens as officers of local affiliates. Seven thousand locals dotted the North by 1863. The national officers and most of the five hundred paid agents of the commission were men; most of the tens of thousands of volunteer workers were women. They held bazaars and "Sanitary Fairs" to raise money. They sent bandages, medicine, clothing, food, and volunteer nurses to army camps and hospitals. They provided meals and lodging to furloughed soldiers going and coming from the front. Because of the close ties between commission leaders and the citizen volunteers who became officers of regiments, the Sanitary helped shape the hygienic conditions of army camps despite the continuing coldness of the Army Medical Bureau. "Sanitary inspectors" from the commission instructed sol-

This appeal to the residents of Bucks County, Pennsylvania, to contribute blankets for Union soldiers is an example of the localized, voluntary nature of mobilization and supply in the early months of the war that became institutionalized in the U.S. Sanitary Commission.

The quarters of the U.S. Sanitary Commission near an army camp in Virginia. The clean and orderly grounds, including the whitewashed picket fence, were meant to serve as an example to the army. The presence of women volunteer nurses helped make the "Sanitary" popular with soldiers.

diers in proper camp drainage, placement of latrines, water supply, and cooking. Many soldiers paid little attention, and suffered the consequences. Others benefited by improved health from following this advice.

The Sanitary won popularity with soldiers and influence with congressmen. By the winter of 1861–62 it had become a power in national politics. It decided to use this power to attack the Medical Bureau's seniority system, which kept young, progressive surgeons down and left the bureau in charge of men like Surgeon General Clement A. Finley, whose antediluvian thinking was geared to the somnolent bureaucracy of a 16,000-man peacetime army. "It is criminal weakness to intrust such responsibilities . . . to a self-satisfied, supercilious, bigoted blockhead, merely because he is the oldest of the old mess-room doctors of the frontier-guard of the country," Olmsted wrote in a private letter. "He knows nothing, and does nothing, and is capable of knowing nothing and doing nothing but quibble about matters of form and precedent." Commission president Bellows drafted a bill to enable Lincoln to bypass the seniority system and promote younger men to top positions in the Medical Bureau.

The army medical establishment fought back against the "sensation preachers, village doctors, and strong-minded women" of the commission. But the bill passed on April 18, 1862. It not only suspended the seniority system but also gave the surgeon general authority to appoint eight medical inspectors with power to institute reforms in army procedures. Lincoln immediately appointed the Sanitary's candidate as the new surgeon general: thirty-three-year-old William Hammond, a progressive, energetic, strong-willed army surgeon. Hammond's appointment marked the end of an adversarial relationship between the army and the commission, and the beginning of an extraordinarily productive partnership between public and private medical enterprise. The army turned over several passenger steamers to the commission, which fitted them up as hospital ships staffed with volunteer nurses for evacuation of wounded from the Peninsula to general hospitals in Washington and New York. The commission had already proved the value of such a policy by chartering its own hospital boats to evacuate wounded men from Shiloh. The Sanitary also pioneered in the development of hospital trains with specially fitted cars for rail transport of wounded.

Surgeon General Hammond was so impressed by the Sanitary Commission nurses who staffed the hospital ships that he issued an order in July 1862 requiring at least one-third of the army nurses in general hospitals to be women. As early as April 1861 the venerable reformer of insane asylums, Dorothea Dix, had been named "Superintendent of Female Nurses" with rather vaguely defined powers. An assertive individualist whose long suit was not administrative ability, Dix worked in uneasy cooperation with the Sanitary Commission to recruit nurses. By the end of the war more than three thousand northern women had served as paid army nurses. In addition, several thousand women continued to work as volunteers and as salaried agents of the Sanitary Commission.

These were not the only means by which northern women and men performed medical services in the war. Some worked for other volunteer agencies such as the Western Sanitary Commission (separate from the U.S.S.C.) in the trans-Mississippi

A photograph of one of the river steamboats purchased or chartered by the Union navy and converted into floating hospitals.

theater, or the Christian Commission, founded by YMCA leaders in November 1861 to provide blankets, clothing, books, and physical as well as spiritual nurture to Union soldiers. And some northern women who earned fame as nurses operated pretty much on their own. One of these was Clara Barton, a forty-year-old spinster working as a clerk in the patent office when the war broke out. She became a one-woman soldiers' aid society, gathering medicines and supplies and turning up on several battlefields or at field hospitals to comfort the wounded and goad careless or indifferent surgeons. Barton's friendship with influential congressmen helped bring political pressure to bear for reforms in army medicine. Her wartime experiences motivated her postwar crusade for American affiliation with the international Red Cross. Another remarkable woman was Mary Ann Bickerdyke, a forty-five-year-

This painting by Eastman Johnson shows a Sanitary Commission volunteer taking dictation from a wounded soldier for a letter to loved ones at home. The soldier has been moved from the hospital tent in the background into the open air. The setting suggests one of the many field hospitals established at Gettysburg after the battle there.

old widow from Illinois who began her service in 1861 at the fever-ridden army base at Cairo. A large, strong, indomitable yet maternal woman, she swept through the camp like an avenging angel. She became the gadfly of obtuse officers and the special champion of enlisted men, who fondly named her "Mother Bickerdyke." She cleaned up the camps and continued on with Grant's and then Sherman's armies from Fort Donelson to Atlanta. Bickerdyke earned the respect of both of these Union generals; she was the only woman that Sherman allowed in his advanced base hospitals.

Not all the female army nurses belonged to that category known in the nineteenth century as

Known as "the Angel of the Battlefield" for her tireless work at field hospitals after and even during several battles in Virginia, Maryland, and South Carolina, Clara Barton was probably the most famous Civil War nurse. Her wartime experiences led her to organize the American Red Cross after the war.

"respectable." Some regiments on both sides sheltered the ancient army institution of "camp followers"—female laundresses or cooks who sometimes doubled as prostitutes and as nurses. Nonetheless, "respectable" women nurses had overcome by 1862 many of the prejudices that had prevailed against them at the war's beginning. They had achieved—with soldiers and the public if not always with surgeons—the status and esteem that Florence Nightingale and her cohorts had earned in Britain. The courage and energy demonstrated by many women chipped away at the weaker-sex image—and prepared the way for the eventual political emancipation and equal empowerment of women in America.

But if the outstanding contributions of women in the service of healing served to transform nursing from a menial service to a genuine profession in the Civil War, the deadly limitations of what passed for medical "science" were made painfully clear. The conflict did produce some important innovations in army medical practice. One was the creation of a special ambulance corps for first-aid treatment of the wounded and their evacuation to field hospitals. Traditional practice in both armies assigned regimental musicians and soldiers "least effective under arms" as stretcher-bearers to carry the wounded from the field and assist the surgeons in field hospitals. Civilian teamsters were expected to double as ambulance drivers. The large-scale fighting in 1862 quickly revealed the defects of this system. Lacking training and *esprit*, the men and boys (many of the bandsmen were under eighteen) assigned to these tasks all too often fled in terror when the shooting started. Even when ambulance drivers remained on duty, there were not enough ambulances. Fighting men often defied orders and dropped out of line to carry wounded friends to the rear because they knew no one else would.

This wretched situation became a scandal in the Union army during the summer of 1862 and caused Surgeon General Hammond to appoint Jonathan K. Letterman as the new medical director of the Army of the Potomac after the Seven Days. This

A nurse at a Union general hospital in Nashville mixes a medication, probably for the soldier on the right. It is not clear whether he is looking at her in appreciation for her soothing presence or at the cup in apprehension of how the medicine might taste.

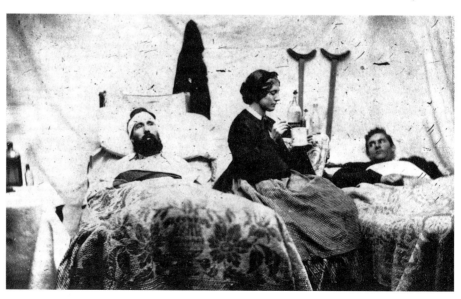

appointment brought improvement. The Sanitary Commission had long advocated the creation of a trained ambulance corps. Letterman instituted such a unit in the Army of the Potomac, from where it spread to other Union armies and was formally mandated by law in 1864. Wearing special uniforms and imbued with high morale, these noncombatant medics risked their lives to reach the wounded in the midst of battle and evacuate them as quickly as possible to surgeons' stations and field hospitals. The ambulance corps became a model for European armies down to World War I; both the Germans and French adopted the system in the Franco-Prussian War. The South evolved a similar "infirmary corps" in 1862 but did not

Experiments during the first year of the war demonstrated that specially designed four-wheeled wagons with oversize springs made the best ambulances. This photograph shows a dozen Union ambulances parked awaiting the call to duty.

institute it on the same scale. The Confederate medical service, like everything else in the southern war effort, did wonders with the resources available but did not have enough men, medicines, or ambulances to match the Union effort. This was one reason why about 18 percent of the wounded rebels died of their wounds compared with 14 percent of the wounded Yankees.

The record of both armies in this respect, of course, was abysmal by twentieth-century standards. In the Korean War only one of every fifty wounded Americans died of his wounds; in Vietnam the proportion was one in four hundred. The Civil War soldier was eight times more likely to die of a wound and ten times more likely to die of disease than an American soldier in World War I. Indeed, twice as many Civil War soldiers died of disease as were killed and mortally wounded in combat. Such a record seems at first glance to justify the conclusion shared by several historians that "the medical services represent one of the Civil War's most dismal failures."

Soldiers at the front knew this even more keenly than those journalists and members of the Sanitary Commission who were reporting horror stories about fetid hospitals, drunken surgeons, and untended sick or wounded soldiers dying in agony. The reputation of many army doctors as "quacks" or "butchers" reflected the generally low repute of the medical profession. Soldiers dreaded hospitals and sometimes went to great lengths to conceal wounds or illnesses in order to avoid them. "I beleave the Doctors kills more than they cour," wrote an Alabama soldier in 1862. "Doctors haint Got half Sence." Yanks were inclined to agree. An Illinois private wrote that "our doctor knows about as much as a ten year old boy," while a Massachusetts officer pronounced his regimental surgeon "a jackass."

Soldiers who believed they were more likely to get well outside a hospital than inside it may have been right. What Louis Pasteur and Joseph Lister revealed about the deadly relationship between microbes, unsterile conditions and disease would be accepted—a few years too late. The discovery of the link between mosquitoes and yellow fever and malaria made possible the control of these killer diseases. But Civil War doctors knew none of these things.

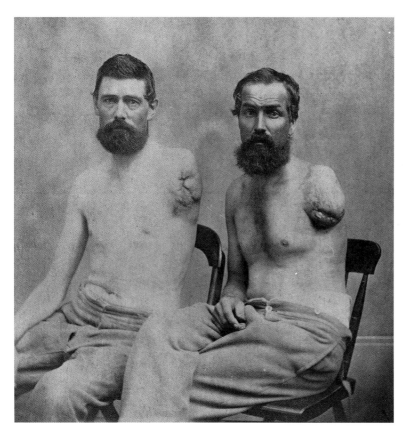

These two amputees had been wounded in the upper arm by bullets that shattered the bone, leaving the surgeon no option but amputation.

In a dreadful sort of synergy, the large caliber and low muzzle velocity of Civil War rifles caused horrible wounds (and collateral, fulminating infection) with the bullet usually remaining in the body rather than going through it. Surgeons knew of few ways except amputation to stop gangrene or osteomyelitis or pyemia. Stomach wounds were generally fatal because there was no known prevention of peritonitis. Chloroform and ether were used as anesthetics, but shortages especially in the South sometimes required soldiers to be dosed with whiskey and literally to bite the bullet during an operation. This was the "heroic age" of medicine in which soldiers who suffered anything from dysentery to constipation to malaria to a cold were dosed with calomel or tartar emetic or quinine or morphine or laudanum. Little wonder that many soldiers preferred to remain out of the clutches of doctors. Little wonder, also, that some became narcotics addicts.

Disease was a greater threat to the health of Civil War soldiers than enemy weapons. Only by twentieth-century standards was Civil War disease mortality high. Nevertheless, despite improvement over previous wars in this respect, disease was a crippling factor in Civil War military operations. At any given time a substantial proportion of men in a regiment might be on the sick list. Disease reduced the size of most regiments from their initial complement of a thousand men to about half that number before the regiment ever went into battle.

Sickness hit soldiers hardest in their first year. The crowding together of thousands of men from various backgrounds into a new and highly contagious disease environment had predictable results. Men (especially those from rural areas) who had never before been exposed to measles, mumps, or tonsilitis promptly came down with these childhood maladies. Though rarely fatal, these illnesses could cripple units for weeks at a time. More deadly were smallpox and erysipelas, which went through some rural regiments like a scythe. If soldiers recovered from these diseases and remained for some time at the training or base camp—where by poor sanitary practices and exposure to changeable weather they fouled their water supply, created fertile breeding grounds for bacteria, and became susceptible to deadly viruses—many of them contracted one of the three principal killer diseases of the war: diarrhea/dysentery, typhoid, or pneumonia. As they marched southward in summer campaigns, many of them caught the fourth most prevalent mortal disease: malaria. A good many Union occupation troops in southern cities as well as Confederate soldiers camped near other cities—especially Richmond—experienced another soldiers' malady, venereal disease, of which there were about as many reported cases as of measles, mumps, and tonsilitis combined.

Disease disrupted several military operations. Lee's West Virginia campaigns of 1861 failed in part because illness incapacitated so many of his men. One reason for the abandonment of the first effort to capture Vicksburg in July 1862 was the sickness of more than half of the Union soldiers and sailors there. Beauregard's decision to abandon Corinth was influenced by illness of epidemic proportions that put more than a third of his army on the sick list. By the time Halleck's Union army had established its occupation of Corinth in early June, a third or more of the Yankee soldiers were also ill. Nearly half of the twenty-nine Union generals came down sick during the Corinth campaign and its aftermath, including Halleck himself and John Pope with what they ruefully called the "Evacuation of Corinth" (diarrhea) and Sherman with malaria. Halleck's failure after Corinth to continue his invasion into Mississippi resulted in part from fears of even greater disease morbidity among unacclimated northern soldiers in a deep-South summer campaign.

Illness also influenced the denouement of the Peninsula campaign in Virginia. The health of McClellan's army, already affected by the heavy rains and humid heat among the Chickahominy swamps in May and June, deteriorated further after the army's arrival at Harrison's Landing in July. Nearly a fourth of the unwounded men were sick. Scores of new cases of malaria, dysentery, and typhoid were reported every day. McClellan himself had not fully recovered from an earlier bout with dysentery. With the sickliest season of the year (August–September) coming on, the administration decided over McClellan's protest to withdraw his army from the Peninsula.

Strategic and political questions also played a part in this decision. Recognizing the drawbacks of trying to function as his own general in chief, Lincoln had called Halleck out of the West to take this post. The president had also formed a new army out of Banks's, Frémont's, and McDowell's corps in northern Virginia and had brought John Pope east to command it. While this was going on, Congress was passing a bill to confiscate the property (including slaves) of Confederates, and Lincoln was making up his mind to issue an emancipation proclamation. The failure of McClellan's Peninsula campaign was not alone a military failure; it represented also the downfall of the limited war for limited ends that McClellan favored. From now on the North would fight not to preserve the old Union but to destroy it and build a new one on the ashes.

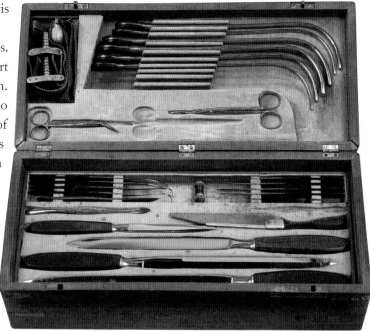

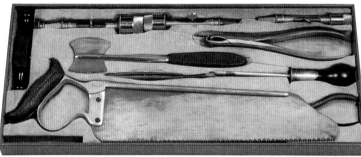

The tools of the surgeon's trade included a saw for amputation, a tourniquet to cut the supply of blood to the wounded area, and various knives and scalpels.

CHAPTER SIXTEEN

☆ ☆ ☆ ☆ ☆

We Must Free the Slaves
or Be Ourselves Subdued

I

If Robert E. Lee was unhappy with the escape of McClellan's army from destruction in the Seven Days, the southern people did not share his discontent. Lee became the hero of the hour. The *Richmond Whig* proclaimed that the quiet Virginian had "amazed and confounded his detractors by the brilliancy of his genius . . . his energy and daring. He has established his reputation forever, and has entitled himself to the lasting gratitude of his country."

This commentator, of course, could not foresee the profound irony of Lee's achievement. If McClellan's campaign had succeeded, the war might have ended. The Union probably would have been restored with minimal destruction in the South. Slavery would have survived in only slightly modified form, at least for a time. By defeating McClellan, Lee assured a prolongation of the war until it destroyed slavery, the Old South, and nearly everything the Confederacy was fighting for.

After the Seven Days, Union policy took a decisive turn toward total war. Northern morale initially plunged downward as far as southern morale ascended skyward. Although depressed by military setbacks, Lincoln did not falter. "I expect to maintain this contest," he informed state governors, "until successful, or till I die, or am conquered . . . or Congress or the country forsakes me."

Lincoln now recognized that the cessation of recruiting in April had been a mistake. But he feared that if he issued a new appeal for recruits in the wake of the Seven Days, "a general panic and stampede would follow." Seward solved this dilemma by persuading northern governors to issue an address (written by Seward) to the president urging him to call on the states for new volunteers to "follow up" the "recent successes of the Federal arms" and "speedily crush the rebellion." Seward backdated this document to June 28 in order to avoid the appearance of a panicked response to McClellan's retreat. In pretended compliance with the governors' appeal, Lincoln on July 2 called for 300,000 new volunteers to bring the war "to a speedy and satisfactory conclusion."

Once again recruiting committees in the North geared up their machinery.

Opposite page: This Allegory of Freedom *by an unknown artist shows a Union officer dragging the Confederate flag in the dirt as he holds the American flag aloft and a black soldier stands next to another flag flying triumphantly in celebration of emancipation.*

THE OVERDUE BILL.

Mr. South to Mr. North. "YOUR 'NINETY DAYS' PROMISSORY NOTE ISN'T TAKEN UP YET, SIRREE!"

This cartoon from the British humor magazine Punch *offers a somewhat uninformed commentary on Lincoln's call for troops in the summer of 1862 to pay the overdue bill the ninety-day militia of 1861 had failed to meet. Lincoln's first call for militia in April 1861 had specified a term of only ninety days not because he expected the war to last no longer than that but because the existing law limited the federal service of state militia to ninety days. Congress extended that limit to nine months in 1862; most Union troops were volunteers (not militia) for a three-year term.*

Governors called on men to join up to fight for "the old flag, for our country, Union, and Liberty." But the parades and rallies of 1862 were a pale imitation of the stirring demonstrations of 1861. The lengthening casualty lists had taught people that war was not a glorious game. Although the North had mobilized only a third of its potential military manpower, a booming war economy and the busy summer season on farms had left few young men at loose ends and ready to volunteer. Moreover, the new recruits, like those already in the army, had to enlist for three years. Governors informed the War Department that they could easily raise enough short-term men to fill their quotas, but getting three-year recruits would be difficult.

In response the government adopted an ingenious carrot-and-stick approach. The carrot was bounties. The War Department authorized payment in advance of $25 of the traditional $100 bounty normally paid in full upon honorable discharge. In addition, some states or cities offered bounties to three-year recruits. The stick was a militia law enacted by Congress on July 17, 1862. This law defined the militia as comprising all able-bodied men between ages eighteen and forty-five and empowered the president to call state militia into federal service for a period of up to nine months. Since the militia in several states had fallen into a comatose condition, a key provision of the act authorized the president to "make all necessary rules and regulations . . . to provide for enrolling the militia and otherwise putting this act into execution." Here was a potential for an enormous expansion of federal power at the expense of the states. The government did not hesitate to use this power to reach across state boundaries and institute a quasi-draft. On August 4 the War Department imposed on the states a levy of 300,000 nine-month militia *in addition to* the 300,000 three-year volunteers called for a month earlier. Secretary of War Stanton softened the blow of this big stick, however, with a regulation stipulating that every three-year volunteer enlisted above quota would be counted as four men against the nine-month militia quota.

Although of dubious legality, this regulation achieved its purpose. Before the end of 1862 this policy had produced 421,000 three-year volunteers and 88,000 militiamen, which according to Stanton's arithmetic exceeded the combined quotas by 45 percent. Most of the volunteers were organized into new regiments, some of which became crack units by 1863—but in the process they had to go through the same high-casualty trial-and-error experiences as their 1861 predecessors.

In several states a militia draft became necessary to fill the quotas. This draft met violent resistance in some areas, especially Irish Catholic neighborhoods in the coalfields of eastern Pennsylvania, Butternut districts in Ohio and Indiana, and German Catholic townships in Wisconsin. Mobs murdered two enrollment officers in Indiana and wounded a commissioner in Wisconsin. The army had to send troops into

all four states to keep order and carry out the draft. On September 24, Lincoln issued a proclamation suspending the writ of habeas corpus and subjecting to martial law "all persons discouraging volunteer enlistments, resisting militia drafts, or guilty of any disloyal practice affording aid and comfort to the rebels." The War Department took off the gloves to enforce this decree. Stanton created a network of provost marshals who arrested and imprisoned without trial several hundred draft resisters and antiwar activists, including five newspaper editors, three judges, and several minor political leaders.

Most of the men arrested were Democrats. Virtually all those who denounced and resisted the militia draft were from the most conservative wing of the party. They also attacked the administration on such issues as emancipation and the financial legislation passed by the Republican Congress in 1862. Opposition to these measures was strongest among Irish and German Catholics and among Butternuts of the southern Midwest whose wealth and income were significantly below the northern median. These groups rioted against the draft while carrying banners proclaiming "The Constitution As It Is, The Union As It Was" and "We won't fight to free the nigger."

Such slogans offer a key to understanding both the motives of antidraft resisters and the Republican response to them. The "copperhead" faction of the northern Democratic party opposed the transformation of the Civil War into a total war—a war to destroy the old South instead of to restore the old Union. In Republican eyes,

Left: The temptation to write poetry and music to encourage men to enlist proved irresistible. At least two bards wrote poems with identical titles in response to Lincoln's call for 300,000 volunteers in July 1862. Three different composers wrote music to fit the verses. The sheet-music cover of the most popular version is shown here.

Right: This broadside offering a $300 bounty from city funds for three-year volunteers in a New York cavalry regiment was an early example of what became a serious problem the following year when ever-growing bounties appealed to greed rather than patriotism as an incentive for enlisting.

opposition to Republican war aims became opposition to the war itself. Opponents therefore became abettors of the rebellion and liable to military arrest. Most such arrests in 1861 had occurred in border states where pro-Confederate sentiment was rife. In 1862 many of the men arrested were northern Democrats whose disaffection from the war had been sparked by Republican adoption that year of emancipation as a war policy.

II

By the beginning of 1862 the impetus of war had evolved three shifting and overlapping Republican factions on the slavery question. The most dynamic and clearcut faction were the radicals, who accepted the abolitionist argument that emancipation could be achieved by exercise of the belligerent power to confiscate enemy property. On the other wing of the party a smaller number of conservatives hoped for the ultimate demise of bondage but preferred to see this happen by the voluntary action of slave states coupled with colonization abroad of the freed slaves. In the middle were the moderates, led by Lincoln, who shared the radicals' moral aversion to slavery but feared the racial consequences of wholesale emancipation. Events during the first half of 1862 pushed moderates toward the radical position.

One sign of this development was the growing influence of abolitionists. The most radical of them all, Wendell Phillips, lectured to packed houses all over the North in the winter and spring of 1862. In March he came to Washington—which he could scarcely have entered without danger to his life a year earlier—and spoke on three occasions to large audiences that included the president and many members of Congress. Phillips also had the rare privilege of a formal introduction on the floor of the Senate. "The Vice-President left his seat and greeted him with marked respect," wrote a reporter for the *New York Tribune*. "The attentions of Senators to the apostle of Abolition were of the most flattering character." This was a change from the previous winter when mobs had attacked abolitionists as troublemakers who had provoked the South to secession. As the *Tribune* observed: "It is not often that history presents such violent contrasts in such rapid succession. . . . The deference and respect now paid to him by men in the highest places of the nation, are tributes to the idea of which he, more than any other one man, is a popular exponent."

There was a growing Republican conviction that the fate of the nation could not be separated from the fate of slavery. In an important House speech on January 14, 1862, radical leader George W. Julian of Indiana set the tone for Republican congressional policy. "When I say that this rebellion has its source and life in slavery, I only repeat a simple truism," declared Julian. The four million slaves "cannot be neutral. As laborers, if not as soldiers, they will be the allies of the rebels, or of the Union." By freeing them the North would convert their labor power from support of treason to support of Union and liberty. This would hasten the day of national triumph, but even if the nation should triumph without such action "the mere suppression of the rebellion will be an empty mockery of our sufferings and sacrifices, if slavery shall be spared to canker the heart of the nation anew, and repeat its diabolical deeds."

By midsummer 1862 all but the most conservative of Republicans had come to a similar conclusion. Given this consensus, antislavery bills poured into the congressional hopper like leaves dropping from trees in autumn. Referred to committees, they met a friendly reception. A unique combination of history and geography had given New England–born radicals extraordinary power in Congress, especially the Senate. New England and the upper tier of states west of the Hudson settled by Yankee emigrants had been the birthplace of abolitionism and free-soil politics. From these regions had come to Washington the earliest and most radical Republicans. Eleven of the twelve New England senators chaired committees, and men born in New England but now representing other states held five of the eleven remaining chairmanships. Five of the ten most prominent radicals in the House, including the speaker and the chairman of the ways and means committee (Galusha Grow and Thaddeus Stevens, both of Pennsylvania), had been born and raised in New England. Little wonder, then, that seven emancipation or confiscation bills were favorably reported out of congressional committees by mid-January and became law during the next six months.

Some of these laws fulfilled long-standing free-soil goals: prohibition of slavery in the territories; ratification of a new treaty with Britain for more effective suppression of the slave trade; and abolition of slavery in the District of Columbia. But while these would have been heralded as great antislavery achievements in peacetime, they scarcely touched the real war issues concerning slavery in 1862. More important was a new article of war passed on March 13 forbidding army officers to return fugitive slaves to their masters. This grappled with the question first raised by Benjamin Butler's "contraband" policy in 1861. Union conquests along the south Atlantic coast and in the lower Mississippi Valley had brought large numbers of slaves into proximity to the Yankees. Many of them escaped their owners and sought refuge—and freedom—in Union camps.

Sometimes their welcome was less than friendly. While northern soldiers had no love for slavery, most of them had no love for slaves either. They fought for Union and against treason; only a minority in 1862 felt any interest in fighting for black freedom. Rare was the soldier who shared the sentiments of a Wisconsin private: "I have no heart in this war if the slaves cannot be free." More common was the conviction of a New York soldier that "we must first conquer & then its time enough to talk about the *dam'd niggers*." While some Yanks treated contrabands with a degree of equity or benevolence, the more typical response was indifference, contempt, or cruelty—including rape and other forms of sexual abuse. Even when Billy Yank welcomed the contrabands, he often did so from utilitarian rather than humanitarian motives. "Officers & men are having an easy time," wrote a Maine soldier from occupied Louisiana in 1862. "We have Negroes to do all fatigue work, cooking and washing clothes."

Before March 1862 Union commanders had no legislative guidelines for dealing with contrabands. Some officers followed Butler's precedent of sheltering them and

By 1862 large numbers of black men were part of both Confederate and Union armies as laborers, teamsters, blacksmiths, servants, cooks—almost everything except soldiers. Most black Confederates were slaves; in the Union army they were "contrabands," as in the case of the two men photographed here with the Army of the Potomac. No longer slaves, they were still in a limbo between slavery and freedom.

turning away white men who claimed to be their owners. The Treasury Department sent agents to the conquered South Carolina sea islands to supervise contraband labor in completing the harvest of cotton for sale to New England mills. Abolitionists organized freedmen's aid societies, which sent teachers and labor superintendents to these islands to launch a well-publicized experiment in free labor and black education. But in other areas, commanding officers refused to admit slaves to Union camps and returned them to owners. In his Western Department, General Halleck ordered contrabands excluded from Union lines on grounds of military security. Though many of Halleck's field commanders honored this order in the breach, its existence produced an outcry from radicals who insisted that the army had no business enforcing the fugitive slave law. Thus Congress enacted the new article of war prohibiting, under penalty of court-martial, the return of fugitives from army camps even to masters who claimed to be loyal.

Here was a measure with large potential for breaking down slavery in the Union as well as the Confederate slave states. This circumstance gave added force to Lincoln's first step in the direction of an emancipation policy. As a gradualist who hoped to end slavery without social dislocation and with the voluntary cooperation of slaveowners, Lincoln in 1862 thought that border-state unionists, aware of the mounting pressure against slavery, might respond positively to an offer of federal compensation for voluntary emancipation of their slaves. On March 6 Lincoln asked Congress to pass a resolution offering "pecuniary aid" to "any state which may adopt gradual abolishment of slavery." This was not merely a humanitarian measure, said the president; it was a means of shortening the war, for if the border states became free the Confederacy would no longer be sustained by the hope of winning their allegiance. To those who might deplore the cost of compensation, Lincoln pointed out that three months of war expenditures would buy all the slaves in the four border states. To slaveholders the president uttered a thinly veiled warning: if they refused this offer "it is impossible to foresee all the incidents which may attend and all the ruin which may follow" a continuation of the war.

Congress adopted Lincoln's resolution on April 10. All Republicans supported it; 85 percent of the Democrats and border-state unionists voted against it. The latter's opposition was a discouraging sign. Lincoln had already held one unsuccessful meeting with border-state congressmen, on March 10, when they questioned the constitutionality of his proposal, bristled at its hint of federal coercion, and deplored the potential race problem that would emerge with a large free black population.

In the months following this meeting the scale of the war and of emancipation sentiment increased. Congress moved toward passage of an act confiscating Confederate property. Tens of thousands more contrabands came under Union army control. On May 9 General David Hunter, commander of Union forces occupying the islands off the South Carolina and Georgia coast, issued a sweeping declaration of martial law abolishing slavery in all three states constituting his "Department of the South" (South Carolina, Georgia, and Florida). Hunter, like Frémont and Cameron before him, had taken this action without informing Lincoln, who first learned of it from the newspapers. "No commanding general shall do such a thing, on *my* responsibility, without consulting me," Lincoln told Treasury Secretary Chase, who had urged approval of Hunter's edict. Lincoln revoked it and rebuked the general. While conservatives applauded this action, they should have noticed the antislavery sting in the tail of Lincoln's revocation. The *substance* of Hunter's order might "become a necessity indispensable to the maintenance of the government," hinted the president, but this was a decision which "I reserve to myself." Lincoln then appealed to border-state unionists to reconsider his offer of compensated, gradual emancipation. The changes produced by such a plan "would come gently as the dews of heaven, not rending or wrecking anything. Will you not embrace it? . . . You can not if you would, be blind to the signs of the times."

But most border-state politicians remained blind to the significance of the new measures of recruitment and mobilization undertaken in response to McClellan's

This photograph shows former slaves on St. Helena Island just off the South Carolina coast cleaning cotton they had picked for the first time as free people.

defeat. Those measures indicated a turn toward total war in which preservation of "the Union as it was" had become an impossible dream.

In July 1862 the 37th Congress climaxed its second session with passage of two laws that signaled the turn toward a harsher war policy. The first was the militia act under which the government subsequently called for a draft of nine-month men. This bill also empowered the president to enroll "persons of African descent" for "any war service for which they may be found competent"—including service as soldiers, a step that would horrify conservatives and that the administration was not yet prepared to take. But the law gave the government revolutionary leverage. As even moderate Republican senators observed, "the time has arrived when . . . military authorities should be compelled to use all the physical force of this country to put down the rebellion." The war must be fought on "different principles"; the time for "white kid-glove warfare" was past.

This theme was underlined by the confiscation act of July 1862, which punished "traitors" by confiscating their property, including slaves who "shall be deemed captives of war and shall be forever free." But this poorly drawn law's provisions for enforcement were vague, consisting of *in rem* proceedings by district courts that were of course not functioning in the rebellious states. Yet the confiscation act was important as a symbol of what the war was becoming—a war to overturn the southern social order as a means of reconstructing the Union.

Major General John Pope was one of the hard-luck commanders of the war. He arrived in the Virginia theater in July 1862 with a high reputation earned by success in the West. Less than three months later he returned to the West with his reputation in tatters. Whether he was a victim of circumstances and intrigue or of his own mistakes is still debated by historians.

The agency for accomplishing this was the executive working through the enforcing power of the army. July 1862 brought a significant hardening of attitude in both army and executive. John Pope arrived from the West to take command of the newly designated Army of Virginia, formed from the divisions of Banks, Frémont, and McDowell that had chased Stonewall Jackson so futilely in the Shenandoah Valley. Irked by this promotion of a junior general over his head, Frémont offered his resignation, which Lincoln gratefully accepted. Although the radical Republicans thereby lost one of their favorite commanders, they soon discovered in Pope a kindred spirit. One of his first acts in Virginia was a series of general orders authorizing his officers to seize rebel property without compensation, to shoot captured guerrillas who had fired on Union troops, to expel from occupied territory any civilians who refused to take the oath of allegiance, and to treat them as spies if they returned.

Southerners erupted in anger toward Pope, whom they execrated with a fury felt toward no other Yankee "vandal" except Butler and, later, Sherman. Robert E. Lee declared that this "miscreant Pope" must be "suppressed." Jefferson Davis threatened retaliation on Union prisoners if captured guerrillas were executed. Pope's orders were undoubtedly ill-advised, but not groundless. Southern civilians behind Union lines did form partisan bands to pick off Yankee stragglers, teamsters, and other rear-area personnel.

Although Pope did not shoot any guerrillas or expel any civilians, his policy concerning southern property was carried out, in Virginia as in other theaters, by privates as well as officers, with or without orders. Large portions of the South were becoming a wasteland. Much of this was the inevitable destruction of war— by both armies. Soldiers have pillaged civilian property since the beginning of

Stripping a rail fence for fires ⟨signature⟩

time. But by midsummer 1862 some of the destruction of southern property had acquired a purposeful, even an ideological, dimension. More and more Union soldiers were writing that it was time to take off the "kid gloves" in dealing with "traitors." It seemed only logical to destroy the property of men who were doing their best to destroy the Union—to "spoil the Egyptians," as Yankee soldiers put it. "This thing of guarding rebel property when the owner is in the field fighting us is played out," wrote the chaplain of an Ohio regiment. "That is the sentiment of every private soldier in the army." It was a sentiment sanctioned from the top. In July, Lincoln called Halleck to Washington to become general in chief. One of Halleck's first orders to Grant, now commander of occupation forces in western Tennessee and Mississippi, was to "take up all active [rebel] sympathizers, and either hold them as prisoners or put them beyond our lines. Handle that class without gloves, and take their property for public use. . . . It is time that they should begin to feel the presence of the war."

Take their property. Here was abolition in action. Emancipation was a *means* to victory, not yet an end in itself. Grant informed his family that his only desire was "to put down the rebellion. I have no hobby of my own with regard to the Negro, either to effect his freedom or to continue his bondage. . . . I am using them as teamsters, hospital attendants, company cooks and so forth, thus saving soldiers to carry the musket. I don't know what is to become of these poor people in the end, but it weakens the enemy to take them from them."

One prominent northerner who deplored this new turn in the war was McClellan.

When Lincoln came down to Harrison's Landing on July 8 to see for himself the condition of McClellan's army, the general handed him a memorandum on the proper conduct of the war. "It should not be a war looking to the subjugation of the [southern] people," McClellan instructed the president. "Neither confiscation of property . . . [n]or forcible abolition of slavery should be contemplated for a moment. . . . It should not be a war upon population, but against armed forces. . . . Military power should not be allowed to interfere with the relations of servitude. . . . A declaration of radical views, especially upon slavery, will rapidly disintegrate our present armies."

Lincoln read these words in McClellan's presence without comment. But the president's thoughts can be reconstructed. Three or four months earlier he would have agreed with McClellan. Now he had become convinced of the necessity for "forcible abolition of slavery" and had begun to draft a proclamation of emancipation. To a southern unionist and a northern Democrat who several days later made the same points as McClellan, the president replied with asperity that the war could no longer be fought "with elder-stalk squirts, charged with rose water. . . . This government cannot much longer play a game in which it stakes all, and its enemies stake nothing. Those enemies must understand that they cannot experiment for ten years trying to destroy the government, and if they fail still come back into the Union unhurt." The demand by border-state slaveowners "that the government shall not strike its open enemies, lest they be struck by accident" had become "the paralysis—the dead palsy—of the government in this whole struggle."

In this mood Lincoln called border-state congressmen to the White House on July 12. Once more he urged favorable action on his plan for compensated emancipation. His revocation of General Hunter's emancipation edict caused "dissatisfaction, if not offense, to many whose support the country cannot afford to lose. And this is not the end of it. The pressure, in this direction, is still upon me, and is increasing." If the border states did not make "a *decision* at once to emancipate *gradually* . . . the institution in your states will be extinguished by mere friction and abrasion—by the mere incidents of the war . . . and you will have nothing valuable in lieu of it." But even this blunt warning fell on mostly deaf ears. Two-thirds of the border-state representatives signed a manifesto rejecting Lincoln's proposal because it would produce too "radical [a] change in our social system"; it was "interference" by the government with a state matter; it would cost too much (a curious objection from men whose states would benefit from a tax that would fall mainly on the free states); and finally, instead of shortening the conflict by depriving the Confederacy of hope for border-state support, it would lengthen the war and jeopardize victory by driving many unionist slaveholders into rebellion.

This response caused Lincoln to give up trying to conciliate conservatives. From then on the president tilted toward the radical position, though this would not become publicly apparent for more than two months. On July 13, the day he received the border-state manifesto, Lincoln privately told Seward and Welles of his intention to issue an emancipation proclamation. As Welles recorded the conversation, Lincoln said that he had decided that emancipation was "a military necessity, absolutely essential to the preservation of the Union. We must free the slaves or be ourselves subdued. The slaves were undeniably an element of strength to those who had their service, and we must decide whether that element should be with us or against us." Lincoln brushed aside the argument of unconstitutionality. This was a *war*, and as commander in chief he could order seizure of enemy slaves just as surely as he could order destruction of enemy railroads. "The rebels . . . could not at the same time throw off the Constitution and invoke its aid. Having made war on the Government, they were subject to the incidents and calamities of war." The border states "would do nothing" on their own; indeed, perhaps it was not fair to ask them to give up slavery while the rebels retained it. Therefore "the blow must fall first and foremost on [the rebels]. . . . Decisive and extensive measures must be adopted. . . . We wanted the army to strike more vigorous blows. The Administration must set an example, and strike at the heart of the rebellion."

McClellan had made it clear that he was not the general to strike this sort of vigorous blow. After giving the president his memorandum on noninterference with slavery, McClellan followed it with a letter to Stanton warning that "the nation will support no other policy. . . . For none other will our armies continue to fight." This was too much for Stanton and Chase. They joined a growing chorus of Republicans who were urging Lincoln to remove McClellan from command. But Lincoln demurred. He may have known that McClellan was privately denouncing the administration as fools and villains for failing to sustain his Peninsula campaign. The general's Democratic partisans were broadcasting such sentiments loudly. Lincoln also knew that prominent New York Democrats including copperhead Fernando Wood had visited McClellan at Harrison's Landing to court him as the party's next presidential nominee. But Lincoln also recognized that soldiers in the Army of the Potomac revered McClellan as the leader who had molded them into a proud army. The enlisted men did not subscribe to Republican criticisms of McClellan, and many of their officers did not share the Republican vision of an antislavery war. Because of this, Lincoln believed that he could not remove McClellan from command without risking demoralization in the army and a lethal Democratic backlash on the home front.

This threat of a Democratic fire in the rear helped delay announcement of an emancipation policy. On July 22 Lincoln informed the cabinet of his intention to issue a proclamation of freedom and invited comment. Only Montgomery Blair dissented, on the ground that such an edict would cost the Republicans control of Congress in the fall elections. Secretary of State Seward approved the proclamation but counseled its postponement "until you can give it to the country supported by military success." The wisdom of this suggestion "struck me with very great force," said the president later. He put his proclamation in a drawer to wait for a victory.

It would prove to be a long wait. Meanwhile the polarization of opinion on the slavery issue reached new extremes. On the left, abolitionists and radicals, notably William Lloyd Garrison and Frederick Douglass, grew abusive of a president who remained publicly uncommitted to emancipation. In a letter to Charles Sumner on August 7, Horace Greeley asked: "Do you remember that old theological book containing this: 'Chapter One—Hell; Chapter Two—Hell Continued.' Well, that gives

This painting by Francis Carpenter of Lincoln reading the first draft of the Emancipation Proclamation to his cabinet on July 22, 1862, is one of the most famous nonmilitary pictures of the Civil War. Carpenter spent six months at the White House in 1864 to make sketches and designs for the painting, which now hangs in the U.S. Capitol. From left to right the cabinet members are Secretary of War Edwin M. Stanton, Secretary of the Treasury Salmon P. Chase, Secretary of the Navy Gideon Welles, Secretary of the Interior Caleb B. Smith, Secretary of State William H. Seward, Postmaster General Montgomery Blair, and Attorney General Edward Bates.

a hint of the way Old Abe *ought to be* talked to in this crisis." Greeley proceeded to give Lincoln hell in the columns of the *New York Tribune*.

Lincoln could stand criticism from this quarter better than the sticks and stones hurled by Democrats. The emergence of slavery as the most salient war issue in 1862 threatened to turn a large element of the Democrats into an antiwar party. This was no small matter. The Democrats had received 44 percent of the popular vote in the free states in 1860. If the votes of the border states are added, Lincoln was a minority president of the Union states. By 1862 some "War Democrats" were becoming Republicans, even radicals—General Butler and Secretary of War Stanton are outstanding examples. Other War Democrats such as McClellan remained in their party and supported the goal of Union through military victory but opposed emancipation. In 1862 a third element began to emerge: the Peace Democrats, or copperheads, who would come to stand for reunion through negotiations rather than victory—an impossible dream, and therefore in Republican eyes tantamount to treason because it played into Confederate hands. Southerners pinned great hopes on the copperhead faction, which they considered "large & strong enough, if left to operate constitutionally, to paralyze the war & majority party."

War and Peace Democrats would maintain a shifting, uneasy, and sometimes divided coalition, but on one issue they remained united: opposition to emancipation. On four crucial congressional roll-call votes concerning slavery in 1862—the war article prohibiting return of fugitives, emancipation in the District of Columbia, prohibition of slavery in the territories, and the confiscation act—96 percent of the Democrats were united in opposition, while 99 percent of the Republicans voted Aye. Seldom if ever in American politics has an issue so polarized the major parties.

Because of secession the Republicans had a huge majority in Congress and could easily pass these measures, but an antiemancipation backlash could undo that majority in the fall elections. This explains Montgomery Blair's concern and Lincoln's caution.

As they had done in every election since the birth of the Republican party, northern Democrats exploited the race issue for all they thought it was worth in 1862. The Black Republican "party of fanaticism" intended to free "two or three million semi-savages" to "overrun the North and enter into competition with the white laboring masses" and mix with "their sons and daughters." "Shall the Working Classes be Equalized with Negroes?" screamed Democratic newspaper headlines. Ohio's soldiers, warned that state's congressman and Democratic leader Samuel S. Cox, would no longer fight for the Union "if the result shall be the flight and movement of the black race by millions northward." And Archbishop John Hughes added his admonition that "we Catholics, and a vast majority of our brave troops in the field, have not the slightest idea of carrying on a war that costs so much blood and treasure just to gratify a clique of Abolitionists."

Until Lincoln made public the Emancipation Proclamation, Frederick Douglass was one of his most outspoken critics. Douglass changed his tune after Lincoln issued the Proclamation, though he continued to prod the president in the direction of equal rights for freed slaves. Born a slave, Douglass combined great eloquence with the authenticity of personal experience in his testimony against slavery and inequality.

With this kind of rhetoric from their leaders, it was little wonder that some white workingmen took their prejudices into the streets. In a half-dozen or more cities, antiblack riots broke out during the summer of 1862. Some of the worst violence occurred in Cincinnati, where the replacement of striking Irish dockworkers by Negroes set off a wave of attacks on black neighborhoods. In Brooklyn a mob of Irish-Americans tried to burn down a tobacco factory where two dozen black women and children were working. The nightmare vision of blacks invading the North seemed to be coming true in southern Illinois, where the War Department transported several carloads of contrabands to help with the harvest. Despite the desperate need for hands to gather crops, riots forced the government to return most of the blacks to contraband camps south of the Ohio River.

Antiblack sentiments were not a Democratic monopoly. The antebellum Negro exclusion laws of several midwestern states had commanded the support of a good many Whigs. In 1862 about two-fifths of the Republican voters joined Democrats to reaffirm Illinois's exclusion law in a referendum. Senator Lyman Trumbull of Illinois, architect of the confiscation act, conceded that "there is a very great aversion in the West—I know it to be so in my State—against having free negroes come among us. Our people want nothing to do with the negro." To placate this aversion, some Republicans maintained that it was *slavery* which forced blacks to flee North toward freedom; emancipation would keep this tropical race in the South by giving them freedom in a congenial clime. This thesis encountered considerable skepticism, however. To meet the racial fears that constituted the party's Achilles' heel, many Republicans turned to colonization.

This solution of the race problem was stated crudely but effectively by an Illinois soldier: "I am not in favor of freeing the negroes and leaving them to run free among us nether is Sutch the intention of Old Abe but we will Send them off and

Artist Edwin White titled this painting Thoughts of Liberia, Emancipation. *The elderly black man bundled against the cold despite the fire under the kettle seems to be contemplating a better life in Liberia than he had in the United States. This conviction underlay Lincoln's support for colonization in 1862. Most African-Americans did not agree, and Lincoln soon changed his mind.*

colonize them." Old Abe did indeed advocate colonization in 1862. From his experience in Illinois politics he had developed sensitive fingers for the pulse of public opinion on this issue. He believed that support for colonization was the best way to defuse much of the antiemancipation sentiment that might otherwise sink the Republicans in the 1862 elections. This conviction underlay Lincoln's remarks to a group of black leaders in the District of Columbia whom he invited to the White House on August 14, 1862. Slavery was "the greatest wrong inflicted on any people," Lincoln told the delegation in words reported by a newspaper correspondent who was present. But even if slavery were abolished, racial differences and prejudices would remain. "Your race suffer very greatly, many of them, by living among us, while ours suffer from your presence." Blacks had little chance to achieve equality in the United States. "There is an unwillingness on the part of our people, harsh as it may be, for you free colored people to remain among us. . . . I do not mean to discuss this, but to propose it as a fact with which we have to deal. I cannot alter it if I would." This fact, said Lincoln, made it necessary for black people to emigrate to another land where they would have better opportunities. The president asked the black leaders to recruit volunteers for a government-financed pilot colonization project in Central America. If this worked, it could pave the way for the emigration of thousands more who might be freed by the war.

Most black spokesmen in the North ridiculed Lincoln's proposal and denounced its author. "This is our country as much as it is yours," a Philadelphia Negro told the president, "and we will not leave it." Frederick Douglass accused Lincoln of "contempt for negroes" and "canting hypocrisy." The president's remarks, said Douglass, would encourage "ignorant and base" white men "to commit all kinds of violence and outrage upon the colored people." Abolitionists and many radical Republicans continued to oppose colonization as racist and inhumane. "How much better," wrote Salmon P. Chase, "would be a manly protest against prejudice against color!—and a wise effort to give free[d] men homes in America!"

But conservatives chided their radical colleagues for ignoring the immutability of racial differences. Abolitionists "may prattle as they wish about the end of slavery being the end of strife," wrote one conservative, but "the great difficulty will then but begin! The question is the profound and awful one of race." Two-thirds of the Republicans in Congress became sufficiently convinced of the need to conciliate this sentiment that they voted for amendments to the District of Columbia emancipation bill and the confiscation act appropriating $600,000 for colonization. As a practical matter, said one Republican, colonization "is a damn humbug. But it will take with the people."

The government managed to recruit several hundred prospective black emigrants. But colonization did turn out to be a damn humbug in practice. The Central American project collapsed in the face of opposition from Honduras and Nicaragua. In 1863 the U.S. government sponsored the settlement of 453 colonists on an island near Haiti, but this enterprise also foundered when starvation and smallpox decimated the colony. The administration finally sent a naval vessel to return the 368 survivors to the United States in 1864. This ended official efforts to colonize blacks. By then the accelerating momentum of war had carried most northerners beyond the postulates of 1862.

Lincoln's colonization activities in August 1862 represented one part of his indirect effort to prepare public opinion for emancipation. Although he had decided to withhold his proclamation until Union arms won a victory, he did drop hints of what might be coming. On August 22 he replied to Horace Greeley's emancipation editorial, "The Prayer of Twenty Millions," with an open letter to the editor. "My paramount object in the struggle *is* to save the Union, and is *not* either to save or to destroy slavery," wrote Lincoln in a masterpiece of concise expression. "If I could save the Union without freeing *any* slave I would do it, and if I could save it by freeing *all* the slaves I would do it; and if I could save it by freeing some and leaving others alone, I would also do that." Here was something for all viewpoints: a reiteration that preservation of the Union remained the purpose of the war, but a hint that partial or even total emancipation might become necessary to accomplish that purpose.

The same intentional ambiguity characterized Lincoln's reply on September 13 to a group of clergymen who presented him a petition for freedom. The president agreed that "slavery is the root of the rebellion" and that emancipation would "weaken the rebels by drawing off their laborers" and "would help us in Europe, and convince them that we are incited by something more than ambition." But in present circumstances, "when I cannot even enforce the Constitution in the rebel states . . . what *good* would a proclamation of emancipation from me do? . . . I do not want to issue a document that the whole world will necessarily see must be inoperative, like the Pope's bull against the comet!" Here too was something for everybody: an assertion that emancipation was desirable though at present futile but perhaps imminent if the military situation took a turn for the better.

Military matters preoccupied Lincoln as he uttered these words. For two months, events in both the western and eastern theaters had been deteriorating to the point where by mid-September three southern armies were on the march northward in a bold bid for victory. But within the next few weeks the Confederate tide receded southward again without prevailing, thus ending the chance for European recognition and giving Lincoln the victory he needed to issue the Emancipation Proclamation.

✫ ✫ ✫ ✫ ✫

CHAPTER SEVENTEEN

Carry Me Back to Old Virginny

I

While Lee was driving McClellan away from Richmond, prospects also began to turn sour for Union forces in the West. Four tasks faced Halleck after his army of 110,000 occupied Corinth at the end of May. 1) Push on south after the retreating rebels and try to capture Vicksburg from the rear. 2) Send a force against Chattanooga to "liberate" east Tennessee. 3) Repair and defend the network of railroads that supplied Federal armies in this theater. 4) Organize occupation forces to preserve order, administer the contraband camps where black refugees had gathered, protect unionists trying to reconstruct Tennessee under military governor Andrew Johnson, whom Lincoln had sent to Nashville, and oversee the revival of trade with the North in occupied areas. In the best of all possible worlds, Halleck would have done all four tasks simultaneously. But he did not have the resources to do so. Secretary of War Stanton and General Grant thought his first priority ought to be the capture of Vicksburg. Halleck's decision to defer this effort in favor of the other three has been the subject of much critical appraisal. An all-out campaign against Vicksburg, according to the critics, might have severed this Confederate artery and shortened the war.

This thesis overlooks some physical, logistical, and political realities. In addition to the impact of disease on unacclimated northern soldiers, an unusually wet spring had turned into a disastrously dry summer. Several cavalry and infantry brigades did pursue the Confederates twenty miles south of Corinth but could go no farther by July for lack of water. Halleck's detachment of several brigades for railroad repair and guard duty was not so obtuse as it is sometimes portrayed, for as the rivers dropped below navigable stage the armies became wholly dependent on rail supply. Any overland campaign against Vicksburg would have been vulnerable to rebel raids on railroads and supply depots, as Grant learned six months later when such raids compelled him to abandon his first campaign against Vicksburg. Other brigades had to be detached from combat forces for the politically necessary tasks of policing and administering occupied territory. Finally, Lincoln's cherished aim of restoring east Tennessee made this political goal into a top military priority.

Opposite page: This watercolor portrays the Union supply depot at Manassas Junction, Virginia. It was painted by the Prince of Joinville, an exiled member of France's deposed royal family who served on McClellan's staff in 1862.

435

Union armies in areas of the South they had conquered learned the hard way to protect bridges essential to keep open the railroads that supplied them. Enemy cavalry raids in their rear repeatedly burned bridges and tore up the rails. This elaborate blockhouse defended the bridge over the Hiawassee River in Tennessee. Every company of Union soldiers detached to garrison such blockhouses weakened the armies' offensive strength.

Like McClellan, Don Carlos Buell found himself out of step with the new "hard war" strategies emerging in 1862. Beginning as an effort to restore the Union, the conflict was evolving into a war to destroy the Old South and give the nation a new birth of freedom. Buell's ideas did not evolve.

Halleck therefore divided the Army of the Tennessee under Grant into several fragments for occupation and railroad-repair duties, detached a division to reinforce Union troops confronting a new threat in Arkansas, and ordered the 40,000 men in the Army of the Ohio under Buell to move against Chattanooga. Buell's campaign—the major Union effort in the West during the summer of 1862—turned out as badly as McClellan's drive against Richmond. As old army friends, Buell and McClellan had much in common. Buell's idea of strategy was similar to McClellan's: "The object is," wrote Buell, "not to fight great battles, and storm impregnable fortifications, but by demonstrations and maneuvering to prevent the enemy from concentrating his scattered forces."

A political conservative, Buell also believed in limited war for limited goals. Despite guerrilla attacks on his supply lines, his belief in a "soft" war precluded a ruthless treatment of the civilian population that sheltered them or a levy upon this population for supplies. Buell therefore could move only as fast as repair crews could rebuild bridges and re-lay rails. He was rebuked by Lincoln when, three weeks after leaving Corinth in early June, he had advanced only ninety miles and was still less than halfway to Chattanooga. By this time the Army of the Ohio was approaching Stevenson, Alabama, where it opened a new rail supply line from Nashville. But Buell's troubles had barely begun. Just as the first trainload of supplies started south from Nashville on July 13, Nathan Bedford Forrest's cavalry struck the Union garrison at Murfreesboro. Forrest captured the garrison, wrecked the railroad, and escaped eastward through the Cumberland Mountains before a division sent by Buell could catch him. When the repair crews finished mending the damage, Forrest struck again, destroying three bridges just south of Nashville and once more escaping the pursuing Federals. Forrest's attacks stalled Buell's creeping advance for more than two weeks. From Washington came further word of "great dissatisfaction." When Buell tried to explain, back came a threat of removal if he did not remedy his "apparent want of energy and activity."

As Buell finally prepared to cross the Tennessee River twenty miles from Chattanooga, disaster struck again in the form of yet another rebel cavalry raid. This time the enemy commander was John Hunt Morgan, a thirty-six-year-old Kentuckian whose style combined elements of Stuart's dash and Forrest's ferocity. Soft-spoken and a fastidious dresser, Morgan had raised a brigade of lean and hard Kentucky horsemen who first achieved fame in July 1862 with a thousand-mile raid through Kentucky and middle Tennessee that captured 1,200 prisoners and tons of supplies at the cost of fewer than ninety Confederate casualties. In mid-August, Morgan's merry men suddenly reappeared in middle Tennessee and blocked the railroad north of Nashville by pushing flaming boxcars into an eight-hundred-foot tunnel, causing the timbers to burn and the tunnel to cave in. This exploit cut Buell off from his main supply base at Louisville.

These cavalry raids illustrated the South's advantage in fighting on the defensive in their own territory. With 2,500 men living off and sheltered by the friendly countryside, Forrest and Morgan had immobilized an invading army of 40,000 and could

This photograph of the rail yard in Nashville during Union occupation shows the splendid state capitol on a hill in the background. Nashville became the most important base for Union operations in the Confederate interior from 1862 to 1865.

In his effectiveness as a leader of cavalry raids in the Union rear, and in the romantic legends that grew up about him, John Hunt Morgan rivaled Jeb Stuart. This engraving shows Morgan and his staff leading one of his fabled raids in Kentucky.

This photograph of a bridge destroyed by Confederate cavalry was taken in Virginia, but it could have been any of the scores of such wrecked bridges in several theaters during 1862. Union engineer units learned from experience how to rebuild such bridges quickly.

strike at times and places of their own choosing. Defending hundreds of miles of railroad and infrastructure against hit-and-run raids was virtually impossible. The only effective counterforce would be Union cavalry of equal ability, troopers who knew the country and could track and intercept rebel cavalry and make raids deep into the Confederate rear. Union commanders learned these things the hard way in 1862. The Yankees did not catch up with the rebels in this respect until 1863, when they finally began to give as good as they got in the war of cavalry raids.

Buell's campaign also illustrated the strengths and weaknesses of railroad logistics. The iron horse could transport more men and supplies farther and faster than the four-legged variety. As an invading force operating on exterior lines over greater distances, Union armies depended more on rail transport than did the Confederates. In January 1862 the northern Congress authorized the president to take over any railroad "when in his judgment the public safety may require it." The government rarely exercised this power in northern states, but in the occupied South the government went into the railroad business on a large scale. In February 1862 Stanton established the U.S. Military Rail Roads and appointed Daniel McCallum superintendent. A former Erie Railroad executive and an efficient administrator, McCallum eventually presided over

This rare photograph of Confederate rail facilities and rolling stock in Louisiana hints at the rundown state of southern railroads by the midpoint of the war. The photograph shows the terminus at Port Hudson, Louisiana, of a short-line railroad from Clinton thirty miles away.

more than two thousand miles of lines acquired, built, and maintained by the U.S.M.R.R. in conquered portions of the South.

The War Department in Richmond did not achieve similar control over southern railroads until May 1863, and thereafter rarely exercised this power. There was no southern counterpart of the U.S.M.R.R. The Confederate government was never able to coax the fragmented, rundown, multigauged network of southern railroads into the same degree of efficiency exhibited by northern roads. This contrast illustrated another dimension of Union logistical superiority that helped the North eventually to prevail.

But in 1862 the dependence of Union armies on railroads proved as much curse as blessing. "Railroads are the weakest things in war," declared Sherman; "a single man with a match can destroy and cut off communications." It was the fate of any "railroad running through a country where every house is a nest of secret, bitter enemies" to suffer "bridges and water-tanks burned, trains fired into, track torn up," and "engines run off and badly damaged." These experiences would ultimately teach Union generals to make their troops live off the country when supply by railroad was interdicted or insufficient. Buell was unwilling to fight this kind of war, and that led to his downfall. Braxton Bragg, the new commander of the Confederate Army of Mississippi (soon to be known as the Army of Tennessee), saw the opening created by Morgan's and Forrest's raids against Buell's supply lines. Bragg decided to leave 32,000 men in Mississippi under Van Dorn and Price to defend Vicksburg and central Mississippi. He planned to take the remaining 34,000 to Chattanooga, from where he would launch an invasion of Kentucky. Bragg hoped to repeat the Morgan and Forrest strategy on a larger scale. Buell would be forced to follow him and might present Bragg an opportunity to hit the Federals in the flank. If Grant moved to Buell's aid, Van Dorn and Price could strike northward to recover western Tennessee. Forrest's and Morgan's cavalry would continue to harass the Union rear, while Bragg was also assured of cooperation from Edmund Kirby Smith's East Tennessee Army of 18,000 men, who had been warily watching Buell's snail-paced advance toward Chattanooga. The Confederates believed Kentuckians to be chafing at the bit to join the southern cause. Bragg requisitioned 15,000 extra rifles to arm the men of the bluegrass he expected to join his army.

Since taking over from the dismissed Beauregard in June, Bragg had been reorganizing and disciplining the army for a new campaign. A sufferer from ulcers and migraine, the short-tempered and quarrelsome Bragg was a hard driver. By executing deserters and imposing other punishments he showed his troops that he was a "man who would do what he said and whose orders were to be obeyed." But another Reb added that "not a single soldier in the whole army ever loved or respected him."

This hardly bothered Bragg; his main problem just now was to get his invasion force from Mississippi to Chattanooga. He came up with an ironic solution: he would send them by rail—not the direct 200-mile route along which

Braxton Bragg was the longest-serving commander of the Confederacy's Army of Tennessee (June 1862–December 1863). But he never won the confidence of his subordinates or the affection of his men.

Buell had been crawling for six weeks, but a 776-mile roundabout journey south to Mobile, northeast to Atlanta, and thence north to Chattanooga. He sent the infantry a division at a time beginning July 23; two weeks later they were all in Chattanooga. It was the largest Confederate railroad movement of the war. By mid-August, Bragg and Smith were ready to march forth on the great invasion. "Van Dorn and Price will advance simultaneously with us from Mississippi on West Tennessee," wrote an enthusiastic Bragg, "and I trust we may all unite in Ohio."

Kirby Smith started first and moved fastest. With 21,000 men (including one of Bragg's divisions) he left Knoxville on August 14 and struck northward toward the Cumberland Gap, which had been captured by a Union force of 8,000 two months earlier. Not wishing to assault this Thermopylae, Kirby Smith bypassed it and continued northward, leaving behind a division to watch the Federals at the Gap. Smith moved with a speed that Lincoln wished his generals could emulate. In two weeks he reached Richmond, Kentucky, 150 miles from Knoxville and only 75 miles south of Cincinnati, whose residents were startled into near panic by the approach of the rebels. At Richmond, Smith encountered his first significant opposition, a division of 6,500 new recruits never before under fire. The southerners surged forward with a rebel yell on August 30 and drove the Yanks back, killing or wounding more than a thousand and capturing most of the rest at a cost of fewer than five hundred southern casualties.

Smith's army occupied Lexington and prepared to inaugurate a Confederate governor in the nearby capital at Frankfort. Meanwhile Bragg's 30,000 had marched northward from Chattanooga on a parallel route about a hundred miles to the west

At the time of the Civil War there was no bridge over the Ohio River at Cincinnati. To get Union troops across the river to defend the city and northern Kentucky, Union engineer troops had to build a pontoon bridge. This lithograph shows the 73rd Illinois crossing the river from Cincinnati on September 12, 1862. The 73rd fought in the battle of Perryville four weeks later.

of Kirby Smith. As they crossed the border into Kentucky, Bragg issued a proclamation encouraging "liberated" Kentuckians to rally to the cause. But few men came forward to fight for the South. Perhaps they understood what Bragg did not— his forces were sufficient for a raid but not an occupation that could withstand aroused Federal countermeasures. These were imminent; Buell had already been reinforced to a strength of 55,000 by two divisions from Grant, with another on the way, while 60,000 new Union recruits were organizing in Louisville and Cincinnati.

Bragg's apparent military success and political failure caused his mood to fluctuate from elation to despondency. On September 18 he wrote to his wife: "We have made the most extraordinary campaign in military history." But a few days later he expressed himself "sadly disappointed in the want of action by our friends in Kentucky."

As Buell's army backtracked toward Louisville, Bragg was in a position to attack its flank. But knowing himself outnumbered, he was eager to unite with Kirby Smith, who was still in the Lexington-Frankfort area a hundred miles to the east. Bragg asked Smith to link up with him at Bardstown, a point halfway between the two Confederate armies and only thirty-five miles south of Louisville. There the combined forces could fight the decisive battle for Kentucky. Meanwhile the two commanders took time out to witness the inauguration of Kentucky's Confederate governor. They hoped that this symbolic action might encourage timid Kentuckians to jump off the fence onto the southern side.

But the ceremony was rudely interrupted by the booming of advancing Union artillery. Goaded by a disgusted Lincoln and an angry northern press, Buell had finally turned to strike his rebel tormentors. For the past month his larger, better-equipped army had seemed to do nothing to stop the Confederate invasion. All through September, Halleck had kept the wires humming with messages prodding Buell to action: "Here as elsewhere you move too slowly. . . . The immobility of your army is most surprising. Bragg in the last two months has marched four times the distance you have." If Buell did not get moving, Halleck warned him, he would be removed. Buell got the point, and in the first week of October he got moving. He had organized his army into a striking force of 60,000 men—fully a third of whom, however, were raw recruits who had not yet fired a shot in anger. Bragg and Smith had 40,000 veterans in the vicinity, but they were scattered across a front of sixty miles from Lexington to Bardstown. Buell sent one division on a feint toward Frankfort (this was the force that disrupted the inauguration) while marching the remainder in three mutually supporting columns toward Bragg's main army at Bardstown. Bragg was deceived by the feint, which pinned nearly half of the Confederate force in the Frankfort area while Buell's three main columns bore down on the rest, commanded in Bragg's absence by Bishop Leonidas Polk. Outnumbered two to one, the bishop retreated and sent appeals to Bragg for reinforcements.

The sequel was much influenced by both armies' search for water in the drought-parched countryside. With only 16,000 men, Polk took up a defensive position just west of the Chaplin River at Perryville on October 7. That evening one Union corps arrived and attacked unsuccessfully to gain control of the few stagnant pools in a tributary of the river. Commanding the most aggressive division in this corps was Philip Sheridan, a small, bandy-legged man whose only dis-

This lithograph of the battle of Perryville shows the 1st Wisconsin defending the left of the Union line against an attack across the fields by part of General Benjamin F. Cheatham's Confederate division. The Badgers held the line, but at the cost of 77 killed and 115 wounded. Note that the soldiers are fighting in two ranks, the front rank kneeling and the rear rank standing, without any cover. This tactical formation helps explain their heavy casualties. Later in the war, soldiers learned to entrench or use the cover of woods, fences, and irregularities in the ground.

tinctions in the prewar army had been pugnacity and a handlebar mustache. The pugnacity served him well once the war gave him a chance. Languishing as a quartermaster captain during the conflict's first year, he obtained field command of a cavalry regiment by a fluke in May 1862 and within weeks had proved himself so able ("he is worth his weight in gold," wrote one superior) that he had been promoted to brigade command and in September to division command. At dawn on October 8, Sheridan's thirsty division attacked again and gained control of the creek as well as the hills beyond. During the day the rest of Buell's main force filed into line on the left and right of Sheridan.

But thereafter Buell lost the initiative in a battle that set a new record for confusion among top brass on both sides. Still believing that the main part of Buell's army was at Frankfort, Bragg ordered Polk's 16,000 to attack the fragment (as he thought) at Perryville. In early afternoon a reluctant Polk sent two of his three divisions against the two divisions holding the Union left. The rebels were in luck, for one of these blue divisions was composed of new troops. They broke, sweeping the other Union division back with them a mile or more before reinforcements halted the rout. Meanwhile in the center, Sheridan attacked the remaining southern division and drove it back through the streets of Perryville. Less than half of the Union army was engaged in this fighting, while a freak combination of wind and topography (known as acoustic shadow) prevented the right wing and Buell himself from hearing the battle a couple of miles away. Not until a courier came pounding back to headquarters on a sweat-lathered horse did the Union commander know that a battle was raging. By then the approaching darkness prevented an attack by the Union right against the lone rebel brigade in its front. Buell ordered an assault all along the line at dawn, but when the Yanks went forward next morning they found the rebels gone. Finally recognizing that he faced three times his numbers at Perryville, Bragg had retreated during the night to link up with Kirby Smith—several days too late.

For both sides this climactic battle of a long campaign turned out to be anticlimactic. Casualties were relatively high in proportion to the numbers engaged—4,200 Federals and 3,400 Confederates—but neither side really "won." Buell missed a chance to wipe out one-third of the rebels who had invaded Kentucky; Bragg and Smith failed to clinch their invasion with a smashing blow that might have won Kentuckians to their side. After Perryville the contending armies maneuvered warily for a few days without fighting. With supplies short, the sick list lengthening, and a larger army in his front, Bragg succumbed to pessimism once again and decided to abandon the campaign, ordering his weary men to retrace their steps to Knoxville and Chattanooga. Despite the failure of his campaign, Davis kept Bragg in command and expressed a confidence in the general shared by a decreasing number of southerners.

Buell followed the retreating rebels gingerly, responding with McClellan-like excuses to telegrams from Washington. Lincoln and Halleck urged him to attack, or at least to drive Bragg out of east Tennessee and accomplish Lincoln's cherished goal of recovering that unionist region. Reflecting Lincoln's impatience, Halleck wired Buell, "You say that [east Tennessee] is the heart of the enemy's resources; make it the heart of yours. Your army can live there if the enemy's can. . . . [The president] does not understand why we cannot march as the enemy marches, live as he lives, and fight as he fights." It was no good. Buell was not the general to march and fight while living off the country. When he made clear his intent to reestablish a base at Nashville instead of going after the rebels, Lincoln removed him and named William S. Rosecrans to command the renamed Army of the Cumberland.

Events three hundred miles away in Mississippi had influenced both Bragg's decision to retreat and Lincoln's decision to appoint Rosecrans. Just after the battle of Perryville, Bragg received word of the defeat of Van Dorn and Price in the battle of Corinth four days earlier. Since Bragg's hope for a successful invasion had been contingent on a similar northward thrust by the troops he had left behind in Mississippi, this defeat compounded his discouragement. The Union commander at Corinth was Rosecrans. While Buell had failed to keep the rebels out of central Tennessee and Kentucky, Rosecrans had earned credit in Lincoln's eyes by keeping them out of west Tennessee.

On September 14 Price's 15,000 troops, as a first step in the contemplated invasion of Tennessee, had driven a small Union force from the railroad town of Iuka in northern Mississippi. Grant, seeing an opportunity to counterattack, devised a plan to trap Price in Iuka between converging Union forces. Grant sent two divisions under General Edward Ord eastward along the railroad from Corinth and ordered

Having been promoted from captain in May 1862 to brigadier general by September, Phil Sheridan had already proved himself one of the most charismatic cavalry leaders in the Union army. In September he was given an infantry division, which he commanded with distinction at Perryville. The porkpie hat became his trademark for the rest of the war.

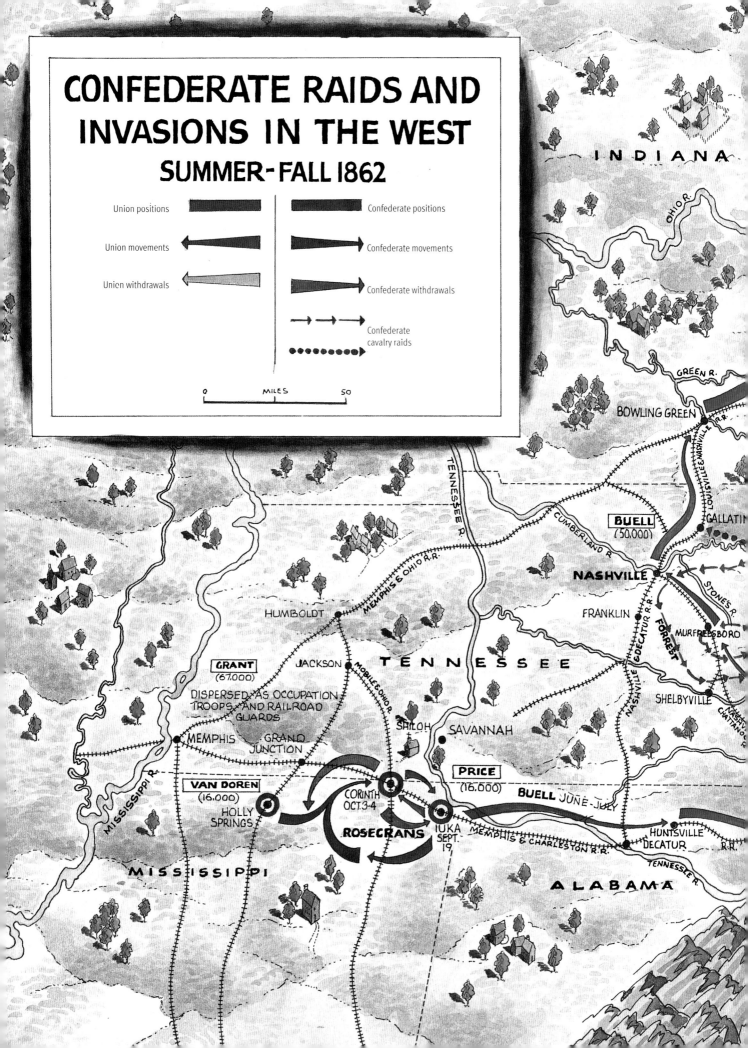

CONFEDERATE RAIDS AND INVASIONS IN THE WEST
SUMMER-FALL 1862

Union positions
Confederate positions
Union movements
Confederate movements
Union withdrawals
Confederate withdrawals
Confederate cavalry raids

0   MILES   50

INDIANA

OHIO R.

GREEN R.

BOWLING GREEN

LOUISVILLE & NASHVILLE R.R.

CUMBERLAND R.

BUELL (50,000)

GALLATIN

TENNESSEE R.

NASHVILLE

FRANKLIN

STONE'S R.

FORREST

MURFREESBORO

NASHVILLE & DECATUR R.R.

NASHVILLE & CHATTANOOGA R.R.

SHELBYVILLE

HUMBOLDT

MEMPHIS & OHIO R.R.

JACKSON

T E N N E S S E E

GRANT (67,000)

MOBILE & OHIO R.R.

DISPERSED AS OCCUPATION TROOPS AND RAILROAD GUARDS

SHILOH

SAVANNAH

MEMPHIS

GRAND JUNCTION

PRICE (16,000)

BUELL JUNE-JULY

MISSISSIPPI R.

VAN DOREN (16,000)

HOLLY SPRINGS

CORINTH OCT. 3-4

ROSECRANS

IUKA SEPT. 19

MEMPHIS & CHARLESTON R.R.

HUNTSVILLE

DECATUR

TENNESSEE R.

R.R.

MISSISSIPPI

ALABAMA

BATTLE OF CORINTH — **OCT. 3**

VAN DORN
PRICE
ROSENCRANS
ENTRENCHMENTS
MEMPHIS & CHARLESTON R.R.
MOBILE & OHIO R.R.
TUSCUMBIA R.
CORINTH
MILE

OCT. 4

PRICE
VAN DORN
ROSECRANS
TUSCUMBIA R.
CORINTH
NEW ENTRENCHMENTS

BUELL
LOUISVILLE
FRANKFORT SEPT. 3
MORGAN
LEXINGTON SEPT. 2
PERRYVILLE OCT. 8
RICHMOND AUG. 30
LEBANON
KENTUCKY R.
MUNFORDSVILLE SEPT. 17
LONDON
KENTUCKY
CUMBERLAND R.
MILL SPRINGS
KIRBY SMITH
CUMBERLAND GAP
TOMKINSVILLE
BRAGG
MORGAN
MORGAN
KIRBY SMITH
(20,000)
LEAVES AUG.14
KNOXVILLE
SPARTA
MORGAN
CUMBERLAND MTS.
TENNESSEE R.
MEMPHIS & CHARLESTON R.R.
APPALACHIAN MOUNTAINS
FORREST
BRAGG
(30,000)
LEAVES AUG. 28
CHATTANOOGA
STEVENSON
GEORGIA

BATTLE OF PERRYVILLE — **OCT. 8**

POLK
BUELL
DOCTOR CR.
BRAGG
SHERIDAN
CHAPLIN HEIGHTS
PERRYVILLE
NOT ENGAGED
CHAPLIN RIVER
MILE

The Town of Corinth

This drawing shows the ammunition limber chests and caissons of a Union artillery battery in the battle of Corinth. Confederate infantry are attacking in line in the middle distance. A Confederate shell has scored a direct hit on one of the limber chests, causing an explosion that has wounded or killed three cannoneers.

two others under Rosecrans to circle up on Iuka from the south for an assault on Price's flank while Ord attacked his front. But this pincers movement went awry, as such maneuvers often did in an era when communications depended on couriers. Smelling the trap, Price attacked Rosecrans's advance units south of town on September 19 while Ord (accompanied by Grant) was still three miles to the west. Here too an acoustic shadow masked all sound of the fighting from Ord, whose troops remained in blissful ignorance of Rosecrans's battle a few miles away. In a short, sharp contest the outnumbered Yankees gave a good account of themselves and inflicted more casualties than they received. But after nightfall Price got away to the south on a road that Rosecrans had neglected to block. When the Union pincers finally closed next morning, they grasped an empty town.

Grant had at least stopped Price's thrust northward. But the enterprising Missouri rebel marched his little army to join Van Dorn for another try. With a combined mobile force of 22,000 they attacked the main Union position at Corinth. The Confederates ran into more than they bargained for—21,000 men commanded by Rosecrans, a tough and skillful fighter. On October 3 the southerners assaulted the outer defenses north of Corinth with the screaming élan and willingness to take high casualties that had become their trademark. During a long, hot day they drove the Yankees back two miles to the inner defenses. Next morning the rebels attacked again, but after early success they succumbed to exhaustion and thirst in the ninety-degree heat. By noon a Union counterattack had put Van Dorn and Price to flight.

Having expressed disappointment after Iuka at "not capturing [Price's] entire army or . . . destroying it, as I hoped to do," Grant tried again after Corinth. He ordered a division from west Tennessee to intercept the escaping Confederates in front while Rosecrans pitched into their rear. But Old Rosy, as his men had begun to call him, was slow in pursuit. Van Dorn's force got away after a sharp fight at a bridge with Grant's intercepting column in which the southerners lost another six hundred men. Despite his admiration for Rosecrans's tenacity as a fighter, Grant was thereafter cool toward the general who he believed had twice let the rebels escape from a trap. Nevertheless, what turned out to be the last Confederate offensive in the Mississippi theater had been thwarted. The initiative went over to Grant, who launched his first (and unsuccessful) campaign against Vicksburg a month later. Rosecrans earned promotion to a new army command. The rebel reverses in Mississippi, coupled with Bragg's retreat from Kentucky, produced discouragement in Richmond and relief in Washington.

Despite their importance in the overall strategic picture, these events in the western theater from June to October faded into the background of public perception, which focused primarily on military developments in the East. The eastern campaigns seemed more crucial because they took place closer to the two capitals and to the major newspapers that dominated the reporting of war news. At the same time that Kirby Smith and Bragg moved north from Knoxville and Chattanooga, Jackson and Lee moved north from Richmond. Although the western invasions covered more territory, the eastern fighting as usual produced more casualties. These simultaneous Confederate northward thrusts represented the South's boldest bid for victory.

When Lincoln appointed Henry Halleck general in chief in July 1862, he hoped that Old Brains would coordinate an offensive by McClellan's 100,000 on the Peninsula with Pope's 50,000 north of Richmond. But three men blighted this hope; their names were Pope, McClellan, and Jackson.

Pope's first act as commander of the newly designated Army of Virginia was to issue an address to his troops in which he boasted about victories in the West and declared, "I am sorry to find so much in vogue amongst you . . . certain phrases [like] . . . 'lines of retreat,' and 'bases of supplies.' . . . Let us study the probable lines of retreat of our opponents, and leave our own to take care of themselves. Let us look before us and not behind. Success and glory are in the advance, disaster and shame lurk in the rear."

This snide denigration of eastern troops won Pope few friends. Fitz-John Porter declared that Pope had "written himself down, what the military world has long known, an Ass." This expressed McClellan's opinion as well. At the same time, Pope believed that McClellan's "incompetency and indisposition to active movements were so great" that little help could be expected from the Army of the Potomac. Lee could hardly have hoped for a more mutually antagonistic pair of opponents had he chosen them himself.

After the Seven Days, McClellan expressed readiness to renew the offensive if Lincoln would send him another 50,000 men. Privately, however, the general was telling a New York Democratic leader that he had "lost all regard and respect" for the administration and doubted "the propriety of my brave men's blood being shed to further the designs of such a set of heartless villains." For his part, Lincoln had lost faith in McClellan's willingness to fight Lee. The president did not have 50,000 men to spare, but even if he could have sent 100,000, he told a senator, McClellan would suddenly discover that Lee had 400,000. At the end of July, Lincoln and Halleck decided to withdraw the Army of the Potomac from the Peninsula to unite it with Pope's force.

Confederate actions had influenced this decision. To counter Pope's threat to the rail junction at Gordonsville northwest of Richmond, Lee had sent Jackson with 12,000 men to that point on July 13. When McClellan remained quiet on the Richmond front, Lee detached A. P. Hill with another 13,000 to join Jackson on July 27. Rumor magnified this force—for in spite of Jackson's failures on the Peninsula his name was worth several divisions—and helped persuade Lincoln of the need to reinforce Pope. As Lee pieced together information about McClellan's withdrawal, he used his interior lines to shift most of his troops by rail sixty miles to Gordonsville. The Army of the Potomac had to travel several times that far by water down the James, along the Chesapeake Bay, and up the Potomac before arriving within marching distance of Pope. The efficiency of this Union movement was not helped by McClellan's bitter protests against it or by his subordinates' distaste for coming under Pope's command. "Pope will be thrashed . . . & be disposed of" by Lee, wrote McClellan to his wife with relish at the prospect. "Such a villain as he is ought to bring defeat upon any cause that employs him."

While McClellan sulked in his tent, Jackson moved against Pope's two advance divisions near Cedar Mountain twenty miles north of Gordonsville. Commanding this Union force was none other than Jackson's old adversary Nathaniel P. Banks. Eager to redeem his reputation, Banks attacked on August 9 even though he knew that Jackson outnumbered him at least two to one. Expecting imminent reinforcements, the Union general sent his two undersize divisions forward in a headlong assault that drove back the surprised rebels and put Jackson's old Stonewall Brigade to flight. Having mishandled the first stage of the fight, Jackson went to the front himself to rally his troops and then watched approvingly as A. P. Hill's division punished the Yankees with a slashing counterattack. Banks fell back several miles to the support of late-arriving reinforcements after losing 30 percent of his force. Within the next two days the rest of Pope's army came up and forced Jackson to pull back to Gordonsville.

The chief result of this battle of Cedar Mountain was to confirm the transfer of operations from the Peninsula to the Rappahannock River halfway between Richmond and Washington. Here for ten days Lee's reunited force of 55,000 (he had left 20,000 around Richmond) carried on a campaign of thrust and parry with Pope's army of equal size. Lee probed for an opening to isolate and attack a portion of the enemy, while Pope maneuvered to hold his position while awaiting the arrival of reinforcements from the Peninsula that would enable him to go over to the offensive. Since that was just what Lee wanted to prevent, he determined on what was becoming a typical

This photograph of a Union artillery battery fording a tributary of the Rappahannock River was taken on August 9, 1862, by Timothy O'Sullivan, a photographer who worked for Mathew Brady. The battery was moving up to the front to take part in the battle of Cedar Mountain.

This contemporary sketch depicts a Union regiment attacking the Confederate line at the edge of the woods in the background at the battle of Cedar Mountain.

This photograph by George N. Barnard shows some of the debris at Manassas Junction after Jackson's troops had departed. The dead horse in the foreground lies next to several pieces of butchered steer. The Confederates had cleaned out the boxcars on the siding but had unaccountably failed to burn them.

Lee stratagem: he divided his army and sent Jackson's corps on a long clockwise flanking march to cut Union rail communications deep in Pope's rear. This maneuver defied military maxims about keeping an army concentrated in the presence of an enemy of equal or greater size. But Lee believed that the South could never win by following maxims. His well-bred Episcopalian demeanor concealed the audacity of a skillful gambler ready to stake all on the turn of a card. The dour Presbyterian who similarly concealed the heart of a gambler was the man to carry out Lee's strategy.

For Jackson had reverted from the sluggard of the Chickahominy to the gladiator of the Valley. Indeed, the Valley was where Pope thought the rebels were heading when his scouts detected Jackson's march northwestward along the Rappahannock on August 25. But Pope's understrength cavalry failed to detect Jackson's turn to the east on August 26, when he marched unopposed along the railroad to Manassas, the main Union supply base twenty-five miles behind Pope. In one of the war's great marches, Jackson's whole corps—24,000 men—had covered more than fifty miles in two days. The hungry, threadbare rebels swooped down on the mountain of supplies at Manassas like a plague of grasshoppers. After eating their fill and taking everything they could carry away, they put the torch to the rest.

The accumulation of supplies at Manassas and the maintenance of the vulnerable single-track line that linked Pope to his base had been the work of Herman Haupt, the war's wizard of railroading. The brusque, no-nonsense Haupt was chief of construction and transportation for the U.S. Military Rail Roads in Virginia. He had brought order out of chaos in train movements. He had rebuilt destroyed bridges in record time. His greatest achievement had been the construction from green logs

and saplings of a trestle eighty feet high and four hundred feet long with unskilled soldier labor in less than two weeks. Haupt developed prefabricated parts for bridges and organized the first of the Union construction corps that performed prodigies of railroad and bridge building in the next three years. As an awed contraband put it, "the Yankees can build bridges quicker than the Rebs can burn them down."

Within four days Haupt had trains running over the line Jackson had cut. But unfortunately for the North, Pope's military abilities did not match Haupt's engineering genius. Still confident and aggressive, Pope saw Jackson's raid as an opportunity to "bag" Jackson before the other half of Lee's army could join him. The only problem was to find the slippery Stonewall. After burning the supply depot at Manassas, Jackson's troops disappeared. Pope's overworked cavalry reported the rebels to be at various places. This produced a stream of orders and countermanding orders to the fragmented corps of three commands: his own, two corps of the Army of the Potomac sent to reinforce him, and part of Burnside's 9th Corps, which had been transferred from the North Carolina coast.

One of the Army of the Potomac units moving up to support Pope was Fitz-John Porter's corps, whose commander had called Pope "an Ass" and who had recently written in another private letter: "Would that this army was in Washington to rid us of incumbents ruining our country." During this fateful August 28, Porter's friend McClellan was at Alexandria resist-

Brigadier General Herman Haupt was one of the foremost engineers of railroad construction in the nineteenth century, and a key asset for Union logistics in the Virginia theater. He supervised the building of this trestle over Potomac Creek in forty hours. After viewing a similar bridge in 1862, President Lincoln said: "I have seen the most remarkable structure that human eyes ever rested upon. That man, Haupt, has built a bridge . . . over which loaded trains are running every hour, and upon my word, gentlemen, there is nothing in it but beanpoles and cornstalks."

ing Halleck's orders to hurry forward another Army of the Potomac corps to Pope's aid. McClellan shocked the president with a suggestion that all available troops be held under his command to defend Washington, leaving Pope "to get out of his scrape by himself." If "Pope is beaten," wrote McClellan to his wife, "they may want me to save Washington again. Nothing but their fears will induce them to give me any command of importance." Almost broken down by worry, Halleck failed to assert his authority over McClellan. Thus two of the best corps in the Army of the Potomac remained within marching distance of Pope but took no part in the ensuing battle.

Meanwhile Jackson's troops had gone to ground on a wooded ridge a couple of miles west of the old Manassas battlefield. Lee and Longstreet with the rest of the army were only a few miles away, having broken through a gap in the Bull Run Mountains which Pope had neglected to defend with a sufficient force. Stuart's cavalry had maintained liaison between Lee and Jackson, so the latter knew that Longstreet's advance units would join him on the morning of August 29.

The previous evening one of Pope's divisions had stumbled onto Jackson's hiding place. In a fierce firefight at dusk the outnumbered bluecoats had inflicted considerable damage before withdrawing in a battered condition themselves. Conspicuous in this action was an all-western brigade (one Indiana and three Wisconsin regiments) that soon earned a reputation as one of the best units in the army and became known as the Iron Brigade. By the war's end it suffered a higher percentage of casualties than any other brigade in the Union armies—a distinction matched by one of the units it fought against on this and other battlefields, the all-Virginia Stonewall Brigade, which experienced more casualties than any other Confederate brigade.

The 2nd Wisconsin was the founding regiment of the famous Iron Brigade. Of the total of 1,203 officers and men who served in this regiment, 753 died or were wounded; 238 of these were killed in action. These respective rates of 63 percent and 20 percent were the highest for any regiment in the Union army. Only 77 died of disease (17 of them while in Confederate prisons), which gave this regiment the lowest ratio of disease to combat mortality of any regiment on either side. Pictured here in 1862 are several field officers of the 2nd, including in the left foreground Colonel Edward O'Connor, who was killed in the evening battle against Jackson's troops on August 28, 1862. The hatless man seated in the center was Lt. Colonel Lucius Fairchild, who succeeded O'Connor as colonel and lost an arm at Gettysburg.

Having found Jackson, Pope brought his scattered corps together by forced marches during the night and morning of August 28–29. Because he thought that Jackson was preparing to retreat toward Longstreet (when in fact Longstreet was advancing toward Jackson), Pope committed an error. Instead of waiting until he had concentrated a large force in front of Jackson, he hurled his divisions one after another in piecemeal assaults against troops who instead of retreating were ensconced in ready-made trenches formed by the cuts and fills of an unfinished railroad. The Yankees came on with fatalistic fury and almost broke Jackson's line several times. But the rebels hung on grimly and threw them back.

Pope managed to get no more than 32,000 men into action against Jackson's 22,000 on August 29. The fault was not entirely his. Coming up on the Union left during the morning were another 30,000 in McDowell's large corps and Porter's smaller one. McDowell maneuvered ineffectually during the entire day; only after dark did a few of his regiments get into a moonlight skirmish with the enemy. As for Porter, his state of mind this day is hard to fathom. He believed that Longstreet's entire corps was in his front—as indeed it was by noon—and therefore with 10,000 men Porter did nothing while thousands of other northern soldiers were fighting and dying two miles away. Not realizing that Longstreet's corps had arrived, Pope ordered Porter in late afternoon to attack Jackson's right flank. Porter could not obey because Longstreet connected with Jackson's flank; besides, Porter had no respect for Pope and resented taking orders from him, so he continued to do nothing. For this he was later court-martialed and cashiered from the service.

While Pope fought only with his right hand on August 29, Lee parried only with his left. When Longstreet got his 30,000 men in line during the early afternoon, Lee asked him to go forward in an attack to relieve the pressure on Jackson. But Longstreet demurred, pointing out that a Union force of unknown strength (Porter and McDowell) was out there somewhere in the woods. Unlike Lee and Jackson, Longstreet preferred to fight on the defensive and hoped to induce these Federals to

This contemporary watercolor sketch by a Union soldier shows one of the unsuccessful northern attacks against Confederate lines along the wooded ridge in the distance at the battle of Second Bull Run on August 29, 1862. One of the Union cannons at right center has suffered a direct hit from a Confederate shell.

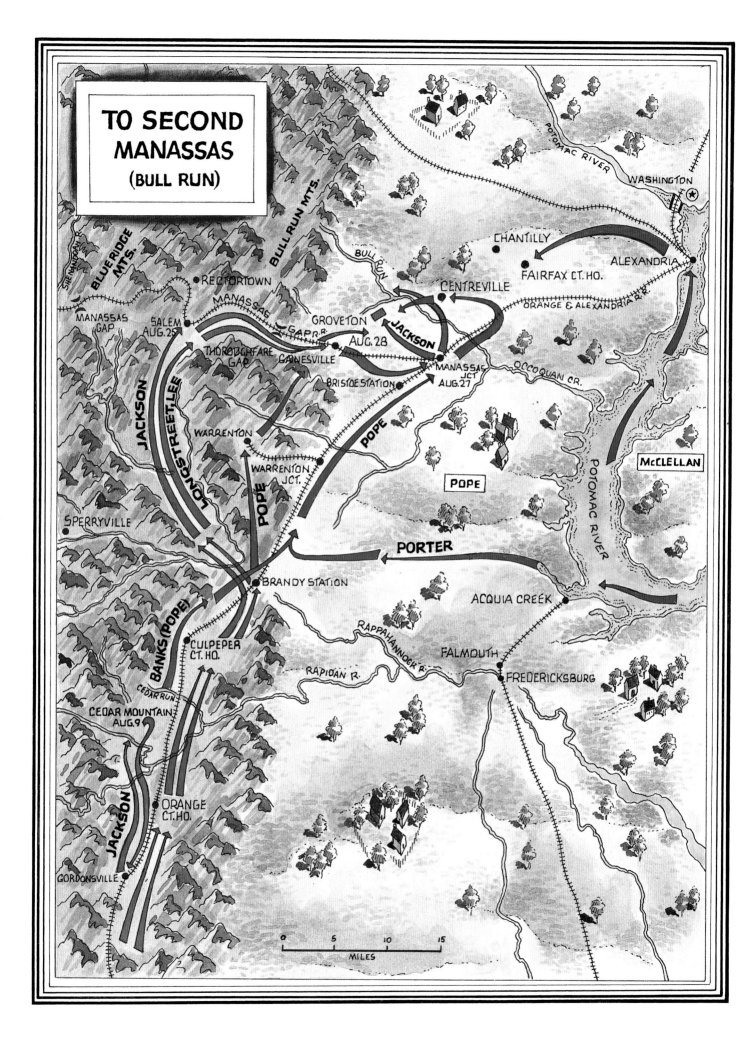

TO SECOND
MANASSAS
(BULL RUN)

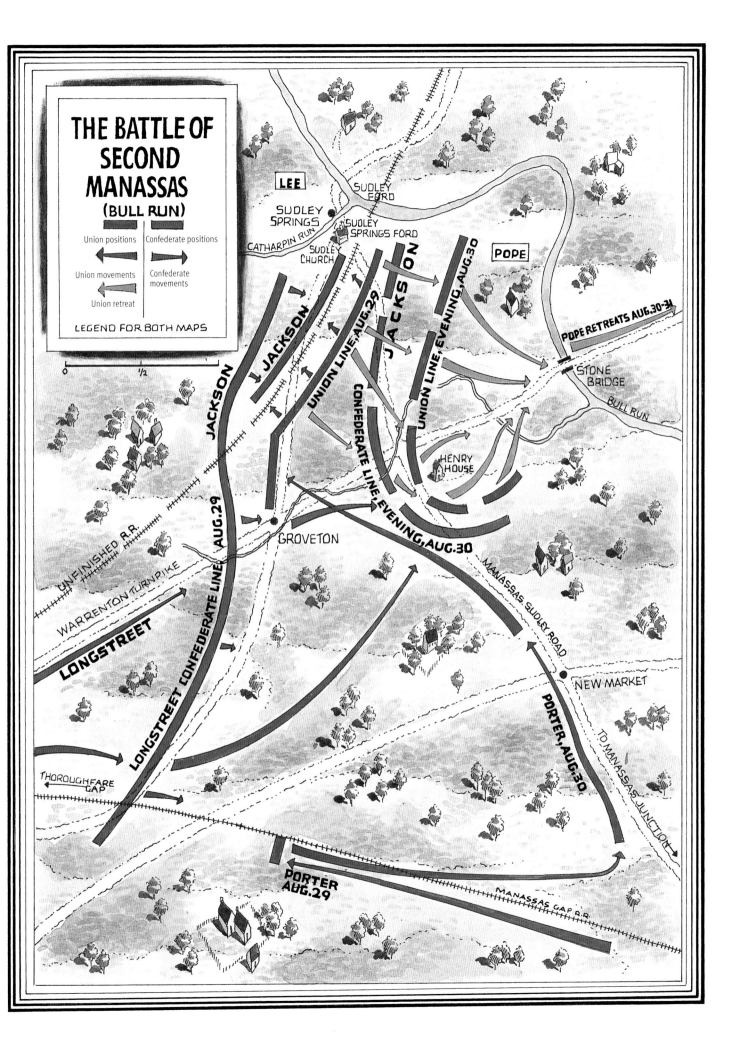

THE BATTLE OF SECOND MANASSAS
(BULL RUN)

Union positions   Confederate positions

Union movements   Confederate movements

Union retreat

LEGEND FOR BOTH MAPS

0   1/2

LEE

SUDLEY FORD

SUDLEY SPRINGS

SUDLEY SPRINGS FORD

CATHARPIN RUN

SUDLEY CHURCH

POPE

JACKSON

JACKSON

JACKSON

UNION LINE, AUG.29

UNION LINE, EVENING, AUG.30

POPE RETREATS AUG.30-31

STONE BRIDGE

BULL RUN

CONFEDERATE LINE, EVENING, AUG.30

HENRY HOUSE

UNFINISHED R.R.

GROVETON

WARRENTON TURNPIKE

LONGSTREET

LONGSTREET CONFEDERATE LINE, AUG.29

MANASSAS SUDLEY ROAD

NEW MARKET

PORTER, AUG.30

TO MANASSAS JUNCTION

THOROUGHFARE GAP

PORTER AUG.29

MANASSAS GAP R.R.

attack *him*. Lee deferred to his subordinate's judgment. Thus while Longstreet's presence neutralized 30,000 Federals, they also neutralized Longstreet.

That night a few Confederate brigades pulled back from advanced positions to readjust their line. Having made several wrong guesses about the enemy's intentions during the past few days, Pope guessed wrong again when he assumed this movement to be preliminary to a retreat. He wanted so much to "see the backs of our enemies"—as he had professed always to have done in the West—that he believed it about to happen. He sent a victory dispatch to Washington and prepared to pursue the supposedly retreating rebels.

But when Pope's pursuit began next day the bluecoats went no more than a few hundred yards before being stopped in their tracks by bullets from Jackson's infantry still holding their roadbed trenches. The Federals hesitated only momentarily before attacking in even heavier force than the previous day. The exhausted southerners bent and almost broke. Some units ran out of ammunition and resorted to throwing rocks at the Yankees. Jackson was forced to swallow his pride and call on Longstreet for reinforcements. Longstreet had a better idea. He brought up artillery to enfilade the Union attackers and then hurled all five of his divisions in a screaming counterattack against the Union left, which had been weakened by Pope's shift of troops to his right for the assaults on Jackson. Once Longstreet's men went into action they hit the surprised northerners like a giant hammer. Until sunset a furious contest raged all along the line. The bluecoats fell back doggedly to Henry House Hill, scene of the hardest fighting in that first battle in these parts thirteen months earlier. Here they made a twilight stand that brought the rebel juggernaut to a halt.

This engraving of the retreat of Pope's army across the stone bridge over Bull Run on the evening of August 30 captures the discouragement and despair of the defeated soldiers.

That night Pope—all boastfulness gone—decided to pull back toward Washington. On September 1 two blue divisions fought a vicious rear-guard action at Chantilly, only twenty miles from Washington, against Jackson's weary corps, which Lee had sent on another clockwise march for one final attempt to hit the retreating Union flank. After warding off this thrust in a drenching thunderstorm, the beaten-down bluecoats trudged into the capital's defenses. During the previous five days they had suffered 16,000 casualties out of a total force of 65,000, while Lee's 55,000 had lost fewer than 10,000 men. Lee's achievement in his second strategic offensive was even more remarkable than in his first. Less than a month earlier the main Union army had been only twenty miles from Richmond. With half as many troops as his two opponents (Pope and McClellan), Lee had shifted the scene to twenty miles from Washington, where the rebels seemed poised for the kill.

Behind Union lines all was confusion. When news of the fighting reached Washington, Secretary of War Stanton appealed for volunteer nurses to go out to help with the wounded. Many government clerks and other civilians responded, but a portion of them—a male portion—turned out to be worse than useless. Some were drunk by the time they reached the front, where they bribed a few ambulance drivers with whiskey to take *them* back to Washington instead of the wounded. To this shameful episode should be contrasted the herculean labors of Herman Haupt, who sent trains through the chaos to bring back wounded men, and the sleepless work of numerous women nurses headed by Clara Barton.

No photographer was on hand to record the aftermath of Second Bull Run. But this drawing by Harper's Weekly *illustrator and cartoonist Thomas Nast depicted the horrors of a battlefield perhaps more graphically than any photograph could have done. In possession of the battlefield, Confederates buried Union dead in mass graves after stripping their bodies of shoes, clothing, and anything else of value. Even civilians participated, at least in Nast's imagination; note the woman searching a corpse in the center foreground.*

The despair of that dark night spread through the North during the first half of September. Army morale also plunged. Although the men had fought well, they knew they had been mishandled. And they knew whom to blame: Pope and McDowell. Baseless rumors of treason rose against McDowell—for no other reason, perhaps, than that this luckless general had commanded the army at First Bull Run and commanded its largest corps in the reprise. Pope and McDowell in turn blamed McClellan and Porter for lack of cooperation and refusal to obey orders.

The administration was inclined to agree with Pope. Lincoln considered McClellan's behavior "unpardonable." He "wanted Pope to fail," the president told his private secretary. The cabinet almost unanimously favored McClellan's dismissal. But the president instead merged Pope's army into the Army of the Potomac, put McClellan in charge of the defense of Washington, sent Pope to Minnesota to pacify Indians, and relieved McDowell of command and ultimately exiled him to California. Stanton and Chase remonstrated against the retention of McClellan. Lincoln himself was "greatly distressed" by having to do it. But while McClellan "had acted badly in this matter," said the president, he "has the Army with him. . . . We must use what tools we have. There is no man in the Army who can lick these troops of ours into shape half as well as he. . . . If he can't fight himself, he excels in making others ready to fight."

Lincoln's judgment was confirmed by an extraordinary incident that occurred during the dispirited retreat of Pope's troops toward Washington on September 2. Stragglers were plodding through the mud when McClellan suddenly rode up. One soldier vividly recalled the moment. As word spread that "Little Mac" had appeared, enlisted men "threw their caps high into the air, and danced and frolicked like school-boys. . . . The effect of this man's presence upon the Army of the Potomac . . . was electrical, and too wonderful to make it worth while attempting to give a reason for it."

Within days McClellan had the army ready for field service again. And they had to take the field immediately, for with scarcely a pause Lee was leading his ragged but confident veterans across the Potomac for an invasion of the North. Most northerners saw this as a calamity. But Lincoln viewed it as an opportunity to cripple Lee's army far from its home base. He told McClellan to go after Lee and "destroy the rebel army, if possible."

Lee and Davis recognized that this could happen, but after weighing the alternatives they had decided that the possible gains outweighed the risk. The weary, ragged, hungry Army of Northern Virginia could not attack the formidable Washington defenses—but it also could not stay where it was, in a fought-over region denuded of supplies at the end of a long and precarious rail line. The safe course was to pull back toward Richmond to rest and refit. But Lee was not the man to choose the safe course; though exhausted, his men were flushed with victory, and the enemy was unnerved by defeat. Lee sensed that this was the North's low-water mark. Kirby Smith and Bragg were marching into Kentucky. Van Dorn and Price were preparing to invade Tennessee. This was no time for the Army of Northern Virginia to rest on its laurels. It must take the war into the North and force the Lincoln government to sue for peace. Maryland like Kentucky beckoned with the prospect of joining her sister slave states. Lee's hungry warriors could feed themselves from the fat farms of Maryland and Pennsylvania while drawing the enemy out of war-ravaged Virginia during the harvest season. At the very least, Lee could cut the B&O and—if things went well—burn the Pennsylvania Railroad bridge over the Susquehanna at Harrisburg, thereby severing Washington's main links with the West. A successful invasion might induce European powers to recognize Confederate nationhood. It might encourage Peace Democrats in the upcoming northern elections. A "proposal of peace" backed by southern armies on northern soil, wrote Lee to Davis on September 8, "would enable the people of the United States to determine at their coming elections whether they will support those who favor a prolongation of the war, or those who wish to bring it to a termination."

For political as well as military reasons, therefore, Lee started his army splashing across the Potomac fords thirty-five miles above Washington on September 4. Reinforced by three divisions called from Richmond, the army numbered some 55,000 men before it crossed the river. But from a variety of causes—exhaustion, hunger, sickness from subsisting on green corn, torn feet from marching barefoot on stony roads—stragglers fell out by the thousands during the next few days.

A drawing by Harper's Weekly *artist Alfred R. Waud of Confederate soldiers crossing at a ford in the Potomac River to Maryland by moonlight on the night of September 4–5, 1862. In the foreground, Union scouts observe the crossing. Their report would reach Washington the next day.*

Most of the soldiers, however, were in high spirits as they entered Frederick on September 6 singing "Maryland, My Maryland." But like Bragg's army in Kentucky, they received a less enthusiastic welcome than they had hoped. This was the unionist part of Maryland. And these rebels did not inspire confidence. One resident of Frederick described them as "the filthiest set of men and officers I ever saw; with clothing that . . . had not been changed for weeks. They could be smelt all over the entire inclosure." Although the men behaved with more restraint toward civilian property than Union soldiers were wont to do, their purchases of supplies with Confederate scrip did not win popularity. Despite the cool reception, Lee doggedly followed President Davis's instructions and issued an address "To the People of Maryland" in which he emphasized their ties with the Confederate states and declared that his army had come "to enable you again to enjoy the inalienable rights of freemen." The silent response of Marylanders was eloquent. It constituted the first failure of the invasion.

The second was caused by a stroke of fate which proved that truth can indeed be stranger than fiction. Although Lee expected his army to live largely off the land, he needed to open a minimal supply line through the Shenandoah Valley, especially for ammunition. But the Union garrison at Harper's Ferry blocked this route. Known as the "railroad brigade," this unit had the duty of protecting the B&O and the Chesapeake and Ohio Canal. When the Confederate invasion cut these arteries east of Harper's Ferry, McClellan urged Halleck to transfer the garrison to the Army of the Potomac, which was marching from Washington to intercept Lee. But Halleck refused—an unsound strategic decision that unwittingly baited a trap for Lee.

To eliminate this garrison in his rear, Lee detached almost two-thirds of his army and sent them in three columns (the largest under Jackson) to converge on the heights overlooking Harper's Ferry. Planning to net the 12,000 bluecoats there like fish in a barrel, Lee intended to reunite his army for a move on Harrisburg before

A satirical cartoon in Harper's Weekly *contrasting the Cavalier self-image of the Confederate "chivalry" with the reality of ragged, dirty Confederate soldiers in Maryland.*

THE REBEL CHIVALRY

As the Fancy of "My Maryland" painted them   As "My Maryland" found them.

A wartime photograph of Harperss Ferry after the Baltimore and Ohio Railroad bridge was rebuilt. The Potomac River is at left, and the Shenandoah River flows into the Potomac from the right beyond the bridge. The Confederates placed artillery on Maryland Heights at left and Loudon Heights at right to command the Union position and compel its surrender on September 15.

McClellan could cross the South Mountain range that protected the rebel flank. For the third time in three campaigns Lee was dividing his army in the presence of a larger enemy. Confident that McClellan's army was demoralized and that their leader would not be prepared for offensive operations for three or four weeks, Lee expected to reach the Susquehanna well before then.

But instead of three of four weeks, Lee had only that many days before the enemy would be upon him. To be sure, McClellan with 70,000 men (soon reinforced to 80,000) was moving cautiously in search of Lee's 50,000 (which he estimated at 110,000). But the bluecoats were no longer demoralized, and on September 13 their nongambling commander hit the all-time military jackpot. In a field near Frederick two Union soldiers found a copy of Lee's orders, wrapped around three cigars lost by a careless southern officer, detailing the objectives for the four separate parts of his army. This fantastic luck revealed to McClellan that each part of the enemy army was several miles from any of the others and that the two largest units were twenty or twenty-five miles apart with the Potomac between them. With his whole force McClellan could push through the South Mountain passes and gobble up the pieces of Lee's army before they could reunite. McClellan recognized his opportunity; to one of his generals he exulted, "Here is a paper with which if I cannot whip 'Bobbie Lee,' I will be willing to go home."

Ever cautious, however, McClellan made careful plans and did not order the men forward until daylight on September 14, eighteen hours after he had learned of Lee's dispositions. As things turned out, this delay enabled Lee to concentrate and save his army. A pro-Confederate citizen of Maryland had witnessed McClellan's response to the finding of the lost orders and had ridden hard to inform Stuart, who passed the information along to Lee on the night of September 13. Lee ordered troops to block the passes through South Mountain. Next day two Union corps fought uphill against D. H. Hill's Confederate division defending Turner's Gap. Taking heavy losses, Hill's hardy band hung on behind stone walls and trees until Longstreet came up with reinforcements and held off the Federals until nightfall. Withdrawing after dark, these outnumbered rebels had given Lee an extra day.

A Union battery going into action at Crampton's Gap on September 14. Two guns at the right have unlimbered and commenced firing, while the gun in the foreground arrives at a gallop.

Meanwhile another Union corps under William B. Franklin had smashed through Crampton's Gap six miles to the south after a sharp firefight with three Confederate brigades. Despite great numerical superiority, Franklin advanced timidly southward toward the forces besieging Harper's Ferry and failed to arrive in time to save the Union garrison at the Ferry.

Although the half of Lee's army north of the Potomac had warded off disaster, the invasion of Maryland appeared doomed. The whole Union army would be across South Mountain next day. The only apparent Confederate option seemed to be retreat into the Shenandoah Valley. But when Lee received word that Jackson expected to capture Harper's Ferry on September 15, he changed his mind about retreating. He ordered the whole army to concentrate at Sharpsburg, a Maryland village about two miles from the Potomac. Lee had decided to offer battle. To return to Virginia without fighting would mean loss of face. It might endanger diplomatic efforts to win foreign recognition. It would depress southern morale. Having beaten the Federals twice before, Lee thought he could do it again—for he still believed the Army of the Potomac to be demoralized.

Lee's estimate of northern morale seemed to be confirmed by Jackson's easy capture of Harper's Ferry. The Union garrison was composed mostly of new troops under a second-rate commander—Colonel Dixon Miles, a Marylander who had been reprimanded for drunkenness at First Bull Run and whose defense of Harper's Ferry was so inept as to arouse suspicions of treason. Killed in the last exchange of fire before the surrender, Miles did not have to defend himself against such a charge.

The various Confederate units that had besieged Harper's Ferry marched as fast as possible for Sharpsburg fifteen miles away. Until they arrived on September 16 and 17, Lee had only three divisions in line with their backs to the Potomac over which only one ford offered an escape in case of defeat. During September 15 the

Army of the Potomac began arriving at Antietam Creek a mile or two east of Lee's position. Still acting with the caution befitting his estimate of Lee's superior force, McClellan launched no probing attacks and sent no cavalry reconnaisance across the creek to determine Confederate strength. On September 16 the northern commander had 60,000 men on hand and another 15,000 within six miles to confront Lee's 25,000 or 30,000. Having informed Washington that he would crush Lee's army in detail while it was separated, McClellan missed his second chance to do so on the sixteenth while he matured plans for an attack on the morrow. Late that afternoon—as two more Confederate divisions slogged northward from Harper's Ferry—McClellan sent two corps across the Antietam north of the Confederate left, precipitating a sharp little fight that alerted Lee to the point of the initial Union attack at dawn next day.

Antietam (called Sharpsburg by the South) was one of the few battles of the war in which both commanders deliberately chose the field and planned their tactics beforehand. Instead of entrenching, the Confederates utilized the cover of small groves, rock outcroppings, stone walls, dips and swells in the rolling farmland, and a sunken road in the center of their line. Only the southernmost of three bridges over the Antietam was within rebel rifle range; this bridge would become one of the keys to the battle. McClellan massed three corps on the Union right to deliver the initial attack and placed Burnside's large 9th Corps on the left with orders to create a diversion to prevent Lee from transferring troops from this sector to reinforce his left. McClellan held four Union divisions and the cavalry in reserve behind the right and center to exploit any breakthrough. He also expected Burnside to cross the

The landscape artist James Hope painted four huge canvases (12 x 5.5 feet) of the battle of Antietam. They can be seen today in the visitor center of Antietam National Battlefield. This scene purports to show the Union attack on the Sunken Road at midday. Many of the details are wrong, but the vista offers a good view of the landscape and terrain of the center of the battlefield.

creek and roll up the Confederate right if opportunity offered. It was a good battle plan, and if well executed it might have accomplished Lincoln's wish to "destroy the rebel army."

But it was not well executed. On the Union side the responsibility for this lay mainly on the shoulders of McClellan and Burnside. McClellan failed to coordinate the attacks on the right, which therefore went forward in three stages instead of simultaneously. This allowed Lee time to shift troops from quiet sectors to meet the attacks. The Union commander also failed to send in the reserves when the blue-coats did manage to achieve a breakthrough in the center. Burnside wasted the morning and part of the afternoon crossing the stubbornly defended bridge when his men could have waded the nearby fords against little opposition. As a result of Burnside's tardiness, Lee was able to shift a division in the morning from the Confederate right to the hard-pressed left, where it arrived just in time to break the third wave of the Union attack. On the Confederate side the credit for averting disaster belonged to the skillful generalship of Lee and his subordinates but above all to the desperate courage of men in the ranks. "It is beyond all wonder," wrote a Union officer after the battle, "how such men as the rebel troops can fight on as they do; that, filthy, sick, hungry, and miserable, they should prove such heroes in fight, is past explanation."

The fighting at Antietam was among the hardest of the war. The Army of the Potomac battled with grim determination to expunge the dishonor of previous defeats. Yankee soldiers were not impelled by fearless bravery or driven by iron discipline. Few men ever experience the former, and Civil War soldiers scarcely knew the latter. Rather, they were motivated in the mass by the potential shame of another defeat and in small groups by the potential shame of cowardice in the eyes of comrades. A northern soldier who fought at Antietam gave as good an explanation of behavior in battle as one is likely to find anywhere. "The truth is, when bullets are whacking against tree-trunks and solid shot are cracking skulls like egg-shells, the consuming passion in the breast of the average man is to get out of the way. Between the physical fear of going forward and the moral fear of turning back, there is a predicament of exceptional awkwardness." But when the order came to go forward, his regiment did not falter. "In a second the air was full of the hiss of bullets and the hurtle of grape-shot. The mental strain was so great that I saw at that moment the singular effect mentioned, I think, in the life of Goethe on a similar occasion—the whole landscape for an instant turned slightly red." This psychological state produced a sort of fighting madness in many men, a superadrenalized fury that turned them into mindless killing machines heedless of the normal instinct of self-preservation. This frenzy seems to have prevailed at Antietam on a greater scale than in any previous Civil War battle.

Joseph Hooker's Union 1st Corps led the attack at dawn by sweeping down the Hagerstown Pike from the north. Rebels waited for them in what came to be known as the West Woods and the Cornfield just north of a whitewashed church of the pacifist Dunkard sect. "Fighting Joe" Hooker—an aggressive, egotistical general who aspired to command the Army of the Potomac—had earned his sobriquet on the Peninsula. He confirmed it here. His men drove back Jackson's corps from the

This drawing of Union attackers entering the famous Cornfield at Antietam was first published in Harper's Weekly *on October 4, 1862. It was subsequently printed as part of a series of images titled* Through the Cornfield.

cornfield and pike, dealing out such punishment that Lee sent reinforcements from D. H. Hill's division in the center and Longstreet's corps on the right. These units counterpunched with a blow that shattered Hooker's corps before the Union 12th Corps launched the second wave of the northern assault. This attack also penetrated the Confederate lines around the Dunkard church before being hurled back with heavy losses, whereupon a third wave led by a crack division of "Bull" Sumner's 2nd Corps broke through the rebel line in the West Woods. Before these bluecoats could roll up the flank, however, one Confederate division that had arrived that morning from Harper's Ferry and another that Lee had shifted from the inactive right near Burnside's Bridge suddenly popped out in front, flank, and rear of Sumner's division and all but wiped it out with a surprise counterattack. Severely wounded and left for dead in this action was a young captain in the 20th Massachusetts, Oliver Wendell Holmes, Jr.

For five hours a dreadful slaughter raged on the Confederate left. Twelve thousand men lay dead and wounded. Five Union and five Confederate divisions had been so cut up that they backed off as if by mutual consent and did no more serious fighting this day. In the meantime Sumner's other two divisions had obliqued left to deal with a threat to their flank from Confederates in a sunken farm road southeast of the Dunkard church. This brought on the midday phase of the battle in which blue and gray slugged it out for this key to the rebel center, known ever after as Bloody Lane. The weight of numbers and firepower finally enabled the blue to prevail. Broken southern brigades fell back to regroup in the outskirts of Sharpsburg itself. A northern war correspondent who came up to Bloody Lane minutes after the

The small church building of the pacifist Dunkard (or Dunker) sect was a focal point of the fighting on the morning of September 17. Alexander Gardner took this photograph two days after the battle. The artillery limber chest (which held ammunition) and some of the dead Confederate soldiers probably belonged to Captain W. W. Parker's Virginia battery.

One of several photographs of Confederate dead in Bloody Lane taken by Alexander Gardner on September 19. Gardner worked for Mathew Brady at the time. A month after the battle, Brady exhibited this and other photographs of "The Dead of Antietam" at his studio in New York City. A reporter for the New York Times was overwhelmed by the exhibit. But "there is one side of the picture that . . . has escaped photographic skill," he wrote. "It is the background of widows and orphans. . . . Homes have been made desolate, and the light of life in thousands of hearts has been quenched forever. All of this desolation imagination must paint—broken hearts cannot be photographed."

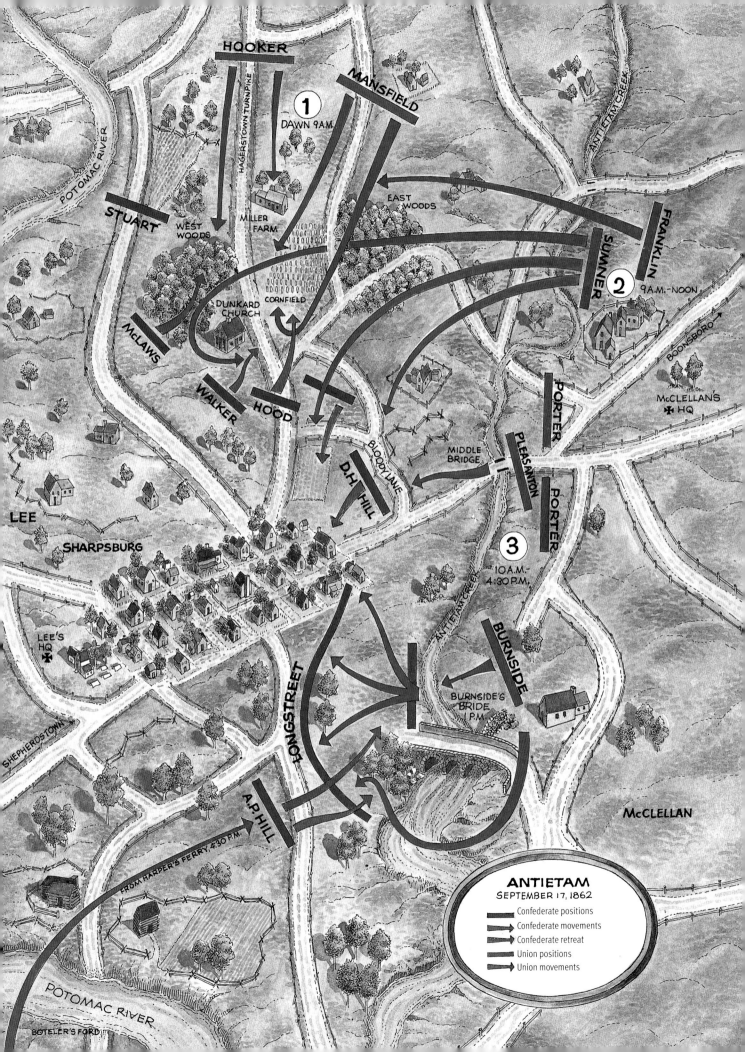

HOOKER

MANSFIELD

① DAWN 9 A.M.

FRANKLIN

SUMNER

② 9 A.M.–NOON

BOONSBORO

HAGERSTOWN TURNPIKE

POTOMAC RIVER

STUART

WEST WOODS

MILLER FARM

EAST WOODS

ANTIETAM CREEK

McCLELLAN'S ✠ HQ

McLAWS

DUNKARD CHURCH

CORNFIELD

WALKER

HOOD

BLOODY LANE

MIDDLE BRIDGE

PORTER

PLEASANTON

PORTER

LEE

D.H. HILL

③ 10 A.M.– 4:30 P.M.

SHARPSBURG

ANTIETAM CREEK

LEE'S ✠ HQ

BURNSIDE

BURNSIDE'S BRIDE 1 P.M.

LONGSTREET

McCLELLAN

SHEPHERDSTOWN

A.P. HILL

FROM HARPER'S FERRY, 4:30 P.M.

POTOMAC RIVER

BOTELER'S FORD

ANTIETAM
SEPTEMBER 17, 1862

▬ Confederate positions
➤ Confederate movements
➤ Confederate retreat
▬ Union positions
➤ Union movements

Federals captured it could scarcely find words to describe this "ghastly spectacle" where "Confederates had gone down as the grass falls before the scythe."

Now was the time for McClellan to send in his reserves. The enemy center was wide open. "There was no body of Confederate infantry in this part of the field that could have resisted a serious advance," wrote a southern officer. "Lee's army was ruined, and the end of the Confederacy was in sight," added another. But the carnage suffered by three Union corps during the morning had shaken McClellan. He decided not to send in the fresh 6th Corps commanded by Franklin, who was eager to go forward. Believing that Lee must be massing his supposedly enormous reserves for a counterattack, McClellan told Franklin that "it would not be prudent to make the attack." So the center of the battlefield fell silent as events on the Confederate right moved toward a new climax.

All morning a thin brigade of Georgians hidden behind trees and a stone wall had carried on target practice against Yankee regiments trying to cross Burnside's

Before the battle of Antietam, this bridge over the creek a mile southeast of town was known as the Rohrbach Bridge, named for a nearby farmer. Ever since the battle it has been known as Burnside's Bridge—in part, perhaps, a mocking reference to General Burnside's obsession with attacking directly across the bridge even though there were nearby fords over the shallow stream. This postbattle photograph was taken from the Confederate side of the bridge.

Bridge. The southern brigade commander was Robert A. Toombs, who enjoyed here his finest hour as a soldier. Disappointed by his failure to become president of the Confederacy, bored by his job as secretary of state, Toombs had taken a brigadier's commission to seek the fame and glory for which he felt destined. Reprimanded more than once by superiors for inefficiency and insubordination, Toombs spent many of his leisure hours denouncing Jefferson Davis and the "West Point clique" who were ruining army and country. For his achievement in holding Burnside's whole corps for several hours at Antietam—and being wounded in the process—Toombs expected promotion, but he did not get it and subsequently resigned to go public with his antiadministration exhortations.

In the early afternoon of September 17 two of Burnside's crack regiments finally charged across the bridge at a run, taking heavy losses to establish a bridgehead on the rebel side. Other units found fords about the same time, and by midafternoon three of Burnside's divisions were driving the rebels in that sector back toward Sharpsburg and threatening to cut the road to the only ford over the Potomac. Here was another crisis for Lee and an opportunity for McClellan. Fitz-John Porter's 5th Corps stood available as a reserve to support Burnside's advance. One of Porter's division commanders urged McClellan to send him in to bolster Burnside. McClellan hesitated and seemed about to give the order when he looked at Porter, who shook his head. "Remember, General," Porter was heard to say, "I command the last reserve of the last army of the Republic." This warning reminded McClellan of the danger from those phantom reserves on the other side, so he refused to give the order.

The Lutheran church in the village of Sharpsburg four days after the battle. On the east side of Sharpsburg, the church was badly damaged by shell fire and later had to be torn down. On the afternoon of September 17, skirmishers from Burnside's division reached the vicinity of the church but were forced to withdraw when McClellan did not send in his reserves and A. P. Hill's counterattack drove back the 9th Corps' advance. At the time of this photograph by Alexander Gardner, the church was being used as a Union field hospital.

Meanwhile Lee looked anxiously to the south, where his right flank seemed to be disintegrating. Suddenly he saw a cloud of dust in the distance that soon materialized as marching men. "Whose troops are those?" Lee asked a nearby lieutenant with a telescope. The lieutenant peered intently for what seemed an eternity, then said: "They are flying the Virginia and Confederate flags, sir." Sighing with relief, Lee observed: "It is A. P. Hill from Harper's Ferry." Indeed it was. Having remained behind to complete the surrender arrangements, Hill had driven his hard-fighting division up the road at a killing pace in response to an urgent summons from Lee. These troops crashed into Burnside's flank in late afternoon just as the Yankees seemed about to crumple Lee's right. Surprised and confused, the Union attackers milled around, stopped, and retreated. The surprise was compounded by the captured blue uniforms many of Hill's men were wearing, which caused four Union flank regiments to hold their fire for fatal minutes.

Night fell on a scene of horror beyond imagining. More than 6,000 men lay dead or dying, and another 16,000 wounded groaned in agony or endured in silence. The casualties at Antietam numbered four times the total suffered by American soldiers at the Normandy beaches on June 6, 1944. More Americans lost their lives in one day at Sharpsburg than fell in combat in the War of 1812, the Mexican War, and the

Spanish-American War *combined*. After dark on September 17 the weary southern corps and division commanders gathered at Lee's headquarters to report losses of 50 percent or more in several brigades. Scarcely 30,000 Confederates remained alive and unwounded. Lee nevertheless stayed in position next day almost as if to dare McClellan to renew the assault. McClellan refused the dare. Although two more fresh Union divisions arrived in the morning, he was still hypnotized by a vision of Lee's limitless legions. The armies remained quiet during the eighteenth, and that night Lee yielded to necessity and ordered his troops back to Virginia. McClellan mounted a feeble pursuit, which A. P. Hill brushed off on September 20, and the Confederates got clean away into the Valley.

McClellan wired news of a great victory to Washington. "Maryland is entirely freed from the presence of the enemy, who has been driven across the Potomac. No fears need now be entertained for the safety of Pennsylvania." Forgotten were Lincoln's instructions to "destroy the rebel army." Secretary of the Navy Welles may have echoed the president's opinion when he wrote two days after the battle: "Nothing from the army, except that, instead of following up the victory, attacking and capturing the Rebels, they . . . are rapidly escaping across the river. . . . Oh dear!" In letters to his wife, McClellan expressed pride in his achievement and pique at such fault-finding. " I feel some little pride in having, with a beaten & demoralized army, defeated Lee so utterly. . . . Well, one of these days history will I trust do me justice."

History can at least record Antietam as a strategic Union success. Lee's invasion of Maryland recoiled more quickly than Bragg's invasion of Kentucky. Nearly one-third of the rebels who marched into Maryland became casualties. When an unwary regimental band struck up "Maryland, My Maryland" after the retreat across the Potomac, men in the ranks hissed and groaned. Seeing the point, the musicians switched to "Carry Me Back to Old Virginny." At Whitehall and the White House the battle of Antietam also went down as a northern victory. It frustrated Confederate hopes for British recognition and precipitated the Emancipation Proclamation. The slaughter at Sharpsburg therefore proved to have been one of the war's great turning points.

A week after the battle of Antietam a newspaper in Hagerstown, Maryland (a dozen miles north of the battlefield), reported that in an area of seventy-five square miles "wounded and dying soldiers are to be found in every neighborhood and in nearly every house. . . . The whole region of country between Boonsboro and Sharpsburg is one vast hospital," and "nearly the whole population" were helping take care of the ten thousand Union wounded and two or three thousand Confederate wounded left behind when their army retreated. The drawing by Alfred R. Waud (opposite) depicts civilian volunteers assisting Union surgeons. The photograph shows a barn that became one of about seventy-five field hospitals in the area.

CHAPTER EIGHTEEN

☆ ☆ ☆ ☆ ☆

John Bull's
Virginia Reel

I

The course of the war in the summer of 1862 revived Confederate hopes for European diplomatic recognition. Lee's offensives convinced British and French leaders that northern armies could never restore the Union. These powers contemplated an offer of mediation, which would have constituted de facto recognition of Confederate independence. Influential elements of British public opinion grew more sympathetic to the southern cause. The Palmerston government seemed to shut its eyes to violations of British neutrality by Liverpool shipbuilders who constructed rebel cruisers to prey on the American merchant marine. The long-awaited cotton famine finally took hold in the summer of 1862. Louis Napoleon toyed with the idea of offering recognition and aid to the Confederacy in return for southern cotton and southern support for French suzerainty in Mexico.

Of all these occurrences, the building of commerce raiders was the only one that generated tangible benefits for the Confederacy. Liverpool was a center of pro-southern sentiment. The city "was made by the slave trade," observed a caustic American diplomat, "and the sons of those who acquired fortunes in the traffic, now instinctively side with the rebelling slave-drivers." Liverpool shipyards built numerous blockade runners. In March 1862 the first warship that the southern agent James D. Bulloch had ordered was also nearing completion. The ship's purpose as a commerce raider was an open secret, owing to the tenacious detective work of the U.S. consul at Liverpool, Thomas H. Dudley.

This combative Quaker was a match for Bulloch. Dudley hired spies and informers to obtain evidence that the Confederacy and British shipyards were violating Britain's Foreign Enlistment Act, which forbade the construction *and* arming of warships in British territory for a belligerent power. Despite Dudley's ultimately successful efforts to convince the British government to regard such activities as contrary to the act's restrictions, Bulloch succeeded in completing construction and delivery to the South of two warships that wreaked havoc on Union shipping. The first began her fearsome career as the *Florida*. She destroyed thirty-eight American

Opposite page: Just as white soldiers had done earlier, one of the first things a black soldier did after he enlisted was to have his picture taken. This is Sergeant J. L. Baldwin of Company G, 56th U.S. Colored Infantry, which fought in the Arkansas theater.

473

merchant vessels before the Union navy captured her by a subterfuge in the harbor of Bahia, Brazil, in October 1864.

The second cruiser evaded the belated application and sanctions of the act, thanks to more bureaucratic negligence, legal pettifoggery, and the Confederate sympathies of the British customs collector at Liverpool. Named the *Alabama*, this cruiser had as her captain Raphael Semmes, who had already proved his prowess as a salt-water guerrilla on the now-defunct C.S.S. *Sumter*. For the next two years Semmes and the *Alabama* roamed the seas and destroyed or captured sixty-four American merchant ships before being sunk by the U.S.S. *Kearsarge* off Cherbourg in June 1864. The *Alabama* and *Florida* were the most successful and celebrated rebel cruisers. Although their exploits did not alter the outcome of the war, they diverted numerous Union navy ships from the blockade, drove insurance rates for American vessels to astronomical heights, forced these vessels to remain in port or convert to foreign registry, and helped topple the American merchant marine from its once-dominant position, which it never regained.

In addition to the escape of the *Alabama* from Liverpool, another straw in the wind seemed to preview a southern tilt in British foreign policy. Henry Hotze, a Swiss-born Alabamian who arrived in London early in 1862, was an effective propagandist for the South. Twenty-seven years old and boyish in appearance, Hotze nevertheless possessed a suavity of manner and a style of witty understatement that appealed to the British upper classes. He successfully stirred up British prejudices against Yankees by writing pro-Confederate editorials for several newspapers and recruiting English journalists to write for a small newspaper he founded to present the southern viewpoint. To liberals he insisted that the South was fighting not for slavery but for self-determination. To conservatives he presented an image of a rural gentry defending its liberties against a rapacious northern government. To

The sharp reduction in cotton imports from the American South had a devastating impact in the textile-manufacturing cities of Britain. Charitable organizations stepped into the breach to distribute food and other necessities to the families of unemployed workers. This drawing in the Illustrated London News portrays the distribution center of the Manchester and Salford Provident Society.

businessmen he promised that an independent Confederacy would open its ports to free trade, in contrast with the Union government, which had recently raised tariffs yet again. To the textile industry he pledged a resumption of cotton exports.

This last prospect had a powerful appeal, for the cotton famine was beginning to pinch. In July 1862 the supply of raw cotton in Britain stood at one-third the normal level. Three-quarters of the cotton-mill workers were unemployed or on short time. Charity and the dole could not ward off hardship and restiveness in Lancashire working-class districts. Young Henry Adams, son and secretary of the American minister in London, conceded as early as May 1862 that "the suffering among the people in Lancashire and in France is already very great and is increasing enormously." Chancellor of the Exchequer William E. Gladstone feared an outbreak of rioting unless something was done to relieve the distress. Gladstone favored British intervention to stop the war and start the flow of cotton across the Atlantic. A British diplomat predicted that "so great a pressure may be put upon the government [that] they will find it difficult to resist."

The attitude of textile workers toward the American war has been something of a puzzle to historians as well as to contemporaries. Henry Hotze confessed frustration at his failure to win support from this class whose economic self-interest would seem to have favored the South. "The Lancashire operatives," wrote Hotze, are the only "class which as a class continues actively inimical to us. . . . They look upon us, and . . . upon slavery as the author and source of their present miseries." The American minister, Charles Francis Adams, echoed this appraisal. "The great body of the aristocracy and the commercial classes are anxious to see the United States go to pieces," wrote Adams in December 1862, while "the middle and lower class sympathise with us" because they "see in the convulsion in America an era in the history of the world, out of

William E. Gladstone was the most powerful British advocate of mediation to bring an end to the Civil War on the basis of Confederate independence. Many years later he expressed regret for his pro-Confederate stance during the war.

Many Britons followed news of the American Civil War with great interest, nowhere more intensely than in the industrial midlands most affected by the cotton famine. In this illustration of the free library in Manchester, people gather around newspapers to read the latest news from America.

which must come in the end a general recognition of the right of mankind to the produce of their labor and the pursuit of happiness."

In this view, the issues of the American Civil War mirrored the issues of class conflict in Britain. The Union stood for popular government, equal rights, and the dignity of labor; the Confederacy stood for aristocracy, privilege, and slavery. Lincoln expressed this theme in his speeches portraying the war as "essentially a People's contest . . . a struggle for maintaining in the world that form and substance of government whose leading object is to elevate the condition of men . . . to afford all an unfettered start, and a fair chance in the race of life." British radicals expounded numerous variations on the theme. For a generation they had fought for democratization of British politics and improved conditions for the working class. For them, America was a "beacon of freedom" lighting the path to reform. The leading British radical, John Bright, passionately embraced the Union cause. "There is no country in which men have been so free and prosperous" as the Union states, declared Bright. "The existence of that free country and that free government has a prodigious influence upon freedom in Europe." Confederates were "the worst foes of freedom the world has ever seen." John Stuart Mill reflected the views of other liberal intellectuals when he declared that a southern victory "would be a victory of the powers of evil which would give courage to the enemies of progress and damp the spirits of its friends all over the civilized world." A German revolutionary living in exile in England also viewed the American war against the "slave oligarchy" as a "world-transforming . . . revolutionary movement." "The working men of Europe," continued Karl Marx, felt a kinship with Abraham Lincoln, "the single-minded son of the working class. . . . As the American War of Independence initiated a new era of ascendancy for the middle class, so the American anti-slavery war will do for the working classes."

But a number of historians have discovered cracks in the apparent pro-Union unity of working men. Indeed, some have gone so far as to maintain that most Lancashire textile workers favored British intervention on behalf of the South to obtain cotton. Pro-Union rhetoric, they maintain, did not truly represent workers' sentiments but was the work of radical intellectuals like Bright or Marx, while mass meetings that passed pro-Union resolutions were engineered by these middle-class outsiders. This revisionist interpretation overcorrects the traditional view. Cotton manufacturing was not the only industry in Britain or even in Lancashire. Workers in wool, flax, armaments, shipping, and other industries prospered from increased wartime trade. And in any case, a good deal of truth still clings to the old notion of democratic principle transcending economic self-interest in Lancashire. As a veteran Chartist leader put it in February 1863: "The people had said there was something higher than work, more precious than cotton . . . it was right, and liberty, and doing justice, and bidding defiance to all wrong."

Much truth also adheres to the notion of British upper-class support for the South—or at least hostility to the North, which amounted to almost the same thing. Well-born Englishmen professed to dislike Yankees as much for their manners as for their dangerous democratic example to the lower orders. The Earl of Shrewsbury looked upon "the trial of Democracy and its failure" with pleasure. "The dissolution of the Union [means] that men now before me will live to see an aristocracy established in America." Similar statements found their way into prominent newspapers, including the London *Morning Post* and the magisterial *Times*, both with close ties to the Palmerston government. If by some remote and hateful chance the North did manage to win, said the *Morning Post*, "who can doubt that Democracy will be more arrogant, more aggressive, more levelling and vulgarizing, if that be possible, than ever before." This war of words against the Yankees contributed to an embitterment of Anglo-American relations for a generation after the *Alabama* had sunk below the waves and the Enfield rifles shipped through the blockade had fallen silent.

In 1862 an incident in New Orleans intensified British upper-class alienation from the North. After a sequence of provocative incidents, when a woman dumped the contents of a chamberpot on Fleet Captain David Farragut's head, the heavy-handed Benjamin Butler issued an order on May 15 that any woman who persisted in the practice of insulting northern soldiers "shall be regarded and held liable to be treated as a woman of the town plying her avocation." Butler's intention was to humiliate southern civilians into decent behavior; southerners and Europeans chose to interpret it as a barbarous license for northern soldiers to treat refined ladies as prostitutes. In an extraordinary statement to the House of Commons, Palmerston branded Butler's conduct "infamous." This was more than Charles Francis Adams could stand. For months he had silently endured the gibes of Englishmen. But this self-righteous condemnation of Butler, with its implied approval of a people who held two million women in slavery, evoked an official protest by Adams. Palmerston's huffy reply caused an estrangement between the two men at a time when Anglo-American relations were entering a critical stage.

The correlation between class and British attitudes toward the American conflict should not be exaggerated. The Union had few warmer friends than the Duke of Argyll, and the same could be said of others whose blood matched the color of northern uniforms. At the same time, several liberals and even radicals were attracted to the South's fight for self-determination. Many Englishmen had cheered the Greek fight for independence or the struggle of Hungary and Italian states to throw off Hapsburg rule. Some viewed the South's revolution against Yankee overlordship in a similar light. Such convictions motivated Russell and Gladstone, the most important members of the Palmerston ministry next to Old Pam himself. "Jefferson Davis and other leaders of the South," said Gladstone in a celebrated speech at Newcastle in October 1862, "have made an army; they are making, it appears, a navy; and they have made what is more than either; they have made a nation."

The canker in this image of southerners as freedom-loving nationalists, of course, was slavery. One thing upon which Englishmen prided themselves was their role in suppressing the transatlantic slave trade and abolishing slavery in the West Indies. To support a rebellion in behalf of slavery would be un-British. To accept

French Emperor Louis Napoleon, sometimes derisively called "Napoleon the Little," was ambitious to reclaim the glory and power that France had known during the reign of his uncle Napoleon Bonaparte. Of all the European monarchs, Louis Napoleon was the most eager advocate of recognizing the Confederacy but was reluctant to act alone.

the notion that the South fought for independence rather than slavery required considerable mental legerdemain. But so long as the North did *not* fight for freedom, many Britons could see no moral superiority in the Union cause. If the North wanted to succeed in "their struggle [for] the sympathies of Englishmen," warned a radical newspaper, "they must abolish slavery."

But these issues of ideology and sentiment played a secondary role in determining Britain's foreign policy. A veteran of a half-century in British politics, Palmerston was an exponent of *Realpolitik*. When prosouthern members of Parliament launched a drive in the summer of 1862 for British recognition of the Confederacy, Palmerston professed not to see the point. As far as Palmerston was concerned, the South could earn recognition only by winning the war: Britain must "know that their separate independence is a truth and a fact" before declaring it to be so.

In France, Louis Napoleon thought he saw a way to get cotton for France and further his imperial ambitions. By 1862 thousands of his soldiers were struggling in Mexico to overthrow the liberal regime of Benito Juarez. The Union supported Juarez but could not do much to help him; the South offered to support Napoleon—for a price. In return for French diplomatic recognition of the Confederacy, in July the South offered him several hundred thousand bales of cotton and an alliance against Juarez. But Napoleon knew that such a move, without Britain at his side, could lead to a disastrous confrontation with the Union's formidable navy. A tentative inquiry to the British government about its reaction to such an alliance evoked a decidedly unfavorable response from Palmerston, ever suspicious of Napoleon's global designs. The British prime minister warded off a parliamentary motion for Confederate recognition in mid-July even though a majority in Commons clearly favored such a step.

But as the summer wore on, Confederate victories seemed likely to fulfill Palmerston's criterion for recognition: establishment of southern nationhood as truth and fact. During 1861 most British observers had assumed as a matter of course that the North could never conquer so large an area and so militant a people. After all, if the redcoats could not prevail over a much weaker nation in 1776, how could the Yankees expect to win? Union victories in the first half of 1862 had threatened this smug assumption, but Jackson and Lee—who became instant legends in Britain—revived and made it stronger than ever. By September, according to the French foreign secretary, "not a reasonable statesman in Europe" believed that the North could win.

Both Whitehall and on the Quai d'Orsay a sentiment favoring an offer of mediation grew stronger as reports of new Confederate victories filtered across the Atlantic. If a combination of major powers proposed mediation, the Union would be under great pressure to accept and the Confederacy would, effectively, secure recognition of its independence. Rumors that such a move was afoot caused euphoria among southern diplomats and plunged the American legation into gloom.

The European belief that defeat might induce Lincoln to accept mediation misjudged his determination to fight through to victory. "I expect to maintain this contest until successful, or till I die," Lincoln had said, and he meant it. Such obstinacy compelled the proponents of mediation to pin their hopes on a Democratic triumph in the northern elections. Betraying a typical British misunderstanding of the American constitutional system, Foreign Minister Russell expected that Democratic control of the House would force Lincoln to change his foreign policy. "The Democratic party may by that time [November] have got the ascendancy," wrote Russell in October. "I heartily wish them success."

So did Robert E. Lee, as he invaded Maryland to conquer a peace. The fate of diplomacy rode with Lee in this campaign. The Federals "got a very complete smashing" at Bull Run, wrote Palmerston to Russell on September 14, "and it seems not altogether unlikely that still greater disasters await them, and that even Washington or Baltimore may fall into the hands of the Confederates. If this should happen, would it not be time for us to consider whether . . . England and France might not address the contending parties and recommend an arrangement upon the basis of separation?" Russell was ready and willing. On September 17—the very day of the fighting at Sharpsburg—he concurred in the plan to offer mediation, adding that if the North refused, "we ought ourselves to recognise the Southern States as an independent State." But when reports of Antietam reached England (news required twelve days or more to cross the Atlantic), Palmerston turned cautious. When he learned of Lee's retreat to Virginia, Palmerston backed off. "These last battles in Maryland have rather set the North up again," he wrote to Russell early in October. "The whole matter is full of difficulty, and can only be cleared up by some more decided events between the contending armies."

But Antietam did not cool the ardor of Russell and Gladstone for recognition. They persisted in bringing the matter before the cabinet on October 28, despite Palmerston's repeated insistence that matters had changed since mid-September, "when the Confederates seemed to be carrying all before them. . . . I am very much come back to our original view that we must continue merely to be lookers-on till the war shall have taken a more decided turn." The cabinet voted Russell and Gladstone down. The French weighed in at this point with a suggestion that Britain, France, and Russia propose a six-month armistice—during which the blockade would be suspended. This so blatantly favored the South that pro-Union Russia quickly rejected it. The British cabinet, after two days of discussion, also turned it down.

Thus ended the South's best chance for European intervention. It did not end irrevocably, for the military situation remained fluid and most Britons remained certain that the North could never win. But at least they had avoided losing. Antietam had, in Charles Francis Adams's understatement, "done a good deal to

A GENTLEMAN IN A FIX—AN UNNATURAL PARENT.

An old woman by the name of Bull recently played a most cruel hoax upon a gentleman, one Mr. Napoleon, of France. It appear that the woman Bull, by means of her tears and lamentations, induced Mr. Napoleon to aid her in carrying her baby Intervention. No sooner, however, had the gentleman taken up the infant than the unprincipled parent ran away, at the same time denying any relationship to her offspring. She is an old offender.

This cartoon in Frank Leslie's Illustrated Newspaper *satirizes Louis Napoleon's eagerness to intervene in the American Civil War. It shows Napoleon holding a baby named "Intervention" as the mother, "Bull" (Britain), runs away.*

restore our drooping credit here." It had done more; by enabling Lincoln to issue the Emancipation Proclamation the battle also ensured that Britain would think twice about intervening against a government fighting for freedom as well as Union.

II

On September 22, five days after the battle of Antietam, Lincoln called his cabinet into session. He had made a covenant with God, said the president, that if the army drove the enemy from Maryland he would issue his Emancipation Proclamation. "I think the time has come," he continued. "I wish it were a better time. I wish that we were in a better condition. The action of the army against the rebels has not been quite what I should have best liked." Nevertheless, Antietam was a victory, and Lincoln intended to warn the rebel states that unless they returned to the Union by January 1 their slaves "shall be then, thenceforward, and forever free." The cabinet approved, though Montgomery Blair repeated his warning that this action might drive border-state elements to the South and give Democrats "a club . . . to beat the Administration" in the elections. Lincoln replied that he had exhausted every effort to bring the border states along. Now "we must make the forward movement" without them. "They [will] acquiesce, if not immediately, soon." As for the Democrats, "their clubs would be used against us take what course we might."

The Proclamation would apply only to states in rebellion on January 1. This produced some confusion, because the edict thus appeared to "liberate" only those slaves beyond Union authority while retaining in bondage all those within the government's reach. A few disappointed radicals and abolitionists looked upon it this way. So did tories and some liberals in England. The conservative British press affected both to abhor and to ridicule the measure: to abhor it because it might encourage a servile rebellion that would eclipse the horrors of the 1857 Sepoy uprising in India; to ridicule it because of its hypocritical impotence. "Where he has no power Mr. Lincoln will set the negroes free; where he retains power he will consider them as slaves," declared the London *Times*. "This is more like a Chinaman beating his two swords together to frighten his enemy than like an earnest man pressing forward his cause."

But such remarks missed the point and misunderstood the president's prerogatives under the Constitution. Lincoln acted under his war powers to seize enemy resources; he had no constitutional power to act against slavery in

One of the arguments of abolitionists during the Civil War was that "slavery is the backbone of the rebellion." This cartoon builds on that theme. It shows Jefferson Davis at left holding the chain of a dog labeled Rebellion. Generals Halleck and McClellan are wielding hammers labeled Skill and Strategy while Secretary of War Stanton holds one labeled Draft. But Lincoln stands by with an axe labeled Emancipation Proclamation, saying to Stanton: "You can try him with that, but I'm afraid this axe of mine is the only thing that will fetch him."

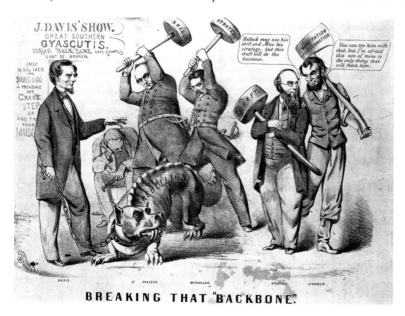

BREAKING THAT "BACKBONE".

areas loyal to the United States. The Proclamation would turn Union forces into armies of liberation after January 1—if they could win the war. And it also invited the slaves to help them win it. Most antislavery Americans and Britons recognized this. "We shout for joy that we live to record this righteous decree," wrote Frederick Douglass, while William Lloyd Garrison considered it "an act of immense historic consequence." A British abolitionist pronounced September 22 "a memorable day in the annals of the great struggle for the freedom of an oppressed and despised race"; a radical London newspaper believed it "a gigantic stride in the paths of Christian and civilized progress." Lincoln's own off-the-record analysis showed how much his conception of the war had changed since ten months earlier, when he had deprecated a "remorseless revolutionary struggle." After January 1, Lincoln told an official of the Interior Department, "the character of the war will be changed. It will be one of subjugation. . . . The [old] South is to be destroyed and replaced by new propositions and ideas."

This cartoon in the satirical British weekly Punch *illustrates the initial reaction of many Britons to the preliminary Emancipation Proclamation, which is portrayed as Lincoln's last desperate card in the deadly game against the Confederacy—the ace of spades with its malevolent black face, implying that the Proclamation was an attempt to set off the gunpowder of a slave insurrection.*

Would the army fight for freedom? From an Indiana colonel came words that could have answered for most soldiers. Few of them were abolitionists, he wrote, but they nevertheless wanted "to destroy everything that in *aught* gives the rebels strength," including slavery, so "this army will sustain the emancipation proclamation and enforce it with the bayonet." General-in-Chief Halleck explained his position to Grant: "The character of the war has very much changed within the last year. There is now no possible hope of reconciliation. . . . We must conquer the rebels or be conquered by them. . . . Every slave withdrawn from the enemy is the equivalent of a white man put *hors de combat*."

But would McClellan and officers of the Army of the Potomac go along with this? Much Republican opposition to McClellan stemmed from the belief that he would not. And indeed, the general's first response to the Proclamation indicated indecision. He considered it "infamous" and told his wife that he "could not make up my mind to fight for such an accursed doctrine as that of a servile insurrection." McClellan consulted Democratic friends in New York, who advised him "to submit to the Presdt's proclamation & quietly continue doing [your] duty as a soldier." But some of McClellan's associates stirred up opposition to the new policy. Fitz-John Porter denounced this "absurd proclamation of a political coward." A staff officer confided to a colleague that Lee's army had not been "bagged" at Sharpsburg because "that is not the game. The object is that neither army shall get much advantage of the other; that both shall be kept in the field till they are exhausted, when we will make a compromise and save slavery." When word of this conversation reached Lincoln he cashiered the officer to "make an example" and put a stop to such "silly,

treasonable expressions." Belatedly awakening to the danger of such loose talk among his officers, McClellan on October 7 issued a general order reminding them of the necessity for military subordination to civil authority. "The remedy for political errors, if any are committed," concluded McClellan with an artful reference to the imminent elections, "is to be found only in the action of the people at the polls."

Democrats scarcely needed this hint. They had already made emancipation the main issue in their quest for control of Congress. The New York Democratic platform denounced the Emancipation Proclamation as "a proposal for the butchery of women and children, for scenes of lust and rapine, and of arson and murder." The party nominated for governor a suave, conservative veteran of thirty years in New York politics, Horatio Seymour, who declared: "If it be true that slavery must be abolished to save this Union, then the people of the South should be allowed to withdraw themselves from the government which cannot give them the protection guaranteed by its terms." Democrats in Ohio and Illinois asserted that if abolition was "the avowed purpose of the war, the South cannot be subdued and ought not to be subdued. . . . In the name of God, no more bloodshed to gratify a religious fanaticism." An Ohio Democrat amended the party's slogan to proclaim "the Constitution as it is, the Union as it was, *and the Niggers where they are.*"

Lincoln's suspension of habeas corpus to enforce the militia draft also hurt the Republicans. "A large majority," declared an Ohio editor, "can see no reason why *they* should be shot for the benefit of niggers and Abolitionists." If "the *despot* Lincoln" tried to ram abolition and conscription down the throats of white men, "he would meet with the fate he deserves: hung, shot, or burned." The arrests of Democrats for antiwar activities and the indictment of forty-seven members of the Knights of the Golden Circle in Indiana probably backfired against Republicans by enabling Democrats to portray themselves as martyrs to civil liberty.

Subsuming all these issues was the war itself. "After a year and a half of trial," admitted one Republican, "and a pouring out of blood and treasure, and the maiming and death of thousands, we have made no sensible progress in putting down the rebellion. . . . The people are desirous of some change, they scarcely know what." This remained true even after northern armies turned back Confederate invasions at Antietam, Perryville, and Corinth. None of these battles was a clear-cut Union victory; the failure to follow them with a blow to the retreating rebels produced a feeling of letdown. In October enemy forces stood in a more favorable position than five months earlier: Bragg's army occupied Murfreesboro in central Tennessee only thirty miles from Nashville, and Lee's army remained only a few miles from Harper's Ferry. Jeb Stuart's cavalry had thumbed their noses at the Yankees again by riding around the entire Army of the Potomac (October 10–12), raiding as far north as Chambersburg, Pennsylvania, and returning to their own lines with 1,200 horses while losing only two men. If anything seemed to underscore northern military futility, this was it.

Democrats scored significant gains in the 1862 elections: the governorship of New York, the governorship and a majority of the legislature in New Jersey, a legislative majority in Illinois and Indiana, and a net increase of thirty-four congressmen. Only the fortuitous circumstance that legislative and gubernatorial elections in Ohio and Pennsylvania were held in odd-numbered years and that the Republican governors of Illinois and Indiana had been elected in 1860 to four-year terms prevented the probable loss of these posts to the Democrats in 1862. Panicky Republicans interpreted the elections as "a great, sweeping revolution of public sentiment," *"a most serious and severe reproof."* Gleeful Democrats pronounced "Abolition Slaughtered." Nearly all historians have agreed: the elections were "a near disaster for the Republicans"; "a great triumph for the Democrats"; "the verdict of the polls showed clearly that the people of the North were opposed to the Emancipation Proclamation."

But a closer look at the results challenges this conclusion. Republicans retained control of seventeen of the nineteen free-state governorships and sixteen of the legislatures. They elected several congressmen in Missouri for the first time, made a net *gain* of five seats in the Senate, and retained a twenty-five-vote majority in the House after experiencing the *smallest* net loss of congressional seats in an off-year election in twenty years. It is true that the congressional delegations of the six lower-North states from New York to Illinois would have a Democratic majority for the next two years. But elsewhere the Republicans more than held their own. And the Democratic margins in most of those six states were exceedingly thin: 4,000 votes in Pennsylvania, 6,000 in Ohio, 10,000 each in New York and Indiana. These majorities could be explained, as Lincoln noted, by the absence of soldiers at the front, for scattered evidence already hinted at a large Republican edge among enlisted men, a hint that would be confirmed in future elections when absentee soldier voting was permitted.

Although disappointed by the elections, Lincoln and the Republicans did not allow it to influence their actions. Indeed, the pace of radicalism increased during the next few months. On November 7 Lincoln removed McClellan from command of the Army of the Potomac. Although military factors prompted this action, it had

This lithograph presents an almost allegorical picture of Lincoln writing the final Proclamation surrounded by items that the artist supposed might have influenced Lincoln to take this step: a Bible on his knee, the scale of justice and a key to the future on the wall behind him, antislavery petitions on his left, George Washington's sword hanging over a map of Europe at the far right, and many other symbolic items.

important political overtones. In December the House decisively rejected a Democratic resolution branding emancipation "a high crime against the Constitution," and endorsed the Emancipation Proclamation by a party-line vote. Congress also passed an enabling act requiring the abolition of slavery as a condition of West Virginia's admission to statehood.

During December the Democratic press speculated that Lincoln, having been rebuked by the voters, would not issue the final Emancipation Proclamation. The president's message to Congress on December 1 fed this speculation. Lincoln again recommended his favorite plan for gradual, compensated emancipation in every state "wherein slavery now exists." Worried abolitionists asked each other: "If the President means to carry out his edict of freedom on the New Year, what is all this stuff about gradual emancipation?" But both the friends and enemies of freedom misunderstood Lincoln's admittedly ambiguous message. Some failed to notice his promise that all slaves freed "by the chances of war"—including his Proclamation—would remain forever free. The Proclamation was a war measure applicable only against states in rebellion; Lincoln's gradual emancipation proposal was a peace measure to *abolish the institution* everywhere by constitutional means. The president's peroration should have left no doubt of his position: "Fellow citizens, *we* cannot escape history. . . . The fiery trial through which we pass, will light us down, in honor or dishonor, to the latest generation. . . . The dogmas of the quiet past, are inadequate to the stormy present. . . . In *giving* freedom to the *slave* we *assure* freedom to the *free*. . . . We must disenthrall ourselves, and then we shall save our country."

On New Year's Day Lincoln ended all speculation. The Proclamation he signed that day exempted the border states along with Tennessee and Union-controlled portions of Louisiana and Virginia. To meet the criticism that the preliminary Proclamation had invited slaves to revolt, the final edict enjoined them to "abstain from all violence." But in other respects this Proclamation went beyond the first one. Not only did it justify emancipation as an "act of justice" as well as a military necessity, but it also sanctioned the enlistment of black soldiers and sailors in Union forces.

Here was revolution in earnest. Armed blacks were truly the *bête noire* of southern nightmares. Despite the service of black soldiers in the Revolution and the War of 1812, Negroes had been barred from state militias since 1792 and the regular army had never enrolled black soldiers. The prejudices of the old order died hard. Lincoln had squelched Secretary of War Cameron's reference to arming slaves in December 1861, and the administration refused at first to accept the organization of black regiments in Kansas, occupied Louisiana, and the South Carolina sea islands during the summer of 1862.

The Union navy, however, had taken men of all colors and conditions from the outset. Blacks at sea served mainly as firemen, coal heavers, cooks, and stewards. But as early as August 1861 a group of contrabands served as a gun crew on the U.S.S. *Minnesota*. In May 1862 a South Carolina slave, Robert Smalls, commandeered a dispatch boat in Charleston harbor and ran it out to the blockading fleet. Smalls became a pilot for the U. S. navy.

Meanwhile black leaders, abolitionists, and radical Republicans continued to push for enlistment of black soldiers. This would not only help the North win the war, they said; it would also help free the slaves and earn equal rights for the whole race. Frederick Douglass made the point succinctly; if a black man fought for the Union there would be "no power on earth which can deny that he has earned the right to citizenship."

As a twenty-three-year-old slave in 1862, Robert Smalls took control of the Confederate dispatch boat Planter *in Charleston harbor and ran her out to the Union blockade fleet with seventeen escaping slaves on board, including Smalls's wife. This daring exploit won him fame and a distinguished political career as a black congressman representing a low-country district during Reconstruction, when this picture was taken.*

The Union navy did not keep accurate records of its sailors by race, so the estimates of the number of black sailors who served in the navy range from 10,000 to 20,000 thousand (out of a total of 115,000). More than two dozen of them are photographed aboard the U.S.S. Vermont *in 1863.*

Helping blacks to earn citizenship was not the main motive for a congressional mandate (in the militia act of July 17, 1862) to enroll Negroes in "any military or naval service for which they may be found competent." Rather, the need for labor battalions to free white soldiers for combat prompted this legislation. The Emancipation Proclamation envisaged a limited role for black soldiers "to garrison forts, positions, stations, and other places" instead of to fight as front-line troops. But reality had a way of surpassing policy. Just as Lincoln, nine days before issuing the preliminary Proclamation, had told a delegation that such an edict would be like the Pope's bull against the comet, so on August 4, three weeks before the War Department authorized enlistment of contrabands as soldiers in occupied South Carolina, he told a delegation that "to arm the negroes would turn 50,000 bayonets against us that were for us." But even as Lincoln uttered these words, a regiment of free Negroes was completing its organization in Louisiana and a regiment of free and contraband blacks was forming in Kansas. Two more Louisiana regiments along with the authorized South Carolina regiment quietly completed their organization during the fall. In October the Kansans saw action in a Missouri skirmish that left ten of them dead—the first black combat casualties of the war.

By the year's end the government was ready to acknowledge the existence of these regiments, a change in policy occasioned, in part, by the actions of Thomas Wentworth Higginson of Massachusetts, whose pen was at least as mighty as his sword. After taking part of his black regiment, the 1st South Carolina Volunteers, on a minor raid along a South Carolina river in January 1863, Higginson wrote an enthusiastic report to the War Department which, as intended, found its way into

the newspapers. "Nobody knows anything about these men who has not seen them in battle," wrote Higginson. "No officer in this regiment now doubts that the key to the successful prosecution of the war lies in the unlimited employment of black troops." The *New York Tribune* commented that such reports were sure "to shake our inveterate Saxon prejudice against the capacity and courage of negro troops." About the time of Higginson's raid, Governor Andrew of Massachusetts squeezed permission from the War Department to raise a black regiment. Commissioning prominent abolitionists as recruiters and officers, Andrew enlisted enough men from northern states for two regiments, the 54th and 55th Massachusetts, the first of which became the most famous black regiment of the war.

The recruitment of black soldiers did not produce an instantaneous change in northern racial attitudes. Indeed, to some degree it intensified the Democratic backlash against emancipation and exacerbated racial tensions in the army. The black regiments reflected the Jim Crow mores of the society that reluctantly accepted them: they were segregated, given less pay than white soldiers, commanded by white officers some of whom regarded their men as "niggers," and intended for use mainly as garrison and labor battalions. One of the first battles these black troops had to fight was for a chance to prove themselves in combat.

The southern response to emancipation and the enlistment of black troops was

On January 1, 1863, thousands of former slaves living on the South Carolina sea islands, now free by the Emancipation Proclamation, celebrate their first Emancipation Day. Sergeant Prince Rivers and Corporal Robert Sutton of the 1st South Carolina Volunteers present the colors while Sergeant Rivers addresses the crowd. Standing between them is the regiment's abolitionist colonel, Thomas Wentworth Higginson. Seated on the platform are white teachers and missionaries from the North.

The 54th and 55th Massachusetts Infantry were the most famous black regiments recruited in the North, but not the only ones. This photograph shows part of what was initially designated the 127th Ohio, which was renamed the 5th U.S. Colored Infantry. It saw a great deal of action in Virginia in 1864–65. The photograph was taken on the main street of Delaware, Ohio, in 1863, before the regiment departed for the front. Four members of the regiment won the Congressional Medal of Honor.

These officers of the 4th U.S. Colored Infantry pose for the camera in April 1865. The war was over, and these men were relaxed, even playful. They had seen hard fighting in 1864, losing 105 men killed in action in less than a year, including three white officers.

ferocious—at least in word and, regrettably, sometimes in deed as well. Jefferson Davis's message to Congress on January 12, 1863, pronounced the Emancipation Proclamation "the most execrable measure in the history of guilty man." Davis promised to turn over captured Union officers to state governments for punishment as "criminals engaged in inciting servile insurrection." The punishment for this crime, of course, was death.

Sober second thoughts prevented the enforcement of such a policy. But the South did sometimes execute captured black soldiers and their officers. Even before official adoption of black enlistment by the Union government, southerners got wind of the premature efforts along this line in occupied Louisiana and South Carolina. From Confederate army headquarters on August 21, 1862, came a general order that such "crimes and outrages" required "retaliation" in the form of "execution as a felon" of any officer of black troops who was captured. When a rebel commando raid seized four blacks in Union uniforms on a South Carolina island in November, Secretary of War James A. Seddon and President Davis approved their "summary execution" as an "example" to discourage the arming of slaves. A month later, on Christmas Eve, Davis issued a general order requiring all former slaves and their officers captured in arms to be delivered up to state officials for trial. On May 30, 1863, the Confederate Congress sanctioned this policy but stipulated that captured officers were to be

MASKS AND FACES.

King Abraham before and after issuing the EMANCIPATION PROCLAMATION.

This cartoon from the Southern Illustrated News *portrays Lincoln as showing his true face—the face of the devil—when he issued the Emancipation Proclamation. In the background is a gallows next to the Confederate flag— presumably to hang devil Lincoln if the Confederates could catch him.*

tried and punished by military courts rather than by the states.

Though the South did not actually do this, considerable evidence indicates that captured officers were sometimes "dealt with red-handed on the field or immediately thereafter," as Secretary of War Seddon suggested to General Kirby Smith in 1863. Black prisoners of war were sometimes shot "while attempting to escape." A Confederate colonel whose regiment captured a squad of black soldiers in Louisiana reported that when some of them tried to escape, "I then ordered every one shot, and with my Six Shooter I assisted in the execution of the order."

Rumors and reports of several such massacres vexed Union authorities through the rest of the war and forced them more than once to threaten retaliation. This was one reason for the hesitation to use black troops in combat, where they ran a heightened risk of capture. The Confederate refusal to treat captured black soldiers as legitimate prisoners of war contributed to the eventual breakdown in prisoner-of-war exchanges that had tragic consequences for both sides.

III

Northern diplomats were disappointed by the initial skeptical response of many Englishmen to the Emancipation Proclamation. But as the real import of the edict sank in, and as Lincoln made clear on January 1 that he really meant it, British antislavery sentiment mobilized for the Union. Mass meetings took place throughout the kingdom. Confederate sympathizers were forced to lie low for a time. The effect of "this development of sentiment," noted Charles Francis Adams happily, "is to annihilate all agitation for recognition." Young Henry Adams wrote to his brother Charles Francis, Jr., a cavalry captain in the Army of the Potomac: "If only you at home don't have disasters, we will give such a checkmate to the foreign hopes of the rebels as they never yet have had."

But the Union armies did have more disasters. The foreign hopes as well as domestic prospects of the rebels rose again during this northern winter of discontent.

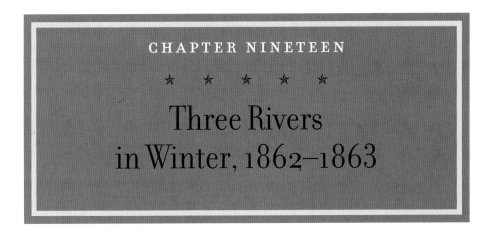

I

A lthough disappointed by McClellan's failure to thrash Lee at Antietam, Lincoln expected the Army of the Potomac to push after the rebels and fight them again while they were far from home. Lincoln visited the army in early October and urged McClellan to get moving before the Confederates could be reinforced and refitted. Upon returning to Washington, the president had Halleck send McClellan an order: "Cross the Potomac and give battle. . . . Your army must move now while the roads are good."

But McClellan as usual protested that he could not act until his supply wagons were full and his soldiers reorganized. Halleck threw up his hands in despair. He knew that the Army of Northern Virginia was in worse shape than the Army of the Potomac. "I am sick, tired, and disgusted" with McClellan's inactivity, wrote Halleck in October. Republicans shared Halleck's impatience. "What devil is it that prevents the Potomac Army from advancing?" asked the editor of the *Chicago Tribune* on October 13. "What malign influence palsies our army and wastes these glorious days for fighting? If it is McClellan, does not the President see that he is a traitor?"

Lincoln too was becoming exasperated with Little Mac and his endless chain of excuses. But instead of removing McClellan he decided to try some fatherly advice. "You remember my speaking to you of what I called your over-cautiousness," Lincoln wrote the general on October 13. "Are you not over-cautious when you assume that you can not do what the enemy is constantly doing?" If McClellan crossed the Potomac quickly and got between the enemy and Richmond he could force Lee into the open for a fight to the finish. "We should not so operate as to merely drive him away. If we can not beat the enemy where he now is [west of Harper's Ferry], we never can. . . . If we never try, we shall never succeed."

But this appeal failed to move McClellan. When little happened for another two weeks except telegrams citing broken-down horses, Lincoln lost patience: "Will you pardon me for asking what the horses of your army have done since the battle of Antietam that fatigues anything?" Such goading made McClellan waspish. "The good of the country," he wrote to his wife, "requires me to submit to all this from

Opposite page: A low point for the Union cause occurred in January 1863 near Fredericksburg, Virginia, when heavy winter rains bogged down the Army of the Potomac in the infamous "Mud March." This is a detail from a painting of Union soldiers slogging through the mud. (See page 506 for full painting.)

men whom I know to be my inferior! . . . There never was a truer epithet applied to a certain individual than that of the 'Gorilla.'" In truth, McClellan had again lost sight of reality. Considering himself the hero of Antietam, he believed he could dictate to the government. "I have insisted that Stanton shall be removed, & that Halleck shall give way to me as Comdr. in Chief," McClellan informed his wife. "The only safety for the country & for me is to get rid of the lot of them."

The Army of the Potomac finally began to cross its namesake river on October 26 but moved so slowly that Lee was able to interpose Longstreet's corps between Richmond and the bluecoats while Jackson remained in the Shenandoah Valley on McClellan's flank. For Lincoln this was the last straw; he was tired of trying to "bore with an auger too dull to take hold." On November 7 he replaced McClellan with Burnside. To his private secretary Lincoln explained that when McClellan kept "delaying on little pretexts of wanting this and that I began to fear that he was play-

This famous photograph of Lincoln and McClellan in McClellan's headquarters tent was taken on October 4, 1862, during Lincoln's visit to the Army of the Potomac near the Antietam battlefield. Note the captured Confederate battle flag at lower left. It was on this occasion that Lincoln urged McClellan to pursue the enemy with celerity and vigor. McClellan seemed not to understand the meaning of these words and did not move for another three weeks.

ing false—that he did not want to hurt the enemy." If he let Lee block an advance toward Richmond "I determined to . . . remove him. He did so & I relieved him."

McClellan's farewell to the army was emotional. A few officers muttered darkly about "changing front on Washington" and "throwing the infernal scoundrels into the Potomac." Nothing came of this, however, and nothing in McClellan's tenure of command became him like his leaving of it. "Stand by General Burnside as you have stood by me, and all will be well," he told the men as they yelled their affection for the leader who had created them as an army. Among those who most regretted McClellan's removal was Burnside himself. Although he was one of the few Union generals in the East with marked successes to his credit—along the coast of North Carolina—Burnside considered himself unqualified to command the Army of the Potomac. This conviction would all too soon be confirmed.

Burnside started well, however. Instead of continuing straight south, using the vulnerable railroad through Manassas as his supply line, he moved the ponderous army of 110,000 men with unwonted speed to Falmouth, across the Rappahannock from Fredericksburg. From there he hoped to cross the river and drive toward Richmond, with his supply line secured by naval control of the rivers flowing into the Chesapeake Bay. The drawback to this strategy was the number of rivers the army would have to cross, beginning with the Rappahannock. By moving quickly, though, Burnside had gotten two advance corps to Falmouth on November 17, before Lee could shift troops to block a crossing. But the pontoons Burnside needed

This woodcut illustration in Harper's Weekly *shows McClellan riding along the line of his assembled troops as he bids them farewell on November 10, 1862.*

to bridge the river did not show up for more than a week—a delay caused by Burnside's unfortunate knack for issuing unclear instructions and Halleck's misunderstanding of where and when Burnside intended to cross the river. As a result, Lee had most of his 75,000 men dug in along the hills south of the Rappahannock by the time the pontoons arrived.

Lee was willing to sit there all winter, but Burnside could not; he decided to move, reckoning that "the enemy will be more surprised by a crossing immediately in our front." Lee was surprised only by the folly of this move. He had Longstreet's corps posted along four miles of high ground overlooking Fredericksburg with a sweeping field of fire over the half-mile of open fields that attacking troops would have to cross. Hoping that the Federals would assault this position, Lee decided to offer just enough resistance to their river crossing to give Jackson's corps time to move upstream and connect with Longstreet to extend the Confederate line another three miles.

In the predawn darkness of December 11, Union engineers began laying three pontoon bridges at Fredericksburg and three more a couple of miles downstream. Covered by artillery, the downstream bridge-builders did their job without trouble. But in Fredericksburg a brigade of Mississippians firing from buildings and rifle-pits picked off the engineers as soon as it became light enough to see. Federal artillery shelled the buildings (most civilians had been evacuated), but the rebel snipers continued to fire from the rubble. Three blue regiments finally crossed in boats and drove them away in house-to-house fighting. After the rest of the army crossed, northern soldiers looted the town, smashing "rebel" furniture, pianos, glassware, and anything else they could find in the abandoned houses.

For many of the looters it was the last night of their lives. The battle of Fredericksburg on December 13 once again pitted great valor in the Union ranks and mismanagement by their commanders against stout fighting and effective generalship on the Confederate side. Burnside's tactics called for the left wing under

This woodcut from the Southern Illustrated News *shows pickets of General William Barksdale's Mississippi brigade waiting to open fire on Union combat engineers constructing a pontoon bridge across the Rappahannock River on December 11, 1862. Most of Barksdale's men were posted in houses and other buildings in Fredericksburg.*

General William B. Franklin to assault the Confederate right commanded by Jackson while the Union right probed Longstreet's defenses on Marye's Heights behind the town. If Franklin managed to roll up Jackson's flank, the Union probe on the right could be converted into a real attack. Whatever slim prospects this plan had were marred by Burnside's confusing written orders to Franklin and the latter's failure to push ahead with his 50,000 infantrymen when opportunity offered.

The fog lifted at midmorning on December 13 to reveal the panoply of Franklin's men advancing across the plain south of Lee's hilltop headquarters. These Federals soon assaulted Jackson's position on Prospect Hill. A division of Pennsylvanians commanded by George Gordon Meade found a seam in Jackson's line along a wooded ravine and penetrated the Confederate defenses. Here was a

Union soldiers apparently subscribed to the ancient military adage that an army that captures a defended city has the right to sack it. This illustration by Harper's Weekly *artist Alfred R. Waud telescopes the street fighting that cleared Barksdale's troops from the town with the looting of civilian property that began soon afterwards.*

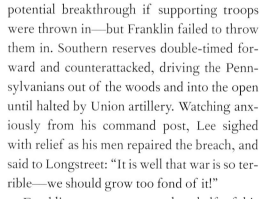

potential breakthrough if supporting troops were thrown in—but Franklin failed to throw them in. Southern reserves double-timed forward and counterattacked, driving the Pennsylvanians out of the woods and into the open until halted by Union artillery. Watching anxiously from his command post, Lee sighed with relief as his men repaired the breach, and said to Longstreet: "It is well that war is so terrible—we should grow too fond of it!"

Franklin never got more than half of his men into action and did not renew the attack despite orders from Burnside to do so. Meanwhile the initial probe by the Union right had turned into a series of brigade-size attacks as courageous and hopeless as anything in the

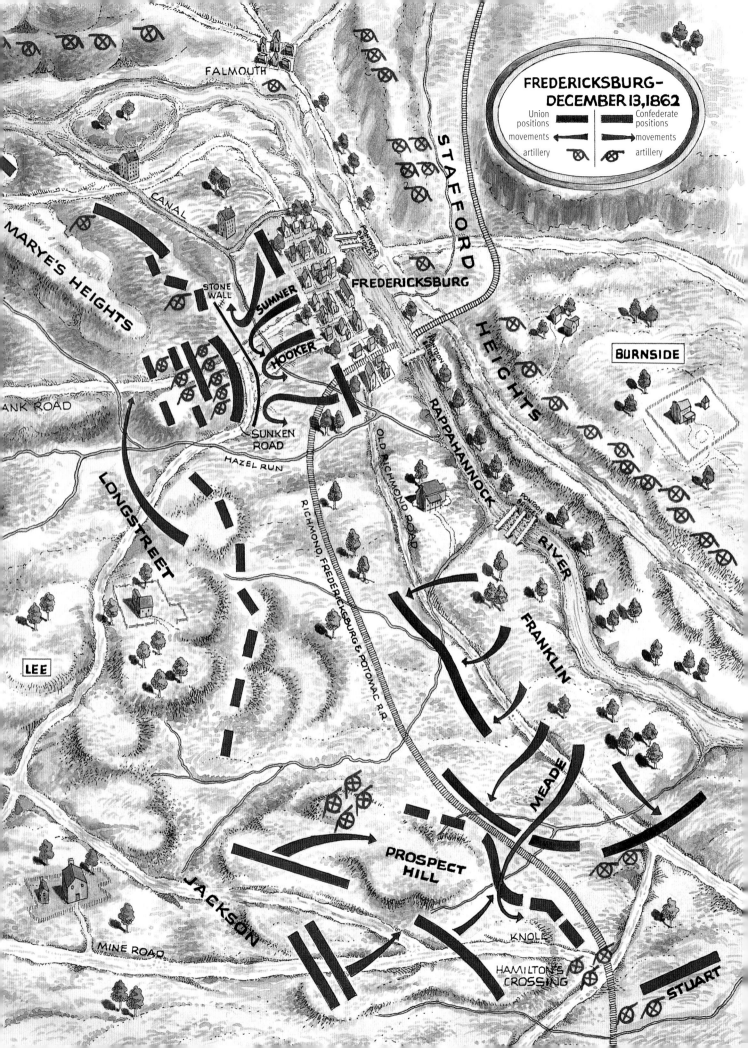

FALMOUTH

MARYE'S HEIGHTS

CANAL

STONE WALL

SUMNER

HOOKER

ANK ROAD

SUNKEN ROAD

HAZEL RUN

LONGSTREET

LEE

FREDERICKSBURG

STAFFORD HEIGHTS

RAPPAHANNOCK

OLD RICHMOND ROAD

RICHMOND, FREDERICKSBURG & POTOMAC R.R.

RIVER

FRANKLIN

MEADE

PROSPECT HILL

JACKSON

MINE ROAD

KNOLL

HAMILTON'S CROSSING

STUART

FREDERICKSBURG—DECEMBER 13, 1862

Union positions | Confederate positions
movements | movements
artillery | artillery

BURNSIDE

This postwar engraving by Confederate veteran C. Redwood shows the South Carolina soldiers of Brigadier General Joseph B. Kershaw's brigade defending the famous stone wall along the sunken road at Fredericksburg.

war. Wave after wave of blue soldiers poured out of the town toward Marye's Heights. Channeled by ravines, a marsh, and a drainage ditch toward a sunken road fronted by a stone fence almost a half-mile long at the base of the hill, these waves broke fifty yards short of the fence, each one leaving hundreds of dead and dying men as it receded. Behind the fence stood four ranks of Georgians and North Carolinians loading and shooting so fast that their firing achieved the effect of machine guns. Still the Yankees surged forward through the short but endless December afternoon, fourteen brigades in all. "It can hardly be in human nature for men to show more valor," wrote a newspaper reporter, "or generals to manifest less judgment."

When the early twilight finally turned to darkness the Union army had suffered one of its worst defeats of the war. Nearly 13,000 Federals were casualties—about the same number as at Antietam—most of them in front of the stone wall at the base of Marye's Heights. Fighting on the defensive behind good cover, the Confederates suffered fewer than 5,000 casualties. Distraught by the disaster, Burnside wanted personally to lead a desperation charge by his old 9th Corps next day but came to his senses and withdrew the army unmolested across the river on the stormy night of December 15.

Yet another drive "On to Richmond" had come to grief. Fredericksburg's carpet of bodies in front of the stone wall brought home the horrors of war to northerners more vividly, perhaps, than any previous battle. This terrible cost with nothing accomplished created a morale crisis in the army and on the homefront. Soldiers wrote home that "my loyalty is growing weak. . . . I am sick and tired of disaster and the fools that bring disaster upon us. . . . All think Virginia is not worth such a loss of life. . . . Why not confess we are worsted, and come to an agreement?" Burnside manfully took the blame, but Lincoln himself became the target for much of the criticism: "If there is a worse place than Hell," said the president upon learning of the disaster at Fredericksburg, "I am in it."

These were dark days in Washington. Among the many strange rumors sweeping the capital was that McClellan would be recalled to head a military government; another claimed that radical Republicans were plotting a coup to reorganize the cabinet. This latter rumor contained some truth. On December 16 and 17 Republican senators met in caucus and with but one dissenting vote decided to urge a reorganization of the cabinet. Seward was the intended victim of this move, which reflected the conflict between conservative and radical Republicans symbolized by a cabinet rivalry between Seward and Chase. Lincoln was "more distressed" by news of the senatorial caucus "than by any event of my life." "What do these men want?" he asked a friend. "They wish to get rid of me, and sometimes I am more than half disposed to gratify them. . . . We are now on the brink of destruction. It appears to me that the Almighty is against us." But the president pulled himself together and handled the affair in a manner that ultimately strengthened his leadership. On December 19 he met with a delegation of Republican senators and listened to speeches "attributing to Mr. Seward a lukewarmness in the conduct of the war," an impression Chase, with an eye to a future presidential nomination, had helped create. Seward had already offered to resign, but Lincoln did not reveal this. Instead he invited the delegation back next day, when they were surprised to find the whole cabinet (except Seward) on hand. Lincoln defended the absent secretary of state and asserted that all members of the cabinet had supported major policy decisions, for which he as president was solely responsible. Lincoln turned to the cabinet for confirmation. Put on the spot, Chase could only mumble assent. Deflated and embarrassed, the senators departed. Next day a chagrined Chase offered his resignation. Lincoln was now master of the situation. The senators could not get rid of Seward without losing Chase as well. The president refused both resignations. The stormy political atmosphere in Washington began to clear. Though military prospects remained bleak, Lincoln had warded off a threat to his political right flank—for the time being.

II

Jefferson Davis also encountered vexing problems during the winter of 1862–63. In November, Joseph E. Johnston had reported himself ready for duty after recovering from his Seven Pines wounds. Because of his earlier differences with Davis, Johnston had become a rallying point for some of the president's critics. Perhaps to confound these critics, Davis on November 24 named Johnston "plenary commander" of a newly formed Department of the West embracing everything between the Mississippi and the Appalachians. Although this new department appeared impressive on paper, Johnston glumly appraised the appointment as an attempt to put him on the shelf with a "nominal and useless" command. This was unfair, because Davis really did want someone to take charge of the strategic problem in the West. Johnston regarded the task as thankless, in part because the Army of Tennessee at Murfreesboro was still riven by dissension between Bragg and his corps commanders, while the new head of the Army of Mississippi at Vicksburg, John C. Pemberton, was unpopular because he was an adoptive southerner, a Philadelphian who had married a Virginian. This curt and

Promoted to lieutenant general in October 1862 and given command of the defenses of Vicksburg, John C. Pemberton had the hard luck to preside over the largest surrender of Confederate troops in the war eight months later. After his exchange he resigned his generalship and accepted an appointment as lieutenant colonel of artillery, four grades below his previous rank.

Like Lincoln, John A. McClernand was born in the Kentucky backwoods and became a lawyer and politician in Illinois. Unlike Lincoln he was a Democrat before the war, but Lincoln appointed him as a brigadier general in May 1861 to help hold his southern Illinois constituency for the Union. McClernand considered himself a better commander than Ulysses S. Grant, whom he hoped to supplant. Grant soon set him straight.

crusty artillery expert had compiled no combat record that justified to Mississippians the assignment of a "Yankee" to defend their state. Indeed, it is hard to understand why Davis appointed Pemberton (instead, for example, of sending Johnston to Vicksburg) except as a way of making room for another problem general, Beauregard. The colorful Creole took Pemberton's place at the defenses of Charleston, where he had become a hero by firing on Fort Sumter and starting the war.

This kettle of catfish in the West prompted Davis to rise from a sickbed to make a December journey to the afflicted theaters. Instead of straightening matters out, however, this trip in some respects made them worse. Without consulting Johnston, Davis ordered a 7,500-man division in Bragg's army transferred to Pemberton. When Bragg and Johnston protested that this would encourage Rosecrans's army at Nashville to attack the weakened Army of Tennessee, Davis responded that Pemberton faced even longer odds and that holding Vicksburg was more vital than defending middle Tennessee. Accompanying Davis to Vicksburg, Johnston disapproved of Pemberton's defensive arrangements and urged a shorter fortified line that could be held by a skeleton force to free most of the army for mobile operations. Johnston also believed that the main Confederate army in Mississippi was too small for success and urged its reinforcement from across the river even if this meant the temporary loss of Arkansas. Though Davis suggested that the Arkansas commander send troops to Vicksburg, he did not *order* it—and it was not done. Johnston tried to resign his nugatory post. The president persuaded him to stay on, but their lack of mutual confidence and their differing concepts of strategy boded ill for the future.

After the battle of Corinth in October, Grant had launched an invasion southward along the Mississippi Central Railroad to capture Vicksburg. Establishing a forward base at Holly Springs, Grant with 40,000 men had advanced to Oxford by early December. But one enemy in front and two in the rear threatened his further progress. In front, Pemberton entrenched 20,000 men along the Yalabusha River at Grenada. Behind Grant, 150 miles of railroad offered a tempting target to enemy cavalry. Deep in his rear—all the way back to Illinois, in fact—Grant faced a potential threat from his former subordinate John A. McClernand, a political general who was organizing a separate army to proceed down the Mississippi for its own attack on Vicksburg. A War Democrat from Lincoln's home state, McClernand had managed to convince the president that he could rekindle the patriotism of Democrats in the Old Northwest if given an independent command. Without informing Grant,

UNION EFFORTS TO GET AT VICKSBURG
WINTER 1862-63

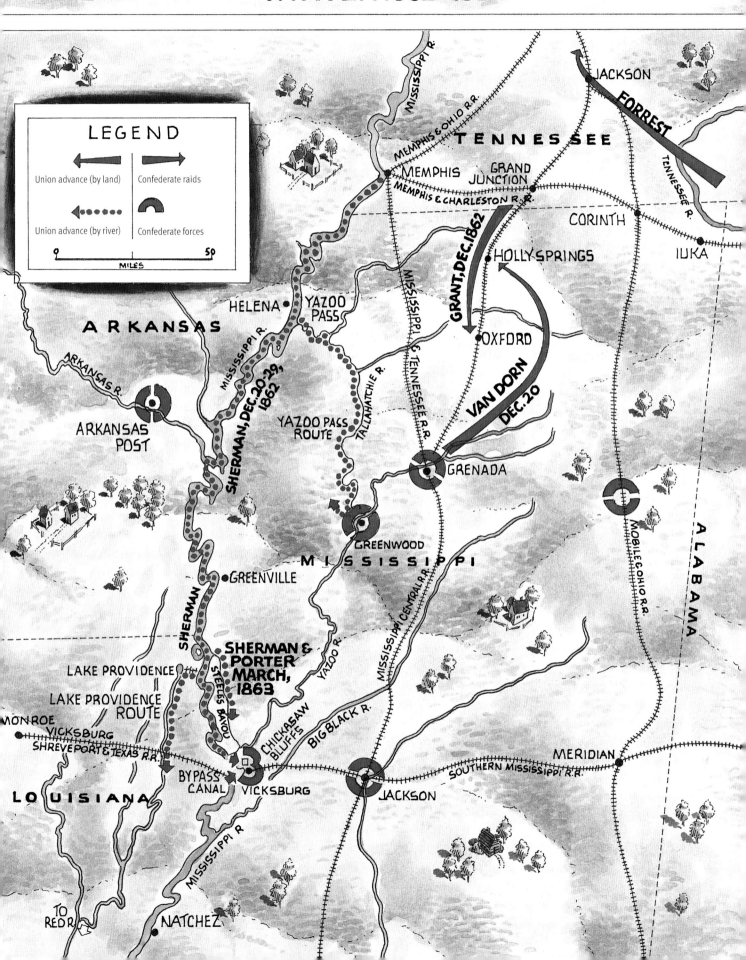

LEGEND

Union advance (by land)

Confederate raids

Union advance (by river)

Confederate forces

0   MILES   50

JACKSON

FORREST

TENNESSEE

MEMPHIS & OHIO R.R.

MISSISSIPPI R.

MEMPHIS

GRAND JUNCTION

TENNESSEE R.

MEMPHIS & CHARLESTON R.R.

CORINTH

IUKA

GRANT, DEC. 1862

HOLLY SPRINGS

ARKANSAS

HELENA

YAZOO PASS

MISSISSIPPI R.

MISSISSIPPI & TENNESSEE R.R.

OXFORD

VAN DORN DEC. 20

ARKANSAS R.

ARKANSAS POST

SHERMAN, DEC. 20-29, 1862

YAZOO PASS ROUTE

TALLAHATCHIE R.

GRENADA

ALABAMA

MOBILE & OHIO R.R.

GREENWOOD

MISSISSIPPI

GREENVILLE

SHERMAN

SHERMAN & PORTER MARCH, 1863

YAZOO R.

MISSISSIPPI CENTRAL R.R.

LAKE PROVIDENCE

STEELE'S BAYOU

LAKE PROVIDENCE ROUTE

MONROE

VICKSBURG

CHICKASAW BLUFFS

BIG BLACK R.

SHREVEPORT & TEXAS R.R.

MERIDIAN

BYPASS CANAL

VICKSBURG

JACKSON

SOUTHERN MISSISSIPPI R.R.

LOUISIANA

MISSISSIPPI R.

TO RED R.

NATCHEZ

This etching by pro-Confederate artist Adalbert Volck of Baltimore suggests that Confederate guerrillas were motivated by a desire for revenge against Union soldiers who destroyed their homes. A man with a rifle stands alongside his wife and child in front of their burned farm, about to join a band of guerrillas under a flag with the slogan "No More Surrenders." In actual fact, most Confederate guerrillas were more proactive than reactive, and they had homes to return to as "innocent civilians" after a raid.

Lincoln told McClernand to go ahead. With great energy fueled by dreams of military glory, McClernand recruited and forwarded to Memphis dozens of new regiments during the fall. Grant got wind of this activity and requested clarification of his authority. General-in-Chief Halleck, who shared Grant's reservations about McClernand, wired Grant that he had full control of all troops in his department. Halleck also ordered the divisions organized by McClernand formed into two corps to be commanded by McClernand and Sherman. When McClernand learned of this, he protested bitterly to Lincoln that a West Point conspiracy had defrauded him of his army. Lincoln upheld Grant and Halleck, however, and advised McClernand for his own good and the good of the country to obey orders and get on with the war.

McClernand's greatest humiliation occurred when he arrived at Memphis on December 28 to find his troops gone. Grant had again outwitted the political general in the game of army politics, with an unwitting assist from none other than Nathan Bedford Forrest. When Grant learned of the new troops arriving at Memphis he sent Sherman to prepare them for a downriver expedition against Vicksburg in tandem with Grant's overland invasion. This two-pronged drive, if successful, would force Pemberton to divide his outnumbered forces and enable the Federal pincers to close on Vicksburg by land and by river. If McClernand reached Memphis before the river expedition left, he would take command by reason of seniority. Sherman therefore sped his preparations and got off on December 20. Meanwhile Grant's telegram to Illinois informing McClernand of the expedition's imminent departure was delayed because Forrest, in one of two cavalry raids on Grant's supply lines, had cut his communications.

Grant had little reason to feel thankful to Forrest, however, because this action and another simultaneous cavalry raid by Van Dorn brought Grant's first Vicksburg campaign to grief. Forrest rode westward from central Tennessee in mid-December with 2,000 men. Picking up local guerrillas along the way, Forrest outfought, outmaneuvered, or outbluffed several Union garrisons and cavalry detachments while tearing up fifty miles of railroad and telegraph line, capturing or destroying great quantities of equipment, and inflicting 2,000 Union casualties. The rebels lost only 500 men, who were more than replaced with new recruits attracted by Forrest's hell-for-leather tactics and inspiring leadership. While this was going on, Earl Van Dorn with another cavalry force of 3,500 rode northward from Grenada, circled behind Grant's army, and wrecked the poorly defended supply depot at Holly Springs on December 20. For good measure Van Dorn tore up several sections of the railroad and returned to Confederate lines before Union horsemen could catch up with him.

Dangling deep in enemy territory without a supply line, Grant called off his

advance on Vicksburg. During the retreat to Tennessee the army lived off food and forage seized along the way. Grant learned a lesson, one that he and Sherman would apply with spectacular results in the future, but just now Grant's retreat left Sherman out on a limb. The latter had taken his (and McClernand's) corps up the Yazoo River a few miles north of Vicksburg for an assault on the Confederate defenses overlooking Chickasaw Bayou. This morass of swamps and waterways offered the only route to high and dry ground for an attack on the northside land defenses of Vicksburg itself. Sherman's plans were based on the assumption that Grant's simultaneous advance would occupy most of Pemberton's troops. The downed telegraph lines prevented Grant from informing Sherman of his withdrawal. On December 29 Sherman managed to get two-thirds of his 32,000 men across the narrow causeways and through the sloughs for an assault on the bluffs. The 14,000 dug-in defenders knocked them down like tenpins. After losing nearly 1,800 men (to the Confederates' 200), Sherman called it quits. The battered and waterlogged bluecoats pulled back to the Mississippi a dozen miles above Vicksburg. News of this repulse added to the gloomy mood in the North.

But tidings soon arrived from Tennessee that relieved some of Lincoln's distress. Since taking over the Union Army of the Cumberland in late October, William S. Rosecrans had built up supplies and reorganized his troops for an advance. Rosecrans was a study in paradox: a man of bulldog courage, he seemed reluctant to get into a fight; slow and methodical in preparation, he moved quickly once he started; a convivial drinking man, he was a devout Catholic who loved to

This wartime sketch of Chickasaw Bayou and the bluffs above it provides a good view of what the Union attackers were up against. After crossing the marshy lowlands and the bayou, they had to advance up the steep bluffs defended by well-fortified Confederate artillery and infantry. It was no contest.

This panel from a huge panoramic painting of the battle of Stones River by the artist William Travis shows Union soldiers in the foreground cheering Rosecrans (at the far right) as he rides up to inspect this part of his line.

argue theology with his staff officers. Rosecrans had gotten his job because Buell was too cautious; Lincoln prodded Old Rosy to march against the rebels at Murfreesboro forthwith if he wanted to keep the job. After exasperating delays, Rosecrans's 42,000 men finally moved out from Nashville the day after Christmas for the showdown with Bragg's Army of Tennessee.

Bragg had 8,000 fewer infantrymen than Rosecrans. But the rebel cavalry evened the odds. Forrest and Morgan raided deep behind Union lines while Bragg's remaining cavalry under twenty-six-year-old Joseph Wheeler slowed the northern infantry with hit-and-run skirmishes. On December 29, Wheeler took off on a ride completely around the enemy rear where he wreaked havoc on supply wagons and captured part of Rosecrans's reserve ammunition. But the Yankees came on relentlessly. On December 30 they moved into line two miles northwest of Murfreesboro to confront Bragg's divisions drawn up astride Stones River. Both commanders formed similar plans for the morrow: to turn the enemy's right, get into his rear, and cut him off from his base. As the two armies bedded down a few hundred yards from each other, their bands commenced a musical battle as prelude to the real thing next day. Northern musicians blared out "Yankee Doodle" and "Hail Columbia," and were answered across the way by "Dixie" and "The Bonnie Blue Flag." One band finally swung into the sentimental strains of "Home Sweet Home"; others picked it up, and soon thousands of Yanks and Rebs who tomorrow would kill each other were singing the familiar words together.

At dawn on December 31 the southerners struck first, catching the bluecoats at breakfast as they had done twice before, at Donelson and Shiloh. This time their initial success was even greater, as 13,000 rebels massed on the left "swooped down on those Yankees like a whirl-a-gust of woodpeckers in a hail storm," in the words of a Tennessee private. In several hours of ferocious fighting the graybacks drove back the Union flank three miles but were stopped short of the railroad and turnpike in

STONES RIVER (MURFREESBORO)
DEC. 31, 1862 – JAN. 2, 1863

LEGEND

Union lines, Dec. 31, A.M.

Union lines, Dec. 31, P.M.

Union lines, Jan. 2

Union artillery, Jan. 2

Confederate lines, Dec. 31, A.M.

Confederate attack, Dec. 31, A.M.

Confederate lines, Dec. 31, P.M.

Confederate attack, Jan. 2

0   MILE   ½

ROSECRANS

FORD

FORD

FORD

FORD

THOMAS

NASHVILLE TURNPIKE

ROUND FOREST

THOMAS

STONES RIVER

BRECKINRIDGE

SHERIDAN

NASHVILLE & CHATTANOOGA R.R.

NASHVILLE TURNPIKE

BRAGG

MURFREESBORO

FRANKLIN ROAD

The lithograph by A. E. Mathews, a Union soldier who fought at Stones River, shows the attack by Breckinridge's division (in the distance at the right) against the Union position defending the Nashville Pike and the railroad. Breckinridge never forgave Bragg for ordering this suicidal attack. In the photograph (opposite page) we can almost see Breckinridge's handlebar mustache twitching in anger.

the Union rear. Rosecrans canceled his attack on the Confederate right and rushed reinforcements to shore up his own crumpled right. Old Rosy was at his bulldog best in this crisis, riding from one part of the line to another, his uniform spattered with blood from a staff officer beheaded by a cannonball while riding alongside Rosecrans.

The Union army was saved from disaster during the morning by the fierce resistance of Philip Sheridan's division in the right center. Anticipating Bragg's tactics, Sheridan had his division awake and under arms by 4:00 A.M.; when the rebels swept down on them after wrecking two other Union divisions, Sheridan's men were ready. They shredded and slowed the rebel attack at heavy cost to themselves as well as to the enemy: all three of Sheridan's brigade commanders were killed and more than one-third of his men became casualties in four hours of fighting. By noon the Union line had been forced into the shape of a bent jackknife. The hinge was located in a patch of woods along the railroad and turnpike known locally as the Round Forest. Believing this position the key to the Union defense, Bragg ordered the division commanded by John C. Breckinridge—Buchanan's vice president and the southern Democratic presidential candidate in 1860—to go forward in a do-or-die attack on the Round Forest. They went, many died, but the Yankees held firm amid firing so deafening that many soldiers stuffed their ears with cotton plucked from the fields.

The darkness of New Year's Eve descended on a scene filled not with the sound of music but with the cries of wounded men calling for help. Bragg believed that he had won a great victory and wired the good news to Richmond, where it produced "great exultation." Bragg's dispatch added that the enemy "is falling back." But this was wishful thinking. During the night Rosecrans held a council of war with his commanders and decided to hold tight. Skirmishes on New Year's Day took a few more lives, but the main action on January 1 was the occupation of a hill east of

Stones River by a Union division. On January 2 Bragg ordered Breckinridge to clear this force off the hill. The Kentuckian protested that such an attack would fail with great loss because Union artillery on high ground across the river would enfilade his line. Bragg insisted; Breckinridge's men swept forward with a yell and routed the bluecoats but then were indeed cut down by fifty-eight Union guns across the river and driven back to their starting point by an infantry counterattack, having lost 1,500 men in an hour. This affair added to the growing tension between Bragg and his generals.

Nonplussed by Rosecrans's refusal to retreat, Bragg seemed not to know what to do. But in truth there was little he could do, for more than a third of his troops had been killed, wounded, or captured. The Yankees had suffered 31 percent casualties, making Stones River the most deadly battle of the war in proportion to numbers engaged. When Bragg awoke on January 3 to find the enemy still in place and receiving reinforcements from Nashville, he knew the game was up. That night the rebels pulled back to a new position behind the Duck River, twenty-five miles to the south. For the second time in three months, the Army of Tennessee had retreated after its commander claimed to have won a victory.

The outcome at Stones River brought a thin gleam of cheer to the North. It blunted, temporarily, the mounting copperhead offensive against the administration's war policy. "God bless you, and all with you," Lincoln wired Rosecrans. "I can never forget, whilst I remember anything," the president wrote later, that "you gave us a hard earned victory which, had there been a defeat instead, the nation could hardly have lived over." The Army of the Cumberland was so crippled by this "victory," however, that Rosecrans felt unable to renew the offensive for several months.

*   *   *   *   *

While Washington breathed a sigh of relief after Stones River, dissension came to a head in the Army of Tennessee. All of Bragg's corps and division commanders vociferously expressed a lack of confidence in their chief. The poisoned relations between Bragg and his generals threatened to do more damage to the army than the Yankees had done. Disheartened, Bragg told a friend that it might "be better for the President to send someone to relieve me," and he wrote Davis to the same effect.

Asked by Davis to recommend a solution to this crippling problem, Johnston reported that many officers were hostile to Bragg but the enlisted men were in good condition with high morale, a dubious discovery. Davis had apparently wanted and expected Johnston to take command himself—but Johnston, who told friends he wanted to return to his old post as head of the Army of Northern Virginia, advised that Bragg retain his command! If the government desired to replace Bragg, he said, let them send Longstreet to Tennessee. And if they thought that Johnston's supervisory role over the whole Western Department was so important, let them put Lee in

This painting by Giovanni Ponticelli captures the depressed spirits of Union soldiers as they trudge through the drenched countryside returning to their camps after the aborted "Mud March."

charge of it. In March the War Department virtually ordered Johnston to take command of the Army of Tennessee. But he demurred on the grounds that to remove Bragg while his wife was critically ill would be inhumane. Johnston himself then fell ill. So Bragg stayed on and continued to feud with his leading subordinates.

Lincoln handled similar disaffection in the Army of the Potomac with more deftness and firmness than Davis had shown. Demoralization reached epidemic proportions in this army after Fredericksburg. Four generals in the 6th Corps headed by William B. Franklin went directly to Lincoln with complaints about Burnside's leadership. McClellan's friends were declaring that "we *must* have McClellan back with unlimited and unfettered powers." Joe Hooker was intriguing to obtain the command for himself. Hooker also told a reporter that what the country needed was a dictator. Men in the ranks were deserting at the rate of a hundred or more every day during January. Thousands of others went on the sick list because slack discipline in regimental camps and corruption in the commissary had produced sanitary and dietary deficiencies. Recognizing that he had lost the army's confidence, Burnside offered to resign—suggesting to Lincoln at the same time that he fire Stanton, Halleck, and several disgruntled generals.

Discord in the Army of the Potomac climaxed with the inglorious "Mud March." Unusually dry January weather encouraged Burnside to plan a crossing of the Rappahannock at fords several miles above Fredericksburg. Success would put the Federals on Lee's flank and force the rebels out of their trenches for a fair fight. Some of Burnside's subordinates openly criticized the move. Franklin "has talked so much and so loudly to this effect," wrote an artillery colonel, "that he has completely demoralized his whole command." Even God seemed to be against Burnside. As soon as the general got his army in motion on January 20 the heavens opened, rain fell in torrents, and the Virginia roads turned into swamps. Artillery carriages sank to their axles, men sank to their knees, mules sank to their ears. Confederate pickets across the river watched this with amusement and held up signs pointing "This Way to Richmond." With his army bogged down in the mud, Burnside on January 22 called the whole thing off.

The mortified and furious commander hastened to Washington and told the president that either Hooker, Franklin, and a half-dozen other generals must go, or he would. Lincoln decided to remove Burnside—probably to the latter's relief. The president also transferred a few other malcontents to distant posts. But Lincoln astonished Burnside by appointing

Hooker as his successor. Fighting Joe was hardly an exemplary character. Not only had he schemed against Burnside, but his moral reputation stood none too high. Hooker's headquarters, wrote Charles Francis Adams, Jr., archly, was "a place which no self-respecting man liked to go, and no decent woman could go. It was a combination of barroom and brothel."

But Hooker proved a popular choice with the men. He took immediate steps to cashier corrupt quartermasters, improve the food, clean up the camps and hospitals, grant furloughs, and instill unit pride by creating insignia badges for each corps. Hooker reorganized the cavalry into a separate corps, a much-needed reform based on the Confederate model. Morale rose in all branches of the army. Sickness declined, desertions dropped, and a grant of amnesty brought many AWOLs back to the ranks. "Under Hooker, we began to *live*," wrote a soldier.

When Lincoln appointed Hooker he handed him a letter which the general later described as the kind of missive that a wise father might write to his son. Hooker should know, wrote the president, "that there are some things in regard to which, I am not quite satisfied with you." In running down Burnside "you have taken counsel of your ambition . . . in which you did a great wrong to the country, and to a most meritorious and honorable brother officer. I have heard, in such way as to believe it, of your recently saying that both the Army and the Government needed a Dictator. Of course it was not *for* this, but in spite of it, that I have given you the command. Only those generals who gain successes, can set up dictators. What I now ask of you is military successes, and I will risk the dictatorship." Two months after appointing Hooker, Lincoln visited the Army of the Potomac on the Rappahannock. The presi-

This photograph of a martial-looking Joe Hooker in dress uniform astride his war horse offers a sharp contrast to the satirical cartoon in the Southern Illustrated News *(below) showing a clown-like (and beardless!) Lincoln, with his Emancipation Proclamation behind him on the wall, manipulating his latest puppet commanding general while discarded puppets lie on the shelf.*

dent was pleased by what he saw, and agreed with Hooker's proud description of it as "the finest army on the planet." Lincoln was less enthusiastic about the general's cockiness. The question, said Hooker, was not *whether* he would take Richmond, but *when*. "The hen is the wisest of all the animal creation," Lincoln remarked pointedly, "because she never cackles until the egg is laid."

III

While the armies in Virginia sat out the rest of the winter and the armies in Tennessee licked their wounds after Stones River, plenty of action but little fighting took place around Vicksburg. After the failure of his first campaign to capture this river citadel, Grant went down the Mississippi to Milliken's Bend to take personal command of a renewed army-navy campaign. Although Union forces controlled the endless rivers and swamps north and west of Vicksburg, continual rains during the winter made army movements almost impossible, and many of Grant's 45,000 men were felled by lethal diseases. High and dry ground east of the city offered the only suitable terrain for military operations. Grant's problem was to get his army to this terrain with enough artillery and supplies for a campaign. Since he had the assistance of the gunboat fleet commanded by David Dixon Porter, Grant hoped to use the high water as an asset. During the winter he launched four separate efforts to flank Vicksburg by water and transport his army to the east bank above or below the city.

The first project was completion of the cutoff canal that would create a new channel out of range of Vicksburg's guns. But even if the effort had succeeded, the rebels could have planted new batteries to dominate the mouth of the canal four miles downstream. After rising waters in February threatened Sherman's men with drowning, Grant pinned his hopes on a second enterprise known as the Lake Providence route. This project became the task of soldiers in the corps of General James B. McPherson, formerly Grant's chief engineer and now next to Sherman his favorite combat officer. This route followed a meandering course from an oxbow lake fifty miles above Vicksburg through Louisiana swamps and bayous to the Mississippi again four hundred river-miles below. But after heroic efforts by soldiers to clear a channel for gunboats and transports, this undertaking was called off because it looked as if it would go on until doomsday.

More promising—or so it appeared at first—were two water routes through the jungle-like Yazoo Delta north of Vicksburg. If gunboats and transports could ferry the army through this maze for a dry-ground landing north of the fortified bluffs, Grant's troops could go to work as soldiers instead of ditch-diggers. Several gunboats and part of McClernand's corps went to Helena, four hundred river-miles above Vicksburg, and blew up a levee to float the gunboats into the flooded Delta rivers. But the fleet soon ran into trouble. Overhanging cypress and cottonwood branches smashed smokestacks, lifeboats, and everything else above deck. Rushing logs carried by the flood crashed into the boats while they maneuvered through channels scarcely wider than their beams. Confederates felled trees across the rivers in front of them. The naval commander in charge of the expedi-

tion began to show signs of a nervous breakdown. When his boats came under fire from a hastily built Confederate fort near Greenwood, Mississippi, he collapsed—and so did the expedition.

Meanwhile another flotilla commanded by Porter himself and carrying a division of Sherman's troops was working its way through a two-hundred-mile tangle of bayous and tributaries just north of Vicksburg. These boats were also immobilized by the jungle's tentacles. Porter's gunboats were in a bad spot by March 20, with Confederate infantry converging on them hopeful of capturing the whole lot. Porter swallowed his naval pride and called on the army for help. He sent a contraband with a note to Sherman a few miles back with the transports:

Dear Sherman,
Hurry up, for Heaven's sake. I never knew how helpless an ironclad could be steaming around through the woods without an army to back her.

Sherman disembarked his men to march through waist-deep swamps and drive off the rebels. Porter's paddle-wheeled monsters backed ignominiously up the choked channels, and another effort to flank Vicksburg came to an end.

For two months Grant's army had been floundering in the mud and suffering

In an effort to get his gunboats and transports south of Vicksburg for a landing on the eastern bank of the Mississippi, Grant put Sherman's soldiers to work on the bypass canal started and abandoned the previous summer. This woodcut in Frank Leslie's Illustrated Newspaper *shows the head of the canal. The river refused to cooperate with this effort to direct it into a new channel.*

many deaths from various diseases. Vicksburg stood defiant as ever. Republicans and Democrats joined in assailing Grant as an incompetent failure—and a drunkard to boot. Although many of their complaints came to Lincoln, he refused to throw Grant to the wolves. "I think Grant has hardly a friend left, except myself," said the president. But "what I want . . . is generals who will fight battles and win victories. Grant has done this, and I propose to stand by him."

This photograph of Vicksburg taken from a vantage point on the Mississippi shows why a frontal attack from the river would have been suicidal. Artillery firing down the streets from the high ground and infantry fighting from building to building would have decimated the attackers. The courthouse is at the top of the bluff in the center.

Complaints about Grant's drinking persisted. According to one story, Lincoln deflected such charges with humor, telling a delegation of congressmen that he would like to know Grant's brand of whiskey so he could send some to his other generals. It is hard to separate fact from fiction in this matter. Many wartime stories of Grant's drunkenness are false; others are at best dubious. Grant's meteoric rise to fame provoked jealousy in the hearts of men who indulged in gossip to denigrate him. Subject to sick headaches brought on by strain and loss of sleep, Grant sometimes acted unwell in a manner to give observers the impression that he had been drinking. But even when the myths have been stripped away, a hard substratum of truth about Grant's drinking remains. He may have been an alcoholic in the medical meaning of that term. He was a binge drinker. For months he could go without liquor, but if he once imbibed it was hard for him to stop. His wife and his chief of staff John A. Rawlins were his best protectors. With their help, Grant stayed on the wagon nearly all the time during the war. If he did get drunk (and this is much disputed by historians) it never happened at a time crucial to military operations. His struggle for self-discipline enabled him to understand and discipline others; the humiliation of prewar failures gave him a quiet humility that was conspicuously absent from so many generals with a reputation to protect; because Grant had nowhere to go but up, he could act with more boldness and decision than commanders who dared not risk failure.

Despite Lincoln's continuing faith in Grant, in March 1863 he permitted Secretary of War Stanton to send Charles A. Dana, former managing editor of the *New York Tribune* and now an assistant secretary of war, to the Mississippi, ostensibly to straighten out the paymaster service in western armies. But Grant was aware of his real mission. Instead of giving Dana the cold shoulder—as some of his staff advised—Grant welcomed him. It was a wise action. Dana sized up the general favorably and began sending a stream of commendatory dispatches to Washington. Grant was "the most modest, the most disinterested and the most honest man I ever knew, with a temper that nothing could disturb," wrote Dana later in summary of his impressions at the time. "Not a great man except morally; not an original or brilliant man, but sincere, thoughtful, deep and gifted with courage that never faltered."

Grant rarely wore his full dress uniform, but allowed himself to do so when he sat for the photographer. But even this formal pose could not disguise the calm, unceremonious, determined quality of his personality and leadership.

Men in the ranks shared Dana's opinion. They appreciated Grant's lack of "superfluous flummery," his tendency to wear a plain uniform "without scarf, sword, or trappings of any sort save the double-starred shoulder straps." A private reported that the men "seem to look upon him as a friendly partner of theirs, not as an arbitrary commander." Instead of cheering him when he rode by, they were likely to "greet him as they would address one of their neighbors at home. 'Good morning, General,' 'Pleasant day, General,' and like expressions are the greetings he meets everywhere. . . . There was no nonsense, no sentiment; only a plain business man of the republic, there for the one single purpose of getting that command over the river in the shortest time possible."

Get them over the river Grant would soon do, with spectacular results. But at the end of March 1863 the northern public could see only the failures of the past four months—on the Mississippi as well as in Virginia. Captain Oliver Wendell Holmes, Jr., recovering from his Antietam wound, wrote dispiritedly that "the army is tired with its hard and terrible experience. . . . I've pretty much made up my mind that the South have achieved their independence." The staunchly loyal Joseph Medill, editor of the *Chicago Tribune*, believed that "an armistice is bound to come during the year '63. The rebs can't be conquered by the present machinery." Into this crisis of confidence slithered the copperheads with their program for peace without victory.

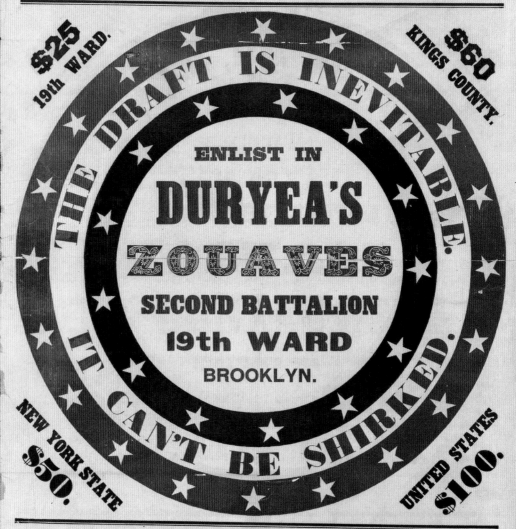

CHAPTER TWENTY

★ ★ ★ ★ ★

Fire in
the Rear

I

Despite his preoccupation with military matters, Lincoln told Charles Sumner in January 1863 that he feared "'the fire in the rear'—meaning the Democracy, especially at the Northwest—more than our military chances." The president had ample grounds for concern. The peace faction of the Democratic party grew stronger with each setback of Union armies. And the enactment of a conscription law in March 1863 gave the antiwar movement additional stimulus.

By 1863 Clement L. Vallandigham had emerged as leader of the Peace Democrats. Only forty-two years old, the handsome Ohio congressman had cut his political eyeteeth on the Jeffersonian philosophy of limited government. "It is the desire of my heart," he declared soon after the outbreak of war, "to restore the Union, the Federal Union as it was forty years ago." To this desire Vallandigham added sympathy for the South produced by descent from a Virginia family and marriage to the daughter of a Maryland planter. Although Ohio Republicans had gerrymandered him into defeat in the 1862 election, Vallandigham went out with a bang rather than a whimper. In a farewell speech to the House on January 14, 1863, and a subsequent tour from New Jersey to Ohio, he set forth his indictment of the war and his proposals for peace.

Vallandigham professed himself a better unionist than the Republicans whose fanaticism had provoked this ruinous war. These same Republicans, he continued, were now fighting not for Union but for abolition. And what had they accomplished? "Let the dead at Fredericksburg and Vicksburg answer." He proposed an armistice and brushed aside the objection that it would preserve slavery. "I see more of barbarism and sin, a thousand times, in the continuance of this war . . . and the enslavement of the white race by debt and taxes and arbitrary power" than in Negro slavery. "In considering terms of settlement we [should] look only to the welfare, peace, and safety of the white race, without reference to the effect that settlement may have on the African."

This became the platform of Peace Democrats for the next two years. During the

Opposite page: By 1863 few volunteers for the Union army were joining up from patriotic motives. So communities, states, and the federal government began offering cash bounties as incentives for enlistment. Those who waited to be drafted would get no bounties.

Clement L. Vallandigham's good looks belied his reputation among Republicans as a Mephistopheles bent on sabotaging the Union by concluding peace with the Confederacy.

early months of 1863 this faction commanded the support of a large minority of the party—perhaps even a majority. A mass meeting of New York Democrats resolved that the war "against the South is illegal, being unconstitutional, and should not be sustained." And while Governor Horatio Seymour of New York promised "to make every sacrifice . . . for the preservation of this Union," he also denounced emancipation as "bloody, barbarous, revolutionary" and pledged to "maintain and defend the sovereignty" of New York against unconstitutional violations by the federal government.

In Butternut regions of the Midwest, economic grievances reinforced the cultural attitudes of people descended from southern settlers. The war had cut off their normal trade routes along the Mississippi and its tributaries, forcing them into dependence on Yankee railroads and canals feeding an east-west pattern of trade. This sense of Butternut identity with the South and hostility to the Northeast gave rise to talk among western Democrats of a "Northwest Confederacy" that would reconstruct a Union with the South, leaving New England out in the cold until she confessed the error of her ways and humbly petitioned for readmission. However bizarre such a scheme appears in retrospect, it commanded much rhetorical support during the war. "The people of the West demand peace, and they begin to more than suspect that New England is in the way," warned Vallandigham in January 1863, and if the war continued the country faced *"eternal divorce between the West and the East."* Though less extreme than Vallandigham, Congressman Samuel S. Cox of Ohio agreed that "the erection of the states watered by the Mississippi and its tributaries into an independent Republic is the talk of every other western man." This threat to reopen the Mississippi by a separate peace generated General McClernand's proposal to reopen it with his separate campaign against Vicksburg. The whole issue lent an urgency to Grant's efforts to capture Vicksburg and a bitter edge to criticisms of his initial failures to do so.

An important law passed by Congress in February 1863 intensified the alienation of western Democrats: the National Banking Act. This measure owed much to Secretary of the Treasury Chase's desire to augment the market for war bonds; it owed even more to the Whiggish Republican desire to rationalize the decentralized, unstable structure of state banks and to create a uniform banknote currency. Treasury notes (greenbacks) provided a national currency, but they circulated alongside several hundred types of banknotes of varying degrees of soundness. No effective national regulation of banking had existed since the Jacksonian era. "The policy of this country," Senate Finance Committee Chairman John Sherman argued, "ought to be to make everything national as far as possible; to nationalize our country so that we shall love our country."

On February 25, 1863, the National Banking Act became law with the affirmative votes of 78 percent of the Republicans overcoming the negative votes of 91 percent of the Democrats. As supplemented by additional legislation the next year, this law authorized the granting of federal charters to banks that met certain standards, required them to purchase U.S. bonds in an amount equal to one-third of their capital, and permitted them to issue banknotes equal to 90 percent of the value of such bonds. Not until Congress drove state banknotes out of circulation with a 10 percent tax levied on them in 1865 did most state banks convert to federal charters. But the 1863 law laid the groundwork for the banking system that prevailed for a half-century after the war. Not surprisingly, Jacksonian Democrats in the Old Northwest denounced "this monstrous Bank Bill" as new evidence of the wartime conspiracy by "the money monopoly of New England" to "destroy the fixed institutions of the States, and to build up a central moneyed despotism."

The years of real passion on the bank issue, however, belonged to the 1830s and 1890s. In 1863 hostility to emancipation was the principal fuel that fired antiwar Democrats. On this issue, also, New England was the main enemy. The "Constitution-breaking, law-defying, negro-loving Phariseeism of New England" had caused the war, said Samuel S. Cox. An Ohio editor branded Lincoln a "half-witted usurper" and his Emancipation Proclamation "monstrous, impudent, and heinous . . . insulting to God as to man, for it declares those 'equal' whom God created unequal."

Did such rhetoric fall within the rights of free speech and a free press? A case can be made that it stimulated desertion from the army and resistance to the war effort. Democratic newspapers that circulated among soldiers contained many editorials proclaiming the illegality of an antislavery war as well as letters allegedly written by family members at home to soldiers in the army. "I am sorry you are engaged in this . . . unholy, unconstitutional and hellish war," a father supposedly wrote to his son, "which has no other purpose but to free the negroes and enslave the whites." Another letter advised an Illinois soldier "to come home, if you have to desert, you will be protected"—by angry citizens prepared to crush the abolitionists. Such propaganda had its intended effect. So many members of two southern Illinois regiments deserted "rather than help free the slaves" that General Grant had to disband the regiments. Soldiers from several other regiments allowed themselves to be captured so they could be paroled and sent home.

Equally serious were the actions of the newly elected Democratic legislatures of Indiana and Illinois. The lower houses in both states passed resolutions calling for an armistice and a peace conference. Both lower houses also demanded retraction of the "wicked, inhuman and unholy" Emancipation Proclamation as the price for continued state support of the war. When the two legislatures began work on bills to take control of state troops away from the Republican governors (elected in 1860), these governors decided to act. With the acquiescence of the Lincoln administration, in June 1863 Richard Yates of Illinois used an obscure clause of the state constitution to prevent the legislature from meeting. Indiana's iron-willed Oliver P. Morton simply persuaded Republican legislators to absent themselves, thereby forcing the legislature into adjournment for lack of a quorum. For the next two years Morton ran the state without a legislature—and without the usual appropriations. He borrowed from banks and businesses, levied contributions on Republican counties, and drew $250,000 from a special service fund in the War Department—all quite extralegal, if not illegal. But Republicans everywhere endorsed the princi-

The placid countenances of Richard Yates (left) and Oliver P. Morton in these photographs belie the truculent manner in which they faced down Democrats in their states.

ple of Morton's action: the Constitution must be stretched in order to save constitutional government from destruction by rebellion.

This reasoning buttressed Lincoln's policy in the most celebrated civil liberties case of the war—the military arrest and conviction of Vallandigham for disloyalty. Vallandigham, eager to play the part of a martyr and advance his languishing candidacy for the Democratic gubernatorial nomination in Ohio, found an unwitting ally in General Burnside. Appointed commander of the Department of the Ohio (embracing states bordering that river) after transfer from the Army of the Potomac, Burnside decided to come down hard on the copperheads. In April 1863 he unwisely issued a general order declaring that any person committing "expressed or implied" treason would be subject to trial by a military court and punishment by death or banishment. What constituted implied treason Burnside did not say, but the country would soon find out.

Vallandigham seized the opportunity and spoke at a rally in Mount Vernon, Ohio, on May 1. After he denounced this "wicked, cruel and unnecessary war" waged "for the purpose of crushing out liberty and erecting a despotism . . . a war for the freedom of the blacks and the enslavement of the whites," Burnside sent a squad of soldiers to arrest Vallandigham at his home in Dayton. In a manner that lent credence to accusations of despotism, soldiers broke down the door in the middle of the night and hustled Vallandigham away, leaving behind his hysterical wife and a terrified sister-in-law. While his supporters rioted and burned down the office of Dayton's Republican newspaper, a military commission met in Cincinnati on May 6 and convicted Vallandigham "of having expressed sympathy" for the enemy and having uttered "disloyal sentiments and opinions, with the object and purpose of weakening the power of the Government [to suppress] an unlawful rebellion." Unwilling to go so far as to put Vallandigham before a firing squad, the commission recommended his imprisonment for the war's duration, and Burnside so ordered. Vallandigham filed for a writ of habeas corpus, which was denied by a federal judge who pointed out that Lincoln had suspended the writ in such cases.

These proceedings produced cries of outrage from Democrats and murmurings of anxiety from many Republicans. The Vallandigham case did indeed raise troubling constitutional questions. Could a speech be treason? Could a military court try a civilian? Did a general, or for that matter a president, have the power to impose martial law or suspend habeas corpus in an area distant from military operations where the civil courts were functioning?

These questions went to the heart of the administration's policy for dealing with the fire in the rear. Lincoln would have preferred not to have had the issue raised by Burnside's unauthorized arrest of Vallandigham, but decided that more damage would be done by repudiating Burnside than by upholding him. In an attempt to minimize the political consequences, however, Lincoln commuted Vallandigham's sentence from imprisonment to banishment. On May 25 Union cavalry escorted the Ohioan under flag of truce to General Bragg's lines south of Murfreesboro, where the reluctant rebels accepted this uninvited guest.

Lincoln's shrewd move failed in one respect: while in exile, Vallandigham rode to the gubernatorial nomination on a wave of sympathy from Ohio Democrats. He made his way to the border city of Windsor in Canada, from which he conducted his campaign for governor. Before leaving the South, he assured several Confederate congressmen and army officers that he was committed to reunion through an armistice and negotiations, but they made it clear that they would accept peace only on the basis of independence. Vallandigham clung to his hope for eventual reunion but, in a confidential interview with a Confederate agent, gave the impression that if the South refused to come back "then possibly he is in favor of recognizing our independence."

While Vallandigham conducted his strange "reunionist" campaign-in-exile for governor, Lincoln sought to defuse the civil liberties issue with two public replies to Democratic critics. He rejected the charge that Vallandigham had been arrested "for no other reason than words addressed to a public meeting." Rather it was "because he was laboring, with some effect, to prevent the raising of troops [and] to encourage desertions. . . . He was damaging the army, upon the existence and vigor of which the life of the nation depends." The president than asked a rhetorical question that turned out to be the most powerful—and famous—part of his argument. "Must I shoot a simple-minded soldier boy who deserts, while I must not touch a hair of a wily agitator who induces him to desert? . . . I think that in such a case to silence the agitator and save the boy is not only constitutional, but withal a great mercy." This "giant

This drawing in Frank Leslie's Illustrated Newspaper *shows a Union officer with a flag of truce delivering Vallandigham to the Confederate picket guard in Tennessee. The Confederates did not particularly want him, nor did he want to stay in the South. Within three weeks Vallandigham escaped on a blockade runner from Wilmington, North Carolina, to Halifax, Canada, and then on to Windsor. There he lived for the next year, running for governor of Ohio and maintaining contact with northern Democrats—and with Confederate agents in Canada.*

At the time of the Civil War the penny bore the head of Miss Liberty on one side. Peace Democrats sought to convert the stigma of the term "copperhead" into a symbol of pride by wearing a badge made from this penny to signify their right to the liberty of dissent. The cartoonist for Frank Leslie's Illustrated Newspaper was having none of that, however; he portrayed the "patriotic storekeeper" as giving the customer (with unmistakable Irish features) who asked for the "copperhead badge" a very different badge that he would wear on his chin for several days.

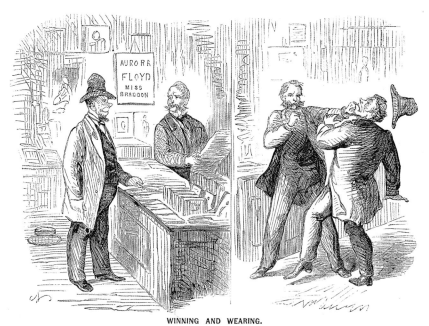

WINNING AND WEARING.

DOUBTFUL CITIZEN—*Sir, do you sell Copperhead Badges? I want one.*   PATRIOTIC STOREKEEPER—*This is the only badge you Copperheads deserve.* (Doubtful citizen wears it for some days.)

rebellion" reached into the North itself, Lincoln continued, where "under cover of 'liberty of speech,' 'liberty of the press,' and '*Habeas corpus*,' [the rebels] hoped to keep on foot amongst us a most efficient corps of spies, informers, suppliers, and aiders and abettors of their cause." Thus the whole country was a war zone and military arrests in areas far from the fighting front were justified. Civil courts were "utterly incompetent" to deal with such a massive threat to the nation's life. This was precisely the contingency that framers of the Constitution foresaw when they authorized suspension of the writ of habeas corpus in cases of rebellion or invasion. With a homely but effective metaphor, Lincoln affirmed that he could no more believe that the necessary curtailment of civil liberties in wartime would establish precedents fatal to liberty in peacetime "than I am able to believe that a man could contract so strong an appetite for emetics during temporary illness, as to persist in feeding upon them through the remainder of his healthful life."

Lincoln's two letters on civil liberties were published far and wide by the newly established Union League clubs and the Loyal Publication Society, both founded by influential businessmen and professional men to fight back against copperheads in secret societies such as the Knights of the Golden Circle and Order of American Knights. These organizations achieved much greater power than the Democratic secret societies, whose supposed legions existed more in the fevered imaginations of Republicans than in fact. The Union Leagues became in effect an auxiliary of the Republican party, which began to call itself the Union party in several states—thereby implying that the opposition was a *dis*-union party.

The first successes of this counterattack against Democratic defeatism came in New Hampshire and Connecticut. These states held gubernatorial elections in the spring. The results in 1863 were closely watched elsewhere as a portent. In both states the Democrats nominated peace men of the Vallandigham stripe, hoping to cash in on voter disillusionment with the war. Republicans and Union Leagues

Titled *"The Copperhead Party—In Favor of a Vigorous Prosecution of Peace!"* this Harper's Weekly *cartoon in February 1863, unsigned but possibly by Thomas Nast, portrays Miss Liberty defending the Union against a pack of copperheads whose program for peace negotiations, it implies, would destroy the Union.*

mobilized to stem the apparent Democratic tide. The War Department helped by granting well-timed furloughs to soldiers who were expected to go home and vote Republican. These efforts succeeded—but just barely. The Republican candidate in Connecticut won with 52 percent of the vote. In New Hampshire the presence of a War Democratic third party prevented any candidate from winning a majority and threw the election into the Republican legislature, which elected their man.

A prime issue in both elections was the draft, enacted by Congress on March 3, 1863. Democrats added conscription to emancipation and military arrests in their catalogue of Republican sins. The Enrollment Act of 1863 was designed mainly as a device to stimulate volunteering by the threat of a draft. As such it worked, but with such inefficiency, corruption, and perceived injustice that it became one of the most divisive issues of the war and served as a model of how *not* to conduct a draft in future wars.

Like the Confederacy in early 1862, the Union army in 1863 faced a serious manpower loss through expiration of enlistments: thirty-eight two-year regiments raised in 1861, and ninety-two nine-month militia regiments organized in 1862, were due to go home during the spring and summer of 1863. This prompted Congress to act.

In its nationalizing tendencies the resulting law was similar to the recently passed Banking Act. State governors had taken the lead in the organization of volunteer regiments in 1861–62. The draft was a national process. Congress authorized a Provost Marshals Bureau in the War Department to enforce conscription in each congressional district by enrolling every male citizen and immigrant who had filed for citizenship aged twenty to forty-five. This became the basis for each district's quota in the four calls for new troops that Lincoln issued after passage of the conscription act in March 1863. In the first draft (July 1863), provost marshals called up 20 percent of the enrollees, chosen by lot in each district. In the three drafts of 1864, the War Department assigned each district a quota determined by its pro rata share of the number of soldiers called for by the president, after adjustment for men who had already enlisted from the district. Each district had fifty days to fill its quota with volunteers. Those that failed to do so then held a lottery draft to obtain a sufficient number of men to meet the quota.

If a man's name was drawn in this lottery, one of several things would happen to him next—the least likely of which was induction into the army. Of the men chosen in the four drafts, more than one-fifth (161,000 of 776,000) "failed to report"—fleeing instead to the West, to Canada, or to the woods. Of those who did report to the provost marshal's office, one-eighth were sent home because of already filled quotas. Three-fifths of the remaining 522,000 were exempted for physical or mental disability or because they convinced the inducting officer that they were the sole means of support for a widow, an orphan sibling, a motherless child, or an indigent parent. Unlike the Confederate Congress, Union lawmakers allowed no occupational exemptions. But a draftee who passed the physical exam and could not claim any dependent relatives still had two options: he could hire a substitute, which exempted him from this and any future draft; or he could pay a commutation fee of $300, which exempted him from this draft but not necessarily the next one. Of the 207,000 men who were drafted, 87,000 paid the commutation fee and 74,000 furnished substitutes, leaving only 46,000 who went personally into the army. The pool of substitutes was furnished by eighteen- and nineteen-year-olds and by immigrants who had not filed for citizenship, who were not liable to conscription.

There were numerous instances of fraud, error, and injustice in this cumbersome and confusing process, and impediments to its implementation. Timid enrollers feared to venture into Butternut counties of the Midwest, coal-mining districts of Pennsylvania, tough neighborhoods in New York, and other areas hostile to the draft and to the war. Many men "skedaddled" to avoid enrollment. Consequently some districts were underenrolled while others had padded lists, with resulting inequities in quotas. Governors and congressmen brought pressure for adjustment of quotas, and some districts had to be reenrolled. Governor Seymour of New York (a Democrat) accused the administration of padding the enrollment in Democratic districts to increase their quotas. Although discrepancies between Democratic and Republican districts did sometimes occur, the usual reason was not a Republican plot but rather a smaller previous enlistment from Democratic districts, leaving a larger quota to be conscripted.

Numerous openings for fraud also existed after enrollment was completed and men whose names had been drawn were called for examination. Surgeons could be bribed, false affidavits claiming dependent support could be filed, and other kinds of under-the-table

Cartoonists had a field day with the efforts of northern men to escape the draft. This lithograph offers a grim satire on the most extreme means of draft evasion. The woman has just severed the index finger of the man in the center, who is hopping with pain, while the man at right extends his right hand, also with the index finger chopped off, and says, "T'wont hurt but a minute and then you can get one of these," referring to an exemption certificate in his left hand signed by "Dr. Syntax."

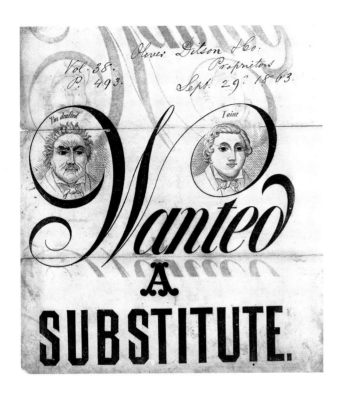

SCENE, FIFTH AVENUE.

He. "Ah! Dearest ADDIE! I've succeeded. I've got a Substitute!"
She. "Have you? What a curious coincidence! And *I* have found one FOR YOU!"

influence could be exerted. Some potential draftees feigned insanity or disease. Others practiced self-mutilation. Some naturalized citizens claimed to be aliens.

In the South, the privilege of hiring a substitute had produced the bitter slogan of "rich man's war and poor man's fight." In the North, commutation was even more unpopular than substitution. The price of commutation amounted to almost a year's wages for an unskilled laborer. "*The rich are exempt!*" proclaimed an Iowa editor. "Did you ever know aristocratic legislation to so directly point out the poor man as inferior to the rich?" On the face of it, the privileges of commutation and substitution did seem to make the conscription act, in the words of a modern historian, "one of the worst pieces of class legislation ever passed by the United States Congress."

But a closer examination challenges this conclusion. Substitution was hallowed by tradition, having existed in European countries (even in France during the *levée en masse*), in American states during the Revolution, in the militia, and in the Confederacy. The Republican architects of the draft law inserted commutation as a means of putting a cap on the price of substitutes. In the South the cost of a substitute had already soared above $1,000. The commutation alternative in the North would prevent the price of a substitute going much higher than $300. Republicans saw this as a way of bringing exemption within reach of men of the working class instead of discriminating against them.

Of course a draft without either substitution or commutation would have been more equitable. But substitution was so deeply rooted in precedent as to be viewed as a right. Civil War experience changed this perception, and after twenty months of such experience the Confederacy repealed substitution in December 1863. But the North retained it through all four of its draft calls (also a period of about twenty months). Commutation remained an alternative in the first two Union drafts (summer 1863 and spring 1864). In these drafts it worked as Republicans said

Although the hiring of substitutes by drafted men was rooted in custom, many journalists and cartoonists criticized those who did so as unpatriotic and condemned the system as discriminatory in favor of those who were wealthy enough to pay for a substitute. "Wanted: A Substitute" was a satirical song composed in 1863. The sheet-music cover shows a man on the left who says "I'm drafted." On the right is a man obviously from a higher class who says "I aint." The Harper's Weekly *cartoon labeled "Scene, Fifth Avenue" shows a well-dressed New York socialite telling his sweetheart, "Ah! Dearest Addie! I've succeeded. I've got a substitute." She replies, "Have you? What a curious coincidence. And I have found one for YOU!"*

it would. Studies of conscription in New York and Ohio have found virtually no correlation between wealth and commutation. Districts in New York with low per capita wealth had about the same percentage of men who paid commutation (or hired substitutes) as those with higher wealth. In four Ohio districts—two rural and two urban—the proportion of unskilled laborers who commuted was 18 percent, compared with 22 percent for skilled laborers, 21 percent for merchants, bankers, manufacturers, doctors, lawyers, and clerks, and 47 percent for farmers and farm laborers. Since skilled and unskilled laborers had the highest percentage of "failure to report" when their names were drawn, it appears that at least in Ohio the laborers and farmers were *more* likely than men in white-collar jobs to avoid the draft. In this respect it does not seem to have been especially a poor man's fight.

Yet the outcry against "blood money" prompted Congress to repeal commutation in July 1864, despite warnings by some Republicans that this would drive the price of substitutes beyond the reach of the poor. The warning proved to be only partly true. The proportion of laborers and farmers who bought their way out of the last two drafts declined by half after the abolition of commutation. But the percentage of exemptions purchased by white-collar and professional classes also declined by almost half. And in the four drafts taken together the poor seem to have suffered little comparative disadvantage. In New York City districts with the highest concentration of Irish immigrants, 98 percent of the men not otherwise exempted paid commutation or hired substitutes. The following table provides a detailed occupational breakdown of men whose names were drawn in four sample Ohio districts:

OCCUPATIONAL CATEGORIES	FAILED TO REPORT	EXEMPTED FOR CAUSE	COMMUTED OR HIRED SUBSTITUTE	HELD TO SERVICE
Unskilled laborer	24.9%	45.1%	24.2%	5.8%
Skilled laborer	25.7	43.8	21.9	8.6
Farmer and farm laborer	16.1	34.1	30.9	18.9
Merchant, manufacturer, banker, broker	22.6	46.3	29.1	2.0
Clerk	26.2	47.7	24.3	1.8
Professional	6.3	48.5	28.9	6.3

How could laborers come up with the price of commutation or a substitute? Few of them did, out of their own pockets. But numerous cities and counties appropriated funds raised by property taxes to pay the $300 for those who could not afford it. Tammany Hall ward committees collected money to hire substitutes for draftees, and political machines elsewhere followed suit. Several factories and businesses and railroads bought exemptions for drafted workers with funds contributed by employers and by a 10 percent levy on wages. Draft insurance societies sprang up everywhere to offer a $300 policy for premiums of a few dollars a

month. In this manner more than three-quarters of all draftees who reported to the provost marshal's office and were not exempted for cause were able to buy their way out of serving.

What kind of conscription was this, in which only 7 percent of the men whose names were drawn actually served? The answer: it was not conscription at all, but a clumsy carrot-and-stick device to stimulate volunteering. The stick was the threat of being drafted and the carrot was a bounty for volunteering. In the end this method worked, for while only 46,000 drafted men served and another 74,000 provided substitutes, some 800,000 men enlisted or reenlisted voluntarily during the two years after passage of the conscription act. While the social and economic cost of this process was high, Americans seemed willing to pay the price because compulsory service was contrary to the country's values and traditions. Alexis de Tocqueville's words a generation earlier were still relevant in 1863: "In America conscription is unknown and men are induced to enlist by bounties. The notions and habits of the people . . . are so opposed to compulsory recruitment that I do not think it can ever be sanctioned by their laws."

Yet in the end, bounty-stimulated volunteering came to seem an even greater evil than the draft. Implicit bounties began in the first days of the war, when soldiers' aid societies raised money to help support the families of men who gave up their jobs to go off to war. States, counties, and municipalities also appropriated funds for this purpose. These patriotic subsidies aroused no controversy. In the summer of 1862, however, several northern localities found it necessary to pay explicit bounties in order to fill quotas under Lincoln's two calls for troops. A year later the shock of the first draft enrollment and lottery, which provoked bitter resistance in many areas, caused communities to resolve to fill future quotas by any means possible to avoid a draft. Lincoln's three calls for troops in 1864 produced a bidding war to buy volunteers. Private associations raised money for bounties. Cities and counties competed

EXTRA BOUNTY!

Families of Recruits provided for. By the liberal contribution of the Grocers' Committee, the

FIFTH METROPOLITAN GUARD

Col. T. W. PARMELE, is enabled to offer an EXTRA CASH BOUNTY of

$10 FOR EACH RECRUIT

in addition to other bounties. The families of recruits are also provided for by the Metropolitan Police Fund, and have the gratuitous services of the Physicians of the Police Department at their own homes.

Headquarters, HOWARD ST., near Broadway.

When the system of local bounties began to grow in the fall of 1862, the justification for them was to provide for the families they left behind, as with this offer of a small supplementary bounty from the Grocers' Committee for recruits to the Fifth Metropolitan Guard (174th New York). Within a year, however, the bidding war of bounties became a scandal.

This cartoon shows a bounty broker telling the barber to rig up the old man with a wig and mustache to make him look like a young recruit for the Union army, promising the barber $50 of the $300 the broker expects to get for the recruit.

THE RECRUITING BUSINESS.

VOLUNTEER-BROKER (*to Barber*) "Look a-here—I want you to trim up this old chap with a flaxen wig and a light mustache, so as to make him look like twenty; and as I shall probably clear three hundred dollars on him, I sha'n't mind giving you fifty for the job."

for recruits. The federal government got into the act in October 1863 with a $300 bounty (financed by the $300 commutation fee) for volunteers and reenlistees.

The half-billion dollars paid in bounties by the North represented something of a transfer of wealth from rich to poor—an ironic counterpoint to the theme of rich man's war/poor man's fight. By 1864 a canny recruit could pyramid local, regional, and national bounties into grants of $1,000 or more. Some men could not resist the temptation to take this money, desert, assume a different name, travel to another town, and repeat the process. Several of these "bounty jumpers" got away with the practice several times. "Bounty brokers" went into business to seek the best deals for their clients—with a cut of the bounty as payment. They competed with "substitute brokers" for a share of this lucrative trade in cannon fodder. Relatively few of the bounty men or substitutes actually became cannon fodder, however, for many deserted before they ever got into action and others allowed themselves to be captured at the first contact with the enemy. Thus while the conscription-substitute-bounty system produced three-quarters of a million new men, they did little to help win the war. This task fell mainly on the prebounty veterans of 1861 and 1862—who with exaggerated contempt viewed many of the bounty men and substitutes of 1864 as "off-scourings of northern slums . . . dregs of every nation . . . branded felons . . . thieves, burglars, and vagabonds."

One notorious facet of the bounty-and-substitute business was the crimping of immigrants. Immigration had declined sharply during the first half of the war, but picked up again in 1863 because of wartime labor shortages. Some of these immigrants came with the intention of joining the army to cash in on bounties or substitute fees. Others were virtually kidnapped into the service by unscrupulous "runners." The substantial number of immigrants in the Union army gave rise to the long-standing southern myth that "the majority of Yankee soldiers were foreign hirelings." But in fact quite the opposite was true. Immigrants were proportionally underrepresented in the Union's armed services. Of some two million white soldiers and sailors, half a million had been born abroad. While immigrants therefore constituted 25 percent of the white servicemen, 30 percent of the males of military age in the Union states were foreign-born. Despite the fighting reputation of the Irish Brigade, the Irish were the most underrepresented group in proportion to population, followed by German Catholics. Other immigrant groups enlisted in rough proportion to their share of the population.

The underrepresentation of Catholic immigrants can be

explained in part by the Democratic allegiance of these groups and their opposition to Republican war aims, especially emancipation. Some of them had not yet filed for citizenship—or claimed not to have done so—and were therefore exempt from the draft. Although this group furnished a large number of substitutes and bounty men during the final year of war—thereby achieving an inglorious visibility—they also furnished a large number of deserters and bounty jumpers. Together with Butternuts from the Ohio River valley, they likewise provided many of those who "skedaddled" to escape the draft. This ethnocultural pattern reinforced economic class, for Butternuts and Catholic immigrants were concentrated in the lower end of the wealth and income scale. Perhaps this confirms the theme of a "rich man's war"—for many of these people wanted no part of the war—but it modifies the "poor man's fight" notion. This modification is borne out by the following table comparing previous occupations of white Union soldiers with the occupational distribution of males in the states from which they came.

OCCUPATIONAL CATEGORIES	UNION SOLDIERS (U.S. SANITARY COMMISSION SAMPLE)	UNION SOLDIERS (BELL WILEY SAMPLE)	ALL MALES (FROM 1860 CENSUS)
Farmer and farm laborer	47.5%	47.8%	42.9%
Skilled laborer	25.1	25.2	24.9
Unskilled laborer	15.9	15.1	16.7
White-collar and commercial	5.1	7.8	10.0
Professional	3.2	2.9	3.5
Miscellaneous and unknown	3.2	1.2	2.0

From this table it might appear that the white-collar class was the most underrepresented group in the army. But this appearance is deceptive, for the median age of soldiers at enlistment was 23.5 years while the occupational data from the census were for all adult males. Two-fifths of the soldiers were twenty-one or younger. Studies of nineteenth-century occupational mobility have shown that 10 percent or more of young men who started out as laborers subsequently moved up the occupational ladder. If one could control for the age of soldiers, it seems likely that the only category significantly underrepresented would be unskilled workers.

Even if the dichotomy rich man's war/poor man's fight lacked objective reality, it remained a powerful symbol to be manipulated by Democrats who made conscription a partisan and class issue. While 100 percent of the congressional Republicans supported the draft bill, 88 percent of the Democrats voted against it. Scarcely any other issue except emancipation evoked such clear-cut partisan division. Indeed, Democrats linked these two issues in their condemnation of the draft as an unconstitutional means to achieve the unconstitutional end of freeing the slaves. A Democratic convention in the Midwest pledged that "we will not render support to the present Administration in its wicked Abolition crusade [and] we will *resist* to the

The draft rioters in New York singled out targets they associated with the draft, the war, and emancipation. The drawing at right shows the lynching of a black man by a mob that included women and children. The one on the opposite page shows the police charging the rioters in front of the Tribune *office.*

death all attempts to draft any of our citizens into the army." Democratic newspapers hammered at the theme that the draft would force white workingmen to fight for the freedom of blacks who would come north and take away their jobs. The editor of New York's leading Catholic weekly told a mass meeting that "when the President called upon them to go and carry on a war for the nigger, he would be d—d if he believed they would go." In a Fourth of July 1863 speech to Democrats in the city, Governor Seymour warned Republicans who pleaded military necessity for emancipation and conscription: "Remember this—that the bloody and treasonable doctrine of public necessity can be proclaimed by a mob as well as by a government."

Such rhetoric inflamed smoldering tensions. Draft-dodgers and mobs killed several enrollment officers during the spring and summer. Anti-Negro violence erupted in a number of cities. Nowhere was the tinder more flammable than in New York City, with its large Irish population and powerful Democratic machine. Crowded into noisome tenements in a city with the worst disease mortality and highest crime rate in the Western world, working in low-skill jobs for marginal wages, fearful of competition from black workers, hostile toward the Protestant middle and upper classes who often disdained or exploited them, the Irish were ripe for revolt against this war waged by Yankee Protestants for black freedom. Wage increases had lagged 20 percent or more behind price increases since 1861. Numerous strikes had left a bitter legacy, none more than a longshoremen's walkout in June 1863 when black stevedores under police protection took the place of striking Irishmen.

Into this setting came draft officers to begin the drawing of names on Saturday, July 11. Most of the militia and federal troops normally stationed in the city were absent in Pennsylvania pursuing Lee's army after the battle of Gettysburg. The first day's drawing went quietly enough, but on Sunday hundreds of angry men congregated in bars and vowed to attack the draft offices next morning. They made good their threat, setting off four days of escalating mob violence that terrorized the city and left at least 105 people dead. It was the worst riot in American history.

Many of the men (and women) in the mobs indulged in indiscriminate looting and destruction. But as in most riots, the mobs singled out certain targets that were related to the underlying causes of the outbreak. Draft offices and other federal property went up in flames early in the rioting. No black person was safe. Rioters beat several, lynched a half-dozen, smashed the homes and property of scores, and burned the Colored Orphan Asylum to the ground. Mobs also fell upon several business establishments that employed blacks. Rioters tried to attack the offices of Republican newspapers and managed to burn out the ground floor of the *Tribune* while howling for Horace Greeley's blood. Several editors warded off the mob by arming their employees with rifles; Henry Raymond of the *Times* borrowed three recently invented Gatling guns from the army to defend his building. Rioters sacked the homes of several prominent Republicans and abolitionists. With shouts of "Down with the rich" and "There goes a $300 man" they attacked well-dressed men who were incautious enough to show themselves on the streets. These hints of class warfare were amplified by assaults on the property of reputed antilabor employers and the destruction of street-sweeping machines and grain-loading elevators that had automated the jobs of some of the unskilled workers who made up the bulk of the rioters. Several Protestant churches and missions were burned by the mobs, whose membership was at least two-thirds Irish.

Untrained in riot control, New York's police fought the mobs courageously but with only partial success on July 13 and 14. Army officers desperately scraped together a few hundred troops to help. The War Department rushed several regiments from Pennsylvania to New York, where on July 15 and 16 they poured volleys into the ranks of rioters. By July 17 an uneasy peace returned to the shattered city. Determined to carry out the draft in New York lest successful resistance there spawn imitation elsewhere, the government built up troop strength in Manhattan to 20,000 men who enforced calm during the resumption of drafting on August 19. By then the city council had appropriated funds to pay the commutation fees of drafted men—including, no doubt, some of the rioters.

The specter of class conflict also haunted the South. As in the North, conscription worsened the friction. Manpower needs had forced the Confederate Congress in September 1862 to raise the upper age limit from thirty-five to forty-five. This made the heads of many poor families suddenly subject to the draft at a time when that summer's drought had devastated food crops. And Congress added insult to injury by a provision to exempt one white man on every plantation with twenty or more slaves.

This controversial exemption was intended to ensure that slaves would not flee but continue working—and to protect white women from them. An Alabama woman, living alone with her two-year-old daughter, wrote a letter to the governor in September 1862 telling him that "I am now surrounded on all sides by plantations of negroes—many of them have not a white [man] on them" and begging him to "give me the power of having my overseer recalled." The Confederacy also needed the food and fiber raised on plantations, and southerners believed that without overseers the slaves would raise nothing. Planters insisted that the exemption of overseers was at least as important to the war effort as the exemption of teachers or apothecaries. In October 1862 Congress concurred, though not without objections by some senators against this legislation "in favour of slave labour against white labour."

By granting a special privilege to a class constituting only 5 percent of the white population, the "twenty-Negro law" became as unpopular in the South as commutation in the North. Although only four or five thousand planters or overseers obtained exemptions under the law—representing about 15 percent of the eligible plantations and 3 percent of the men exempted for all causes—the symbolism of the law was powerful. Many of the men who deserted from Confederate armies during the winter of 1862–63 agreed with a Mississippi farmer who went AWOL because he "did not propose to fight for the rich men while they were at home having a good

One of the key institutions of the antebellum South was the slave patrol, a rotating group of white men authorized to seize slaves who were away from home without a pass signed by their owner. The war put great strain on the patrol, both by absorbing most white men into the army and by increasing the restlessness of slaves. That was one reason why the Confederate Congress enacted the "twenty-Negro" exemption from the draft in 1862. This woodcut from Frank Leslie's Illustrated Newspaper *shows home guard troops in Louisiana fulfilling the function of the old slave patrol by examining the passes of slaves.*

time." Alarmed by what he heard on a trip home from Richmond, on December 9 Mississippi's Senator James Phelan warned his friend Jefferson Davis that men on the home front were banding together to resist the law and that "in the army it is said it only needs some daring men to raise the standard to develop a revolt."

Such protests made limited headway against planter influence. Congress modified but never repealed the twenty-Negro exemption, which remained a divisive issue for the rest of the war. One modification in February 1864 reduced the number of slaves to fifteen but specified that exempted plantations must sell to the government at fixed cost two hundred pounds of meat per slave, part of it for the families of needy soldiers. As this requirement suggests, hunger was a serious factor in the disaffection of yeoman and laboring classes. Despite the conversion of much acreage from cotton to food crops in 1862, the drought and the breakdown of southern transportation—not to mention Union conquest of prime agricultural regions—led to severe food shortages the following winter. The quickening pace of inflation also drove the price of food, even when available, beyond the reach of many. Having doubled in the latter half of 1862, the price index doubled again in the first half of 1863. In Richmond, War Department clerk John Jones saw his salary fall farther and farther behind the cost of living until in March 1863 "the shadow of the gaunt form of famine is upon us." Jones had lost twenty pounds, "and my wife and children are emaciated." Even the rats in his kitchen were so hungry that they ate bread crumbs from his daughter's hand "as tame as kittens. Perhaps we shall have to eat them!"

Women and children on farms suffered as much as those in cities. Some women wrote to Confederate officials pleading for the discharge of their husbands. Such appeals availed little, so thousands of husbands discharged themselves. "There is already a heap of men gone home," wrote a Mississippi private to his wife in November 1862, "and a heap says if their familys get to suffering that they will go [too]." A month later a

THE FOOD QUESTION DOWN SOUTH.
JEFF DAVIS. "See! see! the beautiful Boots just come to me from the dear ladies of Baltimore!"
BEAUREGARD. "Ha! Boots? Boots? When shall we eat them? Now?"

This rather crude cartoon in Harper's Weekly *suggests that even high-ranking southerners were starving in the spring of 1863. General Beauregard, at right, eagerly reaches for the boots Jefferson Davis has received from prosouthern ladies of Baltimore, asking, "When shall we eat them? Now?"*

Northern artist Alfred R. Waud depicts a Confederate deserter who joined one of the guerrilla or bands, or regulators, that infested parts of the Confederacy by 1863.

distressed officer in Bragg's Army of Tennessee declared that "desertions are multiplying so fast in this army that almost one-third of it is gone."

Many of these deserters joined with draft-evaders in backcountry regions to form guerrilla bands that resisted Confederate authority and virtually ruled whole counties. Some of these "regulators" formed ties with the antiwar or unionist secret societies that sprang up in 1862 and 1863 in Arkansas, northern Alabama, and northern Georgia as well as western North Carolina and east Tennessee. The rich man's war/poor man's fight theme stimulated the growth of these societies just as it strengthened copperheads in the North. Although the southern peace societies did not achieve the visibility or influence that an established political party gave northern copperheads, they drained vitality from the Confederate war effort in certain regions and formed the nucleus for a significant peace movement if the war should take a turn for the worse.

Was it especially a poor man's fight in the South? Probably no more than it was in the North, according to the following table based on data from seven Confederate states.

OCCUPATIONAL CATEGORIES	CONFEDERATE SOLDIERS	WHITE MALES (FROM 1860 CENSUS)
Planters, farmers, and farm laborers	61.5%	57.5%
Skilled laborers	14.1	15.7
Unskilled laborers	8.5	12.7
White-collar and commercial	7.0	8.3
Professional	5.2	5.0
Miscellaneous and unknown	3.7	.8

From this sample it appears that, adjusted for age, both skilled and unskilled laborers were underrepresented in the Confederate army while business and professional classes may have been overrepresented. The most important categories in this rural society, however, were farmers and planters. Unfortunately, neither the census nor the regimental muster rolls consistently distinguished between these two classes, so it is impossible to tell whether "planters" were underrepresented. One study of this question found that in three piedmont counties of Georgia the average wealth of men who did not serve in the army was about 20 percent greater than those who did. The pattern indicated by this limited sample may have been counterbalanced for the Confederacy as a whole by the greater tendency of men from its poorest upcountry regions to skedaddle, desert, or otherwise avoid Confederate service.

In any case, the symbolic power of the twenty-Negro law and the actual suffering of poor families gave greater credence to the poor-man's-fight theme in the South than in the North. The government—more particularly state and county governments—recognized this. Most southern states and many counties appropriated funds for assistance to the families of poor soldiers. These expenditures were financed by taxes on slaves and large landholdings, thus representing an attempt to alleviate class discontent by transferring resources from the rich to the poor. The two states that did most in this line were Georgia and North Carolina—the very states whose governors, Joseph Brown and Zebulon Vance, interposed state's-rights roadblocks to the southern war effort. The common people tended to applaud Brown or Vance and to criticize Davis, not necessarily because they favored state's rights at the expense of the Confederacy but because the state helped them while the Richmond government took away their husbands and sons and their livelihood.

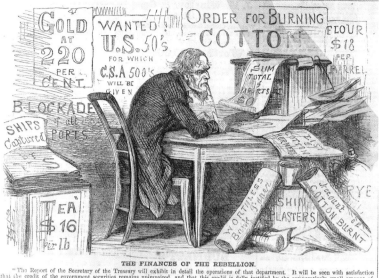

THE FINANCES OF THE REBELLION.

"The Report of the Secretary of the Treasury will exhibit in detail the operations of that department. It will be seen with satisfaction that the credit of the government securities remains unimpaired, and that this credit is fully justified by the comparatively small amount of accumulated debt, notwithstanding the magnitude of our military operations.—(*Extract from* JEFF DAVIS'S *Message*.)

Harper's Weekly *did its best to encourage northern morale by frequently suggesting that the Confederacy was on the verge of collapse from one cause or another. This cartoon of Jefferson Davis trying to figure out how to keep Confederate finances afloat was not far off the mark. Financing the war was one of the Confederacy's greatest headaches.*

The Confederate government's taxes and impressments to sustain the army also caused it to appear as an oppressor. By the spring of 1863, runaway inflation finally compelled Richmond's lawmakers to seek alternatives to the printing press to finance the war. In April they followed the Union example and enacted a comprehensive tax law that included a progressive income tax, an 8 percent levy on certain goods held for sale, excise and license duties, and a 10 percent profits tax on wholesalers intended to take back some of the money that "speculators" had "extorted" from the people. But the notion that these taxes would make the rich pay their share was neutralized by an additional category of items that were taxed and one that was not. Because money had so little value, Congress imposed a 10 percent "tax in kind" on agricultural produce. After reserving a subsistence for his family, each farmer had to turn over 10 percent of the surplus to one of the three thousand agents who fanned out through the South to collect it. Yeoman farmers bitterly resented this levy. Why should the poor husbandman—or rather husbandwoman, since so many men were at the front—have to pay 10 percent, they asked, when a clerk or teacher with a salary of $1,500 paid only 2 percent of his income? More pointedly, why was the chief property of the rich—slaves—*not* taxed? The answer: a tax on slaves was considered a direct tax, constitutionally permissible only after an apportionment on the basis of population. No census could be taken in wartime, hence no direct tax was possible. The relevance of this constitutional inhibition escaped most dirt farmers, who saw only that the revenue agents took their produce while the rich man's slaves escaped taxation.

In practice the tax in kind seemed little different from "impressment" of supplies by the army. Desperate for provisions, commissary and quartermaster officers scoured the countryside for food, fodder, and work animals. They paid whatever price *they* (not the farmer) considered fair with promissory notes that deteriorated in value still further before the farmer could cash them. By the end of the war an estimated half-billion dollars in these worthless IOUs were outstanding. Some army units, especially the cavalry, took what they wanted without even pretending to pay.

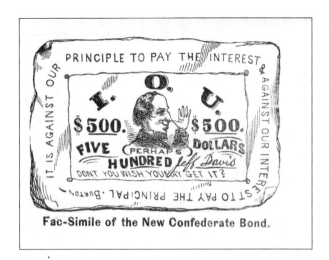

Fac-Simile of the New Confederate Bond.

A satirical cartoon on Confederate bonds and promissory notes that predicts—accurately, as it turned out—that holders of these bonds or notes would never receive either principal or interest.

Despite the notorious reputation of northern invaders in this regard, many southerners believed that "the Yankees cannot do us any more harm than our own soldiers have done." Impressment fell with impartial injustice on the rich and the poor who happened to live near active military operations. But because the family farmer could scarcely afford to lose what little he had, impressment became another source of his alienation from the government and the cause it represented.

Responding to the outcries against impressment, Congress in March 1863 passed a law to regulate it by creating commissions to fix and arbitrate "fair" prices. This law was honored most often in the breach, however, and abuses continued. More successful were revisions of the tax law in February 1864. Suspending the requirement for a census-based apportionment of direct taxes, Congress imposed a 5 percent levy on land and slaves. Families with property worth less than $500 were exempted from the tax in kind. At the same time the revision of the twenty-Negro law that impressed two hundred pounds of meat per slave got the Confederate government into the food-welfare business.

But these measures came too late to avert the most shocking revelation of internal stress—the bread riots in the spring of 1863. In a dozen or more cities and hamlets from Richmond to Mobile, desperate women raided shops or supply depots for food. Many of the riots followed a similar pattern. Groups of women, many of them wives of soldiers and some armed with knives or revolvers, marched in a body to shops owned by "speculators" and asked the price of bacon or flour. When informed, they denounced such "extortion," took what they wanted, and marched away.

By far the largest and most momentous riot occurred in Richmond. Special circumstances made the Confederate capital particularly volatile. Its population had more than doubled since 1861. Military operations had desolated many food-producing areas of Virginia. Lee's army on the Rappahannock, reduced to half-rations by March 1863, competed with the civilian population for dwindling stocks of the previous year's drought-curtailed crops. In late March a freak nine-inch snowfall made roads impassable for several days. Prices for the few goods left on merchants' shelves skyrocketed to famine levels. On April 2 several hundred women—many of them wives of employees at the Tredegar Iron Works—met at a Baptist church and proceeded to the governor's mansion to make known their distress. The governor offered little comfort, and as the delegation moved on it turned into a mob. A middle-class bystander asked one of the members, an emaciated girl of eighteen, what was going on. "We are starving," said the girl. "We are going to the bakeries and each of us will take a loaf of bread. That is little enough for the government to give us after it has taken all our men." Grown to more than a thousand persons, including some men and boys, the mob broke into shops and warehouses. "Bread! Bread!" they shouted. "Our children are starving while the rich roll in wealth." Emboldened by success, some women began to seize clothing, shoes, even jewelry as well as food. The governor and mayor confronted the rioters and called on them to disperse. A hastily mobilized company of militia marched up and loaded their muskets. A few timid souls left, but the majority remained, confident that the militia—which contained friends and perhaps even a few husbands of the rioters—would not obey orders to fire on the crowd.

At this juncture Jefferson Davis himself arrived and climbed onto a cart to address the mob. Taking out his watch, Davis gave the rioters five minutes to disperse before he ordered the troops to fire. This succeeded. The rioters melted away. Davis pocketed his watch and ordered the police to arrest the ringleaders. Several of these were later convicted and briefly imprisoned. Military officials ordered newspapers to make no mention of the riot in order not "to embarrass our cause [or] to encourage our enemies." The lead editorial in the *Richmond Dispatch* next day was entitled "Sufferings in the North."

But the rioters had made their point. The government distributed some of its stock of rice to needy citizens. Apprehensive merchants brought out reserve stocks of food, and prices dropped by half. The Richmond city council expanded its welfare food aid. Other localities did likewise. More acreage than the previous year went over from cotton to corn. But serious problems persisted, and the South was never able to solve

This famous illustration of the Richmond bread riot first appeared in Frank Leslie's Illustrated Newspaper. *It reflects the artist's imagination of what the riot was like, but it was probably not far wrong.*

them. Priorities for military traffic on deteriorating railroads caused food to rot at sidings while thousands went hungry a hundred miles away. Union advances further constricted the food-producing areas of the Confederacy. In July 1863 the commissary general warned of a subsistence crisis for southern armies. A government clerk told of the following exchange between a woman and a shopkeeper in Richmond who asked seventy dollars for a barrel of flour. "My God!" she exclaimed. "How can I pay such prices? I have seven children; what shall I do?" "I don't know, madam," the merchant replied, "unless you eat your children."

The South's food crisis was exacerbated by refugees, who were displaced by battles or fled rather than comply with the orders of commanders of Union occupation forces who insisted that they take the oath of allegiance or leave. As thousands of these fugitives packed the roads and crowded in with friends and relatives or endured cheerless boardinghouses in towns and cities, they taxed the South's ever-decreasing resources and added to the uncounted deaths of white and black civilians from disease and malnutrition—deaths that must be included in any reckoning of the war's human cost.

Most civilians in conquered areas, of course, stayed home and lived better than their compatriots who fled southward. They also enjoyed the benefits of clandestine commerce. In his first inaugural address Lincoln had said, "We cannot remove our respective sections from each other . . . and intercourse, either amicable or hostile, must continue between them." Intercourse both hostile *and* amicable continued for the next four years in ways that neither Lincoln nor anyone else had anticipated. The South needed salt, shoes, clothing, bacon, flour, medicine, gunpowder, lead, and other necessities of war from the outside world. Since the blockade restricted

the flow of these supplies from abroad, canny Confederates sought to flank the blockade by direct trade with the North. Enterprising Yankees were willing to exchange such goods for cotton. Both governments officially banned trade with the enemy. But when the price of a pound of cotton leapt from ten cents to a dollar in the North while the price of a sack of salt jumped from $1.25 to $60 in parts of the South, venturesome men would find a way to trade cotton for salt. An English resident of the Confederacy observed that "a Chinese wall from the Atlantic to the Pacific" could not stop this commerce.

The war's first year witnessed a considerable amount of smuggling between the lines in Kentucky and through southern counties of Maryland. The real bonanza, however, began with the Union conquests in the Mississippi Valley during 1862. First Nashville, then New Orleans and Memphis became centers of a flourishing trade in this region. Some of this exchange was legitimate. Eager to restore commercial activities in occupied areas and to win their inhabitants back to unionism, the Treasury Department issued trade permits to merchants and planters who took an oath of allegiance. Having taken the oath a merchant in Memphis, for example, could sell cotton for cash or credit which he could then use to purchase a cargo of salt, flour, and shoes from Cincinnati for sale within Union-occupied territory. The Treasury Department hoped that trade would follow the flag as northern armies moved south until the whole South was commercially "reconstructed."

The problem was that trade had a tendency to get ahead of the flag. Some southerners within Union lines swore the oath with mental reservations. Others bribed treasury agents to obtain a trading permit. Having sold cotton and bought salt or shoes, these men in turn smuggled the latter to southern armies or to merchants serving the civilian market behind Confederate lines. Some northern traders paid for cotton with gold, which eventually found its way to Nassau in the Bahamas to pay for rifles shipped through the blockade. Traders sometimes bribed Union soldiers to look the other way when cotton or salt was going through the lines. A good many soldiers could not resist the temptation to get in on the profits directly. The "mania for sudden fortunes made in cotton," wrote Charles A. Dana from Memphis in January 1863, "has to an alarming extent corrupted and demoralized the army. Every colonel, captain, or quartermaster is in secret partnership with some operator in cotton; every soldier dreams of adding a bale of cotton to his monthly pay. I had no conception of the extent of this evil until I came and saw for myself."

Similar complaints were made on the Confederate side of the line. The *Richmond Examiner* spoke bitterly in July 1863 of the injury done to the South's cause by "those rampant cotton and sugar planters, who were so early and furiously in the field for secession" but "having taken the oath of allegiance to the Yankees, are now raising cotton in partnership with their Yankee *protectors*, and shipping it to Yankee markets."

In theory the Confederate War Department agreed that all such trade was illegal but in practice recognized that under the circumstances "some barter or trading for the supply of their necessities is almost inevitable." Even the incorruptible Jefferson Davis conceded that such trading might, as a last resort, become necessary, "but the necessity should be absolute." For the Confederacy the necessity was usually absolute. Trade with the Yankees prevented famine in some areas and kept Van Dorn's Army of Mississippi in the field during the fall of 1862. "The alternative," stated the secretary of war starkly, "is thus presented of violating our established policy of withholding cotton from the enemy or of risking the starvation of our armies."

Sherman and Grant issued a stream of regulations to stop the illicit cotton trade and tighten the granting of permits for legal trade. They banished southerners who refused to take the oath and imprisoned some who violated it, required that all payments for cotton be made in U.S. greenbacks (instead of gold that could be converted into guns at Nassau), and tried to prevent the access of unscrupulous northern traders

Before the Civil War, Memphis had been a busy interior river port for the shipment of cotton. After its capture by the Union navy on June 6, 1862, Memphis resumed that function, as portayed in this Harper's Weekly *illustration of cotton being loaded aboard steamboats at the levee for shipment to northern mills. What the illustration does not tell us is where the money went that paid for this cotton.*

to Memphis. But much of this was like Canute trying to hold back the waves. The order banning gold payments was overruled in Washington. And one of Grant's restrictive regulations was also rescinded after achieving an unhappy notoriety.

Several highly visible traders who defied Grant's orders were Jews. Grant and other Union generals had frequently complained about Jewish "speculators whose love of gain is greater than their love of country." When Grant's own father brought three Jewish merchants to Memphis seeking special permits, his son the general lost his temper and on December 17, 1862, issued this order: "The Jews, as a class, violating every regulation of trade established by the Treasury Department, and also Department orders, are hereby expelled from the Department." Jewish spokesmen denounced this "enormous outrage" that punished a whole group for the alleged sins of a few. Lincoln rescinded Grant's order. While he had no objection to expelling dishonest traders, he explained, the order "proscribed a whole class, some of whom are fighting in our ranks." Grant said no more about Jews, but six months later he summed up the frustrations of his efforts to regulate a trade that was making fortunes for opportunists and "is weakening us of at least 33 percent of our force."

Fortunes were made in New Orleans, too, where Benjamin Butler ruled a restive city with a sharp two-edged sword. Cynical, clever, and apparently unscrupulous, Butler in New Orleans presented a paradox. On the one hand his Woman Order, his hanging of a southern gambler who had torn down the U.S. flag at the beginning of the occupation, and his imprisonment of several citizens who defied or displeased him earned everlasting southern hatred of "Beast" Butler. But Butler's martial law gave New Orleans the most efficient and healthy administration it had ever had. Rigorous enforcement of sanitary and quarantine measures cleaned the normally filthy streets and helped ward off the annual scourge of yellow fever—and his troops dealt with human vermin. After three months of martial law even the pro-Confederate *Picayune* had to confess that the city had never been "so free from burglars and cutthroats."

The paradox extended to Butler's economic policies. The Union blockade by sea and the Confederate blockade of river commerce with the North had strangled the city's economy. Most workers were unemployed when Farragut captured the city. Butler distributed Union rations to the poor and inaugurated an extensive public works program financed in part by high taxes on the rich and confiscation of the property of some wealthy rebels who refused to take the oath of allegiance. These procedures earned the general another Confederate cognomen— "Spoons" Butler—for allegedly stealing southerners' silver for the enrichment of himself and his Yankee friends. Some truth stuck to this charge, as Union officers and other northerners who flocked to the city bought confiscated valuables at auction for nominal

One of the first tasks of Union occupation troops in New Orleans commanded by General Benjamin Butler was to feed the civilian population. Butler soon established a system of relief and public works financed by taxation of wealthier residents, which did not increase his popularity with such people.

prices. The northerners included Butler's brother Andrew and other Yankee businessmen who helped the general with his project of obtaining cotton for northern mills. These speculators bribed their way through treasury officials and army officers to make deals with planters and brokers beyond Union lines, trading salt and gold for cotton and sugar. Both sides sometimes used French agents as go-betweens to preserve the fiction of trading with a neutral instead of the enemy. Nothing illegal was proved against Butler himself—an unfriendly treasury officer described him as "such a smart man, that it would, in any case, be difficult to discover what he wished to conceal"—but his brother Andrew returned home several hundred thousand dollars richer than he came.

Butler's notoriety compelled Lincoln to recall him in December 1862. His successor was Nathaniel P. Banks, fresh from defeats by Stonewall Jackson in Virginia. Banks tried to ban trade with the enemy and to substitute conciliation for coercion in ruling the natives—with limited success in both efforts. Treasury regulations and congressional legislation in 1863–64 curtailed the permit system for private traders. The North also began obtaining more cotton from the cultivation of plantations in occupied territory by freed slaves. But none of this seemed to diminish the commerce between the lines. The Davis administration looked the other way out of necessity; the Lincoln administration looked the other way out of policy. The North needed the cotton for its own industry and for export to earn foreign exchange. To one angry general who could not understand this policy, Lincoln explained that the war had driven the gold price of cotton to six times its prewar level, enabling the South to earn as much foreign exchange from the export of one bale through the blockade as it would have earned from six bales in peacetime. Every bale that came north, even by means of "private interest and pecuniary greed," was one less bale for the enemy to export. "Better give him *guns* for it than let him, as now, get both guns and ammunition for it."

Lincoln's rationalization did not satisfy the general, nor does it fully satisfy the historian. Cotton was the great corrupter of the Civil War; as a Confederate general noted, it made "more damn rascals on both sides than anything else." This corrosion in the rear—like the antiwar fire in the rear—grew from a malaise of the flesh in the resource-starved South and a malaise of the spirit in the North. During the winter of 1862–63 this northern malaise, spread by military defeat, appeared more fatal than the South's malaise of the flesh. Military success was a strong antidote for hunger. Buoyed by past victories in Virginia and the apparent frustration of Grant's designs against Vicksburg, the South faced the spring military campaigns with confidence. "If we can baffle them in their various designs this year," wrote Robert E. Lee in April 1863, "next fall there will be a great change in public opinion at the North. The Republicans will be destroyed & I think the friends of peace will become so strong as that the next administration will go in on that basis. We have only therefore to resist manfully . . . [and] our success will be certain."

CHAPTER TWENTY-ONE

★ ★ ★ ★ ★

Long Remember: The Summer of '63

I

Grant's failure during the winter of 1862–63 to get his army on dry land for a drive against Vicksburg bolstered Confederate faith in this "Gibraltar of the West." Believing that the Yankees were giving up, Pemberton on April 11 informed Joseph Johnston that "Grant's forces are being withdrawn to Memphis." Pemberton had earlier sent most of his cavalry to Bragg in Tennessee, where danger appeared more imminent, and he now prepared to dispatch an 8,000-man infantry division to Bragg. Civilians and officers were celebrating their deliverance at a gala ball held in Vicksburg on the night of April 16 when flashes of light and loud explosions suddenly rent the air. Yankee gunboats were running the batteries. Grant had not gone to Memphis; he had only backed up for a better start.

A resolute Grant had decided to march his army down the west bank of the Mississippi to a point below Vicksburg while sending the fleet straight past the batteries to rendezvous with the troops downriver. There they could carry the army across the mile-wide water for a dry-ground campaign against this Gibraltar from the southeast. Apparently simple, the plan involved large risks. The gunboat fleet might be destroyed or crippled. Even if it survived to ferry Grant's soldiers across the river, they would be virtually cut off from their base, for while the ironclads and even some supply transports might get past Vicksburg *down*river with the help of a four-knot current, they would be sitting ducks if they tried to go back up again. The army would have to operate deep in enemy territory without a supply line against a force of unknown strength which held interior lines and could be reinforced.

Grant's staff and his most trusted subordinates, Sherman and McPherson, opposed the plan. But like Lee, Grant believed that success could not be achieved without risk, and he was willing to lay his career on the line to prove it. When Sherman advised him to go back to Memphis and start over again with a secure supply line, Grant told him that such a move would dishearten the country. It was essential to achieve a decisive victory.

Grant's first gamble paid off; all of the gunboats got through on that moonless night. Vicksburg's gunners sank only one of the three transports. A few nights later,

Opposite page: A painting of the famous spoiling attack by eight companies of the 1st Minnesota against an entire Alabama brigade at Gettysburg. Eighty percent of the Minnesotans were killed or wounded.

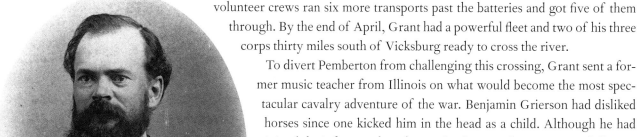

Having graduated first in his West Point class of 1853, James B. McPherson served as Grant's chief engineer officer in the first part of the war. Promoted to brigadier general in August 1862 and to major general two months later, he became one of the youngest corps commanders in the Union army in January 1863. Grant considered him his ablest subordinate next to Sherman.

volunteer crews ran six more transports past the batteries and got five of them through. By the end of April, Grant had a powerful fleet and two of his three corps thirty miles south of Vicksburg ready to cross the river.

To divert Pemberton from challenging this crossing, Grant sent a former music teacher from Illinois on what would become the most spectacular cavalry adventure of the war. Benjamin Grierson had disliked horses since one kicked him in the head as a child. Although he had joined the infantry when the war broke out, the governor of Illinois, in a stroke of genius, assigned this erstwhile bandmaster to the cavalry. Grierson soon became one of the finest horse soldiers in the western theater, where he rose to brigade command in 1862. In the spring of 1863 Grant borrowed a leaf from the enemy's book and ordered Grierson's 1,700-man brigade on an expedition into the heart of Mississippi to tear up Pemberton's supply lines and distract Confederate attention from the Union infantry toiling down the river's west bank. Combining speed, boldness, and cunning, Grierson's troopers swept triumphantly through the entire state of Mississippi during the last two weeks of April, killing or capturing over five hundred rebels at a cost of two dozen casualties and wreaking havoc on three different railroads supplying Pemberton's army. During sixteen days and six hundred miles of marauding Grierson skillfully employed diversions to lure most of Pemberton's depleted cavalry plus a full infantry division into futile pursuit. He more than evened the score against Forrest and Morgan. The Yankees rode through enemy territory, while the southern horsemen raided in Tennessee and Kentucky, where friendly natives aided them. And the strategic consequences of Grierson's foray were greater, perhaps, than those of any other cavalry raid of the war, for it played a vital role in Grant's capture of Vicksburg.

Thanks to Grierson's raid, and thanks also to a feigned attack north of Vicksburg by one of Sherman's divisions, Grant's crossing on April 30 was unopposed. Sherman had landed this division near the site of his Chickasaw Bayou repulse the previous December. For two days Sherman's artillery and a few gunboats shelled

On the night of April 16–17, Commodore David D. Porter's gunboats drifted silently on the current toward Vicksburg with coal barges lashed to their sides and with vulnerable parts of their decks protected by water-soaked cotton bales. Spotted by lookouts who set fires on the banks to illuminate the targets, the seven gunboats and three transports went full steam ahead. They were hit several times by the guns of Vicksburg, shown here firing on the boats as they rounded the S-curve in the river, but all save one transport got through.

Confederate defenses while the infantry deployed as if for attack. Pemberton took the bait. In response to a panicky message from the commander confronting Sherman—"The enemy are in front of me in force such as has never before been seen at Vicksburg. Send me reinforcements"—Pemberton recalled 3,000 troops who had been on their way to challenge Grant.

In a sharp fight on May 1 the 23,000 bluecoats with Grant brushed aside 6,000 rebel infantry at Port Gibson ten miles east of the river. Having established a secure lodgement, Grant sent for Sherman and the rest of his troops, who would bring Union strength east of the river to more than 40,000 to oppose Pemberton's 30,000 scattered in various detachments. Pemberton finally recognized that Grant had crossed his whole army below Vicksburg. But instead of predictably driving straight northward toward Vicksburg, keeping his left flank in contact with the river where he might hope to receive additional supplies from transports that ran the batteries, Grant was focusing on the army Joseph Johnston was trying to scrape together at Jackson, the state capital forty miles east of Vicksburg. If he ignored Johnston and went after Pemberton, the Yankees might suddenly find another enemy on their right flank. So Grant decided to drive eastward, eliminate the Johnston threat before it became serious and before Pemberton realized what was happening, and then turn back west to attack Vicksburg.

As for provisions, Grant remembered what he had learned after Van Dorn's destruction of his supply base the previous December. This time he intended to cut loose from his base, travel light, and live off the country. Although civilians were

Finding his true calling as a cavalry leader instead of a band leader, Grierson aided Grant's Vicksburg campaign with a raid that Sherman later described as "the most brilliant expedition of the war." Grierson stayed in the regular army after the war as commander of the black 10th U.S. Cavalry, one of the best mounted units in the army. We can also be certain that this regiment had an excellent band.

By 1863 one of the most formidable ironclad gunboats on the Mississippi was the U.S.S. Choctaw, *photographed here. Sheathed in iron plate and equipped with a ram, she was also armed with seven big guns. In Sherman's diversionary attack on Chickasaw Bluffs April 30, 1863, the* Choctaw *was struck by Confederate shells fifty-three times but suffered little damage and no injuries to her crew.*

This painting by Owen J. Hopkins, a veteran of the 43rd Ohio in Grant's army, shows members of an artillery battery foraging for food and fodder in Mississippi. Note the private at the far right carrying a chicken.

going hungry in Mississippi, Grant was confident that his soldiers would not. A powerful army on the move could seize supplies that penniless women and children could not afford to buy. For the next two weeks the Yankee soldiers lived well on hams, poultry, vegetables, milk and honey as they stripped bare the plantations in their path. Divided counsels and paralysis in the face of Grant's unexpected and rapid movements crippled the Confederate response. On May 9 the War Department in Richmond ordered Johnston to take overall command of the Mississippi defenses and promised him reinforcements. But Johnston got no farther than Jackson, where he found 25,000 confident Yankees bearing down on the capital after bowling over a small rebel force at Raymond a dozen miles to the west. Coming on

This lithograph of a sketch by A. E. Mathews, a soldier in the 31st Ohio, shows a portion of General McPherson's 17th Corps attacking Confederate defenses during the battle of Jackson on May 14, 1863.

through a rainstorm, Sherman's and McPherson's corps on May 14 launched a straight-ahead attack against the 6,000 entrenched Confederates defending Jackson and sent them flying through the streets out of town. Sherman's corps set to work at a task in which they soon became experts—wrecking railroad facilities and burning foundries, arsenals, factories, and machine shops in the capital along with a fair number of homes that got in the way of the flames, doing their work so thoroughly that Jackson became known to its conquerors as Chimneyville.

Meanwhile Johnston urged Pemberton to unite his troops with Johnston's 6,000 survivors north of Jackson, where with expected reinforcements they would be strong enough to attack Grant. This would leave Vicksburg undefended, but Johnston cared little about that. His strategy was to concentrate superior numbers against Grant and beat him, after which the Confederates could reoccupy Vicksburg at leisure. Pemberton disagreed. He had orders to hold Vicksburg, and he intended to do so by shielding it with his army. Before the two southern generals could agree on a plan, the Yankees made the matter moot by slicing up Pemberton's mobile force on May 16 at Champion's Hill, midway between Jackson and Vicksburg.

This was the key battle of the campaign, involving about 29,000 Federals against 20,000 Confederates. The Union troops were McPherson's and McClernand's corps (Sherman's men were still burning Jackson), which found the rebels posted along four miles of the seventy-foot-high Champion's Hill ridge. While the normally aggressive McClernand showed unwonted caution, McPherson pitched into the enemy left with blows that finally crumpled this flank after several hours of bloody fighting. If McClernand had done his part, Grant believed, the Yankees might have bagged most of Pemberton's army; as it was the bluecoats inflicted 3,800 casualties at the cost of 2,400 to themselves and cut off one whole division from the rest of Pemberton's force.

The main body of Confederates fell back in demoralized fashion to the Big Black River only ten miles east of Vicksburg. Grant's cocky midwesterners came after them on May 17. The rebel position at the Big Black was strong, but an impetuous brigade in McClernand's corps, chafing at its lack of a share in the previous day's glory, swept forward without orders and routed the left of the Confederate line defending the bridge that Pemberton was trying to keep open for his lost division, which unbeknown to him was marching in the opposite direction to join Johnston. The unnerved rebels collapsed once again, losing 1,750 men (mostly prisoners) while Union casualties were only 200. On May 17 Pemberton retreated to Vicksburg, where citizens were shocked by the exhausted countenances of the soldiers.

Thus had Grant wrought in a seventeen-day campaign during which his army marched 180 miles, fought and won five engagements against separate enemy forces which if combined would have been almost as large as his own, inflicted 7,200 casualties at the cost of 4,300, and cooped up an apparently demoralized enemy in the Vicksburg defenses. Of all the tributes Grant received, the one he appreciated most came from his friend Sherman. "Until this moment I never thought your expedition a success," Sherman told Grant on May 18 as he gazed down from the heights where his corps had been mangled the previous December. "I never could see the end clearly until now. But this is a campaign. This is a success if we never take the town."

But Grant hoped to take the town, immediately, while its defenders were still

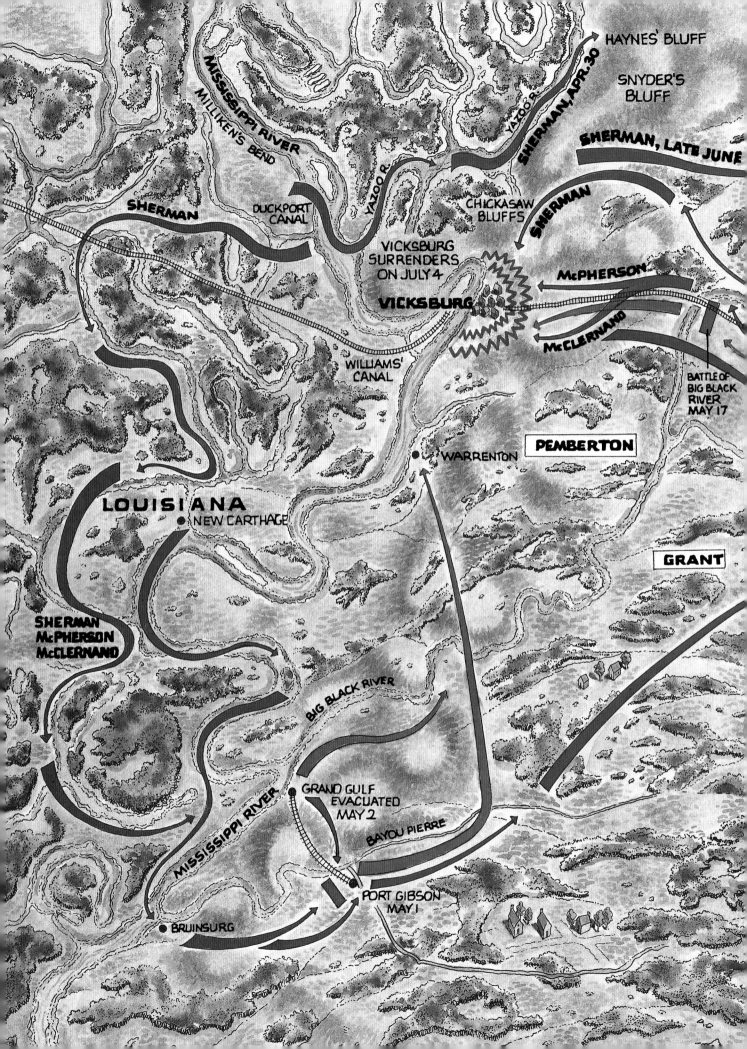

HAYNES' BLUFF

SNYDER'S BLUFF

SHERMAN, APR. 30

SHERMAN, LATE JUNE

MISSISSIPPI RIVER

MILLIKEN'S BEND

SHERMAN

DUCKPORT CANAL

YAZOO R.

YAZOO R.

CHICKASAW BLUFFS

SHERMAN

SHERMAN

McPHERSON

VICKSBURG SURRENDERS ON JULY 4

VICKSBURG

McCLERNAND

WILLIAMS' CANAL

BATTLE OF BIG BLACK RIVER MAY 17

WARRENTON

PEMBERTON

LOUISIANA

NEW CARTHAGE

GRANT

SHERMAN McPHERSON McCLERNAND

BIG BLACK RIVER

MISSISSIPPI RIVER

GRAND GULF EVACUATED MAY 2

BAYOU PIERRE

PORT GIBSON MAY 1

BRUINSBURG

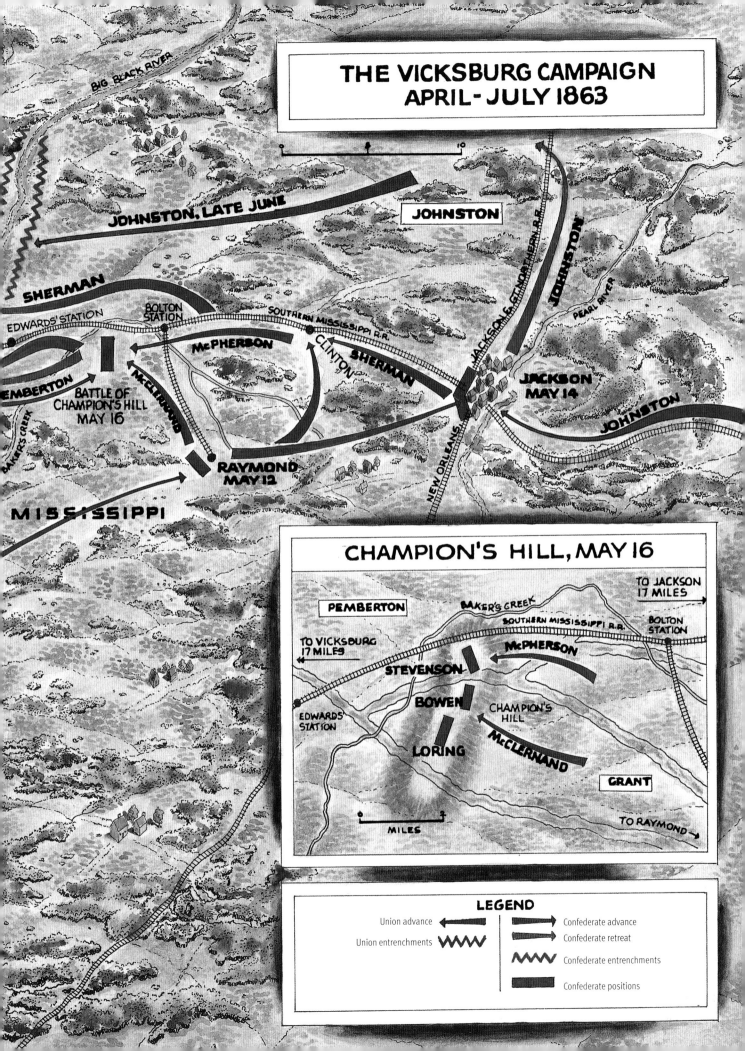

stunned. Without stopping to rest, he ordered an attack by his whole army on May 19. With confidence bred by success, northern boys charged the maze of trenches, rifle-pits, and artillery ringing the landward side of Vicksburg. But as they emerged into the open the rebel line came alive with sheets of fire that stopped the bluecoats in their tracks. Ensconced behind the most formidable works of the war, the rebels had taken heart. They proved the theory that one soldier under cover was the equal of at least three in the open.

Bloodied but still undaunted, the Union troops wanted to try again. Grant planned another assault for May 22, preceded this time by reconnaisance to find weak points in enemy lines (there were few) and an artillery bombardment by two hundred guns on land and one hundred in the fleet. Again the Yankees surged forward against a hail of lead, this time securing lodgement at several points only to be driven out by counterattacks. After several hours of this, McClernand on the Union left sent word of a breakthrough and a request for support to exploit it. Distrustful as ever of McClernand, Grant nevertheless ordered Sherman and McPherson to renew their attacks and send reinforcements to the left. But these efforts, said Grant later, "only served to increase our casualties without giving any benefit." For the second time in four days the southerners threw back an all-out attack, doing much to redeem their earlier humiliation and inflicting almost as many casualties on the enemy as in all five earlier clashes combined.

This painting depicts the most dramatic moment in the May 22 attack on Confederate defenses at Vicksburg. The 22nd Iowa of General McClernand's 13th Corps made a temporary lodgement on the redoubt protecting the rail line into Vicksburg. McClernand exaggerated their success, causing Grant to order renewed attacks elsewhere along the lines, to no avail except to increase Union casualties. The 22nd Iowa suffered the greatest number of casualties that day— 70 killed or mortally wounded, 75 wounded, and 15 missing.

Though they failed, Grant did not consider these assaults a mistake. He had hoped to capture Vicksburg before Johnston could build up a relief force in his rear and before summer heat and disease wore down his troops. Moreover, he explained, the men "believed they could carry the works in their front, and they would not [afterwards] have worked so patiently in the trenches if they had not been allowed to try." After the May repulses the bluecoats dug their own elaborate network of trenches and settled down for a siege. Grant called in reinforcements from Memphis and other points to build up his army to 70,000. He posted several divisions to watch Johnston, who was now hovering off to the northeast with a makeshift army of 30,000, some of them untrained conscripts. Grant had no doubt of ultimate success. On May 24 he informed Halleck that the enemy was "in our grasp. The fall of Vicksburg and the capture of most of the garrison can only be a question of time."

Pemberton thought so too, unless help arrived. Regarding Vicksburg as "the most important point in the Confederacy," he informed Johnston in a message smuggled through Federal lines by a daring courier that he intended to hold it "as long as possible." But Pemberton could hold on only if Johnston pierced the blue cordon constricting him. "The men credit and are encouraged by a report that you are near with a large force." For the next six weeks Pemberton's soldiers and some three thousand civilians trapped in Vicksburg lived in hope of rescue by Johnston.

But Davis had no more reinforcements to send to Johnston. Braxton Bragg had already lent Johnston two divisions and could not spare another. Robert E. Lee insisted that he needed every soldier in Virginia for his impending invasion of Pennsylvania. In Louisiana, General Richard Taylor (son of Mexican War hero Zachary Taylor) reluctantly diverted three brigades from his campaign against Banks to assist Pemberton. Their only accomplishment, however, was to publicize the controversy surrounding northern employment of black troops. In a futile attempt to disrupt Grant's restored supply line, one of Taylor's brigades on June 7 attacked the Union garrison at Milliken's Bend on the Mississippi above Vicksburg. This post was defended mainly by two new regiments of contrabands. Untrained and armed with old muskets, most of the black troops nevertheless fought desperately. With the aid of two gunboats they finally drove off the enemy. For raw troops, wrote Grant, the freedmen "behaved well." Assistant Secretary of War Dana, still with Grant's army, spoke with more enthusiasm. "The bravery of the blacks," he declared, "completely revolutionized the sentiment of the army with regard to the employment of negro troops. I heard prominent officers who formerly in private had sneered at the idea of negroes fighting express themselves after that as heartily in favor of it." But among the Confederates, Dana added, "the feeling was very different." Infuriated by the arming of former slaves, southern troops at Milliken's Bend shouted "no quarter!" and reportedly murdered several captured blacks. If true, such behavior undoubtedly reflected their officers' sentiment: the rebel brigade commander "consider[ed] it an unfortunate circumstance that any negroes were captured," while General Taylor reported that "a very large number of the negroes were killed and wounded, and, unfortunately, some 50, with 2 of their white officers, captured." The War Department in Washington learned that some of the captured freedmen were sold as slaves.

The repulse at Milliken's Bend cut short Confederate attempts to succor Vicksburg from west of the Mississippi. All hopes for relief now focused on Johnston. During the first month of the siege, morale remained good despite around-the-clock Union artillery and gunboat fire that drove civilians into man-made caves that dotted the hillsides.

But as the weeks passed and Johnston did not come, spirits sagged. Soldiers were subsisting on quarter-rations. By the end of June nearly half of them were on the sick list, many with scurvy. Skinned rats appeared beside mule meat in the markets. Dogs and cats disappeared mysteriously. The tensions of living under siege drove people to the edge of madness: if things went on much longer, wrote a Confederate officer, "a building will have to be arranged for the accommodation of maniacs." Johnston had never shared the belief in himself as Deliverer. "I consider saving Vicksburg hopeless," he informed the War Department on June 15. To the government this looked like a western refrain of Johnston's behavior on the

In its issue of May 21, 1864, Harper's Weekly ran an article titled "Rebel Atrocities," which was accompanied by several illustrations of Confederate murders of black soldiers and their white officers after surrender. This woodcut purports to show such an action after the battle of Milliken's Bend. The article stated: "A large number of the negroes were murdered on the field after they had surrendered. . . . Some were crucified and burned. Of those whom this last fate befell, several were white officers in command of the negro troops."

This striking photograph was taken in 1902. It shows T. C. Lewis standing at the entrance of a cave at Vicksburg in which he had lived as a fourteen-year-old with his family from May 18 to July 4, 1863.

Virginia Peninsula in 1862, when he had seemed reluctant to fight to defend Richmond. "Vicksburg must not be lost without a desperate struggle," the secretary of war wired back. But Johnston considered his force too weak. He shifted the burden to Pemberton, urging him to try a breakout attack or to escape across the river (through the gauntlet of Union ironclads!). At the end of June, in response to frantic pressure from Richmond, Johnston began to probe feebly with his five divisions toward seven Union divisions commanded by Sherman which Grant had detached from the besiegers to guard their rear. Johnston's rescue attempt was too little and too late. By the time he was ready to take action, Pemberton had surrendered.

Inexorable circumstances forced Pemberton to this course—though many southerners then and later believed that only his Yankee birth could have produced such poltroonery. All through June, Union troops had dug approaches toward Confederate lines in a classic siege operation. They also tunneled under rebel defenses. To show what they could do, northern engineers exploded mines and blew holes in southern lines on June 25 and July 1, but Confederate infantry closed the breaches. The Yankees readied a bigger mine to be set off July 6 and followed by a full-scale assault. But before then it was all over. Literally starving, "Many Soldiers" addressed a letter to Pemberton on June 28 advising surrender: "This army is now ripe for mutiny, unless it can be fed." Pemberton consulted his division commanders, who assured him that their sick and malnourished men could not attempt a breakout attack. On July 3 Pemberton asked Grant for terms. Living up to his Donelson reputation, Grant at first insisted on unconditional

Under flag of truce, Generals Grant and Pemberton met near Union lines on July 3 for a private conversation, as pictured here. Pemberton resisted Grant's terms of unconditional surrender of Vicksburg and its 30,000 defenders. Pemberton returned to his own lines thinking the siege would continue, but that night Grant sent a note offering to parole the Confederate soldiers. Pemberton accepted, and next day Union soldiers marched into Vicksburg.

surrender. But after reflecting on the task of shipping 30,000 captives north to prison camps when he needed all his transport for further operations, Grant offered to parole the prisoners. With good reason he expected that many of them, disillusioned by suffering and surrender, would scatter to their homes and carry the contagion of defeat with them.

The Fourth of July 1863 was the most memorable Independence Day in American history since that first one four score and seven years earlier. Far away in Pennsylvania the high tide of the Confederacy receded from Gettysburg. Here in Mississippi, white flags sprouted above rebel trenches, the emaciated troops marched out and stacked arms, and a Union division moved into Vicksburg to raise the stars and stripes over the courthouse. To many southerners the humiliation of surrendering on July 4 added insult to injury. The good behavior of the occupation troops, however, mitigated the insult. Scarcely a taunt escaped their lips as Union soldiers marched into the city; on the contrary, they paid respect to the courage of the defenders and shared rations with them. Indeed, the Yankees did what many Vicksburg citizens had wanted to do for weeks—they broke into the stores of "spec-

This painting of the 4th Minnesota entering Vicksburg on July 4, 1863, while black and white civilians look on, was done in 1904 by one of America's foremost artists, Francis Millet, who had been a drummer boy and surgeon's assistant in the Union army. The American flag would soon fly atop the courthouse in the distance. A local woman who watched the Union soldiers march into Vicksburg wrote in her diary: "What a contrast [these] stalwart, well-fed men, so splendidly set up and accoutered [were] to . . . the worn men in gray, who were being blindly dashed against this embodiment of modern power." Millet went down with the Titanic *in 1912.*

One of the best-known women artists in the United States, Lily Martin Spencer, portrayed a northern family celebrating the news of Vicksburg's fall. The mother of eight children, Spencer painted many domestic scenes. In this one the mother holds her infant son while she reads the New York Times*'s story of the "Great Victory" at Vicksburg; her other children march around in celebration as a servant looks on.*

ulators" who had been holding food for higher prices and distributed it to the starving population.

The capture of Vicksburg was the most important northern strategic victory of the war, perhaps meriting Grant's later assertion that "the fate of the Confederacy was sealed when Vicksburg fell." But the Union commander did not intend to rest on his Fourth of July laurels. Johnston still threatened his rear, and the Confederate garrison at Port Hudson 240 river-miles to the south still held out against Nathaniel P. Banks's besieging army. Grant ordered Sherman with 50,000 men to go after Johnston's 31,000 "and inflict all the punishment you can." Grant also prepared to send a division or two to help Banks capture Port Hudson.

In the event, however, Banks needed no more help than the news of Vicksburg's capitulation, which persuaded the southern commander at Port Hudson to surrender his now untenable position. After a two-month campaign to establish Union control of the rich sugar and cotton regions along Bayou Teche, Banks's soldiers aided by Farragut's warships had laid siege to Port Hudson in the last week of May. Outnumbering the Confederate garrison by 20,000 to 7,000, Banks nevertheless had to contend with natural and man-made defenses as rugged as those at Vicksburg. Two head-on northern assaults on May 27 and June 14 produced only a twelve-to-one disparity in casualties. In the attack of May 27 two Union regiments of Louisiana blacks proved that they could die as bravely as white Yankees. After the failure of these assaults, Banks had to rest content with starving the garrison into submission. Port Hudson's defenders lived in the hope that Johnston would rescue them after he had disposed of Grant at Vicksburg. When news came instead that the upriver fortress had fallen, the garrison at Port Hudson—subsisting on mules and rats—did likewise on July 9. A week later an unarmed merchant ship from St. Louis arrived in New Orleans after an unmolested trip down the Mississippi. "The Father

of Waters again goes unvexed to the sea," announced Lincoln. The Confederacy was cut in twain.

Johnston, blamed by Jefferson Davis for the fall of Vicksburg, was also soon disposed of. Retreating to his defenses at Jackson, the cautious southern commander hoped to lure Sherman into a frontal assault. Having learned the cost of such attacks at Vicksburg, Sherman refused the bait. He started to surround the city and cut its communications. Johnston evaded the trap by slipping across the Pearl River on the night of July 16. Unlike Pemberton he had saved his army—an achievement cited by his defenders—but its withdrawal halfway to Alabama abandoned central Mississippi's plantations and railroads to the none-too-tender mercies of Sherman's army. Johnston's retreat came as icing on the cake of Grant's Vicksburg campaign, which Lincoln described as "one of the most brilliant in the world"—a judgment echoed by a good many subsequent military analysts. "Grant is my man," the president declared on July 5, "and I am his the rest of the war."

This photograph of part of the Confederate defenses at Port Hudson after they were surrendered shows why Union forces were not able to carry them by attack. Behind such formidable earthworks and sandbags, one soldier was equal to at least three enemy soldiers in the open.

Important as they were, Grant's achievements in Mississippi took second place in public attention to events in the Virginia theater. The Union ultimately won the war mainly by victories in the West, but the Confederacy more than once came close to winning it in the East. During the spring and summer of 1863, Robert E. Lee scored his greatest success in this effort—followed by his greatest failure.

That Lee could take any initiative at all seemed unlikely in April 1863. Food and forage for his army were in such short supply that men hunted sassafras buds and wild onions to ward off scurvy while horses died for lack of grass. Longstreet had taken two divisions to confront Federal thrusts from Norfolk and the North Carolina coast. These Union movements amounted to little in the end, but Longstreet remained in southeast Virginia through April to harass the enemy and gather supplies from this unscarred region. Without these two divisions, Lee had only 60,000 men along the Rappahannock to watch double that number of bluecoats under their new and dynamic commander, Joseph Hooker. The Confederate cavalry had to disperse over a wide area to find grass for the horses, further weakening southern forces at a time when Hooker had reorganized his cavalry into a single corps better armed and mounted than Jeb Stuart's troopers. The days of easy rebel cavalry superiority were over.

Nevertheless, morale remained high in Confederate ranks, the supplies sent by Longstreet improved their rations, and the elaborate network of trenches they held along twenty-five miles of the Rappahannock near Fredericksburg gave them confidence that they could hold off any number of Yankees. But Hooker had no intention of assaulting those trenches. Having reinvigorated the Army of the Potomac after the Burnside disasters, he planned a campaign of maneuver to force Lee into the open for a showdown fight. Brash and boastful, Hooker reportedly said: "May God have mercy on General Lee, for I will have none."

This drawing by Edwin Forbes depicts part of the Union 5th Corps marching up the north bank of the Rappahannock River to cross at Kelly's Ford and come in behind the Confederates. The regiment in the foreground was one of the colorful Zouave units, probably the 5th New York. General Hooker tried an experiment in this campaign: he had ammunition and other supplies loaded on pack mules, several of which are shown here, rather than in wagons. In theory this method would give the army greater mobility, but in practice it did not work out well. Many of the mules were not accustomed to carrying packs, and many of the teamsters were inexperienced at packing them efficiently. After Chancellorsville the Army of the Potomac went back to wagons.

For a few days at the end of April, Hooker seemed ready to make good his boast. He divided his large army into three parts. Ten thousand blue horsemen splashed across the Rappahannock far upstream and headed south to cut Lee's supply lines. Seventy thousand northern infantry also marched upriver to cross at fords several miles beyond Lee's left flank, while another 40,000 feigned an advance at Fredericksburg to hold Lee in place while the flanking force pitched into his left and rear. The Army of the Potomac carried out these complicated maneuvers swiftly. By the evening of April 30 Hooker had his 70,000 infantry near a crossroads mansion and outbuildings

Edwin Forbes's sketch of the initial encounter between Union and Confederate forces at Chancellorsville on May 1. Even though Hooker had the advantages of numbers and initiative, he lost his nerve and pulled back from this position.

called Chancellorsville, nine miles west of Fredericksburg in the midst of a dense second-growth forest called locally the Wilderness. For once the Yankees had stolen a march on Lee and seemed to have the outnumbered rebels gripped in an iron pincers. Despite his nickname of Fighting Joe, when he saw that Lee intended to fight rather than withdraw Hooker mysteriously lost his nerve. Perhaps his resolve three months earlier to go on the wagon had been a mistake, for he seemed at this moment to need some liquid courage. Or perhaps a trait noted by a fellow officer in the old army had surfaced again: "Hooker could play the best game of poker I ever saw until it came to the point where he should go a thousand better, and then he would flunk." Whatever the reason, when Lee called his bet on May 1, Hooker gave up the initiative to the boldest of gamblers in this deadliest of games.

Guessing correctly that the main threat came from the Union troops at Chancellorsville, Lee left only 10,000 infantry under feisty Jubal Early to hold the Fredericksburg defenses, and put the rest on the march westward to the Wilderness on May 1. At midday they clashed with Hooker's advance units a couple of miles east of Chancellorsville. Here the dense undergrowth gave way to open country, where the Federals' superior weight of numbers and artillery gave them an edge. But instead of pressing the attack, Hooker ordered his troops back to a defensive position around Chancellorsville—where the thick woods evened these odds. Thunderstruck, Union corps commanders protested but obeyed. Sensing his psychological edge, Lee decided to take the offensive despite being outnumbered nearly two to one. On the night of May 1, Jackson and Lee sat on empty hardtack boxes and conferred by firelight. The Federals' entrenched line on high ground around Chancellorsville seemed too strong for a direct assault. The Union left was anchored on the Rappahannock and could not be turned. While the two generals discussed how to get at "those people," Stuart brought reports from his scouts that Hooker's right flank was "in the air" three miles west of Chancellorsville. Here was the opportunity Lee needed, and Jackson was the man to seize it. The only problem was to find a route through the wilderness of scrub oak and thorny undergrowth by which a force could get around to this flank unobserved. One of Jackson's staff officers

To recoup his damaged reputation after acquittal on the charge of murdering his wife's lover, Dan Sickles had raised a whole brigade (five regiments) in New York City and was rewarded with appointment as brigadier general. He proved to be a capable commander as well as a crony of Hooker's and was promoted to major general and to corps command by 1863.

solved this problem by finding a local resident to guide them along a track used to haul charcoal for an iron-smelting furnace.

Screened by Stuart's cavalry, Jackson's 30,000 infantry and artillery left early May 2 for a roundabout twelve-mile march to their attack position. Lee remained with only 15,000 men to confront Hooker's main force. This was the most daring gamble Lee had yet taken. Jackson's flank march across the enemy's front—one of the most dangerous maneuvers in war—left his strung-out column vulnerable to attack. Lee's holding force was likewise in great peril if Hooker should discover its weakness. And Early still faced nearly three times his numbers at Fredericksburg (from which Hooker had called one more corps to Chancellorsville). But Lee counted on Hooker doing nothing while Jackson completed his march; the Union commander fulfilled expectations.

Hooker could not blame his cavalry for failure to detect Jackson's maneuver, for he had sent nearly all of it away on a raid that threw a scare into Richmond but otherwise accomplished little. Besides, Federal infantry units spotted Jackson's movement and reported it to Hooker—who misinterpreted it. Two of Daniel Sickles's 3rd Corps divisions moved out and attacked the tail of Jackson's column. Sickles was a character of some notoriety, the only political general among Hooker's corps commanders, a prewar Tammany Democrat with a reputation for philandering. His wife, perhaps in revenge, had taken a lover whom Sickles shot dead on a Washington street in 1859. He was acquitted of murder after the first successful plea of temporary insanity in the history of American jurisprudence. Rising from colonel to major general in Hooker's old division, Sickles was one of the army commander's favorites. His probing attack on May 2 alerted Hooker to Jackson's movement toward the southwest. Fighting Joe momentarily wondered if the slippery Stonewall was up to his old flanking tricks, but the wishful thought that the rebels must "ingloriously fly" soon convinced him that Lee's whole army was retreating! Hooker therefore failed to prepare for the blow soon to fall on his right.

Commander of the 11th Corps holding the Union right was Oliver O. Howard, the opposite in every respect of Sickles. A West Point professional whose distinguished combat record included loss of an arm at Fair Oaks, Howard was a monogamous teetotaling Congregationalist known as the Christian Soldier. He had little in common with the German-American soldiers who constituted a large part of his corps. This "Dutch" corps, only 12,000 strong, had a poor reputation, having turned in mediocre performances under Frémont in the Shenandoah Valley and Franz Sigel at Second Bull Run. What happened at Chancellorsville did nothing to improve that reputation. All through the afternoon, alarmed pickets sent word to Howard that the rebels were building up to something off to the west. Howard assured Hooker that he was ready for an attack. Yet most of his regiments were facing south, for Howard considered the thick woods to the west impenetrable. And like Hooker he also thought that this enemy activity was designed to cover a retreat. As suppertime approached, many of Howard's troops were relaxing or cooking.

A few hundred yards to the west, Jackson's rugged veterans—their uniforms torn to worse tatters than usual by briars and brush—were deployed for attack at 5:15. Coming through the woods from the west on a front two miles wide and three divisions deep, the yelling rebels hit the south-facing Union regiments endwise and knocked them down like tenpins. Despite wild confusion, some of the 11th Corps brigades and batteries maintained discipline and fought desperately, slowing the Confederate advance but being forced in the end to join the stampede of routed regiments fleeing to the rear. By dusk Jackson had rolled up the Union right for two miles before Howard and Hooker improvised a new line out of troops from four different corps to bring the jubilant but disorganized southerners to a halt. The two divisions remaining with Lee had joined the attack on their front. For several hours, sporadic and disordered fighting flared up in the moon-shadowed woods, with some units firing on their own men in one of the rare night actions of the Civil War.

Misfortune beyond the usual tragedies of war struck the Confederates during this moonlit melee. Determined to keep the Yankees on the run, Jackson and several officers rode ahead of their lines to reconnoiter for a renewed attack. Returning at a trot, they were fired on by nervous rebels who mistook them for Union cavalry. Jackson fell with two bullets in his left arm, which had to be amputated. Stuart took command of his corps and led it well for the rest of the battle. But the loss of Jackson proved to be permanent and irreparable. Pneumonia set in, and the inimitable Stonewall died eight days later.

The morning after Jackson's wounding, May 3, saw the crisis of the battle. Some of the war's hardest fighting took place on two fronts separated by nine miles. During the night Hooker had ordered "Uncle" John Sedgwick (so named by his men for his avuncular manner), commander of the 6th Corps at Fredericksburg, to carry the heights back of the town and push on toward Lee's rear at Chancellorsville. At daybreak Uncle John hurled his three divisions against the trenches and the stone wall below Marye's Heights where Burnside's troops had come to grief the previous December. History appeared to repeat itself as Jubal Early's division threw them back twice. But on the third try, in one of the war's few genuine bayonet charges, the first wave of blue attackers carried the heights, captured a thousand prisoners, and sent the rebels flying.

Meanwhile Hooker at Chancellorsville had remained strangely passive, seeming to expect Sedgwick to do all the army's offensive fighting. Hooker had even ordered Sickles's corps to fall back at dawn from a salient on high ground at Hazel Grove, a mile west of the Chancellorsville crossroads. This allowed Lee and Stuart to reunite the two wings of their army and to mass their artillery at Hazel Grove, one of the few places in the Wilderness where it could be used effectively. The Confederates pressed an all-out attack on the three corps holding the immediate area around Chancellorsville. Hooker kept three other Union corps idle despite openings for them to fall on Lee's flanks. Hooker seemed in a daze even before a cannonball hit his headquarters and knocked him unconscious in midmorning. He recovered in time to retain command—a pity, in the eyes of several subordinates, who had hoped that the ranking corps commander would take charge and launch a counterattack. Instead, Hooker ordered withdrawal a mile or two northward to a contracted defensive line.

This photograph of Major General Oliver Otis Howard was made after his wounded right arm had been amputated in June 1862; the empty sleeve of his uniform hangs limply. The right-handed Howard learned to write with his left hand.

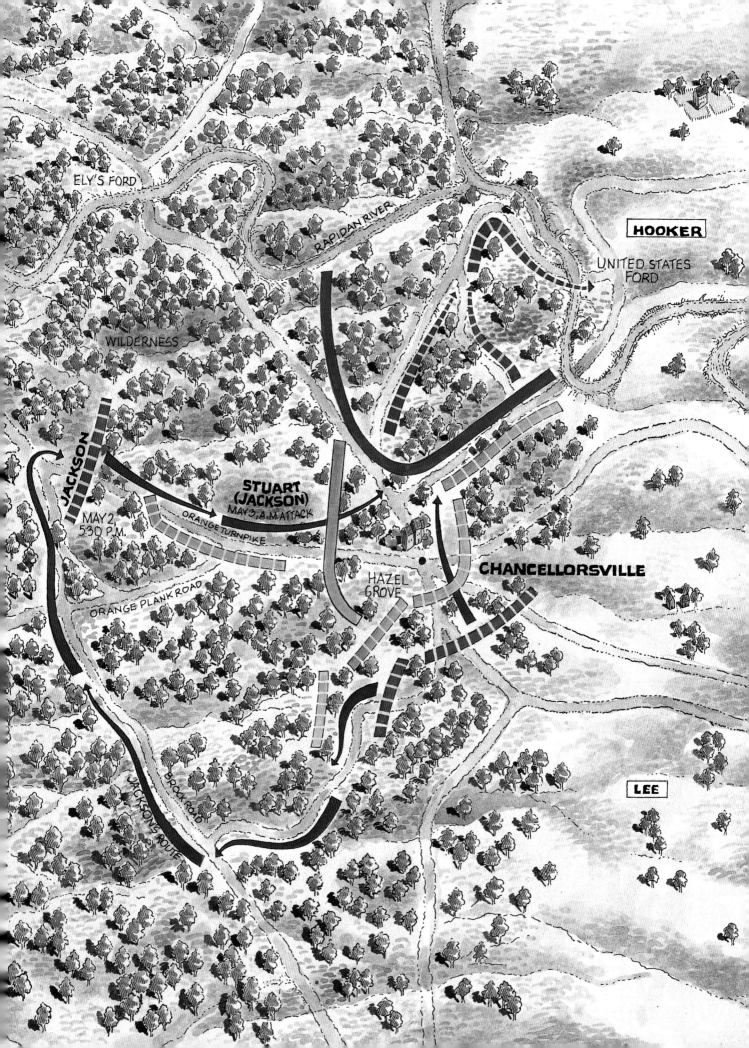

ELY'S FORD

RAPIDAN RIVER

HOOKER

UNITED STATES FORD

WILDERNESS

JACKSON
MAY 2
5:30 P.M.

STUART
(JACKSON)
MAY 3, A.M. ATTACK

ORANGE TURNPIKE

ORANGE PLANK ROAD

HAZEL GROVE

CHANCELLORSVILLE

BROCK ROAD

JACKSON'S ROUTE

LEE

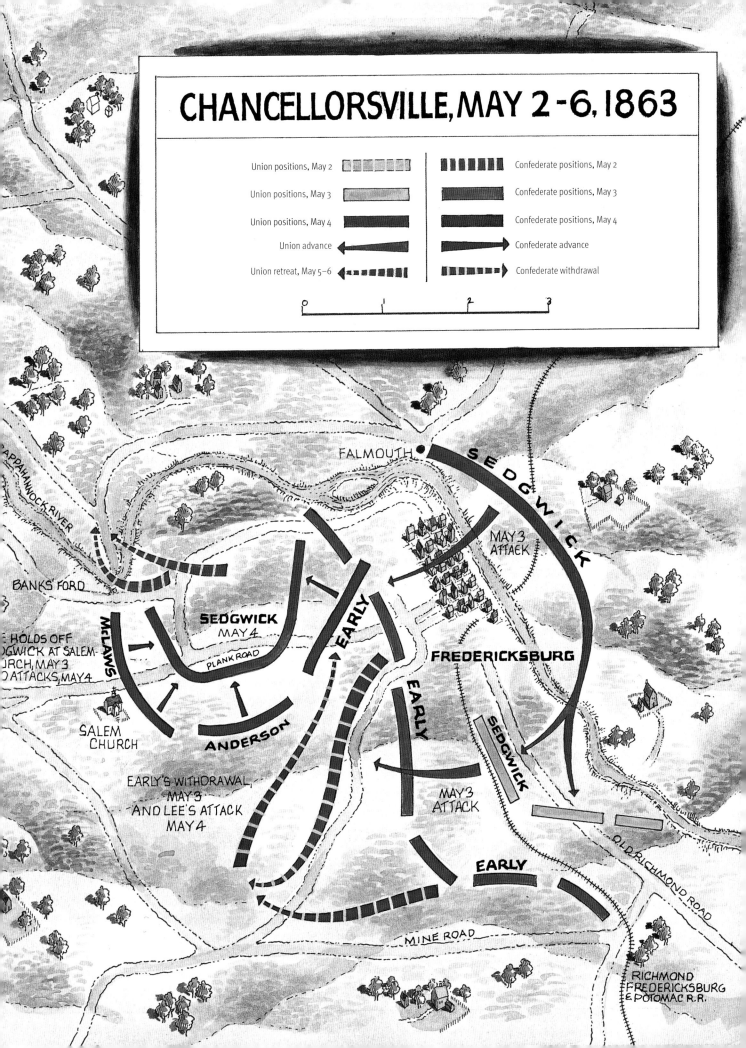

CHANCELLORSVILLE, MAY 2-6, 1863

Union positions, May 2

Union positions, May 3

Union positions, May 4

Union advance

Union retreat, May 5–6

Confederate positions, May 2

Confederate positions, May 3

Confederate positions, May 4

Confederate advance

Confederate withdrawal

0   1   2   3

FALMOUTH

SEDGWICK

RAPPAHANNOCK RIVER

BANKS' FORD

MAY 3 ATTACK

E HOLDS OFF
GWICK AT SALEM
URCH, MAY 3
O ATTACKS, MAY 4

McLAWS

SEDGWICK
MAY 4

PLANK ROAD

EARLY

FREDERICKSBURG

SALEM
CHURCH

ANDERSON

EARLY

SEDGWICK

EARLY'S WITHDRAWAL
MAY 3
AND LEE'S ATTACK
MAY 4

MAY 3
ATTACK

EARLY

OLD RICHMOND ROAD

MINE ROAD

RICHMOND
FREDERICKSBURG
& POTOMAC R.R.

A view of the town of Fredericksburg from across the Rappahannock River on May 3, 1863. Earlier that day the Union artillery in the foreground, now limbered up and ready to move, had supported the infantry assault that carried the heights behind the town.

The exhausted but exultant rebels, who had fought with an élan unprecedented even in this victorious army, cheered wildly as Lee rode into the clearing around the burning Chancellor mansion. It was the Virginian's greatest triumph—but the battle was not yet over. While the two armies around Chancellorsville broke off fighting as if by mutual consent to rescue hundreds of wounded men threatened by brush fires started by exploding shells, Lee received word of Sedgwick's breakthrough at Fredericksburg. Here was a serious threat to his rear even though Hooker seemed cowed in his front. Without hesitation Lee dispatched a division which blunted Sedgwick's advance near a country church midway between Fredericksburg and Chancellorsville. Next day Lee took yet another division from his front to attack Sedgwick. This left only 25,000 Confederates under Stuart to face Hooker's 75,000, but Lee seemed to know that his benumbed adversary would remain passive. In the late afternoon of May 4 a disjointed attack by 21,000 rebels against Sedgwick's equal force was repulsed. Aware that Hooker had given up, however, Sedgwick pulled his troops back over the Rappahannock during the night.

At a council of war that same night, a majority of the Union corps commanders with Hooker voted to counterattack. True to form, Hooker disregarded this vote and decided to retreat across the river. The Army of the Potomac accomplished this difficult task during a rainstorm the next night. Aggressive as ever, Lee had planned another assault on the morning of May 6 and expressed regret, as he had done the previous summer, that the Federals escaped destruction. But by any standard he had won an astounding victory, recognized as such in both North and South. Without Longstreet and with little more than half as many men as an enemy that had initially outmaneuvered him, Lee had grasped the initiative, gone over to the attack, and repeatedly divided and maneuvered his forces in such a way as to give them superiority or equality of numbers at the point of attack. Like a rabbit mesmerized by the gray fox, Hooker was frozen into immobility and did not use half his power at any time in the battle.

The triumph at Chancellorsville, however, came at great cost. The Confederates suffered 13,000 casualties, 22 percent of their force (the Union figures were 17,000 and 15 percent). The most grievous loss was Jackson, who had done so much to make the victory possible. And the boost that the battle gave to southern morale proved in the end harmful, for it bred an overconfidence in their own prowess and a contempt for the enemy that led to disaster. Believing his troops invincible, Lee was about to ask them to do the impossible.

During the battle Lincoln haunted the War Department telegraph office. For several days he received only fragmentary and contradictory reports. When the truth became clear on May 6, the president's face turned "ashen," according to a newspaperman who was present. "My God! my God!" exclaimed Lincoln. "What will the country say?" It said plenty, all of it bad. Copperheads saw in the outcome further proof, if any was necessary, that the North could never cobble the Union together by force. Republicans expressed despair. "Lost, lost, all is lost!" cried Charles Sumner when he heard the news.

Northern morale descended into the slough of despond in the spring of 1863. Reports of Grant's advances in Mississippi were slow in coming and uncertain in meaning, especially after the failure of assaults at Vicksburg on May 19 and 22.

Official Union army photographer Captain A. J. Russell took this photograph of the abandoned winter camp of Confederate soldiers near Fredericksburg soon after Sedgwick's troops had carried the heights. Union soldiers ransacked the camp for anything of value they might be able to find—not much.

Exploding shells and burning wadding from muskets set the dry leaves and pine needles on fire during the fighting on May 3. The fires spread to brush and dead trees. Soldiers on both sides worked desperately to carry wounded men from the path of the fires, as shown in this drawing. Not all of them were rescued.

Rosecrans had done nothing in middle Tennessee since his bloody and ambiguous New Year's victory at Stones River. On April 7, as a first step in an effort to capture Charleston, an attack on Fort Sumter by eight supposedly irresistible ironclads had been repulsed in a manner that gave the Union navy a black eye. The high hopes for naval conquest of the citadel of secession were dashed. Union army troops began a slow, frustrating, and ultimately unsuccessful advance along the coastal islands and through the swamps in an attempt to starve or pound Charleston into submission.

III

The Confederacy could not rest on Lee's laurels in Virginia or Beauregard's at Charleston. Although beaten, Hooker's army still bristled 90,000 strong along the Rappahannock. Grant was on the move in Mississippi. Rosecrans showed signs of motion in middle Tennessee. Pressed on all sides by invading forces, the South needed an offensive-defensive stroke to relieve the pressure. Longstreet was returning with his two detached divisions to rejoin Lee on the Rappahannock when he met with Secretary of War James Seddon in Richmond on May 6 and proposed that he take these two divisions to reinforce Bragg in Tennessee. With additional help from Johnston, they would drive Rosecrans back to the Ohio, thus compelling Grant to break off his campaign against Vicksburg and go to the rescue of the shattered Army of the Cumberland. Seddon liked the idea but suggested that Longstreet go instead to Mississippi to help Johnston and Pemberton smash Grant, after which they could turn their attention to Rosecrans. Jefferson Davis favored this proposal, for he was concerned about his home state and convinced that the retention of Vicksburg was crucial.

But Lee dashed cold water on the enterprise. It would take weeks for Longstreet's divisions to travel nearly a thousand miles to Mississippi over the Confederacy's mangled railroads. If Vicksburg could hold out that long, said Lee, it would be safe without reinforcements, for "the climate in June will force the enemy to retire." In the meantime a reinforced Army of the Potomac might return to the offensive against Lee's depleted forces. Although he had held off Hooker before without these two divisions, Lee now believed that he needed them—and additional troops as well. In sum, he concluded, "it becomes a question between Virginia and Mississippi."

Lee's opinion carried so much weight that Davis felt compelled to concur. The president remained disquieted by news from Mississippi, however, and called Lee to Richmond for a strategy conference on May 15. This time the Virginian dazzled Davis and Seddon with a proposal to invade Pennsylvania with a reinforced army and inflict a crushing defeat on the Yankees in their own backyard. This would remove the enemy threat on the Rappahannock, take the armies out of war-ravaged Virginia, and enable Lee to feed his troops in the enemy's country. It would also strengthen Peace Democrats, discredit Republicans, reopen the question of foreign recognition, and perhaps even conquer peace and recognition from the Union government itself.

The cabinet was awed by this vision. Postmaster General John Reagan, a Texan, dissented because he thought it essential to preserve Vicksburg as a link between the Confederacy's two halves. But Lee convinced the others that even if the climate failed to drive the Yankees out of Mississippi, a successful invasion of Pennsylvania would draw them out. In the post-Chancellorsville aura of invincibility, anything seemed possible. Even Longstreet came around. "When I agreed with [Seddon] and yourself about sending troops west," he wrote to Senator Wigfall of Texas, "it was under the impression that we would be obliged to remain on the defensive here. But the prospect of an advance changes the aspect of affairs."

So Lee set about reorganizing his augmented army into an invasion force of three infantry corps and six cavalry brigades—a total of 75,000 men. A. P. Hill became commander of the new 3rd Corps while Jackson's old 2nd Corps went to Richard Ewell, now sporting a wooden leg as souvenir of Second Manassas. Having used the month after Chancellorsville to rest and refit, the Army of Northern Virginia was much better prepared for this invasion than it had been for the previous one in September 1862. Morale was high, most men had shoes, and few stragglers fell out as Lee edged westward in the first week of June to launch his invasion through the Shenandoah Valley. Ewell's corps led the way, adding to its laurels won in the Valley under Jackson the previous year by capturing 3,500 men in the Union garrisons at Winchester and Martinsburg.

This success and the apparently unimpeded advance of the fearsome rebels into Pennsylvania set off panic in the North and heightened southern euphoria. "From the very beginning the true policy of the South has been invasion," declared an editorial in the *Richmond Examiner* as first reports arrived of a great victory in Pennsylvania, confirming the South's capacity to strike deep into the enemy's territory and compel Lincoln to make peace. Dated July 7, 1863, the editorial's enthusiasm proved grimly premature when the true outcome of the battle at Gettysburg became clear several days later.

Only one untoward event had marred the invasion's success so far. On June 9 the Union cavalry crossed the Rappahannock in force twenty-five miles above Fredericksburg to find out what Lee was up to. Catching Stuart napping, the blue troopers learned that the enemy had begun to move north. The rebel horsemen rallied and finally pushed the Yankees back after the biggest cavalry battle of the war at Brandy Station. The southern press criticized Stuart for the initial surprise of his "puffed up cavalry." His ego bruised, Stuart hoped to regain glory by some spectacular achievement in the invasion. His troopers efficiently screened the infantry's advance. But the improved northern cavalry also kept Stuart from learning of Hooker's movements. To

The Army of Northern Virginia had to ford numerous streams and rivers in its invasion of Pennsylvania. The soldiers removed their shoes and rolled up their trousers to wade this stream. If the water was more than hip deep, they would remove their cartridge pouches (on the right hips of several soldiers here) and hang them from their musket barrels.

break this stalemate, Stuart on June 25 took his three best brigades for another raid around the rear of the Union infantry slogging northward after Lee. In its initial stages this foray caused alarm in Washington and added to the scare in Pennsylvania. But Stuart became separated from the Army of Northern Virginia for a full week. This deprived Lee of intelligence about enemy movements at a crucial time.

Nevertheless these halcyon June days seemed to mark a pinnacle of Confederate success. Lee forbade pillaging of private property in Pennsylvania, to show the world that southern soldiers were superior to the Yankee vandals who had ravaged the South. But not all rebels refrained from plunder and arson. The army destroyed Thaddeus Stevens's ironworks near Chambersburg, wrecked a good deal of railroad property, levied forced requisitions of money from merchants and banks ($28,000 in York, for example), and seized all the shoes, clothing, horses, cattle, and food they could find—giving Confederate IOUs in return. Lee's invasion became a gigantic raid for supplies that stripped clean a large area of south-central Pennsylvania. Southern soldiers also seized scores of black people in Pennsylvania and sent them south into slavery.

One of Lee's purposes in ordering restraint toward (white) civilians, as he explained to Jefferson Davis, was to cultivate the copperheads and encourage the "peace party" in the North, thereby undercutting support for the war. As for the differences between the copperheads' reunion strategy and the South's insistence on independence, when "peace is proposed to us it will be time enough to discuss its terms, and it is not the part of prudence to spurn the proposition in advance, merely because those who made it believe, or affect to believe, that it will result in bringing us back to the Union." Davis did indeed think he saw a chance to carry peace proposals on the point of Lee's sword. In mid-June, Alexander Stephens suggested to Davis that in light of "the failure of Hooker and Grant," this might be the time to make peace overtures. Stephens offered to approach his old friend Lincoln under flag of truce to discuss prisoner-of-war exchanges, which had stopped because of Confederate refusal to exchange blacks. This issue could serve as an entering wedge for the introduction of peace proposals. Davis was intrigued by the idea. He gave Stephens formal instructions limiting his powers to negotiations on prisoner exchanges and other procedural matters. What additional informal powers Stephens carried with him are unknown. On July 3 the vice president boarded a flag-of-truce boat for a trip down the James to Union lines at Norfolk on the first leg of his hoped-for trip to Washington.

Lee's invasion also sparked renewed Confederate hopes for diplomatic recognition. In the wake of Chancellorsville, John Slidell in Paris queried the French whether "the time had not arrived for reconsidering the question of recognition." Napoleon agreed, as usual, but would not act independently of Britain. Southern diplomats and their allies in both countries put forward a plan for a motion in the British Parliament favoring joint Anglo-French steps toward recognition. When the motion was presented, the inadvertent disclosure that Napoleon had given his blessing to the enterprise made it a casualty of an anti-French backlash. But British proponents of recognition eagerly awaited reports of Lee's triumph in Pennsylvania. "Diplomatic means can now no longer prevail," wrote Confederate publicist

Henry Hotze from London on July 11, "and everybody looks to Lee to conquer recognition."

Northerners abroad understood only too well the stakes involved in military operations during June 1863. "The truth is," wrote Henry Adams, "all depends on the progress of our armies." In Washington, Lincoln was not pleased with the progress of Hooker's army. When Hooker first detected Lee's movement in early June, he wanted to cross the Rappahannock and pitch into the rebel rear. Lincoln disapproved and urged Hooker to fight the enemy's main force north of the river instead of crossing it at the risk of becoming "entangled upon the river, like an ox jumped half over a fence and liable to be torn by dogs front and rear without a fair chance to gore one way or kick the other." Hooker seemed unimpressed by this advice, for a few days later he proposed that since the Army of Northern Virginia was moving north, the Army of the Potomac should move south and march into Richmond! Lincoln began to suspect that Hooker was afraid to fight Lee again. "I think *Lee's* Army, and not *Richmond*, is your true objective point," he wired Hooker. "If he comes toward the Upper Potomac, follow on his flank, and on the inside track. . . . Fight him when opportunity offers." With the head of the enemy force at Winchester and the tail still back at Fredericksburg, "the animal must be very slim somewhere. Could you not break him?"

Although Hooker finally lurched the Army of the Potomac into motion, he moved too late to prevent Lee's whole force from crossing the Potomac. But this actually encouraged Lincoln. To Hooker he sent word that this "gives you back the chance [to destroy the enemy far from his base] that I thought McClellan lost last fall." To Secretary of the Navy Welles, Lincoln said that "we cannot help beating them, if we have the man." But Lincoln became convinced that Hooker was not the man. The general began to fret that Lee outnumbered him, that he needed more troops, that the government was not supporting him. Looking "sad and careworn," the president told his cabinet that Hooker had turned out to be another McClellan. On June 28 he relieved Hooker from command and named George Gordon Meade in his place.

If the men in the ranks had been consulted, most of them probably would have preferred the return of McClellan. Although Meade had worked his way up from brigade to corps command with a good combat record, he was an unknown quantity to men outside his corps. By now, though, their training in the school of hard knocks under fumbling leaders had toughened the soldiers to a flinty self-reliance that left many of them indifferent to the identity of their commander. As the army headed north into Pennsylvania, its morale rose with the latitude. "Our men are three times as Enthusiastic as they have been in Virginia," wrote a Union surgeon. "The idea that Pennsylvania is invaded and that we are fighting on our own soil proper, influences them strongly. They are more determined than I have ever before seen them."

When Meade took over the army, its 90,000 effectives were concentrated in the vicinity of Frederick, Maryland. Longstreet's and Hill's Confederate corps were forty miles to the north near Chambersburg,

Major General George Gordon Meade had compiled a solid if not brilliant record as a division and corps commander. He also earned Lincoln's confidence by not taking part in the cliquish rivalries and jealousies that had plagued the officer corps in the Army of the Potomac. Meade's testy temper, however, and his piercing eyes crowned by a high forehead caused one soldier to describe him as an "old goggle-eyed snapping turtle."

Part of the 114th Pennsylvania in their winter camp several months before Gettysburg. This Zouave regiment would be in the thick of the fighting at Gettysburg on July 2 and would suffer nearly 150 casualties.

Pennsylvania. Part of Ewell's corps was at York, threatening a railroad bridge over the Susquehanna, while the remainder was at Carlisle preparing to move on Harrisburg to sever the main line of the Pennsylvania Railroad and capture the state capital. Lee had cut himself off from his faraway Virginia base, as Lincoln had hoped, but he had done so purposely. Like Grant's army in Mississippi, Lee's invaders took enough ammunition for their needs and lived off the country as they moved. Lee's greatest worry was not supplies but rather the absence of Stuart with information about the whereabouts of the enemy. By contrast, Meade obtained accurate intelligence of the rebels' location and moved quickly to confront them.

On the night of June 28, one of Longstreet's scouts brought word that the Army of the Potomac was north of its namesake river. Alarmed by the proximity of a concentrated enemy while his own forces remained scattered, Lee sent couriers to recall Ewell's divisions from York and Carlisle. Meanwhile one of A. P. Hill's divisions learned of a reported supply of shoes at Gettysburg, a prosperous town served by a dozen roads that converged from every point on the compass. Since Lee intended to reunite his army near Gettysburg, Hill authorized this division to go there on July 1 to "get those shoes."

When Hill's would-be Crispins approached Gettysburg that morning, however, they found something more than the pickets and militia they had expected. Two brigades of Union cavalry had arrived in town the previous day. Their commander was weather-beaten, battle-wise John Buford, who like Lincoln had been born in Kentucky and raised in Illinois. Buford had noted the strategic importance of this crossroads village flanked by defensible ridges and hills. Expecting the rebels to come this way, he had posted his brigades with their breech-loading carbines on high ground northwest of town. Buford sent word to John Reynolds, a Pennsylvanian who commanded the nearest infantry corps, to hurry forward to Gettysburg. If there was to be a battle, he said, this was the place to fight it. When A. P. Hill's lead division came marching out of the west next morning, Buford's horse soldiers were ready for them. Fighting dismounted behind fences and trees, they held off twice their numbers for two hours while couriers on both sides galloped up the roads to summon reinforcements. Lee had told his subordinates not to bring on a general engagement until the army was concentrated. But the engagement became general of its own accord as the infantry of both armies marched toward the sound of guns at Gettysburg.

As Buford's tired troopers were beginning to give way in midmorning, the lead division of Reynolds's 1st Corps double-timed across the fields and brought the rebel assault to a standstill. One unit in this division was the Iron Brigade, five midwestern regiments with distinctive black hats who confirmed here their reputation as the hardest-fighting outfit

General John Buford and his staff. Although his aides were young, they were battle-hardened veterans by the time of Gettysburg. Seated in the center, Buford seems almost like a father figure to these men.

in the Army of the Potomac. They also lost two-thirds of the men they took into the battle. The most crucial Union casualty on this first morning of July was John Reynolds—considered by many the best general in the army—drilled through the head by a sharpshooter. About noon, General Howard's "Dutch" 11th Corps arrived and deployed north of town to meet the advance units of Ewell's Confederate 2nd Corps coming fast after a brisk march from the Susquehanna. By early afternoon some 24,000 Confederates confronted 19,000 bluecoats along a three-mile semicircle west and north of Gettysburg. Neither commanding general had yet reached the field; neither had intended to fight there; but independently of their intentions a battle destined to become the largest and most important of the war had already started.

As Ewell's leading divisions swept forward against Howard, Lee rode in from the west. Quickly grasping the situation, he changed his mind about waiting for Longstreet's corps, still miles away, and authorized Hill and Ewell to send in everything they had. With a yell, four southern divisions went forward with the irresistible power that seemed to have become routine. The right flank of Howard's corps collapsed here as it had done at Chancellorsville. When the 11th Corps retreated in disorder through town to Cemetery Hill a half-mile to the south, the right flank of the Union 1st Corps was uncovered and these tough fighters, too, were forced back yard by yard to the hill, where Union artillery and a reserve brigade that Howard had posted there caused the rebel onslaught to hesitate in late afternoon. The battle so far appeared to be another great Confederate victory.

But Lee could see that so long as the enemy held the high ground south of town, the battle was not over. He knew that the rest of the Army of the Potomac must be hurrying toward Gettysburg; his best chance to clinch the victory was to seize those hills and ridges before they arrived. So Lee gave Ewell discretionary orders to

The Philadelphia artist Peter F. Rothermel painted many pictures of the battle of Gettysburg. This one shows stretcher-bearers carrying the body of General John Reynolds toward the rear from where he was killed at the edge of the woods in the middle distance. Confederate attackers had overrun the farm to the right of the woods. In this picture, Union troops of the Iron Brigade are sweeping forward in a counterattack.

attack Cemetery Hill "if practicable." Had Jackson still lived, he undoubtedly would have found it practicable. But Ewell was not Jackson. Thinking the enemy position too strong, he did not attack—thereby creating one of the controversial "ifs" of Gettysburg that have echoed down the years. By the time dusk approached, General Winfield Scott Hancock of the 2nd Corps had arrived and laid out a defense line curling around Culp's and Cemetery hills and extending two miles south along Cemetery Ridge to a hill called Little Round Top. As three more Union corps arrived during the night—along with Meade himself—the bluecoats turned this line into a formidable position. Not only did it command high ground, but its convex interior lines also allowed troops to be shifted quickly from one point to another while forcing the enemy into concave exterior lines that made communication between right and left wings slow and difficult.

Studying the Union defenses through his field glasses on the evening of July 1 and again next morning, Longstreet concluded that this line was too strong for an attack to succeed. He urged Lee to turn its south flank and get between the Union army and Washington. This would compel Meade to attack the Army of Northern Virginia in *its* chosen position. Longstreet liked best the tactical defensive; the model he had in mind was Fredericksburg, where Yankee divisions had battered themselves to pieces while the Confederates had suffered minimal casualties. Longstreet had not been present at Chancellorsville, nor had he arrived at Gettysburg on July 1 until after the whooping rebels had driven the enemy pell-mell through the town. These were the models that Lee had in mind. He had not accomplished the hoped-for "destruction" of the enemy in the Seven Days or at Chancellorsville. Gettysburg presented him with a third chance. The morale of his veteran troops had never been higher; they would regard such a maneuver as Longstreet suggested as a retreat, Lee thought, and

lose their fighting edge. According to a British military observer accompanying the Confederates, the men were eager to attack an enemy "they had beaten so constantly" and for whose fighting capacity they felt "profound contempt." Lee intended to unleash them. Pointing to Cemetery Hill, he said to Longstreet: "The enemy is there, and I am going to attack him there." Longstreet replied: "If he is there, it will be because he is anxious that we should attack him; a good reason, in my judgment, for not doing so." But Lee had made up his mind, and Longstreet turned away sadly with a conviction of impending disaster.

Although aware of Longstreet's reluctance, Lee assigned to him the principal attack duty on July 2. Two of Hill's three divisions had suffered heavy casualties the previous day and could not fight today. Ewell still regarded the Union defenses on Cemetery and Culp's hills as too strong for a successful assault. Lee grudgingly agreed. He therefore ordered Longstreet's two fresh divisions (the third, under George Pickett, had been posted as rear guard and could not arrive in time) to attack the Union left holding the southern end of Cemetery Ridge. The assault would be supported by Hill's one fresh division, while Ewell was to demonstrate against the Union right and convert this demonstration into an attack when Meade weakened his right to reinforce his left. If this plan worked, both enemy flanks would crumble and Lee would have the war-winning Cannae that he sought.

Longstreet's state of mind as he prepared for this attack is hard to fathom. The only non-Virginian holding high command in the Army of Northern Virginia (and the only prominent Confederate general to join the postwar Republican party), Longstreet became the target of withering criticism from Virginians after the war for insubordination and tardiness at Gettysburg. They held him responsible for losing the battle—and by implication the war. Some of this criticism was self-serving, intended to shield Lee and other Virginians (mainly Stuart and Ewell) from blame. But Longstreet did seem to move slowly at Gettysburg. Although Lee wanted him to attack as early in the day as possible, he did not get his troops into position until 4:00 P.M. There were extenuating reasons for this delay: his two divisions had made night marches to reach the vicinity of Gettysburg and were then compelled to countermarch by a circuitous route to reach the attack position because Lee's guide led

This photograph of the town of Gettysburg was taken two weeks after the battle. The camera was located northwest of town on the slope of Seminary Ridge north of the Chambersburg Pike. On the late afternoon of July 1, Union troops holding this position conducted a fighting retreat through town to Cemetery Hill, marked by the tall tree in the distance at right. The hill to its left behind the town is Culp's Hill. There were many orchards near Gettysburg in 1863; several can be seen in the foreground of this photograph.

This print of General James Longstreet at Gettysburg dates from 1900. It shows him on the afternoon of July 2 giving an order to a staff officer to carry to troops fighting in the distance. The hill in the background is probably intended to be Little Round Top.

them initially on a road in sight of an enemy signal post on Little Round Top at the south end of the Union line. Yet Longstreet may have been piqued by Lee's rejection of his flanking suggestion, and he did not believe in the attack he was ordered to make. He therefore may not have put as much energy and speed into its preparation as the situation required.

To compound the problem, Longstreet did not find the Yankee left on Cemetery Ridge where Lee's scout had reported it to be. It was not there because of an unauthorized move by Dan Sickles, commander of the 3rd Corps holding the Union left. Distressed by the exposed nature of the low ground at the south end of Cemetery Ridge before it thrust upward at Little Round Top, Sickles had moved his two divisions a half-mile forward to occupy slightly higher ground along a road running southwest from Gettysburg. There his troops held a salient with its apex in a peach orchard and its left anchored in a maze of boulders locally called Devil's Den, just below Little Round Top. Although this gave Sickles high ground to defend, it left his men unconnected to the rest of the Union line and vulnerable to attack on both flanks. When Meade learned what Sickles had done, it was too late to order him back to the original line. Longstreet had launched his attack.

Sickles's unwise move may have unwittingly foiled Lee's hopes. Finding the Union left in an unexpected position, Longstreet probably should have notified Lee. Scouts reported that Little Round Top and the higher Big Round Top to its south were unoccupied, opening the way for a flanking move around to the Union rear. Longstreet's division commanders urged a change of attack plans to take advantage of this opportunity. But Longstreet had already tried at least twice to change Lee's mind. He did not want to risk another rebuff. Lee had repeatedly ordered him to attack here, and here he meant to attack. At 4:00 P.M. his brigades started forward in echelon from right to left.

During the next few hours some of the war's bloodiest fighting took place in the peach orchard, in a wheat field to the east of the orchard, at Devil's Den, and on Little Round Top. Longstreet's 15,000 yelling veterans punched through the salient with attacks that shattered Sickles's leg and crushed his undersize corps. But with skillful tactics, Meade and his subordinates rushed reinforcements from three other corps to plug the breaks. Part of Hill's fresh division finally joined Longstreet's assault, while at the other end of the line Ewell's men belatedly went forward but achieved only limited gains before Union counterattacks and darkness halted them.

The most desperate struggle occurred on Longstreet's front, where two Union regiments at separated points of this combat zone, the 20th Maine and the 1st Minnesota, achieved lasting fame by throwing back Confederate attacks that came dangerously close to breakthroughs. Rising above the surrounding countryside, the two Round Tops dominated the south end of Cemetery Ridge. If the rebels had gotten artillery up there, they could have enfiladed the Union left. Sickles's advance had

uncovered these hills. A brigade of Alabamians advanced to seize Little Round Top. Minutes earlier nothing but a Union signal station had stood in their way. But Meade's chief of engineers, General Gouverneur K. Warren, discovered this appalling situation as enemy troops were approaching. Acting quickly, Warren persuaded the 5th Corps commander to send a brigade double-timing to the crest of Little Round Top just in time to meet the charging rebels.

Posted at the far left of this brigade was the 20th Maine, commanded by Colonel Joshua L. Chamberlain. A year earlier Chamberlain had been a professor of rhetoric and modern languages at Bowdoin College. Taking a leave of absence ostensibly to

This photograph of Little Round Top (with Big Round Top at right) was taken by one of Mathew Brady's cameramen two weeks after the battle. Brady himself is leaning on the tree at left. The Confederate attack on Little Round Top swept from right to left. By the time this photograph was taken the dead had been buried and the battlefield mostly cleaned up.

This postwar sketch shows the Confederate capture of Devil's Den at about 5:00 p.m. on July 2 after a bitter struggle. A color bearer has planted the Confederate battle flag on one of the granite boulders as several Union soldiers bolt for the rear and others conduct a fighting retreat.

Long Remember   569

study in Europe, he joined the army instead and now found himself responsible for preventing the rebels from rolling up the Union left. The fighting professor and his down-easterners proved equal to the occasion. For nearly two hours they stood off repeated assaults by portions of two Confederate regiments along the rocky, wooded slope filled with smoke, noise, and terror. Their valor seemed in vain. With more than a third of his men down and the remainder out of ammunition—and with the Johnnies forming for another assault—Chamberlain was in a tight spot. But being cool and quick-witted—perhaps a legacy of dealing with fractious students—he ordered his men to fix bayonets on their empty rifles and charge. With a yell, these smoke-grimed Yanks lurched downhill against the surprised rebels. Exhausted by their uphill fighting following a twenty-five-mile march that day to reach the battlefield, and shocked by the audacity of this bayonet assault, the Alabamians surrendered by scores to the jubilant boys from Maine. Little Round Top remained in northern hands. Although Sickles's corps was driven back yard by yard through the peach orchard, the wheat field, and Devil's Den, the Union left on Little Round Top was secure.

A mile to the north, however, another Alabama brigade threatened to puncture the Cemetery Ridge line near its center. Their attack hit a gap in the Union line created by the earlier advance of Sickles's corps to the peach orchard. Winfield Scott Hancock's 2nd Corps occupied this sector, but until Hancock could shift reinforcements to stop the assault he had only eight companies of one regiment on hand to meet the oncoming brigade. The regiment was the 1st Minnesota, veterans of all the army's battles from the beginning at Bull Run. Hancock ordered these 262 men to charge the 1,600 Alabamians and slow them down long enough for reinforcements

Surviving members of the 1st Minnesota gather at Gettysburg on the thirty-fourth anniversary of their sacrificial attack against an entire Alabama brigade.

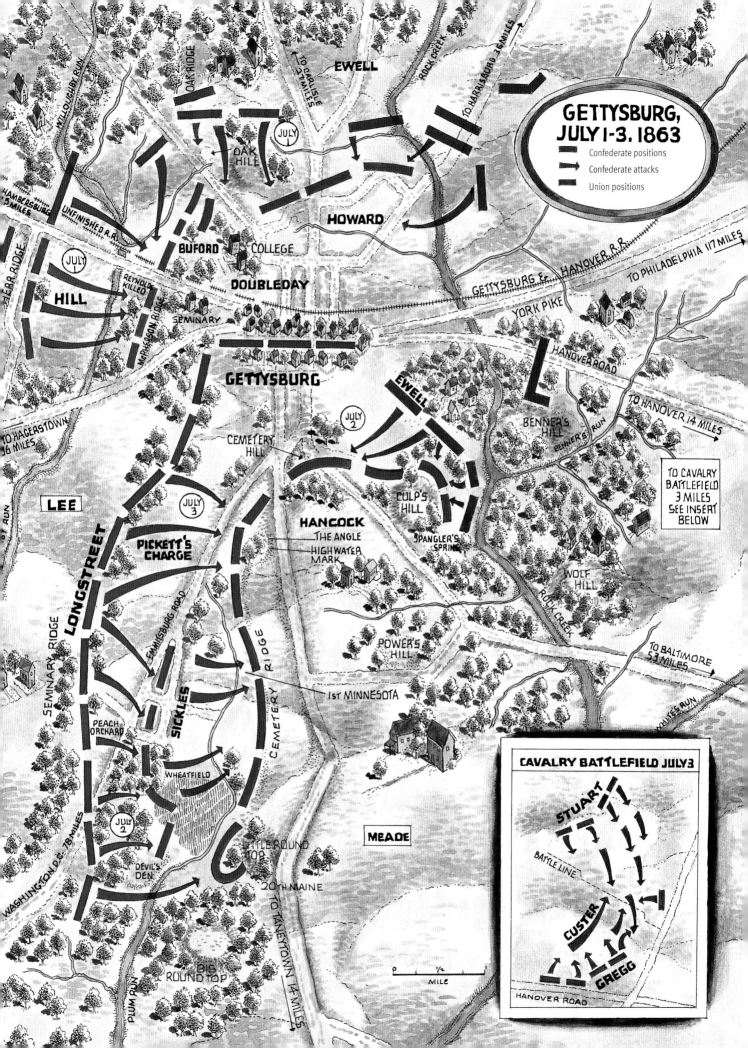

GETTYSBURG,
JULY 1-3, 1863

Confederate positions
Confederate attacks
Union positions

EWELL

OAK RIDGE

WILLOUGHBY RUN

TO CARLISLE 27 MILES

ROCK CREEK

TO HARRISBURG 36 MILES

JULY 1

OAK HILL

HOWARD

UNFINISHED R.R.

CHAMBERSBURG 3 MILES

JULY 1

BUFORD   COLLEGE

DOUBLEDAY

GETTYSBURG & HANOVER R.R.

TO PHILADELPHIA 117 MILES

HILL

REYNOLDS KILLED

McPHERSON RIDGE

SEMINARY

YORK PIKE

HANOVER ROAD

SEMINARY RIDGE

GETTYSBURG

EWELL

TO HANOVER 14 MILES

BENNER'S HILL

BENNER'S RUN

JULY 2

CEMETERY HILL

TO HAGERSTOWN 36 MILES

TO CAVALRY BATTLEFIELD 3 MILES SEE INSERT BELOW

CULP'S HILL

LEE

JULY 3

HANCOCK

THE ANGLE

HIGH WATER MARK

SPANGLER'S SPRING

WOLF HILL

PICKETT'S CHARGE

ROCK CREEK

LONGSTREET

EMMITSBURG ROAD

POWER'S HILL

TO BALTIMORE 53 MILES

SICKLES

CEMETERY RIDGE

1st MINNESOTA

WHITE'S RUN

PEACH ORCHARD

WHEATFIELD

MEADE

CAVALRY BATTLEFIELD JULY 3

JULY 2

LITTLE ROUND TOP

STUART

WASHINGTON D.C. 78 MILES

DEVIL'S DEN

20TH MAINE

TO TANEYTOWN 14 MILES

BATTLE LINE

PLUM RUN

BIG ROUND TOP

0   ½
MILE

CUSTER

GREGG

HANOVER ROAD

These soldiers of the 2nd Georgia Battalion had their pictures taken while they were at Norfolk, Virginia, in the spring of 1862. Their servant "Pink" is at right. The 2nd Battalion attacked Cemetery Ridge near dusk on July 2. Eighty-two of its 173 men were killed, wounded, or missing in the attack.

to arrive. The Minnesotans did the job, but only forty-seven of them came back. Hancock plugged the gap, and the Confederate attack all along the southern half of the battlefield flickered out in the twilight.

To the north the shift of Union troops from Cemetery and Culp's hills to meet Longstreet's assault gave Ewell's corps the opportunity Lee had hoped for to convert its demonstration into an attack. But the opportunity slipped away. Several of Ewell's brigades did finally advance as dusk descended. One of them seized some trenches on Culp's Hill left unoccupied by a Federal unit sent to the other end of the battlefield, but could advance no farther against determined opposition. Two other gray brigades scored a temporary lodgement against the hapless 11th Corps at Cemetery Hill, but a 2nd Corps brigade counterattacked in the gathering darkness and drove them back.

The Confederate assaults on July 2 were uncoordinated and disjointed. The usual skill of generalship in the Army of Northern Virginia was lacking this day. On the Union side, by contrast, officers from Meade down to regimental colonels acted with initiative and coolness. They moved troops to the right spots and counterattacked at the right times. As a result, when night fell the Union line remained firm except for the loss of Sickles's salient. Each side had suffered 9,000 or more casualties, bringing the two-day totals for both armies to nearly 35,000.

It was the heaviest single-battle toll in the war thus far, but the fighting was not over. Despite stout resistance by the Yankees, Lee believed that his indomitable veterans had almost achieved victory. One more push, he thought, and "those people" would break. Lee seemed unusually excited by the supposed success of the past two days. At the same time, however, he was weakened by a bout with diarrhea and irritated by Stuart's prolonged absence (Jeb's tired troopers had finally rejoined the army during the day). In any case, Lee's judgment was not at its best. He had come to Pennsylvania in quest of a decisive victory, and he was determined not to leave

without it. He had attacked both enemy flanks, causing Meade (he believed) to weaken his center. With Pickett's fresh division as a spearhead, therefore, Lee would send three divisions preceded by an artillery barrage against that weakened center on July 3. Stuart would circle around the Union rear and Ewell would assail the right flank to clamp the pincers when Pickett broke through the front. With proper coordination and leadership, his invincible troops could not fail.

Across the way a late-night council of Union generals resolved to stay and fight it out. With prescience, Meade told the general commanding his center that "if Lee attacks to-morrow, it will be in *your front*." At first light, however, fighting broke out at the extreme right of the Union line along the base of Culp's Hill. Units of the Federal 12th Corps, which had been shifted to the left the previous day, came back during the night and attacked at dawn to regain their abandoned trenches now occupied by the rebels. In a seven-hour firefight they succeeded, and thus dimmed Lee's chances for turning the Union right simultaneously with the planned piercing of the center.

While this was going on, Longstreet once more urged Lee to maneuver around Meade's left. Again Lee refused, and ordered Longstreet to attack the Union center with Pickett's division and two of Hill's—fewer than 15,000 men to advance three-quarters of a mile across open fields and assault dug-in infantry supported by ample artillery. "General Lee," Longstreet later reported himself to have said, "there never was a body of fifteen thousand men who could make that attack successfully." Lee impatiently replied that his magnificent army had done it before and could do it again. "My heart was heavy," wrote Longstreet subsequently. "I could see the desperate and hopeless nature of the charge and the hopeless slaughter it would cause. . . . That day at Gettysburg was one of the saddest of my life."

In this mood Longstreet ordered a concentration of Confederate artillery—some

This lithograph by Edwin Forbes shows a counterattack by Colonel Samuel Carroll's brigade of the Union 2nd Corps near the cemetery gate on East Cemetery Hill against a Louisiana brigade that had achieved a breakthrough and captured a battery. The bluecoats recaptured the battery and drove back the Louisianians.

Severely wounded in the battle of Gaines's Mill (June 27, 1862), George E. Pickett and his division had been involved only in skirmishing and support duties since he had returned to duty in October. His division would experience almost as many casualties in a half-hour on July 3 as it did in the entire rest of the war.

150 guns—for the largest southern bombardment of the war, to soften up the enemy at the point of attack. At 1:07 P.M. Longstreet's guns shattered the uneasy silence that had followed the morning's fight on the Union right. For almost two hours an artillery duel among nearly 300 guns filled the Pennsylvania countryside with an ear-splitting roar heard as far away as Pittsburgh. Despite this sound and fury, the Union infantry lying behind stone walls and breastworks suffered little, for the rebel aim was high.

Pickett's all-Virginia division waited with nervous impatience to go in and get it over with. Thirty-eight years old, George Pickett had graduated last in the same West Point class as George McClellan (who graduated second). Pickett did well in the Mexican War, but in the present conflict he had enjoyed few chances to distinguish himself. His division did not fight at Chancellorsville and marked time guarding supply wagons during the first two days at Gettysburg. With his long hair worn in ringlets and his face adorned by a drooping mustache and goatee, Pickett looked like a cross between a Cavalier dandy and a riverboat gambler. He affected the romantic style of Sir Walter Scott's heroes and was eager to win everlasting glory at Gettysburg.

Finally, about 3:00 P.M., Longstreet reluctantly ordered the attack. The Confederate bombardment seemed to have disabled the enemy's artillery; it was now or never. With parade-ground precision, Pickett's three brigades moved out joined by six more from Hill's division on their left and two others in reserve. It was a magnificent mile-wide spectacle, a picture-book view of war that participants on both sides remembered with awe until their dying moment—which for many came within the next hour. Pickett's charge represented the Confederate war effort in microcosm: matchless valor, apparent initial success, and ultimate disaster. As the gray infantry poured across the gently undulating farmland with seemingly irresistible force, northern artillery suddenly erupted in a savage cascade, sending shot and shell among the southern regiments and changing to canister as they kept coming. The Union guns had not been knocked out after all; their canny chief of artillery, General Henry J. Hunt, had ordered them to cease firing to lure on the rebels and conserve ammunition to welcome them. Yankee infantry behind stone walls opened up at two hundred yards while Vermont,

Ohio, and New York regiments on the left and right swung out to rake both flanks of the attacking force. The southern assault collapsed under this unbearable pressure from front and flanks. Two or three hundred Virginians and Tennesseeans with General Lewis A. Armistead breached the first Union line, where Armistead was mortally wounded with his hand on a Yankee cannon and his followers fell like leaves in an autumn wind. In half an hour it was all over. Of the 14,000 Confederates who had gone forward, scarcely half returned. Pickett's own division lost two-thirds of its men; his three brigadiers and all thirteen colonels were killed or wounded.

As the dazed survivors stumbled back to their starting point, they met Lee and Longstreet working to form a defensive line against Meade's expected counterattack. "It's all my fault," said Lee as he rode among his men. "It is I who have lost this fight, and you must help me out of it the best way you can. All good men must rally." Rally they did—some of them, at least. But Meade did not counterattack. For this he has been criticized down the years. Hancock, despite being wounded in the repulse of Pickett's assault, urged Meade to launch the 15,000 fresh reserves of the 5th and 6th Corps in pursuit of Lee's broken brigades. But a heavy load of responsibility weighed on Meade's shoulders. He had been in command only six days. For three of them his army had been fighting for the nation's life, as he saw the matter, and had narrowly saved it. Meade could not yet know how badly the enemy was hurt, or that rebel artillery was low on ammunition. He did know that Stuart was loose in his rear, but had not yet learned that a division of blue troopers had stopped the southern cavalry three miles east of Gettysburg—thus foiling the third part of Lee's three-pronged plan for Meade's undoing. Meanwhile two Union

This painting of the beginning of Pickett's charge on July 3 was done by Edwin Forbes. From the vantage point of Seminary Ridge, Confederate attackers sweep forward toward Cemetery Ridge, crowned by the trees in Ziegler's Grove in the left distance and the famous copse of trees in the right distance. Union artillery has opened fire on the Confederate infantry as it emerges from the treeline where the viewer of this scene would be standing.

This photograph taken by Alexander Gardner on July 5 was long thought to show Union dead from the first day's fighting near the spot where General Reynolds was killed. Later research indicated these these dead are from General Sickles's 3rd Corps and were photographed near the Rose farm south of the peach orchard. Note that all of the feet have been stripped of their shoes by needy Confederates. These five men were among the 3,155 Union soldiers killed in three days; almost 2,000 more would die of their wounds.

Confederate sharpshooters firing from Devil's Den took a large toll of Union soldiers, especially officers, on Little Round Top on July 2. Union sharpshooters did their best to retaliate, and in at least one case they succeeded. Alexander Gardner photographed this Confederate sharpshooter at Devil's Den on July 5.

cavalry regiments on the left flank south of the Round Tops charged the rebel infantry in anticipation of orders for a counterattack, but were badly shot up by the alert enemy. In late afternoon a few units from the 5th and 6th Corps advanced over the scene of the previous day's carnage in Devil's Den and the wheat field. They flushed out the rear guard of Longstreet's two divisions, which were pulling back to a new line. Meade apparently did have some idea of attacking in this vicinity next day—the Fourth of July—but a heavy rainstorm that began shortly after noon halted the move.

Meade's lack of aggressiveness was caused by his respect for the enemy. He could scarcely believe that he had beaten the victors of Chancellorsville. Meade also explained later that he had not wanted to follow "the bad example [Lee] had set me, in ruining himself attacking a strong position." "We have done well enough," he said to a cavalry officer eager to do more. In a congratulatory telegram, a former corps commander expressed a widely felt astonishment that the long-suffering Army of the Potomac had actually won a big victory: "The glorious success of the Army of the Potomac has electrified all. I did not believe the enemy could be whipped."

The news did indeed electrify the North. "VICTORY! WATERLOO ECLIPSED!" shouted a headline in the *Philadelphia Inquirer*. The glad tidings reached Washington the day after Pickett's repulse, making this the capital's most glorious Fourth ever. "I *never* knew such excitement in Washington," wrote one observer. When word arrived three days later of the surrender at Vicksburg, the excitement doubled. Lincoln appeared on a White House balcony to tell a crowd of serenaders that this "gigantic Rebellion" whose purpose was to "overthrow the principle that all men are created equal" had been dealt a crippling blow. In New York the diarist George Templeton Strong rejoiced that

> the results of this victory are priceless. . . . The charm of Robert Lee's invincibility is broken. The Army of the Potomac has at last found a general that can handle it, and has stood nobly up to its terrible work in spite of its long disheartening list of hard-fought failures. . . . Copperheads are palsied and dumb for the moment at least. . . . Government is strengthened four-fold at home and abroad.

Strong's final sentence was truer than he could know. Confederate Vice President Stephens was on his way under flag of truce to Union lines at Norfolk as the battle of Gettysburg reached its climax. Jefferson Davis had hoped that Stephens would reach Washington from the south while Lee's victorious

This Harper's Weekly *cartoon comments satirically on rumors that Alexander Stephens had intended to present Lincoln with the Confederacy's peace terms when he sought permission to travel to Washington under flag of truce. The cartoon shows an arrogant Jefferson Davis sitting on a barrel of gunpowder drafting his peace terms, unaware of Confederate defeats at Gettysburg and Vicksburg and the graves of thousands of southern soldiers behind him.*

The too Confiding South DRAFTING TERMS OF PEACE with the Federal Government.

army was marching toward it from the north. Reports of Stephens's mission and of Gettysburg's outcome reached the White House at the same time. Lincoln thereupon sent a curt refusal to Stephens's request for a pass through the lines. In London the news of Gettysburg and Vicksburg gave the *coup de grâce* to Confederate hopes for recognition. "The disasters of the rebels are unredeemed by even any hope of success," crowed Henry Adams. "It is now conceded that all idea of intervention is at an end."

The victory at Gettysburg was purchased at high human cost: 23,000 Union casualties, more than one-quarter of the army's effectives. Yet the cost to the South was greater: 28,000 men killed, wounded, or missing, more than a third of Lee's army. As the survivors began their sad retreat to Virginia in the rain on July 4, thousands of wounded men suffered torture as ambulances and commandeered farm wagons bounced along rutted roads. Seven thousand rebel wounded were left behind to be attended by Union surgeons and volunteer nurses who flocked to Gettysburg. Lee was depressed by the outcome of his campaign to conquer a peace. A month later he offered his resignation to Jefferson Davis. Of course Davis refused to accept his resignation. Lee and his men would go on to earn further laurels. But they never again possessed the power and reputation they carried into Pennsylvania those palmy midsummer days of 1863. Though the war was destined to continue for

This etching by the prominent artist Thomas Hovenden shows a wounded Confederate soldier being treated by a Union surgeon in the home of a Gettysburg family. The surgeon himself seems to have a scalp wound, and the Union officer seated at the desk had also been wounded. Note the portrait of Lincoln and the American flag on the wall. This sentimental scene suggests that all is forgiven and that this Confederate, at least, has rejoined the Union.

More than 20,000 wounded men of both armies were left behind at Gettysburg when their comrades marched away. Almost every farmhouse and barn and many buildings in town became hospitals, and hundreds of tents were set up around the battlefield as field hospitals. This photograph, taken a week after the battle, shows several tents of the 2nd Corps field hospital in Ziegler's Grove, near the site of the modern cyclorama building.

almost two more bloody years, Gettysburg and Vicksburg proved to have been its crucial turning point.

Perceptive southerners sadly recognized this. The fall of Vicksburg "is a terrible blow, and has produced much despondency," wrote War Department clerk John Jones when he heard the news on July 8. Next day his spirits sank lower, for "the news from Lee's army is appalling. . . . This [is] the darkest day of the war." And the usually indefatigable Josiah Gorgas, chief of Confederate ordnance, sat down on July 28 and wrote a diary entry whose anguish echoes across the years:

> Events have succeeded one another with disastrous rapidity. One brief month ago we were apparently at the point of success. Lee was in Pennsylvania, threatening Harrisburgh, and even Philadelphia. Vicksburgh seemed to laugh all Grant's efforts to scorn. . . . Port Hudson had beaten off Banks' force. . . . Now the picture is just as sombre as it was bright then. . . . It seems incredible that human power could effect such a change in so brief a space. Yesterday we rode on the pinnacle of success—today absolute ruin seems to be our portion. The Confederacy totters to its destruction.

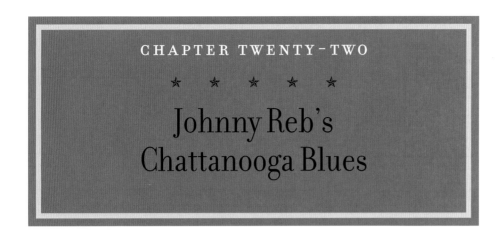

★ ★ ★ ★ ★

CHAPTER TWENTY-TWO

Johnny Reb's Chattanooga Blues

I

Lincoln also believed that the victories at Gettysburg and Vicksburg had set the Confederacy tottering. One more push might topple it. But Lincoln was doomed to disappointment. Although Lee was in a tight spot after Gettysburg, the old Gray Fox once again gave the blue hounds the slip.

It was a near thing, however. A Union cavalry raid wrecked the Confederate pontoon bridge across the Potomac, and days of heavy rain that began July 4 made the swollen river unfordable. The rebels were compelled to stand at bay with their backs to the Potomac while engineers tore down warehouses to build a new bridge. The tired soldiers fortified a defensive perimeter at Williamsport and awaited Yankee attack. But no attack came. Having given Lee a two-day head start from Gettysburg, Meade did not get his reinforced army into line facing the Confederates at Williamsport until July 12. In Washington an "anxious and impatient" Lincoln awaited word of Lee's destruction. As the days passed and no word arrived, the president grew angry. When Meade finally telegraphed on July 12 that he intended "to attack them tomorrow, unless something intervenes," Lincoln commented acidly: "They will be ready to fight a magnificent battle when there is no enemy there to fight." Events proved him right. A pretended deserter (a favorite southern ruse) had entered Union lines and reported Lee's army in fine fettle, eager for another fight. This reinforced Meade's wariness. He allowed a majority of his corps commanders to talk him out of attacking on the thirteenth. When the Army of the Potomac finally groped forward on July 14, it found nothing but a rear guard. The slippery rebels had vanished across a patched-together bridge during the night.

"Great God!" cried Lincoln when he heard this news. "What does it mean? . . . There is bad faith somewhere. . . . Our Army held the war in the hollow of their hand & they would not close it." Lincoln's estimate of the situation at Williamsport was not quite accurate. An attack on the strong Confederate position might have succeeded—with heavy casualties—or it might not. In either case, the destruction of Lee's veteran army was scarcely a sure thing. When word of Lincoln's dissatisfaction reached Meade, the testy general offered his resignation. But Lincoln could

Opposite page: This painting depicts Union troops trying to hold back a Confederate attack on September 20, 1863, at Kelly's Field, one of the few clearings in the wooded terrain of the Battle of Chickamauga.

Confederate artillery posted in part of the nine miles of entrenchments covering Williamsport, Maryland, with both flanks on the Potomac during the second week of July 1863. These formidable earthworks gave Meade pause; he did not attack.

hardly afford to sack the victor of Gettysburg, so he refused to accept it. On July 14 he sat down to write Meade a soothing letter. "I am very—*very*—grateful to you for the magnificent success you gave the cause of the country at Gettysburg," said the president. But he could not refrain from pointing out that the opportunity to crush Lee's army and end the war had been lost: "As it is, the war will be prolonged indefinitely." Upon reflection, Lincoln concluded that this letter was unlikely to mollify Meade, so he did not send it. And the war continued.

Lincoln's temper soon recovered thanks to victories west of the Mississippi and Rosecrans's expulsion of Bragg's army from middle Tennessee as well as the capture of Vicksburg and Port Hudson.

With a countenance befitting his name, Major General James G. Blunt commanded the most multicultural army of the Civil War in the Missouri–Arkansas–Indian Territory theater, consisting of white, black, and Indian regiments.

The transfer of Van Dorn's Confederate army to Mississippi in the spring of 1862 had left northern Arkansas shorn of defenders. Samuel R. Curtis's small Union force began advancing toward Little Rock but was deflected by Thomas C. Hindman, a political general five feet tall who made up in energy what he lacked in size, and his hastily conscripted 20,000-man army, which went over to the offensive in the fall,

Little Rock, Arkansas, photographed after its capture by Union forces in September 1863. The Arkansas River is in the background at the upper right.

driving the Federals northward almost to Missouri. But then the initiative went over to the Yankees. Their leader was General James G. Blunt, a Maine-born Kansas abolitionist who had learned his fighting with John Brown. While Blunt and Hindman were sparring in northwest Arkansas during the first week of December, two small Union divisions marched 110 miles in three days from Missouri to help Blunt. Turning to attack this force at Prairie Grove on December 7, Hindman suddenly found himself attacked in front and flank by three converging Yankee divisions. Forced to retreat in freezing weather, the diminutive Arkansan watched helplessly as his conscript army melted away.

In the spring of 1863 Jefferson Davis reorganized the trans-Mississippi Department by assigning overall command to Edmund Kirby Smith and sending Sterling Price to Little Rock. Both generals did well with their small resources. Kirby Smith turned the trans-Mississippi into a virtually autonomous region after it was cut off from the rest of the Confederacy by the loss of Vicksburg. But Price could not stop the blue invaders who advanced toward Little Rock from two directions in midsummer. Blunt led a multiracial force of white, black, and Indian regiments down the Arkansas River from Honey Springs in Indian Territory, where they had defeated a Confederate army of white and Indian regiments on July 17. In early September Blunt occupied Fort Smith, while another Union army approached Little Rock from the east and captured it on September 10. The rebels fled to the southwest corner of the state, yielding three-quarters of Arkansas to Union control—though southern guerrillas and the small number of occupation troops made that control tenuous in large areas.

In Tennessee, however, Rosecrans failed to advance in concert with Grant's movements in Mississippi and Hooker's in Virginia. Such an advance would have achieved Lincoln's strategy of concurrent pressure on all main Confederate armies to prevent one of them from reinforcing another. But the memory of the New Year's Eve bloodbath at Stones River convinced Rosecrans that he must not attack without sufficient resources to ensure success. His delays enabled Bragg to send

This panoramic photograph of Knoxville was taken in the fall of 1863 after Burnside's small army captured the city. Forts on the hill across the Holston River at the extreme right and on the two hills seen dimly in the distance at left were part of the defensive works built by Union forces.

reinforcements to Mississippi, an action that increased Lincoln's exasperation. But when Rosecrans finally made his move on June 24, his careful planning produced a swift and almost bloodless success. Each of the four northern infantry corps and one cavalry corps burst through a different gap in the Cumberland foothills south of Murfreesboro. Having confused Bragg with feints, Rosecrans got strong forces on both Confederate flanks in the Duck River Valley. Despite constant rain that turned roads to gluten, the Yankees kept moving. One blue brigade of mounted infantry armed with seven-shot Spencer rifles got in the rebel rear and threatened to cut their rail lifeline. At the beginning of July, Bragg decided to fall back all the way to Chattanooga rather than risk a battle.

In little more than a week of marching and maneuvering, the Army of the Cumberland had driven its adversary eighty miles at the cost of only 570 casualties. Rosecrans was annoyed by Washington's apparent lack of appreciation. On July 7 Secretary of War Stanton sent Rosecrans a message informing him of "Lee's army overthrown; Grant victorious. You and your noble army now have the chance to give the finishing blow to the rebellion. Will you neglect the chance?" Rosecrans shot back: "You do not appear to observe the fact that this noble army has driven the rebels from Middle Tennessee. . . . I beg in behalf of this army that the War Department may not overlook so great an event because it is not written in letters of blood."

Bragg's retreat offered two rich prizes to the Federals if they could keep up the momentum: Knoxville and Chattanooga. The former was the center of east Tennessee unionism, which Lincoln had been trying to redeem for two years. Chattanooga had great strategic value, for the only railroads linking the eastern and

western parts of the Confederacy converged there in the gap carved through the Cumberlands by the Tennessee River. Having already cut the Confederacy in two by the capture of Vicksburg, Union forces could slice up the eastern portion by penetrating into Georgia via Chattanooga.

For these reasons Lincoln urged Rosecrans to push on to Chattanooga while he had the enemy off balance. From Kentucky General Burnside, now commanding the small Army of the Ohio, would move forward on Rosecrans's left flank against the 10,000 Confederate troops defending Knoxville. But once again Rosecrans dug in his heels. He could not advance until he had repaired the railroad and bridges in his rear, established a forward base, and accumulated supplies. July passed as General in Chief Halleck sent repeated messages asking and finally ordering Rosecrans to get moving. On August 16, after more delays, he did.

Rosecrans repeated the deceptive strategy of his earlier advance, feinting a crossing of the Tennessee above Chattanooga (where Bragg expected it) but sending most of his army across the river at three virtually undefended points below the city. Rosecrans's objective was the railroad from Atlanta. His 60,000 men struck toward it in three columns through gaps in the mountain ranges south of Chattanooga. At the same time, a hundred miles to the north Burnside's army of 24,000 also moved through mountain passes in four columns like the fingers of a hand reaching to grasp Knoxville. The outnumbered defenders, confronted by Yankees soldiers in front and unionist partisans in the rear, abandoned the city without firing a shot. Burnside rode into town on September 3 to the cheers of most citizens. His troops pushed patrols toward the North Carolina and Virginia borders to consolidate their

The first of Longstreet's troops from Virginia detraining near Ringgold, Georgia on September 18, 1863. They had been on the road for nine days, riding in and on top of boxcars as shown here. They had not lost any of their fighting edge during this slow trip, however, and two days later they formed the spearhead of a Confederate breakthrough at Chickamauga.

hold on east Tennessee, while the rebel division that had evacuated Knoxville moved south to join Bragg just in time to participate in the evacuation of Chattanooga on September 8. With Rosecrans on his southern flank, Bragg had decided to pull back to northern Georgia before he could be trapped in this city enfolded by river and mountains.

In this dark hour of defeat desertions from the southern armies rose alarmingly. But it had been almost as dark after Union victories in early 1862, until Jackson and Lee had rekindled southern hopes. Davis was determined to make history repeat itself. Lee had turned the war around by attacking McClellan; Davis instructed Bragg to try the same strategy against Rosecrans. To aid that effort, two divisions had already joined Bragg from Joseph Johnston's idle army in Mississippi. This brought Bragg's numbers almost equal to Rosecrans's. Concerned by the low morale in the Army of Tennessee, though, Davis knew that something more was required at this critical moment, so he asked Lee to go south in person to take over Bragg's augmented army. Lee demurred and also objected at first to Longstreet's renewed proposal to reinforce Bragg with his corps. Instead, Lee wanted to take the offensive against Meade on the Rappahannock. But this time Davis overruled Lee and ordered Longstreet to Georgia with two of his divisions (the third, Pickett's, had not yet recovered from Gettysburg). The first of Longstreet's 12,000 veterans entrained on September 9. Because of Burnside's occupation of east Tennessee, the direct route of 550 miles was closed off. Instead, the soldiers had to make a roundabout 900-mile excursion through both Carolinas and Georgia over eight or ten different lines. Only half of Longstreet's men got to Chickamauga Creek in time for the ensuing battle—but they helped win a stunning victory over Longstreet's old West Point roommate Rosecrans.

With help on the way, Bragg went over to the offensive. To lure Rosecrans's three

separated columns through the mountains where he could pounce on them individually in the valley south of Chattanooga, Bragg sent sham deserters into Union lines bearing tales of Confederate retreat. Rosecrans took the bait and pushed forward too eagerly. But Bragg's subordinates failed to spring the traps. Three times from September 10 to 13 Bragg ordered attacks by two or more divisions against outnumbered and isolated fragments of the enemy. But each time the general assigned to make the attack, considering his orders discretionary, found reasons for not doing so. Warned by these maneuvers, Rosecrans concentrated his army in the valley of West Chickamauga Creek during the third week of September.

Angered by the intractability of his generals—who in turn distrusted his judgment—Bragg nevertheless devised a new plan to turn Rosecrans's left, cut him off from Chattanooga, and drive him southward up a dead-end valley. With the arrival on September 18 of the first of Longstreet's troops under the fighting Texan John Bell Hood, with his arm in a sling from a Gettysburg wound, Bragg was assured of numerical superiority. If he had been able to launch his attack that day, he might have succeeded in rolling up Rosecrans's flank, for only one Union corps stood in his way. But Yankee cavalry with repeating carbines blunted the rebels' sluggish advance. That night Virginia-born George Thomas's large Union corps made a forced march to strengthen the Union left. Soon after dawn on September 19, enemy patrols bumped into each other just west of Chickamauga Creek, setting off what became the bloodiest battle in the western theater.

Bragg persisted in trying to turn the Union left. All through the day the rebels made savage division-size attacks mostly against Thomas's corps through woods and undergrowth so thick that units could not see or cooperate with each other. Rosecrans fed reinforcements to Thomas, who held the enemy to minimal gains, at

This drawing by Harper's Weekly *artist Alfred R. Waud depicts a Confederate attack on General George Thomas's lines at Chickamauga on September 19. Note the open, park-like nature of the woods, where the underbrush had been kept cleared by grazing livestock.*

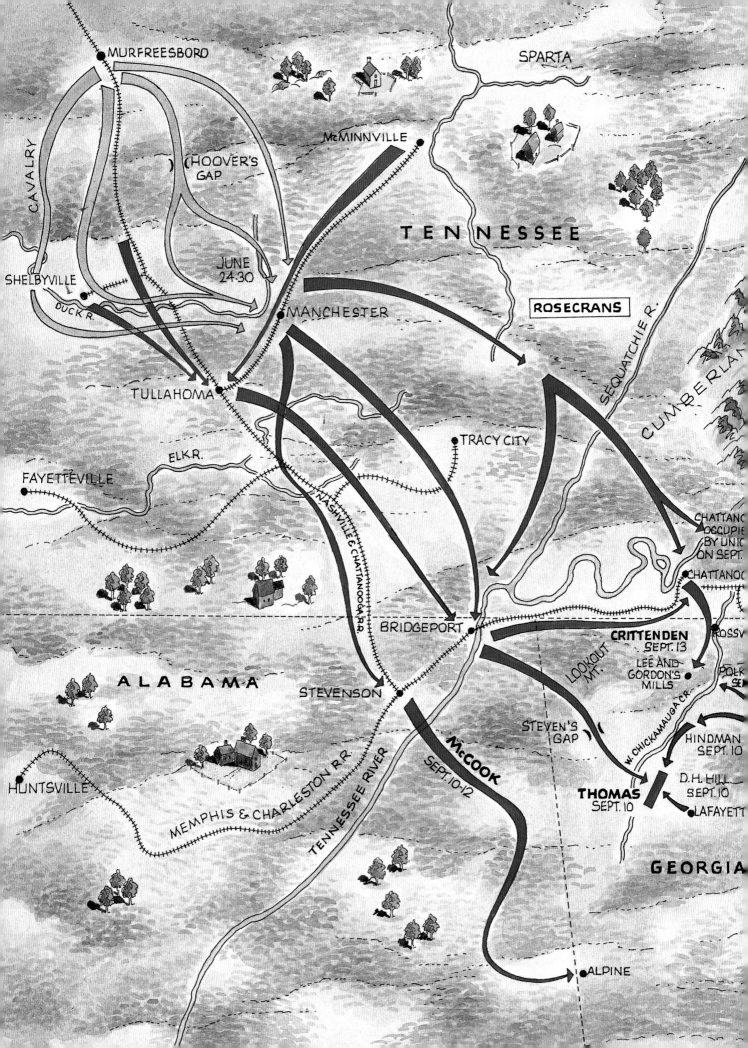

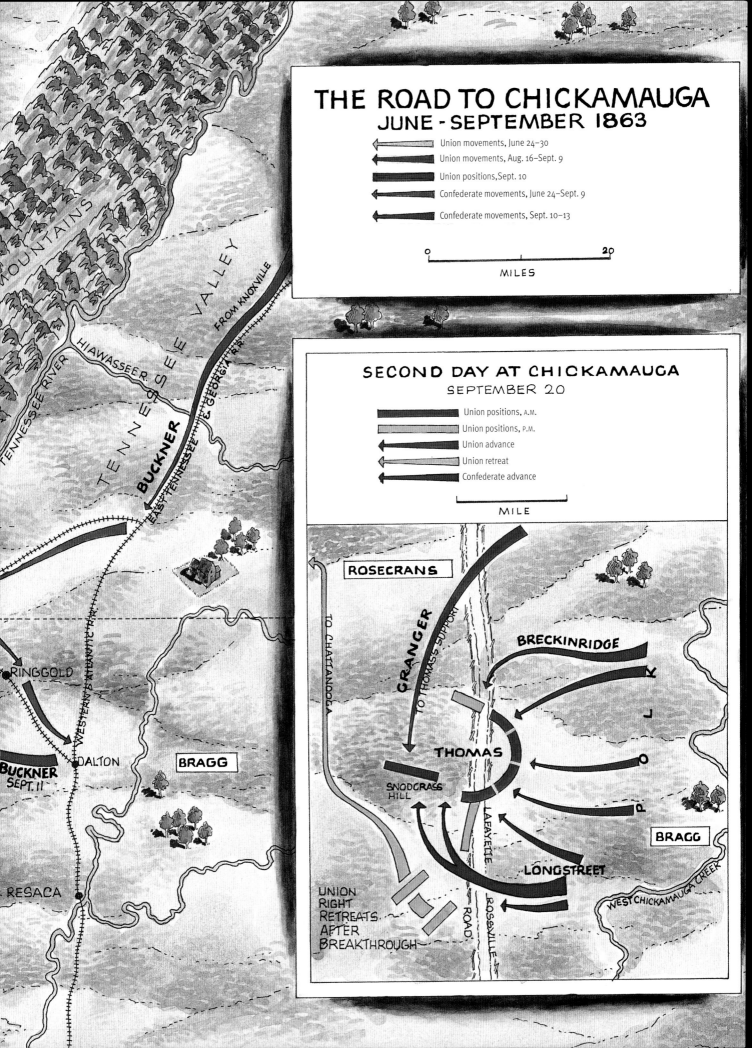

THE ROAD TO CHICKAMAUGA
JUNE - SEPTEMBER 1863

Union movements, June 24–30
Union movements, Aug. 16–Sept. 9
Union positions, Sept. 10
Confederate movements, June 24–Sept. 9
Confederate movements, Sept. 10–13

0   20
MILES

SECOND DAY AT CHICKAMAUGA
SEPTEMBER 20

Union positions, A.M.
Union positions, P.M.
Union advance
Union retreat
Confederate advance

MILE

ROSECRANS

GRANGER

TO THOMAS'S SUPPORT

BRECKINRIDGE

THOMAS

SNODGRASS HILL

LONGSTREET

UNION RIGHT RETREATS AFTER BREAKTHROUGH

LAFAYETTE ROAD

ROSSVILLE ROAD

TO CHATTANOOGA

BRAGG

WEST CHICKAMAUGA CREEK

MOUNTAINS

TENNESSEE RIVER

HIAWASSEE R.

TENNESSEE VALLEY

FROM KNOXVILLE

EAST TENNESSEE & GEORGIA RR.

BUCKNER

RINGGOLD

WESTERN & ATLANTIC RR.

BUCKNER SEPT. 11

DALTON

BRAGG

RESACA

harsh cost to both sides. That evening Longstreet arrived personally with two more of his brigades. Bragg organized his army into two wings, gave Longstreet command of the left and Leonidas Polk of the right, and ordered them to make an echelon attack next morning from right to left. Polk's assault started several hours late—a failing that had become a habit—and made little headway against Thomas's stubborn defenders fighting behind breastworks they had built overnight. Exasperated, Bragg canceled the echelon order of attack and told Longstreet to go forward with everything he had. At 11:30 A.M. Longstreet complied, and charged into one of the greatest pieces of luck in the war.

Over on the Union side, Rosecrans had been shifting reinforcements to his hard-pressed left. During this confusing process a staff officer, failing to see a blue division concealed in the woods on the right, reported a quarter-mile gap in the line at that point. To fill this supposedly dangerous hole, Rosecrans ordered another division to move over, thus creating a real gap in an effort to remedy a nonexistent one. Into this breach unwittingly marched Longstreet's veterans from the Army of Northern Virginia, catching the Yankees on either side in the flank and spreading a growing panic. More gray soldiers poured into the break, rolling up Rosecrans's right and sending one-third of the blue army—along with four division commanders, two corps commanders, and a traumatized Rosecrans, whose headquarters had been overrun—streaming northward toward Chattanooga eight miles away. Here were the makings of the decisive victory that had eluded western Confederate armies for more than two years.

Recognizing the opportunity, Longstreet sent in his reserves and called on Bragg for reinforcements. But the commander said he could not spare a man from his fought-out right, so a disgusted Longstreet had to make the final push with what he had. By this time, however, the Federals had formed a new line along a ridge at right angles to their old one. George Thomas took charge of what was left of the army and organized it for a last-ditch stand. For his leadership this day he won fame as

A native of Virginia who had married a New Yorker, George H. Thomas remained loyal to the United States when his native state seceded. None of his Virginia relatives ever spoke to him again. A large, portly man and a deliberate commander, Thomas was known by the rather unflattering nickname of "Old Slow Trot." His tenacious stand at Chickamauga, however, earned him distinction forever after as "the Rock of Chickamauga."

"the Rock of Chickamauga." Thomas got timely help from another northern battle hero, Gordon Granger, commander of the Union reserve division posted several miles to the rear. On his own initiative Granger marched toward the sound of the guns and arrived just in time for his men to help stem Longstreet's repeated onslaughts. As the sun went down, Thomas finally disengaged his exhausted troops for a nighttime retreat to Chattanooga. There the two parts of the army—those who had fled and those who had stood—were reunited to face an experience unique for Union forces, the defense of a besieged city.

Longstreet and Forrest wanted to push on next morning to complete the destruction of Rosecrans's army before it could reorganize behind the Chattanooga fortifications. But Bragg was more appalled by the wastage of his own army than impressed by the magnitude of its victory. In two days he had lost 19,000 killed, wounded, and missing—nearly 30 percent of his effectives. Ten Confederate generals had been killed or wounded, including Hood, who narrowly survived amputation of a leg. Although the rebels had made a rich haul in captured guns and equipment, Bragg's immediate concern was the ghastly spectacle of dead and wounded lying thick on the ground. Half of his artillery horses had also been killed. Thus he refused to heed the pleas of his lieutenants for a rapid pursuit—a refusal that laid the groundwork for bitter recriminations that swelled into an uproar during the coming weeks. "What does he fight battles for?" asked an angry Forrest, and soon many others in the South were asking the same question. The tactical triumph at Chickamauga seemed barren of strategic results so long as the enemy held Chattanooga.

Bragg hoped to starve the Yankees out. By mid-October he seemed likely to succeed. The Confederates planted artillery on the commanding height of Lookout Mountain south of Chattanooga, infantry along Missionary Ridge to the east, and infantry on river roads to the west. This enabled them to interdict all of Rosecrans's supply routes into the city except a tortuous wagon road over the forbidding Cumberlands to the north. Mules consumed almost as much forage as they could haul over these heights, while rebel cavalry raids picked off hundreds of wagons. Union horses starved to death in Chattanooga while men were reduced to half rations or less.

Rosecrans seemed unequal to the crisis. The disaster at Chickamauga and the shame of having fled the field while Thomas stayed and fought unnerved him. Lincoln considered Rosecrans "confused and stunned like a duck hit on the head." The Army of the Cumberland clearly needed help. Even before Chickamauga, Halleck had ordered Sherman to bring four divisions from Vicksburg to Chattanooga, rebuilding the railroad as he went. But the latter task would take weeks. So, on September 23, Stanton pressed a reluctant Lincoln to transfer the understrength 11th

This drawing by an illustrator for Frank Leslie's Illustrated Newspaper *who was present depicts a Confederate attack on a Union wagon train carrying supplies to Chattanooga. Repeated raids like this one kept Union soldiers on a near-starvation diet in Chattanooga.*

This cartoon from the Southern Illustrated News *shows Braxton Bragg and James Longstreet kicking a hapless General Rosecrans into Chattanooga, where the Confederates bottled him up. The contemporary media misspelled "Rosecrans" in several different ways; the caption writer here also found a new way to spell "supersedure."*

CAUSE OF ROSECRANZ'S SUPERCEDURE!

ROSECRANZ'S ADDRESS TO HIS SOLDIERS:
"We have fought the Battle of Chickamauga to gain our position at Chattanooga, AND HERE WE ARE!!!"

This photograph taken from the heights of Lookout Mountain shows Chattanooga across the Tennessee River. The "cracker line" opened by Union troops in late October bridged the river around the bend at the upper left, out of range of Confederate artillery on the mountain.

and 12th Corps by rail from the Army of the Potomac to Rosecrans. Lincoln finally consented and dispatched an expeditionary force under Joe Hooker. Eleven days later, after Stanton organized dozens of railroad trains to convey the force over a route 1,233 miles long, more than 20,000 men had arrived at the rail-head near Chattanooga with their artillery, horses, and equipment. It was an extraordinary feat of logistics—the longest and fastest movement of such a large body of troops before the twentieth century.

But there was no point putting these men into Chattanooga when the soldiers already there could not be fed. And there seemed to be no remedy for that problem

without new leadership. In mid-October, Lincoln took the matter in hand. He created the Division of the Mississippi, embracing the whole region between that river and the Appalachians, and put Grant in command "with his headquarters in the field." The field just now was Chattanooga, so there Grant went. On the way he authorized the replacement of Rosecrans with Thomas as commander of the Army of the Cumberland. Within a week of Grant's arrival on October 23, Union forces had broken the rebel stranglehold on the road and river west of Chattanooga and opened a new supply route dubbed the "cracker line" by hungry bluecoats. The inspiration of Grant's presence seemed to extend even to the 11th Corps, which had suffered disgrace at Chancellorsville and Gettysburg but fought well during a night action October 28–29 to open the cracker line. By mid-November, Sherman had arrived with 17,000 troops from the Army of the Tennessee to supplement the 20,000 men Hooker had brought from the Army of the Potomac to reinforce the 35,000 infantry of

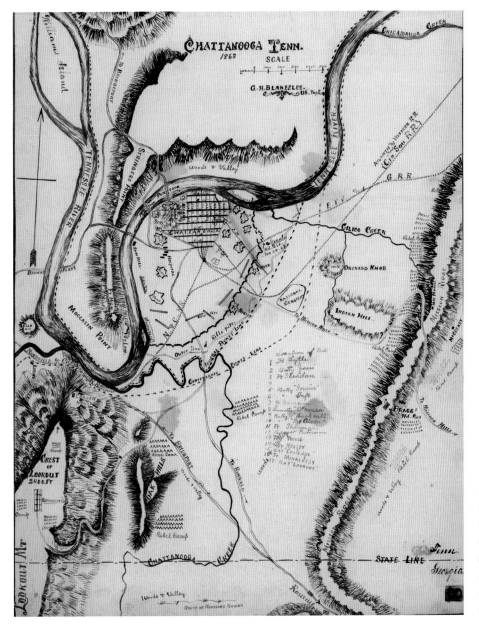

This contemporary map of the Union and Confederate positions at Chattanooga was drawn by a Northern topographer who was penned up there by the Confederate siege. Confederate positions on Lookout Mountain (left) and Missionary Ridge (right) commanded rail and river approaches to Chattanooga as well as all roads except the one from the north.

Thomas's Army of the Cumberland. Though Bragg still held Lookout Mountain and Missionary Ridge, his immediate future began to look cloudy.

This cloudiness stemmed in part from continuing internecine warfare within Bragg's command. Soon after Chickamauga, Bragg suspended Polk and two other generals for slowness or refusal to obey crucial orders before and during the battle. The hot-blooded Forrest, bitter about failure to follow up the victory, refused to serve any longer under Bragg and returned to an independent command in Mississippi. Longstreet wrote to the secretary of war with a lugubrious prediction that "nothing but the hand of God can save us or help us as long as we have our present commander."

Twice before—after Perryville and Stones River—similar dissensions had erupted in the Army of Tennessee. On October 6 a weary Jefferson Davis boarded a special train for the long trip to Bragg's headquarters where he hoped to straighten out the mess. In Bragg's presence all four corps commanders told Davis that the general must go. After this embarrassing meeting, Davis considered various replacements for Bragg (Longstreet's recommendation of Johnston was quickly rejected) but finally concluded that there seemed no alternative but to retain him. In an attempt to reduce friction within the army, Davis authorized the transfer of several generals to other theaters. He also counseled Bragg to detach Longstreet with 15,000 men for a campaign to recapture Knoxville—an ill-fated venture that accomplished nothing while depriving Bragg of more than a quarter of his strength. Indeed, none of Davis's decisions during this maladroit visit had a happy result. The president left behind a sullen army as he returned to Richmond.

With Longstreet's departure in early November the Confederates yielded the initiative to Grant. As soon as Sherman's reinforcements arrived, Grant set in motion a plan to drive the rebels away from Chattanooga and open the gate to Georgia. As usual the taciturn general's offensive succeeded, but this time not in quite the way he had planned. Grant rejected the idea of a frontal assault against the triple line of trenches on Missionary Ridge as suicidal. He intended to attack both ends of Bragg's line to get on the enemy's flanks. Believing that Thomas's Army of the Cumberland was still demoralized from their shock at Chickamauga and "could not be got out of their trenches to assume the offensive," Grant assigned them the secondary role of merely threatening the Confederate center on Missionary Ridge while Sherman's and Hooker's interlopers from the Armies of the Tennessee and the Potomac did the real fighting on the flanks. By this plan Grant unwittingly applied a goad to Thomas's troops that would produce a spectacular though serendipitous success.

Hooker carried out the first part of his job with a flair. On November 24 he sent the better part of three divisions against three Confederate brigades holding the northern slope of Lookout Mountain. The Yankee infantry scrambled uphill over boulders and fallen trees through an intermittent fog that in later years became romanticized as the "Battle Above the Clouds." With surprisingly light casualties (fewer than 500), Hooker's troops drove the rebels down the reverse slope, forcing Bragg that night to evacuate his defenses on Lookout and pull the survivors back to Missionary Ridge.

During the night the skies cleared to reveal a total eclipse of the moon; next morning a Kentucky Union regiment clawed its way to Lookout's highest point and raised a huge American flag in sunlit view of both armies below. For the South these were ill omens, though at first it did not appear so. On the other end of the line Sherman had found the going hard. When his four divisions pressed forward on November 24 they quickly took their assigned hill at the north end of Missionary Ridge—and found that it was not part of the ridge at all, but a detached spur separated by a rock-strewn ravine from the main spine. The latter they attacked with a will on the morning of November 25 but were repeatedly repulsed by Irish-born Patrick Cleburne's oversize division, the best in Bragg's army. Meanwhile Hooker's advance toward the opposite end of Missionary Ridge was delayed by obstructed roads and a wrecked bridge.

The right wing of Hooker's attack against Confederate forces on November 24 swept across the rugged slopes of Lookout Mountain, shown in this photograph. The bend in the Tennessee River with Chattanooga at its right can be seen dimly in the distance.

His plan not working, Grant in midafternoon ordered Thomas to launch a limited assault against the first line of Confederate trenches in the center to prevent Bragg from sending reinforcements to Cleburne. Thomas made the most of this opportunity to redeem his army's reputation. He sent four divisions, 23,000 men covering a two-mile front, across an open plain straight at the Confederate line. It looked like a reprise of Pickett's charge at Gettysburg, with blue and gray having switched roles. And this assault seemed even more hopeless than Pickett's, for the rebels had had two months to dig in and Missionary Ridge was much higher and more rugged than Cemetery Ridge. Yet the Yankees swept over the first line of trenches with astonishing ease, driving the demoralized defenders pell-mell up the hill to the second and third lines at the middle and top of the crest.

Having accomplished their assignment, Thomas's soldiers did not stop and await orders. For one thing, they were now sitting ducks for the enemy firing at them from above. For another, these men had something to prove to the rebels in front of them and to the Yankees on their flanks. So they started up the steep ridge, first by platoons and companies, then by regiments and brigades. Soon sixty regimental flags seemed to be racing each other to the top. At his command post a mile in the rear, Grant watched with bewilderment. "Thomas, who ordered those men up the ridge?" he asked angrily. "I don't know," replied Thomas. "I did not." Someone would catch hell if this turned out badly, Grant muttered as he clamped his teeth on a cigar. But he need not have worried. Things turned out better than anyone at Union headquarters could have expected—the miracle at Missionary Ridge, some of them were calling it by sundown. To the Confederates it seemed a nightmare. As the Yankees kept coming up the hill the rebels gaped with amazement, panicked, broke, and fled. "Completely and frantically drunk with excitement," blueclad soldiers yelled "Chickamauga! Chickamauga!" in derisive triumph at the backs of the disap-

CHATTANOOGA
OCT.– NOV. 1863

Union advance | Confederate retreat

Union positions | Confederate positions

MILES
0   1   2   3

GRANT

SHERMAN
NOV. 23-24

TENNESSEE RIVER

RACCOON MOUNTAINS

BROWN'S FERRY

CHATTANOOGA

UNION CRACKER LINE OPENED OCT. 28

TO BRIDGEPORT
UNION RAILROAD

KELLEY'S FERRY

MOCCASIN POINT

WAUHATCHIE

LOOKOUT CREEK

HOOKER NOV. 24

WALTHALL BRIGADE
NOV. 24

NIGHT OF NOV.

STEVENSON
DIVISION
NOV. 24

NASHVILLE & CHATTANOOGA R.R.

LOOKOUT VALLEY

LOOKOUT MOUNTAIN

CHATTANOOGA CREEK

GEORGIA

TENNESSEE

TENNESSEE RIVER

SOUTH CHICKAMAUGA CREEK

SHERMAN
NOV. 24-25

CLEBURNE
NOV. 25

EAST TENNESSEE & GEORGIA R.R.

RAILROAD
TUNNEL

WESTERN ATLANTIC R.R.

CHICKAMAUGA
STATION

THOMAS
NOV. 25

RIDGE

NOV. 25

ORCHARD
KNOB

BRAGG

HOOKER NOV. 25

MISSIONARY

ROSSVILLE

This lithograph of a painting by Swedish-born American artist Thure de Thulstrup shows General Ulysses S. Grant watching through binoculars as Union soldiers move forward up the slopes of Missionary Ridge in the distance. General George Thomas stands to Grant's right.

pearing enemy. Darkness and a determined rear-guard defense by Cleburne's division, which had not broken, prevented effective pursuit. But Bragg's army did not stop and regroup until it had retreated thirty miles down the railroad toward Atlanta.

Union soldiers could hardly believe their stunning success. When a student of the battle later commented to Grant that southern generals had considered their position impregnable, Grant replied with a wry smile: "Well, it *was* impregnable." Bragg himself wrote that "no satisfactory excuse can possibly be given for the shameful conduct of our troops. . . . The position was one which ought to have been held by a line of skirmishers." Perhaps the ultimate explanation was the Army of Tennessee's dispirited morale, which had spread downward from back-biting generals to the ranks. Bragg conceded as much in a private letter to Jefferson Davis tendering his resignation. "The disaster admits of no palliation," he wrote. "I fear we both erred in the conclusion for me to retain command here after the clamor raised against me." As the army went into winter quarters, Davis grasped the nettle and grudgingly appointed Johnston to the command.

Meanwhile the repulse on November 29 of Longstreet's attack against Knoxville deepened Confederate woes. In Virginia a campaign of maneuver by Lee after the 11th and 12th Corps left the Army of the Potomac also turned out badly. During October, Lee tried to turn the Union right and get between Meade and Washington. Having foiled that move, Meade in November attempted to turn Lee's right on the

Rapidan. Though unsuccessful, the Federals inflicted twice as many casualties as they suffered during these maneuvers, subtracting another 4,000 men from the Army of Northern Virginia it could ill afford to lose.

The glimmer of southern optimism that had flared after Chickamauga died in November. At the end of 1863 diarist Mary Chesnut found "gloom and unspoken despondency hang[ing] like a pall everywhere."

II

In foreign policy, too, the second half of 1863 brought cruel disappointment to the South. Not only had dreams of British recognition gone glimmering after Vicksburg and Gettysburg, but hopes for a new super weapon to break the blockade were also dashed.

Encouraged by British laxity in allowing the commerce raiders *Florida* and *Alabama* to escape from Liverpool, Confederate naval envoy James Bulloch contracted with the Laird firm in the summer of 1862 for construction of two armor-plated vessels carrying turrets for nine-inch guns and a seven-foot iron spike attached to the prow to pierce wooden ships below the waterline. These fearsome "Laird rams" were expected to raise havoc with the blockade fleet, perhaps even to steam into New York harbor and hold the city for ransom.

In the face of strenuous protests and warnings to the Foreign Office by Charles Francis Adams, Bulloch arranged the rather transparent subterfuge of transferring ownership of the vessels to a French firm which was ostensibly buying them for His Serene Highness the Pasha of Egypt. The diplomatic tension escalated as the ships neared completion in midsummer 1863. A court ruling against the Palmerston government's seizure in April of the commerce raider *Alexandra* seemed to clear the

A photograph of the Wivern, *one of the two "Laird rams" built for the Confederacy in 1863 but never delivered. When completed and armed, these two vessels would have been the most lethal warships in the world, with two gun turrets, 4.5 inches of armor plating, and a reinforced bow holding a seven-foot iron spike for ramming.*

Archduke Ferdinand Maximilian was the younger brother of Emperor Franz Joseph of Austria. As naval minister, Maximilian had little to do, so he was quite happy to become emperor of Mexico, supported by the presence of 35,000 French troops in that country. Maximilian's Mexican empire was short-lived, however, and so was he. Under pressure from the United States, Napoleon pulled his troops out of Mexico in 1866, whereupon Benito Juarez's republican forces overthrew Maximilian and executed him in 1867.

way for Bulloch to sail his unarmed rams out of Liverpool through a loophole in British law. Adams's protests culminated with a declaration to Foreign Secretary Russell on September 5: "It would be superfluous in me to point out to your Lordship that this is war." Unknown to Adams, the Palmerston ministry had decided to detain the ships even before receiving this note. But when the diplomatic correspondence was later published, Adams became a hero at home for apparently forcing John Bull to give in. Union diplomacy had won a victory that Henry Adams described as "a second Vicksburg."

A disheartened James Bulloch transferred his efforts to France, where during 1863 the Confederates contracted for four commerce raiders and two double-turreted ironclad rams. Louis Napoleon continued to nurture southern hopes for recognition. He was still trying to restore a French empire in the new world. In June 1863 a French army of 35,000 men captured Mexico City and overthrew the republican government of Benito Juarez. Meanwhile the Confederates had formed alliances with anti-Juarez chieftains in provinces bordering Texas to foster the contraband trade across the Rio Grande. When Napoleon made clear his intent to set up the Hapsburg Archduke Ferdinand Maximilian as emperor of Mexico, Confederate envoys made contact with Maximilian and offered to recognize him if he would help obtain French recognition of the South. Maximilian was willing, but by January 1864 Napoleon seemed to have lost interest in the scheme.

A combination of Union diplomacy and European great-power politics had produced this outcome. The United States was friendly to the Juarez government. When it was overthrown, the Lincoln administration called home the American minister and refused to recognize the French-installed provisional government. Lincoln also modified Union military strategy in order to show the flag in Texas as a warning to the French. After the capture of Vicksburg and Port Hudson, Grant and Banks wanted to mount a campaign against Mobile. But for purposes of diplomacy, the government ordered Banks to move against Texas instead. After the failure of an initial attack at Sabine Pass on the Texas-Louisiana border in November, Banks captured Brownsville and made a token lodgement near the Mexican border for Napoleon to ponder.

Ponder it he did, for he wanted no trouble with the United States at a time when his intricate house of cards in European diplomacy seemed about to collapse. Part of Napoleon's purpose in setting Maximilian on the Mexican throne was to extract favors from Austria in the delicate but deadly game of diplomacy and war among the Continental powers as each sought to protect its flanks while trying to defend or gobble up parts of Poland, Italy, and Denmark. Austria's alliance with Prussia in a war against Denmark by which Prussia gained Schleswig-Holstein cooled Napoleon's ardor for the Hapsburg connection. In early 1864 he scaled down the French commitment to Maximilian and spurned Confederate attempts to use Mexico as bait for French recognition. Napoleon's foreign ministry also shut down Bulloch's efforts to build a navy in France. The six ships contracted for by the South were sold instead to Peru, Prussia, and Denmark.

For the Lincoln administration, victories on the battlefield translated into political success at home as well as abroad in 1863. Several state elections occurred during the fall, of which the most important were the gubernatorial contests in Ohio and Pennsylvania. A year earlier the Republicans had suffered a setback in congressional elections. The issues in 1863 remained the same: the conduct of the war; emancipation; civil liberties; and conscription. On the war issue Republicans seemed in good shape, for Chickamauga only barely dimmed the luster of Gettysburg, Vicksburg, and other triumphs. Nevertheless Lincoln was nervous about the Ohio and Pennsylvania elections because the Democrats in both states had nominated copperheads for governor. The election of either would revive sagging Confederate morale and might depress the northern will to win.

Clement Vallandigham conducted his campaign for the Ohio governorship from exile in Windsor, Canada. George W. Woodward remained in dignified silence on his bench as a state supreme court judge in Pennsylvania while the party ran his campaign for governor. But a little investigative reporting by Republicans dug up information about his views on the war, which were similar to Vallandigham's. "Slavery was intended as a special blessing to the people of the United States," believed Woodward. "Secession is not disloyalty," he had written in 1860, for the election of Lincoln had destroyed the old Union of consent and comity. "I cannot in justice condemn the South for withdrawing. . . . I wish Pennsylvania could go with them." A prominent Democrat campaigning for Woodward declared that when elected he would unite with Governors Vallandigham of Ohio and Seymour of New York (representing together nearly half of the North's population) "in calling from the army troops from their respective States for the purpose of compelling the Administration to invite a convention of the States to adjust our difficulties."

Both Woodward and Vallandigham had been nominated before the Union triumphs at Gettysburg and Vicksburg. These battles undercut their theme of the war's failure. Though neither candidate changed his personal views, the party recognized that excessive antiwar statements would alienate War Democrats whose votes were necessary for victory. It came hard for War Democrats to swallow Vallandigham, but Woodward proved more digestible. He published a statement condemning the rebellion. And on election eve the party achieved a coup by persuading McClellan (who resided in neighboring New Jersey) to write a letter stating that if he could vote in Pennsylvania he would "give to Judge Woodward my voice and my vote."

Because of Republican advantages on the war question, however, Democrats concentrated mainly on such tried-and-true issues as emancipation. In Ohio the party portrayed the contest as an "'irrepressible conflict' between white and black laborers. . . . Let every vote count in favor of the *white* man, and against the Abolition hordes, who would place negro children in your schools, negro jurors in your jury boxes,

Judge George W. Woodward, Democratic candidate for governor of Pennsylvania in 1863, was next in prominence as a copperhead only to Clement L. Vallandigham. Ironically, his son Orpheus E. Woodward was an officer in the 83rd Pennsylvania, one of the Army of the Potomac's best regiments; he became its colonel in March 1864. One can readily imagine the arguments that took place between father and son.

and negro votes in your ballot boxes!" Party orators lampooned the portly Republican gubernatorial candidate John Brough as a "fat Knight of the corps d'Afrique." Similar though less strident outcries against "political and social equality" also typified the Pennsylvania campaign.

But antiabolitionism and racism seemed to have lost potency as Democratic shibboleths. Two almost simultaneous events in July 1863 were largely responsible for this phenomenon. The first was the New York draft riot, which shocked many northerners into a backlash against the consequences of virulent racism. The second was a minor battle in the campaign against Charleston. At dusk on July 18 two Union brigades assaulted Fort Wagner, a Confederate earthwork defending the entrance to Charleston harbor. Leading the attack was the 54th Massachusetts Infantry. This was not unusual in itself: Bay State regiments fought in the hottest part of many battles, and the combat casualties of Massachusetts were among the highest for Union states. But the 54th was the North's showcase black regiment. Its colonel and lieutenant colonel were sons of prominent abolitionist families. More was riding on the 54th's first big action than the capture of a fort, important as that might be. Colonel Robert Gould Shaw had implored his brigade commander to give the regiment a chance to prove its mettle. The general responded by assigning Shaw to lead the frontal assault across a narrow spit of sand against this strong earthwork. The result was predictable; the rebels drove back the attacking brigades and inflicted heavy losses.

This lithograph of the attack on Fort Wagner by the 54th Massachusetts is the best of many illustrations of that famous event. At the top of the rampart Colonel Robert Gould Shaw is shot through the heart while Sergeant William Carney, carrying the flag, is wounded next to him. Carney kept the flag and brought it back after the attack, for which he won the Congressional Medal of Honor.

The 54th took the largest casualties, losing nearly half of its men, including Colonel Shaw with a bullet through his heart. Black soldiers gained Wagner's parapet and held it for an hour in the flame-stabbed darkness before falling back. The achievements and losses of this elite black regiment, much publicized by the abolitionist press, wrought a dramatic change in northern perceptions of black soldiers.

This apotheosis of Shaw and his men took place just after Democratic rioters in New York had lynched black people and burned the Colored Orphan Asylum. Few Republican newspapers failed to point the moral: black men who fought for the Union deserved more respect than white men who fought against it. Lincoln expressed this theme in a public letter of August 26 addressed to Democrats. "You are dissatisfied with me about the negro," wrote the president. But "some of the commanders of our armies in the field who have given us our most important successes, believe the emancipation policy, and the use of colored troops, constitute the heaviest blow yet dealt to the rebellion." "You say you will not fight to free negroes," continued Lincoln. "Some of them seem willing to fight for you; but, no matter. Fight you, then, exclusively to save the Union. I issued the proclamation on purpose to aid you in saving the Union." When this war was won, concluded the president, "there will be some black men who can remember that, with silent tongue, and clenched teeth, and steady eye, and well-poised bayonet, they have helped mankind on to this great consummation; while, I fear, there will be some white ones, unable to forget that, with malignant heart, and deceitful speech, they have strove to hinder it."

Lincoln's letter set the tone for Republicans in the 1863 campaign. Many of them had previously felt defensive about emancipation; now they could put Democrats on the defensive. Opposition to emancipation became opposition to northern victory. Linking abolition and Union, Republicans managed to blunt the edge of Democratic racism in Ohio, Pennsylvania, and New York (where legislative elections were held in 1863). The party carried two-thirds of the legislative districts in New York. In Ohio it buried Vallandigham under a victory margin of 100,000 votes, winning an unprecedented 61 percent of the ballots. Especially gratifying to Republicans was their 94 percent share of the absentee soldier vote. Efforts to persuade soldiers to "vote as they shot" paid off in a big way. Significantly, in an opinion written by none other than George Woodward, the Pennsylvania Supreme Court had ruled a year earlier that soldiers could not vote outside their home districts. Since only a few thousand Pennsylvania soldiers could be furloughed home for the election, their votes contributed only a small part of the Republicans' 15,000-vote victory (51.5 percent) over Woodward.

Republicans additionally scored significant gains in state and local elections elsewhere. They interpreted these results as signs of a transformation of public opinion toward emancipation. The Emancipation Proclamation had been "followed by dark and doubtful days," admitted Lincoln in his annual message to Congress on December 8, 1863. But now "the crisis which threatened the friends of the Union is past." If Lincoln's optimism proved premature, it nevertheless mirrored the despair that threatened to undermine the southern will to continue fighting.

CHAPTER TWENTY-THREE

When This Cruel War Is Over

I

In the Confederate congressional elections in the fall of 1863 the Davis administration suffered a more severe rebuke from voters than the Lincoln administration had sustained the previous year in a similar situation. The difference resulted not only from the greater calamity to Confederate arms but also from the different political structures in North and South.

Formal political parties did not exist in the Confederacy. Below the surface of southern politics Whiggery persisted in the form of memory and sentiment, but the most assiduous researchers employing the tools of roll-call analysis have been unable to identify party organizations or significant partisan patterns of voting in the Confederate Congress from 1861 through 1863.

Southerners considered this circumstance a source of strength. But in fact, as historians now recognize, the absence of parties was a source of weakness. In the North the two-party system disciplined and channeled political activity. The Republican party, closing ranks against Democratic opposition, became the means for mobilizing war resources, raising taxes, creating a new financial system, initiating emancipation, and enacting conscription. Because measures were supported or opposed by *parties*, voters could identify those responsible for them and register their approval or disapproval at the polls by voting a party ticket. Both parties, of course, used their well-oiled machinery to rally voters to their side. In the Confederacy, by contrast, the Davis administration had no such means to mobilize support. Opposition to the Davis administration became personal or factional and therefore difficult to deal with.

In the North, where nearly all state governors were Republicans, the ties of party bound them to the war effort. In the South the obstructionist activities of several governors hindered the centralized war effort because the centrifugal tendencies of state's rights were not restrained by the centripetal force of party. The Confederate Constitution limited the president to a single six-year term, so Davis had no reason to create a party organization for reelection. Such government policies as conscription, impressment, the tax in kind, and management of finances were the main issues

Opposite page: This photograph shows freed slaves in Richmond in 1865, but it could have been taken in any of several southern cities where slaves were liberated during the war itself.

A native of South Carolina, where he fought several duels and killed a man, Louis T. Wigfall moved to Texas in 1846. Elected to the U.S. Senate in 1859, he was one of the leading "fire-eaters" advocating secession. As a senator in the Confederate Congress he was initially a strong supporter of President Davis, but he turned against Davis in 1863 and became one of the sharpest thorns in the president's side. After the war Wigfall fled to England, where he tried to foment a war with the United States to enable the South to rise again. When that scheme failed, he returned to Texas to die in 1874.

in the congressional elections of 1863. Opposition candidates ran on an individual rather than a party basis, and the government could not muster political artillery to shoot at all these scattered targets.

Historians have identified "proto-parties" emerging in the Confederacy by 1863. Former Whigs were most prominent in the crystallizing opposition, but the lack of a definite pattern was illustrated by the prominence of Louis T. Wigfall and the private influence of General Joseph E. Johnston among Davis's adversaries. A fire-eating Democrat who had served briefly under Johnston as a general in Virginia before being elected by Texas to the Senate in 1862, Wigfall became a bitter critic of Davis's "pigheadiness and perverseness" in 1863. While Davis blamed Johnston for the loss of Vicksburg, Johnston and Wigfall blamed Davis for the ambiguous command structure in the West that had led to disaster. Although Johnston did not speak out publicly, his letters to friends made no secret of his opinions. By the fall of 1863 Johnston had become, in the words of another Confederate general, a "shield" behind which critics of the administration "gathered themselves . . . and shot arrows at President Davis."

Worsening inflation and shortages heaped fuel on the fires of political opposition. In the four months after Gettysburg, prices jumped nearly 70 percent, producing misery and encouraging theft. The head of the War Department's administrative bureau, a loyal Davis man, confessed in November that "the irretrievable bankruptcy of the national finances, the tenacity with which the President holds to men in whom the country has lost all confidence, the scarcity of means of support . . . are producing deep disgust. . . . my faith [in the cause] . . . is yielding to a sense of hopelessness."

In this atmosphere the congressional elections took place. They produced an increase of openly antiadministration representatives from 26 to 41 (of 106). Twelve of the twenty-six senators in the next Congress were identified with the opposition. The proportion of former Whigs and conditional unionists in Congress grew from one-third to half. Erstwhile Whigs won several governorships in 1863, including those of Alabama and Mississippi for the first time ever. Although the administration did preserve a narrow majority in Congress, this margin rested on an ironic anomaly. Support for the Davis government was strongest among congressmen from areas under Union occupation: Kentucky, Missouri (both considered part of the Confederacy and represented in its Congress), Tennessee, and substantial portions of Louisiana, Arkansas, Mississippi, and Virginia. Regular elections were impossible in these areas, of course, so the incumbents merely continued themselves in office or were "elected" by a handful of refugees from their districts. These irredentist congressmen had the strongest of motives for supporting "war to the last ditch." They constituted the closest thing to an administration party that existed in the Confederacy. They provided the votes for higher taxes that would not be levied on their constituents and for tougher conscription laws that would take no men from their districts. The areas of the South still under Confederate control, by contrast, sent an antiadministration majority to Congress. From the two largest such constituencies, North Carolina and Georgia, sixteen of the nineteen new congressmen opposed the government.

As in the North, the opposition took two forms. Most antiadministration southerners backed the government's war aims but dissented from some of the total-war measures intended to achieve those aims. Other opponents, however, branded the war a failure and demanded peace through negotiations even if this risked the country's war aims. In the North such men were called copperheads; in the South they were known as reconstructionists or tories. In both North and South the peace faction grew stronger when the war went badly.

The prowar but antiadministration faction was most outspoken in Georgia. There the triumvirate of Vice President Alexander Stephens, ex-general Robert Toombs, and Governor Joseph E. Brown turned their opposition into a personal vendetta against Davis. Stephens likened the president to "my poor old blind and deaf dog." Resentful of the "West Point clique" that had blocked his rise to military glory, Toombs in 1863 lashed out at Davis as a "false and hypocritical . . . wretch" who had "neither the ability nor the honesty to manage the revolution." The government's financial policy, said Toombs, was "pernicious," "ruinous," "insupportable"; the impressment of farm products was "force and fraud"; conscription had "outraged justice and the constitution." Governor Brown did more than speak against the draft. He appointed several thousand new constables, militia officers, justices of the peace, coroners, and county surveyors to exempt them from conscription.

A Georgia crisis erupted in February 1864 when the lame-duck session of the old Confederate Congress authorized the president to suspend the writ of habeas corpus to suppress disloyalty and enforce the draft. Both of Georgia's senators voted against the bill. Vice President Stephens condemned it as a "blow at the very 'vitals of liberty'" by a president "aiming at absolute power." Stephens also helped write an address by Brown to the Georgia legislature denouncing the law as a step toward "military despotism" and a threat to the very liberties the South was fighting for. The legislature passed resolutions written by Stephens's brother condemning suspension of the writ of habeas corpus as unconstitutional.

From Richmond's viewpoint all this was bad enough, but worse was a proposal by

Elected governor of Georgia in 1857, Joseph E. Brown was reelected several times and served in that post through the entire Civil War. Of all southern governors, he gave Jefferson Davis the most grief. Union troops arrested Brown in May 1865 but soon let him go. During Reconstruction he became a Republican and served as chief justice of the state supreme court, but switched back to the Democrats when they returned to power. Cat-like, he landed on his feet and was a powerful figure in Georgia politics until his death in 1894.

Brown for peace negotiations, apparently supported by Stephens. His brother introduced additional resolutions in the legislature urging the people "through their state organizations and popular assemblies" to bring pressure on the government to end the war. This had an ominous ring. It smacked of treason. In reality, Brown and Stephens wanted to begin negotiations *after* the next Confederate victory, with independence as a precondition of peace. No one, Stephens included, expected Lincoln to negotiate on such conditions. The resolutions were intended to divide northern opinion and strengthen the Peace Democrats for the 1864 election by giving the impression of a southern willingness to negotiate. But this subtlety escaped most southerners, who regarded Brown and Stephens as reconstructionists advocating peace at any price. Instead of dividing and conquering the North, their peace gambit seemed likely to play into the hands of Yankees hoping to divide and conquer the South.

Most of the southern press, even in Georgia, reprimanded the vice president. Georgia regiments at the front passed resolutions condemning Brown and the legislature. Georgia's senators privately slapped Stephens's wrist. "You have allowed your antipathy to Davis to mislead your judgment," Senator Herschel Johnson told the vice president. "You are wrong in view of your official position; you are wrong because the whole movement originated in a mad purpose to make war on Davis & Congress;—You are wrong because the movement is joyous to the enemy, and they are already using it in their press." The legislature hastily passed a resolution pledging Georgia's continuing support for the war.

In North Carolina, the last state to secede, the commitment to the Confederacy had remained shaky. While it had contributed more soldiers than any other state save Virginia, it also accounted for more deserters than any other. Its western portion resembled east Tennessee and West Virginia in socioeconomic structure and unionist leanings. The inaccessibility of this region to northern armies, however, inhibited the development there of a significant unionist political movement before 1863. In that year the Order of the Heroes of America, a secret peace society, attained a large, war-weary following in piedmont and upcountry North Carolina after Gettysburg. Thousands of returning deserters allied with tories and draft-dodgers gained virtual control of whole counties.

North Carolina's most powerful political leaders were Zebulon B. Vance and William W. Holden. An antebellum Whig and in 1861 a conditional unionist, Vance commanded a regiment in the Army of Northern Virginia before winning the governorship in 1862. Though he feuded with Davis over

Zebulon B. Vance, pictured here, was initially allied with William W. Holden's Conservative party in North Carolina. When Holden seemed to turn against the Confederacy, however, Vance repudiated him with the words: "I will see the Conservative party blown into a thousand atoms and Holden and his understrappers in hell before I will consent to a course which would bring dishonor and ruin upon both state and Confederacy." Reelected governor by a landslide over Holden in 1864, Vance dominated North Carolina politics for a generation after Reconstruction.

matters of state versus Confederate authority, Vance backed the war effort and continued to "fight the Yankees and fuss with the Confederacy" until the end. Holden was of another stripe. Beginning his career as a Whig, he became a Democratic secessionist in the 1850s but broke with the party and resisted secession until the last moment in 1861. As editor of the Raleigh *North Carolina Standard* he championed civil liberties and attacked administration policies during the war. Emphasizing the rich man's war/poor man's fight theme, Holden won a large following among yeoman farmers and workingmen. His "Conservative party," composed mainly of old Whigs and conditional unionists, had supported Vance for governor on a platform of state sovereignty within the Confederacy. By the summer of 1863, however, Holden became convinced that the South could not win the war and that conscription, impressment, "military despotism," and economic ruin represented a greater threat to North Carolinians than reunion with the United States.

Aided by the Heroes of America, Holden and his associates held meetings in the western part of the state and advocated opening negotiations for an "honorable peace." Another reason for grave concern in Richmond was that at least five and perhaps eight of the congressmen elected from North Carolina in 1863 were "reported to be in favor of peace." After the elections Holden began to call for North Carolina to invoke its sovereignty and open separate negotiations with the North, a move that, he insisted, would produce Confederate independence.

Vance became convinced that Holden and his party wanted the take North Carolina out of the Confederacy. He feared that a majority in the state supported Holden. Vance urged Jefferson Davis to outflank Holden by making a show of negotiating with the North "on the basis of independence" with the expectation that the initiative would be rejected by the Union, thereby intensifying North Carolinians' support for the war and the government.

Davis failed to appreciate the Machiavellian subtlety of this gambit. He admonished Vance that Lincoln would see it as a sign of weakness and an opportunity to reiterate that peace would come only by the South's "emancipating all our slaves, swearing allegiance and obedience to him and his proclamations, and becoming in point of fact the slaves of our own negroes." The only path to peace was to continue the war and demonstrate that the Confederacy would not accept such "subjugation." North Carolina must do her part in this struggle; instead of dallying with traitors, Vance must "abandon a policy of conciliation and set them at defiance."

Taking his own advice, on February 3, 1864, Davis urged Congress to pass a law suspending habeas corpus to enable the government to deal with "citizens of well-known disloyalty" who were seeking to "accomplish treason under the form of the law." Holden knew this meant him. On February 24 he announced that he was suspending publication of the *Standard* because, he later explained, "if I could not continue to print as a free man I would not print at all." But this did not stop the peace movement; on the contrary, a week later Holden announced his intention to run against Vance for governor in the midsummer election.

Holden's expected victory would pose the most serious internal threat to the Confederacy so far. But Vance outmaneuvered him and managed to capture most of the peace vote on a war platform. Holden's "reconstructionist" plan, Vance argued, would lead North Carolina back into the Union; its sons would be drafted "to fight alongside of [Lincoln's] negro troops in exterminating the white men, women, and children of the South." The only way to obtain peace was to win the war despite its mismanagement by Richmond.

Late in the campaign the exposure of the Heroes of America as a treasonable organization secretly aiding Holden gave the editor's candidacy the *coup de grâce*. Few believed Holden's denial of any connection with the society. North Carolina soldiers at the front damned Holden for disgracing the state. On election day Vance smothered Holden, winning 88 percent of the soldier vote and 77 percent of the civilian vote. North Carolina remained safe for the Confederacy.

II

The signs of southern disaffection in the fall of 1863 encouraged Lincoln to announce a policy for the reconstruction of recanting Confederates. "Whereas it is now desired by some persons heretofore engaged in said rebellion to resume their allegiance to the United States, and to reinaugrate loyal State governments," declared the president in a proclamation on December 8, he offered pardon and amnesty to such persons who took an oath of allegiance to the United States and to all of its laws and proclamations concerning slavery. (Confederate government officials and high-ranking military officers were exempted from this blanket offer of amnesty.) Whenever the number of persons in any state taking the oath reached 10 percent of the number of voters in 1860, this loyal nucleus could form a state government which would be recognized by the president. To Congress, of course, belonged the right to decide whether to seat the senators and representatives elected from such states.

This document was a distillation of two previous years of experience and debate that led to a consensus among Republicans that the pieces of the old Union could not be cobbled together. One piece lost but not lamented was slavery; another that must go was the prominent role played in southern politics by the old state's-rights secessionists. Beyond this, however, a spectrum of opinions could be found in the Republican party concerning both the process and substance of reconstruction.

Lincoln never deviated from the theory that secession was illegal and southern states therefore remained in the Union. Rebels had temporarily taken over their governments; the task of reconstruction was to return "loyal" officials to power. At one level all Republicans subscribed to this theory of indestructible states in an indissoluble Union; to believe otherwise would stultify their war aims. But at another level, no one could deny that the southern states had gone *out* of the Union and had formed a new government with all the attributes of a nation. A few radical Republicans led by Thaddeus Stevens boldly insisted that they had therefore ceased to exist as legal states. When invaded and controlled by the Union army they became "conquered provinces" subject to the conqueror's will. But most Republicans were unwilling to go this far. Instead, many of them subscribed to one variant or another of a theory that by attempting the treasonable act of secession, southern states had committed "state suicide" (Charles Sumner's phrase) or had "forfeited" their rights as states and reverted to the condition of territories.

Discussion of these theories consumed much time and energy in Congress. Lincoln impatiently noted the general agreement that the seceded states were "out of their proper practical relation with the Union; and that the sole object of the government . . . is to again get them into that proper practical relation." What Lincoln well understood, but did not acknowledge, was that conflicting reconstruction theories concealed a power struggle between Congress and the Executive over control of the process. If the southern states had reverted to the status of territories, Congress had the right to frame the terms of their readmission under its constitutional authority to govern territories and admit new states. If, on the other hand, the states were indestructible and secession was the act of individuals, the president had the power to prescribe the terms of restoration under his constitutional authority to suppress insurrection and to grant pardons and amnesty.

Underlying this conflict over procedure was a significant difference of opinion about substance. Of Kentucky birth and moderate antislavery persuasion, Lincoln had been a Whig and had maintained cordial relations with southern Whigs and unionists almost to the end in 1861. He believed that these men had been swept into secession against their better judgment and were ready by 1863 to return like prodigal sons. By offering them pardons on the conditions of Union and emancipation, Lincoln hoped to set in motion a snowballing defection from the Confederacy and a state-by-state reconstruction of the Union.

Despite the exclusion of top Confederate leaders from Lincoln's blanket offer of amnesty, his policy would preserve much of the South's old ruling class in power. To most abolitionists and radical Republicans this was unacceptable. They insisted that simply to abolish slavery without also destroying the economic and political structure of the old order would merely convert black people from slaves to landless serfs and leave the political power of the planter class untouched. By restoring property and the franchise to Confederates, said Wendell Phillips, the president's amnesty program "leaves the large landed proprietors of the South still to domineer over its politics, and makes the negro's freedom a mere sham." Phillips and other radicals envisaged reconstruction as a revolution. "The whole system of the Gulf States [must] be taken to pieces," said Phillips. "The war can be ended only by annihilating that Oligarchy which formed and rules the South and makes the war—by annihilating a state of society." Similar rhetoric came from Chairman Thaddeus Stevens of the House ways and means committee. Reconstruction must "revolutionize Southern institutions, habits, and manners," said Stevens. "The foundation of their institutions . . . must be broken up and relaid, or all our blood and treasure have been spent in vain."

Although Stevens and Lincoln had different visions of the South's future, Congress and Executive had not yet become polarized on this issue. For his part, Lincoln remained flexible toward reconstruction as he had done earlier toward emancipation. While his plan of amnesty and restoration "is the best the Executive can present, with his present impressions," he said, "it must not be understood that no other mode would be acceptable." For their part, most congressional Republicans also entertained a range of shifting and flexible opinions less radical than those of Phillips and Stevens. But many moderates as well as radicals believed that some way must be found to ensure political domination by genuine unionists in the South. This, in turn, led to a growing number of Republicans favoring at least partial enfranchisement of freed slaves to offset the voting power of former Confederates. Believing that Lincoln lagged behind them by only a few months on this matter as on emancipation, most Republicans responded favorably at first to his amnesty and reconstruction proclamation. And indeed, about a month later Lincoln did write privately to a New York Republican that, having offered amnesty to whites, he also favored suffrage for blacks, "at least, suffrage on the basis of intelligence and military service." Both Lincoln and congressional moderates stepped warily around this issue in public, however. Black men could vote in only six northern states, and the possibility of them doing so elsewhere was no more popular among many northern voters than the prospect of emancipation had been a year or two earlier.

On theoretical and procedural questions, Lincoln and congressional Republicans had also moved closer together by 1863. Several bills to provide territorial governments for rebellious states had come before the previous Congress. More than two-thirds of House Republicans favored this concept. But the remainder along with Democrats and border-state unionists produced enough votes to defeat the one measure that came to a vote. Sobered by this experience, a majority of Republicans turned to a new approach that combined the view of indestructible states with a notion of congressional power to intervene in the affairs of these states under extraordinary circumstances. Article IV, Section 4, of the Constitution stipulates

The first large-scale fighting by black soldiers was the attack by two Louisiana Union regiments on Confederate defenses at Port Hudson on May 27, 1863. This illustration shows the temporary penetration of the Confederate lines by the 2nd Louisiana. The New York Times *commented that this attack "settles the question that the negro race can fight. . . . It is no longer possible to doubt the bravery and steadiness of the colored race." Such convictions supported the idea that blacks deserved the right to vote.*

that "the United States shall guarantee to every state in this Union a republican form of government." Here was a concept of sufficient ambiguity to attract supporters of various viewpoints. A "republican form of government" might mean Negro suffrage; it could be construed to prohibit slavery; it certainly discountenanced rebellion. And best of all, the Constitution did not state whether Congress or the Executive had the principal responsibility in this matter, and earlier Supreme Court interpretations had suggested dual responsibility. Thus the "republican form of government" clause became by 1863 the basis for both presidential and congressional approaches to reconstruction.

In the matter of intervening in the affairs of states the president as commander in chief had an inherent advantage over Congress in time of war. While Congress had debated in 1862, Lincoln had acted. He appointed military governors for the portions of Tennessee, Louisiana, and Arkansas that came under Union control, and he authorized them to prepare for the restoration of civil government. The continuation of active fighting in all three states postponed this prospect for a year or more. But with the capture of Port Hudson, the expulsion of Bragg from Tennessee, and the occupation of Little Rock in the latter part of 1863, Lincoln urged his military governors to begin the process of reconstruction. He intended his amnesty proclamation and 10 percent proposal to serve as "a rallying point—a plan of action."

Louisiana seemed to offer the best prospect for an early test of Lincoln's policy. The citizens of New Orleans had voted overwhelmingly for Bell or Douglas. The city's prosperous and well-educated light-skinned free black community, which had furnished two regiments to fight at Port Hudson, supported Republican principles. Many of the wealthy sugar and cotton planters along the bayous had been Whigs

and conditional unionists. They readily took the oath of allegiance—if only to obtain trade permits to sell cotton. In Nathaniel Banks, veteran Republican who commanded the occupation forces, and George F. Shepley, prewar Maine Democrat who became a radical Republican and military governor of occupied Louisiana, Lincoln had political generals eager to aid the reconstruction process.

Banks, once his operation in Texas had been successfully concluded, had to steer a careful course between two factions. The first and smaller one, composed of planters who had reluctantly accepted quasi-emancipation, had found Lincoln unwilling to endorse their proposal in June 1863 to elect a new state government under the existing Louisiana constitution because Lincoln suspected their underlying intent was to preserve slavery. They continued, however, to advocate this means of reconstruction.

The second and more dynamic faction was led by lawyers, doctors, and entrepreneurs most of whom had been born in the North or abroad but had resided in New Orleans for many years before the war. They had opposed secession, and some had gone into exile rather than support the Confederacy. They organized a Union Association and proposed to hold a state convention to adopt a new constitution abolishing slavery, paving the way for election of state officials and congressmen in a purified Louisiana that could rejoin the Union.

Lincoln, having approved this procedure in the summer of 1863, pressed Banks and Shepley to get on with registering voters. Even though less than half of the state was under Union military control, he wanted Banks to create a "tangible nucleus" of voters, which "the rest of the State may rally around as fast as it can, and which I can at once recognize and sustain as the true State government." To implement this promptly, Lincoln defined the "tangible nucleus" at 10 percent of a state's 1860 voters.

Banks responded swiftly to Lincoln's prodding, bypassing a convention and ordering the election of state officials in February 1864 under the existing constitution. It would be followed in April by a convention. As for slavery, he simply issued an order declaring the institution "inoperative and void." If Lincoln wanted prompt restoration, assured emancipation, and participation by at least 10 percent of the voters, insisted Banks, the election of state officials must be held first and the convention later. Convinced by these arguments, Lincoln told the general to "proceed with all possible dispatch."

Banks considered the unionists' recently organized Free State General Committee, which advocated limited Negro suffrage, too radical and ready to go farther than most Louisiana whites—or even northern whites—would accept. Their leader, a lawyer named Thomas J. Durant, rivaled Wendell Phillips in fervor for "equality and fraternity" and proclaimed that "there could be no middle ground in a revolution. It must work a radical change in society; such had been the history of every great revolution." But Banks had his own view of revolutions, writing to Lincoln that "the *history* of the world shows that Revolutions which are not controlled, and held within reasonable limits, produce counter Revolutions." To prevent the radicals from provoking such a counterrevolution he had implemented a policy that ultimately split the Free State Committee into radical and moderate factions, each of which nominated

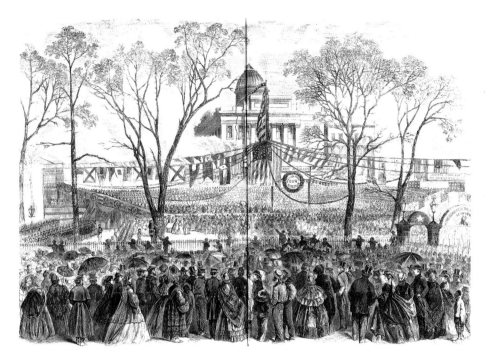

candidates for governor and other state offices in the February 22 election. Enjoying the support of Banks and most federal officials in New Orleans, the moderates won a vote greater than the radicals and conservatives combined; the total vote amounted to nearly a quarter of the total recorded for the entire state in 1860.

It seemed a triumph for Lincoln's 10 percent policy. Meanwhile in Arkansas a convention of unionists representing half the state's counties adopted a new constitution repudiating secession and abolishing slavery. A vote equal to almost one-quarter of the 1860 total ratified the constitution and elected a state government in March. But this success remained almost unnoticed in the shadow cast by events in Louisiana—and in Tennessee, where quarrels between ironclad unionists and recanting Confederates delayed action through most of 1864. This problem plus continuing controversy over affairs in Louisiana drove a wedge into the Republican party that threatened a serious split between the president and Congress. Four related issues emerged in this conflict: the fate of slavery; the political role of blacks in reconstruction; the definition of loyalty; and the status of free black labor in the new order. As each issue generated heat in Louisiana, the temperature also rose in Congress where Republican lawmakers sought to frame their own approach to reconstruction.

The doom of slavery was their first concern. As military measures, both Lincoln's Emancipation Proclamation and Banks's edict declaring slavery "void" in Louisiana would have precarious legal force when the war was over—a problem anticipated by the Louisiana radicals. Many congressional Republicans also feared a revival of slavery if conservatives should gain control of a reconstructed Louisiana. The best solution for this problem was a national constitutional amendment abolishing slavery. All Republicans including Lincoln united in favor of this in 1864. But the problem persisted. The Senate quickly mustered the necessary two-thirds majority for a Thirteenth Amendment abolishing slavery, but Democratic gains in the 1862 congressional elections prevented similar success in the House, where a 93 to 65 vote for the Amendment on June 15 fell thirteen votes short of success. In an attempt to ensure that emancipation became part of reconstruction, therefore, the Wade-Davis bill passed by Congress on July 2 included a provision outlawing slavery in Confederate states as a condition of their return to the Union.

Fears that moderates and conservatives in Louisiana might make a deal to preserve slavery proved groundless. Despite the refusal of many radicals to participate in the election of a convention in March 1864, that body, meeting from April to July, wrote a prohibition of slavery into Louisiana's fundamental law. It also mandated public schools for all children, opened the militia to blacks, and provided equal access to the courts for both races. In the context of Louisiana's previous history, these were indeed revolutionary achievements. Lincoln described the constitution as "excellent . . . better for the poor black man than we have in Illinois."

But on the matter that would emerge as the central issue of postwar reconstruction, Negro suffrage, the convention balked. A Louisiana moderate probably spoke with accuracy when he said that scarcely one in twenty white men favored suffrage even for literate, cultured Creoles—much less for newly freed field hands. Nevertheless, pressures for enfranchisement of blacks continued to grow. Abolitionists and radicals won converts among congressional Republicans with their argument that it was not only immoral but also fatuous to grant the ballot to former rebels and withhold it from loyal blacks. In January 1864 the "free people of color" in New Orleans drew up a petition asking for the right to vote. This memorial bore the signatures of more than a thousand men. Twenty-seven of them had fought with Andrew Jackson to defend New Orleans against the British in 1815; many others

A crowd of Louisiana blacks both free and recently freed, civilians and soldiers, turned out to hear Adjutant General Lorenzo Thomas address them in the fall of 1864 on the duties and opportunities of freedom. Thomas had supervised the recruitment and organization of many black regiments in the lower Mississippi Valley.

had sons or brothers in the Union army. Two delegates carried the petition to Washington, where radical congressmen praised them and Lincoln welcomed them to the White House. Impressed by their demeanor, the president wrote to the newly elected governor of Louisiana, Michael Hahn, a letter whose diffident wording conveyed a plain directive. When the forthcoming convention took up the question of voter qualifications, said Lincoln, "I barely suggest for your private consideration, whether some of the colored people may not be let in—as, for instance, the very intelligent, and especially those who have fought gallantly in our ranks. They would probably help, in some trying time to come, to keep the jewel of liberty in the family of freedom." Hahn and Banks got the message. But persuading a convention of Louisiana whites, even unionists who had swallowed emancipation, to confer political equality on blacks was uphill work. The best that the governor and general could do by cajolery, threats, and patronage was to reverse an initial vote for a clause *for-bidding* Negro suffrage and secure instead a clause authorizing the legislature to enfranchise blacks if it saw fit.

Unaware of these efforts by Banks and Hahn, several radicals denounced the Louisiana constitution for its "spirit of caste." Regarding Louisiana as "Mr. Lincoln's model of reconstruction . . . which puts all power in the hands of an unchanged white race," a number of congressional Republicans turned against Lincoln's policy in the spring of 1864. Yet in the matter of Negro suffrage, Congress could do no better. The initial version of the House reconstruction bill included a requirement for the registration of "all loyal male citizens." This phrase had become a Republican code for black enfranchisement. But moderates were not ready for such a step, so they modified the bill by adding the word "white." When the measure came to the Senate, Benjamin Wade's Committee on Territories deleted "white." But after counting heads, Wade added it again before passage on July 2 "because, in my judgment, [black suffrage] will sacrifice the bill." Some radicals expressed outrage at such a surrender to expediency.

The Negro suffrage issue was part of a larger debate over who constituted the "loyal" population of a state for purposes of reconstruction. Radicals considered blacks and unionist whites who had never supported the Confederacy to be the only true loyalists. Some moderates went along with Lincoln in wishing to include whites who repudiated their allegiance to the Confederacy and took an oath of future loyalty to the Union. But the unionism of these "galvanized" rebels was suspect in the eyes of many Republicans, who therefore wanted to enfranchise blacks to ensure a unionist majority. If blacks could not vote, then neither should recanting whites—at least not until the war was won and all danger of their relapse into rebellion was over. Moreover, congressional Republicans considered 10 or even 25 percent of a state's *white* voters too slender a basis for reconstruction—especially when, as they saw it, that process in Louisiana had been "imposed on the people by military orders under the form of elections."

The fourth area of contention concerned the degree of freedom in the free-labor system to replace slavery. "Any provision which may be adopted . . . in relation to the freed people" by new state governments, declared Lincoln in his proclamation of amnesty and reconstruction, "which shall recognize and declare their permanent

Many contrabands came within Union lines as northern armies occupied large parts of the lower Mississippi Valley. This photograph shows several slave cabins on a plantation near Helena, Arkansas, which the Union army converted into a contraband camp, photographed here in 1864.

freedom, provide for their education, and which may yet be consistent, as a tempo-rary arrangement, with their present condition as a laboring, landless, and homeless class, will not be objected to by the national Executive." Here in a nutshell was the problem that would preoccupy the South for generations after the war. How "tem-porary" would this suggested system of apprenticeship turn out to be? What kind of education would freed slaves receive? How long would their status as a "laboring, landless, and homeless class" persist? These were questions that could not be fully resolved until after the war—if then. But they had already emerged in nascent form in the army's administration of contraband affairs in the occupied South.

A Union army at war had few resources to provide for the several hundred thou-sand contrabands under their control; minimal food and shelter was made available, but disease, malnutrition, exposure and poor sanitation took an appalling toll that accounted for a large part of the civilian casualties suffered by the South.

A degree of order gradually emerged from this chaos. Northern philanthropy stepped into the breach and sent clothing, medicine, emergency economic aid, and teachers to the contrabands. Supported by numerous organizations both religious and secular, hundreds of missionaries and schoolma'ams followed Union armies into the South to bring material aid, spiritual comfort, and the three *R*'s to freed slaves. Forerunners of a larger invasion that occurred after the war, these emissaries of Yankee culture—most of them women—saw themselves as a peaceful army come to elevate the freedmen and help them accomplish the transition from slavery to a prosperous freedom.

Of predominantly New England heritage and abolitionist conviction, these reformers exerted considerable influence in certain quarters of the Union govern-ment. In 1863 they persuaded the War Department to create a Freedmen's Inquiry

Commission, whose recommendations eventually led to establishment of the Freedmen's Bureau in the last days of the war. They also managed to secure the appointment of sympathetic army officers to administer freedmen's affairs in several parts of the occupied South—particularly General Rufus Saxton on the South Carolina sea islands and Colonel John Eaton, whom Grant named superintendent of contrabands for the Mississippi Valley in November 1862. By 1863 the army had put many freedmen to work on "home farms" to provide some of their own support; others worked for the army or joined black regiments.

The need of northern and British textile mills for cotton also caused the army to put many freed people to work growing cotton—often on the same plantations where they had done the same work as slaves. Some of these plantations remained in government hands and were administered by "labor superintendents" sent by northern freedmen's aid societies. Others were leased to Yankee entrepreneurs who hoped to make big money raising cotton with free labor. Still others remained in the hands of their owners, who took the oath of allegiance and promised to pay wages to workers who had recently been their slaves. Some land was leased by the freedmen themselves, who farmed it without direct white supervision and in some cases cleared a handsome profit that enabled them subsequently to buy land of their own. The outstanding example of a self-governing black colony occurred at Davis Bend, Mississippi, where former slaves of the Confederate president and his brother leased their plantations (from the Union army, which had seized them) and made good crops.

The quality of supervision of contraband labor ranged from a benign to a brutal paternalism, prefiguring the spectrum of labor relations after the war. Part of the freedmen's wages was often withheld until the end of the season to ensure that they stayed on the job, and most of the rest was deducted for food and shelter. Many contrabands, understandably, could see little difference between this system of "free" labor and the bondage they had endured all their lives. Nowhere was the apparent similarity greater than in occupied Louisiana, where many planters took the oath of allegiance and continued to raise cotton or sugar under regulations issued by General Banks. Because of the national political focus on the reconstruction process in

Northern teachers and missionaries went south during the war to establish schools for contrabands in areas occupied by Union forces. Many of their students were black soldiers, who had been prohibited from learning to read as slaves. This photograph shows eighteen soldiers with a white officer and white teachers standing behind them. Some of the soldiers are holding books.

Louisiana, these regulations became another irritant between radical and moderate Republicans and another issue in the controversy between Congress and president. By military fiat Banks fixed the wages for plantation laborers and promised that the army would enforce "just treatment, healthy rations, comfortable clothing, quarters, fuel, medical attendance, and instruction for children." But further regulations ensured that some of these promises were likely to be honored in the breach. A worker could not leave the plantation without a pass and must sign a contract to remain for the entire year with his employer, who could call on provost marshals to enforce "continuous and faithful service, respectful deportment, correct discipline and perfect subordination." This system amounted to a virtual "reestablishment of slavery," charged abolitionists. It "makes the [Emancipation] Proclamation of 1863 a mockery and delusion," said Frederick Douglass.

In 1864 the controversy over freedmen's policy in Louisiana added its force to the process by which Congress hammered out a reconstruction bill. As finally passed after seemingly endless debate, the Wade-Davis bill reached Lincoln's desk on the Fourth of July. By limiting suffrage to whites it did not differ from the president's policy. In another important respect—the abolition of slavery—it only appeared to differ. While the bill mandated emancipation and Lincoln's policy did not, the president's offer of amnesty required recipients of pardon to swear their support for all government actions on slavery. Two states thus far "reconstructed," Louisiana and Arkansas, had abolished the institution. Nevertheless a fear persisted among some Republicans that a residue of slavery might survive in any peace settlement negotiated by Lincoln, so they considered abolition by statute vital.

More significant were other differences between presidential and congressional policy: the Wade-Davis bill required 50 percent instead of 10 percent of the voters to swear an oath of allegiance, specified that a constitutional convention must take place *before* election of state officers, and restricted the right to vote for convention delegates to men who could take the "ironclad oath" that they had never voluntarily supported the rebellion. No Confederate state (except perhaps Tennessee) could meet these conditions; the real purpose of the Wade-Davis bill was to postpone reconstruction until the war was won. Lincoln by contrast wanted to initiate reconstruction immediately in order to convert lukewarm Confederates into unionists as a means of winning the war.

Lincoln pocket-vetoed the bill and issued a statement denying the right of Congress to abolish slavery by statute. To assert such a right would "make the fatal admission" that these states were out of the Union and that secession was therefore legitimate. The pending Thirteenth Amendment, said the president, was the only constitutional way to abolish slavery. Lincoln also refused "to be inflexibly committed to any single plan of restoration" as required by the bill, since this would destroy "the free-state constitutions and governments, already adopted and installed in Arkansas and Louisiana."

Because Congress, then in recess, had no official way to respond to this quasi-veto message, Wade and Davis decided to publish their own statement in the press. As they drafted it, their pent-up bitterness toward "Executive usurpation" carried them into rhetorical excess. "This rash and fatal act of the President," they declared, was "a blow at the friends of his Administration, at the rights of humanity, and at the principles of Republican Government." The congressional bill would ensure the protection of loyalists and prevent those who had fomented the rebellion from returning to power and perpetuating slavery. If Lincoln wanted Republican support for his reelection, "he must confine himself to his Executive duties—to obey and execute, not make the laws—to suppress by arms armed rebellion, and leave political reorganization to Congress."

That final clause provides a key to understanding this astonishing attack on a president by leaders of his own party. The reconstruction issue had become tangled with intraparty political struggles in the Republican presidential campaign of 1864. The Wade-Davis manifesto was part of a movement to replace Lincoln with a candidate more satisfactory to the radical wing of the party.

III

Lincoln's renomination and reelection were by no means assured. No incumbent president had been renominated since 1840, and none had been reelected since 1832. Even the war did not necessarily change the rules of this game. If matters were going badly at the front, voters would punish the man in charge. And if the man in charge was not conducting affairs to the satisfaction of his party, he might fail of renomination. The Republican party contained several men who in 1860 had considered themselves better qualified for the presidency than the man who won it. In 1864 at least one of them had not changed his opinion: Salmon P. Chase.

He was an ambitious as well as an able man. The republic rewarded him with many high offices: governor, senator, secretary of the treasury, chief justice. But the highest office eluded him despite a most assiduous pursuit of it. Chase had no doubts about his qualifications for the job; as his friend Benjamin Wade said of him, "Chase is a good man, but his theology is unsound. He thinks there is a fourth person in the Trinity."

Chase used Treasury Department patronage to build a political machine for his nomination in 1864. The emergence of dissatisfaction with Lincoln's reconstruction policy strengthened his cause. In December 1863 a Chase committee headed by Senator Samuel C. Pomeroy of Kansas issued a "circular" declaring that Lincoln's "manifest tendency toward temporary expedients" made "the 'one-term principle' absolutely essential" to ensure a victorious war and a just peace. Chase was the man to achieve these goals.

This attempt to promote a Chase boom backfired. Once again, as in the cabinet crisis of December 1862, the secretary proved no match for the president in the game of politics. While Chase had filled the Treasury Department with his partisans, Lincoln had not neglected the patronage. Postmaster General Montgomery Blair did yeoman service for the president in this respect. And his brother Frank Blair, on leave from corps command in Sherman's army to take a seat in Congress, functioned in a capacity that a later generation would describe as "hatchet man" for the administration. A week after the Pomeroy Circular appeared, Frank Blair caused an uproar with a blistering anti-Chase speech in the House that among other things charged widespread Treasury corruption in the issuance of cotton-trading permits. Many radical

Republicans never forgave the Blair family for this climactic event in a series of intra-party dogfights which found the Blairs leading the conservative faction. Meanwhile Republican state committees, legislatures, newspapers, and Union Leagues throughout the North—including Chase's home state of Ohio—passed resolutions endorsing Lincoln's renomination. Embarrassed by this boomerang destruction of his aspirations, Chase disingenuously disavowed any connection with the Pomeroy Circular, withdrew his name from consideration for the presidency, and offered to resign from the cabinet. For his part the president—perhaps with equal disingenuousness—disavowed any connection with Blair's attack and refused to accept Chase's resignation. Describing Chase's ambition for the presidency as a form of "mild insanity," Lincoln considered him less dangerous inside the government than out of it.

Although most Republicans climbed aboard the Lincoln bandwagon, some of them did so with reluctance. As the reconstruction issue drove its wedge deeper into party unity, several radicals continued to hope that the bandwagon could be stopped. Horace Greeley futilely urged postponement of the national convention from June until September in a Micawber-like hope that something might turn up. Others launched trial balloons for an unlikely series of candidates including Grant, Butler, and Frémont. Of these only Frémont's balloon became airborne, carrying as strange a group of passengers as American politics ever produced.

Bitter toward a president who did not reassign him to an important military command, Frémont like McClellan had been "awaiting orders" since 1862. Indeed, these two disgruntled generals represented the foremost political dangers to Lincoln. Of the two, McClellan posed the greater threat because he seemed likely to become the Democratic nominee later in the summer. In the meantime Frémont attracted a coalition of abolitionists and radical German-Americans into a third party. A few Republicans lent behind-the-scenes support to this movement, hoping to use it as a cat's-paw to scratch Lincoln from the main party ticket and bring Chase back to life. But the sparsely attended convention that met in Cleveland on May 31 to nominate Frémont contained not a single influential Republican. The most prominent supporter of this nomination was Wendell Phillips, whose letter to the convention proclaimed that Lincoln's reconstruction policy "makes the freedom of the negro a sham, and perpetuates slavery under a softer name." The convention adopted an apparently radical platform that called for a constitutional amendment to abolish slavery and "secure to all men absolute equality before the law." The platform also asserted that Congress rather than the president must control reconstruction and urged confiscation of land owned by "rebels" for redistribution "among the soldiers and actual settlers." At the same time, however, the platform denounced Lincoln's suspension of habeas corpus and suppression of free speech. This of course was the main Democratic indictment of the administration. The convention also nominated a Democrat for vice president, and the new party called itself the Radical *Democratic* party.

This cartoon in Harper's Weekly *attributes the motive for Frémont's presidential campaign to pique with Lincoln for failing to give him another important military command after Frémont resigned in 1862. The significance of the black doll that Frémont is holding is not clear; perhaps it is perhaps meant to suggest that the "equality before the law" plank in Frémont's platform was not seriously meant.*

THAT'S WHAT'S THE TROUBLE WITH JOHN C.

Mrs. Columbia. "Tell me, Doctor, what is the *matter* with him? Do you think his Brain is affected?"

Doctor Jonathan. "Oh! no, my dear Madam; it's only a rather aggravated case of Sore Head!"

Thereby hung a tale—and a tail that soon began to wag the dog. Frémont unwisely accepted a predictable Democratic offer to make an alliance against Lincoln. His acceptance letter repudiated the confiscation plank and ignored the "equality before the law" plank but dwelt at length on Lincoln's misconduct of the war and violation of civil liberties. As the Democratic game of using Frémont to divert a few thousand Republican votes to a third party in close states became evident, most radicals (but not Phillips) renounced the venture and concluded that they had no alternative but Lincoln.

The Republican convention in Baltimore during the second week of June exhibited the usual hoopla and love-feast unity of a party renominating an incumbent. The assemblage called itself the National Union convention to attract War Democrats and southern unionists who might flinch at the name Republican. But it nevertheless adopted a down-the-line Republican platform, including endorsement of unremitting war to force the "unconditional surrender" of Confederate armies and the passage of a constitutional amendment to abolish slavery. When this latter plank was presented, "the whole body of delegates sprang to their feet . . . in prolonged cheering," according to William Lloyd Garrison, who was present as a reporter for his newspaper *The Liberator*. "Was not a spectacle like that rich compensation for more than thirty years of personal opprobrium?"

The platform dealt with the divisive reconstruction issue by ignoring it. Delegations from the Lincoln-reconstructed states of Louisiana, Arkansas, and Tennessee were admitted, while with the president's covert sanction the convention made a gesture of conciliation to radicals by seating an anti-Blair delegation from Missouri, which cast a token ballot for Grant before changing its vote to make Lincoln's nomination unanimous. The only real contest at the convention was generated by the vice-presidential nomination. The colorless incumbent, Hannibal Hamlin, would add no strength to the ticket. The attempt to project a Union party image seemed to require the nomination of a War Democrat from a southern state. Andrew Johnson of Tennessee best fitted this bill. After backstairs maneuvers whose details still remain obscure, Johnson received the nomination on the first ballot. This nomination had a mixed impact on radical-moderate tensions in the party. On the one hand, Johnson had dealt severely with "rebels" in Tennessee. On the other, he embodied Lincoln's executive approach to reconstruction.

The unanimity at Baltimore only temporarily papered over cracks in the party. By the time of Benjamin Wade's and Henry Winter Davis's angry manifesto against the president's reconstruction policy two months later, those cracks had become so wide that a serious move was afoot to replace Lincoln with another candidate. But the pressures that produced this astounding development arose less from controversy over what to do with the South when the war was won than from despair about whether it could be won at all. A Confederacy that had seemed on the ropes at the end of 1863 had come back fighting and appeared likely to survive after a season of slaughter whose toll eclipsed even that of the terrible summers of '62 and '63.

When Republicans nominated Andrew Johnson for vice president in 1864, they could not know that this southern Democrat would become president in 1865 and prove so defiant toward Republican reconstruction polities that they would ultimately impeach him. Johnson was saved from removal from office by a single vote in the Senate.

CHAPTER TWENTY-FOUR

★ ★ ★ ★ ★

If It Takes All Summer

I

"Upon the progress of our arms," said Lincoln late in the war, "all else chiefly depends." Never was this more true than in 1864, when "all else" included Lincoln's own reelection as well as the fate of emancipation and of the Union.

In the spring of 1864 the progress of Union arms seemed assured. Congress had revived the rank of lieutenant general (last held by George Washington), and Lincoln had promoted Grant to this rank with the title of general in chief. Henry W. Halleck stepped down to the post of chief of staff. Grant designated Sherman as his successor to command western armies and came east to make his headquarters with the Army of the Potomac. Though Meade remained in charge of this army subject to Grant's strategic orders, Phil Sheridan also came east to take over its cavalry. With the Union's three best generals—Grant, Sherman, Sheridan—in top commands, the days of the Confederacy appeared numbered.

Given their losses in 1863, the Confederacy abolished substitution and stretched the draft's upper and lower age limits to fifty and seventeen. Despite this and other measures, in the spring of 1864 southern forces numbered fewer than half the enemy's. But the Union's successes made it necessary to detach many northern divisions as occupation forces in 100,000 square miles of conquered territory and the border slave states, as well as assign other troops to guard supply lines against cavalry and guerrilla raids. This reduction in the number of Union soldiers available for battle was a boon for the Confederacy and for the Army of Northern Virginia, whose morale remained high; many of its lean, tough veterans had reenlisted before Congress required them to do so on February 17. These soldiers shared a powerful sense of comradeship and devotion to Lee; they also shared his sentiments, on the eve of the 1864 military campaign, that "if victorious, we have everything to hope for in the future. If defeated, nothing will be left for us to live for." Johnston had not been able to instill the same *esprit* in the army he inherited from Bragg. But he had done more in that direction by May 1864 than anyone who watched these troops flee

This dramatic painting of Union Troops Capturing a Confederate Fort *by G. DeNigri portrays the kind of attack that Northern soldiers had to make all too often in 1864–65, at heavy cost.*

By 1864 the Confederacy's desperate need for soldiers forced its armies to "rob the cradle and the grave," as one unhappy southerner put it. This Confederate soldier looks even younger than the specified minimum age of seventeen.

from Missionary Ridge the previous November would have thought possible.

Most of the Confederate soldiers were veterans. Many of the veterans in the Union army were due to go home in 1864 when their three-year enlistments were up. If this happened, the South might well seize victory from the jaws of defeat. The Union Congress regarded their veterans' three-year terms as a contract and rather than abrogate it relied on persuasion and inducements to reenlist such as granting them a special chevron to wear on their sleeves, a thirty-day furlough, and a $400 federal bounty plus local and state bounties. If three-quarters of the men in a regiment re-enlisted, that regiment would retain its identity and thus its unit pride, which in turn created effective peer pressure on holdouts to re-enlist.

Some 136,000 veterans reenlisted. Another 100,000 or so decided not to. This latter group experienced the usual aversion to risk-taking during their final weeks in the army, thus limiting their combat capacity and damaging the morale of their reenlisted comrades at crucial times during the summer of 1864. To replace wounded, killed, and discharged soldiers the Union armies mustered conscripts, substitutes, and bounty men who had been obtained by the first draft in 1863. This procedure affected most the Army of the Potomac, which had suffered higher casualties than any other army and had a reenlistment rate of only 50 percent. Veteran officers and men regarded most of these new recruits with contempt. A Connecticut soldier described the new men in his regiment as "bounty jumpers, thieves, and cutthroats"; a Massachusetts officer reported that 40 of the 186 "substitutes, bounty-jumpers . . . thieves and roughs" who had been assigned to his regiment disappeared the first night after they arrived. This he considered a blessing, as did a Pennsylvania officer who wrote that the deserting "gamblers, thieves, pickpockets and blacklegs" given to his charge "would have disgraced the regiment beyond all recovery had they remained." Much of the North's apparent superiority in numbers thus dissolved during 1864.

Southern leaders hoped to exploit the Union's problem in such a manner as to influence the 1864 presidential election in the North. If southern armies could hold out until the election, war-weariness in the North might cause the voters to elect a Peace Democrat who would negotiate Confederate independence. Recognizing "the importance of this [military] campaign to the administration of Mr. Lincoln," Lee intended to "resist manfully" in order to undermine the northern war party. "If we can break up the enemy's arrangements early, and throw him back," explained

Longstreet, "he will not be able to recover his position or his morale until the Presidential election is over, and then we shall have a new President to treat with."

*　　*　　*　　*　　*

Grant was well aware of these southern hopes. But he intended to crush rebel armies and end the war before November. Eastern Yankees curious about the secret of this western general's success thought they saw the answer in his unpretentious but resolute demeanor. This "short, round-shouldered man" with "a slightly seedy look," according to an observer in Washington who saw Grant for the first time, nevertheless possessed "a clear blue eye" and "an expression as if he had determined to drive his head through a brick wall, and was about to do it."

Grant did not confine his attention solely to Virginia. Instead, believing that the various northern armies in the past had "acted independently and without concert, like a balky team, no two ever pulling together," he worked out plans for coordinated advances on several fronts to prevent any one of the Confederate armies from reinforcing another. "Lee's Army will be your objective point," Grant instructed Meade. "Wherever Lee goes, there will you go also." Sherman received orders to destroy Johnston's army and inflict all possible damage on the enemy's resources for making war. These two main Union armies would have a numerical advantage of nearly two to one over their adversaries, but Grant issued additional orders to increase the odds. On the periphery of the main theaters stood three northern

This lithograph depicts a recruiting office in New York City in 1864, where a volunteer could parlay the various bounties listed here into almost $700— nearly two years' wages for an unskilled laborer. Few of these bounty men made good soldiers; many of them deserted before they ever saw a Confederate. " Out of five reported North as having enlisted," complained General Grant, "we don't get more than one effective soldier."

The U.S.S. Mound City, *pictured here, was one of the thirteen ironclads and several other gunboats supporting General Banks's campaign up the Red River toward Shreveport in April 1864.*

Lieutenant General Richard Taylor, commander of the Confederate forces in Louisiana in 1864. From his father he inherited military ability as well as several Louisiana sugar plantations and hundreds of slaves. He did not, however, inherit his father's patriotic American nationalism.

armies commanded by political generals whose influence prevented even Grant from getting rid of them: Benjamin Butler's Army of the James on the Peninsula; Franz Sigel's scattered forces in West Virginia and the Shenandoah Valley; and Nathaniel Banks's Army of the Gulf in Louisiana. Grant directed Banks to plan a campaign to capture Mobile, after which he was to push northward and prevent rebel forces in Alabama from reinforcing Johnston. At the same time Butler was to advance up the James to cut the railroad between Petersburg and Richmond and threaten the Confederate capital from the south, while Sigel moved up the Valley to pin down its defenders and cut Lee's communications to that region.

The first to fail meeting Grant's expectations was Banks. The administration shared responsibility for this outcome, for it diverted Banks from the attack on Mobile to a drive up the Red River in Louisiana to seize cotton and expand the area of Union political control in the state. Only after achieving these objectives was he to turn eastward against Mobile. As it turned out, Banks achieved none of the goals except the seizure of a little cotton—along with the wanton destruction of much civilian property, an outcome that hardly won the hearts and minds of Louisianians for the Union.

Banks's nemesis was Richard Taylor (the son of Zachary Taylor), who had learned his fighting trade as a brigade commander under Stonewall Jackson in 1862. Taking command of some 15,000 men after the loss of southern Louisiana to the Union, Taylor prepared to defend what was left of the state in which he had gained wealth as a planter. Banks had been humiliated in Virginia by Jackson; he suffered the same fate a thousand miles away at the hands of Stonewall's protégé. On April 8 Taylor struck the vanguard of Banks's army at Sabine Cross-roads thirty-five miles south of the Union objective of Shreveport. Driving the routed Yankees pell-mell back to their supports, Taylor came on and attacked again next day at Pleasant Hill. This time the bluecoats held, forcing the rebels in turn to recoil after taking sharp punishment.

Despite this success, Banks was unnerved by the nonarrival of a

These Union transport steamboats tied up at the wharf in Alexandria, Louisiana, were temporarily trapped there by low water in the Red River. (So were the gunboats, not pictured.)

cooperating Union force pushing south from Little Rock (it had been deflected by guerrillas and cavalry harassment) and by the abnormally low Red River, which threatened to strand the already damaged Union gunboat fleet above the rapids at Alexandria. Banks decided to retreat. Disaster to the gunboats was averted by the ingenuity of a Wisconsin colonel who used his lumbering experience to construct a series of wing dams that floated the fleet through the rapids. The dispirited army did not get back to southern Louisiana until May 26, a month too late to begin the aborted Mobile campaign. As a consequence Joseph Johnston received 15,000 reinforcements from Alabama. Moreover, 10,000 soldiers that Banks had borrowed from Sherman for the Red River campaign never rejoined the Union army in Georgia. Instead they remained in the Tennessee-Mississippi theater to cope with threats by Forrest against Sherman's rail communications. Banks was superseded as department commander and returned to his controversial role as military administrator of Louisiana's reconstruction.

Butler and Sigel fared no better than Banks in their assignments to pin down potential reinforcements for Lee and Johnston. Butler had a real chance to achieve the glory that had eluded him since the war's early days. With 30,000 men drawn from coastal operations in the Carolinas he steamed up the James River and landed midway between Richmond and Petersburg on May 5. The two cities were defended by only 5,000 troops plus hastily mobilized government clerks serving as militia. Their commander—none other than P.G.T. Beauregard, who was transferred from Charleston to southside Virginia—had not yet arrived on the scene. If Bulter had moved quickly to cut the railroad

A photograph of the wing dams built by Union soldiers and sailors under the direction of Lieutenant Colonel Joseph Bailey to save the Union fleet of thirty-three vessels that might otherwise have fallen into Confederate hands or have been destroyed. By forcing the current into a narrow channel between the two dams, Bailey's ingenious construction white-watered the whole fleet to safety. Bailey earned the Thanks of Congress for this feat—one of only fifteen officers who received this distinction.

Part of the camp of Butler's troops where they were "corked" by the Confederate defenses across the neck between the James and Appomattox rivers. Note the shelter tents, each intended to hold two men for sleeping. Soldiers derisively called them "dog tents"; in World War II the words had become "pup tents."

This famous painting by Benjamin West Clinedinst portrays the V.M.I. cadets attacking across a waterlogged field against the Union position at New Market. The painting measures 18 by 23 feet and hangs in V.M.I.'s Jackson Memorial Hall.

between Petersburg and Richmond he might have smashed into the capital against little opposition. Lee could have done nothing to prevent this, for he was otherwise engaged with the Army of the Potomac sixty miles to the north. But the squint-eyed Union commander fumbled his chance. Instead of striking fast with over-helming force, he advanced cautiously with detached units, which managed to tear up only a few miles of track while fending off rebel skirmishers. Not until May 12, a week after landing, did Butler get his main force on the march for Richmond. By then Beauregard had brought reinforcements from the Carolinas and was ready to meet Butler on almost even terms. On May 16 the Confederates attacked near Drewry's Bluff, eight miles south of Richmond. After severe casualties on both sides, the rebels drove Butler's men back to their trenches across a neck between the James and Appomattox rivers. There the southerners entrenched their own line and sealed off Butler's army, in Grant's caustic words, "as if it had been in a bottle strongly corked."

Grant received the news of Butler's corking about the same time he learned of a similar setback to Franz Sigel in that vale of Union sorrows, the Shenandoah Valley. With 6,500 men Sigel had advanced up the Valley to capture Staunton, whence Lee's army received some of its meager supplies. Before Sigel could get there, however, former U.S. vice president John C. Breckinridge, now commanding a scraped-together rebel force of 5,000, attacked Sigel at New Market on May 15 and drove him back. This small battle was marked on one side by Sigel's skill at retreating and on the other by a spirited charge of 247

V.M.I. cadets aged fifteen to seventeen, who were ever after immortalized in southern legend. Convinced that Sigel "will do nothing but run; he never did anything else," Halleck and Grant prevailed upon Lincoln to remove him from command.

The failure of Grant's subordinates in Virginia complicated the task of assaulting Lee. The Armies of the Potomac and of Northern Virginia had wintered a dozen miles apart on opposite sides of the Rapidan. As the dogwood bloomed, Grant prepared to cross the river and turn Lee's right. He hoped to bring the rebels out of their trenches for a showdown battle somewhere south of the Wilderness, that gloomy expanse of scrub oaks and pines where Lee had mousetrapped Joe Hooker exactly a year earlier. Remembering that occasion, Lee decided not to contest the river crossing but instead to hit the bluecoats in the flank as they marched through the Wilderness, where their superiority in numbers—115,000 to 64,000— would count for less than in the open.

Accordingly on May 5 two of Lee's corps coming from the west ran into three Union corps moving south from the Rapidan. For Lee this collision proved a bit premature, because Longstreet's corps had only recently returned from Tennessee and could not come up in time for this first day of the battle of the Wilderness. The Federals thus managed to get more than 70,000 men into action against fewer than 40,000 rebels. But the southerners knew the terrain, and the Yankees' preponderance of troops produced only immobility in these dense, smoke-filled woods where soldiers could rarely see the enemy, units blundered the wrong way in the directionless jungle, friendly troops fired on each other by mistake, and gaps in the opposing line went unexploited because unseen, while muzzle flashes and exploding shells set the underbrush on fire to threaten wounded men with a fiery death. Savage fighting surged back and forth near two road intersections that the bluecoats needed to hold in order to continue their passage southward. They held on and by dusk had gained a position to attack Lee's right.

Grant ordered this done at dawn next day. Lee likewise planned a dawn assault in the same sector to be spearheaded by Longstreet's corps, which was on the march and expected to arrive before light. The Yankees attacked first and nearly

The wagon train of the 5th Corps, Army of the Potomac, crossing the Rapidan River on May 4, 1864, at the beginning of the campaign that, as General Grant later wrote, was "destined to result in the capture of the Confederate capital and the army defending it"—but not for eleven months.

These three skeletons were the remains of Union soldiers killed in the battle of Chancellorsville a year before the Union army returned to the same "Wilderness," where the fighting on May 5 and 6, 1864, would turn 4,000 of them into skeletons as well.

achieved a spectacular success. After driving the rebels almost a mile through the woods, they emerged into a small clearing where Lee had his field headquarters. Agitated, the gray commander tried personally to lead a counterattack at the head of one of Longstreet's arriving units, a Texas brigade. "Go back, General Lee, go back!" shouted the Texans as they swept forward. Lee finally did fall back as more of Longstreet's troops double-timed into the clearing and brought the Union advance to a halt.

The initiative now shifted to the Confederates. By midmorning Longstreet's fresh brigades drove the bluecoats in confusion almost back to their starting point. The southerners' local knowledge now came into play. Unmarked on any map, the roadbed of an unfinished railroad ran past the Union left. Vines and underbrush had so choked the cut that an unwary observer saw nothing until he stumbled into it. One of Longstreet's brigadiers knew of this roadbed and suggested using it as a concealed route for an attack against the Union flank. Longstreet sent four brigades on this mission. Shortly before noon they burst out of thickets and rolled up the surprised northern regiments. Then tragedy struck the Confederates as it had done a year earlier only three miles away in this same Wilderness. As the whooping rebels drove in from the flank they converged at right angles with Longstreet's other units attacking straight ahead. In the smoke-filled woods Longstreet went down with a bullet in his shoulder fired by a Confederate. Unlike Jackson he recovered, but he was out of the war for five months.

With Longstreet's wounding the steam went out of this southern assault. Lee straightened out the lines and renewed the attack in late afternoon. Combat raged near the road intersection amid a forest fire that ignited Union breastworks. The Federals held their ground, and the fighting gradually died toward evening as survivors sought to rescue the wounded from cremation. At the other end of the line General John B. Gordon, a rising brigadier from Georgia, discovered that Grant's right flank was also exposed. After trying for hours to get his corps commander Richard Ewell to authorize an attack, Gordon went to the top and finally obtained Lee's permission to pitch in. The evening assault achieved initial success and drove the Federal flank back a mile while capturing two northern generals. Panic spread all the way to Grant's headquarters, where a distraught officer galloped up on a lathered horse to tell the Union commander that all was lost—that Lee was repeating

Jackson's tactics of a year earlier in these same woods. But Grant did not share the belief in Lee's superhuman qualities that seemed to paralyze so many eastern officers. "I am heartily tired of hearing what Lee is going to do," Grant told the officer. "Some of you always seem to think he is suddenly going to turn a double somersault, and land on our rear and on both our flanks at the same time. Go back to your command, and try to think what we are going to do ourselves, instead of what Lee is going to do."

Grant soon showed that he meant what he said. Both flanks had been badly bruised, and his 17,500 casualties in two days exceeded the Confederate total by at

Many buildings in Fredericksburg were turned into hospitals during the battle of the Wilderness. Convalescent Union soldiers rest in the shade outside one of those buildings.

least 5,000. Under such circumstances previous Union commanders in Virginia had withdrawn behind the nearest river. Men in the ranks expected the same thing to happen again. But Grant had told Lincoln that "whatever happens, there will be no turning back." While the armies skirmished warily on May 7, Grant prepared to march around Lee's right during the night to seize the crossroads village of Spotsylvania a dozen miles to the south. If successful, this move would place the Union army closer to Richmond than the enemy and force Lee to fight or retreat. All day Union supply wagons and the reserve artillery moved to the rear, confirming the soldiers' weary expectation of retreat. After dark the blue divisions pulled out one by one. But instead of heading north they turned *south*. A mental sunburst brightened their minds. It was not "another Chancellorsville . . . another skedaddle" after

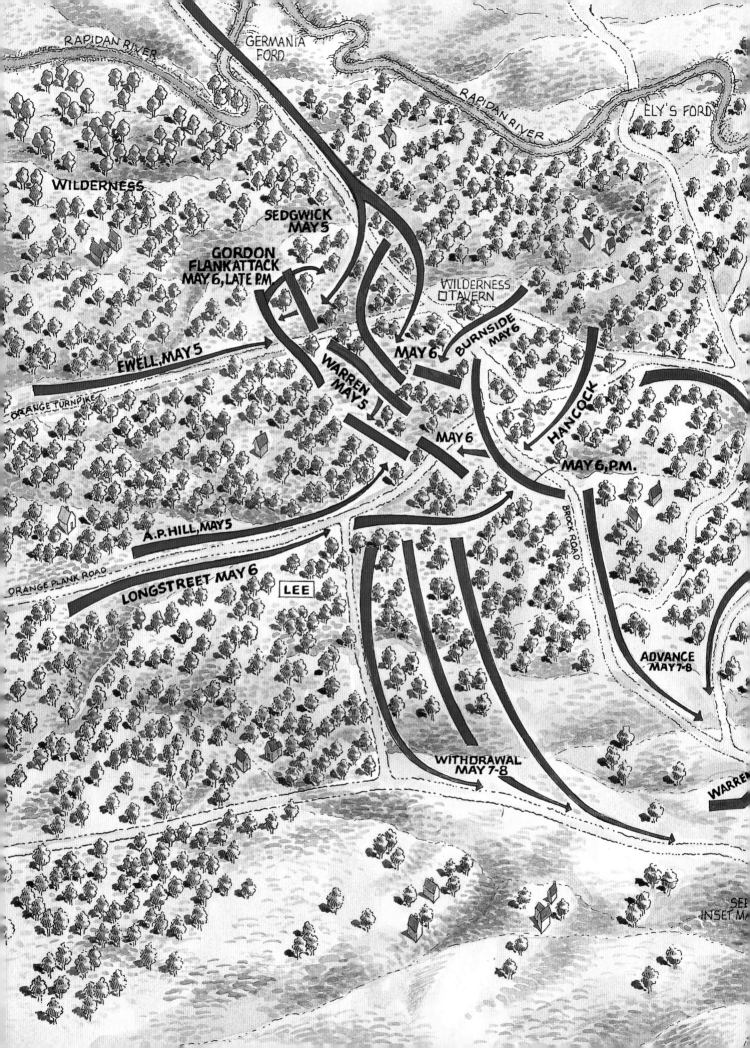

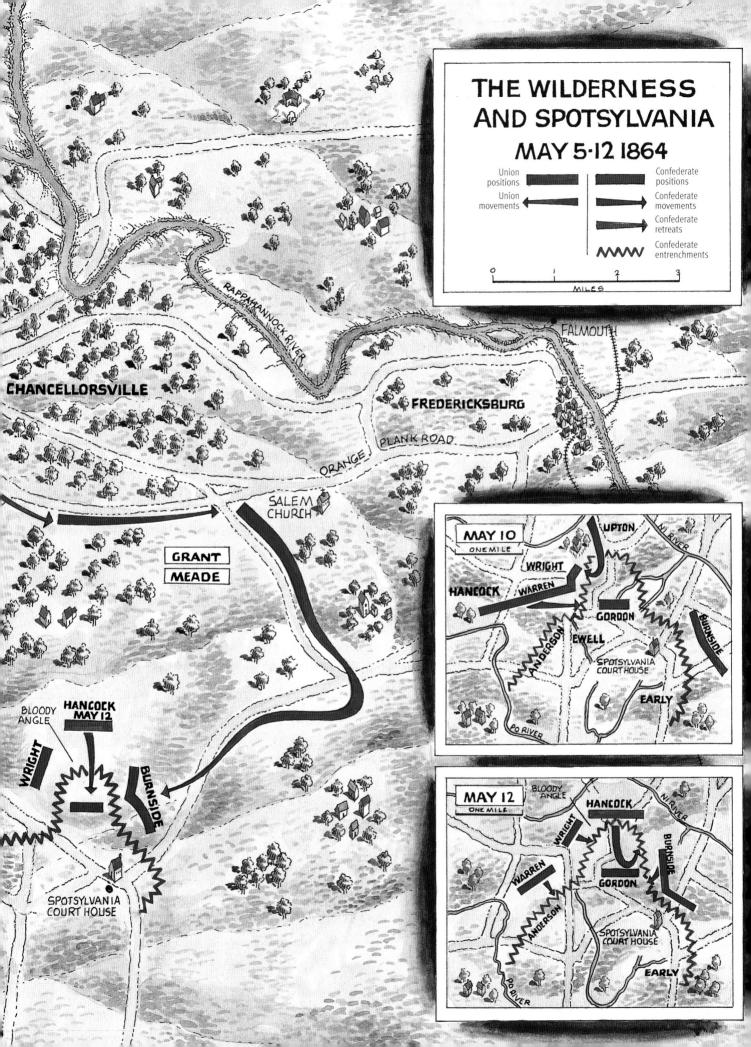

THE WILDERNESS AND SPOTSYLVANIA
MAY 5·12 1864

Union positions
Union movements
Confederate positions
Confederate movements
Confederate retreats
Confederate entrenchments

0   1   2   3
MILES

CHANCELLORSVILLE

RAPPAHANNOCK RIVER

FALMOUTH

FREDERICKSBURG

PLANK ROAD

ORANGE

SALEM CHURCH

GRANT
MEADE

BLOODY ANGLE

HANCOCK MAY 12

WRIGHT

BURNSIDE

SPOTSYLVANIA COURT HOUSE

MAY 10
ONE MILE

UPTON
NI RIVER
WRIGHT
HANCOCK
WARREN
GORDON
BURNSIDE
ANDERSON
EWELL
SPOTSYLVANIA COURT HOUSE
EARLY
PO RIVER

MAY 12
ONE MILE

BLOODY ANGLE
NI RIVER
HANCOCK
WRIGHT
WARREN
GORDON
BURNSIDE
ANDERSON
SPOTSYLVANIA COURT HOUSE
EARLY
PO RIVER

As Grant and his staff cantered south on the night of May 7 instead of retreating north across the Rapidan, his weary soldiers cheered him to the echo. It was probably the first time these soldiers willingly cheered a commander since McClellan's departure. A contemporary sketch captures that dramatic moment.

all. "Our spirits rose," recalled one veteran who remembered this moment as a turning point in the war. Despite the terrors of the past three days and those to come, "we marched free. The men began to sing." For the first time in a Virginia campaign the Army of the Potomac stayed on the offensive after its initial battle.

Sheridan's cavalry had thus far contributed little to the campaign. Their bandy-legged leader was eager to take on Jeb Stuart's fabled troopers. Grant obliged Sheridan by sending him on a raid to cut Lee's communications in the rear while Grant tried to pry him out of his defenses in front. Aggressive as always, Sheridan took 10,000 horsemen at a deliberate pace southward with no attempt at deception, challenging Stuart to attack. The plumed cavalier chased the Yankees with only half his men (leaving the others to patrol Lee's flanks at Spotsylvania), nipping at Sheridan's heels but failing to prevent the destruction of twenty miles of railroad, a quantity of rolling stock, and three weeks' supply of rations for Lee's army. On May 11 Stuart made a stand at Yellow Tavern, only six miles north of Richmond. Outnumbering the rebels by two to one and outgunning them with rapid-fire carbines, the blue troopers rolled over the once-invincible southern cavalry and dispersed them in two directions. A grim bonus of this Union victory was the mortal wounding of Stuart—a blow to Confederate leadership next only to the death of Jackson a year and a day earlier.

While the cavalry played its deadly game of cut and thrust near Richmond, the infantry back at Spotsylvania grappled like muscle-bound giants. By this stage of the war the spade had become almost as important for defense as the rifle. Wherever they stopped, soldiers quickly constructed elaborate networks of trenches, breast-

This bridge of the Richmond and Fredericksburg Railroad over the North Anna River fell victim to Sheridan's troopers during their raid deep into Lee's rear almost to Richmond. The photographer arrived in time to take his picture while the ruins of the bridge were still smoking.

works, artillery emplacements, traverses, a second line in the rear, and a cleared field of fire in front with the branches of felled trees (abatis) placed at point-blank range to entangle attackers. At Spotsylvania the rebels built the strongest such fieldworks in the war so far. Grant's two options were to flank these defenses or smash through them; he tried both. On May 9 he sent Winfield Scott Hancock's 2nd Corps to turn the Confederate left. But this maneuver required the crossing of a meandering river twice, giving Lee time to shift two divisions on May 10 to counter it. Believing that this weakening of the Confederate line made it vulnerable to assault, Grant ordered five divisions to attack the enemy's left-center on a mile-wide front during the afternoon of May 10. But they found no weakness, for Lee had shifted those reinforcements from his right.

Farther along toward the center of the line, however, on the west face of a salient jutting out a half-mile along high ground and dubbed the Mule Shoe because of its shape, a Union assault achieved a potentially decisive breakthrough. Here Colonel Emory Upton, a young and intensely professional West Pointer who rarely restrained his impatience with the incompetence he found among fellow officers, made a practical demonstration of his theory on how to attack trenches. With twelve picked regiments formed in four lines, Upton took them across two hundred yards of open ground and through the abatis at a run. Not stopping to fire until they reached the trenches, screaming like madmen and fighting like wild ani-

A drawing of Confederate trenches at Spotsylvania. Troops dug these trenches quickly and set logs with sharpened ends facing toward the enemy to impale attackers who had not been shot down before they got there.

mals, the first line breached the defenses and fanned left and right to widen the breach while the following line kept going to attack the second network of trenches a hundred yards farther on. The third and fourth lines came on and rounded up a thousand dazed prisoners. The road to Richmond never seemed more open. But the division assigned to support Upton's penetration came forward halfheartedly and retreated wholeheartedly when it ran into massed artillery fire. Stranded without support a half-mile from their own lines, Upton's regiments could not withstand a withering counterattack by rebel reinforcements. The Yankees fell back in the gathering darkness after losing a quarter of their numbers.

Their temporary success, however, won Upton a battlefield promotion and persuaded Grant to try the same tactics with a whole corps backed by follow-up attacks all along the line. As a cold, sullen rain set in next day (May 11) to end two weeks of hot weather, reports by rebel patrols of Union supply wagons moving to the rear caused Lee to make a wrong guess about Grant's intentions. Believing that the wagon traffic presaged another flanking maneuver, Lee ordered the removal of twenty-two guns in preparation for a quick countermove. The apex of the salient defended by these guns was exactly the point that Hancock's corps planned to hit at dawn on May 12. Too late the guns were ordered back—just in time to be captured by yelling bluecoats as 15,000 of them swarmed out of the mist and burst through the Confederate trenches. Advancing another half-mile and capturing most of the famed Stonewall division, Hancock's corps split Lee's army in two. At this crisis the southern commander came forward with a reserve division. As he had done six days previously in the Wilderness, Lee started to lead them himself in a desperate counterattack. Again the soldiers—Virginians and Georgians this time—shouted "General Lee to the rear!" and vowed to drive back "those people" if Marse Robert would only stay safely behind. Lee acceded, and the division swept forward. Their counterattack benefited from the very success of the Yankees, whose

Marked on the maps as the McCoul House, this farmhouse was within the Confederate Mule Shoe salient. Hancock's attack on May 12 penetrated a quarter-mile past the house before the Confederate counterattack drove the Yankees back. Heavy fighting swirled around the house and outbuildings; most of the battle detritus had been cleared up by the time this photograph was taken two weeks after the battle.

rapid advance in rain and fog had jumbled units together in a disorganized mass beyond control of their officers. Forced back to the toe of the Mule Shoe, bluecoats rallied in the trenches they had originally captured and there turned to lock horns with the enemy in endless hours of combat across a no-man's land at some places but a few yards wide.

While this was going on the Union 5th and 9th Corps attacked the left and right of the Confederate line with little success, while the 6th Corps came in on Hancock's right to add weight to a renewed attempt to crush the salient. Here was the famous Bloody Angle of Spotsylvania. For eighteen hours in the rain, from early morning

to midnight, some of the war's most horrific fighting raged along a few hundred yards of rebel trenches. "The flags of both armies waved at the same moment over the same breastworks," recalled a 6th Corps veteran, "while beneath them Federal and Confederate endeavored to drive home the bayonet through the interstices of the logs." Impelled by a sort of frenzy, soldiers on both sides leaped on the parapet and fired down at enemy troops with bayoneted rifles handed up from comrades, hurling each empty gun like a spear before firing the next one until shot down or bayoneted themselves. So intense was the firing that at one point just behind the southern lines an oak tree nearly two feet thick was cut down by minié balls.

Hand-to-hand fighting like this usually ended quickly when one side broke and ran; but today neither line broke and few men ran. It became an atavistic territorial battle. Blood flowed as copiously as the rain, turning trench floors into a slimy ooze where dead and wounded were trampled down by men fighting for their lives. "I never expect to be fully believed when I tell what I saw of the horrors of Spotsylvania," wrote a Union officer, "because I should be loath to believe it myself were the

case reversed." Long after nightfall Lee finally sent word to exhausted Confederate survivors to fall back to a new line a half-mile in the rear which his engineers had worked feverishly to fortify. Next morning the Bloody Angle contained only corpses; Union soldiers on a burial detail found 150 dead southerners piled several deep in one area of trench measuring two hundred square feet, and buried them by simply pushing in the parapet on top of them.

As the armies battered each other in Virginia, citizens back home crowded newspaper and telegraph offices in a mood of "painful suspense [that] unfits the mind for mental activity." These were "fearfully critical, anxious days," wrote a New Yorker, in which "the destines of the continent for centuries" would be decided. In Richmond, elation at the first reports of Lee's victories in the Wilderness turned to

These two photographs depict part of the grim harvest of death at Spotsylvania. The top picture shows a Union burial detail preparing to inter a comrade whose arm points skyward in rigor mortis. The bottom photograph portrays seven Confederate soldiers lined up for mass burial.

"grave apprehension" and "feverish anxiety" as his army fell back to Spotsylvania while Butler and Sheridan approached Richmond. The day before the Bloody Angle, Grant had sent a dispatch to Washington declaring that "I propose to fight it out on this line if it takes all summer." Newspapers picked up this phrase and made it as famous as Grant's unconditional-surrender note at Fort Donelson. Coupled with reports describing the Union advance southward from the Wilderness, Grant's dispatch produced jubilant headlines in northern newspapers: "Glorious Successes"; "Lee Terribly Beaten"; "The End Draws Near." A veteran newspaper reporter recalled that "everybody seemed to think that Grant would close the war and enter Richmond before the autumn leaves began to fall."

When it became clear by May 17 that Grant had not broken Lee's lines at Spotsylvania and that Butler had been "bottled up" south of Richmond, the northern mood turned "despondent and bad." This was exactly what Lincoln had feared—that overly optimistic expectations would make bad news seem even worse. The price of gold, an inverse barometer of public opinion, rose from 171 to 191 during the last two weeks of May. The appalling casualty reports that began to filter up from Virginia did not help morale. From May 5 through May 12 the Army of the Potomac lost some 32,000 men killed, wounded, and missing—a total greater than for all Union armies *combined* in any previous week of the war. As anxious relatives scanned the casualty lists, a pall of gloom settled over hundreds of northern communities.

Lee's casualties had been proportionately as great—about 20,000—and his loss of twenty of fifty-seven commanders of infantry corps, divisions, and brigades was devastating. Yet it could truly be said that both sides had just begun to fight. Each army made good about half of its losses by calling in reinforcements. Six brigades from the Richmond front and two from the Shenandoah Valley joined Lee. Grant received a few thousand new recruits and combed several heavy artillery regiments out of the Washington defenses and converted them to infantry. Lee's replacements were higher in quality though lower in number than Grant's, for the southerners were combat veterans, while the "heavies" from Washington had seen no real fighting during their two or three years of garrison duty. And even as the Union reinforcements came forward, the first of the thirty-six regiments whose time would expire in the next six weeks began to leave the army. While the available manpower pool in the North was much larger, therefore, Lee could more readily replace his losses with veterans than Grant could during these crucial weeks of May and June.

After the Bloody Angle, Grant wasted no time licking his wounds. During the next week he tried several maneuvers on Lee's flanks and another assault up the middle. Aided by rains that slowed Union movements, the rebels countered all these moves. All that the Yankees could show for these six days of maneuvering and fighting were three thousand more casualties. Recognizing the impossibility of loosening the Confederate hold on Spotsylvania by head-on attacks or short-range flanking efforts, Grant decided to lure Lee out by another race twenty-five miles south toward a rail junction just beyond the North Anna River. Lee detected the move by a reconnaissance in force on May 19 that cost him a thousand men and blooded one of Grant's converted heavy artillery divisions.

Holding the inside track, Lee got his army behind the North Anna River before the Union vanguard arrived. Entrenching a strong position on the south bank, the Confederates fought several small actions against probing bluecoats. Grant decided to move twenty miles downriver for another attempt to get around Lee's right.

A Union pontoon bridge across the Pamunkey River, where part of the Army of the Potomac crossed on May 28, 1864, bringing them within a dozen miles of Richmond.

The Federals crossed the Pamunkey River unscathed, only to find the rebels, who again moved on shorter interior lines, entrenched behind Totopotomy Creek nine miles northeast of Richmond. Although half-starved from lack of rations, the southerners were still full of fight. After two days of skirmishing at the end of May the Yankees sidled southward once more—moving to their left as always, to maintain a short, secure supply line via the tidal rivers controlled by the navy.

Grant's objective was a dusty crossroads named Cold Harbor near the Gaines's Mill battlefield of 1862. Sheridan's cavalry seized the junction after an intense fight on May 31 with southern horsemen commanded by Lee's nephew Fitzhugh Lee. Next day Sheridan's troopers held on against an infantry counterattack until Union infantry came up and pushed the rebels back. During the night of June 1–2 the remainder of both armies arrived and entrenched lines facing each other for seven miles from the Totopotomy to the Chickahominy. To match additional southern reinforcements from south of the James, Grant pried one of Butler's corps from the same sector. At Cold Harbor, 59,000 Confederates confronted 109,000 Federals. Both armies had thus built themselves back up almost to the numbers with which they started the campaign four long weeks earlier.

These four weeks had been exhausting as well as bloody beyond all precedent. The Federals had suffered some 44,000 casualties, the Confederates about 26,000. This was a new kind of relentless, ceaseless warfare. These two armies had previously fought several big set-piece battles followed by the retreat of one or the other behind the nearest river, after which both sides rested and recuperated before going at it again. Since the beginning of this campaign, however, the armies had never been out of contact with each other. Some kind of fighting along with a great deal of marching and digging took place almost every day and a good many nights as well. Mental and physical exhaustion began to take a toll; officers and men suffered what in World War I would be called shell shock. Two of Lee's unwounded corps commanders, A. P. Hill and Richard Ewell, broke down for a time during the campaign, and Ewell had to be replaced by Jubal Early. Lee fell sick for a week. On the Union side an officer noted that in three weeks men "had grown thin and haggard. The experience of those twenty days seemed to have added twenty years to their age." "Many a man," wrote Captain Oliver Wendell Holmes, Jr., "has gone crazy since this campaign began from the terrible pressure on mind & body."

All of this was on Grant's mind as he pondered his next move. Another flanking maneuver to the left would entangle his army in the Chickahominy bottomlands where McClellan had come to grief. And it would only drive Lee back into the Richmond defenses, which had been so strengthened during the past two years that the usual defensive advantage of fieldworks would be doubled. Another dozen Union regiments were scheduled to leave the army when their time expired in July; this factor also argued against postponement of a showdown battle. Grant's purpose was not a war of attrition—though numerous historians have mislabeled it thus. From the outset he had tried to maneuver Lee into open-field combat, where Union superiority in numbers and firepower could cripple the enemy. It was Lee

In this photograph taken in late May near a country church in Virginia midway between Fredericksburg and Richmond, General Grant consults with his senior commanders on plans for the next move in the campaign. Grant is leaning over one of the church pews brought outside, looking at a map held by General Meade, sitting in the pew.

who turned it into a war of attrition by skillfully matching Grant's moves and confronting him with an entrenched defense at every turn. Although it galled Lee to yield the initiative to an opponent, his defensive strategy exacted almost two enemy casualties for every one of his own. This was a rate of attrition that might stun northern voters into denying Lincoln reelection and ending the war. It was to avoid such a consequence that Grant had vowed to fight it out on this line if it took all summer. "This line" had now become Cold Harbor, and the results of a successful attack there might win the war. If beaten, the Confederates would be driven back on the Chickahominy and perhaps annihilated. Grant knew that the rebels were tired and hungry; so were his own men, but he believed that they had the edge in morale. So Grant ordered an assault at dawn on June 3.

The outcome revealed his mistake in two crucial respects. Lee's army was not whipped, nor did Grant's men attack with confidence. Indeed, hundreds of them pinned slips of paper with name and address on their uniforms so their bodies could be identified after the battle. At dawn came the straight-ahead assault delivered primarily by three corps on the left and center of the Union line. A sheet of flame greeted the blue uniforms with names pinned on them. The rebels fought from trenches described by a newspaper reporter as "intricate, zig-zagged lines within lines, lines protecting flanks of lines, lines built to enfilade opposing lines . . . works within works and works without works." Although a few regiments in Hancock's 2nd Corps—the same that had breached the Angle at Spotsylvania—managed to penetrate the first line of trenches, they were quickly driven out at the cost of eight colonels and 2,500 other casualties. Elsewhere along the front the result was worse— indeed it was the most shattering Union repulse since the stone wall below Marye's Heights at Fredericksburg. The Yankees suffered 7,000 casualties this day; the Confederates fewer than 1,500. By early afternoon Grant admitted defeat and called off

During the campaigning and fighting in May and June 1864, the two sides occasionally called a truce of an hour or more so that soldiers could bring back to their own lines the dead and wounded from no-man's land between the armies. This poignant illustration shows a soldier searching for his buddy, hoping against hope that he will find him wounded instead of dead.

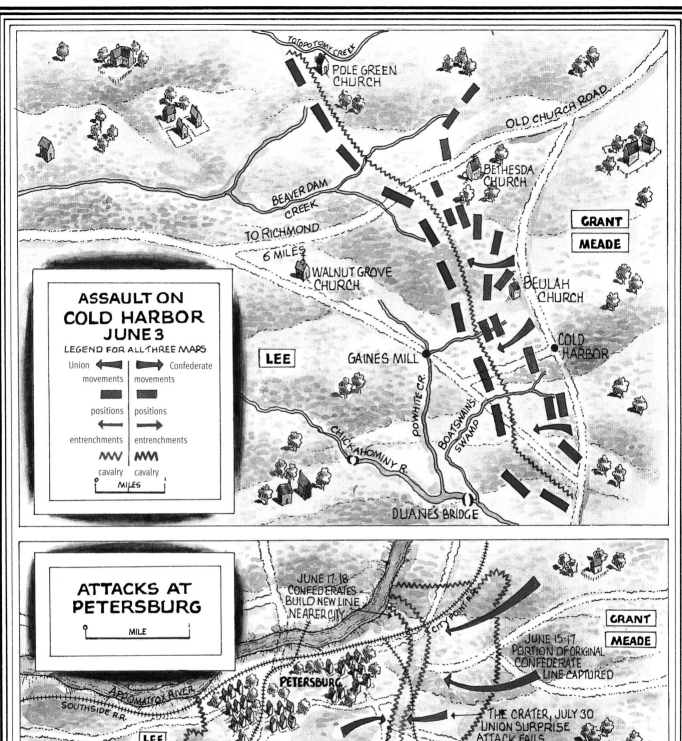

ASSAULT ON COLD HARBOR JUNE 3

LEGEND FOR ALL THREE MAPS

Union		Confederate
← movements		movements →
positions		positions
← entrenchments		entrenchments →
⋙ cavalry		⋙ cavalry

0 _____ MILES

TOTOPOTOMY CREEK

POLE GREEN CHURCH

OLD CHURCH ROAD

BEAVER DAM CREEK

BETHESDA CHURCH

GRANT

MEADE

TO RICHMOND
6 MILES

WALNUT GROVE CHURCH

BEULAH CHURCH

LEE

GAINES MILL

COLD HARBOR

POWHITE CR.

CHICKAHOMINY R.

BOATSWAINS' SWAMP

DUANES BRIDGE

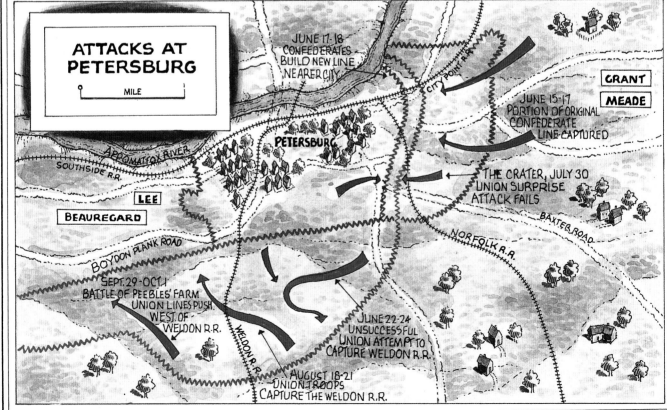

ATTACKS AT PETERSBURG

0 _____ MILE

JUNE 17-18 CONFEDERATES BUILD NEW LINE NEAR CITY

CITY POINT R.R.

GRANT

MEADE

JUNE 15-17 PORTION OF ORIGINAL CONFEDERATE LINE CAPTURED

PETERSBURG

APPOMATTOX RIVER

SOUTHSIDE R.R.

THE CRATER, JULY 30 UNION SURPRISE ATTACK FAILS

LEE

BEAUREGARD

BAXTER ROAD

NORFOLK R.R.

BOYDON PLANK ROAD

SEPT. 29-OCT.1 BATTLE OF PEEBLES' FARM UNION LINES PUSH WEST OF WELDON R.R.

WELDON R.R.

JUNE 22-24 UNSUCCESSFUL UNION ATTEMPT TO CAPTURE WELDON R.R.

AUGUST 18-21 UNION TROOPS CAPTURE THE WELDON R.R.

further efforts. "I regret this assault more than any one I have ever ordered," he said that evening. "I think Grant has had his eyes opened," Meade wrote dryly to his wife, "and is willing to admit now that Virginia and Lee's army is not Tennessee and Bragg's army."

The horrors of this day, added to those of Spotsylvania, created something of a Cold Harbor syndrome in the Army of the Potomac. Men in the ranks had learned what European armies on the Western Front a half-century later would have to learn all over again about trench warfare. "The men feel at present a great horror and dread of attacking earthworks again" was how one officer put it. So Grant devised a new three-part plan to cut Lee's supply lines and flank him out of his trenches. He ordered the army in the Shenandoah Valley, now led by David Hunter, to renew Sigel's aborted effort to move up the Valley (southward) and destroy its railroads, cross the Blue Ridge to smash the Confederate supply depot at Lynchburg, and continue east toward Richmond, wrecking the railroads and the James River Canal. At the same time Sheridan was to take two cavalry divisions westward on a raid to lay waste the same railroads from the other end and link up with Hunter midway for a grand climax of demolition before rejoining the Army of the Potomac somewhere south of Richmond. While all this was going on, Grant planned to disengage from Cold Harbor, march swiftly to cross the James, seize Petersburg with its hub of railroads linking Richmond to the South, and force Lee into the open.

Federal units carried out handsomely the first step in each part of this intricate plan. But thereafter the vigorous Confederate responses plus failures of nerve by subordinate Union commanders brought all three efforts to a halt. Out in the Valley, Hunter's 15,000 men constituted his first field command since he had been wounded at Bull Run in 1861. His main distinction in the war stemmed from his abortive attempt in 1862 to abolish slavery along the south Atlantic coast and to raise the first black regiment there. He was eager to achieve a military success. On June 5 at Piedmont, Virginia—halfway between Harrisonburg and Staunton—his men got him off on the right foot by overrunning a smaller rebel force, killing its commander, and capturing more than a thousand prisoners. Hunter moved on through Staunton to Lexington, home of the Virginia Military Institute.

Along the way his soldiers destroyed a good deal more than military property. Many of them had spent the war fighting guerrillas in western Virginia. The foremost of such enemies was John Singleton Mosby. A diminutive but fearless man who a decade earlier had been expelled from the University of Virginia and jailed for shooting a fellow student, Mosby studied law in prison, received a pardon from the governor, and became a lawyer. After serving as a cavalry scout for Jeb Stuart, Mosby raised a guerrilla company under the Partisan Ranger Act of April 1862. His fame spread with such exploits as the capture of a northern general in bed ten miles from Washington in March 1863. Never totaling more than 800 men, Mosby's partisans operated in squads of twenty to eighty and attacked Union outposts, wagon trains, and stragglers with such fury and efficiency that whole counties in northern Virginia became known as Mosby's Confederacy. No Union supplies could move in this area except under heavy guard.

Southerners lionized Mosby's partisans and numerous other guerrilla bands in Virginia for their boldness and dash. Northern soldiers had quite a different view of Mosby and his raiders. They were "'honest farmers' who have taken the oath of allegiance [to the Union] a few times" and then, arming themselves with whatever weapon came to hand, ambushed supply trains whenever they "find them unguarded or broken down, and he generally takes them without loss of a man. Now and then an ambulance or two, full of sick men, is taken by him without loss."

Union soldiers were not likely to treat with kid gloves any guerrillas they caught or the civilian population that sheltered them. As Hunter marched up the Valley guerrilla attacks got worse; for a month after May 20 only one wagon train got through. Getting angrier as they grew hungrier, Hunter's men foraged savagely from civilians and burned what they did not take. By the time they reached Lexington on June 12 the soldiers were in a foul mood. Looting escalated to terrorizing of citizens; destruction of military property escalated to the burning of

Although John Singleton Mosby was not a big man, the photographer makes him look tall and imposing in this picture. Union officers whose commands were bedeviled by Mosby's guerrillas would have confirmed that he was very big indeed.

This drawing by an artist for the Illustrated London News *shows several of Mosby's partisans at a moonlight rendezvous in a pass of the Blue Ridge Mountains for a raid into the Shenandoah Valley. For his British audience the artist exaggerated the ruggedness of the mountains.*

Many of the officers in the Army of Northern Virginia were graduates of Virginia Military Institute, which became for the other side a master symbol of rebellion and treason. They had it in for V.M.I., which looked like this after Hunter's troops burned it.

V.M.I. and the home of the current governor—who had recently called on civilians to take up arms as guerrillas. Justifying their behavior, one Union soldier wrote: "Many of the women look sad and do much weeping over the destruction that is going on. We feel that the South brought on the war and the State of Virginia is paying dear for her part."

Short of ammunition because none could get through, Hunter left Lexington in flames and moved on toward Lynchburg. Lee regarded this threat to his rear as most serious. To meet it he sent Jubal Early with Jackson's old corps back to the vicinity of their great achievements two years earlier. Though reduced by casualties to 10,000 men, Early's veterans brought Confederate strength at Lynchburg equal to Hunter's 15,000. Hunter tapped at the Lynchburg defenses on June 17–18, learned of Early's arrival, pondered his shortage of ammunition, and decided to retreat. And he did so *westward*, into West Virginia, rather than risk a movement back down the Valley with guerrillas on his flanks and Early in his rear. This path of retreat left the Valley open to the Confederates. Believing that Early would draw more strength away from Grant by staying there than by returning to the Richmond front, Lee authorized him to emulate Jackson by using the Valley as an avenue to threaten Maryland and Washington. Hunter spent the rest of the war rationalizing his decision to retreat into West Virginia, but he soon lost his command as well as his reputation.

Sheridan's raid fared only slightly better than Hunter's expedition. Lee sent 5,000 of his cavalry to head off Sheridan's 7,000. The rebel horsemen were now commanded by Wade Hampton, a South Carolina planter reputed to be the richest man in the South, who had already been wounded three times in this war. Catching up with the Federals sixty miles northwest of Richmond, the gray troopers slugged it out with Sheridan's men for two days near Trevilian Station on June 11–12. With casualties of 20 percent on each side, this was the bloodiest cavalry action of the war. On the Union side a Michigan brigade commanded by George Armstrong Custer did the hardest fighting. Sheridan managed to keep the graybacks at bay while he tore up the railroad, but he abandoned the plan to link up with Hunter, and the southerners soon repaired the railroad.

While all this was going on, the whole Army of the Potomac withdrew from Cold Harbor on the night of June 12–13. While one corps went around to the James by water, the other four marched overland, screened by the one cavalry division that Sheridan had left behind. So smoothly was the operation carried out, with feints toward Richmond to confuse Lee, that the Confederate commander remained puzzled for several days about Grant's intentions. Meanwhile Union engineers built perhaps the longest pontoon bridge in military history, 2,100 feet, anchored to hold against strong tidal currents and a four-foot tidal rise and fall. Bluecoats began crossing the James on June 14, and next day two corps approached Petersburg, which was held by Beauregard with a scratch force of 2,500. Grant had borrowed a leaf from his Vicksburg campaign and gotten in the enemy's rear before his opponent realized what was happening.

But the denouement was different from Vicksburg, because Grant's corps commanders failed him here and because Beauregard and Lee were not Pemberton and Johnston. The first Union troops to reach Petersburg were the 18th Corps, which Grant had borrowed from Butler two weeks earlier for the Cold Harbor assault. Their commander was William F. "Baldy" Smith, who had quarreled with Butler and had not distinguished himself in this theater. With a chance to retrieve his reputation, Smith became cautious as he approached Petersburg and surveyed the formidable defensive line: ten miles of twenty-foot-thick breastworks and trenches fronted by fifteen-foot ditches and linking fifty-five artillery redans bristling with cannon. Having seen at Cold Harbor what happened to soldiers attacking much less imposing works, Smith paused, not realizing that Beauregard had only a handful of men to hold them. The Union forces finally went forward near sundown and easily captured more than a mile of line and sixteen guns. One of Smith's three divisions

A photograph of the pontoon bridge over the James River that carried 50,000 troops and all their artillery in two days without mishap.

Part of the Confederate defenses at
Petersburg, Fort Mahone, photographed
here, sheltered a concentration of
artillery that wreaked such havoc
against attacking Yankees that they
named it "Fort Damnation." Note the
complete absence of trees, which had all
been cut down to create fields of fire and
to feed soldiers' campfires.

was composed of black troops who tasted here their first combat and performed
well. As a bright moon lighted the captured trenches, Smith took counsel of rumors
that reinforcements from Lee had arrived and failed to push on. "Petersburg at that
hour," wrote Beauregard after the war, "was clearly at the mercy of the Federal
commander, who had all but captured it."

More such missed opportunities crowded the next three days. On the night of
June 15–16, Beauregard's survivors desperately entrenched a new line while two
rebel divisions from north of the James came to bolster it. Next day another two
Union corps arrived, and in late afternoon 48,000 bluecoats seized more of Beauregard's lines but did not achieve a breakthrough. By June 17 Lee recognized that
Grant was bringing almost his whole army south of the James. Although the Union
forces that day missed a chance to turn the Confederate right, their disjointed
attacks did force Beauregard to pull his whole line back at night almost to the outskirts of Petersburg while proclaiming, melodramatically, that "the last hour of the
Confederacy had arrived." At dawn on June 18 some 70,000 Federals stumbled forward but overran nothing but empty trenches. By the time they got into position
again for an attack on the new rebel line, Lee with most of his troops had arrived to
defend it.

The Cold Harbor syndrome inhibited Union soldiers and their commanders
from pressing home their assaults. General Meade's famous temper snapped on the
afternoon of June 18. "What additional orders to attack you require I cannot imagine," he railed at one hapless commander by field telegraph. To another: "Finding it
impossible to effect cooperation by appointing an hour for attack, I have sent an
order to each corps commander to attack at all hazards and without reference to
each other." But men who had survived previous assaults on trenches were not

eager to try it again. In one 2nd Corps brigade, veterans wriggled forward under cover but refused to get up and charge across bullet-swept open ground. Next to them one of the converted heavy artillery regiments, the 1st Maine, prepared to sweep ahead in 1861 picture-book style. "Lie down, you damn fools," called the veterans. "You can't take them forts!" But the heavies went in anyway and were shot to pieces, losing 632 of 850 men in this one action. Meade finally called off the futile assaults because "our men are tired and the attacks have not been made with the vigor and force which characterized our fighting in the Wilderness; if they had been, I think we should have been more successful." Grant concurred: "We will rest the men and use the spade for their protection until a new vein has been struck."

Thus ended a seven-week campaign of movement and battle whose brutal intensity was unmatched in the war. Little wonder that the Army of the Potomac did not fight at Petersburg with "the vigor and force" it had shown in the Wilderness—it was no longer the same army. Many of its best and bravest had been killed or wounded; thousands of others, their enlistments expired or about to expire, had left the war or were unwilling to risk their lives during the few days before leaving. Some 65,000 northern boys were killed, wounded, or missing since May 4. This figure amounted to three-fifths of the total number of combat casualties suffered by

The French artist André Castaigne painted this dramatic picture of the 22nd U.S. Colored Infantry attacking part of the Confederate lines at Petersburg on June 15, 1864. The Confederates had cut down all the trees along their position to create an open field of fire. Nevertheless, the attack succeeded. One of the white officers in this regiment, Lieutenant Luther Osborn, was the author's great grandfather.

the Army of the Potomac during the *previous three years*. No army could take such punishment and retain its fighting edge. "For thirty days it has been one funeral procession past me," cried General Gouverneur K. Warren, commanding the 5th Corps, "and it has been too much!"

Could the northern people absorb such losses and continue to support the war? Financial markets were pessimistic; gold shot up to the ruinous height of 230. A Union general home on sick leave found "great discouragement over the North, great reluctance to recruiting, strong disposition for peace." Democrats began denouncing Grant as a "butcher." Even Benjamin Butler's wife wondered, "What is all this struggling and fighting for? This ruin and death to thousands of families? . . . What advancement of mankind to compensate for the present horrible calamities?"

To the universal question, "When is the war to end?" Lincoln replied in a speech on June 16: "We accepted this war for [the] worthy object . . . of restoring the national authority over the whole national domain . . . and the war will end when that object is attained. Under God, I hope it never will until that time. [Great Cheering) . . . General Grant is reported to have said, I am going through on this line if it takes all summer. (Cheers) . . . I say we are going through on this line if it takes three years more."

In his speech Lincoln praised Grant for having gained "a position from whence he will never be dislodged until Richmond is taken." And indeed, despite its horrendous losses the Army of the Potomac had inflicted a similar percentage of casualties (at least 35,000) on Lee's smaller army, had driven them south eighty miles, cut part of Lee's communications with the rest of the South, pinned him down in defense of Richmond and Petersburg, and smothered the famed mobility of the Army of Northern Virginia. Lee recognized the importance of these enemy achievements. At the end of May he had told Jubal Early: "We must destroy this army of Grant's before it gets to the James River. If he gets there it will become a siege, and then it will be a mere question of time."

II

In the long run, to be sure, Lee and the South could not withstand a siege. But in the short run—three or four months—time was on the Confederacy's side, for the northern presidential election was approaching. In Georgia as well as Virginia the rebels were holding out for time. At the end of June, Joe Johnston and Atlanta still stood against Sherman despite an eighty-mile penetration by the Yankees in Georgia to match their advance in Virginia.

While Grant and Lee sought to destroy or cripple each other's army, Sherman and Johnston engaged in a war of maneuver seeking an advantage that neither found. While Grant continually moved around Lee's right after hard fighting, Sherman continually moved around Johnston's left without as much fighting. Differences in terrain as well as in the personalities of commanders determined these contrasting strategies. Unlike Lee, whom necessity compelled to adopt a defensive strategy, Johnston by temperament preferred the defensive. He seemed to share with his prewar friend George McClellan a reluctance to commit troops to all-out combat unless he had all possible conditions in his favor; perhaps for that reason Johnston was idolized by his men as McClellan had been. In Virginia in 1862, Johnston had retreated from Manassas without a battle and from Yorktown almost to Richmond with little fighting. In Mississippi he never did come to grips with Grant at Vicksburg. In the spring of 1864 Jefferson Davis prodded Johnston to make some move against Sherman before Sherman attacked him. But Johnston preferred to wait in his prepared defenses until Sherman came so close that he could not miss.

Sherman refused to oblige him. Despite his ferocious reputation, "Uncle Billy" (as his men called him) had little taste for slam-bang combat: "Its glory is all moonshine; even success the most brilliant is over dead and mangled bodies, with the anguish and lamentation of distant families." Sherman's invasion force consisted of three "armies" under his single overall command: George Thomas's Army of the Cumberland, now 60,000 strong including the old 11th and 12th Corps of the Army of the Potomac reorganized as the 20th Corps; 25,000 men in the Army of the Tennessee, which had been first Grant's army and then Sherman's and was now commanded by their young protégé James B. McPherson; and John M. Schofield's 13,000-man corps, called the Army of the Ohio, which had participated in the liberation of east Tennessee the previous autumn. This composite army was tied to a vulnerable single-track railroad for its supplies. The topography of northern Georgia favored the defense even more than in Virginia. Steep, rugged mountains interlaced by swift rivers dominated the landscape between Chattanooga and Atlanta. Johnston's army of 50,000 (soon to be reinforced to 65,000 by troops from Alabama) took position on Rocky Face Ridge flanking the railroad twenty-five miles south of Chattanooga and dared the Yankees to come on.

Sherman declined to enter this "terrible door of death." Instead, like a boxer he jabbed with his left—Thomas and Schofield—to fix Johnston's attention on the ridge, and sent McPherson on a wide swing to the right through mountain gaps to hit the railroad at Resaca, fifteen miles in the Confederate rear. Through an oversight by Johnston's cavalry, Snake Creek Gap was almost unguarded when McPherson's fast-marching infantry poured through on May 9. Finding Resaca protected by strong earthworks, however, McPherson skirmished cautiously, overestimated the force opposing him (there were only two brigades), and pulled back without reaching the railroad. Alerted to this threat in his rear, Johnston sent additional troops to Resaca and then retreated with his whole army to this point on the night of May 12–13. Sherman's knockout punch never landed. "Well, Mac," he told the chagrined McPherson, "you missed the opportunity of your life."

For three days Sherman's whole force probed the Resaca defenses without finding a weak spot. Once again part of McPherson's army swung southward by the right flank, crossed the Oostanaula River, and threatened Johnston's railroad lifeline. Disengaging skillfully, the southerners withdrew down the tracks, paused

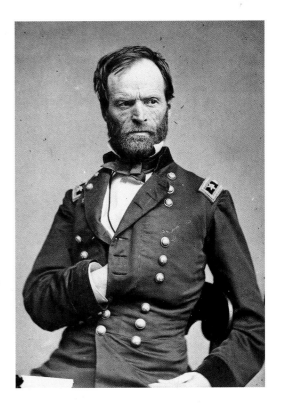

As the 1864 military campaigns began, General William T. Sherman was not widely known outside his own army. That would soon change, as Sherman earned a reputation in the North second only to Grant's and an enmity in the South second to none.

Resaca, Georgia, the site of the first major battle in Sherman's Atlanta campaign. George N. Barnard, the most prolific photographer in the last year of the war, took this picture during the winter of 1864–65, after the armies were long gone, leaving behind burned buildings, Confederate earthworks (right rear), and the stumps of trees felled to create a field of clear fire.

briefly fifteen miles to the south for an aborted counterpunch against the pursuing Yankees, then continued another ten miles to Cassville, where they turned at bay. The rebels wrecked the railroad as they retreated, but Uncle Billy's repair crews had it running again in hours and his troops remained well supplied. In twelve days of marching and fighting, Sherman had advanced halfway to Atlanta at a cost of only four or five thousand casualties on each side. The southern government and press grew restive at Johnston's retreats without fighting.

Johnston's most impatient subordinate was John Bell Hood. The crippling of Hood's left arm at Gettysburg and the loss of his right leg at Chickamauga had done

Part of the Resaca battlefield, with graves of Confederate soldiers killed there marked by wooden headboards in the foreground.

nothing to abate his aggressiveness. Schooled in offensive tactics under Lee, Hood had remained with the Army of Tennessee as a corps commander after recovering from his wound at Chickamauga, where his division had driven home the charge that ruined Rosecrans. Eager to give Sherman the same treatment, Hood complained behind his commander's back to Richmond of Johnston's Fabian strategy.

At Cassville, Johnston finally thought the time had come to fight. But ironically it was Hood who turned cautious and let down the side. Sherman's pursuing troops were spread over a front a dozen miles wide, marching on several roads for better speed. Johnston concentrated most of his army on the right under Hood and Leonidas Polk to strike two of Sherman's corps isolated seven miles from any of the others. On May 19 Johnston issued an inspirational order to the troops: "You will now turn and march to meet his advancing columns. . . . Soldiers, I lead you to battle." This seemed to produce the desired effect. "The soldiers were jubilant," recalled a private in the 1st Tennessee. "We were going to whip and rout the Yankees." But confidence soon gave way to dismay. Alarmed by reports that the enemy had worked around to *his* flank, Hood pulled back and called off the attack. The Union threat turned out to have been only a cavalry detachment. But the opportunity was gone; the rebels took up a defensive position and that night pulled back another ten miles to a line (constructed in advance by slaves) overlooking the railroad and the Etowah River through Allatoona Pass.

This latest retreat proved a serious blow to morale. Blaming Hood, Johnston's chief of staff wrote that "I could not restrain my tears when I found we could not strike." Mutual recrimination among Johnston and his corps commanders began to

Allatoona Pass in the distance with the Etowah River in the foreground and the rebuilt trestle of the Western and Atlantic Railroad at the right. Instead of attacking the strong Confederate defenses protecting the pass, Sherman cut loose from the railroad and launched a long flanking march to the right with his whole army.

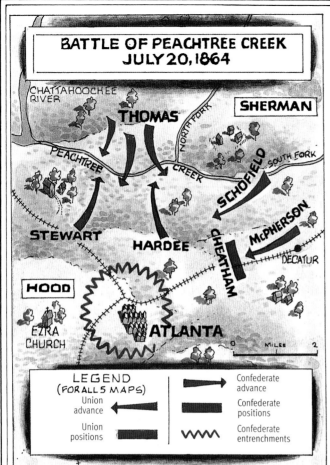

BATTLE OF PEACHTREE CREEK
JULY 20, 1864

CHATTAHOOCHEE RIVER

SHERMAN

THOMAS

NORTH FORK

SCHOFIELD

SOUTH FORK

PEACHTREE CREEK

STEWART

HARDEE

McPHERSON

CHEATHAM

DECATUR

HOOD

EZRA CHURCH

ATLANTA

0   MILES   2

LEGEND
(FOR ALL 5 MAPS)

Union advance → | Confederate advance →
Union positions ▬ | Confederate positions ▬
| Confederate entrenchments ∿∿∿

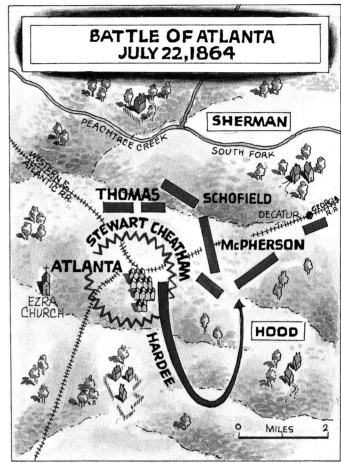

BATTLE OF ATLANTA
JULY 22,1864

PEACHTREE CREEK

SHERMAN

SOUTH FORK

WESTERN & ATLANTIC R.R.

THOMAS

SCHOFIELD

DECATUR

GEORGIA R.R.

STEWART CHEATHAM

McPHERSON

ATLANTA

EZRA CHURCH

HARDEE

HOOD

0   MILES   2

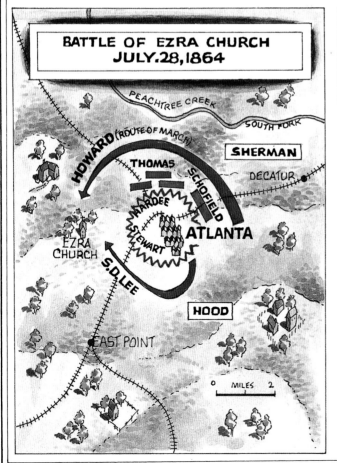

BATTLE OF EZRA CHURCH
JULY 28, 1864

PEACHTREE CREEK

SOUTH FORK

HOWARD (ROUTE OF MARCH)

THOMAS

SCHOFIELD

SHERMAN

DECATUR

HARDEE

EZRA CHURCH

STEWART

ATLANTA

S.D. LEE

HOOD

EAST POINT

0   MILES   2

BATTLE OF JONESBORO
AUG.-SEPT. 1,1864

HOOD

DECATUR

EZRA CHURCH

ATLANTA

CHATTAHOOCHEE R.

SANDTOWN

HOWARD

THOMAS

SCHOFIELD

HARDEE

EAST POINT

ROUGH & READY

FLINT R.

FAIRBURN

THOMAS

HOWARD

HARDEE

SHERMAN

JONESBORO

0   MILES   6

THE
CAMPAIGN
FOR ATLANTA
MAY-SEPT. 1864

0   MILES   20

TENNESSEE

CHATTANOOGA

TENNESSEE R.

LOOKOUT MT.

MISSIONARY RIDGE

WEST CHICKAMAUGA CREEK

RINGGOLD

SCHOFIELD

ROCKY FACE RIDGE

THOMAS

DUG GAP

DALTON MAY 7

SCHOFIELD

THOMAS

LA FAYETTE

GEORGIA

SNAKE CREEK GAP

RESACA MAY 14-15

McPHERSON

THOMAS

ADAIRSVILLE

SCHOFIELD

OOSTANAULA R.

ROME

CASSVILLE MAY 19

KINGSTON

COOSA R.

ETOWAH R.

ALLATOONA PASS

SHERMAN

ALLATOONA

JOHNSTON

WESTERN & ATLANTIC R.R.

THOMAS

SCHOFIELD

McPHERSON

McPHERSON

THOMAS

KENNESAW MT. JUNE 27

McPHERSON

PINE MOUNTAIN

PUMPKINVINE CR.

MARIETTA

SCHOFIELD JULY 9

DALLAS MAY 25-28

NEW HOPE CHURCH

SMYRNA

PEACHTREE CREEK

SCHOFIELD

THOMAS

JULY 8

CHATTAHOOCHEE R.

DECATUR

ATLANTA

Part of the Confederate breastworks near New Hope Church, photographed by George Barnard after the armies had fought there, buried their dead, and moved on.

plague the army with the same factionalism that had nearly wrecked it under Bragg. Opinion in the government and press was similarly divided: Davis's supporters criticized Johnston, while the anti-Davis faction censured the government for fostering intrigue against the general. In northern Georgia people voted with their feet and took to the roads as refugees, abandoning farms that could have produced food and forage the South desperately needed. In Atlanta a note of apprehension began to creep into the newspapers, though most of them continued to praise Johnston as a "masterful" strategist who was luring Sherman ever deeper into a trap to make his destruction more certain.

But Johnston could not spring the trap at Allatoona, for Sherman never came near the place. Instead he paused to rest his men, repair the railroad, bring up twenty days of supplies, and cut loose from the railroad for another flanking move around Johnston's left. Sherman's objective was a road junction in the piney woods at Dallas, twenty miles in Johnston's rear and not much farther from Atlanta itself. But Johnston's cavalry detected the move in time for the rebels to fall back on the inside track and entrench another line before the Yankees got there. Sharp fighting took place on May 25 and 27 near New Hope Church before both armies settled in for weeks of skirmishing and sniping (in which Leonidas Polk was killed) as each vainly sought an opening for attack or maneuver. "A big Indian war," the frustrated Sherman called it as continual rains turned red clay roads to soft grease. The two armies

Confederate artillerymen dragging a cannon up Kenesaw Mountain. The slope was too steep and rocky for horses, so the men themselves had to tail onto a long rope, called a prolonge, to drag the gun up the mountain.

gradually moved their lines eastward until both were astride the railroad just north of Marietta, where the Confederates entrenched a formidable position along Kenesaw Mountain and its spurs.

Sherman chafed during this impasse. His concern focused not only on the rebels in his front but also on others three hundred miles to the rear. Any significant interference with his rail supply line through Tennessee would cripple Sherman's campaign as decisively as a defeat here in Georgia. And with Nathan Bedford Forrest loose in Mississippi, anything might happen. This hard-bitten cavalryman had mauled the Yankees so often that—as Forrest himself would have said—he had "put the skeer on 'em." Forrest's most recent exploit had been the destruction on

This lithograph is an imaginative rendering of the Union attack in the battle of Kenesaw Mountain. The mountain itself looks more like it belongs in the Alps than the Appalachians.

April 12 of the Union garrison at Fort Pillow on the Mississippi River, where some of his men had murdered black soldiers after they surrendered. When Sherman began his campaign in Georgia, Johnston urged "the immediate movement of Forrest into Middle Tennessee" to cut the railroad. To prevent this, Sherman ordered the garrison commander at Memphis to send out 8,000 men to chase Forrest down. The Federals marched into Mississippi, found Forrest, fought him, and were routed at Brice's Crossroads on June 10 by a force little more than half their size. It was the most humiliating Union defeat in the western theater, but it did divert Forrest from the railroad in Tennessee. Nevertheless, an angry Sherman ordered another and larger expedition out of Memphis to "follow Forrest to the death, if it cost 10,000 lives and breaks the Treasury. There never will be peace in Tennessee till Forrest is dead." This time 14,000 Federals lured half as many rebels into an attack at Tupelo, Mississippi, on July 14 and repulsed them at a high cost in southern casualties, including Forrest himself, who was wounded.

This enabled Sherman to breathe easier about Tennessee—for the time being. The guards he had dropped off along the railroad between Chattanooga and Marietta also managed to keep Johnston's cavalry under Joe Wheeler from doing much damage. But the main rebel force at Kenesaw Mountain appeared to have him stymied as Lee had stalled Grant at Petersburg. Another flanking move on the glutinous roads seemed impossible—it was hard enough to move supplies only six miles from the railhead to the Union right wing. Sherman also feared that constant maneuver and entrenchment without battle was dulling his army's fighting edge. "A fresh furrow in a plowed field will stop the whole column, and all begin to entrench," he grumbled. "We are on the offensive, and . . . must assail and not defend." Reasoning that Johnston expected another turning movement, Sherman decided to "feign on both flanks and assault the center. It may cost us dear but in results would surpass an attempt to pass around."

It cost him dear, but the results were nil. On June 27 several Union divisions assaulted the southern spurs of Kenesaw Mountain near the points where small streams divided Johnston's center from his two wings. As the temperature rose toward a hundred in the shade, Yankees recoiled from breastworks that rivaled those at Petersburg. After the attacks had been beaten back, a Confederate soldier looked around at his fellows. "I never saw so many broken down and exhausted men in my life," he wrote years later. By early afternoon Sherman recognized failure and called off the operation. He had lost 3,000 killed and wounded—small numbers compared with battles in Virginia, but the largest for any engagement so far in Georgia—while inflicting only a fifth as many on the enemy.

Perhaps worse, from the Union viewpoint, the battle of Kenesaw Mountain bolstered southern morale and increased northern frustration. "Everyone feels unbounded confidence in General Johnston," wrote an Atlanta woman, while one of the city's newspapers declared Sherman's army "whipped" and soon to be "cut to pieces." Admittedly the invaders had suffered altogether fewer than 17,000 casualties in the campaign while driving to within twenty miles of Atlanta. But Johnston had lost only 14,000 men compared with Lee's 35,000, and morale in the Army of Tennessee was reported to be "as good as could be desired." After two months of fighting and 90,000 casualties on all fronts, Union armies seemed little if any closer to winning the war than when they started. "Who shall revive the withered hopes that bloomed at the opening of Grant's campaign?" asked the Democratic *New York World*. Even Republicans seemed "discouraged, weary, and faint-hearted," reported a New York diarist. "They ask plaintively, 'Why don't Grant and Sherman do something?'"

CHAPTER TWENTY-FIVE

★ ★ ★ ★ ★

After Four Years of Failure

I

Atlanta was a great prize. Its population had doubled to 20,000 during the war as foundries, factories, munitions plants, and supply depots sprang up at this strategic railroad hub. The fall of Atlanta, said Jefferson Davis, would "open the way for the Federal Army to the Gulf on the one hand, and to Charleston on the other, and close up those rich granaries from which Lee's armies are supplied. It would give them control of our network of railways and thus paralyze our efforts." Because the South invested so much effort in defending the city, Atlanta also became a symbol of resistance and nationality second only to Richmond. As the Petersburg front stabilized to trench warfare, concern in the Confederate capital shifted to Georgia, where mobile warfare resumed as the rains ceased.

Slaves had prepared two more defensive positions between Kenesaw Mountain and the Chattahoochee River, which flowed from northeast to southwest only eight miles from Atlanta. Johnston had told a senator who visited his headquarters on July 1 that he could hold Sherman north of the Chattahoochee for two months. By the time Davis received word of this assurance on July 10, the Yankees had crossed the river. Once again Sherman had sent McPherson swinging around Johnston's left, forcing the rebels to fall back six miles on July 3 and another six to the river on the fourth. Sherman now reached deeper into his bag of tricks. Having always moved around the enemy's left, he instructed McPherson and a cavalry division to make a feint in that direction while another cavalry division and Schofield's infantry corps moved secretly upriver several miles above Johnston's right for a surprise crossing against a handful of cavalry pickets. At one point Yankee troopers swam the river naked except for their cartridge belts and captured the bemused pickets. At another ford, blue horsemen waded dismounted through neck-deep water with their Spencer carbines. "As the rebel bullets began to splash around pretty thick," recalled a Union officer, northern soldiers discovered that they could pump the waterproof metal cartridges into the Spencer's chamber underwater; "hence, all along the line you could see the men bring their guns up, let the water run from the muzzle a

Opposite page: One of Winslow Homer's best Civil War paintings, Defiance: Inviting a Shot Before Petersburg *shows a Confederate soldier standing atop the parapet of his trench, daring Union sharpshooters in the distance to take a shot at him. Homer based this painting on an actual incident; a split second after the moment depicted in the painting, the soldier fell dead with a bullet in his head.*

moment, then take quick aim, fire his piece and pop down again." The astonished rebels called to each other: "Look at them Yankee sons of bitches, loading their guns under water! What sort of critters be they, anyhow?" The pickets surrendered to this submarine assault; Sherman had part of his army across the river on Johnston's flank by July 9. The Confederates pulled back to yet another fortified position behind Peachtree Creek, only four miles from downtown Atlanta. Civilians scrambled for space on southbound trains. Newspapers in the city still uttered defiance, but they packed their presses for a quick departure.

In Richmond, seeking a way to avert calamity, Davis unwisely sent a most trouble-

In this remarkable photograph, Union artillery and infantry of Schofield's corps cross the Chattahoochee River on July 9 on a canvas-covered pontoon boat (an innovation developed by Union engineers) after the cavalry had driven away Confederate pickets and secured the crossing.

some troubleshooter to Georgia on a fact-finding mission. Braxton Bragg, lately Davis's military adviser, consulted mainly with Hood, who was clearly angling for the command and advocated a robust attack. After hearing out Bragg, who urged Davis to appoint Hood in Johnston's place, as well as Lee, who thought Hood aggressive but reckless, Davis decided to give Johnston one last chance: on July 16 he telegraphed the general a request for "your plan of operations." Johnston replied that his plan "must depend upon that of the enemy. . . . We are trying to put Atlanta in condition to be held by the Georgia militia, that army movements may be freer and wider." This hint of an intention to give up Atlanta was the final straw. Next day the thirty-three-year-old Hood replaced Johnston.

This action stirred up a controversy that has echoed down the years. Like Lincoln's removal of McClellan, the removal of Johnston was supported by the cabinet and by the proadministration faction in Congress but condemned by the opposition and deplored in the army. For his part, Sherman professed to be "pleased at this change." "This was just what we wanted," declared Sherman after the war, "to fight on open ground, on any thing like equal terms, instead of being forced to run up against prepared intrenchments." So he said, with benefit of hindsight. But Davis, like Lincoln, preferred generals who would fight. To have lost Atlanta without a battle would have demoralized the South. And whatever else Hood's appointment meant, it meant fight.

Sure enough, two days after taking command Hood tried to squash the Yankees. As events turned out, however, it was the rebels

who got squashed. After crossing the Chattahoochee, Sherman had again sent McPherson on a wide swing—this time to the left—to cut Atlanta's last rail link with the upper South. Schofield followed on a shorter arc, while Thomas's Army of the Cumberland, separated from Schofield by a gap of two miles, prepared to cross Peachtree Creek directly north of Atlanta. Hood saw his chance to hit Thomas separately, but the attack on July 20 started several hours too late to catch the bluecoats in the act of crossing the stream. Five Union divisions drove an equal number of rebels back after the bloodiest combat in the campaign thus far.

Not succeeding at first, Hood tried again. On July 21 he pulled the army back into elaborate defenses ringing the city. After dark Hood sent one corps on an exhausting all-night march to attack the exposed south flank of McPherson's Army of the Tennessee on July 22. They did, but found the flank less exposed than expected. After recovering from their initial surprise the bluecoats fought with ferocity and inflicted half as many casualties on Hood's army in one afternoon as it had suffered in ten weeks under Johnston. But the Confederates exacted a price in return: the death of McPherson, shot from his saddle when he refused to surrender after riding blindly into Confederate lines while trying to restore his own.

Though grieved by the loss of his favorite subordinate, Sherman wasted no time getting on with the job. He gave command of the Army of the Tennessee to Oliver O. Howard, a transplant from the Army of the Potomac. The one-armed Christian General from Maine took his profane midwesterners on another wide swing around the Confederate left and headed south to tear up the one remaining open railroad out of Atlanta. Hood sent a corps to stop them and readied another to follow up with a counterattack. But the Federals handled them so roughly at the Ezra Church crossroads two miles west of the city on July 28 that the rebels had to entrench instead of continuing the attack. Nevertheless, they kept the bluecoats off the railroad.

In three battles during the past eight days Hood's 15,000 casualties were two and one-half times Sherman's 6,000. But southern valor did seem to have stopped the inexorable Yankee advance on Atlanta. Union infantry and artillery settled down for a siege, while Sherman sent his cavalry on raids to wreck the railroad far south of the city. One division of northern horsemen headed for Andersonville to liberate Union captives at the notorious prison, but rebel cavalry headed them off halfway. Six hundred of these Yankee troopers did reach Andersonville—as prisoners. Confederate cavalry and militia prevented other Union detachments from doing more than minimal damage to the railroad, while southern raids in turn on Sherman's supply line fared little better.

Civilians continued to flee the city; some of those who remained were killed by northern shells that rained down on their streets. "War is war, and not popularity-seeking," wrote Sherman in pursuance of his career as Georgia's

This sketch of the site where General McPherson fell was published in Harper's Weekly *soon after he was killed. Note the battlefield debris: two wheels and the limber chest of a disabled cannon; the skeleton of a horse; several cannonballs and an unexploded shell. The sign on the tree and the legend carved into the trunk announce McPherson's death on July 22, 1864.*

SCENE OF M'PHERSON'S DEATH.

most unpopular visitor. The defiant courage of Atlantans who stayed raised the spirits of southerners everywhere. Much of the Confederate press viewed Hood's attacks as victories. The *Atlanta Intelligencer* (published in Macon) predicted that "Sherman will suffer the greatest defeat that any Yankee General has suffered during the war. . . . The Yankee forces will disappear before Atlanta before the end of August."

Opinion north of the Potomac reflected the other side of this coin of southern euphoria. As Sherman closed in on Atlanta during July, northern newspapers had daily predicted the city's capture before the next edition. By early August the forecast had moderated to "a question of a few days," and one reporter confessed himself "somewhat puzzled at the stubborn front presented by the enemy." By the middle of the month a Boston newspaper expressed "much apprehension" while the *New York Times* warned against "these terrible fits of despondency, into which we plunge after each of our reverses and disappointments." In New York a prominent member of the Sanitary Commission feared that "both Grant and Sherman are on the eve of disaster."

II

Indeed, Grant's siege of Petersburg seemed even less successful during those dog days of summer than Sherman's operations against Atlanta. Soldiers on both sides burrowed ever deeper in the trenches at Petersburg to escape the daily toll exacted by sharpshooters and mortars. Grant did not cease his efforts to interdict Lee's supply lines and break through the defenses. During the latter half of June the rebels turned back an infantry drive and a cavalry raid that tried to cut Richmond's remaining three railroads, though the Yankees managed to break all three temporarily. In these actions many of the exhausted veterans and inexperienced new troops in

the Army of the Potomac performed poorly. The vaunted 2nd Corps, bled to a shadow of its former self, made an especially bad showing. And soon afterward Grant had to send away his best remaining unit, the 6th Corps.

This happened because Jubal Early's 15,000 rebels, after driving David Hunter away from Lynchburg in June, had marched down the Shenandoah Valley and crossed the Potomac on July 6. They bowled over a scratch force of Federals at the Monocacy River east of Frederick on July 9 and marched unopposed toward Washington. This seemed a stunning reversal of the fortunes of war. Northern hopes of capturing Richmond were suddenly replaced by fears for the safety of their own capital. The rebels appeared in front of the Washington defenses five miles north of the White House on July 11. Except for convalescents, militia, and a few odds and ends of army units there were no troops to man them, for Grant had pulled the garrison out for service in Virginia. But the fortifications ringing the capital were immensely strong, and Grant, in response to frantic appeals from the War Department, quickly sent the 6th Corps to Washington. These hardened veterans filed into the works just in time to discourage Early from assaulting them.

During the skirmishing on July 12 a distinguished visitor complete with stovepipe hat appeared at Fort Stevens to witness for the first time the sort of combat into which he had sent a million men over the past three years. Despite warnings, President Lincoln repeatedly stood to peer over the parapet as sharpshooters' bullets whizzed nearby. Out of the corner of his eye a 6th Corps captain—Oliver

During the long siege of Petersburg (June 1864–April 1865), both sides extended, deepened, and improved their trenches and earthwork fortifications, anticipating the elaborate trench network on the Western Front in World War I. Seven Union soldiers take a break to pose for the camera while working on the trenches at Petersburg.

Wendell Holmes, Jr.—noticed this ungainly civilian popping up. Without recognizing him, Holmes shouted, "Get down, you damn fool, before you get shot!" Amused by this irreverent command, Lincoln got down and stayed down. With the 6th Corps in his front and other Union troops gathering in his rear, Early wisely decided that it was time to return to Virginia. He did so with only a few scratches, much to Grant's and Lincoln's disgust, because the forces chasing him were divided among four command jurisdictions that could never quite coordinate their efforts.

During their raid some of Early's soldiers partly replenished the Confederacy's coffers; they levied $20,000 on Hagerstown and $200,000 on Frederick, while also drinking up the contents of Francis Preston Blair's wine cellar, burning down the Silver Spring home of his son Montgomery, the postmaster general, and putting the torch to the private residence of Maryland's governor. To add further injury to insult, on July 30 two of Early's cavalry brigades rode into Pennsylvania, demanded $500,000 from the citizens of Chambersburg as restitution for Hunter's pillaging in Virginia, and burned the town when they refused to pay.

Early's foray to the outskirts of Washington could not have come at a more inopportune time. Gold soared to 285—and on July 18 Lincoln issued a new call for

The sketch (opposite page) by Charles Reed, a Union soldier, shows General Jubal Early demanding $200,000 from citizens of Frederick on July 9, 1864. They paid, and the town was spared. Three weeks later Early's cavalry demanded $500,000 from Chambersburg, Pennsylvania, and burned the town when the locals could not raise this sum. The two photographs show some of the ruins of Chambersburg. In the picture with horses in the foreground (above) the columns of the burned-out courthouse are in the left background. The other photograph (left) shows the shell of the Baptist church and the remnants of the gas works along Conococheague Creek.

500,000 men, with quota deficiencies to be filled by a draft just before the fall elections. "Lincoln is deader than dead," chortled a Democratic editor.

Angered by the inability of fragmented Union forces to run Early down, Grant cut through the Washington red tape and put Phil Sheridan in charge of a newly created Army of the Shenandoah consisting of the 6th Corps, several brigades from David Hunter's former Army of West Virginia, two divisions recently transferred from Louisiana, and two divisions of Sheridan's own cavalry. Grant ordered Sheridan to go after Early "and follow him to the death." Sheridan was just the man for the job, but it would take him time to organize this composite army. Meanwhile Grant suffered another frustration in his attempt to break Lee's lines at Petersburg.

This was the famous battle of the Crater. In conception it bid fair to become the most brilliant stroke of the war; in execution it became a tragic fiasco. A section in the center of the Union line at Petersburg held by Burnside's 9th Corps lay within 150 yards of an enemy salient on high ground where the rebels had built a strong redoubt. One day in June, Colonel Henry Pleasants of the 48th Pennsylvania, a Schuylkill County regiment containing many coal miners, overheard one of his men growl: "We could blow that damn fort out of existence if we could run a mine shaft under it." A prewar mining engineer, Pleasants liked the idea and proposed it to his division commander, who submitted it to Burnside, who approved it. Pleasants put his regiment to work excavating a tunnel more than five hundred feet long. They did so with no help from the army's engineers, who scoffed at the project as "claptrap and nonsense" because ventilation problems had limited all previous military tunnels in history to less than four hundred feet. Meade consequently put no faith in the enterprise. Nevertheless, the 48th Pennsylvania improvised its own tools and found its own lumber to timber the shaft. Burnside borrowed an old-fashioned theodolite from a civilian so Pleasants could triangulate for distance and direction. Pleasants also rigged a coal-mining ventilation shaft with a fire at the base to create a draft and pull in fresh air through a tube. In this manner the colonel confounded the skeptics. His men dug a shaft 511 feet long with lateral galleries at the end each nearly forty feet long under the Confederate line in which they placed four tons of gunpowder. Reluctantly converted, Meade and Grant authorized Burnside to spring the mine and attack with his corps through the resulting gap.

The sidewhiskered general's enthusiasm for the project had grown steadily from the time it began on June 25. Here was a chance to redeem his failure at Fredericksburg by cap-

These drawings show the various cross-sections and diagrams of the tunnel and gallery for the mine to be exploded under Confederate lines at Petersburg.

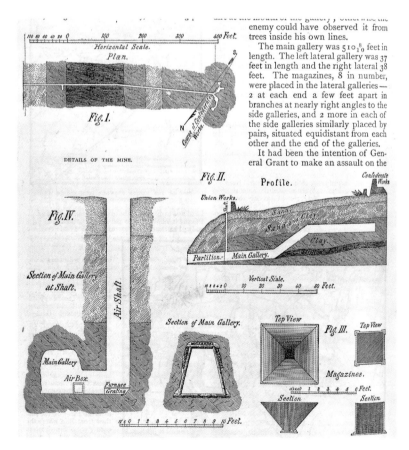

enemy could have observed it from trees inside his own lines.

The main gallery was $510\frac{8}{10}$ feet in length. The left lateral gallery was 37 feet in length and the right lateral 38 feet. The magazines, 8 in number, were placed in the lateral galleries — 2 at each end a few feet apart in branches at nearly right angles to the side galleries, and 2 more in each of the side galleries similarly placed by pairs, situated equidistant from each other and the end of the galleries.

It had been the intention of General Grant to make an assault on the turing Petersburg and winning the war. Burnside's corps contained four divisions. Three had been worn down by combat since the Wilderness; the fourth was fresh, having seen no action except guarding rear-area supply lines. It was a black division, and few officers in the Army of the Potomac from Meade down yet believed in the fighting capacity of black troops. Burnside was an exception, so he designated this fresh division to lead the assault. The black soldiers received special tactical training for this task. Their morale was high; they were eager "to show the white troops what the colored division could do," said one of their officers. Grant arranged a diversion by Hancock's corps north of the James which pulled several of Lee's divisions away from the Petersburg front. Everything seemed set for success when the mine was scheduled to explode at dawn on July 30.

Only hours before this happened, however, Meade—with Grant's approval—ordered Burnside to send in his white divisions first. Meade's motive seems to have been lack of confidence in the inexperienced black troops, though in later testimony before the Committee on the Conduct of the War Grant mentioned another reason as well: if things went wrong, "it would then be said . . . that we were shoving these people ahead to get killed because we did not care anything about them. But that could not be said if we put white troops in front."

Apparently demoralized by the last-minute change of his battle plan, Burnside lost all control over the operation. The commander of the division designated to lead the assault (chosen by drawing straws!), James H. Ledlie, had a mediocre

This drawing by Harper's Weekly *artist Alfred R. Waud, who was present, shows the advance on the crater by black soldiers. Note the flags planted on the edge of the crater by the white troops who had attacked earlier, and the church spires of Petersburg in the distance.*

record and an alcohol problem. During the assault he stayed behind in the trenches drinking rum cadged from the surgeon. With no preparation and without leadership, his men attacked in disordered fashion. The explosion blew a hole 170 feet long, 60 feet wide, and 30 feet deep. One entire rebel regiment and an artillery battery were buried in the debris. Confederate troops for a couple of hundred yards on either side of the crater fled in terror. When Ledlie's division went forward, its men stopped to gawk at the awesome spectacle. Mesmerized by this vision of what they supposed Hell must be like, many of them went *into* the crater instead of fanning out left and right to roll up the torn enemy flanks. The two following white divisions did little better, degenerating into a disorganized mob as rebel artillery and mortars found the range and began shooting at the packed bluecoats in the crater as at fish in a barrel. Frantic officers, with no help from Burnside or from division commanders, managed to form fragments of brigades for a further penetration. But by midmorning a southern division commanded by William Mahone was ready for a counterattack. The black troops who had finally pushed their way through the milling or retreating white Yankees caught the brunt of Mahone's assault. As on other fields, rebel soldiers enraged by the sight of black men in uniform murdered several of them who tried to surrender. When it was all over, the 9th Corps had nothing to show for its

This photograph shows some of the survivors of the black division's attack on the crater. They look discouraged, as well they might, given the mismanagement of the attack by the high command.

This photograph of the crater was made in April 1865 after the Confederates abandoned Petersburg. The soldier sitting in the left center, at the end of one of the shafts where gunpowder was set off, shows the scale of the explosion and destruction.

big bang except 4,000 casualties (against fewer than half as many for the enemy), a huge hole in the ground, bitter mutual recriminations, and new generals commanding the corps and one of its divisions. Grant pronounced the epitaph in a message to Halleck: "It was the saddest affair I have witnessed in the war. Such opportunity for carrying fortifications I have never seen and do not expect again to have."

III

The months of July and August 1864 brought a greater crisis of northern morale than the same months in 1862. Even the spectacular achievement of David Farragut's fleet in Mobile Bay did little at first to dispel northern depression. As the fog lifted on the morning of August 5, Farragut took his fourteen wooden ships and four Monitors past the largest of the three forts guarding the entrance to Mobile Bay. During a terrific duel between fort and fleet, Farragut climbed the mainmast to see what was going on above the smoke from the guns of his flagship U.S.S. *Hartford*. A quartermaster lashed the admiral to the rigging and thereby created an unforgettable image in the rich traditions of the U.S. navy. Farragut soon added a memorable phrase as well. The rebels had scattered mines across the channel. One of them blew up the leading Monitor and sent her to the bottom with more than ninety of her crew. This halted the whole fleet under the punishing guns of the fort. Refusing to countenance retreat, Farragut shouted, "Damn the torpedoes! Full speed ahead." He took his flagship through the minefield safely, followed by the rest of the fleet. When they reached the bay they pounded into submission a rebel flotilla led by the giant ironclad C.S.S. *Tennessee*, the most redoubtable but also one of the most unwieldy ships afloat. During the next three weeks, combined operations by the navy and one army division captured the three forts. Though the city of Mobile thirty miles to the north at the head of the bay remained in Confederate hands, this last blockade-running port in the Gulf east of Texas was out of business.

The dimensions of Farragut's victory were more apparent to the North in retrospect than in August, when so much dismal attention was focused on the apparent lack of progress in Virginia and Georgia. Defeatism and a desire for peace spread from the copperheads like

This famous lithograph shows Admiral Farragut lashed to the rigging of his flagship U.S.S. Hartford *during the battle of Mobile Bay. The Monitor U.S.S.* Tecumseh *had just been sunk by a Confederate mine, and Farragut is shouting to his helmsman: "Damn the torpedoes! Full speed ahead," to lead the rest of the Union warships through the minefield.*

The C.S.S. Tennessee *was photographed after her capture in the battle of Mobile Bay. Armed with six rifled canons and sheathed in iron armor, she gave Farragut's fleet a hard fight but surrendered after several Union ships closed on her and cut her rudder chains.*

widening rings from a stone thrown in the water. By the beginning of August the veteran Republican leader Thurlow Weed was convinced that "Lincoln's reelection [is] an impossibility. . . . The people are wild for peace."

Clement L. Vallandigham had returned from his Canadian exile in June to attend an Ohio Democratic convention which denounced this "unnecessary war" and adopted resolutions calling for an "immediate cessation of hostilities" to negotiate "a just and lasting peace." Not wishing to revive Vallandigham's martyrdom, Lincoln decided to leave him alone. Aware that the Ohio copperhead had been elected "Grand Commander" of a shadowy organization known as the Sons of Liberty—which Republican propaganda pumped up to a vast pro-Confederate conspiracy—the administration probably hoped that if given enough rope he would hang himself. Instead, Vallandigham's return seemed to kindle a forest fire of peace resolutions in Democratic district conventions throughout the North. It appeared that the peace faction would control the party's national convention beginning in Chicago on August 29.

Believing that all was lost, the mercurial Horace Greeley wrote to the president in July. "Our bleeding, bankrupt, almost dying country," he declaimed, "longs for peace—shudders at the prospect of fresh conscriptions, of further wholesale devastations, and of new rivers of human blood." Greeley had learned that two Confederate envoys were at Niagara Falls, Canada, supposedly bearing peace proposals from Jefferson Davis. "I entreat you," Greeley wrote Lincoln, "to submit overtures for pacification to the Southern insurgents." The president responded immediately, authorizing Greeley to bring to Washington under safe conduct "any person anywhere professing to have any proposition of Jefferson Davis in writing, for peace, embracing the restoration of the Union and abandonment of slavery."

Lincoln knew perfectly well that Davis had not authorized negotiations on such conditions. He also knew that the rebel agents had come to Canada not to negotiate peace but to stir up antiwar opposition in the North. Union detectives had infiltrated copperhead groups that were in contact with these agents in Canada. The detectives had uncovered a series of bizarre plots linked to the Richmond government. Confederate leaders shared with Republicans the conviction that a potent fifth column of southern sympathizers in the Midwest stood poised for an uprising to take their states out of the Union and establish a separate peace with the Confederacy. That this "Northwest Conspiracy" existed only in the dreams of fringe elements among the Peace Democrats did not prevent it from becoming a crucial factor in the calculations of both governments in 1864.

To the War and State departments in Richmond came reports from Confederate spies of "a perfect organisation . . . of formidable character" in the lower Midwest variously known as the Knights of the Golden Circle, the Order of American Knights, or the Sons of Liberty and containing half a million members "for the purpose of revolution and the expulsion or death of the abolitionists and free negroes." Perhaps the most influential such report came from Captain Thomas C. Hines, a Kentuckian and a scout with John Hunt Morgan's cavalry brigade which had done so much damage behind Union lines in Kentucky during 1862–63. In July 1863 Morgan had led a raid across the Ohio River into the North. After a long chase through southern Indiana and Ohio, Union cavalry had finally captured Morgan and most of his men, including Hines. Imprisoned in the Ohio penitentiary, Morgan and Hines along with several other officers made a spectacular tunnel escape in November 1863. They returned to the Confederacy after thrilling adventures of derring-do. These credentials helped Hines persuade southern leaders of the potential for Canadian-based sabotage operations against the North. In a secret session on February 15, 1864, the Confederate Congress appropriated $5 million for this purpose. Jefferson Davis dispatched Hines to Canada with instructions to take charge of other escaped rebel prisoners there and to carry out "appropriate enterprises of war against our enemies." On his way through the North, Hines was to "confer with the leading persons friendly or attached to the cause of the Confederacy, or who may be advocates of peace, and do all in your power to induce our friends to organize and prepare themselves to render such aid as circumstances may allow."

The Confederate government also sent a number of civilian agents by blockade runner to Canada. Leaders of this group were Jacob Thompson, a former U.S. secretary of the interior in the Buchanan administration, and Clement C. Clay, former U.S. senator from Alabama. Both men had many friends among northern Democrats. During the summer of 1864 these rebel agents conferred with dozens of Peace Democrats (including Vallandigham before he returned to the United States) at various cities in Canada, especially St. Catharines near Niagara Falls. They plotted a fantastic variety of activities ranging from Confederate subsidies of Democratic newspapers and of peace candidates for state offices to the capture of a Union gunboat on Lake Erie and the liberation of Confederate prisoners at Johnson's Island on that lake and at Camp Douglas near Chicago. Some of these operations actually occurred. Thompson channeled funds to newspapers, to organizers of peace rallies, and to the Democratic candidate for governor in Illinois. Rebel agents distributed weapons and canisters of "Greek fire" to copperheads. Hines's arson squad of southern soldiers who had escaped from Union prisons filtered back into the states and managed to destroy or damage a half-dozen military steamboats at St. Louis, an army warehouse at Mattoon, Illinois, and several hotels in New York City. They also carried out a daring raid

Mississippian Jacob Thompson had served six terms in the U.S. Congress before becoming secretary of the interior in the Buchanan administration. He resigned in January 1861 to join the Confederacy. From Canada in 1864 he tried to incite armed uprisings by escaped Confederate prisoners of war and copperheads in Northern states, without success. He blamed his failure on the arrest of several copperheads by federal agents.

across the border to rob the banks of St. Albans, Vermont. The success of Canadian-based rebel operations, however, was inhibited by two contradictions. First, Hines and his colleagues were trying to prod *Peace* Democrats into *war* against their own government. A few bellicose copperheads did hide caches of arms in anticipation of the glorious day of insurrection against Union arsenals and POW camps. But that day never came, for these "leaders" could not mobilize their followers. The vast army of Sons of Liberty ready to rise and overthrow Lincoln's tyranny turned out to be a phantom. No fewer than five planned "uprisings" died a-borning.

The first was intended to coincide with Vallandigham's return to Ohio in June. His expected arrest was to be the signal. But the administration left Vallandigham alone. Hopes next turned to the Democratic convention scheduled to open in Chicago on July 4. Anticipating an attempt by the government or by Republican vigilantes to interfere with the gathering, the Canadian plotters intended to fan the ensuing riot into a rebellion. But the uncertain military situation caused the Democratic National Committee to postpone the convention until August 29. Impatient Confederate agents now demanded action on July 20, after Lincoln announced his expected draft call. Hines and his ex-soldiers would "start the ball," and the legions of copperheads would take their arms out of hiding to "join in the play." Thompson was confident of success; a Chicago Democrat had promised two regiments "eager, ready, organized, and armed"; Indiana Sons of Liberty were prepared "to seize and hold Indianapolis and release the prisoners there." Lincoln did issue a draft call on July 18, but copperhead leaders were getting cold feet. One of them confessed himself "overwhelmed with the responsibility of speedy action on so momentous a subject." Others echoed this sentiment; with a groan of exasperation, the rebel agents called off the operation and summoned a half-dozen Sons of Liberty to St. Catharines for a meeting.

The southerners insisted on an irrevocable date of August 16 for an uprising. Again the copperheads demurred, fearing that Federal troops would easily crush them unless a Confederate invasion of Kentucky or Missouri took place at the same time. Unable to promise such an undertaking, the agents agreed to a final postponement until August 29, when the throngs at the Democratic convention would provide a cover for Hines's commandos and Sons of Liberty to gather for an attack on Camp Douglas to release the prisoners. Hines brought seventy men armed with revolvers to Chicago, where they mixed with the crowds and hunted in vain for their allies. They found only a few, who explained that infiltration by Union agents had led to the arrest of several leaders and the strengthening of the guard at Camp Douglas. The plot collapsed. One disappointed copperhead declared angrily that there were "too many political soldiers in the Sons of Liberty. It is as hard to make a real soldier out of a politician as it is to make a silk purse out of a sow's ear."

In truth, the mainstream Peace Democrats shrank from violent counterrevolution in part because their chances of overthrowing Lincoln by legitimate political means seemed ever brighter as the weeks passed. The civilian Confederate agents in Canada recognized this and encouraged the process with rebel gold. But here a second contradiction arose. For Confederates the goal of peace was independence. But most northern Democrats viewed an armistice as the first step toward negotiations for reunion. Thompson and his fellow agents tried to resolve this contradiction with vague doubletalk about an armistice now, to be followed by a cooling-off period, knowing that whatever Peace Democrats wanted to believe might come of such a process, any cessation of the fighting, in the context of midsummer 1864, would be tantamount to a Confederate victory.

Lincoln understood this too; that was why he insisted in his letter to Greeley on reunion and emancipation as *prior conditions* of peace negotiations. Knowing full well that Jefferson Davis insisted on independence and slavery as prior conditions, Lincoln hoped to provoke the southern agents into saying so and thereby demonstrate to the northern people that peace with Union was possible only through military victory. But on this occasion the rebels outmaneuvered Lincoln.

THE COPPERHEAD PLAN FOR SUBJUGATING THE SOUTH.
War and Argument—Cold Steel and Cool Reason—having failed to restore the Union, it is supposed that the South may be *bored* into coming back.
Our Picture represents the successful operation of this exceedingly humane and ingenious device.

This Harper's Weekly *cartoon ridiculed the Democratic plans for bringing the South back into the Union. Humbling themselves before a caricatured southern rebel, northern Democrats plead with him to come back, promising to do anything he wants. Bored by their incessant toadyism, he agrees, just to get rid of them. The short man at the left, with a braying donkey's head above him, is General McClellan, lumped here with the copperheads.*

On July 18 Greeley and John Hay, the president's private secretary, met in Niagara Falls, Canada, with Confederate agents Clement Clay and James Holcombe. Hay handed them a letter from Lincoln offering them safe conduct to Washington to discuss "any proposition which embraces the restoration of peace, the integrity of the whole Union, and the abandonment of slavery." Clay and Holcombe had no authority to negotiate *any* peace terms—that was not their purpose in Canada—much less these terms, which amounted to Confederate surrender. So the Niagara Falls conference came to nothing. But the southerners saw a chance to score a propaganda triumph by "throw[ing] upon the Federal Government the odium of putting an end to all negotiation." They sent a report of the conference to the Associated Press. Saying nothing of southern conditions for peace, they accused Lincoln of deliberately sabotaging the negotiations by prescribing conditions he knew to be unacceptable. "If there be any citizen of the Confederate States who has clung to the hope that peace is possible," wrote Clay and Holcombe, Lincoln's terms "will strip from their eyes the last film of such delusion." And if there were "any patriots or Christians" in the North "who shrink appalled from the illimitable vistas of private misery and public calamity" presented by Lincoln's policy of perpetual war, let them "recall the abused authority and vindicate the outraged civilization of their country."

The response was all the Confederates could have hoped for. Zebulon Vance exploited the affair in his gubernatorial campaign against peace candidate William Holden in North Carolina. Southern newspapers used it to paint lurid new strokes in their portrait of Lincoln the monster. In the North, reported Clay with delight, "all the Democratic presses denounce Mr. Lincoln's manifesto in strong terms, and many Republican presses (among them the New York Tribune) admit it was a blunder. . . . From all that I can see or hear, I am satisfied that this correspondence has tended strongly toward consolidating the Democracy and dividing the Republicans." Greeley did indeed scold Lincoln for giving "to the general eye" the impression that the rebels were "anxious to negotiate, and that we repulse their advances." If nothing was done to correct this impression, "we shall be beaten out of sight next November."

Jefferson Davis did something to neutralize the southern propaganda victory by his response to a simultaneous but less publicized, unofficial peace overture to Richmond by two northerners: James R. Gilmore, a free-lance journalist, and James Jaquess, colonel of an Illinois regiment and a Methodist clergyman. Although conferring on them no official status, Lincoln permitted them to pass through the lines with the renewed hope that they could smoke out Davis's intransigent peace terms. Unwilling to be seen by those in the Confederate peace movement as spurning an opportunity for negotiations, a reluctant Davis and Secretary of State Judah Benjamin talked with Gilmore and Jaquess on July 17. The northerners informally reiterated the same terms Lincoln had stated in his reconstruction proclamation the previous December: reunion, abolition, and amnesty. Davis scorned these terms. "Amnesty, Sir, applies to criminals," he declared. "We have committed no crime. . . . At your door lies all the misery and crime of this war. . . . We are fighting for INDEPENDENCE and that, or extermination, we will have. . . . You may 'emancipate' every negro in the Confederacy, but *we will be free*. We will govern ourselves . . . if we have to see every Southern plantation sacked, and every Southern city in flames."

With Lincoln's agreement, Gilmore published a brief report of this meeting in northern newspapers. His account appeared at the same time as the story of Greeley's meeting with rebel agents at Niagara Falls. After all the publicity, no one could doubt that Davis's irreducible condition of peace was disunion while Lincoln's was Union. This served Lincoln's purpose of discrediting copperhead notions of peace *and* reunion through negotiations. As the president later put it in a message to Congress, Davis "does not attempt to deceive us. He affords us no excuse to deceive ourselves. He cannot voluntarily reaccept the Union; we cannot voluntarily yield it. Between him and us the issue is distinct, simple, and inflexible. It is an issue which can only be tried by war, and decided by victory."

But in the dejected state of northern morale during August, Democratic newspapers were able to slide around the awkward problem of Davis's conditions by pointing to Lincoln's second condition—emancipation—as the real stumbling block to peace. "Tens of thousands of white men must yet bite the dust to allay the negro mania of the President," according to a typical Democratic editorial. "Is there any man that wants to be shot down for a niger?" asked a Connecticut soldier. "That is what we are fighting for now and nothing else." Even staunch Republicans condemned Lincoln's "blunder" of making emancipation "a fundamental article," for it "has given the disaffected and discontented a weapon that doubles their power of mischief." Henry J. Raymond, editor of the *New York Times* and chairman of the Republican National Committee, told Lincoln on August 22 that "the tide is setting strongly against us." If the election were held now, party leaders in crucial states believed they would lose.

These reports filled Lincoln with dismay. He denied that he was "now carrying on this war for the sole purpose of abolition. It is & will be carried on so long as I am President for the sole purpose of restoring the Union. But no human power can subdue this rebellion without using the Emancipation lever as I have done." Lincoln pointed out to War Democrats that some 130,000 black soldiers and sailors were fighting for the Union: "If they stake their lives for us they must be prompted by the strongest motive—even the promise of freedom. And the promise being made, must be kept." To abandon emancipation "would ruin the Union cause itself. All recruiting of colored men would instantly cease, and all colored men now in our service would instantly desert us. And rightfully too. Why should they give their lives for us, with full notice of our purpose to betray them? . . . Abandon all the posts now possessed by black men, surrender all these advantages to the enemy, & we would be compelled to abandon the war in 3 weeks." Besides, there was the moral question: "There have been men who have proposed to me to return to slavery the black warriors of Port Hudson & Olustee [a battle in Florida in which black soldiers fought]. I should be damned in time & in eternity for so doing. The world shall know that I will keep my faith to friends & enemies, come what will."

This seemed clear enough. But the pressure to back away from a public commitment to abolition as a condition for negotiations grew almost irresistible. At the same time Lincoln was well aware of a move among some Republicans to call a new convention and nominate another candidate. The motive force of this drive was a belief that Lincoln was a sure loser; but many of its participants were radicals who considered his reconstruction and amnesty policy too *soft* toward rebels. These crosscutting pressures during August made Lincoln's life a hell; no wonder his photographs from this time show an increasing sadness of countenance; no wonder he could never escape that "tired spot" at the center of his being.

This most familiar of Lincoln photographs was taken at Mathew Brady's studio in Washington on January 8, 1864. It was the model for Daniel Chester French's sculpture in the Lincoln Memorial on the Mall in Washington.

Lincoln almost succumbed to demands for the sacrifice of abolition as a stated condition of peace. On August 17 he drafted a letter to a War Democrat saying that if Davis wanted to know what he would do if Davis offered peace and reunion, "saying nothing about slavery, let him try me." Then, on August 22, the Republican National Committee met in New York. Speaking through Henry Raymond, they urged Lincoln to send a commissioner *"to make distinct proffers of peace to Davis . . . on the sole condition of acknowledging the supremacy of the constitution,*—all the other questions to be settled in a convention of the people of all the States." The idea was to make a public relations gesture, not an abandonment of emancipation, which would meet a rebuff from Davis and thus "plant seeds of disaffection in the south, dispel all the delusions about peace that prevail in the North . . . and reconcile public sentiment to the War, the draft, & the tax as inevitable *necessities.*"

Lincoln initially authorized Raymond himself to go to Richmond and "propose, on behalf [of] this government, that upon the restoration of the Union and the national authority,

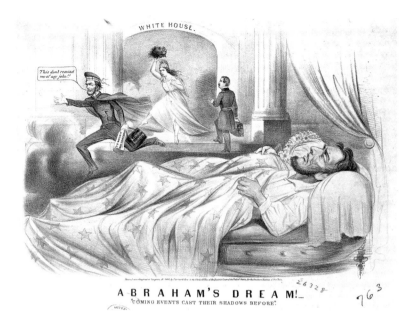

ABRAHAM'S DREAM!—
"COMING EVENTS CAST THEIR SHADOWS BEFORE".

This Democratic cartoon was published before the Union military victories in September that turned around prospects for Lincoln's reelection. While Lincoln sleeps, he has a nightmare in which the Goddess of Liberty emerges from the White House bearing the severed head of a black man, which she seems ready to throw at the fleeing Lincoln while General McClellan walks calmly into the White House to claim the presidency.

the war shall cease at once, all remaining questions to be left for adjustment by peaceful modes"—but then pulled back. On August 25 he met with Raymond and convinced him that "to follow his plan of sending a commission to Richmond would be worse than losing the Presidential contest—it would be ignominiously surrendering it in advance." Whatever the purport of this ambiguous statement, recorded by one of Lincoln's private secretaries, Raymond did not go to Richmond, nor did Lincoln send his "let Jefferson Davis try me" letter. His peace terms remained Union *and* emancipation. The president fully anticipated defeat in November on this platform. "I am going to be beaten," he told an army officer, "and unless some great change takes place *badly* beaten." On August 23 he wrote his famous "blind memorandum" and asked cabinet members to endorse it sight unseen: "This morning, as for some days past, it seems exceedingly probable that this Administration will not be re-elected. Then it will be my duty to so co-operate with the President elect, as to save the Union between the election and the inauguration; as he will have secured his election on such ground that he can not possibly save it afterwards."

Lincoln expected George B. McClellan to be the next president. McClellan was the most popular Democrat and the most powerful symbol of opposition to Lincoln's war policies. But there was uncertainty about his position on the peace plank to be submitted by Vallandigham, chairman of the resolutions subcommittee of the platform committee. In a recent address at West Point, McClellan had seemed to sanction the cause of Union through military victory. This caused the Peace Demo-

This anti-McClellan broadside draws a stark contrast between a future of Union and Liberty under Lincoln and one of Union and Slavery under McClellan. Lincoln shakes the hand of an honest free laborer (symbolized by his cap and the saw in his hand) while black and white children issue forth from a schoolhouse. The contrasting scene shows McClellan shaking hands with Jefferson Davis while slaves are auctioned in the background. This positive portrayal of an integrated school as a Republican goal was extremely unusual in 1864.

UNION AND LIBERTY!   AND   UNION AND SLAVERY!

Published by M. W. Siebert, Printer, 25 Centre Street, Cor. of Reade.

crats to look elsewhere, though they could apparently find no one except Thomas Seymour of Connecticut, who had lost the gubernatorial election in 1863, or Governor Horatio Seymour of New York—who refused to be a candidate. Nevertheless, the peace faction would command close to half of the delegates and might jeopardize McClellan's chances by bolting the party if the convention nominated him. Behind the scenes, McClellan's principal adviser assured doubters that "the General is for peace, not war. . . . If he is nominated, he would prefer to restore the Union by peaceful means, rather than by war." McClellan himself reportedly told a St. Louis businessman on August 24: "If I am elected, I will recommend an immediate armistice and a call for a convention of all the states and insist upon exhausting all and every means to secure peace without further bloodshed."

Doubts about McClellan's peace credentials persisted, however, so the party "bridged the crack" between its peace and war factions by nominating the general on a peace platform and giving him as a running mate Congressman George Pendleton of Ohio, a close ally of Vallandigham. Scion of an old Virginia family, Pendleton had opposed the war from the start, had voted against supplies, and expressed sympathy with the South. The platform condemned the government's "arbitrary military arrests" and "suppression of freedom of speech and of the press." It pledged to preserve "the rights of the States unimpaired" (a code phrase for slavery). On these matters all Democrats could agree. More divisive (but adopted almost unanimously) was the plank drafted by Vallandigham: "After four years of failure to restore the Union by the experiment of war . . . [we] demand that immediate efforts be made for a cessation of hostilities, with a view to an ultimate convention of the states, or other peaceable means, to the end that, at the earliest practicable moment, peace may be restored on the basis of the Federal Union."

This crucial resolution made peace the first priority and Union a distant second. Republicans and Confederates alike interpreted it thus, and responded accordingly. "It contemplates surrender and abasement," wrote a New York Republican. "Jefferson Davis might have drawn it." Alexander Stephens declared joyfully that "it presents . . . the first ray of real light I have seen since the war began." The *Charleston Mercury* proclaimed that McClellan's election on this platform "must lead to peace and our independence . . . [provided] that for the next two months *we hold our own and prevent military success by our foes*."

But . . . From the diary of George Templeton Strong, September 3, 1864: "Glorious news this morning—Atlanta taken at last!!! . . . It is (coming at this political crisis) the greatest event of the war."

Or as a Republican newspaper headlined the news:

VICTORY

IS THE WAR A FAILURE?

OLD ABE'S REPLY TO THE CHICAGO CONVENTION

CONSTERNATION AND DESPAIR AMONG THE COPPERHEADS

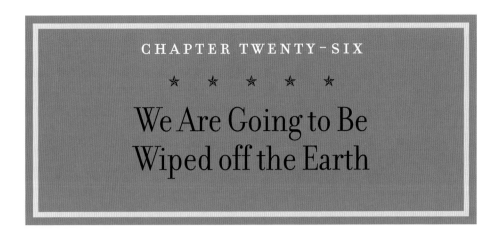

CHAPTER TWENTY-SIX

★ ★ ★ ★ ★

We Are Going to Be Wiped off the Earth

I

It happened this way. While Sherman's and Hood's cavalry had gone off on futile raids into each other's rear during the first half of August, the Union infantry had continued to probe unsuccessfully toward the railroad south of Atlanta. When all but one blue corps suddenly disappeared on August 26, Hood jubilantly concluded that Sherman had retreated. But celebrations by Atlantans proved premature. Sherman had withdrawn nearly all of his army from the trenches, all right, but they were marching *south* to slice across the roads and railroads far beyond Confederate defenses. As the Democrats met in Chicago to declare the war a failure, northern soldiers seven hundred miles away were making "Sherman neckties" out of the last open railroad into Atlanta by heating the rails over a bonfire of ties and twisting the iron around trees.

Hood woke up to the truth a day too late. On August 30 he sent two corps against the enemy at Jonesborough twenty miles south of Atlanta. They found the Yankees too strong and were repulsed with heavy loss. Next day Sherman counterattacked and mauled the rebels. To avoid being cut off and trapped, Hood evacuated Atlanta on September 1 after destroying everything of military value in it. Next day the bluecoats marched in with bands blaring Union songs and raised the American flag over city hall. Sherman sent a jaunty wire to Washington: "Atlanta is ours, and fairly won."

The impact of this event cannot be exaggerated. Cannons boomed hundred-gun salutes in northern cities. Newspapers that had bedeviled Sherman for years now praised him as the greatest general since Napoleon. In retrospect the victory at Mobile Bay suddenly took on new importance as the first blow of a lethal one-two punch. "Sherman and Farragut," exulted Secretary of State Seward, "have knocked the bottom out of the Chicago platform." The *Richmond Examiner* reflected glumly that "the disaster at Atlanta" came "in the very nick of time" to "save the party of Lincoln from irretrievable ruin. . . . [It] obscures the prospect of peace, late so bright. It will also diffuse gloom over the South." Gloom became a plentiful commodity indeed. "Never until now did I feel hopeless," wrote a North Carolinian,

Opposite page: Sherman and his troops were not the first to burn a large part of Atlanta. When the Confederates evacuated the city on the night of September 1–2, 1864, General Hood ordered the destruction of everything of military value that could not be carried away. The Confederates destroyed a rolling mill and blew up an ammunition train, leaving a landscape in Atlanta's industrial district that looked like this.

This drawing shows how soldiers made "Sherman neckties" of southern railroads. In the background, several soldiers are prying up the rails while another group heats them over a bonfire of ties. In the foreground, soldiers wrap the heated rails around trees to make "neckties."

"but since God seems to have forsaken us I despair." The South Carolina diarist Mary Boykin Chesnut saw doom approaching. "Since Atlanta I have felt as if all were dead within me, forever," she wrote. "We are going to be wiped off the earth."

Far to the north George B. McClellan digested the news of Atlanta as he wrote his letter accepting the Democratic nomination. If he endorsed the platform, or said nothing about it, he would by implication commit himself to an armistice and negotiations. McClellan felt great pressure from the party's peace faction to do just that.

But McClellan's "Eastern friends"—War Democrats including the banker August Belmont, chairman of the Democratic National Committee—convinced him that if once stopped, the war could not be started again; an armistice without conditions would mean surrender of the Union. After Atlanta such a proposal would stultify his candidacy. So McClellan's letter released on September 8 repudiated the "four years of failure" plank. "I could not look in the faces of gallant comrades of the army and navy . . . and tell them that their labor and the sacrifice of our slain and wounded brethren had been in vain," he wrote. No, when "our present adversaries are ready for peace, on the basis of the Union," negotiations could begin in "a spirit of conciliation and compromise. . . . The Union is the one condition of peace—we ask no more."

Peace Democrats fumed that McClellan had betrayed them. They held hurried meetings to consider nominating another candidate. But nobody seemed to want this dubious honor, and the revolt subsided. Most Peace Democrats including Vallandigham eventually returned to the fold—though they campaigned mainly for the party and its platform rather than for McClellan.

A similar process occurred in the Republican party. The news from Atlanta dissolved the movement for a new convention to replace Lincoln. The president was now a victorious leader instead of a discredited loser. Only John C. Frémont's splinter candidacy stood in the way of a united party. Behind the scenes, radicals negotiated Frémont's withdrawal on September 22 in return for Montgomery Blair's resignation from the cabinet. Though some radicals remained less than enthusiastic about Lincoln, they willingly went forth to assail the Democratic party's platform.

After a slow start in the Shenandoah Valley, Phil Sheridan soon gave Republicans more cheering news. Mindful of Grant's injunction to follow Jubal Early "to the death," Sheridan was also aware of the long record of Union disasters in the Valley. Therefore his Army of the Shenandoah sparred carefully with Early's rebels for six weeks without driving them any farther south than Winchester. Intelligence reports

LET THE PLATFORM ALONE
IF YOU DONT LIKE IT DONT
MEDDLE WITH IT

Maj. Gen. George B. McClellan Whitewashing the Chicago Platform.

This Republican cartoon shows McClellan trying in vain to whitewash the Democratic platform's peace plank while vice-presidential nominee George Pendleton looks on as devilish copperheads (Vallandigham at left) demand that McClellan leave the platform alone and a copperhead snake looks malevolently at McClellan.

of the reinforcement of Early by four divisions from Lee (in fact he had received only two) added to Sheridan's unwonted caution. Taking advantage of this weakening of the Petersburg defenses, Grant in late August had cut the railroad linking the city to the blockade-running port of Wilmington. Forced to lengthen his lines and protect wagon trains hauling supplies around this break, Lee recalled one division from the Valley. Learning of this from Rebecca Wright, a Quaker schoolteacher and Union sympathizer in Winchester, Sheridan decided to strike. On September 19 his 37,000 bluecoats attacked the 15,000 Confederates at Winchester. The wagon train of one Union corps tangled up the troops of another and almost halted the assault before it began. But with much energy and profanity Sheridan straightened out the jam, got his troops into line, and led them forward in an irresistible wave. Northern

The thundering cavalry charge at the climax of the third battle of Winchester on September 19 deserved a heroic color illustration, and here it is. This was one of the few times in the Civil War that a mounted attack against infantry actually succeeded.

We Are Going to Be Wiped off the Earth

cavalry with their rapid-firing carbines played a conspicuous role; two divisions of horsemen even thundered down on Early's left in an old-fashioned saber charge and captured the bulk of the 2,000 rebels who surrendered. "We have just sent them whirling through Winchester," wired Sheridan's chief of staff in a phrase that looked good in the newspapers, "and we are after them to-morrow."

Having lost one-fourth of his army, Early retreated twenty miles to a strong defensive position on Fisher's Hill just south of Strasburg. Sheridan indeed came "after them tomorrow." On September 22 two corps made a feint against Early's entrenched line while a third—mostly West Virginians and Ohioans who had fought through this rugged terrain for three years—worked their way up mountain paths to hit the Confederate left end-on. Bursting out of thick woods with the setting sun at their backs, they crumbled the surprised southern flank like a dry leaf. The Federals again sent Early "whirling" southward some sixty miles to a pass in the Blue Ridge where the rebels holed up to lick their wounds.

"Sheridan has knocked down gold and G. B. McClellan together," wrote a New York Republican. "The former is below 200 [for the first time since May], and the latter is nowhere." Grant weighed in with renewed attacks on both ends of Lee's line south and north of the James River. Though failing to score a breakthrough, Union forces advanced another two miles southwest of Petersburg and captured an important fort only six miles from Richmond. Panic gripped the Confederate capital as provost guards rounded up every able-bodied male under fifty they could find—including two indignant cabinet members—to put them into the trenches. But Lee's veterans stopped the Yankees before they reached these inner defenses. Northern newspapers nevertheless puffed this action into a great victory—pale though it was in comparison with Sheridan's triumphs.

Having followed Early almost to the death, Sheridan proceeded to carry out the second part of Grant's instructions: to render the Valley useless as a highway of

Harper's Weekly *artist Alfred R. Waud made this drawing of Union troops in the field as they advanced against Confederate positions at Fisher's Hill on September 22, 1864.*

invasion into the North and to turn "the Shenandoah Valley [into] a barren waste," thereby depriving the Confederate armies in Virginia of a large part of their food supplies. By October 7 Sheridan could report that they had "destroyed over 2,000 barns filled with wheat, hay, and farming implements; over seventy mills filled with flour and wheat; have driven in front of the army over 4,000 head of stock, and have killed and issued to the troops not less than 3,000 sheep." But this was just the beginning. By the time he was through, Sheridan promised, "the Valley, from Winchester up to Staunton, ninety-two miles, will have little in it for man or beast."

This was playing for keeps. Northern barnburners made little distinction between rebel farmers and those who claimed to be loyal to the Union. The grain and fodder of both would go to the Confederates if not seized or destroyed, or it would be consumed by the guerrillas who swarmed around the army's flanks and rear and tried to sting it to death. One Union officer claimed that Sheridan's swath of destruction had finally "purified" the Valley of partisan bands: "As our boys expressed it, 'we burned out the hornets.'"

It was a hard war and would soon become even harder, down in Georgia and South Carolina. Meanwhile the rebels decided that they could not give up the Shenandoah Valley without another fight. Lee reinforced Early with an infantry division and a cavalry brigade, which caused Sheridan to postpone the planned return of the 6th Corps to the Petersburg front. Leaving his army camped near Cedar Creek fifteen miles south of Winchester, Sheridan entrained for Washington on October 16 for a strategy conference to decide what to do next. While he was gone, Early borrowed a leaf from the book of his mentor Stonewall Jackson and decided to make a surprise attack. On the night of October 18–19 four Confederate divisions silently moved into position for a dawn assault on the two left-flank Union divisions. The surprise was complete. The rudely awakened bluecoats fell back on the next two divisions, communicating their panic and causing the whole Army of the Shenandoah to retreat in a rout four miles down the Valley after losing 1,300 prisoners and eighteen guns.

Early believed he had won a great victory. So did his hungry soldiers, who broke

As Sheridan's men swept through the Shenandoah Valley, they packed everything useful they could in their large wagon train and destroyed the rest. This practice of "area denial" of potential resources to the enemy meant hardship and hunger to the Valley's residents, unionist and Confederate alike.

The hill in the middle distance anchored the Union left near Cedar Creek on the morning of October 19, 1864. Confederate attackers struck this flank at dawn and routed it.

A pencil drawing of Sheridan's famous ride, made at the time by Alfred R. Waud. Meeting Union stragglers, Sheridan cajoled and shamed them into turning around to rejoin the fight.

ranks to forage in the Union camps. But it was only ten o'clock in the morning. The Union cavalry and the 6th Corps, which had not been routed, remained intact with remnants of four broken divisions scattered behind them. And Sheridan was coming. He had returned to Winchester the previous evening. Puzzled at breakfast by the ominous rumbling of artillery off to the south, he saddled up and began his ride into legend. As Sheridan approached the battlefield, stragglers recognized him and began to cheer. "God *damn* you, don't cheer me!" he shouted at them. "If you love your country, come up to the front! . . . There's lots of fight in you men yet! Come up, God damn you! Come up!" By dozens and then hundreds they followed him. Sheridan's performance this day was the most notable example of personal battle-

field leadership in the war. A veteran of the 6th Corps recalled: "Such a scene as his presence and such emotion as it awoke cannot be realized but once in a century."

While across the way Early seemed mesmerized by his victory, Sheridan reorganized his army during the hazy autumn afternoon and sent it forward in a counterattack. With cavalry slashing in from the flanks and infantry rolling ahead like ocean surf, Sheridan's assault sent Early's graybacks reeling back over the morning's battleground. Driving the rebels across Cedar Creek, bluecoats captured a thousand prisoners along with the eighteen guns they lost in the morning and twenty-three more for good measure. Early's army virtually disintegrated as it fled southward in the gathering darkness with blue cavalry picking off most of its wagon train. Within a few hours Sheridan had converted the battle of Cedar Creek from a humiliating defeat into one of the more decisive Union victories of the war.

To follow it up, Grant tried another double swipe at both ends of Lee's line at Petersburg and Richmond. Though unsuccessful, this forced Lee to lengthen his defenses further, until they now stretched thirty-five miles from a point east of Richmond to another one southwest of Petersburg. This line was so thin, Lee informed Davis, that, unless he could get more troops, "I fear a great calamity will befall us."

II

Republicans not only were invigorated by these military triumphs (which led veterans to reenlist and relieved the pressure of the draft) but they also knew how to make the best use of evidence, real and imagined, of continued Democratic involvement with rebel schemes hatched in Canada. The aborted uprising at the Chicago Democratic convention did not put an end to such enterprises. The most bizarre was a botched attempt by rebel agents and northern sympathizers on September 19 to capture the U.S.S. *Michigan*, the sole navy gunboat on Lake Erie, where it guarded the prisoner of war camp at Johnson's Island near Sandusky, and to liberate the prisoners.

More ambitious but equally abortive was a plot for an uprising by copperheads in Chicago and New York on election day. Once again southern agents, assured by a few Democratic desperadoes that—this time—a peace movement uprising would succeed, infiltrated dozens of Confederate ex-soldiers into Chicago, New York and other cities. These infiltrators and their supporters were undone by secret service operatives, who penetrated the loose security of the Sons of Liberty. Federal authorities arrested more than a hundred copperheads and rebels in Chicago and seized a cache of arms. In New York, Benjamin Butler arrived with 3,500 soldiers and ensured a tranquil election day.

In the copperhead stronghold of southern Indiana, provost marshals reportedly uncovered hiding places containing weapons and arrested several prominent members of the Sons of Liberty. When those arrested went on trial in October before a military court, Union agents who had infiltrated the Sons of Liberty implicated prominent Democrats including Vallandigham. Republican newspapers had a field day. Four conspirators were condemned to death; a postwar Supreme Court ruling

General Henry B. Carrington,
photographed here in a Napoleonic pose,
made his most important contributions to
Union victory behind the scenes. A native
of Connecticut, a graduate of Yale, and a
successful lawyer, Carrington moved in
1848 to Ohio where he was an active
abolitionist and a founder of the
Republican party. In 1861 Carrington
recruited several Ohio regiments that
played an important part in securing
West Virginia for the Union. Named
colonel of the 18th Infantry (regular
army), he did not serve with that
regiment in the field during the war.
Instead, he organized Ohio and later
Indiana regiments, earning promotion to
brigadier general for his skills in that
capacity. In 1863–64 he established a
corps of agents who infiltrated the Sons
of Liberty and other copperhead
organizations. These agents supplied
evidence for Carrington to prosecute and
convict several members of these groups
in military courts. The U.S. Supreme
Court later overturned these convictions.

ultimately set them free. But in October 1864 all that lay in the future. Simultaneously with the Indiana treason trials, U.S. Judge-Advocate General Joseph Holt released a report on the Sons of Liberty that portrayed them as a disciplined, powerful organization armed to the teeth and in the pay of Jefferson Davis to help him destroy the Union. The Republican party used the report as a highly effective weapon against the Democrats, equating the opposition party with copperheadism and copperheadism with treason. Democrats condemned the report and the testimony of government detectives as "absolute falsehoods and fabrications . . . too ridiculous to be given a moment's credit."

Lincoln himself did not take the conspiracy threat seriously—and a number of modern scholars take a similar view. The leading historian of midwestern copperheads brands "the great Civil War myth of conspiracies and subversive secret societies" as a "fairy tale," a "figment of Republican imagination" compounded of "lies, conjecture and political malignancy."

This carries revisionism a bit too far. The Sons of Liberty and similar organizations did exist. A few of their leaders—perhaps only a lunatic fringe—did conspire with rebel agents in Canada, receive arms for treasonable purposes, and plot insurrections against the government. Although Vallandigham and other prominent Democrats probably did not participate actively in these plots, some of them did confer with Jacob Thompson in Canada. Vallandigham was "Supreme Grand Commander" of the Sons of Liberty, and he lied under oath when he denied all knowledge of conspiracies at the treason trials of the Chicago conspirators in early 1865. As Thompson wrote in the final report on his Canadian mission, "I have so many papers in my possession, which would utterly ruin and destroy very many of the prominent men in the North."

Whatever the true extent of pro-Confederate activity in the Old Northwest may have been, no one could deny its potency and danger in Missouri. There the shadowy "Order of American Knights" established connections with various guerrilla bands that ravaged the state. Confederate General Sterling Price was designated "military commander" of the O.A.K. In September 1864, Price coordinated an invasion of Missouri with guerrilla attacks behind northern lines that represented a greater threat to Union control there than all the cloudy conspiracies in other parts of the Midwest.

Partisan warfare along the Kansas-Missouri border continued the violence that had begun in 1854. The vicious conflicts between border ruffians and free soil "Jayhawkers" expanded a hundredfold after 1861 as they gained sanction from Confederate and Union governments. The guerrilla fighting in Missouri produced a form of terrorism that exceeded anything else in the war. Jayhawking Kansans and bushwhacking Missourians took no prisoners, killed in cold blood, plundered and pillaged and burned (but almost never raped) without stint. Jayhawkers initiated a scorched-earth policy against rebel sympathizers three years before Sheridan practiced it in the Shenandoah Valley. Guerrilla chieftains, especially the infamous William Clarke Quantrill, initiated the slaughter of unarmed soldiers as well as civilians, whites as well as blacks, long before Confederate troops began murdering captured black soldiers elsewhere. Guerrilla bands in Missouri provided a training ground for outlaw gangs that emerged after the war—most notably the James and Younger brothers.

The war of raid and ambush in Missouri seemed often to have little relation to the larger conflict of which it was a part. But the hit-and-run tactics of the guerrillas, who numbered only a few thousand, tied down tens of thousands of Union soldiers and militia who might otherwise have fought elsewhere. The guerrillas' need for sanctuary in the countryside and the army's search-and-destroy missions forced civilians to choose sides or else suffer the consequences—usually both. Confederate generals frequently attached guerrilla bands to their commands or requested these bands to destroy Union supply lines and bases in conjunction with orthodox operations against northern forces. In August 1862 Quantrill's band captured Independence, Missouri, as part of a raid by rebel cavalry from Arkansas. As a reward Quantrill received a captain's commission in the Confederate army—and thereafter claimed to be a colonel.

The motives of guerrillas and Jayhawkers alike sometimes seemed nothing more than robbery, revenge, or nihilistic love of violence. But ideology also played a part. Having battled proslavery Missourians for nearly a decade, many Jayhawkers were hardened abolitionists intent on destroying slavery and the social structure that it sustained. The notorious 7th Kansas Cavalry—"Jennison's Jayhawkers"—that plundered and killed their way across western Missouri were commanded by an abolitionist colonel, with Susan B. Anthony's brother as lieutenant colonel and John Brown, Jr., as captain of a company. To a man the soldiers were determined to exterminate rebellion and slaveholders in the most literal manner possible. On the other side, guerrilla outlaws such as the James brothers have been celebrated in myth, by Hollywood films, and by some scholars as Robin Hood types or "primitive rebels" who defended small farmers by attacking the agencies of Yankee capitalism—the Union army during the war, banks and railroads afterwards. But in reality the guerrillas tended to be the sons of farmers and planters of southern heritage who were three times more likely to own slaves and possessed twice as much wealth as the average Missourian. To the extent that ideology motivated their depredations, they fought for slavery and Confederate independence.

The most notorious of their leaders was William Clarke Quantrill. The son of an Ohio schoolteacher, Quantrill had drifted around the West until the war came along to give full rein to his particular talents. Without any ties to the South or to slavery, he chose the Confederacy apparently because in Missouri this allowed him to attack all symbols of authority. He attracted to his gang some of the most psychopathic killers in American history. In kaleidoscopic fashion, groups of these men would split off to form their own bands and then come together again for larger raids. An eruption of such activities along Missouri's western border in the spring of 1863 infuriated the Union commander there, Thomas Ewing. A brother-in-law of

These men do not look dangerous, but in this case looks are indeed deceiving. They were hardened killers who rode with Quantrill. Sitting in the center is Frank James; the tall man standing at right is his younger brother Jesse.

An artist for Harper's Weekly *sketched this drawing of Lawrence, Kansas, after Quantrill's raid.*

William T. Sherman, Ewing had learned what Sherman was learning—that this was a war between peoples, not simply between armies. The wives and sisters of Quantrill's men fed and sheltered the guerrillas. Ewing arrested these women and lodged them under guard in Kansas City. There on August 14 a building containing many of them collapsed, killing five of the women.

'This tragedy set in motion a greater one. Inflamed by a passion for revenge, the raiders combined in one large band of 450 men under Quantrill (including the Younger brothers and Frank James) and headed for Lawrence, Kansas, the hated center of free soilism since Bleeding Kansas days. After crossing the Kansas line they kidnapped ten farmers to guide them toward Lawrence and murdered each one after his usefulness was over. Approaching the town at dawn on August 21, Quantrill ordered his followers: "Kill every male and burn every house." They almost did. The first to die was a United Brethren clergyman, shot through the head while he sat milking his cow. During the next three hours Quantrill's band murdered another 182 men and boys and burned 185 buildings in Lawrence. They rode out of town ahead of pursuing Union cavalry and after a harrowing chase made it back to their Missouri sanctuary, where they scattered to the woods.

This shocking act roused the whole country. A manhunt for Quantrill's outlaws netted a few of them, who were promptly hanged or shot. An enraged General Ewing issued his famous Order No. 11 for the forcible removal of civilians from

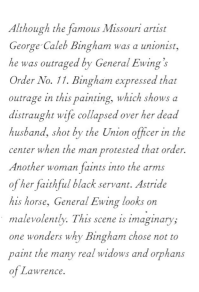

Although the famous Missouri artist George Caleb Bingham was a unionist, he was outraged by General Ewing's Order No. 11. Bingham expressed that outrage in this painting, which shows a distraught wife collapsed over her dead husband, shot by the Union officer in the center when the man protested that order. Another woman faints into the arms of her faithful black servant. Astride his horse, General Ewing looks on malevolently. This scene is imaginary; one wonders why Bingham chose not to paint the many real widows and orphans of Lawrence.

large parts of four Missouri counties bordering Kansas. Union soldiers ruthlessly enforced this banishment of ten thousand people, leaving these counties a wasteland for years. None of this stopped the guerrillas, however. Quite the contrary, their raids became more daring and destructive during the following year.

General Sterling Price, who longed to redeem Missouri from the Yankees, was impressed by Quantrill's prowess. Guerrilla chieftains convinced Price that Missourians would rise *en masse* if a Confederate army invaded the state, which had been denuded of first-line Union troops to deal with Forrest in Tennessee. Scraping together 12,000 cavalry from the trans-Mississippi, Price moved northward through Arkansas and entered Missouri in September 1864. He instructed partisan bands to spread chaos in the Union rear, while the Order of American Knights mobilized civilians to welcome the invaders. The latter enterprise came to nothing, for when Union officers arrested the O.A.K.'s leaders the organization proved to be an empty shell. The guerrillas were another matter. Raiding in small bands all over central Missouri, they brought railroad and wagon transportation to a standstill and even halted boat traffic on the Missouri River.

The most effective partisan was "Bloody Bill" Anderson, who had split from Quantrill with about fifty followers—all of them pathological killers like their leader. Through August and September, Anderson's band struck isolated garrisons and posts, murdering and scalping teamsters, cooks, and other unarmed personnel as well as soldiers. The climax of this saturnalia came at Centralia on September 27. With eighty men including Frank and Jesse James, Bloody Bill rode into town, burned a train and robbed its passengers, and murdered twenty-three unarmed northern soldiers traveling home on furlough. Chased out of town by three companies of militia,

Left: Price's invasion and the swarming bands of Confederate guerrillas forced hundreds of unionist families to flee their farms for refuge in St. Louis. Pictured here is one such family, with the wagons of other refugees in the background.

Right: William C. Anderson was proud of his sobriquet of "Bloody Bill." He expressed that pride in this pose for the photographer.

This painting portrays the 2nd Kansas State Militia crossing the state line into Missouri in October 1864 to join the forces gathering to fight Price's army.

the guerrillas picked up 175 allies from other bands, turned on their pursuers, and slaughtered 124 of the 147 men, including the wounded, whom they shot in the head.

That same day, September 27, Price's invasion met its first setback 140 miles to the south at Pilot Knob, Missouri. There a Union force of 1,000 men under Thomas Ewing held a fort against assaults by 7,000 rebels and inflicted on them 1,500 casualties at the cost of only 200. Deflected by this action from his initial objective of St. Louis—which was filling up with Union reinforcements—Price turned westward toward the capital at Jefferson City. Here he expected to inaugurate a Confederate governor who had accompanied him. But the Federals had strengthened its defenses, so the rebels continued to plunder their way westward along the south bank of the Missouri. Recruits and guerrilla bands swelled Price's ranks—he welcomed Bloody Bill Anderson to Boonville on October 11—but now they were beginning to think of flight rather than attack. Missouri and Kansas militia were swarming in their front; Union cavalry were coming up from behind; and a veteran infantry division was marching fast to cut off escape to the south. In skirmishes and battles east and south of Kansas City from October 20 to 28, these Union forces pummeled Price and drove him south along the border all the way back to Arkansas via the Indian Territory and Texas. Although Price put the best possible face on his invasion—boasting that he had marched 1,400 miles from beginning to end, far more than any other Confederate army—it was a greater disaster than any other southern foray into Union territory. Though he had started with 12,000 men and picked up thousands of recruits along the way, he returned to Arkansas with fewer than 6,000. Organized Confederate resistance in Missouri came to an end.

Best of all from a Union standpoint, the fighting had wrecked most of the guerrilla bands and killed many of their leaders, including Bloody Bill Anderson. Quantrill left Missouri and headed east with the avowed intent of assassinating Lincoln. But he ran afoul of a Union patrol in Kentucky and was killed. In the presidential election, meanwhile, Lincoln had carried Missouri with 70 percent of the vote (most southern sympathizers, of course, were excluded from the polls by refusal or inability to take the loyalty oath). The radical Republican faction triumphed over the conservatives and called a constitutional convention which abolished slavery in Missouri in January 1865. The state's troubles were not over, however, for when the war ended the James and Younger brothers along with other surviving guerrillas were allowed to surrender as soldiers and go free.

III

Sensational revelations of copperhead activities in Missouri helped the Republican effort to discredit the opposition as disloyal. Democrats fought back with their tried-and-true weapon—racism. On this issue the party remained united and consistent. Sixty-five of sixty-eight Democratic congressmen had voted against the Thirteenth Amendment, denying it the necessary two-thirds majority in the House. These congressmen also published a manifesto denouncing the enlistment of black soldiers as a vile Republican scheme to establish "the equality of the black and white races." Democratic opposition forced compromises in a Republican bill to equalize the pay of black and white soldiers. Under the terms of the militia act passed in July 1862, blacks enrolled in the army were regarded as laborers and paid several dollars a month less than white soldiers. A concession to prejudice, this provision was blatantly inconsistent with the combat status of 100,000 black soldiers by 1864. In response to bitter protests by abolitionists and incipient mutiny among black troops, Republicans sponsored a law for retroactive equalization of pay. But a coalition of Democrats who opposed any equalization and conservative Republicans who questioned the retroactive clause prevented passage. To satisfy the latter and enact the bill, Congress made equal pay retroactive only to January 1, 1864—except for blacks who had been free before the war, who received equal pay from date of enlistment.

Having gained votes in 1862 by tarring Republicans with the brush of racial equality, Democrats expected to do the same in 1864. The vulgarity of their tactics almost surpasses belief. An editor and a reporter for the *New York World*, McClellan's most powerful newspaper supporter, coined a new word with their anonymous pamphlet *Miscegenation: The Theory of the Blending of the Races*. Pretending to be Republicans, the authors recommended "miscegenation" as a solution of the race problem. This fusion, the pamphlet declared, would particularly "be of infinite service to the Irish." If the Republicans were reelected they would prosecute the war to "its final fruit, to the blending of the white and the black." Although the Democratic press tried to pump up this hoax into a serious Republican program, few readers except confirmed copperheads seemed to take it seriously.

Democrats nevertheless exploited the miscegenation issue *ad nauseam*. The Emancipation Proclamation became the Miscegenation Proclamation. The "Benediction" of a leaflet entitled "Black Republican Prayer" invoked "the blessings of Emancipation throughout our unhappy land" so that "illustrious, sweet-scented Sambo [may] nestle in the bosom of every Abolition woman, that she may be quickened by the pure blood of the majestic African." Campaign pamphlets and newspapers reported that Butler's occupation of New Orleans had led to the birth of "a great many" mixed-race infants and that five thousand mulatto babies had been born in Washington since 1861. This, declared a Democratic pamphlet, was "what the President means by 'Rising to the Occasion.'"

"Abraham Africanus the First" was of course the chief target of the tar brush. "Passing the question as to his taint of negro blood," commented a Catholic weekly,

This crude racist cartoon reflects one of the dominant themes of Democratic campaign rhetoric during the 1860s. It purports to show a "miscegenation ball" at the headquarters of the Lincoln Central Campaign Club in New York City. White men and women dance with black partners while off to the side, under a Lincoln banner, interracial couples kiss and fondle each other.

THE MISCEGENATION BALL

"Abe Lincoln . . . is brutal in all his habits. . . . He is obscene. . . . He is an animal. . . . Filthy black niggers, greasy, sweaty, and disgusting, now jostle white people and even ladies everywhere, even at the President's levees." Commenting on petitions to suspend the draft, a Pennsylvania newspaper urged citizens to "go a step further, brethren, and suspend Old Abe—by the neck if necessary to stop the accursed slaughter of our citizens."

For all their stridency, Democrats appear to have profited little from the race issue in this election. For most undecided voters, the success or failure of the war was more salient than the possibility of blacks marrying their sisters. Republicans were far more successful in pinning the label of traitor on Democrats than the latter were in pinning the label of miscegenationist on Republicans. If anything, racism may have boomeranged against the Democrats this time, for after Sherman's and Sheridan's victories many northern voters began to congratulate themselves on the selflessness of their sacrifices in this glorious war for Union *and* freedom.

On one issue tangentially linked to racial policy—the prisoners of war issue—the Democrats undoubtedly suffered a backlash, for northerners embittered by the condition of Union soldiers in southern prisons were not likely to favor a party stereotyped as prosouthern. The Democratic platform contained a plank condemning the administration's "shameful disregard" of "our fellow-citizens who now are, and long have been, prisoners of war in a suffering condition." When this plank was written, the overcrowding and shocking circumstances at Andersonville in particular had already become notorious. The anger evoked by this situation opens a window on one of the most emotional issues of the war.

After the relative trickle of prisoners in 1861, the South found itself having to feed and detain a rising flood of thousands and understandably pressed for a formal exchange cartel. The Lincoln administration was reluctant to grant the official recognition that such a cartel might imply but finally succumbed to growing northern pressure for regularized exchanges. Taking care to negotiate with a belligerent *army*, not government, the Union army accepted an exchange cartel on July 22,

The steamboat lying at Aiken's Landing on the James River in the illustration at left has delivered Confederate prisoners of war who were exchanged for the Union prisoners lined up to board the boat for return to their own regiments or for hospitalization or discharge. Below is a drawing of jubilant Confederate prisoners celebrating their exchange.

1862. Specifying a rank weighting whereby a noncommissioned officer was equal to two privates, a lieutenant to four, and so on up to a commanding general who was worth sixty privates, this cartel specified a man-for-man exchange of all prisoners. The excess held by one side or another were to be released on parole (that is, they promised not to take up arms until formally exchanged). For ten months this arrangement worked well enough to empty the prisons except for captives too sick or wounded to travel.

But two matters brought exchanges to a halt during 1863. First was the northern response to the southern threat to reenslave or execute captured black soldiers and their officers. When the Confederate Congress in May 1863 authorized this policy, which Jefferson Davis had announced four months earlier, the Union War Department suspended the cartel in order to hold southern prisoners as hostages against fulfillment of the threat. A trickle of informal exchanges continued, but the big battles in the second half of 1863 soon filled makeshift prisons with thousands of men. Grant averted an even greater problem by paroling the 30,000 Vicksburg captives; Banks followed suit with the 7,000 captured at Port Hudson. But the South's handling of these parolees provoked a second and clinching breakdown in exchange negotiations. Alleging technical irregularities in their paroles, the Confederacy arbitrarily declared many of them exchanged (without any real exchange taking place) and returned them to duty. Grant was outraged when the Union army recaptured some of these men at Chattanooga.

Attempts to renew the cartel foundered on the southern refusal to treat freedmen soldiers as prisoners of war or to admit culpability in the case of the Vicksburg parolees. By the

A GROUP OF EXCHANGED REBEL PRISONERS

Among this group of Confederate soldiers captured in the battles around Chattanooga November 23–25, 1863, were probably some men previously captured and paroled at Vicksburg but—in the opinion of Union officials—never officially exchanged. The captives are awaiting transportation to northern prison camps.

end of 1863 the Confederacy expressed a willingness to exchange black captives whom it considered to have been legally free when they enlisted. But the South would "die in the last ditch," said the Confederate exchange commissioner, before "giving up the right to send slaves back to slavery as property recaptured." Very well, responded Union Secretary of War Stanton. The 26,000 rebel captives in northern prisons could stay there. For the Union government to accede to Confederate conditions would be "a shameful dishonor. . . . When [the rebels] agree to exchange all alike there will be no difficulty." After becoming general in chief, Grant confirmed this hard line. "No distinction whatever will be made in the exchange between white and colored prisoners," he ordered on April 17, 1864. And there must be "released to us a sufficient number of officers and men as were captured and paroled at Vicksburg and Port Hudson. . . . Non-acquiescence by the Confederate authorities in both or either of these propositions will be regarded as a refusal on their part to agree to the further exchange of prisoners." Confederate authorities did not acquiesce.

The South's actual treatment of black prisoners is hard to ascertain. Even the number of Negro captives is unknown, for in refusing to acknowledge them as legitimate prisoners the Confederates kept few records. Many black captives never made it to prison camp. In the spirit of Secretary of War Seddon's early directive that "we ought never to be inconvenienced with such prisoners . . . summary execution must therefore be inflicted on those taken," hundreds were massacred at Fort Pillow, Poison Springs, the Crater, and elsewhere.

Black prisoners who survived the initial rage of their captors sometimes found themselves returned as slaves to their old masters or, occasionally, sold to a new one. While awaiting this fate they were often placed at hard labor on Confederate fortifications. The *Mobile Advertiser and Register* of October 15, 1864, published a list of 575 black prisoners in that city working as laborers until owners claimed them.

What to do about the murder or enslavement of black captives presented the Union government with a dilemma. At first Lincoln threatened an eye-for-an-eye retaliation. "For every soldier of the United States killed in violation of the laws of war," he ordered on July 30, 1863, "a rebel soldier shall be executed; and for every one enslaved by the enemy or sold into slavery, a rebel soldier shall be placed at hard

labor on the public works." But this was easier said than done; as Lincoln himself put it, "the difficulty is not in stating the principle, but in practically applying it." After the Fort Pillow massacre the cabinet decided to retaliate against actual offenders from Forrest's command, if any were captured, and to warn Richmond that a certain number of southern officers in northern prisons would be set apart as hostages against such occurrences in the future.

But no record exists that either recommendation was carried out. As Lincoln sadly told Frederick Douglass, "if once begun, there was no telling where [retaliation] would end." Lincoln's policy, in effect, became one of winning the war to free Union prisoners. Union field commanders in South Carolina and Virginia carried out the only official retaliation for southern treatment of black prisoners. When Confederates at Charleston and near Richmond put captured Negroes to work on fortifications under enemy fire in 1864, northern generals promptly placed an equal number of rebel prisoners at work on Union facilities under fire. This ended the Confederate practice. Some black soldiers did their own retaliating. After Fort Pillow several Negro units vowed to take no prisoners and yelled "Remember Fort Pillow" when they went into action.

Although Union threats of retaliation did little to help ex-slaves captured by Confederates, they appear to have forced southern officials to make a distinction between former slaves and free blacks. "The serious consequences," wrote Secretary of War Seddon to South Carolina's governor, "which might ensue from a rigid enforcement of the act of Congress" (which required *all* captured blacks to be turned over to states for punishment as insurrectionists) compel us "to make a distinction between negroes so taken who can be recognized or identified as slaves and those who were free inhabitants of the Federal States." The South generally treated the latter—

This photograph shows Elmira, New York, prison as it looked during the fall of 1864. Some prisoners lived in the tents in the distance, but by the winter most were housed in the barracks. They nevertheless suffered much sickness, in part because the prison was poorly sited in the floodplain of the Chemung River, causing a lagoon of stagnant water to form (not shown in the picture). Of the 12,122 prisoners at Elmira, 2,917 died—24 percent compared with about 29 percent at Andersonville.

along with white officers of black regiments—as prisoners of war. This did not necessarily mean equal treatment. Prison guards singled out black captives for latrine and burial details or other onerous labor. In South Carolina, for example, captured black soldiers from the 54th Massachusetts and other northern units were kept in the Charleston jail rather than in a POW camp.

They probably fared as well in jail as—if not better than—their white fellows in war prisons. The principal issue that aroused northern emotions was not the treatment of black prisoners but the treatment of all Union prisoners. As the heavy fighting of 1864 piled up captives in jerry-built prisons, grim stories of disease, starvation, and brutality began to filter northward. The facility at Andersonville in southwest Georgia, a stockade camp of sixteen acres designed for 10,000 prisoners, soon became overcrowded with captives from Sherman's army as well from the eastern theater. It was enlarged to twenty-six acres, in which 33,000 men were packed by August 1864—an average of thirty-four square feet per man—without shade in a deep South summer and with no shelter except what they could rig from sticks, tent flies, blankets, and odd bits of cloth. (By way of comparison, the Union prison camp at Elmira, New York, generally considered the worst northern prison, provided barracks for the maximum of 9,600 captives living inside a forty-acre enclosure—an average of 180 square feet per man.) During some weeks in the summer of 1864 more than a hundred prisoners died every day in Andersonville. Altogether 13,000 of the 45,000 men imprisoned there died of disease, exposure, or malnutrition.

Andersonville was the most extreme example of what many northerners regarded as a fiendish plot to murder Yankee prisoners. After the war a Union military commission tried and executed its commandant, Henry Wirz, for war crimes—the only such trial to result from the Civil War. Whether Wirz was actually guilty of anything worse than bad temper and inefficiency remains controversial today. In any case, he served as a scapegoat for the purported sins of the South. The large genre of prisoner memoirs, which lost nothing in melodramatics with passage of time, kept alive the bitterness for decades after the war. During 1864 a crescendo rose in the northern press demanding retribution against rebel prisoners to coerce better treatment of

This postwar lithograph offers the artist's bird's-eye view of Andersonville prison looking from the southeast. Note the double stockade fence with guard towers at regular intervals along the interior fence and the "dead line" inside this fence, which prisoners were forbidden to pass at the risk of being shot. Fortifications with cannons pointing at the prison are at lower left, lower center, upper right, and upper left. Guards lived in the tents at lower right. The stream running through the center was polluted with the waste and garbage of 30,000 prisoners.

Union captives. When a special exchange of sick prisoners in April returned to the North several living skeletons, woodcut copies of their photographs appeared in illustrated papers and produced a tidal wave of rage. What else could one expect of slaveholders "born to tyranny and reared to cruelty?" asked the normally moderate *New York Times*. The Committee on the Conduct of the War and the U.S. Sanitary Commission each published an account of Confederate prison conditions based on intelligence reports and on interviews with exchanged or escaped prisoners. "The enormity of the crime committed by the rebels," commented Secretary of War Stanton, "cannot but fill with horror the civilized world. . . . There appears to have been a deliberate system of savage and barbarous treatment." An editorial in an Atlanta

This drawing of emaciated Union POWs at Andersonville burying even more emaciated corpses against a backdrop of thousands of graves dates from 1885. It illustrates the degree to which the bitter memories of Andersonville were kept alive by prisoner memoirs and other northern media.

These woodcut copies of photographs of sick Union POWs exchanged in the spring of 1864 were published in Frank Leslie's Illustrated Newspaper. *They fed the growing northern outrage over conditions in southern prisons. As in all times and places, the press tended to portray the extreme as typical.*

newspaper during August made its way across the lines and was picked up by the northern press: "During one of the intensely hot days of last week more than 300 sick and wounded Yankees died at Andersonville. We thank Heaven for such blessings."

This was the sort of thing that convinced otherwise sensible northerners of the necessity for retaliation. The Union War Department did institute a limited retaliation. In May 1864 Stanton reduced prisoner rations to the same level that the Confederate army issued to its own soldiers. In theory this placed rebel prisoners on the same footing as Yankee prisoners in the South, who in theory received the same rations as Confederate soldiers. But in practice few southern soldiers ever got the official ration by 1864—and Union prisoners inevitably got even less—so most rebel captives in the North probably ate better than they had in their own army. Nevertheless, the reduction of prisoner rations was indicative of a hardening northern attitude. Combined with the huge increase in the number of prisoners during 1864, this produced a deterioration of conditions in northern prisons until the suffering, sickness, and death in some of them rivaled that in southern prisons—except Andersonville, which was in a class by itself.

This state of affairs produced enormous pressures for a renewal of exchanges. Many inmates at Andersonville and other southern prisons signed petitions to Lincoln asking for renewal, and the Confederates allowed delegations of prisoners to bear these petitions to Washington. Nothing came of them. Entries in prison diaries at Andersonville became increasingly bitter as the summer wore on: "What can the Government be thinking of to let soldiers die in this filthy place?" "We are losing all trust in old Abe." A spokesman for a group of clergymen and physicians implored Lincoln in September 1864: "For God's sake, interpose! . . . We know you can have them exchanged if you give your attention to it. It is simple murder to neglect it longer." From local Republican leaders came warnings that many good Union men "will work and vote against the President, because they think sympathy with a few negroes, also captured, is the cause of a refusal" to exchange.

Lincoln could indeed have renewed the exchange if he had been willing to forget about ex-slave soldiers. But he no more wanted to concede this principle than to renounce emancipation as a condition of peace. On August 27 Benjamin Butler, serving as a special exchange agent, wrote a letter (widely reprinted in newspapers) to his Confederate counterpart specifying that the Lincoln administration would renew exchanges only when the Confederacy agreed to exchange *all* classes of prisoners. He was willing to do anything to effect the liberation of imprisoned, suffering

Union soldiers except to dishonor his government's solemn pledge to "the colored soldiers in its ranks," a position consistent with "national faith and justice."

In the same month General Grant had privately enunciated another argument against exchange: it would strengthen enemy armies more than Union armies. Most exchanged rebels—"hale, hearty, and well-fed" as northerners believed them to be—would "become active soldier[s] against us at once" while "the half-starved, sick, emaciated" Union prisoners could never fight again. "We have got to fight until the military power of the South is exhausted," wrote Grant, "and if we release or exchange prisoners captured it simply becomes a war of extermination."

A good many historians—especially those of southern birth—have pointed to Grant's remarks as the real reason for the North's refusal to exchange. Concern for the rights of black soldiers, in this view, was just for show. The northern strategy of a war of attrition, therefore, was responsible for the horrors of Andersonville and the suffering of prisoners on both sides. This position is untenable. Grant expressed his opinion more than a year after the exchange cartel had broken down over the Negro prisoner question. And an opinion was precisely what it was; Grant did not *order* exchanges prohibited for purposes of attrition, and the evidence indicates that if the Confederates had conceded on the issue of ex-slaves the exchanges would have resumed. In October 1864, General Lee proposed an informal exchange of prisoners captured in recent fighting on the Richmond-Petersburg front. Grant agreed, on condition that blacks be exchanged "the same as white soldiers." If this had been done, it might have provided a precedent to break the impasse that had by then penned up more than a hundred thousand men in POW camps. But Lee replied that "negroes belonging to our citizens are not considered subjects of exchange and were not included in my proposition." Grant thereupon closed the correspondence by saying that because " [my] Government is bound to secure to all persons received into her armies the rights due to soldiers," Lee's refusal to grant such

Originally a training camp for Ohio soldiers, Camp Chase near Columbus became a prison camp in 1863 that housed as many as 8,000 prisoners. This photograph shows prisoners in the exercise yard between rows of huts while a Union guard walks the walls.

Many prisoners whiled away the hours by carving trinkets or making useful items out of whatever material came to hand. These chess pieces and the leather pouch were created in Libby Prison, Richmond, by Captain Nathaniel Rollins of the 2nd Wisconsin.

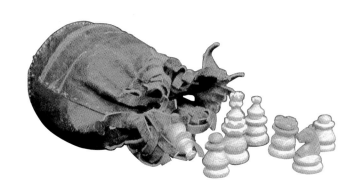

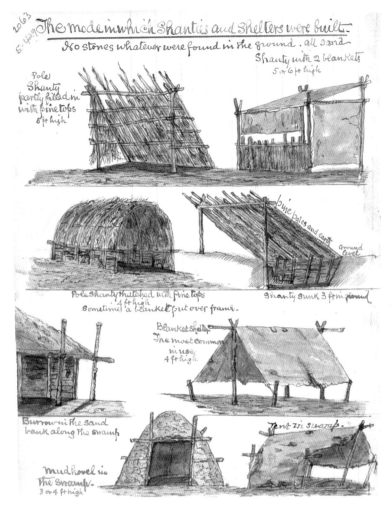

The mode in which Shanties and Shelters were built.

No stones whatever were found in the ground, all sand

Pole Shanty partly filled in with pine tops 6 ft high

Shanty with 2 blankets 5 or 6 ft high

Pole Shanty thatched with pine tops 4 ft high sometimes a blanket put over frame.

pine poles and earth
Ground level
Shanty sunk 3 ft in ground

Blanket shelter. The most common in use 4 ft high

Burrow in the sand bank along the swamp

Mud hovel in the Swamp. 3 or 4 ft high

Tent in swamp.

rights to former slaves "induces me to decline making the exchanges you ask."

In January 1865 the rebels finally gave in and offered to exchange "all" prisoners. Hoping soon to begin recruiting black soldiers for their own armies, Davis and Lee suddenly found the Yankee policy less barbaric. The cartel began functioning again and several thousand captives a week were exchanged over the next three months, until Appomattox liberated everyone.

Few if any historians would now contend that the Confederacy deliberately mistreated prisoners. Rather, they would concur with contemporary opinions—held by some northerners as well as southerners—that a deficiency of resources and the deterioration of the southern economy were mainly responsible for the sufferings of Union prisoners. The South could not feed its own soldiers and civilians; how could it feed enemy prisoners? Because Confederates kept expecting exchanges to be resumed, they made no long-range plans. The matter of shelter at Andersonville affords an example of shortages

These watercolor sketches of the flimsy shelters that Andersonville prisoners rigged up were made by Robert Sneden, a Union private who survived a year in Andersonville and other prisons. An architecture student before the war, Sneden enlisted in the 40th New York in 1861. His draftsman skills brought him to the attention of headquarters, and he became a mapmaker for the Army of the Potomac in 1862. In November 1863, however, a raid behind Union lines by Mosby's guerrillas netted Sneden and other prisoners, who were taken first to the Belle Isle prison camp on the James River and then to Andersonville in February 1864. There Sneden drew many sketches such as these showing various "shanties and shelters" (above) built by the prisoners and his own "shanty and burrow" (right) overlooked by a Confederate guard and with a prisoner "dying alone" at lower right.

Sketch made May 10 1864 of R.K. SNEDEN'S SHANTY and Surroundings ANDERSONVILLE PRISON &c
(Copy of original)

and lack of foresight. Although the South had plenty of cotton, it did not have the industrial capacity to turn enough of that cotton into tent canvas. Prisoners could have hewn logs for huts from the pine forests surrounding Andersonville, but no one thought to supply axes, and the young boys and the old men who guarded the prisoners were too inexperienced to prevent escapes from work details outside the stockade. So the prisoners broiled in the sun and shivered in the rain. Union cap-

In April 1864 Confederates at Andersonville built a "dead line" around the interior twenty feet from the stockade. Commandant Henry Wirz warned prisoners that if they tried to pass the dead line, the guards would shoot them. Robert Sneden sketched this watercolor of a prisoner shot by a guard when he tried to take a rail of the dead line for firewood.

tives at other enlisted men's prison camps endured a similar lack of shelter—in contrast to northern prisons, all of which provided barracks except Point Lookout in Maryland, where prisoners lived in tents. During the war numerous southerners criticized their own prisons. One young Georgia woman voiced grave apprehension after a visit to Andersonville: "I am afraid God will suffer some terrible retribution to fall upon us for letting such things happen. If the Yankees ever should come to South-West Georgia . . . and see the graves there, God have mercy on the land!"

"And yet, what can we do?" she asked herself. "The Yankees themselves are really more to blame than we, for they won't exchange these prisoners, and our poor, hard-pressed Confederacy has not the means to provide for them, when our own soldiers are starving in the field." This defensive tone became dominant in southern rhetoric after the war. One former Andersonville guard argued that the suffering at his prison camp was no worse than that at Johnson's Island in the North.

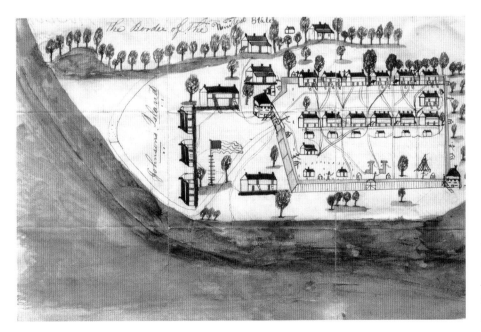

This watercolor depiction of the prison for Confederate officers at Johnson's Island in Lake Erie, just offshore from Sandusky, Ohio, was painted by a prisoner on the back of a letter home.

In their memoirs Jefferson Davis and Alexander Stephens maintained that the death rate at southern prisons was actually lower than at northern prisons. And the responsibility for "all this sacrifice of human life," asserted Stephens, "rests *entirely* on the Authorities at Washington" who refused to exchange prisoners. The state of Georgia placed two historical markers near Andersonville declaring that wartime shortages caused the suffering there, which thus cannot be blamed on anybody, and that "deaths among the prison guards were as high as among the prisoners." In 1909 the United Daughters of the Confederacy erected a monument to Henry Wirz proclaiming that this "hero-martyr" was "judicially murdered" by Yankees whose general in chief prevented the exchange of prisoners.

These defenders of the South doth protest too much. Readers of this book will form their own conclusions about responsibility for the breakdown in prisoner exchanges. As for the comparison of Andersonville with Johnson's Island, the mortality of southern prisoners at the latter was 2 percent—and at Andersonville, 29 percent. The percentage of deaths among inmates at Andersonville was in fact five or six times higher than among guards. Davis and Stephens were also wide of the mark. Because of the loss or destruction of many Confederate records, the actual number of Union dead in all southern prisons can never be known. The best estimate based on existing records finds that 30,218 (15.5 percent) of the 194,743 northern inmates of southern prisons died there, compared with 25,976 (12 percent) of 214,865 southerners who died in northern prisons. The figure for Union prisoners is undoubtedly too low. In any event, the treatment of prisoners during the Civil War was something that neither side could be proud of.

IV

In the end the POW issue played a minor role in the presidential election. The principal issue was the war itself, and how it should be ended. In this matter the Republicans managed to get a patent on the policy of peace through victory. Even McClellan could not escape the copper taint of peace without victory. Most Confederates saw McClellan's candidacy that way, after some initial hesitation caused by the general's warlike letter of acceptance. If McClellan was elected, predicted a War Department clerk in Richmond, "we shall have peace and independence." War-weary rebel soldiers hoped fervently for McClellan and peace. "The enemy are exceedingly anxious to hold out until after the Presidential election," reported Grant from the Petersburg front. "Deserters come into our lines daily who tell us that the men are nearly universally tired of the war, and that desertions would be much more frequent, but they believe peace will be negotiated after the fall elections." Such sentiments provoked opposite feelings among Union soldiers. Although "many leading officers" in the Army of the Potomac were still "McClellanized," according to a general in another Union army, most men in the ranks no longer favored their former commander. "Not that the soldiers dislike the man so much as the company he keeps," wrote one enlisted man. "I had rather stay out here a lifetime (much as I dislike it)," wrote another soldier, a former Democrat, "than consent to a division of our country. . . . We all want peace, but none *any* but an *honorable* one."

Many Union soldiers had a chance to register their opinions at the ballot box. Here was a bold experiment in democracy: allowing fighting men to vote in what amounted to a referendum on whether they should continue fighting. But as Grant put it, "they are American citizens, [and] they have as much right to [vote] as those citizens who remain at home. Nay, more, for they have sacrificed more for their country." By 1864 nineteen states had enacted provisions for soldiers to vote in the field. Of the states that had not, the three most important were Indiana, Illinois, and New Jersey, where Democratic legislatures had blocked the measure. Although much rhetoric about "proconsular rule" and "Caesarism" had accompanied this opposition, the true reason was the recognition by Democrats that the army had become overwhelmingly Republican—or at least "Union," as the Republican party styled itself in 1864.

A Harper's Weekly *drawing of Confederate deserters surrendering to a Union picket post in 1864.*

Twelve of the states allowing absentee voting provided for the separate tabulation of soldier ballots. Lincoln received 119,754 of them to McClellan's 34,291, a majority of 78 percent for the president compared with 54 percent of the civilian vote in those states. The absentee soldier-vote majority for Republicans in the other seven states was probably at least as great. Of the states that did not permit absentee

This pencil sketch by William Waud shows Pennsylvania soldiers standing in line to cast their ballots in 1864.

ELECTION-DAY.

8ᵗʰ NOVEMBER

NO COMPROMISE.

1864

THE VETERAN'S VOTE.

In this panel of illustrations for Harper's Weekly, *Thomas Nast left little doubt of his sentiments toward the election of 1864. In the upper panel, Columbia with sword and shield proudly casts her vote for Lincoln while copperheads in devil's form skulk behind the fallen angel of the Democratic party. In the lower left panel, soldiers vote for Lincoln as they take time out from beating the rebels in battle (center panel); in the lower right panel, respectable civilians vote for Lincoln and an Irishman obediently votes for McClellan.*

voting, the contest was particularly close and important in Indiana. As commander in chief, the president could help along his cause there and did not shrink from doing so. "The loss of [Indiana] to the friends of the Government," Lincoln wrote to General Sherman in Atlanta, "would go far towards losing the whole Union cause," so the president would be pleased if the general could furlough as many Indiana soldiers as possible to go home and vote. Several thousand soldiers did get to Indiana to vote; the War Department also combed military hospitals for convalescent Indiana soldiers well enough to travel. Some members of a Massachusetts regiment temporarily stationed in Indiana may have added their votes to the Republican total there.

In none of the states with separately tabulated soldier ballots did this vote change the outcome of the presidential contest—Lincoln would have carried all of them except Kentucky in any case. But in two close states where soldier votes were lumped with the rest, New York and Connecticut, these votes may have provided the margin of Lincoln's victory. The men in blue also decided the outcome in several congressional districts, and the votes of Maryland soldiers for a state constitutional amendment abolishing slavery more than offset the slight majority of the home vote against it.

Lincoln's popular-vote majority of half a million translated into an electoral count of 212 to 21. The president won all the states but Kentucky, Delaware, and New Jersey; his party also captured control of the governorships and legislatures of all but those states. The next Congress would have a Republican majority of three-fourths. The similarity between the "Union" vote of 1864 and the Republican vote of 1860 in the northern states was remarkable. Lincoln received virtually the same 55 percent from the same regions and constituencies within these states that he had received four years earlier. Republicans continued to draw their greatest support from native-born and British Protestant farmers, skilled workers, and white-collar voters especially in New England and the greater New England of the upper North. Democrats remained strongest among unskilled workers, immigrant Catholics, and Butternuts in the southern Midwest. As the "Union" party, Republicans expanded their base beyond 1860 in the border states (including West Virginia), where they won 54 percent of the vote (compared with about 9 percent in 1860) and drew most of their support from the urban middle class and prosperous nonslaveholding farmers. Democrats retained the slaveholders, immigrants, and poorer farmers.

Contemporaries interpreted the election of 1864 as a triumph for Lincoln's policy

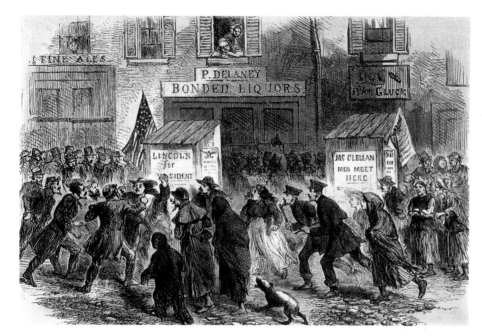

of compelling the unconditional surrender of the Confederacy. "I am astonished," wrote the American correspondent of the *London Daily News*, at "the extent and depth of [this] determination . . . to fight to the last. . . . [The northern people] are in earnest in a way the like of which the world never saw before, silently, calmly, but desperately in earnest."

But Jefferson Davis was also in earnest. He had never shared southern hopes for the election of McClellan and a negotiated peace. "We are fighting for existence; and by fighting alone can independence be gained," Davis had told audiences during a morale-building tour of the lower South after the fall of Atlanta. The Confederacy remained "as erect and defiant as ever," he informed Congress in November. "Nothing has changed in the purpose of its Government, in the indomitable valor of its troops, or in the unquenchable spirit of its people." It was to quench this spirit that Sherman set forth on his march from Atlanta to the sea.

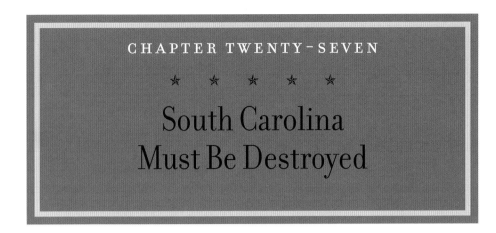

CHAPTER TWENTY-SEVEN

★ ★ ★ ★ ★

South Carolina
Must Be Destroyed

I

John B. Hood's Army of Tennessee did not crawl into the woods and die after losing Atlanta. Quite the contrary; inspired by a visit from Jefferson Davis, the aggressive Hood planned to circle around to Sherman's rear, cut his rail lifeline from Chattanooga, and pounce at leisure on the fragments of the stricken and starving Yankee army. Meanwhile Forrest had returned to his wonted occupation of smashing up Union railroads and supply depots in Tennessee. President Davis told cheering crowds in Georgia and South Carolina what to expect next. "I see no chance for Sherman to escape from a defeat or a disgraceful retreat," he declared a month after Atlanta's fall. His army, like Napoleon's retreating from Russia, would be destroyed. Then the South would "march into Tennessee" where "we will draw from twenty thousand to thirty thousand to our standard, and . . . push the enemy back to the banks of the Ohio and thus give the peace party of the North an accretion no puny editorial can give."

This glorious prospect may have pumped new life into flagging southern spirits. But when Grant read of Davis's speeches he snorted: "Who is to furnish the snow for this Moscow retreat?" A clever riposte; but in truth Sherman was vulnerable to enemy harassment. Having attained one of his objectives—the capture of Atlanta—he had not achieved the other, the destruction of Hood's army. Forty thousand strong, these tired but game rebels moved along the railroad to Chattanooga during October attacking targets of opportunity. Sherman left a corps to hold Atlanta and pursued Hood with the rest of his army. Skirmishing and fighting northward over the terrain they had conquered while marching southward four months earlier, the Yankees finally drove Hood's graybacks into Alabama and repaired the railroad.

Sherman grew exasperated with this kind of warfare. To continue chasing Hood would play the rebel game. "It will be a physical impossibility to protect the [rail]roads," Sherman told Grant, "now that Hood, Forrest, and Wheeler, and the whole batch of devils, are turned loose, without home or habitation. By attempting to hold the roads, we will lose a thousand men monthly and will gain no result."

Opposite page: Sherman's march through South Carolina left behind a wide swath of destruction, but the ruins in Charleston photographed here were produced by Confederate soldiers when they blew up or set fire to everything of military value before evacuating the city on February 13, 1865.

711

One of the elite units in the Confederate army was the Washington Artillery, whose men came from the middle and upper classes of New Orleans society. Batteries of this outfit fought in both the Army of Northern Virginia and the Army of Tennessee. This photograph of four tentmates in the Washington Artillery dates from 1861; by 1864 the survivors would be hardened, begrimed, ragged veterans.

On November 11, 1864, Sherman sent his last telegram from Atlanta to Washington and then cut the wire before moving out. Note also the rails twisted around the pole in Sherman neckties.

Instead, Sherman wanted to ignore Hood and march through the heart of Georgia to the coast. "I could cut a swath through to the sea," he assured Grant, "divide the Confederacy in two, and come up on the rear of Lee." Lincoln, Halleck, and even Grant resisted this idea at first. To leave Hood loose in his rear while the Union army abandoned its supply lines in the midst of enemy territory seemed doubly dangerous. But Sherman intended to station George Thomas in Tennessee with 60,000 men, more than enough to cope with anything the rebels might try. Sherman's own army of 62,000 hardened campaigners could find plenty to eat in the interior of Georgia. If he slashed his way through to the sea it would b "a demonstration to the world, foreign and domestic, that we have a power which Davis cannot resist. . . . I can make the march, and make Georgia howl!"

Sherman persuaded Grant, who in turn persuaded a still skeptical Lincoln. Sherman returned to Atlanta and prepared to move out a week after the presidential election. Like Lincoln, he believed in a hard war and a soft peace. "War is cruelty and you cannot refine it," Sherman had told Atlanta's mayor after ordering the civilian population expelled from the occupied city. But "when peace does come, you may call on me for anything. Then will I share with you the last cracker." Until then, though, he was fighting not only hostile armies but a hostile people; Union forces must devastate the South's capacity to wage war and the will to resist by making war so terrible that "generations would pass away before they would again appeal to it."

In this spirit Sherman's soldiers put the torch to everything of military value (by a broad definition) that Hood had left standing in Atlanta and marched out on November 15. As Sherman started south, Hood prepared to move north from Alabama into Tennessee, creating the odd spectacle of two contending armies turning their backs on each other and marching off in opposite directions. As it turned out, there was more method in Sherman's madness than in Hood's.

No enemy stood between Sherman's army and Savannah 285 miles away except several thousand Georgia militia and 3,500 rebel cavalry commanded by Joseph Wheeler. Union cavalry kept the gray horsemen at bay while weaving back and forth across the flanks of four infantry corps spread over a front varying from twenty-five to sixty miles wide. The militia attacked a rear-guard Union infantry brigade on November 22, but after suffering 600 casualties to the Yankees' 60 they made no more such efforts. Southerners wrecked bridges, burned provisions, toppled trees and planted mines on the roads ahead of the Yankees, but this accomplished little except to make them more vengeful. In truth, nothing could stop the bluecoats' relentless pace of a dozen miles a day. For most northern soldiers the march became a frolic, a moving feast in which they "foraged liberally on the country" and destroyed everything of conceivable military value—along with much else—that they did not consume.

Groups of foraging soldiers, soon called "bummers," roamed through the countryside and found more than enough food for their regiments. Under slack discipline, they helped themselves to anything they wanted from farms, plantations, even slave cabins. The pillage of Sherman's bummers has become legendary; like most legends it has some basis in fact. Not all the bummers were Yankees, however. Georgia unionists and liberated slaves hung on the flanks and rear of the army and lost few chances to despoil their rebel neighbors and former masters. Confederate deserters and stragglers from Wheeler's cavalry were perhaps even worse. Southern newspapers complained of "the destructive lawlessness" of Wheeler's troopers. "I do not think the Yankees are any worse than our own army," said a southern soldier. They "steal and plunder indiscriminately regardless of sex."

The worst havoc, nevertheless, was caused by Sherman's soldiers, who, in the words of one of them, "destroyed all we could not eat, stole their niggers, burned their cotton & gins, spilled their sorghum, burned & twisted their R. Roads and raised Hell generally." The hell-raising became grimmer after an incident at Milledgeville, the state capital. The soldiers' Thanksgiving Day feast there was interrupted by the arrival of several prisoners who had escaped from Andersonville. Hollow-cheeked, emaciated, with nothing but rags on their backs, these men wept uncontrollably at the sight of food and the American flag. This experience "sickened and infuriated" Sherman's soldiers, who thought "of the tens of thousands of their imprisoned comrades, slowly perishing with hunger in the midst of . . . barns bursting with grain and food to feed a dozen armies."

An Alabama-born major on Sherman's staff censured the vandalism committed by bummers. But he recognized that only a thin line separated such plundering from the destruction of enemy resources and morale necessary to win the war. "It is a ter-

A major general and commander of the Army of Tennessee's cavalry corps by the age of twenty-six, Joseph Wheeler survived the war, later served eight terms in Congress from Alabama, and fought in the U.S. army as a major general of volunteers in the Spanish-American War of 1898.

rible thing to consume and destroy the sustenance of thousands of people," the major wrote in his diary. But if inflicting such misery, terror, and grief would help "to paralyze their husbands and fathers who are fighting us . . . it is mercy in the end."

As the Yankees closed in on Savannah in mid-December and the 10,000 rebel soldiers defending it escaped before they could be trapped, Sherman sent one of his sportive telegrams to Lincoln: "I beg to present you, as a Christmas gift, the city of Savannah, with 150 heavy guns and . . . about 25,000 bales of cotton." The president responded with "many, many thanks" to Sherman and his army for their "great success," especially when "taking the work of Gen. Thomas into the count," which had brought "those who sat in darkness, to see a great light."

Thomas had indeed weighed in with an achievement equaling Sherman's—the virtual destruction of Hood's Army of Tennessee. Hood's activities after Sherman left Atlanta seemed to have been scripted in never-never land. Although he faced Union forces under Thomas totaling more than 60,000 men with only 40,000 of his own—one-fourth of them wearing shoes so rotten that by December they would march barefoot—Hood hoped to drive through Tennessee into Kentucky, where he expected to pick up 20,000 recruits and smash Thomas. Then, Hood fantasized, he would move eastward to Virginia, combine with Lee, and defeat Grant and Sherman in turn.

This enterprise started well. Moving into Tennessee during the last week of November, Hood tried to get between Thomas's advance force of 30,000 commanded by John Schofield at Pulaski and the 30,000 at Nashville seventy-five miles to the north. Schofield detected this effort in time to fall back to the Duck River at Columbia, where Hood skirmished with the Federals, November 24–27. Not wishing to risk a frontal assault, Hood sent Forrest's cavalry and two infantry corps on a deep flanking march to get into Schofield's rear, hoping to emulate "the grand results achieved by the immortal Jackson in similar maneuvers." But Union horse-

men spotted this move, and Schofield rushed two divisions to hold the turnpike in his rear at the crossroads village of Spring Hill. Uncoordinated rebel attacks failed to dislodge these Yankees—and nothing went right for Hood's army ever again.

During the night of November 29–30 Schofield pulled his whole force back and entrenched a line covering the crossings of the Harpeth River at Franklin, fifteen miles south of Nashville. On November 30 Hood followed Schofield to Franklin and ordered his infantry to make a head-on assault, almost as if by such punishment to purge them of their supposed timidity. Hood's corps commanders protested this order to attack equal numbers who were dug in with strong artillery support, while nearly all the Confederate artillery and part of the infantry were far in the rear and could not arrive in time for action on this short November afternoon. Their protests only confirmed Hood's feelings that his subordinates had failed him at Spring Hill, bolstered his belief that Johnston had sapped the army's elan, and stiffened his determination to force it to fight. He had broken the enemy line at Gaines's Mill and at Chickamauga; he would do it again here.

Twenty-two thousand southern soldiers swept forward in the slanted sunlight of an Indian summer afternoon. Parts of Patrick Cleburne's hard-hitting division and another gray division temporarily broke the Union line but were driven out with heavy losses in hand-to-hand combat as fierce as anything at the Bloody Angle of Spotsylvania. For hours after dark the firing raged until toward midnight the bluecoats broke off and headed north to Nashville. Hood could hardly claim a victory, however, for his 7,000 casualties were three times the enemy total. Hood lost more men killed at Franklin than Grant at Cold Harbor or McClellan in all of the Seven Days. A dozen Confederate generals fell at Franklin, six of them killed including Cleburne and a fire-eating South Carolinian by the name of States Rights Gist. No fewer than fifty-four southern regimental commanders, half of the total, were casualties. Having proved even to Hood's satisfaction that they would assault breastworks, the Army of Tennessee had shattered itself beyond the possibility of ever doing so again. Southerners were appalled by the news from Franklin of "fearful loss and no results."

The lack of results galled Hood too as he prodded his battered troops northward toward Nashville, where they entrenched a defensive line along the hills four miles south of Tennessee's capital. Like Micawber, Hood seemed to be waiting for some-

The Confederate attack at Franklin initially struck Union troops posted in advance of the main line along the stone wall in the near distance. Overrunning the position, the southerners were hurled back with great loss when they struck the main line along the high ground visible in the distance.

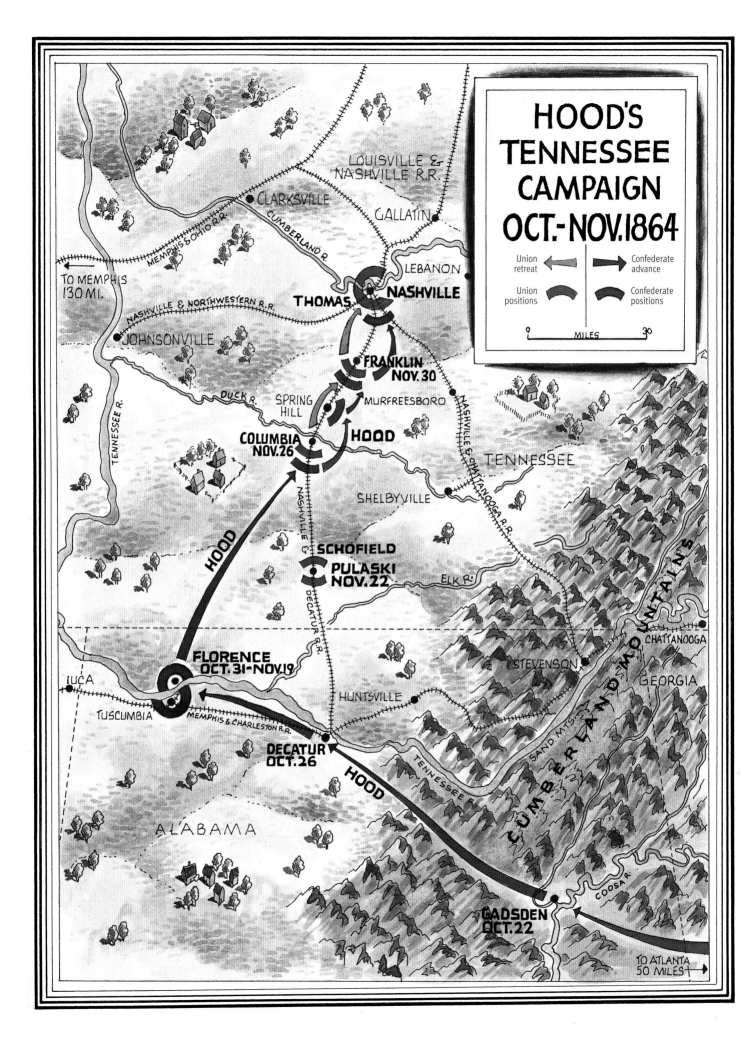

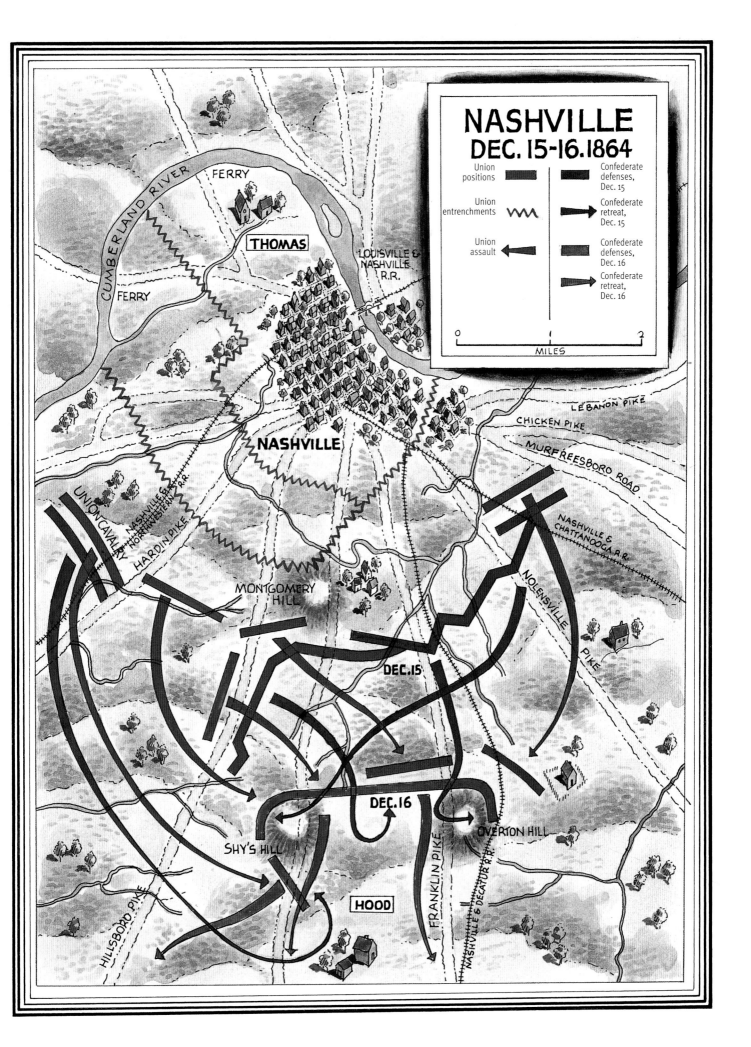

NASHVILLE
DEC. 15-16.1864

Union positions

Union entrenchments

Union assault

Confederate defenses, Dec. 15

Confederate retreat, Dec. 15

Confederate defenses, Dec. 16

Confederate retreat, Dec. 16

0   1   2
MILES

CUMBERLAND RIVER

FERRY

FERRY

THOMAS

LOUISVILLE & NASHVILLE R.R.

NASHVILLE

LEBANON PIKE

CHICKEN PIKE

MURFREESBORO ROAD

NASHVILLE & NORTHWESTERN R.R.

HARDIN PIKE

UNION CAVALRY

MONTGOMERY HILL

NASHVILLE & CHATTANOOGA R.R.

NOLENSVILLE PIKE

DEC.15

DEC.16

SHY'S HILL

OVERTON HILL

HOOD

FRANKLIN PIKE

NASHVILLE & DECATUR R.R.

HILLSBORO PIKE

A view to the southwest from the Tennessee capitol building in Nashville. The main Union attacks against Hood's lines on December 15–16 swept straight ahead and then to the left in the distance.

thing to turn up—specifically, reinforcements from across the Mississippi. But Union gunboats prevented that. Afraid that a retreat to Alabama would trigger wholesale desertions by Tennessee soldiers, Hood hunkered down and waited for Thomas to attack. So did an impatient General Grant. Unaware of the crippled condition of Hood's army, northern leaders far from the scene feared that this rebel raid, like Jubal Early's the previous summer, might undo all the results of recent Union successes. While Thomas methodically prepared to attack, Stanton fumed that "this looks like the McClellan and Rosecrans strategy of do nothing and let the rebels raid the country." Grant bombarded Thomas with telegraphic exhortations to action, and he had started for Nashville himself to relieve the ponderous general from command when news came that Thomas had finally made his move.

When he did, it turned out like Joe Louis's second fight with Max Schmeling—a devastating knockout that almost annihilated the adversary. The analogy is appropriate, for Thomas's battle plan called for one division (including two brigades of black soldiers) to pin down Hood's right with a left jab while three Union infantry corps and the cavalry smashed the other flank with a roundhouse right. All worked as planned, though it took two winter days to finish the job. On December 15 the lifting fog at midmorning revealed 50,000 bluecoats coming on against Hood's 25,000 (most of Forrest's cavalry was thirty miles away watching a small Union force at Murfreesboro). All day the rebels hung on by their fingernails against the feinting jabs at their right and sledgehammer blows at their left. As darkness began to fall the fingernails on the left let go, and during the night Hood pulled his army back two miles to a new and shorter line anchored by hills on both ends.

The Federals moved forward with titanic inexorability next day and repeated the tactics of left jab and right uppercut. Again the Confederates parried groggily until late afternoon. But dismounted Union cavalrymen with rapid-firing carbines had worked around to the rear of Hood's left while two infantry corps hit this flank head-on. When the collapse finally came during a drenching rain and gathering darkness, it came with calamitous suddenness. From left to right, southern brigades toppled like dominoes. Thousands of rebels surrendered, and others streamed southward, throwing away their arms and equipment to make better time. Officers tried to rally them, "but the line they formed," a private recalled, "was like trying to stop the current of the Duck River with a fish net."

Yankee cavalrymen scrambled to find their horses and take up the pursuit over roads shin-deep in mud. For nearly two weeks the chase continued from one river to the next through Tennessee into Alabama and Mississippi. At each river or creek Forrest's cavalry would make a stand and fall back, while the exhausted infantry—half of them now without shoes—leaked stragglers and deserters by the hundreds. By the beginning of 1865 the remnants of Hood's army had fetched up at Tupelo,

Mississippi, where a head count found barely half of the 40,000 who had marched northward seven weeks earlier. Heartsick and broken, Hood resigned his command on January 13—a Friday.

The news of Hood's "irretrievable disaster" and of Savannah's surrender to Sherman spread dejection through the South. This was "one of the gloomiest [days] in our struggle," wrote Ordnance Chief Josiah Gorgas on December 19. As the full extent of Hood's defeat became known and as shortages exacerbated by Sherman's and Sheridan's ravages became more serious, the head of the Confederate War Bureau conceded that "things are getting worse very rapidly. . . . Ten days ago the last meat ration was issued [to Lee's army] and not a pound remained in Richmond. . . . The truth is we are prostrated in all our energies and resources." The price of gold rose to 5,000, and the value of the Confederate dollar slipped to less than 2 percent of its 1861 level. The heretofore resolute General Gorgas, who had performed miracles to keep rebel armies supplied with arms and ammunition, wondered in January 1865: "Where is this to end? No money in the Treasury—no food to feed Gen. Lee's army—no troops to oppose Gen. Sherman. . . . Is the cause really hopeless? Is it to be lost and abandoned in this way? . . . Wife and I sit talking of going to Mexico to live out there the remnant of our days."

The upbeat tone of Lincoln's annual message to Congress on December 6 provided a northern counterpoint to southern gloom. "The purpose of the people . . . to maintain the integrity of the Union, was never more firm, nor more nearly unanimous, than now," said Lincoln. And the resources to do the job "are unexhausted, and, as we believe, inexhaustible." With 671 warships the navy was the largest in the world. With a million men in uniform the army was larger and better equipped than ever. And despite the deaths of over 300,000 soldiers, immigration and natural increase had more than made up the loss. Thus while "material resources are now more complete and abundant than ever," we also "have more men now than we had when the war began. . . . We are gaining strength, and may, if need be, maintain the contest indefinitely."

These were chilling words to the South. Josiah Gorgas noted in his diary that "Lincoln's message spawns nothing but subjugation." Nor was the president's talk of abundant and inexhaustible resources mere gasconade. On the contrary, the demands of war had boosted the northern economy to new heights of productivity following the temporary setback of 1861–62 caused by departure of the South with its markets and raw materials. Coal and iron production declined in the first year or so of the war but increased by 1864 to higher levels than ever before. Iron production in the Union states was 29 percent higher in 1864 than for the whole country in the previous record year of 1856; coal production in the North during the four war years was 21 percent greater than in the highest four peacetime years for both North and South. The North built more merchant ship tonnage during the war than the whole country had built in any comparable peacetime period despite the crippling of the transatlantic merchant marine by southern commerce raiders and the competing demands of the navy on shipbuilding capacity. Although new railroad construction slowed during the war, the amount of traffic over existing lines increased by 50 percent or more, absorbing the excess capacity created by the railroad-building boom of the 1850s. Traffic on the Erie Canal also increased by more than 50 percent during the war. Despite a drastic decline of 72 percent in the North's leading industry, cotton textiles, the overall manufacturing index stood 13 percent higher in 1864 for the Union states alone than for the entire country in 1860. The North had to import hundreds of thousands of rifles in the first year or two of the war; by 1864 the firearms industry was turning out more than enough rifles and artillery for the large Union army.

And the northern economy churned out plenty of butter as well as guns. Despite the secession of southern states, war in the border states, and the absence of a half-million farmers in the army, Union states grew more wheat in both 1862 and 1863 than the entire country had grown in the previous record year of 1859. Despite the food needs of the army and the civilian population, the United States actually doubled its exports of wheat, corn, pork, and beef during the war to help fill the void created by crop failures in western Europe during the early 1860s. It was an impressive achievement made possible by the stimulus of war production, by mechanization of agriculture, and by the expanded employment of women as well as machines in northern industry. In the contrasting impact of the war on the northern and southern economies could be read not only the final outcome of the war but also the future economic health of those regions.

The North had enough manpower and energy left over from the war effort to continue the process of westward expansion. As Lincoln noted in his 1864 message, a hundred miles of the eastern end of the transcontinental railroad had been surveyed and twenty miles of tracks already laid on the other end in California. Gold production held steady during the war, copper increased by 50 percent, and silver quadrupled as new mines were opened, especially in Nevada, which entered the Union as a state in 1864. Western growth had its dark side, of course: many of the

new settlers were draft-dodgers from states east of the Mississippi; the politics of federal aid to railroad construction were none too scrupulous; and worst of all, the extinguishment of Indian titles to the land proceeded ruthlessly, accompanied by bloody fighting in Minnesota, Colorado, and elsewhere during the war.

New industries also blossomed in the hot-house climate of the southern wartime economy. Gunpowder mills, ordnance plants, machine shops, and the like sprang up at Augusta, Selma, Atlanta, and numerous other places, while the Tredegar Works in Richmond turned out iron for every conceivable military use. But Yankee invasions and raids sooner or later destroyed most of this new industry, along with anything else of economic value within reach, so that by war's end much of the South was an economic desert. The war not only killed one-quarter of the Confederacy's white men of military age. It also killed two-fifths of southern livestock, wrecked half of the farm machinery, ruined thousands of miles of railroad, left scores of thousands of farms and plantations in weeds and disrepair, and destroyed the principal labor system on which southern productivity had been based. Two-thirds of assessed southern wealth vanished in the war. The wreckage of the southern economy caused the 1860s to become the decade of least economic growth in American history before the 1930s. It also produced a wrenching redistribution of wealth and income between North and South. As measured by the census, southern agricultural and manufacturing capital declined by 46 percent between 1860 and 1870, while northern capital increased by 50 percent. In 1860 the southern states had contained 30 percent of the national wealth; in 1870, only 12 percent. Per capita commodity output (including agriculture) was almost equal in North and South in 1860; by 1870 the North's per capita output was 56 percent greater. In 1860 the average per capita income of southerners including slaves was about two-thirds of the northern average; after the war southern income dropped to less than two-fifths of the northern average and did not rise above that level for the rest of the nineteenth century. Such were the economic consequences of the South's bid for independence.

This photograph shows the smoldering ruins of the Tredegar Works in Richmond, which the Confederates destroyed when they evacuated the city on April 2, 1865. Note the guns and their carriages in the foreground. The James River, which supplied water power to this industrial complex, flows by at the left.

II

Despite Confederate disasters in the last months of 1864, the war was not yet over—at least Jefferson Davis and his colleagues refused to admit that it was over. To persuade them, the Yankees put the finishing touches on Winfield Scott's Anaconda Plan, conceived nearly four years earlier, by capturing Fort Fisher in January 1865. By then Robert E. Lee's Army of Northern Virginia was the only substantial military force left in the Confederacy, and the Carolinas were just about the only region from which it could draw supplies. Many of these came on blockade runners that were still getting into Wilmington, twenty miles up the Cape Fear River from Fort Fisher. This massive L-shaped fort, almost a mile long on its seaward face, represented a new version of an ancient idea in fortifications. Instead of masonry, it was built of sand and dirt over a log framework. Twenty-five feet thick and ten to thirty feet high, sodded with tough marsh grass, it absorbed shot and shell as a pillow absorbs punches—unlike, for example, Fort Sumter, which had been blasted to rubble by Union guns. Fort Fisher's forty-seven big guns threatened dire punishment to any Union warship that tried to close in on blockade runners weaving their way through the treacherous shoals and channels at the mouth of the Cape Fear River.

Union strategists were slow to make the capture of Fort Fisher a top priority. In 1863 the wasteful diversion of resources to the futile attempt to seize Charleston delayed the project. Finally in the fall of 1864 Admiral David D. Porter assembled the largest fleet of the war—nearly sixty warships plus troop transports to carry 6,500 soldiers—for an all-out effort against Fort Fisher. Commander of the infantry was Benjamin Butler, who by virtue of his early, politically motivated promotion to major general outranked everyone in the eastern theater except Grant. Butler conceived the idea of loading an old ship with 215 tons of gunpowder, running it into the shallows near the fort, and exploding it with the expectation that the blast would damage the fort and stun its garrison. Storms delayed the project until Christmas Eve day. The exploding ship did virtually no damage, the open air having absorbed the shock wave. The fleet then pummeled the fort with the heaviest bombardment of the war but managed to damage only a few of its guns. Butler got part of his infantry onto the beach but called off the attack when he found the parapet bristling with artillery and the approaches mined with "torpedoes."

This fiasco provided Grant with the excuse he had been looking for to get rid of Butler. With the election safely over, Lincoln could disregard the political influence that had kept Butler in the army so long; on January 8, 1865, the Massachusetts general was relieved of his command. Grant ordered a second attempt against Fort Fisher, this time with the bright young General Alfred Terry in command of a beefed-up infantry force of 8,000. On January 13 they waded ashore through the surf and worked their way down the narrow peninsula toward the fort's north face while the fleet opened a barrage that rained eight hundred tons of shot and shell on the defenders. This time the navy's big guns disabled nearly all of those in the fort and cut the detonating wires for the mines, preparing the way for an assault on January 15 by 4,500 infantrymen against the north face while 2,000 sailors and marines stormed the bastion from the seaward side. Although the attackers took more than a thousand casualties, the army troops finally broke through and captured the fort along with its garrison of 2,000 men. Wilmington was cut off from the sea, and Lee's soldiers in the trenches at Petersburg would have to tighten further their belts whose buckles were already scraping their backbones.

Wilmington itself soon fell, and most of coastal North Carolina was in Yankee hands. Desertions from Lee's army, especially of North Carolina troops, rose to disastrous levels. "Hundreds of men are deserting nightly," reported Lee in February.

In a single month the army lost 8 percent of its strength by desertion. Most of these men went home to protect and sustain their families; some went over to the enemy, where they knew they could find food and shelter. Confederate officers recognized that "the depressed and destitute conditions of the soldiers' families was one of the prime causes of desertion," but that "the chief and prevailing reason was a conviction among them that our cause was hopeless and that further sacrifices were useless." Whatever the reasons for this "epidemic" of desertions, wrote Lee, "unless it can be changed, [it] will bring us calamity."

Confederate officials regarded the loss of Fort Fisher as a "stunning" blow. Alexander Stephens pronounced it "one of the greatest disasters that had befallen our Cause from the beginning of the war." The southern Congress, then in session, stepped up its attacks on the administration. Secretary of War Seddon succumbed to the pressure and resigned. Some congressmen even called on Davis to step down in favor of Robert E. Lee as dictator, and in fact Congress did pass a law creating the post of general in chief. Although Davis recognized this as a gesture of nonconfidence in his own leadership, he appointed Lee to the position. Davis and Lee maintained their cordial relationship, and both vowed to fight on until victory. But the fall of Fort Fisher had convinced many congressmen that "we cannot carry on the war any longer" and should "make terms with the enemy, on the basis of the old Union."

In this climate of opinion another movement for peace negotiations flared up and then fizzled out. The old Jacksonian Francis Preston Blair became convinced that the North and South could be reunited by proposing a joint campaign to throw the French out of Mexico. Lincoln, who wanted no part of this hare-brained scheme, nevertheless decided to see what might develop and let Blair pass through the lines

This lithograph shows part of the Union fleet standing almost a mile offshore bombarding Fort Fisher in the distance. The four ships closer to the fort (less than a half mile) were ironclads.

to present this proposal to Jefferson Davis. The Confederate president expected all this to yield only a reiteration of Lincoln's previous demands for humiliating "unconditional submission." He nevertheless thought that eliciting Lincoln's demands publicly might both discredit the peace movement and stiffen southerners' resolve to fight on. Davis therefore sent word through Blair that he was ready to "enter into conference with a view to secure peace to the two countries." Lincoln responded promptly that he too was ready to receive overtures "with the view of securing peace to the people of our one common country."

Davis appointed a three-man commission consisting of prominent advocates of negotiations: Vice-President Stephens, President Pro Tem of the Senate Robert M. T. Hunter, and Assistant Secretary of War John A. Campbell, a former U.S. Supreme Court justice. Their proposed conference with William H. Seward, whom Lincoln had sent to Hampton Roads to meet with them, almost aborted because of the irreconcilable differences between the agendas for "two countries" and "our one common country." But after talking with Stephens and Hunter and becoming convinced of their sincere desire for peace, General Grant telegraphed Washington that to send them home without a meeting would leave a bad impression. On the spur of the moment Lincoln decided to journey to Hampton Roads and join Seward for a face-to-face meeting with the Confederate commissioners.

This dramatic confrontation took place February 3 on the Union steamer *River Queen*. Lincoln's earlier instructions to Seward formed the inflexible Union position during four hours of talks: "1) The restoration of the National authority throughout all the States. 2) No receding by the Executive of the United States on the Slavery question. 3) No cessation of hostilities short of an end of the war, and the disbanding of all forces hostile to the government." In vain did Stephens try to divert Lincoln by bringing up Blair's Mexican project. Equally unprofitable was Hunter's proposal for an armistice and a convention of states. No armistice, said Lincoln; surrender was the only means of stopping the war. But even Charles I, said Hunter, had entered into agreements with rebels in arms against his government during the English Civil War. "I do not profess to be posted in history," replied Lincoln. "All I distinctly recollect about the case of Charles I, is, that he lost his head."

On questions of punishing rebel leaders and confiscating their property Lincoln promised generous treatment based on his power of pardon. On slavery he even suggested the possibility of compensating owners to the amount of $400 million (about 15 percent of the slaves' 1860 value). Some uncertainty exists about exactly what Lincoln meant in these discussions by "no receding . . . on the Slavery question." At a minimum he meant no going back on the Emancipation Proclamation or on other wartime executive and congressional actions against slavery. No slaves freed by these acts could ever be reenslaved. But how many had been freed by them? asked the southerners. All of the slaves in the Confederacy, or only those who had come under Union military control after the Proclamation was issued? As a war measure, would it cease to operate with peace? That would be up to the courts, said Lincoln. And Seward informed the commissioners that the House of Representatives had just passed the Thirteenth Amendment. Its ratification would make all

other legal questions moot. If southern states returned to the Union and voted against ratification, thereby defeating it, would such action be valid? That remained to be seen, said Seward. In any case, remarked Lincoln, slavery as well as the rebellion was doomed. Southern leaders should cut their losses, return to the old allegiance, and save the blood of thousands of young men that would be shed if the war continued. Whatever their personal preferences, the commissioners had no power to negotiate such terms. They returned dejectedly to Richmond.

But they rebuffed Davis's attempt to add language to their report on negotiations expressing resentment of "degrading submission" and "humiliating surrender" since they knew that the president wished to use the phrases to discredit the whole idea of negotiations. So Davis added them himself in a message to Congress on February 6 accompanying the commissioners' report. The South must fight on, said Davis that evening in a public speech which bristled with "unconquerable defiance," according to press reports. We will never submit to the "disgrace of surrender," he declared and predicted that Lincoln and Seward would find that "they had been speaking to their masters," for southern armies would yet "compel the Yankees, in less than twelve months, to petition us for peace on our own terms."

The press and public—in Richmond at least—took their cue from Davis. "To talk now of any other arbitrament than that of the sword is to betray cowardice or treachery," proclaimed the *Whig*, while war clerk John B. Jones asserted: "Valor alone is relied upon now for our salvation. Every one thinks the Confederacy will at once gather up its military strength and strike such blows as will astonish the world."

The River Queen, *where the Hampton Roads Conference took place on February 3, 1865, served during the war as a sort of presidential yacht for Lincoln on several of his trips to the front in Virginia.*

III

If William Tecumseh Sherman had read these words he would have uttered a sigh of exasperation. Having bent but apparently not broken the South's "unconquerable defiance," his army was now smashing and burning its way through South Carolina to finish the job.

At the beginning of 1865 the only sizable portions of the Confederate heartland

Major General Edward R. S. Canby (top) probably covered more distance than any other Union commander in the war. In 1861–62 he countered a Confederate invasion of New Mexico and drove the survivors back to Texas. The middle part of the war found him in a staff position in Washington. In 1864 he went to Louisiana and then to Alabama, where he led the forces that captured Mobile in 1865 and then drove inland, while Brigadier General James H. Wilson (bottom) led a cavalry raid into Alabama from Tennessee. Wilson's troopers pushed on to Georgia and captured a fleeing Jefferson Davis on May 10.

still untouched by invading Yankees were the interior of the Carolinas and most of Alabama. Grant and Thomas planned a two-pronged campaign to deal with the latter. Using troops drawn from the Army of the Gulf and from Thomas's force in Tennessee, General E.R.S. Canby was to invade southern Alabama through Mobile. At the same time twenty-seven-year-old James H. Wilson, who had risen to command of Thomas's cavalry, was to take 13,000 troopers armed with repeating carbines on a strike from Tennessee into Alabama to destroy the munitions complex at Selma and seize the original Confederate capital of Montgomery. Both operations got under way in March; both were complete successes, especially Wilson's raid. Brushing aside Forrest's outmanned and outgunned horsemen, the blue cavalry burned or smashed or blew up great quantities of cotton, railroads, bridges, rolling stock, factories, niter works, rolling mills, arsenals, a navy yard, and captured Montgomery, while Mobile fell to Canby's infantry in April.

Destructive as these enterprises were, they became a sideshow to Sherman's march through South Carolina. As his army had approached Savannah in December 1864, Georgians said to Sherman: "Why don't you go over to South Carolina and serve them this way? They started it." Sherman had intended to do so all along. He converted Grant to the idea, and on February 1 Sherman's 60,000 blue avengers left Savannah for their second march through the heart of enemy territory. This one had two strategic purposes: to destroy all war resources in Sherman's path; and to come up on Lee's rear to crush the Army of Northern Virginia in a vise between two larger Union armies and "wipe out Lee," in Grant's succinct phrase.

Sherman's soldiers had a third purpose in mind as well: to punish the state that had hatched this unholy rebellion. The soldiers' temper was not improved by the taunts of southern newspapers against this "grand army of Mudsills." One of the mudsills, an Ohio private, vowed to make South Carolina "suffer worse than she did at the time of the Revolutionary War. We will let her know that it isn't so sweet to secede as she thought it would be." A South Carolina woman whose house was plundered recalled that the soldiers "would sometimes stop to tell me they were sorry for the women and children, but South Carolina must be destroyed."

Destroyed it was, through a corridor from south to north narrower than in Georgia but more intensely pillaged and burned. Not many buildings remained standing in some villages after the army marched through. The same was true of the countryside. "In Georgia few houses were burned," wrote an officer; "here few escaped." A soldier felt confident that South Carolina "will never want to seceed again. . . . I think she has her 'rights' now." When the army entered North Carolina the destruction of civilian property stopped. "Not a single column of the fire or smoke which a few days ago marked the positions of heads of column, can be seen on the horizon," noted an officer after two days in

North Carolina. "Not a house was burned, and the army gave to the people more than it took from them."

The war of plunder and arson in South Carolina was not pretty, and hardly glorious, but Sherman considered it effective. The terror his bummers inspired "was a power, and I intended to utilize it. . . . My aim then was to whip the rebels, to humble their pride, to follow them to their inmost recesses, and make them fear and dread us." It seemed to work: "All is gloom, despondency, and inactivity," wrote a South Carolinian on February 28. "Our army is demoralized and the people panic stricken. . . . The power to do has left us . . . to fight longer seems to be madness."

Even more important, perhaps, than the destructive vengeance of Sherman's army in spreading this demoralization was its stunning logistical achievements. Sherman himself later rated the march through the Carolinas as ten times more important in winning the war than the march from Atlanta to the sea. It was also ten times more difficult. Terrain and weather posed much greater problems in South Carolina than in Georgia. The march from Atlanta to Savannah proceeded 285 miles parallel to major rivers in dry autumn weather against token opposition. The march northward from Savannah was aimed at Goldsboro, North Carolina, 425 miles away, where Sherman expected to be resupplied by Union forces moving inland from Wilmington. Sherman's soldiers would have to cross nine substantial rivers and scores of their tributaries during what turned out to be the wettest winter in twenty years.

Confederate defenders expected the swamps in tidewater South Carolina to stop Sherman before he got fairly started. Indeed, so far under water were the roads in this region that Union scouts had to reconnoiter some of them in canoes. But Sherman organized "pioneer battalions" of soldiers and freedmen (some of the latter recruited from the thousands of contrabands who had trailed the army to Savannah) to cut saplings and trees to corduroy the roads, build bridges, and construct causeways. Meeting resistance from Wheeler's cavalry at some rain-swollen streams and rivers, the bluecoats sent out flanking columns that waded through water up to their armpits, brushing aside alligators and snakes, and drove the rebels away. Northward lapped the blue wave at a rate of nearly ten miles a day for forty-five days including skirmishing and fighting. Rain fell during twenty-eight of those days, but this seemed to benefit South Carolina only by slightly damping

This etching provides a good illustration of the corduroying of a dirt road through wet or muddy spots so that wheels did not sink to the axles in mud.

the style of Sherman's arsonists. "When I learned that Sherman's army was marching through the Salk swamps, making its own corduroy roads at the rate of a dozen miles a day," said Joseph Johnston, "I made up my mind that there had been no such army in existence since the days of Julius Caesar."

Johnston soon acquired the dubious honor of trying to stop these latter-day legions. One of Lee's first acts as general in chief was to persuade Davis to appoint Johnston on February 22 to command all Confederate troops in the Carolinas. There were not many of them, and they had already been flanked out of South Carolina by Sherman's feints and fast marching. The four Union corps moved northward on separate roads in a Y formation with the forward units pointing toward Augusta and Charleston and the inner corps in a position to reinforce them quickly in case of trouble. The rebels had scraped together about 20,000 troops plus Wheeler's cavalry to resist Sherman. They consisted of the demoralized remnants of Hood's Army of Tennessee, the Charleston garrison reinforced by Hardee's troops that had evacuated Savannah, and a brigade of South Carolina cavalry that Lee sent from Virginia along with Wade Hampton to rally faltering morale in his home state. Some 10,000 of these troops were stationed in Augusta and about the same number in Charleston with the expectation that Sherman would attack one or both cities—Augusta because of its gunpowder and munitions plants, Charleston because of its symbolic value. Sherman kept up the feint toward both but went near neither. Instead he sliced through the center of the state, destroying the railroad between them and heading for the capital at Columbia. With their communications cut and an enemy army of 60,000 in their rear, the defenders of Charleston evacuated the city on February 18. The rebel troops at Augusta also slogged northward to combine with Hardee's divisions now under Johnston's overall command to offer some resistance when Sherman reached North Carolina.

Charleston was fortunate that it was occupied by troops from the Department of the South (including black regiments), who put out fires started when departing rebels blew up military supplies, instead of by Sherman's bummers, who probably would have started new fires of their own. Columbia was not so fortunate. Units from two of Sherman's corps occupied the capital on February 17; by next morning almost half of the city was rubble and ashes. The greatest atrocity charged against Sherman, the burning of Columbia also provoked an ongoing controversy about responsibility for the tragedy. The fullest and most dispassionate study of this controversy blames all parties in varying proportions—including the Confederate authorities for the disorder that characterized the evacuation of Columbia, leaving

The 55th Massachusetts Infantry, a black regiment in which one of the sons of famous abolitionist William Lloyd Garrison was an officer, was one of the first Union regiments to enter Charleston. The local black population greeted them joyfully, as portrayed in this illustration.

Artist William Waud sketched this dramatic scene of the city of Columbia, South Carolina, on fire during the night of February 17–18, 1865. Note the almost horizontal direction of the smoke and flames, from the gale-force winds that drove the fire out of control.

thousands of cotton bales in the streets (some of them burning) and huge quantities of liquor undestroyed. It turned some of the Union soldiers into inebriated incendiaries. In fact, Sherman did not deliberately burn Columbia; a majority of Union soldiers including the general himself worked through the night to put out the fires, although only the abatement of gale-force winds after 3:00 A.M. prevented more of the city from going up. In any event, the fate of Columbia was not inconsistent with the scorched-earth policy experienced by other parts of South Carolina.

Sherman kept the enemy guessing about his ultimate objective until mid-March, when it became clear that he was headed for Goldsboro and a junction with 30,000 additional bluecoats moving in from the coast. In the forlorn-hope style that had become southern strategy, Johnston planned to attack one wing of Sherman's army and try to cripple it before the remainder could come up in support. On March 16 two of Johnston's divisions fought a delaying action against four of Sherman's at Averasborough, thirty-odd miles south of Raleigh. From this affair the rebels learned that the two wings of Sherman's army were separated by a dozen or more miles. Johnston concentrated his infantry (17,000 men) to ambush about the same number of Federals strung out on the road in the advance of the left wing near Bentonville on March 19. The attackers achieved some initial success, but the Yankees dug in and repulsed several assaults during the afternoon. That night and next day the rest of Sherman's army was hard on the march to reinforce the left wing. On March 21 a Union division drove in the Confederate left, but Sherman called off the attack and let Johnston slip away during the night.

What prompted this reluctance to finish off an opponent he outnumbered by three to one? Sherman wanted to get his road-weary troops to Goldsboro to replenish equipment and supplies after seven weeks of the most strenuous campaigning of the war. Beyond that, despite his ferocious reputation Sherman was careful with the lives of his soldiers. "I don't want to lose men in a direct attack when it can be avoided," he said. He would rather win by strategy and maneuver than by battle. He was confident that the war was nearly over and that his destruction of enemy resources had done much to win it. Johnston's small and demoralized force, in Sherman's view, hardly mattered anymore. The important thing was to rest and refit his army for the move up to Virginia to help Grant "wipe out Lee."

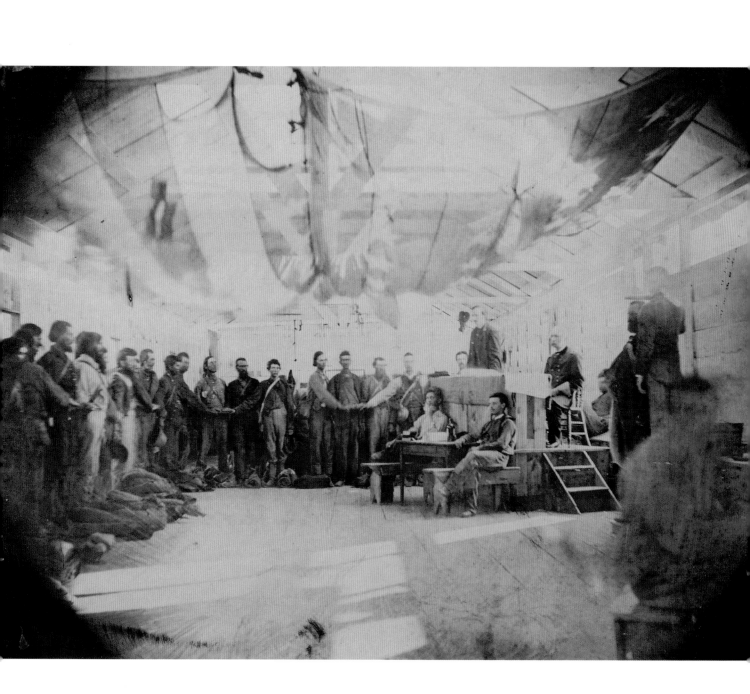

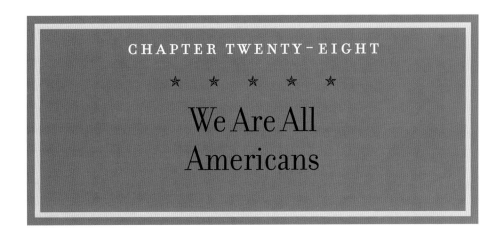

CHAPTER TWENTY-EIGHT

We Are All Americans

I

After the fall of Vicksburg and the defeat at Gettysburg, certain southerners began to entertain a notion that would formerly have been unthinkable—and regarded as treasonous by a president who had denounced the North's emancipation and recruitment of slaves. Several newspaper editors in Mississippi and Alabama began speaking out in extraordinary fashion. "We are forced by the necessity of our condition," they declared, "to take a step which is revolting to every sentiment of pride, and to every principle that governed our institutions before the war." It would be better for the South to use its slaves for defense than let the North use them to make war. Indeed, "we can make them fight better than the Yankees are able to do." Masters and overseers could make slaves fight just as effectively as they had made slaves work. It was true, admitted the *Jackson Mississippian*, that "such a step would revolutionize our whole industrial system" and perhaps lead to universal emancipation, "a dire calamity to both the negro and the white race." But losing the war would mean the end of slavery, so it came down to a matter of necessity, a choice of evils. "We must . . . save ourselves from the rapacious North, WHATEVER THE COST."

General Patrick Cleburne had been thinking along similar lines. He wrote down his ideas and presented them to division and corps commanders in the Army of Tennessee in January 1864. The South was losing the war, said Cleburne, because it lacked the North's manpower and because "slavery, from being one of our chief sources of strength at the commencement of the war, has now become, in a military point of view, one of our chief sources of weakness." The Emancipation Proclamation had given the enemy a moral cause to justify his drive for conquest, Cleburne continued, had made the slaves his allies, undermined the South's domestic security, and turned European nations against the Confederacy. Hence we are threatened with "the loss of all we now hold most sacred—slaves and all other personal property, lands, homesteads, liberty, justice, safety, pride, manhood." To save the rest of these cherished possessions we must sacrifice the first. Let us recruit an army of slaves, concluded Cleburne, and "guarantee free-

Opposite page: Union officials gave Confederate POWs the opportunity to obtain release from prison if they took an oath of allegiance to the United States. Many did so, including those photographed here at the Point Lookout (Maryland) prison camp, where each prisoner taking the oath stands with his hand on a Bible as a Union officer at the podium administers the oath under a huge American flag stretched across the ceiling. Released prisoners from areas still under Confederate control could not go home; many of them enlisted in the Union army instead. These "galvanized Yankees" went west to fight Indians.

A native of Ireland, where he had served a three-year enlistment in the British army, Patrick Cleburne emigrated to the United States in 1849. After a career as a pharmacist and lawyer in Arkansas, he joined the Confederate army and became one of only two foreign-born officers to attain the rank of major general. He might have risen higher had it not been for the hostile response to his proposal to enlist slave soldiers and give them freedom.

dom within a reasonable time to every slave in the South who shall remain true to the Confederacy."

Twelve brigade and regimental commanders in Cleburne's division endorsed his proposal, which was potentially explosive because it came from men fighting for the survival of the South and raised questions about a fundamental ambiguity in the Confederacy's *raison d'être*. Had secession been a means to the end of preserving slavery? Or was slavery one of the means for preserving the Confederacy, to be sacrificed if it no longer served that purpose? Few southerners in 1861 would have recognized any dilemma: slavery and independence were each a means as well as an end in symbiotic relationship with the other, each essential for the survival of both. By 1864, however, southerners in growing numbers were beginning to wonder if they might have to make a choice between them. "Let not slavery prove a barrier to our independence," intoned the *Jackson Mississippian*. "Although slavery is one of the principles that we started to fight for . . . if it proves an insurmountable obstacle to the achievement of our liberty and separate nationality, away with it!"

At the time of Cleburne's proposal, however, such opinions still seemed dangerous. Most generals in the Army of Tennessee disapproved of Cleburne's action, some of them vehemently. A corps commander abhorred it as "at war with my social, moral, and political principles." A shocked and angry brigadier insisted that "we are not whipped, & cannot be whipped. Our situation requires resort to no such remedy. . . . Its propositions contravene the principles upon which we fight."

Convinced that the "promulgation of such opinions" would cause "discouragements, distraction, and dissension" in the army, Jefferson Davis ordered the generals to stop discussing the matter. So complete was their compliance that the affair remained unknown outside this small circle of southern officers until the U. S. government published the war's *Official Records* a generation later. The only consequence of Cleburne's action seemed to be denial of promotion to this ablest of the army's division commanders, who was killed ten months later at the battle of Franklin.

By then the South's dire prospects had revived the notion of arming blacks. In September 1864 the governor of Louisiana declared that "the time has come for us to put into the army every able-bodied negro man as a soldier." A month later the governors of six more states, meeting in conference, enigmatically urged the impressment of slaves for "the public service as may be required." When challenged, all but two of the governors (those of Virginia and Louisiana) hastened to deny that they meant the *arming* of slaves. On November 7 Jefferson Davis urged Congress to purchase forty thousand slaves for work as teamsters, pioneers, and laborers with the promise of freedom after "service faithfully rendered." But this cautious proposal proved much too radical for most of the press and Congress. It would crack the door of Abolition, declared the *Richmond Whig*. The idea of freeing slaves who performed faithfully was based on the false assumption "that the condition of freedom is so much better for the slave than servitude, that it may be bestowed upon him as a reward." This was "a repudiation of the opinion held by the whole South . . . that servitude is a divinely appointed condition for the highest good of the slave."

Congress did not act on the president's request. But the issue would not go away. Although Davis in his November 7 message had opposed the notion of arming blacks *at that time*, he added ominously: "Should the alternative ever be presented of subjugation or the employment of the slave as a soldier, there seems no reason to doubt what should then be our decision." Within three months the alternative stared the South starkly in the face. The president and his cabinet made their choice. "We are reduced," said Davis in February 1865, "to choosing whether the negroes shall fight for or against us." And if they fought for us, echoed some newspapers, this would not necessarily produce wholesale abolition. Perhaps those who fought must be offered freedom, but that would only "affect units of the race and not the whole institution." By enabling the South to whip the Yankees, it was the only way to *save* slavery. "If the emancipation of a part is the means of saving the rest, then this partial emancipation is eminently a pro-slavery measure." Some advocates went even further and said that discipline rather than the motive of freedom was sufficient to make slaves fight. "It is not true," declared General Francis Shoup, "that to make good soldiers of these people, we must either give or promise them freedom. . . . As well might one promise to free one's cook . . . with the expectation of thereby securing good dinners."

Such talk prompted one exasperated editor to comment that "our Southern people have not gotten over the vicious habit of not believing what they don't wish to believe." Most participants in this debate recognized that if slaves became soldiers, they and probably their families must be promised freedom or they might desert to the enemy at first opportunity. If one or two hundred thousand slaves were armed (the figures most often mentioned), this would free at least half a million. Added to the million or so already liberated by the Yankees, asked opponents of the proposal, how could the institution survive?

These opponents remained in the majority until February 1865. Yet with the Yankees thundering at the gates, their arguments took flight into an aura of unreality. We can win without black help, they said, if only the absentees and stragglers return to the ranks and the whole people rededicate themselves to the Cause. "The freemen of the Confederate States must work out their own redemption, or they must be the slaves of their own slaves," proclaimed the *Charleston Mercury* edited by those original secessionists the Robert Barnwell Rhetts, father and son. "The day that the army of Virginia allows a negro regiment to enter their lines as soldiers they

Despite evidence to the contrary, southern whites long persisted in the belief that most slaves liked being slaves and also liked their masters. This drawing of a slave woman concealing her master from a Union search party reflected that belief.

will be degraded, ruined, and disgraced," roared Robert Toombs. His fellow Georgian Howell Cobb agreed that "the moment you resort to negro soldiers your white soldiers will be lost to you. . . . The day you make soldiers of them is the beginning of the end of the revolution. If slaves will make good soldiers our whole theory of slavery is wrong."

And was not that the theory the South fought for? "It would be the most extraordinary instance of self-stultification the world ever saw" to arm and emancipate slaves, declared the Rhetts. "It is abolition doctrine . . . the very doctrine which the war was commenced to put down," maintained a North Carolina newspaper. It would "surrender the essential and distinctive principle of Southern civilization," agreed the *Richmond Examiner*. Many southerners apparently preferred to lose the war than to win it with the help of black men. "Victory itself would be robbed of its glory if shared with slaves," said a Mississippi congressman. Senator Louis Wigfall of Texas "wanted to live in no country in which the man who blacked his boots and curried his horse was his equal." "If such a terrible calamity is to befall us," declared the *Lynchburg Republican*, "we infinitely prefer that Lincoln shall be the instrument of our disaster and degradation, than that we ourselves should strike the cowardly and suicidal blow."

But the shock effect of Lincoln's insistence at Hampton Roads on unconditional surrender helped the Davis administration make headway against these arguments. During February many petitions and letters from soldiers in the Petersburg trenches poured into Richmond to challenge the belief that white soldiers would refuse to fight alongside blacks. Robert E. Lee's opinion would have a decisive influence. For months rumors had circulated that he favored arming the slaves. Lee had indeed expressed his private opinion that "we should employ them without delay [even] at the risk which may be produced upon our social institutions." On February 18 he broke his public silence with a letter to the congressional sponsor of a Negro soldier bill. This measure was "not only expedient but necessary," wrote Lee. "The negroes, under proper circumstances, will make efficient soldiers. I think we could at least do as well with them as the enemy. . . . Those who are employed should be freed. It would be neither just nor wise . . . to require them to serve as slaves."

Lee's great prestige carried the day—but just barely. By a vote of 40 to 37 the House passed a bill authorizing the president to requisition a quota of black soldiers from each state. In deference to state's rights, the bill did not mandate freedom for slave soldiers. The Senate nevertheless defeated the measure by a single vote, with both senators from Lee's own state voting No. The Virginia legislature meanwhile enacted its own law for the enlistment of black soldiers—without, however, requiring the emancipation of those who were slaves—and instructed its senators to vote for the congressional bill. They did so, enabling it to pass by 9 to 8 (with several abstentions) and become law on March 13. In the few weeks of life left to the Confederacy no other state followed Virginia's lead. The two companies of black soldiers hastily organized in Richmond never saw action. Nor did most of these men obtain freedom until the Yankees—headed by a black cavalry regiment—marched into the Confederate capital on April 3.

A last-minute diplomatic initiative to secure British and French recognition in return for emancipation also proved barren of results. The impetus for this effort came from Duncan F. Kenner of Louisiana, a prominent member of the Confederate Congress and one of the South's largest slaveholders. Convinced since 1862 that slavery was a foreign-policy millstone around the Confederacy's neck, Kenner had long urged an emancipationist diplomacy. His proposals got nowhere until December 1864, when Jefferson Davis, though aware he would ultimately need approval from Congress and state legislatures, called Kenner in and conceded that the time had come to play this last card. Consequently, Kenner traveled to Paris and London as a special envoy to offer abolition for recognition. His difficulties in getting out of the Confederacy foretokened the fate of his mission. The fall of Fort Fisher prevented his departure on a blockade runner. Forced to make his way in disguise to New York, Kenner sailed to France only to find that Louis Napoleon as usual would not act without Britain. So James Mason accompanied Kenner to London, where on March 14 they presented the proposition to Palmerston. Once again the Confederates learned the hard lesson of diplomacy: nothing succeeds like military success. The South had never been able to convince the British government that independence was within its grasp, an essential prerequisite for recognition. Recent setbacks, Mason reported to Secretary of State Benjamin, "increased rather than diminished" Britain's reluctance to grant recognition.

II

While the South debated the relationship of slavery to its Cause, the North acted. Lincoln interpreted his reelection as a mandate for passage of the thirteenth Amendment to end slavery forever. The voters had retired a large number of Democratic congressmen. But until the thirty-eighth Congress expired on March 4, 1865, they retained their seats and could block House passage of the amendment by the necessary two-thirds majority. In the next Congress the Republicans would have a three-quarters House majority and could easily pass it. Lincoln intended to call a special session in March if necessary to do the job. But he preferred to accomplish it sooner, by a bipartisan majority, as a gesture of wartime unity in favor of this measure that Lincoln considered essential to Union victory. "In a great national crisis, like ours," he told Congress in his message of December 6, 1864, "unanimity of action among those seeking a common end is very desirable—almost indispensable." This was an expression of an ideal rather than reality, since most war measures, especially those concerning slavery, had been passed by a strictly Republican vote. For the historic achievement of terminating the institution, however, Lincoln appealed to Democrats to recognize the "will of the majority" as expressed by the election.

But most Democrats preferred to stand on principle in defense of the past. Even if the war had killed slavery, they refused to help bury it. The party remained officially opposed to the thirteenth Amendment as "unwise, impolitic, cruel, and unworthy of the support of civilized people." A few Democratic congressmen believed otherwise, however. The party had suffered disaster in the 1864 election, said one,

The central panel of this Thomas Nast drawing shows a family of freed slaves enjoying their new status. At left are scenes of slavery—fugitive slaves hunted down in a swamp, a black man sold apart from his wife and children, a slave woman whipped, and a man branded. At right Nast portrays his optimistic view of freedom—a black mother sending her children to school and a black man receiving wages for his labor.

"because we [would] not venture to cut loose from the dead carcass of negro slavery." Another declared that to persist in opposition to the amendment "will be to simply announce ourselves a set of impracticables no more fit to deal with practical affairs than the old gentleman in Copperfield." Encouraged by such sentiments, the Lincoln administration targeted a dozen or so lame-duck Democratic congressmen and subjected them to a barrage of blandishments. Secretary of State Seward oversaw this lobbying effort. Some congressmen were promised government jobs for themselves or relatives; others received administration favors of one sort or another.

This arm-twisting and log-rolling paid off. Sixteen of the eighty Democrats finally voted for the amendment; fourteen of them were lame ducks. Eight other Democrats had absented themselves. This enabled the amendment to pass with two votes to spare, 119 to 56. When the result was announced, Republicans on the floor and spectators in the gallery broke into prolonged—and unprecedented—cheering, while in the streets of Washington cannons boomed a hundred-gun salute. By acclamation the House voted to adjourn for the rest of the day "in honor of this immortal and sublime event."

The Thirteenth Amendment sped quickly through Republican state legislatures that were in session; within a week eight states had ratified it, and during the next two months another eleven did so. Ratification by five additional northern states was certain as soon as their legislatures met. Of the Union states only those carried by McClellan in the presidential election—New Jersey, Kentucky, and Delaware—held out. The "reconstructed" states of Louisiana, Arkansas, and Tennessee ratified readily. Since the Lincoln administration had fought the war on the theory that states could not secede, it considered ratification by three-quarters of *all* the states including those in the Confederacy to be necessary. One of the first tasks of reconstruction would be to obtain the ratification of at least three more ex-Confederate states to place the amendment in the Constitution.

Among the spectators who cheered and wept for joy when the House passed the Thirteenth Amendment were many black people. Their presence was a visible symbol of the revolutionary changes signified by the amendment, for until 1864 Negroes had not been allowed in congressional galleries. Blacks were also admitted to White House social functions for the first time in 1865, and Lincoln went out of his way to welcome Frederick Douglass to the inaugural reception on March 4. Congress and northern states enacted legislation that began to break down the pattern of second-class citizenship for northern Negroes: admission of black witnesses to federal courts; repeal of an old law that barred blacks from carrying mail; prohibition of segregation on streetcars in the District of Columbia; repeal of black laws in several northern states that had imposed certain kinds of discrimination against Negroes or barred their entry into the state; and steps to submit referendums to the voters of several states to grant the ballot to blacks (none of these referendums passed until 1868).

Perhaps the most dramatic symbol of change occurred on February 1, the day after House passage of the Thirteenth Amendment. On that day Senator Charles Sumner presented Boston lawyer John Rock for admission to practice before the Supreme Court, and Chief Justice Salmon P. Chase swore him in. There was nothing unusual in this except that Rock was a black man, the first Negro accredited to the highest court, which eight years earlier had denied U.S. citizenship to his race. The Court had been virtually reconstructed by Lincoln's appointment of five new justices including Chase. The transition from Roger Taney to Chase as leader of the Court was itself the most sweeping judicial metamorphosis in American history.

Important questions concerning emancipation and reconstruction

This contemporary engraving portrays the celebration on the floor of the House and in the galleries when Congress finally passed the Thirteenth Amendment on January 31, 1865.

A man of learning and eloquence, John Rock had graduated from the American Medical College in Philadelphia and had practiced as a physician while reading law and becoming a member of the Massachusetts Bar. He could read French and German. In the Dred Scott decision in 1857, the Supreme Court had declared that such men as Rock were not citizens of the United States; in 1865 Rock was certified to argue cases before the same court. Three of the justices who had participated in the Dred Scott decision were still there.

Thousands of slaves of all ages and both sexes followed Sherman's army as it marched through Georgia. Most fell out along the way; some died; others were captured by Confederate cavalry and returned to slavery. But almost seven thousand made it to Savannah with the army.

were sure to come before this new Court. Two such questions might well grow out of actions taken in the area of freedmen's affairs during the winter of 1864–65. Thousands of contrabands had attached themselves to Sherman's army on its march from Atlanta to the sea. Reports filtered northward of Sherman's indifference to their welfare and of ill-treatment of them by some officers and men. To sort out the rumors and problems, Secretary of War Stanton journeyed to Savannah in January for a talk with Sherman and an interview with black leaders, most of them former slaves. Among the questions Stanton asked these men was how best they could support their families in freedom. "The way we can best take care of ourselves," they answered, "is to have land, and turn in and till it by our labor. . . . We want to be placed on land until we are able to buy it, and make it our own."

Stanton and Sherman thought this a good idea, so the conservative general prepared the most radical field order of the war. Issued January 16, Sherman's "Special Field Orders, No. 15" designated the sea islands and the rich plantation areas bordering rivers for thirty miles inland from Charleston down to Jacksonville for settlement by freedmen. Each head of family could be granted forty acres of land, to which he would be given a "possessory title" until Congress "shall regulate their title." This land had of course belonged to slaveholders. Their dispossession of it by Sherman's order, like Lincoln's dispossession of their slaves by the Emancipation Proclamation, was a military measure carried out under "war powers." The Thirteenth Amendment confirmed Lincoln's action; it remained to be seen how Court, Congress, and Executive would deal with the consequences of Sherman's Order No. 15. The army did not wait, however. During the next several months General Rufus Saxton, an abolitionist who commanded the Union occupation forces on the South Carolina sea islands, supervised the settlement of forty thousand freedmen on land designated in Sherman's order.

The wartime experience of Union army officers who governed occupied territory, of treasury agents who had charge of abandoned plantations, and of freedmen's aid societies that sent missionaries and teachers to the freed slaves made clear the need for a government agency to coordinate their efforts. All too often these various groups pulled in different directions—and the freedmen themselves in still another direction. In 1863 Congress first considered legislation to create a Freedmen's Bureau. Disagreement whether this agency should be part of the War or the Treasury Department prevented final enactment of a bill until March 3, 1865. By then Chase was no longer secretary of the treasury, so radical Republicans who had wanted him in charge of the Bureau were now willing to place it in the War Department. The function of the Bureau (formally called the Bureau of Refugees, Freedmen, and Abandoned Lands) would be to dispense rations and relief to the hundreds of thousands of white as well as black refugees uprooted by the war and to assist the freedmen during the difficult transition from slavery to freedom. Congress also gave the Bureau control of "abandoned" land with the provision that individual freedmen "shall be assigned not more than forty acres" of such land at rental for three years and an option to buy at the end of that time with "such title thereto as the United States can convey." Here was Sherman's Order No. 15 writ large. Whether Congress would be able to convey any title was a troublesome question, given the constitutional ban on bills of attainder and the presidential power of pardon and restoration of property. In any event, the Freedmen's Bureau represented an unprecedented extension of the federal government into matters of social welfare and labor relations—to meet unprecedented problems produced by the emancipation of four million slaves and the building of a new society on the ashes of the old.

The success or failure of the Freedmen's Bureau would be partly determined by the political terms of reconstruction. This matter occupied much of Congress's time during the winter of 1864–65. Prospects seemed good for a compromise with the

When the Freedmen's Bureau came into existence in March 1865, it inherited many "freedmen's villages" such as this one near Arlington, Virginia. One of the Bureau's main functions was the support of northern missionary education societies that sent teachers and books to educate the former slaves, several dozen of whom posed with books in hand for the photographer.

president. The afterglow of a Republican electoral sweep had dissolved the bitterness that had crested with Lincoln's pocket veto of the Wade-Davis bill. Chase's elevation to the Court was another step toward rapprochement between Lincoln and radical Republicans. The president's reference to reconstruction in his message to Congress on December 6 hinted at the likelihood of "more rigorous measures than heretofore." This willingness to meet Congress halfway set the stage for an attempt to enact a new reconstruction bill. The outlines of such legislation soon emerged in negotiations between Lincoln and congressional leaders: Congress would accept the already reconstructed regimes of Louisiana and Arkansas (soon to be joined by Tennessee) in return for a presidential promise to sign legislation similar to the Wade-Davis bill for the other Confederate states.

As first introduced in the House this new bill enfranchised "all male citizens"—including blacks. Lincoln persuaded the committee chairman in charge of the bill to modify it to limit this provision to black soldiers. During the next two months the measure went through a bewildering series of revisions and amendments in committee and on the House floor. Democrats voted with moderate Republicans to defeat the more radical versions of the bill and joined radicals to defeat the more conservative versions. Consequently no bill could be passed. Not wishing to create a precedent for Executive reconstruction by seating Louisiana's senators and representatives in Congress, radicals teamed with Democrats to deny them admission. Thus the 38th Congress expired without any further action on reconstruction. Radical Republicans thought this just as well. The next Congress would have more radicals and fewer Democrats, noted one of them, and "in the meantime I hope the nation may be educated up to our demand for universal suffrage."

The prospect of "educating" Lincoln up to this demand seemed promising. He had moved steadily leftward on emancipation during the war, which suggested that he might move to a broader platform of equal suffrage by the time the war ended. The entreaty in Lincoln's second inaugural address for "malice toward none" and "charity for all" provided few clues on this question, though it seemed to endorse generous treatment of ex-rebels. At the same time this address left no doubt of Lincoln's intention to fight on until slavery was crushed forever. "Fondly do we hope—fervently do we pray—that this mighty scourge of war may speedily pass away," said the nation's sixteenth president at the beginning of his second term. "Yet if God wills that it continue, until all the wealth piled up by the bondman's two hundred and fifty years of unrequited toil shall be sunk, and until every drop of blood drawn with the lash, shall be paid by another drawn with the sword, as was said three thousand years ago, so it must be said 'the judgments of the Lord, are true and righteous altogether.'"

III

Ulysses S. Grant was determined that it should not take that long. During the winter, Union forces at Petersburg had fought their way westward to cut off the last road into town from the south and threaten the last open railroad. With Lee's army of 55,000 melting away by desertions while the oncoming spring dried

roads after an exceptionally raw, wet winter, the final success of Grant's 120,000 seemed only a matter of time. Sherman could be expected on Lee's rear by late April, but Grant wanted the Army of the Potomac to "vanquish their old enemy" without help that might produce future gloating by Sherman's veterans. "I mean to end the business here," the general in chief told Phil Sheridan. Grant's main concern now was that he might wake one morning to find Lee gone to join Johnston's 20,000 for an attack on Sherman. Lee had precisely that in mind. In his effort to accomplish it, however, he gave Grant a long-sought opportunity to drive the ragged rebels from their trenches into the open.

By March, Lee had become convinced that he must soon abandon the Petersburg lines to save his army from encirclement. This would mean the fall of Richmond, but better that than loss of the army which was the only thread holding the Confederacy together. To force Grant to contract his lines and loosen the stranglehold blocking a rebel escape, Lee planned a surprise attack on the enemy position just east of Petersburg. Southern corps commander John B. Gordon sent false deserters to fraternize with Yankee pickets in front of Fort Stedman on the night of March 24–25. The "deserters" suddenly seized the dumbfounded pickets, and Gordon's divisions swarmed into sleepy Fort Stedman. Capturing several batteries and a half-mile of trenches, the Confederates seemed to have achieved a smashing breakthrough. But a northern counterattack recaptured all lost ground plus the forward trenches of the Confederate line, trapping many of the rebels and forcing them to surrender. Lee lost nearly 5,000 men; Grant only 2,000. Instead of compelling Grant to shorten his lines, Lee had to thin his own to the breaking point. And Grant lost little time in breaking them.

These veteran soldiers of the Army of the Potomac await the beginning of Grant's spring offensive. Like Grant, they appear determined "to end the business here."

One of the strongpoints of the Confederate defenses at Petersburg was Fort Gregg. Alfred R. Waud drew this sketch of the successful Union attack against this position on the morning of April 2, 1865.

On March 29 he ordered an infantry corps and Sheridan's cavalry, recently returned from the Shenandoah Valley, to turn the Confederate right ten miles southwest of Petersburg. Lee sent George Pickett with two divisions of infantry through a drenching downpour to help the worn-down rebel cavalry counter this move. Hard fighting across a sodden landscape on the last day of March stopped the Federals temporarily. But next afternoon they launched an enveloping attack against Pickett's isolated force at the road junction of Five Forks. Sheridan's rapid-firing troopers, fighting on foot, attacked head-on, while Gouverneur K. Warren's 5th Corps moved sluggishly against Pickett's flank. Storming up and down the line cajoling and god-damning the infantry to move faster and hit harder, Sheridan finally coordinated an assault that achieved the most one-sided Union victory since the long campaign began eleven months earlier in the Wilderness. Pickett's divisions collapsed, half of their men surrendering to the whooping Yankees and the other half running rearward in rout. When the news reached Grant that evening, he ordered an assault all along the line next morning, April 2.

At dawn it came, with more élan and power than the Army of the Potomac had shown for a long time. And the Army of Northern Virginia—weary, hungry, shorn of more than one-fifth of its strength by the fighting on March 25 and April 1— could no longer hold the Yankees off. Sheridan got astride the last railroad into Petersburg, and the blue infantry punched through Confederate lines at several places southwest of the city. The rebels fought desperately as they fell back, but it was only to hold on to the inner defenses until dark in order to get away.

For Lee knew that he must pull out. As Jefferson Davis worshiped at St. Paul's Church in Richmond this balmy Sunday, a messenger quietly gave him a telegram from Lee; Richmond must be abandoned. Parishioners read the message on his face, and the news spread quickly through the city. Everyone who could beg, borrow, or steal a conveyance left town. Government officials crowded aboard ramshackle trains headed for Danville with the Treasury's remaining gold and as much of the archives as they could carry, the rest being put to the torch. So was every-

thing of military and industrial value in Richmond. As night came and the army departed, mobs took over and the flames spread. Southerners burned more of their own capital than the enemy had burned of Atlanta or Columbia. When the Yankees arrived next morning, their first tasks were to restore order and put out the flames. Among the troops who marched into Richmond as firemen and policemen were units from the all-black 25th Corps.

Following the northern soldiers into Richmond came Abraham Lincoln, who wanted to witness the apparently imminent end of this terrible conflict. Commander in chief and general in chief entered Petersburg on April 3 only hours after the Army of Northern Virginia had left. Grant soon rode west on the chase to head off Lee. Lincoln returned to the Union base on the James River and told Admiral David D. Porter: "Thank God I have lived to see this. It seems to me that I have been

This dramatic drawing by Thomas Nast depicts Lincoln's walk through the streets of Richmond on April 4 surrounded by wildly cheering black people. Note the scowling white couple at the right and two Union sailors armed with carbines at left.

dreaming a horrid dream for four years, and now the nightmare is gone. I want to see Richmond." On April 4 Porter took Lincoln upriver to the enemy capital, where the president of the United States sat down in the study of the president of the Confederate States forty hours after Davis had left it.

Lincoln's visit to Richmond produced the most unforgettable scenes of this unforgettable war. With an escort of only ten sailors, the president walked the streets while Porter peered nervously at every window for would-be assassins. But the Emancipator was soon surrounded by an impenetrable cordon of black people shouting, "Glory to God! Glory! Glory! Glory!" and "Bless the Lord! The great Messiah! I knowed him as soon as I seed him. He's been in my heart four long years. Come to free his children from bondage. Glory, Hallelujah!" Several freed slaves touched Lincoln to make sure he was real. "I know I am free," shouted an old woman, "for I have seen Father Abraham and felt him." Overwhelmed by rare emotions, Lincoln said to one black man who fell on his knees in front of him: "Don't kneel to me. That is not right. You must kneel to God only, and thank Him for the liberty you will enjoy hereafter."

*   *   *   *   *

For Robert E. Lee and his army the retreat from Richmond turned into a nightmare. Reduced to 35,000 men, the scattered divisions from Petersburg and Richmond rendezvoused at Amelia Courthouse thirty-five miles to the west, where the starving men expected to find a trainload of rations. Because of a mixup they found ammunition instead, the last thing they needed since the worn-out horses could scarcely pull the ordnance the army was carrying. A delay to forage the countryside for food proved fatal. Lee had intended to follow the railroad down to Danville, where he could link up with Johnston and where Jefferson Davis on April 4 issued a rallying cry to his people: "Relieved from the necessity of guarding cities . . . with our army free to move from point to point . . . and where the foe will be far removed from his own base . . . nothing is now needed to render our triumph certain, but . . . our own unquenchable resolve." But the foe was closer to Danville than Lee's army was. Racing alongside the retreating rebels a few miles to the south were Sheridan's cavalry and three infantry corps. On April 5 they cut the Danville railroad, forcing Lee to change direction toward Lynchburg and the Blue Ridge passes beyond.

But this goal too was frustrated by the weariness of Lee's despondent men and the speed of Union pursuers who sniffed victory and the end of the war. Stabbing attacks by blue cavalry garnered scores of prisoners, while hundreds of other southerners collapsed in exhaustion by the roadside and waited for the Yankees to pick them up. Along an obscure stream named Sayler's Creek on April 6, three Union

Union attacks at Sayler's Creek on April 6, 1865, cut off and captured most of Richard Ewell's corps. This contemporary sketch shows the surrender of some of these men.

corps cut off a quarter of Lee's army, captured 6,000 of them, and destroyed much of their wagon train. "My God!" exclaimed Lee when he learned of this action. "Has the army been dissolved?"

Not yet, but it soon would be. As the remaining rebels trudged westward on April 7, Grant sent Lee a note under flag of truce calling on him to surrender. Lee responded with a feeler about Grant's terms. The northern commander offered the same terms as at Vicksburg: parole until exchanged. Since Lee's surrender would virtually end the war, the part about exchange was a mere formality. As the tension mounted on April 8—Grant had a splitting headache, and Meade suffered from nausea—Lee parried with a vague proposal to discuss a general "restoration of peace," a political matter on which Grant had no authority to negotiate. Grant shook his aching head and commented: "It looks as if Lee meant to fight."

Lee did have that notion, intending to try a breakout attack against Sheridan's troopers blocking the road near Appomattox Courthouse on the morning of April 9. For the last time rebel yells shattered the Palm Sunday stillness as the gray scarecrows drove back Union horsemen—only to reveal two Yankee infantry corps coming into line behind them. Two other Union corps were closing in on Lee's rear. Almost surrounded, outnumbered by five or six to one in effective troops, Lee faced up to the inevitable. One of his subordinates suggested an alternative to surrender: the men could take to the woods and become guerrillas. No, said Lee, who did not want all of Virginia devastated as the Shenandoah Valley had been; "we would bring on a state of affairs it would take the country years to recover from." With a heavy heart Lee decided that "there is nothing left for me to do but go and see General Grant, and I would rather die a thousand deaths."

Lee sent a note through the lines offering to surrender. Grant's headache and Meade's illness vanished. The bleeding and dying were over; they had won. To the

This etching of Wilmer McLean's parlor at Appomattox is one of many such scenes portrayed by artists (no photographer was present). Lee sits at left as Colonel Charles Marshall of his staff leans against the mantel; Grant sits at center writing the terms of surrender. The other Union officers in the room include General Philip Sheridan at the far right.

home of Wilmer McLean went Lee and Grant for the surrender formalities. In 1861 McLean had lived near Manassas, where his house was a Confederate headquarters and a Yankee shell had crashed into his kitchen. He moved to this remote village in southside Virginia to escape the contending armies only to find the final drama of the war played out in his living room. The vanquished commander, six feet tall and erect in bearing, arrived in full-dress uniform with sash and jeweled sword; the victor, five feet eight with stooped shoulders, appeared in his usual private's blouse with mud-spattered trousers tucked into muddy boots—because his headquarters wagon had fallen behind in the race to cut off the enemy. There in McLean's parlor the son of an Ohio tanner dictated surrender terms to the scion of a First Family of Virginia.

The terms were generous: officers and men could go home "not to be disturbed by U.S. authority so long as they observe their paroles and the laws in force where they may reside." This clause had great significance. Serving as a model for the subsequent surrender of other Confederate armies, it guaranteed southern soldiers immunity from prosecution for treason. Lee asked another favor. In the Confederate army, he explained, enlisted men in the cavalry and artillery owned their horses; could they keep them? Yes, said Grant; privates as well as officers who claimed to own horses could take them home "to put in a crop to carry themselves and their families through the next winter." "This will have the best possible effect upon the men," said Lee, and "will do much toward conciliating our people." After signing the papers, Grant introduced Lee to his staff. As he shook hands with Grant's military secretary Ely Parker, a Seneca Indian, Lee stared a moment at Parker's dark features and said, "I am glad to see one real American here." Parker responded, "We are all Americans."

Colonel Ely Parker, Grant's military secretary, who copied out Grant's surrender terms in his elegant handwriting. When introduced to Parker, General Lee initially mistook him for an African-American, then realized his mistake. This photograph was taken several years after the war when Parker was commissioner of Indian affairs during Grant's presidency.

The surrender completed, the two generals saluted somberly and parted. Having given birth to a reunited nation, Grant experienced a postpartum melancholy. "I felt . . . sad and depressed," Grant wrote, "at the downfall of a foe who had fought so long and valiantly, and had suffered so much for a cause, though that cause was, I believe, one of the worst for which a people ever fought." As news of the surrender spread through Union camps, batteries began firing joyful salutes until Grant ordered them stopped. "The war is over," he said; "the rebels are our countrymen again, and the best sign of rejoicing after the victory will be to abstain from all demonstrations." To help bring those former rebels back into the Union, Grant sent three days' rations for 25,000 men across the lines. This perhaps did something to ease the psychological as well as physical pain of Lee's soldiers.

So did an important symbolic gesture at a formal ceremony three days later when Confederate troops marched up to stack arms and surrender their flags. As they came, many among them shared the sentiments of one officer: "Was this to be the end of all our marching and fighting for the past four years? I could not keep back the tears." The Union officer in charge of the surrender ceremony was Joshua L. Chamberlain, the fighting professor from Bowdoin who won a medal of honor for Little Round Top, had been twice wounded since then, and was now a major general. Leading the southerners as they marched toward two of Chamberlain's

Even before the rations arrived that Grant ordered sent to the Confederate camp at Appomattox, many Union soldiers shared their own rations with the famished and now vanquished enemy soldiers, as shown in this sketch made at the time.

brigades standing at attention was John B. Gordon, one of Lee's hardest fighters, who now commanded Stonewall Jackson's old corps. First in line of march behind him was the Stonewall Brigade, five regiments containing 210 ragged survivors of four years of war. As Gordon approached at the head of these men with "his chin drooped to his breast, downhearted and dejected in appearance," Chamberlain gave a brief order, and a bugle call rang out. Instantly the Union soldiers shifted from order arms to carry arms, the salute of honor. Hearing the sound, General Gordon looked up in surprise, and with sudden realization turned smartly to Chamberlain, dipped his sword in salute, and ordered his own men to carry arms. These enemies in many a bloody battle ended the war not with shame on one side and exultation on the other but with a soldier's "mutual salutation and farewell."

The news of Lee's surrender traveled through a North barely recovered from boisterous celebrations of Richmond's capture. The fall of the rebel capital had merited a *nine-hundred* gun salute in Washington; the surrender of Lee produced another five hundred. "From one end of Pennsylvania Avenue to the other," wrote a reporter, "the air seemed to burn with the bright hues of the flag. . . . Almost by magic the streets were crowded with hosts of people, talking, laughing, hurrahing and shouting in the fullness of their joy. Men embraced one another, 'treated' one another, made up old quarrels, renewed old friendships, marched arm-in-arm singing." The scene was similar on Wall Street in New York, where "men embraced and hugged each other, *kissed* each other, retreated into doorways to dry their eyes and came out again to flourish their hats and hurrah," according to an eyewitness.

Another observer commented that the intensity of feeling was "founded on memories of years of failure, all but hopeless, and the consciousness that national victory was at last secured."

Lincoln shared this joyous release of pent-up tension, but he was already thinking more of the future than of the past. On April 11 he delivered from a White House balcony a carefully prepared speech on peace and reconstruction to a crowd celebrating Union victory. "There is no authorized organ for us to treat with," he said—thereby disposing of state governments as well as Jefferson Davis's fugitive government. "We must simply begin with, and mould from, disorganized and discordant elements." This he had done in Louisiana, Arkansas, and Tennessee. Defending the government of Louisiana, Lincoln conceded that he would prefer it to have enfranchised literate Negroes and black veterans. He hoped that it would soon do so; as for the unreconstructed states, Lincoln promised an announcement soon of a new policy for their restoration to the Union.

At least one listener interpreted this speech as moving Lincoln closer to the radical Republicans. "That means nigger citizenship," snarled John Wilkes Booth to a companion. "Now, by God, I'll put him through. That is the last speech he will ever make."

Lined up opposite General Chamberlain and his troops at the formal surrender ceremony on April 12, Confederate soldiers have stacked their arms and are furling their shot-torn battle flag for the last time.

EPILOGUE

★ ★ ★ ★ ★

To the Shoals of Victory

The weeks after Booth fulfilled his vow on Good Friday passed in a dizzying sequence of events. Jarring images dissolved and re-formed in kaleidoscopic patterns that left the senses traumatized or elated: Lincoln lying in state at the White House on April 19 as General Grant wept unabashedly at his catafalque; Confederate armies surrendering one after another as Jefferson Davis fled southward hoping to reestablish his government in Texas and carry on the war to victory; Booth killed in a burning barn in Virginia; seven million somber men, women, and children lining the tracks to view Lincoln's funeral train on its way back home to Springfield; the steamboat *Sultana* returning northward on the Mississippi with liberated Union prisoners of war blowing up on April 27 with a loss of life equal to that of the *Titanic* a half-century later; Jefferson Davis captured in Georgia on May 10, accused (falsely) of complicity in Lincoln's assassination, imprisoned and temporarily shackled at Fortress Monroe, Virginia, where he remained for two years until released without trial to live on until his eighty-first year and become part of the ex-Confederate literary corps who wrote weighty tomes to justify their Cause; the Army of the Potomac and Sherman's Army of Georgia marching 200,000 strong in a Grand Review down Pennsylvania Avenue on May 23–24 in a pageantry of power and catharsis before being demobilized from more than 1,000,000 soldiers to fewer than 80,000 a year later and an eventual peacetime total of 27,000; weary, ragged Confederate soldiers straggling homeward begging or stealing food from dispirited civilians who often did not know where their own next meal was coming from; joyous black people celebrating the jubilee of a freedom whose boundaries they did not yet discern; gangs of southern deserters, guerrillas, and outlaws ravaging a region that would not know real peace for many years to come.

The terms of that peace and the dimensions of black freedom would preoccupy the country for a decade or more. Meanwhile the process of chronicling the war and reckoning its consequences began immediately and has never ceased. More than 620,000 soldiers lost their lives in four years of conflict—360,000 Yankees and at least 260,000

Opposite page: The armed might of the victorious republic marches in review down Pennsylvania Avenue past the White House in celebration of Union victory.

rebels. The number of southern civilians who died as a direct or indirect result of the war cannot be known; what *can* be said is that the Civil War's cost in American lives was almost as great as in all of the nation's other wars combined through Vietnam. Was the liberation of four million slaves and the preservation of the Union worth the cost? That question too will probably never cease to be debated—but in 1865 few black people and not many northerners doubted the answer.

In time even a good many southerners came to agree with the sentiments of Woodrow Wilson (a native of Virginia who lived four years of his childhood in wartime Georgia) expressed in 1880 when he was a law student at the University of Virginia: "*Because* I love the South, I rejoice in the failure of the Confederacy. . . . Conceive of this Union divided into two separate and independent sovereignties! . . . Slavery was enervating our Southern society. . . . [Nevertheless] I recognize and pay loving tribute to the virtues of the leaders of secession . . . the righteousness of the cause which they thought they were promoting—and to the immortal courage of the soldiers of the Confederacy." Wilson's words embodied themes that would help reconcile generations of southerners to defeat: their glorious forebears had fought courageously for what they believed was right; perhaps they deserved to win; but in the long run it was a good thing they lost. This Lost Cause mentality took on the proportions of a heroic legend, a southern *Götterdämmerung* with Robert E. Lee as a latter-day Siegfried.

But a persistent question has nagged histo-

By 1865, hundreds of thousands of soldiers had been hastily buried in battlefield graves or near military hospitals, such as this cemetery near the general hospital at the Union supply base of City Point (today Hopewell), Virginia. The names of most of those buried here were known; more than half of those in battlefield graves were unknown. Most Union dead were eventually reinterred in two dozen or more national military cemeteries; Confederate dead were reinterred in scores of local cemeteries throughout the South.

rians and mythologists alike: if Marse Robert was such a genius and his legions so invincible, why did they lose? The answers, though almost as legion as Lee's soldiers, tend to group themselves into a few main categories. One popular answer has been phrased, from the northern perspective, by quoting Frederick the Great's aphorism that God was on the side of the heaviest battalions. For southerners this explanation usually took some such form as these words of a Virginian: "They never whipped us, Sir, unless they were four to one. If we had had anything like a fair chance, or less disparity of numbers, we should have won our cause and established our independence." The North had a potential manpower superiority of more than three to one (counting only white men), and Union armed forces had an actual superiority of two to one during most of the war. In economic resources and logistical capacity the northern advantage was even greater. Thus, in this explanation, the Confederacy fought against overwhelming odds; its defeat was inevitable.

But this explanation has not satisfied a good many analysts. History is replete with examples of peoples who have won or defended their independence against greater odds: the Netherlands against the Spain of Philip II; Switzerland against the Hapsburg Empire; the American rebels of 1776 against mighty Britain; North Vietnam against the United States of 1970. Given the advantages of fighting on the defensive in its own territory with interior lines in which stalemate would be victory against a foe who must invade, conquer, occupy, and destroy the capacity to resist, the odds faced by the South were not formidable. Rather, as another category of interpretations has it, internal divisions fatally weakened the Confederacy: the state's-rights conflict between certain governors and the Richmond government; the disaffection of nonslaveholders from a rich man's war and poor man's fight; libertarian opposition to necessary measures such as conscription and the suspension of habeas corpus; the lukewarm commitment to the Confederacy by quondam Whigs and unionists; the disloyalty of slaves who defected to the enemy whenever

This painting by a Northern artist (Henry Mosler) in 1868 portrays a grimmer and less heroic version of the Lost Cause than later became popular in the South. This is an image of death and despair, as the Confederate veteran returns to his home to find everything in ruins and his family gone, probably dead.

they had a chance; growing doubts among slaveowners themselves about the justice of their peculiar institution and their cause. "So the Confederacy succumbed to internal rather than external causes," according to numerous historians. The South suffered from a "weakness in morale," a "loss of the will to fight." The Confederacy did not lack "the means to continue the struggle" but "the will to do so."

The "internal division" and "lack of will" explanations for Confederate defeat, while not implausible, are not very convincing either. The problem is that the North experienced similar internal divisions, and if the war had come out differently the Yankees' lack of unity and will to win could be cited with equal plausibility to explain that outcome. The North had its large minority alienated by the rich man's war/poor man's fight theme; its outspoken opposition to conscription, taxation, suspension of habeas corpus, and other war measures; its state governors and legislatures and congressmen who tried to thwart administration policies. If important elements of the southern population, white as well as black, grew disaffected with a war to preserve slavery, equally significant groups in the North dissented from a war to abolish slavery. One critical distinction between Union and Confederacy was the institutionalization of obstruction in the Democratic party in the North, compelling the Republicans to close ranks in support of war policies to overcome and ultimately to discredit the opposition, while the South had no such institutionalized political structure to mobilize support and vanquish resistance.

Nevertheless, the existence of internal divisions on both sides seemed to neutralize this factor as an explanation for Union victory, so a number of historians have looked instead at the quality of leadership both military and civilian. There are several variants of an interpretation that emphasizes a gradual development of superior northern leadership. In Beauregard, Lee, the two Johnstons, and Jackson the South enjoyed abler military commanders during the first year or two of the war, while Jefferson Davis was better qualified by training and experience than Lincoln to lead a nation at war. But Lee's strategic vision was limited to the Virginia theater, and the Confederate government neglected the West, where Union armies developed a strategic design and the generals to carry it out, while southern forces floundered under incompetent commanders who lost the war in the West. By 1863 Lincoln's remarkable abilities gave him a wide edge over Davis as a war leader, while in Grant and Sherman the North acquired commanders with a concept of total war and the necessary determination to make it succeed. At the same time, in Edwin M. Stanton and Montgomery Meigs, aided by the entrepreneurial talent of northern businessmen, the Union developed superior managerial talent to mobilize and organize the North's greater resources for victory in the modern industrialized conflict that the Civil War became.

This interpretation comes closer than others to credibility. Yet it also commits the fallacy of reversibility—that is, if the outcome had been reversed some of the same factors could be cited to explain Confederate victory. If the South had its bumblers like Bragg and Pemberton and Hood who lost the West, and Joseph Johnston who fought too little and too late, the North had its McClellan and Meade who threw away chances in the East and its Pope and Burnside and Hooker who nearly lost the war in that theater where the genius of Lee and his lieutenants nearly won it, despite all the South's disadvantages. If the Union had its Stanton and Meigs, the Confederacy had its Josiah Gorgas and other unsung heroes who performed miracles of organization and improvisation. If Lincoln had been defeated for reelection in 1864, as he anticipated in August, history might record Davis as the great war leader and Lincoln as an also-ran.

Most attempts to explain southern defeat or northern victory lack the dimension of *contingency*—the recognition that at numerous critical points during the war things might have gone altogether differently. Four major turning points defined the eventual outcome. The first came in the summer of 1862, when the counteroffensives of Jackson and Lee in Virginia and Bragg and Kirby Smith in the West arrested the momentum of a seemingly imminent Union victory. This assured a prolongation and intensification of the conflict and created the potential for Confederate success, which appeared imminent before each of the next three turning points.

The first of these occurred in the fall of 1862, when battles at Antietam and Perryville threw back Confederate invasions, forestalled European mediation and recognition of the Confederacy, perhaps prevented a Democratic victory in the northern elections of 1862 that might have inhibited the government's ability to carry on the war, and set the stage for the Emancipation Proclamation which enlarged the scope and purpose of the conflict. The third critical point came in the summer and fall of 1863, when Gettysburg, Vicksburg, and Chattanooga turned the tide toward ultimate northern victory.

One more reversal of that tide seemed possible in the summer of 1864, when appalling Union casualties and apparent lack of progress especially in Virginia brought the North to the brink of peace negotiations and the election of a Democratic president. But the capture of Atlanta and Sheridan's destruction of Early's army in the Shenandoah Valley clinched matters for the North. Only then did it become possible to speak of the inevitability of Union victory. Only then did the South experience an irretrievable "loss of the will to fight."

Of all the explanations for Confederate defeat, the "loss of will" thesis suffers most from its own particular fallacy of reversibility—that of putting the cart before

The Civil War is the most memorialized event in American history. Thousands of monuments to northern and southern soldiers stand in town squares and county seats or on one of several dozen battlefields preserved as national, state, or private parks. Two monuments are pictured here: the Union soldiers and sailors monument at Indianapolis and the Virginia monument at Gettysburg battlefield with Robert E. Lee astride his horse Traveller.

the horse. Defeat causes demoralization and loss of will; victory pumps up morale and the will to win. Nothing illustrates this better than the radical transformation of *northern* will from defeatism in August 1864 to a "depth of determination . . . to fight to the last" that "astonished" a British journalist a month later. The southern loss of will was a mirror image of this northern determination. These changes of mood were caused mainly by events on the battlefield. Northern victory and southern defeat in the war cannot be understood apart from the contingency that hung over every campaign, every battle, every election, every decision during the war. This phenomenon of contingency can best be presented in a narrative format—a format this book has tried to provide.

Arguments about the causes and consequences of the Civil War, as well as the reasons for northern victory, will continue as long as there are historians to wield the pen—which is, perhaps even for this bloody conflict, mightier than the sword. But certain large consequences of the war seem clear. Secession and slavery were killed, never to be revived during the century and a third since Appomattox. These results signified a broader transformation of American society and polity punctuated if not alone achieved by the war. Before 1861 the two words "United States" were generally rendered as a plural noun: "the United States *are* a republic." The war marked the transition of the United States to a singular noun. The "Union" also became the nation, and Americans now rarely speak of their Union except in an historical sense. Lincoln's wartime speeches betokened this transition. In his first inaugural address he used the word "Union" twenty times and the word "nation" not once. In his first message to Congress, on July 4, 1861, he used "Union" thirty-two

times and "nation" three times. In his letter to Horace Greeley of August 22, 1862, on the relationship of slavery to the war, Lincoln spoke of the "Union" eight times and of the "nation" not at all. Little more than a year later, in his address at Gettysburg, the president did not refer to the "Union" at all but used the word "nation" five times to invoke a new birth of freedom and nationalism for the United States. And in his second inaugural address, looking back over the events of the past four years, Lincoln spoke of one side seeking to dissolve the *Union* in 1861 and the other accepting the challenge of war to preserve the *Nation*.

This bird's-eye view of Washington in 1871, looking west toward the Potomac, symbolized the renewed unity and new power of the nation and its government.

The old federal republic in which the national government had rarely touched the average citizen except through the post office gave way to a more centralized polity that taxed the people directly and created an internal revenue bureau to collect these taxes, drafted men into the army, expanded the jurisdiction of federal courts, created a national currency and a national banking system, and established the first national agency for social welfare—the Freedmen's Bureau. Eleven of the first twelve amendments to the Constitution had limited the powers of the national government; six of the next seven, beginning with the Thirteenth Amendment in 1865, vastly expanded those powers at the expense of the states.

This change in the federal balance paralleled a radical shift of political power from South to North. During the first seventy-two years of the republic down to 1861 a slaveholding resident of one of the states that joined the Confederacy had been president of the United States for forty-nine of those years—more than two-thirds of the time. In Congress, twenty-three of the thirty-six speakers of the House

This painting by New Jersey artist Mary Nimmo Moran done in 1880 and the photograph of a southern textile mill taken in 1908 by the New York photographer Lewis Hine (opposite) illustrate facets of the emergence of the United States as an industrial giant in the generations after the Civil War. The painting depicts Newark as viewed from marshes and meadows across the Passaic River, juxtaposing bucolic nature with modern industry.

and twenty-four of the presidents pro tem of the Senate had been southerners. The Supreme Court always had a southern majority; twenty of the thirty-five justices to 1861 had been appointed from slave states. After the war a century passed before a resident of an ex-Confederate state was elected president. For half a century only one of the speakers of the House and none of the presidents pro tem of the Senate came from the South, and only five of the twenty-six Supreme Court justices appointed during that half-century were southerners.

These figures symbolize a sharp and permanent change in the direction of American development. Through most of American history the South has seemed different from the rest of the United States, with "a separate and unique identity . . . which appeared to be out of the mainstream of American experience." But when did the northern stream become the mainstream? From a broader perspective it may have been the *North* that was exceptional and unique before the Civil War. The South more closely resembled a majority of the societies in the world than did the rapidly changing North during the antebellum generation. Despite the abolition of legal slavery or serfdom throughout much of the western hemisphere and western Europe, most of the world—like the South—had an unfree or quasi-free labor force. Most societies in the world remained predominantly rural, agricultural, and labor-intensive; most, including even several European countries, had illiteracy rates as high as or higher than the South's 45 percent; most like the South remained bound by traditional values and networks of family, kinship, hierarchy, and patriarchy. The North—along with a few countries of northwestern Europe—hurtled forward eagerly toward a future of industrial capitalism that many southerners

In the textile industry that developed from the 1880s on in the New South, a majority of workers were women and children, as dramatically shown here. Sometime in the 1880s the United States surpassed Britain to become the world's leading industrial nation; by 1913 American manufacturing output equaled that of Britain, Germany, and France combined.

found distasteful if not frightening; the South remained proudly and even defiantly rooted in the past before 1861.

Thus when secessionists protested that they were acting to preserve traditional rights and values, they were correct. They fought to protect their constitutional liberties against the perceived northern threat to overthrow them. The South's concept of republicanism had not changed in three-quarters of a century; the North's had. With complete sincerity the South fought to preserve its version of the republic of the founding fathers—a government of limited powers that protected the rights of property and whose constituency comprised an independent gentry and yeomanry of the white race undisturbed by large cities, heartless factories, restless free workers, and class conflict. The accession to power of the Republican party, with its ideology of competitive, egalitarian, free-labor capitalism, was a signal to the South that the northern majority had turned irrevocably toward this frightening, revolutionary future. Indeed, the Black Republican party appeared to the eyes of many southerners as "essentially a revolutionary party" composed of "a motley throng of Sans culottes . . . Infidels and freelovers, interspersed by Bloomer women, fugitive slaves, and amalgamationists." Therefore secession was a preemptive counterrevolution to prevent the Black Republican revolution from engulfing the South. "*We* are not revolutionists," insisted James B. D. De Bow and Jefferson Davis during the Civil War. "We are resisting revolution. . . . We are conservative."

Union victory in the war destroyed the southern vision of America and ensured that the northern vision would become the American vision. Until 1861, however, it was the North that was out of the mainstream, not the South. Of course the northern states, along with Britain and a few countries in northwestern Europe, were cutting a new channel in world history that would doubtless have become the

Winslow Homer titled this painting, which he completed in 1876, A Visit from the Old Mistress. The rich canvas captured the essence of changes in race relations brought about by the war. The three black women and the child turn toward the white woman who formerly owned them, but they meet now as equals. The aproned matriarch and the mother and child anchor the center of the picture; the white mistress is marginalized. In this painting Homer blended past and present, but for him, as for his subjects, the future remained unknown.

mainstream even if the American Civil War had not happened. Russia had abolished serfdom in 1861 to complete the dissolution of this ancient institution of bound labor in Europe. But for Americans the Civil War marked the turning point. A Louisiana planter who returned home sadly after the war wrote in 1865: "Society has been completely changed by the war. The [French] revolution of '89 did not produce a greater change in the 'Ancien Régime' than this has in our social life." And four years later George Ticknor, a retired Harvard professor, concluded that the Civil War had created a "great gulf between what happened before in our century and what has happened since, or what is likely to happen hereafter. It does not seem to me as if I were living in the country in which I was born." From the war sprang the great flood that caused the stream of American history to surge into a new channel and transferred the burden of exceptionalism from North to South.

What would be the place of freed slaves and their descendants in this new order? In 1865 a black soldier who recognized his former master among a group of Confederate prisoners he was guarding called out a greeting: "Hello, massa; bottom rail on top dis time!" Would this new arrangement of rails last? Will a nation "conceived in liberty and dedicated to the proposition that all men are created equal" continue to evolve in accordance with that fundamental "proposition"? This is a question that can be answered only by generations yet to come.

INDEX

Note: Page numbers in *italics* refer to illustrations and associated captions.

abolitionists, 47, *480*; and 1860 election, 174, 179; on breakup of slave families, 31–32; growing influence of, 422; and issue of nonviolence, 159–60; oppose colonization, 432–33; resist fugitive slave law, 67–68; and Second Great Awakening, 8; on slavery and the war, 252, 290–93, 294–95; women and, 29. *See also* antislavery movement; emancipation of slaves; Thirteenth Amendment

Adams, Charles Francis, *321*; and 1860 election, 178, 183; on British attitudes toward war, 475; on Compromise of 1850, 63; on consequences of Antietam, 479–80; on consequences of Emancipation Proclamation, 489; and Free Soil party, 52; and Know Nothings, 108; Laird rams, 599; minister to Britain, 321–22; rebukes Palmerston, 477; in secession crisis, 200

Adams, Charles Francis, Jr., 489, 507

Adams, Henry: on cotton famine, 475; on Emancipation Proclamation, 489; on Gettysburg and Vicksburg, 578; on Laird rams, 599; on Roebuck motion, 563; on settlement of *Trent* crisis, 323

advertisements: bounties, *513*; fugitive slaves, *67*; railroad service, *77*; recruitment, *217*, *251*, *421*, *512*; slave trade, *33*; for supplies, *411*

African Labor Supply Association, 82

agriculture: mechanical reaper machines, *13*; scientific, *81*; self-sufficient farming, *14*. *See also* cotton

Aiken's Landing, *697*

Alabama, C.S.S., 5, 254, *256*, 474, *474*, 477, 599

Alabama brigade, *539*

Allatoona Pass, *655*

Allegory of Freedom (unknown), *419*

ambulances, *415*

American Anti-Slavery Society, *8*

American party: in 1856, 120; disappearance of, 147; splits on slavery issue, 109

American Red Cross, *414*

American Republican Association, *26*

"American system of manufactures," 15–17

amputees, *416*

"Anaconda Plan," 271–73; *272*, *273*, 721

Anderson, Robert, *209*; and Fort Sumter, 208–16; recruits Kentucky unionists, 234

Anderson, William C. "Bloody Bill," *693*, 693–94

Andersonville prison, 666, *701*, *704*, *705*; conditions at, 700; controversies about, 701–2, 704–6, 713; mortality at, 700, 705–6

Andrew, John: and 1860 election, 179; and General Stone, 297; raises black regiments, 487; sends regiments to Washington, 217, 226

Anthony, Susan B., 691

anti-Catholic sentiment, 26, *26*–27, *103*, 103–4, 110, 121–22, *123*

Antietam, battle of, 463–71, *465*, *467*, *469*, *471*, 480, 492, 496; Antietam National Battlefield, *463*; consequences of, 479–80, 483, 755

antislavery movement, *8*, *67*, *114*; and free soil sentiment in 1840s, 47–48; and nativism, 107; origins of, 8, 71; and Whig party, 70–71. *See also* abolitionists; Free Soil party; Republican party

Appomattox Courthouse, 746, *746*, *748*, 748–49

Appomattox River, *630*

"area denial," *687*

Arkansas, C.S.S., 355, *355*

Arkansas River, *583*

Armistead, Lewis A., 575

army, Confederate: black servants, *291*, *424*; "chivalry" cartoon, *460*; class composition of, 530; conscription, *626*; deserters, *529*, *707*; discipline and training, 268–70; election of officers, 267–68; guerrilla warfare, *500*; organization and mobilization of, 256–60; origins, *197*; political generals, 267–68; raids and invasions, *444–45*; reenlistment of soldiers required in 1864, 626; strategy, 274–75; tactics, 401–7. *See also* conscription in Confederacy; desertions from Confederate army; *specific armies; specific battles; specific commanders; specific units*

army, Union, *231*; black laborers, *424*; discipline and training, 268–70; election of officers, 266; encampments, *265*; ethnic and class composition, 524–25; expanded by Lincoln's call for new troops, 419–21, 435; organization and mobilization of, 252–53, 260–66, 284–85; political generals, 267–68; size of, when secession begins, 195–96, *196*; strategy, 270–74; tactics, 401–7; veteran reenlistments, 626. *See also* black soldiers in Union army; conscription in Union; desertions from Union army; *specific battles; specific commanders; specific units*

Army of the Cumberland, 222, 560; crippled by Stones River, 505; designation of, 443, 501; in Georgia campaign, 653, 666; reinforced after Chickamauga, 591–92; Thomas takes

Benton, Thomas Hart, 42, *56*, 121, 124, 289

Bentonville, battle of, 729

Bermuda, *315, 316*

Bickerdyke, Mary Anne, 413

Bickley, George, 90–91

Big Black River, battle of, 543

Bingham, George Caleb, *692*

Black, Jeremiah, 209

Black Hawk, 39, *39*

black laws: in Illinois, 431; in Kansas, 124; in northern states, 71; repeal of, during and after war, 737

black sailors in Union navy, 485–86, *486*

black soldiers in Union army, 485–87; *Allegory of Freedom, 419*; in Arkansas, *473*, 583; with Army of the Potomac, *424*, 671; assault on Fort Wagner, 602; 1862 militia act, 426; authorized by Emancipation Proclamation, 485; in battle of Nashville, 718; at battle of the Crater, *671*, 671–72, *672*, 698; contrabands as, 547; education for, *619*; equal pay issue, 695; 5th U.S. Colored Infantry, *488*; 55th Massachusetts Infantry, 487, *488*, *728*; 54th Massachusetts Infantry, 69, 487, *488*, *602*; 1st South Carolina Volunteers, 486–87, *487*; first regiments organized, 485–86; 4th U.S. Colored Infantry, *488*; history of, 485; Lincoln on contributions of, 679; at Milliken's Bend, 547; murdered after capture, 547, *547*, 660, 698–99, *699*; and northern racial attitudes, 487; number from upper South, 247; at Port Hudson, 550, *612–13*; portraits, *473*; and prisoners of war issue, 489, 562, 697–700; southern response to, 487–89; 10th U.S. Cavalry, *541*; 22nd U.S. Colored Infantry, *651*

black suffrage: as an issue of reconstruction, 612, 614, 616–17, 740; defeated in New York, 107, 124–25, 176–77

blacksmiths, *19*

Blackwell, Elizabeth, 410

Blair, Austin, 179

Blair, Francis Preston: in 1856 election, 120; in 1860 election, 170, 204; and Hampton Roads conference, 723

Blair, Francis Preston, Jr.: appointed general, 268; attacks Chase, 621–22; and struggle for Missouri, 229–31, 623

Blair, Montgomery, *212, 430*; and Fort Sumter, 212; opposes Emancipation Proclamation, 429, 480; postmaster general, 204, 205; role in Lincoln's reelection, 621

blockade of southern ports, *314, 318*; effectiveness of, 315–16; and foreign relations, 316–17, 318–21; initiation of, 253–54, 255, 273, 286–87, 290; operation of, 303, 306–7, 313–14

blockade runners, 314, *315, 316*, 319, 473–74, *517*

blockhouses, *436*

"Blood Tubs," *226*

Bloody Angle, *639*, 639–40

Bloody Lane, *466*

Blue Ridge Mountains, *647*

Blunt, James G., *582*, 583

Book of Mormon, *37*

Boonville, *232*

Booth, John Wilkes, 749, 751

border states: dilemma of, after Sumter, 219; importance of, 247; issue of emancipation in, 424–25, 428; remain under tenuous Union control, 224–36

Botts, John Minor, 366

Brady, Mathew, *85, 222, 235, 240, 466, 569, 679*

Bragg, Braxton, *439, 504*, 539, 560, *592*; approves Brooks's assault on Sumner, 118; battle of Murfreesboro, 502; battle of Perryville, 442–43; at Chattanooga, 586, 591, 593–94, 613; Chickamauga campaign and battle, 586–91; as Davis's military adviser, 665; dissension with corps commanders, 497–98, 505–6; evaluation of, 755; Kentucky invasion, 439–41, 447, 458, 460, 471, 755; in Mexican War, 5; at Murfreesboro, 497; new quarrels with generals, 594, 658; relieved of command, 598, 625; replaces Beauregard as commander, 350; sends reinforcements to Johnston, 546–47; Shiloh campaign, 338; Tullahoma campaign, 583–84

Bragg, C.S.S., *352*

Brandy Station, battle of, 561–62

bread riots, *533*, 532–33

breastworks, *658*

Breckinridge, John C., *169, 181, 186, 504*; battle of New Market, 630; dislike of Bragg, 505; division commander at Murfreesboro, 504; joins Confederacy, 235; presidential candidacy, 169, 175, 180, 182, 196, 225; as vice president, 151

Brice's Crossroads, battle of, 660

bridges: B&O Railroad, 240, *461*; Burnside's Bridge, *468*; destroyed by Confederates, 240, *438*; "Grapevine Bridge," *389, 390*; Lick Creek, *245*; pontoon bridges, *440, 494, 641, 649*; protecting, *436*; Richmond and Fredericksburg Railroad, *637*; Rohrbach Bridge, *468*; train trestles, *451, 461, 655*

Bright, John, 476

Britain: and Confederate commerce raiders, 474–75; cotton famine, 474–75; and Emancipation Proclamation, 479–81, *481*, 489; issue of recognizing Confederacy, 320–22, 471; Kenner mission, 735; Laird rams, 599; mediation moves by, in 1862, 473, 478–80; and *Monitor-Virginia* battle, 313; public opinion in, toward American war, 474–78; and Roebuck motion, 562–63; and slavery as issue in war, 251; and southern cotton, 317–19; and *Trent* crisis, 321–22; and Union blockade, 314, 317, 318–19, 319–20

Broadway Landing, Va., *363*

Brock Road, *633*

Brooks, Preston, 117–19, *118*

Brough, John, 602

Brown, Albert Gallatin, 84, 139

Brown, George, 229

Brown, Isaac Newton, 355

Brown, John, 69, *159, 164, 180*; Harper's Ferry raid, 157, 159–62, *161, 163*; in Kansas, *119*, 119–20, 131, 159; trial and aftermath, 84–86; trial, execution and aftermath, 162–67, *163*, 165–67, 170, 174, 179

Brown, John, Jr., 691
Brown, Joseph E., *607*; critic of Davis, 607–8; and martial law, 366; opposes conscription, 607; and secession, 190–91; wartime aid to poor families, 531
Browning, Oliver, 206–7, 293
Brownlow, William G. ("Parson"), 244, 246
Brownlow, William S., *244*
Bryant, William Cullen, 48; on Dred Scott decision, 138; on John Brown, 165; on secession, 191
Buchanan, James, 38, 49, *122*, 175, *208*, 504; advocates compromise, 195–97; and corruption issue in 1860, 177–78, 331; denies legality of secession, 192–93; Dred Scott case, 136, 139, 140; 1852 election, 94; 1856 election, 122–23; 1858 elections, 146–47; favors acquisition of Cuba, 152; and Forts Moultrie and Sumter, 208–10; and Lecompton, 127–30; opposes "coercion," 194; and Ostend Manifesto, 86–87; vetoes by, 152
Buckingham Hall, *73*
Buckner, Simon Bolivar, 331–35
Bucks County, Pennsylvania, *411*
Buell, Don Carlos, *436*; Chattanooga campaign, 436–40; Corinth campaign, 349; occupies Nashville, 336; Perryville campaign, 441–43; relieved of command, 443, 502; at Shiloh, 339, 341–43, 347; Union commander in Kentucky, 245–46, 301, 327–28, 328, 330
Buford, John, 564–65, *565*
Bull Run, 1st and 2nd battles of. *See* Manassas, 1st and 2nd battles of
Bulloch, James D.: and commerce raiders, 473; Confederate naval agent, 253–54, 259; efforts in France, 599–600; Laird rams, 599
burial details, *397, 640*
Burlingame, Anson, 108
Burns, Anthony, 95, *95*, 160
Burnside, Ambrose E., *306, 469*; Antietam, 463–64, 465, 468–69; arrests Vallandigham, 516; battle of the Crater, 670–71; commands Army of

Potomac, 492; evaluation of, 755; 1st Bull Run, 279; Fredericksburg, 493–96, 555; Mud March, 506–7; North Carolina operations, 306; occupies Knoxville, 585; relieved of command, 507
Burnside's Bridge, *468*
Burton, James H., 404
Butler, Andrew P. (Benjamin's brother), 96, 117, 536–37
Butler, Benjamin F., *227, 291*, 355, 430, *536*, 652; battle of Drewry's Bluff, 629–31, 640; and contrabands, 290–93, 423; Fort Fisher fiasco, 722; Hatteras Inlet, 304; keeps peace in New York City, 689; in Maryland, 226; occupies New Orleans, 353–54; Petersburg campaign, 649; political general, 268; presidential politics (1864), 622; and prisoner of war exchanges, 702; strategic role of (1864), 628; trading between lines, 536–37; unpopularity in South, 426; Woman Order issued by, 477, 536
"Butternuts": antiwar opposition, 420, 514; definition of, and culture, 25; draft resistance, 525; racism, 71
bypass canal at Vicksburg, 508, *509*

Cable, George Washington, 354
Cairo, Ill.,325, *326*
caissons, *362, 446*
Calhoun, John C., *58, 59*; and Compromise of 1850, 57, 59, 60; proslavery argument, 48; slavery expansion, 49–50, 55
California: American settlement in, 35; and Compromise of 1850, 57–63; and gold rush, 37, 53–54, *54*, 156; and slavery expansion issue, 54–55; statehood controversy, 55–56, *56*; 70, 84; U.S. annexation of, 41, 42
California Trail, *36*
Cambridge, U.S.S., *316*
Cameron, Simon, *212, 263*; and 1860 election, 170, 173; and arming of slaves, 294, 425, 485; inefficiency and corruption of, 253, 257, 260–63; secretary of war, 204, 213; and U.S. Sanitary Commission, 411

Camp Chase, *703*
camp meetings, *30*
Campbell, John A., 724
Canada and fugitive slaves, 66, 68, *68*, 69–70, 131, 160
Canby, Edward R. S., 726, *726*
Capitol, U.S., 206, *757*
Carney, William, *602*
Carnifex Ferry, 242
Carondelet, U.S.S., *348*, 349, *349, 352*, 355
Carpenter, Francis, *430*
Carrington, Henry B., 689
Carroll, Samuel, *573*
cartoons: "Anaconda Plan," *272, 273*; Beauregard, P.G.T., *529*; Bell, John, *181*; Boonville victory, *232*; Breckinridge, John C., *169, 181*; Buchanan's concilliation, *194*; California's admission, *56*; Cass, Lewis, *49, 51*; Confederacy and foreign countries, *319*; Confederate bonds, *532*; Confederate "chivalry," *460*; Confederate currency, *371*; Confederate finances, *531*; Confederate losses and peace terms, *577*; "contrabands," *293*; copperheads, *518, 519, 677, 685*; Crittenden Compromise, *198*; Cuba annexation, *49, 152*; Davis, Jefferson, *157, 273, 319, 480, 529, 531, 577, 680*; Democratic 1864 platform, *685*; Democratic racist rhetoric, *696*; draft-dodgers, *520*; draft substitutes, *524*; Emancipation Proclamation, *481, 507*; Free Soil party, *51*; Frémont's campaigns, *123, 622*; Frémont's emancipation edict, *289*; Greeley, Horace, *53, 94, 157, 172*; Hooker, Joseph, *507*; Internal Revenue Act, *377*; Jefferson Davis, *319*; Know Nothing movement, *107*; Lewis Cass, *49*; Lincoln, *172, 181, 289, 489, 507, 680*; Louis Napoleon, *479*; McClellan, George B., *480, 677, 680, 685*; McClellan's "change of base," *396*; Magoffin, Beriah, *234*; northern wealth, *372*; Panic of 1857, *148*; Pendleton, George, *685*; Raymond, Henry J., *94, 172*; reconciliation with South, *677*; recruitment, *365, 420, 524*; Rosecrans, William,

274–75; names Johnston to succeed Bragg, 598; names Lee general in chief, 723; opposition to, in Confederate politics, 607–8; and peace movements, 608; "peace negotiations" (1864), 677–78, 679–81; and Peninsula campaign, 361; and political generals, 267–68; qualities of, compared with Lincoln, 755; question of British recognition, 477; and rebel agents in Canada, 674–75; relations with A. S. Johnston, 327, 338, *339*; relations with Beauregard and Joe Johnston, 299–300, 330, 357; relieves Beauregard of command, 350; reorganizes Trans-Mississippi Department, 583; response to Emancipation Proclamation and black Union soldiers, 488; Richmond bread riot, 532–33; Seven Pines, 389–90; and Sherman's march, 711–12; southern criticism of, 363, 469; and southern mobilization, 257, 258; on strategy after Chancellorsville, 560; threatens retaliation against Pope's orders, 426; on trade with enemy, 535, 537; and treasury notes, 370; and treatment of black prisoners of war, 697–98, 704; treatment of other Union prisoners, 706; on Union blockade, 316; and unpopularity of the draft, 529, 531; urges conscription, 363, 365; and Vicksburg campaign, 546, 550; visits Hood's army, 711; and western Virginia, 242; will fight to last ditch, 709, 721–22, 725

Davis, Theodore R., *209*

Davis, Varina Howell, 363

Davis Bend (Miss.), freedmen's colony at, 619

Dayton, William, 121

De Bow, James B. D.: champions southern commercial development, 75–76, 77; proslavery polemics of, 79, 81; and reopening of slave trade, 82; on secession as counterrevolution, 759

De Bow's Review, 75–76, *76*, 79, 81; and annexation of slave territory, 84; on John Brown, 166

"The Dead of Antietam" (Brady), *466*

Dee (ship), *316*

defensive structures, *551, 625, 650*

Defiance: Inviting a Shot Before Petersburg (Homer), *663*

Democratic party and Democrats: and banks, 22–23; Barnburner faction, *51*, 51–52, 94, *110*; constituency of, 24–25, 27, 176, 708; 1860 convention, 167–69, *168*; impact of Kansas-Nebraska Act on, 97, 101; and Indians, 38–39; and Manifest Destiny, 41–42, 85–86, 152; and Mexican War, 4, 41–44; and nativism, 106; racism of, 24, 110, 124–25, 143, 176–77, 431, 601, 695–96; role of, as opposition party in wartime North, 605; and slavery, 24, 46–47, 49–50, 55; southern domination of, 46, 101; split by Lecompton, 129–30, 146–47, 167; and Thirteenth Amendment, 735–36; "Union procession," *177*; War Democrats, 430. *See also* copperheads; elections

Dennison, William, 237–38

desertions from Confederate army, *529, 707*; in 1863, 586; and civilian suffering, 371, 530; epidemic of (1865), 722–23, 740–41; of North Carolina troops, 608; and twenty-Negro law, 528–29

desertions from Union army: after Fredericksburg, 506, 507; of substitutes and bounty men, 524, 626

Devil's Den, *569, 576*

disease in Civil War armies, 401, 415–17, 435, 510. *See also* medical care in Civil War armies

Dix, Dorothea, 412

Dobbin, James, 97

dog tents, *630*

domestic scenes, *550*

Doolittle, James, 140

Douglas, Stephen A., *61*, 84–85, *143, 157, 167, 176, 181*; and Compromise of 1850, 57, 61–62; debates with Lincoln (1858), *132–33*, 141–46, *142, 143, 144*, 155, 171–72; on Dred Scott decision, 139–40, 142; 1852 election, 94; 1854 election, 99–101; 1860 election, 167–69, 176–82, *176, 177, 181*, 613; and federal slave code issue, 152–53; on John Brown, 166; on Kansas, 114–15, 122; Kansas-Nebraska Act, 96–97; and Lecompton, 129–30; on Lincoln's inaugural address, 207; and secession, 198; supports war for Union, 217

Douglas and Stanton hospital, *408*

Douglass, Frederick, 144, *431*, 699; attends inaugural reception, 737; on black soldiers, 485–86; criticizes Lincoln, 429, 432; 1856 election, 125; 1860 election, 179; on emancipation, 290, 481; on freedmen's policy in Louisiana, 620; on fugitive slave law, 69; and John Brown, 161; on nonviolence, 159–60; opposes concessions to secessionists, 197

draft. *See* conscription in Confederacy; conscription in Union

Dred Scott v. Sandford, *737*; background, 133–36; justices' opinions, *136*, 136–38, 141; public reaction, *138*, 138–40, 142–43, 147

Drewry's Bluff, battle of, 361, *361*, 630–31

Du Pont, Samuel, 305

Dudley, Thomas H., 473

Duncanson, Robert S., *7*

Dunker sect, *466*

Durant, Thomas J., 614

Eads, James B., 325

Eads, Samuel, *327*

Early, Jubal, 652, *669*; and Cedar Creek, 687–89, 755; at Chancellorsville, 553–54; gets corps command, 642; invasion of Maryland, 668–70, 718; routed by Sheridan at Winchester and Fisher's Hill, 684–85; stops Hunter in Valley, 648

East Cemetery Hill, *573*

east Tennessee: guerrilla and military actions, 245–46; Union capture of Knoxville and Chattanooga, 585–86; unionism in, 244, 435

Eaton, John, 619

economy, U.S.: and "American system of manufactures," 15–17; antebellum economic development, 7–8, 9–10; Civil War and transformation of,

Fillmore, Millard, *56, 58*; American party nominee in 1856, 120, 123, 170; and Compromise of 1850, 61–62; fails of renomination, 93; and fugitive slave law, 68, 69

finance of war, *73*; in Confederacy, 367–72, 373–74, 530–32, *531, 532*; election issue in 1863, 605, 607; in Union, 372–77, 379–81, 514–15. *See also* inflation

Finley, Clement A., 412

"fire-eaters" (southern nationalists), 57, *606*; on Compromise of 1850, 62–63; and fugitive slave law, 70; and Lecompton, 130; strategy in 1860, 185; urge attack on Fort Sumter, 215

fires, *559, 633, 682*

1st Indian Brigade, *337*

1st Massachusetts Light Artillery, *271*

1st Michigan Volunteer Infantry, *216*

1st Minnesota, *539, 570*, 570, 572

1st South Carolina Volunteers, 486–87, *487*

1st Wisconsin, *442*

Fisher's Hill, battle of, 686, *686*

Fitzhugh, George, 154, 156

"The Flag of Our Union" (song), *62*

flags, 281, *281, 400, 419*

Florida, C.S.S., 254, 473–74, 599

Floyd, John B.: Confederate general, *242*, 268; corruption of as secretary of war, 178, *179*; at Fort Donelson, 331, 334; operations in western Virginia, 242, 306

"Flying Artillery," *256*

Foote, Andrew Hull, 325, *326*, 328; and capture of Fort Henry, 329; and Fort Donelson, 331; Island No. 10, 349

Foote, Henry S., 56, *56*

Forbes, Edwin, *386, 552, 553, 573, 575*

Forney, John, *167*

Forrest, Nathan Bedford, 219, *335*, 540, 693; Brice's Crossroads, 660; at Chickamauga, 590–91; at Fort Donelson, 335; Fort Pillow massacre, 660, 699; and Hood's invasion of Tennessee, 714, 718; quarrels with Bragg, 594; raids foil Union advances in Tennessee, 436–38, 439; raids in Grant's rear, 500; raids in

Rosecrans's rear, 502; raids in Tennessee, 711, 712; and Shiloh, 343–46; threats to Sherman's supply line, 629; Tupelo, 660; and Wilson's raid, 726

Fort Clark, *304*

Fort Donelson, Union capture of, 330–35, *334*, 339, 349, 502; consequences of, 336, 347, 363

Fort Fisher, battles of, 721–22, 723, *723*, 735

Fort Gregg, *742*

Fort Hatteras, *304*

Fort Henry, Union capture of, 328, 329–30, *330*; consequences of, 336

Fort Jackson, *354*

Fort Mahone, *650*

Fort Moultrie, *209, 214*

Fort Pickens, *207*, 210, 211, *213*, 213–14

Fort Pillow: massacre at, 660, 698–99, *699*; Union capture of, 350

Fort St. Philip, *354*

Fort Slemmer, *358*

Fort Stedman, battle of, 741

Fort Sumter, *185, 209, 213, 214, 215, 219, 281*; northern response to firing upon, 216–17, 249; and secession crisis, 207–17, 498; southern response, 219–20; Union attack (1863), 560

Fort Wagner, battle of, 602, *602*

Fortress Monroe, *752*

42nd Illinois, *348*

43rd Ohio, *542*

4th Minnesota, *549*

4th U.S. Colored Infantry, *488*

Fox, Claiborne, *232*

Fox, Gustavus V., *253*; and Fort Sumter, 212–15

France: and blockade, 318; and Kenner mission, 735; and mediation moves in 1862, 473, 475, 478; Mexican adventures of, 600, *600*; and question of Confederate recognition, 317, 318, *319*, 562–63

Franklin, battle of, 715, *715*

Franklin, William B., 462, 468, 494, 506–7

Franz Joseph of Austria, *600*

Frederick the Great, 753

Fredericksburg, battle of, *491*, 493–96, *494, 495, 496*, 513, *558*, 566, *633*, 643, *669*, 671

free-labor ideology: and slavery, 33, 47–48; and social mobility, 23

Free Soil party, *50, 51, 110*; in 1852, 94; birth of, 52; and Compromise of 1850, 63; election of 1848, 53, 55–56, 107; and Kansas-Nebraska Act, 97; Republicans absorb, 98

freedmen: freedmen villages, *739*; freedmen's aid societies, 424, 618; in future of South, 617–20; land for, and Sherman's Order No. 15, 738; policy toward, and reconstruction issue in Louisiana, 615–17; at Port Royal, 305

Freedmen's Bureau, 619, 739, *739*, 757

Freedom. *See* emancipation of slaves; liberty

Freeport doctrine, 139, 142–43, 168

Frémont, Jessie Benton, 121, 289

Frémont, John C., *121, 123, 622*; and California, 42; 1856 presidential candidacy, 121–26; 1864 presidential candidacy, 622; emancipation edict, 288–89, 292–94, 425; given western Virginia command, 358–59; and Jackson's Shenandoah Valley campaign, 384, 417, 554; military commander in Missouri, 286–87; relieved of command, 290, 327–28; resigns command, 426; withdraws candidacy, 684

Fry, David, *245*

Fugitive Slave Act, 68

Fugitive Slave Law, 34, 62, 63, *67*, 68, *69, 70, 323*; background, 65–66; northern resistance to, 67–70, 95; operation of, 67–68, 71, 93, 95; southern insistence on enforcement of, 70–71; and *Uncle Tom's Cabin,* 71–72

Fulton, Robert, 10

Gadsden, James, and Gadsden Purchase, 85–86

Gaines's Mill, battle of, 396–97, *397*, 400, *401, 406, 574, 641, 715*

"galvanized Yankees," *731*

Gardner, Alexander, *466, 469, 576*

Garnett, Robert S., 238–41

Garrett, John W., 227

Garrison, William Lloyd, 69, 160, *728*; and

mudsill speech, 153–54; on Lecompton, 130; sectional champion, 48

Hammond, William, 412

Hampton, Wade, 257, 279, 648, 728

Hampton Roads Conference, *302*, 723–25, *725*, 734–35

Hancock, Winfield Scott: at Cold Harbor, 643; at Gettysburg, 566, 570, 575; in Mexican War, 4; on Petersburg front, 671; at Spotsylvania, 637–38

Hardee, William J., 727–28, 728–29

Harper's Ferry, *461*; capture of by Jackson (1862), 460–63, *461*, 470; John Brown raid, *119*, 159–62, *162*, *163*, *221*; Virginia militia seizes, 220, *221*, *240*, *249*, 259

Harrison, William Henry, 171

Hartford, U.S.S., 354, *354*, 673, *673*

Hastings, Lansford, *36*

Hatteras Inlet, Union capture of, 303–4, 306, 311

Haupt, Herman, 450–51, *451*, 457

Havelock, Henry, *241*

Hawthorne, Nathaniel, 30

Hay, John, 677

Healy, George P. A., *42*

Helena (Ark.), *618*

Helper, Hinton Rowan, 155–57, 190

Henry, Judith, 279, *279*

Heroes of America, 608–9

Hesler, Alexander, *170*

Hibernia Hose Company, *26*

Hickok, "Wild Bill," 337

Hicks, Thomas, 225, 227

Higginson, Thomas Wentworth: attempted rescue of Burns, 95; commands black regiment, 486–87, *487*; and John Brown, 160, 163–64

Hill, Ambrose Powell, 219, *469*; at Antietam, 470; breaks down in Wilderness campaign, 642; Cedar Mountain, 448–49; gains corps command, 561; at Gettysburg, 565, 567–68, 573; and Seven Days battles, 393–96, 398

Hill, Benjamin H., 180

Hill, Daniel Harvey, 219; and Antietam, 465; battle of South Mountain, 461; on Gaines's Mill, 407; and Malvern Hill, 399–400

Hindman, Thomas C., 582

Hine, Lewis, *758*

Hines, Thomas C., 675, 676

H. L. Hunley (ship), *255*

Holden, William W., *608*, 608–10, 677

Holmes, Oliver Wendell, Jr., 465, 511, 642, 668–69

Holston River, *584–85*

Holt, Joseph, 209, 690

Holt, Michael, 178

Holt, R. S., 180

Homer, Winslow, *405*, *663*, *760*

Homestead Act: defeated by South, 98, 147, 150–51, 152; endorsed by Republican platform, 174, 177; passed during war, 378–79

homesteads, *378*

Hood, John Bell, 219, *665*, *683*, *716–17*; army scattered, 728; in Atlanta campaign, 655; attacks Sherman's supply line, 711–12; battle of Franklin, 715; battles around Atlanta, 666–67; at Chickamauga, 587, 590; evacuation of Atlanta, 683, 712–13; at Gaines' Mill, 396; invades Tennessee, 713, 714; named to command army, 665; and Nashville, 715–18

Hooker, Joseph, *507*, *553*; and ambition for top command, 506–7, 507–8; at Antietam, 464–65; battle of Lookout Mountain, 594; and Chancellorsville, 552–59, 562, 583, 631; to Chattanooga, 592; evaluation of, 755; and Gettysburg campaign, 560, 562; in Mexican War, 4–5; replaced by Meade, 563

Hope, James, 277, 463

Hopewell, Virginia, 753

hospital boats, *413*

hospitals, *408*, *409*, *471*, *579*, *633*, *753*

Hotchkiss, Jedediah, *384*

Hotze, Henry, 474–75, 563

House of Representatives, 110–11, *111*, *737*

Hovendens, Thomas, *578*

Howard, Oliver Otis, *555*; at Chancellorsville, 554–55; at 1st Bull Run, 279; at Gettysburg, 565; named commander of Army of the Tennessee, 666

Howe, Elias, 17, *17*

Howe, Samuel Gridley, 160, 163

Howells, William Dean, 165

Huger, Benjamin, 397

Hughes, John, 431

Hunley, Horace, and C.S.S. *Hunley*, 254

Hunt, Henry J., 574

Hunter, David, *646*; emancipation edict of, revoked by Lincoln, 425, 428; Shenandoah Valley campaign of, 646–48, 668, 670

Hunter, Robert M. T., 48; favors Davis for C.S.A. president, 203; at Hampton Roads peace conference, 724; and slavery in Kansas, 96, 113

Huse, Caleb, 259

immigrants and immigration, *20*, 34, *102*; elections and, *106*, *107*; Five Points neighborhood, *103*, *709*; and nativism, 7, 19, 25–27, 103–5; politics of, 25–27, 106; and population growth, 9, 19, *20*; travel conditions, *26*; underrepresentation of, in Union army, 524–25

impressment of supplies in South, 531–32, 607, 609

inaugurations, *206*

Indians, *38*; Indian regiments in Civil War, 336–37, 583; victims of U.S. expansion, 7, 38–39, 42

industrialization: 13–17, *13*, *14*, *15*, *17*, 758–59, *758*, *759*; Arcadian America before, 7; in antebellum South, 78–79, *155*; and banks, 22; and labor, *13*, *14*, 16–22, *19*; and women, *14*, 27–28, *28*, *759*

inflation: in Confederacy, 368–71, 376; and Confederate shortages, 371–72; food shortages and, 529; in Union, 376–77

Internal Revenue Act, *377*

Irish Americans, *20*, *103*, 266; and blacks, 107, 431; growing antiwar opposition of, in North, 420–21; and nativism, 26, 102, 107, 108; and New York draft riots, 526–27; and temperance, 104–5; underrepresented in Union army, 524

Iron Brigade, *452*, *566*; at Gettysburg, 565; at 2nd Bull Run, 452

Lincoln, Abraham (*continued*)
    campaign, 357, 389–96; and McClel-
        lan, 296, 299, 448, 491–92, *492*; and
        McClernand, 498–500; military
        strategy, 273–74, 286–87, 328; and
        Monitor, 309; names Grant general in
        chief, 625; names Hooker to com-
        mand Army of Potomac, 506, *507*;
        on northern overoptimism, 640; and
        peace issue in 1864, 674, 677–80; pol-
        icy of unconditional surrender,
        719–20, 724, 725, 740; and political
        generals, 267–68; proclaims block-
        ade, 253, 290; prods Rosecrans,
        583–84; puts Grant in command at
        Chattanooga, 593; relieves Butler of
        command, 722; relieves McClellan of
        command, 483–84, 492, 665; removes
        Buell, 443; removes Sigel, 631; reor-
        ganizes Union command in East,
        417, 429; replaces Hooker with
        Meade, 563; rescinds Grant's "Jew
        order," 536; response to 1st Bull
        Run, 284; restores McClellan's com-
        mand, 458; in Richmond, *744*; on
        Rosecrans in Chattanooga, 591–92;
        Sherman's march to the sea, 712,
        714; on Sons of Liberty, 690; south-
        ern response to militia call, 219–20,
        223; on southern treatment of black
        prisoners, 698–99; and Stephens's
        mission, 562, 578; suspends writ of
        habeas corpus, 228, 365–66, 482;
        thanks Rosecrans for Stones River,
        505; and trade between the lines, 533,
        537; urges Meade to pursue Lee,
        581–82; and U.S. Sanitary Commis-
        sion, 411, 412; visits Richmond,
        743–44, *744*
Lincoln, Abraham, as wartime political
        leader, 679; 1863 state elections, 601;
        ability to express Union war aims,
        249–50, 476; appoints military gover-
        nors, 435; cabinet crisis of Dec. 1862,
        497; capture of Atlanta raises
        prospects, 681; carries Missouri, 694;
        copperheads attack "tyranny" of,
        676; on 1862 elections, 483–84, 605;
        expects to lose 1864 election, 680,
        680; foreign policy, 321; leadership

qualities compared with Davis's, 363,
        755; policy toward Mexico, 600; pub-
        lic letter to Democrats, 602–3;
        reelected, 708; renomination (1864),
        621–23; southern hopes for defeat of,
        626, 643; target of Democratic racist
        attacks, 695–96; copperheads attack
        him, 515; and *Trent* affair, 322–23;
        and Vallandigham, 516–18; and war
        finance, 372, 374, 375; and western
        Virginia, 237; wins soldier vote,
        707–8, *708*
Lincoln Memorial, *679*
Lister, Joseph, 415
Little Rock (Ark.), *583*
Little Round Top, *568, 569. See also* Get-
        tysburg, campaign and battle of
Logan, John A., 268
Logan's Cross Roads (Mill Springs), battle
        of, 246
Longfellow, Henry Wadsworth, 73, 165
Longstreet, James, 505, *568, 592*; and
        Antietam, 465, 492; and battle of the
        Wilderness, 631–32; at Chicka-
        mauga, 590; confronts Federals in
        southside Virginia, 552, 558; criti-
        cizes Bragg, 594; at Fredericksburg,
        493–94; at Gaines's Mill, 396; to
        Georgia, 586; at Gettysburg,
        564–75; given corps command, 401;
        at Glendale, 398; hopes for election
        of northern peace president,
        626–27; and Knoxville, 594, 598; at
        Malvern Hill, 399; in Mexican War,
        4; and Pennsylvania invasion,
        560–61, *561*; at 2nd Manassas,
        452–56; at Seven Pines, 389; sug-
        gests western strategy, 560; at
        Williamsburg, 361
Lookout Mountain, *592, 593, 595*
Lopez, Narciso, *83*, 83–84, 86
Loudon Heights, *461*
Louis Napoleon, *319*, 478, *478, 479*
Louisiana, *188*, 613–18, 620–21, *629*, 740
Lowell Offering, *28*
Lowell (Mass.), *28*
lower Hudson Valley, *16*
lower Mississippi Valley, *618*
Luray Valley, *384*
lynching, *8, 526*

Lyon, Nathaniel, *230, 231, 288*; and strug-
        gle for Missouri, 229–31, 273; and
        Wilson's Creek, 287

McCallum, Daniel, 438–39
McCauley, Charles, 221
McClellan, George B., 193, *240, 241, 277,
        285, 359, 360, 398, 493*, 497, 563, 653,
        708*, 718; acceptance letter, 684; and
        Antietam, 460–71, 491–92; candi-
        dacy of, hurt by Union victories,
        686; cartoon depictions, *396, 480,
        677, 680, 685*; "change of base," *396*;
        comparison with Grant, 329; Con-
        federate hopes for election of, 706,
        709; contracts typhoid, 300–301; cre-
        ates Army of Potomac, 285–86;
        defects of military and political acu-
        men, 296–99, 374; defects of person-
        ality, 295–96; Democratic presiden-
        tial nominee, 680–81; on
        Emancipation Proclamation,
        481–82; endorses Woodward for
        governor, 601; evaluation of gener-
        alship, 755; with Lincoln, *492*; loses
        soldier vote, 707–8; in Mexican War,
        4; opposes emancipation, 428;
        Peninsula campaign, 356–57, 367,
        383, 386, 389; relieved of and
        restored to command, 458, 483–84,
        506, 622, 665; rivalry with Pope, 448;
        and 2nd Bull Run, 452, 457; and
        Seven Days battles, 390–99, 417,
        419, 425–26, 435, 436, 642, 715; and
        Seven Pines, 389; in western Vir-
        ginia, 238–41, 273; wins three states,
        737; withdrawn from Peninsula,
        448–49
McClernand, John A., *498*; at Fort Donel-
        son, 331–34; political general, 268;
        and Vicksburg campaigns, 498–500,
        501, 508–9, 514, 543–44
McCormick Harvesting Machinery Com-
        pany, *9*
McCoul House, *638*
McCulloch, Ben, 287, 336–37
McDowell, battle of, 383–84
McDowell, Irvin: campaign and battle,
        277–83, 339; corps commander, 359,
        383; and Jackson's Shenandoah Val-

Toombs, Robert (*continued*)
124; on John Brown, 166; opposes arming of slaves, 734; political general, 268; and secession, 55–57, *57*, 70, 198; and Taylor administration, 55–57

trade between the lines during war, 534–37

transportation: and economic growth, 10–11, 19, 24; and southern economy, 74–77. *See also* railroad

Traveller (horse), *756*

traveling salesmen, *27*

Travis, William, *502*

Tredegar Iron Works (Richmond), 77, 222, 259, 721, *721*

trenches, *637*

Trent affair, 300, *322*, 322–23, 374

Trevilian Station, battle of, 648

Trist, Nicholas, 3, 44

Trumbull, Lyman: on black rights, 124; elected senator, 102, 171; on midwestern racism, 431

tunnels, *670*

Tupelo, battle of, 660

"twenty-Negro" exemption, *528*, 528–29, 530

22nd Iowa, *546*

22nd U.S. Colored Infantry, *651*

Tycoon (ship), *346*

Tyler, John, 201

Uncle Tom's Cabin Contrasted with Buckingham Hall, the Planter's Home (Criswell), *73*

Uncle Tom's Cabin (Stowe), 32, 71–74, *72*, *73*, 97

underground railroad, 66, 66–70

unemployment, *320*

uniforms, 262, 281–82, *282*, 287, 470; Confederate, 257, *257*, 262, *406*; "Flying Artillery," *256*; 9th Mississippi, *258*; "Wisconsin gray," *262*; Zouave units, 262, *282*, *552*, *564*

Union Leagues, 518, 622

Union Pacific Railroad, *380*

Union Press, *233*

Union soldiers and sailors monument (Indianapolis), *756*

United States Military Rail Roads, 438–39, 450–51

United States Sanitary Commission, *411*, *413*, 652; formation of, 262; influence and achievements, 411–15; investigates war prisons, 701; women and, 410

University of Wisconsin, *379*

Upton, Emory, 637

urbanization, 6–7, 9, *9*

U.S. Supreme Court, 34, 131, *690*, *737*; and fugitive slave laws, 65–66, 68; Taney Court, *135*. *See also Dred Scott v. Sanford*

Vallandigham, Clement L., *514*, *517*, *685*; arrest and exile, 516, 518; candidate for governor, 517, 601, 603; and McClellan, 684; and Northwest Confederacy, 514; peace program of, 513, 518; peace sentiments in 1864, 674; with rebel agents, 675, 689, 690; returns to U.S., 676; role at Democratic convention, 680–81

Van Buren, Martin, *51*; Free Soil nominee in 1848, 52; and slavery expansion, 46, 47

Van Dorn, C.S.S., *352*

Van Dorn, Earl: attack on Baton Rouge, 356; and Corinth, 350, 443–47; defense of Vicksburg, 354; Holly Springs raid, 500, 541; Mississippi command of, 439, 440, 458, 582; and Pea Ridge, 336–37; and trade with enemy, 535

Van Evrie, John H., *136*

Vance, Zebulon, *608*; denounces impressment, 531–32; and home-front economic distress, 531; loyal opposition of, 608–9; reelected governor, 609–10, 677

Vanderbilt, Cornelius, 88, 89

Vanity Fair, *167*, *172*

Vermont, U.S.S., *486*

Vicksburg, *355*, 499, *510*, *540*, 544–45, *546*, *548*, *549*, *550*; defies first Union attacks, 354, 417, 435; failure of Grant's first campaign against, 498–500; and Grant's spring 1863 campaign, 540–49, 560, 649; maneuvers against in winter 1863, 508–10, 513, 514, 539; plans for defense of, 498–500; surrender of, consequences

of, 550–51, 578–79, 583, 599, 600, 601, 606, 731, 755

Victoria (Queen of England), *319*

Virginia, C.S.S., *255*, *303*, *308*, *309*, *310*, *312*, 355; attacks Union fleet at Hampton Roads, 310–11, 351; fight with *Monitor*, 311–13; rebuilt from *U.S.S. Merrimack*, 221, 254, 307–8; scuttled, 361

Virginia Military Institute (VMI), *266*, *648*; cadets at New Market, 630–31; graduates of, in Confederate army, 267; Hunter burns, 647–48

Virginia monument at Gettysburg, *756*

A Visit from Old Mistress (Homer), *760*

Volck, Adalbert, *371*, *500*

Wade, Benjamin, 152, 179; antislavery Whig, 71; chairman of Committee on Conduct of War, 297; on Chase, 621; response to Lincoln's veto, 620, 623; in secession crisis, 198; and Wade-Davis bill, 616, 617, 620, 740

wages: antebellum, 10, 13, 19; and free-labor ideology, 23; inflation and, in Confederacy, 371; inflation and, in Union, 377; and "wage slavery," 20–21, 78, *79*

wagon ambulances, *415*

wagon trains, 36, *383*, *591*, *631*

Walke, Henry, *352*

Walker, Leroy P., *204*, 257, 260

Walker, Robert J., *127*, 127–29

Walker, William, 87, 87–91, *89*, *91*

Wall, James, 367

Wall Street, *22*

Wallace, Lewis, 268, 339–43

Wanderer (ship), 82

"Wanted: A Substitute" (song), *521*

War Democrats, 430

Warren, Gouverneur K., 569, 652, 742

Washburne, Elihu, 268

Washington, D.C., *358*, *751*, *757*

Washington, George, 145, 162, 216–17, 222, 274, 625

Washington, Lewis, *163*

Washington Artillery, *712*

Washington Light Infantry, *196*

Washington Peace Convention (1861), 201

Watie, Stand, *337*

ILLUSTRATION CREDITS

Project Management: Susan C. Day
Design and Composition: Facedancer
  Design
Maps: Hal Just, © 2003 Oxford University
  Press

A grateful acknowledgment to the
staffs at historical societies, libraries,
and museums who assisted with
research and art, and especially to
Marty Baldessari.

ABBREVIATIONS

B&L: *Battles and Leaders of the Civil War*,
  1887, The Century Co.
BMC: Anne S. K. Brown Military
  Collection, Brown University Library,
  Providence R.I.
CHS: Chicago Historical Society
DAS: Documenting the American South,
  (http://docsouth.unc.edu), The
  University of North Carolina at
  Chapel Hill Libraries
DU: Duke University, Rare Book,
  Manuscript, and Special Collections
  Library, Durham, North Carolina
GC: The Granger Collection, New York
ISHL: Illinois State Historical Library,
  Springfield, Ill.
KSHS: Kansas State Historical Society
LC: Library of Congress
MC: Museum of the Confederacy,
  Richmond, Va.
MFA/MK: Museum of Fine Arts, Boston,
  Karolik Collection, © Museum of Fine
  Arts, Boston
MHS: Minnesota Historical Society
MMA: The Metropolitan Museum of Art,
  Gift of I.N. Phelps Stokes, Edward S.
  Hawes, Alice Mary Hawes, and Marion

Augusta Hawes, 1937. © The
  Metropolitan Museum of Art
NM: The Newark Museum, Newark, New
  Jersey/Art Resource, New York
NARA: U.S. National Archives and
  Records Administration
NHC: U.S. Naval Historical Center
NPG: National Portrait Gallery, Smith-
  sonian Institution, Washington
  D.C./Art Resource, New York
NYHS: New-York Historical Society
NYPL: The New York Public Library,
  Prints and Photographs Division
PH: Picture History
SAAM: Smithsonian American Art
  Museum, Washington D.C./Art
  Resource, New York
SINMAH: Smithsonian Institution,
  National Museum of American History
USAMHI: U.S. Army Military History
  Institute
WP: West Point Museum Art Collection,
  United States Military Academy

ENDPAPERS
DU

TITLE PAGE
ii–iii USAMHI

PROLOGUE
2 LC; 4 LC; 5 LC

CHAPTER ONE
6 SAAM; 8 LC; 9 NYPL; 10 GC; 11
MFA/KC (48.471); 13 top LC, 13 bottom
LC; 14 top SAAM, 14 bottom GC; 15 LC;
16 LC; 17 LC; 19 (all) LC; 20 LC; 22 PH;
25 (both) LC; 26 top LC, 26 bottom (left
and right) The Historical Society of Pennsylvania; 27 NM; 28 GC; 29 LC; 30 top

LC, 30 bottom MMA (37.14.22) © 1995;
31 LC; 32 LC; 33 top DU, 33 bottom GC;
35 LC; 36 (both) LC; 37 top LC, 37 bottom
Utah State Historical Society; 38 SAAM;
39 LC

CHAPTER TWO
40 LC; 42 top James K. Polk Memorial
Association, Columbia, Tennessee;, 42
bottom LC; 44 (both) LC; 46 LC; 47 LC;
48 GC; 49 LC; 51 LC; 52 LC; 53 LC; 54
MFA/KC (50.3844); 56 LC; 57 NARA; 58
LC; 59 NARA (all); 61 LC; 62 (both) LC

CHAPTER THREE
64 Philbrook Museum of Art, Tulsa, Okla.;
66 Cincinnati Art Museum (1927.26), Sub-
scription Fund Purchase; 67 (both) LC; 68
NYPL Schomburg Center; 69 (both) LC;
70 LC; 72 left MMA, right LC; 73 top
NYHS, bottom PH; 75 NYPL; 76 LC; 77
DU; 78 GC; 79 LC; 81 DU; 82 NYHS; 83
LC; 85 (both) LC; 87 LC; 89 LC; 91 LC

CHAPTER FOUR
92 GC; 94 LC; 95 LC; 96 LC; 97 Corbis; 99
LC; 102 NYHS; 103 (both) LC; 104 LC;
105 LC; 106 LC; 107 GC; 108 NARA; 110
LC; 111 LC

CHAPTER FIVE
112 KSHS; 114 (both) GC; 115 top GC,
bottom LC; 116 KSHS; 118 LC; 119 LC;
121 GC; 122 LC; 123 LC; 125 LC; 126 LC;
127 LC; 129 LC

CHAPTER SIX
132 PH; 134 (both) LC; 135 LC; 136 LC;
138 Lincoln University of Pennsylvania
Archives, Langston Hughes Memorial
Library Special Collections, Lincoln Uni-

versity, Penn.; 142 PH; 143 ISHL; 144 PH; 146 LC; 148 (both) LC; 150 LC; 151 LC; 152 LC; 153 LC; 155 LC; 157 LC

CHAPTER SEVEN
158 NPG; 160 LC; 162 NYPL; 163 (both) LC; 164 LC; 167 LC; 168 LC; 169 LC; 170 LC; 171 CHS; 172 (both) LC; 173 LC; 174 top LC, bottom NYHS; 175 LC; 176 ISHL; 177 NYHS; 178 LC; 179 LC; 180 Bostonian Society; 181 LC; 182 NYHS; 183 LC

CHAPTER EIGHT
184 NARA; 186 (both) LC; 188 LC; 190 MC, Photography by Katherine Wetzel; 191 Georgia Historical Society; 194 LC; 196 LC; 197 LC; 198 LC; 202 LC; 203 (all) LC; 204 LC; 206 LC; 208 LC; 209 top LC, bottom American Heritage Picture Collection; 210 LC; 211 LC; 212 LC; 213 top LC, bottom NARA; 214 Collections of Henry Ford Museum & Greenfield Village; 215 Fort Sumter National Monument, National Park Service; 216 Burton Historical Collection, Detroit Public Library; 217 NYHS

CHAPTER NINE
218 Tennessee Historical Society; 221 Harper's Ferry Historical Assn.; 222 Robert E. Lee Memorial Assn.; 226 LC; 227 top MFA/KC (51.2785, cat. no. 961, fig. 194), bottom LC; 228 LC; 229 LC; 230 LC; 231 (both) LC; 232 LC; 233 top LC, bottom Kentucky Historical Society; 234 LC; 235 top LC, bottom USAMHI; 237 NYHS; 238 LC; 240 (both) LC; 241 LC; 242 B&L; 243 MC; 244 LC; 245 LC; 246 LC

CHAPTER TEN
248 MFA/KC (55.880, Karolik cat. no. 1002); 250 top Indianapolis Museum of Art, bottom Birmingham Museum of Art; 251 DAS; 253 LC; 254 LC; 255 MC; 256 top NHC, bottom LC; 257 Gettysburg National Military Park, Courtesy Harper's Ferry Design Center; 258 LC; 259 LC; 260 LC; 261 NYHS; 262 Wisconsin Veterans Museum; 263 (both) LC; 264 LC; 265 LC;

266 LC; 267 VMI Museum, Lexington, Va.; 269 LC; 271 USAMHI; 272 LC; 273 LC; 274 LC

CHAPTER ELEVEN
276 MFA/KC (45.890); 278 LC; 279 top USAMHI, bottom USAMHI; 281 left MC, Photography by Katherine Wetzel, right Fort Sumter National Monument, courtesy Harper Ferry's Design Center; 282 LC; 284 LC; 285 USAMHI; 286 MC; 288 Missouri State Capitol, photography by Zeal Wright; 289 top B&L, bottom LC; 291 top Valentine Museum, Richmond History Center, bottom B&L; 292 American Heritage Picture Collection; 293 LC; 294 LC; 297 LC; 298 White House Historical Assn.

CHAPTER TWELVE
302 WP; 304 LC; 305 USAMHI; 306 LC; 307 top LC, 307 bottom MC; 308 B&L; 309 (both) Mariners' Museum, Newport News, Va.; 310 WP, photography by Anthony Mairo; 312 top Franklin Roosevelt Library, bottom USAMHI; 314 USAMHI; 315 WP; 316 USAMHI; 318 Western Reserve Historical Society; 319 LC; 320 LC; 321 LC; 322 LC; 323 (both) LC

CHAPTER THIRTEEN
324 NHC; 326 top LC, bottom NARA; 327 NHC; 328 top B&L, bottom LC; 330 LC; 334 CHS; 335 LC; 337 left NARA, right North Carolina Office of Archives and History; 338 B&L; 339 NARA; 340 top B&L, bottom LC; 341 LC; 342 USAMHI; 343 CHS; 346 top USAMHI, bottom B&L; 347 B&L; 348 top LC, bottom LC; 349 USAMHI; 350 LC; 351 LC; 352 B&L; 353 LC; 354 Historic New Orleans Collection; 355 NHC; 357 LC; 358 (both) LC; 359 LC; 360 (both) LC; 361 LC

CHAPTER FOURTEEN
362 LC; 364 DAS; 365 LC; 368 USAMHI; 369 (both) DAS; 370 (both) DAS; 371 NYHS; 372 LC; 373 LC; 375 SINMAH; 376 LC; 377 LC; 378 MHS; 379 Wisconsin Historical Society, Madison, Wisc., Whi-1885; 680 LC

CHAPTER FIFTEEN
382 Fenton History Center, Jamestown, N.Y.; 384 top left LC, top right LC, bottom USAMHI; 385 Virginia Museum of Fine Arts, Richmond. Gift of Mrs. Hugh L. Macneil in memory of Mrs. Charles E. Bolling. Photo Wen Hwa Ts'ao. © Virginia Museum of Fine Arts; 386 top NARA, bottom LC; 388 LC; 389 LC; 390 LC; 391 top (both) LC; 392 (both) LC; 393 LC; 396 NYPL; 397 LC; 398 LC; 399 (both) LC; 400 LC; 401 LC; 402 LC; 403 LC; 404 (all) SINMAH; 405 top MC, bottom Portland Museum of Art; 406 MC; 407 LC; 408 LC; 409 top MC, bottom LC; 410 MCNY (38.120.3); 411 top NYHS, bottom LC; 413 top NHC, bottom MFA/KC (48.434); 414 top LC, bottom USAMHI; 415 LC; 416 LC; 417 MC

CHAPTER SIXTEEN
418 GC; 420 LC; 421 left DU, right LC; 424 LC; 425 USAMHI; 426 LC; 427 LC; 430 U.S. Capitol; 431 NPG; 432 NYHS

CHAPTER SEVENTEEN
434 Réunion des Musées Nationaux/Art Resource, N.Y.; 436 top USAMHI, bottom LC; 437 top LC, bottom LC; 438 USAMHI, bottom ISHL; 439 MC, photograph by George S. Cook; 440 LC; 442 BMC; 443 NPG; 446 MFA/KC, (55.819, Karolik cat. no. 993); 447 LC; 449 top 383 USAMHI, bottom LC; 450 USAMHI; 451 (both) LC; 452 Wisconsin Historical Society, Madison, Wisc., Whi-1908; 453 GLC 6106 p. 14. Henry Berckhoff. Drawing: Battle on Manassas plains, 2nd Bull Run, 29 August 1862 (The Gilder Lehrman Collection); 456 B&L; 457 LC; 459 LC; 460; 461 Antietam National Park; 462 B&L; 463 Antietam National Park; 465 LC; 466 top USAMHI, bottom LC; 468 LC; 469 USAMHI; 470 LC; 471 LC

CHAPTER EIGHTEEN
472 CHS; 474 NHC; 475 top Courtesy Sandra J. Still and the BeckCenter, Emory University, Atlanta, Ga., bottom LC; 476 Corbis; 478 LC; 479 LC; 480 LC; 481 LC;

482 LC; 484 LC; 485 LC; 486 USAMHI; 487 LC; 488 top Ohio Historical Society, bottom USAMHI; 489 LC

CHAPTER NINETEEN
490 WP; 492 LC; 493 LC; 494 (both) LC; 496 B&L; 498 (both) LC; 500 NYHS; 501 B&L; 502 SINMAH; 504 BMC; 505 LC; 506 WP; 507 (both) LC; 509 LC; 510 Old Courthouse Museum, Vicksburg, Miss.; 511 USAMHI

CHAPTER TWENTY
512 NYHS; 514 LC; 516 left ISHL, right Indiana Historical Society (C5831); 517 LC; 518 LC; 519 LC; 520 LC; 521 (both) LC; 523 LC; 524 top NYHS, bottom LC; 526 NYHS; 527 LC; 528 LC; 529 (both) LC; 531 LC; 532 NYHS; 533 LC; 534 LC; 535 LC ; 536 LC

CHAPTER TWENTY-ONE
538 MHS (Artist: Rufus Zogbaum); 540 top USAMHI, bottom LC; 541 top LC, bottom LSU Libraries Special Collections, Baton Rouge, La.; 542 top OHS, bottom LC; 546 LC; 547 LC; 548 top Old Courthouse Museum, Vicksburg, Miss., bottom LC; 549 MHS (Artist: Francis Millet); 550 NM; 551 NARA; 552 LC; 553 LC; 554 NARA; 555 LC; 558 LC; 559 top CHS, bottom B&L; 561 B&L; 563 USAMHI; 564 USAMHI; 565 LC; 566 State Museum of Pennsylvania, Pennsylvania Historical and Museum Commission; 567 USAMHI; 568 LC; 569 top USAMHI, bottom B&L; 570 MHS; 572 NARA; 573LC; 574 LC; 575 LC; 576 (both) LC; 577 LC; 578 LC; 579 Gettysburg National Military Park

CHAPTER TWENTY-TWO
580 MHS (Artist: Henry J. Kellogg); 582

(both) LC; 583 NARA; 584–85 NARA; 586 LC; 587 LC; 590 LC; 591 LC; 592 top LC, bottom USAMHI; 593 LC; 595 MHS; 598 LC; 599 Imperial War Museum, London, U.K.; 600 LC; 601 LC; 602 LC

CHAPTER TWENTY-THREE
604 CHS; 606 PH; 607 PH; 608 PH; 612–13 LC; 615 LC; 616 LC; 618 MHS; 619 LC; 622 LC; 623 LC

CHAPTER TWENTY-FOUR
624 WP; 626 GC; 627 BMC; 628 top NHC, bottom CHS; 629 (both) USAMHI; 630 top LC, bottom VMI Museum, Lexington, Va.; 631 USAMHI; 632 USAMHI; 633 top LC, bottom USAMHI; 636 LC; 637 top LC, bottom B&L; 638 USAMHI; 639 top B&L, bottom USAMHI; 640 top LC, bottom USAMHI; 641 USAMHI; 642 LC; 643 B&L; 646 WRHS; 647 top Valentine Museum, Richmond History Center, bottom LC; 648 VMI Museum, Lexington, Va.; 649 LC; 650 NARA; 651 WP; 6553 LC; 654 top USAMHI, bottom WRHS; 655 USAMHI; 658 USAMHI; 659 B&L; 660 LC

CHAPTER TWENTY-FIVE
662 Detroit Institute of Arts (51.66), Photograph © 1989 Detroit Institute of Arts; 664–65 (all) LC; 666 LC; 667 LC; 668 top USAMHI, bottom LC; 669 (both) LC; 670 LC; 671 LC; 672 top LC, bottom LC; 673 LC; 674 NARA; 675 LC; 677 LC; 679 LC; 680 top LC, bottom GC

CHAPTER TWENTY-SIX
682 LC; 684 B&L; 685 top BMC, bottom LC; 686 LC; 687 LC; 688 top USAMHI, bottom LC; 690 PH; 691 State Historical

Society of Missouri; 692 top LC, bottom Cincinnati Art Museum (1958.515), The Edwin and Virginia Irwin Memorial; 693 left LC, right State Historical Society of Missouri; 694 KSHS; 696 LC; 697 (both) LC; 698 LC; 699 LC; 700 LC; 701 top LC, bottom Andersonville National Park, courtesy Harper's Ferry Design Center; 702 LC; 703 top OHS, bottom Wisconsin Veterans Museum; 704 (both) Virginia Historical Society; 705 top Virginia Historical Society, bottom Sandusky Library Follett House Museum Archives; 707 top NYHS, bottom LC; 708 NYHS; 709 GC

CHAPTER TWENTY-SEVEN
710 CHS; 712 top USAMHI, bottom B&L; 713 LC; 714 B&L; 715 USAMHI; 718 USAMHI; 719 LC; 721 LC; 723 LC; 725 USAMHI; 726 top LC, bottom NARA; 727 B&L; 728 MFA/KC (59.940); 729 LC

CHAPTER TWENTY-EIGHT
730 NYHS; 732 LC; 733 LC; 736 LC; 737 (both) LC; 738 B&L; 739 USAMHI; 741 LC; 742 LC; 743 B&L; 744 Union League Club, N.Y., photography by Arthur Lawrence; 745 B&L; 746 B&L; 747 NARA; 748 B&L; 749 WP, photography by Anthony Mairo

EPILOGUE
750 LC; 752 top National Museum of Health and Medicine, bottom LC; 753 NYHS; 754 Kentucky Historical Society; 756 left LC, right MC, photography by Katherine Wetzel; 757 LC; 758 NM; 759 © Museum of Modern Art/Licensed by SCALA/Art Resource, N.Y.; 760 SAAM